ABOUT THE AUTHORS

BILL FLEISCHMAN

Bill Fleischman has been a member of the *Philadelphia Daily News* sports staff for more than 30 years. During the 1970s he covered the Philadelphia Flyers (authoring a book on Flyers' goaltender Bernie Parent called *Bernie, Bernie*), and since then he has served as an assistant sports editor, covering auto racing, tennis, sports on television, and hockey. He is past president of the Philadelphia Sports Writers Association and the Professional Hockey Writers Association. Since 1981 he has served as an adjunct professor of journalism at the University of Delaware. He has written for *Inside Sports* and *PhillySports* magazines, and he also has the best answering machine messages in the business.

AL PEARCE

Al Pearce saw his first NASCAR race in 1966 when he attended the Daytona 500. He has been a sportswriter since 1969 and has covered NASCAR for nearly as long for the *Newport News (VA) Daily Press*. He has traveled to France, Japan, and Australia to cover the Winston Cup cars and can tell you a story about every track and every driver on the circuit. He has contributed to a number of other books on NASCAR and has been the NASCAR correspondent for leading car magazine *Autoweek* for more than 32 years. In his travels while covering races, Al has been to every state in the continental United States except Wyoming.

THE UNAUTHORIZED
NASCAR®
FAN GUIDE
2004

THE UNAUTHORIZED
NASCAR®
FAN GUIDE
2004

BILL FLEISCHMAN

AND

AL PEARCE

CHECKERED
FLAG PRESS™

Detroit

The Unauthorized NASCAR Fan Guide 2004

This edition published by Checkered Flag Press™ by arrangement with Visible Ink Press®.

Copyright 2004 by Visible Ink Press®

Checkered Flag Press
43311 Joy Rd. #414
Canton, MI 48187-2075

Cover photo reprinted by permission of AP/Wide World Photos.
Back cover photo reprinted by permission of W. Dennis Winn.

ISBN 0-681-27587-1

Cataloging-in-Publication Data is on file with the Library of Congress.

Printed in the United States of America
All rights reserved
10 9 8 7 6 5 4 3 2 1

CONTENTS

year breakdown of rank, events run, poles, wins, top-10 finishes, and earnings, as well as lifetime totals in those categories.

Profiles of the leading Nextel Cup teams that are expected to compete in the 2004 season. Includes the team name, a profile of the team owner(s), and a listing of the team's driver, crew chief, and primary sponsor, when that information is available. Also includes the address and phone number for each team, when available. Teams are listed in car number order (as available at press time).

It had to happen eventually. With the U.S. automobile market filled with foreign carmakers, it was only a matter of time before one of them decided to give NASCAR a try, and Toyota decided there was no better time than the present to make its debut. The Japanese automaker will run its Tundra trucks—which, by the way, are made in the United States—in the Craftsman Truck Series in 2004; learn how this is almost certainly a stepping stone to the Nextel Cup.

First there was Big Bill, then there was Bill Jr. (who wasn't really a Jr., but that's another story), and now there's Brian. As NASCAR moves into a new era with lead sponsor Nextel, see why most observers feel that new chairman and chief executive officer Brian France is the perfect choice to lead stock car racing to the next level.

No one has ever doubted NASCAR's commitment to safety, but in 2004, racing's ruling body will devote more attention than ever to keeping its drivers safe and sound behind the wheel. All the new innovations are covered in this chapter: the use of SAFER foam barriers at more and more tracks, the opening of NASCAR's state-of-the-art Research and Development/Safety Center in Charlotte, North Carolina, and much more.

While there is no question NASCAR's roots are firmly planted in the southern United States, the NASCAR of the twenty-first century is hardly just a southern playground. This chapter shows how many of today's best young drivers grew up and learned to race in the Midwest, West, and Northeast.

A two-part review of the history of NASCAR begins with a look back at the sport's early days, from the time Bill France Sr. founded NASCAR in a Florida restaurant in 1949 until the end of the Grand National days in 1970. This comprehensive review covers the birth of the superspeedway and the death of the dirt tracks, NASCAR's first superstars, the very first Daytona 500, and the final years before R.J. Reynolds formed the Winston Cup.

The two-part review concludes with a look at the period from 1971 until 2003, when the big money that RJR brought and the spread of big-name sponsorship changed the sport forever—and raised the bar for Nextel as it takes over from RJR in 2004. Read about Richard Petty and David Pearson's classic 1970s duels, NASCAR "hitting" the television airwaves with the contentious 1979 Daytona 500, Jeff Gordon's meteoric rise as four-time Winston Cup champion, and more as NASCAR becomes a modern sports phenomenon.

11 AT A GLANCE: YEAR-BY-YEAR SUMMARIES
From 1949 until 2003, a year-by-year look back at each season on NASCAR's top circuit. Each year includes an "At a Glance" feature that lists that season's champion, top rookies, and notable events, followed by more in-depth information on the year's best races, leading personalities, and top news stories. The chapter concludes with a look at the exciting 2003 season, the last to give away the Winston Cup.

12 DID YOU KNOW?
Impress your friends and family with your newfound knowledge of even the most obscure bits of NASCAR trivia by reading this collection of short bits and bites from the Winston Cup scene. Features more than 50 facts that are new to this edition.

13 THE BUSCH GRAND NATIONAL
A look at the Nextel Cup's main "farm system," where young drivers learn what it takes to make it on the top circuit and veteran drivers fight to stay near the top. Includes highlights of the 1999 through 2003 seasons and all-time driver records.

14 THE CRAFTSMAN TRUCK SERIES
Explores the birth and extraordinary growth of the series many thought would never come to pass and examines the how the circuit has overcome problems that threatened its existence. Includes highlights of the 1999 through 2003 season and all-time driver records.

15 RACE RESULTS: 1949–2002
Contains race results for every Strictly Stock, Grand National, and Winston Cup race that has been held between NASCAR's first full season in 1949 and the 2002 season; results for 2003 can be found in Chapter 2. Because early records are incomplete, only the race winners are listed from 1949 until 1971. Beginning with the first Winston Cup season of 1972, complete, race-by-race results are provided, including date, location, race name, time of race, average speed, margin of victory, finish position, driver name, and type of car driven.

Where to find more information about NASCAR and stock car racing in general, including videos; books; magazines; associations; fan clubs; and driver, team, and general interest Web sites.

PREFACE

by Al Pearce

Welcome to NASCAR, 2004. Take a good, hard look, because you might not recognize what you see. Never in its 54-year history has the Daytona Beach-based organization entered a season with such a new look. Let us count the changes between late in the 2003 season and the season-opening Daytona 500:

• Of course, there's the most prominent change: Nextel replaces Winston as sponsor of NASCAR's top series. Despite generating reams of publicity, the Nextel-for-Winston change will have almost no impact on the racing. After all, a rose by any other name…

• The point system used to determine the champion, which has been in place since 1975, was changed to create a new and dramatically different method for selecting who will raise the Nextel Cup at the end of the year. To call it "controversial" could be the understatement of the year.

• The formula for awarding provisional starting positions at the 36 major races was changed. Although relatively minor, the change will almost certainly impact which teams qualify and which ones go home early.

• The schedule was revised. California Speedway got a second date at the expense of North Carolina Speedway, which lost a race. NASCAR squeezed in three open weekends early in the season, but only one in the final 25 weekends. The fall race at Darlington Raceway was moved to mid-November.

• Pontiac left NASCAR's top series, the first time since the early 1980s it hasn't been involved in NASCAR racing. General Motors announced in October of 2003 that it would no longer provide financial, technical, or administrative support for Pontiac teams and was delighted when they all switched to Chevrolet.

• As Pontiac exited, Toyota entered. For the first time, a non-U.S. automaker will race in one of NASCAR's three main divisions. The Japanese carmaker will support several teams running Tundra trucks in the Craftsman Truck Series, with an eye on eventually competing in the Nextel Cup Series.

• Sunoco became NASCAR's new fuel supplier. It replaced Pure/Union 76/Unocal, which had been around almost forever since NASCAR founder

Bill France Sr. once owned a Pure franchise in Daytona Beach.

• Brian Z. France, 42, became NASCAR's new chief executive officer and chairman of the board. He replaced his father, Bill France Jr., who replaced his father, Big Bill, in January of 1972. Wisely, Brian surrounded himself with age, experience, and knowledge—including his father, sister (Lesa), and uncle (Jim)—just down the hallway.

"I don't think we've ever had a season when so much new was coming all at once," said Richard Petty, a seven-time NASCAR champion and its most recognizable figure. "We've had personnel changes and sponsorship changes and rules changes and stuff like that, but never at the same time. Just about everything will be different. It's going to take some getting used to."

CROWNING A NEW CHAMPION

Without question, the biggest change is the points system used to crown the first Nextel Cup champion.

When suggestions were first made in December of 2003 that it was time to make a change, there was an immediate outcry by traditionalists. That didn't stop the NASCAR brain trust, however. In mid-January, at a gathering near Charlotte, Brian France and NASCAR president Mike Helton spelled out how the new system would work. The plan calls for 26 "regular-season" races, followed by a 10-race "playoff season" to determine the champion. Only drivers among the top-10 in points after the September 11 race at Richmond (plus anyone within 400 points of first-place) will advance to the "Chase for the Championship." This represents a drastic change from the old system, which counted all 36 races equally and used the same scoring system for all of those races.

When the "chase" begins, regardless of the lead the frontrunner built from February 15 (the Daytona 500) through September 11 (the Chevy Monte Carlo 400), the points leader enters the "playoffs" with 5,050 points. The driver in second place enters with 5,045 points, third-place with 5,040, fourth with 5,035, and so on through the list of the championship contenders. While the system allows for more than 10 drivers to qualify for the chase (if a driver is within 400 points of first, he qualifies), past results indicate that it is likely that no more than 10 will be eligible. Every team is eligible for, and will run, the final 10 races, but only the drivers who qualify for the chase can win the title. Separate standings will be kept during the chase: one for drivers in the hunt for the Nextel Cup, and one for everyone else. Each driver in the final top-10 gets at least $1 million from the points fund, while the 11th-place finisher gets a $250,000 payoff and special recognition at the awards banquet in New York City. The first Nextel Cup champion gets $5 million.

Officials hope the new system will create more interest in the Nextel Cup in the fall, when football and the World Series often upstage racing, especially in years when a driver has built a huge points lead by that time. "We need a different approach to enhance the excitement and interest in our racing," Brain France said at the press conference. "This will give more drivers an opportunity to race for the championship. Our goal is to create better racing, and this makes a good system a great system. It adds more urgency in the spring and summer for teams to be in the transfer position. We want to capture sports fans' attention all the time."

The change also awards drivers with five more points for winning a race. That means the winner gets 180 points instead of 175, plus five bonus points for leading a lap (which, obviously, every winner does), and perhaps another five for leading the most laps. Under the old system, a runner-up who led the most laps got the same 180 points as the winning driver. Now, the first-to-second spread can range from 5 to 20 points instead of 0 to 15 points. "We want consistency to still matter, that's why we didn't add more to win," said France. "We could have made it a bigger number (to win), but that would have taken us away from what we wanted. And we're not giving qualifying points because our races have always counted for points, but qualifying never has."

Many feel the system was changed because Matt Kenseth won the 2003 Cup in runaway fashion even though he won only one race the entire season. After winning the third race of the year in Las Vegas in March, he steadily built his lead with 20 top-10 finishes in the next 25 races. That didn't make for the most exciting racing for fans at the track, nor did it boost the television ratings. NBC and TNT, which have the rights for this year's final 18 races, say they didn't influence the changes to the scoring system, but they do applaud them.

When the changes were announced, many drivers played it safe by saying, "Let's wait and see." But a few were openly against it, including Kenseth.

"It's worse than I thought," he said. "I felt they might knock it down to 100 points (for the leader) if you had a 300-point lead after 26 races. But I'm not in favor of it because five points per position isn't that big a deal. There was talk about putting more emphasis on winning, but I don't think this does that. They didn't do anything to take away consistency. It's probably more about consistency now because you can concentrate on having solid finishes (the first 26 races) and making sure you're in the top 10 for the final 10.

"This is entertainment driven," he continued, "nothing like when racing started for most of us. I understand the need to keep people interested and understand there has to be entertainment value. But from my point of view as a racer, I'm disappointed. I feel this takes away from winning. A lot of guys will have the feeling of not wanting to make a mistake and concentrate on making sure they're in the top 10. I think it takes the emphasis away from winning."

Second-year driver Greg Biffle fears the change will affect sponsor and driver contracts, but not how teams prepare. "We try to win every week," he said. "That's what everybody does. No matter if you're in a tight points race or not, you can't crash out. You're not going to do stupid stuff. You try to use the same mindset every week, and that's get yourself in the top 10, be consistent, and stay on the lead lap. Once you get into the top 5, you're there for the wins."

Dale Earnhardt Jr. worried that the change would cause fans to compare champions, judging some more worthy than others. His father, the late Dale Earnhardt, won seven Cups under the previous system. Junior felt fans and the media would have a "yeah, but" attitude toward champions under the new system.

"It's important to see how mine—if I'm ever fortunate enough to win one—is compared to his," Junior said of his father. "Were his better, the same as, or not as good as the ones under this system? And people will talk about two champions: the one who is and the one who would have been under the old system. Sure, I'd be upset if I had a 400-point lead after Richmond and had it cut to five points for the last 10. But what if I'm way behind and get to catch up after Richmond? Overall, though, I'm not for it. I wish it had stayed the way it was."

Dale Jarrett, the 1999 Winston Cup champion, took a different approach. "My father (Ned Jarrett) won two championships (1961 and 1965) and nobody ever compared mine to his," he said. "Nobody will compare this year's to last year's, and I don't think anybody compared Richard Petty's championships under different systems in the 1960s and 1970s. I didn't like the new deal at first, but I spoke before I knew the facts. This is more exciting than anything NASCAR's ever done, so I retract what I said before now."

Team owner Ray Evernham said the new system will crown a "10-race champion, not a full-season champion." Jeff Burton called it "the right thing to do," and Elliott Sadler said, "a clean sheet with 10 races left is good for the sport." Jimmie Johnson would have been the 2003 champion under the new system. "I feel better about it knowing it can work," he said. Teammate Jeff Gordon, a four-time champion, said the increased degree of difficulty will make this year's title more prestigious than in past years.

"This is a perfect time for it to happen," Gordon said in mid-January. "It'll be very exciting and let us compete with other entertainment mediums."

Or, as most drivers said, "Let's wait and see."

In this year's other major changes:

• Only five owner-point provisionals will be available at Nextel Cup races, two fewer than last year. Thirty-eight drivers will qualify on speed and five will get provisional, a change from the old 36-7 system.

• The 54-year-old Labor Day weekend race was moved from Darlington (S.C.) Raceway to California Speedway near Fontana. NASCAR, wanting two races in the lucrative Southern California market, took the fall date from North Carolina Speedway at Rockingham, a small market with no clout. In payment for losing its Labor Day tradition, Darlington got Rockingham's fall date.

• Five teams switched from Pontiac to Chevy in the winter: Morgan-McClure with Kevin Lepage, MBV with Scott Riggs, MB2 with Joe Nemechek, PPI with Ricky Craven, and Haas-CNC with Ward Burton.

• In August of '03, Sunoco signed a 10-year deal worth a reported $150 million to provide fuel for Nextel, Busch, and Craftsman races. Sunoco becomes the second "official fuel" in NASCAR's 54-year history, replacing the Conoco Phillips/Unocal 76 brand. All told, Sunoco provides fuel at 400 tracks from its manufacturing facility at Marcus Hook, New Jersey.

• Brian France succeeded his father as NASCAR's CEO in September of 2003. Within weeks, he implemented the long-awaited ban on racing back to the caution flag and began tweaking the new points system. If nothing else, those initiatives showed cynical NASCAR-watchers that this isn't his father's NASCAR.

• R.J. Reynolds Inc. ended its long association with NASCAR after last season. During their 33-season marriage, RJR paid $135 million–plus in purses, post-season awards, special event purses, and bonuses. Two factors led to its departure: the annual $45 million sponsorship grew excessive at a time when the tobacco industry was in trouble, and the 1999 Master Tobacco Settlement made it difficult for RJR to use motorsports to advertise its product.

• Nextel survived the corporate battle to replace RJR, beating out (at least, reportedly) Coca-Cola, McDonald's, VISA, and Gillette. Exact figures are closely guarded secrets, but it's thought the wireless giant pledged $75 million a year for 10 years. Much of that was earmarked for mass media advertising and cross-promotion of its products with NASCAR.

GIBBS TRIES TO REVITALIZE THE REDSKINS

There was, of course, one more fairly significant event that occurred just before the start of the 2004 season: Joe Gibbs turned over control of his multilevel NASCAR empire to eldest son J. D. and returned to the Washington Redskins as the team's head coach. He'd left that same job in 1992 with three Super Bowl rings, shocking many by announcing that he was going to form a NASCAR racing organization. Really, though, no one should have been surprised when Gibbs showed that his success on the gridiron could be transferred to NASCAR: Gibbs's team won NASCAR titles with Bobby Labonte in 2000 and Tony Stewart in 2002. All told, Joe Gibbs Racing won 31 poles, 40 races, two titles, and almost $63 million with drivers Dale Jarrett (1992–1994), Labonte (1995–present), and Stewart (1999–present).

"My race team was getting ready to roll me over in a corner," the 63-year-old Gibbs said early in January. "The first time J. D. said, 'No, we're not doing that,' I thought, 'I've gotta go someplace where they'll listen to me.'" That was Washington, the city that grieved deeply when he left and celebrated wildly when he announced his return.

The return to Washington almost didn't happen. The Atlanta Falcons were courting Gibbs the very day Steve Spurrier quit after two ill-fated years in the nation's capital. It took only eight days for Redskins owner Daniel Snyder to complete his coast-to-coast "search" and introduce Gibbs as his $5 million-a-year coach.

Nobody at JGR expects any appreciable drop-off in performance. "I'm excited and I know he's excited," Labonte said of Gibbs. "In the past few years he's let J. D. do more in the office. He's still got the management team to take care of whatever comes up and plan for the future. He wouldn't be doing this if it were five or seven years ago, but Joe feels the timing is right to coach and be out of the shop. He can feel comfortable because of the people at the shop. He knows they can get by day-to-day without him."

"I'm very happy for him," said Stewart. "He's always been a coach, and football has always been very close to him. After working with Joe for a number of years, I know his commitment to winning is unmatched. Fans of the Redskins should be very happy."

Happy Redskins fans? After the rough seasons they've endured the past few years, that would represent *another* major change for 2004.

INTRODUCTION

by Bill Fleischman

After more than 30 years of stability and continuity, 2004 will bring about some of the most sweeping changes in NASCAR history, both on the track and in the boardroom. With sponsorship changes, scoring changes, new leaders, new teams, and more, stock car racing fans will need *The Unauthorized NASCAR Fan Guide* by their side to keep track of who's who and what's what.

In 1971, RJR announced that it would lend its Winston brand name to NASCAR's top racing circuit, and the Winston Cup was born. RJR was great for the sport, but increased government pressure on tobacco companies made it increasingly difficult for RJR to advertise the way it wanted to, and the company decided it was time to take a smaller role in the sport it revolutionized. In its place, telecommunications giant Nextel quickly threw its hat into the ring, and after all the *i*'s were dotted and *t*'s crossed, the new NASCAR Nextel Cup Series was born.

Support for Nextel has been widespread, as team owners, drivers, and fans all expect the action on the track to remain as intense as ever. However, there are large changes afoot there as well. For the first time in 29 years, NASCAR officials made changes to the season scoring system in order to reward drivers for actually winning races. The old system rewarded consistency and finishing in the top 10 more than it did winning—Ryan Newman easily led all drivers with eight victories in 2003, but he finished in sixth in the final Cup standings, far behind. Reaction to the new system—which will create a "playoff" style finish to the season—has been mixed, but everyone agrees that NASCAR has definitely shaken things up.

The sponsorship and scoring changes are just the biggest in a series of changes that fans will notice in 2004 (see the Preface preceding this Introduction for a rundown of all the major changes). But no matter how much the sport changes, one thing will remain the same: NASCAR fans are among the most knowledgeable, loyal, and passionate in the sporting world, and *The Unauthorized NASCAR Fan Guide* is once again here to serve as a fact- and fun-filled companion to the first Nextel Cup season.

Among the new features in this year's edition of the *Guide:*

• Read in the opening chapter about how the Nextel-NASCAR partnership came to be, as authors

Al Pearce and Bill Fleishman give you the inside story on how the cutting-edge telecommunications company came to replace longtime sponsor R.J. Reynolds.

- Learn why the Big Three American automakers are getting company in 2004, as Toyota will become the first non-U.S. carmaker to race in one of NASCAR's top three circuits when the Toyota Tundra runs in the Craftsman Truck Series.

- Get to know Brian France, the latest member of the NASCAR-founding France family to take over the top spot in NASCAR's front office. Learn how he plans to expand on his father and grandfather's vision and lead the sport into a new era of prosperity.

- See what innovations NASCAR has in store this year on the safety front as its newly opened Research and Development/Safety Center in Charlotte, North Carolina, strives to find ways to make racing even safer.

- Learn where your favorite driver got his start in racing—odds are it wasn't in the Southeast. An in-depth look at the origins of Nextel Cup drivers shows that stock car racing has become a truly national sport, as most of today's leading young drivers grew up racing in the Midwest, West, Northeast, and just about everywhere else.

New sidebars and new photos add even more value to this edition.

Along with all the new material, all of the *Fan Guide*'s favorite sections are back for another season: read a race-by-race summary of the thrilling 2003 season; check out your favorite driver in the Driver Register; learn which teams will be running in 2004 in the Team Directory; read about the exciting, down-to-the-wire action in the Busch series and Craftsman Truck series; and learn everything there is to know about NASCAR history, including a season-by-season summary and the season standings for every NASCAR season from 1949 to 2003; and much more.

For the avid fan, the comprehensive Race Results chapter presents every race winner from NASCAR's vintage Strictly Stock and Grand National days from 1949 to 1971, and then complete race results for every race run during the Winston Cup era from 1972 to 2002 (2003 results can be found in Chapter 2).

Finally, informative appendices cover resources for race fans, including books, videos, magazines, fan clubs, web sites, and more; a comprehensive list of car numbers and the name of every driver to use that number for even one race; and 2004 schedules for the Nextel Cup, Busch, and Craftsman series.

The Unauthorized NASCAR Fan Guide has something to interest every stock car racing fan. Coauthor Al Pearce and I are proud of the book and hope you'll enjoy it and find it useful as you follow NASCAR. We suggest you take the book with you when you attend races and keep it nearby as you watch races on television. We always carry the book with us, and it's become a must-have in the media tent at races.

In addition, we'd love to hear from our readers. Spot something you think requires correction, or have an idea for a new feature? Then drop us a line at our email addresses. I can be reached at bill_fanguide@yahoo.com; Al's address is al_fanguide@yahoo.com.

ACKNOWLEDGMENTS

Al and I could never have created this book on our own, so there are many people we'd like to thank. If we leave anyone out, please forgive us and accept our thanks for helping to make this book happen. Among the people I'd like to thank are:

- Photographer Dennis Winn for once again creating wonderful images just for this book, and Marcia Schiff at the Associated Press for her help in gathering the historical photographs. Thanks too for Robert Huffman's for his extraordinary help this year in preparing the photos for publication.

- Editor Brad Morgan for his help and guidance through each edition of the *Guide,* and Marty

Connors, Roger Jänecke, and Christa Gainor for their perseverance in ensuring that a new edition would see the light of day. And thanks to Tom Connors for initially suggesting the idea for a book on stock car racing.

• Jim Craddock for his help with the proofreading and Carol Morgan for help with the indexing.

• Mary Claire Krzewinski for her wonderful cover, back cover, and page design.

• All of the public relations people at NASCAR and the numerous Nextel Cup teams who provided information and assistance when needed, often on short notice.

• Executive Sports Editor Pat McLoone and Sports Editor Caesar Alsop of the *Philadelphia Daily News* who, while not racing enthusiasts, have recognized the growing interest in NASCAR.

• And last but not least, my family. My wife, Barbara, for being patient while I devoted time to the book and for providing such invaluable computer expertise whenever I required it; our daughter, Jill, and her husband, Roger Herr, for their support and enthusiasm about the book; and our late daughter, Heather, whose spirit is always with us. She was a racing fan: I'm sure she would be proud of this book

Al Pearce echoes these words of thanks and would also like to provide his own note of gratitude:

• Special thanks to my wife, Francie, for putting up (mostly without complaint) with my late days at the office, my all-night drives back from races and my uncanny knack of being gone at the precise moment things break at home. And extra-special thanks to Annie, whose fledgling careers as a show-rider and tireless stall-mucker put my meager writing efforts to shame.

PASSING THE TORCH: FROM RJR TO NEXTEL

The timing was not good. With the United States economy in a prolonged slump and business declining for the R.J. Reynolds Tobacco Co., RJRT executives informed NASCAR late in 2002 that it would like an early out from its contract as sponsor of the Winston Cup series. RJRT (known in racing circles as RJR) was in its 33rd year with NASCAR and had paid more than $100 million in points-fund money. With RJR at the helm, NASCAR had gone from backwoods to Madison Avenue.

People might think such news would send frantic NASCAR officials bouncing off the walls of their offices. Instead, NASCAR calmly began a search for a new sponsor. Months later, NASCAR held a press conference in New York City to announce that, starting in 2004, communications giant Nextel would sponsor the top series in stock car racing for 10 years thanks to a deal that reportedly was worth $750 million. For NASCAR, it would be big business as usual. Maybe back in the day finding a replacement for RJR might have been hard, but with today's high-pressure blend of sports and marketing, NASCAR officials knew they wouldn't have to look far to find a company that was willing to take the sport into the next decade.

A MUTUAL ADMIRATION SOCIETY

When NASCAR approached Nextel about succeeding RJR as the sponsor of its top series, Nextel officials already knew about NASCAR. "NASCAR is something we had been looking at," said Michael Robichaud, Nextel's director of sports and event marketing. "We would have been involved (in 2004), probably more in a primary sponsorship." Before the larger opportunity became available, Robichaud said, Nextel had spoken with three teams about sponsorship deals. "NASCAR was always on our radar," he said. "It was just a matter of the dollars needed to invest to do it right."

Like other sponsors in NASCAR, Nextel isn't spending millions because it has an affection for stock car racing. Nextel is in the sport because the company believes the relationship will be good for its business. "It was the right opportunity at the right time," Robichaud said. "The stars aligned."

One reason that Nextel is in NASCAR is to increase its visibility and thereby boost its share of the cellular phone market. In mid-2003, Nextel's share of the United States wireless market was 7.5 percent. According to a Technology Business Research *Mobile Operators Benchmark Report,* Nextel ranked behind Verizon (22.9 percent), Cingular (15.4), AT&T (14.7), and Sprint (10.4).

In the summer of 2002, Nextel's stock had plummeted to about $2.50 a share. As of late 2003, it was up to $22 per share. "We had taken some pretty aggressive action in dealing with our debt," Robichaud explained. "Our business was at a major turning point. Our cash flow was starting to be positive. Our business was taking off. (In 2003) we were able to launch our nationwide direct-connect (cellular phone) product. We went from regional to nationwide with push-to-talk. As big as NASCAR is, the biggest thing to happen to Nextel (in 2003) is definitely (that) launch." (Direct Connect is a digital walkie-talkie system inside every Nextel phone that allows customers to speak instantly to others at the push of a button.)

THE NASCAR NEXTEL CUP: IT WILL GROW ON YOU

And just like that, the Winston Cup—that near-mythical championship that had been the not-so-secret desire of every driver who ever climbed behind the wheel of a stock car—was history. In it's place: the NASCAR Nextel Cup. With drivers now pursuing that new top trophy, racing fans can expect to see an enthusiastic sponsor who wants to help keep the sport on a high level while also paying attention to the sport's traditions. Sound familiar? This is exactly what NASCAR officials have been saying as the Cup series moves into larger markets.

"What we're excited to bring is our technology, to improve the communication at the tracks," Robichaud said. "We're going to do it in a next-generation way. We'll try to add products and services via wireless data applications (where fans) can get more information about a race or the sport.

We're big fans, from a marketing point of view, of what RJR did. They set the bar high. The good things that they did we absolutely want to pick up.

"We have tremendous admiration and respect for (NASCAR's) loyal fans. They love the product that they've grown accustomed to. NASCAR is working hard to maintain that product. Now, they've taken it to bigger cities. The (loyal fans) were there first: they were the smart ones, they got it. Now, the rest of the country is getting it."

According to *NASCAR Winston Cup Scene,* the popular weekly newspaper, NASCAR was thinking about signing up a new series sponsor as early as 1998. George Pyne, then NASCAR's vice president of marketing, asked a colleague, "What do you think about one day selling the biggest deal in the history of pro sports?" Pyne, now chief operating officer of NASCAR, described the eventual deal as a "game changer" because it would involve megabucks and probably introduce a corporate sponsor for auto racing from a nontraditional field.

Research identified about 60 companies that might be interested in partnering with NASCAR. Brian Corcoran, NASCAR's director of corporate marketing, launched the process that would lead to Nextel.

Tim Donahue, Nextel's president and chief executive officer, believes that his company and NASCAR share similarities. "Both of our organizations began as upstarts," Donahue said at the New York press conference. "To be candid, not a lot of people took us seriously. But, look at us now. America's No. 1 spectator sport and America's most successful wireless company joining forces."

Since many teenagers and college students carry cellular phones, Nextel will use its association with NASCAR to appeal to the youth market. Said Tim Kelly, NASCAR's chief operating officer, "Sixteen-to-twenty year olds don't remember a time when there were not wireless phones. That shows that wireless is becoming a pervasive technology: you couldn't kill it if you tried." Kelly sees Nextel integrating its technolo-

Tim Donahue (left), CEO of Nextel, holds up a Nextel cell phone painted to resemble a NASCAR stock car while NASCAR drivers Jeff Gordon (center) and Dale Earnhardt Jr. look on. The occasion was a June 19, 2003 press conference at which it was announced that Nextel would take over primary sponsorship of NASCAR's top racing circuit, ending more than 30 years of involvement by the R.J. Reynolds Tobacco Co. Later it was announced that the top series would change names from the Winston Cup to the NASCAR Nextel Cup.

gy with NASCAR by helping drivers communicate with their pit crews and by making it easier for track operations people to communicate with staff at the tracks. Nextel also expects more interaction with fans during telecasts.

Commenting on the new deal, Bill France Jr., then NASCAR's chairman and chief executive officer, said, "Nextel is a perfect fit for NASCAR because technology is an untapped growth area for our sport. Nextel will be able to promote our drivers, teams, and tracks in all forms of media and to all NASCAR fans."

Jim Hunter, NASCAR's vice president for corporate communications, has worked with Bill France Jr. and Brian through the RJR years. Like the Frances, Hunter is excited to have Nextel on board. "We've got such a great product," Hunter said, "and Nextel is such an innovative company. To me, it's a perfect fit. We all hate to see Winston leave, but Nextel is a perfect partner for this day and age. Their technology appeals to a broad range of people, especially young people. Nextel is going to take us places we've never been with their advertising and promotions. Tobacco was so restricted by regulations. There are no restrictions on Nextel."

ANOTHER MEMBER OF THE OLD GUARD CALLS IT QUITS

RJR wasn't the only long-time sponsor exiting NASCAR after 2003.

Union 76, the official fuel of NASCAR for more than 40 years, also bowed out.

Enter, Sunoco. Philadelphia-based Sunoco signed a 10-year deal in August 2003 to be the official fuel supplier for NASCAR's three national series (Nextel Cup, Busch Grand National, and Craftsman Truck). Said Robert Owens, Sunoco's senior vice president of marketing, "When we read that Unocal would be leaving, we looked at this as an opportunity to showcase the quality of our products. Moving up to the big leagues gives us the opportunity to participate in the top venue in motorsports today."

Sunoco supplies fuel to more than 400 race tracks across the United States. The company also fuels about 80 percent of the Dodge Weekly Series.

ConocoPhillips, owner of the 76 brand, left NASCAR because it decided to shift its marketing strategy and focus following the merger of the two companies in 2002.

Sunoco's 4,500 retail outlets are in 23 states throughout the East and Midwest. Owens said the company has no plans to go national.

Bill France Jr. recalled a comment by his father, Bill Sr., during the founding of NASCAR in 1947. "I believe stock car racing can become a nationally recognized sport. We do not know how big it can be if it's handled properly." It took a few decades for NASCAR to grow nationally, but it's there now, thanks to skilled drivers, team owners, and track operators; NASCAR's management; and media coverage and RJR's promotional work. Referring to his father, Bill Jr. said, "I'd like to think he'd be proud of how we have handled the sport so far."

DRIVERS ARE OPTIMISTIC BUT WARY

Driver Jeff Burton is one person who expects some bumps in the road as Nextel begins its association with NASCAR. Burton sees NASCAR heading into "uncharted territory that, for a time, will be a little painful. Not everything will work like we thought it was going to work because there are so many unknowns. But I think, in the long run, I think it will be positive for the sport." Referring to RJR, Burton said, "The legislation that has been passed and the continued pressure on the tobacco companies has created a situation where they can't do successful sports marketing. As good as Winston has been for the sport, with all that's going on, I don't think the sport can return the favor. A company that doesn't have all those issues is better for the sport. They can promote the sport in ways that R.J. Reynolds couldn't. Times change and when it's time to move on, it's time to move on. That's the position that we got in."

Burton was impressed with how quickly NASCAR found a new sponsor for its top series after RJR declared its wish to bow out. "The strength of our sport was shown through that," Burton said.

RJR: AN IMPORTANT LEGACY

During the 2003 racing season, NASCAR paid tribute to RJR for what it did for stock car racing. RJR spent about $80 million annually on NASCAR. The 2003 points fund was worth $17 million, with the champion receiving $4.25 million. No wonder champion Matt Kenseth, as well as every other driver, drove as fast as they could.

After signing on in December 1970 to sponsor NASCAR's top racing series, RJR helped racetracks improve their facilities. It was esti-

NASCAR's Winston Cup drivers gather to say "Thanks, and so long," to R.J. Reynolds Tobacco Co. and the Winston Cup racing series before the final race of the 2003 season at the Homestead-Miami Speedway in Homestead, Florida. After being involved in NASCAR racing since 1971, RJR ended its sponsorship of the Winston Cup, stock car racing's top trophy.

mated that RJR annually purchased about 300,000 gallons of paint (RJR red and white, of course). The company's Ralph Seagraves and T. Wayne Robertson had an enormous influence on increasing NASCAR's visibility nationwide. Seagraves was the first manager of RJR's special events department, which eventually became Sports Marketing Enterprises (SME). Under the direction of Seagraves, national billboards promoting the Winston Cup series were erected. The company also began advertising in newspapers and magazines.

Veteran drivers like Rusty Wallace appreciate what RJR did for the sport. "Winston has done so much for the sport and so much for me personally. There are a lot of friendships there. I could talk forever about the R.J. Reynolds guys. I hope we're able to develop the same type of relationship with the Nextel guys." Referring to RJR, Wallace said, "They always did a lot of nice things for you. You called them up and you needed some support for a charity event, and they always did that. I know corporate America has gotten very corporate these days. R.J. Reynolds guys weren't like that. They were just really nice, fun, relaxing people to hang out with."

T. Wayne Robertson was one of those guys. Hired by Seagraves to drive Winston show cars,

Robertson later became president of SME. Both Robertson and Seagraves were "people persons" who, in their day, attended a party or two (hundred). Robertson, known as "T. Wayne," was always open to new ideas. H. A. "Humpy" Wheeler, the president and general manager of Lowe's Motor Speedway near Charlotte, North Carolina, recalls attending a meeting with Robertson in 1991. The topic was The Winston all-star race, which the Concord, North Carolina, speedway hosted. Richmond International Raceway was also interested in hosting the race. With the meeting going nowhere, Wheeler finally blurted, "We'll light the place (Lowe's) and run the race on Saturday night." Robertson smiled and said, "Now you're thinking."

Sadly, Robertson died much too soon in a boating accident in January 1998 while he and five others were duck hunting in Louisiana. Robertson was only 48.

Now, RJR is gone and it's a new era, the Nextel era, in NASCAR. Nextel has a tough act to follow.

2

2003 RACE RESULTS

RACE 1—DAYTONA 500

Daytona International Speedway
Daytona Beach, Florida
February 16
Pole winner: Jeff Green (186.606 mph)
Race winner: Michael Waltrip (133.870 mph)

Michael Waltrip's first Daytona 500 victory in 2001 was memorable for two reasons. First, it was his initial Winston Cup win in 463 starts. More memorably (for all the wrong reasons), Dale Earnhardt, the man who hired him to drive the No. 15 NAPA Chevrolet, was killed on the last lap of the race. Even though the 2003 race was halted by rain after 109 laps and thus became the shortest Daytona 500 in history, Waltrip could finally celebrate Earnhardt's faith in him as a racer without the shadow of the 2001 tragedy hanging over him. Just as they had in 2001, Dale Earnhardt Inc. (DEI) cars dominated the race, with Waltrip pacing 68 laps and teammate Dale Earnhardt Jr. leading 22 laps. Waltrip took the lead for the final time just one lap before a caution flag came out due to debris on the track—then the rains came. Kurt Busch was runner-up in a race that featured a tumbling, spinning crash by Ryan Newman, who wasn't injured. By the time the race was over, few remembered that Jeff

Green was the surprising fastest qualifier. He was involved in an accident and finished 39th.

Daytona 500

Time of Race: 2 hours, 2 minutes, 8 seconds
Average Speed: 133.870 mph
Margin of Victory: Under caution

FINISH	DRIVER	CAR
1.	Michael Waltrip	Chevrolet
2.	Kurt Busch	Ford
3.	Jimmie Johnson	Chevrolet
4.	Kevin Harvick	Chevrolet
5.	Mark Martin	Ford
6.	Robby Gordon	Chevrolet
7.	Tony Stewart	Chevrolet
8.	Jeremy Mayfield	Dodge
9.	Mike Wallace	Dodge
10.	Dale Jarrett	Ford
11.	Jeff Burton	Ford
12.	Jeff Gordon	Chevrolet
13.	Kyle Petty	Dodge
14.	Jack Sprague	Pontiac
15.	Ricky Rudd	Ford
16.	Kenny Wallace	Dodge
17.	Sterling Marlin	Dodge
18.	Todd Bodine	Ford
19.	Johnny Benson	Pontiac
20.	Matt Kenseth	Ford
21.	Greg Biffle	Ford
22.	Joe Nemechek	Chevrolet
23.	Elliott Sadler	Ford
24.	Dave Blaney	Ford
25.	Rusty Wallace	Dodge
26.	Ricky Craven	Pontiac
27.	Casey Mears	Dodge
28.	Jerry Nadeau	Pontiac
29.	Steve Park	Chevrolet
30.	Terry Labonte	Chevrolet
31.	Jamie McMurray	Dodge
32.	Bill Elliott	Dodge
33.	Tony Raines	Chevrolet
34.	John Andretti	Dodge

Ryan Newman had a terrific year in 2003, but it got off to a bit of a rough start at the Daytona 500. Coming out of turn 4, Newman's right rear wheel came off, sending him tumbling end over end in a spectacular crash. Newman, who was uninjured in the crash, climbed out of the car on his own and waved to the crowd. "We went for a heck of a ride," said Newman after the race.

35.	Christian Fittipaldi	Chevrolet
36.	Dale Earnhardt Jr.	Chevrolet
37.	Mike Skinner	Pontiac
38.	Ward Burton	Dodge
39.	Jeff Green	Chevrolet
40.	Jimmy Spencer	Dodge
41.	Bobby Labonte	Chevrolet
42.	Ken Schrader	Dodge
43.	Ryan Newman	Dodge

RACE 2—SUBWAY 400

North Carolina Speedway
Rockingham, North Carolina
February 23
Pole winner: Dave Blaney (154.683 mph)
Race winner: Dale Jarrett (117.852 mph)

One of the year's best races saw Dale Jarrett and Kurt Busch battle hard at the end before Jar-rett pulled out the win. Busch led laps 310–383; Jarrett, 384–388; and Busch again on lap 389. However, Jarrett rallied past Busch and led the final four laps to take his only victory in what would become a disappointing season. Dave Blaney got his first career Winston Cup pole, but led only the first eight laps before fading to 10th at the finish. Six of the top-15 finishers started well back in the race, proving that unrestricted racing on midlength tracks can be thoroughly entertaining. For example, Busch started 27th, Jimmie Johnson moved up from 37th to 8th, Ricky Rudd from 28th to 11th, Jeff Burton from 38th to 12th, Ryan Newman from 21st to 14th, and Jeff

Gordon from 23rd to 15th. All told, 11 drivers swapped the lead 20 times, with Rusty Wallace leading the most, 4 times for 182 laps. All but 4 of the 43 starters were running at the finish. Matt Kenseth finished third to reach sixth in the overall point standings, 67 behind leader Busch.

Subway 400

Time of Race: 3 hours, 23 minutes, 29 seconds
Average Speed: 117.852 mph
Margin of Victory: 0.966 seconds

FINISH	DRIVER	CAR
1.	Dale Jarrett	Ford
2.	Kurt Busch	Ford
3.	Matt Kenseth	Ford
4.	Ricky Craven	Pontiac
5.	Jamie McMurray	Dodge
6.	Rusty Wallace	Dodge
7.	Mark Martin	Ford
8.	Jimmie Johnson	Chevrolet
9.	Elliott Sadler	Ford
10.	Dave Blaney	Ford
11.	Ricky Rudd	Ford
12.	Jeff Burton	Ford
13.	Johnny Benson	Pontiac
14.	Ryan Newman	Dodge
15.	Jeff Gordon	Chevrolet
16.	Bobby Labonte	Chevrolet
17.	Mike Skinner	Pontiac
18.	Ward Burton	Dodge
19.	Michael Waltrip	Chevrolet
20.	Tony Stewart	Chevrolet
21.	Steve Park	Chevrolet
22.	Greg Biffle	Ford
23.	Joe Nemechek	Chevrolet
24.	Ken Schrader	Dodge
25.	Kevin Harvick	Chevrolet
26.	Jerry Nadeau	Pontiac
27.	Terry Labonte	Chevrolet
28.	Jimmy Spencer	Dodge
29.	Robby Gordon	Chevrolet
30.	Casey Mears	Dodge
31.	Jeff Green	Chevrolet
32.	Bill Elliott	Dodge
33.	Dale Earnhardt Jr.	Chevrolet
34.	Jack Sprague	Pontiac
35.	Kyle Petty	Dodge
36.	Larry Foyt	Dodge
37.	Tony Raines	Chevrolet
38.	Kenny Wallace	Dodge
39.	John Andretti	Dodge
40.	Sterling Marlin	Dodge
41.	Jeremy Mayfield	Dodge
42.	Todd Bodine	Ford
43.	Derrike Cope	Chevrolet

RACE 3—
UAW-DAIMLERCHRYSLER 400

Las Vegas Motor Speedway
Las Vegas, Nevada
March 2
Pole winner: Bobby Labonte (173.016 mph)
Race winner: Matt Kenseth (132.934 mph)

Matt Kenseth became the third Roush Racing driver to win at Las Vegas, joining Jeff Burton (1999 and 2000) and Mark Martin (1998, the first Winston Cup race held at the track). In winning

by a comfortable 9.104 seconds over Dale Earnhardt Jr., Kenseth led 88 laps to Earnhardt's race-best 97. After starting 17th, Kenseth had moved into the top 10 by lap 40, aided by some efficient work by his pit crew, which was breaking in several new members. Pole-sitter Bobby Labonte finished fourth. Winner of the most races (five) during the 2002 season, Kenseth left Las Vegas second in points, just three behind Michael Waltrip.

UAW-DaimlerChrysler 400

Time of Race: 3 hours, 0 minutes, 46 seconds
Average Speed: 132.934 mph
Margin of Victory: 9.104 seconds

FINISH	DRIVER	CAR
1.	Matt Kenseth	Ford
2.	Dale Earnhardt Jr.	Chevrolet
3.	Michael Waltrip	Chevrolet
4.	Bobby Labonte	Chevrolet
5.	Tony Stewart	Chevrolet
6.	Jeff Burton	Ford
7.	Ryan Newman	Dodge
8.	Sterling Marlin	Dodge
9.	Joe Nemechek	Chevrolet
10.	Steve Park	Chevrolet
11.	Jimmie Johnson	Chevrolet
12.	Johnny Benson	Pontiac
13.	Kevin Harvick	Chevrolet
14.	Bill Elliott	Dodge
15.	Casey Mears	Dodge
16.	Terry Labonte	Chevrolet
17.	Jimmy Spencer	Dodge
18.	John Andretti	Dodge
19.	Ricky Rudd	Ford
20.	Todd Bodine	Ford
21.	Jeremy Mayfield	Dodge
22.	Jerry Nadeau	Pontiac
23.	Robby Gordon	Chevrolet
24.	Tony Raines	Chevrolet
25.	Ward Burton	Dodge
26.	Jack Sprague	Pontiac
27.	Jeff Green	Chevrolet
28.	Ken Schrader	Dodge
29.	Derrike Cope	Chevrolet
30.	Kenny Wallace	Dodge
31.	Kyle Petty	Dodge
32.	Jamie McMurray	Dodge
33.	Hideo Fukuyama	Ford
34.	Dave Blaney	Ford
35.	Larry Foyt	Dodge
36.	Ricky Craven	Pontiac
37.	Jeff Gordon	Chevrolet
38.	Kurt Busch	Ford
39.	Mike Skinner	Pontiac
40.	Rusty Wallace	Dodge
41.	Dale Jarrett	Ford
42.	Elliott Sadler	Ford
43.	Mark Martin	Ford

RACE 4—
BASS PRO SHOPS/MBNA 500

Atlanta Motor Speedway
Hampton, Georgia
March 9
Pole winner: Ryan Newman (191.417 mph)
Race winner: Bobby Labonte (146.048 mph)

It's always a good bet Bobby Labonte will do well at Atlanta Motor Speedway (AMS). His victory in this spring race was his 6th in his last 15 AMS starts, and he finished in the top five in 4 of the remaining 9 races. After starting fourth, Labonte led nine times for 172 of the 325 laps, including the last 11 after he passed Jeff Gordon. He also led laps 21–36, 56–57, 69–118, 121–136, 138–175, 177–185, and 41 of the final 44 in one of the year's most dominating performances. Except for Jimmie Johnson, who blew an engine with 17 laps remaining en route to a 32nd-place finish, every lap leader finished among the top 10. Pole-sitter Ryan Newman led the first 20 laps and one other, but he was a lap down in 10th place at the finish. After a total of only two blown engines in the first three races, there were nine at AMS, a track where engines turn high RPMs almost from start to finish. Matt Kenseth finished fourth to take the overall point lead (by 49 points) over defending Winston Cup champion Tony Stewart.

Bass Pro Shops/MBNA 500

Time of Race: 3 hours, 25 minutes, 37 seconds
Average Speed: 146.048 mph
Margin of Victory: 1.274 seconds

FINISH	DRIVER	CAR
1.	Bobby Labonte	Chevrolet
2.	Jeff Gordon	Chevrolet
3.	Dale Earnhardt Jr.	Chevrolet
4.	Matt Kenseth	Ford
5.	Tony Stewart	Chevrolet
6.	Elliott Sadler	Ford
7.	Jimmy Spencer	Dodge
8.	Dave Blaney	Ford
9.	Joe Nemechek	Chevrolet
10.	Ryan Newman	Dodge
11.	Johnny Benson	Pontiac
12.	Ricky Craven	Pontiac
13.	Greg Biffle	Ford
14.	Sterling Marlin	Dodge
15.	Rusty Wallace	Dodge
16.	Steve Park	Chevrolet
17.	Robby Gordon	Chevrolet
18.	Ward Burton	Dodge
19.	Kevin Harvick	Chevrolet
20.	Terry Labonte	Chevrolet
21.	Dale Jarrett	Ford
22.	Jeremy Mayfield	Dodge
23.	Casey Mears	Dodge
24.	Tony Raines	Chevrolet
25.	Jeff Green	Chevrolet
26.	Kenny Wallace	Dodge
27.	Michael Waltrip	Chevrolet
28.	Todd Bodine	Ford
29.	John Andretti	Dodge
30.	Mike Skinner	Pontiac
31.	Jerry Nadeau	Pontiac
32.	Jimmie Johnson	Chevrolet
33.	Jeff Burton	Ford
34.	Kyle Petty	Dodge
35.	Ricky Rudd	Ford
36.	Jamie McMurray	Dodge
37.	Jack Sprague	Pontiac
38.	Ken Schrader	Dodge
39.	Bill Elliott	Dodge
40.	Kurt Busch	Ford
41.	Brett Bodine	Ford
42.	Mark Martin	Ford
43.	Larry Foyt	Dodge

RACE 5—CAROLINA DODGE DEALERS 400

Darlington Raceway
Darlington, South Carolina
March 16
Pole winner: Elliott Sadler (170.147 mph)
Race winner: Ricky Craven (126.214 mph)

Two-thousandths of a second—or 0.002 for you number gurus. That was the slim margin of victory in Ricky Craven's memorable win over Kurt Busch at legendary Darlington. Their cars were locked together door-to-door as they roared across the finish line—talk about trading paint! It turned out to be the closest finish since electronic timing and scoring were introduced in the Winston Cup series, beating the previous best of 0.005, which was set by Dale Earnhardt over Ernie Irvan at Talladega in July 1993. For the final three laps at Darlington, Craven attempted to pass Busch but was unable to nudge ahead of him until just before the finish line. "It's the most fun I've ever had in my life," Craven said after the record finish. In other highlights, Dave Blaney finished a career-high third, while Matt Kenseth, who had taken over the points lead after the Atlanta race, was eighth. Kenseth increased his overall lead over runner-up Tony Stewart to 57 points. Pole-sitter Elliott Sadler finished seventh.

Carolina Dodge Dealers 400

Time of Race: 3 hours, 10 minutes, 16 seconds
Average Speed: 126.214 mph
Margin of Victory: .002 seconds

FINISH	DRIVER	CAR
1.	Ricky Craven	Pontiac
2.	Kurt Busch	Ford
3.	Dave Blaney	Ford
4.	Mark Martin	Ford
5.	Michael Waltrip	Chevrolet
6.	Dale Earnhardt Jr.	Chevrolet
7.	Elliott Sadler	Ford
8.	Matt Kenseth	Ford
9.	Bill Elliott	Dodge
10.	Tony Stewart	Chevrolet
11.	Mike Skinner	Pontiac
12.	Greg Biffle	Ford
13.	Joe Nemechek	Chevrolet
14.	Ryan Newman	Dodge
15.	Ricky Rudd	Ford
16.	Rusty Wallace	Dodge

Even though they just crossed the finish line, Kurt Busch (right, near wall) and Ricky Craven continue to bang into each other after one of the most exciting races in NASCAR history. The two were locked together as they came to the finish line, and it took the sophisticated electronic timing equiptment and a photo finish to determine that Craven had won the race by two-thousandths (0.002) of a second.

17.	Ken Schrader	Dodge
18.	Dale Jarrett	Ford
19.	Jeff Green	Chevrolet
20.	Jimmy Spencer	Dodge
21.	Steve Park	Chevrolet
22.	Jamie McMurray	Dodge
23.	Kenny Wallace	Dodge
24.	Terry Labonte	Chevrolet
25.	Johnny Benson	Pontiac
26.	Jimmie Johnson	Chevrolet
27.	Kyle Petty	Dodge
28.	Robby Gordon	Chevrolet
29.	Ward Burton	Dodge
30.	Jeremy Mayfield	Dodge
31.	Brett Bodine	Ford
32.	Larry Foyt	Dodge
33.	Jeff Gordon	Chevrolet
34.	Casey Mears	Dodge
35.	Jerry Nadeau	Pontiac
36.	Kevin Harvick	Chevrolet
37.	Bobby Labonte	Chevrolet
38.	John Andretti	Dodge
39.	Sterling Marlin	Dodge
40.	Jack Sprague	Pontiac
41.	Tony Raines	Chevrolet
42.	Jeff Burton	Ford
43.	Todd Bodine	Ford

RACE 6—FOOD CITY 500

Bristol Motor Speedway
Bristol, Tennessee
March 23
Pole winner: Ryan Newman (128.709 mph)
Race winner: Kurt Busch (76.185 mph)

Kurt Busch backed up his 2002 victory at Bristol with another strong run in the year's first short-track race. He qualified ninth, dropped back early, then ran top 10 most of the afternoon. Busch led twice for 116 laps—from 359 to 377 and 404 to 500—beating series leader Matt Kenseth by a fraction of a second in a race slowed 17 times for 121 laps. Kyle Petty was among two dozen drivers who spun or crashed, and he was examined and released from a local hospital after a vicious late-race crash in turn 1. Only seven drivers shared the lead, swapping it 11 times. Ironically, pole-winner Ryan Newman wasn't among them, but number two starter Jeff Gordon led all drivers with 174 laps in front. On lap 422, Busch was able to make his final pit stop on a caution when Petty's crash occurred just before Busch was ready to go in. Leading at the time, Busch was able to cruise to victory after he returned to the track. The win allowed Busch to surge into second-place in the overall standings, 138 points behind Kenseth, who finished second in the race.

Food City 500

Time of Race: 3 hours, 29 minutes, 53 seconds
Average Speed: 76.185 mph
Margin of Victory: 0.390 seconds

FINISH	DRIVER	CAR
1.	Kurt Busch	Ford
2.	Matt Kenseth	Ford
3.	Bobby Labonte	Chevrolet
4.	Ricky Rudd	Ford
5.	Greg Biffle	Ford
6.	Sterling Marlin	Dodge
7.	Kevin Harvick	Chevrolet
8.	Jimmie Johnson	Chevrolet
9.	Jeff Gordon	Chevrolet
10.	Kenny Wallace	Dodge
11.	Jamie McMurray	Dodge
12.	Jimmy Spencer	Dodge
13.	Rusty Wallace	Dodge
14.	Jeff Burton	Ford
15.	Ricky Craven	Pontiac
16.	Dale Earnhardt Jr.	Chevrolet
17.	Robby Gordon	Chevrolet
18.	Bill Elliott	Dodge
19.	Johnny Benson	Pontiac
20.	Jeff Green	Chevrolet
21.	Elliott Sadler	Ford
22.	Ryan Newman	Dodge
23.	Jeremy Mayfield	Dodge
24.	Brett Bodine	Ford
25.	Tony Stewart	Chevrolet
26.	Michael Waltrip	Chevrolet
27.	Joe Nemechek	Chevrolet
28.	Jerry Nadeau	Pontiac
29.	Mark Martin	Ford
30.	Steve Park	Chevrolet
31.	John Andretti	Dodge
32.	Ward Burton	Dodge
33.	Kyle Petty	Dodge
34.	Casey Mears	Dodge
35.	Jack Sprague	Pontiac
36.	Dale Jarrett	Ford
37.	Ken Schrader	Dodge
38.	Dave Blaney	Ford
39.	Terry Labonte	Chevrolet
40.	Todd Bodine	Ford
41.	Mike Skinner	Pontiac
42.	Tony Raines	Chevrolet
43.	Derrike Cope	Chevrolet

RACE 7—SAMSUNG/RADIO SHACK 500

Texas Motor Speedway
Fort Worth, Texas
March 30
Pole winner: Bobby Labonte (193.514 mph)
Race winner: Ryan Newman (134.517 mph)

It took a few races until Ryan Newman's crew figured out their new Dodge, but once they did, good things started to happen in a hurry. Newman's team believed that it could have already won a couple of the early races, but strategy errors and mediocre pits stops had kept that from happening. Finally, at Texas, everything worked and Newman cruised to victory. On lap 324 of the 334-lap race, Newman passed Dale Earnhardt Jr. to take a lead he held until the checkered flag. Earlier, Newman led from lap 224 until a caution period that began on lap 283. During the pit stop on that yellow flag, Newman's crew changed just right-side tires while Earnhardt Jr. took four new tires. Newman and his crew chief, Matt Borland, wanted to hold their track position, and the gamble paid off, as Newman was first out of the pits. The victory was the first in what would develop into an outstanding season for Newman. Earnhardt Jr. was runner-up, 3.405 seconds back. Jeff Gordon finished third. Points leader Matt Kenseth's sixth place finish gave him a 155-point advantage over Kurt Busch; Kenseth led 65 laps.

Samsung/Radio Shack 500

Time of Race: 3 hours, 43 minutes, 28 seconds
Average Speed: 134.517 mph
Margin of Victory: 3.405 seconds

FINISH	DRIVER	CAR
1.	Ryan Newman	Dodge
2.	Dale Earnhardt Jr.	Chevrolet
3.	Jeff Gordon	Chevrolet
4.	Jerry Nadeau	Pontiac
5.	Mark Martin	Ford
6.	Matt Kenseth	Ford
7.	Jeff Green	Chevrolet
8.	Jimmie Johnson	Chevrolet
9.	Kurt Busch	Ford
10.	Jamie McMurray	Dodge
11.	Todd Bodine	Ford
12.	Ward Burton	Dodge
13.	Dale Jarrett	Ford
14.	Rusty Wallace	Dodge
15.	Kevin Harvick	Chevrolet
16.	Terry Labonte	Chevrolet
17.	Michael Waltrip	Chevrolet
18.	Robby Gordon	Chevrolet
19.	John Andretti	Dodge
20.	Jeff Burton	Ford
21.	Ricky Craven	Pontiac
22.	Jack Sprague	Pontiac

Joe Nemechek's day comes to an end in the MBNA America 400 at Dover International Speedway on September 21 after a crash knocked him out of the race in lap 78.

23.	Kenny Wallace	Dodge
24.	Ken Schrader	Dodge
25.	Jeremy Mayfield	Dodge
26.	Ricky Rudd	Ford
27.	Casey Mears	Dodge
28.	Greg Biffle	Ford
29.	Sterling Marlin	Dodge
30.	Larry Foyt	Dodge
31.	Brett Bodine	Ford
32.	Johnny Benson	Pontiac
33.	Jimmy Spencer	Dodge
34.	Tony Stewart	Chevrolet
35.	Joe Nemechek	Chevrolet
36.	Dave Blaney	Ford
37.	Bobby Labonte	Chevrolet
38.	Christian Fittipaldi	Dodge
39.	Steve Park	Chevrolet
40.	Mike Skinner	Pontiac
41.	Elliott Sadler	Ford
42.	Tony Raines	Chevrolet
43.	Bill Elliott	Dodge

RACE 8—AARON'S 499

Talladega Superspeedway
Talladega, Alabama

April 6
Pole winner: Jeremy Mayfield (186.489 mph)
Race winner: Dale Earnhardt Jr. (144.625 mph)

Fair pass or illegal move that the officials excused? That was the question after Dale Earnhardt Jr. got his fourth consecutive Talladega victory with a late-race pass in the year's second restrictor-plate race. He led nine times for 34 of 188 laps, including the final two. "Junior's" longest lap-led streak was just 10, from lap 144 to 154. His controversial maneuver came on lap 186 when he passed several cars by sweeping low in turn 3. Replays showed that during the pass, the left side of his car dipped below the yellow line at the bottom of the track, which is illegal. However, officials did not penalize Earnhardt Jr. because they felt he was forced down below the line, which is not illegal. Other drivers and crews disagreed, claiming that Earnhardt Jr. received the favorable no-call because of who he is (son of late star Dale Sr.). The judges weren't swayed, and the victory stood. The race was slowed by cautions 6 times for 32 laps, and 16 drivers swapped the lead 43 times. Jimmie Johnson led the most, 10 times for 65 laps, but he slipped to 15th after a 360-degree spin on the next-to-last lap nearly took him all the way off the lead lap. A ninth-place finish was good enough for Matt Kenseth to build his overall lead to 129 points over Earnhardt Jr.

Aaron's 499

Time of Race: 3 hours, 27 minutes, 28 seconds
Average Speed: 144.625 mph
Margin of Victory: .125 seconds

FINISH	DRIVER	CAR
1.	Dale Earnhardt Jr.	Chevrolet
2.	Kevin Harvick	Chevrolet
3.	Elliott Sadler	Ford
4.	Ricky Craven	Pontiac
5.	Terry Labonte	Chevrolet
6.	Sterling Marlin	Dodge
7.	Ward Burton	Dodge
8.	Jeff Gordon	Chevrolet
9.	Matt Kenseth	Ford
10.	Robby Gordon	Chevrolet
11.	Kyle Petty	Dodge
12.	Dale Jarrett	Ford
13.	Bill Elliott	Dodge
14.	John Andretti	Dodge
15.	Jimmie Johnson	Chevrolet
16.	Tony Raines	Chevrolet
17.	Kenny Wallace	Dodge
18.	Jeremy Mayfield	Dodge
19.	Kurt Busch	Ford
20.	Steve Park	Chevrolet
21.	Joe Nemechek	Chevrolet
22.	Greg Biffle	Ford
23.	Dave Blaney	Ford
24.	Michael Waltrip	Chevrolet
25.	Tony Stewart	Chevrolet
26.	Mark Martin	Ford
27.	Jamie McMurray	Dodge
28.	Todd Bodine	Ford
29.	Jeff Green	Chevrolet
30.	Mike Wallace	Dodge
31.	Mike Skinner	Pontiac
32.	Bobby Labonte	Chevrolet
33.	Ken Schrader	Dodge
34.	Jack Sprague	Pontiac
35.	Jeff Burton	Ford
36.	Jerry Nadeau	Pontiac
37.	Rusty Wallace	Dodge
38.	Jimmy Spencer	Dodge
39.	Ryan Newman	Dodge
40.	Casey Mears	Dodge
41.	Johnny Benson	Pontiac
42.	Ricky Rudd	Ford
43.	Hermie Sadler	Chevrolet

RACE 9—VIRGINIA 500

Martinsville Speedway
Martinsville, Virginia
April 13

Pole winner: Jeff Gordon (94.307 mph)
Race winner: Jeff Gordon (75.557 mph)

"That was hard racing: that was good clean fun," Bobby Labonte said after his runner-up finish to Jeff Gordon. On lap 487 of the 500-lap event, Gordon bumped Labonte and passed him on the inside on his way to his first victory of the season. Afterward, Labonte visited Gordon in victory lane—to offer congratulations, not a right to the jaw (which sometimes happens after a close race!). Prior to the decisive pass, Gordon and Labonte raced together ahead of the pack. On lap 475, Gordon tapped Labonte, but it took 12 more laps before Gordon was able to repeat the move and finally pass Labonte. Earlier in the season, the same two drivers had dueled down the stretch at Atlanta, with Labonte coming out on top that time. The Martinsville race ended under caution after Kurt Busch spun out on the next-to-last lap. Matt Kenseth finished in 22nd place, which allowed Dale Earnhardt Jr. to trim Kenseth's series lead to 51.

Virginia 500

Time of Race: 3 hours, 28 minutes, 51 seconds
Average Speed: 75.557 mph
Margin of Victory: Under caution

FINISH	DRIVER	CAR
1.	Jeff Gordon	Chevrolet
2.	Bobby Labonte	Chevrolet
3.	Dale Earnhardt Jr.	Chevrolet
4.	Jeff Burton	Ford
5.	Elliott Sadler	Ford
6.	Tony Stewart	Chevrolet
7.	Sterling Marlin	Dodge
8.	Rusty Wallace	Dodge
9.	Jimmie Johnson	Chevrolet
10.	Ken Schrader	Dodge
11.	Ricky Rudd	Ford
12.	Kenny Wallace	Dodge
13.	Bill Elliott	Dodge
14.	Terry Labonte	Chevrolet
15.	Joe Nemechek	Chevrolet
16.	Kevin Harvick	Chevrolet
17.	Mark Martin	Ford
18.	Greg Biffle	Ford
19.	Jimmy Spencer	Dodge
20.	Dale Jarrett	Ford
21.	Robby Gordon	Chevrolet
22.	Matt Kenseth	Ford
23.	Michael Waltrip	Chevrolet
24.	Steve Park	Chevrolet
25.	Ward Burton	Dodge
26.	Jeff Green	Chevrolet
27.	Ricky Craven	Pontiac
28.	Kurt Busch	Ford
29.	Jack Sprague	Pontiac
30.	John Andretti	Dodge
31.	Dave Blaney	Ford
32.	Johnny Benson	Pontiac
33.	Tony Raines	Chevrolet
34.	Kyle Petty	Dodge
35.	Mike Skinner	Pontiac

FINISH	DRIVER	CAR
36.	Casey Mears	Dodge
37.	Todd Bodine	Ford
38.	Ryan Newman	Dodge
39.	Jamie McMurray	Dodge
40.	Jeremy Mayfield	Dodge
41.	Jerry Nadeau	Pontiac
42.	Derrike Cope	Chevrolet
43.	Hermie Sadler	Chevrolet

RACE 10—AUTO CLUB 500

California Speedway
Fontana, California
April 27
Pole winner: Steve Park (186.838 mph)
Race winner: Kurt Busch (140.111 mph)

Kurt Busch didn't lead often or for many laps, but he still earned his second victory of the season for Roush Racing. After starting 16th, the Bristol winner led only twice for 27 of 250 laps—laps 131–145 and 239–250. He passed leader Jamie McMurray on lap 239 and then pulled away the rest of the way for a winning margin of 2.294 seconds. It was Busch's sixth career Cup victory, his first in a full 500-mile race. Each of the top-five finishers led laps, as did Cup leader Matt Kenseth, Dave Blaney, Ricky Craven, and Tony Stewart. Pole-winner Steve Park and number four starter Ryan Newman wrecked on the first lap, then Larry Foyt, Dale Jarrett, Johnny Benson, and Jeremy Mayfield crashed near the halfway point and called it a day. Stewart led three times for 100 laps, more than any other driver, but dropped out near the race's midpoint with a blown engine. Kenseth's ninth-place finish (plus five bonus points for leading two laps) kept him in first place in the points race, although his lead over Dale Earnhardt Jr. slipped to only 44 points.

Auto Club 500

Time of Race: 3 hours, 34 minutes, 07 seconds
Average Speed: 140.111 mph
Margin of Victory: 2.294 seconds

FINISH	DRIVER	CAR
1.	Kurt Busch	Ford
2.	Bobby Labonte	Chevrolet
3.	Rusty Wallace	Dodge
4.	Bill Elliott	Dodge
5.	Jamie McMurray	Dodge
6.	Dale Earnhardt Jr.	Chevrolet
7.	Michael Waltrip	Chevrolet
8.	John Andretti	Dodge
9.	Sterling Marlin	Dodge
10.	Matt Kenseth	Ford
11.	Jeff Gordon	Chevrolet
12.	Terry Labonte	Chevrolet
13.	Dave Blaney	Ford
14.	Jerry Nadeau	Pontiac
15.	Ricky Craven	Pontiac
16.	Jimmie Johnson	Chevrolet
17.	Mark Martin	Ford
18.	Greg Biffle	Ford
19.	Jeff Burton	Ford
20.	Mike Skinner	Pontiac
21.	Ward Burton	Dodge
22.	Kenny Wallace	Dodge
23.	Elliott Sadler	Ford
24.	Ricky Rudd	Ford
25.	Todd Bodine	Ford
26.	Jeff Green	Chevrolet
27.	Robby Gordon	Chevrolet
28.	Kyle Petty	Dodge
29.	Kevin Harvick	Chevrolet
30.	Ken Schrader	Dodge
31.	Tony Raines	Chevrolet
32.	Joe Nemechek	Chevrolet
33.	Jimmy Spencer	Dodge
34.	Casey Mears	Dodge
35.	Jeremy Mayfield	Dodge
36.	Johnny Benson	Pontiac
37.	Dale Jarrett	Ford
38.	Larry Foyt	Dodge
39.	Jack Sprague	Pontiac
40.	Steve Park	Chevrolet
41.	Tony Stewart	Chevrolet
42.	Ryan Newman	Dodge
43.	Derrike Cope	Chevrolet

RACE 11—PONTIAC EXCITEMENT 400

Richmond International Raceway
Richmond, Virginia
May 3
Pole winner: Terry Labonte (126.511 mph)
Race winner: Joe Nemechek (86.783 mph)

Joe Nemechek made his third Winston Cup victory a memorable one by overcoming a mistake regarding a crucial pit stop. After starting second, Nemechek led 91 of the first 228 laps. When the leaders pitted during a caution period on lap 226, Nemechek was speaking with crew chief Peter Sospenzo and missed the entrance to pit road. Forced to pit out of sequence, Nemechek dropped back in the field. Furious at the blunder, Nemechek aggressively worked his way back to the front of the pack, passing Robby Gordon for the lead on lap 331. When rain began falling with seven laps to go, the race was put under a final caution, giving Nemechek the hard-earned victory. Points leader Matt Kenseth saw his overall lead continue to disappear, as his seventh-place finish in the race allowed Dale Earnhardt Jr. (third in the race) to cut the margin to a mere 20 points. The racing community at Richmond was concerned for Jerry Nadeau, who was seriously injured in a practice-run accident the day before the race. Nadeau faced a long rehabilitation after his accident, but he is hoping to race again in 2004.

Bill Elliott (No. 9) pulls ahead of Kenny Wallace (No. 23) during the MBNA America 400 at Dover International Speedway.

Pontiac Excitement 400

Time of Race: 3 hours, 23 minutes, 47 seconds
Average Speed: 86.783 mph
Margin of Victory: Under caution

FINISH	DRIVER	CAR
1.	Joe Nemechek	Chevrolet
2.	Bobby Labonte	Chevrolet
3.	Dale Earnhardt Jr.	Chevrolet
4.	Robby Gordon	Chevrolet
5.	Mark Martin	Ford
6.	Kevin Harvick	Chevrolet
7.	Matt Kenseth	Ford
8.	Kurt Busch	Ford
9.	Jeff Burton	Ford
10.	Rusty Wallace	Dodge
11.	Ward Burton	Dodge
12.	Michael Waltrip	Chevrolet
13.	Sterling Marlin	Dodge
14.	Johnny Benson	Pontiac
15.	Tony Raines	Chevrolet
16.	Greg Biffle	Ford
17.	Jeff Gordon	Chevrolet
18.	Dave Blaney	Ford
19.	Jimmie Johnson	Chevrolet
20.	Bill Elliott	Dodge
21.	Terry Labonte	Chevrolet
22.	Todd Bodine	Ford
23.	Jamie McMurray	Dodge
24.	Ken Schrader	Dodge
25.	Jeremy Mayfield	Dodge
26.	Jack Sprague	Pontiac
27.	Kenny Wallace	Dodge
28.	Kyle Petty	Dodge
29.	Casey Mears	Dodge
30.	John Andretti	Dodge
31.	Brett Bodine	Ford
32.	Jason Keller	Pontiac
33.	Larry Foyt	Dodge
34.	Ricky Rudd	Ford
35.	Mike Skinner	Pontiac
36.	Dale Jarrett	Ford
37.	Elliott Sadler	Ford
38.	Ricky Craven	Pontiac
39.	Ryan Newman	Dodge
40.	Jeff Green	Chevrolet
41.	Tony Stewart	Chevrolet
42.	Jimmy Spencer	Dodge
43.	Steve Park	Chevrolet

RACE 12—COCA-COLA 600

Lowe's Motor Speedway
Concord, North Carolina
May 25
Pole winner: Ryan Newman (185.312 mph)
Race winner: Jimmie Johnson (126.198 mph)

The year's second rain-shortened race went to Jimmie Johnson, who led only twice but still managed to earn his first 2003 victory. He led laps 242 to 264, yielded to Bobby Labonte for 265, then led again from 266 to 276. That was all it took—scheduled for 400 laps (600 miles), the race was stopped after lap 276 (414 miles) and Johnson declared the winner. Even though the race was shortened, it was an impressive win for Johnson, as he started 43rd (last) after a prerace engine change. He was briefly lapped, but well-timed caution periods and quicker pit stops by his crew gave him the lead at lap 242. A short pit stop on lap 265 cost Johnson the lead, but only briefly. A caution flag on the next lap allowed him to make a very quick pit stop while all the other drivers were taking longer pit stops (since they hadn't pitted just one lap earlier like Johnson). The faster stop under caution allowed him to get back on the track in first place, a spot he never gave up over the race's last 10 laps. Eight drivers led: Johnson, Matt Kenseth, Labonte, pole-winner Ryan Newman, Kevin Harvick, Kurt Busch, Elliott Sadler, and Tony Stewart. The race was first stopped for rain around lap 104, and when rain hit for the second time on lap 276 at 9:30 p.m., NASCAR quickly called the race because it was past the halfway point and more rain was on the way; many fans felt NASCAR should have waited more than a few minutes before making the call to end the race. Series leader Matt Kenseth led the most—four times for 82 laps—en route to a second-place finish that built his advantage over Dale Earnhardt Jr. to 160 points.

Coca-Cola 600

Time of Race: 3 hours, 16 minutes, 50 seconds

Average Speed: 126.198 mph
Margin of Victory: Under caution

FINISH	DRIVER	CAR
1.	Jimmie Johnson	Chevrolet
2.	Matt Kenseth	Ford
3.	Bobby Labonte	Chevrolet
4.	Jimmy Spencer	Dodge
5.	Ryan Newman	Dodge
6.	Michael Waltrip	Chevrolet
7.	Sterling Marlin	Dodge
8.	Jeff Gordon	Chevrolet
9.	Dale Jarrett	Ford
10.	Ward Burton	Dodge
11.	Joe Nemechek	Chevrolet
12.	Rusty Wallace	Dodge
13.	Kevin Harvick	Chevrolet
14.	Dave Blaney	Ford
15.	Kurt Busch	Ford
16.	Greg Biffle	Ford
17.	Robby Gordon	Chevrolet
18.	Jeff Burton	Ford
19.	Jeff Green	Chevrolet
20.	Mike Skinner	Pontiac
21.	Terry Labonte	Chevrolet
22.	Jack Sprague	Pontiac
23.	Todd Bodine	Ford
24.	Johnny Benson	Pontiac
25.	Jamie McMurray	Dodge
26.	Bill Elliott	Dodge
27.	Steve Park	Chevrolet
28.	Ken Schrader	Dodge
29.	Mark Martin	Ford
30.	Kyle Petty	Dodge
31.	Mike Wallace	Pontiac
32.	Kevin Lepage	Ford
33.	Ricky Rudd	Ford
34.	Larry Foyt	Dodge
35.	Casey Mears	Dodge
36.	Elliott Sadler	Ford
37.	Tony Raines	Chevrolet
38.	Ricky Craven	Pontiac
39.	John Andretti	Dodge
40.	Tony Stewart	Chevrolet
41.	Dale Earnhardt Jr.	Chevrolet
42.	Kenny Wallace	Dodge
43.	Jeremy Mayfield	Dodge

RACE 13—MBNA ARMED FORCES FAMILY 400

Dover International Speedway
Dover, Delaware
June 1
Pole winner: Ryan Newman (158.716 mph)
Race winner: Ryan Newman (106.896 mph)

Lack of power steering didn't prevent Ryan Newman from collecting his second victory of the season. Newman moved to the front on lap 328 of the 400-lap race and led all but three of the remaining laps; in total, he led 162 laps. He won by 0.834 of a second over Jeff Gordon. On a restart with six laps to go, Gordon had his chance to seize the lead, but Newman blocked the four-time Cup champion and stayed in front until the end. If the race had lasted 10 more laps, Tony Stewart may have overtaken Newman, as Stewart was closing fast and had the faster car. However, Stewart had earlier been penalized a lap for pitting just outside his stall, and he could do no better than fourth before he ran out of laps. Stewart was upset with Newman for not giving him his lap back—while leading, Newman could have slowed down slightly and let Stewart pass him to get back on the lead lap, but he did not. Bobby Labonte finished third to gain his fifth consecutive top-five finish (three seconds, two thirds). Following the race, Matt Kenseth (seventh place) was 171 points ahead of Dale Earnhardt Jr. (ninth place) in the season standings.

MBNA Armed Forces Family 400

Time of Race: 3 hours, 44 minutes, 31 seconds
Average Speed: 106.896 mph
Margin of Victory: 0.834 seconds

FINISH	DRIVER	CAR
1.	Ryan Newman	Dodge
2.	Jeff Gordon	Chevrolet
3.	Bobby Labonte	Chevrolet
4.	Tony Stewart	Chevrolet
5.	Johnny Benson	Pontiac
6.	Rusty Wallace	Dodge
7.	Matt Kenseth	Ford
8.	Ricky Craven	Pontiac
9.	Dale Earnhardt Jr.	Chevrolet
10.	Robby Gordon	Chevrolet
11.	Terry Labonte	Chevrolet
12.	Todd Bodine	Ford
13.	Jamie McMurray	Dodge
14.	Jeff Burton	Ford
15.	Kurt Busch	Ford
16.	Michael Waltrip	Chevrolet
17.	Ricky Rudd	Ford
18.	Mark Martin	Ford
19.	Mike Wallace	Pontiac
20.	Dave Blaney	Ford
21.	Jeremy Mayfield	Dodge
22.	Bill Elliott	Dodge
23.	Kenny Wallace	Dodge
24.	Joe Nemechek	Chevrolet
25.	Jeff Green	Chevrolet
26.	Ken Schrader	Dodge
27.	Kevin Harvick	Chevrolet
28.	Larry Foyt	Dodge
29.	Jimmy Spencer	Dodge
30.	Greg Biffle	Ford
31.	Tony Raines	Chevrolet
32.	Steve Park	Chevrolet
33.	Elliott Sadler	Ford
34.	John Andretti	Dodge
35.	Sterling Marlin	Dodge
36.	Mike Skinner	Pontiac
37.	Ward Burton	Dodge
38.	Jimmie Johnson	Chevrolet
39.	Dale Jarrett	Ford
40.	Casey Mears	Dodge
41.	Jack Sprague	Pontiac
42.	Brett Bodine	Ford
43.	Kyle Petty	Dodge

RACE 14—POCONO 500

Pocono Speedway
Pocono, Pennsylvania
June 8
Pole winner: Jimmie Johnson (170.645 mph)
Race winner: Tony Stewart (134.892 mph)

It took defending Winston Cup champion Tony Stewart 14 starts to get his first victory of the 2003 season. He started fourth, led five times for 37 laps and was ahead when the 200-lap, 500-mile race went under caution for the fifth and final time. That final yellow flag occurred after a late-race accident involving Kurt Busch, Mike Skinner, and Jeff Green. It was Stewart's 16th career victory, but his first in a 500-mile race that went the full distance. His other 15 victories all came on short tracks or road courses, in 300- or 400-mile races, and in the rain-shortened 500-mile race in November 2002 at Atlanta Motor Speedway. Stewart led laps 54–55, 90–91, and 126–127 by being in the right place when other drivers took pit stops, then led laps 156–175 and finally 190–200 on his own merits. He was among 16 drivers (including the top nine finishers) who swapped the lead 28 times. Sterling Marlin led the most, twice for 44 laps, showing just how competitive the race was. Nineteen drivers finished on the lead lap and 11 more were only one lap down.

Pocono 500:

Time of Race: 3 hours, 42 minutes, 24 seconds.
Average Speed: 134.892 mph
Margin of Victory: Under caution

FINISH	DRIVER	CAR
1.	Tony Stewart	Chevrolet
2.	Mark Martin	Ford
3.	Matt Kenseth	Ford
4.	Dale Earnhardt Jr.	Chevrolet
5.	Ryan Newman	Dodge
6.	Sterling Marlin	Dodge
7.	Terry Labonte	Chevrolet
8.	Ward Burton	Dodge
9.	Elliott Sadler	Ford
10.	Ricky Craven	Pontiac
11.	Todd Bodine	Ford
12.	Jimmie Johnson	Chevrolet
13.	Jeff Gordon	Chevrolet
14.	Jeff Burton	Ford
15.	Jeremy Mayfield	Dodge
16.	Rusty Wallace	Dodge
17.	Bobby Labonte	Chevrolet
18.	Michael Waltrip	Chevrolet
19.	Bill Elliott	Dodge
20.	Greg Biffle	Ford
21.	Casey Mears	Dodge
22.	Jack Sprague	Pontiac
23.	John Andretti	Dodge
24.	Kevin Harvick	Chevrolet
25.	Johnny Benson	Pontiac
26.	Dave Blaney	Ford
27.	Kyle Petty	Dodge
28.	Robby Gordon	Chevrolet
29.	Kenny Wallace	Dodge
30.	Tony Raines	Chevrolet
31.	Mike Wallace	Pontiac
32.	Jamie McMurray	Dodge
33.	Jeff Green	Chevrolet
34.	Mike Skinner	Pontiac
35.	Steve Park	Chevrolet
36.	Kurt Busch	Ford
37.	Ricky Rudd	Ford
38.	Joe Nemechek	Chevrolet
39.	Jimmy Spencer	Dodge
40.	Casey Atwood	Dodge
41.	Larry Foyt	Dodge
42.	Dale Jarrett	Ford
43.	Ken Schrader	Dodge

RACE 15—SIRIUS SATELLITE RADIO 400

Michigan International Speedway
Brooklyn, Michigan
June 15
Pole winner: Bobby Labonte (190.365 mph)
Race winner: Kurt Busch (131.219 mph)

Kurt Busch gave Ford and Jack Roush something special to celebrate with Busch's third victory of the year. Ford Motor Company, in the midst of observing its 100th anniversary as a carmaker, had a special event planned for the day after the race at its Dearborn, Michigan, headquarters, which is approximately 90 miles from the track in Brooklyn. To add to the hometown feel, Roush's company is based in Livonia, Michigan, which is only a few minutes from Ford headquarters. Not only did Busch provide Roush, a former Ford employee, with his sixth win at Michigan International Speedway, but Roush teammates Matt Kenseth, Mark Martin, and Jeff Burton all placed in the race's top 11. All in all, it was a spectacular weekend of racing and celebration for both Ford and Roush. Busch won by 0.774 of a second over pole-sitter Bobby Labonte, who also held onto fourth place in the overall points chase. Busch gained the lead for the first time on lap 177 when he passed Jeff Gordon. Tony Stewart (eighth place) led 51 laps. Kenseth's fourth-place finish enabled him to increase his lead over Dale Earnhardt Jr. to 185 points.

Sirius Satellite Radio 400

Time of Race: 3 hours, 2 minutes, 54 seconds
Average Speed: 131.219 mph
Margin of Victory: 0.774 seconds

FINISH	DRIVER	CAR
1.	Kurt Busch	Ford
2.	Bobby Labonte	Chevrolet
3.	Jeff Gordon	Chevrolet
4.	Matt Kenseth	Ford
5.	Michael Waltrip	Chevrolet
6.	Sterling Marlin	Dodge
7.	Dale Earnhardt Jr.	Chevrolet

Ford Motor Company threw a huge party the weekend of the Sirius Satellite Radio 400 to celebrate its 100th year making automobiles. Here, fans at the company's Dearborn, Michigan, headquarters look at cars driven by Dave Blaney (front) and Ricky Rudd (rear) while the race is broadcast on the large screen in the background. The weekend got even better for Ford when Kurt Busch drove his Jack Roush-owned Ford to victory in the race.

8.	Tony Stewart	Chevrolet
9.	Mark Martin	Ford
10.	Terry Labonte	Chevrolet
11.	Jeff Burton	Ford
12.	Rusty Wallace	Dodge
13.	Jeremy Mayfield	Dodge
14.	Jamie McMurray	Dodge
15.	Ricky Craven	Pontiac
16.	Jimmie Johnson	Chevrolet
17.	Elliott Sadler	Ford
18.	Kevin Harvick	Chevrolet
19.	Jack Sprague	Pontiac
20.	Casey Mears	Dodge
21.	Joe Nemechek	Chevrolet
22.	Robby Gordon	Chevrolet
23.	Mike Wallace	Pontiac
24.	Bill Elliott	Dodge
25.	Kenny Wallace	Dodge
26.	Johnny Benson	Pontiac
27.	Steve Park	Chevrolet
28.	Jeff Green	Chevrolet
29.	Jimmy Spencer	Dodge
30.	Ward Burton	Dodge
31.	Greg Biffle	Ford
32.	Dale Jarrett	Ford

33.	Tony Raines	Chevrolet
34.	Kyle Petty	Dodge
35.	Christian Fittipaldi	Dodge
36.	Hermie Sadler	Chevrolet
37.	Todd Bodine	Ford
38.	Dave Blaney	Ford
39.	Geoffrey Bodine	Ford
40.	Derrike Cope	Chevrolet
41.	Ryan Newman	Dodge
42.	Ken Schrader	Dodge
43.	Ricky Rudd	Ford

RACE 16—DODGE/SAVE MART 350

Infineon Raceway
Sears Point, California
June 22
Pole winner: Boris Said (93.620 mph)
Race winner: Robby Gordon (73.821 mph)

The year's most one-sided race saw only six lead changes among four drivers. Pole-winner Boris Said led the first lap, race winner Robby Gordon led three times for 81 of 110 laps, road racer Ron Fellows twice for 21 laps, and Johnny Benson once for 7 laps. Gordon was stout, leading laps 2–30, 35–56, and 80–110 for his first victory of 2003 and the second of his career. His winning pass came as he and teammate Kevin Harvick approached the caution flag at lap 79. Instead of falling in line behind the leader, Gordon squeezed past Harvick to take the lead for good. Harvick later complained about the somewhat-unusual move, but it was perfectly legal. Several teams hired road racers specifically to drive in this race: Said in the No. 01 Pontiac, Fellows in the No. 1 Chevrolet, Johnny Miller in the No. 4 Pontiac, and Scott Pruett in the No. 09 Dodge. Said and Fellows finished 6th and 7th, respectively, Miller was 24th, and Pruett 34th. Despite finishing a lead-lap 14th, Matt Kenseth's overall series lead was cut to 174 points over Jeff Gordon, who finished second in the race.

Dodge/Save Mart 350

Time of Race: 2 hours, 57 minutes, 55 seconds
Average Speed: 73.821 mph
Margin of Victory: 0.553 seconds

FINISH	DRIVER	CAR
1.	Robby Gordon	Chevrolet
2.	Jeff Gordon	Chevrolet
3.	Kevin Harvick	Chevrolet
4.	Bill Elliott	Dodge
5.	Ryan Newman	Dodge
6.	Boris Said	Pontiac
7.	Ron Fellows	Chevrolet
8.	Rusty Wallace	Dodge
9.	Bobby Labonte	Chevrolet
10.	Jeremy Mayfield	Dodge
11.	Dale Earnhardt Jr.	Chevrolet
12.	Tony Stewart	Chevrolet
13.	Michael Waltrip	Chevrolet
14.	Matt Kenseth	Ford
15.	Ricky Rudd	Ford
16.	Ward Burton	Dodge
17.	Jimmie Johnson	Chevrolet
18.	Sterling Marlin	Dodge
19.	Mark Martin	Ford
20.	Jamie McMurray	Dodge
21.	Ricky Craven	Pontiac
22.	Elliott Sadler	Ford
23.	Todd Bodine	Ford
24.	Johnny Miller	Pontiac
25.	Terry Labonte	Chevrolet
26.	Casey Mears	Dodge
27.	Kyle Petty	Dodge
28.	Kurt Busch	Ford
29.	Kenny Wallace	Dodge
30.	Johnny Benson	Pontiac
31.	Tony Raines	Chevrolet
32.	Dave Blaney	Ford
33.	Ken Schrader	Dodge
34.	Scott Pruett	Dodge
35.	Joe Nemechek	Chevrolet
36.	Jimmy Spencer	Dodge
37.	Greg Biffle	Ford
38.	Jeff Burton	Ford
39.	Jack Sprague	Pontiac
40.	Christian Fittipaldi	Dodge
41.	Steve Park	Chevrolet
42.	Dale Jarrett	Ford
43.	Hideo Fukuyama	Ford

RACE 17—PEPSI 400

Daytona International Speedway
Daytona Beach, Florida
July 5
Pole winner: Steve Park (184.752 mph)
Race winner: Greg Biffle (166.109 mph)

"Surprised." That's how rookie Greg Biffle described himself after winning his first Winston Cup race. After all, if you're going to win your first Cup race, Daytona—in prime-time no less—is the place to do it. Biffle's 4.102-second victory over Roush Racing teammate Jeff Burton was achieved with subtle pit strategy. Biffle made a pit stop on lap 75 under caution, then returned two laps later to top off his fuel. The Vancouver, Washington, native thus had enough fuel to make just one more pit stop while most other drivers required two. Biffle, who only led the last 21 laps, was so overwhelmed at winning that he thought Matt Kenseth, another Roush teammate, had finished second. Kenseth actually was sixth, which allowed him to leave Daytona with a 180-point advantage over Dale Earnhardt Jr.

Pepsi 400

Time of Race: 2 hours, 24 minutes, 29 seconds
Average Speed: 166.109 mph
Margin of Victory: 4.102 seconds

FINISH	DRIVER	CAR
1.	Greg Biffle	Ford
2.	Jeff Burton	Ford
3.	Ricky Rudd	Ford
4.	Terry Labonte	Chevrolet
5.	Bobby Labonte	Chevrolet
6.	Matt Kenseth	Ford
7.	Dale Earnhardt Jr.	Chevrolet
8.	Jeremy Mayfield	Dodge
9.	Kevin Harvick	Chevrolet
10.	Dale Jarrett	Ford
11.	Michael Waltrip	Chevrolet
12.	Jimmy Spencer	Dodge
13.	Todd Bodine	Ford
14.	Jeff Gordon	Chevrolet
15.	Kenny Wallace	Dodge
16.	Bill Elliott	Dodge
17.	Buckshot Jones	Dodge
18.	Jimmie Johnson	Chevrolet
19.	Sterling Marlin	Dodge
20.	Mark Martin	Ford
21.	Tony Stewart	Chevrolet
22.	Ryan Newman	Dodge

With his crew celebrating in the foreground, Kevin Harvick burns out along the main straightaway after winning the Brickyard 400 at Indianapolis Motor Speedway. It was Harvick's first win of the year.

23.	Kyle Petty	Dodge
24.	Elliott Sadler	Ford
25.	Casey Mears	Dodge
26.	Mike Bliss	Chevrolet
27.	Johnny Benson	Pontiac
28.	Rusty Wallace	Dodge
29.	Jeff Green	Chevrolet
30.	Ward Burton	Dodge
31.	Jack Sprague	Pontiac
32.	David Green	Chevrolet
33.	Stacy Compton	Pontiac
34.	Larry Foyt	Dodge
35.	Dave Blaney	Ford
36.	Kurt Busch	Ford
37.	Jamie McMurray	Dodge
38.	Joe Nemechek	Chevrolet
39.	Steve Park	Chevrolet
40.	Robby Gordon	Chevrolet
41.	Ken Schrader	Dodge
42.	Mike Wallace	Pontiac
43.	Ricky Craven	Pontiac

RACE 18—TROPICANA 400

Chicagoland Speedway
Joliet, Illinois

July 13
Pole winner: Tony Stewart (184.786 mph)
Race winner: Ryan Newman (134.059 mph)

Ryan Newman, the year's winningest driver, got the third of his eight victories by leading 66 of the final 77 laps on the three-year-old track near Chicago. He started 14th, but quickly raced his way into the top 10. Two-time Chicagoland winner Kevin Harvick and pole-winner Tony Stewart ruled the first 127 laps before Jeff Gordon and Jimmie Johnson led 61 of the next 62. That's when Newman made his move, leading laps 190 to 198 before yielding to Johnson and Gordon for 11 laps, then regaining the lead for the final 58 laps. His margin of victory was 2.633 seconds over Stewart, who led three times for 80 laps (most of any driver). The race went under caution seven times for 36 of its 267 laps. Bobby Labonte took the day's scariest ride when his car backed hard into the turn 3 wall and burst into flames. Luckily, he was shaken but uninjured. Matt Kenseth finished one lap off the pace in 12th, the only time in the first 18 races he did not finish on the lead lap. Even with that lower-than-normal finish, his overall points lead still stood at 165 over Jeff Gordon.

Tropicana 400

Time of Race: 2 hours, 59 minutes, 15 seconds
Average Speed: 134.059 mph
Margin of Victory: 2.633 seconds

FINISH	DRIVER	CAR
1.	Ryan Newman	Dodge
2.	Tony Stewart	Chevrolet
3.	Jimmie Johnson	Chevrolet
4.	Jeff Gordon	Chevrolet
5.	Michael Waltrip	Chevrolet
6.	Jeff Burton	Ford
7.	Robby Gordon	Chevrolet
8.	Jamie McMurray	Dodge
9.	Elliott Sadler	Ford
10.	Jeremy Mayfield	Dodge
11.	Bill Elliott	Dodge
12.	Matt Kenseth	Ford
13.	Ricky Rudd	Ford
14.	Mark Martin	Ford
15.	Terry Labonte	Chevrolet
16.	Jeff Green	Chevrolet
17.	Kevin Harvick	Chevrolet
18.	Johnny Benson	Pontiac
19.	Ward Burton	Dodge
20.	Greg Biffle	Ford
21.	Sterling Marlin	Dodge
22.	Tony Raines	Chevrolet
23.	Jimmy Spencer	Dodge
24.	Kenny Wallace	Dodge
25.	Ricky Craven	Pontiac
26.	Steve Park	Chevrolet
27.	Kyle Petty	Dodge
28.	Ken Schrader	Dodge
29.	Christian Fittipaldi	Dodge
30.	Dale Jarrett	Ford
31.	Dave Blaney	Ford
32.	Rusty Wallace	Dodge
33.	Todd Bodine	Ford
34.	Casey Mears	Dodge
35.	Johnny Sauter	Pontiac
36.	Bobby Labonte	Chevrolet
37.	Mike Wallace	Pontiac
38.	Dale Earnhardt Jr.	Chevrolet
39.	Kurt Busch	Ford
40.	Jack Sprague	Pontiac
41.	Larry Foyt	Dodge
42.	Joe Nemechek	Chevrolet
43.	Derrike Cope	Chevrolet

RACE 19—NEW ENGLAND 300

New Hampshire International Speedway
Loudon, New Hampshire
July 20
Pole winner: Rained out; starting lineup determined by points standings
Race winner: Jimmie Johnson (96.924 mph)

Flat tracks like New Hampshire aren't Jimmie Johnson's specialty. As a result, winning the summer race at NHIS definitely gave him a feeling of accomplishment. Johnson credited his success to all the experience he had gained in his second full season in Winston Cup racing. After starting sixth, Johnson led laps 80 to 100. Later, he had to pass Kevin Harvick just before the last caution on lap 233 to temporarily regain the top spot. Finally, Johnson surged past leader Ryan Newman on lap 264 and then stayed in front for the final 37 laps, earning his second victory of the season. Jeff Gordon led the most laps in the race (133), but finished a disappointing 24th when fuel mileage problems and fading power in his Chevrolet pushed him back in the pack. A third-place finish boosted Matt Kenseth's points lead to a season-high 234 over Jeff Gordon.

New England 300

Time of Race: 3 hours, 16 minutes, 29 seconds
Average Speed: 96.924 mph
Margin of Victory: 1.582 seconds

FINISH	DRIVER	CAR
1.	Jimmie Johnson	Chevrolet
2.	Kevin Harvick	Chevrolet
3.	Matt Kenseth	Ford
4.	Ryan Newman	Dodge
5.	Robby Gordon	Chevrolet
6.	Dale Earnhardt Jr.	Chevrolet
7.	Dale Jarrett	Ford
8.	Steve Park	Chevrolet
9.	Jeff Burton	Ford
10.	Greg Biffle	Ford
11.	Kurt Busch	Ford
12.	Ricky Rudd	Ford
13.	Dave Blaney	Ford
14.	Bobby Labonte	Chevrolet
15.	Jimmy Spencer	Dodge
16.	Casey Mears	Dodge
17.	Rusty Wallace	Dodge
18.	Mark Martin	Ford
19.	Todd Bodine	Ford
20.	Terry Labonte	Chevrolet
21.	Ricky Craven	Pontiac
22.	Tony Stewart	Chevrolet
23.	Johnny Sauter	Pontiac
24.	Jeff Gordon	Chevrolet
25.	Ward Burton	Dodge
26.	Johnny Benson	Pontiac
27.	Elliott Sadler	Ford
28.	Michael Waltrip	Chevrolet
29.	Joe Nemechek	Chevrolet
30.	Jeff Green	Chevrolet
31.	Bill Elliott	Dodge
32.	Kyle Petty	Dodge
33.	Tony Raines	Chevrolet
34.	Jeremy Mayfield	Dodge
35.	Derrike Cope	Chevrolet
36.	Ken Schrader	Dodge
37.	Christian Fittipaldi	Dodge
38.	Kenny Wallace	Dodge
39.	Sterling Marlin	Dodge
40.	Jamie McMurray	Dodge
41.	John Andretti	Pontiac
42.	Mike Wallace	Pontiac
43.	Morgan Shepherd	Ford

RACE 20—PENNSYLVANIA 500

Pocono Raceway
Pocono, Pennsylvania
July 27
Pole winner: Ryan Newman (170.358 mph)
Race winner: Ryan Newman (127.705 mph)

Five mediocre to poor finishes early in the season and five more bad runs before midseason virtually ended Ryan Newman's championship hopes. But when he and his Penske South team did manage to finish a race, they generally finished very well. Newman's victory in the year's second Pocono race was his series-leading fourth, all in a span of 14 races. Even so, the 0.307-second victory left him mired in ninth place in the season points race, 614 behind leader (and one-race winner) Matt Kenseth. After winning his series-leading fifth pole, Newman led the first 31 laps and also laps 38 to 50. He regained the top spot on lap 157 and led the rest of the 200-lap race. His 88 laps in front were the most by any of the 11 drivers who led the race. The others were Kurt Busch, Dale Earnhardt Jr., Michael Waltrip, Jeff Burton, Rusty Wallace, Matt Kenseth, Johnny Benson, Jimmy Spencer, Casey Mears, and Tony Stewart (who won the June Pocono race). Kenseth led two early laps and finished a lead-lap 13th, which cut his series lead to 232 points over Earnhardt Jr.

Pennsylvania 500

Time of Race: 3 hours, 54 minutes, 55 seconds
Average Speed: 127.705 mph
Margin of Victory: 0.307 seconds

FINISH	DRIVER	CAR
1.	Ryan Newman	Dodge
2.	Kurt Busch	Ford
3.	Dale Earnhardt Jr.	Chevrolet
4.	Michael Waltrip	Chevrolet
5.	Terry Labonte	Chevrolet
6.	Jeff Burton	Ford
7.	Joe Nemechek	Chevrolet
8.	Todd Bodine	Ford
9.	Dave Blaney	Ford
10.	Sterling Marlin	Dodge
11.	Rusty Wallace	Dodge
12.	Kevin Harvick	Chevrolet
13.	Matt Kenseth	Ford
14.	Elliott Sadler	Ford
15.	Jimmie Johnson	Chevrolet
16.	Tony Raines	Chevrolet
17.	Bill Elliott	Dodge
18.	Robby Gordon	Chevrolet
19.	Ward Burton	Dodge
20.	Johnny Benson	Pontiac
21.	Dale Jarrett	Ford
22.	Jimmy Spencer	Dodge
23.	Mike Wallace	Pontiac
24.	Christian Fittipaldi	Dodge
25.	Steve Park	Chevrolet
26.	Ken Schrader	Dodge
27.	Greg Biffle	Ford
28.	Jamie McMurray	Dodge
29.	Larry Foyt	Dodge
30.	Bobby Labonte	Chevrolet
31.	Jeff Green	Chevrolet
32.	Kenny Wallace	Dodge
33.	John Andretti	Pontiac
34.	Kyle Petty	Dodge
35.	Casey Mears	Dodge
36.	Jeff Gordon	Chevrolet
37.	Tony Stewart	Chevrolet
38.	Jeremy Mayfield	Dodge
39.	Ricky Rudd	Ford
40.	Ricky Craven	Pontiac
41.	Mark Martin	Ford
42.	Derrike Cope	Chevrolet
43.	Morgan Shepherd	Ford

RACE 21—BRICKYARD 400

Indianapolis Motor Speedway
Indianapolis, Indiana
August 3
Pole winner: Kevin Harvick (184.343 mph)
Race winner: Kevin Harvick (134.554 mph)

Richard Childress won the second Brickyard 400 in 1995 with Dale Earnhardt driving. After Earnhardt died in the 2001 Daytona 500, Childress wasn't sure he'd ever celebrate another Brickyard victory. Enter Kevin Harvick. Running a terrific race, Harvick became the first Brickyard pole winner to also win the race. Harvick led for the first 17 laps, then settled back into the top 10. By lap 145 he was second behind rookie Jamie McMurray. On a restart following a caution, McMurray drove high and was caught behind slower traffic. Harvick went low and found himself alone in front. "It was like the sea just parted," Harvick said. McMurray finished third, behind points leader Matt Kenseth. After making the traditional kiss of the bricks at the start/finish line, a smiling Childress said, "I've never had a cold kiss like that, that felt so good." Tony Stewart led the most laps (60), but finished 12th. Kenseth's points lead over Dale Earnhardt Jr. increased to a season-high 286.

Brickyard 400

Time of Race: 2 hours, 58 minutes, 22 seconds.
Average Speed: 134.554 mph.
Margin of Victory: 2.758 seconds

FINISH	DRIVER	CAR
1.	Kevin Harvick	Chevrolet
2.	Matt Kenseth	Ford
3.	Jamie McMurray	Dodge
4.	Jeff Gordon	Chevrolet
5.	Bill Elliott	Dodge
8.	Jimmy Spencer	Dodge
9.	Mark Martin	Ford
10.	Rusty Wallace	Dodge

At the Brickyard 400, Dale Jarrett's crewmen have to scramble to safety when Jarrett spins out of control into the pit area during the race at Indianapolis Motor Speedway.

11.	Ryan Newman	Dodge
12.	Tony Stewart	Chevrolet
13.	Johnny Benson	Pontiac
14.	Dale Earnhardt Jr.	Chevrolet
16.	Michael Waltrip	Chevrolet
18.	Jimmie Johnson	Chevrolet
19.	Terry Labonte	Chevrolet
20.	Jeff Green	Chevrolet
21.	Greg Biffle	Ford
22.	Bobby Labonte	Chevrolet
23.	Todd Bodine	Ford
24.	Kenny Wallace	Dodge
25.	Tony Raines	Chevrolet
26.	Ward Burton	Dodge
27.	Jeff Burton	Ford
28.	Dave Blaney	Ford
29.	Casey Mears	Dodge
30.	Kevin Lepage	Ford
32.	Larry Foyt	Dodge
33.	Jason Leffler	Pontiac
34.	Sterling Marlin	Dodge
35.	Mike Skinner	Pontiac
36.	Derrike Cope	Chevrolet
37.	Joe Nemechek	Chevrolet
38.	Ricky Rudd	Ford
39.	Dale Jarrett	Ford
40.	Kyle Petty	Dodge
41.	Jeremy Mayfield	Dodge
42.	Elliott Sadler	Ford
43.	John Andretti	Chevrolet

RACE 22—SIRIUS AT THE GLEN

Watkins Glen International
Watkins Glen, New York
August 10
Pole winner: Jeff Gordon (124.580 mph)
Race winner: Robby Gordon (90.441 mph)

Robby Gordon proved to be NASCAR's road racing king—for 2003, anyway—by winning at Watkins Glen seven weeks after dominating and winning the other road race at Sears Point, California. Gordon wasn't as dominant as he was in California, but the result was the same. He started 14th and led only the final 30 laps, winning by 2.335 seconds. He was one of eight lap leaders, but three of them—Bobby Labonte, Ricky Rudd, and Jamie McMurray—led only during pit stop cycles. The other leaders were Gordon, runner-up Scott Pruett, third-place Dale Earnhardt Jr., Greg Biffle, and Jeff Burton. Much like at Sears Point, road racers Pruett, P. J. Jones, Paul Menard, Johnny Miller, Ron Fellows, and Boris Said were brought in to help Cup teams with their road-racing effort. Pole-starter Jeff Gordon had a bad day. He did manage to overcome a first-lap spin to reach the top five during the race's final laps, but he ultimately finished a lap-down in 33rd place after he made contact with Kevin Harvick on the last lap while heading for the checkered flag. Points leader Matt Kenseth started seventh, finished eighth, and left with a 258-point lead over Earnhardt Jr.

Sirius at The Glen

Time of Race: 2 hours, 26 minutes, 17 seconds.
Average Speed: 90.441 mph
Margin of Victory: 2.335 seconds

FINISH	DRIVER	CAR
1.	Robby Gordon	Chevrolet
2.	Scott Pruett	Dodge
3.	Dale Earnhardt Jr.	Chevrolet
4.	Jimmie Johnson	Chevrolet
5.	Kevin Harvick	Chevrolet
6.	Ward Burton	Dodge
7.	Dale Jarrett	Ford
8.	Matt Kenseth	Ford
9.	Ryan Newman	Dodge
10.	Mark Martin	Ford
11.	Tony Stewart	Chevrolet
12.	Kurt Busch	Ford
13.	Michael Waltrip	Chevrolet
14.	Bobby Labonte	Chevrolet
15.	Elliott Sadler	Ford
16.	Jeremy Mayfield	Dodge
17.	Joe Nemechek	Chevrolet
18.	Terry Labonte	Chevrolet
19.	John Andretti	Pontiac
20.	Bill Elliott	Dodge
21.	Ricky Rudd	Ford
22.	Casey Mears	Dodge
23.	Jamie McMurray	Dodge
24.	Jimmy Spencer	Dodge
25.	P. J. Jones	Pontiac
26.	Dave Blaney	Ford
27.	Steve Park	Chevrolet
28.	Johnny Benson	Pontiac
29.	Ricky Craven	Pontiac
30.	Paul Menard	Chevrolet
31.	Greg Biffle	Ford
32.	Jeff Burton	Ford
33.	Jeff Gordon	Chevrolet
34.	Kenny Wallace	Dodge
35.	Todd Bodine	Ford
36.	Johnny Miller	Pontiac
37.	Rusty Wallace	Dodge
38.	Ron Fellows	Chevrolet
39.	Boris Said	Pontiac
40.	Christian Fittipaldi	Dodge
41.	Tony Raines	Chevrolet
42.	Kyle Petty	Dodge
43.	Sterling Marlin	Dodge

RACE 23—GFS MARKETPLACE 400

Michigan International Speedway
Brooklyn, Michigan
August 17

Pole winner: Bobby Labonte (190.240 mph)
Race winner: Ryan Newman (127.310 mph)

The victory was Ryan Newman's series-high fifth of the year, but the race will always be remembered more for the Jimmy Spencer–Kurt Busch skirmish than for who won. Spencer and Busch had been involved in several other confrontations during previous races. After they made contact on the track, the two continued to battle after the race was over. Busch's car stalled in the garage area. Spencer rammed him, then climbed out of his car and punched Busch. Later, a tape of Busch's comments during the race indicated that he intended to flatten a fender on Spencer's car. NASCAR fined Spencer $25,000 and suspended him for one race. Both drivers were placed on probation until December 31. Busch led laps 157 to 197 of the 200-lap event, then was passed by Newman, who led the final three laps. Busch was running out of gas as Newman accelerated past him. After the race, Matt Kenseth held a 329-point lead over Dale Earnhardt Jr. in the Winston Cup race.

GFS Marketplace 400

Time of Race: 3 hours, 8 minutes, 31 seconds
Average Speed: 127.310 mph
Margin of Victory: 1.652 seconds

FINISH	DRIVER	CAR
1.	Ryan Newman	Dodge
2.	Kevin Harvick	Chevrolet
3.	Tony Stewart	Chevrolet
4.	Greg Biffle	Ford
5.	Steve Park	Chevrolet
6.	Robby Gordon	Chevrolet
7.	Michael Waltrip	Chevrolet
8.	Ken Schrader	Dodge
9.	Matt Kenseth	Ford
10.	Johnny Benson	Pontiac
11.	Jeff Burton	Ford
12.	Elliott Sadler	Ford
13.	Terry Labonte	Chevrolet
14.	Bill Elliott	Dodge
15.	Kyle Petty	Dodge
16.	Mark Martin	Ford
17.	Kurt Busch	Ford
18.	Sterling Marlin	Dodge
19.	Joe Nemechek	Chevrolet
20.	Jeff Green	Chevrolet
21.	Mike Skinner	Pontiac
22.	Dale Jarrett	Ford
23.	Tony Raines	Chevrolet
24.	Dave Blaney	Ford
25.	Jimmy Spencer	Dodge
26.	Jimmie Johnson	Chevrolet
27.	Jeremy Mayfield	Dodge
28.	Ricky Rudd	Ford
29.	Jeff Gordon	Chevrolet
30.	Kevin Lepage	Ford
31.	Dale Earnhardt Jr.	Chevrolet
32.	Christian Fittipaldi	Dodge
33.	Derrike Cope	Chevrolet

Christian Fittipaldi loses control of his car and slams into the foam safety cushion in turn 11 during the Sirius at The Glen race in Watkins Glen, New York. Fittipaldi, who was unhurt in the accident, finished in 40th place.

35.	Jason Leffler	Pontiac
36.	Jamie McMurray	Dodge
37.	Bobby Labonte	Chevrolet
38.	Rusty Wallace	Dodge
39.	Larry Foyt	Dodge
40.	Ricky Craven	Pontiac
41.	Casey Mears	Dodge
42.	Kenny Wallace	Dodge
43.	Todd Bodine	Ford

RACE 24—SHARPIE 500

Bristol Motor Speedway
Bristol, Tennessee
August 23
Pole winner: Jeff Gordon (127.597 mph)
Race winner: Kurt Busch (77.421 mph)

Kurt Busch put aside his problems with Jimmy Spencer and NASCAR to sweep the season's two races at Bristol. He came to the half-mile bullring under close scrutiny following the ugly incident with Spencer the previous week in Michigan. How-ever, Busch qualified fifth and led the final 121 laps for the last of his four victories. In the spring race at Bristol, he'd been equally dominant, leading twice for 116 laps en route to his first victory of the season. Pole-winner Jeff Gordon seemed in command of this race, leading three times for 174 of the first 225 laps, but he finished 28th after going behind the wall for repairs following a mid-race crash. Sterling Marlin, Mark Martin, Ryan Newman, and Kevin Harvick swapped the lead after Gordon's crash (lap 225) until Busch took over for good at lap 380. Busch finished ahead of Harvick, Jamie McMurray, points leader Matt Kenseth, and Jimmie Johnson. Eight drivers swapped the lead 11 times in a race slowed 20 times for 119 of the 500 laps. Kenseth's points lead rose to 351 points.

Sharpie 500

Time of Race: 3 hours, 26 minutes, 32 seconds
Average Speed: 77.421 mph
Margin of Victory: 0.818 seconds

FINISH	DRIVER	CAR
1.	Kurt Busch	Ford
2.	Kevin Harvick	Chevrolet
3.	Jamie McMurray	Dodge
4.	Matt Kenseth	Ford
5.	Jimmie Johnson	Chevrolet
6.	Ryan Newman	Dodge
7.	Dale Jarrett	Ford
8.	Ricky Craven	Pontiac
9.	Dale Earnhardt Jr.	Chevrolet
10.	Jeremy Mayfield	Dodge
11.	Terry Labonte	Chevrolet
12.	Ken Schrader	Dodge
13.	Ward Burton	Dodge
14.	Johnny Benson	Pontiac
15.	Kenny Wallace	Dodge
16.	Bill Elliott	Dodge
17.	Sterling Marlin	Dodge
18.	Mike Skinner	Pontiac
19.	Joe Nemechek	Chevrolet
20.	Tony Raines	Chevrolet
21.	Casey Mears	Dodge
22.	Greg Biffle	Ford
23.	Tony Stewart	Chevrolet
24.	Scott Wimmer	Dodge
25.	Johnny Sauter	Pontiac
26.	Jason Leffler	Pontiac
27.	Bobby Labonte	Chevrolet
28.	Jeff Gordon	Chevrolet
29.	Steve Park	Chevrolet
30.	Dave Blaney	Ford
31.	Ted Musgrave	Dodge
32.	Jeff Burton	Ford
33.	Ricky Rudd	Ford
34.	Kyle Petty	Dodge
35.	Robby Gordon	Chevrolet
36.	Mark Martin	Ford
37.	Todd Bodine	Ford
38.	Elliott Sadler	Ford
39.	Larry Foyt	Dodge
40.	Jeff Green	Chevrolet
41.	Christian Fittipaldi	Dodge
42.	Michael Waltrip	Chevrolet
43.	Rusty Wallace	Dodge

RACE 25—MOUNTAIN DEW SOUTHERN 500

Darlington Raceway
Darlington, South Carolina
August 31
Pole winner: Ryan Newman (169.048 mph)
Race winner: Terry Labonte (120.744 mph)

The final Southern 500 on Labor Day weekend at Darlington thankfully had a touch of history. Veteran Terry Labonte gained his 22nd career victory and his first in 156 races. Labonte made his first Winston Cup start in the Southern 500 in 1978, finishing an impressive fourth. Racing traditionalists are upset that the Labor Day Winston Cup date will shift to California starting in 2004. Labonte, who hadn't won since the 1999 Texas race, actually came close to cracking the top 10 in the Cup standings after the race, rising to 11th, just

one point out of 10th. Labonte led only the final 33 laps. He moved to the front when he beat Kevin Harvick off pit road after a caution flag on lap 334. Harvick finished second for the third consecutive week. Ryan Newman led the most laps (120), but he lost eight laps when he inadvertently hit the kill switch on his Dodge during a pit stop. Greg Biffle was runner-up in laps led (70). Points leader Matt Kenseth hit the wall during the race and had to settled for 14th place, but his lead in the Cup race still grew from 351 to 389 lead over Dale Earnhardt Jr.

Mountain Dew Southern 500

Time of Race: 4 hours, 9 minutes, 7 seconds
Average Speed: 120.744 mph
Margin of Victory: 1.651 seconds

FINISH	DRIVER	CAR
1.	Terry Labonte	Chevrolet
2.	Kevin Harvick	Chevrolet
3.	Jimmie Johnson	Chevrolet
4.	Jamie McMurray	Dodge
5.	Bill Elliott	Dodge
6.	Jeremy Mayfield	Dodge
7.	Bobby Labonte	Chevrolet
8.	Ricky Craven	Pontiac
9.	Elliott Sadler	Ford
10.	Greg Biffle	Ford
11.	Jeff Burton	Ford
12.	Tony Stewart	Chevrolet
13.	Kurt Busch	Ford
14.	Matt Kenseth	Ford
15.	Kevin Lepage	Pontiac
16.	Ricky Rudd	Ford
17.	Todd Bodine	Ford
18.	Jeff Green	Chevrolet
19.	Ward Burton	Dodge
20.	Steve Park	Chevrolet
21.	Joe Nemechek	Chevrolet
22.	Jimmy Spencer	Dodge
23.	Ryan Newman	Dodge
24.	Kenny Wallace	Dodge
25.	Dale Earnhardt Jr.	Chevrolet
26.	Jason Leffler	Pontiac
27.	Kyle Petty	Dodge
28.	Robby Gordon	Chevrolet
29.	Mike Skinner	Pontiac
30.	Dave Blaney	Ford
31.	Sterling Marlin	Dodge
32.	Jeff Gordon	Chevrolet
33.	Mark Martin	Ford
34.	Dale Jarrett	Ford
35.	Casey Mears	Dodge
36.	Rusty Wallace	Dodge
37.	Michael Waltrip	Chevrolet
38.	Ken Schrader	Dodge
39.	Derrike Cope	Chevrolet
40.	Johnny Benson	Pontiac
41.	Hermie Sadler	Pontiac
42.	Tony Raines	Chevrolet
43.	Christian Fittipaldi	Dodge

RACE 26—CHEVY ROCK & ROLL 400

Richmond International Raceway
Richmond, Virginia
September 6
Pole winner: Mike Skinner (125.792 mph)
Race winner: Ryan Newman (94.945 mph)

Ryan Newman got his first-ever Winston Cup short-track victory by leading twice for 125 of the 400 laps around the three-quarter-mile track. Before Richmond, all six of his Cup victories had come on superspeedways. Newman qualified fourth, led lap 65 during an exchange of pit stops, then settled comfortably into the top 10. He led from lap 277 to the finish, beating Jeremy Mayfield, Ricky Rudd, Jeff Burton, and Rusty Wallace in the year's fifth short-track race. Twelve drivers swapped the lead 20 times, with Jeff Gordon leading the most, four times for 126 laps. The race featured a five-lap sprint to the finish after then–second-place Kevin Harvick crashed following contact with third-place Ricky Rudd on lap 392. Security guards and NASCAR officials broke up an angry post-race gathering between Harvick and several of Rudd's crewmen near the latter's car. Twelve drivers exchanged the lead 20 times, but only Newman, Dale Earnhardt Jr., and Gordon led after the halfway point. Series leader Matt Kenseth started 18th and finished 7th to build his margin over Earnhardt Jr. to 418 points.

Chevy Rock & Roll 400

Time of Race: 3 hours, 9 minutes, 35 seconds
Average Speed: 94.945 mph
Margin of Victory: 0.159 seconds

FINISH	DRIVER	CAR
1.	Ryan Newman	Dodge
2.	Jeremy Mayfield	Dodge
3.	Ricky Rudd	Ford
4.	Jeff Burton	Ford
5.	Rusty Wallace	Dodge
6.	Bobby Labonte	Chevrolet
7.	Matt Kenseth	Ford
8.	Terry Labonte	Chevrolet
9.	Johnny Benson	Pontiac
10.	Jeff Gordon	Chevrolet
11.	Jimmie Johnson	Chevrolet
12.	Mike Wallace	Dodge
13.	Mark Martin	Ford
14.	John Andretti	Chevrolet
15.	Ward Burton	Dodge
16.	Kevin Harvick	Chevrolet
17.	Dale Earnhardt Jr.	Chevrolet
18.	Mike Skinner	Pontiac
19.	Jamie McMurray	Dodge
20.	Greg Biffle	Ford
21.	Dale Jarrett	Ford
22.	Sterling Marlin	Dodge
23.	Kenny Wallace	Dodge
24.	Kurt Busch	Ford
25.	Ken Schrader	Dodge
26.	Joe Nemechek	Chevrolet
27.	Tony Stewart	Chevrolet
28.	Jason Leffler	Pontiac
29.	Robby Gordon	Chevrolet
30.	Ricky Craven	Pontiac
31.	Steve Park	Chevrolet
32.	Michael Waltrip	Chevrolet
33.	Dave Blaney	Ford
34.	Kyle Petty	Dodge
35.	Tony Raines	Chevrolet
36.	Jimmy Spencer	Dodge
37.	Bill Elliott	Dodge
38.	Johnny Sauter	Pontiac
39.	Elliott Sadler	Ford
40.	Hermie Sadler	Chevrolet
41.	Casey Mears	Dodge
42.	Todd Bodine	Ford
43.	Christian Fittipaldi	Dodge

RACE 27—NEW HAMPSHIRE 300

New Hampshire International Speedway
Loudon, New Hampshire
September 14
Pole winner: Ryan Newman (133.357 mph)
Race winner: Jimmie Johnson (106.580 mph)

Jimmie Johnson completed his sweep of both New Hampshire races by working his way through the field. Johnson led only 12 laps, but 11 of them were near the end of the race, including the last 7. Dale Earnhardt Jr. led the most laps (120). With 30 laps to go, Michael Waltrip was in front. However, he needed a final pit stop, which proved disastrous. During that last stop on lap 272, the gas can stuck in the car, forcing Waltrip to return to the pits for a stop-and-go penalty. Johnson took the lead, then relinquished it four laps later when he pitted. Johnson regained the lead for good on lap 294. The victory was the sixth of Johnson's three-year Winston Cup career. Earlier, during the first caution on lap 127, Jeff Gordon was pulling into the pits when he made contact with Michael Waltrip's car. Gordon's Chevrolet spun and hit three members of Johnson's crew. The three—Cory Quick, Ryan McCray, and Chris Anderson—completed their work and then were treated at the infield care center. Points leader Matt Kenseth headed for Dover with a 404-point lead over Earnhardt Jr.

New Hampshire 300

Time of Race: 2 hours, 58 minutes, 41 seconds
Average Speed: 106.580 mph
Margin of Victory: 6.240 seconds

FINISH	DRIVER	CAR
1.	Jimmie Johnson	Chevrolet
2.	Ricky Rudd	Ford
3.	Joe Nemechek	Chevrolet
4.	Bill Elliott	Dodge
5.	Dale Earnhardt Jr	Chevrolet
6.	Rusty Wallace	Dodge
7.	Matt Kenseth	Ford
8.	Elliott Sadler	Ford
9.	Ryan Newman	Dodge
10.	Jamie McMurray	Dodge

Members of Terry Labonte's crew climb the fence at Darlington Raceway to celebrate Labonte's victory in the Mountain Dew Southern 500. The victory ended a four-year winless drought for Labonte, a two-time Winston Cup champion.

11.	Jeremy Mayfield	Dodge
12.	John Andretti	Chevrolet
13.	Kevin Harvick	Chevrolet
14.	Dave Blaney	Ford
15.	Kurt Busch	Ford
16.	Bobby Labonte	Chevrolet
17.	Casey Mears	Dodge
18.	Terry Labonte	Chevrolet
19.	Jeff Gordon	Chevrolet
20.	Tony Stewart	Chevrolet
21.	Robby Gordon	Chevrolet
22.	Mike Skinner	Pontiac
23.	Jimmy Spencer	Dodge
24.	Scott Wimmer	Chevrolet
25.	Johnny Benson	Pontiac
26.	Michael Waltrip	Chevrolet
27.	Jason Leffler	Pontiac
28.	Mark Martin	Ford
29.	Sterling Marlin	Dodge
30.	Kyle Petty	Dodge
31.	Christian Fittipaldi	Dodge
32.	Johnny Sauter	Pontiac
33.	Tony Raines	Chevrolet
34.	Steve Park	Chevrolet
35.	Todd Bodine	Ford
36.	Kenny Wallace	Dodge
37.	Ken Schrader	Dodge
38.	Ricky Craven	Pontiac
39.	Ward Burton	Dodge
40.	Hermie Sadler	Pontiac
41.	Dale Jarrett	Ford
42.	Jeff Burton	Ford
43.	Greg Biffle	Ford

RACE 28—MBNA AMERICA 400

Dover International Speedway
Dover, Delaware
September 21
Pole winner: Rained out; starting lineup determined by points standings.
Race winner: Ryan Newman (108.802 mph)

Hours after criticizing a new rule giving the highest-scored lapped driver his lap back under caution, Ryan Newman used it en route to his seventh victory of the season. The rule lets one driver regain his lost lap without having to race the leader to the caution flag. NASCAR preferred that to having lapped drivers battling the leader to the flag, with both drivers often having to steer clear of the accident that caused the caution in the first place. The rule freezes the field and requires drivers to slow down immediately instead of racing to the flag while jockeying for position. Newman started fifth and led laps 12 to 44, but he was later lapped when he suffered a flat tire and had to pit under green after 150 laps. He regained the lost lap at lap 328 when he was the highest scoring driver to be one-lap down at the start of a caution, which invoked the new rule. When Newman decided not to pit during the caution—all the leaders did pit—he suddenly found himself in first place, a spot he held for the last 63 laps. He finished just ahead of

Jeremy Mayfield, Tony Stewart, Kevin Harvick, and Jeff Gordon. Ninth-place Matt Kenseth's series lead was 436 points over Harvick. Dale Earnhardt Jr. dropped out of the second-place slot in the season standings and was briefly hospitalized after a late-race crash; he finished 37th in the race.

MBNA America 400

Time of Race: 3 hours, 40 minutes, 35 seconds
Average Speed: 108.802 mph
Margin of Victory: 1.152 seconds

FINISH	DRIVER	CAR
1.	Ryan Newman	Dodge
2.	Jeremy Mayfield	Dodge
3.	Tony Stewart	Chevrolet
4.	Kevin Harvick	Chevrolet
5.	Jeff Gordon	Chevrolet
6.	Jamie McMurray	Dodge
7.	Greg Biffle	Ford
8.	Jimmie Johnson	Chevrolet
9.	Matt Kenseth	Ford
10.	Rusty Wallace	Dodge
11.	Ricky Rudd	Ford
12.	Jeff Burton	Ford
13.	Sterling Marlin	Dodge
14.	Bill Elliott	Dodge
15.	Jimmy Spencer	Dodge
16.	Jeff Green	Dodge
17.	Todd Bodine	Ford
18.	Dale Jarrett	Ford
19.	Elliott Sadler	Ford
20.	Terry Labonte	Chevrolet
21.	Johnny Benson	Pontiac
22.	Mark Martin	Ford
23.	Robby Gordon	Chevrolet
24.	Dave Blaney	Ford
25.	Jason Leffler	Pontiac
26.	Steve Park	Chevrolet
27.	Kevin Lepage	Pontiac
28.	Kenny Wallace	Dodge
29.	Ward Burton	Dodge
30.	Tony Raines	Chevrolet
31.	Bobby Labonte	Chevrolet
32.	Kyle Petty	Dodge
33.	Ken Schrader	Dodge
34.	John Andretti	Chevrolet
35.	Derrike Cope	Chevrolet
36.	Casey Mears	Dodge
37.	Dale Earnhardt Jr.	Chevrolet
38.	Kurt Busch	Ford
39.	Hermie Sadler	Pontiac
40.	Ricky Craven	Pontiac
41.	Mike Skinner	Pontiac
42.	Michael Waltrip	Chevrolet
43.	Joe Nemechek	Chevrolet

RACE 29—EA SPORTS 500

Talladega Superspeedway
Talladega, Alabama
September 28
Pole winner: Elliott Sadler (189.943 mph)
Race winner: Michael Waltrip (156.045 mph)

So what if Michael Waltrip only wins on restrictor-plate tracks? Waltrip sure isn't complaining about that, and neither is Dale Earnhardt Inc., the owner of Waltrip's car. Waltrip's victory at Talladega gave DEI its ninth victory in plate races

Dale Earnhardt Jr. (No. 8), one of NASCAR's most popular young drivers, leads a pack of cars out of the turn at Dover International Speedway during the running of the MBNA America 400 on September 21.

in the last 12. Waltrip edged teammate Dale Earnhardt Jr., who had won the last four Cup races at Talladega. Junior was runner-up in the race, just 0.095 of a second behind Waltrip. Following his fourth career win, Waltrip celebrated by popping out of the alternate escape roof hatch, the only car in the race with such a device. He needed the win because he had dropped from 5th in the points standings after the Brickyard 400 to 11th before Talladega. Waltrip survived a penalty for a catch-can violation during a pit stop between laps 144 and 148. He led the final nine laps (16 total). Jeff Gordon led the most laps (47).

Just after Waltrip took the lead on lap 181, Elliott Sadler's Ford was tapped by Kurt Busch,

sending Sadler airborne. His car flipped five times before stopping. Sadler was not injured. Points leader Matt Kenseth suffered his first "did not finish" (DNF) of the year. The engine on his Ford quit with 30 laps to go, relegating Kenseth to 33rd. He still led Kevin Harvick by 354 points. Afterward, many drivers complained about the racing conditions. By opening the restrictor plate slightly and raising the rear spoiler one-half inch, NASCAR hoped to give the cars more horsepower. The idea was to create more passing and cut down on the major wrecks that had been commonplace during races at Talladega. The drivers felt that the rule adjustment didn't work and that the proof was easy to see—their cars were just as banged up and damaged as they were during the rough-and-tumble short-track races at Bristol and Martinsville.

EA Sports 500

Time of Race: 3 hours, 12 minutes, 17 seconds
Average Speed: 156.045 mph
Margin of Victory: 0.095 seconds

FINISH	DRIVER	CAR
1.	Michael Waltrip	Chevrolet
2.	Dale Earnhardt Jr.	Chevrolet
3.	Tony Stewart	Chevrolet
4.	Ryan Newman	Dodge
5.	Jeff Gordon	Chevrolet
6.	Kurt Busch	Ford
7.	Kevin Harvick	Chevrolet
8.	Ricky Craven	Pontiac
9.	Rusty Wallace	Dodge
10.	Mike Wallace	Dodge
11.	Bobby Labonte	Chevrolet
12.	Robby Gordon	Chevrolet
13.	Bill Elliott	Dodge
14.	Ward Burton	Dodge
15.	John Andretti	Chevrolet
16.	Jamie McMurray	Dodge
17.	Dave Blaney	Dodge
18.	Jeff Green	Dodge
19.	Dale Jarrett	Ford
20.	Kenny Wallace	Dodge
21.	Ken Schrader	Dodge
22.	Terry Labonte	Chevrolet
23.	Mark Martin	Ford
24.	Greg Biffle	Ford
25.	Joe Nemechek	Chevrolet
26.	Jason Keller	Chevrolet
27.	Mike Skinner	Pontiac
28.	Christian Fittipaldi	Dodge
29.	Jason Jarrett	Ford
30.	Elliott Sadler	Ford
31.	Tony Raines	Chevrolet
32.	Jeff Burton	Ford
33.	Matt Kenseth	Ford
34.	Jimmie Johnson	Chevrolet
35.	David Green	Chevrolet
36.	Ricky Rudd	Ford
37.	Casey Mears	Dodge
38.	Jeremy Mayfield	Dodge
39.	Sterling Marlin	Dodge
40.	Buckshot Jones	Chevrolet
41.	Johnny Benson	Pontiac
42.	Jimmy Spencer	Dodge
43.	Larry Foyt	Dodge

RACE 30—BANQUET 400

Kansas Speedway
Kansas City, Kansas
October 5
Pole winner: Jimmie Johnson (180.373 mph)
Race winner: Ryan Newman (121.630 mph)

Bill Elliott was understandably miffed after finishing just behind winner Ryan Newman at the 1.5-mile track. Elliott led a race-high four times for 115 of 267 laps, but still he couldn't overcome Newman's better fuel efficiency. Newman led only once, but it was for the final 28 laps, during which time most of his rivals made late-race stops for tires and gas. Newman stayed on the track and elected to try to stretch his last 22 gallons for 78 laps, much

farther than anyone else had done. Elliott and Jeff Gordon (among many) questioned how Newman could run 117 miles on that much gas. Newman's eighth—and final—victory of 2003 was just ahead of Elliott and teammate Jeremy Mayfield, then Tony Stewart and Gordon. The front three all led laps, as did pole winner Jimmie Johnson, Rusty Wallace, Bobby Labonte, Dale Earnhardt Jr., Mike Skinner, Jason Leffler, Dale Jarrett, and Kurt Busch. It was a bad day for series leader Matt Kenseth. He crashed in practice, took a provisional to start 37th, then crashed again en route to a 36th-place finish. He lost 95 points, but still left Kansas City leading Kevin Harvick by 259 points.

Banquet 400

Time of Race: 3 hours, 17 minutes, 34 seconds
Average Speed: 121.630 mph
Margin of Victory: 0.863 seconds

FINISH	DRIVER	CAR
1.	Ryan Newman	Dodge
2.	Bill Elliott	Dodge
3.	Jeremy Mayfield	Dodge
4.	Tony Stewart	Chevrolet
5.	Jeff Gordon	Chevrolet
6.	Kevin Harvick	Chevrolet
7.	Jimmie Johnson	Chevrolet
8.	Jamie McMurray	Dodge
9.	Rusty Wallace	Dodge
10.	Ricky Rudd	Ford
11.	Todd Bodine	Ford
12.	Greg Biffle	Ford
13.	Jeff Burton	Ford
14.	Bobby Hamilton Jr.	Ford
15.	Jimmy Spencer	Dodge
16.	Terry Labonte	Chevrolet
17.	Bobby Labonte	Chevrolet
18.	Dale Earnhardt Jr.	Chevrolet
19.	John Andretti	Chevrolet
20.	Mark Martin	Ford
21.	Ward Burton	Dodge
22.	Steve Park	Chevrolet
23.	Kyle Petty	Dodge
24.	Casey Mears	Dodge
25.	Robby Gordon	Chevrolet
26.	Tony Raines	Chevrolet
27.	Jeff Green	Dodge
28.	Ken Schrader	Dodge
29.	Mike Skinner	Pontiac
30.	Jason Leffler	Pontiac
31.	Kenny Wallace	Dodge
32.	Mike Wallace	Dodge
33.	Dale Jarrett	Ford
34.	Sterling Marlin	Dodge
35.	Johnny Benson	Pontiac
36.	Matt Kenseth	Ford
37.	Joe Nemechek	Chevrolet
38.	Derrike Cope	Chevrolet
39.	Michael Waltrip	Chevrolet
40.	Kurt Busch	Ford
41.	Ricky Craven	Pontiac
42.	Elliott Sadler	Ford
43.	Dave Blaney	Ford

RACE 31—UAW-GM QUALITY 500

Lowe's Motor Speedway

Members of Jimmie Johnson's pit crew quickly fill his No. 48 Chevrolet so he can get back into the Pop Secret Microwave Popcorn 400 at North Carolina Speedway in the next-to-last race of the season. Johnson's crew did its job well, as Johnson finished second behind Cup veteran Bill Elliott.

Concord, North Carolina
October 11
Pole winner: Ryan Newman (186.657 mph)
Race winner: Tony Stewart (142.871 mph)

Tony Stewart won, and he had fun doing it. "It's about time in the Winston Cup series that the fastest car wins the race," Stewart said after gaining his second victory of the year. The reigning Cup champion was referring to Ryan Newman's second-half dominance that was at least partially due to Newman's superior fuel-mileage management. Stewart led the most laps (149) and finally passed pole-sitter Newman on lap 327 of the 334-lap race. Newman made his final pit stop on lap 267, while Stewart's last pit stop was on lap 296. When Stewart wheeled his Joe Gibbs-owned Chevrolet back on the track following that final stop, he trailed Newman by about eight seconds. No problem— Stewart slowly reeled in Newman, who was running the same line as Stewart, and passed him with seven laps to go. Jimmie Johnson led the second most laps (104) and finished third. Points leader Matt Kenseth, 33rd and 36th in his previous two races, placed eighth. Following the race, he held a 267-point advantage over Kevin Harvick.

UAW-GM Quality 500

Time of Race: 3 hours, 30 minutes, 24 seconds
Average Speed: 142.871 mph
Margin of Victory: 0.608 seconds

FINISH	DRIVER	CAR
1.	Tony Stewart	Chevrolet
2.	Ryan Newman	Dodge
3.	Jimmie Johnson	Chevrolet
4.	Bill Elliott	Dodge
5.	Jeff Gordon	Chevrolet
6.	Bobby Labonte	Chevrolet
7.	Jamie McMurray	Dodge
8.	Matt Kenseth	Ford
9.	Dale Earnhardt Jr.	Chevrolet
10.	Kevin Harvick	Chevrolet
11.	Mark Martin	Ford
12.	Jeremy Mayfield	Dodge
13.	Rusty Wallace	Dodge
14.	Michael Waltrip	Chevrolet
15.	Sterling Marlin	Dodge
16.	Johnny Benson	Pontiac
17.	Greg Biffle	Ford
18.	Terry Labonte	Chevrolet
19.	Ricky Craven	Pontiac
20.	Jeff Burton	Ford
21.	Kevin Lepage	Pontiac
22.	Dale Jarrett	Ford
23.	Ricky Rudd	Ford
24.	Dave Blaney	Ford
25.	Tony Raines	Chevrolet
26.	Jimmy Spencer	Dodge
27.	Jeff Green	Dodge
28.	Ward Burton	Dodge
29.	Todd Bodine	Ford
30.	John Andretti	Chevrolet
31.	Joe Nemechek	Chevrolet
32.	Kenny Wallace	Dodge
33.	Brian Vickers	Chevrolet
34.	Christian Fittipaldi	Dodge
35.	Jason Leffler	Pontiac
36.	Steve Park	Chevrolet
37.	Derrike Cope	Chevrolet
38.	Robby Gordon	Chevrolet
39.	Mike Skinner	Pontiac
40.	Kyle Petty	Dodge
41.	Kurt Busch	Ford
42.	Casey Mears	Dodge
43.	Elliott Sadler	Ford

RACE 32—SUBWAY 500

Martinsville Speedway
Martinsville, Virginia
October 19
Pole winner: Jeff Gordon (93.650 mph)
Race winner: Jeff Gordon (67.653 mph)

Jeff Gordon completed a rare "double sweep" by winning the pole and race, a feat he'd also performed in the spring at the half-mile bullring. He led the first 107 laps and the final 206, easily beating Jimmie Johnson, Tony Stewart, Dale Earnhardt Jr., and Ryan Newman. Gordon floundered somewhat between laps 125 and 290 after being forced high shortly after a restart, which cost him valuable track position. His 313 laps led were 118 more than any driver led in any other race all season. The only other leaders were Stewart, Earnhardt Jr., Rusty Wallace, Terry Labonte, Kurt Busch, Joe Nemechek, and Kevin Harvick. Gordon's biggest challenge faded when Earnhardt Jr. lost two seconds trying to pass Newman for fourth. Earnhardt Jr. had moved up from 12th to 5th after stopping under caution on lap 405, and he seemed capable of catching Gordon. Earnhardt's threat passed, however, when he needed 10 laps just to pass Newman. Series leader Matt Kenseth (by 240 over Kevin Harvick) was a nonfactor in the race, finishing 13th. The race was slowed 15 times for a track-record 117 laps.

Subway 500

Time of Race: 3 hours, 53 minutes, 15 seconds
Average Speed: 67.653 mph
Margin of Victory: 1.036 seconds

FINISH	DRIVER	CAR
1.	Jeff Gordon	Chevrolet
2.	Jimmie Johnson	Chevrolet
3.	Tony Stewart	Chevrolet
4.	Dale Earnhardt Jr.	Chevrolet
5.	Ryan Newman	Dodge
6.	Terry Labonte	Chevrolet
7.	Kevin Harvick	Chevrolet
8.	Jamie McMurray	Dodge

Prerace preparations involve the whole team, as it takes a great deal of teammwork to keep a Nextel Cup team running smoothly. Here, Terry Labonte's crew works on the right-side tires before the Pop Secret Microwave Popcorn 400 at North Carolina Speedway.

9.	Bill Elliott	Dodge
10.	Jeff Burton	Ford
11.	Dale Jarrett	Ford
12.	Steve Park	Chevrolet
13.	Matt Kenseth	Ford
14.	Mark Martin	Ford
15.	Ricky Rudd	Ford
16.	Kenny Wallace	Dodge
17.	Casey Mears	Dodge
18.	Ward Burton	Dodge
19.	Greg Biffle	Ford
20.	Joe Nemechek	Chevrolet
21.	Mike Skinner	Pontiac
22.	Ken Schrader	Dodge
23.	Tony Raines	Chevrolet
24.	Jeff Green	Dodge
25.	Kyle Petty	Dodge
26.	Michael Waltrip	Chevrolet
27.	Jason Leffler	Pontiac
28.	Elliott Sadler	Ford
29.	Rusty Wallace	Dodge
30.	Hermie Sadler	Pontiac
31.	John Andretti	Chevrolet
32.	Ricky Craven	Pontiac
33.	Jeremy Mayfield	Dodge
34.	Johnny Benson	Pontiac
35.	Kevin Lepage	Pontiac

36.	Robby Gordon	Chevrolet
37.	Dave Blaney	Ford
38.	Jimmy Spencer	Dodge
39.	Kurt Busch	Ford
40.	Todd Bodine	Ford
41.	Bobby Labonte	Chevrolet
42.	Derrike Cope	Chevrolet
43.	Sterling Marlin	Dodge

RACE 33—BASS PRO SHOPS/MBNA 500

Atlanta Motor Speedway
Hampton, Georgia
October 27
Pole winner: Ryan Newman (194.295 mph)
Race winner: Jeff Gordon (127.769 mph)

Jeff Gordon didn't mind waiting a day to win his third race of the season and 64th of his Winston Cup career. After rain forced postponement of the race until Monday—Kevin Harvick was leading after 40 laps when the delay occurred—Gordon went on to take consecutive races for the 18th time in his career. Efficient pit stops helped Gordon stay up front with Tony Stewart, who led for 109 laps, Bobby Labonte (66 laps led), Harvick (41 laps led) and Dale Earnhardt Jr. (32 laps led). On lap 232 of the 325-lap event, Labonte passed Gordon for the lead; Earnhardt moved in front seven laps later. Earhardt didn't last long—Labonte regained the lead five laps later. On lap 277, Gordon took the lead for good. Ryan Newman won his series-leading ninth pole of the year. Newman, however, did not leave the track happy. With four laps to go, Newman's Dodge wobbled and appeared to be tapped by Earnhardt. The race ended under caution as Newman walked up the track and gestured at Earnhardt as he drove past. An 11th-place finish enabled points leader Matt Kenseth to hold a 258-point lead over Earnhardt.

BASS Pro Shops/MBNA 500

Time of Race: 3 hours, 55 minutes, 2 seconds
Average Speed: 127.769 mph
Margin of Victory: Under caution

FINISH	DRIVER	CAR
1.	Jeff Gordon	Chevrolet
2.	Tony Stewart	Chevrolet
3.	Jimmie Johnson	Chevrolet
4.	Bill Elliott	Dodge
5.	Bobby Labonte	Chevrolet
6.	Dale Earnhardt Jr.	Chevrolet
7.	Jeremy Mayfield	Dodge
8.	Kurt Busch	Ford
9.	Jimmy Spencer	Dodge
10.	Joe Nemechek	Pontiac
11.	Matt Kenseth	Ford
12.	Dale Jarrett	Ford
13.	Ward Burton	Pontiac
14.	Kevin Lepage	Pontiac
15.	Jamie McMurray	Dodge
16.	Sterling Marlin	Dodge
17.	Elliott Sadler	Ford
18.	Tony Raines	Chevrolet
19.	Rusty Wallace	Dodge
20.	Kevin Harvick	Chevrolet
21.	Robby Gordon	Chevrolet
22.	John Andretti	Chevrolet
23.	Jeff Burton	Ford
24.	Johnny Benson	Pontiac
25.	Kyle Petty	Dodge
26.	Ken Schrader	Dodge
27.	Bobby Hamilton Jr.	Ford
28.	Casey Mears	Dodge
29.	Ryan Newman	Dodge
30.	Kenny Wallace	Dodge
31.	Ricky Rudd	Ford
32.	Scott Wimmer	Dodge
33.	Terry Labonte	Chevrolet
34.	Greg Biffle	Ford
35.	Ricky Craven	Pontiac
36.	Steve Park	Chevrolet
37.	Dave Blaney	Ford
38.	Michael Waltrip	Chevrolet
39.	Mark Martin	Ford
40.	Derrike Cope	Chevrolet
41.	Hermie Sadler	Chevrolet
42.	Todd Bodine	Ford
43.	Brian Vickers	Chevrolet

RACE 34—CHECKER AUTO PARTS 500

Phoenix International Raceway
Avondale, Arizona
November 2
Pole winner: Ryan Newman (133.675 mph)
Race winner: Dale Earnhardt Jr. (93.984 mph)

The rap against Dale Earnhardt Jr. (by some NASCAR-watchers, anyway) was that he was a one-trick pony, and that trick was winning restrictor-plate races at Daytona Beach and Talladega. Going into 2003, four of his seven victories had come at those tracks. That went to five-of-eight when he won the spring race at Talladega. However, Junior had the last laugh by winning the fall race at Phoenix, a 1-mile, flat, oddly shaped track that requires skill and finesse. After starting 11th, he led three times for 125 of 312 laps, including the final 51. He beat Jimmie Johnson by 0.735 seconds, withstanding everything Johnson threw at him down the stretch. Pole-winner Ryan Newman, Kurt Busch, and Michael Waltrip rounded out the top five. Champion-in-waiting Matt Kenseth started 37th, but (typically) drove a smart and steady race and finished sixth. Accidents sidelined or slowed Jimmy Spencer, Ricky Craven, Steve Park, Ward Burton, Kevin Harvick, Rusty Wallace, and Bobby Labonte, and engine problems eliminated Jeremy Mayfield and Casey Mears, as well as Petty Enterprises teammates Jeff Green and Kyle Petty.

Checker Auto Parts 500

Time of Race: 3 hours, 19 minutes, 11 seconds
Average Speed: 93.984 mph
Margin of Victory: 0.735 seconds

FINISH	DRIVER	CAR
1.	Dale Earnhardt Jr.	Chevrolet
2.	Jimmie Johnson	Chevrolet
3.	Ryan Newman	Dodge
4.	Kurt Busch	Ford
5.	Michael Waltrip	Chevrolet
6.	Matt Kenseth	Ford
7.	Jeff Gordon	Chevrolet
8.	Jeff Burton	Ford
9.	Scott Wimmer	Dodge
10.	Mark Martin	Ford
11.	Sterling Marlin	Dodge

As Matt Kenseth slows down after crossing the finish line, his team catches up with him, fists raised in celebration after their driver clinched his first Winston (now Nextel) Cup title with a fourth-place finish in the season's next-to-last race, the Pop Secret Microwave Popcorn 400 at North Carolina Speedway.

12.	Jamie McMurray	Dodge
13.	Brian Vickers	Chevrolet
14.	Bill Elliott	Dodge
15.	Greg Biffle	Ford
16.	John Andretti	Chevrolet
17.	Ricky Rudd	Ford
18.	Tony Stewart	Chevrolet
19.	Tony Raines	Chevrolet
20.	Elliott Sadler	Ford
21.	Johnny Benson	Pontiac
22.	Todd Bodine	Ford
23.	Kevin Lepage	Pontiac
24.	Dave Blaney	Ford
26.	Mike Wallace	Dodge
27.	Ken Schrader	Dodge
28.	Larry Foyt	Dodge
29.	Dale Jarrett	Ford
30.	Terry Labonte	Chevrolet
31.	Joe Nemechek	Pontiac
32.	Robby Gordon	Chevrolet
33.	Rusty Wallace	Dodge
34.	Kevin Harvick	Chevrolet
35.	Kyle Petty	Dodge
36.	Bobby Labonte	Chevrolet
37.	Jeff Green	Dodge
38.	Ricky Craven	Pontiac
39.	Steve Park	Chevrolet

40.	Jimmy Spencer	Dodge
41.	Ward Burton	Pontiac
42.	Casey Mears	Dodge
43.	Jeremy Mayfield	Dodge

RACE 35—POP SECRET MICROWAVE POPCORN 400

North Carolina Speedway
Rockingham, North Carolina
November 9
Pole winner: Ryan Newman (155.577 mph)
Race winner: Bill Elliott (111.677 mph)

The final fall Winston Cup race at the "Rock" was significant for two reasons: Matt Kenseth clinched his first Winston Cup championship with a fourth-place finish and Bill Elliott gained his first win since the Brickyard 400 in 2002. Kenseth left Rockingham with a 226-point lead over Jimmie Johnson (151 points are the most a driver can earn in a race). Kenseth became only the sixth Ford driver to win a Winston Cup title, and the win also gave Jack Roush his first Winston Cup title as a team owner. After starting 23rd, Kenseth moved into the top 10 just past the halfway mark. For Elliott, the win was the 44th of his career. After qualifying fifth in an Evernham Motorsports Dodge, Elliott led 140 laps: 186–243, 245–254, 320–329, 331–368, and 370–393. With six top-10 finishes in his last seven starts, Elliott, 48, was racing like a young driver, not one who was set to retire after the season's final race. Ryan Newman (11th pole of the season) finished fifth. He collided with Jeff Gordon early in the race, then was spun out by Gordon. Jeremy Mayfield had a strong race and finished third. Mayfield, Elliott's teammate at Evernham Motorsports, led laps 78–169, plus 171–173 and 244. Tony Raines, driving an unsponsored Chevrolet for BACE Motorsports, finished a season-best sixth.

Pop Secret Microwave Popcorn 400

Time of Race: 3 hours, 34 minutes, 44 seconds
Average Speed: 111.677 mph
Margin of Victory: 1.230 seconds

FINISH	DRIVER	CAR
1.	Bill Elliott	Dodge
2.	Jimmie Johnson	Chevrolet
3.	Jeremy Mayfield	Dodge
4.	Matt Kenseth	Ford
5.	Ryan Newman	Dodge
6.	Tony Raines	Chevrolet
7.	Jeff Burton	Ford
8.	Bobby Labonte	Chevrolet
9.	Tony Stewart	Chevrolet
10.	Sterling Marlin	Dodge
11.	Greg Biffle	Ford
12.	Terry Labonte	Chevrolet
13.	Dale Earnhardt Jr.	Chevrolet
14.	Jimmy Spencer	Dodge
15.	Kevin Harvick	Chevrolet
16.	Todd Bodine	Ford
17.	Kurt Busch	Ford
18.	Ward Burton	Pontiac
19.	Jeff Green	Dodge
20.	Robby Gordon	Chevrolet
21.	Elliott Sadler	Ford
22.	Jeff Gordon	Chevrolet
23.	Rusty Wallace	Dodge
24.	Brian Vickers	Chevrolet
25.	Joe Nemechek	Pontiac
26.	Scott Wimmer	Dodge
27.	Dave Blaney	Ford
28.	Larry Foyt	Dodge
29.	Johnny Benson	Pontiac
30.	John Andretti	Chevrolet
31.	Kenny Wallace	Dodge
32.	Kyle Petty	Dodge
33.	Casey Mears	Dodge
34.	Steve Park	Chevrolet
35.	Jamie McMurray	Dodge
36.	Ken Schrader	Dodge
37.	Michael Waltrip	Chevrolet
38.	Dale Jarrett	Ford
39.	Ricky Craven	Pontiac
40.	Ricky Rudd	Ford
41.	Mark Martin	Ford
42.	Kevin Lepage	Pontiac
43.	Derrike Cope	Chevrolet

RACE 36—FORD 400

Homestead-Miami Speedway
Homestead, Florida
November 16
Pole winner: Jamie McMurray (171.111 mph)
Race winner: Bobby Labonte (116.868 mph)

Bill Elliott was a mile from his second victory of 2003—his second straight and the 45th of his career—until a flat right-rear tire gave Bobby Labonte his second victory of the season. International Speedway Corporation and Bill France Jr. spent $12 million reconfiguring the track, repaving its 1.5 miles, increasing its banking from 6 to 20 degrees, and shaping three distinctive grooves. It worked: 12 drivers swapped the lead 21 times compared to 6 drivers swapping it 12 times in 2002. Unlike previous years, when the track was flat, cars ran faster and raced harder. Elliott dominated, leading six times for 189 laps before the flat tire. (Michael Waltrip, Brian Vickers, Greg Biffle, Jeremy Mayfield, Rusty Wallace, Ricky Craven, and Jeff Burton also had tire issues.) Labonte led only the 267th lap in beating Kevin Harvick, Jimmie Johnson, Johnny Benson, Jeff Gordon, Jeremy Mayfield, Tony Stewart, and Elliott. Champion Matt Kenseth blew up early and finished a season's-worst 43rd. Ryan Newman crashed early, finished 37th, and dropped from fourth to sixth in points.

Ford 400

Time of Race: 3 hours, 25 minutes, 37 seconds
Average Speed: 116.868 mph
Margin of Victory: 1.749 seconds

FINISH	DRIVER	CAR
1.	Bobby Labonte	Chevrolet
2.	Kevin Harvick	Chevrolet
3.	Jimmie Johnson	Chevrolet
4.	Johnny Benson	Pontiac
5.	Jeff Gordon	Chevrolet
6.	Jeremy Mayfield	Dodge
7.	Tony Stewart	Chevrolet
8.	Bill Elliott	Dodge
9.	Jamie McMurray	Dodge
10.	Sterling Marlin	Dodge

In just his fourth year of full-time Cup racing, 31-year-old Matt Kenseth claimed his first championship. While he won only a single race during the year, he was the most consistent driver and easily claimed the title, which was also the first Winston (now Nextel) Cup championship for owner Jack Roush. Here, Kenseth hoists the winner's trophy after clinching the title at the Pop Secret Microwave Popcorn 400 at North Carolina Speedway on November 9.

11.	Todd Bodine	Ford
12.	Scott Wimmer	Dodge
13.	Tony Raines	Chevrolet
14.	Jeff Burton	Ford
15.	Terry Labonte	Chevrolet
16.	Larry Foyt	Dodge
17.	Joe Nemechek	Pontiac
18.	Kevin Lepage	Pontiac
19.	Steve Park	Chevrolet
20.	Ron Hornaday	Chevrolet
21.	Elliott Sadler	Ford
22.	Kenny Wallace	Dodge
23.	Rusty Wallace	Dodge
24.	Dale Earnhardt Jr.	Chevrolet
25.	Jimmy Spencer	Dodge
26.	Dale Jarrett	Ford
27.	Casey Mears	Dodge
28.	Dave Blaney	Ford
29.	Ricky Craven	Pontiac
30.	Robby Gordon	Chevrolet
31.	Ricky Rudd	Ford
32.	Ward Burton	Pontiac
33.	Mark Martin	Ford
34.	Brian Vickers	Chevrolet
35.	Greg Biffle	Ford
36.	Kurt Busch	Ford
37.	Ryan Newman	Dodge
38.	Hermie Sadler	Chevrolet
39.	Mike Skinner	Chevrolet
40.	Jeff Green	Dodge
41.	Michael Waltrip	Chevrolet
42.	John Andretti	Chevrolet
43.	Matt Kenseth	Ford

2003 WINSTON CUP STANDINGS

	DRIVER	STARTS	WINS	POINTS	MONEY
1.	Matt Kenseth	36	1	5,022	4,038,120
2.	Jimmie Johnson	36	3	4,932	5,517,850
3.	Dale Earnhardt Jr.	36	2	4,815	4,923,500
4.	Jeff Gordon	36	3	4,785	5,107,760
5.	Kevin Harvick	36	1	4,770	4,994,250
6.	Ryan Newman	36	8	4,711	4,827,380
7.	Tony Stewart	36	2	4,549	5,227,500
8.	Bobby Labonte	36	2	4,377	4,745,260
9.	Bill Elliott	36	1	4,303	4,321,190
10.	Terry Labonte	36	1	4,162	3,643,690
11.	Kurt Busch	36	4	4,150	5,020,480
12.	Jeff Burton	36	0	4,109	3,846,880
13.	Jamie McMurray	36	0	3,965	2,699,970
14.	Rusty Wallace	36	0	3,950	3,766,740
15.	Michael Waltrip	36	2	3,934	4,463,840
16.	Robby Gordon	36	2	3,856	3,705,320
17.	Mark Martin	36	0	3,769	4,048,850
18.	Sterling Marlin	36	0	3,745	3,960,810
19.	Jeremy Mayfield	36	0	3,736	2,962,230
20.	Greg Biffle	35	1	3,696	2,410,050
21.	Ward Burton	36	0	3,550	3,500,160
22.	Elliott Sadler	36	0	3,525	3,660,170
23.	Ricky Rudd	36	0	3,521	3,106,610
24.	Johnny Benson	36	0	3,448	3,411,790
25.	Joe Nemechek	36	1	3,426	2,560,480
26.	Dale Jarrett	36	1	3,358	4,055,490
27.	Ricky Craven	36	1	3,334	3,116,210
28.	Dave Blaney	36	0	3,194	2,828,690
29.	Jimmy Spencer	35	0	3,147	2,565,800
30.	Kenny Wallace	36	0	3,061	2,480,490
31.	Todd Bodine	35	0	2,976	2,521,720
32.	Steve Park	35	0	2,923	2,686,910
33.	Tony Raines	35	0	2,772	2,122,740
34.	Jeff Green	31	0	2,656	2,693,530
35.	Casey Mears	36	0	2,638	2,639,180
36.	Ken Schrader	32	0	2,451	2,007,420
37.	Kyle Petty	33	0	2,414	2,293,220
38.	John Andretti	29	0	2,379	2,577,620
39.	Mike Skinner	26	0	1,960	1,782,800
40.	Jack Sprague	18	0	1,284	1,187,830
41.	Larry Foyt	20	0	1,228	1,180,990
42.	Mike Wallace	14	0	1,189	1,031,100
43.	Kevin Lepage	11	0	877	742,077
44.	Christian Fittipaldi	15	0	857	1,265,830
45.	Jerry Nadeau	10	0	844	861,628
46.	Derrike Cope	18	0	822	1,030,690
47.	Jason Leffler	10	0	764	594,500
48.	Scott Wimmer	6	0	599	479,504
49.	Brian Vickers	5	0	379	263,484
50.	Hermie Sadler	10	0	373	552,741

3

DRIVER REGISTER

JOHN ANDRETTI

Born: March 12, 1963
Bethlehem, PA
Family: wife, Nancy; children,
Jarett, Olivia and Amelia
No. 1 Chevrolet Monte Carlo

Career highlights: Faces an uncertain 2004 since (at press time) he doesn't have a full-time ride ... will almost certainly get plenty of calls for fill-in or "one-off" rides ... opened 2003 with Petty Enterprises, but was released in June after the team struggled at almost every venue ... ran most of the second half of the season with Dale Earnhardt Inc., plus ran one race each with owners Richard Childress, Michael Waltrip, and Gene Haas ... got first Winston Cup victory in July of 1997 at Daytona Beach for owner Cale Yarborough, then won the 1999 spring race at Martinsville, Virginia, for Petty Enterprises ... got the first of four poles in the 1995 Southern 500 at Darlington, South Carolina ... former Indy car driver who maintains close friendships in open-wheel racing ... first Indy car victory was in Australia in 1991 ... finished 10th in the 1994 Indianapolis 500 and 36th in the Coca-Cola 600 on the same day ... nephew of Mario Andretti and cousin of Indy car driver Michael Andretti ... co-driving with them, placed sixth in the 24 Hours of LeMans race in 1988 ... has degree in business management from Moravian College in Bethlehem ... godfather is A. J. Foyt.

YEAR	PTS. POS.	EVENTS	POLES	WINS	TOP 10	MONEY
1993	50	4	0	0	0	24,915
1994	32	29	0	0	0	391,920
1995	18	31	1	0	5	593,542
1996	31	30	0	0	3	688,511
1997	23	32	1	1	4	1,143,725
1998	11	33	1	0	10	1,838,379
1999	17	34	1	1	10	2,001,832
2000	23	34	0	0	2	2,035,902
2001	31	35	0	0	2	2,873,184
2002	28	36	0	0	1	2,954,229
2003	38	29	0	0	1	2,577,616
Lifetime		327	4	2	37	$17,123,755

JOHNNY BENSON

Born: June 27, 1963
Grand Rapids, MI
Family: wife, Debbie;
children, Katelyn and Mikayla
Plans were uncertain at
press time

Career highlights: Lost ride in the No. 10 Valvoline Pontiac Grand Prix team (which has since switched to Chevrolet) after the 2003 season ... was replaced at MBV Motorsports by Busch Series star Scott Riggs, who is eight years younger ... Benson drove for MBV for three-plus seasons with respectable results ... was 11th, 29th, and 24th in points in the three full seasons, and he won the fall of 2002 race at Rockingham, North Carolina ... didn't win a pole or race in 2003, but was fifth at Dover in June and fourth in the finale at Homestead in November ... other top-10s were at Michigan in August and Richmond in September ... started second at Rockingham in February, tenth at Charlotte in May, and ninth at Richmond in September ... came to NASCAR after successful Late Model and ASA career in the Midwest ... was 1994 Busch Series Rookie of the Year and 1995 champion, then 1996 Winston Cup Rookie of the Year with Bahari Racing, who he raced with in 1996 and 1997 ... spent 1998 and 1999 with Roush Racing, then split 2000 between Tim Beverley and Nelson Bowers ... got first of his two career Cup poles at Atlanta in March of 1996 in fourth Cup start for Bahari.

YEAR	PTS. POS.	EVENTS	POLES	WINS	TOP 10	MONEY
1996	21	30	1	0	6	947,080
1997	11	32	1	0	8	1,256,457
1998	20	32	0	0	10	1,360,335
1999	28	34	0	0	2	1,567,668
2000	13	33	0	0	7	1,841,324
2001	11	36	0	0	14	2,573,569
2002	29	31	0	1	7	2,791,879
2003	24	36	0	0	4	3,544,793
Lifetime		264	2	1	58	$16,204,439

GREG BIFFLE

Born: December 23, 1969
Vancouver, WA
Family: Single
No. 16 National Guard
Ford Taurus

Career highlights: Got his breakthrough victory in the Pepsi 400 at Daytona Beach in July 2003 ... led only the final 21 laps and had a relatively easy last lap when Bobby Labonte, who was running second at the time, ran out of gas on the backstretch ... that race was among three top-5s and six top-10s in his rookie year ... was in a strong rookie class that included Rookie of the Year winner Jamie McMurray, Casey Mears, Tony Raines, and Larry Foyt ... worked his way from weekly short-track racing in the Northwest, through the Raybestos Brakes Northwest Series, the Craftsman Truck Series, and then the Busch Series before reaching Winston Cup ... was 1998 CTS Rookie of the Year, then won the championship in 2000 ... moved to the Busch Series after 12 poles and 16 victories in just over three full years in the CTS ... finished fourth in points in 33 Busch Series races in 2001 (when he was Rookie of the Year) and won the 2002 championship for team owner Jack Roush ... won five poles and four Busch Series races in clinching the championship in the next-to-last race of the season at Phoenix, Arizona ... made seven Winston Cup starts in 2002—one for Roush Racing, four for Andy Petree while Bobby Hamilton recovered from early-September injuries, then two late-season starts in Petty Enterprises' No. 44 Dodge.

YEAR	PTS. POS.	EVENTS	POLES	WINS	TOP 10	MONEY
2002	48	7	0	0	0	394,773
2003	20	35	0	1	6	2,805,673
Lifetime		42	0	1	6	$3,200,446

DAVE BLANEY

Born: October 24, 1962
Sharon, PA
Family: wife, Lisa; children, Emma, Ryan and Erin

Career highlights: Another driver facing an uncertain 2004 after he lost his ride with the Jasper team when Roger Penske bought it and merged it with the Dodges run by Rusty Wallace and Ryan Newman ... as late as mid-December 2003, Blaney had no idea what his plans were for 2004 ... got first career pole at Rockingham in February and had top-10 starts at Charlotte in May, Chicago in July, Michigan in August, and

Jeff Burton (No. 99) leads two other drivers past a piece of history at North Carolina Speedway. Starting in 2004, R.J. Reynolds will no longer sponsor NASCAR's main racing circuit, meaning the word "Winston" will become nearly extinct at the racetrack.

Phoenix in November ... best finishes were tenth at Rockingham in February, eighth at Atlanta and third at Darlington in back-to-back spring races, and ninth at Pocono in July ... an outstanding Sprint Car driver who came to NASCAR via the Bill Davis-owned Busch Series team in 1999 ... was 1995 World of Outlaws series champion and is a multiple winner of most major Sprint Car races ... ran five Cup races for Davis in 1999 before going full-time in 2000 ... was seventh in 1999 Busch Series points based on five top five finishes (including two seconds) and seven other top-10 finishes ... replaced Robert Pressley at Jasper Engines for 2002 and 2003 when Davis was uncertain of sponsorship possibilities.

YEAR	PTS. POS.	EVENTS	POLES	WINS	TOP 10	MONEY
1992	N/A	1	0	0	0	4,500
1999	N/A	5	0	0	0	212,170
2000	31	33	0	0	2	1,272,689
2001	22	36	0	0	6	1,788,146
2002	19	36	0	0	5	2,978,593
2003	28	36	1	0	4	2,838,692
Lifetime		147	1	0	17	$9,124,540

BRETT BODINE

Born: January 11, 1959
Elmira, NY
Family: Single;
daughter, Heidi
No. 11 Ford Taurus

Career highlights: Made only 6 of the first 13 races before sponsorship woes sidelined him the rest of the year ... finished between 24th and 42nd in those six races ... incorrectly thought he had a solid sponsor for the final third of the season ... isn't sure of his 2004 plans, but thinks he'll somehow make it work, if only part-time ... 2003 was his eighth year as owner/driver, the last such combination on the circuit ... bought team from Junior Johnson late in 1995 ... drove for Johnson that season after five years with Kenny Bernstein ... started Cup racing in 1988 with Bud Moore after successful Modified and Busch career ... runner-up for the 1986 Busch title ... began racing at the Chemung (New York) Speedrome, where older brother, Geoffrey, had started and where younger brother, Todd, would also race ... only victory came at North Wilkesboro in 1990 ... graduate of New York State University at Alfred with an associate degree in mechanical engineering ... second-best racing moment was finishing second in the inaugural Brickyard 400 in 1994.

YEAR	PTS. POS.	EVENTS	POLES	WINS	TOP 10	MONEY
1986	92T	1	0	0	0	10,100
1987	32	14	0	0	0	51,145
1988	20	29	0	0	5	433,658
1989	19	29	0	0	6	281,274
1990	12	29	1	1	9	422,681
1991	19	29	1	0	6	376,220
1992	15	29	1	0	13	495,224
1993	20	29	2	0	9	582,014
1994	19	31	0	0	6	791,444
1995	20	31	0	0	2	893,029
1996	24	30	0	0	1	767,716
1997	29	31	0	0	2	936,694
1998	25	33	0	0	0	1,281,673
1999	35	32	0	0	0	1,321,396
2000	35	29	0	0	0	1,020,659
2001	30	36	0	0	2	1,740,526
2002	36	32	0	0	0	1,766,82
2003	52	6	0	0	0	383,718
Lifetime		480	5	1	61	$13,575,991

TODD BODINE

Born: February. 27. 1964
Elmira, NY
Family: wife, Lynn;
child, Ashlyn
Plans uncertain at press time

Career highlights: A rough 2003 with Travis Carter's underfunded team meant that Bodine's 2004 plans were still uncertain at press time ...

the Carter team went into the Christmas/New Year's break without solid backing in place and was shut down, pending sponsorship ... team was 31st in 2003 points with only one top-10 in 35 starts (eighth at Pocono in July) ... Bodine generally qualified in the 20s, 30s, or 40s, and finished in the 20s or 30s ... followed older brothers Geoffrey and Brett into Cup racing after starting in Modifieds and the Busch Series ... ran a limited Cup schedule in 1992 and 1993 before going full-time for Butch Mock in 1994 and 1995 ... raced for 11 other Cup owners from 1996 through 2001, when he gained a full-time ride with Travis Carter and Carl Haas ... resume includes 14 Busch Series victories (the most recent one in 2002) and seven top-10 finishes in points ... was second to Randy LaJoie in the 1997 Busch season standings ... father and grandfather owned the Chemung (New York) Speedrome ... Todd built race cars before he started racing them.

YEAR	PTS. POS.	EVENTS	POLES	WINS	TOP 10	MONEY
1992	87T	1	0	0	0	3,485
1993	40	10	0	0	0	63,245
1994	20	30	0	0	7	494,316
1995	33	28	0	0	3	664,620
1996	40	10	0	0	1	198,525
1997	52	5	1	0	0	125,845
1998	41	14	0	0	2	378,766
1999	46	7	0	0	0	208,382
2000	49	5	0	0	1	234,065
2001	29	35	3	0	2	1,740,315
2002	38	24	1	0	4	1,879,760
2003	31	35	0	0	1	2,521,724
Lifetime		204	5	0	21	$8,513,055

JEFF BURTON

Born: June 29, 1967
South Boston, VA
Family: wife, Kim; children,
Kimberle and Harrison
No. 99 Ford Taurus

Career highlights: Missed out on a spot in the top 10 of the overall standings for just the third time in seven years with Roush Racing ... finished 12th, with no poles, no victories, only three top-5 finishes and 11 top-10s ... finished strong, with three top-10s in the last four races in October and November ... came to Cup racing from weekly short tracks, which led to the Busch

Driver Scott Wimmer talks to one crew member while another pushes his car into place before the Pop Secret Microwave Popcorn 400 at North Carolina Speedway on November 9.

Series and a one-ride Cup deal in 1993 with owner Fil Martocci ... drove without distinction in 1994 and 1995 for the Stavola Brothers ... had 12 top-10s in his first year with Roush (1996), more than twice as many as with Martocci and the Stavolas combined ... earned his first victory in the inaugural race at the new Texas track in 1997, and also won at New Hampshire and Martinsville that year ... in 1998, won twice, at New Hampshire and Richmond ... won six races in 1999 and four in 2000 before dropping off to just two in 2001 and none in 2002 and 2003 ... younger brother of Ward Burton ... outstanding athlete in high school, where he played basketball and soccer ... his favorite sports team is the Duke University men's basketball squad ... had seven top-10

qualifying runs in 2003, including seventh-place starts at Las Vegas and Richmnond ... best finish was second behind Roush Racing teammate Greg Biffle at Daytona Beach in July ... one of four Roush Racing drivers to finish outside the top-10 in final points, although teammate Matt Kenseth helped offset that by claiming the final Winston Cup championship ... team went into the Christmas/New Years break without a solid sponsor, leaving the unlikely possibility that the team might have to run a limited schedule in 2004.

YEAR	PTS. POS.	EVENTS	POLES	WINS	TOP 10	MONEY
1993	83T	1	0	0	0	9,550
1994	24	30	0	0	3	594,700
1995	32	29	0	0	2	630,770

YEAR	PTS. POS.	EVENTS	POLES	WINS	TOP 10	MONEY
1996	13	30	1	0	12	884,303
1997	4	32	0	3	18	2,296,614
1998	5	33	0	2	23	2,626,987
1999	5	34	0	6	23	5,725,399
2000	3	34	1	4	22	5,959,439
2001	10	36	0	2	16	3,866,333
2002	12	36	0	0	14	3,863,220
2003	12	36	0	0	11	4,384,752
Lifetime		331	2	17	144	$31,588,107

WARD BURTON

Born: October 25, 1961
Danville, VA
Family: wife, Tabitha;
children, Sarah, Jeb,
and Everett
No. 0 NetZero Chevrolet
Monte Carlo

Career highlights: Won the 2002 Daytona 500 and that season's July race at Loudon, New Hampshire, bringing his career victory total to five ... 2003 had promise, but internal strife and poor performances divided the Bill Davis-owned team, and Burton left in the fall to drive for Gene Haas on the No. 0 NetZero Pontiac (now a Chevrolet) ... best qualifying effort of 2003 was second for the fall race at Martinsville, his last start with Davis and crew chief Frankie Stoddard ... in addition to Martinsville, had three other top-10 qualifying runs to go with four top-10 finishes in what was generally an unpleasant season ... went from go-karts and Late Model cars to the Busch Series, which led to a Cup ride in 1994 with owner Alan Dillard ... older brother of Cup driver Jeff Burton ... all five Cup victories were with Bill Davis Racing: Rockingham in 1995, Darlington in 2000 and 2001, and Daytona Beach and Loudon in 2002 ... graduated from Hargrave Military Academy and attended Elon College for two years ... sponsors the Ward Burton Wildlife Foundation at Patrick Henry School for Boys and Girls.

YEAR	PTS. POS.	EVENTS	POLES	WINS	TOP 10	MONEY
1994	35	26	1	0	2	304,700
1995	22	29	0	1	6	634,655
1996	33	27	1	0	4	873,619
1997	24	31	1	0	7	1,004,944
1998	16	33	0	0	5	1,516,183
1999	9	34	0	0	16	2,405,913
2000	10	34	0	1	17	2,699,604
2001	14	36	0	1	10	3,293,599
2002	25	36	1	2	8	4,849,880
2003	21	36	0	0	4	3,628,600
Lifetime		322	7	5	79	$21,211,697

KURT BUSCH

Born: August 4, 1978
Las Vegas, NV
Family: Single
No. 96 Sharpie Ford Taurus

Career highlights: Had an eventful year with Roush Racing, a year that featured four victories and some well-publicized run-ins with fellow drivers and NASCAR officials ... won both races at Bristol, Tennessee, and one each at Fontana, California (April), and Michigan (June) ... lost to Ricky Craven by inches in the spring at Darlington in what turned out to be the closest finish in Winston Cup racing since NASCAR started using electronic timers ... that was one of nine top-5 finishes and 14 top-10s ... surprisingly, all of those strong finishes only earned an 11th-place finish in the final Cup standings ... began racing in Dwarf and Legend cars in Las Vegas ... won the 1999 NASCAR Southwest Tour title and was hired by Jack Roush for the Craftsman Truck Series in 2000 ... had a successful first CTS season, winning four poles and four races, finishing second in points, and earning Rookie of the Year honors ... ran seven Cup races late in 2000 in preparation for full run in 2001 ... qualified for 35 of 36 races in his rookie year, missing only the fall event near Atlanta ... was 27th in points and lost Rookie of the Year honors to ninth-ranked Kevin Harvick ... was fined and placed on NASCAR probation for the balance of the season after getting into a scrap with Jimmy Spencer (who also was fined and put on probation) following the August race in Michigan ... later, Busch again drew NASCAR's ire after apparently oiling down pit road and driving recklessly at Martinsville in October.

YEAR	PTS. POS.	EVENTS	POLES	WINS	TOP 10	MONEY
2000	48	7	0	0	0	311,915
2001	27	35	1	0	6	2,170,629
2002	3	36	1	4	20	3,723,650
2003	11	36	0	4	14	5,587,384
Lifetime		114	2	8	40	$11,793,578

RICKY CRAVEN

Born: May 24, 1966
Newburgh, ME
Family: wife, Cathleen;
children, Riley and Richard
No. 32 Tide Chevrolet
Monte Carlo

Career highlights: Won in one of NASCAR's closest-ever finishes (and closest since the advent of electronic timers), beating Kurt Busch in a down-to-the-line, beatin' and bangin' shootout at Darlington in March ... the margin of victory was inches, almost unrecognizable to the unaided eye ... that was the unquestioned highlight in an otherwise mediocre year that saw Craven slip from 7th in points in May to 27th in the final accounting ... he won no poles, had just the one memorable victory, and claimed three top-5 finishes and eight top-10s in 36 starts ... Cal Wells–owned team switched from Pontiac to Chevrolet in the off-season after General Motors announced that it would no longer support the Pontiac nameplate in NASCAR ... career began on short tracks in Maine in mid-1980s ... advanced through several support series to get full-time Cup ride in 1995 with Larry Hedrick ... was 1995 Rookie of the Year, adding to his collection of those awards that began with the 1990 Busch North and 1992 Busch Series rookie titles ... spent 1995–1996 with Hedrick before going to Hendrick Motorsports ... was third in the 1997 Daytona 500, behind teammates Jeff Gordon and Terry Labonte ... injured in practice at Texas and missed much of the 1998 season ... left Hedrick after eight races in 1998 and briefly drove for Nelson Bowers ... spent frustrating 1999 and 2000 with Scott Barbour and Hal Hicks on underfunded teams ... determination led to a call from Cal Wells to replace Scott Pruett for 2001 ... 2004 will be his fourth consecutive season with Wells.

YEAR	PTS. POS.	EVENTS	POLES	WINS	TOP 10	MONEY
1991	N/A	1	0	0	0	3,750
1995	24	31	0	0	4	597,054
1996	20	31	2	0	5	941,959
1997	19	30	0	0	7	1,259,550
1998	46	11	1	0	1	506,230
1999	41	24	0	0	0	853,835
2000	44	16	0	0	0	363,562
2001	21	36	1	1	7	1,923,981
2002	15	36	2	0	9	2,493,722
2003	27	36	0	1	8	3,216,211
Lifetime		252	6	2	41	$12,159,854

DALE EARNHARDT JR.

Born: October 10, 1974
Kannapolis, NC
Family: Single
No. 8 Budweiser Chevrolet
Monte Carlo

Career highlights: The tour's most popular driver—both unofficially and in season-long fan balloting—had a somewhat bittersweet year ... he didn't win any poles, but he won at Talladega in the spring and Phoenix in the fall and finished third in the overall points race, never dropping out of the top five in points the entire season ... it was his first top-5 points finish and his second top-10 in four full seasons ... his spring victory at Talladega was his fourth consecutive at the track where his late father always had so much success ... regardless of his on-track performance, he is NASCAR's most heavily-marketed driver ... began racing at Concord (North Carolina) Speedway in 1991 at age 17 ... progressed to the Busch Series, where he debuted at Myrtle Beach (South Carolina) Speedway in 1997 ... won the 1998 and 1999 Busch titles in cars prepared by Dale Earnhardt Inc. ... won 8 poles and 13 races in those championship seasons ... ran five Cup races for DEI in 1999 and the full 34-race season in 2000 ... first victories were at Texas in April 2000 and Richmond in May the same year ... finished second to Matt Kenseth for 2000 Rookie of the Year honors ... sponsor Budweiser is making sure everyone knows he's their man with an aggressive marketing campaign ... to some, he's an incredible talent destined to win one championship after another; to others, he's an overhyped driver, no better or worse than a dozen other drivers who aren't marketed and promoted nearly as much.

YEAR	PTS. POS.	EVENTS	POLES	WINS	TOP 10	MONEY
1999	N/A	5	0	0	1	162,095
2000	16	34	2	2	5	2,801,880

2001	8	36	2	3	15	5,384,627
2002	11	36	2	2	16	4,570,980
2003	3	36	0	2	21	6,980,807
Lifetime		147	6	9	58	$20,742.359

BILL ELLIOTT

Born: October 8, 1955
Cumming, GA
Family: wife, Cindy; children,
Starr, Chase, and Brittany
No. 91 Dodge

Career highlights: Won the late-season race at Rockingham and came within a mile of winning the following weekend in the season-finale at Homestead, Florida ... while well ahead on the last lap at Homestead, a cut right-rear tire foiled his nearly flawless run and cost him seven positions ... finished ninth in points, his 14th top-10 points finish since 1983 ... announced after the season that he planned to reduce his workload and run a limited 2004 schedule, yielding his No. 9 Dodge to rookie Kasey Kahne (Elliott will race a different car the weeks he decides to participate) ... the Rockingham victory was the 44th of his career and his 4th since joining Ray Evernham and his Dodge-sponsored team for the 2001 season ... had 15 top-10 starts, 9 top-5 finishes, and 12 top-10 finishes ... despite only four victories since 1995, he remains one of racing's most popular drivers ... came out of the Georgia backwoods in 1976 with a family-owned team that got its big break when the late Harry Melling bought the team and began sponsoring it in 1982 ... Elliott got his first career victory in 1983, then won 11 races and the first Winston Million in 1985 ... won the 1988 championship, one of 13 times he was top-10 in points ... voted Most Popular Driver a record 15 times in 17 tries, including every year between 1991 and 2000 ... drove three years for Junior Johnson after leaving Melling following the 1991 season ... drove for his own team for six years (1995–2000), and was glad to get out from under that burden ... voted American Driver of the Year in 1985 and 1988 ... has fastest qualifying lap in NASCAR history, 212.809 mph at Talladega in 1987, a lap that likely will never be challenged.

YEAR	PTS. POS.	EVENTS	POLES	WINS	TOP 10	MONEY
1976	41	7	0	0	0	11,635
1977	35	10	0	0	2	20,575
1978	33	10	0	0	5	42,065
1979	28	14	0	0	5	57,450
1980	34	12	0	0	4	42,545
1981	30	13	1	0	6	70,320
1982	25	21	1	0	9	226,780
1983	3	30	0	1	22	479,965
1984	3	30	4	3	24	680,266
1985	2	28	11	11	18	2,433,187
1986	4	29	4	2	16	1,069,142
1987	2	29	8	6	20	1,612,210
1988	1	29	6	6	22	1,574,639
1989	6	29	2	3	14	854,570
1990	4	29	2	1	16	1,090,730
1991	11	29	2	1	12	705,605
1992	2	29	2	5	17	1,692,381
1993	8	30	2	0	15	955,859
1994	10	31	1	1	12	936,779
1995	8	31	2	0	11	996,816
1996	30	24	0	0	6	716,506
1997	8	32	1	0	14	1,607,827
1998	18	32	0	0	5	1,618,421
1999	21	34	0	0	2	1,624,101
2000	21	34	0	0	0	2,580,823
2001	15	36	2	1	9	3,337,671
2002	13	36	4	2	13	3,753,490
2003	9	36	0	1	12	5,008,530
Lifetime		731	55	44	319	$36,427,403

BRENDAN GAUGHAN

Born: July 10, 1975
Las Vegas, NV
Family: Single
No. 77 Kodak
Dodge Intrepid

Career highlights: Moves from the Craftsman Truck Series to drive a Dodge for the new Roger Penske/Jasper Motorsports team ... replaces Dave Blaney, who ran the 2002 and 2003 seasons for Jasper and owner Doug Bawel after two-plus seasons at Bill Davis Racing ... Gaughan ran a handful of CTS races between 1997 and 2001, then was Rookie of the Year in 2002 when he won 2 races in 22 starts ... backed that up with a series-high six CTS victories in 2003, but crashed in the finale at Homestead and finished only fourth in overall points ... his 2003 line was impressive: 6 victories, 14 top-5 finshes, and 18 top-10s in 24 starts ... all told, has 8 victories, 21 top-5 finishes, and 30 top-10s in 64 career starts ... he was the 2000 and 2001 NASCAR Winston West champion and an outstanding off-road racer ... played football and basketball at Georgetown University, where he was a teammate with current NBA superstar Allen Iverson.

NASCAR officials inspect every last detail of every car both before and after each race to make sure that drivers and crew chiefs are following all NASCAR rules. Here they use pre-made templates to check the specifications on Tony Stewart's car.

YEAR	PTS. POS.	EVENTS	POLES	WINS	TOP 10	MONEY

No Cup experience

JEFF GORDON

Born: August 4, 1971
Vallejo, CA
Family: Single
No. 24 Du Pont Chevrolet
Monte Carlo

Career highlights: Another solid year for one of NASCAR's best drivers and best teams ... 4 poles, 3 victories, 15 top-5 finshes, and 20 top-10s got him to fourth in overall points, his 10th consecutive year finishing in the top 10 in the Winston Cup race ... moved from fifth to fourth in the season-finale at Homestead, Florida ... was second in points at midseason, but nine mediocre finishes during an eleven-race stretch cost him any shot at his fifth championship ... has 64 career victories and 46 career poles, and has won on almost every Cup track ... has won every major race at least once, including three Brickyard 400s, three Coca-Cola 600s, and two Daytona 500s ... began racing go-karts and quarter-midgets at age 5 ... was 1979 and 1981 national quarter-midget champion ... won the 1991 USAC Silver Crown title before casting his lot with stock cars ... was 11th in points and was 1991 Busch Series Rookie

![Bill Elliott (No. 9) maintains a slight lead over fellow veteran driver Ricky Craven (No. 32) during the MBNA America 400 at Dover International Speedway]

Bill Elliott (No. 9) maintains a slight lead over fellow veteran driver Ricky Craven (No. 32) during the MBNA America 400 at Dover International Speedway. After the 2003 season ended, 26-year-veteran Elliott announced that he would run only a partial Cup schedule in 2004.

of the Year, then won three races and a record 11 Busch poles in 1992, when he finished fourth in points ... Rick Hendrick hired him that year, and Gordon ran the season-finale near Atlanta ... was 14th in points, won a Daytona 125-mile qualifier and was 1993 Cup Rookie of the year ... won an amazing 33 Cup races in 96 starts in 1996–1998 ... stepfather, John Bickford, moved family from California to Indiana so Jeff, then 13, could race ... storybook marriage to Brooke, a stunning former Miss Winston, ended in 2002.

YEAR	PTS. POS.	EVENTS	POLES	WINS	TOP 10	MONEY
1992	79T	1	0	0	0	6,285

1993	14	30	1	0	11	765,168
1994	8	31	1	2	14	1,799,523
1995	1	31	8	7	23	4,347,343
1996	2	31	5	10	24	3,428,485
1997	1	32	1	10	23	6,375,658
1998	1	33	0	13	28	9,306,584
1999	6	34	7	7	21	5,858,633
2000	9	34	3	3	22	3,001,144
2001	1	36	6	6	24	6,649,076
2002	4	36	3	3	20	4,981,170
2003	4	36	4	3	20	6,622,002.
Lifetime		365	46	64	210	$58,525,057

ROBBY GORDON

Born: January 2, 1969
Bellflower, CA
Family: Single
No. 31 Cingular Chevrolet
Monte Carlo

Career highlights: Swept both of 2003's road races, winning at Sonoma, California, in June and two months later at Watkins Glen, New York, to claim his only victories of the season ... had 4 top-5 finishes and 10 top-10 finishes ... had four top-10 qualifying efforts: second at Sonoma, third in the Daytona 500 and at Michigan in August, and sixth at Talladega in the spring ... an outstanding off-road, stadium, and open-wheel Indy car driver ... has been with 10 different Cup teams since his NASCAR debut in 1991 with Junie Donlavey ... the 2003 season with Richard Childress Racing was the first time Gordon was with the same team for the entire duration of two consecutive years ... consistent winner in long-distance off-road races and in the Mickey Thompson Stadium Series ... also accomplished IMSA and SCCA sports car road racer ... came within a lap of winning the 1999 Indianpolis 500 before running out of fuel while leading the race ... victory at Loudon, New Hampshire, in November 2001 came five days after not qualifying near Atlanta, where he won his only Cup pole in 1997.

YEAR	PTS. POS.	EVENTS	POLES	WINS	TOP 10	MONEY
1991	55	2	0	0	0	27,265
1993	94	1	0	0	0	17,665
1994	N/A	1	0	0	0	7,665
1996	57	3	0	0	0	23,365
1997	40	20	1	0	1	622,439
1998	67	1	0	0	0	24,765
2000	43	17	0	0	1	620,781
2001	44	17	0	1	3	1,371,900
2002	20	36	0	0	5	3,054,240
2003	16	36	0	2	10	4,157,064
Lifetime		134	1	3	21	$10,226,462

JEFF GREEN

Born: September 6, 1962
Owensboro, KY
Wife: Michelle
Children: None
No. 43 Cheerios
Dodge Intrepid

Career highlights: In 2004, Green returns to Petty Enterprises, which hired him in September 2003 after he started the season in the No. 30 AOL Chevrolet owned by Richard Childress Rac-

ing ... that relationship lasted until May, when Green replaced Steve Park in Dale Earnhardt Inc.'s No. 1 Pennzoil Chevrolet (Park went from DEI to RCR in an even-up driver swap) ... Green then ran eight late-season races for the Pettys, who were so impressed they hired him for the 2004 season ... Green ran 20 of 31 Cup races in 1997 for Gary Bechtel, then 22 of 32 in 1998 for Bechtel, Felix Sabates, and Chuck Rider ... made the jump to NASCAR following an outstanding go-cart and short-track career in Kentucky and Tennessee ... made his Busch Series debut in 1990 and ran a limited schedule until going full-time in 1995 for Dale Earnhardt Inc. ... drove in the Busch Series for Bechtel in 1996 and 1997, and ran a few races for Ricky Craven in 1998 ... broke through in 1999 with three Busch victories, then won six more races in 2000 en route to the Busch title, winning by a record 616 points over teammate Jason Keller ... made a strong run at the 2001 Busch title, but didn't have enough to catch new Cup teammate Kevin Harvick ... ran a few Cup races for RCR in 2001 even while he was primarily busy chasing the Busch title ... he and older brother, David, are the only siblings to win Busch Series titles.

YEAR	PTS. POS.	EVENTS	POLES	WINS	TOP 10	MONEY
1994	N/A	3	0	0	0	20,270
1996	49	4	0	0	0	46,875
1997	39	20	0	0	2	434,685
1998	40	22	0	0	0	589,841
1999	60	1	0	0	1	62,921
2001	48	8	1	0	1	441,449
2002	17	36	0	0	6	2,531,339
2003	34	31	1	0	1	2,693,533
Lifetime		125	2	0	10	$6,830,913

KEVIN HARVICK

Born: December 8, 1975
Bakersfield, CA
Wife: DeLana
Children: None
No. 29 Goodwrench
Chevrolet Monte Carlo

Career highlights: Finished a career-best fifth in points, a nice comeback after finishing 21st in 2002 ... before 2003, his best points finish was ninth in his Rookie of the Year–winning season of 2001, when he succeeded the late Dale Earnhardt at Richard Childress Racing … both of 2003's highlights came on the same weekend in August when he won the pole and the race in the Brickyard 400 at Indianapolis Motor Speedway … had 12 total top-10 starts and 18 total top-10 finishes in 36 starts … won his third-ever Cup start (near Atlanta in March 2001) and also won at Chicagoland later that season … also won five races and the Busch Series title in 2001 … first driver to run the full Busch and Winston Cup schedules in the same season … named 1995 NASCAR Southwest Tour Rookie of the Year, even as he raced a limited Craftsman Truck Series schedule in 1995 and 1996 … in 1997–1998 ran CTS and Winston West, then full CTS schedule in 1999 … 2000 Busch Series Rookie of the Year for Childress based on three victories and a third-place points finish … all told, already has 28 NASCAR victories: 3 on the Southwest Tour, 10 in Winston West, 10 in Busch, 4 in Winston Cup, and 1 in Craftsman … 2003 was his first official "full season" of Winston Cup racing; in 2001, he didn't run the Daytona 500 (the day Earnhardt was killed), and in 2002, he was "parked" by NASCAR officials and forced to sit out the spring Martinsville race after being cited for rough driving in the previous day's Craftsman Series race.

YEAR	PTS. POS.	EVENTS	POLES	WINS	TOP 10	MONEY
2001	9	35	0	2	16	3,716,633
2002	21	35	1	1	8	3,849,216
2003	5	36	1	1	18	6,237,119
Lifetime		106	2	4	42	$14,388,537

DALE JARRETT

Born: November 26, 1956
Newton, NC
Family: wife, Kelley; children, Jason, Natalee, Karsyn, and Zachary
No. 88 UPS Ford Taurus

Career highlights: The 2003 season started out fine—tenth in the Daytona 500 and victory a week later in the Subway 400 at Rockingham—but not much went right after that and Jarrett finished a career-worst 26th in the points race … that snapped his streak of eight consecutive top-10 finishes in the Winston Cup race … Rockingham was his only top-5 finish of 2003 and he had only five more top-10s after the first two weekends … the second son to join his father (Ned, who won in 1961 and 1965) as Winston Cup champion, following Lee and Richard Petty … won the Cup in 1999, his fifth year with Robert Yates Racing (RYR) … began racing in the late 1970s at hometown Hickory (North Carolina) Motor Speedway … moved up through the Busch Series, with occasional Cup races for many different owners, during the 1980s … first quality ride was with Cale Yarborough in 1988–1989, then in 1990–1991 he drove for the Wood Brothers … from 1992 to 1994, he drove for Joe Gibbs, then moved to RYR to replace the injured Ernie Irvan … was top 10 in points eight of his first nine years with Yates … first driver to win the Daytona 500 and Brickyard 400 in the same season (1999) … won at least one race every year between 1993 and 2003 … an excellent golfer and star high school football and basketball player … very active in the Susan G. Komen Breast Cancer Foundation.

YEAR	PTS. POS.	EVENTS	POLES	WINS	TOP 10	MONEY
1984	N/A	3	0	0	0	7,345
1986	N/A	1	0	0	0	990
1987	26	24	0	0	2	143,405
1988	23	29	0	0	1	118,640
1989	24	29	0	0	5	232,317
1990	25	24	0	0	7	214,495
1991	17	29	0	1	8	444,256
1992	19	29	0	0	8	418,648
1993	4	30	0	1	18	1,242,394
1994	16	30	0	1	9	871,754
1995	3	31	1	1	14	1,363,158
1996	3	31	2	4	21	2,985,418
1997	2	32	3	7	23	3,240,542
1998	3	33	0	3	22	4,019,657
1999	1	34	0	4	24	6,649,596
2000	4	34	3	2	24	5,934,475
2001	5	36	4	4	19	4,608,366
2002	9	36	1	2	18	4,421,951
2003	26	36	0	1	7	4,121,487
Lifetime		531	15	31	235	$41,818,270

JIMMIE JOHNSON

Born: September 17, 1975
El Cajon, CA
Family: Single
No. 48 Lowe's Chevrolet Monte Carlo

Career highlights: Followed his outstanding 2002 rookie season with two poles, three victories, and a career-best second-place finish in the points race ... finished just 90 points behind champion Matt Kenseth, but he (along with everyone else) never had a realistic chance to catch the consistent Kenseth over the final third of the season ... Johnson won poles at Pocono in June and Kansas City in October, and won the spring 600-mile race near Charlotte and both the July and September races in New Hampshire ... had 19 other top-10 qualifying efforts and 17 other top-10 finishes ... despite a great rookie season, he lost a classic Rookie of the Year battle to Ryan Newman ... brought an impressive resume to Winston Cup racing, including success on off-road and stadium tracks and in the Busch Series ... won the Mickey Thompson Stadium title in 1992, 1993, and 1994; the 1994 SCORE Desert title; the 1996–1997 SODA Winter Series title; and the 1995 SCORE Trophy ... was 1998 ASA Rookie of the Year ... has only one Busch Series victory, but was top 10 in points in 2000 and 2001 ... made Cup debut at Charlotte in fall 2001, then made his second and third starts at Homestead and Atlanta ... four-time Cup champion Jeff Gordon and Rick Hendrick are co-owners of Johnson's car.

YEAR	PTS. POS.	EVENTS	POLES	WINS	TOP 10	MONEY
2001	52	3	0	0	0	122,320
2002	5	36	4	3	21	3,788,268
2003	2	36	2	3	20	7,745,530
Lifetime		75	6	6	41	$11,656,118

KASEY KAHNE

Born: April 10, 1980
Enumclaw, WA
Family: Single
No. 9 Dodge Dealers Dodge

Career highlights: Was named in December 2003 to run the full 2004 season for Ray Evernham as Bill Elliott's replacement ... Elliott will run a limited schedule, with Kahne in the No. 9 Dodge for owner-points provisionals ... came up through open-wheel ranks in the Northwest, then ran United States Auto Club (USAC) events in the Midwest in 2000 ... highly successful in Midget, Sprint, and Silver Crown cars ... came to NASCAR in 2002 with a limited Busch Series schedule in a Ford prepared by Robert Yates ... finished seventh in the 2003 Busch standings, winning the final race of the season at Homestead and adding three other top-5 finishes and 13 other top-10s ... Evernham and Dodge lured him away from Ford, which thought it had him secured and locked up for a future Cup ride.

YEAR	PTS. POS.	EVENTS	POLES	WINS	TOP 10	MONEY
No Cup experience						

MATT KENSETH

Born: March 10, 1972
Cambridge, WI
Family: wife, Katie;
child, Ross
No. 17 DeWalt Ford Taurus

Career highlights: Shocked almost everyone—probably even himself and team owner Jack Roush—by winning his first Winston Cup title in workmanlike fashion ... even more notable because it is the last Winston Cup title, with Nextel taking over series sponsorship in 2004 ... almost no preseason talk centered on Kenseth and crew chief Robbie Reiser as a championship caliber team, and even their season numbers weren't spectacular: no poles and only one victory ... however, the team was consistently near the top, finishing with 11 top-5 finishes and 25 top-10s ... Kenseth also made sure he was always on the track at the end of nearly every race, suffering only two DNFs all year—one at Talladega in October and the other in the season finale at Homestead when the title was already clinched ... ironically, he led the tour with five victories in 2002, but finished only eighth in points ... raced on several short-track and lower-level Midwestern series before Bill Elliott tapped him in 1998 to be his substitute in a Cup race at Dover, Delaware, while Elliott attended his mother's funeral ... ran

With his championship trophy proudly displayed on the roof of his No. 17 Ford, Matt Kenseth poses for photos after clinching the Winston (now Nextel) Cup title at the Pop Secret Microwave Popcorn 400 at North Carolina Speedway.

21 Busch races in 1997 with moderate success, then won a pole and three races en route to a second-place finish in the 1998 Busch standings ... won four more Busch races and finished third (behind Dale Earnhardt Jr. and Jeff Green) in 1999 ... ran five Cup races for Roush Racing in 1999 in preparation for his 2000 Rookie of the Year season ... that year he won the Coca-Cola 600 near Charlotte and had 10 other top-10s in beating Earnhardt Jr. for top rookie honors ... the 2001 season wasn't nearly as successful: no top-10 starts, 11 provisionals, and only 9 top-10 finishes ... rebounded nicely in 2002 with Roush and Reiser.

YEAR	PTS. POS.	EVENTS	POLES	WINS	TOP 10	MONEY
1998	57	1	0	0	1	42,340
1999	49	5	0	0	1	143,561
2000	14	34	0	1	11	2,408,138
2001	13	36	0	0	9	2,265,839
2002	8	36	1	5	19	4,514,203
2003	1	36	0	1	25	9,422,764
Lifetime		148	1	7	66	$19,096,585

BOBBY LABONTE

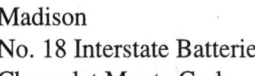

Born: May 8, 1964
Corpus Christi, TX
Family: wife, Donna;
children, Robert and
Madison
No. 18 Interstate Batteries
Chevrolet Monte Carlo

Career highlights: Rebounded nicely after a mediocre 2002 season, when he was 16th in points and won only once ... in 2003, had 4 poles, 2 victories, 12 top-5 finishes, and 17 top-10s, roughly twice as well as he had done the year before ... finished eight in the points race, his seventh top-10 finish in nine years with Joe Gibbs Racing ... poles came at Las Vegas and Bristol in the spring, then at both Michigan races ... won the spring race near Atlanta and the season finale at Homestead, Florida, in November when race leader Bill Elliott had a flat tire on the last lap ... qualified on the outside pole at Atlanta and Homestead in the fall and finished second on three consecutive spring weekends, first at Martinsville, then Fontana, California,

Bobby Labonte, 2000 Winston Cup champion and two-time winner in 2003.

and Richmond, Virginia; also finished in second at Michigan in June ... began racing in quarter-midgets in Texas, then worked with several teams while running Late Models (and winning a track title) in the late 1980s in North Carolina ... was full-time in the Busch Series from 1990 to 1992, winning the 1991 title and finishing second in 1992 ... went Cup racing with Bill Davis in 1993–1994, then joined Joe Gibbs Racing when Dale Jarrett left prior to 1995 ... his relationship with Gibbs has produced 24 poles, 21 victories, and 6 top-10 point finishes ... highlight of racing career was claiming the 2000 Winston Cup title with crew chief Jimmy Makar ... biggest victory was the 2000 Brickyard 400 at Indianapolis ... has been remarkably successful at Atlanta Motor Speedway, where he has six career victories, including the November 1996 race in which his older brother, Terry, clinched his second straight Winston Cup with a fifth-place finish ... was runner-up to Jeff Gordon in the 1993

DEFINING MOMENTS:
TERRY LABONTE

"When I first started, I came to North Carolina and ran four or five races. I thought, 'This is really neat.' I finished fourth at Darlington in my first race (in 1978). Then at Richmond I finished seventh and I thought, 'Gosh, I'm going to like this. This was a lot of fun.'

"(In Texas) I won some track championships. I thought, 'I could stay there and win more of these.' Then I had the opportunity (from Billy Hagan) to run some Winston Cup races. I thought, 'I've got to do it. I've got to go see (if I'm any good).'

"I never thought about it as a job. I've always looked at it as being pretty fortunate to make a living at doing something that I love to do."

Cup Rookie of the Year standings ... was the team owner when David Green won the 1994 Busch Series title ... he and Terry are the only brothers to win Winston Cup titles.

YEAR	PTS. POS.	EVENTS	POLES	WINS	TOP 10	MONEY
1991	66	2	0	0	0	8,350
1993	19	30	1	0	6	395,660
1994	21	31	0	0	14	550,305
1995	10	31	2	3	14	1,413,682
1996	11	31	4	1	14	1,475,196
1997	7	32	3	1	18	2,217,999
1998	6	33	3	2	18	2,980,052
1999	2	34	5	5	27	4,763,615
2000	1	34	2	4	24	7,361,386
2001	6	36	1	2	20	4,139,851
2002	16	36	0	1	7	4,183,715
2003	8	36	4	2	17	5,505,018
Lifetime		366	25	21	166	$35,641,757

TERRY LABONTE

Born: Nov. 16, 1956
Corpus Christi, TX
Family: wife, Kim; children, Justin and Kristen
No. 5 Kellogg's Chevrolet Monte Carlo

Career highlights: Clearly the comeback driver of 2003 ... after finishing 12th, 17th, 23rd, and

24th in the points race in the previous four seasons, "Texas Terry" finished 10th, the 17th time in 25 full seasons that he accomplished a top-10 finish ... won the pole at Richmond in the spring and thrilled old-timers everywhere by winning the Southern 500 at Darlington on Labor Day weekend ... had seven other top-10 qualifying runs and eight other top-10 finishes ... earned his top-10 status in the season standings by finishing 15th in the season finale at Homestead, Florida, where top-10 challenger Kurt Busch finished 37th to end up in 11th place ... won the 1984 and 1996 Winston Cup titles, the longest break between championships ever ... had made a record 655 consecutive Cup starts until injuries kept him out of the Brickyard 400 in August 2000; he also missed the following week's race at Watkins Glen before returning to the track ... his 514th consecutive Cup start at Martinsville in 1996 broke Richard Petty's record of 513 ... wrapped up his second title near Atlanta in 1996 by finishing fifth in a race won by his brother Bobby ... first Cup victory was in 1980 at Darlington for Billy Hagan ... a year earlier, he had finished fourth in first-ever Cup race at the same track ... spent nine seasons with Hagan, three with Junior Johnson, one with Richard Jackson, and three more with Hagan before joining Hendrick Motorsports in 1994 ... began racing in quarter-midgets in 1964 in Texas, where he eventually became a short-track star in stock cars ... moved to North Carolina in 1977, followed shortly by his mother, father, and brother ... won the 1989 IROC championship, a 1990 race in Australia, and the 1999 Winston All-Star race near Charlotte.

YEAR	PTS. POS.	EVENTS	POLES	WINS	TOP 10	MONEY
1978	39	5	0	0	3	20,545
1979	10	31	0	0	13	130,057
1980	8	31	0	1	16	215,889
1981	4	31	2	0	18	344,987
1982	3	30	2	0	21	363,970
1983	5	30	3	1	20	362,790
1984	1	30	2	2	24	713,010
1985	7	28	4	1	17	694,510
1986	12	29	1	1	10	522,235
1987	3	29	4	1	22	825,369
1988	4	29	1	1	18	950,781
1989	10	29	0	2	11	704,806
1990	15	29	0	0	9	450,230
1991	18	29	1	0	7	348,898
1992	8	29	0	0	16	600,381
1993	18	30	0	0	10	531,717
1994	7	31	0	3	14	1,125,921
1995	6	31	1	3	17	1,558,659

1996	1	31	4	2	24	4,030,648
1997	6	32	0	1	12	2,270,144
1998	9	33	0	1	15	2,054,163
1999	12	34	0	1	7	2,475,365
2000	17	32	1	0	6	2,239,716
2001	23	36	0	0	3	2,972,901
2002	24	36	0	0	4	3,244,240
2003	10	36	1	1	9	4,283,625
Lifetime		781	27	22	353	$34,064,557

KEVIN LEPAGE

Born: June 26, 1962
Shelburne, VT
Family: wife, Donna;
children, Amadee
and Roxann
Plans were uncertain at
press time

Career highlights: Ran 11 races in 2003, including the final eight in the No. 4 Morgan-McClure Kodak Pontiac ... had three finishes in the teens, three in the 20s, one in the 30s and an engine-related 42nd ... even though Kodak is leaving the team, Lepage hopes to return to the No. 4 for 2004 ... went from Vermont short tracks to the American-Canadian Tour, then Busch North to Busch, where he won twice ... ran limited Cup schedules in 1997 and 1998 before two full seasons with Roush Racing ... runner-up to Tony Stewart in 1999 Rookie of the Year standings ... won only pole to date in 1999 finale near Atlanta ... ran only three races in 2002 and was largely inactive in 2003 until Morgan-McClure called him back.

YEAR	PTS. POS.	EVENTS	POLES	WINS	TOP 10	MONEY
1997	56	3	0	0	0	20,975
1998	35	27	0	0	2	851,971
1999	25	34	1	0	6	1,587,841
2000	28	32	0	0	3	1,679,186
2001	36	29	0	0	1	1,424,852
2002	N/A	3	0	0	0	142,459
2003	43	11	0	0	0	742,077
Lifetime		139	1	0	8	$5,887,238

STERLING MARLIN

Born: June 30, 1957
Franklin, TN
Family: wife, Paula; children,
Steadman and Sutherlin
No. 40 Coors Light
Dodge Intrepid

Career highlights: Endured his sixth mediocre season out of the previous seven, finishing 18th in points ... starting in 1997, his final Cup position was 25th, 13th, 16th, 19th, 3rd (tying his career-best finish), 18th, and 18th again ... didn't have a pole, a victory, or a top-5 finish in 2003, and claimed only 11 top-10 finishes ... best start was fourth, which he accomplished three times—at Rockingham in February, Daytona Beach in July, and Talladega in September ... best finish was sixth, which happened four times—at Bristol in March, Talladega in April, and Pocono and Michigan in June ... also had top-10 finishes at Las Vegas, Martinsville, and near Charlotte in the spring; Pocono in July; and Rockingham and Homestead, Florida, in November ... was headed for a top-10 finish in the 2002 points race until a fall accident sidelined him for the final seven races ... gave Dodge its first two "second generation" victories at Michigan and Charlotte in 2001 ... he was Dodge's lead driver when the automaker returned to Winston Cup racing in 2001 after being absent since the late 1980s ... two-time Daytona 500 winner (1994 and 1995), with the first of his 10 career victories being the 1994 season-opener ... started out on short tracks around Nashville, Tennessee, where his father "Coo Coo" had starred before making the jump to Winston Cup himself ... Sterling followed in his father's footsteps and ran his first full Cup season in 1983 ... raced a full Cup schedule every year since 1987 ... has raced full-time for Roger Hamby, Billy Hagan, Junior Johnson, the Stavola Brothers, Morgan-McClure, and, since 1998, for Felix Sabates and Chip Ganassi ... 1983 Cup Rookie of the Year has been top 10 in final points six times ... collects Civil War artifacts ... son, Steadman, ran a handful of Busch races in 2003 with an eye toward running a more complete schedule in 2004.

YEAR	PTS. POS.	EVENTS	POLES	WINS	TOP 10	MONEY
1976	101	1	0	0	0	565
1978	67	2	0	0	1	10,170
1979	85	1	0	0	0	505
1980	49	5	0	0	2	29,810
1981	93	2	0	0	0	1,955
1982	NR	1	0	0	0	4,015
1983	19	30	0	0	1	143,564

YEAR	PTS. POS.	EVENTS	POLES	WINS	TOP 10	MONEY
1984	37	14	0	0	2	54,355
1985	37	8	0	0	0	29,805
1986	36	10	0	0	4	113,070
1987	11	29	0	0	8	306,412
1988	10	29	0	0	13	521,464
1989	12	29	0	0	13	473,267
1990	14	29	0	0	10	369,167
1991	7	29	2	0	15	633,690
1992	10	29	5	0	13	649,048
1993	15	30	0	0	8	628,835
1994	14	31	1	1	11	1,127,683
1995	3	31	1	3	22	2,253,502
1996	8	31	0	2	10	1,588,425
1997	25	32	0	0	6	1,301,370
1998	13	32	0	0	6	1,350,161
1999	16	34	1	0	5	1,797,416
2000	19	34	0	0	7	1,992,301
2001	3	36	1	2	20	3,361,662
2002	18	29	0	2	14	4,228,889
2003	18	36	0	0	11	4,384,491
Lifetime		604	11	10	203	$28,512,919

MARK MARTIN

Born: January 9, 1959
Batesville, AR
Family: wife, Arlene;
children, Amy, Rachel,
Heather, Stacey, and Matthew
No. 6 Viagra Ford Taurus

Career highlights: In almost every sense, 2003 was Mark Martin's worst season since returning to Winston Cup with Jack Roush in 1988 ... the series veteran didn't win a pole, didn't win a race, and had only five top-5 finishes and ten top-10s en route to a 17th-place finish in the points race, the worst full-season ranking of his career ... the only bright spot was his partial ownership of the Cup-winning team of driver Matt Kenseth and crew chief Robbie Reiser ... Martin's best 2003 start was second at Bristol in August, and his best finish was second at Pocono in June ... all five top-5 finishes and seven of his top-10s came in the first half of the season ... had only one top-10 finish in the last 14 races, and that was a 10th at Phoenix in November ... compare 2003 to 2002, when Martin won a race, had 22 top-10 finishes, and finished second overall to Cup champion Tony Stewart ... that was Martin's fourth runner-up points finish, and he's ended up in the top five six other times ... generally recognized as the best driver without a Winston Cup title on his resume ... came to NASCAR in 1981 after winning three American Speed Association (ASA) titles; he won another in 1986 ... ran a few Winston Cup races in 1981, ran the full 1982

schedule, and then 16 races in 1983 before temporarily returning to ASA ... returned to Cup racing in 1988 with Roush, and they've been together ever since ... second to Geoffrey Bodine in the 1982 Rookie of the Year chase ... was 1989 Driver of the Year after winning six poles and one race and finishing third in points ... four-time IROC champion and winningest driver (with 45) in Busch Series history ... first Cup victory was at Rockingham in the fall of 1989 ... finished second in the Cup standings in 1990 to Dale Earnhardt, losing by fewer points than he'd been penalized for a minor, early-season rules infraction ... one of Cup racing's most versatile drivers, he has four road race victories, seven on short tracks, two on restrictor-plate tracks, and twenty on unrestricted superspeedways ... son Matthews's fledgling racing career is Mark's newest and most compelling obsession.

YEAR	PTS. POS.	EVENTS	POLES	WINS	TOP 10	MONEY
1981	42	5	2	0	2	13,950
1982	14	30	0	0	8	1266550
1983	30	16	0	0	3	99,655
1986	48	5	0	0	0	20,515
1987	101T	1	0	0	0	3,550
1988	15	29	1	0	10	223,630
1989	3	29	6	1	18	1,019,250
1990	2	29	3	3	23	1,302,958
1991	6	29	5	1	17	1,039,991
1992	6	29	1	2	17	1,000,571
1993	3	30	5	5	19	1,657,662
1994	2	31	1	2	20	1,628,906
1995	4	31	4	4	22	1,893,519
1996	5	31	4	0	23	1,887,396
1997	3	32	3	4	24	2,532,484
1998	2	33	3	7	26	4,309,006
1999	3	34	1	2	26	3,509,744
2000	8	34	0	1	20	3,098,874
2001	12	36	2	0	15	3,487,719
2002	2	36	0	1	22	7,004,893
2003	17	36	0	0	10	4,486,560
Lifetime		566	41	33	325	$40,656,775

JEREMY MAYFIELD

Born: May 27, 1969
Owensboro, KY
Family: Wife, Shana
No. 19 Dodge
Dealers Intrepid

Career highlights: Rallied nicely in 2003, moving up from 30th in points in August to finish 19th, a showing that saved Mayfield's ride for another year ... he and owner Ray Evernham seemed about done with each other until Mayfield and crew chief Ken Francis strung together 8 top-10 finishes in their last 13 starts ... all told, they won a pole at Talladega in April and had 4 top-5 finishes and 12 top-10 finishes ... had eight other top-10 qualifying runs in addition to the Talladega pole ... his top-10 finishes in 2003: Daytona Beach in the spring; Sonoma, California; Daytona Beach again in midseason; Chicago and Bristol in the summer; then the fall races at Darlington, Richmond, Dover, Kansas City, Atlanta, Rockingham, and Homestead ... late in the year, Mayfield and Evernham extended their own working arrangement and also their partnership with Dodge ... arrived in the Winston Cup in 1993 after racing go-karts and short track cars in Kentucky and Tennessee ... also raced ARCA before his Cup debut with owner Earl Sadler at Charlotte in fall 1993 ... ran a partial season with several owners in 1994, then a full season in 1995 with Cale Yarborough before splitting 1996 between Yarborough and Michael Kranefuss ... was part of the Kranefuss-Penske organization until leaving late in 2001 ... got first of his seven career poles at Talladega in 1996 and first of his three victories at Pocono in 1998 ... also won at Fontana, California, and Pocono, Pennsylvania, in 2000 ... inspired to get into racing by fellow Kentucky native Darrell Waltrip.

YEAR	PTS. POS.	EVENTS	POLES	WINS	TOP 10	MONEY
1993	74T	1	0	0	0	4,830
1994	37	20	0	0	0	226,265
1995	31	27	0	0	1	436,875
1996	26	30	1	0	2	592,853
1997	13	32	0	0	8	1,067,203
1998	7	33	1	1	16	2,332,034
1999	11	33	0	0	12	2,125,227
2000	24	32	4	2	10	2,169,251
2001	35	28	0	0	7	2,682,603
2002	26	36	0	0	4	2,494,583
2003	19	36	1	0	12	3,371,879
Lifetime		309	7	3	74	$17,595,675

JAMIE MCMURRAY

Born: June 6, 1976
Joplin, MO
Family: Single
No. 42 Texaco Havoline
Dodge Intrepid

Throughout the 1990s, NASCAR started to attract many nontraditional sponsors to the sport, expanding beyond the typical automotive companies and breweries. That trend was still going strong in 2003, as seen here on one of Tony Stewart's crew members: 15 years ago, it's almost certain that Pop Tarts would have never been seen on a NASCAR uniform.

Career highlights: Even though some may say 2003 was a disappointment, McMurray easily won the Raybestos Rookie of the Year honor and had some good runs ... beat out teammate Casey Mears, Jack Sprague, Greg Biffle, Tony Raines, and Larry Foyt for the rookie honor ... got his first career pole at the November season finale at Homestead, where he finished a lead-lap ninth ... that was one of 13 top-10 finishes that helped him finish 13th in the overall point standings ... also had top-10 qualifying runs at Rockingham in February, Daytona Beach and Chicago in July, and at New Hampshire and Talladega in September ... best finish was third in the Brickyard 400 at Indianapolis in August ... also finished top 10 at Rockingham, Fort Worth, and Fontana in the spring; at Chicago and Bristol in the summer; and at Darlington, New Hampshire, Dover, Kansas City, Charlotte, Martinsville, and Homestead in the fall ... he was the top-finishing rookie 21 times, 12 more than Biffle, 17 more than Raines, and 20 more than Mears and Sprague ... he had 320.25 rookie points to Biffle's

283.25 ... was hired in the fall of 2002 to drive the third Ganassi-Sabates Dodge team ... he subbed for the injured Sterling Marlin late in 2002, winning the fall race near Charlotte in only his second career start ... rose quickly from weekly short-track racing, through lower NASCAR series, and then up to the Busch Series in 2002 ... won 2 Busch races in 19 starts in 2003..

YEAR	PTS. POS.	EVENTS	POLES	WINS	TOP 10	MONEY
2002	46	6	0	1	2	717,942
2003	13	36	1	0	13	3,258,806
Lifetime		42	1	1	15	$3,876,748

CASEY MEARS

Born: March 12, 1978
Bakersfield, CA
Family: Single
No. 41 Target Dodge Intrepid

Career highlights: Had a rough rookie season, failing to win a pole or a race, or earn a top 5 or top 10 finish ... he hung around the 30s in the points standings all season and never had a real chance of finishing much higher than he did ... ran in all 36 races, but needed provisionals to get into three of them ... best starting position was fourth at Chicago in July, one of five top-10 efforts ... his best finish was 15th at Las Vegas in March—he had 13 finishes in the 20s, another 13 in the 30s, and 6 in the 40s ... part of the "3-M" team with Sterling Marlin and Jamie McMurray ... team co-owners Chip Ganassi and Felix Sabates shocked everyone when they hired Mears to replace Jimmy Spencer as one of their drivers ... son of Roger Mears and nephew of Indy 500 star Rick Mears, he was winless in 35 career Busch Series starts and had only one top-5 finish and two top-10s ... came to NASCAR after some success in a brief Indy Lights and CART Indy car career ... finished well behind McMurray and Greg Biffle and just behind Tony Raines in the Rookie of the Year race.

YEAR	PTS. POS.	EVENTS	POLES	WINS	TOP 10	MONEY
2003	35	36	0	0	0	2,639,178
Lifetime		36	0	0	0	$2,639,178

JERRY NADEAU

Born: September 9, 1970
Danbury, CT
Resides: Charlotte, NC
Family: wife, Jada
Plans were uncertain at press time

Career highlights: Missed most of 2003 after crashing during final practice at Richmond in May ... suffered life-threatening head and internal injuries ... unsure when or if he'll ever race again ... his fourth-place finish at Texas in March was his only top 10 in the first 10 races of 2003 ... was in first season for U.S. Army-backed No. 01 Pontiac team of MB2 Motorsports ... drove for Hendrick Motorsports in 2000 and 2001, and part of 2002 ... outstanding road racer came to Cup in 1997 after limited experience in Busch and ARCA ... in 1998 drove for Bill Elliott-Dan Marino part of the year, then for Harry Melling ... drove for Melling and Nelson Bowers in 1999, then joined Hendrick ... only Cup victory was in 2000 finale at Atlanta ... would have won there in fall of 2001 if he hadn't run out of gas on the last lap ... finished second in a go-kart race on ice in Russia in 1992.

YEAR	PTS. POS.	EVENTS	POLES	WINS	TOP 10	MONEY
1997	54	5	0	0	0	118,545
1998	36	30	0	0	0	804,167
1999	34	34	0	0	2	$1,370,229
2000	20	30	0	1	5	2,164,778
2001	17	36	0	0	10	$2,246,774
2002	37	28	0	0	1	1,606,133
2003	45	10	0	0	1	861,628
Lifetime		177	0	1	19	$9,634,007

JOE NEMECHEK

Born: September 26, 1963
Naples, FL
Family: wife, Andrea; children, John Hunter and Blair Makenzie
No. 01 U.S. Army Chevrolet Monte Carlo

Career highlights: Picked up his third career victory in the spring 400-lap race at Richmond ... even with that win, he lost his No. 25 Chevrolet ride with Hendrick Motorsports in the fall so that Busch star Brian Vickers could begin prepping for his run at the 2004 Rookie of the Year title ... Nemechek quickly signed to finish the season in the No. 01 Pontiac (now, Chevrolet) owned by Nelson Bowers ... that ride had been passed around since May, when Jerry Nadeau was critically injured in a practice incident in Richmond ... Nemechek earned the ride for 2004 after running some solid races in the fall ... all told, he had 10 top-10 qualifying runs (including the last four races) and 6 top-10 finishes, including the Richmond victory ... first race for Bowers was the November race at Atlanta ... got his first career victory at New Hampshire in the fall of 1999 for owner Felix Sabates and his second at Rockingham in November 2001 ... ironically, both came in late-season races on 1-mile tracks in what amounted to "lame-duck" team situations ... has six career poles, the most recent at Talladega in the fall of 2000 for owner Andy Petree ... 1990 Busch Series Rookie of the Year, 1992 Busch champion, and 1992–1993 Busch Most Popular Driver ... began racing motorcross at age 13, winning more than 300 races in six years ... started racing stock cars in 1986 ... was champion and Rookie of the Year in Southeastern Mini-Stocks in 1987 and repeated those dual titles in 1988 in the United States Auto Racing Series and in 1989 in the All-Pro Late Models series ... ran a limited Cup schedule in 1993, then the full schedule for Larry Hedrick in 1994 ... fielded his own cars in 1995 and 1996, then drove for Sabates from 1997 to 1999 and Petree in 2000 and 2001 ... spent 2002 with Travis Carter and Bowers before going to Hendrick at midseason.

YEAR	PTS. POS.	EVENTS	POLES	WINS	TOP 10	MONEY
1993	44	5	0	0	0	56,580
1994	27	29	0	0	3	389,565
1995	28	29	0	0	4	428,925
1996	34	29	0	0	2	666,247
1997	28	30	2	0	3	732,194
1998	26	32	0	0	4	1,343,991
1999	30	34	3	1	3	1,643,946
2000	15	34	1	0	9	2,105,041
2001	28	31	0	1	4	2,510,723
2002	34	33	0	0	3	2,454,482
2003	25	36	0	1	6	2,626,484
Lifetime		322	6	3	41	$14,982,115

RYAN NEWMAN

Born: December 8, 1977
South Bend, IN
Family: Single
No. 12 Alltell
Dodge Intrepid

Career highlights: A star was born in 2003, one that likely will shine for years to come ... despite finishing sixth in the points race, Newman had an unforgettable season ... first, there were the 11 poles he won: Atlanta, Bristol, and Charlotte in the spring; at Dover and Pocono in the summer; and at Darlington, New Hampshire, Charlotte, Atlanta, Phoenix, and Rockingham in the fall ... then, of course, there's the eight victories, by far the most of any driver in 2003: Texas in the spring; Dover, Chicago, Pocono, and Michigan in the summer; then Richmond, Dover, and Kansas City in the fall ... Newman didn't finish higher than sixth overall because he was a little inconsistent—in addition to his victories, he also had three finishes in the 40s, four in the 30s, and four in the 20s ... he ranged from 43rd in points after the Daytona 500 to 4th as late as the Phoenix race in November ... in 2002, he and Jimmie Johnson formed one of the strongest rookie duos in NASCAR history ... Newman won a rookie-record six poles that year, won the fall race at Loudon, was sixth in the season standings, and won the Rookie of the Year award ... like Tony Stewart and Jeff Gordon before him, he was an intense and fiercely competitive open-wheel star ... spent 2001 getting experience in ARCA, Busch Series, and Winston Cup races in preparation for 2002, where he joined veteran Rusty Wallace on the Penske South Racing team ... already had a Cup pole and a top-five finish to his credit before his official rookie year ... graduated from Purdue University in the spring of 2001 ... won in all three major USAC divisions in 1999, when he was Silver Bullet champion ... is a member of the Quarter-Midget Racing Hall of Fame ... has two open-wheel national championships and 100-plus career victories.

YEAR	PTS. POS.	EVENTS	POLES	WINS	TOP 10	MONEY
2000	70	1	0	0	0	37,825
2001	49	7	1	0	1	465,276

Ryan Newman (left) and Jimmie Johnson (right) share a laugh after Newman won the pole for the Coca-Cola 600 at Lowe's Motor Speedway. Newman led all drivers with eight wins.

2002	6	36	6	1	22	5,346,651
2003	6	36	11	8	22	6,100,877
Lifetime		80	18	9	46	$11,950,629

STEVE PARK

Born: August 23, 1967
Islip, NY
Family: Single
Plans were uncertain at press time

Career highlights: Split 2003 between the No. 1 Chevrolet of Dale Earnhardt Inc. and the No. 30 Chevrolet of Richard Childress Racing … many feel he's still affected by 2001 Busch crash that cost him the last third of that season and the early stages of 2002 … only highlights in 2003 were poles at Fontana in April and Daytona Beach in July … finished 40th at Fontana and 39th at Daytona Beach, 2 of his 14 finishes in the 30s and 40s … was fifth at Michigan in August, tenth at Las Vegas in March, and eighth at New Hampshire in July … DEI let him go in June and RCR announced in November he wouldn't return … got first career victory at Watkins Glen in 2000, then won emotional race at Rockingham the weekend after team owner Dale Earnhardt died in the 2001 Daytona 500 … came to Cup racing after outstanding Modified and Busch career … 1995 and 1996 Most Popular Driver in Modified, then won three races and was 1997 Busch Series Rookie of the Year for Dale Earnhardt Inc. … ran five Cup races in 1997, but following season was shortened after crashing during Atlanta weekend in March … returned for the Brickyard 400 and ran well until crashing late … lost to Kenny Irwin for Rookie of the Year in a season that saw Irwin start all but one race and Park only 17 … was 14th in points in 1999 and 11th in 2000, and seemed on track for a top 10 finish in 2001 until he was sidelined by his terrible accident … neighborhood pal of rock diva Mariah Carey on Long Island … loyal supporter of Kyle Petty's annual cross-country charity motorcycle ride.

YEAR	PTS. POS.	EVENTS	POLES	WINS	TOP 10	MONEY
1997	51	5	0	0	0	74,120
1998	42	17	0	0	0	487,265
1999	14	34	0	0	0	1,767,690

DEFINING MOMENTS: RYAN NEWMAN

"There was no one defining moment. There were a lot of distinct moments. Winning my first Winston Cup race (September 2002 race at New Hampshire) was a huge one. And my winning my first Busch race (at Michigan in 2001) was a huge moment for me, as well as my family, to achieve some of our goals. Winning The Winston (2002) was our greatest win as a team to this day."

2000	11	34	2	1	13	2,283,629
2001	32	24	0	1	12	2,496,490
2002	33	32	0	0	2	2,681,594
2003	32	35	2	0	3	2,686,915
Lifetime		181	4	2	35	$12,477063

KYLE PETTY

Born: June 2, 1960
Randleman, NC
Family: wife, Pattie; children, Austin and Montgomery Lee; (Adam, d. 2000)
No. 45 Georgia-Pacific Dodge Intrepid

Career highlights: It was another tough year for Petty and Petty Enterprises … he missed the Texas race in the spring and the fall races at Talladega and Homestead after failing to qualify and not having any provisionals … his best start was eighth at Richmond in the spring, but most of his starts were in the 30s and 40s … his best finish was 11th at Talladega in the spring, but most of those were in the 20s and 30s … after showing considerable progress with Robin Pemberton serving as team manager in 2002, Petty Enterprises moved backward in 2003 … even so, it remains one of the best-known organizations in NASCAR racing … Kyle returned to the family-owned team in 1997 after seven years with Sabco Racing … he then brought the family's far-flung teams together under one roof at the family's famous headquarters in Level Cross, North Carolina … he was the first third-generation driver to win in Winston Cup, following the traditions started by his grandfather Lee and father Richard … his best points finish was fifth in 1992 and 1993 … won his first stock car race, the ARCA 200, at Daytona Beach in 1979, one week before Richard won his record seventh Daytona 500 … has eight career poles and eight career victories, but none for Petty Enterprises … has also driven for Rahmoc, Hoss Ellington, the Wood Brothers, and Felix Sabates … his teenage son, Adam, died during a Busch practice session at Loudon, New Hampshire in May 2000, a devastating blow to the family and a setback for the company, which was rebuilding around Adam, who was a budding star.

YEAR	PTS. POS.	EVENTS	POLES	WINS	TOP 10	MONEY
1979	N/A	5	0	0	1	10,810
1980	28	15	0	0	6	36,350
1981	12	31	0	0	10	112,289
1982	15	29	0	0	4	120,730
1983	13	30	0	0	2	157,820
1984	16	30	0	0	6	324,555
1985	9	28	0	0	12	296,367
1986	10	29	0	1	14	403,242
1987	7	29	0	1	13	544,437
1988	13	29	0	0	8	377,092
1989	30	19	0	0	5	117,022
1990	11	29	2	1	4	746,326
1991	31	18	2	1	4	413,727
1992	5	29	3	2	17	1,107,063
1993	5	30	1	1	15	914,662
1994	15	31	0	0	7	806,332
1995	30	30	0	1	5	698,875
1996	27	28	0	0	2	689,041
1997	15	32	0	0	9	984,314
1998	30	33	0	0	2	1,287,731
1999	26	32	0	0	9	1,278,953
2000	41	19	0	0	1	894,911
2001	43	24	0	0	0	1,008,919
2002	22	36	0	0	1	2,198,073
2003	37	33	0	0	0	2,293,222
Lifetime		678	8	8	168	$17,822,863

TONY RAINES

Born: April 14, 1964
LaPorte, IN
Family: wife, Susan; child, Lee
No. 74 Outdoor Life Chevrolet

Career highlights: Made 35 of 36 starts on underfunded Chevrolet team of owner Bill Baumgardner Jr. … finished behind Jamie McMurray and Greg Biffle in the Rookie of the Year standings … only DNQ was at Daytona Beach in July … only top-10 start was a good one: fourth at Rockingham in November … best finish was a career-best sixth in the same race … came to Cup racing from ASA, All-Pro, Craftsman, and Busch racing … ran six full ASA seasons and won the 1996 title … won four Craftsman Truck Series races in 1997 and 1998 before going Busch racing in 1999, when he won Rookie of the Year … made seven Cup starts in 2002 in preparation for full 2003 effort … also ran 12 Busch races in 2003 … all told, has 42 Cup starts, 52 in Craftsman, and 142 in Busch.

YEAR	PTS. POS.	EVENTS	POLES	WINS	TOP 10	MONEY
2002	51	7	0	0	0	326,042
2003	33	35	0	0	1	2,122,739
Lifetime		42	0	0	1	$2,448,781

SCOTT RIGGS

Born: January 1, 1971
Bahama, NC
Family: wife, Jai; son, Lane
No. 10 Valvoline Chevrolet Monte Carlo

Career highlights: Another Busch Series graduate gets a good Cup ride in 2004 at the cost of a series veteran … Riggs is part of the rookie Class of 2004 that also includes Kasey Kahne, Brian Vickers, Johnny Sauter, Scott Wimmer, and Brendan Gaughan … ran only two full Busch seasons, finishing 10th in points and winning twice in 2002 and sixth in points and winning twice in 2003 … all told, he has 4 victories, 19 top-5 finishes, and 30 top-10s in 68 Busch starts … an outstanding Late Model driver in North Carolina and Virginia, he did some All-Pro and Craftsman Series racing before arriving in the Busch Series in 2002, when he was Rookie of the Year … takes over the ride formerly held by Johnny Benson, who had it three-and-a-half seasons and gave the team its only victory, at Rockingham, in the fall of 2002.

YEAR	PTS. POS.	EVENTS	POLES	WINS	TOP 10	MONEY
No Cup experience						

RICKY RUDD

Born: September. 12, 1956
Chesapeake, VA
Family: wife, Linda; child,
Landon Lee
No. 21 Motorcraft
Ford Taurus

Career highlights: Rudd's first year with the legendary Wood Brothers team had its ups and downs, but unfortunately for Rudd, more downs than ups ... he turned in 4 top-5 finishes and 5 top-10s in 36 starts and finished 23rd in points, the fourth-lowest ranking of his 29-year career ... Rudd started top 10 in three races, but he also used eight provisionals to extend his consecutive-start streak to a record 716 ... the streak, which was still intact as the 2004 season began, dates back to January 1979 ... he was fourth at Bristol in March; third at Daytona Beach in July; third and then second in back-to-back September races, the first in Richmond and the second in New Hampshire; then tenth at Kansas City in October ... was involved in a nasty postrace scrap with Kevin Harvick after Harvick crashed following contact with Rudd's car late in the fall race at Richmond ... Rudd ended a bittersweet three-year run with Robert Yates Racing (RYR) to drive for the Wood Brothers ... the biggest of Rudd's 23 victories was the 1997 Brickyard 400 at Indianapolis ... winner of the 1977 Rookie of the Year award, Rudd had never raced a stock car before his 1975 debut at Rockingham ... he spent his early years on a family-owned team and driving for Junie Donlavey and DiGard Racing ... earned victories with Richard Childress, Bud Moore, Kenny Bernstein, Hendrick Motorsports, his own RPM team, and RYR ... was 1992 IROC champion despite not winning any of the four races ... won at least once a year from 1983 through 1998, but never won more than two races in a single season ... has six road-course victories and five on short tracks ... entering second year of his three-year deal with the Woods, meaning 2005 likely will be his final year.

YEAR	PTS. POS.	EVENTS	POLES	WINS	TOP 10	MONEY
1975	47	4	0	0	1	4,345
1976	53	4	0	0	1	7,525
1977	17	25	0	0	10	68,448
1978	31	13	0	0	4	49,610
1979	9	28	0	0	17	146,302
1980	35	13	0	0	13	50,500
1981	6	31	3	0	17	381,968
1982	9	30	2	0	13	201,130
1983	9	30	4	2	14	257,585
1984	7	30	4	1	16	476,602
1985	6	28	0	1	19	512,441
1986	5	29	1	2	17	671,548
1987	6	29	0	2	13	653,508
1988	11	29	2	1	11	410,954
1989	8	29	0	1	15	533,624
1990	7	29	2	1	15	573,650
1991	2	29	1	1	17	1,093,765
1992	7	29	1	1	18	793,903
1993	10	30	0	1	14	752,562
1994	5	31	1	1	15	1,044,441
1995	9	31	2	1	16	1,337,703
1996	6	31	0	1	16	1,503,025
1997	17	32	0	2	11	1,975,981
1998	22	33	0	1	5	1,602,895
1999	31	34	1	0	5	1,632,011
2000	5	34	2	0	19	2,914,970
2001	4	36	1	2	22	3,976,203
2002	10	36	1	1	12	4,444,614
2003	23	36	0	0	5	3,240,614
Lifetime		803	28	23	361	$32,215,451

ELLIOTT SADLER

Born: April 30, 1975
Emporia, VA
Family: Single
No. 38 M&Ms Ford Taurus

Career highlights: Didn't come close to having the kind of year he expected in his debut with Robert Yates Racing ... he did win two poles, but he didn't win a race and had only two top-5 finishes and nine top-10s ... the two poles—which were the first of his career—came at Darlington in March and Talladega in September ... finished top 10 at Rockingham, Atlanta, Darlington, Talladega, and Martinsville in the spring, Pocono in the summer, then Darlington and New Hampshire in the fall ... crashed hard in three consecutive fall races at Talladega, Kansas City, and Charlotte, which accounted for three of the seven wreck-related DNFs that he suffered ... despite the early lack of results, signing with RYR in 2003 *did* signal a major career upturn ... only career victory through 2003 came in the spring of 2001 at Bristol with the Wood Brothers ... came to Cup racing after prepping in go-karts and weekly Late Models in Virginia, and in the Busch Series ... ran two Cup races for Gary Bechtel in 1998 before going to the Woods for four years ... has five Busch victories, plus a career-best fifth-place finish in the Busch points race in 1998 ... was part of the strong 1999 Rookie of the Year class that included Tony Stewart and Buckshot Jones.

YEAR	PTS. POS.	EVENTS	POLES	WINS	TOP 10	MONEY
1998	59	2	0	0	0	45,325
1999	24	34	0	0	1	1,589,221
2000	29	33	0	0	1	1,579,656
2001	20	36	0	1	2	2,525,007
2002	23	36	0	0	7	3,491,694
2003	21	36	2	0	9	3,795,174
Lifetime		177	2	1	20	$13,184,295

JOHNNY SAUTER

Born: May 1, 1978
Necedah, WI
Family: Single
No. 30 AOL Chevrolet
Monte Carlo

Career highlights: Tapped by team owner Richard Childress to move from Busch Series to the Nextel Cup in 2004, replacing several drivers who had the No. 30 car in 2003 ... Sauter is from a long line of successful racers, including his father, Jim, and brothers Jay and Tim ... was the 2001 ASA Rookie of the Year and series champion, which earned him a ride on RCR's Busch team ... ran five Busch races late in 2001 and the full 2002 and 2003 schedules ... all told, has 2 victories, 10 top-5 finishes, and 21 top-10s in 72 starts ... was 15th in 2002 points and 9th in 2003.

YEAR	PTS. POS.	EVENTS	POLES	WINS	TOP 10	MONEY

No Cup experience

KEN SCHRADER

Born: May 29, 1955
St. Louis, MO
Family: wife, Ann; children, Dorothy and Sheldon
No. 49 BAM Dodge Intrepid

Career highlights: Struggled through a tough 2003 with the underfunded and mostly unsponsored BAM team owned by Beth Ann and Tony

Morgenthau ... made 32 of the 36 races, missing Indy and Watkins Glen in August, Charlotte in October, and the finale at Homestead in November ... had no poles, no victories, and no top-5 finishes to show for his efforts, but he did earn top-10 finishes at Martinsville in April and Michigan in August ... finished 36th in points, the lowest ranking of his full-schedule career ... will race almost anything, anywhere, anytime ... huge fan base comes from racing different types of cars at different tracks all over the United States ... spent eight years at Hendrick Motorsports, where he had 17 of his 23 poles and all 4 victories ... has impressive resume in open-wheel dirt cars and in CART-type Indy cars, but has been primarily a NASCAR driver since the late 1980s ... hasn't won since June 1991 at Dover ... won three consecutive Daytona 500 poles (1988 to 1990) ... was 1985 Rookie of the Year driving for Junie Donlavey ... first Cup victory was at Talladega in 1988 ... drove USAC midgets, Sprint cars, and Silver Crown cars ... 1982 Silver Crown champion ... 1983 Sprint Car champion ... his 2004 team didn't have a sponsor as of early January, leading to many questions about its future—and Schrader's.

YEAR	PTS. POS.	EVENTS	POLES	WINS	TOP 10	MONEY
1984	53	5	0	0	0	16,425
1985	16	28	0	0	3	211,523
1986	16	29	0	0	4	235,904
1987	10	29	1	0	10	375,918
1988	5	29	2	1	17	631,544
1989	5	29	4	1	14	1,039,941
1990	10	29	3	0	14	769,934
1991	9	29	0	2	18	772,434
1992	17	29	1	0	14	639,679
1993	9	30	6	0	15	952,748
1994	4	31	0	0	18	1,171,062
1995	17	31	1	0	10	886,566
1996	12	31	0	0	10	1,089,603
1997	10	32	2	0	8	1,355,292
1998	12	33	2	0	11	1,907,399
1999	15	34	1	0	6	1,939,147
2000	18	34	0	0	2	1,711,476
2001	19	36	0	0	5	2,254,390
2002	30	36	0	0	0	2,460,140
2003	36	32	0	0	2	2,007,424
Lifetime		596	23	4	178	$22,567,845

JIMMY SPENCER

Born: February 15, 1957
Berwick, PA
Family: wife, Pat; children, James and Katrina
No. 7 Dodge Intrepid

NASCAR is known as one of the most fan-friendly professional sports, and here driver Jimmy Spencer takes time to sign autographs before the MBNA America 400 at Dover International Speedway.

Career highlights: Questions surrounded Spencer's team for the 2004 Nextel Cup season, as it was still unsponsored as of early January ... Spencer wanted to return for owner Jimmy Smith, but primary sponsor Sirius Satellite Radio and crew chief Tommy Baldwin left in the winter ... it was likely that the No. 7 team would exist in some form in 2004, but it was uncertain if Spencer would be a part of that team ... he ran 35 of 36 races in 2003, missing only the Bristol race in August ... did turn in six top-10 qualifying efforts: Atlanta, Darlington, and Bristol in the spring; Michigan in the summer; and Martinsville and Rockingham in the fall ... only top-5 finish was at Charlotte on Memorial Day weekend, added top-10s at both Atlanta races and at Indianapolis ...

got unwanted publicity at Michigan in August when he punched Kurt Busch after they rubbed fenders on the track and traded barbs in the garage afterward ... came up through the Modified and Busch Series ranks, where he enjoyed great success ... has 15 Modified victories, 12 in the Busch Series, and 1 (in 2003 in New Hampshire) in the Craftsman Series ... was the 1986–1987 Modified champion and was top 10 in Busch Series points in 1988 ... drove his first Cup race in 1989 for Buddy Baker ... also drove for Rod Osterlund and Dick Moroso before working one full season each for Junior Johnson and Bobby Allison ... was with the Carl Haas–Travis Carter team from 1995 through 2001 ... his 2 Cup victories in 439 career starts were both in 1994 while racing for Johnson—the first at Talladega and the second at Daytona Beach in the summer race.

YEAR	PTS. POS.	EVENTS	POLES	WINS	TOP 10	MONEY
1989	34	17	0	0	3	121,065
1990	24	26	0	0	2	219,775
1991	25	29	0	0	6	283,620
1992	33	12	0	0	3	186,085
1993	12	30	0	0	10	686,026
1994	29	29	1	2	4	479,235
1995	26	29	0	0	4	507,210
1996	15	31	0	0	9	1,090,876
1997	20	32	0	0	4	1,073,779
1998	14	31	0	0	8	1,741,012
1999	20	34	0	0	3	1,752,299
2000	22	34	0	0	5	1,936,762
2001	16	36	2	0	8	2,398,939
2002	27	34	0	0	6	2,136,792
2003	29	35	0	0	4	2,565,803
Lifetime		439	3	2	80	$17,449,977

TONY STEWART

Born: Columbus, IN
Family: Single
No. 20 Home Depot
Chevrolet Monte Carlo

Career highlights: The 2002 Winston Cup champion didn't come close to defending his title in 2003 ... had claimed the pole at Chicago in July, and won races at Pocono in June and Charlotte in October, but that was it for the year ... despite the two wins, Stewart did manage to finish in seventh place in the season's point race ... all told, had 14 top-10 qualifying runs, 12 top-5 finishes, and 18 top-10 finishes ... five DNFs hurt his cause, including consecutive 41sts at California and Richmond, and a 40th at Charlotte in the spring ... had 10 other finishes in the 20s and 30s ... the 2002 title came in his fourth season with Joe Gibbs Racing ... one of NASCAR's most outspoken and controversial figures, he maintained a fairly low profile and behaved himself in 2003 ... fiercely independent and single-minded, he's easily irritated by rules and regulations that he sees as unreasonable ... major go-kart titles in 1987 and 1993 foreshadowed greatness ... he was the 1994 USAC Midget champion and 1995 Midget, Sprint Car, and Silver Crown champion ... 1996 Indy Racing League (IRL) and Indy 500 Rookie of the Year, and 1997 IRL champion ...

ran a few Busch races in 1996, 1997, and 1998, the latter for Joe Gibbs ... won two Cup poles, a rookie-record three races, finished fourth in points, and was 1999 Rookie of the Year ... finished ninth in the 1999 Indy 500 and fourth in the Coca-Cola 600 at Charlotte on the same day ... did it again in 2001, finishing sixth at Indy and third at Charlotte ... to some, seventh in points was a down year; after all, he was fourth, sixth, second, and first in his previous Cup seasons ... pledged $1 million for the Victory Junction Gang Camp being built by the Petty family for children with chronic or life-threatening illnesses.

YEAR	PTS. POS.	EVENTS	POLES	WINS	TOP 10	MONEY
1999	4	34	2	3	21	3,190,149
2000	6	34	2	6	22	3,642,348
2001	2	36	0	3	22	3,493,043
2002	1	36	2	3	21	9,163,761
2003	7	36	1	2	18	6,131,633
Lifetime		176	7	17	104	$27,069,354

BRIAN VICKERS

Born: October 24, 1983
Thomasville, NC
Family: Single
No. 25 UAW-GM Chevrolet
Monte Carlo

Career highlights: Another member of the strong rookie class of 2004 that includes fellow Busch Series graduates Scott Riggs, Kasey Kahne, Johnny Sauter, and Scott Wimmer, plus Craftsman Series driver Brendan Gaughan ... in September 2003 was named as the replacement for veteran Joe Nemechek at Hendrick Motorsports, where his teammates will be Jeff Gordon, Jimmie Johnson, and Terry Labonte ... won the 2003 Busch Series title as part of a Hendrick-owned Chevrolet team that won 3 races, had 13 top-5 finishes, and 21 top-10s ... victories came at Clermont, Indiana, in August, then at Darlington and Dover in September ... made late-season Cup starts at Charlotte, Atlanta, Phoenix, Rockingham, and Homestead ... qualified top four in the last four, including the outside pole at both Rockingham and Phoenix, but he finished poorly in all but the Phoenix race, where he ended up a

Jeremy Mayfield's pit crew springs into action as his No. 19 Dodge slides into its slot along pit road during the Pop Secret Microwave Popcorn 400 at North Carolina Speedway.

respectable 13th ... came up through go-karts and weekly Late Model stock cars to the Hooters Pro Cup Series in 2000 and the Busch Series in 2001.

YEAR	PTS. POS.	EVENTS	POLES	WINS	TOP 10	MONEY
2003	49	5	0	0	0	263,484
Lifetime		5	0	0	0	$263,484

RUSTY WALLACE

Born: August 14, 1956
St. Louis, MO
Family: wife, Patti; children, Greg, Katie, and Stephen
No. 2 Miller Lite
Dodge Intrepid

Career highlights: Second consecutive poor season stretched his losing streak to a career-worst 98 races and kept him out of the top 10 in points for only the second time in 13 years with owner Roger Penske ... the season didn't look any better when compared to that of his teammate, Ryan Newman, who won 11 poles and 8 races with equipment from the same shop ... Wallace's last victory, which was the 54th of his career, came in April 2001 at Fontana ... didn't have any poles or victories in 2003, and his only top-5 finishes were at Fontana in April and Richmond in September ... had 12 top-10s, but almost half of his 378 laps led (182) came at Rockingham in February, when he finished sixth ... went through several crew chiefs and a manufacturer change in the early 2000s, leading to some team instability … he was the 1989 Winston Cup champion, edging Dale Earnhardt by 12 points … Cup runner-up in 1988 and 1993 … won the inaugural NASCAR exhibition race in Japan in 1996 … USAC Rookie of the Year in 1979, ASA champion in 1983, and 1984 Winston Cup Rookie of the Year … 1991 IROC champion … finished second in his first Cup race, at Atlanta in 1980, driving for Penske … has his pilot's license and owns a fleet of planes … father was a champion racer in the St. Louis area … middle of three racing Wallace brothers: older brother is Mike, younger brother is Kenny … other than himself, has driven for only five owners in a 23-year Cup career: Ron Benfield, John Childs, Cliff Stewart, Raymond Beadle, and Penske … son Stephen is beginning to make his own name as a short-track racer in North Carolina.

YEAR	PTS. POS.	EVENTS	POLES	WINS	TOP 10	MONEY
1980	57	2	0	0	1	22,760
1981	64	4	0	0	1	12,895
1982	65	3	0	0	0	7,655
1983	NR	0	0	0	0	1,100
1984	14	30	0	0	4	195,927
1985	19	28	0	0	8	233,670
1986	6	29	0	2	16	557,354
1987	5	29	1	2	16	690,652
1988	2	29	2	6	23	1,411,567
1989	1	29	4	6	20	2,247,950
1990	6	29	2	2	16	954,129
1991	10	29	2	2	14	502,073
1992	13	29	1	1	12	657,925
1993	2	30	3	10	21	1,702,154
1994	3	31	2	8	20	1,914,072
1995	5	31	0	2	19	1,642,837
1996	7	31	0	5	18	1,665,315
1997	9	32	1	1	12	1,705,625
1998	4	33	4	1	21	2,667,889
1999	8	34	4	1	16	2,454,050
2000	7	34	9	4	20	3,621,468
2001	7	36	0	1	14	4,272,406
2002	7	36	1	0	17	4,785,134
2003	14	36	0	0	12	4,246,547
Lifetime		634	36	54	321	$38,689,400

MICHAEL WALTRIP

Born: April 30, 1963.
Owensboro, KY
Family: wife, Buffy; children, Caitlin and Margaret Carol
No. 15 NAPA Chevrolet
Monte Carlo

Career highlights: The good news was his second Daytona 500 victory and a fall victory at Talladega … the bad news was his late-season drop from a possible top 10 in the points race to a mediocre 15th, his 17th consecutive season of finishing 12th or worse … didn't win a pole, but had 12 top-10 starts … won the rain-shortened Daytona race and had five other top-10 finishes in the first half of the season, but had only five top-10s—including the Talladega victory—in the second half … was 10th in points with nine races remaining, but six finishes in the 20s, 30s, and 40s ensured his drop down the points ladder … all four of his career Cup victories have come on a restrictor-plate track: three at Daytona Beach and one at Talladega … followed older brother, Darrell, into racing in the early 1980s on Kentucky short tracks … 1983 champion and 1983–1984 Most Popular Driver in the Dash Series … ran part of the 1985 Cup season and all of the 1986 and 1987 campaigns for Bob Bahre … runner-up to Alan Kulwicki for the 1986 Rookie of the Year award … spent eight years with Chuck Rider, three with the Wood Brothers, and two with Jim Mattei/Jim Smith before going to Dale Earnhardt Inc. in 2001 … first career victory was the 2001 Daytona 500, the race in which the legendary Dale Earnhardt died on the last lap … won the 1991 and 1992 Winston Open nonpoints races at Charlotte and the 1996 Winston All-Star race … first of two career Cup poles came at Dover in 1991 … remains active in the Busch Series, where he has ten victories, including one in 2003 … has run in several long-distance races, including the Boston Marathon.

YEAR	PTS. POS.	EVENTS	POLES	WINS	TOP 10	MONEY
1985	57	5	0	0	0	9,540
1986	19	28	0	0	0	108,767
1987	20	29	0	0	1	205,370
1988	18	29	0	0	3	240,400
1989	18	29	0	0	5	249,233
1990	16	29	0	0	10	395,507
1991	15	29	2	0	12	440,812
1992	23	29	0	0	2	410,545
1993	17	30	0	0	5	529,923
1994	12	31	0	0	9	706,426
1995	12	31	0	0	8	898,338
1996	14	31	0	0	11	1,182,811
1997	18	32	0	0	6	1,135,509
1998	17	32	0	0	5	1,508,680
1999	29	34	0	0	1	1,702,460
2000	27	34	0	0	0	1,690,821
2001	24	36	0	1	3	3,373,394
2002	14	36	0	1	10	3,185,969
2003	15	36	0	2	11	4,929,620
Lifetime		570	2	4	114	$22,945,465

SCOTT WIMMER

Born: January 26, 1976.
Wausau, WIS
Family: Single
No. 22 Caterpillar
Dodge Intrepid

Career highlights: In 2004, goes full-time Cup racing as a member of a rookie class that also includes Johnny Sauter, Kasey Kahne, Scott Riggs, Brian Vickers, and Brendan Gaughan ... started Cup races at Bristol in August and New Hampshire in September in the Bill Davis-owned No. 27 Dodge, then replaced Ward Burton in the Davis-owned No. 22 Dodge for the last four races of the season ... made one Cup start in 2000 and three more for Davis in 2002 ... ran the Hooters Pro Cup and ASA series before coming to the Busch Series to drive for Davis late in 2000 ... was 11th, 3rd, and 9th in three full Busch seasons, winning five races, including the July 2003 clash at Pikes Peak, Colorado ... breakout season was 2002, when he won late-season Busch races at Dover, Memphis, Phoenix, and Homestead en route to his third-place finish in the points race.

YEAR	PTS. POS.	EVENTS	POLES	WINS	TOP 10	MONEY
2000	N/A	1	0	0	0	37,789
2002	56	3	0	0	0	143,110
2003	48	6	0	0	1	487,060
Lifetime		10	0	0	1	$667,959

4

TEAM DIRECTORY

NO. 0—HAAS CNC RACING

Car: No. 0 Chevrolet
Driver: Ward Burton
Owner: Gene Haas
Crew Chief: Tony Furr
Sponsor: Net Zero
Address: 6780 Hudspeth Rd.
Harrisburg NC 28075
Telephone: (704)454-5381

About Gene Haas: In 1983 he founded Haas Automation, Inc., the largest machine tool manufacturing company in the United States. He's also a technical partner of another NASCAR team, Hendrick Motorsports. His Cup team made its first start at Kansas in 2002. The next year, the team used Jack Sprague as its driver for the whole season. Starting in 2004, Ward Burton takes over behind the wheel for the initial Nextel Cup battle. In 2004, Haas will also have a Busch Grand National team, featuring driver Jason Leffler. Haas and codriver Joe Custer won the best-in-class championship in the 2001 Best of the Desert Off-Road Truck Series.

NO. 01—MB2 MOTORSPORTS

Car No. 01 Chevrolet

Driver: Joe Nemechek
Owners: Nelson Bowers, Tom Beard, Read Morton Jr.
Crew Chief: Ryan Pemberton
Sponsor: U.S. Army
Address: 7065 Zephyr Pl. NW,
Concord, N.C. 28027
Telephone: (704)664-7416

About the MB2 owners: See No. 10 car for information on Nelson Bowers, Tom Beard, and Read Morton Jr.

NO. 1—DALE EARNHARDT, INC.

Car: No. 1 Chevrolet Monte Carlo
Driver: John Andretti
Owner: Dale Earnhardt, Inc.
Crew Chief: Tony Gibson
Sponsor: Pennzoil
Address: 1675 Coddle Creek Hwy.
Mooresville, NC, 28115
Telephone: (704)662-8000

About DEI: Founded by seven-time Winston Cup champion Dale Earnhardt, DEI also fields cars for Dale Earnhardt Jr. and Michael Waltrip. Earnhardt's widow, Teresa, and Ty Norris, executive vice president of motorsports, are heavily involved in the day-to-day operation of DEI.

NO. 2—PENSKE RACING SOUTH

Car: No. 2 Dodge
Driver: Rusty Wallace
Owner: Roger Penske
Crew Chief: Larry Wallace
Sponsor: Miller Lite
Address: 136 Knob Hill Rd.
Mooresville, NC 28117
Telephone: (704)662-8000

About Roger Penske: Perhaps best known for his success in Indy car racing, Penske began his Winston Cup involvement in 1972 on a limited basis. His drivers were the late Mark Donohue, Dave Marcis, and Donnie Allison. He also fielded cars for George Follmer, Bobby Allison, the late Neil Bonnett, and Gary Bettenhausen. Penske returned to NASCAR in 1991 with a team built around Rusty Wallace. By 2004, the team had won 37 races and often contended for the Winston Cup championship. Penske owned speedways in Pennsylvania, Michigan, North Carolina, and California before selling them to the International Speedway Corp. (ISC). Penske's Indy car resume includes a record 119 victories, 11 national titles, and 13 Indianapolis 500 wins. Among those who have raced Indy cars for Penske are Donohue, Bettenhausen, Mario Andretti, Rick Mears, Al and Bobby Unser, Emerson Fittipaldi, Gil de Ferran, Helio Castroneves, and Danny Sullivan. Penske, a graduate of Lehigh University, is founder and chairman of the Penske Corp. diversified transportation services company.

NO. 4—MORGAN-MCCLURE MOTORSPORTS

Car: No. 4 Chevrolet
Driver: Kevin Lepage
Owner: Larry McClure
Crew Chief: Tim Brewer

Sponsor: Unkown at press time
Address: 26502 Newbanks Rd.
Abingdon, VA 24210
Telephone: (540)628 3683

About Larry McClure: He cofounded the team in 1983 with Charles Morgan. As of the start of the 2004 season, the team had 14 victories and 13 poles. The team experienced its greatest success with Ernie Irvan driving, grabbing seven victories from 1990 through late 1993, when Irvan left to drive for Robert Yates. Sterling Marlin won two Daytona 500s (1994 and 1995) driving for Morgan-McClure. Before Irvan, Bobby Hamilton drove for the team from 1998 through 2000. Robby Gordon began 2001 in the No. 4 Chevy, then was replaced by Bobby Hamilton Jr. McClure is highly visible and active with the team.

NO. 5—HENDRICK MOTORSPORTS

Car: No. 5 Chevrolet
Driver: Terry Labonte
Owner: Rick Hendrick
Crew Chief: Jim Long
Sponsor: Kellogg's
Address: 4414 Papa Joe Hendrick Blvd.
Charlotte, NC 28262
Telephone: (704)455-0309

About Rick Hendrick: Few owners in the history of NASCAR have gone through the highs and lows that Rick Hendrick has experienced in the last few years. He's been plagued by extensive legal and medical problems—including a battle with cancer—that often seemed insurmountable. On the racing front, his organization won the 1995, 1997, and 1998 Winston Cup titles with Jeff Gordon, and the 1996 title with Terry Labonte. Hendrick Motorsports won 57 races in the 1990s while fielding teams for such stars as Darrell Waltrip, Ken Schrader, Ricky Rudd, Gordon, and Labonte. The Hendrick empire began taking shape in 1984 when Hendrick, owner of several dozen automobile dealerships, started a team with Geoffrey Bodine. Since then, the team

When a driver wins a Winston Cup championship, it means his entire team has worked hard and done all the little things that it takes to race competitively each week. So naturally, the winning team members also gets to enjoy the celebration surrounding their driver's victory. Here, the men and women of the No. 17 Roush Racing team celebrate as Matt Kenseth crosses the finish line and clinches his first championship in the Pop Secret Microwave Popcorn 400 at North Carolina Speedway.

has produced 92 victories, four championships, and more than $125 million in earnings.

NO. 6—ROUSH RACING

Car: No. 6 Ford
Driver: Mark Martin
Owner: Jack Roush
Crew Chief: Pat Tryson
Sponsor: Viagra
Address: 7020 Aviation Blvd.
Concord, NC 28027
Telephone: (704)632-1600

About Jack Roush: One of the most innovative and single-minded owners in the sport, he won his first Winston Cup title in 2003 with Matt Kenseth. Roush got his start in stock car racing with a modest one-team effort in 1988 that featured driver Mark Martin. Four years later, Roush added a second car for Wally Dallenbach Jr. (replaced after two years by Ted Musgrave and then by Kevin Lepage). Roush added a third car for Jeff Burton in 1996, then brought Chad Little and Johnny Benson to his stable in 1998. Michigan-based Roush Racing has also been active in the Craftsman Truck Series and the Trans-Am Series.

Roush was rescued by ex-Marine Larry Hicks in April 2002 after Roush's plane crashed on the way to the Winston Cup race in Talladega, Alabama. Roush was seriously injured in the crash but was back on the track as soon as his doctors allowed.

NO. 7—ULTRA MOTORSPORTS

Car: No. 7 Dodge
Driver: Jimmy Spencer
Owners: Jim Smith
Crew Chief: Gene Nead
Sponsor: Unavailable at press time
Address: 222 Raceway Dr.
Mooresville, NC 28115
Telephone: (704)662-8655

About Jim Smith: Entered NASCAR with a background in off-road racing. In 1991 he was the SCORE/HDRA Class 1 champion and recipient of the True Grit Award, given to the driver covering all the racing miles in the fastest average speed. In 1994 he was named Off-Roadsman of the Year after winning the Baja 1000 and finishing second in the standings. Also owns a NASCAR Craftsman Truck Series team. Smith's Ultra Wheel Co., based in Buena Park, California, is one of the largest custom wheel manufacturers in the nation.

NO. 8—DALE EARNHARDT, INC.

Car: No. 8 Chevrolet
Driver: Dale Earnhardt Jr.
Owner: Teresa Earnhardt
Crew Chief: Tony Eury Sr.
Sponsor: Budweiser
Address: 1675 Coddle Creek Hwy.
Mooresville, NC 28115
Telephone: (704)662-8000

About DEI: See the No. 1 team for information on Dale Earnhardt, Inc..

NO. 9—EVERNHAM-ELLIOTT MOTORSPORTS

Car: No. 9 Dodge

Driver: Kasey Kahne
Owner: Ray Evernham
Crew Chief: Tommy Baldwin
Sponsor: Dodge
Address: 160 Munday Rd.
Statesville, NC 28677
Telephone: (704)924-9404

About Ray Evernham: He made his first mark in Winston Cup as crew chief for Jeff Gordon, guiding Gordon to three Cup championships and 47 wins. As a result of that success, he was named Crew Chief of the Decade by *NASCAR Winston Cup Scene* magazine. In the fall of 1999, Dodge executives selected Evernham to lead the manufacturer back into Winston Cup racing in 2001 after a long hiatus. In that first season with Dodge, Evernham chose veteran Bill Elliott and rookie Casey Atwood as his two drivers. Evernham was born in Hazlet, New Jersey, and grew up in the central Jersey area. His start in racing came as a Modified driver. He and his wife, Mary, and son Ray Jr. live in Harrisburg, North Carolina.

NO. 10—VALVOLINE RACING

Car: No. 10 Pontiac
Driver: Scott Riggs
Owner: Valvoline
Crew Chief: Doug Randolph
Sponsor: Valvoline
Address: 7065 Zephyr Place NW
Concord, NC 28027
Telephone: (704)454-5638

About Valvoline Racing: Nelson Bowers, Tom Beard, and Reed Morton share ownership of the team with the Valvoline Co. All three men are graduates of the University of Georgia. Bowers is a successful entrepreneur in the retail automotive industry and owns and operates automobile dealerships and collision centers in Chattanooga, Tennessee. Beard is managing director of an Atlanta bank. A former Army infantry officer, Beard was deputy assistant to President Jimmy Carter from 1976 to 1980. Morton is a senior partner with an Atlanta law firm. James J. O'Brien is president of the Valvoline Oil Co.

NO. 12—PENSKE SOUTH RACING

Car: No. 12 Dodge
Driver: Ryan Newman
Owner: Roger Penske
Crew Chief: Matt Borland
Sponsor: AllTel
Address: 136 Knob Hill Rd.
Mooresville, NC 28117
Telephone: (704)664-2300

About Roger Penske: See the No. 2 team for information on Roger Penske.

NO. 14—A. J. FOYT

Car: No. 14 Chevrolet
Driver: Larry Foyt
Owner: A. J. Foyt
Crew Chief: Greg Connors
Sponsor: Harrah's
Address: 128 Commercial Dr.
Mooresville, NC 28115
Telephone: (704)799-1414

About A. J. Foyt: He's one of the true legends of American racing. The first four-time winner of the Indianapolis 500, Foyt also won more Indy car races (67) than any other driver. The seven-time national Indy car driving champion has raced almost every type of car, from midgets to stock cars (he won the Daytona 500 in 1972). He also won the 24 Hours of Le Mans. In 1999, Kenny Brack gave Foyt his first Indy 500 victory as a car owner. The tough Texan's business interests include auto dealerships, oil investments, and raising thoroughbred horses.

NO. 15—DALE EARNHARDT, INC.

Car: No. 15 Chevrolet
Driver: Michael Waltrip
Owner: Dale Earnhardt, Inc.
Crew Chief: Richard "Slugger" Labbe

Jack Roush, owner of four Nextel Cup teams, earned his first Cup championship in 2003 when Matt Kenseth drove the No. 17 DeWalt Ford to the title.

Sponsor: NAPA Auto Parts
Address: 1675 Coddle Creek Hwy.
Mooresville, NC 28115
Telephone: (704)662-8000

About DEI: See the No. 1 team for information on Dale Earnhardt, Inc.

NO. 16—ROUSH RACING

Car: No. 16 Ford
Driver: Greg Biffle

Owner: Jack Roush
Crew Chief: Randy Goss
Sponsor: Army National Guard and Subway
Address: 7020 Aviation Blvd.
Concord, NC 28027
Telephone: (704)632-1600

About Jack Roush: See the No. 6 team for information on Jack Roush.

NO. 17—ROUSH RACING

Car: No. 17 Ford
Driver: Matt Kenseth
Owner: Jack Roush/Mark Martin
Crew Chief: Robbie Reiser
Sponsor: DeWalt Industrial Tools
Address: 7050 Aviation Blvd.
Concord, NC 28027
Telephone: (704)632-1500

About Jack Roush: See the No. 6 team for information on Jack Roush. For more information on Mark Martin, see the Driver Register (Chapter 3).

NO. 18—JOE GIBBS RACING

Car: No. 18 Chevrolet
Driver: Bobby Labonte
Owner: Joe Gibbs
Crew Chief: Michael "Fatback" McSwain
Sponsor: Interstate Batteries
Address: 13415 Reese Blvd. West
Huntersville, NC 28078
Telephone: (704)944-5000

About Joe Gibbs: (Editor's Note: At press time, the Joe Gibbs Racing team was in transition because Gibbs had accepted an offer to return as head coach of the Washington Redskins in the National Football League.) Until Bobby Labonte won the 2000 Winston Cup championship, Gibbs was better known to American sports fans as the coach of three Washington Redskins Super Bowl teams. The Redskins won the biggest game around in 1982 (over Miami), 1987 (over Denver), and 1991 (over Buffalo). In 12 seasons under Gibbs, Washington's record was 140-65 (regular season and playoffs). He retired in 1992, but in January 2004, Redskins' owner Daniel Snyder lured Gibbs back to the gridiron with a reported five-year contract worth $25 million, making Gibbs one of the highest paid coaches in the league.

When Gibbs left football, he chose Dale Jarrett as his first full-time Winston Cup driver. In addition to Labonte's Winston Cup title, Gibbs also guided Tony Stewart to the crown in 2002, giving Joe Gibbs racing two championships in three years. A native of North Carolina, Gibbs moved with his family to California when he was still in elementary school. There, he became a fan of all types of motorsports. Gibbs also owned teams on the National Hot Rod Association (NHRA) drag racing circuit until withdrawing a few years ago. Both his sons, J. D. and Coy, are involved in Gibbs Racing. J. D., a former William & Mary football player, is president, while Coy, who played football at Stanford, is a driver (2003 was his second year on the Craftsman Truck Series). Having Joe Gibbs in Winston Cup as an owner helped spread the appeal of the series.

NO. 19—EVERNHAM MOTORSPORTS

Car: No. 19 Dodge
Driver: Jeremy Mayfield
Owner: Ray Evernham
Crew Chief: Kenny Francis
Sponsor: Dodge
Address: 160 Munday Rd.
Statesville, NC 28677
Telephone: (704)924-9404

About Ray Evernham: See the No. 9 team for information on Ray Evernham.

NO. 20—JOE GIBBS RACING

Car: No. 20 Chevrolet
Driver: Tony Stewart
Owner: Joe Gibbs
Crew Chief: Greg Zipadelli
Sponsor: Home Depot

After more than a decade of competing at NASCAR's highest level, team owner Joe Gibbs decided to go back to his first love in 2004 and return as the head coach of the NFL's Washington Redskins. Between 1980 and 1992, Gibbs led the Redskins to 140 wins and three Super Bowl championships. Here, Gibbs—standing behind the three Super Bowl trophies—is introduced to the media as the 'Skins new coach on January 8, 2004.

Address: 13415 Reese Blvd. West
Huntersville, NC 28078
Telephone: (704)944-5000

About Joe Gibbs: See the No. 18 team for more information on Joe Gibbs.

NO. 21—WOOD BROTHERS RACING

Car: No. 21 Ford
Driver: Ricky Rudd
Owner: Glen Wood
Crew Chief: Ben Leslie

Sponsor: Motorcraft Quality Parts
Address: 21 Performance Dr.
Stuart, VA 24171
Telephone: (540)694-2121

About the Wood Brothers: Glen and Len Wood are two of NASCAR's legendary figures. Both have been part of the sport since the early 1950s. Glen competed as a driver from 1953 until 1965, when he and his family began fielding cars for some of racing's biggest names, including Dan Gurney, Curtis Turner, Parnelli Jones, A. J. Foyt, LeeRoy Yarbrough, Cale Yarborough, and Marvin Panch. Later, the team featured David

Pearson, Neil Bonnett, Buddy Baker, Kyle Petty, Dale Jarrett, Morgan Shepherd, and Michael Waltrip. The organization's record is among the most impressive in NASCAR history: more than 1,000 starts, 116 poles, 97 victories, and more than $16 million in earnings through the 2003 season. Glen's son, Eddie, and Eddie's wife, Kim, are co-owners of the team; Eddie is a chassis expert. The team was moving its racing operation to Mooresville, North Carolina, in 2004.

NO. 22—BILL DAVIS RACING

Car: No. 22 Dodge
Driver: Scott Wimmer
Owner: Bill Davis
Crew Chief: Frank Stoddard
Sponsor: Caterpillar
Address: 300 Old Thomasville Rd.
High Point, N.C. 27260
Telephone: (336)887-2222

About Bill Davis: After fielding Busch Grand National series cars for such drivers as Mark Martin and Jeff Gordon, Davis moved to the Winston Cup series in 1993. Bobby Labonte, a two-time Grand National titlist, drove for Davis for two seasons. Randy LaJoie, Jimmy Hensley, and Wally Dallenbach shared time in 1995 before Ward Burton joined the team for the final nine races. Burton, who earned his first Cup victory at Rockingham in 1995, was Davis's driver until 2004, when Scott Wimmer took over the No. 22 Dodge. Davis is a native of Arkansas.

NO. 23—BILL DAVIS RACING

Car: No. 23 Dodge
Driver: Kenny Wallace
Owner: Bill Davis
Crew Chief: Philippe Lopez
Sponsor: Stacker 2
Address: 300 Old Thomasville Rd.
High Point, NC 27127
Telephone: (336)887-2222

About Bill Davis: See the No. 22 team for information on Bill Davis.

NO. 24—HENDRICK MOTORSPORTS

Car: No. 24 Chevrolet
Driver: Jeff Gordon
Owner: Rick Hendrick
Crew Chief: Robbie Loomis
Sponsor: Du Pont Automotive Finishes
Address: 4433 Papa Joe Hendrick Blvd.
Charlotte, N.C. 28262
Telephone: (704)455-0324

About Rick Hendrick: See the No. 5 team for information on Rick Hendrick.

NO. 25—JOE HENDRICK MOTORSPORTS

Car: No. 25 Chevrolet
Driver: Brian Vickers
Owner: Joe Hendrick
Crew Chief: Peter Sospenzo
Sponsor: UAW-Delphi
Address: 4423 Papa Joe Hendrick Blvd.
Charlotte, N.C. 28262
Telephone: (704)455-0326

About Joe Hendrick: Affectionately known as "Papa Joe," Hendrick began racing Modifieds in the early 1960s. With Ray Hendrick (no relation) as the driver, the team, based in South Hill, Virginia, won races all across its home state. Hendrick's sons, Rick and John, rode to races in the back of the family pickup truck before moving up in the family business. The main road through the Hendrick Motorsports complex near Charlotte is named Papa Joe Hendrick Boulevard. Joe continues to work on restoring cars.

NO. 29—RICHARD CHILDRESS RACING

Car: No. 29 Chevrolet.
Driver: Kevin Harvick
Owner: Richard Childress
Crew Chief: Todd Berrier
Sponsor: GM Goodwrench Service
Address: P.O. Box 1189

236 Industrial Dr.
Welcome, NC 27374-1189
Telephone: (336)731-3334

About Richard Childress: A former Winston Cup racer himself, Childress finished in the top 10 in points five times (his best finish was fifth in 1975). While he was still racing the Cup circuit, he signed Dale Earnhardt in 1981. Together, they won six Winston Cup titles before Earnhardt's untimely death in 2001. Childress retired as a driver in 1981. As an owner, he expanded to the NASCAR Crafstman Truck series in 1995. With Mike Skinner driving, the Childress team won the first truck series title. Childress also owns 200 acres of farmland and is the principle owner in a merchandise and apparel business. Some of the company's employees have been with Childress Racing for more than 20 years. Childress and his wife, Judy, have one daughter, Tina Lynn Dillon. Tina's husband, Mike, drives in the Busch Grand National series.

NO. 30—RICHARD CHILDRESS RACING

Car: No. 30 Chevrolet
Driver: Johnny Sauter
Owner: Richard Childress
Crew Chief: Kevin Hamlin
Sponsor: AOL
Address: P.O. Box 1189
236 Industrial Dr.
Welcome, NC 27374-1189
Telephone: (336)731-4594

About Richard Childress: See the No. 29 team for information on Richard Childress.

NO. 31—RICHARD CHILDRESS RACING

Car: No. 31 Chevrolet.
Driver: Robby Gordon.
Owner: Richard Childress
Crew Chief: Chris Andrews
Sponsor: Cingular Wireless
Address: P.O. Box 1189

Frank Stoddard, crew chief for the No. 22 team owned by Bill Davis, preparing for the 2003 MBNA America 400 at Dover International Speedway.

236 Industrial Dr.
Welcome, N.C. 27374-1189
Telephone: (336)731-3334

About Richard Childress: See the No. 29 team for information on Richard Childress.

NO. 32—PPI MOTORSPORTS

Car: No. 32 Ford
Driver: Ricky Craven
Owner: Cal Wells III
Crew Chief: David Charpentier
Sponsor: Tide
Address: 3051 First Ave. Ct. SE
Hickory, NC 28602
Telephone: (828)267-0250

About Cal Wells III: With a background in Indy car and off-road racing, Wells moved to

NASCAR in 2000 with former CART driver Scott Pruett as his driver. Pruett was replaced by Andy Houston for the season's five final races. Wells's team improved in 2001 when he moved to North Carolina from California, where his CART Indy car team was headquartered. Wells volunteered and worked at off-road shops in his native California before building his own off-road truck at age 15. He raced until his late teens. At age 24, Wells and a partner hired a mechanic and started Precision Preparation, Inc., concentrating on off-road racing. Wells joined Toyota in 1982 and collected more than 75 off-road wins.

NO. 38—ROBERT YATES RACING

Car: No. 38 Ford
Driver: Elliott Sadler
Owner: Robert Yates
Crew Chief: Todd Parrott
Sponsor: Texaco Havoline.
Address: 292 Rolling Hills Rd.
Mooresville, N.C. 28117
Telephone: (704)662-8600

About Robert Yates: Established a reputation as one of the top engine builders in Winston Cup racing before becoming a team owner. Built engines for Junior Johnson in the early 1970s, and in 1972, Bobby Allison won 10 races for Johnson with engines built by Yates. In 1976, Yates joined the DiGard team during Darrell Waltrip's first full Winston Cup season. He left DiGard in 1986 to work with Ranier/Lundy Racing as team manager; Cale Yarborough was the team's driver. The following year, Davey Allison was named the team's driver, and he became the first driver in Winston Cup history to win twice as a rookie. In 1988 Yates purchased the team from Harry Ranier. The team has persevered through the death of Allison (1993) in a helicopter crash and Ernie Irvan's near-fatal practice crash at Michigan in 1994. Dale Jarrett joined the team as the driver of the No. 88 Ford, and in 1996 Jarrett became the first driver to win the Daytona 500 and the Brickyard 400 at Indianapolis in the same year. Yates is the ninth, and youngest, child of a prominent Southern Baptist minister in Charlotte. Twin brother Richard is the business manager for Yates Racing. Robert and his wife, Carolyn, have two children: Doug and Amy.

NO. 40—CHIP GANASSI RACING

Car: No. 40 Dodge
Driver: Sterling Marlin
Owner: Chip Ganassi
Crew Chief: Lee McCall
Sponsor: Coors Light
Address: 114 Meadow Hill Circle
Mooresville, N.C. 28117
Telephone: (704)662-9642

About Chip Ganassi: After winning four consecutive titles in the CART Fed Ex Indy car series and five overall in the 1990s, Ganassi bought 80 percent of the Felix Sabates Winston Cup operation. Ganassi's goal is to be as successful in Winston Cup as he was in CART. Sterling Marlin delivered the first victory for Ganassi and Dodge at Michigan in August 2001. Ganassi's Indy car streak began with Jimmy Vasser in 1996; Alex Zanardi followed with championships in 1997 and 1998, and Juan Montoya completed the run in 1999. Ganassi is a former CART driver. He was the fastest rookie qualifier for the Indianapolis 500 in 1982. The Pittsburgh native is executive vice president of the FRG Group, a holding company with interests in telecommunications, manufacturing, and computer businesses. Ganassi is also a partner in the Pittsburgh Pirates ownership group and is president of Chicago Motor Speedway. Ganassi is a graduate of Duquesne University.

NO. 41— CHIP GANASSI RACING

Car: No. 41 Dodge
Driver: Casey Mears
Owner: Chip Ganassi
Crew Chief: Jimmy Elledge
Sponsor: Target Stores
Address: 114 Meadow Hill Circle
Mooresville, NC 28817
Telephone: (704)662-9642

About Chip Ganassi: See the No. 40 team for information on Chip Ganassi.

NO. 42—CHIP GANASSI RACING

Car: No. 42 Dodge
Driver: Jamie McMurray
Owner: Chip Ganassi
Crew Chief: Donnie Wingo
Sponsor: Texaco Havoline
Address: 114 Meadow Hill Circle
Mooresville, NC 28117
Telephone: (704)662-9642

About Chip Ganassi: See the No. 40 team for information on Chip Ganassi.

NO. 43—PETTY ENTERPRISES

Car: No. 43 Dodge
Driver: Jeff Green
Owner: Richard Petty.
Crew Chief: Gary Putnam
Sponsor: Cheerios
Address: 311 Branson Mill Rd.
Randleman, N.C. 27317
Telephone: (336)498-1443

About Richard Petty: One of the most popular drivers ever in any racing series, Petty holds the record for most Winston Cup race victories (200) and most Daytona 500 wins (7). Shares with Dale Earnhardt the mark for most Winston Cup titles (7). Only driver to win the Daytona 500 in four different automobile brands: Plymouth, Dodge, Oldsmobile, and Buick. His fender-denting duels with Bobby Allison, Cale Yarborough, David Pearson, and others are at the core of NASCAR's history. President George Bush helped Petty celebrate his 55th birthday at Daytona in 1992, the year Petty retired as a driver. President Reagan attended the Firecracker 400 at Daytona in 1984 when Petty won his final race. Followed his father, Lee, into Winston Cup racing. Early in Richard's career he won a convertible division race by a few inches, but the runner-up protested; officials upheld the protest and gave the victory to the second-place

Chad Knaus, crew chief for the No. 48 car owned by Rick Hendrick and Jeff Gordon and driven by Jimmie Johnson.

finisher, who just happened to be Lee Petty. Richard's trademarks include a cowboy hat and sunglasses. Petty is interested in politics and has served as a county commissioner in Randolph County, North Carolina. The No. 43 car and STP have been associated since 1972. Nicknamed "King Richard" He and his wife, Lynda, have four children: Kyle, Sharon, Lisa, and Rebecca.

NO. 45—PETTY ENTERPRISES

Car: No. 45 Dodge
Driver: Kyle Petty
Owner: Petty Enterprises/Patricia Huffman Petty
Crew Chief: Greg Steadman
Sponsor: Georgia Pacific
Address: 110 Sunrise Center Drive
Thomasville, NC 27360
Telephone: (336)498-1443

About Petty Enterprises: See the No. 43 team for information on Petty Enterprises.

NO. 48—HENDRICK MOTORSPORTS

Car: No. 48 Chevrolet
Driver: Jimmie Johnson
Owners: Rick Hendrick, Jeff Gordon
Crew Chief: Chad Knaus
Sponsor: Lowe's Home Improvement Warehouse
Address: 4414 Papa Joe Hendrick Blvd.
Charlotte, NC 28262
Telephone: (704)455-0309

About Rick Hendrick and Jeff Gordon: See the No. 5 team for information on Rick Hendrick. For information on Jeff Gordon, see his bio in the Driver Register (Chapter 3).

NO. 49—BAM RACING

Car: No. 49 Dodge
Owner: Beth Ann Morgenthau
Crew Chief: Scott Eggleston
Sponsor: Schwan Food Service
Address: BAM Racing
11881 Vance Davis Dr.
Charlotte, NC 28269
Telephone: (704)947-9696

About Beth Ann Morgenthau: Her No. 49 team entered Winston Cup racing in 2001 with a limited schedule. Shawna Robinson was the team's driver for a part-time schedule in 2002. Morgenthau and her husband own an investment banking firm and live in Coral Gables, Florida.

NO. 54—BEL CAR RACING

Car: No. 54 Ford
Driver: Todd Bodine
Owners: Sam Belnavis and Travis Carter
Crew Chief: Gary Cogswell
Sponsor: Unknown at press time
Address: 2668 Peachtree Rd.
Statesville, NC 28265
Telephone: (704)873-2310

About Sam Belnavis and Travis Carter: Belnavis is the only full-time African American owner in the Nextel Cup series. A native of Brooklyn, New York, Belnavis got his start in racing in 1979 as the sports marketing director at Miller Brewing Co. He is a graduate of Manhattan College. Carter is a NASCAR veteran. Before becoming a team owner in 1989, Carter gained experience as a crew chief with two Cup-winning teams: 1973, with Benny Parsons driving for L. G. DeWitt; and 1978, with the Cale Yarborough team owned by Junior Johnson. Carter also has worked with such drivers as Bobby Allison, Dave Marcis, Harry Gant, Morgan Shepherd, and Rick Mast. Carter had two stints with Jimmy Spencer: all of 1991 and part of 1992, then again in 1995 through 2001. As a team owner, Carter is still searching for his first victory.

NO. 74—BACE MOTORSPORTS

Car: No. 74 Chevrolet
Driver: Tony Raines
Owner: Bill Baumgardner
Crew Chief: Larry Carter
Sponsor: Unknown at press time
Address: 117 Luma Hill Ct.
Mooresville, NC 28117
Telephone: (704)664-7440

About Bill Baumgardner: Success in the Busch Grand National series with Randy Lajoie preceded his team's entry into Winston Cup in 2003. Only team to win three consecutive Busch titles (1995 to 1997). Team is named after his children: Brian, Anna, Carrie, and Emily. In 1992 Baumgardner founded StaffAmerica, a professional employer organization that specializes in the general administration services industy. He is a graduate of the University of North Carolina-Charlotte.

NO. 77 PENSKE SOUTH/ JASPER MOTORSPORTS

Car: No. 77 Dodge
Driver: Brendan Gaughan
Owners: Doug Bawel, Mark Wallace, Mark Harrah

Crew Chief: Shane Wilson
Sponsors: Kodak Film
Address: 110 Knob Hill Rd.
Mooresville, N.C. 28117
Telephone: (704)662-6222

About Bawel, Wallace, and Harrah: Doug Bawel has been involved in the automotive business since he began selling cars at a Ford dealership while he was a student at the University of Evansville. Bawel joined Jasper Engines and Transmissions as a sales trainee and worked his way up as advertising manager, sales manager, and vice president before he was elected president in 1987. He and his associates purchased the company from founder Alvin Ruxer in 1987. Jasper sponsored Ken Ragan in Winston Cup in 1989. In 1993, Bawel became a partner with D. K. Ulrich, fielding a Ford for Greg Sacks in 1994. Davy Jones and Bobby Hillin Jr. later drove for Jasper. In 1995, Bawel bought Ulrich's interest in Jasper Motorsports and formed a partnership with Wallace and Harrah. They are owners of Jasper distributorships, Wallace in Atlanta and Harrah in Greensboro, North Carolina. In 2003, Bawel was named Business Leader of the Year by the Indiana Chamber of Commerce.

NO. 88—ROBERT YATES RACING

Car: No. 88 Ford
Driver: Dale Jarrett
Owner: Robert Yates
Crew Chief: Mike Ford
Sponsor: UPS
Address: 115 Dwelle St.
Charlotte, N.C. 28208
Telephone: (704)392-8184

About Robert Yates: See the No. 28 team for information on Robert Yates.

NO. 91—EVERNHAM MOTORSPORTS

Car: No. 91 Dodge
Driver: Bill Elliott
Owner: Ray Evernham
Crew Chief: Sammy Johns
Sponsor: Unknown at press time
Address: 160 Munday Rd.
Statesville, NC 28677
Telephone: (704)924-9404

About Ray Evernham: See the No. 9 team for information on Evernham.

NO. 97—ROUSH RACING

Car: No. 97 Ford
Driver: Kurt Busch
Owner: Georgetta Roush
Crew Chief: Jimmy Fennig
Sponsor: Sharpie/Rubbermaid
Address: 7050 Aviation Blvd.
Concord, NC 28027
Telephone: (704)632-1500

About Roush Racing: See the No. 6 team for information on Roush Racing.

NO. 99—ROUSH RACING

Car: No. 99 Ford
Driver: Jeff Burton
Owner: Jack Roush
Crew Chief: Paul Andrews
Sponsor: Citgo
Address: 7020 Aviation Blvd.
Concord, NC 28027
Telephone: (704)632-1600

About Jack Roush: See the No. 6 team for information on Roush Racing.

5

TOYOTA

NASCAR has always prided itself as being the all-American sport. Since its founding by "Big Bill" France in 1948, the Daytona Beach, Florida-based organization has presented American cars from American teams with American drivers racing at American tracks in front of flag-waving American fans.

In fact, NASCAR's rule book used to restrict models eligible for competition to "American-manufactured." Well, with one notable exception.

Somehow, a Jaguar slipped in and won the June 13, 1954 Grand National race (later, Winston Cup and Nextel Cup) at Linden, New Jersey. The 50-lap, 100-mile race around the Linden Airport was NASCAR's first road race and is still the only victory by a foreign-made car. Al Keller won it, followed by three other Jaguars in the top six and nine more scattered throughout the 43-car field. In addition, five MGs, an Austin Healy, and a Porsche also competed in the race. Before that race, American-built cars had won the first 156 NASCAR races, and since then, they've won the 1,864 held through 2003. That means that, for now, Keller and his Jaguar remain footnotes to history and the answer to a

good trivia question. However, that could all change in 2004.

TOYOTA'S BIG NEWS

In February 2003 at Daytona International Speedway, officials from Toyota Racing Development (TRD) confirmed plans to field factory-supported, V-8 Tundras in the 2004 Craftsman Truck Series. Rumors of the Japanese manufacturer's involvement had first surfaced in June 2002. Rumor then turned into solid speculation in December of that year and became fact in January 2003. As expected, everyone said the right things during the press conference. Toyota was "delighted to join NASCAR" and "looked forward to getting competitive." NASCAR was "happy to welcome Toyota to our family" and "looked forward to years of working together." Left unsaid was the obvious: Toyota Racing Development wasn't going to be content just to race trucks in NASCAR's third-tier series. Clearly, the prestigious Nextel Cup Series was the real goal.

Bill France Jr., chairman and CEO of NASCAR at the time, downplayed the possibility of backlash from fans who didn't want anything Japanese in their red, white, and blue sport. "But Tundra trucks are built in America," France countered. "They come from Indiana and their engines come from California. Their bodies fit our templates and their engines will be push–rod V-8s with carburetors, just like the other engines in the series. Toyota has 100,000 people building cars and trucks [and] engines in this country and they're our fans. We're in the middle of a worldwide economy and this is part of it. I don't see any negatives."

Jim Aust, Motorsports Vice President of Toyota U.S.A. and head of TRD, said his company had no illusions of immediate grandeur. After all, Fords, Chevrolets, and Dodges have spent years in the truck series. Toyota's only stock car involvement had been three years with Robert Huffman racing Celicas in the lower-level Goody's Dash Series. But what a three years: Huffman won 10 races and was third, fourth, and first in points. "It'll be a tough challenge for Tundra to get competitive in the Craftsman Series," Aust said in Daytona Beach, "but we'll eventually make it."

TOYOTA CHOOSES ITS TEAMS

Toyota kept a fairly low profile throughout 2003. It received 80 serious inquiries from Cup, Busch, and Craftsman owners hoping to become part of the grassroots program. Toyota Racing Development officials interviewed 30 of them and asked 16 to submit detailed proposals. All the while, its engineers were submitting prototype bodies and engines for approval and keeping Craftsman Series officials updated on wind tunnel and dyno results. The only public hiccup came in June, when it was learned that long-time Winston Cup and Busch Series owner Bill Davis had agreed to help Toyota with its start-up efforts. Not surprisingly, Dodge Motorsports quickly withdrew all financial and technical support from Bill Davis Racing and filed suit for breech of contract.

Toyota Racing Development waited until the 2003 season finale in November at Homestead,

Florida, to officially introduce this year's CTS lineup. Bill Davis Racing will field Tundras for drivers Shelby Howard and Craftsman Series veteran Bill Lester. Bang Racing co-owners Larry McReynolds and Alex Meshkin have signed 1995 series champion Mike Skinner and 2003 champion Travis Kvapil. The Innovative Motorsports team of George di Bidart will field trucks for Huffman and Hank Parker Jr. And Darrell Waltrip Motorsports will have a full-time truck for David Reutimann and a part-time truck for Waltrip.

Just as in February, questions arose about Toyota's long-range plan in NASCAR. "The first thing we've got to find out is whether we can do a good job in the trucks," Aust said. "We're off to a great start, so obviously we're looking down the road. At this particular time, though, we've got our hands full with trucks and the Indy Racing League (IRL). No decision (about the Nextel Cup) has been made and I honestly can't tell you when it might. It's on the horizon and something we'll keep looking at. The best I can tell you at this point is that it's years down the road."

Aust wouldn't comment on the cost of bringing Toyota into the relatively inexpensive Craftsman Series. "I'd like to tell you (what TRD is spending), but then you'd know the rest of the story," he quipped, "We'll be sponsoring the No. 12 truck (for Huffman) and the No. 42 truck (for Parker Jr.). And we'll provide some additional sponsorship for the rest of the teams. That includes engines and chassis support, and that's about as far as I'd like to go into it."

NASCAR-watchers feel the company will almost certainly push up the cost of doing business for all teams. They cite its willingness to help Bill Davis Racing weather the financial hit when Dodge withdrew its support and filed the lawsuit in the summer of 2003. They also realize that any company willing to pour tens of millions of dollars into CART and IRL open-wheel racing won't be shy about spending at least that much in NASCAR.

That's especially bad news for long-time Ford loyalist Jack Roush, whose Winston Cup team won the 2003 championship with Matt

Kenseth. Roush isn't happy that Toyota is going NASCAR racing, and he foresees a major economic impact.

"I don't want to be seen as a guy who's laid himself on the tracks and said we shouldn't have Japanese cars in stock car racing," he said last fall. "But I do hope that NASCAR and fans and everybody involved will take stock of what's good for our economy in their purchases of consumer goods. We're not doing the right thing for our country when we're faced with the prospect of somebody coming into our world and stripping our economy of its essence and conveying that for interests abroad."

NASCAR IS JUST THE NEXT STEP FOR TOYOTA

The company's four-team, seven-driver foray into the Craftsman Truck Series is the latest in its long and successful association with American racing. It began in 1967, when the company had legendary driver/builder/owner Carroll Shelby develop a Toyota 2000-GT for the Sports Car Club of America's (SCCA) C-Production class. It wasn't long before the car was earning victories and challenging chief rival Porsche on American road courses. Even so, the program wasn't renewed for a second season.

Toyota reappeared in American racing in 1976 by introducing a Celica GT Liftback as the pace car of the Long Beach Grand Prix. In addition, six identically tuned Liftbacks were fielded for an exhibition race featuring three professional female drivers and three men from major automotive publications. The "Race for Youth" generated $12,000 for several Los Angeles-area youth organizations. It led to the Toyota Pro/Celebrity Race that's been part of the Long Beach GP weekend for 29 years. The race has raised more than $1 million for children's hospitals in Southern California in the last decade.

The Celica returned to professional racing in 1983 with Dan Gurney in the International Motor Sports Association's (IMSA) GTU class. Three years later, it moved to the turbo-charged GTO class, then graduated into IMSA's top-level GTP class in 1989. At every level and with almost every driver, the team won poles and races, as well as manufacturer's and driver's titles. In 1983, the first year in IMSA, Toyota also began working with Cal Wells on trucks for desert and stadium off-road events. For the next 12 years the team dominated, winning 11 manufacturer's titles and 9 driver's championships. The team also won 27 races and 7 titles in SCORE off-road desert racing.

Toyota moved into open-wheel racing in 1989 by becoming sponsor of what became known as the Toyota Atlantic Series. Among the notable graduates of this Indy car training ground were Michael Andretti, Bobby Rahal, Jimmy Vasser, Jacques Villeneuve, and Sam Hornish Jr. As of 2004, Toyota still sponsored the series and provided spec (identical) engines for its cars.

It was seven more years before Toyota made the huge leap into the Championship Auto Racing Team (CART) Indy car circuit for owners Gurney and Wells. The factory-backed effort struggled mightily until Juan-Pablo Montoya won the 2000 race at Milwaukee for Chip Ganassi. Toyota's CART program peaked in 2002 when Cristiano da Matta won seven poles and seven races to claim the CART championship. Da Matta's title for the Paul Newman/Mario Andretti-owned team snapped Honda's six-year (1996–2001) stranglehold on the series title. Toyota didn't stop there: Bruno Junqueira, driving for Chip Ganassi, raced his Toyota to two victories and a second-place finish in the points race, and another Ganassi driver, Kenny Brack, also won a late-season race. Overall, Toyota-powered cars won 21 races its last three seasons in CART.

In 2003, Toyota moved to the Indy Racing League with an immediate and spectacular impact. Scott Dixon won two races and the series title for Ganassi. Gil de Ferran won three races (including the Indianapolis 500) and was second for Roger Penske. His teammate, Helio Castroneves, won two races and was third in points. In addition, Toyota drivers Al Unser Jr., Tomas

Toyota will race its Tundra truck—shown here during initial track tests—in the Craftsman Truck Series for the first time in 2004.

Scheckter, and Scott Sharp were sixth, seventh, and eighth, respectively, and Japanese driver Toranosuke Takagi was tenth.

And as if that wasn't impressive enough, Toyota has also won seven titles in the truck-based Championship Off-Road Racing Series with teammates Johnny Greaves and Jeff Kincaid. From 1994 through 2000, Celica driver Ron Millen won six Unlimited Class championships in the Pikes Peak International Hill Climb. Finally, 2004 will be Toyota's second year supporting a Celica-based funny car for Alan Johnson Racing on the National Hot Rod Association (NHRA) drag racing circuit.

Les Unger, Toyota's National Motorsports Manager, knows reaction to his company's plans to go NASCAR racing have been mixed. "Obviously, there's enthusiasm coming from fans and spectators, and obviously from the sanctioning body," he said last fall. "There have been some negative responses, but it's not something we're surprised about. I think it's probably difficult to warm up to a new face since we're the first new entry in NASCAR since it started back in the late '40s.

"By the same token, it'll be a win-win with our teams and with the drivers who'll hit the tracks. With the advertising support and promotional support Toyota will bring—and has already started bringing—it's good for everybody involved. It will certainly make for more exciting racing, and that's what it's all about."

6

BRIAN FRANCE: THE NEXT GENERATION TAKES CHARGE

At first glance, Brian France doesn't appear to be the likely person to lead the premier auto racing organization in the United States. One might expect the leader of such an organization to be a forceful, imposing, high-energy figure. After all, managing a racing business—especially one as big as NASCAR—is not an easy job. You are dealing with independent thinkers, from team owners to sponsors. In addition, most of the owners are wealthy and accustomed to having things their way.

France, however, has a youthful, rather privileged, suburban appearance. A common first impression would be: here's a tall guy who is perhaps a stockbroker, sitting behind a desk most of the time, working the phones and computers.

In September 2003, Brian, 41, succeeded his father, Bill France Jr., as chairman and chief executive officer of NASCAR. Previously, as senior vice president of NASCAR, Brian had been influential in the marketing and television areas of the organization. When the change was announced, Bill Jr. came out firmly in support of his son: "In the past years we've seen a lot of innovations and new thinking (in NASCAR). Many of these inno-

vations happened because of Brian's prodding and passion for our sport. Brian has worked long and hard for this opportunity, just as I had. He has worked in about every area (of racing) and he has exceeded my expectations every time—and I'm a pretty tough critic. I have total confidence in what he can do. He's loaded with street smarts."

With Brian guiding NASCAR, leadership of the organization remains in the France family. In 1972, Bill France Jr. replaced his father, Bill Sr., as NASCAR's chairman.

GROWING UP IN NASCAR

Brian has a solid background in racing. Growing up, he performed numerous jobs around racetracks. After attending the University of Central Florida in Orlando, he was national tour director of NASCAR's Weekly Racing Series. He also was general manager of Tucson Raceway Park in Arizona.

Over the last several years, Brian has concentrated on NASCAR's marketing efforts. He is credited with paving the way on the lucrative television contract with Fox and NBC/Turner

Brian France walks through the garage area on race day at Dover International Speedway before the MBNA America 400 on September 21, 2003. France carried on his family's leadership role in NASCAR by succeeding his father as chairman and chief executive officer of NASCAR in 2003.

Broadcasting and with steering NASCAR toward Nextel as the new sponsor of stock car racing's top series.

Ty Norris, executive vice president of Dale Earnhardt Inc. (DEI), is a contemporary of Brian France. "Brian has grown up in the sport, and he's made a real effort, I've noticed, over the last few years to get to know the inner workings of the sport," Norris told *NASCAR Winston Cup Scene*. "He's been pretty dedicated to the future of the sport by trying to understand how other sports made themselves better. He's studied the success stories of the NFL, Major League Baseball, and the NBA. He's taken the good from those case studies and applied them to NASCAR. He's seen the bad in those studies and tried to keep that out of NASCAR. He's done a lot of things behind the scenes that a lot of people in the garage aren't even aware of."

Many in NASCAR are glad that control of the organization is staying in the family. Mike Helton, NASCAR president, and George Pyne, chief operating officer, are two outsiders who have risen to power in the organization. But Bill Jr. and his brother, Jim, as well as Brian and Lesa France Kennedy (Bill Jr.'s daughter) are the real forces in NASCAR. Jim is president of the International Speedway Corp. (ISC) and executive vice president and secretary of NASCAR. Lesa is executive vice president of ISC.

Ray Evernham is among those who like the "all in the family" theme. "I feel more comfortable with the France family continuing to run it than a board of businessmen," the president of Evernham Motorsports told *Winston Cup Scene*'s Mark Ashenfelter. "The France family made this what it is and I think they need to remain in control of it. This thing can't grow until it's just a business. It's got to retain some tradition, some history to keep it going and I think the France family will provide that."

Geoff Smith, president of Roush Racing, respects the France style of doing business. "They do have a methodical, business-like way of approaching issues of succession and management

development, overall, that they believe is going to be in the best interest of continuing the sport," Smith said. "If you address succession early enough, with management in place, you have a chance to evaluate it while there are still senior family members around to guide it in case it doesn't work out. I think it's all reflecting on good planning."

Leonard Wood, one of the famed racing Wood brothers, told *NASCAR Winston Cup Scene*, "We've known the France family ever since we started. You basically know where you stand with them." Referring to the transition in 1972, when Bill Jr. succeeded his father, Wood said, "As far as Big Bill (Sr.), you had extremely big shoes to fill. He was a man that spoke with authority. He just had a way of persuading people without saying that much. A very stern person when he wanted to be. It was also like that with Bill Jr. If you had a legitimate gripe, he would go to bat for you. There were no real feelings of concern (over Bill Jr.'s rise) because (he) had been around for a while."

NASCAR wisely has surrounded Brian with many sharp racing and business people. Before Bill France Jr. decided that Brian was ready to succeed him, he rounded up people such as Mike Helton, George Pyne, and John Darby. Helton, NASCAR's president, is an imposing man with a dark walrus mustache. He handles the daily racing issues for NASCAR. As NASCAR's chief operating officer. Pyne, a former Brown University football player, focuses on the business and marketing side. Darby is the Nextel Cup Series competition director. Brian will lean on Helton, Pyne, and Darby for advice. Brian plans to be a good listener, but says he is up to making tough decisions.

WHAT DOES THE FUTURE HOLD?

What can racing fans expect under Brian's leadership? His plans include continuing NASCAR's strong racing heritage. He will follow the "realignment" plan started by his father and continue to take NASCAR to major markets in

The NASCAR brain trust discusses new safety measures to be implemented in the 2003 season at a press conference in Concord, North Carolina. From left to right are Brian France, chairman and chief executive officer; George Pyne, chief operating officer; and Mike Helton, president.

the United States. Does this mean some traditional tracks will lose race dates? Undoubtedly—in fact, it will already happen in 2004, when Darlington loses its annual Labor Day race. NASCAR also will be marketed and promoted more than ever before. And, Brian plans to make NASCAR more diverse than ever.

"'Grow' to me means several things," Brian said. "It means focusing on our core product, which is delivering thrilling, exciting race competition. Also, it means reaching new markets and venues. It also means a more diverse audience. We're an American sport. We have to embrace everyone in this country to be as excited as we

are about NASCAR." Brian makes the point that he wants to work with the existing racetracks. "We don't want our tracks looking over their shoulders, wondering if NASCAR thinks a date might work better (elsewhere)," he said.

Jim Hunter, NASCAR's vice president of corporate communications, is as respected as anyone in NASCAR. Hunter has held a variety of racing jobs, from track promoter to—horrors!—sportswriter. He has seen Brian develop into a leadership role. Referring to Nextel's selection as the new sponsor of NASCAR's top racing series, Hunter said, "It's noteworthy that Brian led the charge to go out and find a company that fits with NASCAR today. It's indicative of the kind of leadership he's going to show. He's going to be creative."

Regarding long overdue diversity in NASCAR, Hunter said, "Brian has developed a plan over two, five, ten years to put young people of color in position to either make it or not make it as drivers, crew members, engine builders, PR people. NASCAR's grassroots program (involving some team owners, drivers, and crew chiefs) is a way to get four drivers a year into the sport. The key is the lasting commitment on this from Brian." That grassroots plan includes helping with sponsorship in all areas of the United States.

H. A. "Humpy" Wheeler, the president and general manager of Lowe's Motor Speedway, likes Brian's vision. "He's open to new things (such as) changing the points system (and) expanding to different markets." Wheeler, like many others, reminds France to "concentrate on competition. The sport needs exciting dramatic races."

In an effort to gain more exposure for NASCAR, Bill Jr. brought the season-ending Winston Cup festivities to New York City each year. Even though the weather in New York in early December is very un-Daytona like, people in NASCAR like spending time in New York. The Cup champion makes television appearances (*Live with Regis and Kelly* and other morning shows) and NASCAR does business with the Madison Avenue advertisers. Brian says he plans to continue the New York festivities, as NASCAR likes the media attention it receives. What he should say is the television attention. The New York newspapers—busy with their coverage of the NFL's Giants and Jets, the NBA's Knicks and Nets, the NHL's Rangers, Devils, and Islanders, and college basketball—pay virtually no attention to the annual NASCAR invasion.

One problem that Brian has is that he is not well known in the garage area. Previously, he spent most of his time marketing the sport. Toward the end of the 2003 season, Brian spent more time at the racetracks, getting to know drivers, team owners, and crew members. However, with Helton still in charge of NASCAR's day-to-day operations, Brian doesn't need to be everybody's pal. However, he will gain greater acceptance and have more impact if the drivers, team owners, and crews feel comfortable around him.

What happens now to Bill Jr.? At age 70, with a battle against cancer presumably won, Bill Jr. has mellowed. He no longer is the "benevolent dictator" of NASCAR, as his father, Bill Sr., was before him. Bill Jr. occasionally even lets his sense of humor surface, When asked what his role will be, he replied, "That hasn't quite been defined yet. I'll try to stay out of the way and keeps my hands off things. I'm walking around with a little knowledge from the old days. If somebody wants to ask, I will try to answer." Pausing, he added, with a twinkle in his eye, "If it's important enough, I might even suggest it."

A typical Bill Jr. scene occurred during the 2003 media tour held in January in the Charlotte area. As NASCAR officials were presenting their realignment plan during a press conference, Brian was attempting to handle a question about which tracks may lose a race. Suddenly, Bill Jr. stood up in the audience, grabbed a microphone and said, "Let me help Brian out here." He then proceeded to name the four tracks in danger of losing one of their two races: Atlanta, Darlington, Rockingham, and Martinsville.

With Brian France at the helm of NASCAR and Tony George supervising the Indianapolis Motor Speedway (IMS) and the Indy Racing League (IRL), auto racing in the United States is now in the hands of younger, forward-looking men from two of the first families of racing. George, 43, is the grandson of Tony Hulman, the man who revived IMS after World War II and brought NASCAR to Indy in 1993. The Brickyard 400 is now one of the top races on the NASCAR Nextel Cup schedule.

It's interesting that Brian France and Tony George are maintaining family traditions in racing. When George assumed command of IMS, there were many skeptics who doubted his ability to handle the job. Not only has IMS prospered under George with the addition of the Brickyard

400 and the United States Grand Prix Formula One race, he has turned the IRL into a viable series. Many people think Brian France will do the same for NASCAR.

7

SAFETY NEVER
TAKES A BACKSEAT

Some NASCAR watchers feel the biggest story of 2003 was the July announcement that Nextel would replace Winston as stock car racing's main sponsor in 2004. Others feel it was Brian France's appointment as CEO and chairman of the board. Still others favor Toyota's introduction as the major moment in 2003. Some may even say it was Bill Elliott's "semiretirement" announcement in New York City in December.

But clearer heads agree on this: the biggest story was NASCAR's renewed commitment to all things safety-related. Among the significant safety improvements made in 2003 were the installation of the new SAFER barriers at three tracks, the debut of the Research and Development/Safety Center near Charlotte, and the development of roof-mounted escape hatches and rear-end fire extinguishers. Not to be overlooked was the new rule barring drivers from racing back to the caution flag, a change that allows safety vehicles to reach accident scenes much faster.

Terrible accidents led to the SAFER walls at three tracks, and another accident proved how valuable they are. A third accident led to the rule barring racing back to the caution flag. And several accidents led to the escape hatch and fire-suppression system. In their own way, each helped make NASCAR safer than ever.

NADEAU'S ACCIDENT:
A NEAR TRAGEDY

The first accident was on May 2, during Winston Cup practice at Richmond International Raceway. It began when Jerry Nadeau abruptly lost traction approaching turn 1 of the ¾-mile, D-shaped track. Without warning, his Grand Prix snapped to the right, looped about 180 degrees and slid viciously into the turn 2 wall. It impacted the unprotected concrete wall almost flush, driver's side first. Those watching immediately knew it was a very, very bad accident.

Rescue workers needed 15 minutes to stabilize Nadeau. When all else failed—after all, the car's left side was flush against the wall—they removed the roof and lifted him out, unconscious and strapped to a backboard. One worker held an oxygen bag attached to a breathing bag over Nadeau's nose and mouth. After a cursory stop at the infield medical center, workers put him into a helicopter for the short flight to the nearby Medical College of Virginia. Word quickly spread that he was alive, but barely.

The 32-year-old racer had massive injuries to the left side of his body. Broken left collarbone, shoulder blade, ribs, and a collapsed lung. The worst injury was what doctors called a "moderate to severe" closed head injury. Nadeau was in intensive care, listed as "critical but stable" in an induced coma. His mother, father, and sister were summoned from Connecticut, his wife from North Carolina. Four days later he was upgraded to "serious but stable," and then to "fair" a week later. Despite being "semiconscious" and "not verbally responsive," he went from ICU into a private room. A week later, two weeks after the accident, he began responding to commands with hand squeezes and facial expressions. He suddenly awoke and began talking on May 22, feeling so good he called MB2 Racing team manager Jay Frye and crew chief Ryan Pemberton.

In late May, he was flown from Richmond to the Charlotte Institute of Rehabilitation for a week of intense inpatient physical and speech therapy. He went home in early June after beginning a five-day-a-week regimen of outpatient therapy at CIR. His rehab schedule eventually was reduced to three days a week, then to monthly. Although almost 100 percent, he knows he's not ready to race again. MB2 and the U.S. Army team hired Joe Nemechek to sub for Nadeau for this year's full 36-race season. Ironically, Nemechek won at RIR the night after Nadeau was injured.

KELLER'S ACCIDENT: WHAT A DIFFERENCE A WALL MAKES

The second accident involved Busch Series driver Jason Keller and was in the Funai Busch Series 250. It was also at Richmond International Raceway (RIR), but a very different Richmond than the one that had nearly claimed Nadeau's life just four months earlier. By the time Keller's crash occurred on September 5, one significant change had been made at RIR—the new, high-speed safety walls knows as SAFER barriers had been installed.

Nadeau's accident had been the catalyst for installing the new walls. Shortly after his crash, RIR and International Speedway Corp. officials agreed to install the new "soft walls" that had recently been introduced. Richmond fit the profile that most safety experts said was ideal for the technology: fairly high cornering speeds, moderate banking, and tight turns with almost no room to scrub off speed. With Nadeau's accident fresh in their memories, everyone agreed that the track needed SAFER barriers.

SAFER stands for "steel and foam energy-reduction." The system was developed by Dr. Dean Sicking at the University of Nebraska, who began designing and testing his idea in the late 1990s with a grant from NASCAR and the Indy Racing League.

Workers began installing the walls in mid-August, three weeks before the Craftsman, Busch, and Winston Cup triple-header weekend. They began by unloading a fleet of 18-wheelers that carried enough steel, Styrofoam, and fasteners to cushion 1,200 feet of concrete at each end of the 3,960-foot track. SAFER barriers don't replace existing walls—rather, they are attached to them. When secured to the walls, SAFER barriers offer a 30-inch, energy-absorbing cushion between race car and concrete wall. The 1,197-foot section padding turns 3 and 4 started 50 feet before the outside wall began turning and ended near the crossover gate in turn 4. The section padding turns 1 and 2—where Nadeau and several others had crashed so hard—began opposite the last pit box and ended where the backstretch wall began straightening out in turn 2.

Each 28-foot section was assembled from $\frac{3}{16}$-inch steel and backed with 22-inch wide bundles of energy-absorbing Styrofoam placed every 10 feet between the steel and existing concrete walls. When painted and lettered, the 41-inch high barriers are almost indistinguishable from standard concrete walls.

Richmond was the first short track and second overall to implement the SAFER barriers. After a brief tryout on the inside wall off turn 4, they were installed at each end of the Indianapo-

Terry Labonte speeds through turn 1 at Indianapolis Motor Speedway, past corner walls that are fitted with the new SAFER (Steel and Foam Energy-Reduction) energy-absorbing barrier. The SAFER walls were first installed at Indianapolis before the 2002 Indianapolis 500 IRL race.

lis Motor Speedway prior to the 2002 Indianapolis 500 and Brickyard 400. Richmond was among three NASCAR venues—joining tracks at Loudon, New Hampshire, and Homestead, Florida—to add the SAFER walls in 2003. Phoenix added the walls in early 2004.

DRIVERS ARE HAPPY WITH THE NEW SYSTEM

In an unusual show of unity, every poll of drivers at Richmond last fall showed unconditional approval of the barriers. Clearly, RIR and its ISC parent company had done something very

right. "I'd like to see them at every track," said two-time Richmond winner and four-time Winston Cup champion Jeff Gordon. "Once everybody feels comfortable with test results, they should go up everywhere. Nobody realized how fast we ran or how hard we hit until Jerry's crash. It's amazing how hard we hit here because we're carrying so much speed into the corners and get to the wall really fast."

Perhaps surprisingly, Richmond had developed a reputation for uncommonly hard hits (surprising because Richmond is a short track, where speeds are slower than the superspeedways). Johnny Benson suffered season-interrupting injuries in a Busch crash there. Bobby Hamilton broke his hand and missed five Cup races after crashing there in a Craftsman race. Derrike Cope was briefly hospitalized after a Busch crash, while Sterling Marlin took what he called "my hardest hit ever" in a Cup crash, and Ashton Lewis Jr. suffered minor burns in a spectacular back-in Busch crash.

It didn't take drivers long to test the new SAFER barriers. Five Craftsman Series drivers crashed in practice and four more in the Thursday night race. Two drivers crashed in Cup practice, and half-a-dozen Busch drivers crashed either in practice or in the Friday night race. Capping off a week of crashes, more than a dozen Cup drivers crashed during the Saturday night race. Despite heavy damage to cars and trucks, there were no injuries: the barriers had worked.

Keller's crash late in the Friday night Busch race was a real eye-opener. He lost control after hard left-rear contact from Shane Hmiel, a relatively inexperienced series newcomer. Keller's car lost traction, looped to the right. and slid driver's side-first into the turn 3 wall, hitting the wall in much the same way Nadeau had four months earlier. Unlike Nadeau, though, Keller had no injuries whatsoever. Later, after studying "black box" data from Keller's car, NASCAR president Mike Helton said the driver's compartment of Keller's car recorded 70 percent less G-forces than Nadeau's car in May.

"I've never been in an accident at that angle where the driver's side door hits against the wall like that," Keller said several days after the RIR crash. "I honesty believe I'd still be in a hospital at Richmond if the SAFER barrier wasn't in place. I'll never say anything negative about that technology except that it's not at every track."

John Nemechek died in a left-side impact crash in a Craftsman Series race at Homestead in 1997. Adam Petty and Kenny Irwin died in similar left-side crashes in the same turn at Loudon in 2000, Petty during Busch practice and Irwin two months later during Cup practice. And, of course, there was Nadeau's left-side crash at Richmond.

But Keller—almost certainly because of a SAFER barrier—walked away without a scratch from his similar Richmond crash.

While NASCAR officials are always looking for new ways to increase safety, the addition of the SAFER barriers could go down as one of the most significant improvements in many years.

A SIMPLE RULE CHANGE DRASTICALLY IMPROVES SAFETY

The most popular NASCAR rule in years was introduced in 2003 in the week between the September 14 race at Loudon and the September 21 race at Dover, Delaware. The new rule prohibits drivers from racing at speed back to the start/finish line once the yellow caution lights are displayed. The goal is to prevent a serious or fatal collision with a driver whose car is wrecked or disabled on the track, or with a medical crew that has started to move onto the track. This allows medical personnel to get to accident scenes quicker. Before the rule, the ambulances and other vehicles had been told to stay put until the field was slowed behind the pace car.

For years, the "no racing back" suggestion had been a hot-button issue. However, no steps were ever made to officially do something about it until September 2003. At the Loudon race on September 14, Dale Jarrett's No. 88 Ford sat disabled in turn 4 as traffic rushed at him. He'd been hit and turned sideways, sitting motionless on the track; it seemed as if half the field barely missed him as drivers raced the leader back to the start/finish line to avoid going a lap down. Replays of the incident show several cars coming dangerously close to slamming into Jarrett's driver's-side door, which almost certainly would have resulted in a fatal crash. Within days, NASCAR issued a technical bulletin outlining the new "no racing back" rule.

"I don't know anyone who's not happy about this," said Jarrett, who downplayed his role in the rule change. "I'm happy, my owner and my crew are happy, and I think the rest of the competitors

The HANS device—or, head and neck support—is one of NASCAR's most important recent safety innovations. The device, which keeps the head and neck from moving during an accident, was made mandatory in the aftermath of Dale Earnhardt's fatal 2001 crash.

are happy about it. I know my wife and family and my parents are happy about it. Last weekend (at Loudon) was pretty scary. I'm sitting there with nowhere to go, and here comes half the field trying to get that lap back. I didn't have anything to do with it except I was the guy sitting there when somebody noticed how dangerous it was."

At Dover the week following Jarrett's near-disaster, officials patiently explained how the new rule would work. First, the race's running order would be "frozen" the instant the yellow was displayed. Using whatever means available—spotters around the track, television replays, scoring monitors, or officials atop the grandstand—

NASCAR hoped to ensure that nobody gained or lost a position under caution. No longer would a driver be able to make a last-second surge just as the yellow light came on in an effort to avoid going a lap down or to otherwise improve position. Pit stops would be handled as always, and drivers choosing not to pit didn't have to.

The second part of the rule change was that the highest-running lapped driver would be given a "free pass" to get his lap back at the end of the lead-lap line. This quickly became known as the "lucky dog" award because the one driver who got back his spot on the lead lap had definitely received a lucky break; some web sites even created

To demonstrate it's renewed commitment to safety, NASCAR opened a new, 61,000-square foot Research and Development/Safety Center in Concord, North Carolina. Clearly visible in this car housed at the center are the driver's roll cage, meant to protect the driver in a collision, and the roof escape hatch, a new feature implemented for the first time in 2003.

a "lucky dog" statistical entry. Before the rule, when the caution flag came out, leaders had often slowed down and allowed lapped drivers to pass them so that driver could regain his lost lap at the yellow flag. The practice generally followed team or manufacturer lines, and occasionally tempted lapped drivers to race hard through an accident scene to catch the slowing leader. The rule change made that unnecessary, thus ending that temptation and protecting drivers—like Jarrett—who were disabled and in the face of oncoming traffic.

Amazingly, the rule played a major part in the very first race in which it was used, the MBNA America 400 at Dover on September 21. Following a late-race accident, the caution flag came out and the field was frozen. As the highest scoring "lapped" driver, Ryan Newman was allowed to reclaim a spot on the lead lap. When Newman elected not to pit on the caution while every other driver did, he suddenly found himself leading the race—a lead he never relinquished. The ironic part was that Newman had criticized the new rule before the race.

Perhaps surprisingly, the rule didn't cause even a ripple of discontent in the last nine races. Drivers followed the spirit and the letter of the rule, immediately slowing and falling into single-file formation the instant the yellow appeared. Drivers unsure of their position in relationship to those around them generally fell in where officials told them. With the ban on racing back to the flag, medical and safety teams were noticeable quicker getting to accident scenes. One series-watcher even quipped that NASCAR safety and medical crews were finally getting to accident scenes in NHRA- and IRL-like times.

OTHER IMPROVEMENTS IN 2003

Three other safety-related advances appeared in 2003:

• After several brief, but spectacular, fires from rear-first impacts, safety guru Gary Nelson and his staff developed a driver-activated fire suppression system in the trunk/fuel cell area. It is designed to handle fires caused by damage to fuel cells or broken fuel lines. Nelson concentrated on the project after rear-impact fires involving Ken Schrader and Dale Jarrett at Pocono, Bobby Labonte at Chicago, and Ryan Newman at Michigan.

• In the spring, Nelson and his staff opened the 61,000-square foot Research and Development/Safety Center near Concord Regional Airport, north of Charlotte. The $10 million facility serves as NASCAR's headquarters for all things related to safety, technology, competition, or rules enforcement. Among its ongoing projects: development of composite-material seats, cockpit carbon monoxide filters, incident data-gathering boxes (black boxes) activated by contact, and continued research into head-and-shoulder restraint devices;

• Funny car–like roof hatches became an option for drivers during 2003, with an eye toward making the hatches mandatory in 2004. Several larger drivers—chiefly, Michael Waltrip and Jimmy Spencer—struggled to exit their car if they were involved in a left-side first accident into a wall. NASCAR approved the hatch in the summer, but only Dale Earnhardt Inc. installed one, in Waltrip's car. To show that the hatch worked like a charm, Waltrip popped out of it like a Jack-in-the-box after winning at Talladega in September. "I hope I never have to use it," he said then, "but it's cool to know it works."

8

NEXTEL CUP: HOW DID THEY GET THERE?

Here's a little-known fact about NASCAR: The first winner in what is now the Nextel Cup series was from the wilds of far-away Kansas. Not, as most might expect, from North Carolina or Georgia or Alabama. Rather, Jim Roper towed his No. 34 Lincoln from Great Bend, Kansas, to Charlotte, North Carolina, for a race on June 19, 1949. Despite running only 197 of the 200 laps and apparently finishing second on the half-mile dirt track, he was declared the winner when flagged winner Glenn Dunnaway was disqualified for using illegal suspension parts.

Want more? Here's yet another little-known fact: NASCAR's second major champion was from upstate New York. Bill Rexford won the 1950 Grand National title (later, Winston Cup; now, Nextel Cup) in the No. 60 Oldsmobile owned and prepared by Julian Buesink.

Imagine that: a Midwesterner winning NASCAR's first stock car race and a Yankee winning its second championship. Beating the good ol' boys at their own game is like a bunch of rebels beating the Swedes in the Olympic downhill.

But Roper and Rexford weren't unique in major league stock car racing. Indeed, the Day-

tona Beach-based sanctioning body has awarded countless race trophies and eight of its premier series championship trophies to drivers from outside what is generally considered "stock car country." All told, those eight "outsiders" have won twelve championships including the last four and eight of the last nine. In addition, 25 of the 47 Grand National/Winston Cup/Nextel Cup Rookie of the Year winners have come from outside the Southeast.

NASCAR OFFICIALS AREN'T SURPRISED BY THE DIVERSITY

"People may not realize it, but we've always been a broad-based sport," said Jim Hunter, NASCAR's vice president of communications and one of stock car racing's most knowledgeable historians. "We've always had owners and crewmen and drivers from every part of the country, not just from the Southeast. Look at race reports from as far back as the 1950s and you'll find plenty of drivers from places other than Florida, Georgia, Alabama, the Carolinas, Virginia, and Tennessee. We've never been as regional as some people think. One of the biggest factors in our na-

A trio of drivers from "nontraditional" NASCAR states battles it out during the MBNA America 400 at Dover International Speedway. Johnny Benson (No. 10) is from Michigan, Jeremy Mayfield (No. 19) is from Kentucky, and Ricky Craven (No. 32) is from Maine.

tional appeal is that our competitors come from everywhere. That gives fans a connection with our drivers and owners and crew chiefs."

NASCAR's first major champion in 1949 was Red Byron, a World War II tailgunner from Anniston, Alabama. He won the organization's first race, for Modifieds, on the famous Daytona Beach road/beach course in 1948 and won the sixth race in the eight-race schedule during the 1949 "Strictly Stock" season. It would be another 34 years—1983—before another Alabama driver won NASCAR's biggest prize. To this day, Bobby Allison of Hueytown remains one of the sport's most beloved figures.

After Rexford in 1950, the next 33 championships went to drivers from the Deep South: twenty-one to North Carolinians, six to South Carolinians, two each to Virginians and to drivers from Kentucky, and one each to drivers from Alabama and Georgia. Texas native Terry Labonte interrupted that streak by taking the 1984 Winston Cup with owner Billy Hagan. The next four Cups went to southerners before Missouri native Rusty Wallace won the title in 1989.

SOUTHERN STREAK ENDS

Other than seven-time champion Dale Earnhardt and 1999 champion Dale Jarrett—both born

Matt Kenseth spins his car through an infield donut after clinching his first Winston (now Nextel) Cup title at the Pop Secret Microwave Popcorn 400 at North Carolina Speedway. Kenseth, who grew up racing in Wisconsin, is a key member of the young group of non-Southern drivers.

into North Carolina racing families—every Cup winner since Wallace in 1989 was born and reared outside the South. The list of winners includes Alan Kulwicki from Wisconsin in 1992; Jeff Gordon from California and Indiana in 1995, 1997, 1998, and 2001; Texan Bobby Labonte in 2000; Tony Stewart from Indiana in 2002; and Matt Kenseth, another Wisconsin native, in 2003. Who would have imagined that NASCAR would have crowned more championship drivers from Wisconsin than from Florida, Tennessee, or Virginia? Or as many champions from Wisconsin as from Alabama, Georgia, South Carolina, or Texas?

What's more, only two of the top 10 in the final 2003 standings are from the South: third-ranked Dale Earnhardt Jr. from North Carolina and ninth-ranked Bill Elliott from Georgia. The other eight were born, reared, and honed their racing skills in the Midwest or Southwest, or on the West Coast. Runner-up Jimmie Johnson is from California, as are fourth-ranked Gordon and fifth-ranked Kevin Harvick. Sixth-ranked Ryan Newman and seventh-ranked Stewart are from Indiana, and, as noted, the Labonte brothers—Bobby was ranked 8th and brother, Terry, was 10th—are from Texas.

"Almost no matter where we have fans, there are local drivers they can pull for in Nextel Cup," Hunter said. "People in California have the Gordons, Casey Mears, Kevin Harvick, and Jimmie

Johnson. Greg Biffle and Derrike Cope are from Washington state and Kurt Busch is from out in Las Vegas. The Labonte brothers and Larry Foyt are from Texas, and Mark Martin is from Arkansas. Look at all the drivers we have from the Midwest and the ones from New England. It's the same way in the Busch and Craftsman series, too. And we make it a point to publicize where our competitors are from. We want people to understand that we're not just about the Southeast."

The list of drivers from the Midwest is filled with some of the best young drivers in all of NASCAR. Besides 2003 champion Kenseth, there's eight-race winner Ryan Newman, 2002 champion Tony Stewart, and a group of drivers hoping to break through in 2004, including Jamie McMurray, Scott Wimmer, Johnny Sauter, Tony Raines, and Dave Blaney. A number of Nextel Cup veterans round out the Midwest group: John Andretti, Johnny Benson, Ken Schrader, and the Wallace brothers, Rusty, Kenny, and Mike.

The Northeast isn't nearly as loaded as the Midwest, but it does have some strong regional favorites. Among those from that region are Todd, Geoff, and Brett Bodine; Steve Park; Jimmy Spencer; Kevin Lepage; and Ricky Craven.

2003 WAS A BANNER YEAR FOR THOSE FROM OUTSIDE THE SOUTH

Drivers from outside the Southeast won 29 of 2003's 36 Winston Cup races, or 80 percent. Upholding southern pride were Earnhardt Jr. and Michael Waltrip, who each won twice, and one-time winners Elliott, Jarrett, and Joe Nemechek. Not surprisingly, the Midwest led with 11 victories; followed by the West Coast with 10; Las Vegas (specifically, Kurt Busch) with 4; Texas, in the form of the Labonte brothers, with 3; and the Northeast (Craven), with 1.

Non-southern drivers might have had a particularly strong 2003, but in reality, that year was closer to the norm than most people might think. In fact, it's been years since drivers born, reared,

and trained in the Southeast have won more Cup races than drivers from the rest of the country—2003 just took that trend to an extreme.

"There's a lot of good racing in other areas, not just in the Southeast," said Kenseth, one of three Wisconsin natives (along with Johnny Sauter and Scott Wimmer) expected to run the full 36-race Nextel Cup schedule in 2004. "Tracks in the North and Midwest don't open as early in the year or stay open as late as tracks in the Southeast. But there's racing almost every night during the spring and summer in the Midwest. It's tough racing, too. Alan Kulwicki came from Wisconsin, and he encouraged a lot of drivers to try to make it in Cup racing after he won his title in 1992. Dave Marcis was the first to come south and make it, and now a lot of young drivers from the upper Midwest are trying to get to Cup racing."

Kenseth is right to say that a lot of young drivers are making the jump to the Nextel Cup. The last 9 drivers and 10 of the last 11 named Rookie of the Year came from outside the Southeast, meaning that fans should accept the fact that teams from outside that region are going to be strong for years to come. Jeff Gordon started the trend in 1993, followed by Virginia native Jeff Burton in 1994. The top rookies from 1995 through 2003 were hardly from the heart of stock car country. In chronological order, Craven came from Maine, Johnny Benson from Michigan, Mike Skinner from California, the late Kenny Irwin and Tony Stewart from Indiana, Kenseth from Wisconsin, Kevin Harvick from California, Ryan Newman from Indiana, and current ROTY Jamie McMurray from Missouri.

The 2003 rookie class, in fact, was a particularly strong group that included McMurray, Greg Biffle from Washington, Larry Foyt from Texas, Casey Mears from California, Jack Sprague from Michigan, and Tony Raines from Indiana. In 2002, drivers from Indiana and California battled it out for Rookie of the Year honors. The 2001 award came down to a trio from California and one driver each from Nevada and Tennessee. Fans can expect more of the same from the 2004 rook-

Jeff Gordon, shown here in the Pop Secret Microwave Popcorn 400 at North Carolina Speedway, is the most successful of the new breed of drivers who were not born and raised in the South. Indiana-born and California-bred, Gordon has won four Winston (now Nextel) Cup championships.

ie class, which includes two drivers each from Wisconsin and North Carolina and one each from Nevada and Washington.

HOW DO THE DRIVERS REACH THE NEXTEL CUP?

Almost as diverse as their birthplaces is the path that drivers took to reach the Nextel Cup circuit. Many used the traditional training ground, going from weekly short-track, Late Model racing to the Busch Series, then to the Cup. That's how it worked for established stars Jarrett, Earnhardt Jr., Jeff and Ward Burton, Sterling Marlin, Bobby Labonte, and Elliott Sadler. A few drivers—notably the Bodine brothers, Jimmy Spencer, and Steve Park—came from the Northeastern-based Modified series, then through Busch and into Cup racing. Michael Waltrip went from the Goody's Dash series to Busch to the Nextel Cup, while Ricky Craven started in the Busch North, then moved on to Busch, then to the Cup. Ricky Rudd took the most direct route available: straight from motocross to Winston Cup, without any lower-level stock car racing at all.

Those routes to the Cup are all slightly different, but all are considered "normal." However, more and more drivers are reaching the Cup level

Kevin Harvick, shown here in the MBNA America 400 at Dover International Speedway, is a prime example of how most hot young drivers are from somewhere other than the South. Harvick, from Bakersfield, California, gained most of his early racing experience on the West Coast.

with resumes that some might consider a bit unusual. Among the featured stops: Sprint Cars, Midgets, Indy cars, long-distance off-road races, dirt Modifieds, sports cars, and the Craftsman Truck Series. Many drivers get to Cup racing after prepping in the American Speed Association, the Hooters Pro Cup, or any number of lesser-known NASCAR touring series.

2003: AN EXAMPLE OF THE RECENT TREND

For proof that drivers are taking a diverse paths to the sports highest level, one only needs to look as far as the 2003 top 10, starting at the top:

• Champion Kenseth prepped in the ARTGO, Hooters Pro Cup, NASCAR All-Pro, and ASA tours in the early- to mid-1990s. He ran the full 1998 and 1999 Busch seasons even while running a few Cup races. He got his full-time Winston Cup ride with Roush Racing in 2000 and won the title last year. Most of his stock car "training" came on tracks far from the Southeast.

• Jimmie Johnson began racing motocross in California at age four, then progressed through several West Coast off-road and stadium truck series through his teenage years. His success in the Midwest-based ASA circuit in 1998 led to several Busch rides in 1999, and then to the Cup in 2001 with Hendrick Motorsports.

- Jeff Gordon's background is well known. He enjoyed great success in go-karts and ¾-midgets in California, which led to an outstanding open-wheel career in Indiana. He spurned Indy cars by entering the Busch series full-time in 1991 and 1992 and then the Winston Cup series full-time in 1993. Like so many other Cup drivers, he discovered racing and got most of his early training far from "NASCAR country."

- Like Johnson and Gordon, Kevin Harvick got most of his early racing experience on the West Coast. He progressed from go-karts to weekly Late Models to the Winston West and Southwest tours, finally arriving at the Craftsman Series in 1999. His success there led to Busch, which led (sooner than expected), to Cup racing when Dale Earnhardt died in the 2001 Daytona 500.

- Newman spent most of the 1990s winning Midget, Sprint Car, Silver Crown, and USAC open-wheel races in the Midwest. Amazingly, he even found time to earn a bachelor degree from Purdue University along the way!. His impressive resume earned a 2000–2001 ABC (ARCA, Busch, Cup) tryout with Penske South Racing. That led to his 2002 Rookie of the Year Cup season, then his dominant 11-pole, 8-victory season of 2003.

- Tony Stewart followed a similar path to the Cup. He won countless go-kart, Midget, Sprint Car, Silver Crown, and USAC open-wheel races in the Midwest during the 1990s. He ran in the Indy Racing League racing in 1996 and 1997, but managed to fit in a few Busch races those years. He ran more Busch races in 1998 before going full-time Cup racing with Joe Gibbs Rac-

ing in 1999. When he won the Cup in 2002, he became the first driver to win major Indy car and stock car titles in a career.

- Bobby Labonte accompanied his parents from Texas to North Carolina in the mid-1970s when they followed their other son, Terry, into "NASCAR land." Bobby had started racing quarter-midgets in Texas, and he continued his career in weekly Late Model races in the Carolinas in the late 1980s. He went full-time on the Busch series in 1990, winning the title in 1991 and finishing second in 1992. He then went full-time Cup racing in 1993 and won the title in 2000 with Joe Gibbs Racing.

- Elliott trained on Southeastern dirt tracks until his family could cobble together a Winston Cup ride for a few races in 1976. They were a part-time team until Michigan businessman Harry Melling assumed ownership and bankrolled the full 1983 schedule. Despite a thin resume with no Busch or weekly paved-track Late Model experience, Elliott became one of NASCAR's all-time best drivers—witness the 1988 championship.

- Terry Labonte's resume was even thinner than Elliot's. He won some quarter-midget and dirt-track stock car races in Texas in the 1970s, then jumped to Cup racing in 1978 with hardly any paved weekly Late Model experience. Even so, he finished in the top 10 in three of his first five races on the Winston Cup circuit in 1978, a sign of things to come. He went on to win the 1984 and 1996 championships, the longest spell between titles in NASCAR history.

As that look at the 2003 top 10 shows, NASCAR-watchers have been right for years: once you reach the Nextel Cup level, geography and resumes don't count nearly as much as talent.

9

THE HISTORY OF NASCAR:
BEFORE RJR JOINED THE PARTY

It can be said with some certainty that big-time stock car racing began because one man grew tired of shyster promoters who promised this and delivered that. He was concerned about rules not being evenly applied across the board, and he'd had his fill of rough and rutty speedways that weren't close to being major league. Mostly, he was tired of the daily uncertainties surrounding this new sport that held so much hope and promise in post–World War II America.

The man's name was William Henry Getty France. Later, "Big Bill" would do nicely, thank you.

More than anyone in American history, NASCAR founder William H. G. France created a successful sport from scratch. That, and from his own will and grit and stubbornness. He conceived and delivered stock car racing, and he nursed it through its childhood of the late 1940s and 1950s. He guided it into its adolescence of the 1960s and watched in 1972 as his son, Bill France Jr., became its guiding hand. The elder France never strayed far as his sons—Bill Jr. and Jim—built NASCAR into one of America's most successful and popular businesses. The France

family quit counting how often Bill Jr. and Jim asked their father for his wise counsel.

A man of considerable stature, Big Bill was a racer, mechanic, team owner, and sponsor before he became an organizer/promoter. In his mind, his years of experience before and after World War II gave him the right to some say-so in racing's future. He'd seen its potential and noticed how Southerners embraced it as their own. There was a passion from drivers in their souped-up "street" cars and a similar passion from their brand-loyal fans. At a time when much of America considered the region a primitive backwater, the rural South considered racing *its* sport.

That's ironic, because France wasn't a Southerner. Born in Washington, D.C., he lived there until the promise of better things lured him southward in 1934. The son of a banker, he'd held several jobs before operating his own service station in metropolitan D.C. He built his customer base by rising before dawn in the dead of winter to help white-collar bureaucrats crank their cars. Although it was steady work that paid relatively well, France wanted more for his wife, Anne, and their infant firstborn, William Clay France. So it

Curtis Turner crosses over from the beach to the highway portion of the famous Daytona Beach highway-beach racetrack in 1959. During the 1950s, convertible races were popular, especially in the warm weather southern states.

was they left Washington in 1934, headed for Miami Beach or Tampa, only to settle in Daytona Beach for the rest of their lives.

Here, myth and rumor mingle. Some have suggested the Frances stayed in Daytona Beach because they were broke. Others have said Anne wanted to stay put because she had a sister in nearby New Smyrna Beach. One popular story said their aging car wouldn't take them any farther. Years later, Bill France Jr. set the record straight. No, there wasn't a sister urging them to stay put. He didn't know if his parents were too broke to keep going, but he knew a broken-down

car wouldn't have stopped them. His father was good enough with his hands and his toolbox to fix anything that needed fixing.

It's been said that nothing special kept the Frances in Daytona Beach. As the story goes, they arrived when the weather was especially ideal. After years in Washington, the family was deeply enamored of Florida's mild temperatures and soft breezes. Daytona Beach was small and relatively undeveloped, and it moved to a comfortable pace. It wasn't paradise, but it was the closest the Frances had come in their years together. Clearly, there was no need to go any farther south.

AN IDEAL TRACK

There may be another reason the Frances stayed. His name was Sir Malcolm Campbell, and he was the fastest man on four wheels. For years, the hard-packed beach sand between Daytona Beach and Ormond Beach had hosted automotive speed trials. They began with Ransom Olds and Alexander Winton in 1902, became more frequent around World War I, and reached their zenith in the 1930s. The 20-mile stretch of beach was perfect for cars routinely trying to reach 300 miles per hour.

It was reported that Campbell was bringing his legendary Bluebird to Daytona Beach early in 1935 in search of 300 miles per hour. Big Bill was a racer at heart, so it's altogether likely that he and Anne added Campbell's spring visit to their list of reasons to stay. Alas, Campbell didn't reach 300 during what turned into the last round of Florida speed trials. He reached a disappointing 276.82 miles per hour on March 7, then said his future land-speed efforts would be on the Bonneville Salt Flats in Utah. In a way, the sand that produced so many records was killed by its success. Technology was so precise that winds and tides made it difficult to get a safe grip on the beach. In addition, years of use had left the sand rough and rutted.

Herb Thomas (left) and his mechanic, Smokey Yunnick (right), show just how far the NASCAR safety uniform has come as they pose with the trophy that Thomas just won for finishing first in the Southern 500 at Darlington Raceway on September 6, 1954.

After Campbell left, government officials vowed to keep bringing speed-related events to the area. Speed had helped establish the identity of the Ormond Beach–Daytona Beach area and had helped bring midwinter income into area hotels and restaurants. City leaders asked former dirt-track star and Daytona Beach resident Sig Haugdahl to promote a stock car race along a 3.2-mile course that included parts of Highway A1A and the hard-packed beach that had hosted speed trials. The City of Daytona Beach hosted a $5,000 purse and AAA sanctioned the 78-lap, 250-mile event for sedans built in 1935 and 1936.

Things couldn't have gone much worse. Revenue was lost when some ticket-takers arrived long after thousands of fans had wandered into the area and found viewing areas. The turns became virtually impassable, leading to stalled or stuck cars. Mercifully, the race was stopped after 75 laps with Milt Marion declared the winner. Not surprisingly, second-place Ben Shaw and third-place Tommy Elmore protested, but their appeals were squashed. The AAA officials had seen enough to know they'd better get gone. (France, still quite a driver in his own right, finished fifth behind Marion, Shaw, Elmore, and Sam Purvis).

Considering its reported $22,000 loss, it's no surprise the City of Daytona Beach vowed never to promote another race. But Haugdahl wasn't discouraged. He and France had become friends, and they talked the Elks Club into helping promote a stock car race over Labor Day weekend of 1937. Even with a paltry $100 purse and improved management, promotion, and track conditions, the Elks Club also lost money. When Haugdahl quit after his second failure, France was the last hope to keep racing alive in Daytona Beach.

More than anyone, he saw a bright future for stock car racing. He knew what drivers wanted and needed, but he wasn't able to pay the purse, advertise, promote, and pay the city for its services. He found a willing partner in Charlie Reese, a popular restaurateur who agreed to post a $1,000 purse if France would recruit drivers and spread the word. Danny Murphy beat France in the 150-mile race that generated just enough profit to convince Reese and France to try again.

They did well on Labor Day weekend of 1938, then again in March, July, and September of 1939 and 1940. Their expanded 1941 schedule included two March races and one each in July and August. They were planning their 1942 schedule when the Japanese hit Pearl Harbor on December 7, 1941, stopping all major racing. France spent four years in the Daytona Boat Works, all the while contemplating how to make racing more popular. His outline was shaping up when he realized he was a better promoter/organizer than driver. When one door closed, another opened.

He quit the boat works after World War II and set about creating a new stock car racing organization. He wanted one that sanctioned and promoted stock cars, but also brought uniformity to procedures and rules. He envisioned an association with a membership benefit/insurance fund, and one that kept its word about purses and postseason awards. Mostly, he wanted an organization that would crown an undisputed national champion through a clearly defined points system.

At the time, several groups claimed to do that. The AAA was one, but it was more concerned with champ-cars that evolved into USAC/CART. The United Stock Car Racing Association, the National Auto Racing League, and the American Stock Car Racing Association also claimed to promote races that led to a single national champion. The Daytona Beach Racing Association promoted within the city and thus made no claim of a national champion. In fact, France's own National Championship Stock Car Circuit didn't do it . . . which is why he turned his attention in June of 1947 from driving to creating NASCAR.

NASCAR IS BORN

France began his quest with a "summit meeting" in December of 1947 in the Streamline Hotel of Daytona Beach. It attracted three dozen men representing owners, track operators, drivers, technical inspectors, mechanics, businessmen, and lawyers. France was in charge, a role he played from that meeting until the day he died in 1992. It took three days to cobble together the National Association of Stock Car Auto Racing. Its stated goals were uniform rules, a point fund with postseason bonuses, a driver's insurance and benevolence fund, a points system to crown a national champion, and stronger promotions and more media attention.

France was elected president. (You were maybe expecting someone else?) Cannonball Baker was the national commissioner, Eddie Bland the vice president, Bill Tuthill the treasurer, and Marshall Teague the secretary. NASCAR

Johnny Beauchamp (No. 73) slightly trails Lee Petty (No. 42) early on in the first Daytona 500 ever held. Beauchamp was initially declared the winner of the race, which was held on February 22, 1959, but after a long review period, that decision was reversed after it was determined that Petty had actually finished first.

sanctioned its first race on the Daytona Beach road/beach course in February of 1948, several days before it was incorporated. More than 14,000 fans watched Red Byron beat Teague, Raymond Parks, Buddy Shuman, and Swayne Pritchett in a Modified 150-miler on the now-famous beach/highway course south of Daytona Beach proper.

France's idea was for NASCAR to promote Strictly Stock, Modified, and Roadster races. Perhaps surprisingly, Modifieds and Roasters were expected to be more popular than Strictly Stocks. As things turned out, though, NASCAR's first audience shunned the Roadsters. At the same time,

Strictly Stock was delayed while automakers converted from military to family vehicles. Demand outstripped supply, and France didn't want new models racing until they were available in showrooms. So the heart and soul of early NASCAR were pre–World War II cars that France let compete with major engine and bodywork changes. The 1948 Modified schedule showed 52 dirt-track races, with Red Byron its first national championship.

Things changed dramatically in 1949. In February, France staged a 20-mile Strictly Stock exhibition race near Miami. In June, realizing he'd better run a points race or risk losing the se-

Fan-favorite Fonty Flock snaps on his helmet and prepares to tackle the famed highway-beach course in Daytona Beach, Florida, on February 26, 1956.

ries, he scheduled a 200-lap, 150-miler around a ¾-mile dirt track in Charlotte, North Carolina. It paid a $5,000 purse and featured 33 street-legal sedans built after the war. Pole-sitter Bob Flock led the first 5 laps in a 1946 Hudson, Bill Blair led 6-150 in a 1949 Lincoln, then Glenn Dunnaway led 151-200 in his 1947 Ford.

But after tech inspectors caught Dunnaway with illegal rear springs, they moved him from first to last on the rundown sheet. That elevated Roper to victory and moved Fonty Flock, Red Byron, Sam Rice, and Tim Flock into the top 5. Even though he'd been caught red handed, team owner Hubert Westmoreland tried to sue NASCAR for $10,000. A North Carolina judge dismissed it, saying the organization could make and enforce its own rules without outside interference. For not the first time in their lives, France and NASCAR won their day in court.

The race drew 13,000-plus fans, far more than anyone expected. All told, France's new organization staged seven races that year, two each in North Carolina and Pennsylvania, and one each in Florida, New York, and Virginia. Just as in 1947 in the Modified class, Byron won the Strictly Stock (later, Grand National and Winston Cup) championship. Fifty drivers ran at least one race, and between 16 and 45 cars showed up for each of the seven short-track events.

BRASINGTON'S FOLLY

Despite its early success, NASCAR needed something to grab the nation's attention. USAC had its Indianapolis 500, and NASCAR's Modified and Sportsman cars had their annual beach/road races in Daytona Beach. Strictly Stock didn't have a spotlight event until South Carolina native Harold Brasington built a 1.25-mile speedway near Darlington. He stunned everyone by paving it and saying he wanted a run 500-miler for stock cars. A retired racer, Brasington had come to know and respect France during their racing days. He'd quit driving in the late 1940s to tend his farm and construction business,

but he still followed racing. He knew France wanted to expand its image, and he felt a 500-miler would do the trick.

Brasington began planning his speedway after watching the 1948 Indy 500 and seeing the size of the crowd. "If Tony Hulman can do it here," he thought while in Indy, "I can do it back home." In 1949, after buying 70 acres of farmland, he began carving out a speedway. Instead of a true oval, though, he created an egg-shaped facility with one end tighter and more banked than the other. He did so after promising the previous landowner that he wouldn't disturb a nearby minnow pond. So, after he shaped the east end sweeping and flat he shaped the west end narrow and tight.

In the summer of 1950, even as Sam Nunis prattled on about a 500-miler at Lakewood Speedway in Atlanta, Brasington and France agreed to a Labor Day race at Darlington. The inaugural Southern 500 paid $25,000 and was promoted by NASCAR and the Central States Racing Association. When all 9,000 seats were sold, about 6,000 other fans jammed into the infield for the Monday race. Winner Johnny Mantz drove a 1950 Plymouth owned by France, Westmoreland, driver Curtis Turner, and NASCAR official Alvin Hawkins. Despite complaints from some also-rans, Mantz's car passed tech inspection. And if France thought it odd to be owner/promoter and associate with a known cheater like Westmoreland, he didn't let on.

That 500-miler got NASCAR going. With few exceptions, the 1950s featured short races on dirt tracks and home-grown stars like Lee Petty, the Flocks, Buck Baker, the Thomases, Joe Weatherly, Speedy Thompson, Curtis Turner, Rex White, Fireball Roberts, and Ned Jarrett. But there was hardly any coverage from the mainstream media, which still considered stock car racing little more than junk cars driving on cow pasture tracks for the amusement of rednecks. The Southern 500 was NASCAR's only paved-track event in 1950, and there were only four paved races in 1951, two in Dayton, and one each at Darlington and Thompson, Connecticut.

It might not have been comfortable, but the seat that Cale Yarborough (left) and Bobby Isaacs (right) selected gave them the view they needed to personally check out the lap times of cars preparing for the 1969 Daytona 500 at Daytona International Speedway.

Paved tracks didn't gain widespread acceptance until the late 1950s. Darlington and the half-miler at Dayton each had two races in 1952, and Darlington and the new one-mile track at Raleigh, North Carolina, each had one date in 1953. Darlington, Raleigh, and the paved road course at Linden, New Jersey, had races in 1954, and a half-miler at Martinsville, Virginia, joined Darlington (one race) and Raleigh (two) in 1955. The future began emerging in 1956, when France and NASCAR sanctioned 11 paved-track races. The number grew to 14 in 1957 and 24 in 1958. In addition to ovals, NASCAR went road racing at Watkins Glen and Bridgehampton in New York, and at Elkhart Lake in Wisconsin. Almost overnight, stock car racing became a national series rather than one with regional ties. That had been France's vision all along, so his plan was working.

GROWING PAINS

But, like anyone born into an unfamiliar culture, NASCAR didn't always coordinate its parts and pieces. All hell broke loose when scheduling conflicts, cheating scandals, charges of rough driving with intent to injure, and cries of brand-based favoritism got in the way of each other. But things worked in perfect harmony most of the time, as precisely as if an unseen hand were pulling all the right strings. By the way . . . did we mention that "Big Bill" oversaw all issues, great and small? His care, concern, and attention to detail were everywhere as NASCAR moved into the 1960s.

There never was a shortage of men and women racers in the early years. Some were simply foolish thrill seekers with nothing else to do. Others were World War II or Korea veterans, bored by the workaday life they'd returned to find. After all they'd been through, why not race? Why, indeed, since their beloved South had fallen in love with racing to the virtual exclusion of everything except college football and outdoor sports. The South didn't get its first stick-and-ball teams until 1966, when the Braves and Falcons arrived in Atlanta. Two years later, the Hawks be-

Ned Jarrett poses before his automobile in 1965, the year he claimed his second NASCAR Grand National championship.

came the South's first professional basketball team. So from 1948 until 1966, NASCAR and minor-league baseball (and the Masters each spring) were the South's only professional sports.

France saw this and acted quickly. He knew Southerners loved their cars only slightly less than they loved God, country, and family. He knew that, given the opportunity, almost all of them would try racing at least once. It was easy to find dates and places since almost every county had a fairground with a speedway. First used during the 1930s and 1940s for minor-league horse racing, these dirt ovals hosted hundreds of races and bred many stars. In the 1950s and early 1960s, almost every corner of the South had at least one NASCAR track.

In southeastern Virginia, for example, there were tracks in Hampton, Newport News, Norfolk,

LeeRoy Yarbrough takes a break from running test laps at the Daytona International Speedway on June 6, 1962. Yarbrough was at Daytona to practice for the Daytona Firecracker 250, which was scheduled to be held on July 4.

and Virginia Beach. Richmond had three tracks, and there were tracks near Washington and in Roanoke, South Boston, Danville, and Martinsville. North Carolina had tracks from Moyock on the Atlantic Coast to Asheville-Weaverville in the Appalachians. In between were Concord, Fayetteville, Raleigh, Greensboro, North Wilkesboro, Charlotte, Gastonia, Spring Lake, Wilson, Hillsborough, Jacksonville, Shelby, Winston-Salem, High Point, and Randleman.

South Carolina couldn't keep up with its northern neighbor. Its NASCAR tracks were at Darlington, Newberry, Columbia, Spartanburg, Lancaster, Sumter, Hartsville, and Myrtle Beach. Georgia had tracks at Augusta, Macon, Savannah, and Atlanta, and Alabama had them at Birmingham, Huntsville, and Montgomery. NASCAR had

Tennessee tracks at Nashville, Bristol, Newport, and Chattanooga, and Florida had Jacksonville, West Palm Beach, Pensacola, Titusville, and the beach/highway course at Daytona Beach.

A SHOWPLACE IS BORN

Despite 100 or so venues in the 1950s and 1960s, NASCAR still didn't have a showplace. It was evident in the early 1950s that Daytona Beach's highway/beach course was done. Nobody had to remind France to do something quickly, lest Daytona Beach lose racing. He approached city officials in 1953 with talk of a huge speedway west of town. Without such a track, he said, it was doubtful the annual Speed Week program would return. When nothing happened, France promoted what he called his "final" highway/beach races in 1954. He hoped the word "final" would spur the city into action. When it didn't, 1954 became the first of his "final" races in Daytona Beach.

No progress in 1955 meant another threat and another "final" highway/beach race. France said 1956 would be his last promotion, then repeated that threat in 1957. But like the boy who cried wolf, he knew that someday the "last highway/beach race" would indeed happen. As optimistic as he was, he simply couldn't continue working with an increasingly busy public highway and an increasingly crowded beach. Frustrated and willing to go out on a limb, France approached the Daytona Beach Racing and Recreation Facilities Authority in the fall of 1957. He presented a $27,000 check from the Daytona Beach International Speedway Corporation, the down payment on a 50-year lease of 450 acres near the airport. He broke ground in November of 1957 and said that Daytona International Speedway would be a NASCAR showplace by February of 1959. The 1958 Speed Week program was the last major race on the highway-beach course that had served France, Daytona Beach, and racing so well for so long.

It's almost impossible to underestimate the impact of Daytona International Speedway on stock car racing. Finally, NASCAR and France could begin their 11th season with a showplace to call their own. Well, maybe. DIS had an open-air press box and concession stands, and steel railing atop its high-banked turns. But its length and massive turns made up for what it lacked in creature comforts. Once again—as he had so many times—Big Bill France had shown he was a man of uncommon vision.

It would be years before DIS could call itself "The World Center of Racing." But after years of half-mile and shorter dirt tracks (and a few paved tracks), the speedway west of Daytona Beach briefly mesmerized the men and women racing on it. Charles Moneypenny designed it at 2.5 miles and banked it an unprecedented 31 degrees. The frontstretch was bowed out, giving fans an unobstructed view of cars coming and going. The 4,000-foot backstretch was almost flat, and there were almost geometrically perfect transitions from flat sections to banked turns. More than anything he'd done since leaving Washington 25 years ago, Daytona International Speedway put France's personal stamp on American motorsports for all time.

Speeds for Grand National cars approached 145 miles per hour when the track opened for the 1959 Speed Week in February. By comparison, the fastest qualifier for the previous year's Southern 500 ran a mere 118 miles per hour. Bob Welborn won the first DIS race, a 100-mile qualifier. Shorty Rollins won a 100 for Convertibles, Banjo Matthews a 200 for Modified/Sportsman, and Jack Smith the 25-mile Grand National consolation race. As exciting as they were, they were just a warm-up for the inaugural Daytona 500.

A RACE FOR THE AGES

It was a race for the ages, without serious incident but marred somewhat by a major scoring flap. Lee Petty's margin of victory over Johnny Beauchamp was certified at two feet after France spent three days studying it. Joe Weatherly's lapped car was beside Petty and Beauchamp in all

What more could a guy ask for? Pete Hamilton enjoys his trophy, a giant wreath, and a visit from Miss Paul Revere, Debbie Aimes, after winning the third annual Paul Revere 250 Grand Touring race at Daytona International Speedway on July 4, 1969.

photos, muddling the debate. Seconds after the photo finish, Beauchamp was declared the winner and sent to Victory Lane to enjoy the fruits of success. But Petty begged to differ, and his impassioned appeal was supported by reporters who'd seen the finish from above the track. When they said Petty had won by a yard, France had no choice but to reconsider.

The next day, even as news accounts painted glowing pictures of the track and the race, France sought anyone with positive proof of the winner. As stills and motion picture footage arrived, he studied them for three days. (Whether he needed that long is debatable. Even if he'd had proof Sunday night, why not let the suspense grow and the publicity build?) After further review, France knew the first call was wrong. Petty got the win-

Benny Parson's pit crew makes sure they are in racing form by practicing their pit stops before the ARCA 300 at Daytona International Speedway on February 14, 1970.

ner's trophy and a permanent place in NASCAR history. If ever there had been doubts about France and his Midas touch, the first Daytona 500 removed them. In late January of 1960, for the first time, CBS televised Daytona 500 pole qualifying as part of its "Sports Spectacular." In July, also for the first time, ABC presented the 12-day-old Firecracker 400 on "Wide World of Sports."

BEYOND DAYTONA

Consider this startling fact: Only four of the 100 or so tracks with Grand National races (Martinsville, Virginia; Darlington, South Carolina; Richmond, Virginia; and Daytona Beach, Florida) in 1959 still had those dates in 2003. The other 96

or so were left behind as NASCAR moved toward the 1960s and 1970s. Seven tracks that helped shape the sport were built in the 1960s: Atlanta Motor Speedway and Charlotte Motor Speedway in 1960; Bristol Motor Speedway in 1961; North Carolina Motor Speedway in 1965; and Michigan International Speedway, Dover International Speedway, and Talladega Superspeedway in 1969.

NASCAR's unprecedented growth also was reflected in the demand for its product. The 1959 and 1960 schedules showed 44 races. There were 52 events in 1961, 53 the next year, 55 the next season, 62 in 1964, and 55 races in the 1965 season. More mainstream media outlets (newspapers, magazines, radio, and television) covered stock car racing in the early 1960s than in all of the 1950s. And auto manufacturers began using racing to boost brand awareness with its "Win on Sunday, Sell on Monday" mantra. France and NASCAR did their part, keeping competition as close as they could, catering first to one brand and then to another. Perhaps ironically, the ex-driver who ran NASCAR never hesitated to change the rules on the fly to ensure a "level playing field." He also didn't mind flashing some iron when unsure of his audience. He used it to "dissuade" drivers from joining the Teamsters Union in the early 1960s.

The 1960s also saw the emergence of some of NASCAR's best drivers and greatest teams. Richard Petty won two of his seven championships in that decade, and David Pearson won all three of his. Ned Jarrett won his two in the 1960s, and Joe Weatherly won his in back-to-back seasons. Fred Lorenzen was among the era's biggest stars, and Bobby Allison, Donnie Allison, Cale Yarborough, and LeeRoy Yarbrough got their breakthrough victories in the 1960s. Holman-Moody, Bud Moore Engineering, Petty Enterprises, and the Wood Brothers enjoyed great success. They found that after running very stock cars throughout the previous dozen or so years, NASCAR began letting them race purpose-built cars. But the first half of the 1960s was also a time for reflection after Joe Weatherly, Fireball Roberts, Jimmy Pardue, and Billy Wade died in separate on-track incidents. Granted, safety improvements came from each tragedy (better seat belts, fuel cells, and tire inner liners), but the cost seemed much too high.

The close of the decade brought about one of NASCAR's most important moments. In 1970, driver-turned-owner Junior Johnson drove from his North Wilkesboro, North Carolina farm to the R.J. Reynolds Tobacco Company in nearby Winston-Salem. There, he tried to convince long-time friend Ralph Seagraves that the giant cigarette-maker should sponsor his Grand National team for the upcoming 1971 season. Seagraves said no, but that if RJR did anything in motorsports, it would be on a grand scale. After all, the new ban on all TV advertising had abruptly freed up millions upon millions of advertising dollars. The prospect of selling its flagship Winston brand through NASCAR appealed to Seagraves, who came to terms with Big Bill France. The series was called NASCAR Winston Cup Grand National Division until 1986, when it was renamed Winston Cup.

10

THE HISTORY OF NASCAR: WINSTON CUP COMES TO TOWN

To some, the 1971 marriage of NASCAR and the R. J. Reynolds Tobacco Co. remains the most important business relationship in the history of American motorsports. Not only did it finally introduce NASCAR to OPM (Other People's Money), it debunked the long-held belief that the only people who cared about stock car racing were those in the automobile industry. In 1970, the year before RJR and NASCAR became bedfellows, only a few teams had major sponsors of any kind, let alone nonautomotive sponsors. But once the tobacco giant nudged open the door, dozens of "mainstream" companies walked through and began changing racing for all time.

Among those first sponsors to come on board in the 1970s were the cola companies, including Coca-Cola, RC Cola, and Pepsi-Cola; the beer companies, including Falstaff, Carling, Olympia, Busch, and Old Milwaukee; and many others, including King's Row Fireplace Shops, Burger King, Holly Farms, Gatorade, First National City, Hawaiian Tropic, Shoney's, Truxmore Industries, Kelly Girl, Russ Togs, and Bearfinder.

The success of those pioneers in the 1970s of course meant that even more firms were going to try their hands at racing in the 1980s. Sure enough, new companies such as Piedmont Airlines; Mountain Dew; the smokeless tobacco companies, including Skoal, Levi Garrett, Kodiak, and Copenhagen; 7-Eleven; Wrangler; Pet Dairy; more beer companies, including Coors, Budweiser, and Miller High Life; Chameleon; Hardee's; Northwestern Security Insurance; Crisco; Tide; Folger's; Kodak; Red Baron; Dominos; and Freedlander Financial Services.

RJR TAKES THE PLUNGE

The RJR-NASCAR deal was brokered by bootlegger-turned-driver-turned-owner Junior Johnson. He asked R. J. Reynolds late in 1970 to sponsor his team for the 1971 season. The company said no, and indicated it was looking for something flashier for its marketing bucks than simply one racing team. Johnson passed that on to NASCAR founder Bill France Sr., and he eventually worked out a much bigger deal with the tobacco company. RJR began by giving signage, promotional materials, print ads, and thousands of gallons of red and white paint to NASCAR tracks. Its Winston cigarette brand sponsored the May race at Talladega,

Cale Yarborough's car looks more like a bus than a NASCAR Winston Cup National car as Yarborough gives his crew a ride to the victory circle after winning the Winston Western 500 at Riverside International Raceway on January 22, 1978.

Alabama, and the June race at Riverside, California. The company also put up $100,000 for NASCAR's postseason point fund, including $40,000 for the season champion, who turned out to be Richard Petty. In recognition of its benefactor, NASCAR renamed its top series "Winston Cup Grand National" and called its championship the "Winston Cup." Early in 1972, with the RJR-NASCAR relationship solidly into its second year, William Henry Getty France retired as president of NASCAR and put his sons in charge.

It was a key moment, as RJR's money, promotional outreach, and advertising expertise spurred stock car racing's growth. At the time, NASCAR's media-PR-marketing staff was woefully undermanned. RJR, on the other hand, had offices filled with advertising and marketing experts with time on their hands. Many had worked with the television networks before a 1970 Congressional ban on cigarette ads put an end to that. "RJR came in and brought an awful lot of things to the table other than just money," said Bruton Smith, owner of five NASCAR tracks. "They also brought in experience in marketing. That started moving stock car racing up the ladder. That helped give it some growth."

The 1971 season was NASCAR's last "long season." It featured 48 races—finally, all were on paved tracks —dragging on from January 10 at Riverside, California, to December 12 at College

Station, Texas. Sixteen of the races were on short tracks that wouldn't return in 1972, the result of RJR's preference for a shorter schedule of races measuring 250 or more miles. That decision took precious, long-held dates from three short tracks in North Carolina; two each in South Carolina, Tennessee, and New York; and one each in Virginia, Georgia, and Texas. After 24 years of being fairly true to its roots, NASCAR was beginning to yield to money and sponsors.

But the post-RJR 1970s brought far more positives than negatives. The Motor Racing Network debuted in 1971, making Winston Cup Grand National the only racing series with live coverage of every major event. Pocono Raceway got its first Cup race in 1974, bringing NASCAR to the Philadelphia-Baltimore market. Network television took an interest, as seen by ABC's live coverage of the final laps of the 1976 Daytona 500 and CBS's complete coverage of the 1979 Daytona 500. Cars, drivers, crews, and owners became more professional and more aware of the media and the role it could play. With the schedule limited to 30 or so races, each one was a major event, and RJR spared no expense getting out the word that the "stars and cars" were coming to town. The point fund grew from $100,000 to $175,000 and the champion's share grew from $40,000 to $49,000. And in perhaps its most visible sign of national respect, First Lady Rosalyn Carter hosted a huge NASCAR gathering at The White House in September of 1978. President Jimmy Carter, a long-time race fan, begged off to oversee delicate Mideast peace talks at Camp David.

The stars of that decade were a who's who of racing: Richard Petty, Bobby Allison, Cale Yarborough, David Pearson, Buddy Baker, Donnie Allison, Dave Marcis, Benny Parsons, Neil Bonnett, and Bobby Isaac. The next generation of stars, the ones who would dominate the 1980s, also made their debuts in the late 1970s, including Dale Earnhardt, Darrell Waltrip, Ricky Rudd, Terry Labonte, Sterling Marlin, and Bill Elliott. At the end of the decade, it was obvious that RJR and Winston had advanced the sport further and faster than anyone might have imagined. RJR was

Even when he wasn't on the track, Darrell Waltrip was thinking about racing. Here, he reads a racing-related newspaper after qualifying in third position for the Pocono 500 at Pocono International Raceway on July 28, 1979.

happy, NASCAR was happy, and the public was happy. It had been quite a 10-year run.

THE FUN CONTINUES

The rapid growth continued throughout the 1980s. RJR-Winston boosted the season-ending point fund from $210,000 in 1980 to an astonishing $2,500,000 in 1989. The champion's share went from a mere $49,500 in 1980 to an even million dollars in 1989. Darrell Waltrip won the first Winston all-star race in 1985, the same year Bill Elliott took the first Winston Million bonus for winning three of NASCAR's four "crown jewel" races. By now, "Winston Cup Grand National" had become simply "Winston Cup" as RJR and its flagship brand poured more and more money into NASCAR. It must have worked, because the new tracks that

Another generation of the Petty family enters the Winston Cup scene as father Richard (left) hands over the keys of his famous No. 43 to his son Kyle before the Winston Western 500 in November 1981. Petty switched to the No. 42 car until his retirement several years later.

came aboard reflected the sport's geographic diversity: Watkins Glen, New York, in 1986; Phoenix, Arizona, in 1988; and Sonoma, California, in 1989. In the mid-1980s, qualifying speeds topped the 200 mph mark until restrictor plates slowed cars and kept insurance underwriters happy.

What a decade for competition! Darrell Waltrip and Dale Earnhardt each won three championships. The other four went to Bobby Allison, and relative newcomers Terry Labonte, Bill Elliott, and Rusty Wallace. Cale Yarborough and Richard Petty remained competitive, as the racing world saw when the two staged a slugfest in the 1984 Firecracker 400 in front of President Ronald

Reagan. Long-time Sportsman favorites Harry Gant, Morgan Shepherd, and Jody Ridley became Cup favorites, and Ricky Rudd, Neil Bonnett, Tim Richmond, Geoff (later, Geoffrey) Bodine, Kyle Petty, Ken Schrader, and Sterling Marlin began building their resumes. With almost every race televised, NASCAR felt good enough about itself and its product. To prove it, it moved the annual postseason awards banquet from Daytona Beach during Speed Week to New York's famous Waldorf-Astoria Hotel in December. The city didn't even look up, but race fans in the rest of the country were amazed. And why not: In less than a decade, NASCAR had left every other racing series—including Indy car—in its dust.

THE BRICKYARD AND MORE

Some will say NASCAR's most important decade was the 1990s. In 1993 the New Hampshire International Speedway at Loudon opened up the New England market to the NASCAR marketing team. In 1994 mainstream American finally awoke to the phenomenon when NASCAR ran the inaugural Brickyard 400. Not since the first Daytona 500 had there been anything quite like that first stock car race at the Indianapolis Motor Speedway. It had been a long time coming, this union of American's most popular series and the world's most famous venue. NASCAR president Bill France Jr. and speedway president Tony George announced the race in April 1993, fully 16 months ahead of time. Even so, more than 250,000 tickets were sold within days. It happened because France and George knew a nationally-televised race before a sold-out house would help everyone. For NASCAR, Indy meant acceptance by those who looked down their nose at "taxi cab racing," as some Indy car fans referred to stock-car racing. To Indy, it meant another sellout crowd just weeks after its showcase Indy 500.

It's been said the Brickyard 400 finally put NASCAR on America's motorsports radar. Quite the contrary: Thanks to RJR and Winston, stock-car racing was alive and well long before August 1994 at Indy. And Indy—still the world's famous speedway and one of its greatest sports venues overall—was doing fine, too. All of which leads to this conclusion: The Brickyard 400 was good for everyone. Let it go at that.

The 1990s saw several other new venues besides Indy. Those that opened in 1997 again reflected NASCAR's geographic diversity: the 1.5-mile Texas Motor Speedway near Fort Worth opened in April and the 2-mile California Speedway at Fontana opened in June. The addition of a second race in New Hampshire and single races at Texas and California—and the loss of two dates at North Wilkesboro—fattened the schedule to 32 races in 1997. Las Vegas made it 33 the next year, then Homestead pushed it to 34 in 1999.

Suddenly and perhaps inexplicably, NASCAR was chic. Oh, the Westminster Dog Show and The

DEFINING MOMENT: JEFF GORDON

"The day I graduated from high school, I drove in a World of Outlaws sprint car race in Bloomington, Indiana, I qualified second and finished fourth. All the heavy hitters were there. That was a very special time in my career. I said, 'All right, I've graduated from high school. I either have to go to college, or I can continue this racing thing, and I'd sure like to do this racing thing. If it works out, I'm going to stick with it.' That night kind of told me to stick with the racing thing. (I thought) 'It might work out for you.'"

Metropolitan Opera and Broadway needn't worry. Neither should the major "stick and ball sports," with their huge fan base and betting lines. But stock-car racing was inching more and more into the mainstream media. The National Press Club hosted Bill France Jr. and Dale Earnhardt. National Public Radio examined the sport's growth. The Smithsonian and George Washington University brought officials and drivers together for a public forum. Even weekly news magazines occasionally took note.

While media exposure and new tracks did much to fuel NASCAR's growth, driver Jeff Gordon can also take a great deal of credit. In the telegenic Gordon, NASCAR had its best combination of driver, spokesman, sponsor rep, and goodwill ambassador since Richard Petty. Even the wildly talented Gordon couldn't create on-track interest in the sport by himself. Earnhardt was still the master, but a slew of talented drivers, including Rusty Wallace, Bill Elliott, Dale Jarrett, Tony Stewart, the Burton brothers, the Labonte brothers, Mark Martin, Ernie Irvan, Ricky Rudd, and the late Davey Allison and Alan Kulwicki were also successful, well-known, and popular. Oh, yeah, one more thing: RJR's point-fund payout grew from $2.5 million in 1990 ($1,000,000 for the champion) to $5,000,000 (including $3 million for the champion) in 1999.

Rusty Wallace goes for a wild ride as his No. 2 Miller Genuine Draft Pontiac gets airborne after being involved in a crash during the Daytona 500 on February 14, 1993. Lake Speed (left, back end of car showing) and Terry Labonte (No. 14) try to avoid the out-of-control Wallace.

THE NEW MILLENNIUM

The turn of the century has already brought profound changes. Dale Earnhardt died in the 2001 Daytona 500, an unfathomable tragedy that led to a year's worth of agonizing questions and soul-searching. Fox and NBC paid NASCAR several billion dollars for the rights to its Cup races, even as poor health pushed Bill France Jr. closer to retirement. Two new heartland tracks were added in 2001: The 1.5-mile Chicagoland Motor Speedway opened in July, and the 1.5-mile Kansas City Speedway opened in September.

While many stars are well past age 40 and getting closer to retirement age—Mark Martin, Terry Labonte, Ricky Rudd, Rusty Wallace, Sterling Marlin, Dale Jarrett, Bill Elliott, Ken Schrader, and Kyle Petty among them—the top new youngsters aren't willing to wait for a changing of the guard and have already burst onto the scene. Bobby Labonte (Terry's younger brother) won the 2000 title, Jeff Gordon took it in 2001, Tony Stewart in 2002,and Matt Kenseth won in 2003. Beyond them, Jamie McMurray, Jerry Nadeau, Dale Earnhardt Jr., Ryan Newman, Jimmie Johnson, Kurt Busch, Kevin Harvick, and Elliott Sadler have already won, and none is over 35. And how strong is the RJR-NASCAR connection: RJR put an astonishing $37.2 million into the 2000, 2001, and 2002 point funds, including more than $6 million for each year's champion.

Tony Stewart climbs into his car at Pocono Raceway in 2002, the year he won his first Winston (now Nextel) Cup championship.

New stars, new venues, new sponsors from outside motorsports—that was NASCAR early in the twenty-first century. Back in 1990, people wondered if racing could get much bigger. Now, with the Nextel Cup schedule at 36 races (plus two nonpoints races), they're wondering if the circuit has topped out. A few Cup races are having trouble selling out, and the schedule-related stress on drivers and crews has reached the crisis point. The economy is also a great concern. Unlike the booming 1990s, when sponsors were practically everywhere, an economic downturn has left some teams searching for sponsors heading into 2004. Fielding a Nextel Cup team yet more expensive each year which has left some companies reluctant to invest in full sponsorship deals.

NASCAR also must do a better job with diversity. In 2002, Bill Lester was the only African American racing regularly in NASCAR's top three series. He drove a Dodge for Bobby Hamilton in the Craftsman Truck Series. NASCAR also needs people of color as owners. Joe Washington, a former NFL running back, and basketball great Julius Erving owned a Busch Series team in 1998, but it folded. Former track great Jackie Joyner-Kersey planned to form a Busch team, but she and her fellow investors never fulfilled their goal. A number of sports stars talk a good game

Dale Earnhardt enjoys a conversation with two of New York's finest while making an appearance with is famed black No. 3 "Intimidator" in New York's Central Park on December 5, 1990. Earnhardt was in New York for the annual NASCAR awards dinner, where he would collect $1 million for winning his fourth Winston Cup championship.

when it comes to Cup racing, but so far, only former NFL head coach Joe Gibbs (already a two-time Cup championship owner) has lasted.

THE END OF AN ERA

As the 2003 season drew to a close at the last race of the season at the Homestead-Miami Speedway in Homestead, Florida, Winston Cup's top drivers gathered for a historic photo shoot. With onlookers watching, the drivers stood behind a banner that said simply "Thanks Winston." After 33 years of sponsoring the Winston Cup, NASCAR's top series, the R.J. Reynolds Tobacco

Co. had decided to pull the plug on one of its best-known marketing endeavors.

Why that had to happen is a complicated question that could be debated for hours, but in the end, it was one simple thing that led to the break-up of one of sport's best partnerships—the continued attacks on tobacco in the United States. A June 1997 agreement between the tobacco industry and the states' attorneys general had laid the groundwork for the end of motorsports sponsorship by tobacco companies, but then everyone relaxed when nothing happened. Just as people thought that RJR might be able to escape the growing national antismoking/antitobacco sentiment, officials at that company decided that the economy had gotten too tough, and the company was losing too much money. The decision was made: end the Winston Cup sponsorship.

For NASCAR officials, the end of the Winston Cup era is bittersweet. While there is no question that NASCAR experienced its greatest growth while sponsored by RJR (the 2003 points fund, for example, was over $17 million), it is equally certain that partnering with Nextel instead of RJR will be a little easier for NASCAR. No longer will the organization have to look over its shoulder and wonder if this is the year that Congress steps in and forces the end of tobacco sponsorship. Instead, NASCAR can look to the future with a partner that is tied into one of the fastest-growing segments of the national economy, cellular communcations. That should lead to good things in the future, but only time will tell.

OTHER PROBLEMS AHEAD?

Now that the "tobacco question" has been answered, there is still one significant issue looming on the horizon for NASCAR. Mainly, how will it manage its rapid expansion. First, how will it find enough dates to go around? With 36 events, the season already stretches from mid-February to late November, by far the longest season of any major sport. With no open weekends left, many traditionalists feared NASCAR would take races away from the older tracks, and in 2004 that fear will finally be realized. For years, Labor Day weekend meant one thing to NASCAR fans—the Southern 500 at Darlington. Not anymore. Start-ing in 2004, the Labor Day race will be held in California. Darlington will still get to hold two races, but its longstanding Labor Day tradition will now disappear. The other older tracks that hold two races—Rockingham and Atlanta to name just two—are worried that they're next in line. Unfortunately, they're probably right. If NASCAR hopes to keep spreading the sport to new parts of the country, it will limit some tracks to just one race a year. It remains to be seen how old guard stock car fans will handle that news, but check back in September.

While keeping long-time track operators and fans happy is one issue tied to expansion, the other directly involves the drivers. Driver fatigue as a result of the expanded schedule is a definite concern among NASCAR officials. While it's true NASCAR often ran 50 or 60 races in the 1950s and 1960s, times were different. Most of the tracks that hosted those races could be reached by a reasonable drive, and it wasn't essential for drivers to race in every event to stay in the points race. That's not true today—tracks are coast-to-coast and drivers must compete in every race if they hope to stay in the Winston Cup championship hunt. This situation bears watching, especially as new tracks are added in new cities, requiring drivers to travel even more.

The most successful era in NASCAR history has ended. With Nextel signing a 10-year contract for sponsorship of racing's top series, only time will tell if the next chapter in the NASCAR saga is even better than that authored by RJR. With a strong fan base, an exciting sport, and big-money sponsors, most observers are betting that NASCAR is poised to build on its continued success.

11

AT A GLANCE:
YEAR-BY-YEAR SUMMARIES

1949

AT A GLANCE:

Strictly Stock Champion: Red Byron

Notable Event: A Greensboro, North Carolina, judge refused to intervene when team owner Hubert Westmoreland sued NASCAR over a rules interpretation. The ruling set a precedent (recognized to this day) that allows NASCAR to make its rules and enforce them, generally without outside interference.

NASCAR's first Strictly Stock points race (there had been an exhibition early in the year near Miami) went for 200 laps around a ¾-mile dirt track in Charlotte. NASCAR president Bill France posted a $5,000 purse for 33 street-legal sedans, all of them built after World War II. Glenn Dunnaway led the final 49 laps in a 1947 Ford that failed postrace inspection because it had illegal rear springs. When Jim Roper inherited the victory, it gave birth to NASCAR's first great trivia question: Why was the winner of the very first Winston Cup race (even though it wasn't called Winston Cup until years later) disqualified?

The event drew 13,000-plus fans on a Sunday afternoon, far more than France or any of his lieutenants expected. Buoyed by that unexpected success, NASCAR scheduled seven more races for that summer: two each in North Carolina and Pennsylvania, and one each in Florida, New York, and Virginia. Red Byron and Bob Flock each won twice, and Lee Petty, Curtis Turner, and Jack White split the other three. Byron was NASCAR's first champion by 117.5 points over Petty, with Bob Flock ranked third, Bill Blair fourth, and Fonty Flock fifth.

STRICTLY STOCK STANDINGS

	DRIVER	STARTS	WINS	POINTS	MONEY
1.	Red Byron	6	2	842.5	5,800
2.	Lee Petty	6	1	725	3,855
3.	Bob Flock	6	2	704	4,870
4.	Bill Blair	6	0	567.5	1,280
5.	Fonty Flock	6	0	554.5	2,015
6.	Curtis Turner	6	1	430	2,675
7.	Ray Erickson	4	0	422	1,460
8.	Tim Flock	5	0	421	1,510
9.	Glenn Dunnaway	6	0	384	810
10.	Frank Mundy	4	0	370	1,160
11.	Bill Snowden	4	0	315	660
12.	Bill Rexford	3	0	286	785
13.	Sara Christian	6	0	282	760
14.	Clyde Minter	0	0	280	760
15.	Gober Sosebee	3	0	265	1,305
16.	Jim Raper	2	1	253	2,130
17.	Sam Rice	2	0	231	680
18.	Jack White	1	1	200	1,580
19.	Dick Linder	3	0	180.5	1,305
20.	Billy Rafter	1	0	160	480
21.	Archie Smith	2	0	145	225
22.	Joe Littlejohn	1	0	140	300
23.	Jack Russell	3	0	140	175
24.	Mike Eagan	1	0	140	300

25.	Herb Thomas	4	0	132	225
26.	Sterling Long	2	0	100	150
27.	Frank Christian	1	0	100	175
28.	Frankie Schneider	1	0	100	150
29.	Lloyd Moore	1	0	100	150
30.	Roy Hall	1	0	100	150
31.	Slick Smith	4	0	99	275
32.	Al Keller	1	0	90	200
33.	John Wright	1	0	80	100
34.	Al Bonnell	2	0	80	150
35.	Otis Martin	4	0	69.5	200
36.	Jimmy Thompson	2	0	65	175
37.	Charles Muscatel	1	0	60	75
38.	Raymond Lewis	1	0	60	75
39.	Al Wagoner	1	0	60	75
40.	George Lewis	1	0	40	50
41.	Lou Volk	1	0	30	125
42.	Buddy Helms	1	0	27.5	75
43.	Bob Apperson	3	0	25	150
44.	Bill Bennett	1	0	24	100
45.	Ted Chamberlain	2	0	24	100
46.	Buck Baker	2	0	20	50
47.	Jack Etheridge	1	0	20	75
48.	Ellis Pearce	1	0	20	50
49.	Bobby Greene	2	0	19.5	50
50.	Ken Wagner	3	0	19	100

1950

AT A GLANCE:

Grand National Champion: Bill Rexford

Notable Event: After realizing that "Strictly Stock" sounded more like a rule than a series, France renamed his ever-growing stock car series "Grand National." He liked its sophistication, particularly the image it portrayed as a quality product. It remained Grand National until the early 1970s, when NASCAR renamed its main series "Winston Cup" in recognition of its new patron, R.J. Reynolds' Winston cigarettes brand.

The popularity of stock car racing took a quantum leap when ex-racer Harold Brasington mounted a bulldozer and carved a 1¼-mile, high-banked, egg-shaped speedway in Darlington, South Carolina. He then stunned almost everyone by paving the track and saying it would host America's first 500-mile race for street-legal family sedans. He and France agreed that just such an event over Labor Day weekend would generate enormous attention for the series and for Darlington.

The inaugural Southern 500 boasted a NASCAR-record $25,000 purse and an unprecedented 75-car field. Brasington aligned them three-wide for 25 rows, like the Indianapolis 500 grid. All 9,000 seats were quickly filled, leaving 6,000 late-comers to jam themselves into the track's vast infield. Johnny Mantz needed more than six hours to cover the distance in a 1950 Plymouth that was owned by France, Westmoreland

(the owner who'd been DQ'ed at Charlotte in 1949), driver Curtis Turner, and Alvin Hawkins. Fireball Roberts finished second, Red Byron third, Bill Rexford fourth, and Chuck Mahoney fifth. Despite some suspicions that Mantz's car was illegal, it passed a cursory technical inspection and the victory stood.

There were 18 other races that year, but none attracted the national attention generated at Darlington. Not only was it America's first 500-mile stock car race, but it drew a capacity crowd and was run to its conclusion with few serious incidents. The other 18 races were on dirt tracks, most of them measuring less than a mile. Thirteen drivers won races, including multiple winners Turner (four victories) and Dick Linder (three). Rexford won only one race in 17 starts, but he was consistent enough (5 top-5s and 11 top-10s) to beat Fireball Roberts, Lee Petty, Lloyd Moore, and Turner for the championship. Other winners included Harold Kite, Tim Flock, Fonty Flock, Bill Blair, Jimmy Florian (the first Cup winner in a Ford), Leon Sales, Herb Thomas, Lloyd Moore, Roberts, and Petty.

GRAND NATIONAL STANDINGS

	DRIVER	STARTS	WINS	POINTS	MONEY
1.	Bill Rexford	17	1	1,959	5,750
2.	Fireball Roberts	9	1	1,848.5	6,800
3.	Lee Petty	17	1	1,590	7,120
4.	Lloyd Moore	16	1	1,398	5,235
5.	Curtis Turner	16	4	1,375.5	8,080
6.	Johnny Mantz	3	1	1,282	10,810
7.	Chuck Mahoney	11	0	1,217.5	2,250
8.	Dick Linder	13	3	1,121	5,695
9.	Jimmy Florian	10	1	801	2,730
10.	Bill Blair	16	1	766	4,400
11.	Herb Thomas	13	1	590.5	2,645
12.	Buck Baker	9	0	531.5	2,145
13.	Cotton Owens	3	0	500	1,100
14.	Fonty Flock	7	1	458.5	2,195
15.	Weldon Adams	4	0	440	1,205
16.	Tim Flock	12	1	437.5	3,980
17.	Clyde Minter	8	0	427	1,155
18.	Dick Burns	8	0	341.5	780
19.	Art Laney	4	0	320	655
20.	Bob Flock	4	0	314	1,155
21.	George Hartley	8	0	298	875
22.	Gayle Warren	10	0	287	550
23.	Frank Mundy	8	0	275.5	550
24.	Jim Paschal	6	0	220.5	850
25.	Jack White	7	0	211.5	525
26.	Pappy Hough	5	0	207.5	325
27.	Ray Duhigg	5	0	202.5	450
28.	Leon Sales	2	0	200	1,000
29.	Jimmy Thompson	4	0	200	525
30.	Harold Kite	3	1	187	1,550
31.	Neil Cole	2	0	183.5	300
32.	Jack Smith	3	0	180	775
33.	Bucky Sager	2	0	180	750
34.	Red Harvey	1	0	180	750
35.	Ted Swaim	1	0	180	750
36.	Buck Barr	2	0	180	575
37.	Pepper Cunningham	2	0	177.5	300
38.	Ewell Weddle	3	0	173.5	600

39.	Donald Thomas	2	0	164	300
40.	Bill Snowden	4	0	163	325
41.	Jimmie Lewallen	3	0	140	400
42.	Chuck James	1	0	140	400
43.	Dick Clothier	5	0	133.5	350
44.	Paul Parks	6	0	124.5	375
45.	Al Gross	3	0	124	550
46.	Jack Reynolds	2	0	120	300
47.	Jim Delaney	2	0	114	175
48.	Carl Renner	2	0	108	250
49.	Jack Holloway	2	0	107.5	225
50.	Bob Dickson	6	0	105	275
51.	J. C. Van Landingham	1	0	105	450

1951

AT A GLANCE:

Grand National Champion: Herb Thomas

Notable Event: To debunk the perception that NASCAR was a southern and eastern pastime, France scheduled 5 races in California and another in Arizona; 15 more were held above the Mason-Dixon line. Perhaps the year's most important event was a 250-miler held in Detroit, home of the Big Three automakers, as part of that city's 250th anniversary. It was the first time automotive executives had a firsthand look at this new-fangled sport.

If it was the birth of a trend, hardly anyone noticed. After visiting only one paved track in its first two seasons, the 1951 schedule included trips to two more paved tracks, with a total of four races held at the three tracks. Four paved-track races didn't really make a dent in the schedule, but it was a glimpse of where the sport was headed. Two of the races were held at the half-mile track in Dayton, Ohio; another on the half-miler at Thompson, Connecticut; and the other at Darlington. The series continued to expand, moving into eight states for the first time, six of them outside the Southeast. The number of races also expanded dramatically, more than doubling to 41.

Herb Thomas (7 victories and 19 top-10 finishes) entered 33 of the 41 races and won the title over eight-time winner Fonty Flock, seven-time winner Tim Flock, one-time winner Lee Petty, and three-time winner Frank Mundy. In an effort to promote as many races as possible, NASCAR often scheduled conflicting events. On April 8, for example, it sanctioned races in Alabama and California. It did so again on April 29, September 23, and November 11, and even scheduled three races on October 14. There were few complaints, however, since nobody expected to run all the races, anyway, and everyone

agreed NASCAR needed all the exposure it could get. The other winners in 1951 were Marshall Teague, Curtis Turner, Lou Figaro, Tommy Thompson, Bob Flock, Neil Cole, Marvin Burke, Danny Weinberg, Pappy Hugh, and Bill Norton.

GRAND NATIONAL STANDINGS

	DRIVER	STARTS	WINS	POINTS	MONEY
1.	Herb Thomas	35	7	4,208.45	20,850
2.	Fonty Flock	34	8	4,062.25	15,200
3.	Tim Flock	0	7	3,722.5	14,545
4.	Lee Petty	32	1	2,392.25	7,340
5.	Frank Mundy	27	3	1,963.5	7,085
6.	Buddy Shuman	7	0	1,368.75	2,830
7.	Jesse James Taylor	10	0	1,214	3,750
8.	Dick Rathmann	15	0	1,040	3,225
9.	Bill Snowden	12	0	1,009.25	2,640
10.	Joe Eubanks	12	0	1,005.5	3,415
11.	Lloyd Moore	22	0	996.5	2,600
12.	Fireball Roberts	9	0	930	1,190
13.	Jimmie Lewallen	12	0	874.25	2,430
14.	Bob Flock	17	1	869	3,680
15.	Jim Paschal	16	0	858.5	2,450
16.	Bill Blair	18	0	840	2,710
17.	Gober Sosebee	10	0	784	2,710
18.	Erick Erickson	12	0	723.5	2,435
19.	Tommy Thompson	5	1	755	5,510
20.	Donald Thomas	17	0	743.5	2,060
21.	Johnny Mantz	6	0	725	2,025
22.	Lou Figaro	13	1	684.2	2,135
23.	Buck Baker	11	0	644.5	1,650
24.	Dick Meyer	6	0	626.5	1,650
25.	Harold Kite	2	0	625	800
26.	Billy Carden	11	0	509.75	1,460
27.	Jimmy Florian	9	0	462.5	1,100
28.	Jim Fiebelkorn	17	0	455	1,355
29.	Ronnie Kohler	5	0	432	1,100
30.	Danny Weinberg	6	1	423.5	1,470
31.	Pappy Hugh	9	1	423	760
32.	Woody Brown	3	0	421	1,125
33.	Neil Cole	5	1	382	2,050
34.	Paul Newkirk	0	0	375	500
35.	John McGinley	6	0	372.5	1,300
36.	Marvin Panch	3	0	371.5	1,075
37.	Oda Greene	6	0	366.5	825
38.	Jack Goodwin	3	0	362.5	725
39.	Jack Smith	7	0	360.5	1,275
40.	Robert Caswell	3	0	350	1,325
41.	Lloyd Dane	7	0	323.5	975
42.	Cotton Owens	5	0	312.5	225
43.	Fred Steinbroner	6	0	306.5	700
44.	Ewell Weddle	7	0	293.5	435
45.	George Seeger	9	0	278	910
46.	Sam Hawks	3	0	262.5	650
47.	Don Bailey	10	0	239.5	625
48.	Bud Farrell	5	0	227.5	700
49.	Harvey Riley	8	0	262.5	475
50.	Fred Lee	6	0	224	450

1952

AT A GLANCE:

Grand National Champion: Tim Flock

Notable Event: Until now, many automotive-related companies had taken a "wait-and-see" attitude about NASCAR. But in 1952, for the first time, companies like Pure Oil Co. (later Union 76 and Unocal) and Champion Spark Plug Inc. began paying contingency awards in exchange for publicity generated by drivers using their products.

Three of NASCAR's true pioneers gather on the victory stand after sweeping the top spots in the Convertible stock car race in Daytona Beach, Florida, on February 25, 1956. Herb Thomas (left) finished in third place, Glenn "Fireball" Roberts (center) took second, and Curtis Turner (right) claimed the first-place trophy.

In a startling turnabout, NASCAR moved away from scheduling conflicting events. Except for June 1—when it sent cars to Ohio and Georgia—drivers found the schedule easier to take. The 34 races were spread among 33 dates, giving eight-time winner and series champion Tim Flock the flexibility to make 33 starts. Herb Thomas, also an eight-time winner, started 32 races, as did three-time winner Lee Petty. Rounding out the top 5 in points were Fonty Flock (2 victories in 27 starts) and Dick Rathmann (5 victories in 27 starts). As usual, all but four of the races—two each at Dayton and Darlington—were on dirt.

From the beginning, France's goal had been to create an organization that would crown a single national champion. His plan to have the best stock car drivers facing each other on a regular basis had been undermined by 1952's conflicting scheduling. Granted, a driver in Georgia wouldn't tow to California if there was a race closer to home, but the perception was that NASCAR sometimes didn't present the best fields it could. It was a situation that convinced France to move toward single-date scheduling. Other 1952 winners were Marshall Teague, Buck Baker, Bill Blair, Gober Sosebee, Buddy Shuman, Bob Flock, and Donald Thomas.

GRAND NATIONAL STANDINGS

	DRIVER	STARTS	WINS	POINTS	MONEY
1.	Tim Flock	8	8	6,858.5	22,890
2.	Herb Thomas	32	8	6,752.5	18,965
3.	Lee Petty	32	3	6,498.5	16,876

4.	Fonty Flock	29	2	5,183.5	19,112
5.	Dick Rathmann	27	5	3,952.5	11,248
6.	Bill Blair	19	1	3,449	7,899
7.	Joe Eubanks	19	0	3,090.5	3,630
8.	Ray Duhigg	18	0	2,986.5	3,811
9.	Donald Thomas	21	1	2,574	4,477
10.	Buddy Shuman	15	1	2,483	4,587
11.	Ted Chamberlain	18	0	2,208	1,277
12.	Buck Baker	14	1	2,159	3,187
13.	Perk Brown	19	0	2,151.5	2,187
14.	Jimmie Lewallen	20	0	2,033	2,052
15.	Bub King	10	0	1,993	2,737
16.	Herschel Buchanan	0	0	1,868	2,468
17.	Johnny Patterson	5	0	1,708	3,618
18.	Jim Paschal	15	0	1,694	1,483
19.	Neil Cole	11	0	1,618	1,793
20.	Lloyd Moore	8	0	1,513.5	2,193
21.	Gene Comstock	8	0	1,339	785
22.	Banjo Matthews	3	0	1,240	1,000
23.	Ralph Ligouri	12	0	1,230	920
24.	Jack Reynolds	10	0	1,177.5	1,450
25.	Dick Passwater	6	0	1,148	945
26.	Bucky Sager	10	0	1,119.5	710
27.	Frankie Schneider	6	0	931	1,350
28.	Otis Martin	5	0	873.5	275
29.	Coleman Lawrence	8	0	846	375
30.	Ed Samples	8	0	827	1,535
31.	Fred Dove	0	0	780	390
32.	Slick Smith	5	0	746	725
33.	Iggy Katona	5	0	742	525
34.	Jack Smith	8	0	729	820
35.	Tommy Moon	6	0	726	1,145
36.	Rollin Smith	1	0	700	350
37.	Speedy Thompson	2	0	656	305
38.	Jimmy Thompson	0	0	650	300
39.	Bud Farrell	6	0	648	325
40.	Weldon Adams	6	0	634	275
41.	Clyde Minter	5	0	632	375
42.	Elton Hildreth	6	0	614	375
43.	Dave Terrell	5	0	612	475
44.	Tommy Thompson	5	0	602.5	525
45.	Bob Moore	5	0	579.5	575
46.	Jim Reed	7	0	567	475
47.	E. C. Ramsey	7	0	560	260
48.	Jimmy Florian	6	0	551	175
49.	Ed Benedict	5	0	526	360
50.	Curtis Turner	7	0	505	265

1953

AT A GLANCE:

Grand National Champion: Herb Thomas

Notable Event: Until 1953, drivers earned points based on finish position—period. No questions asked. But as star power became an issue, NASCAR decreed that drivers who didn't pre-enter a race (and thus make themselves available for prerace publicity) wouldn't earn points. Thus it remains to this day.

The much-heralded "Fabulous Hudson Hornet" lived up to its reputation in 1953. Series champion Herb Thomas used one to run all 37 races (the first time anyone ran the full schedule), won 12, and had 31 top-10 finishes. Second-ranked Lee Petty won five races, third-ranked Dick Rathmann won five, fourth-ranked Buck Baker won four, and fifth-ranked Fonty Flock also won four. All told, Hudsons won 22 races, including 16

of 20 during the heart of the season. The Hudson lineup included Thomas, Rathmann, and Tim and Fonty Flock, and the success of racing Hudsons spurred sales of their street-legal cousins.

As part of NASCAR's ever-growing scope, many teams took a three-race swing into South Dakota, Nebraska, and Iowa in late July and early August. Thomas won in South Dakota and Iowa, and Rathmann in Nebraska. A week later they were back home racing in the Southeast. As if anyone ever had any doubts, NASCAR racing was moving from its infancy to a healthy, precocious childhood. In addition to Thomas, Petty, Rathmann, Baker, and the Flock brothers, 1953 winners included Jim Paschal, Curtis Turner, Speedy Thompson, and Bill Blair.

GRAND NATIONAL STANDINGS

	DRIVER	STARTS	WINS	POINTS	MONEY
1.	Herb Thomas	37	12	8,460	28,910
2.	Lee Petty	36	5	7,814	18,447
3.	Dick Rathmann	34	5	7,362	20,245
4.	Buck Baker	33	4	6,713	18,167
5.	Fonty Flock	33	4	6,174	17,756
6.	Tim Flock	1	1	5,011	8,282
7.	Jim Paschal	24	1	4,211	5,571
8.	Joe Eubanks	24	0	3,603	5,254
9.	Jimmie Lewallen	22	0	3,508	4,222
10.	Curtis Turner	19	1	3,373	4,347
11.	Speedy Thompson	7	2	2,958	6,547
12.	Slick Smith	23	0	2,670	2,302
13.	Elton Hildreth	25	0	2,625	1,997
14.	Gober Sosebee	17	0	2,525	2,722
15.	Bill Blair	21	1	2,457	4,535
16.	Fred Dove	0	0	1,997	1,240
17.	Bub King	14	0	1,624	1,036
18.	Gene Comstock	13	0	1,519	990
19.	Donald Thomas	17	0	1,408	1,765
20.	Ralph Liguori	12	0	1,336	1,098
21.	Pop Mcginnis	13	0	1,113	975
22.	Otis Martin	8	0	1,068	610
23.	Andy Winfree	7	0	954	300
24.	Bob Welborn	11	0	761	1,160
25.	Johnny Patterson	11	0	753	645
26.	Ted Chamberlain	9	0	738	500
27.	Neil Roberts	2	0	738	400
28.	Buddy Shuman	5	0	713	395
29.	Arden Mounts	10	0	644	395
30.	Bobby Myers	2	0	644	390
31.	Clyde Minter	8	0	636	405
32.	George Osborne	2	0	612	300
33.	Jim Reed	3	0	590	635
34.	Gordon Bracken	6	0	538	215
35.	Don Oldenberg	4	0	527	375
36.	C. H. Dingler	5	0	520	250
37.	Elbert Allen	4	0	488	250
38.	Mike Magill	3	0	486	235
39.	Lloyd Hulette	1	0	486	250
40.	Bill Harrison	3	0	480	450
41.	Tommy Thompson	3	0	463	865
42.	Coleman Lawrence	8	0	446	250
43.	Dub Livingston	6	0	435	225
44.	Buck Smith	5	0	400	175
45.	Jimmy Ayers	4	0	384	150
46.	Bob Walden	4	0	356	250
47.	Eddie Skinner	4	0	352	200
48.	Bill Adams	2	0	346	250
49.	Mel Krueger	3	0	336	175
50.	Johnny Beauchamp	3	0	328	150

Bobby Allison gets some advice from a pit crew member during the Atlanta 500 at Atlanta International Raceway, advice that helped him win the March 29, 1970, race. The win snapped Cale Yarborough's three-year winning streak in that race.

1954

AT A GLANCE:

Grand National Champion: Lee Petty ·

Notable Event: After running only oval-track races since 1949, NASCAR hosted its first road race on June 13. It was on a 2-mile course at the airport in Linden, New Jersey. Al Keller earned his second and final Grand National victory in, perhaps appropriately in light of the type of course, a Jaguar.

After being one of NASCAR's most popular and successful drivers since its inception, Lee Petty won the first of his two championships. He won "only" 7 races, but was consistent enough to have 32 top-10 finishes. Herb Thomas won 12 races, but had 7 fewer top-10s and lost the title by 283 points. Buck Baker, destined to become one of NASCAR's all-time greats, won four times and was third in points, just ahead of Dick Rathmann and Joe Eubanks. After being twelfth in 1952 and fourth in 1953, Baker was steadily moving toward the top.

If nothing else, 1954 proved what later became common knowledge: NASCAR was bigger than any of its stars. Early in the season, when Tim Flock was disqualified at Daytona Beach, he quit the circuit. Later that spring, Fonty Flock, Al Keller, and Hershel McGriff quit for various reasons. But the season-long scrap between Petty and Thomas—as well as the presence of Baker and Rathmann—kept stock car racing alive and well. The year's winners included Petty, Thomas, Baker, Rathmann, McGriff, Keller, Jim Paschal, Curtis Turner, Gober Sosebee, John Soares, and Danny Letner.

GRAND NATIONAL STANDINGS

	DRIVER	STARTS	WINS	POINTS	MONEY
1.	Lee Petty	34	7	8,649	21,127
2.	Herb Thomas	34	12	8,366	30,975
3.	Buck Baker	34	4	6,893	19,368
4.	Dick Rathmann	32	3	6,760	16,264
5.	Joe Eubanks	33	0	5,467	8,559
6.	Hershel McGriff	24	4	5,137	13,250
7.	Jim Paschal	27	1	3,903	5,451
8.	Jimmie Lewallen	22	0	3,233	4,694
9.	Curtis Turner	10	1	2,994	10,120
10.	Ralph Liguari	23	0	2,905	3,495
11.	Blackie Pitt	27	0	2,661	1,925
12.	Dave Terrell	30	0	2,645	2,225
13.	Bill Blair	19	0	2,362	2,650
14.	Laird Bruner	24	0	2,243	2,080
15.	Gober Sosebee	18	1	2,114	3,150
16.	John Soares	9	1	2,072	3,262
17.	Marvin Panch	10	0	1,925	4,747
18.	Eddie Skinner	15	0	1,794	1,017
19.	Joel Million	9	0	1,779	1,092
20.	Elton Hildreth	14	0	1,710	1,152
21.	Arden Mounts	12	0	1,705	875
22.	Fireball Roberts	5	0	1,648	1,080
23.	Speedy Thompson	7	0	1,480	1,165
24.	Johnny Patterson	4	0	1,417	1,240
25.	Erick Erickson	6	0	1,337	1,365
26.	Ray Duhigg	12	0	1,245	1,375
27.	Slick Smith	6	0	1,122	950
28.	Clyde Minter	12	0	1,116	900
29.	Gwyn Staley	2	0	1,088	670
30.	Lloyd Dane	4	0	984	1,600
31.	Donald Thomas	9	0	980	1,675
32.	Ted Chamberlain	10	0	920	475
33.	Danny Letter	4	1	915	1,975
34.	Elmo Langley	2	0	864	450
35.	Tim Flock	5	0	860	1,050
36.	Fred Dove	0	0	832	525
37.	Bill Widenhouse	6	0	805	425
38.	Gene Comstock	1	0	780	400
39.	Walt Flinchum	8	0	756	425
40.	Charlie Cregar	5	0	716	405
41.	Bill Amick	6	0	700	250
42.	Harvey Eakin	7	0	698	425
43.	Lou Figaro	3	0	690	425
44.	Ken Fisher	5	0	668	400
45.	Jim Reed	9	0	631	965
46.	Russ Hepler	6	0	624	525
47.	Allen Adkins	2	0	624	1,150
48.	Van Van Wey	3	0	602	495
49.	Tony Nelson	3	0	568	325
50.	John Dodd Jr.	1	0	552	150

1955

AT A GLANCE:

Grand National Champion: Tim Flock

Notable Event: The phrase "Win on Sunday, Sell on Monday" began making the rounds as executives at Ford and Chevrolet took tentative steps toward the factory backing of teams. However, in one of the sport's most ironic twists, Chrysler products won 27 races—even though the company did nothing to back Chrysler drivers.

Tim Flock and NASCAR had made up late in 1954 and Flock was ready when the tour reached Daytona Beach in February. He returned with a flourish, winning 18 races, easily the most dominating Grand National season to that point. He had 14 other top-5s and another top-10, and beat 3-race winner Buck Baker by 508 points. Even though Lee Petty won 6 races and was third in the final standings, he was an astonishing 2,402 points behind Flock. Bob Welborn and Herb Thomas were fourth and fifth in points.

The champion drove potent Chrysler 300s for Carl Kiekhaefer, a wealthy Wisconsin businessman who invaded NASCAR bent on outspending and outpreparing everyone. In addition to Tim Flock, Kiekhaefer's Mercury Marine–sponsored stable included Fonty Flock, Speedy Thompson, and Norm Nelson. The owner was so obsessed with winning that he owned or sponsored seven cars in a late-season race in Arkansas. He hoped Tim Flock would lead the race, separated from his nearest title challenger by a squadron of his own cars.

And it worked—well, sort of. Flock finished fourth, his teammate and brother Bob finished fifth, and Buck Baker was sixth in a self-owned Ford that Kiekhaefer was sponsoring. All told, Kiekhaefer had the winning driver (Speedy Thompson), Tim and Bob Flock, and Baker in the top 10. Banks Simpson, Norm Nelson, and Fonty Flock were the other drivers in the field who were associated with Kiekhaefer in one way or another. The season's winners included Tim and Fonty Flock, Baker, Petty, Junior Johnson, Jim Paschal, Danny Letner, Nelson, Thompson, and Thomas.

GRAND NATIONAL STANDINGS

	DRIVER	STARTS	WINS	POINTS	MONEY
1.	Tim Flock	18	5	9,596	37,780
2.	Buck Baker	32	3	8,088	19,771
3.	Lee Petty	42	6	7,194	18,920
4.	Bob Welborn	32	0	5,460	10,147
5.	Herb Thomas	23	3	5,186	18,024
6.	Junior Johnson	36	5	4,810	13,803
7.	Eddie Skinner	38	0	4,652	4,737
8.	Jim Paschal	36	5	4,572	10,586
9.	Jimmie Lewallen	33	0	4,526	6,440
10.	Gwyn Staley	24	0	4,360	6,547
11.	Fonty Flock	31	3	4,266	13,100
12.	Dave Terrell	25	0	3,170	3,655
13.	Jimmy Massey	11	0	2,924	3,510
14.	Marvin Panch	10	0	2,812	4,385
15.	Speedy Thompson	15	2	2,452	7,090
16.	Jim Reed	14	0	2,416	2,703

17.	Gene Simpson	22	0	2,388	2,158
18.	Dick Rathmann	20	0	2,298	4,368
19.	Ralph Liguori	12	0	2,124	1,973
20.	Joe Eubanks	14	0	2,028	2,008
21.	Blackie Pitt	20	0	1,992	1,785
22.	Harvey Henderson	17	0	1,930	1,810
23.	Banks Simpson	7	0	1,852	870
24.	Dink Widenhouse	0	0	1,752	1,660
25.	John Dodd Jr.	13	0	1,496	1,695
26.	Bill Widenhouse	5	0	1,444	1,065
27.	Lou Spears	3	0	1,272	810
28.	Larry Flynn	1	0	1,260	1,175
29.	Cotton Owens	2	0	1,248	900
30.	Gordon Smith	15	0	1,212	975
31.	Billy Carden	13	0	1,172	1,340
32.	Arden Mounts	12	0	1,170	1,025
33.	Joel Milton	8	0	1,136	1,685
34.	Curtis Turner	9	0	1,120	2,605
35.	John Lindsay	6	0	1,052	575
36.	Nace Mattingly	3	0	992	700
37.	Bill Blair	12	0	974	440
38.	Donald Thomas	10	0	932	1,240
39.	Ed Cole Jr.	13	0	924	645
40.	Mack Hanbury	8	0	900	575
41.	Danny Letter	4	1	892	1,780
42.	George Parrish	12	0	880	750
43.	Banjo Matthews	3	0	860	745
44.	Carl Krueger	7	0	748	585
45.	Ted Cannady	9	0	744	450
46.	Allen Adkins	4	0	740	1,160
47.	Joe Weatherly	6	0	724	2,575
48.	John McVitty	7	0	684	550
49.	Lloyd Dane	5	0	674	780
50.	Fred Dove	0	0	668	750

1956

AT A GLANCE:

Grand National Champion: Buck Baker

Notable Event: As if going 22-of-40 in 1955 wasn't enough of a thrill, Carl Kiekhaefer assembled an even more formidable stable for 1956. Even so, he found that success didn't always bring happiness. After winning the 1955 and 1956 titles, he abruptly left the sport he had ruled for two years.

It shouldn't have surprised anyone when Buck Baker won the 1956 championship. After all, he had been steadily climbing in the points: fourth in 1953, third in 1954, then second in 1955. He was almost assured the 1956 title when Kiekhaefer hired him to join Tim Flock and Speedy Thompson as part of his powerful stable. The organization—it has been compared to today's Hendrick Motorsports—won 30 of 56 races, including 21 of the first 25 and 16 straight during the middle of the season. Baker beat fellow top five drivers Herb Thomas, Speedy Thompson, Lee Petty, and Jim Paschal for the championship.

But all was not well. Feeling poorly and blaming it on the unrelenting pressure to excel, Tim Flock quit the team in April and moved into

a Mercury owned by Bill Stroppe. Herb Thomas replaced Flock on Kiekhaefer's team, but soon tired of the owner's stern and demanding manner. Thomas quit in July and began preparing cars and driving for himself, and it looked briefly like he might upstage his former boss by beating Baker for the championship.

Thomas led by 246 points entering a late-season race in Shelby, North Carolina, an "add-on" date that Kiekhaefer convinced NASCAR to schedule. Thomas's season and title hopes ended when he was critically injured in a controversial incident with Thompson. After winning the championship by 586 points, Baker and Kiekhaefer were vilified by people who thought Thompson intentionally crashed into Thomas to give Baker a better shot at the title. There's nothing to indicate the accident was deliberate, but the criticism so stung Kiekhaefer that he shut down and left NASCAR as quickly as he had come.

A then-record 17 drivers won races in 1956: Baker, Thomas, Thompson, Petty, Paschal, Billy Myers, Fireball Roberts, Ralph Moody, Tim Flock, Fonty Flock, Marvin Panch, Paul Goldsmith, Curtis Turner, Jack Smith, Lloyd Dane, Eddie Pagan, and John Kieper. The schedule showed 56 races, almost a quarter of them west of the Mississippi River, including 5 in car-crazy California.

GRAND NATIONAL STANDINGS

	DRIVER	STARTS	WINS	POINTS	MONEY
1.	Buck Baker	48	14	9,252	34,077
2.	Speedy Thompson	42	8	8,788	27,169
3.	Herb Thomas	48	5	8,710	19,352
4.	Lee Petty	47	2	8,324	15,338
5.	Jim Paschal	42	1	7,878	17,204
6.	Billy Myers	42	2	6,976	15,830
7.	Fireball Roberts	33	5	5,794	14,742
8.	Ralph Moody	35	4	5,528	15,493
9.	Tim Flock	4	1	5,062	15,769
10.	Marvin Panch	20	1	4,680	11,520
11.	Rex White	24	0	4,642	5,334
12.	Johnny Allen	32	0	4,024	4,559
13.	Paul Goldsmith	9	1	3,788	8,569
14.	Gwyn Staley	22	0	3,550	5,159
15.	Joe Eubanks	26	0	3,284	5,584
16.	Joe Weatherly	17	0	3,084	5,251
17.	Bill Amick	13	0	3,048	5,381
18.	Jim Reed	11	0	2,890	5,077
19.	Tiny Lund	0	0	2,754	2,811
20.	Curtis Turner	13	1	2,580	14,541
21.	Jack Smith	15	1	2,320	3,825
22.	Billy Carden	23	0	2,108	2,175
23.	Lloyd Dane	10	2	2,106	4,370
24.	Frank Mundy	9	0	1,836	3,585
25.	Bobby Johns	9	0	1,832	1,450
26.	Blackie Pitt	27	0	1,760	1,545
27.	Harold Hardesty	9	0	1,724	2,380

28.	Al Watkins	14	0	1,710	1,185
29.	Chuck Meekins	7	0	1,656	2,815
30.	Harvey Henderson	18	0	1,634	1,310
31.	Bill Champion	14	0	1,632	1,570
32.	Eddie Pagan	8	1	1,598	4,095
33.	Pat Kirkwood	3	0	1,540	2,025
34.	Clyde Palmer	11	0	1,516	2,755
35.	John Kieper	8	1	1,506	3,250
36.	Johnny Dodson	11	0	1,488	1,450
37.	Bill Blair	9	0	1,284	1,005
38.	Junior Johnson	13	0	1,272	1,350
39.	Ed Cole	12	0	1,200	950
40.	Brownie King	15	0	1,140	925
41.	Scotty Cain	4	0	1,124	1,235
42.	Allen Adkins	6	0	1,104	1,465
43.	Bobby Keck	15	0	1,076	950
44.	Gordon Haines	7	0	1,066	1,500
45.	Bob Keefe	7	0	1,066	1,040
46.	Dick Beaty	15	0	1,036	910
47.	Jim Blomgren	6	0	992	475
48.	Ed Negre	5	0	952	1,255
49.	Jimmy Massey	7	0	950	1,545
50.	Fonty Flock	7	1	946	1,780

1957

AT A GLANCE:

Grand National Champion: Buck Baker

Notable Event: The Automobile Manufacturers Association decided early in 1957 that its members should distance themselves from motorsports. In addition, after formerly providing financial and administrative support for Ford, GM, and Chrysler teams, the factories got skittish and left racing after a car went in the stands at Martinsville, Virginia, injuring five spectators, including a small boy. Late in 1957, a spectator at North Wilkesboro, North Carolina, was killed by a wheel thrown from Tiny Lund's car.

Glenn "Fireball" Roberts mingles with the crowd while he enjoys the trophy he just earned for winning the first-ever Firecracker 250 at Daytona International Speedway on July 4, 1959. The win was one of eight victories for Roberts in 1957, when he finished sixth in the season's points race.

Buck Baker won his second consecutive championship, one that wasn't the least bit tainted. Not that his 1956 title was, but some series watchers still recalled how teammate Speedy Thompson had wrecked Herb Thomas the previous year when Thomas was in second place in points. This time, preparing and driving his own Chevrolets, Baker won 10 times in 40 starts. He backed that with 28 other top-10 finishes and won the title by 760 points. Six-time winner Marvin Panch was second, two-time winner Speedy Thompson was third, four-time winner Lee Petty was fourth, and fellow four-time winner Jack Smith was fifth.

The schedule featured a diverse lineup of venues. There were 14 paved-track races, the most in NASCAR history. Darlington had always been paved, but it seemed that more dirt tracks were converting to asphalt. The popular half-milers at Martinsville, North Wilkesboro, and Weaverville

were among the first to make the switch. The 1957 schedule also featured NASCAR's first trip to the Watkins Glen, New York, road course. Additional paved tracks included a 2-mile road circuit at Willow Springs, California; a 1.6-mile road circuit at Titusville, Florida; and a 1-mile oval at Raleigh, North Carolina.

Baker, Panch, Thompson, Petty, and Smith were among 18 race winners. The other 13 were Fireball Roberts, Paul Goldsmith, Cotton Owens, Eddie Pagan, Bill Amick, Lloyd Dane, Ralph Moody, Gwyn Staley, Danny Graves, Bob Welborn, Marvin Porter, Parnelli Jones, and Art Watts. Six of the year's 53 races were in California, with 3 in Oregon and 1 in Washington.

GRAND NATIONAL STANDINGS

	DRIVER	STARTS	WINS	POINTS	MONEY
1.	Buck Baker	40	10	10,716	30,764
2.	Marvin Panch	42	6	9,956	24,307
3.	Speedy Thompson	38	2	8,560	26,841
4.	Lee Petty	41	4	8,528	18,326
5.	Jack Smith	39	4	8,464	14,562
6.	Fireball Roberts	42	8	8,268	19,829
7.	Johnny Allen	42	0	7,068	9,815
8.	L. D. Austin	40	0	6,532	6,485
9.	Brownie King	36	0	5,740	5,589
10.	Jim Paschal	35	0	5,124	7,079
11.	Tiny Lund	32	0	4,848	6,424
12.	Billy Myers	28	0	4,640	6,566
13.	Paul Goldsmith	25	4	4,188	12,734
14.	Cotton Owens	17	1	4,032	12,784
15.	Eddie Pagan	15	3	3,612	7,274
16.	Bill Amick	21	1	3,512	8,073
17.	Dick Beaty	20	0	3,220	3,648
18.	Jim Reed	6	0	2,836	3,408
19.	Clarence DeZalia	25	0	2,828	3,308
20.	Frankie Schneider	10	0	2,516	4,588
21.	Rex White	9	0	2,508	3,870
22.	Curtis Turner	10	0	2,356	4,830
23.	George Green	17	0	2,216	2,240
24.	Whitey Norman	13	0	1,920	3,390
25.	Lloyd Dane	10	1	1,852	4,985
26.	Jimmie Lewallen	7	0	1,796	1,030
27.	Johnny Mackinson	5	0	1,764	1,330
28.	Bobby Keck	16	0	1,740	1,525
29.	Billy Carden	3	0	1,600	1,675
30.	Bill Benson	11	0	1,592	1,090
31.	Dick Getty	10	0	1,504	1,890
32.	Scotty Cain	11	0	1,492	1,165
33.	Roy Tyner	10	0	1,468	1,020
34.	T. A. Toomes	11	0	1,404	1,450
35.	Possum Jones	6	0	1,360	2,375
36.	Huck Spaulding	8	0	1,240	1,120
37.	Ralph Earnhardt	9	0	1,180	1,150
38.	George Seeger	6	0	1,108	2,740
39.	Ken Rush	16	0	1,104	2,045
40.	Peck Peckham	10	0	1,064	950
41.	Bill Champion	10	0	956	1,125
42.	Chuck Hansen	7	0	900	510
43.	Danny Graves	7	1	880	1,895
44.	Marvin Porter	6	1	872	1,770
45.	Eddie Skinner	4	0	848	605
46.	Jimmy Thompson	2	0	816	325
47.	Parnelli Jones	10	1	812	1,625
48.	Bobby Johns	1	0	800	225
49.	Don Porter	6	0	784	810
50.	Joe Weatherly	14	0	776	5,240

1958

AT A GLANCE:

Grand National Champion: Lee Petty

Notable Event: On July 19, at the ⅓-mile paved oval at Exposition Speedway in Toronto, Ontario, Canada, the 21-year-old son of two-time NASCAR champion Lee Petty made his NASCAR debut. Richard Petty started 7th, crashed near the halfway point, and finished 17th in the 19-car field. Needless to say, it was not a sign of things to come for the winningest driver in NASCAR history.

You have to wonder how the final standings would have looked if Junior Johnson or Fireball Roberts had run the full 51-race schedule. Johnson won 6 races in 27 starts and finished 8th in points.

Roberts was even more efficient: 6 wins in 10 starts, but that put him only 11th in points. That compared to Lee Petty, who won 7 of 50 races, had 37 other top-10 finishes and won the championship. He beat Buck Baker (3 victories in 44 starts, with 32 other top-10s) by 644 points. Speedy Thompson, who won 4 of 36 starts, was third, then Shorty Rollins and Jack Smith. As for that young Petty kid: he ran 9 races, had 1 top-10 finish, was 36th in points, and earned $760 in prize money.

All told, 19 drivers won Grand National races in 1958: top-5 ranked Petty, Baker, Thompson, Rollins, and Smith, plus Rex White, Bob Welborn, Jim Reed, Frankie Schneider, Paul Goldsmith, Cotton Owens, Curtis Turner, Joe Weatherly, Parnelli Jones, Joe Eubanks, Jim Paschal, Eddie Gray, Roberts, and Johnson.

GRAND NATIONAL STANDINGS

	DRIVER	STARTS	WINS	POINTS	MONEY
1.	Lee Petty	50	7	12,232	26,565
2.	Buck Baker	44	3	11,588	25,841
3.	Speedy Thompson	37	4	8,792	17,295
4.	Shorty Rollins	29	1	8,124	13,399
5.	Jack Smith	39	2	7,666	12,634
6.	L. D. Austin	46	0	6,972	6,246
7.	Rex White	22	2	6,552	12,233
8.	Junior Johnson	27	6	6,380	13,809
9.	Eddie Pagan	27	0	4,910	7,472
10.	Jim Reed	17	4	4,762	9,644
11.	Fireball Roberts	10	6	4,420	32,219
12.	Bobby Keck	30	0	4,240	3,459
13.	Herman Beam	20	0	4,224	2,599
14.	Herb Estes	11	0	4,048	2,509
15.	Clarence DeZalia	27	0	3,948	3,004
16.	Doug Cox	14	0	3,736	3,404
17.	Cotton Owens	29	1	3,716	6,579
18.	Marvin Panch	11	0	3,424	4,114
19.	Billy Rafter	19	0	2,916	2,799
20.	Curtis Turner	17	3	2,856	10,029
21.	Lloyd Dane	5	0	2,844	2,490
22.	Bob Duell	7	0	2,740	2,415
23.	Jimmy Thompson	8	0	2,540	3,275
24.	Fred Harb	25	0	2,484	3,320
25.	Tiny Lund	22	0	2,436	3,155
26.	Bill Poor	24	0	2,292	3,115
27.	Gene White	9	0	2,040	1,400
28.	Joe Weatherly	15	1	2,032	6,330
29.	Johnny Mackison	11	0	1,680	1,255
30.	Jim Parsley	10	0	1,488	1,135
31.	Al White	9	0	1,464	920
32.	Jimmy Massey	9	0	1,300	1,625
33.	Parnelli Jones	3	1	1,140	1,010
34.	Joe Eubanks	7	1	1,120	2,070
35.	Brownie King	24	0	1,116	3,045
36.	G. C. Spencer	1	0	1,040	315
37.	Richard Petty	9	0	1,016	760
38.	Billy Carden	13	0	1,012	815
39.	Elmo Langley	9	0	980	1,090
40.	Buzz Woodward	9	0	964	1,195
41.	Possum Jones	11	0	960	1,790
42.	Jim Paschal	6	1	928	1,670
43.	Chuck Hansen	7	0	916	580
44.	Eddie Gray	3	1	910	3,375
45.	Peck Peckham	11	0	868	835
46.	Lennie Page	8	0	836	760
47.	Bob Keefe	2	0	782	925
48.	R. L. Combs	9	0	760	805
49.	Volney Shultze	7	0	680	490
50.	Dean Layfield	7	0	664	370

1959

AT A GLANCE:

Grand National Champion: Lee Petty

Notable Event: One of racing's most unusual stats is that neither of the first two races at Daytona International Speedway was slowed by caution flags. The February 22 Daytona 500 and the July 4 Firecracker 250 were incident-free. No other track has ever had two caution-free races in the same season. Oh, as if the opening of the 2.5-mile, high-banked track in Daytona Beach, Florida, wasn't a big enough news story on its own.

Top Newcomers: Richard Petty was 0-for-21, but he had 6 top-5 finishes and 8 top-10s. Rookie of the Year was the first of dozens of honors he'd receive throughout his NASCAR career. Buddy Baker also made his NASCAR debut and Ned Jarrett got the first 2 of his 50 career victories.

Lee Petty dominated the season, winning 11 times in 42 starts (there were 44 races in total) and finishing among the top 10 two dozen other times. Among his biggest victories: the inaugural Daytona 500 in February and a 150-miler in June on a 1-mile track in Atlanta. That's where Richard, his 21-year-old son, was flagged the winner, only to have Lee protest the scoring. He was proved right when a careful recheck of the cards showed father winning and son finishing second. Lee Petty also won twice at North Wilkesboro and Columbia, and once each at Martinsville and numerous tracks in North Carolina, including Weaverville, Charlotte, Hickory, and Hillsborough. After being steady but unspectacular throughout the season, he won four of the last eight races, including two of the last three to clinch his third championship.

A dozen drivers won at least once, but nobody came close to Lee Petty's 11 victories. Rex White and Junior Johnson each won five, but didn't run nearly enough to contend for the title. One-time winner Cotton Owens finished second in points, 1,830 behind Lee Petty. Third-place Speedy Thompson and fourth-place Herman Beam were winless, with fifth-place Buck Baker winning just once. Other winners as NASCAR closed out its first full decade: Tom Pistone, Jack Smith, Jim Reed, Johnny Beauchamp, Parnelli Jones, Joe Lee Johnson, Eddie Gray, Rex White,

WHERE ARE THEY NOW: CALE YARBOROUGH

One of the best drivers in NASCAR history won three consecutive Winston Cup championships from 1976 to 1978, and his 83 race victories rank fifth on the all-time list. After his racing career was over, the four-time Daytona 500 winner (1968, 1977, 1983, and 1984) moved into team ownership, fielding Winston Cup teams for several seasons. After phasing out that part of his career, Yarborough became the owner of a Mazda/Honda dealership in Florence, South Carolina, and also purchased real estate and farming interests. However, the past champion couldn't abandon racing altogether—as of 2002, he was involved in a racing school in Lakeland, Florida.

Junior Johnson, Fireball Roberts, Bob Welborn, Curtis Turner, and Jarrett.

GRAND NATIONAL STANDINGS

	DRIVER	STARTS	WINS	POINTS	MONEY
1.	Lee Petty	42	11	11,792	49,220
2.	Cotton Owens	37	1	9,962	14,640
3.	Speedy Thompson	29	0	7,684	6,816
4.	Herman Beam	30	0	7,396	6,380
5.	Buck Baker	35	1	7,170	11,061
6.	Tom Pistone	22	2	7,050	12,725
7.	L. D. Austin	35	0	6,519	4,671
8.	Jack Smith	21	4	6,150	13,290
9.	Jim Reed	14	3	5,744	23,534
10.	Rex White	23	5	5,526	12,360
11.	Junior Johnson	28	5	4,864	9,675
12.	Shep Langdon	21	0	4,768	3,526
13.	G. C. Spencer	28	0	4,260	3,701
14.	Tommy Irwin	25	0	3,876	9,190
15.	Richard Petty	21	0	3,694	8,111
16.	Fireball Roberts	8	1	3,676	10,661
17.	Bob Welborn	29	3	3,588	6,491
18.	Joe Weatherly	17	0	3,404	9,816
19.	Bobby Jones	1	0	2,732	5,951
20.	Tiny Lund	27	0	2,634	4,941
21.	Bob Burdick	6	0	2,392	10,050
22.	Larry Frank	15	0	2,256	5,993
23.	Bobby Keck	18	0	2,186	1,270
24.	Curtis Turner	10	2	2,088	3,845
25.	Jim Paschal	6	0	1,792	2,980
26.	Buddy Baker	12	0	1,692	1,705
27.	Shorty Rollins	10	0	1,600	1,500
28.	Elmo Langley	13	0	1,568	2,286
29.	Jimmy Thompson	5	0	1,528	1,580
30.	Brownie King	18	0	1,480	1,875
31.	Tim Flock	2	0	1,464	850
32.	Joe Eubanks	13	0	1,432	2,000
33.	Roy Tyner	28	0	1,416	5,425
34.	Charlie Cregar	3	0	1,408	550
35.	Dick Freeman	3	0	1,352	475
36.	Raul Cilloniz	2	0	1,272	550
37.	Ned Jarrett	17	2	1,248	3,860
38.	Dave White	5	0	1,228	660
39.	Dick Joslin	4	0	1,224	485
40.	Tommy Thompson	3	0	1,168	510
41.	Harvey Hege	10	0	1,152	955

42.	Eduardo Dibos	3	0	1,128	1,050
43.	Bill Champion	1	0	1,120	500
44.	Joe Caspolich	1	0	1,040	470
45.	Jim Austin	5	0	1,016	440
46.	Marvin Porter	7	0	984	1,940
47.	Jim McGuirk	4	0	928	325
48.	Harlan Richardson	10	0	924	1,120
49.	Al White	5	0	872	575
50.	Richard Riley	10	0	760	910

1960

AT A GLANCE:

Grand National Champion: Rex White

Notable Events: NASCAR was moving away from short dirt ovals to more paved superspeedways that were faster, more dangerous, and attracted far more fans and sponsors. By 1960, paved superspeedways were all the rage in Daytona Beach; Darlington; Hanford, California; and near Charlotte and Atlanta. The 44-race schedule included 23 races on pavement, to that point, the most in NASCAR history.

Top Newcomers: Rookie of the Year David Pearson emerged from the weekend bullrings in the Carolinas to run 22 Grand National races. He was runner-up at Sumter, South Carolina; fourth at Hickory; and fifth in his hometown of Spartanburg, South Carolina. He also had four other finishes between 6th and 10th, and was 23rd in points. An Illinois native by the name of Fred Lorenzen was top 10 in half of his 10 starts, a sign of things to come.

Unlike the previous season, when Lee Petty dominated, there was more parity in the first year of the 1960s. Rex White won his first and only championship with 6 victories, 25 top-5, and 35 top-10s in 40 starts. He won the title by 3,936 points over 3-race winner Richard Petty, with 1-time winner Bobby Johns third in points, 2-time winner Buck Baker fourth, and 5-time winner Ned Jarrett. Two-time champion Lee Petty won 5 times, but inconsistency left him sixth in points.

Richard Petty got the first 3 of his record-setting 200 victories, first in February at Charlotte, then in April at Martinsville, and finally in September at Hillsborough. Buddy Baker, another second-generation driver (Buck Baker's son), was winless in 15 starts. All told, 15 drivers won races: White, the Pettys, Johns, Buck Baker, Jarrett, Junior Johnson, Johnny Beauchamp, Joe Lee Johnson, Glen Wood, John Rostek, Marvin Porter, Jack Smith, Joe Weatherly, Speedy Thompson, Fireball Roberts, Cotton Owens, and Jim Cook.

GRAND NATIONAL STANDINGS

	DRIVER	STARTS	WINS	POINTS	MONEY
1.	Rex White	40	6	21,164	57,525
2.	Richard Petty	40	3	17,228	41,873
3.	Bobby Johns	19	1	14,964	46,115
4.	Buck Baker	37	2	14,674	38,399
5.	Ned Jarrett	40	5	14,660	25,438
6.	Lee Petty	39	5	14,510	31,283
7.	Junior Johnson	34	3	9,932	38,990
8.	Emanuel Zervakis	14	0	9,720	12,124
9.	Jim Paschal	10	0	8,968	15,096
10.	Banjo Matthews	12	0	8,458	15,617
11.	Johnny Beauchamp	11	1	8,306	17,374
12.	Herman Beam	26	0	7,776	5,916
13.	Joe Lee Johnson	22	1	7,352	34,519
14.	Jack Smith	13	3	6,944	24,721
15.	Fred Lorenzen	10	0	6,764	9,136
16.	Bob Welborn	15	0	6,732	6,194
17.	Jimmy Pardue	32	0	6,682	5,610
18.	Tom Pistone	21	0	6,572	6,714
19.	Johnny Allen	10	0	6,506	14,789
20.	Joe Weatherly	24	3	6,380	20,124
21.	Doug Yates	24	0	6,374	5,205
22.	L. D. Austin	27	0	6,180	4,785
23.	David Pearson	22	0	5,956	5,030
24.	Gerald Duke	11	0	5,950	5,930
25.	Speedy Thompson	9	2	5,658	18,035
26.	Marvin Panch	11	0	5,268	3,225
27.	Paul Lewis	22	0	5,212	3,535
28.	Curtis Crider	24	0	4,720	3,645
29.	Fireball Roberts	9	2	4,700	19,895
30.	Shorty Rollins	4	0	4,374	2,120
31.	Possum Jones	13	0	4,270	6,330
32.	Tiny Lund	8	0	4,124	2,440
33.	G. C. Spencer	26	0	3,986	3,910
34.	Larry Frank	10	0	3,634	2,440
35.	Herb Tillman	9	0	3,504	2,605
36.	Curtis Turner	9	0	3,300	3,220
37.	Bunkie Blackburn	20	0	3,252	3,400
38.	Buddy Baker	15	0	3,070	1,745
39.	Cotton Owens	14	1	3,050	14,065
40.	Charley Griffith	5	0	2,684	1,300
41.	Wilbur Rakestraw	12	0	2,676	2,695
42.	Jimmy Massey	6	0	2,662	3,310
43.	Jimmy Thompson	9	0	2,472	1,940
44.	Jim Reed	8	0	2,340	2,240
45.	Jim Cook	3	1	2,178	1,600
46.	Ernie Gahan	2	0	2,080	625
47.	Elmo Henderson	6	0	2,072	1,425
48.	Bob Burdick	2	0	1,970	850
49.	Roz Howard	3	0	1,810	1,490
50.	Bob Potter	3	0	1,800	640

1961

AT A GLANCE:

Grand National Champion: Ned Jarrett

Notable Event: If there was ever any doubt, Bill France proved who was the boss of southern-style stock car racing. When the Teamsters Union tried to organize the drivers (and perhaps bring in betting) France suspended maverick drivers and threatened to disband the series rather than give in to union pressure. He quickly reinstated several drivers who'd leaned toward the union, but he waited five years before reinstating Curtis Turner, the union's primary loyalist.

Top Newcomers: Woody Wilson had a short and not-to-sweet career. He ran only five races in 1961 (one top-10 finish) and was 41st in the standings, then never raced Grand National again.

Lee Petty, head of the most famous racing family in American automotive history, stands outside his car at an unknown location in 1960.

Ned Jarrett proved that consistency and determination were as valuable as speed and handling. He started 46 of 52 races and won only once (at Birmingham, Alabama, in June), but finished top 10 in 33 others. That earned him the championship by 830 points over 7-time winner Rex White. Emanuel Zervakis won twice in 38 starts and stood third in points. Joe Weatherly (9 victories in 25 starts) and Fireball Roberts (2 victories in 22 races) were fourth and fifth in the final accounting.

Most of the racing world's attention continued to be focused on the high-speed races at superspeedways. While short tracks and sprint races made up the bulk of the schedule, it was the long-distance events at Daytona Beach, Darlington, Charlotte, and Atlanta that caught the nation's fancy. Marvin Panch and David Pearson won on the 2½-mile track at Daytona Beach; Bob Burdick, Fred Lorenzen, and Pearson won on the 1½-mile track near Atlanta; Lorenzen and Nelson Stacy won at the venerable 1¼-mile track at Darlington; and Pearson and Weatherly won on a 1½-mile track near Charlotte. The other winners were Lee Petty, Cotton Owens, Junior Johnson, Richard Petty, Lloyd Dane, Eddie Gray, Jim Paschal, Jack Smith, and Buck Baker.

GRAND NATIONAL STANDINGS

	DRIVER	STARTS	WINS	POINTS	MONEY
1.	Ned Jarrett	46	1	27,272	41,056
2.	Rex White	47	7	26,442	56,395
3.	Emanuel Zervokis	38	2	22,312	27,281

4.	Joe Weatherly	25	9	17,894	47,079
5.	Fireball Roberts	22	2	17,600	50,267
6.	Junior Johnson	41	7	17,178	28,541
7.	Jack Smith	25	2	15,186	21,410
8.	Richard Petty	42	2	14,984	25,239
9.	Jim Paschal	23	2	13,922	18,100
10.	Buck Baker	42	1	13,746	13,697
11.	Jimmy Pardue	44	0	13,408	10,562
12.	Johnny Allen	22	0	13,114	13,127
13.	David Pearson	19	3	13,088	51,911
14.	Bob Welborn	14	0	12,570	13,487
15.	Herman Beam	41	0	11,382	9,392
16.	Nelson Stacy	15	1	10,436	27,608
17.	Ralph Earnhardt	8	0	10,182	11,473
18.	Marvin Panch	9	1	9,392	30,478
19.	Fred Lorenzen	15	3	9,316	30,395
20.	G. C. Spencer	31	0	9,128	7,363
21.	Curtis Crider	41	0	8,414	7,420
22.	Cotton Owens	17	4	8,032	11,890
23.	Tiny Lund	10	0	7,740	5,545
24.	Bobby Johns	14	0	7,590	5,010
25.	L. D. Austin	20	0	7,306	4,530
26.	Tommy Irwin	26	0	7,300	7,170
27.	Doug Yates	32	0	5,878	1,090
28.	Paul Lewis	21	0	5,712	4,095
29.	Bob Barron	31	0	5,412	3,725
30.	Elmo Langley	15	0	5,376	3,530
31.	Banjo Matthews	14	0	4,924	5,560
32.	Wendell Scott	23	0	4,726	3,240
33.	Jim Reed	8	0	4,705	3,350
34.	Fred Harb	27	0	4,526	3,460
35.	Darel Dieringer	7	0	4,416	3,150
36.	Bob Burdick	5	1	4,382	18,750
37.	Lee Reitzel	17	0	4,380	2,910
38.	Tom Pistone	4	0	3,766	2,050
39.	Buddy Baker	14	0	3,668	4,965
40.	Roscoe Thompson	6	0	3,602	2,535
41.	Woodie Wilson	5	0	3,580	2,625
42.	Larry Frank	8	0	3,162	2,380
43.	Larry Thomas	14	0	3,140	2,015
44.	Harry Leake	15	0	3,092	2,000
45.	Paul Goldsmith	2	0	2,930	6,050
46.	Joe Lee Johnson	9	0	2,700	2,615
47.	Bill Morgan	5	0	2,430	1,900
48.	Theodore Hunt	7	0	2,430	2,750
49.	Marvin Porter	8	0	2,326	2,070
50.	Joe Eubanks	2	0	2,320	1,475

1962

AT A GLANCE:

Grand National Champion: Joe Weatherly

Notable Events: After turning a blind eye to racing for several years, Ford Motor Co. and Chrysler Corp. began offering "engineering assistance" to selected NASCAR teams. Little wonder: Pontiacs (12) and Chevrolets (6) had won 18 of the season's first 20 races. Only Richard Petty's two wins in a Plymouth could break GM's stranglehold. Things quickly changed, though: Fords and Plymouths won 15 of the final 33 after their factories took a renewed interest in NASCAR.

Top Newcomers: Tom Cox was 0-for-42 and finished 18th in points, which may not look impressive. But he was among the top 10 in 20 of his starts, and only six of the drivers who finished ahead of him in points (all of them race winners and established stars) had more top-10s.

Finally, a championship battle in which five drivers—not just one or two or even three—were winners. Joe Weatherly, the self-styled "Clown Prince of Racing," won 9 races in 52 starts and had 45 top-10 finishes. He won the title by 2,396 points over 8-time winner Richard Petty, with 6-time winner Ned Jarrett ranked third. Five-time winner Jack Smith was fourth and 8-time winner Rex White was fifth. The season featured 53 races, all of them in Virginia, the Carolinas, Georgia, Tennessee, Alabama, and Florida.

Combined, Weatherly, Petty, Jarrett, Smith, and White combined to win 34 of the season's 53 races. The other 19 victories were spread among veteran Jim Paschal, Fred Lorenzen, Fireball Roberts, Larry Frank, Jimmy Pardue, Junior Johnson, Nelson Stacy, Johnny Allen, Bobby Johns, and Cotton Owens. Six drivers won the 10 superspeedway races that were becoming such an important part of stock car racing. Roberts won the Daytona 500 and Firecracker 250 in Daytona Beach; Stacy won the 600-mile race near Charlotte and the 300-mile race at Darlington; Johnson won near Charlotte; and White and Lorenzen won near Atlanta. Frank won the Southern 500 after an extensive scoring recheck moved him from fourth to first, ahead of Johnson, Marvin Panch, David Pearson, and Richard Petty.

GRAND NATIONAL STANDINGS

	DRIVER	STARTS	WINS	POINTS	MONEY
1.	Joe Weatherly	52	9	30,836	70,743
2.	Richard Petty	52	8	28,440	60,764
3.	Ned Jarrett	52	6	25,336	43,444
4.	Jack Smith	51	5	22,870	34,748
5.	Rex White	37	8	19,424	36,246
6.	Jim Paschal	39	4	18,128	27,348
7.	Fred Lorenzen	19	2	17,554	46,100
8.	Fireball Roberts	19	3	16,380	66,152
9.	Marvin Panch	17	0	15,138	26,746
10.	David Pearson	12	0	14,404	19,032
11.	Herman Beam	51	0	13,650	12,571
12.	Curtis Crider	52	0	13,050	12,016
13.	Buck Baker	37	0	12,838	12,787
14.	Larry Frank	19	1	12,814	32,987
15.	Bob Welburn	25	0	12,368	10,347
16.	George Green	46	0	12,132	9,221
17.	Larry Thomas	37	0	11,946	9,486
18.	Thomas Cox	42	0	11,688	10,181
19.	Jimmy Pardue	29	1	11,414	12,066
20.	Junior Johnson	23	1	11,140	34,841
21.	Nelson Stacy	15	3	10,934	43,080
22.	Wendell Scott	41	0	9,906	7,133
23.	Buddy Baker	31	0	9,828	7,578
24.	G. C. Spencer	42	0	9,788	7,995
25.	Bunkie Blackburn	10	0	8,016	5,890
26.	Johnny Allen	20	1	7,602	7,230
27.	Emanuel Zervakis	11	0	6,406	4,545
28.	Bobby Johns	13	1	5,670	15,863
29.	Ralph Earnhardt	17	0	5,472	4,545
30.	Cotton Owens	16	0	4,984	5,905

31.	Banjo Matthews	5	0	4,956	11,375
32.	Sherman Utsman	12	0	4,896	3,580
33.	Darel Dieringer	14	0	4,548	4,880
34.	Tiny Lund	10	0	4,384	2,880
35.	Stick Elliott	21	0	4,254	3,928
36.	LeeRoy Yarbrough	12	0	4,240	3,285
37.	Tommy Irwin	20	0	3,980	3,305
38.	Ed Livingston	13	0	3,604	2,940
39.	Fred Harb	21	0	3,430	2,220
40.	Elmo Langley	6	0	2,556	1,795
41.	Bill Morton	5	0	2,522	1,350
42.	Speedy Thompson	3	0	2,522	1,400
43.	Jimmy Thompson	3	0	2,346	1,650
44.	Red Foote	4	0	2,274	1,600
45.	Ernie Gahan	3	0	2,092	725
46.	Billy Wade	4	0	2,008	1,350
47.	Jim Cushman	4	0	1,954	850
48.	Bill Wimble	2	0	1,944	675
49.	Troy Ruttman	1	0	1,890	1,750
50.	Cale Yarborough	8	0	1,884	2,725

1963

AT A GLANCE:

Grand National Champion: Joe Weatherly

Notable Event: Given the biggest opportunity of his life, Tiny Lund didn't blow it. The Iowa native got the Wood Brothers' Ford in the Daytona 500 after pulling assigned driver Marvin Panch from his burning sports car 10 days before the 500. Lund made one fewer pit stop, didn't change tires, and led the final eight laps to beat fellow Ford drivers Fred Lorenzen and Ned Jarrett.

Top Newcomers: Billy Wade came out of Texas to run 31 of the year's 55 races. And although he didn't win, he had 5 top-5 finishes and 15 top-10s. And after running only a handful of races the previous few years, a South Carolina farmboy named Cale Yarborough and a North Carolina short-track star named Bobby Isaac became tour regulars.

Seldom has any champion done more with less than Joe Weatherly in 1963. He opened the season lacking a full-time ride, but managed to beg, borrow, and steal(?) enough to run 53 races. He did most of them in Bud Moore-owned Pontiacs and Mercurys, but also raced twice in Dodges and once each in a Plymouth and Chrysler. Weatherly won only 3 times (at Richmond, Darlington, and Hillsborough), but had 20 top-5 finishes and 35 top-10s. That paled beside Richard Petty's 14 victories, 30 top-5s, and 34 top-10s, but Weatherly's top-5 and top-10s were better than Petty's top-5 and top-10s.

Without question, the real star of the season was Fred Lorenzen. Granted, he ran only 29 races and finished third in points (behind Weatherly and Petty, but ahead of Ned Jarrett and Fireball Roberts), but he won major superspeedway races

near Atlanta and Charlotte and short-track races at Martinsville, Huntington, North Wilkesboro, and Weaverville. The so-called "Golden Boy" had 21 top-5s and top-10s, and won a then-record $122,587. It was the first time a NASCAR racer had reached six figures in a season, another sign that the sport was growing up.

The 55-race season featured 15 winners: Weatherly, Petty, Lorenzen, Jarrett, Roberts, Pardue, Darel Dieringer, Dan Gurney, Glen Wood, Johnny Rutherford, Buck Baker, Junior Johnson, Marvin Panch, Jim Paschal, and Lund. The 55 races made up the longest schedule to that point in NASCAR history, making it easier for Indy car drivers Gurney, Rutherford, A. J., Foyt and Parnelli Jones to fit stock car racing into their schedules.

GRAND NATIONAL STANDINGS

	DRIVER	STARTS	WINS	POINTS	MONEY
1.	Joe Weatherly	53	3	33,398	74,624
2.	Richard Petty	54	14	31,170	55,964
3.	Fred Lorenzen	29	6	29,684	122,587
4.	Ned Jarrett	53	8	27,214	45,844
5.	Fireball Roberts	20	4	22,642	73,060
6.	Jimmy Purdue	52	1	22,228	20,359
7.	Darel Dieringer	20	1	21,418	29,725
8.	David Pearson	41	0	21,156	24,986
9.	Rex White	25	0	20,976	27,241
10.	Tiny Lund	22	1	19,624	49,397
11.	Buck Baker	47	1	18,114	18,616
12.	Junior Johnson	33	7	17,720	67,351
13.	Marvin Panch	12	1	17,156	39,102
14.	Nelson Stacy	12	0	14,794	18,266
15.	Wendell Scott	47	0	14,814	10,966
16.	Billy Wade	31	0	14,646	15,204
17.	Curtis Crider	49	0	13,996	11,644
18.	G. C. Spencer	31	0	13,744	13,514
19.	Jim Paschal	32	5	13,456	20,979
20.	Bobby Isaac	27	0	12,858	9,529
21.	Bobby Johns	12	0	12,652	15,915
22.	Larry Thomas	32	0	11,010	8,945
23.	Stick Elliott	28	0	9,582	6,235
24.	Jack Smith	29	0	8,218	8,645
25.	Cale Yarborough	18	0	8,062	5,550
26.	LeeRoy Yarbrough	14	0	7,872	6,680
27.	Herman Beam	25	0	7,742	5,255
28.	Larry Frank	11	0	7,582	5,450
29.	Larry Manning	23	0	6,952	5,405
30.	Ed Livingston	20	0	6,818	4,930
31.	Neil Castles	28	0	5,928	5,165
32.	Tommy Irwin	7	0	5,176	2,655
33.	Reb Wickersham	14	0	4,812	3,800
34.	Worth McMillion	15	0	4,614	3,145
35.	Bob James	10	0	4,316	3,375
36.	Roy Mayne	20	0	4,188	3,490
37.	Bob Cooper	9	0	4,164	3,115
38.	Jimmy Massey	15	0	4,016	2,870
39.	Elmo Langley	11	0	3,982	2,170
40.	Bob Welborn	11	0	3,484	4,830
41.	Fred Harb	16	0	3,286	2,720
42.	Dave MacDonald	2	0	2,944	5,330
43.	Major Melton	17	0	2,806	1,910
44.	Sal Tavella	3	0	2,570	1,300
45.	Ron Hornaday	2	0	2,520	1,600
46.	J. D. McDuffie	12	0	2,498	1,620
47.	Bob Perry	5	0	2,478	1,550
48.	Bunkie Blackburn	7	0	2,454	2,525
49.	Bill Foster	10	0	2,168	1,410
50.	Bud Harless	5	0	2,156	1,550

1964

AT A GLANCE:

Grand National Champion: Richard Petty

Notable Event: After years of relatively safe racing, NASCAR faced tragedy when two-time champion Joe Weatherly, Fireball Roberts, and Jimmy Pardue were killed. Weatherly died at Riverside in January, Roberts died in July of burns and injuries suffered near Charlotte in May, and Pardue died in a tire-testing crash near Charlotte in September. NASCAR took a long look at safety, especially at ways to slow cars and keep them under control. It is a search that continues to this day.

Top Newcomer: Doug Cooper ran 39 of the year's 62 races, had 4 top-5 finishes and 11 top-10s.

Richard Petty got the first of his seven titles with a performance that was more workmanlike than spectacular. He was 9-of-61, had 37 top-5s, 43 top-10s, and earned $114,772, the second NASCAR driver to top $100,000 in a season. Ned Jarrett had a better season —15 victories, 40 top-5s, and 45 top-10s in 59 starts—but wasn't nearly as consistent. Third-ranked David Pearson won 8 races, Billy Wade was fourth in points, and Pardue was fifth, even though he was killed 50 races into the season.

The sport reeled when Weatherly was killed, staggered when Roberts finally died of his injuries, and went to its knees when Pardue died. Weatherly's head and left shoulder apparently came out the driver's side window and hit the wall when he crashed at Riverside. Roberts survived his fiery crash, but died of pneumonia and burn-related infections six weeks later. And Pardue was helping develop new and safer tires when a tire failure sent his Plymouth over the turn 3 wall and tumbling outside the Charlotte Motor Speedway grounds at almost 150 miles per hour.

Petty ran 61 of the year's 62 races and was among 17 drivers with victories. The others were Jarrett, Pearson, Wade, Jim Paschal, Buck Baker, Marvin Panch, Dan Gurney, A. J. Foyt, Cotton Owens, Darel Dieringer, Wendell Scott, Fred Lorenzen, Junior Johnson, LeeRoy Yarbrough, Bobby Isaac and Roberts. The victory for Scott was the first (and, still, only) for an African-American driver in any of NASCAR's top series.

GRAND NATIONAL STANDINGS

	DRIVER	STARTS	WINS	POINTS	MONEY
1.	Richard Petty	61	9	40,252	114,772
2.	Ned Jarrett	59	15	34,950	71,925
3.	David Pearson	61	8	32,146	45,542
4.	Billy Wade	35	4	28,474	36,095
5.	Jimmy Pardue	50	0	26,570	41,598
6.	Curtis Crider	59	0	25,606	22,171
7.	Jim Paschal	22	1	25,450	60,116
8.	Larry Thomas	43	0	22,950	21,226
9.	Buck Baker	34	2	22,366	43,781
10.	Marvin Panch	31	3	21,480	34,836
11.	Darel Dieringer	27	1	19,972	20,685
12.	Wendell Scott	56	1	19,574	16,495
13.	Fred Lorenzen	16	8	18,098	73,860
14.	Junior Johnson	29	3	17,066	26,975
15.	LeeRoy Yarbrough	34	2	16,172	16,630
16.	Roy Tyner	46	0	13,922	11,488
17.	Neil Castles	58	0	13,372	14,318
18.	Bobby Isaac	19	1	13,252	26,733
19.	Cale Yarborough	24	0	12,618	10,378
20.	Tiny Lund	22	0	12,598	9,913
21.	Doug Cooper	39	0	11,942	10,445
22.	Paul Goldsmith	14	0	11,700	20,835
23.	J. T. Putney	17	0	10,744	7,295
24.	Larry Frank	12	0	10,314	7,830
25.	Jack Anderson	31	0	10,040	8,510
26.	G. C. Spencer	20	0	10,012	9,490
27.	Fireball Roberts	9	1	9,900	28,345
28.	Rex White	6	0	8,222	12,310
29.	Dave MacDonald	5	0	7,650	9,195
30.	Worth McMillion	18	0	7,586	4,700
31.	Buddy Baker	33	0	7,314	8,460
32.	Bunkie Blackburn	14	0	7,264	6,630
33.	Bill McMahan	20	0	7,240	7,205
34.	Buddy Arrington	27	0	6,364	4,715
35.	Earl Balmer	10	0	6,170	5,795
36.	Bob Derrington	18	0	5,896	2,755
37.	Bobby Johns	12	0	5,436	5,700
38.	E. J. Trivette	26	0	5,118	5,495
39.	Doug Moore	24	0	4,970	5,175
40.	Ken Spikes	6	0	4,934	3,100
41.	Earl Brooks	28	0	4,820	3,925
42.	Elmo Langley	14	0	4,400	3,905
43.	Roy Mayne	14	0	4,278	4,705
44.	Gene Hobby	18	0	4,054	2,795
45.	Doug Yates	15	0	3,778	3,290
46.	Ralph Earnhardt	11	0	3,720	3,290
47.	Bob Cooper	13	0	3,602	3,360
48.	Joe Weatherly	5	0	3,132	5,290
49.	Sam McQuagg	5	0	2,928	1,700
50.	Bobby Keck	10	0	2,754	2,850

1965

AT A GLANCE:

Grand National Champion: Ned Jarrett

Notable Event: Another new superspeedway sprang up in 1965, this one near Rockingham. Not only was its opening a big deal, but it featured the superspeedway return of fan favorite Curtis Turner. He'd been suspended from NASCAR since 1961, when Bill France banned him for trying to help the Teamsters Union organize the drivers. Turner came back in style, winning the 500-mile race in a Ford.

Top Newcomer: Sam McQuagg, a Georgia native, ran only 15 of the year's 55 races, but he had a pair of top-5 finishes and 5 top-10s, winning just $10,555. He got his only career victory the following year in the Firecracker 400 at Daytona Beach.

Three Ford drivers dominated the 55-race season while many teams with Chrysler equipment boycotted NASCAR because of a rules dispute. When Bill France banned Mopar's powerful Hemi engine, Richard Petty and David Pearson (among others) sat out rather than lose to Ford and Mercury drivers. By the time France adjusted the rules to bring Chrysler teams back, Fords had won 34 races and Jarrett had a near-insurmountable points leads. Petty won 4 of the last 21 races and Pearson 2, but both finished well down in the standings.

Jarrett won 13 races, had 42 top-5s, and 45 top-10s, but still didn't reach $100,000 in winnings. Second-ranked Hutcherson won 9 races in a Ford, third-ranked Darel Dieringer 1, fourth-ranked G. C. Spencer was winless, and fifth-ranked Panch won 4 times. Johnson also won 13 times in a Ford, but ran only 36 races and finished a distant 12th in points. Cale Yarborough, destined to become one of the sport's all-time winners, earned his first victory in late-June at Valdosta, Georgia. Other winners included Dan Gurney, Fred Lorenzen (soon to retire), Tiny Lund, A. J. Foyt, and Turner.

LeeRoi Yarbrough doesn't seem too interested in the celebration going on around him as his dad, LeeRoy, enjoys the aftermath of his victory in the Permatex 300 at Daytona International Speedway on February 22, 1969.

GRAND NATIONAL STANDINGS

	DRIVER	STARTS	WINS	POINTS	MONEY
1.	Ned Jarrett	54	13	38,824	93,625
2.	Dick Hutcherson	52	9	35,790	57,851
3.	Darel Dieringer	35	1	24,696	52,214
4.	G. C. Spencer	47	0	24,314	29,775
5.	Marvin Panch	20	4	22,798	64,027
6.	Bob Derrington	51	0	21,394	20,120
7.	J. T. Putney	40	0	20,928	22,329
8.	Neil Cates	51	0	20,848	22,329
9.	Buddy Baker	42	0	20,672	26,837
10.	Cale Yarborough	46	1	20,192	26,587
11.	Wendell Scott	52	0	19,902	18,639
12.	Junior Johnson	36	13	18,486	60,216
13.	Fred Lorenzen	17	4	18,448	80,615
14.	Paul Lewis	24	0	18,118	13,247
15.	E. J. Trivette	39	0	13,450	13,248
16.	Larry Hess	10	0	13,148	9,260
17.	Buck Baker	31	0	13,136	21,580
18.	Jimmy Helms	30	0	12,996	12,050
19.	Doug Cooper	30	0	12,920	12,380
20.	Bobby Johns	13	0	12,842	24,930
21.	Tiny Lund	30	1	12,820	11,750
22.	Buddy Arrington	31	0	11,744	11,600
23.	Earl Balmer	9	0	11,636	19,045
24.	Sam McQuagg	14	0	11,460	10,555
25.	Elmo Langley	34	0	10,982	10,555
26.	Henley Gray	38	0	9,552	8,320
27.	Roy Mayne	14	0	8,838	9,060
28.	Junior Spencer	21	0	8,436	9,345
29.	H. B. Bailey	5	0	7,340	5,000
30.	Wayne Smith	25	0	7,326	6,790
31.	Donald Tucker	9	0	7,118	5,680
32.	Tom Pistone	33	0	6,598	10,050
33.	Bub Strickler	9	0	6,540	5,275

34.	Bobby Allison	8	0	6,152	4,780
35.	Jim Paschal	10	0	6,046	7,805
36.	Roy Tyner	28	0	5,882	6,505
37.	LeeRoy Yarbrough	14	0	5,852	5,905
38.	Richard Petty	14	4	5,638	16,450
39.	Curtis Turner	7	1	5,542	17,440
40.	David Pearson	14	2	5,464	8,925
41.	Clyde Lynn	24	0	5,414	4,545
42.	Gene Block	18	0	4,970	6,080
43.	Ned Setzer	8	0	4,828	4,805
44.	Stick Elliott	15	0	4,332	4,985
45.	Reb Wickersham	7	0	4,322	4,410
46.	Frank Warren	4	0	3,814	2,880
47.	Worth McMillion	10	0	3,794	2,590
48.	Lionel Johnson	8	0	3,510	3,105
49.	Bud Moore	14	0	3,216	3,434
50.	Sonny Hutchins	10	0	3,118	3,780

1966

AT A GLANCE:

Grand National Champion: David Pearson

Notable Event: That'll show 'em. After winning only 6 times in 1965, Chrysler products combined for 34 victories in 49 races in 1966. David Pearson won 15 in Dodges, Richard Petty 8 in Plymouths, Paul Goldsmith 3 in Plymouths, Jim Paschal 2 in Plymouths, and Earl Balmer, Sam McQuagg, and LeeRoy Yarbrough 1 each in Dodges. Jim Hurtabise, Marvin Panch, and Paul Lewis each won once in Plymouths.

Top Newcomers: South Carolina native James Hylton proved that championship-caliber drivers and winners could be mutually exclusive. He was winless in 41 starts, but his 20 top-5s and 32 top-10s helped him finish second in the points race, just behind 15-time winner David Pearson but ahead of Richard Petty, Henley Gray, and Paul Goldsmith. To prove it wasn't a fluke, Hylton was 0-for-46 and also finished second the following year.

David Pearson got the first of his three titles with one of the best seasons in NASCAR history. At the time, his 15 victories was second only to Tim Flock's 18 in winning the 1955 championship. Pearson had 26 top-5s and 33 top-10s and beat Hylton by 1,950 points. Nobody else reached double-figures in victories: Petty won eight; Goldsmith, Dick Hutcherson, Bobby Allison, and Darel Dieringer three each; and Elmo Langley, Fred Lorenzen, and Jim Paschal two wins apiece. Single victories went to Marvin Panch, Paul Lewis, Sam McQuagg, Tiny Lund, LeeRoy Yarbrough, and Earl Balmer.

GRAND NATIONAL STANDINGS

	DRIVER	STARTS	WINS	POINTS	MONEY
1.	David Pearson	42	15	35,638	78,194
2.	James Hylton	41	0	33,688	38,723
3.	Richard Petty	39	8	22,952	94,666
4.	Henley Gray	45	0	22,468	21,901
5.	Paul Goldsmith	21	3	22,078	54,609
6.	Wendell Scott	45	0	21,702	23,052
7.	John Sears	46	0	21,432	25,192
8.	J. T. Putney	39	0	21,208	18,653

9.	Neil Castles	41	0	20,446	19,035
10.	Bobby Allison	33	3	19,910	23,420
11.	Elmo Langley	47	2	19,116	22,455
12.	Darel Dieringer	25	3	18,214	52,530
13.	Ned Jarrett	21	0	17,616	23,255
14.	Jim Paschal	18	2	16,404	30,985
15.	Sam McQuagg	16	1	16,000	29,530
16.	Paul Lewis	21	1	15,352	17,827
17.	Marvin Panch	14	1	15,308	38,432
18.	Cale Yarborough	14	0	15,188	24,077
19.	G. C. Spencer	20	0	15,028	26,722
20.	Clyde Lynn	40	0	14,856	13,222
21.	Buck Baker	36	0	14,504	13,860
22.	Buddy Baker	41	0	14,302	21,325
23.	Fred Lorenzen	11	2	12,454	36,310
24.	Curtis Turner	21	0	12,266	16,890
25.	Roy Mayne	18	0	11,074	9,940
26.	LeeRoy Yarbrough	9	1	10,528	23,925
27.	J. D. McDuffie	36	0	9,572	8,545
28.	Dick Hutcherson	14	3	9,392	22,985
29.	Tiny Lund	31	1	9,332	11,880
30.	Blackie Watt	20	0	8,518	7,000
31.	Frank Warren	11	0	8,334	6,740
32.	Buddy Arrington	25	0	7,636	8,510
33.	Jimmy Helms	29	0	7,442	9,835
34.	Jimmy Helms	29	0	6,530	5,815
35.	Stick Elliott	19	0	6,358	7,335
36.	Earl Balmer	9	1	5,794	7,935
37.	Tom Pistone	28	0	5,788	7,765
38.	Johnny Wynn	21	0	5,644	4,650
39.	Larry Manning	13	0	4,964	3,920
40.	Larry Hess	13	0	4,928	5,290
41.	Roy Tyner	26	0	4,248	4,435
42.	Bill Seifert	15	0	4,128	3,830
43.	Bob Derrington	11	0	4,122	2,730
44.	Joel Davis	21	0	4,066	4,685
45.	Paul Connors	3	0	3,986	2,820
46.	Jabe Thomas	13	0	3,820	3,580
47.	Doug Cooper	21	0	3,808	5,185
48.	Junior Johnson	7	0	3,750	3,610
49.	Larry Frank	2	0	3,738	1,575

1967

AT A GLANCE:

Grand National Champion: Richard Petty

Notable Events: Mario Andretti, better known for Indy car and Grand Prix racing, did pretty well in his first NASCAR race. Given a shot with the potent Holman-Moody team, he used every bit of asphalt in winning the Daytona 500. Thirty years later his nephew, John, earned his first NASCAR victory in the midsummer Pepsi 400 on the same track.

Top Newcomer: Donnie Allison became the latest in a series of brothers to run the tour, joining his brother Bobby as a full-timer. Donnie won Rookie of the Year based on 20 starts, 4 top-5s, and 4 top-10s.

It takes only two words to describe the 49-race 1967 season: Richard Petty. He won his second championship based on 27 victories in 48 starts, including 10 in a row between August and early October. As if that wasn't enough, he added 11 more top-5s and 2 more top-10s, and beat winless James Hylton by 6,028 points. Two-time winner Dick Hutcherson was third, six-time winner Bobby Allison was fourth, and winless John Sears finished fifth in the final accounting.

There was no secret to Petty's success—he and his blue No. 43 Plymouth were simply better than everyone else. He won 16 races on asphalt and 11 on dirt. He won four superspeedway races (two at Darlington and one each at Rockingham and Trenton) and won on tracks as short as $\frac{1}{5}$-mile (Islip, New York). His 10-race winning streak began August 12 at Winston-Salem and continued in Columbia, Savannah, Darlington, Hickory, Richmond, North Wilkesboro, Hillsborough, Martinsville, and Beltsville (Maryland). That performance remains the most dominating season in NASCAR history.

With Petty winning 27 times, there weren't many races for anyone else. Bobby Allison won six times; Jim Paschal four; Hutcherson, Cale Yarborough, and David Pearson twice each; and Parnelli Jones, LeeRoy Yarbrough, Fred Lorenzen, Buddy Baker, and Darel Dieringer once each. Baker joined Richard Petty as the only second-generation drivers to win a NASCAR race. Baker's father, Buck, was a two-time champion and a strong driver in his own right.

GRAND NATIONAL STANDINGS

	DRIVER	STARTS	WINS	POINTS	MONEY
1.	Richard Petty	48	27	42,472	150,197
2.	James Hylton	46	0	36,444	49,732
3.	Dick Hutcherson	33	2	33,658	85,160
4.	Bobby Allison	45	6	30,812	58,250
5.	John Sears	41	0	29,078	28,937
6.	Jim Paschal	45	4	27,624	60,123
7.	David Pearson	22	2	26,302	72,651
8.	Neil Castles	36	0	23,218	20,683
9.	Elmo Langley	45	0	22,286	23,998
10.	Wendell Scott	45	0	20,700	19,510
11.	Paul Goldsmith	21	0	20,402	38,732
12.	Darel Dieringer	19	1	19,698	34,710
13.	Clyde Lynn	44	0	18,600	19,520
14.	Bobby Isaac	12	0	18,298	24,475
15.	Buddy Baker	20	1	17,502	46,950
16.	Donnie Allison	20	0	16,752	17,614
17.	Henley Gray	43	0	16,292	15,987
18.	J. T. Putney	29	0	16,228	15,687
19.	Tiny Lund	19	0	15,240	17,332
20.	Cale Yarborough	16	2	14,676	57,912
21.	G. C. Spencer	29	0	11,444	20,225
22.	Bill Seifert	41	0	9,992	11,905
23.	Charlie Glotzbach	9	0	9,952	14,790
24.	Frank Warren	12	0	9,768	9,185
25.	Earl Brooks	34	0	9,450	8,610
26.	Buddy Arrington	15	0	9,372	7,720
27.	Buck Baker	21	0	9,268	7,560
28.	Wayne Smith	27	0	9,262	10,225
29.	Fred Lorenzen	5	1	9,078	17,875
30.	Roy Mayne	14	0	8,820	8,830
31.	Bobby Wawak	14	0	8,492	8,070
32.	Friday Hassler	21	0	8,448	10,265
33.	Paul Lewis	14	0	7,812	8,620
34.	Sonny Hutchins	7	0	7,400	6,385
35.	Bud Moore	6	0	7,012	7,200
36.	Sam McQuagg	15	0	5,850	9,845
37.	LeeRoy Yarbrough	15	1	5,676	15,325
38.	Don Biederman	22	0	5,434	5,935
39.	Ramo Stott	3	0	5,254	3,335
40.	George Davis	21	0	5,006	4,400
41.	Jack Harden	10	0	4,936	4,450
42.	Paul Dean Holt	24	0	4,040	4,220
43.	Roy Tyner	27	0	3,954	8,170
44.	Bill Champion	11	0	3,780	6,205
45.	Dick Johnson	23	0	3,730	5,070
46.	George Poulos	23	0	3,780	3,040
47.	Bill Dennis	3	0	3,730	2,335
48.	Doug Cooper	21	0	3,666	5,665
49.	Ed Negre	14	0	3,578	3,805
50.	H. B. Bailey	3	0	3,482	3,850

1968

AT A GLANCE:

Grand National Champion: David Pearson

Notable Event: Cale Yarborough began the season with three career victories and ended it with three times that many. He burst into the spotlight by winning both races at Daytona Beach, one each near Atlanta and at Darlington, and one each on short tracks at Martinsville and Jefferson (Georgia).

Top Newcomer: Pete Hamilton was one of the first college graduates to come into big-time stock car racing. The University of Massachusetts grad headed south from Dedham, Massachusetts, and went Grand National racing after making his mark in NASCAR's Sportsman division.

Two future Hall of Fame drivers made 1968 their personal playground. David Pearson and Richard Petty each won 16 of the season's 49 races (more than everyone else combined) and finished first (Pearson) and third (Petty) in points. And despite winning only three times and not having as many top-5s and top-10s, Bobby Isaac was second in points. Winless drivers Clyde Lynn and John Sears were fourth and fifth in points. In fact, other than Pearson, Isaac, and Petty, nobody else in the top 10 won a race. Cale Yarborough won six, LeeRoy Yarbrough and Bobby Allison two each, and Donnie Allison, Buddy Baker, and Charlie Glotzbach one each.

By now, the move toward paved tracks had become inevitable. Indeed, only 5 of the season's 49 races were on dirt: 2 each at Greensville and Columbia, and the spring race at Richmond. When the tour returned to Richmond in the fall, it too had been paved. But while asphalt was replacing dirt, most of the NASCAR tracks were still less than a mile long. Only 7 of the 24 Grand National facilities were superspeedways. In fact, it was commonplace for teams to race on a $\frac{1}{2}$-mile or shorter track at midweek and at a superspeedway three days later.

GRAND NATIONAL STANDINGS

	DRIVER	STARTS	WINS	POINTS	MONEY
1.	David Pearson	48	16	3,499	133,065
2.	Bobby Isaac	49	3	3,373	60,342
3.	Richard Petty	49	16	3,123	99,535
4.	Clyde Lynn	49	0	3,041	29,226
5.	John Sears	49	0	3,017	29,179
6.	Elmo Langley	48	0	2,823	25,832
7.	James Hylton	41	0	2,719	32,608
8.	Jabe Thomas	48	0	2,687	21,166
9.	Wendell Scott	48	0	2,685	20,498
10.	Roy Tyner	8	0	2,504	20,247
11.	Bobby Allison	37	2	2,454	52,288
12.	Neil Castles	44	0	2,330	19,507
13.	Buddy Baker	38	1	2,310	56,023
14.	Bill Seifert	44	0	2,175	18,403
15.	Earl Brooks	40	0	1,957	14,233
16.	LeeRoy Yarbrough	26	2	1,894	87,920
17.	Cale Yarborough	21	6	1,804	138,052
18.	Paul Dean Holt	40	0	1,723	8,986
19.	Charlie Glotzbach	22	1	1,693	43,101
20.	Henley Gray	30	0	1,559	12,566
21.	Darel Dieringer	18	0	1,525	28,215
22.	Tiny Lund	7	0	1,443	17,775
23.	G. C. Spencer	26	0	1,401	10,120
24.	J. D. McDuffie	32	0	1,370	8,335
25.	Donnie Allison	13	1	1,307	50,815
26.	Stan Meserve	31	0	1,274	7,475
27.	Friday Hassler	20	0	1,224	12,000
28.	Bill Champion	18	0	1,155	10,170
29.	Bud Moore	16	0	1,086	12,325
30.	Paul Goldsmith	15	0	1,020	24,365
31.	Ed Negre	24	0	928	4,985
32.	Pete Hamilton	16	0	919	7,920
33.	Wayne Smith	18	0	901	7,235
34.	Dave Marcis	10	0	851	7,099
35.	Don Tarr	12	0	827	7,510
36.	E. J. Trivette	13	0	821	8,295
37.	Dick Johnson	11	0	735	5,920
38.	Bob Cooper	14	0	668	4,485
39.	Buck Baker	17	0	650	3,580
40.	Walson Gardner	14	0	640	4,275
41.	Larry Manning	12	0	640	6,995
42.	Frank Warren	10	0	611	5,365
43.	Jerry Grant	7	0	559	5,665
44.	Frog Fagan	12	0	531	3,680
45.	Richard Brickhouse	7	0	514	7,190
46.	Jim Hurtubise	6	0	504	4,490
47.	Curtis Turner	6	0	456	5,850
48.	Bobby Johns	7	0	453	5,010
49.	Eddie Yarboro	6	0	447	2,255
50.	Red Farmer	7	0	407	4,810

1969

AT A GLANCE:

Grand National Champion: David Pearson

Notable Event: The only organized driver boycott in NASCAR history marred the opening of the 2.66-mile superspeedway at Talladega, Alabama. Many of NASCAR's top stars left early rather than risk running laps in excess of 200 miles per hour on tires they considered dangerously inadequate. But the show went on and unheralded Richard Brickhouse got his only victory in a winged Dodge Daytona.

Top Newcomers: Dick Brooks came from the mountains around Porterville, California, with nothing but dreams and determination. He fielded his own cars when he could and found enough other rides to start 28 races. He had 3 top-5s and 12 top-10s. And after testing the waters in 1968, Wisconsin native Dave Marcis moved south to become a NASCAR regular in 1969.

David Pearson won his third and final championship, but that was only half the story. New superspeedways were everywhere, and NASCAR moved to gain a foothold in areas once thought off-limits. Bill France opened the 2.66-mile track at Talladega and a new 1-mile track opened in Dover, Delaware. Teams made their first trip to a year-old, 2-mile speedway just west of Detroit and to a similar 2-mile track near College Station, Texas. Again, there were only 5 dirt-track races on the 54-race schedule: 2 each at two tracks in South Carolina and 1 in North Carolina.

Pearson won 11 races in 51 starts, had 42 top-5s, 44 top-10s, and won a then-record $229,760. Petty won 10 times in 50 starts, third-ranked James Hylton was 0-for-52, fourth-ranked Neil Castles was 0-for-53, and fifth-ranked Elmo Langley was 0-for-54. The most successful driver of the season was sixth-ranked Bobby Isaac, who won 17 races, had 29 top-5s, and 33 top-10s in 50 starts. LeeRoy Yarbrough won 7 races, Bobby Allison 5, Cale Yarborough 2, and Donnie Allison and Richard Brickhouse 1 each.

GRAND NATIONAL STANDINGS

	DRIVER	STARTS	WINS	POINTS	MONEY
1.	David Pearson	51	11	4,170	229,760
2.	Richard Petty	50	10	3,813	129,906
3.	James Hylton	52	0	3,750	114,416
4.	Neil Castles	51	0	3,530	54,367
5.	Elmo Langley	52	0	3,383	73,092
6.	Bobby Isaac	50	17	3,301	92,074
7.	John Sears	52	0	3,166	52,281
8.	Jabe Thomas	51	0	3,103	44,989
9.	Wendell Scott	51	0	3,015	47,451
10.	Cecil Gordon	51	0	3,002	39,679
11.	E. J. Trivette	49	0	2,988	35,896
12.	Bill Champion	49	0	2,813	33,656
13.	Bill Seifert	50	0	2,765	44,361
14.	J. D. McDuffie	50	0	2,741	30,861
15.	Ben Arnold	48	0	2,736	33,256
16.	LeeRoy Yarborough	30	7	2,712	193,211
17.	Henley Gray	48	0	2,517	29,335
18.	Earl Brooks	49	0	2,454	34,793
19.	Dave Marcis	37	0	2,348	32,383
20.	Bobby Allison	27	5	2,055	69,483
21.	Dick Brooks	28	0	1,780	28,187
22.	Buddy Baker	18	0	1,769	62,928
23.	Cale Yarborough	19	2	1,715	74,240
24.	Donnie Allison	16	1	1,662	78,055
25.	Richard Brickhouse	24	1	1,660	45,637
26.	G. C. Spencer	26	0	1,562	21,660
27.	Ed Negre	31	0	1,465	15,160
28.	Friday Hassler	18	0	1,421	17,690
29.	Frank Warren	23	0	1,299	15,677
30.	Hass Ellington	15	0	1,210	16,552
31.	Roy Tyner	21	0	1,191	12,302
32.	Ed Hessert	16	0	1,113	17,690
33.	Buddy Arrington	16	0	1,099	12,975
34.	Dick Johnson	22	0	1,055	11,182
35.	Buddy Young	21	0	981	15,542
36.	Dub Simpson	20	0	959	12,915
37.	Charlie Glotzbach	12	0	944	36,090
38.	Roy Mayne	13	0	922	10,340

Tiny Lund, who operated a fishing camp in South Carolina when he wasn't racing, proudly shows off his new Chevy Camaro in this June 1971 photo.

39.	Wayne Smith	16	0	922	10,610
40.	Paul Goldsmith	11	0	892	22,305
41.	Don Tarr	12	0	855	13,720
42.	Ken Meisenhelder	16	0	627	5,630
43.	Pete Hazelwood	16	0	598	4,160
44.	Sonny Hutchins	8	0	535	9,552
45.	Wayne Gillette	16	0	509	5,827
46.	Paul Dean Holt	14	0	485	4,442
47.	Johnny Holford	8	0	465	4,200
48.	Ray Elder	4	0	433	7,200
49.	John Kennedy	9	0	417	6,462
50.	Dick Poling	12	0	408	5,467

1970

AT A GLANCE:

Grand National Champion: Bobby Isaac

Notable Events: Richard Petty (who else, right?) made history on September 30 with his 117th career victory, this one at the ½-mile State Fairgrounds Speedway in Raleigh. The Home State 200 was the third dirt-track race of the season and the last in Grand National history.

Top Newcomers: Bill Dennis graduated from weekend races on Virginia's short tracks and made 25 starts in his cars and those of several owners. He didn't win or get any top-5s, but had five top-10s. He was seen by many at NASCAR as more media-presentable than Minnesota native Joe Frasson (22 starts and 2 top-10s) his chief rival for Rookie of the Year.

After being second in 1968 and sixth in 1969, Bobby Isaac, crew chief Harry Hyde, and owner Nord Krauskopf had a storybook season. They won 11 races in 47 starts and backed that up with 32 top-5s and 38 top-10s. Three-time winner Bobby Allison was a closer-than-expected second, falling only 51 points short despite running one fewer race. James Hylton, who finally got his first Grand National victory at Richmond in the spring and also had 38 other top-10 finishes, was third. Eighteen-time winner Richard Petty was fourth (he missed six races due to injuries and sat out two more) and winless Neil Castles was fifth.

With Isaac (11 wins) and Petty (18 wins) dominating the season, it was up to everyone else to get whatever leftovers he could. In addition to Allison and Hylton, that meant Pete Hamilton (three superspeedway victories as Petty's teammate); Buddy Baker, LeeRoy Yarbrough, and David Pearson (one victory each), Cale Yarborough and Donnie Allison (three each), and two for Charlie Glotzbach.

GRAND NATIONAL STANDINGS

	DRIVER	STARTS	WINS	POINTS	MONEY
1.	Bobby Isaac	47	11	3,911	199,600
2.	Bobby Allison	46	3	3,860	149,745
3.	James Hylton	47	1	3,788	78,201
4.	Richard Petty	40	18	3,447	151,124
5.	Neil Castles	47	0	3,158	49,746
6.	Elmo Langley	47	0	3,154	45,193
7.	Jabe Thomas	46	0	3,120	42,958
8.	Benny Parsons	45	0	2,993	59,402
9.	Dave Marcis	47	0	2,820	41,111
10.	Frank Warren	46	0	2,697	35,161
11.	Cecil Gordon	44	0	2,514	32,713
12.	John Sears	40	0	2,465	32,675
13.	Dick Brooks	34	0	2,460	53,754
14.	Wendell Scott	41	0	2,425	28,518
15.	Bill Champion	38	0	2,350	30,943
16.	J. D. McDuffie	36	0	2,079	24,905
17.	Ben Arnold	29	0	1,997	25,805
18.	Bill Seifert	39	0	1,962	25,647
19.	Henley Gray	34	0	1,871	23,130
20.	Friday Hassler	26	0	1,831	27,535
21.	Pete Hamilton	16	3	1,819	131,406
22.	Joe Frasson	21	0	1,723	20,172
23.	David Pearson	19	1	1,716	87,118
24.	Buddy Baker	18	1	1,555	63,510
25.	Bill Dennis	25	0	1,432	15,630
26.	Ed Negre	31	0	1,413	14,580
27.	G. C. Spencer	20	0	1,410	17,915
28.	Charlie Glotzbach	19	2	1,358	50,649
29.	Roy Mayne	16	0	1,333	16,910
30.	Bill Shirley	29	0	1,244	12,215
31.	Raymond Williams	21	0	1,204	12,535
32.	Larry Baumel	23	0	1,138	16,645
33.	Buddy Arrington	19	0	1,087	16,845
34.	Cale Yarborough	19	3	1,016	115,875
35.	Don Tarr	17	0	995	16,592
36.	Johnny Halford	25	0	975	15,645
37.	Earl Brooks	21	0	884	10,340
38.	Coo Coo Marlin	13	0	876	14,799
39.	Ron Keselowski	17	0	855	11,985
40.	Donnie Allison	19	3	841	96,081
41.	Ken Meisenhelder	19	0	812	7,020
42.	Roy Tyner	14	0	631	5,565
43.	LeeRoy Yarbrough	19	1	625	61,930
44.	Dick May	16	0	551	4,510
45.	Jim Vandiver	14	0	519	16,080
46.	John Kenney	11	0	457	4,115
47.	Dub Simpson	6	0	367	4,510
48.	Lee Roy Carrigg	9	0	355	4,130
49.	Joe Phipps	7	0	325	4,090
50.	Wayne Smith	8	0	300	4,505

1971

AT A GLANCE:

Grand National Champion: Richard Petty

Notable Event: That sigh of relief was from drivers, crewmen, and fans exhaling after years of 40-, 50-, and 60-race seasons. Finally, after being obsessed with presenting as much of its product as possible, NASCAR chose to make 1971 the last of its "long" seasons. No more midweek races on backwater short tracks and no more multirace weeks. Finally, NASCAR and its new sponsor—the R. J. Reynolds Co.—created a national series that made sense.

Top Newcomers: Walter Ballard was the latest in a long line of Texans (after Shorty Rollins and Billy Wade) to come to the Southeast to race. He started 41 of 48 races, had 3 top-5s, and 11 top-10s. He was NASCAR's second rookie (after James Hylton) to finish among the top 10 in points. Another relative newcomer who began making himself more obvious was Richard Childress.

Richard Petty (21) and Bobby Allison (11) dominated, combining to win 32 of the year's 48 races. The other 16 were divided among Bobby Isaac (4); 2-time winners David Pearson, A. J. Foyt, and Tiny Lund; and 1-time winners Pete Hamilton, Buddy Baker, Benny Parsons, Donnie Allison, Charlie Glotzbach, and Ray Elder. And just how dominant were Petty and Allison? They combined for 17 victories in 20 races during one stretch of the season and ended the season winning 7 of 8. Petty won the championship after Allison missed 14 races and finished a distant fourth. Winless James Hylton and Cecil Gordon were second and third, respectively, and Elmo Langley was fifth.

At the end of the season, 13 short tracks were cut from the schedule. It had been a good run, but NASCAR had to move ahead. It needed new venues with tens of thousands of seats and better facilities for the print media and, perhaps most importantly, better ability to accommodate the increasingly important presence of television. And it was clear by the early 1970s that while long-distance superspeedway racing might not be as exciting as 30 cars on a ⅓-mile track, it was the future of the sport. In Daytona Beach, they called it progress.

GRAND NATIONAL STANDINGS

	DRIVER	STARTS	WINS	POINTS	MONEY
1.	Richard Petty	46	21	4,435	351,071
2.	James Hylton	46	0	4,071	90,282
3.	Cecil Gordon	46	0	3,677	69,080
4.	Bobby Allison	42	11	3,636	254,316
5.	Elmo Langley	46	0	3,356	57,037
6.	Jabe Thomas	43	0	3,200	48,241
7.	Bill Champion	45	0	3,058	43,769
8.	Frank Warren	47	0	2,886	40,072

9.	J. D. McDuffie	43	0	2,862	35,578
10.	Walter Ballard	41	0	2,633	30,974
11.	Benny Parsons	35	1	2,611	55,896
12.	Ed Negre	43	0	2,528	29,738
13.	Bill Seifert	37	0	2,403	33,220
14.	Henley Gray	39	0	2,392	31,789
15.	Buddy Baker	19	1	2,358	115,150
16.	Friday Hassler	29	0	2,277	37,305
17.	Earl Brooks	35	0	2,205	25,360
18.	Bill Dennis	28	0	2,181	29,420
19.	Wendell Scott	37	0	2,180	21,701
20.	John Sears	37	0	2,167	26,735
21.	Dave Marcis	29	0	2,049	37,582
22.	Neil Castles	38	0	2,036	22,939
23.	Bobby Isaac	25	4	1,819	106,526
24.	Pete Hamilton	22	1	1,739	60,440
25.	Joe Frasson	17	0	1,619	20,975
26.	Ben Arnold	18	0	1,618	18,491
27.	Ron Keselowski	20	0	1,446	17,680
28.	Bill Shirley	27	0	1,303	9,160
29.	Donnie Allison	13	1	1,280	69,995
30.	Dean Dalton	19	0	1,276	13,910
31.	Raymond Williams	20	0	1,270	14,585
32.	Dick May	22	0	1,090	9,225
33.	Charlie Roberts	19	0	1,053	12,470
34.	G. C. Spencer	17	0	1,008	11,470
35.	Richard Brown	13	0	967	11,940
36.	Dick Brooks	20	0	939	32,921
37.	Larry Baumel	16	0	904	10,910
38.	Maynard Troyer	13	0	879	13,115
39.	Roy Mayne	11	0	852	10,330
40.	Ken Meisenhelder	15	0	797	5,405
41.	Tommy Gade	9	0	729	8,800
42.	Charlie Glotzbach	20	1	699	38,605
43.	Bill Hollar	11	0	644	4,275
44.	Marv Acton	11	0	627	8,620
45.	Fred Lorenzen	14	0	611	45,100
46.	Richard Childress	12	0	601	3,855
47.	Paul Tyler	10	0	561	6,360
48.	Jim Vandiver	7	0	553	13,575
49.	Coo Coo Marlin	12	0	527	9,085
50.	Eddie Yarboro	7	0	497	3,685

1972

AT A GLANCE

Winston Cup Champion: Richard Petty

Notable Events: The first year of the Winston Cup series featured a $100,000 point fund based on a driver's standing after the 31 "major" events, all 250 miles or more. The season also saw the January transfer of power from NASCAR founder and president Bill France Sr., 62, to his 28-year-old son, Bill Jr.

Top Newcomers: Rookie of the Year Larry Smith, from Lenoir, North Carolina, had seven top-10s. Tragically, he was killed just a year later in August 1973 during a race at Talladega. The 1972 season also saw Kentucky native Darrell Waltrip run several races in preparation for taking the tour by storm in a few years.

On the track, the Richard Petty–Bobby Allison feud heated up. Allison, in a Chevrolet, and Petty, in a Plymouth, frequently dented each other's cars. It happened in the fall at Richmond and Martinsville, where Petty beat Allison both times after serious contact. A few weeks later, at North Wilkesboro, they traded the lead 10 times before Petty won by two car lengths. Afterward,

the two were fuming. Said Petty: "There's not going to be any trouble until he hurts me. He's playing with my life out there. If I had films of this, I could sue him for assault with intent to kill, or something close to that." Replied Allison: "He hit me so hard that it bent my fender in. When he did that, I just ran back into him.".

Allison led the tour with 10 victories (including 7 on superspeedways) but still lost the championship to Petty by 128 points. Petty won 8 times, David Pearson 6, and Buddy Baker and A. J. Foyt twice each. James Hylton, Bobby Isaac, and California driver Ray Elder also won 1 race each. In addition to the most victories, Allison also led with 11 poles in 31 attempts. He and Petty each led in 30 of the 31 races, 10 more than Isaac.

WINSTON CUP STANDINGS

	DRIVER	STARTS	WINS	POINTS	MONEY
1.	Richard Petty	31	8	8,701	339,405
2.	Bobby Allison	31	10	8,573	348,939
3.	James Hylton	31	1	8,158	126,705
4.	Cecil Gordon	31	0	7,326	73,126
5.	Benny Parsons	31	0	6,844	102,043
6.	Walter Ballard	31	0	6,781	59,745
7.	Elmo Langley	30	0	6,656	59,644
8.	John Sears	28	0	6,298	51,314
9.	Dean Dalton	29	0	6,295	42,299
10.	Ben Arnold	26	0	6,179	44,547
11.	Frank Warren	30	0	5,788	45,048
12.	Jabe Thomas	28	0	5,772	43,438
13.	Bill Champion	29	0	5,740	42,242
14.	Raymond Williams	28	0	5,712	37,000
15.	Dave Marcis	27	0	5,459	45,012
16.	Charlie Roberts	26	0	5,354	32,488
17.	Henley Gray	28	0	5,093	38,461
18.	J. D. McDuffie	27	0	5,075	36,883
19.	Bobby Isaac	27	1	5,050	133,257
20.	David Pearson	17	6	4,718	142,440
21.	Ed Negre	26	0	4,696	30,538
22.	Buddy Arrington	20	0	4,555	28,700
23.	Larry Smith	23	0	4,173	24,215
24.	Buddy Baker	17	2	3,936	102,540
25.	Coo Coo Marlin	20	0	3,852	28,124
26.	David Ray Boggs	24	0	3,739	19,489
27.	Ron Keselowski	22	0	3,475	21,905
28.	Joe Frasson	16	0	3,152	21,570
29.	Richard Brown	16	0	2,939	19,283
30.	Neil Castles	21	0	2,789	18,760
31.	Jim Vandiver	16	0	2,514	27,983
32.	Clarence Lovell	12	0	2,360	10,770
33.	David Sisco	12	0	2,310	13,700
34.	LeeRoy Yarbrough	18	0	2,157	40,705
35.	George Althiede	11	0	1,916	10,405
36.	Donnie Allison	10	0	1,849	16,826
37.	Richard Childress	15	0	1,521	7,245
38.	Bill Shirley	13	0	1,468	8,070
39.	Fred Lorenzen	8	0	1,333	19,075
40.	Wendell Scott	6	0	1,317	5,830
41.	Tommy Gale	6	0	1,298	7,197
42.	Bill Dennis	11	0	1,279	9,604
43.	G. C. Spencer	10	0	1,238	8,040
44.	Dick May	6	0	1,229	5,370
45.	Hershel McGriff	4	0	1,199	12,290
46.	Les Covey	7	0	1,128	5,070
47.	Johnny Halford	5	0	1,103	4,955
48.	Pete Hamilton	5	0	1,083	8,005
49.	Dick Brooks	14	0	1,023	14,146
50.	Eddie Yarboro	6	0	1,007	3,435

During the 1970s and 1980s, this certainly became a common photo—Richard Petty celebrating a victory in the Daytona 500. Here, he poses with the Governor's Cup after winning the 1971 race on February 15. The win was Petty's third of what would become a record-setting seven Daytona 500 crowns.

1973

AT A GLANCE

Winston Cup Champion: Benny Parsons

Notable Events: The carburetor "sleeves" were replaced by restrictor plates for the July 4 race at Daytona. The change reflected an effort (ongoing, by the way) to limit the speed of cars in hopes they would be safer for fans and competitors.

Top Newcomers: Rookie of the Year Lennie Pond, from Petersburg, Virginia (one top-5 finish, nine top-10s); Richard Childress (one top-5, two top-10s); Darrell Waltrip (one top-5, five top-10s).

David Pearson won 11 of the 18 races he started for the Wood Brothers but wasn't a Winston Cup contender because of his limited schedule. Richard Petty won 6 races and Cale Yarborough (back in NASCAR after an ill-fated Indy car career), won 4. Buddy Baker and Bobby Allison each won 2, and series champion Benny Parsons, Indy car star Mark Donohue, and journeyman driver Dick Brooks 1 each.

When NASCAR ruled that restrictor plates, which limit the air and fuel intake in an engine and thus result in lower speeds, would be used starting with the Firecracker 400 at Daytona, Harry Hyde was furious. Hyde, the crew chief on Buddy Baker's K & K Insurance Dodge, said, "We are being unfairly penalized. If everybody did things like NASCAR, pro basketball would make Wilt Chamberlain play on his knees."

Parsons took a 194-point lead over Petty into the finale at Rockingham. On lap 13, Parsons wrecked with Johnny Barnes. Parsons's severely damaged car appeared to be done for the day, but members of other crews helped patch it and Parsons cruised around the track, finishing 28th. When Petty dropped out on lap 133, it helped Parsons win his only championship by 67 points over Yarborough.

WINSTON CUP STANDINGS

	DRIVER	STARTS	WINS	POINTS	MONEY
1.	Benny Parsons	28	1	7,173	182,321
2.	Cale Yarborough	28	4	7,106	267,513
3.	Cecil Gordon	28	0	7,046	102,120
4.	James Hylton	28	0	6,972	82,512
5.	Richard Petty	28	6	6,877	234,389

6.	Buddy Baker	27	2	6,327	190,531
7.	Bobby Allison	27	2	6,272	161,818
8.	Walter Ballard	28	0	5,955	53,875
9.	Elmo Langley	27	0	5,826	49,542
10.	J. D. McDuffie	27	0	5,743	56,140
11.	Jabe Thomas	25	0	5,637	42,955
12.	Buddy Arrington	26	0	5,483	40,877
13.	David Pearson	18	11	5,382	228,408
14.	Henley Gray	24	0	5,215	34,112
15.	Richard Childress	25	0	5,169	37,880
16.	Frank Warren	26	0	4,992	36,551
17.	David Sisco	23	0	4,986	36,205
18.	Ed Negre	24	0	4,942	34,235
19.	Dean Dalton	26	0	4,712	35,954
20.	Charlie Roberts	24	0	4,695	32,144
21.	Bill Champion	26	0	4,447	31,828
22.	Coo Coo Marlin	21	0	4,233	29,997
23.	Lennie Pond	23	0	4,013	25,155
24.	Dave Marcis	23	0	3,973	30,253
25.	Raymond Williams	22	0	3,708	22,728
26.	Bobby Isaac	19	0	3,352	84,550
27.	Dick Brooks	14	1	3,200	55,369
28.	Darrell Waltrip	19	0	2,968	42,466
29.	Joe Frasson	14	0	2,952	25,834
30.	Vic Parsons	18	0	2,929	18,200
31.	Jim Vandiver	10	0	2,508	18,586
32.	John Sears	17	0	2,465	16,890
33.	Larry Smith	11	0	2,367	14,090
34.	Rick Newsom	12	0	1,931	8,530
35.	Donnie Allison	14	0	1,755	41,246
36.	D. K. Ulrich	11	0	1,543	3,955
37.	G. C. Spencer	10	0	1,503	12,013
38.	Mel Larson	10	0	1,182	8,235
39.	Johnny Barnes	8	0	1,174	8,585
40.	Eddie Bond	6	0	1,163	6,901
41.	Earle Canavan	5	0	1,144	4,980
42.	Earl Brooks	9	0	1,075	4,880
43.	Charlie Glotzbach	5	0	903	6,451
44.	Randy Tissat	3	0	887	4,245
45.	Ron Keselowski	5	0	879	6,060
46.	Jimmy Crawford	4	0	846	4,059
47.	Richard Brown	13	0	827	7,340
48.	Clarence Lovell	4	0	813	9,175
49.	Bill Dennis	4	0	809	4,225
50.	Jack McCoy	3	0	793	5,270

1974

AT A GLANCE

Winston Cup Champion: Richard Petty

Notable Event: The point system was altered to base points on prize money to encourage drivers to win races or finish high in each event. As it turned out, the system rewarded drivers who finished up front in the big-money races. By midseason, everyone realized the system wasn't working, and NASCAR announced it would be changed.

Top Newcomers: Rookie of the Year Earl Ross from Canada had one win, four top-5s, nine top-10s, and finished eighth in the points standings. Second-generation driver Richie Panch had two top-5s and seven top-10s.

This was the year of the Daytona 450. With the United States facing a fuel crisis, NASCAR moved quickly to avoid being shut down. Led by Bill France Sr., a committee was formed to complete a study on fuel consumption. Its figures showed auto racing ranked seventh in fuel consumption. Vacation travel was first. A government official praised the committee's findings, saying the motorsports group's figures were the best available. Responding to the government's directive to reduce fuel usage by 20 to 25 percent, the Frances canceled the 24 Hours of Daytona and NASCAR trimmed the distances of its races. Richard Petty won the first and only Daytona 450. By midseason, the crisis had eased and normal race distances were restored.

Petty and Cale Yarborough tied for most victories with 10. The other 10 victories in the 30-race season went to David Pearson (7), Bobby Allison (2), and Ross (1). The series continued to move into the Northeast, running at Pocono, Pennsylvania, for the first time. It was becoming clear that only a handful of well-sponsored teams with high-tech parts and equipment could win. The five winners in 1974 were the fewest since five drivers won in the inaugural eight-race NASCAR season of 1949.

WINSTON CUP STANDINGS

	DRIVER	STARTS	WINS	POINTS	MONEY
1.	Richard Petty	30	10	5,037	432,020
2.	Cale Yarborough	30	10	4,470	363,782
3.	David Pearson	19	7	2,389	252,819
4.	Bobby Allison	27	2	2,019	178,437
5.	Benny Parsons	30	0	1,591	185,080
6.	Dave Marcis	30	0	1,378	83,377
7.	Buddy Baker	19	0	1,016	151,025
8.	Earl Ross	21	1	1,009	81,199
9.	Cecil Gordon	30	0	1,000	66,166
10.	David Sisco	28	0	956	58,313
11.	James Hylton	29	0	924	61,385
12.	J. D. McDuffie	30	0	920	59,535
13.	Frank Warren	29	0	820	55,779
14.	Richie Panch	28	0	775	52,713
15.	Walter Ballard	27	0	748	54,039
16.	Richard Childress	29	0	735	50,249
17.	Donnie Allison	21	0	728	60,315
18.	Lennie Pond	22	0	723	55,990
19.	Darrell Waltrip	16	0	609	67,775
20.	Tony Bettenhausen Jr.	27	0	601	38,995
21.	Jackie Rogers	22	0	587	32,367
22.	Coo Coo Marlin	23	0	581	41,759
23.	Ed Negre	26	0	534	24,622
24.	Bob Burcham	20	0	445	27,923
25.	Elmo Langley	23	0	433	24,722
26.	Charlie Glotzbach	14	0	293	33,072
27.	Dick Brooks	16	0	267	22,760
28.	Joe Frasson	14	0	240	22,629
29.	George Follmer	13	0	230	53,780
30.	Buddy Arrington	16	0	221	21,510
31.	Bill Champion	18	0	207	13,480
32.	D. K. Ulrich	15	0	155	11,955
33.	Bobby Isaac	11	0	152	22,642
34.	Travis Tiller	14	0	146	11,410
35.	Roy Mayne	11	0	141	15,284
36.	Dean Dalton	14	0	125	12,375
37.	Neil Castles	14	0	123	12,479
38.	G. C. Spencer	10	0	96	12,985
39.	Ramo Stott	6	0	82	23,705
40.	Jim Vandiver	7	0	71	15,909
41.	Dan Daughtry	8	0	63	12,413
42.	Jabe Thomas	10	0	49	7,445
43.	Gary Bettenhausen	5	0	49	10,350

44.	A. J. Foyt	4	0	41	15,560
45.	Jerry Schlid	5	0	35	8,395
46.	Earle Canavan	6	0	34	6,570
47.	Dick Trickle	3	0	24	10,828
48.	Marty Robbins	4	0	23	5,734
49.	Alton Jones	5	0	20	4,080
50.	Hershel McGriff	5	0	20	8,585

1975

AT A GLANCE

Winston Cup Champion: Richard Petty

Notable Events: The current points system was introduced, one that awarded equal point value to all races. Bonus points for leading laps and the most laps also were involved. The new system encouraged teams to enter all races.

Top Newcomers: Rookie of the Year Bruce Hill from Topeka, Kansas, had 3 top-5s, 11 top-10s, and finished 16th in points. Ricky Rudd made his stock car racing debut with four starts and a 47th-place finish in points.

Concerned about escalating costs, NASCAR instituted an Awards and Achievement Plan, also known as deal money. The teams featuring Richard Petty, Cale Yarborough, Buddy Baker, and Dave Marcis got $3,000 for each superspeedway race and $2,000 for each short-track event. Top-20 independent teams would receive $500 per superspeedway race and $250 for short-track races. The Yarborough and Baker teams, both of them lacking full-season sponsors, balked at entering all 30 races.

Petty set a modern-era record with 13 victories and Baker won 4 races in a team car. One of Petty's victories was in the World 600 at Charlotte, marking his first long-distance win at the 1 ½-mile trioval. In the Daytona 500, David Pearson was leading with three laps remaining when he spun out, allowing Benny Parsons to gain his only 500-mile win at Daytona. Elsewhere, Darrell Waltrip continued to command attention. In May, the 28-year-old won his first race in 50 career starts on his home track in Nashville. Later, Waltrip signed with the DiGard Team after Donnie Allison was released. In October, at Richmond, Waltrip won his first race for DiGard.

During the Talladega 500 in August, NASCAR lost one of its most popular drivers when Tiny Lund was killed. Lund, 42, spun and stopped on the backstretch, where he was hit on the driver's side by rookie Terry Link. Lund died of massive chest injuries. All told, eight drivers won: in addition to Petty's 13 and Baker's 4 wins, Pearson, Yarborough and Bobby Allison each won 3 times, Waltrip won twice, and Parsons and Marcis once each.

WINSTON CUP STANDINGS

	DRIVER	STARTS	WINS	POINTS	MONEY
1.	Richard Petty	30	13	4,783	481,751
2.	Dave Marcis	30	1	4,061	240,646
3.	James Hylton	30	0	3,914	113,642
4.	Benny Parsons	30	1	3,820	214,354
5.	Richard Childress	30	0	3,818	96,780
6.	Cecil Gordon	30	0	3,702	101,467
7.	Darrell Waltrip	28	2	3,462	160,192
8.	Elmo Langley	29	0	3,399	67,600
9.	Cale Yarborough	27	3	3,295	214,691
10.	Dick Brooks	25	0	3,182	93,001
11.	Walter Ballard	30	0	3,151	55,696
12.	Frank Warren	27	0	3,148	55,671
13.	David Sisco	28	0	3,116	62,186
14.	David Pearson	21	3	3,057	192,141
15.	Buddy Baker	23	4	3,050	236,351
16.	Bruce Hill	26	0	3,002	79,428
17.	Ed Negre	29	0	2,982	49,629
18.	J. D. McDuffie	26	0	2,745	50,937
19.	Buddy Arrington	25	0	2,654	45,893
20.	Coo Coo Marlin	23	0	2,584	60,013
21.	Lennie Pond	22	0	2,540	59,265
22.	Jabe Thomas	21	0	2,252	22,390
23.	Carl Adams	20	0	2,182	24,865
24.	Bobby Allison	19	3	2,181	122,435
25.	Bruce Jacobi	15	0	1,732	29,455
26.	Dean Dalton	16	0	1,486	19,430
27.	D. K. Ulrich	16	0	1,453	16,525
28.	Donnie Allison	14	0	1,376	45,595
29.	Richie Panch	14	0	1,243	32,585
30.	Jim Vandiver	13	0	1,228	24,200
31.	Bill Champion	13	0	1,218	11,300
32.	Earle Canavan	12	0	1,062	9,725
33.	Grant Adcox	11	0	1,020	16,540
34.	Joe Mihalic	10	0	957	12,910
35.	Joe Frasson	9	0	939	11,975
36.	Travis Tiller	10	0	922	7,780
37.	Rick Newsom	10	0	877	9,370
38.	Ferrel Harris	10	0	797	16,165
39.	Henley Gray	9	0	747	8,785
40.	G. C. Spencer	9	0	634	14,945
41.	Dick May	9	0	631	11,020
42.	Earl Brooks	7	0	534	4,900
43.	Neil Castles	7	0	529	4,190
44.	Jackie Rodgers	8	0	502	11,000
45.	Harry Jefferson	5	0	455	11,395
46.	Tommy Gale	5	0	437	6,570
47.	Ricky Rudd	4	0	431	4,345
48.	Bobby Isaac	6	0	405	6,695
49.	Dick Skillen	5	0	389	4,865
50.	Ray Elder	3	0	372	8,020

1976

AT A GLANCE

Winston Cup Champion: Cale Yarborough

Notable Event: Presidential candidate Jimmy Carter attended the Atlanta 500, bringing even more attention to the ever-growing sport. Carter, a Georgian, knew his way around the track since he was a former ticket-taker. Since then, dozens (hundreds?) of candidates for political office ranging from sheriff to president have courted the vote of NASCAR fans.

Top Newcomers: Rookie of the Year Skip Manning, from Bogalusa, Louisiana, finished in the top 10 four times and finished 18th in points. And Bill Elliott ran eight unremarkable races and used up his Rookie of the Year eligibility.

Daytona 500 qualifying was in turmoil when A. J. Foyt, Darrell Waltrip, and Dave Marcis ran up to seven miles per hour faster than anyone else. After a lengthy inspection, NASCAR disallowed their times after finding that their fuel lines contained nitrous oxide, which provides sudden bursts of horsepower. Accepting the decision, Waltrip uttered a quote that did not go over big in NASCAR's offices. "In Grand National racing," he said, "there are a lot of things you have to do to keep up with the competition. It's common knowledge that cheating, in one form or another, is part of it. If you don't cheat, you look like an idiot."

It was a very interesting season: David Pearson won 10 times, but Cale Yarborough won his first title by winning 9. Richard Petty and Marcis each won 3 times, Parsons twice, and Buddy Baker, Donnie Allison, and Waltrip once each. In one of the wildest Daytona 500 finishes, Petty and Pearson were dueling on the final lap. Pearson passed Petty on the backstretch, but in turn 4 their cars touched and they spun into the infield a few hundred feet from the finish line. Petty was unable to restart his car, but Pearson cranked up his car and crawled across the finish line at 15 to 20 miles per hour. Janet Guthrie made her Winston Cup debut by qualifying 27th in a Chevrolet and fin-

Janet Guthrie wasn't the first woman to race at NASCAR's top level, but she was one of the most well-known. Here, she pulls on her fire-resistant gloves as she prepares to run in the Firecracker 400 on July 2, 1976 at Daytona International Speedway.

ished 15th in May in the World 600 at Charlotte Motor Speedway.

WINSTON CUP STANDINGS

	DRIVER	STARTS	WINS	POINTS	MONEY
1.	Cale Yarborough	30	9	4,644	453,405
2.	Richard Petty	30	3	4,449	374,806
3.	Benny Parsons	30	2	4,304	270,043
4.	Bobby Allison	30	0	4,097	230,170
5.	Lennie Pond	30	0	3,930	159,701
6.	Dave Marcis	30	3	3,875	218,250
7.	Buddy Baker	30	1	3,745	239,922
8.	Darrell Waltrip	30	1	3,505	204,193
9.	David Pearson	22	10	3,483	346,890

10.	Dick Brooks	28	0	3,447	111,880
11.	Richard Childress	30	0	3,428	85,780
12.	J. D. McDuffie	30	0	3,400	82,240
13.	James Hylton	30	0	3,380	78,705
14.	D. K. Ulrich	30	0	3,280	69,435
15.	Cecil Gordon	30	0	3,247	73,830
16.	Frank Warren	30	0	3,240	67,732
17.	David Sisco	28	0	2,994	62,622
18.	Skip Manning	27	0	2,931	61,537
19.	Ed Negre	28	0	2,709	50,919
20.	Buddy Arrington	25	0	2,573	56,647
21.	Terry Bivins	18	0	2,099	44,070
22.	Bobby Wawak	19	0	2,062	31,415
23.	Bruce Hill	22	0	1,995	43,705
24.	Jimmy Means	19	0	1,752	20,945
25.	Dick May	18	0	1,719	29,425
26.	Walter Ballard	14	0	1,554	16,380
27.	Henley Gray	16	0	1,425	15,090
28.	Coo Coo Marlin	12	0	1,412	39,485
29.	Gary Myers	15	0	1,296	11,430
30.	Jackie Rogers	11	0	1,173	21,215
31.	Grant Adcox	11	0	1,163	25,715
32.	Neil Bonnett	14	0	1,130	31,800
33.	Tommy Gale	12	0	1,005	18,955
34.	Donnie Allison	9	1	988	48,455
35.	Joe Mihalic	9	0	981	12,925
36.	Elmo Langley	7	0	824	7,515
37.	Travis Tiller	9	0	816	6,310
38.	Sonny Easley	7	0	772	11,290
39.	Joe Frasson	9	0	707	12,075
40.	Jabe Thomas	6	0	648	6,160
41.	Bill Elliott	8	0	635	11,635
42.	Dean Dalton	6	0	633	7,245
43.	Earle Canavan	7	0	610	6,035
44.	Rick Newsom	7	0	607	5,520
45.	Tighe Scott	6	0	566	15,520
46.	Terry Ryan	5	0	558	24,940
47.	Darrell Bryant	8	0	546	11,925
48.	Buck Baker	8	0	513	12,655
49.	Chuck Bown	5	0	481	5,480
50.	Baxter Price	6	0	479	3,010

1977

AT A GLANCE

Winston Cup Champion: Cale Yarborough

Notable Event: NASCAR had used several points systems for its Grand National/Winston Cup Series, but the existing system had been in place for three years when Cale Yarborough accomplished the unthinkable. He scored exactly 5,000 points in 30 races, a figure that would remain magical until Jeff Gordon scored 5,328 points in 1998 (in three more races).

Top Newcomers: Rookie of the Year Ricky Rudd, from Chesapeake, Virginia, had 1 top-5 and 10 top-10s. Neil Bonnett also did well, finishing with 2 wins, 5 top-5s, and 9 top-10s.

Taking his second consecutive championship, Yarborough won nine races, followed by Darrell Waltrip with six. Richard Petty won five and Benny Parsons four, and Bonnett, a fresh face in the "Alabama Gang" that featured the Allison brothers, won twice. After failing to win in 1976, Bobby Allison left Roger Penske's team and was replaced by Dave Marcis. Allison was winless again in 1977, as were Marcis and Buddy Baker. After the season, Penske briefly left NASCAR to concentrate on his successful Indy car teams.

In his spring victory at Darlington, Waltrip showed the talent that was moving him into the elite level occupied by Petty, Pearson, and Yarborough. With seven laps to go, Waltrip trailed Pearson, Petty, and Bobby Allison, who had relieved his brother, Donnie. When two cars collided in front of the leaders, Waltrip dashed through the wreckage and outran Allison to the caution flag. The race ended under caution. "There was a perception that nobody could beat those guys," Waltrip said. "They were the sport and no one else mattered. I knew that if you were ever going to prove yourself in this business, you had to win Darlington. Winning Darlington makes people take you seriously."

WINSTON CUP STANDINGS

	DRIVER	STARTS	WINS	POINTS	MONEY
1.	Cale Yarborough	30	9	5,000	561,642
2.	Richard Petty	30	5	4,614	406,608
3.	Benny Parsons	30	4	4,570	359,341
4.	Darrell Waltrip	30	6	4,498	324,814
5.	Buddy Baker	30	0	3,961	224,847
6.	Dick Brooks	29	0	3,742	151,374
7.	James Hylton	30	0	3,476	108,392
8.	Bobby Allison	30	0	3,467	94,575
9.	Richard Childress	30	0	3,463	97,012
10.	Cecil Gordon	30	0	3,294	86,312
11.	Buddy Arrington	28	0	3,247	88,887
12.	J. D. McDuffie	30	0	3,236	85,227
13.	David Pearson	22	2	3,227	221,272
14.	Skip Manning	28	0	3,120	111,317
15.	D. K. Ulrich	30	0	2,901	69,677
16.	Frank Warren	29	0	2,876	67,945
17.	Ricky Rudd	25	0	2,810	75,905
18.	Neil Bonnett	23	2	2,649	122,615
19.	Jimmy Means	26	0	2,640	52,505
20.	Tighe Scott	26	0	2,628	63,225
21.	Sam Sommers	23	0	2,517	54,525
22.	Ed Negre	24	0	2,214	42,665
23.	Janet Guthrie	19	0	2,037	37,945
24.	Donnie Allison	17	2	1,970	146,435
25.	Dave Marcis	18	0	1,931	72,605
26.	Tommy Gale	18	0	1,689	39,190
27.	Dick May	13	0	1,324	21,690
28.	Henley Gray	14	0	1,214	18,610
29.	Bruce Hill	16	0	1,213	25,035
30.	Lennie Pond	14	0	1,193	49,440
31.	Butch Hartman	11	0	1,116	18,615
32.	Ferrel Harris	11	0	1,088	19,365
33.	Baxter Price	12	0	1,086	10,890
34.	Coo Coo Marlin	11	0	1,004	42,450
35.	Bill Elliott	10	0	926	20,075
36.	Gary Myers	10	0	888	10,975
37.	David Sisco	10	0	847	13,920
38.	Terry Bivins	8	0	841	14,920
39.	G. C. Spencer	8	0	785	15,755
40.	Terry Ryan	7	0	702	12,405
41.	Joe Mihalic	8	0	683	7,650
42.	Elmo Langley	7	0	634	5,855
43.	Dean Dalton	8	0	620	6,255
44.	Earl Brooks	6	0	552	3,045
45.	Bobby Wawak	8	0	522	13,455
46.	Harold Miller	6	0	470	8,480
47.	Junior Miller	5	0	467	2,475
48.	Ramo Scott	5	0	440	10,170
49.	Grant Adcox	6	0	413	8,750
50.	Sonny Easley	3	0	386	9,490

1978

Ten-time winner Cale Yarborough set a record with his third consecutive NASCAR title. Darrell Waltrip won six races and was third in points. Yarborough and team owner Junior Johnson switched to Oldsmobiles, as did Benny Parsons and owner L. G. DeWitt and Buddy Baker and owner M. C. Anderson. Richard Petty decided to stay with the Dodge Magnum but, after failing to finish four of the first five races, switched to Chevrolet. Bobby Allison, driving for Bud Moore, won his first Daytona 500. Two weeks later at Rockingham, David Pearson got his 100th career Winston Cup victory.

Cale Yarborough and team owner Junior Johnson are pleased to see the results that their competition is turning in during qualifying runs for the Winston 500 at Talladega's Alabama International Raceway on May 4, 1978.

Prior to the World 600 at Charlotte in May, master promoter Humpy Wheeler arranged a ride for Willy T. Ribbs, then 23 and America's most promising African-American driver. Ribbs, an outstanding road racer, was scheduled to drive a Ford owned by Will Cronkite. Since everyone thought Ribbs would need extra practice in a heavy car on a superspeedway, Wheeler set up two practice sessions. Ribbs never showed for either one, and eventually was involved in an incident with the Charlotte police department's traffic division. With Ribbs unavailable, Cronkite gave the ride to a successful, young, local Sportsman driver from nearby Kannapolis named Dale Earnhardt.

WINSTON CUP STANDINGS

	DRIVER	STARTS	WINS	POINTS	MONEY
1.	Cale Yarborough	30	10	4,841	623,506
2.	Bobby Allison	40	5	4,367	335,636
3.	Darrell Waltrip	30	6	4,362	413,908
4.	Benny Parsons	30	3	4,350	329,993
5.	Dave Marcis	30	0	4,335	205,871
6.	Richard Petty	30	0	3,949	242,273
7.	Lennie Pond	28	1	3,794	181,096
8.	Dick Brooks	30	0	3,769	137,590

9.	Buddy Arrington	30	0	3,626	112,960
10.	Richard Childress	30	0	3,566	108,702
11.	J. D. McDuffie	30	0	3,255	86,857
12.	Neil Bonnett	30	0	3,129	167,742
13.	Tighe Scott	29	0	3,110	87,912
14.	Frank Warren	30	0	3,036	68,173
15.	Dick May	28	0	2,936	65,291
16.	David Pearson	22	4	2,756	198,775
17.	Jimmy Means	27	0	2,756	61,725
18.	Ronnie Thomas	27	0	2,733	75,815
19.	Cecil Gordon	26	0	2,641	53,815
20.	Tommy Gale	26	0	2,639	60,765
21.	Roger Hamby	26	0	2,617	41,315
22.	D. K. Ulrich	22	0	2,452	54,550
23.	Baxter Price	24	0	2,418	36,560
24.	Buddy Baker	19	0	2,130	111,765
25.	Donnie Allison	17	1	1,993	127,475
26.	James Hylton	19	0	1,965	48,045
27.	Gary Myers	19	0	1,915	22,140
28.	Ed Negre	21	0	1,857	28,995
29.	Skip Manning	17	0	1,802	55,470
30.	Grant Adcox	14	0	1,802	37,100
31.	Ricky Rudd	13	0	1,260	50,630
32.	Bruce Hill	14	0	1,214	25,770
33.	Bill Elliott	10	0	1,176	42,215
34.	Al Holbert	12	0	1,142	31,075
35.	Ferrel Harris	14	0	1,066	39,685
36.	Coo Coo Marlin	9	0	765	19,415
37.	Blackie Wangerin	10	0	760	13,515
38.	Bobby Wawak	8	0	680	5,870
39.	Terry Labonte	5	0	659	21,395
40.	Ralph Jones	7	0	634	6,305
41.	Janet Guthrie	7	0	592	17,120
42.	Earl Canavan	9	0	559	8,740
43.	Dale Earnhardt	5	0	558	20,745
44.	Roland Wlodyka	6	0	549	9,910
45.	Joe Frasson	5	0	533	9,210
46.	Nelson Oswald	6	0	501	2,955
47.	Joe Mihalic	6	0	419	6,030
48.	Jim Thirkettle	3	0	389	6,850
49.	Jimmy Insolo	3	0	369	8,665
50.	Satch Worley	4	0	368	6,205

1979

AT A GLANCE

Winston Cup Champion: Richard Petty

Notable Event: The Daytona 500 is credited for launching NASCAR's national popularity. Live from start to finish on CBS-TV, it featured Cale Yarborough and Donnie Allison wrecking on the backstretch and ending up in the turn 3 wall on the last lap. Richard Petty, Darrell Waltrip, and A. J. Foyt bypassed the melee and finished 1-2-3. Meanwhile, Allison and Yarborough climbed from their cars, removed their helmets and began arguing. When Allison's brother, Bobby, parked his car and joined the debate, fists started flying. Petty used the victory as a springboard to his seventh championship—but it wasn't easy.

Top Newcomers: Dale Earnhardt (7th), Ricky Rudd (9th), and Terry Labonte (10th) all cracked the top 10 in points for the first time. In addition, relative newcomer Joe Millikan finished sixth in points (5 top-5 finishes, 20 top-10s) and Kyle Petty made his stock car racing debut.

With seven races remaining, Petty trailed Waltrip by 187 points for the championship, but he had managed to trim that to just 17 points with three races left. Petty then won at Rockingham to take the lead, but Waltrip regained control and led

by 2 going to the finale at Ontario, California. There, Petty finally secured his seventh title (by an 11-point margin, the closest ever in Winston Cup) by finishing fifth, three spots ahead of Waltrip. This even though Waltrip had more victories (seven), followed by Petty and Bobby Allison (each with five). Cale Yarborough won four times, Buddy Baker and Neil Bonnett three each, Benny Parsons twice, and Dale Earnhardt and David Pearson one each.

Pearson's lone victory was for owner Hoss Ellington at Darlington in September, when Pearson was subbing for the injured Donnie Allison. It was sweet redemption for Pearson, who had botched a pit stop at Darlington in the spring, an uncharacteristic mistake that hastened his departure from the famous Wood Brothers team. Earnhardt, a rookie in only his 16th start, won his first race (at Bristol, Tennessee) in the spring. And another Petty emerged on the Winston Cup scene: Richard's son, Kyle, finished ninth in the Talladega 500.

WINSTON CUP STANDINGS

	DRIVER	STARTS	WINS	POINTS	MONEY
1.	Richard Petty	31	5	4,830	561,934
2.	Darrell Waltrip	31	7	4,819	557,012
3.	Bobby Allison	31	5	4,633	428,801
4.	Cale Yarborough	31	4	4,604	440,129
5.	Benny Parsons	31	2	4,256	264,930
6.	Joe Millikan	31	0	4,014	229,713
7.	Dale Earnhardt	27	1	3,749	274,810
8.	Richard Childress	31	0	3,735	132,922
9.	Ricky Rudd	28	0	3,642	150,898
10.	Terry Labonte	31	0	3,615	134,653
11.	Buddy Arrington	31	0	3,589	131,833
12.	D. K. Ulrich	31	0	3,508	113,458
13.	J. D. McDuffie	31	0	3,473	113,478
14.	James Hylton	30	0	3,405	97,428
15.	Buddy Baker	26	3	3,249	342,148
16.	Frank Warren	31	0	3,199	94,539
17.	Ronnie Thomas	30	0	2,912	100,079
18.	Tommy Gale	27	0	2,795	72,809
19.	Cecil Gordon	28	0	2,737	66,275
20.	Dave Marcis	25	0	2,736	56,434
21.	Harry Gant	25	0	2,664	47,185
22.	Dick Brooks	27	0	2,622	61,985
23.	Jimmy Means	27	0	2,575	55,560
24.	Donnie Allison	20	0	2,508	144,770
25.	Baxter Price	24	0	2,364	45,165
26.	Neil Bonnett	21	3	2,223	151,235
27.	Tighe Scott	17	0	1,879	88,010
28.	Bill Elliott	14	0	1,548	58,200
29.	Lennie Pond	15	0	1,415	42,970
30.	Dick May	19	0	1,390	26,345
31	Roger Hamby	12	0	1,231	21,000
32.	David Pearson	9	1	1,203	99,180
33.	Coo Coo Marlin	7	0	613	27,540
34.	Bruce Hill	7	0	594	17,260
35.	Blackie Wangerin	7	0	571	14,300
36.	Grant Adcox	6	0	560	15,290
37.	Kyle Petty	5	0	559	10,810
38.	Chuck Bown	7	0	523	31,380
39.	John Anderson	4	0	496	11,210
40.	Ralph Jones	6	0	477	12,785
41.	Earle Canavan	7	0	456	6,675

42.	Slick Johnson	4	0	431	5,360
43.	Nelson Oswald	6	0	431	3,610
44.	Dave Watson	4	0	413	7,170
45.	Al Holbert	6	0	402	14,170
46.	Bobby Wawak	4	0	376	7,295
47.	Jody Riley	3	0	374	11,245
48.	Bill Hollar	5	0	371	2,545
49.	Rick Newsom	4	0	355	5,530
50.	Bill Schmitt	3	0	342	11,695

1980

AT A GLANCE

Winston Cup Champion: Dale Earnhardt

Notable Event: Prior to the April race at Martinsville, NASCAR, seeking to reduce expenses for the teams, ruled that no tires could be changed under caution flags. Teams violating this rule would be penalized two laps.

Top Newcomers: Rookie of the Year Jody Ridley, from Chatsworth, Georgia, had 2 top-5s, 18 top-10s, and finished seventh in points. Harry Gant had 9 top-5s, 14 top-10s, and finished 11th in points.

Dale Earnhardt won the first of his seven titles, edging Cale Yarborough by 19 points. He thus became the first driver to win the Cup the year after being Rookie of the Year. Prior to the season, Earnhardt signed for five years with California real estate developer Rod Osterlund, a deal that barely lasted the season. Several major teams began looking to the future: Cale Yarborough and Junior Johnson said 1980 would be their last together; Bobby Allison and Bud Moore said the same thing; Osterlund and Earnhardt were about done; and Waltrip and DiGard would split up after the season. Not surprisingly, Waltrip and Johnson immediately made plans to hook up for 1981 and beyond.

Entering the year's final race at Ontario, California, Earnhardt led Yarborough by 29 points. Yarborough, in his last race for Johnson, finished third in the race while Earnhardt finished fifth. That was good enough for Earnhardt to hang on and win the championship by 19 points. Yarborough won six races; Earnhardt and Waltrip five each; Allison four; Benny Parsons three; Richard Petty, Buddy Baker, and Neil Bonnett two each; and Terry Labonte and David Pearson one each. NASCAR was already seeing how important live television was to its success, especially the dedicated coverage from new cable network ESPN.

WINSTON CUP STANDINGS

	DRIVER	STARTS	WINS	POINTS	MONEY
1.	Dale Earnhardt	31	5	4,661	671,991
2.	Cale Yarborough	31	6	4,642	567,891
3.	Benny Parsons	31	3	4,278	411,519
4.	Richard Petty	31	2	4,255	397,318
5.	Darrell Waltrip	31	5	4,239	405,711
6.	Bobby Allison	31	4	4,019	378,970
7.	Jody Ridley	31	0	3,972	204,883
8.	Terry Labonte	31	1	3,766	222,502
9.	Dave Marcis	31	0	3,745	150,165
10.	Richard Childress	31	0	3,742	157,420
11.	Harry Gant	31	0	3,703	177,150
12.	Buddy Arrington	31	0	3,461	120,355
13.	James Hylton	31	0	3,449	109,230
14.	Ronnie Thomas	30	0	3,066	94,730
15.	Cecil Gordon	29	0	2,933	83,300
16.	J. D. McDuffie	31	0	2,968	82,402
18.	Tommy Gale	29	0	2,885	84,279
19.	Neil Bonnett	22	2	2,865	231,854
20.	Roger Hamby	25	0	2,606	51,534
21.	Buddy Baker	19	2	2,603	275,200
22.	Lake Speed	19	0	1,853	69,670
23.	Slick Johnson	18	0	1,851	35,460
24.	John Anderson	20	0	1,805	48,265
25.	Bobby Wawak	19	0	1,742	21,080
26.	Donnie Allison	18	0	1,730	92,640
27.	Dick Brooks	19	0	1,698	60,700
28.	Kyle Petty	15	0	1,690	36,045
29.	Baxter Price	18	0	1,689	26,615
30.	Lennie Pond	17	0	1,558	62,265
31.	Junior Miller	16	0	1,402	23,420
32.	Dick May	21	0	1,323	42,945
33.	Joe Millikan	12	0	1,274	74,765
34.	Bill Elliott	12	0	1,232	42,545
35.	Ricky Rudd	13	0	1,213	50,500
36.	Bill Elswick	12	0	1,053	15,600
37.	David Pearson	9	1	1,004	102,730
38.	D. K. Ulrich	11	0	935	23,055
39.	Tighe Scott	10	0	791	21,925
40.	Frank Warren	7	0	559	18,375
41.	Tim Richmond	5	0	527	14,925
42.	Bill Schmitt	4	0	503	21,610
43.	Buck Simmons	6	0	495	6,365
44.	Rick Newsom	6	0	483	3,830
45.	Dave Dion	4	0	441	5,015
46.	Don Whittington	7	0	429	17,610
47.	Steve Moore	4	0	412	9,040
48.	Tommy Houston	4	0	396	5,020
49.	Sterling Marlin	5	0	387	29,810
50.	Bruce Hill	6	0	348	7,540

1981

AT A GLANCE

Winston Cup Champion: Darrell Waltrip

Notable Event: With Detroit manufacturers downsizing cars, NASCAR mandated that cars must have a 110-inch wheelbase. Also, when it became apparent the Pontiac LeMans was too fast, NASCAR adjusted the size of its spoilers, effectively discouraging use of that model.

Top Newcomer: Two rookies won their first races: Ron Bouchard at Talladega and Morgan Shepherd at Martinsville. Bouchard, from Fitchburg, Massachusetts, was Rookie of the Year; Shepherd was 13th on the money list ($170,473). In addition, future superstar Mark Martin won his first pole.

Storming back from a huge deficit midway through the season, Darrell Waltrip won the first

To race fans, this is one of the most beautiful sights in the world—the full field rounding the final corner before the green flag is dropped and another Daytona 500 is underway. It's Bill Elliott at the front of the pack here just before the 1987 race roars into action. At the end of the race, Elliott was in the same position, winning the race with an average speed just over 176 mph.

of his three titles, all within a span of four seasons. Driving for Junior Johnson, he dominated with 12 victories. Bobby Allison was a distant second with 5 victories, and Richard Petty, Benny Parsons, and Neil Bonnett each won twice. Jody Ridley, Shepherd, and Bouchard each won once, which was each driver's first career victory.

After Petty won his seventh Daytona 500, his crew chief, Dale Inman, stunned everyone by re-signing and moving to the Rod Osterlund–Dale Earnhardt team. But Osterlund sold his team to J. D. Stacy, a Kentucky native who'd been in Winston Cup racing in the 1970s. Following the Tal-

ladega 500 in August, Earnhardt quit Stacy's team and signed on with Richard Childress, a veteran driver-turned-owner, for the rest of the season. Nobody knew it at the time, but that pairing was the start of something special.

Bobby Allison's season-opening victory in the Ranier-owned 1977 Chevrolet Monte Carlo was the last Cup race for the full-size cars. After he then won the Daytona 500 pole at 194.624 mph in a Pontiac LeMans, NASCAR attempted to slow that model down and keep the field competitive by enlarging all spoilers from 216 to 250 square inches. In the 500, Allison led 117 laps but lost by 3.5 seconds after Petty took fuel only during his last stop, two laps after Allison had taken more time to take fuel and tires.

WINSTON CUP STANDINGS

	DRIVER	STARTS	WINS	POINTS	MONEY
1.	Darrell Waltrip	31	12	4,880	799,134
2.	Bobby Allison	31	5	4,827	680,957
3.	Harry Gant	31	0	4,210	280,047
4.	Terry Labonte	31	0	4,052	348,703
5.	Jody Ridley	31	1	4,002	267,605
6	Ricky Rudd	31	0	3,988	395,685
7.	Dale Earnhardt	31	0	3,975	353,972
8.	Richard Petty	31	3	3,880	396,072
9.	Dave Marcis	31	0	3,507	162,213
10.	Benny Parsons	31	3	3,449	311,093
11.	Buddy Arrington	31	0	3,381	133,928
12.	Kyle Petty	31	0	3,335	117,433
13.	Morgan Shepherd	29	1	3,261	170,473
14.	Jimmy Means	30	0	3,142	105,628
15.	Tommy Gale	30	0	3,140	110,518
16.	Tim Richmond	29	0	3,091	96,448
17.	J. D. McDuffie	28	0	2,996	105,499
18.	Lake Speed	27	0	2,817	94,069
19.	James Hylton	28	0	2,753	87,305
20.	Joe Millikin	23	0	2,682	148,400
21.	Ron Bouchard	22	1	2,594	152,855
22.	Neil Bonnett	22	3	2,449	181,670
23.	Cecil Gordon	25	0	2,320	55,980
24.	Cale Yarborough	18	2	2,201	150,840
25	Richard Childress	21	0	2,144	71,125
26.	Ronnie Thomas	23	0	2,138	53,605
27.	Buddy Baker	16	0	1,904	115,095
28.	Joe Ruttman	17	0	1,851	137,275
29.	Mike Alexander	19	0	1,784	34,055
30.	Bill Elliott	13	0	1,442	70,320
31.	Bobby Wawak	14	0	1,212	21,790
32.	D. K. Ulrich	15	0	1,191	38,095
33.	Johnny Rutherford	12	0	1,140	29,045
34.	Lennie Pond	12	0	1,100	29,045
35.	Elliott Forbes-Robinson	11	0	1,020	27,350
36.	Rick Newsom	9	0	768	8,625
37.	Dick May	9	0	754	26,380
38.	Stan Barrett	10	0	718	28,540
39.	Connie Saylor	7	0	664	19,715
40.	Gary Balough	10	0	656	34,430
41.	Rick Wilson	8	0	639	15,625
42.	Mark Martin	5	0	615	13,950
43.	Bruce Hill	8	0	596	15,485
44.	Donnie Allison	6	0	527	38,745
45.	Geoff Bodine	5	0	420	15,000
46.	Joe Fields	6	0	418	7,750
47.	Jack Ingram	5	0	377	9,965
48.	Randy Ogden	4	0	367	3,905
49.	Jim Robinson	3	0	351	9,505
50.	Don Waterman	3	0	351	8,570

1982

AT A GLANCE

Winston Cup Champion: Darrell Waltrip

Notable Event: Dave Marcis set a record of sorts at Richmond in February by winning a Winston Cup race without having led a green-flag lap. He was running fifth when a caution came out shortly past the halfway point. Everyone else pitted immediately, but Marcis was going to wait another lap to get the five-point lap leader bonus. By the time he circled the half-mile track again, rain began falling so he stayed out. When the race was stopped for rain, he found himself the winner for the fifth and final time in his career.

Top Newcomers: Rookie of the Year Geoff Bodine, from

Chemung, New York, had 4 top-5s and 10 top-10s. Mark Martin ran his first full season (but wasn't eligible for the rookie award).

Waltrip repeated as champion and again won 12 races. Bobby Allison was runner-up in victories with 8, and nobody else was even close. Cale Yarborough won 3, Harry Gant and Indy car refugee Tim Richmond 2 each, and Marcis, Dale Earnhardt, and Neil Bonnett 1 each. Allison led Terry Labonte by 50 points and Waltrip by 120 with 10 races remaining. But Waltrip pulled within 101 points with six races remaining and within 37 points with four races to go. When Waltrip beat Allison by 18 positions at Martinsville, Waltrip moved ahead of his rival by 37 points with three races to go.

In one of NASCAR's best two-man battles, Waltrip and Allison stayed even after running 1-2 at Rockingham. (Allison led the most laps, thus the equal points.) Allison won the next race near Atlanta, while Waltrip finished third and lost 15 points. However, Waltrip and team owner Junior Johnson won their second consecutive championship by finishing 3rd in the season finale at Riverside, where Allison finished 16th. The final margin of victory was 72 points, and Allison was runner-up for the fifth time in his NASCAR career.

WINSTON CUP STANDINGS

	DRIVER	STARTS	WINS	POINTS	MONEY
1.	Darrell Waltrip	30	12	4,489	923,151
2.	Bobby Allison	30	8	4,417	795,078
3.	Terry Labonte	30	0	4,211	398,635
4.	Harry Gant	30	2	3,877	337,582
5.	Richard Petty	30	0	3,814	465,793
6.	Dave Marcis	30	1	3,666	249,027
7.	Buddy Arrington	30	0	3,642	178,159
8.	Ron Bouchard	30	0	3,545	375,759
9.	Ricky Rudd	30	0	3,537	217,140
10.	Morgan Shepherd	29	0	3,451	166,030
11.	Jimmy Means	30	0	3,423	154,460
12.	Dale Earnhardt	30	1	3,402	400,800
13.	Jody Ridley	30	0	3,333	308,664
14.	Mark Martin	30	0	3,042	142,710
15.	Kyle Petty	29	0	3,024	126,285
16.	Joe Ruttman	29	0	3,021	191,634
17.	Neil Bonnett	25	1	2,996	158,197
18.	Benny Parsons	23	0	2,892	252,267
19.	J. D. McDuffie	30	0	2,886	112,744
20.	Lake Speed	30	0	2,850	118,457
21.	Tommy Gale	26	0	2,698	101,485
22.	Geoff Bodine	25	0	2,654	247,750
23.	Buddy Baker	23	0	2,591	253,675
24.	D. K. Ulrich	25	0	2,566	78,120
25.	Bill Elliott	21	0	2,558	201,030
26.	Tim Richmond	26	2	2,497	175,980
27.	Cale Yarborough	16	3	2,022	231,590
28.	James Hylton	13	0	1,514	49,130
29.	Slick Johnson	17	0	1,261	44,190
30.	Ronnie Thomas	18	0	1,093	23,570

	DRIVER	STARTS	WINS	POINTS	MONEY
31.	Bobby Wawak	10	0	1,002	23,660
32.	Brad Teague	9	0	966	14,300
33.	Lennie Pond	13	0	756	45,715
34.	Rick Wilson	8	0	731	33,230
35.	Joe Millikan	8	0	678	56,230
36.	Rick Newsom	8	0	619	12,390
37.	David Pearson	6	0	613	55,945
38.	Gary Balough	5	0	564	35,735
39.	Lowell Cowell	5	0	554	26,215
40.	Philip Duffie	5	0	542	10,910
41.	H. B. Bailey	6	0	462	9,455
42.	Butch Lindley	4	0	435	16,695
43.	Dean Combs	5	0	431	7,940
44.	Delma Cowart	5	0	410	11,855
45.	Donnie Allison	9	0	406	38,180
46.	Bobby Hillin Jr.	5	0	379	9,830
47.	Roy Smith	3	0	375	26,770
48.	Dick Brooks	5	0	347	9,470
49.	Connie Saylor	7	0	335	16,225
50.	Darryl Sage	5	0	324	4,970

1983

AT A GLANCE

Winston Cup Champion: Bobby Allison

Notable Event: The 1983 season had several cases of creative engineering. The most notable involved Richard Petty, who won the fall race near Charlotte. It was his 198th career victory, but was it fair and above board? NASCAR officials said no after discovering that Petty's crew had used four left-side tires on the final pit stop. What's more, the winning engine was 381.983 cubic inches, well over the 358.1 CID limit. Petty kept the victory, but lost 104 points and paid a $35,000 fine. Several weeks later, Petty announced he'd leave Petty Enterprises and drive next season for Californian Mike Curb. Petty's son, Kyle, would continue racing for Petty Enterprises.

Top Newcomers: Bill Elliott, in his first full year in the series, finished third in points and won his first race; Lake Speed recorded two top-5s and five top-10s and Sterling Marlin ran his first full season.

Bobby Allison captured his first, and only, Winston Cup by 47 points over two-time and defending champion Darrell Waltrip. They tied for the most wins, six apiece, two more than Cale Yarborough and three more than Petty. Two-time winners were Neil Bonnett, Dale Earnhardt and Ricky Rudd, and Elliott, Buddy Baker, Harry Gant, Terry Labonte, and Tim Richmond each won once.

For the third consecutive year, Allison and Waltrip came down to the last race of the season scrapping for the Winston Cup. Allison's lead had been 61 points with 10 remaining, 56 with 8 remaining, and 101 with 6 remaining. But Allison had been in that position before and wasn't taking anything for granted. He beat Waltrip at Mar-

tinsville, but finished behind him at Charlotte and Rockingham, which cut his lead down to 27 points. But Allison hung tough, gaining 37 points near Atlanta to take a 64-point lead to the finale at Riverside. There, Allison finished ninth to Waltrip's sixth, thus earning his only Cup by 47 points.

WINSTON CUP STANDINGS

	DRIVER	STARTS	WINS	POINTS	MONEY
1.	Bobby Allison	30	6	4,667	883,010
2.	Darrell Waltrip	30	6	4,620	865,185
3.	Bill Elliott	30	1	4,279	514,030
4.	Richard Petty	30	3	4,042	508,884
5.	Terry Labonte	30	1	4,004	388,419
6.	Neil Bonnett	30	2	3,842	453,586
7.	Harry Gant	30	1	3,790	414,353
8.	Dale Earnhardt	30	2	3,732	465,203
9.	Ricky Rudd	30	2	3,693	275,400
10.	Tim Richmond	30	1	3,612	262,139
11.	Dave Marcis	30	0	3,361	306,355
12.	Joe Ruttman	30	0	3,342	223,809
13.	Kyle Petty	30	0	3,261	163,848
14.	Dick Brooks	30	0	3,230	180,556
15.	Buddy Arrington	30	0	3,158	138,429
16.	Ron Bouchard	28	0	3,113	159,173
17.	Geoff Bodine	28	0	3,019	209,611
18.	Jimmy Means	28	0	2,983	132,915
19.	Sterling Marlin	30	0	2,980	148,253
20.	Morgan Shepherd	25	0	2,733	287,326
21.	Buddy Baker	21	1	2,621	216,355
22.	Ronnie Thomas	26	0	2,515	47,190
23.	Tommy Gale	28	0	2,507	88,305
24.	D. K. Ulrich	22	0	2,400	85,245
25.	Trevor Boys	23	0	2,293	87,555
26.	J. D. McDuffie	25	0	2,197	73,425
27.	Lake Speed	18	0	2,114	78,220
28.	Cale Yarborough	16	4	1,960	265,035
29.	Benny Parsons	16	0	1,657	129,760
30.	Mark Martin	16	0	1,627	99,055
31.	Ronnie Hopkins Jr.	13	0	1,147	26,455
32.	Jody Ridley	10	0	1,050	45,710
33.	David Pearson	10	0	943	71,720
34.	Lennie Pond	10	0	887	41,530
35.	Ken Ragan	8	0	836	27,905
36.	Bobby Wawak	9	0	825	19,130
37.	Bobby Hillin Jr.	12	0	737	30,275
38.	Slick Johnson	10	0	705	13,665
39.	Mike Potter	11	0	662	20,375
40.	Cecil Gordon	8	0	649	17,340
41.	Rick Newsom	6	0	573	14,445
42.	Dean Combs	5	0	500	21,370
43.	Phil Parsons	5	0	458	23,850
44.	Bob Senneker	5	0	436	11,355
45.	Jerry Bowman	5	0	419	8,610
46.	Clark Dwyer	5	0	411	14,570
47.	Greg Sacks	5	0	359	8,060
48.	Rick McCray	4	0	313	3,710
49.	Delma Cowart	4	0	277	7,750
50.	Philip Duffie	4	0	265	6,480

1984

AT A GLANCE

Winston Cup Champion: Terry Labonte

Notable Event: Richard Petty got his 200th career victory in the July 4 Firecracker 400 at Daytona Beach with President Ronald Reagan watching in person. Reagan had given the command to start engines from Air Force One en route Daytona Beach. He arrived in time to see a wreck with three laps remaining cause a caution flag as Petty and Cale Yarborough raced back to the finish line. Petty edged Yarborough by about one foot, and more than 80,000 fans stood and cheered for the final two laps because they knew they were witnessing history.

Top Newcomer: Rookie of the Year Rusty Wallace had two top-5 finishes, four top-10s, and was 14th in points.

Terry Labonte, driving for Billy Hagan, only won at Riverside and Bristol, but his consistency paid off as he used 17 top-5s to top Harry Gant by 65 points and become the youngest Winston Cup champion. For the sixth consecutive year, the championship wasn't decided until the season finale at Riverside. Labonte regained the lead from Dale Earnhardt by winning at Bristol in August. His lead stayed between 15 and 91 points for several races, dipped to 86, then fell for three straight weeks until it was only 42 points before the final race. However, Labonte finished third in the road race and took the first of his two titles by 65 points.

Darrell Waltrip led the tour with seven victories, but finished only fifth in points. Geoff Bodine, Bill Elliott, Harry Gant, and Yarborough each won three times, and Bobby Allison, Richard Petty, Dale Earnhardt, and Labonte each won two. Single victories went to Benny Parsons, Tim Richmond, and Ricky Rudd. Rookie Terry Schoonover became the first fatality at Atlanta when he crashed in the fall race.

WINSTON CUP STANDINGS

	DRIVER	STARTS	WINS	POINTS	MONE
1.	Terry Labonte	30	2	4,508	767,716
2.	Harry Gant	30	3	4,443	673,060
3.	Bill Elliott	30	3	4,377	680,344
4.	Dale Earnhardt	30	2	4,265	634,671
5.	Darrell Waltrip	30	7	4,230	731,023
6.	Bobby Allison	30	2	4,094	641,049
7.	Ricky Rudd	30	1	3,918	497,779
8.	Neil Bonnett	30	0	3,802	282,533
9.	Geoff Bodine	30	3	3,734	413,748
10.	Richard Petty	30	2	3,643	257,932
11.	Ron Bouchard	30	0	3,609	246,510
12.	Tim Richmond	30	1	3,505	345,848
13.	Dave Marcis	30	0	3,416	330,766
14.	Rusty Wallace	30	0	3,316	201,739
15.	Dick Brooks	30	0	3,265	192,407
16.	Kyle Petty	30	0	3,159	329,920
17.	Trevor Boys	30	0	3,040	165,376
18.	Joe Ruttman	29	0	2,945	168,433
19.	Greg Sacks	29	0	2,545	75,184
20.	Buddy Arrington	26	0	2,504	128,802
21.	Buddy Baker	21	0	2,477	151,635
22.	Cale Yarborough	16	3	2,448	403,853
23.	Clark Dwyer	26	0	2,477	114,335
24.	Phil Parsons	22	0	2,290	90,700
25.	Jimmy Means	22	0	2,218	105,105
26.	Lake Speed	19	0	2,023	98,320
27.	Benny Parsons	14	1	1,865	241,665
28.	Mike Alexander	19	0	1,862	94,820
29.	Morgan Shepherd	20	0	1,811	59,670
30.	Ronnie Thomas	21	0	1,775	79,325
31.	Tommy Ellis	20	0	1,738	44,315
32.	Bobby Hillin Jr.	16	0	1,477	45,020
33.	Tommy Gale	16	0	1,426	69,385
34.	J. D. McDuffie	16	0	1,366	50,320
35.	Jody Riley	14	0	1,288	64,135
36.	Doug Heveron	16	0	1,265	39,950
37.	Sterling Marlin	14	0	1,207	54,355
38.	Lennie Pond	12	0	923	54,200
39.	Dean Combs	12	0	903	22,385
40.	Ken Ragan	10	0	873	37,045
41.	David Pearson	11	0	812	54,125
42.	D.K. Ulrich	9	0	810	31,040
43.	Connie Saylor	8	0	367	19,675
44.	Jerry Bowman	5	0	362	6,265
45.	Elliott Forbes-Robinson	5	0	349	11,335
46.	Jeff Hooker	4	0	322	4,495
47.	Bobby Wawak	4	0	307	8,575
48.	Dick May	3	0	300	5,325
49.	Dean Roper	3	0	294	19,150
50.	Bobby Gerhart	4	0	262	7,585

1985

AT A GLANCE

Winston Cup Champion: Darrell Waltrip

Notable Events: With Fords having a clear advantage, NASCAR mandated in late April that all cars must have a roof height of 50.5 inches. Fords were required to raise their cars a half-inch and General Motors cars could lower their cars a half-inch, thereby improving their aerodynamics. Also, at the banquet leading into the 1985 season, R. J. Reynolds Inc. announced a program that would pay a $1 million bonus if anyone could win three of four major races: the Daytona 500, Winston 500, World 600, and Southern 500.

Top Newcomers: Rookie of the Year was Ken Schrader, from Fenton, Missouri, who had three top-10s and placed 16th in points. Greg Sacks won the July 4th race at Daytona for his first, and only, victory. With a great name for racing, Lake Speed was second at Daytona and 10th in earnings ($300,326). Finally, Bobby Hillin Jr. collected five top-10 finishes.

In only his third full season, Bill Elliott attracted unprecedented attention when he collected $1 million for winning three of the four "crown jewel" events. "Awesome Bill from Dawsonville" won the Daytona 500, the Winston 500, and the Southern 500 to claim the money. The R.J. Reynolds Co. had offered $1 million to the driver who could win three of the series' top four races: the World 600 at Charlotte was the fourth.

After winning two of the first three legs, Elliott went to Darlington for his last chance at the $1 million. He battled Cale Yarborough in the latter portion of the race and was running second with 43 laps left. When Yarborough's car lost its power steering fluid, Elliott avoided it and went on to win the race and the million. He led the points race by 206 at that time but would win only one more race and lose the Cup to Waltrip (a three-race winner) by 101 points. Some decried the apparent flaw in the points system, but NASCAR vetoed the idea when Bill France Jr. reminded fans that, in the seven previous years, the championship wasn't decided until the final race.

WINSTON CUP STANDINGS

	DRIVER	STARTS	WINS	POINTS	MONEY
1.	Darrell Waltrip	28	3	4,292	1,318,375
2.	Bill Elliott	28	11	4,191	2,433,187
3.	Harry Gant	28	3	4,003	804,287
4.	Neil Bonnett	28	2	3,902	530,145
5.	Geoff Bodine	28	0	3,862	565,868
6.	Ricky Rudd	28	1	3,857	512,441
7.	Terry Labonte	28	1	3,683	694,510
8.	Dale Earnhardt	28	4	3,561	546,596
9.	Kyle Petty	28	0	3,528	296,367
10.	Lake Speed	28	0	3,507	300,326
11.	Tim Richmond	28	0	3,413	290,284
12.	Bobby Allison	28	0	3,312	272,536
13.	Ron Bouchard	28	0	3,267	240,304
14.	Richard Petty	28	0	3,140	306,142
15.	Bobby Hillin Jr.	28	0	3,091	145,070
16.	Ken Schrader	28	0	3,024	211,523
17.	Buddy Baker	28	0	2,986	235,480
18.	Dave Marcis	28	0	2,871	173,467
19.	Rusty Wallace	28	0	2,867	233,670
20.	Buddy Arrington	26	0	2,780	153,222
21.	Phil Parsons	28	0	2,740	104,840
22.	Clark Dwyer	28	0	2,641	128,710
23.	Jimmy Means	28	0	2,548	132,130
24.	Eddie Bierschwale	26	0	2,396	102,620
25.	Greg Sacks	20	1	1,944	234,141
26.	Cale Yarborough	16	2	1,861	310,465
27.	J. D. McDuffie	23	0	1,853	84,965
28.	Trevor Boys	20	0	1,461	76,325
29.	Benny Parsons	14	0	1,427	94,450
30.	Joe Ruttman	16	0	1,410	81,425
31.	Morgan Shepherd	16	0	1,406	55,985
32.	Bobby Wawak	14	0	1,226	42,165
33.	Lennie Pond	12	0	1,107	70,640
34.	Tommy Ellis	14	0	1,100	27,695
35.	Mike Alexander	11	0	1,046	43,765
36.	David Pearson	12	0	879	55,625
37.	Sterling Marlin	8	0	645	31,155
38.	Don Hume	7	0	637	22,230
39.	Ronnie Thomas	7	0	631	10,505
40.	Alan Kulwicki	5	0	509	10,230
41.	Rick Newsom	6	0	450	8,690
42.	Mike Potter	6	0	443	10,855
43.	Jerry Bowman	5	0	434	8,665
44.	Bobby Gerhart	5	0	422	7,400
45.	A. J. Foyt	7	0	410	29,750
46.	Phil Good	4	0	406	6,870
47.	Ken Ragan	7	0	356	35,995
48.	Slick Johnson	6	0	343	24,995
49.	Connie Saylor	5	0	296	8,915
50.	Jim Sauter	3	0	267	15,465

1986

AT A GLANCE

Winston Cup Champion: Dale Earnhardt

Notable Event: Prior to the end of the 1985 season, Bill France Jr. had announced that "Grand National" would be dropped as the name of NASCAR's top title. From now on, the series would be known strictly as "Winston Cup" in even greater recognition of its affiliation with the flagship Winston brand of R.J. Reynolds. NASCAR's Sportsman series would now be the Busch Grand National series.

On the way to the second of his record-tying seven Winston Cup championships, Dale Earnhardt won five races: Darlington, Charlotte twice, Atlanta, and North Wilkesboro. Tim Richmond led the tour with seven victories, but finished third in points. Darrell Waltrip was second in points, Bill Elliott was fourth, and Ricky Rudd was fifth. Earnhardt's reputation as "The Intimidator" remained strong; witness his late-race accident with Waltrip at Richmond in February that wrecked them both and handed the victory to Kyle Petty. NASCAR handed Earnhardt a $5,000 fine and put him on probation for a year, a penalty that later was softened to $3,000 and no probation.

The second half of the season belonged to Richmond, who would make 1986 his final full season as the AIDS virus began to take over his life. With Harry Hyde as crew chief and Rick Hendrick as team owner, Richmond won both races at Pocono, the July race in Daytona Beach, the road race at Watkins Glen, back-to-back fall races at Darlington and Richmond, and the season-finale at Riverside. In addition to Earnhardt, Waltrip, Elliott, and Rudd, winners included Geoff Bodine, Terry Labonte, Morgan Shepherd, Rusty Wallace (at Bristol in the spring, the first of his career), Bobby Allison, Bobby Hillin Jr. (at Talladega, his first and only), and Neil Bonnett.

WINSTON CUP STANDINGS

	DRIVER	STARTS	WINS	POINTS	MONEY
1.	Dale Earnhardt	29	5	4,468	1,768,880
2.	Darrell Waltrip	29	3	4,180	1,099,735
3.	Tim Richmond	29	7	4,174	973,221
4.	Bill Elliott	29	2	3,844	1,049,142
5.	Ricky Rudd	29	2	3,823	671,548
6.	Rusty Wallace	29	2	3,762	557,354
7.	Bobby Allison	29	1	3,698	503,095
8.	Geoff Bodine	29	2	3,678	795,111
9.	Bobby Hillin Jr.	29	1	3,546	448,452
10.	Kyle Petty	29	1	3,537	403,242
11.	Harry Gant	29	0	3,498	583,024
12.	Terry Labonte	29	1	3,473	522,235
13.	Neil Bonnett	28	1	3,369	485,930
14.	Richard Petty	29	0	3,314	280,657
15.	Joe Ruttman	29	0	3,295	259,263
16.	Ken Schrader	29	0	3,052	235,904
17.	Dave Marcis	29	0	2,912	220,461
18.	Morgan Shepherd	27	1	2,896	244,146
19.	Michael Waltrip	28	0	2,853	108,767

During a spectacular six-car crash, Richard Petty's No. 43 Pontiac goes airborne and begins to break up along the wall during the 1988 Daytona 500 on February 14. Petty's car eventually flipped seven times before coming to a rest. Petty was taken the local hospital, where it was determined that he had a badly broken ankle.

20.	Buddy Arrington	26	0	2,776	186,588
21.	Alan Kulwicki	23	0	2,705	94,450
22.	Jimmy Means	26	0	2,495	157,940
23.	Tommy Ellis	24	0	2,393	78,310
24.	Buddy Baker	17	0	1,924	138,600
25.	Eddie Bierschwale	24	0	1,860	98,110
26.	J. D. McDuffie	20	0	1,825	106,115
27.	Phil Parsons	17	0	1,742	84,680
28.	Rick Wilson	17	0	1,698	88,820
29.	Cale Yarborough	16	0	1,642	137,010
30.	Benny Parsons	16	0	1,555	176,985
31.	Ron Bouchard	17	0	1,533	106,835
32.	Chet Fillip	17	0	1,433	36,110
33.	Jody Ridley	12	0	1,213	84,380
34.	Trevor Boys	14	0	1,064	74,645
35.	Doug Heveron	13	0	1,052	74,030
36.	Sterling Marlin	10	0	989	113,070
37.	D. K. Ulrich	10	0	804	47,795
38.	Pancho Carter	9	0	706	56,335
39.	Ken Ragan	7	0	627	33,890
40.	Lake Speed	5	0	608	82,800
41.	Greg Sacks	8	0	579	64,810
42.	Ronnie Thomas	6	0	504	25,215
43.	Bobby Wawak	6	0	480	10,155
44.	Rodney Combs	5	0	421	12,180
45.	Derrike Cope	5	0	400	8,025
46.	James Hylton	4	0	386	22,090
47.	Davey Allison	5	0	364	24,190
48.	Mark Martin	5	0	364	20,515
49.	Jim Sauter	8	0	361	52,020
50.	A. J. Foyt	5	0	355	24,135

1987

AT A GLANCE

Winston Cup Champion: Dale Earnhardt

Notable Event: Local favorite Bobby Allison was involved in a terrifying crash that tore away part of the grandstand fence near the start-finish line during the spring 500-mile race at the Alabama International Motor Speedway at Talladega. There were several injuries in the grandstands and the race was delayed for more than two hours while the fence was repaired. The sight of Allison's car sailing backward into the fencing caused NASCAR to reexamine ways to control speeds. That Winston 500 (which was won by Allison's son, Davey), was the last time Cup cars raced without restrictor plates at Talladega or Daytona Beach.

Top Newcomers: Bobby Allison's son, Davey, driving for Harry Ranier, won two races—Talladega and Dover. He also had 9 top-5s and 10 top-10s to finish 21st in points. Dale Jarrett ran 24 races, by far the most in his career to that point.

In winning 11 races en to route his third championship, Dale Earnhardt was streaky. He swept six of seven early in the season, including Darlington, North Wilkesboro, Bristol, and Martinsville in succession. Later, he took Bristol, Darlington, and Richmond in succession. Bill Elliott was runner-up in wins with six, including the Daytona 500. Tim Richmond, clearly in bad health at this time, came back at midseason to win at Pocono and Riverside before dropping off the circuit several months later. He died two years later of AIDS, thus far the only major motorsports star the disease has claimed.

Richmond, Davey Allison, Ricky Rudd, and Rusty Wallace each won twice, and Kyle Petty, Bobby Allison, Darrell Waltrip, and Terry Labonte once each. Earnhardt clinched the championship at Rockingham, holding an insurmountable 515-point lead with two races left. It was clear by now that the Earnhardt–Richard Childress Racing combination was working well, a fact that would remain crystal clear into the twenty-first century.

WINSTON CUP STANDINGS

	DRIVER	STARTS	WINS	POINTS	MONEY
1.	Dale Earnhardt	29	11	4,696	2,069,243
2.	Bill Elliott	29	6	4,207	1,599,210
3.	Terry Labonte	29	1	4,007	805,054
4.	Darrell Waltrip	29	1	3,911	511,768
5.	Rusty Wallace	29	2	3,818	690,652
6.	Ricky Rudd	29	2	3,742	653,508
7.	Kyle Petty	29	1	3,737	544,437
8.	Richard Petty	29	0	3,708	445,227
9.	Bobby Allison	29	1	3,530	515,894
10.	Ken Schrader	29	0	3,405	375,918
11.	Sterling Marlin	29	0	3,381	306,412
12.	Neil Bonnett	26	0	3,352	401,541
13.	Geoff Bodine	29	0	3,328	369,889
14.	Phil Parsons	29	0	3,327	180,261
15.	Alan Kulwicki	29	0	3,238	369,889
16.	Benny Parsons	29	0	3,215	566,484
17.	Morgan Shepherd	29	0	3,099	317,034
18.	Dave Marcis	29	0	3,080	256,354
19.	Bobby Hillin Jr.	29	0	3,027	346,735
20.	Michael Waltrip	29	0	2,840	205,370
21.	Davey Allison	22	2	2,824	361,060
22.	Harry Gant	29	0	2,725	197,645
23.	Jimmy Means	28	0	2,483	154,055
24.	Buddy Baker	20	0	2,373	255,320
25.	Buddy Arrington	20	0	1,885	115,300
26.	Dale Jarrett	24	0	1,840	143,405
27.	Steve Christman	20	0	1,727	54,965
28.	Rick Wilson	19	0	1,723	65,935
29.	Cale Yarborough	16	0	1,450	111,025
30.	J. D. McDuffie	17	0	1,361	45,555
31.	Lake Speed	13	0	1,345	110,810
32.	Brett Bodine	14	0	1,271	71,460
33.	Greg Sacks	16	0	1,200	54,815
34.	Eddie Bierschwale	14	0	1,162	66,790
35.	Rodney Combs	14	0	1,098	90,990
36.	Tim Richmond	8	2	1,063	151,850
37.	Derrike Cope	11	0	797	33,750
38.	Mark Stahl	9	0	687	32,850
39.	Bobby Wawak	8	0	638	22,525
40.	D. K. Ulrich	7	0	625	30,915
41.	Ken Ragan	6	0	549	30,575
42.	Connie Saylor	10	0	486	59,455
43.	Jerry Crammer	5	0	482	20,660
44.	Trevor Boys	10	0	460	59,240
45.	Mike Potter	6	0	456	13,290
46.	Slick Johnson	8	0	444	40,630
47.	Ron Bouchard	5	0	440	24,105
48.	H. B. Bailey	5	0	428	18,885
49.	A. J. Foyt	6	0	409	21,075
50.	Larry Pearson	4	0	401	18,555

1988

AT A GLANCE

Winston Cup Champion: Bill Elliott

Rusty Wallace (left) hugs crew chief Barry Dodson on October 10, 1988, after winning the Oakwood Homes 500 at Charlotte Motor Speedway

Notable Event: Goodyear, NASCAR's only tire supplier for decades, was challenged by Hoosier. The small, Bob Newton-owned company from Indiana had built racing tires for years, and Winston Cup was its ultimate accomplishment. At separate points of the season, Goodyear and Hoosier had their tires banned because they failed a NASCAR test. At year's end, Hoosiers had won 9 of 29 races, but the company quit its Winston Cup effort midway through the 1989 season.

Top Newcomers: Former Modified star Ken Bouchard was Rookie of the Year, matching his brother Ron, who was Rookie of the Year in 1981; as of 2003, they were still the only siblings win the top rookie honor. Ken had one top-10 in 24 starts.

For the first time, three Winston Cup drivers surpassed $1 million in earnings in a season: Elliott with $1,574,639; Wallace with $1,411,567, and Earnhardt with $1,214,089. Elliott and Wallace each won six races (twice as many as Earnhardt), and Neil Bonnett, Davey Allison, and Darrell Wal-

trip each won twice. The list of one-time winners was long: Bobby Allison (the Daytona 500 victory over Davey was his last), Terry Labonte, Phil Parsons (brother of 1973 champion Benny Parsons), Lake Speed, Geoffrey Bodine, Ken Schrader, Ricky Rudd, and Alan Kulwicki. In June, Bobby Allison's career ended in a first-lap crash at Pocono that came perilously close to killing him. The 1988 victories for Speed (at Darlington) and Parsons (at Talladega) were their and first and only, and the Talladega victory was the first of Schrader's career.

WINSTON CUP STANDINGS

	DRIVER	STARTS	WINS	POINTS	MONEY
1.	Bill Elliott	29	6	4,488	1,574,639
2.	Rusty Wallace	29	6	4,484	1,411,567
3.	Dale Earnhardt	29	3	4,256	1,214,089

4.	Terry Labonte	29	1	4,007	950,781
5.	Ken Schrader	29	1	3,858	631,544
6.	Geoff Bodine	29	1	3,779	570,643
7.	Darrell Waltrip	29	2	3,764	731,659
8.	Davey Allison	29	2	3,631	844,532
9.	Phil Parsons	29	1	3,630	532,043
10.	Sterling Marlin	29	0	3,621	521,464
11.	Ricky Rudd	29	1	3,547	410,954
12.	Bobby Hillin Jr.	29	0	3,446	330,217
13.	Kyle Petty	29	0	3,296	377,092
14.	Alan Kulwicki	29	1	3,176	448,547
15.	Mark Martin	29	0	3,142	223,630
16.	Neil Bonnett	27	2	3,040	440,139
17.	Lake Speed	29	1	2,984	260,500
18.	Michael Waltrip	29	0	2,949	240,400
19.	Dave Marcis	29	0	2,854	212,485
20.	Brett Bodine	29	0	2,828	433,658
21.	Rick Wilson	28	0	2,762	209,925
22.	Richard Petty	29	0	2,644	190,155
23.	Dale Jarrett	29	0	2,622	118,640
24.	Benny Parsons	27	0	2,559	210,755
25.	Ken Bouchard	24	0	2,378	109,410
26.	Ernie Irvan	25	0	2,319	96,370
27.	Harry Gant	24	0	2,266	173,325
28.	Morgan Shepherd	23	0	2,193	197,425
29.	Buddy Baker	17	0	2,056	184,200
30.	Jimmy Means	27	0	2,045	139,290
31.	Derrike Cope	26	0	1,985	132,835
32.	Mike Alexander	16	0	1,931	200,709
33.	Bobby Allison	29	1	1,654	409,295
34.	Eddie Bierschwale	20	0	1,481	59,355
35.	Rodney Combs	19	0	1,468	54,150
36.	Brad Noffsinger	17	0	1,316	54,645
37.	Greg Sacks	15	0	1,237	105,579
38.	Cale Yarborough	10	0	940	66,065
39.	Joe Ruttman	12	0	803	46,455
40.	Brad Teague	13	0	802	53,105
41.	Jimmy Horton	8	0	647	23,575
42.	A. J. Foyt	7	0	523	29,660
43.	H. B. Bailey	7	0	478	15,775
44.	Jim Sauter	9	0	463	35,040
45.	Chad Little	4	0	405	14,225
46.	Buddy Arrington	4	0	352	22,165
47.	Ken Ragan	5	0	314	15,755
48.	Dana Patten	4	0	313	9,595
49.	Rick Jeffrey	4	0	307	25,535
50.	Mickey Gibbs	5	0	283	12,850

1989

AT A GLANCE

Winston Cup Champion: Rusty Wallace.

Notable Event: Good, bad, or somewhere in the middle, the movie *Days of Thunder* exposed NASCAR to millions of Americans. It starred Tom Cruise and Nicole Kidman, and followed a fairly predictable story line. The on-track racing footage shot during the 1989 season was laughable to those who know anything about racing, but neither Paramount nor NASCAR passed it off as a great work of art. Rather, the film brought stock car racing reams of attention it might not have received otherwise.

Top Newcomers: Dick Trickle, at age 47, was the Rookie of the Year. The Wisconsin Rapids, Wisconsin, veteran had raced intermittently in NASCAR while concentrating on smaller Midwestern circuits. In 1989, he had six top-5 finishes and nine top-10s and was 15th in points. Bobby Hamilton made his debut in a Rick Hendrick-owned car that was part of the *Days of Thunder* lineup.

Every sport experiences periods when stars retire and new faces reign. That's what happened to Winston Cup racing in 1989. Bobby Allison

and Buddy Baker were forced into retirement by accident-related medical conditions, and Cale Yarborough and Benny Parsons also retired prior to the season. Combined, they took five Winston Cup titles and 313 victories with them. So it was with hardware, too: Goodyear said goodbye to its tried-and-true bias-ply tires and introduced radials in the spring. And shortly after, Chevrolet fielded its final Monte Carlo (of that vintage, anyway) and introduced its new Lumina model.

Talk about close races: Rusty Wallace edged Dale Earnhardt for his first championship by a mere 12 points, the closest finish since Richard Petty beat Darrell Waltrip by 11 points in 1979. Despite legal wrangling with owner Raymond Beadle and his Blue Max team, Wallace stayed in the points race all season. He trailed Earnhardt by 102 points with seven races remaining, but forged a 35-point lead when Earnhardt was an early Did Not Finish at Charlotte in October. Wallace moved ahead by 37 with three races remaining and 109 with two to go. But an incident with a lapped car in the next-to-last race at Phoenix cost him 10 finish positions and 30 points. He went to the finale at Atlanta needing to finish 18th or better to secure his first title, and he got it by finishing a hard-fought 15th-place while Earnhardt kept the pressure on by winning the race.

Wallace and Waltrip each won six races in 1989, and Earnhardt five. Bill Elliott won three, Davey Allison and Terry Labonte two, and Ricky Rudd, Harry Gant, Ken Schrader, Geoffrey Bodine, and Mark Martin one each. Martin's victory in the fall at Rockingham was his first with team owner Jack Roush. It was a year of sweeps: Wallace won both races at Richmond, Waltrip both at Martinsville, and Earnhardt both races at Dover. And it was a year for mind-staggering numbers: Wallace won $2.2 million and Earnhardt, Waltrip, Schrader, and Martin all won more than a million each.

WINSTON CUP STANDINGS

	DRIVER	STARTS	WINS	POINTS	MONEY
1.	Rusty Wallace	29	6	4,176	2,237,950
2.	Dale Earnhardt	29	5	4,164	1,432,230
3.	Mark Martin	29	1	4,053	1,016,850
4.	Darrell Waltrip	29	6	3,971	1,312,479
5.	Ken Schrader	29	1	3,876	1,037,941
6.	Bill Elliott	29	3	3,774	849,370

7.	Harry Gant	29	1	3,610	639,792
8.	Ricky Rudd	29	1	3,608	533,624
9.	Geoff Bodine	29	1	3,600	619,494
10.	Terry Labonte	29	2	3,569	703,806
11.	Davey Allison	29	2	3,481	640,956
12.	Sterling Marlin	29	0	3,422	473,267
13.	Morgan Shepherd	29	0	3,403	544,255
14.	Alan Kulwicki	29	0	3,236	501,295
15.	Dick Trickle	28	0	3,203	343,728
16.	Bobby Hillin Jr.	28	0	3,139	283,181
17.	Rick Wilson	29	0	3,119	312,402
18.	Michael Waltrip	29	0	3,057	249,233
19.	Brett Bodine	29	0	3,051	281,274
20.	Neil Bonnett	26	0	2,995	271,628
21.	Phil Parsons	29	0	2,933	285,012
22.	Ernie Irvan	29	0	2,919	155,329
23.	Larry Pearson	29	0	2,860	156,060
24.	Dale Jarrett	29	0	2,789	232,317
25.	Dave Marcis	27	0	2,715	196,161
26.	Hut Stricklin	27	0	2,705	152,504
27.	Lake Speed	24	0	2,550	201,977
28.	Derrike Cope	23	0	2,180	125,630
29.	Richard Petty	25	0	2,148	133,050
30.	Kyle Petty	19	0	2,099	117,027
31.	Jimmy Means	22	0	1,698	65,005
32.	Greg Sacks	20	0	1,565	113,535
33.	Jim Sauter	17	0	1,510	73,832
34.	Jimmy Spencer	17	0	1,445	121,065
35.	Rick Mast	13	0	1,315	128,102
36.	Eddie Bierschwale	16	0	1,306	82,695
37.	Ben Hess	9	0	921	48,490
38.	Chad Little	8	0	602	44,690
39.	Butch Miller	9	0	576	22,520
40.	A. J. Foyt	7	0	527	31,995
41.	Mickey Gibbs	7	0	508	27,040
42.	Rodney Combs	9	0	470	36,090
43.	Joe Ruttman	9	0	469	64,645
44.	J. D. McDuffie	7	0	457	27,720
45.	Phil Barkdoll	4	0	378	29,050
46.	Jimmy Horton	5	0	377	19,232
47.	Dick Johnson	4	0	322	11,515
48.	Ken Bouchard	4	0	313	33,930
49.	Terry Byers	3	0	306	15,400
50.	Darin Brassfield	3	0	306	10,852

1990

AT A GLANCE

Winston Cup Champion: Dale Earnhardt

Notable Events: At 50, Harry Gant became the oldest driver to win a Winston Cup race when he prevailed at Pocono in the summer. Morgan Shepherd won near Atlanta in the fall, his first victory since 1986. First-time winners included Brett Bodine in the spring at North Wilkesboro, Derrike Cope in the spring at Daytona Beach and Dover, and Ernie Irvan at Bristol in the summer.

Top Newcomers: It was a slim year for new drivers, as Rob Moroso needed only one top-10 finish to take home Rookie of the Year honors. He was killed in a highway accident in the fall and was honored posthumously. Long-time NASCAR Modified star Jimmy Spencer ran his first full season for Rod Osterlund, the owner who helped Dale Earnhardt win his first race in 1979 and his first championship in 1980.

Like so many other seasons, 1990 began on a frustrating note for Earnhardt. Once again, he failed to win the Daytona 500, extending his winless streak in NASCAR's top race to 0-for-his-career. This one was unbelievably wrenching, as he was leading on the last lap when he cut a tire and Cope passed him in turn 3 for his first career victory. A week later, at Richmond, Mark Martin beat Earnhardt by three seconds but was fined $40,000 and docked 46 points for a very minor rules infraction. At the end of the season, when Earnhardt won the Winston Cup by just 26 points over Martin, that easily forgotten penalty became very large, indeed.

With two races remaining, Martin's lead over Earnhardt was 45 points. But Earnhardt won at Phoenix and moved ahead by 6 points over Martin, who finished 10th-place in the race. In the season finale at Atlanta, Morgan Shepherd won for the first time since 1986, while Earnhardt was third and Martin sixth, just enough to give Earnhardt his final 26-point margin. Earnhardt led the tour with nine victories to the three of Martin and Geoffrey Bodine. Two-race winners included Cope, Rusty Wallace, and Davey Allison, and eight drivers won one race each: Shepherd, Irvan, Brett Bodine, Kyle Petty, Harry Gant, Ricky Rudd, Bill Elliott, and Alan Kulwicki. It was the first full winless season for Darrell Waltrip, who missed six races after crashing hard in the midsummer race at Daytona Beach.

WINSTON CUP STANDINGS

	DRIVER	STARTS	WINS	POINTS	MONEY>
1.	Dale Earnhardt	29	9	4,430	3,308,056
2.	Mark Martin	29	3	4,404	1,302,958
3.	Geoffrey Bodine	29	3	4,017	1,131,222
4.	Bill Elliott	29	1	3,999	1,090,730
5.	Morgan Shepherd	29	1	3,689	666,915
6.	Rusty Wallace	29	2	3,676	954,129
7.	Ricky Rudd	29	1	3,601	573,650
8.	Alan Kulwicki	29	1	3,599	550,936
9.	Ernie Irvan	29	1	3,593	535,280
10.	Ken Schrader	29	0	3,572	769,934
11.	Kyle Petty	29	1	3,501	746,326
12.	Brett Bodine	29	1	3,440	442,681
13.	Davey Allison	29	2	3,423	640,684
14.	Sterling Marlin	29	0	3,387	369,167
15.	Terry Labonte	29	0	3,371	450,230
16.	Michael Waltrip	29	0	3,251	395,507
17.	Harry Gant	28	1	3,182	522,519
18.	Derrike Cope	29	2	3,140	569,451
19.	Bobby Hillin Jr.	29	0	3,048	339,366
20.	Darrell Waltrip	23	0	3,013	520,420
21.	Dave Marcis	29	0	2,944	242,724
22.	Dick Trickle	29	0	2,863	350,990
23.	Rick Wilson	29	0	2,666	242,067
24.	Jimmy Spencer	26	0	2,579	219,775
25.	Dale Jarrett	24	0	2,558	214,495
26.	Richard Petty	29	0	2,556	169,465
27.	Butch Miller	23	0	2,377	151,941
28.	Hut Stricklin	24	0	2,316	169,199
29.	Jimmy Means	27	0	2,271	135,165
30.	Rob Moroso	25	0	2,184	162,002
31.	Rick Mast	20	0	1,719	112,875
32.	Greg Sacks	16	0	1,663	216,148
33.	Chad Little	18	0	1,632	80,140
34.	Jack Pennington	14	0	1,278	95,860

Todd Bodine (No. 26) loses control and slides up into the wall during the MBNA Platinum 400 at Dover International Speedway, while Robby Gordon (No. 31) and Terry Labonte (No. 5) have a little better luck and manage to avoid the accident.

35.	Larry Pearson	9	0	822	72,305
36.	Jimmy Horton	9	0	756	72,375
37.	Mickey Gibbs	9	0	755	38,665
38.	Mike Alexander	7	0	682	41,080
39.	Phil Parsons	9	0	632	90,010
40.	J. D. McDuffie	8	0	557	26,170
41.	Buddy Baker	8	0	498	40,085
42.	Lake Speed	6	0	479	75,537
43.	Neil Bonnett	5	0	455	62,600
44.	Mark Stahl	5	0	371	18,470
45.	Bill Venturini	4	0	349	22,970
46.	Rodney Combs	5	0	323	23,365
47.	Irv Hoerr	2	0	281	14,775
48.	Tommy Kendall	3	0	281	14,120
49.	Ted Musgrave	4	0	280	17,190
50.	Chuck Brown	3	0	276	10,150

1991

AT A GLANCE

Winston Cup Champion: Dale Earnhardt

Notable Events: Long-time NASCAR driver J. D. McDuffie was killed at Watkins Glen, Harry Gant won four consecutive races, Dale Jarrett got his first career victory, the legendary Bill Elliott-Harry Melling relationship ended, and NASCAR gave Davey Allison the summer victory at Sears Point after apparent winner Ricky Rudd was disqualified for a late-race, bump-and-run pass.

Top Newcomers: Rookie of the Year Bobby Hamilton had four top-10 finishes and finished 22nd in points. Terry Labonte's brother Bobby made his Cup debut, and Kenny Wallace also began to make a name for himself in the Cup garages.

Dale Earnhardt again was in contention to win the Daytona 500, but someone else grabbed the brass ring. Late in the race, while Ernie Irvan led, Earnhardt and Davey Allison touched and spun while battling for second. The race ended under caution, with Irvan winning his first Daytona 500. Earnhardt won the following weekend at Richmond, the first of four victories that helped bring home his fifth Winston Cup championship. He also won at Martinsville in the spring, Talladega in the summer, and North Wilkesboro in the fall. Even so, he didn't win any poles, a far cry from the four poles he won the previous year. He won the Winston Cup title by merely starting the season-ending race at Atlanta.

Gant's remarkable four-race winning streak tied the modern record for consecutive victories. The 51-year-old driver won at Darlington, Richmond, Dover, and Martinsville on consecutive weekends in September. He was a lap or so from winning at North Wilkesboro the last Sunday in September when brake problems slowed him, allowing Earnhardt to win. Even though they finished third and fourth in points behind Earnhardt and Ricky Rudd, five-race winners Davey Allison and Gant led the tour. Ernie Irvan, Ken Schrader, Rusty Wallace, and Darrell Waltrip each won twice. Rudd, Kyle Petty, Mark Martin, Dale Jarrett, Geoffrey Bodine, and Bill Elliott were one-time winners.

WINSTON CUP STANDINGS

	DRIVER	STARTS	WINS	POINTS	MONEY>
1.	Dale Earnhardt	29	4	4,287	2,416,685
2.	Ricky Rudd	29	1	4,092	1,093,765
3.	Davey Allison	29	5	4,088	1,712,924
4.	Harry Gant	29	5	3,985	1,194,033
5.	Ernie Irvan	29	2	3,925	1,079,017
6.	Mark Martin	29	1	3,914	1,039,991
7.	Sterling Marlin	29	0	3,839	633,690
8.	Darrell Waltrip	29	2	3,711	604,854
9.	Ken Schrader	29	2	3,690	772,434
10.	Rusty Wallace	29	2	3,582	502,073
11.	Bill Elliott	29	1	3,535	705,605
12.	Morgan Shepherd	29	0	3,438	521,147
13.	Alan Kulwicki	29	1	3,354	595,614
14.	Geoffrey Bodine	27	1	3,277	625,256
15.	Michael Waltrip	29	0	3,254	440,812
16.	Hut Stricklin	29	0	3,199	426,524
17.	Dale Jarrett	29	1	3,124	444,256
18.	Terry Labonte	29	0	3,024	348,898
19.	Brett Bodine	29	0	2,980	376,220
20.	Joe Ruttman	29	0	2,938	361,661
21.	Rick Mast	29	0	2,918	344,020
22.	Bobby Hamilton	28	0	2,915	259,105
23.	Ted Musgrave	29	0	2,841	200,910
24.	Richard Petty	29	0	2,817	268,035
25.	Jimmy Spencer	29	0	2,790	283,620
26.	Rick Wilson	29	0	2,723	241,375
27.	Chad Little	28	0	2,678	184,190
28.	Derrike Cope	28	0	2,516	419,380
29.	Dave Marcis	27	0	2,374	219,760
30.	Bobby Hillin Jr.	22	0	2,317	251,645
31.	Kyle Petty	18	1	2,078	413,727
32.	Lake Speed	20	0	1,742	149,300
33.	Jimmy Means	20	0	1,562	111,210
34.	Mickey Gibbs	15	0	1,401	100,360
35.	Dick Trickle	14	0	1,258	129,125
36.	Stanley Smith	12	0	893	56,915
37.	Larry Pearson	11	0	848	56,570
38.	Wally Dallenbach Jr.	11	0	803	54,020
39.	Greg Sacks	11	0	791	84,215
40.	Buddy Baker	6	0	552	58,060
41.	Jimmy Hensley	4	0	488	32,125
42.	Eddie Bierschwale	5	0	431	55,025
43.	Jim Sauter	6	0	423	47,395
44.	Kenny Wallace	5	0	412	58,325
45.	Jeff Purvis	6	0	399	42,910
46.	Phil Barkdoll	4	0	364	41,655
47.	Mike Chase	5	0	356	22,700
48.	J. D. McDuffie	5	0	335	19,795
49.	Bill Sedgwick	3	0	324	15,150
50.	Randy Lajoie	4	0	304	23,875

1992

AT A GLANCE

Winston Cup Champion: Alan Kulwicki

Notable Events: In a thrilling duel, the championship race featured the closest finish ever among Alan Kulwicki, Davey Allison, and Bill Elliott. Seven-time champion Richard Petty made his last start in the same race that future champion Jeff Gordon made his first. And Bill France Sr., the man who made it all possible, died during the season after a long illness.

Top Newcomer: Rookie of the Year Jimmy Hensley posted four top-10 finishes and finished 28th in the points race.

Alan Kulwicki's championship wasn't decided until the season's final race—the Hooters 500 in Atlanta the third Sunday in September—and even then, things weren't fully settled until Kulwicki led the most laps and finished second to Bill Elliott. Elliott and Allison each won five races but finished second and third behind Kulwicki, a two-race winner. Ernie Irvan and Darrell Waltrip each won three times (the last wins in Waltrip's career) and Geoffrey Bodine, Harry Gant, Mark Martin, and Kyle Petty each won twice. Dale Earnhardt, Ricky Rudd, and Rusty Wallace were one-time winners.

Elliott opened the season strong, winning the spring races at Rockingham, Richmond, near Atlanta, and Darlington. However, Allison and Kulwicki were more consistent, and when the final race of the year began, Allison was actually the favorite, as he only needed to finish sixth or better to win the Cup. It wasn't to be, though, as his season ended on lap 253 after a frontstretch crash with Ernie Irvan. Elliott and Kulwicki ran 1-2 most of the race, leading some to realize that the five bonus points for leading the most laps might be crucial. Elliott won the race, but runner-up Kulwicki led one more lap, 103 to 102, to take the big hardware by 10 points, the closest finish in NASCAR history. After Kulwicki circled the track in the opposite direction in his "Polish victory lap," Richard Petty also took a solo farewell lap to cap his final race. Early in the race, Petty had been involved in an accident that ignited flames under the hood of his STP Pontiac. Said Petty: "I wanted to go out in a blaze of glory: I just forgot the glory part." A footnote to NASCAR history: Gordon's 31st-place finish was largely overlooked in light of everything else that went on.

WINSTON CUP STANDINGS

	DRIVER	STARTS	WINS	POINTS	MONEY>
1.	Alan Kulwicki	29	2	4,078	2,322,561
2.	Bill Elliott	29	5	4,068	1,692,381
3.	Davey Allison	29	5	4,015	1,955,628
4.	Harry Gant	29	2	3,955	1,122,776
5.	Kyle Petty	29	2	3,945	1,107,063
6.	Mark Martin	29	2	3,887	1,000,571
7.	Ricky Rudd	29	1	3,735	793,903
8.	Terry Labonte	29	0	3,674	600,381
9.	Darrell Waltrip	29	3	3,659	876,492
10.	Sterling Marlin	29	0	3,603	649,048
11.	Ernie Irvan	29	3	3,580	996,885
12.	Dale Earnhardt	29	1	3,574	915,463
13.	Rusty Wallace	29	1	3,556	657,925
14.	Morgan Shepherd	29	0	3,549	634,222
15.	Brett Bodine	29	0	3,491	495,224
16.	Geoffrey Bodine	29	2	3,437	716,583
17.	Ken Schrader	29	0	3,404	639,679
18.	Ted Musgrave	29	0	3,315	449,121
19.	Dale Jarrett	29	0	3,251	418,648
20.	Dick Trickle	29	0	3,097	429,521
21.	Derrike Cope	29	0	3,033	277,215
22.	Rick Mast	29	0	2,830	350,740
23.	Michael Waltrip	29	0	2,825	410,545
24.	Wally Dallenbach Jr.	29	0	2,799	220,245
25.	Bobby Hamilton	29	0	2,787	367,065
26.	Richard Petty	29	0	2,731	348,870
27.	Hut Stricklin	28	0	2,689	336,965
28.	Jimmy Hensley	22	0	2,410	247,660
29.	Dave Marcis	29	0	2,348	218,045
30.	Greg Sacks	20	0	1,759	178,120
31.	Chad Little	19	0	1,669	145,805
32.	Jimmy Means	22	0	1,531	133,160
33.	Jimmy Spencer	12	0	1,284	183,585
34.	Bobby Hillin Jr.	13	0	1,135	102,160
35.	Stanley Smith	14	0	959	89,650
36.	Mike Potter	11	0	806	74,710
37.	Jim Sauter	9	0	729	56,045
38.	Lake Speed	9	0	726	49,545
39.	Jimmy Horton	9	0	660	50,125
40.	Bob Schacht	9	0	611	58,815
41.	Charlie Glotzbach	7	0	592	48,060
42.	James Hylton	8	0	476	37,910
43.	Andy Belmont	8	0	467	39,820
44.	Jeff Purvis	6	0	453	45,545
45.	Dave Mader III	5	0	436	69,635
46.	Jerry O'Neil	6	0	429	32,370
47.	Eddie Bierschwale	4	0	277	25,995
48.	Buddy Baker	3	0	255	49,500
49.	Rich Bickle	3	0	252	13,370
50.	Mike Wallace	3	0	249	17,415

1993

AT A GLANCE

Winston Cup Champion: Dale Earnhardt

Notable Events: Aviation accidents took the lives of Alan Kulwicki and Davey Allison, leaving a huge void in the future of the sport. Kulwicki died when the plane he was in crashed on final approach to a Tennessee airport in April. Four months later, Allison died when the helicopter he was flying crashed on the infield of the Talladega Superspeedway. It happened the day after he had finished third in the inaugural Cup race at the 1-mile track in Loudon, New Hampshire.

Top Newcomer: Jeff Gordon began his phenomenal career by earning the Rookie of the Year award after claiming 1 pole, 7 top-5s, and 11 top-10s, good for 14th in the final standings. John Andretti, Jeff Burton, and Joe Nemechek all made their Cup debuts, and Bobby Labonte and Kenny Wallace ran their first full Cup seasons.

Nothing on the track could possibly ease the terrible pain of losing Kulwicki and Allison, but the show went on as scheduled. The year began with a familiar story in the Daytona 500: Dale Earnhardt led the most laps, but not the last one. On the 200th and last lap, Dale Jarrett passed Earnhardt and won for owner Joe Gibbs. It was Jarrett's only victory of the year, but Earnhardt won six races and two poles en route to his sixth championship, his fifth for owner Richard Childress. The team took a 126-point lead into the Atlanta finale and needed to finish only 34th or better. Wallace won the race and led the most laps, but Earnhardt finished 10th to win the Cup by 80 points.

It was a year of streaks: Wallace won three and two races in a row, Earnhardt had a pair of two-race streaks, and Mark Martin had a record-tying four-race streak in the summer. Wallace led the tour with 10 victories (including Bristol, North Wilkesboro, and Martinsville in the spring) and was second in points for owner Roger Penske. Martin won five times and Ernie Irvan three. The last of Allison's 19 career victories was at Richmond in the spring, but Kulwicki didn't win in the five starts he made before his fatal air crash. Jarrett, Geoffrey Bodine, Ricky Rudd, Kyle Petty, and Morgan Shepherd were one-race winners. As of 2002, it was the last Cup victory for Shepherd.

WINSTON CUP STANDINGS

	DRIVER	STARTS	WINS	POINTS	MONEY>
1.	Dale Earnhardt	30	6	4,526	3,353,789
2.	Rusty Wallace	30	10	4,446	1,702,154
3.	Mark Martin	30	5	4,150	1,657,662
4.	Dale Jarrett	30	1	4,000	1,242,394
5.	Kyle Petty	30	1	3,860	914,662
6.	Ernie Irvan	29	3	3,834	1,400,468
7.	Morgan Shepherd	30	1	3,807	782,523
8.	Bill Elliott	30	0	3,774	955,859

9.	Ken Schrader	30	0	3,715	952,748
10.	Ricky Rudd	30	1	3,644	752,562
11.	Harry Gant	30	0	3,524	772,832
12.	Jimmy Spencer	30	0	3,496	686,026
13.	Darrell Waltrip	30	0	3,479	746,646
14.	Jeff Gordon	30	0	3,447	765,168
15.	Sterling Marlin	30	0	3,355	628,835
16.	Geoffrey Bodine	30	1	3,338	783,762
17.	Michael Waltrip	30	0	3,291	529,923
18.	Terry Labonte	30	0	3,280	531,717
19.	Bobby Labonte	30	0	3,221	395,660
20.	Brett Bodine	29	0	3,183	582,014
21.	Rick Mast	30	0	3,001	568,095
22.	Wally Dallenbach Jr.	30	0	2,978	474,340
23.	Kenny Wallace	30	0	2,893	330,325
24.	Hut Stricklin	30	0	2,866	494,600
25.	Ted Musgrave	29	0	2,853	458,615
26.	Derrike Cope	30	0	2,787	402,515
27.	Bobby Hillin Jr.	30	0	2,717	263,540
28.	Rick Wilson	29	0	2,647	299,725
29.	Phil Parsons	26	0	2,454	293,725
30.	Dick Trickle	26	0	2,224	24,065
31.	Davey Allison	16	1	2,104	513,585
32.	Jimmy Hensley	21	0	2,001	368,150
33.	Dave Marcis	23	0	1,970	202,305
34.	Lake Speed	21	0	1,956	319,800
35.	Greg Sacks	19	0	1,730	168,055
36.	Jimmy Means	18	0	1,471	148,205
37.	Bobby Hamilton	15	0	1,348	142,740
38.	Jimmy Horton	13	0	841	115,105
39.	Jeff Purvis	8	0	774	108,545
40.	Todd Bodine	10	0	715	62,245
41.	Alan Kulwicki	5	0	625	165,470
42.	P. J. Jones	6	0	498	53,370
43.	Joe Ruttman	5	0	417	70,700
44.	Joe Nemechek	5	0	389	56,580
45.	Loy Allen Jr.	5	0	362	34,695
46.	Mike Wallace	4	0	343	30,125
47.	Jim Sauter	4	0	295	48,860
48.	Rich Bickle	5	0	292	36,095
49.	Rick Carelli	3	0	258	30,125
50.	John Andretti	4	0	250	24,915

1994

AT A GLANCE

Winston Cup Champion: Dale Earnhardt.

Notable Event: History was made when NASCAR arrived at the Indianapolis Motor Speedway for the first stock car race at the famous home of the Indy 500. Rick Mast won the pole for owner Richard Jackson at 172.414 mph. Jeff Gordon, who was reared in nearby Pittsboro as a teenager, won the Brickyard 400 by a half-second over Brett Bodine. Ernie Irvan was leading late, but a flat tire knocked him out of contention. The race drew a sellout crowd of more than 300,000 and generated enormous worldwide interest.

Top Newcomers: Rookie of the Year Jeff Burton posted two top-5 finishes and three top-10s, while Joe Nemechek had three top-10s. Loy Allen became the first rookie to win the Daytona 500 pole. Ward Burton, older brother of Jeff, also ran his first full Cup season, as did Nemechek.

Dale Earnhardt won his seventh championship, which tied him with Richard Petty for the all-time lead. He did it by winning early season races at Darlington and Bristol, the May race at Talladega, and the fall race at Rockingham. He also had 21 other top-5s and basically coasted in

"You gotta see the loser..." That old boxer's saying is the first thing that comes to mind when viewing the wreck that is Terry Labonte's car, as that wreck somehow won the Goody's 500 in Bristol, Tennessee, on August 27, 1995. Labonte and his crew celebrate their unlikely victory after the race.

after Irvan was sidelined by serious injuries at Michigan in August. At the time, Earnhardt led Irvan by 79 points. That lead grew to 201 at Bristol, 227 at Darlington, and 232 at Richmond. It dipped slightly at Dover, Martinsville, and North Wilkesboro, but jumped to a near-insurmountable 321 after Charlotte in the fall. He ended up winning the Cup by 444 points over Mark Martin and 487 over Wallace. Earnhardt dedicated his win to the late Neil Bonnet, one of his few close racing friends, who died practicing for the Daytona 500.

Gordon earned his first two career victories, including the inaugural Brickyard 400. Jimmy Spencer and Martin were also two-time winners. Wallace led the tour with eight victories, including three straight in June and back-to-back victories in September. Earnhardt won four times, and Irvan, Geoffrey Bodine, and Terry Labonte three times each. Single victories went to Ricky Rudd, Bill Elliott, Dale Jarrett (bound for Robert Yates Racing after three years with Gibbs Racing), and career first-timer Sterling Marlin.

WINSTON CUP STANDINGS

	DRIVER	STARTS	WINS	POINTS	MONEY>
1.	Dale Earnhardt	31	4	4,694	3,400,733
2.	Mark Martin	31	2	4,250	1,678,906
3.	Rusty Wallace	31	8	4,207	1,959,072
4.	Ken Schrader	31	0	4,060	1,211,062
5.	Ricky Rudd	31	1	4,050	1,079,441
6.	Morgan Shepherd	31	0	4,029	1,119,038
7.	Terry Labonte	31	3	3,876	1,150,921
8.	Jeff Gordon	31	2	3,776	1,799,523
9.	Darrell Waltrip	31	0	3,688	854,280
10.	Bill Elliott	31	1	3,617	951,679
11.	Lake Speed	31	0	3,565	845,963
12.	Michael Waltrip	31	0	3,512	720,426
13.	Ted Musgrave	31	0	3,477	669,687
14.	Sterling Marlin	31	1	3,443	1,140,683
15.	Kyle Petty	31	0	3,339	818,832
16.	Dale Jarrett	30	1	3,298	893,754
17.	Geoffrey Bodine	31	3	3,297	1,287,626
18.	Rick Mast	31	0	3,238	733,361
19.	Brett Bodine	31	0	3,159	801,944
20.	Todd Bodine	30	0	3,048	504,316
21.	Bobby Labonte	31	0	3,038	550,305
22.	Ernie Irvan	20	3	3,026	1,311,522
23.	Bobby Hamilton	30	0	2,749	514,520
24.	Jeff Burton	30	0	2,726	594,700
25.	Harry Gant	30	0	2,720	556,200
26.	Hut Stricklin	29	0	2,711	333,495
27.	Joe Nemechek	29	0	2,673	386,315
28.	Steve Grissom	27	0	2,660	300,915
29.	Jimmy Spencer	29	2	2,613	479,235
30.	Derrike Cope	30	0	2,612	398,436
31.	Greg Sacks	31	0	2,593	411,728
32.	John Andretti	29	0	2,229	391,920
33.	Mike Wallace	22	0	2,191	265,115
34.	Dick Trickle	25	0	2,019	244,806
35.	Ward Burton	26	0	1,971	304,700
36.	Dave Marcis	23	0	1,910	261,650
37.	Jeremy Mayfield	20	0	1,673	226,265
38.	Wally Dallenbach Jr.	14	0	1,493	241,492
39.	Loy Allen Jr.	19	0	1,468	216,751
40.	Kenny Wallace	12	0	1,413	235,005
41.	Jimmy Hensley	17	0	1,394	203,520
42.	Chuck Brown	13	0	1,211	225,260
43.	Rich Bickle	12	0	849	115,575
44.	Bobby Hillin Jr.	9	0	749	125,340
45.	Brad Teague	8	0	548	59,990
46.	Jeff Purvis	7	0	484	78,755
47.	Billy Standridge	8	0	404	56,405
48.	Randy Lajoie	3	0	312	30,565
49.	Rick Carellli	4	0	283	31,975
50.	Phil Parsons	3	0	243	21,415

1995

AT A GLANCE

Winston Cup Champion: Jeff Gordon

Notable Events: Sterling Marlin won a second consecutive Daytona 500 and finished a career-high third in points. Ted Musgrave (7th) and Bobby Labonte (10th) cracked the top 10 in points for the first time. Ernie Irvan returned from his near-fatal crash the year before, and at Rockingham in the fall, Ward Burton and owner Bill Davis won for the first time after just seven races together

Top Newcomers: Rookie of the Year Ricky Craven earned four top-10 finishes, while Jeremy Mayfield and Robert Pressley each had one top-10 finish.

Jeff Gordon overtook Sterling Marlin mid-way through the season, then held on down the stretch for his first championship. He led everyone with seven victories, two more than series runner-up Dale Earnhardt and three more than Mark Martin. The Labonte brothers and Marlin each won three times, and Rusty Wallace won twice. Burton, Dale Jarrett, Kyle Petty, and Ricky Rudd were one-time winners. The June victory at Dover was the last (through 2003, anyway) for Petty.

Marlin joined Richard Petty and Cale Yarborough as the only back-to-back Daytona 500 winners. Marlin also won at Darlington in the spring and Talladega in July. Among Earnhardt's five victories were Sears Point in May (the first road course victory of his career) and the second annual Brickyard 400. The Labonte brothers—Bobby and Terry—were 1-2 in the May race near Charlotte. Gordon took a 147-point lead into the season-finale near Atlanta, needing only to finish 41st or lead a lap to clinch. Earnhardt led the most laps and won the race while Gordon struggled to a 32nd-place finish, but Earnhardt's best wasn't enough, as Gordon won his first Cup by 34 points.

WINSTON CUP STANDINGS

	DRIVER	STARTS	WINS	POINTS	MONEY>
1.	Jeff Gordon	31	7	4,614	4,347,343
2.	Dale Earnhardt	31	5	4,580	3,154,241
3.	Sterling Marlin	31	3	4,361	2,253,502
4.	Mark Martin	31	4	4,320	1,893,519
5.	Rusty Wallace	31	2	4,240	1,642,837
6.	Terry Labonte	31	3	4,146	1,558,659
7.	Ted Musgrave	31	0	3,949	1,147,445
8.	Bill Elliott	31	0	3,746	996,816
9.	Ricky Rudd	31	1	3,734	1,337,703
10.	Bobby Labonte	31	3	3,718	1,413,682
11.	Morgan Shepherd	31	0	3,618	996,374
12.	Michael Waltrip	31	0	3,601	898,338
13.	Dale Jarrett	31	1	3,584	1,363,158
14.	Bobby Hamilton	31	0	3,576	804,505
15.	Derrike Cope	31	0	3,384	683,075
16.	Geoffrey Bodine	31	0	3,357	1,011,090
17.	Ken Schrader	31	0	3,221	886,566
18.	John Andretti	31	0	3,140	593,542
19.	Darrell Waltrip	31	0	3,075	850,632
20.	Brett Bodine	31	0	2,958	893,029
21.	Rick Mast	31	0	2,984	749,550
22.	Ward Burton	29	1	2,926	634,655
23.	Lake Speed	31	0	2,921	529,435
24.	Ricky Craven	31	0	2,883	597,054
25.	Dick Trickle	31	0	2,875	694,920
26.	Jimmy Spencer	29	0	2,809	504,560
27.	Steve Grissom	29	0	2,757	509,047
28.	Joe Nemechek	29	0	2,742	428,925
29.	Robert Pressley	31	0	2,663	695,875
30.	Kyle Petty	30	1	2,635	698,875
31.	Jeremy Mayfield	27	0	2,637	436,805
32.	Jeff Burton	29	0	2,556	628,270
33.	Todd Bodine	28	0	2,372	664,620
34.	Mike Wallace	26	0	2,175	428,006
35.	Dave Marcis	28	0	2,126	337,853
36.	Hut Stricklin	24	0	2,052	486,065
37.	Bobby Hillin Jr.	18	0	1,888	244,270
38.	Elton Sawyer	20	0	1,499	416,490
39.	Greg Sacks	20	0	1,349	323,720

40.	Randy Lajoie	14	0	1,133	281,945
41.	Loy Allen Jr.	11	0	890	186,670
42.	Kenny Wallace	11	0	878	151,700
43.	Chuck Brown	9	0	818	99,995
44.	Jimmy Hensley	9	0	558	161,025
45.	Rich Bickle	8	0	538	153,250
46.	Davey Jones	7	0	520	109,925
47.	Jeff Purvis	7	0	391	93,875
48.	Ernie Irvan	3	0	354	54,875
49	Steve Kinser	5	0	287	105,224
50.	Wally Dallenbach Jr.	2	0	221	63,900

1996

AT A GLANCE

Winston Cup Champion: Terry Labonte

Notable Events: Jeff Gordon, at age 25, won more races (10) and poles (5) than any other driver, but finished second to teammate Terry Labonte in the final championship standings. It was the second of four consecutive Winston Cups for owner Rick Hendrick. Bobby Hamilton won his first Cup race, providing Richard Petty with his first victory as a car owner.

Top Newcomer: Rookie of the Year Johnny Benson had one pole, one top-5, and six top-10s after coming to Winston Cup racing with the 1995 Busch Series title on his resume.

The long wait finally ended for Terry Labonte, who got his second Cup 12 years after he won his first in 1984. Labonte won only twice, but his consistency paid off as he finished 37 points ahead of 10-race winner Gordon. Rusty Wallace was second with only five victories and Daytona 500 winner Dale Jarrett won four races. The list of two-time winners included Earnhardt, Labonte, Sterling Marlin, and Ernie Irvan (after a remarkable recovery from injuries he suffered in 1994), and the one-timers included Bobby Labonte, Ricky Rudd, Geoffrey Bodine, and Hamilton, who won for Petty Enterprises at Phoenix in the fall. Gordon had two two-race winning streaks and a three-race streak, but he also dropped out of five races (compared to three DNFs for Labonte) and had two other finishes outside the top 10.

In the final Winston Cup race to be held at North Wilkesboro Speedway, Gordon gained his 10th victory of 1996. The popular ⅝ths-mile track in the foothills of the North Carolina mountains had been a NASCAR fixture since 1949 and had seen some of the tour's best races (and some of its best postrace fights) through its four decades of existence. However, when the track was sold to rival owners Bob Bahre and Bruton Smith, it was decided that the two race dates the track had each year could best be used elsewhere. Bahre had strong ties to NASCAR and the France family, who wanted the date to be moved to Bahre's track in New Hampshire, while Smith decided on his own that the other date would be perfect to bring Winston Cup racing back to Texas at his new 1.5-mile speedway near Fort Worth.

WINSTON CUP STANDINGS

	DRIVER	STARTS	WINS	POINTS	MONEY>
1.	Terry Labonte	31	2	4,657	4,030,648
2.	Jeff Gordon	31	10	4,620	3,428,485
3.	Dale Jarrett	31	4	4,568	2,985,418
4.	Dale Earnhardt	31	2	4,327	2,285,926
5.	Mark Martin	31	0	4,278	1,887,396
6.	Ricky Rudd	31	1	3,845	1,503,025
7.	Rusty Wallace	31	5	3,717	1,665,315
8.	Sterling Marlin	31	2	3,682	1,588,425
9.	Bobby Hamilton	31	1	3,639	1,151,235
10.	Ernie Irvan	31	2	3,632	1,683,313
11.	Bobby Labonte	31	1	3,590	1,475,196
12.	Ken Schrader	31	0	3,540	1,089,603
13.	Jeff Burton	30	0	3,538	884,303
14.	Michael Waltrip	31	0	3,535	1,182,811
15.	Jimmy Spencer	31	0	3,476	1,090,876
16.	Ted Musgrave	31	0	3,466	961,512
17.	Geoffrey Bodine	31	1	3,218	1,031,762
18.	Rick Mast	31	0	3,190	924,559
19.	Morgan Shepherd	31	0	3,133	719,059
20.	Ricky Craven	31	0	3,078	941,959
21.	Johnny Benson Jr.	30	0	3,004	947,080
22.	Hut Stricklin	31	0	2,854	631,055
23.	Lake Speed	31	0	2,834	817,175
24.	Brett Bodine	30	0	2,814	767,716
25.	Wally Dallenbach Jr.	30	0	2,786	837,001
26.	Jeremy Mayfield	30	0	2,721	592,853
27.	Kyle Petty	28	0	2,696	689,041
28.	Kenny Wallace	30	0	2,694	457,665
29.	Darrell Waltrip	31	0	2,657	740,185
30.	Bill Elliott	24	0	2,627	716,506
31.	John Andretti	30	0	2,621	688,511
32.	Robert Pressley	30	0	2,485	690,465
33.	Ward Burton	27	0	2,411	873,619
34.	Joe Nemechek	29	0	2,391	666,247
35.	Derrike Cope	29	0	2,374	675,781
36.	Dick Trickle	26	0	2,131	404,927
37.	Bobby Hillin Jr.	26	0	2,128	395,224
38.	Dave Marcis	27	0	2,047	435,177
39.	Steve Grissom	13	0	1,188	314,983
40.	Todd Bodine	10	0	991	198,525
41.	Mike Wallace	11	0	799	169,082
42.	Greg Sacks	9	0	710	207,755
43.	Elton Sawyer	9	0	705	129,618
44.	Chad Little	9	0	627	164,752
45.	Loy Allen Jr.	9	0	603	130,667
46.	Gary Bradberry	9	0	591	155,785
47.	Mike Skinner	5	0	529	65,850
48.	Jeff Purvis	4	0	328	91,127
49.	Jeff Green	4	0	247	46,875
50.	Randy MacDonald	3	0	228	33,910

1997

AT A GLANCE

Winston Cup Champion: Jeff Gordon

Notable Events: In the most important expansion in years, NASCAR returned to the Southern California market with a race

Richard Petty, left, definitely shouldn't quit his day job, as it appears working as a Vegas showgirl like Aki (from the show "Enter the Night") is out of the question. Petty was in Las Vegas to attend a press conference on August 12, 1997, at which NASCAR announced that Las Vegas Motor Speedway would host its first Winston Cup race in 1998.

at the 2-mile California Speedway near Fontana. Earlier in the year, the tour went back into Texas after a long absence, this time to a 1.5-mile track in the Fort Worth-Dallas-Denton area. The tour also made a second trip to the New Hampshire International Speedway at Loudon.

Top Newcomers: Mike Skinner, a former Craftsman Truck Series champion, was Rookie of the Year with owner Richard Childress. He was the pole-sitter for the Daytona 500 and Pepsi 400, the first time a rookie had won both Daytona Beach poles. The only other rookies who ran the full schedule were former Busch Series champion David Green and Indy car driver Robby Gordon. New England natives Jerry Nadeu and Steve Park also made their Cup debuts.

Jeff Gordon continued to cut a wide swath through NASCAR, winning his second championship in three years. He won 10 races in 32 starts, had 22 top-5s, and 23 top-10s. He won the

Daytona 500 and the race at Rockingham one week later, then went back-to-back at Bristol and Martinsville in April, won at Charlotte in May, and at Pocono and Fontana in June. He tailed off a little after that, winning only at Watkins Glen in August and at Darlington (worth an extra $1 million from R.J. Reynolds Inc.) and Loudon in September. Despite that record, he won the Cup by only 14 points over seven-time race winner Dale Jarrett.

Mark Martin won four times, Jeff Burton three (the first three of his career), Ricky Rudd twice, and the Labonte brothers, Rusty Wallace, Ernie Irvan, Bobby Hamilton, and John Andretti

With all of its top drivers on hand to mark the occasion, Ford Motor Company unveils the new 2000 Ford NASCAR Taurus during a Ford Fan Appreciation Day at the RCA Dome in Indianapolis on August 4, 1999. Among the drivers on hand were, from left to right, Dale Jarrett, Rusty Wallace, Bill Elliott, Ricky Rudd, and Darrell Waltrip. At far right is Jeff Burton.

(the first of his career) once each. Several drivers had modest winning streaks: Gordon had a pair of two-race streaks, while Jarrett and Martin each had a two-race streak. One of Gordon's victories was the Daytona 500, where he led a 1-2-3 sweep (with teammates Terry Labonte and Ricky Craven) for Hendrick Motorsports. Ten months later, NASCAR showed up for its annual finale near Atlanta, where Gordon needed to finish 18th or better to win the title. He barely made it, starting 37th in his backup car and finishing 17th, well behind winner Bobby Labonte, runner-up Jarrett, and third-place Martin. Still, that was good enough for his final 14-point spread over Jarrett, who was 15 points ahead of third-place Martin.

WINSTON CUP STANDINGS

	DRIVER	STARTS	WINS	POINTS	MONEY>
1	Jeff Gordon	32	10	4,710	4,201,227
2	Dale Jarrett	32	7	4,696	2,512,382
3	Mark Martin	32	4	4,681	1,877,139
4	Jeff Burton	32	3	4,285	1,858,234
5	Dale Earnhardt	32	0	4,216	1,663,019
6	Terry Labonte	32	1	4,177	1,951,844
7	Bobby Labonte	32	1	4,101	1,943,239
8	Bill Elliott	32	0	3,836	1,377,607
9	Rusty Wallace	32	1	3,598	1,505,260
10	Ken Schrader	32	0	3,576	1,109,782
11	Johnny Benson	32	0	3,575	1,120,814
12	Ted Musgrave	32	0	3,556	1,128,404
13	Jeremy Mayfield	32	0	3,547	943,794
14	Ernie Irvan	32	1	3,534	1,492,739
15	Kyle Petty	32	0	3,455	834,639
16	Bobby Hamilton	32	1	3,450	1,350,335
17	Ricky Rudd	32	2	3,330	1,863,040
18	Michael Waltrip	32	0	3,173	1,015,384
19	Ricky Craven	30	0	3,108	1,139,860
20	Jimmy Spencer	32	0	3,079	1,016,109
21	Steve Grissom	31	0	3,061	1,045,374
22	Geoffrey Bodine	29	0	3,046	1,021,114
23	John Andretti	32	1	3,019	1,115,725

24	Ward Burton	31	0	2,987	977,044
25	Sterling Marlin	32	0	2,954	1,287,570
26	Darrell Waltrip	31	0	2,942	946,179
27	Derrike Cope	31	0	2,901	707,404
28	Joe Nemechek	30	0	2,754	732,194
29	Brett Bodine	31	0	2,716	936,694
30	Mike Skinner	31	0	2,669	791,819
31	Dick Trickle	28	0	2,629	656,189
32	Rick Mast	29	0	2,569	829,339
33	Kenny Wallace	31	0	2,462	926,501
34	Hut Stricklin	29	0	2,423	802,904
35	Lake Speed	25	0	2,301	715,074
36	Chad Little	27	0	2,081	555,914
37	David Green	26	0	2,038	483,833
38	Morgan Shepherd	23	0	2,033	662,999
39	Jeff Green	20	0	1,624	434,685
40	Robby Gordon	20	0	1,495	622,439
41	Wally Dallenbach Jr.	22	0	1,475	461,279
42	Dave Marcis	19	0	1,405	427,364
43	Robert Pressley	14	0	984	252,478
44	Gary Bradberry	16	0	868	251,930
45	Greg Sacks	12	0	778	320,714
46	Mike Wallace	7	0	541	159,303
47	Bobby Hillin Jr.	10	0	511	211,978
48	Lance Hooper	6	0	402	134,150
49	Kenny Irwin	4	0	390	61,230
50	Billy Standridge	6	0	366	149,824

1998

AT A GLANCE

Winston Cup Champion: Jeff Gordon

Notable Events: It was NASCAR's 50th anniversary season and it threw itself quite a party. Season-long events commemorated its successful past, and champion Jeff Gordon made sure the present and future looked rosy. In perhaps the most dominating performance in NASCAR history, he won 13 races to easily claim his second consecutive championship and third overall. The highlight of the year, though, came in the first race when Dale Earnhardt FINALLY won the Daytona 500 after coming so close on so many previous occasions.

Top Newcomer: Rookie of the Year Kenny Irwin crashed in his first race (a 125-mile qualifier at Daytona) but rebounded to post one top-5 finish and four top-10s, finishing 28th in points for owner Robert Yates.

Based on his 1998 performance, some NASCAR-watchers feel Jeff Gordon can claim a spot right next to "King Richard" Petty as having perhaps the best season in series history. Gordon started right, winning the spring races at Rockingham, Bristol, and Charlotte. He won the summer races at Sears Point, Pocono, Indianapolis, Watkins Glen, Michigan, and Loudon, and the fall races at Darlington (worth a $1 million bonus from R. J. Reynolds Co.) and Daytona Beach (rescheduled from July because of fires). Gordon closed the season with victories at Rockingham (it clinched the title) and near Atlanta. The season included a four-race winning streak in July and August, and a pair of two-race streaks.

Gordon was a good story, but the best story was Dale Earnhardt finally winning the Daytona 500. In perhaps NASCAR's most welcomed and satisfying victory in decades, the seven-time champion garnered the one trophy that had eluded him. He started fourth and led 105 of 200 laps, winning when a late-race incident caused the race to end under caution. After he took the checkered flag and cut some donuts in the trioval grass, crewmen from every team lined pit row to applaud his victory and congratulate him.

Gordon dominated the season and Earnhardt won the 500, but other drivers also had good seasons. Martin won seven times, Dale Jarrett won three races, and Jeff Burton and Bobby Labonte each won twice. Single winners included Bobby Hamilton, Terry Labonte, Jeremy Mayfield (his breakthrough victory at Pocono), and Ricky Rudd. One of Martin's victories was in the inaugural spring race at Las Vegas Motor Speedway, a 1.5-mile, Bruton Smith-owned track. LVMS further expanded NASCAR into America's largest and most popular areas, all in the name of marketing and demographics.

WINSTON CUP STANDINGS

	DRIVER	STARTS	WINS	POINTS	MONEY>
1	Jeff Gordon	33	13	5328	6,175,867
2	Mark Martin	33	7	4964	3,279,370
3	Dale Jarrett	33	3	4619	3,368,735
4	Rusty Wallace	33	1	4501	2,133,435
5	Jeff Burton	33	2	4415	2,114,597
6	Bobby Labonte	33	2	4180	2,648,970
7	Jeremy Mayfield	33	1	4157	1,970,521
8	Dale Earnhardt	33	1	3928	2,611,100
9	Terry Labonte	33	1	3901	1,838,415
10	Bobby Hamilton	33	1	3786	1,789,180
11	John Andretti	33	0	3682	1,642,700
12	Ken Schrader	33	0	3675	1,729,881
13	Sterling Marlin	32	0	3530	1,180,740
14	Jimmy Spencer	31	0	3464	1,600,236
15	Chad Little	32	0	3423	1,321,786
16	Ward Burton	33	0	3352	1,396,633
17	Michael Waltrip	32	0	3340	1,360,385
18	Bill Elliott	32	0	3305	1,454,465
19	Ernie Irvan	30	0	3262	1,476,141
20	Johnny Benson	32	0	3160	1,286,971
21	Mike Skinner	30	0	3153	1,205,581
22	Ricky Rudd	33	1	3131	1,564,145
23	Ted Musgrave	32	0	3124	1,215,626
24	Darrell Waltrip	33	0	2957	998,530
25	Brett Bodine	33	0	2907	1,245,173
26	Joe Nemechek	32	0	2897	1,343,991
27	Geoffrey Bodine	32	0	2864	1,247,255
28	Kenny Irwin	32	0	2760	1,433,567
29	Dick Trickle	32	0	2678	1,207,471
30	Kyle Petty	33	0	2675	1,262,731
31	Kenny Wallace	31	0	2615	995,216
32	Robert Pressley	30	0	2388	996,721
33	Rick Mast	30	0	2296	894,327
34	Steve Grissom	27	0	2215	1,030,041
35	Kevin Lepage	27	0	2196	852,721
36	Jerry Nadeau	30	0	2121	804,867

37	Derrike Cope	38	0	2065	956,980
38	Wally Dallenbach Jr.	23	0	1832	807,856
39	Rich Bickle	21	0	1773	682,255
40	Jeff Green	22	0	1687	589,841
41	Todd Bodine	14	0	1322	378,766
42	Steve Park	17	0	1322	487,265
43	Lake Speed	16	0	1297	552,521
44	David Green	15	0	1014	441,121
45	Dave Marcis	13	0	949	444,946
46	Ricky Craven	11	0	907	506,230
47	Morgan Shepherd	12	0	843	364,541
48	Gary Bradberry	13	0	787	341,307
49	Randy LaJoie	9	0	768	336,905
50	Hut Stricklin	13	0	700	337,106

1999

AT A GLANCE

Winston Cup Champion: Dale Jarrett

Notable Events: After finishing top three in points for three consecutive years, Dale Jarrett finally got his Winston Cup. He joined seven-time champion Richard Petty as only the second driver to follow his father as NASCAR champion. (Lee Petty won in 1954, 1958, and 1959, and Ned Jarrett won in 1961 and 1965.) DJ won 4 of 34 races and backed that up with 20 more top-5s and 5 more top-10s. One of the year's biggest stories was the late-season departure of Hendrick Motorsports fixture Ray Evernham to lead Dodge's 2001 return to Winston Cup.

Top Newcomers: Rookie of the Year wasn't much of an issue. Tony Stewart won two poles and three races and finished fourth in points. His breakthrough victory came at Richmond in September, then he won back-to-back at Phoenix and Homestead late in the year. His $3,190,149 more than doubled the previous earnings record by a rookie. Former Busch Series star Elliott Sadler was the only other rookie to run the full schedule.

Dale Jarrett had run 188 races for nine owners over seven years before joining a team that was good enough to win a championship. But even though he and Joe Gibbs Racing had their moments, things never quite worked out and they never won the elusive Winston Cup. So Jarrett left after 1994 to join Robert Yates Racing. He won once in 1995 and was 13th in points, four times in 1996 and was 3rd in points, then seven times in 1997 and was 2nd in points. He won three times and finished 3rd 1998, but things finally came together in 1999. He won 4 races, had 24 top-5s, and 29 top-10s in 34 starts. Ironically, the man he beat for the title was Bobby Labonte, who'd replaced him on Gibbs's team.

Jarrett didn't win until Richmond in May, but that night victory vaulted him into the lead by 63 points, a lead he wouldn't lose. He also won at Michigan in June, Daytona Beach in July, and In-

dianapolis in August. The lead reached 240 points in July and 314 in August, as Jarrett kept racking up top-5 and top-10 finishes to increase his lead. The fall portion of the schedule saw Jarrett's team take a defensive stance, picking and choosing their spots and carefully managing each race. They didn't completely lay back, but Jarrett raced smart and stayed out of trouble to protect his lead. He clinched the championship at Homestead, building a 211-point lead that was more than Labonte could overcome in the finale near Atlanta. Ironically, they finished 1-2 in the last race, and Jarrett and team owner Robert Yates had their Cup by 201 points. Yates had been close twice before with the late Davey Allison, and in 1994, a midseason accident had taken Ernie Irvan out of the running. No wonder he was moved to tears after finally claiming the title.

Gordon led the tour with seven victories, two of them after Evernham left in September to begin preparing his Dodge team. Jeff Burton won six races, while Bobby Labonte won five, Earnhardt and Stewart each won three, and Mark Martin two. Joe Nemechek (his first career victory), Andretti (his second), Rusty Wallace, and Terry Labonte each won once. In keeping with its recent policy, NASCAR moved into a new, high-profile, TV-friendly market. This one was South Florida, where Homestead-Miami Speedway welcomed Winston Cup after prepping for several years with Busch Series, Craftsman Truck, and various Indy car races.

WINSTON CUP STANDINGS

	DRIVER	STARTS	WINS	POINTS	MONEY>
1.	Dale Jarrett	34	4	5262	3,608,829
2.	Bobby Labonte	34	5	5061	3,550,341
3.	Mark Martin	34	2	4943	2,783,296
4.	Tony Stewart	34	3	4774	2,615,226
5.	Jeff Burton	34	6	4733	5,211,301
6.	Jeff Gordon	34	7	4620	5,281,361
7.	Dale Earnhardt	34	3	4492	2,712,089
8.	Rusty Wallace	34	1	4155	2,167,429
9.	Ward Burton	34	0	4062	2,115,824
10.	Mike Skinner	34	0	4003	2,222,321
11.	Jeremy Mayfield	34	0	3743	1,944,589
12.	Terry Labonte	34	1	3580	2,303,104
13.	Bobby Hamilton	34	0	3564	1,846,454
14.	Steve Park	34	0	3481	1,609,808
15.	Ken Schrader	34	0	3479	1,787,184
16.	Sterling Marlin	34	0	3397	1,651,371
17.	John Andretti	34	1	3394	1,861,706
18.	Wally Dallenbach	34	0	3367	1,604,968
19.	Kenny Irwin	34	0	3338	1,995,821
20.	Jimmy Spencer	34	0	3312	1,629,928
21.	Bill Elliott	34	0	3246	1,581,501

A view from atop Martinsville Speedway gives a big-picture view of one of NASCAR's oldest tracks in 2002.

22.	Kenny Wallace	34	0	3210	1,376,708
23.	Chad Little	34	0	3193	1,585,976
24.	Elliott Sadler	34	0	3191	1,551,221
25.	Kevin Lepage	34	0	3185	1,552,841
26.	Kyle Petty	32	0	3103	1,278,953
27.	Geoffrey Bodine	34	0	3053	1,257,494
28.	Johnny Benson	34	0	3012	1,567,668
29.	Michael Waltrip	34	0	2974	1,701,160
30.	Joe Nemechek	34	1	2956	1,634,946
31.	Ricky Rudd	34	0	2922	1,632,011
32.	Rick Mast	34	0	2845	1,290,143
33.	Ted Musgrave	32	0	2689	1,162,403
34.	Jerry Nadeau	34	0	2686	1,370,229
35.	Brett Bodine	32	0	2351	1,321,396
36.	David Green	32	0	2320	1,079,536
37.	Darrell Waltrip	27	0	2158	973,133
38.	Rich Bickle	24	0	2149	892,456
39.	Robert Pressley	28	0	2050	1,033,223
40.	Ernie Irvan	21	0	1915	1,073,775
41.	Ricky Craven	24	0	1513	853,835
42.	Dave Marcis	20	0	1324	731,221
43.	Hut Stricklin	10	0	918	378,942
44.	Derrike Cope	15	0	915	617,976
45.	Buckshot Jones	10	0	676	345,128
46.	Todd Bodine	7	0	529	208,382
47.	Dick Trickle	9	0	528	275,364
48.	Dale Earnhardt	5	0	500	162,095
49.	Matt Kenseth	5	0	434	143,561
50.	Steve Grissom	6	0	336	193,529

2000

AT A GLANCE

Winston Cup Champion: Bobby Labonte

Notable Events: Tragedy struck when Busch driver Adam Petty, Cup driver Kenny Irwin, and Craftsman Truck racer Tony Roper died in separate accidents. Petty, the first fourth-generation professional athlete in American sports, died in May during practice for a Mother's Day weekend race at Loudon, New Hampshire. Several months later, Irwin also died at Loudon, (ironically at the same end of the track as Petty) during practice for a Cup race. Roper died during a CTS race at Fort Worth in the fall. Each died of head injuries, leading some drivers to embrace head-and-neck devices well before NASCAR made them mandatory.

Top Newcomers: Dale Earnhardt Jr. had the sparkling resume (two Busch Series titles), but Matt Kenseth won their Rookie of the Year battle. He won 1 race, had 10 other top-10s, was 14th in points, and was the leading rookie in 17 of 34 starts. He beat two-race winner (and 16th-place finisher) Earnhardt Jr. by 42 rookie points. Dave Blaney was third in rookie points, followed by Scott Pruett and Mike Bliss.

Except for two setbacks, Bobby Labonte had improved in points every year throughout his Cup career. He'd dipped from 19th to 21st in 1993–1994 with owner Bill Davis, then from 10th to 11th in 1995–1996 with owner Joe Gibbs. However, he moved from seventh, to sixth, to second in 1997, 1998, and 1999, respectively. Therefore, it wasn't terribly surprising when he won the 2000 title, thus joining older brother Terry (1984 and 1996) as the only sibling champions. Bobby won 2 poles and 4 races, and backed that up with 3 outside poles, 15 more top-5s, and 5 more top-10s. He won at Rockingham in the spring, Indianapolis in the summer, Darlington on Labor Day weekend, then near Charlotte in October. He won the Cup by 265 points over Earnhardt Sr.

Second-year driver Tony Stewart (Bobby's teammate) led with six victories, but five DNFs left him sixth in points behind Labonte, Earnhardt Sr., Jeff Burton, defending champion Dale Jarrett, and Ricky Rudd. Besides Labonte, Jeff Burton and Rusty Wallace also won four races, while Jeff Gordon won three times in his first full year without long-time crew chief Ray Evernham. Jeremy Mayfield, Jarrett, Earnhardt Sr. and Earnhardt Jr. were two-time winners, while Kenseth, Mark Martin, Ward Burton, Steve Park, and Jerry Nadeau all won once.

WINSTON CUP STANDINGS

	DRIVER	STARTS	WINS	POINTS	MONEY>
1.	Bobby Labonte	34	4	5130	4,041,750
2.	Dale Earnhardt	34	2	4865	3,701,390
3.	Jeff Burton	34	4	4836	5,121,350
4.	Dale Jarrett	34	2	4684	5,225,500
5.	Ricky Rudd	34	0	4575	2,385,400
6.	Tony Stewart	34	6	4570	3,200,190
7.	Rusty Wallace	34	4	4544	3,037,720
8.	Mark Martin	34	1	4410	2,763,540
9.	Jeff Gordon	34	3	4361	2,703,590
10.	Ward Burton	34	1	4152	2,385,330
11.	Steve Park	34	1	3934	2,052,830
12.	Mike Skinner	34	0	3898	1,985,590
13.	Johnny Benson	33	0	3716	1,627,870
14.	Matt Kenseth	34	1	3711	2,150,760
15.	Joe Nemechek	34	0	3534	1,907,280
16.	Dale Earnhardt Jr.	34	2	3516	2,610,400
17.	Terry Labonte	32	0	3433	2,043,090
18.	Ken Schrader	34	0	3398	1,530,840
19.	Sterling Marlin	34	0	3363	1,819,640
20.	Jerry Nadeau	34	1	3273	2,038,670
21.	Bill Elliott	32	0	3267	2,447,790
22.	Jimmy Spencer	34	0	3188	1,858,760

Crew members from Michael Waltrip's team retrieve the car he used to win the 2001 Daytona 500, as tradition dictates that the winner's car be displayed at the track until the following year's season-opening race, at which time the car is returned.

23.	John Andretti	34	0	3169	1,964,400
24.	Jeremy Mayfield	32	2	3156	2,090,500
25.	Robert Pressley	34	0	3055	1,427,820
26.	Kenny Wallace	34	0	2874	1,723,970
27.	Michael Waltrip	34	0	2797	1,689,420
28.	Kevin Lepage	32	0	2795	1,679,190
29.	Elliott Sadler	33	0	2762	1,578,360
30.	Bobby Hamilton	34	0	2715	1,619,770
31.	Dave Blaney	33	0	2656	1,272,690
32.	Chad Little	27	0	2634	1,418,880
33.	Rick Mast	29	0	2366	1,156,430
34.	Wally Dallenbach	30	0	2344	1,169,070
35.	Brett Bodine	29	0	2145	1,020,660
36.	Darrell Waltrip	29	0	1981	1,246,280
37.	Scott Pruett	28	0	1879	1,135,850
38.	Stacy Compton	27	0	1857	1,069,650
39.	Mike Bliss	25	0	1748	953,948
40.	Ted Musgrave	18	0	1614	827,216
41.	Kyle Petty	19	0	1441	894,911
42.	Kenny Irwin	17	0	1440	949,436
43.	Robby Gordon	17	0	1309	620,781
44.	Ricky Craven	16	0	1175	636,562
45.	Geoffrey Bodine	14	0	1039	704,981
46.	Dave Marcis	11	0	723	405,572
47.	Kurt Busch	7	0	613	311,915
48.	Todd Bodine	5	0	456	234,065
49.	Hut Stricklin	7	0	436	255,200
50.	Dick Trickle	6	0	423	233,865

2001

AT A GLANCE

Winston Cup Champion: Jeff Gordon

Notable Event: The sport was shocked beyond words when seven-time champion Dale Earnhardt died in a multi-car crash in turn 4 on the last lap of the Daytona 500. Running third—ironically chasing fellow Dale Earnhardt Inc. employees Michael Waltrip and Dale Earnhardt Jr.—the legendary racer died when his car crashed almost head-on into the outside wall after contact from Sterling Marlin. An instant before impact with the wall, the No. 3 Goodwrench Chevrolet was hit in its right-front by Ken Schrader's No. 36 Pontiac. It was later determined that Earnhardt's seat belt had broken sometime during the incident, a revelation that led to a season-long investigation on safety.

Top Newcomers: Kevin Harvick, whose previous experience had been in Busch and Craftsman Truck races, got the Richard Childress-owned Goodwrench Chevrolet that was renumbered from 3 to 29. He won in the spring near Atlanta and in the summer near Chicago, was ninth in points and easily claimed Rookie of the Year honors. He also ran the full Busch Series and easily won that championship. Fellow rookies Kurt Busch and Casey Atwood also ran the full Cup season, but they couldn't overcome Harvick.

After finishing an uncharacteristic ninth with new crew chief Robbie Loomis the previous season, Gordon had a solid season to win his fourth title. He and Loomis assumed the points lead for good at Pocono in July, eventually building their lead to 349 points. They clinched it by finishing sixth in the next-to-last race near Atlanta in November. Gordon won at Las Vegas in March, Dover and Michigan in June, Indianapolis and Watkins Glen in August, then at Kansas City in August. It was the fourth consecutive season in which the Cup was decided before the final race after several years of down-to-the-wire championship finishes.

Former champion Dale Jarrett won four times, Tony Stewart and Dale Earnhardt Jr. three times each, and Harvick, Jeff Burton, Bobby Labonte, Sterling Marlin, and Ricky Rudd twice each. One-time winners were Ward Burton, Ricky Craven, Bill Elliott, Robby Gordon, Bobby Hamilton, Joe Nemechek, Steve Park, Elliott Sadler, Rusty Wallace, and Michael Waltrip. It was the first career Cup victory each for Waltrip, Harvick, Sadler, Craven, and Robby Gordon and the first in several years for Elliott and Hamilton. There were 19 different winners, five more than in 2000, when a then-record 14 drivers won.

WINSTON CUP STANDINGS

	DRIVER	STARTS	WINS	POINTS	MONEY
1.	Jeff Gordon	36	6	5,112	6,649,080
2.	Tony Stewart	36	3	4,763	3,493,040
3.	Sterling Marlin	36	2	4,741	3,361,660
4.	Ricky Rudd	36	2	4,706	3,976,200
5.	Dale Jarrett	36	4	4,612	4,608,370
6.	Bobby Labonte	36	2	4,561	4,139,850
7.	Rusty Wallace	36	1	4,481	4,272,410
8.	Dale Earnhardt, Jr.	36	3	4,460	5,384,630
9.	Kevin Harvick	35	2	4,406	3,716,630
10.	Jeff Burton	36	2	4,394	3,866,330
11.	Johnny Benson	36	0	4,152	2,573,570
12.	Mark Martin	36	0	4,095	3,487,720
13.	Matt Kenseth	36	0	3,982	2,265,840
14.	Ward Burton	36	1	3,846	3,293,600
15.	Bill Elliott	36	1	3,824	3,337,670
16.	Jimmy Spencer	36	0	3,782	2,398,940
17.	Jerry Nadeau	36	0	3,675	2,246,770
18.	Bobby Hamilton	36	1	3,575	2,275,900
19.	Ken Schrader	36	0	3,480	2,254,390
20.	Elliott Sadler	36	1	3,471	2,525,010
21.	Ricky Craven	36	1	3,379	1,923,980
22.	Dave Blaney	36	0	3,303	1,788,150
23.	Terry Labonte	36	0	3,280	2,972,900
24.	Michael Waltrip	36	1	3,159	3,373,390
25.	Robert Pressley	34	0	3,156	2,100,020
26.	Casey Atwood	35	0	3,132	1,797,110
27.	Kurt Busch	35	0	3,081	2,170,630
28.	Joe Nemechek	31	1	2,994	2,510,720
29.	Todd Bodine	35	0	2,960	1,740,310
30.	Brett Bodine	36	0	2,948	1,740,530
31.	John Andretti	35	0	2,943	2,873,180
32.	Steve Park	24	1	2,859	2,385,970
33.	Stacy Compton	34	0	2,752	1,704,960
34.	Mike Wallace	29	0	2,693	2,075,040
35.	Jeremy Mayfield	28	0	2,651	2,682,600
36.	Kevin Lepage	29	0	2,461	1,424,850
37.	Jason Leffler	30	0	2,413	1,724,690
38.	Ron Hornaday	32	0	2,305	1,435,860
39.	Kenny Wallace	24	0	2,054	1,507,920
40.	Mike Skinner	23	0	2,029	1,921,190
41.	Buckshot Jones	30	0	1,939	1,631,490
42.	Hut Stricklin	22	0	1,770	1,006,020
43.	Kyle Petty	24	0	1,673	1,008,920
44.	Robby Gordon	17	1	1,552	1,371,900
45.	Rick Mast	17	0	1,187	680,321
46.	Andy Houston	17	0	1,123	865,263
47.	Bobby Hamilton Jr.	10	0	748	546,847
48.	Jeff Green	8	0	539	441,849
49.	Ryan Newman	7	0	497	465,276
50.	Boris Said	2	0	272	124,340

2002

AT A GLANCE

Winston Cup Champion: Tony Stewart

Notable Events: After a restart, Ward Burton led the final three laps to claim his first every Daytona 500; Tony Stewart finished last in the race, which was definitely *not* a sign of things to come. The new single-engine rule—which says a team has to race with the same engine it qualified with—changes race strategy immensely. Any team that changes engines for any reason has to start the race from the last row.

Top Newcomers: 2002 presented race fans with one of the best collections of young talent to ever hit the track at the same time. Four drivers won their first race, including three-time winner and Rookie of the Year Jimmie Johnson and four-time winner Kurt Busch. Ryan Newman and Jamie McMurray also won for the first time.

Tony Stewart, who had been NASCAR's next big thing ever since he began racing, fully lived up to all the hype, claiming his first Cup title. Stewart won three races, and by the season's

It looks like Ryan Newman's day is about to come to an end as he begins to lose control of his car, but he came out of the skid before he reached the wall or the infield grass and instead sailed to his series-leading eight victory of the season in the Pop Secret Microwave Popcorn 400 at North Carolina Speedway on November 9, 2003. It was the next-to-last race before the end of the 2003 season and the start of the Nextel era in NASCAR racing.

final race in Miami, had compiled so many points that he needed only to finish 22nd or better to claim the Cup, which he did by finishing 18th. Known almost as much for his outspokenness as for his driving talent, Stewart had to overcome off-track controversy to win the title. After the Brickyard 400 on August 4, Stewart shoved a photographer, which led to disciplinary action—but no suspension—from NASCAR officials.

Kevin Harvick wasn't as lucky as Stewart. Warned repeatedly by Winston Cup officials for bumping other drivers, Harvick became the first driver to ever be suspended before a race for an inci-

dent in another race. After bumping another driver in a Craftsman Truck Series race on April 13, Harvick was suspended for the next day's Virginia 400. In other racing news, veteran Sterling Marlin led the Cup standings for much of the year before sitting out the season's last seven races with a neck injury; he finished 18th in the final standings. Another veteran, Mark Martin, also had an excellent year and finished second to Stewart overall. Matt Kenseth had his best season ever, winning a series-high six races. Other multiple winners included Busch (four); three-time winners Jeff Gordon and Jimmie Johnson; and dual winners Ward Burton, Marlin, Dale Earnhardt Jr., Dale Jarrett, and Bill Elliott, Single-race winners in 2002 included Bobby Labonte, Mark Martin, Ricky Rudd, Michael Waltrip, Kevin Harvick, Ryan Newman, and Johnny Benson.

WINSTON CUP STANDINGS

	DRIVER	STARTS	WINS	POINTS	MONEY
1.	Tony Stewart	36	3	4800	4,695,150
2.	Mark Martin	36	1	4762	5,279,400
3.	Kurt Busch	36	4	4641	3,723,650
4.	Jeff Gordon	36	3	4607	4,981,170
5.	Jimmie Johnson	36	3	4600	2,847,700
6.	Ryan Newman	36	1	4593	4,373,830
7.	Rusty Wallace	36	0	4574	4,090,050
8.	Matt Kenseth	36	5	4432	3,888,850
9.	Dale Jarrett	36	2	4415	3,935,670
10.	Ricky Rudd	36	1	4323	4,009,380
11.	Dale Earnhardt Jr.	36	2	4270	4,570,980
12.	Jeff Burton	36	0	4259	3,863,220
13.	Bill Elliott	36	2	4158	3,753,490
14.	Michael Waltrip	36	1	3985	2,829,180
15.	Ricky Craven	36	0	3888	2,493,720
16.	Bobby Labonte	36	1	3810	3,851,770
17.	Jeff Green	36	0	3704	2,135,820
18.	Sterling Marlin	29	2	3703	3,711,150
19.	Dave Blaney	36	0	3670	2,677,710
20.	Robby Gordon	36	0	3632	3,054,240
21.	Kevin Harvick	35	1	3501	3,748,100
22.	Kyle Petty	36	0	3501	1,995,820
23.	Elliott Sadler	36	0	3418	3,390,690
24.	Terry Labonte	36	0	3417	3,143,990
25.	Ward Burton	36	2	3362	4,849,880
26.	Jeremy Mayfield	36	0	3309	2,494,580
27.	Jimmy Spencer	34	0	3187	2,136,790
28.	John Andretti	36	0	3161	2,954,230
29.	Johnny Benson	31	1	3132	2,746,670
30.	Ken Schrader	36	0	2954	2,460,140
31.	Mike Skinner	36	0	2886	2,094,230
32.	Bobby Hamilton	31	0	2832	2,196,960
33.	Steve Park	32	0	2694	2,681,590
34.	Joe Nemechek	33	0	2682	2,453,020
35.	Casey Atwood	35	0	2621	1,988,250
36.	Brett Bodine	32	0	2276	1,766,820
37.	Jerry Nadeau	28	0	2250	1,801,760
38.	Todd Bodine	24	0	1987	1,879,770
39.	Kenny Wallace	21	0	1868	1,379,800
40.	Hut Stricklin	22	0	1781	1,313,550
41.	Mike Wallace	21	0	1551	1,273,240
42.	Stacy Compton	21	0	1527	1,185,710
43.	Geoffrey Bodine	10	0	803	1,224,500
44.	Steve Grissom	10	0	769	529,781
45.	Hermie Sadler	10	0	688	473,290
46.	Jamie McMurray	6	1	679	669,097
47.	Rick Mast	9	0	576	469,843
48.	Greg Biffle	7	0	570	394,773
49.	Buckshot Jones	7	0	559	394,223
50.	Ted Musgrave	5	0	452	283,770

2003

AT A GLANCE

Winston Cup Champion: Matt Kenseth

Notable Event: Michael Waltrip started the year off by showing that his 2001 win in the Daytona 500 wasn't a fluke by winning his second showcase event in two years. This one was the shortest 500 ever thanks to a persistent rainstorm, but a win's a win, and Waltrip will definitely take it. Ryan Newman suffered a spectacular crash at Daytona, but that was NOT a sign of things to come—he had a breakthrough season, winning eight races and finishing sixth in the points standings. Ricky Craven and Kurt Busch staged the closest finish in NASCAR since the introduction of electronic timing when Craven beat Busch by

two-thousandths of a second. Bill Elliott and Terry Labonte showed that the veterans weren't going to be pushed aside just yet by winning their first races in some time. The "lost lap" caution rule was instituted that allowed the highest scoring driver not on the lead lap to regain a spot on that lead lap when a caution flag went out. Designed to help prevent accidents, the rule came into play immediately when Newman regained a lap under a caution period then went on to win the MBNA America 400. Matt Kenseth might have only won a single race in 2003, but he finished in the top 10 enough times—25—to take home his first Winston Cup championship, the last before NASCAR switched to the Nextel Cup.

Top Newcomers: Biffle was the only rookie to win a race in 2003, one year after four rookies claimed their first victories. Biffle made sure the win was high-profile by winning the Pepsi 400 under the lights at Daytona in July. Jamie McMurray didn't win, but he did post 13 top-10 finishes to claim the Raybestos Rookie of the Year award.

Matt Kenseth acted out his own personal version of the tortoise and the hare, and the result matched that found in the classic fairy tale. The 30-year-old driver won only one race in his fourth year on the Winston Cup circuit, but he consistently finished near the top in almost every other race to easily outdistance the rest of the field, including three-time winners Jimmie Johnson and Jeff Gordon, who finished second and fourth, respectively. Perhaps more impressive was the fact that Kenseth even finished ahead of Ryan Newman, who easily led all drivers with eight victories. However, Newman managed to DNF several races throughout the year and the best he could do with his eight wins was a sixth-place finish. Rounding out the top 10 in the Winston Cup standings were Dale Earnhardt Jr. in third, Kevin Harvick in fifth, then Tony Stewart, Bobby Labonte, Bill Elliott, and Terry Labonte in seventh through tenth.

Some observers might look at Kenseth's single win and wonder how he pulled off the Cup championship. However, one look at the weekly results shows that Kenseth actually turned in one of the most dominant performances of recent years. He took the points lead for the first time in the season's fourth race, finishing fourth in the Bass Pro Shops/MBNA 500 at Atlanta to take a 49-point lead over Tony Stewart. And that, essentially, was that. Kenseth never trailed in the points race for the rest of the season—no one even got within 100 points of first place. Kenseth simply plugged away each week, a model of consistency that suffered a DNF in only two races all season—and the second came in the season's final race at Homestead, long after he had clinched the title. That, combined with 11 top-5 finishes and 25 top-10s made it easy for Kenseth to claim the final Winston Cup championship. Shortly after the season was over, NASCAR officials announced that R.J. Reynolds Tobacco Co. was ending its three-decade reign as chief NASCAR sponsor and handing its top spot over to telecommunications company Nextel. Beginning in 2004, the Winston Cup would be renamed the NASCAR Nextel Cup.

And that's not the only change that came about after the season. For the first time since 1975, there were changes made to the NASCAR scoring system. Many NASCAR fans felt that Kenseth's win was the straw that broke the camel's back. For years some fans had complained that drivers did not receive a big enough reward for winning, that drivers who took things cautiously and finished in the top 10 were rewarded more than those who drove all-out and pushed hard for first place. Those fans pointed to Kenseth's one victory and Newman's eight wins and said "something's got to change." NASCAR, which had seen major league baseball experience one of its most thrilling postseason's in history in 2003, decided for the first time that those fans were right. The result? A 10-race sprint for the title in 2004 that would feature only the top 10 drivers—plus ties—as of the season's 26th race. Those drivers would be given new point totals, with only five points separating first from second, second from third, and on down the line. This essentially created a playoff (although don't whisper that word around NASCAR officials) in which only those 10 drivers (plus ties!) could win the championship. No matter how big a lead the

series leader had built by the end of race 26, come the following Monday, his lead would be five points, and the chase would be on. To say there was mixed reaction to the new system would be an understatement—some loved it, some hated it. It will definitely make for interesting racing at the end of the 2004 season, but whether or not it actually works as planned remains to be seen.

WINSTON CUP STANDINGS

	DRIVER	STARTS	WINS	POINTS	MONEY
1.	Matt Kenseth	36	1	5,022	4,038,120
2.	Jimmie Johnson	36	3	4,932	5,517,850
3.	Dale Earnhardt Jr.	36	2	4,815	4,923,500
4.	Jeff Gordon	36	3	4,785	5,107,760
5.	Kevin Harvick	36	1	4,770	4,994,250
6.	Ryan Newman	36	8	4,711	4,827,380
7.	Tony Stewart	36	2	4,549	5,227,500
8.	Bobby Labonte	36	2	4,377	4,745,260
9.	Bill Elliott	36	1	4,303	4,321,190
10.	Terry Labonte	36	1	4,162	3,643,690
11.	Kurt Busch	36	4	4,150	5,020,480
12.	Jeff Burton	36	0	4,109	3,846,880
13.	Jamie McMurray	36	0	3,965	2,699,970
14.	Rusty Wallace	36	0	3,950	3,766,740
15.	Michael Waltrip	36	2	3,934	4,463,840
16.	Robby Gordon	36	2	3,856	3,705,320
17.	Mark Martin	36	0	3,769	4,048,850
18.	Sterling Marlin	36	0	3,745	3,960,810
19.	Jeremy Mayfield	36	0	3,736	2,962,230
20.	Greg Biffle	35	1	3,696	2,410,050
21.	Ward Burton	36	0	3,550	3,500,160
22.	Elliott Sadler	36	0	3,525	3,660,170
23.	Ricky Rudd	36	0	3,521	3,106,610
24.	Johnny Benson	36	0	3,448	3,411,790
25.	Joe Nemechek	36	1	3,426	2,560,480
26.	Dale Jarrett	36	1	3,358	4,055,490
27.	Ricky Craven	36	1	3,334	3,116,210
28.	Dave Blaney	36	0	3,194	2,828,690
29.	Jimmy Spencer	35	0	3,147	2,565,800
30.	Kenny Wallace	36	0	3,061	2,480,490
31.	Todd Bodine	35	0	2,976	2,521,720
32.	Steve Park	35	0	2,923	2,686,910
33.	Tony Raines	35	0	2,772	2,122,740
34.	Jeff Green	31	0	2,656	2,693,530
35.	Casey Mears	36	0	2,638	2,639,180
36.	Ken Schrader	32	0	2,451	2,007,420
37.	Kyle Petty	33	0	2,414	2,293,220
38.	John Andretti	29	0	2,379	2,577,620
39.	Mike Skinner	26	0	1,960	1,782,800
40.	Jack Sprague	18	0	1,284	1,187,830
41.	Larry Foyt	20	0	1,228	1,180,990
42.	Mike Wallace	14	0	1,189	1,031,100
43.	Kevin Lepage	11	0	877	742,077
44.	Christian Fittipaldi	15	0	857	1,265,830
45.	Jerry Nadeau	10	0	844	861,628
46.	Derrike Cope	18	0	822	1,030,690
47.	Jason Leffler	10	0	764	594,500
48.	Scott Wimmer	6	0	599	479,504
49.	Brian Vickers	5	0	379	263,484
50.	Hermie Sadler	10	0	373	552,741

12

DID YOU KNOW

NASCAR is full of juicy little trivia tidbits that are easily forgotten or never thought of. In addition, there are thousands of things that the average fan doesn't even know that he or she doesn't know. Follow us on that one? Instead of sprinkling these little trivia nuggets and factoids throughout the book, we thought we'd bring them all together in one convenient chapter. Here, you can learn dozens of items to dazzle your NASCAR buddies and win numerous bar bets. For example, did you know …

• Brothers have finished 1–2 in 25 Winston Cup races from 1949 through the 2003 season. The most recent "brother sweep" came in October 1999 when Jeff and Ward Burton finished 1–2 at the North Carolina Speedway near Rockingham. There has never been a 1–2–3 sweep, but the Flock brothers (Bob, Tim and Fonty) were 1–2–4 in August 1951 at Greenville-Pickens Speedway in South Carolina. Future two-time champion (1956 and 1957) Buck Baker was third.

• The late Adam Petty was America's first fourth-generation athlete at his sport's highest level. His great-grandfather, Lee, was a three-time NASCAR champion; his grandfather, Richard, was a seven-time champion; and his father, Kyle, has raced full-time since 1981. Adam was killed in a single-car accident during a Busch Series practice session at Loudon, New Hampshire, in May 2000.

• Matt Kenseth won the 2003 Winston Cup title with just one race victory. Three other drivers won their Cup title with a single race victory: Bill Rexford in 1950, Ned Jarrett in 1961, and Benny Parsons in 1972.

• Only two sons have joined their father as Winston Cup champion: Lee Petty won three and his son, Richard, won seven. Ned Jarrett won two championships and his son, Dale, one.

• The 2003 season was the first time since 1988 that Robert Yates Racing didn't field a number 28 Ford. When Elliott Sadler replaced Ricky Rudd and Texaco Havoline left RYR, the organization assigned Sadler number 38. Teammate

Dale Jarrett kept 88, leaving 28 off the track for the first time in 15 years.

- Going into the 2004 season, Ryan Newman has won as many races (9) in his last 46 starts as Dale Earnhardt Jr. has won in his 147 career starts. Newman was actually ahead, 9–8, until Earnhardt Jr. won late in the 2003 season at Phoenix.

- A. J. Foyt is Larry Foyt's biological grandfather and his legal father by adoption

- As of the end of the 2003 season, North Carolina had hosted 497 Winston Cup races, far more than any other state. Virginia was second with 242, then South Carolina with 209, Georgia with 148, and Florida with 144. Nine states have hosted one race: Iowa, Kentucky, Louisiana, Massachusetts, Nebraska, Oklahoma, South Dakota, Washington, and Wisconsin. Canada has hosted two races.

- Cale Yarborough is the only driver to win three consecutive Winston Cups. He did it in 1976, 1977, and 1978 with owner Junior Johnson, who later won three more titles (but not consecutively) with Darrell Waltrip.

- The first live, superspeedway test of the so-called "soft wall" technology was on the inside wall exiting turn 4 at the Indianapolis Motor Speedway. Arie Luyendyk crashed his IROC car into the barrier in August 1998 and Indy car driver Hideshi Matsuda crashed into it during practice for the 1999 Indy 500. Despite heavy damage to their cars, both drivers escaped without serious injury.

- Only two drivers—unrelated, but with the same last name—have swept the road races at Sears Point, California, and Watkins Glen, New York. Jeff Gordon won both races in 1998 and 1999, then Robby Gordon did it in 2003. Jeff Gordon's two sweeps came during a six-race winning streak on the road courses. He won the 1997 race at Watkins Glen, swept the 1998 and 1999 races, then won at Sears Point in 2000.

- Richard Petty still holds the NASCAR record for top-10 points finishes. He ended the year in the top 10 after 25 seasons, five more than the late Dale Earnhardt, six more than Ricky Rudd, and seven more than the late Davey Allison and retired driver Darrell Waltrip.

- Ten drivers among the top forty in career Winston Cup earnings have two or fewer victories. Jimmy Spencer, John Andretti, Ricky Craven, and Steve Park have two; Johnny Benson, Brett Bodine, and Jerry Nadeau have one; and Mike Skinner, Kenny Wallace, and Rick Mast (No. 40 at $9 million-plus) are winless.

- In 2003, Jamie McMurray became the first Winston Cup Rookie of the Year since the late Kenny Irwin in 1998 to win the honor without winning a race. Tony Stewart won three in 1999, Matt Kenseth one in 2000, Kevin Harvick two in 2001, and Ryan Newman one in 2002. Stewart's three in 1999 is the all-time Winston Cup Rookie of the Year record.

- Two Winston Cup champions drove for more than one owner in their championship season. Lee Petty won in 1954 driving No. 42 for himself and No. 92 for owner/driver Herb Thomas. Joe Weatherly won the 1963 title in the Wood Brothers' No. 21 and Bud Moore's No. 8.

- It's been more than 14 years since a father beat his son 1–2 in a Winston Cup race. It last happened in the 1988 Daytona 500, when Bobby Allison beat his son, Davey. It also happened in June 1959 at Lakewood Speedway in Atlanta and in July 1960 at Heidleberg Speedway near Pittsburgh. In each case, Lee Petty beat his son, Richard.

- Only one non-GM driver has won a Busch Series championship since the series began in 1982. Greg Biffle's 2002 title for Jack Roush in a Ford snapped a 20-year run by GM, 11 of those years by a Chevrolet driver. Alas, Brian Vickers returned Chevy to its accustomed place by winning the 2003 Busch title for Hendrick Motorsports.

- In 2003 Jimmy Spencer became the latest driver to earn a victory in all three of NASCAR's top classes. He has 2 Winston Cup victories, and 12 in the Busch Series, and his victory at Loudon, New Hampshire, was his first in the Craftsman Series. Bobby Hamilton, Kevin Harvick, Greg Biffle, Kurt Busch, Ken Schrader, Mark Martin, and Terry Labonte also have won in NASCAR's top three classes.

- Many fathers have raced their sons in Winston Cup, but only twice has a father raced two sons: Richard and Maurice Petty raced their father, Lee, in August 1960 at Dixieland Speedway in Alabama, and Dale Earnhardt raced his sons, Dale Jr. and Kerry, at Michigan Speedway in August 2000.

- Despite never having won a race through the 2003 season, Tony Raines is in the top 15 in all-time Busch Series earnings with almost $3 million. That's by far the most among winless Busch Series drivers.

- Brian Vickers became the youngest major series champion in NASCAR history when he won the 2003 Busch Series title. He was a few weeks past his 20th birthday when he clinched the title in the season-ending race at Homestead, Florida. That made him too young to legally enjoy the series sponsor's product.

- The historic relationship between STP and Richard Petty almost ended before it began. After agreeing to a sponsorship deal prior to the 1972 season, Petty and STP president Andy Granatelli clashed over the color of Petty's No. 43 Plymouth. Petty wanted it primarily Petty-blue, but Granatelli insisted it be mostly STP-red. Petty was walking out the door, willing to sacrifice the deal, when Granatelli called him back. They compromised on a red-and-blue color scheme that was part of their association until STP became an associate sponsor in the early 1990s.

- Hendrick Motorsports, Roush Racing, and Richard Childress Racing are the only organizations with championships in NASCAR's top three series. Hendrick has five Winston Cup titles, three in the Craftsman Series, and one in Busch. RCR has six Cup titles and one each in Craftsman and

Did you know ... that a NASCAR helmet, such as this one from Michael Waltrip's team, are designed to withstand up to 300 G's (300 times the force of gravity)

Busch. Roush has one championship in each series. Dale Earnhardt Inc. has two each in Craftsman and Busch, but none on the Cup circuit.

- Championship-winning crew chief Ray Evernham—now a successful team owner—was a noted short-track racer in New Jersey from the mid-1970s until the early 1990s. He quit driving after a serious accident in 1991 and moved to North Carolina to work in Winston Cup. He briefly worked for the late Alan Kulwicki and on the Busch team of Bill Davis/Jeff Gordon. That led to his seven-year, four-Cup run with Gordon at Hendrick Motorsports. Evernham left Hendrick late in the 2000 season to oversee Dodge's return to Winston Cup.

- Bobby and Terry Labonte are the last brothers to win Winston Cup races on consecutive weekends. Bobby won at Brooklyn, Michigan, in August 1995 and Terry six days later at Bristol, Tennessee. All told, seven sets of two brothers have Cup victories: Bobby and Terry Labonte, Herb and Donald Thomas, Darrell and Michael Waltrip, Bobby and Donnie Allison, Geoff and Brett Bodine, Jeff and Ward Burton, and Benny

DID YOU KNOW ... HOW JAYSKI.COM GOT ITS START?

When people involved in NASCAR log on to their computers each day, they don't necessarily head right to nascar.com. Nope, quite often one of their first destinations is www.jayski.com. Jayski is where they get the latest NASCAR news.

Jayski information includes driver and crew changes, sponsorship news, links to newspaper and magazine stories, fan club information, and information on new books. In other words, everything people want to know about NASCAR.

Jayski is Jay Adamczyk. Since jayski.com is all-NASCAR, all the time, you might think he would be based in the South. Wrong. For years, Adamczyk, 41, originally produced the site from his home near Atlantic City, New Jersey. In 2004, Adamczyk finally gave in and moved to Mooresville. North Carolina, to be closer to the action.

Adamczyk launched his site in 1996 because he couldn't find much NASCAR information on the Internet. Three years later, he left his job as a computer programmer to devote full time to jayski.com. He spends 12 to 15 hours daily inputting information into the site that receives about 150,000 hits daily.

In 2001, jayski.com was added to the thatsracin.com site owned by the Knight-Ridder newspaper chain. Adamczyk says the only revenue he receives is from the advertising on thatsracin.com

Adamczyk has developed excellent sources in NASCAR. "They came to me," he told the *Philadelphia Daily News.* "If I post something and it's not right, someone from the team will email me and say, 'This is the right (news).'"

Why jayski? When Adamczyk was stationed at Dover Air Base in the 1980s, during roll call his sergeant struggled pronouncing his name. Said Adamczyk: "He'd say things like Adamski. I'd always correct him. Finally, he said, 'I'm just going to call you Jayski.' All the other guys started calling me that."

For several years, Adamczyk was a man of mystery, and it was thought that he preferred not being recognized. After a couple television networks did feature segments on him, however, his photo began appearing with newspaper stories.

---

and Phil Parsons. Three Flock brothers also won races: Tim, Fonty, and Bob.

- Jeff Gordon holds the record for most consecutive races running at the finish. His 56-race streak began at Bristol in March 2001 and extended through the September 2002 race at Darlington, South Carolina.

- Through 2003, Winston Cup rookies had started 1–2 only once in NASCAR's modern era (since 1972). Jimmie Johnson and Ryan Newman pulled off that feat at Richmond, Virginia, in September 2002. Newman won six poles that year to set a rookie record.

- The Petty Enterprises racing complex has been on the same site at Level Cross, North Carolina, since Lee Petty began racing in the late 1940s. No other active team in American racing has been at one site nearly as long.

- Aline Ingram is the only female to own a championship-winning team at one of NASCAR's highest levels. She was the owner of record when her husband, Jack, won the 1982 and 1985 Busch Series titles. Jack also won NASCAR titles in the old Late Model Sportsman class in 1972, 1973, and 1974.

- The slowest-ever Busch Series race had an average speed of 48.8742 mph at Orange County Speedway in Rougemont, North Carolina, in August 1982. The fastest was 169.571 mph in the caution-free race at Brooklyn, Michigan, in August 1995.

Did you know ... that this is what the tires used on NASCAR Nextel Cup cars look like when they are brand new (top), and then what they turn into after a day of hard driving on the track (bottom)?

- Drivers in Chevrolets won eight of the first nine Craftsman Truck Series championships after the series debuted in 1995. Mike Skinner won in 1995; Ron Hornaday in 1996 and 1998; Jack Sprague in 1997, 1999, and 2001; Mike Bliss in 2002; and Travis Kvapil in 2003. Greg Biffle is the only driver to overcome the Chevy dominance, as he piloted his Ford to the title in 2000.

- Three Winston Cup drivers are listed as the driver-owner on championship winning teams? Herb Thomas was the driver-owner in 1951 and 1953, Buck Baker in 1957, and Alan Kulwicki in 1992. Lee Petty won two of his championships with Petty Enterprises and his son, Richard Petty, won all seven of his for Petty Enterprises.

- Jim Fitzgerald was 66 when he drove his last Winston Cup race? It was at Riverside, California, in June 1987, and he finished 17th in a Chevrolet. According to NASCAR records, Fitzgerald was the oldest man to start one of its Cup races. He died in a 1987 sports car road race in Florida.

- Bobby and Terry Labonte are the only brothers to win the Winston Cup? Older brother Terry did it in 1984 for Billy Hagan and in 1996 for Rick Hendrick, and Bobby did it in 2000 for Joe Gibbs.

- Davey Allison won the last "unrestricted" race at the Talladega Superspeedway? It was May 1987 and the race was the Winston 500; Allison's father, Bobby, had taken out half the field in an early-race accident on the front stretch. Davey's victory marks the last time Winston Cup cars raced the 2.66-mile track without the power-robbing and speed-limiting carburetor restrictor plates that are now mandatory on superspeedways.

- The Flock family holds the record for most siblings in a Winston Cup race? Tim, Fonty, Bob, and their sister, Ethel all raced in the 1949 highway-beach race in February at Daytona Beach, Florida.

- Mario Andretti and A. J. Foyt are the only Indianapolis 500 winners to also win the Daytona 500? Andretti did it for Holman-Moody in 1967, and Foyt did it for the Wood Brothers in 1972. Foyt also won the 1964 and 1965 Firecracker 400 summer races at Daytona International Speedway.

- Bobby Allison was NASCAR's oldest Winston Cup champion when he won the 1983 title? He was 45 years and 11 months when that season ended, three months older than Lee Petty when Petty won his third and final title in 1959. The youngest champion was Bill Rexford, who was 23 when he won the 1950 title.

- Rick Hendrick and Carl Kiekhaefer are the only Winston Cup team owners to win consecutive championships with different drivers? Kiekhaefer won in 1955 with Tim Flock and in 1956 with Buck Baker. Forty years later, Hendrick won with Jeff Gordon in 1995 and Terry Labonte in 1996. (Hendrick also won championships with Gordon in 1997, 1998, and 2001.)

- Two women have competed in the Daytona 500? Janet Guthrie was 12th in 1977 and 11th in 1980, and Shawna Robinson was 24th in 2002. Guthrie (40th), Christine Beckers (37th), and Lella Lombardi (31st) all raced in the 1977 Pepsi 400 at Daytona Beach. Sarah Christian, Ethel Mobley, and Louise Smith raced together on the highway-beach course race at Daytona Beach in 1949. A year later, Smith, Christian, and Ann Chester raced together at Hamburg Speedway in New York.

- Cale Yarborough and Tony Stewart are the only drivers to finish last in the season-opening Daytona 500 and still win that year's Winston Cup? Yarborough did it in 1976 and Stewart in 2002.

- Dave Marcis started 33 Daytona 500s between 1968 and 2002, missing only in 2000 and 2001? That's the most starts for anyone in NASCAR's showcase event, two more than Richard Petty ran between 1962 and 1992.

- Ricky Rudd and Rusty Wallace share the modern-era record for winning at least one race in

Did you know ... that patriotism and NASCAR go hand in hand? In the wake of the September 11, 2001 terrorist attacks, the American flag has been a prominent part of each racing weekend on the Winston (now Nextel) Cup. Here, a color guard carries in a parade of flags before the start of the Pop Secret Microwave 400 at North Carolina Speedway.

16 consecutive seasons? Rudd's streak began for owner Richard Childress in 1983 and ended in 1999 after Rudd had taken over as his own team owner. Wallace's streak began in 1986 for Raymond Beadle and ended when he didn't win for Roger Penske in 2002. Overall, Richard Petty holds the record with victories in 18 consecutive seasons from 1960 through 1977. David Pearson is second with victories in 17 consecutive seasons from 1964 through 1980.

• It's been almost 10 years since anyone lapped the field in a Winston Cup race? Geoffrey Bodine did it at North Wilkesboro, North Carolina, in October 1994.

• The longest Winston Cup speedway measured 4.176 miles? A combination highway/beach course in Daytona Beach, Florida, hosted one race a year from 1949 through 1958. Cars raced southward along public highway A1A, turned left between sand dunes near Ponce Inlet, then raced northward along the hard-packed sand until turning left to rejoin A1A between two more dunes. The 2.5-mile Daytona International Speedway replaced the highway/beach course in 1959.

• The Tidewater 300 on November 22, 1970 at Langley Field Speedway in Hampton, Virginia, was the last NASCAR race prior to the arrival of R. J. Reynolds Tobacco Co., as the organization's major sponsor? Beginning at Riverside (California) Raceway in January 1971, the former Grand National Series was known as Winston Cup. In 2003. the Ford 400 at Homestead-Miami Speedway earned the distinction of being the last race of the RJR era. Bobby Labonte won that final race before the start of the Nextel Cup era.

• Terry Labonte's two Winston Cups came 12 years apart (1984 and 1996), the longest stretch between anyone's first and second titles?

• Richard Petty's first Winston Cup start came in Canada? It was in Toronto, Ontario, on July 18, 1958. He started seventh on the 17-car grid, crashed out after 55 of 100 laps and finished 17th. His father, Lee, started third, led the final 29 laps, and won the race.

• The winner of the very first Winston Cup race (Jim Roper in June 1949 at Charlotte, North Carolina) got the victory after the apparent winner (Glenn Dunnaway) was disqualified for using illegal suspension parts in his car?

• Martinsville Speedway in Virginia is the only track still on the Cup schedule that was part of the inaugural Cup season of 1949? The other seven tracks in order of their races: Charlotte (but not the current Lowe's Motor Speedway); Daytona Beach (but not the current Daytona International Speedway); Hillsboro, North Carolina; Langhorne, Pennsylvania; Hamburg, Pennsylvania; Martinsville, Heidelberg, Pennsylvania; and North Wilkesboro, North Carolina.

• The largest field for a Winston Cup race was 75 cars at the inaugural Southern 500 on Labor Day at Darlington Raceway? Similar to the Indianapolis 500 (which inspired Harold Brasington to build stock car racing's first large superspeedway), the cars started the race three-wide for 25 rows.

• One reigning and four future Winston Cup champions drove in NASCAR's first paved, superspeedway, 500-mile race at Darlington in the fall of 1950? Red Byron (1949 champion) finished third, Bill Rexford (1950) finished 4th, Lee Petty (1954, 1958, and 1959) finished 6th,

Tim Flock (1952 and 1955) finished 11th, and Buck Baker (1956 and 1957) finished 69th.

• Dale Jarrett won more in the 1996 Daytona 500 than his father, Ned, won in his entire career? Dale earned $360,775 for that victory, while Ned brought in only $298,146 for a career that included the 1961and 1965 NASCAR championships, 351 starts, and 50 victories.

• A speedway's length of record is determined by measuring 15 feet in from the outside retaining wall?

• Dale Earnhardt won the first-ever Busch Series race? It was at Daytona Beach in February 1982. All told, Earnhardt won 21 Busch Series races.

• P. J. Jones (son of legendary racer Parnelli Jones) won the first Craftsman Truck Series race? It was at Mesa Marin Raceway at Bakersfield, California, in July 1994. But you won't find it among the CTS records because it was the first of four nonpoint, exhibition races. The first official Craftsman Truck Series race was at Phoenix International Raceway in February 1995. Mike Skinner beat Terry Labonte to the finish line en route to winning the first championship by 126 points over Joe Ruttman.

• The 1979 Daytona 500 was the first major stock car race to be televised live, from start to finish? It was a CBS telecast, and it featured the famous last-lap crash between Cale Yarborough and Donnie Allison that opened the door for Richard Petty's record seventh Daytona 500 victory.

• Ricky Craven of Newburgh, Maine, is the Winston Cup winner with the northernmost hometown? He earned that distinction by winning the 2001 fall race at Martinsville.

• NASCAR legend Junior Johnson served time in the mid-1950s in an Ohio federal prison for making and distributing illegal liquor in North Carolina? His life was the subject of the movie *Last American Hero*.

• Richard Petty was the first NASCAR driver to win $1 million in his career? He reached that mark in the summer race at Atlanta Motor Speedway in 1971.

Did you know ... that if a car has to have its engine replaced between its qualifying run and the actual race, then that car has to start the race in the last row? As Jeff Burton's team inspects his car before the MBNA America 400, they are definitely hoping that they will not have to replace the engine.

• Legendary owner/mechanic/crew chief Walter "Bud" Moore is a highly-decorated World War II veteran? He was only 18 when he joined allied forces in storming the beach at Normandy in June 1944.

• The organizational meeting that gave birth to NASCAR was in the Ebony Room of The Streamline Hotel in Daytona Beach? The meetings were held in mid-December 1947, but it wasn't until June 1949 that the first race in what is now the Winston Cup Series was run. At that first meeting, the first official rules were written down on a cocktail napkin.

• The smallest field for a Winston Cup race was 12 cars? It happened twice: For 200 laps on the half-mile dirt track at Hickory, North Carolina, in August 1953 and for 200 laps on the half-mile dirt track in Oklahoma City, Oklahoma, in August 1956.

• Bill Elliott still holds the record for fastest qualifying lap for a Winston Cup race? He ran 212.809 mph in time trials for the 1987 Winston 500 at the Talladega Superspeedway. He's also run the second-fastest lap, 212.229 mph, in qualifying for the 1988 Winston 500 at Talladega. As long as restrictor plates are used in super-

Did you know ... that NASCAR fans, such as the ones enjoying their day at Dover International Speedway for the MBNA America 400, have been found by marketing experts to be the most brand-loyal of any sport in America? In other words, if their driver drives a Ford and drinks Coca Cola, then odds are they will drive a Ford and drink Coke, too.

speedway races, Elliott's record will never be broken.

- Journeyman H. B. Bailey was the first driver to make a qualifying run for the inaugural Brickyard 400 in August of 1994? He didn't make the field, but lives with the distinction of being the first driver to have his car number atop the scoring pylon—if only for a few seconds.

- Neil Bonnett once hit a deer during a qualifying run for a Winston Cup race at Pocono Raceway. Bonnett was fine; the deer wasn't.

- President Ronald Reagan used a phone from Air Force One to give the command to start engines for the 1984 Pepsi 400 on July 4 in Daytona Beach? He flew in and arrived at the track in time to see Richard Petty beat Cale Yarborough in one of NASCAR's most famous finishes. It was Petty's 200th and final Winston Cup victory.

- The first Winston Cup race run west of the Mississippi River was at Gardena, California, in April 1951? Marshall Teague won it in an Oldsmobile at 61.047 mph.

- Ricky Rudd had never raced a car at any level when he made his NASCAR debut at Rockingham in March 1975. He started 26th and finished 11th in a No. 10 Ford owned and prepared by long-time racer and family friend Bill Champion.

- Cale Yarborough retired with more 200-plus mph qualifying laps than anyone in NASCAR history? He topped 200 mph 15 times, once more than Bill Elliott, twice more than Terry Labonte, and four times more than Dale Earnhardt.

- Hollywood actor Skeet Ulrich is the son of former driver D. K. Ulrich and the nephew of long-time Winston Cup star Ricky Rudd?

- NASCAR's last dirt-track race was at Raleigh, North Carolina, on September 30, 1970. It was for 200 laps around the half-mile track at the State Fairgrounds. Plymouth driver Richard Petty won it at 63.376 mph, a victory worth $1,000.

- Six sons have upheld their family name by winning NASCAR races? Richard Petty won after Lee; Kyle Petty won after Richard; Buddy Baker won after Buck; Davey Allison won after Bobby; Dale Jarrett won after Ned; and Dale Earnhardt Jr. won after Dale Earnhardt.

- Hollywood star Bert Reynolds and legendary stuntman Hal Needham were co-owners of the No. 33 Skoal Bandit car that Harry Gant raced in the 1980s?

- Other than Hawaii and Alaska, only nine states have not hosted Winston Cup races? They are Rhode Island, Missouri, Colorado, Utah, Idaho, Montana, Wyoming, New Mexico, and North Dakota.

- The first road race for the Busch Series was July 6, 1986 at Road Atlanta at Flowery Branch, Georgia. Darrell Waltrip won the 74-lap, 186-mile race ahead of Terry Labonte, Dale Earnhardt, Haskell Willingham, and L. D. Ottinger.

- There once was a speedway at Moyock, North Carolina, called Dog Track Speedway and one in Sumter, South Carolina, called Gamecock Speedway? And how about these somewhat-unusual names: Rambi Race Track in Myrtle Beach, South Carolina; Starlite Speedway in Monroe, North Carolina; Shangri-La Speedway in Owego, New York; Funk's Speedway at Winchester, Indiana, Hayloft Speedway in Augusta, Ga., Tucson Rodeo Grounds in Tucson, Arizona, Tar Heel Speedway in Randleman, North Carolina, and Dixie Speedway in (where else?) Birmingham, Alabama.

13

THE BUSCH GRAND NATIONAL SERIES

Ol' Rick Hendrick down in Charlotte, North Carolina, has a pretty good eye for talent, doesn't he? Remember that Tim Richmond fellow he recruited and signed in 1986, long before anyone else realized Richmond could drive a stock car? What about snatching up Jeff Gordon in 1992, before most people (Bill Davis *not* among them, by the way) had any clue how good he'd become? Or when Hendrick signed Jimmie Johnson, whose stock car resume gave no hint of what was to come? And hasn't Hendrick fielded cars for seven other winning drivers: Geoff Bodine, Darrell Waltrip, Ken Schrader, Joe Nemechek, Ricky Rudd, Terry Labonte, and Jerry Nadeau?

So is it any surprise his latest "unknown" won the 2003 Busch Series title and immediately set his sights on being the inaugural Nextel Cup Rookie of the Year in 2004? Given Rick's track record, you shouldn't have been surprised at all.

North Carolina native Brian Vickers, a veritable child at age 20, went from go-karts to major-league stock cars in only seven seasons. He won three World Karting Association national titles in from 1994 to 1997, and five Allison Legacy Series feature races for smaller stock cars in

1998. He drove in NASCAR's weekly Late Model class in 1999, then won poles and races on the Hooters Pro Cup series in 2000 and 2001. He also ran a limited Busch schedule in 2001 and then ran most of the Busch scheduled in 2002. When Hendrick's son Ricky decided to stop driving the No. 5 car and instead become its full-time owner, he signed Vickers to be his driver for the full 2003 season.

Late in 2003, with the Busch title still very much undecided, the elder Hendrick announced that Vickers would run some late-season Winston Cup races for Hendrick Motorsports. Within days, he added that Vickers would replace Nemechek in the No. 25 UAW-GM Chevrolet Monte Carlo for the full 2004 Nextel Cup Series. There, Vickers will join Scott Riggs, Kasey Kahne, Scott Wimmer, Johnny Sauter, and Brendan Gaughan in one of the most impressive and highly anticipated rookie classes in years.

Vickers will have to go quite a ways to match the first-year Cup exploits of other recent Busch champions. Greg Biffle, the 2002 titleist, won a race in his rookie Winston Cup season. Kevin Harvick, the 2001 Busch champion and Cup

Brian Vickers escapes trouble and takes a familiar position at the front of the pack during the Aaron's 312 race at Talladega Superspeedway on April 5, 2003. Vickers, who was only 20 years old at the time, became the youngest champion of any NASCAR series when he claimed the Busch title in 2003, finishing 14 points ahead of David Green. Vickers will race full time in the Nextel Cup series in 2004.

rookie of the year the same year, won twice his first season. And 1998–1999 Busch champion Dale Earnhardt Jr. also won twice in his rookie Cup season of 2000. Since 1995, in fact, every Busch champion except Jeff Green and Randy LaJoie has won at least one race in his rookie Cup season.

Vickers should be up for the challenge. He won three Busch races in 2003 and had 13 top-5 finishes and 21 top-10s in his 34 starts. His breakthrough victory came in the August race at Indianapolis Raceway Park at Clermont, Indiana. Several weeks later he won at venerable Darling-

ton (South Carolina) Raceway, then won again just two weeks later at Dover, Delaware. He rallied from fifth to first in the point race late in the season, coming from 49 behind after the Atlanta race, to 21 behind after Phoenix, to 22 ahead after Rockingham, and, finally, 14 ahead after the season finale at Homestead.

"This is everything I've dreamed of and everything I've worked for my whole life." Vickers said after becoming NASCAR's youngest-ever champion of a major series. "I'm so proud to give Rick, Papa Joe, and Ricky Hendrick their first Busch title. I wouldn't have wanted to win it with anybody else. This race (the finale) was probably one of the most nerve-wracking I've ever been in. There seemed to be always something going on. It was like a game of cat and mouse. When (title challenger) David Green passed a car, I had to pass a car, too. I'm just relieved that it's over and we won."

Vickers beat Green, the 1994 series champion, by 14 points in one of NASCAR's closest multidriver battles ever. Ron Hornaday was 46 points behind Vickers, second-generation driver Bobby Hamilton Jr. 49, and fifth-place Jason Keller 109. The rest of the top 10: Scott Riggs, Kasey Kahne, Johnny Sauter, Scott Wimmer, and Mike Bliss. As late as Phoenix in November, any of the top six drivers still had a shot at the title.

Vickers and Green each won three times, Hornaday once, Hamilton Jr. four times, Keller once, Riggs twice, and Kahne, Sauter, and Wimmer once each. Seven other drivers—all of them full-time Winston Cup drivers who occasionally ran in Busch events—also won in 2003. Joe Nemechek, Harvick, and Earnhardt Jr. each won three times; Biffle, Jamie McMurray, and Matt Kenseth each won twice; and Todd Bodine and Michael Waltrip once each.

The 2004 Busch Series lineup will look dramatically different from 2003's. Vickers, Riggs, Kahne, Sauter, and Wimmer all moved up to Nextel Cup, but they left behind some pretty good drivers. Green returns with Brewco Motorsports, Hornaday with Richard Childress Racing, Hamilton Jr. with owner Ed Rensi, Keller with the potent PPC team, and Bliss with Joe Gibbs Racing. It's fair to assume all five of those drivers and their teams are capable of winning the Busch Series title.

In addition, Jason Leffler, Casey Atwood, David Stremme, Kenny Wallace, Stacy Compton, Ashton Lewis Jr., and Tim Fedewa will also run the full Busch schedule. The Rookie of the Year class will feature Martin Truex Jr. with Dale Earnhardt Inc., Paul Menard with Andy Petree Racing, and Kyle Busch with the same No. 5 Chevy team that won the 2003 title for Vickers.

Kahne and Sauter are scheduled to run the full Busch and Cup schedules, but those ambitious plans may change.

BUSCH: THE LAUNCHING PAD

The Busch Series is to NASCAR what other "developmental" leagues are to stick-and-ball sports. The NFL has its European and Arena football leagues, not to mention those Saturday afternoon games on college campuses. Similarly, the NBA has the National Basketball Development League and the NCAA to train its future stars. And Major League Baseball and the National Hockey League have high schools, colleges, and minor league systems to train their talent. Almost everybody has spent time in the minors, preparing for The Show, no matter what the sport.

But what about NASCAR and its major league series? Where will it find the next Ryan Newman or Jeff Gordon? How does it develop another Dale Earnhardt Jr., Tony Stewart, and Mark Martin? At a time when some fear the supply of quality talent is dwindling, where are the next superstars? For many, it's the Busch Series. Even though NASCAR and Anheuser-Busch have tinkered with the name, the series traces its roots to 1950, when Bill France Sr. named his second-level series the Sportsman Division. It was intended to be a relatively inexpensive alternative to Strictly Stock, which became Grand National, then the Winston Cup, and finally, the Nextel Cup. "Sportsman" was renamed "Late Model Sportsman" in 1968 and "Grand National" in 1982. Budweiser was initially the series's primary sponsor before Anheuser-Busch in St. Louis decided to make Busch the sponsor.

THE STARTING POINT

With few exceptions, all of NASCAR's leading Nextel Cup drivers spent time on the farm. Gordon raced for Bill Davis before getting a call from Rick Hendrick to go Cup racing. "It was great experience, invaluable experience, something I really learned from," the four-time champion said of his years in Busch. "[Nextel] Cup is so difficult and competitive, it's good to have had a series that helped prepare for that. It helped me in so many ways, and I look back on those days as a tremendous learning experience."

Dale Jarrett raced his own Busch car for years before getting his first full-time Cup ride with owner Cale Yarborough. Dale Earnhardt started in the Late Model Sportsman division (where his late father, Ralph, had been a two-time champion) and his son, Dale Jr., was a two-time Busch champion before moving to Cup racing in 2000. Matt Kenseth, 2003 Winston Cup champion, had Busch experience, as did eight-time Cup winner Ryan Newman. Many other top drivers for 2003—including Jeff Gordon, Jimmie Johnson, and Tony Stewart—also spent time on the developmental circuit.

Like their leading colleagues, Earnhardt Jr., Jeff and Ward Burton, Bobby Labonte, Johnny Benson, Michael Waltrip, Jimmy Spencer, Geoff, Brett and Todd Bodine, Ricky Craven, Mike and Kenny Wallace, Kevin Harvick, Joe Nemechek, Michael Waltrip, and Elliott Sadler also spent time in Busch. There are, of course, exceptions—Terry Labonte, Jeremy Mayfield, Bill Elliott, Kyle Petty, John Andretti, Dave Blaney, Robby Gordon, and Ken Schrader lead the group of successful drivers that never raced in the Busch series.

For years, young drivers dreaming of making it into Cup racing had few options. They could walk in and try starting at the top (no longer allowed), or run weekly short-track races in hopes of going from there to Late Model Sportsman to the Cup. When NASCAR created the Busch Series, it eased the transition from those ⅓-mile weekend bullrings to the Saturday afternoon superspeedways. Late Model Sportsman cars of the 1960s and 1970s weren't nearly as fast, sophisticated, or costly as Cup cars. They ran mostly 100- or 200-lap races at backwater short tracks that didn't have Cup dates. The atmosphere generally was low-key (competitive, but more friendly), the purses modest, and media attention almost nonexistent. But that circuit of weekend races wasn't the ideal training ground.

Tracks were so widely scattered that the best New England drivers seldom faced the Carolinas' best. Competition was diluted more because every track operated on Friday or Saturday, forcing promoters to offer secret financial deals to attract stars. What's more, a local backmarker might discover where the regional stars were going, then make plans to be somewhere else. In some cases, the national LMS champion was the driver who started the most races and finished the best. The level of competition seldom had anything to do with it.

CROWNING A TRUE NATIONAL CHAMPION

That changed with the Busch Series. Instead of 55 to 65 races for the national championship, NASCAR created a touring series of 28 to 32 races and called it Grand National. Except for the costs and the tracks it visited, it was similar to what was then the Winston Cup. (To stay alive when NASCAR scrapped the LMS division, local short tracks created their own Late Model Stock Car class.) In Grand National, the top drivers faced each other each weekend. That welcomed change ended the deal-money era that often created hard feelings. And instead of varying rules depending on the track, Grand National rules were uniform and were enforced by the same inspectors and officials at each event. NASCAR even created a separate marketing and public relations division for Grand National.

Even as the Winston Cup began growing in the 1980s, Busch racing began coming of age. It did so by running more Saturday afternoon races on the Busch–Cup doubleheader program, in which the Busch race was held on the same track as that weekend's Cup race, but one day earlier. That brought more Cup drivers into Busch racing, since another few hours of "live practice" before the Cup race never hurt. Cup drivers in the Busch races meant larger crowds attended those races, which led to larger purses, which led to more teams, which led to more sponsors, which led to an even healthier series. In 2003, the great majority of Busch races were same-weekend races at the Winston Cup site.

Whether that's good or bad depends on your outlook. Old-timers who embrace the racing on the vintage ¼-mile, ⅓-mile, and ⅝-mile tracks bemoan the loss of traditional stops at Myrtle Beach, Orange County, Hickory, South Boston, Langley, Volusia County, and Lanier. If they wanted to see superspeedway racing, these folks say, they'd go to a Cup race on Sunday afternoon. Busch, they argue, was never designed as a condensed version of Cup, no more than Single-A ball is supposed to be a scaled-down example of Major League Baseball.

Others argue that the increasing cost of racing demands bigger sponsors, more TV and contingency money, and larger purses. They say the only answer is longer races at larger venues with more seats, more radio and TV coverage, and more hospitality and catering facilities. Besides, supporters add, why not visit Las Vegas, Miami, St. Louis, Milwaukee, and Nashville? Each has an acceptable track, but with the exception of Las Vegas and Miami, none gets a Cup race. The only way to improve the series, say Busch fans, is to expose it to new markets, new sponsors, and new fans.

BOOM TIMES FOR BUSCH

They must be right, because except for a few worries, the series is healthy. A huge crowd watches the season-opener at Daytona Beach, while crowds of 100,000 and more are common at Bristol, Talladega, Dover, and Charlotte. All told, the series drew more than 4.1 million fans in 2003. That's in stark contrast to the half-million or so at Grand National races between 1982 and, say, 1990. Many of the races in those days were at rough little weekly tracks that seemed to look backward rather than forward. None of the drivers from the inaugural 1982 season are still active. The top four in points that year—Jack Ingram, Sam Ard, Tommy Ellis, and Tommy Houston—have long-since retired. Likewise, series regulars Ronnie Silver, L. D. Ottinger, Bosco

---

DEFINING MOMENT: BRIAN VICKERS

Vickers won the 2003 Busch Grand National title as a 20-year-old rookie. He is the youngest Busch series champion in 20 years. Vickers is driving the No. 25 Chevrolet for Hendrick Motorsports in the 2004 Nextel Cup series. In the closing races of the 2003 Winston Cup season in the No. 25 Chevy, Vickers qualified second twice (Phoenix and Rockingham) and third (Homstead).

"There's never been a moment where I thought 'I'm really good at this.' Over time, you run a lot of races, you love it, you do it a lot. You think, 'Maybe I can do this for a living if I can get an opportunity.'

"My parents are a racing family. If I played baseball, they would've supported me. But I got into racing. It's something we can all be involved in." (Vickers father, Clyde owns CV Products, a race-equipment supply company based in North Carolina.)

Lowe, Joe Thurman, Larry Pollard, and Mike Alexander haven't raced in years. For some, the hassle of towing to far-away races and trying to make every event to stay in the title chase was too much. For others, the cost of "tour racing" and keeping up with the better-financed teams went beyond their means.

Two-time champion Larry Pearson (1986 and 1987) went from Busch to Winston Cup, but came back a few years later. Since then, he hasn't been able to reestablish himself anywhere. Rob Moroso, the 1988 champion, died in a highway accident in 1990, the year he was named Winston Cup rookie of the year. Ellis, the 1989 champion, quit in the early 1990s, and 1990 champion Chuck Bown went to Winston Cup, got hurt at Pocono, then briefly ran CTS before retiring for good. With two exceptions, every champion between 1991 and 1995 is in Winston Cup: Bobby Labonte (1991), Joe Nemechek (1992), and Johnny Benson (1995). Steve Grissom (1993) and David Green (1994) have had Cup and Busch rides, and likely will run Busch again in 2004. Two-time champion (1996–1997) Randy LaJoie made an early '90s foray from Busch to Cup, came back, then won consecutive Busch titles. Earnhardt Jr. won in 1998 and 1999 before going to Cup. Jeff Green, the 2000 champion, has found a home in the Nextel Cup, and 2001 champion Harvick did well enough to be named the 2001 Winston Cup Rookie of the Year. Greg Biffle, the 2002 champion, showed he was ready for Cup racing in 2003 by winning a race during his rookie season at that level.

To the casual fan, Busch cars look similar to Nextel Cup cars. There are crucial differences between the cars used on each circuit, however. The wheelbase of a Busch car is five inches shorter (105 vs. 110), but they're both powered by 12-to-1 compression ratio engines. Busch cars weigh 100 pounds less (3,300 vs. 3,400 lbs.) and their engines generate about 710 horsepower, about 50 less than Cup. Speeds are comparable at most tracks, as weight and wheelbase of the Busch cars almost make up for their weaker engines.

The future of the Busch Series depends on what NASCAR wants. Is its role to provide an intermediate step for young drivers between weekly racing and Cup, or to give promoters an attractive Saturday afternoon support race? As of 2003, all indicators point to the Busch Series filling the role it's filled since the 1980s, with no major changes on the horizon. Only time will tell if that

philosophy will change. Whatever happens, this much is evident: Bill France Sr. would be stunned to see how grown-up and sophisticated his old "Sportsman Division" has become.

Come to think of it, even those who've been around since 1982 and watch the series grow and mature are pretty stunned by how far it's come in the past 21 years.

BUSCH SERIES RECORDS
Top-10 career starts

Tommy Houston	417
Elton Sawyer	392
Dale Jarrett	324
Jason Keller	322
Randy LaJoie	309
Todd Bodine	302
Mike McLaughlin	302
David Green	287
Phil Parsons	285
Tim Fewada	278
Kenny Wallace	278

Top-10 career poles

Tommy Ellis	28
Mark Martin	27
Sam Ard	24
Jeff Green	23
David Green	21
Tommy Houston	18
Joe Nemechek	17
Brett Bodine	16
Jimmy Hensley	15
Michael Waltrip	15

Top-10 career victories

Mark Martin	45
Jack Ingram	31
Tommy Houston	24
Sam Ard	22
Tommy Ellis	22
Dale Earnhardt	21
Harry Gant	21
Jeff Burton	20
Dale Earnhardt Jr.	18
Jeff Green	16

14

THE CRAFTSMAN TRUCK SERIES

It took Travis Kvapil slightly more than the 25 scheduled races to win the 2003 Craftsman Truck Series championship. The circuit's ninth season opened at Daytona Beach in mid-February and ended almost exactly nine months later about 380 miles south in Homestead, Florida.

For Kvapil, however, the season lasted 9 months, 25 races, and 10 minutes. And it's those 10 minutes that remain the talk of the CTS tour.

Four drivers went to Homestead chasing the CTS title. Dodge driver Brendan Gaughan led fellow Dodge driver Ted Musgrave by 14 points. Chevrolet driver Kvapil was 34 behind and fourth-ranked Dennis Setzer, also in a Chevy, was 39 behind. It was the closest first-to-fourth championship scrap in NASCAR history.

Gaughan was the first to fall. In lap 101, he crashed in turn 4 after contact with Marty Houston and Bryan Reffner. He was running well enough to win the title, but finished 29th in the race and 4th in points. Afterward, he disparaged Houston and Houston's team-owner, Jim Smith, even using some rather "colorful" language in suggesting certain actions Smith might want to take. This, of course, did not go over to well with

NASCAR officials. After being fined $10,000 for his language, a contrite Gaughan apologized during the series' awards banquet in Miami. "To the families that watched," he said, "I deeply apologize. I hope you continue to watch what I feel is the most exciting and most fan-friendly sport in the world."

That left Musgrave, Kvapil, and Setzer to decide the title in the final 33 laps. A late caution for Scott Lynch's blown motor set up a green-white-checkered finish. Bobby Hamilton, Rick Crawford, David Starr, Andy Houston, and Jack Sprague were top-five for the last restart, followed by Kvapil, Setzer, and Musgrave. According to the scoring system, Setzer had to pass Kvapil for the title and Musgrave needed to pass them both. Kvapil would be champion by finishing where he was.

With that set-up in place, no one could have imagined how wild the finish would be. It's a lock that race fans will talk for years about the final restart of the Ford 200 and how it affected the series title.

Kvapil briefly slowed nearing the green, forcing Setzer to also slow for an instant. When they slowed, Musgrave cut left and passed them before the start/finish line. He was originally scored sixth behind Hamilton, Crawford, Starr, Houston and Sprague, good enough for the title. But officials delayed everything to review TV tapes of the restart. It's illegal to pass on the left before the flag, but did Kvapil and Setzer snooker Musgrave by tricking him into it? The answer to that question would determine the 2003 Craftsman Series championship. Would it be Musgrave for owners Jim/Marlene Smith, or Kvapil for owner Steve Coulter? (no matter what the officials decided, Setzer couldn't win—he was going to be either second or third for owners David Dollar/Rob Morgan).

While Hamilton went to Victory Lane, seventh-place Kvapil sat in his truck for 10 minutes. He refused to exit until someone told him with certainty where he stood. Officials in race control saw clearly that Musgrave had jumped the restart. If allowed to keep sixth, he would have been the champion by 16 points over Kvapil and 21 over Setzer. Instead, he was penalized to 13th, the last driver on the lead lap. That meant Kvapil was the champion by 9 points over Setzer and 18 over Musgrave.

"This is crazy," Kvapil said when the word finally came that he was the champion. "We would have had it for sure if that last caution hadn't come out. We were going to finish two spots ahead of Ted, so he was desperate to make up two spots to beat me (for the title). It wasn't going to happen. He took a chance that didn't pay off. He had to pass the 46 (Setzer) and me, and that was his only chance on a green-white-checkered restart. I guess that's what the rule book is for."

Not too surprisingly, Musgrave didn't agree. "We're coming to the green and I don't know if (Kvapil) spun his wheels or hit the brakes," he said later, clearly steamed at what had just happened. "I was on the gas and had to turn left to avoid Setzer, knowing it's going to draw a penalty. All I can say is next year you're going to see a whole new Ted Musgrave. He's going to be the dirtiest son of a (gun) out there and you might as well throw that rule book away. I ain't going by it no more."

Hamilton's largely overlooked victory was his second during a season that saw 12 drivers divide 25 races. Gaughan won six and Musgrave, Setzer, and runaway Rookie of the Year winner Carl Edwards three each. Jon Wood won two and Kvapil, Crawford, and Leffler one each. In addition, Winston Cup drivers made their presence felt, as Tony Stewart, Kevin Harvick, and Jimmy Spencer each won once.

No matter how hot the action is on the track in 2004, the biggest story will be the introduction of Toyota as the first foreign truck manufacturer to compete full-time in a major NASCAR series. (See Chapter 5 for the full story of Toyota's decision to join NASCAR.) There will be seven teams running Toyota Tundra trucks in 2004, and as the season approached in January, it appeared there would be only a dozen or so other fully funded teams ready to run a full CTS schedule. That number should rise as the season-opener draws closer, as there are roughly two dozen additional teams that are prepared to run the majority of the CTS races. However, several teams have major financial and personnel gaps to fill, so it's impossible to guess how many teams might really compete for the 2004 title.

Hamilton, veteran Chad Chaffin, and new teammate Chase Montgomery will drive for Hamilton's Dodge-based team. Musgrave and new teammate Andy Houston will drive Dodges for Jim and Marlene Smith. Team owner Michael Gaughan will replace his Cup-bound son, Brendan, in the No. 62 Dodge for at least part of the season. Wood and Edwards will return to Roush Racing in Fords. Tour veteran Crawford is back in a Ford for Tom Mitchell and Rick Sanders, while rookie Randy Briggs and veterans Lance Hooper and Morgan Shepherd hope to run at least part of the schedule in Fords.

The Chevrolet lineup features Jack Sprague for championship owner Steve Coulter, Setzer for the David Dollar/Rob Morgan team, David Starr for Wayne Spears, and Phil Bonifield running his own team. Randy MacDonald hopes to get enough backing for his self-owned team, and

Travis Kvapil enjoys a champagne shower as he raises the 2003 championship trophy for the Craftsman Truck Series over his head. After a wild finish that took officials more than 10 minutes to sort out, Kvapil was declared champion after finishing sixth in the season-ending Ford 200 at Homestead-Miami Speedway on November 14.

Matt Crafton will drive for Nextel Cup driver and ex-CTS star Kevin Harvick.

Toyota announced their teams at the end of the 2003 season. Bill Davis Racing will field Tundras for drivers Shelby Howard and Craftsman Series veteran Bill Lester. Bang Racing co-owners Larry McReynolds and Alex Meshkin have signed 1995 series champion Mike Skinner and 2003 champion Travis Kvapil. The Innovative Motorsports team of George di Bidart will field trucks for Huffman and Hank Parker Jr. And Darrell Waltrip Motorsports will have a full-time truck for David Reutimann and a part-time truck for Waltrip.

THE BIRTH OF THE CRAFTSMAN SERIES

The future looked bright when NASCAR created its series late in 1994. Times were good, and Americans loved their pickup. Given the choice of a foreign compact or a Detroit pickup, more and more buyers were choosing the latter. Trucks enjoyed great success in the early days, mainly because they looked dramatically different from Cup and Busch cars. But the racing was good, three manufacturers were represented, and drivers and owners were happy to promote their series. And the presence of big-time owners Richard Childress, Joe Gibbs, Rick Hendrick, Dale Earnhardt, Richard Petty, and Jack Roush didn't hurt.

After eight seasons, things weren't quite as rosy at the start of the 2003 season. In 2002, the CTS consisted of a 22-race schedule, which was down from the 24 of 2001 and 2000, the 25 of 1999, and the 27 of 1998. Several of the series' biggest stars are older drivers coming off failed Busch or Cup careers, and most of its younger drivers want to move up and out. Childress, Dale Earnhardt Inc., Petty Enterprises, and Joe Gibbs Racing have gotten out of the series, and many teams are struggling to find sponsorship.

Things did improve in 2003. The number of races jumped back up to 25, and the fantastic finish to the points race had NASCAR fans everywhere focusing on the CTS. The Speed Channel took over television coverage of the CTS, and that helped give the circuit a distinctive voice and its own "home" channel. The competition from race-to-race was also excellent—12 different drivers made it to Victory Lane, and the winner's circle featured a nice mix of young stars, veteran drivers, and even Winston Cup stars who crossed over. Four drivers had a chance to win the season title in the last race of the season, and their battle literally came down to the last lap. With competition like that, things do seem to be looking up for 2004. Combine that with the unbelievable amount of attention the CTS series will receive thanks to Toyota's presence, and the stage is set for the series to experience a definite renaissance.

HISTORY OF THE CRAFTSMAN SERIES

At first, the idea seemed too "red-neck" for even the most devoted motorsports fan to take seriously. Truck racing? Did they say truck racing, as in pickup truck? Man, you gotta be kidding.

No, they weren't kidding. Pickup truck is exactly what they meant. Adding to the American racing landscape, several off-road racers from Southern California came up with the idea of putting the body of a street-legal pickup atop the chassis and roll cage of a Winston Cup car. They had to endure the jokes about what they thought was a perfectly good idea. For example:

1) By rule, each truck would carry a gun rack and Confederate flag. Whether there would be guns aboard (loaded or not) would be determined by the chief steward and/or each driver's probation officer.

2) Each driver would carry his favorite dog and make him hang out the right-side window. The dog would be walked during pit stops, but only in the presence of a crewman with a pooper-scooper. Drivers would be penalized a lap for each "deposit" left untended.

3) Each truck would carry two of three NASCAR-approved bumper stickers. Either RUSH IS RIGHT or the bandy-legged and grizzled old Confederate vet saying FORGET, HELL or the one urging fans to SEE ROCK CITY. The sticker warning IF YOU CAN READ THIS YOU'RE TOO DAMNED CLOSE would be optional for night races.

4) Finally, all trucks would haul a load of peat moss and fertilizer in the spring and a cord of firewood in the fall. For races on holiday weekends, the load must include an inner tube and cooler of Bud Lite.

Funny stuff, huh? But seriously now...

SUPERTRUCKS TAKE THE TRACK

Veteran off-road racers Dick Landfield, Jimmy Smith, Jim Venable, and Scoop Vessels embraced the idea of racing trucks on paved, oval speedways. They liked it so much, in fact, they built a prototype truck in 1993 and asked NASCAR early in 1994 to sanction several demonstration races. That May, during the Winston Cup weekend at Sonoma, California, NASCAR president Bill France Jr. announced creation of the SuperTruck Series by Craftsman, later renamed the Craftsman Truck Series. The first exhibition was at Bakersfield, California, in July 1994. NASCAR announced a 20-race, 1995 schedule that featured a $1.6 million purse and a television contract. Suddenly, the "redneck" jokes about gun racks, dogs, and bumper stickers weren't so funny.

Seldom has any NASCAR series grown faster or been accepted more openly than CTS. Many races in 1995 were sold out or close to it, and the media attention was more than anyone at NASCAR could have expected. It was almost like every Craftsman-related meeting in Daytona Beach began and ended with this mantra: "It must not fail … It will not fail." To that end, NASCAR gave the series its own radio network, offered extraordinary coverage in its publications, and made sure no race fan in America could say, "Wow, I never knew they raced pickup trucks."

So enthusiastic was NASCAR over the trucks that some Busch teams became jealous. They had been number two for years, but were now being pushed down in the pecking order.

FROM SKINNER TO BLISS: 1995 TO 2002

The first season in 1995 had 20 races at 15 tracks (Phoenix got three and Bakersfield two) in 13 states. The schedule ranged from 1-mile ovals at Phoenix and Milwaukee to the ⅓-mile track at Santa Clarita, California. To make things interesting, the tour went road racing at Topeka and Sonoma. Mike Skinner won eight poles and eight races to take the CTS title by 126 points over Joe Ruttman. The postseason awards banquet was at The Fairmont Hotel in San Francisco.

The 1996 schedule was expanded to 24 races at 23 tracks (Phoenix got two) in 18 states, including stops in the extreme corners of the country. The tour ran its first 1.5-mile tracks (Homestead and Las Vegas), returned to Topeka and Sonoma, and added the Watkins Glen road circuit in New York. More than Cup or Busch, it became evident that CTS would test man and machine on almost every conceivable type of track, and with a cross-country schedule only a World of Outlaw racer could love. Ron Hornaday won two poles and four races en route to the 1996 title by 53 points over Jack Sprague.

There was no letup in 1997. In fact, the schedule was expanded to 26 races at 25 tracks in 19 states. The purse grew to more than $6 million, impressive when you realize the long-established Busch Series raced for just $10 million. But it also ran a half-dozen superspeedway races in support of Winston Cup dates. The series visited the new 1.5-mile track at Fort Worth, the 2-mile track at Fontana, California, and the 1-mile Disney World Speedway in Orlando. Sprague won the title by a series-record 232 points over Rich Bickle.

The 1998 champion wasn't decided until the last lap of the last race on the 27-race schedule.

After 26 races and almost 5,000 laps, Ron Hornaday needed to pass two rivals to win the title by three points. He did it, passing Greg Biffle and Joe Ruttman on the last lap at Las Vegas to finish behind race-winner Jack Sprague. "The whole season came down to the last lap of the last race," said Sprague, whose next-to-last-lap pass of Biffle put him in position to win the title. "I did all I could do—I won the pole and the race— but it still wasn't enough."

While Rick Hendrick is best known for Winston Cup, his Craftsman Truck Series teams have always been strong. Two years after giving Hendrick the 1997 title, Sprague did it again in 1999. He won one pole and three races in beating Biffle by eight points. But Biffle came back in 2000 with four poles and five victories en route to winning the title by 230 points, second-largest margin in series history. Sprague rebounded in 2001, winning seven poles and four races on the way to winning his third championship, this one by 73 points over Ted Musgrave.

Mike Bliss, who had made ill-fated attempt at Winston Cup racing with owner A. J. Foyt in 2000 then raced when he could in 2001 when he didn't have a regular ride, decided to come back to the Craftsman series in 2002. Turns out that was the best decision Skinner could have made, as he made the most of his chance and won the Pikes Peak race in May, then also won at Kansas City and Kentucky in July, Nashville in August, and South Boston in September en route to the series title. All told, he had 12 top-5 finishes, 18 top-10s, and led the standings for the last 10 races. He was virtually bullet-proof, finishing top-10 in his last 8 and in 13 of his last 14 starts.

REACHING NEW HEIGHTS

After nine years of racing, it's obvious that Landfield, Smith, Venable, and Vessels knew their stuff when they approached NASCAR in 1994. "This series has risen in only 18 months to a level it took Nextel Cup 20 years to reach," France said at the 1995 awards banquet in San Francisco. "It

can only be described as a national phenomenon." NASCAR vice-president Dennis Huth called the truck series "a natural entertainment and marketing opportunity since 89 percent of all truck owners enjoy some sort of motorsports."

But why does it work? What is there about pickup trucks on ovals or road courses that bring in American race fans in ever-increasing numbers? Certainly it's more than an "entertainment and marketing opportunity." Ask around and you'll get several answers:

Don't dismiss the novelty of truck racing. Only the most discerning NASCAR fan can tell a Nextel Cup car from a Busch Series car at speed. There are differences, but they're so small that Saturday afternoons aren't all that different from Sunday afternoons. There are, on the other hand, no similarities between a Cup or Busch car and a Craftsman truck. They look different and they sound different, and fans don't need to look twice to realize that.

Another factor is the fierce loyalty of truck buyers. In the fall of 1996, for the first time in American automotive history, light and heavy trucks (combined with sport utility vehicles) accounted for 50 percent of the country's new vehicle registrations. As the Craftsman information booklet explains, half the new cars in this country aren't cars at all. While passenger car sales have declined in recent years, the market for full-sized pickups is the largest segment of the truck industry.

Another reason is the competition among brands. Each of the Big Three manufacturers— General Motors, Ford, and Chrysler—has a truck body similar to one of the other two. It's been proven that fans in the stands readily identify with "their" brand over the others. Chrysler was still not a part of the then–Winston Cup when it joined the truck circuit, but the presence of Dodge Ram trucks rekindled emotions for Dodge to return to Cup racing ... which it did with some success in 2001. It will be very interesting to see how longtime fans react to Toyota's presence in 2004, and also to see if Toyota owners will become NASCAR fans now that their brand is on the track.

And don't discount the gentle persuasion that France and his people applied to convince owners like Childress, Roush, Petty, and Hendrick to get involved. From there, it was easier to convince Winston Cup drivers like Earnhardt, Schrader, Labonte, Darrell Waltrip, Geoff Bodine, Johnny Benson, A. J. Foyt, Harry Gant, Ernie Irvan, Bobby Hamilton, and Jimmy Hensley to get involved in the series.

Much like Busch, the Craftsman tour often sends its drivers up the line. Skinner went from being 1995 CTS champion and third in 1996 points to a regular Cup ride. Hornaday went from being the 1996 and 1998 champion to Busch and Cup rides. Jimmy Hensley, Kenny Irwin and Stacy Compton had extensive truck experience before going to Cup. Kevin Harvick, Greg Biffle, Kurt Bush, Jamie McMurray, and Scott Riggs moved up after enjoying CTS success. Brendan Gaughan, 2003 champion, will try to make the jump from CTS to the Nextel Cup in 2004.

The bottom line: Craftsman Truck Series racing is among the best in any NASCAR division. Its drivers and teams are hungry and competitive, and they certainly don't mind beating and banging, and leaning on each other. Truck racing may be the best value in American motorsports. Now, if only more fans will pay attention.

CAREER RECORDS
Top-10 career victories

Ron Hornaday	26
Jack Sprague	23
Greg Biffle	16
Mike Skinner	16
Ted Musgrave	13
Joe Ruttman	13
Mike Bliss	12
Dennis Setzer	10
Brendan Gaughan	8
Scott Riggs	5

Top-10 career starts

Rick Crawford	173
Jack Sprague	172
Joe Ruttman	168
Terry Cook	165
Lance Norick	153
Jimmy Hensley	146
Mike Bliss	144
Dennis Setzer	142
Rick Carelli	134
Brian Reffner	125

Top-10 career poles

Jack Sprague	26
Mike Bliss	18
Joe Ruttman	17
Mike Skinner	15
Greg Biffle	12
Ron Hornaday	11
Jason Leffler	10
Stacy Compton	9
Ted Musgrave	9
Terry Cook	7

15

RACE RESULTS:
1949-2002

This chapter contains race results for every NASCAR Strictly Stock, Grand National, and Winston Cup race run through the 2001 season. Between the years 1949 and 1971, as many as 60 races were held in a single season and records were not kept as tightly as they are today. For this reason, only the race winner is listed for those years. Starting in 1972, when R. J. Reynolds took over as primary sponsor and the Winston Cup circuit was created, the season was shortened to a more manageable number of approximately 30 races. Complete race results are included from 1971 to 2001, including a listing of all finishers, time of race, average speed, and, when available, margin of victory. Race-by-race results for 2002 are included in Chapter 2, "2002 Race Results."

1949

RACE WINNERS

RACE	DRIVER	CAR
Charlotte, NC	Jim Roper	Lincoln
Daytona Beach, FL	Red Byron	Oldsmobile
Hillsboro, NC	Bob Flock	Oldsmobile
Langhorne, PA	Curtis Turner	Oldsmobile
Hamburg, NY	Jack White	Lincoln
Martinsville, VA	Red Byron	Oldsmobile
Heidelberg, PA	Lee Petty	Plymouth
N. Wilkesboro, NC	Bob Flock	Oldsmobile

1950

RACE WINNERS

RACE	DRIVER	CAR
Daytona Beach, FL	Harold Kite	Lincoln
Charlotte, NC	Tim Flock	Lincoln

Langhorne, PA	Curtis Turner	Oldsmobile
Martinsville, VA	Curtis Turner	Oldsmobile
Canfield, OH	Bill Rexford	Oldsmobile
Vernon, NY	Bill Blair	Mercury
Dayton, OH	Jimmy Florian	Ford
Rochester, NY	Curtis Turner	Oldsmobile
Charlotte, NC	Curtis Turner	Oldsmobile
Hillsboro, NC	Fireball Roberts	Oldsmobile
Dayton, OH	Dick Linder	Oldsmobile
Hamburg, NY	Dick Linder	Oldsmobile
Darlington, SC	Johnny Mantz	Plymouth
Langhorne, PA	Fonty Flock	Oldsmobile
N. Wilkesboro, NC	Leon Sales	Plymouth
Vernon, NY	Dick Linder	Oldsmobile
Martinsville, VA	Herb Thomas	Plymouth
Winchester, IN	Lloyd Moore	Mercury
Hillsboro, NC	Lee Petty	Plymouth

1951

RACE WINNERS

RACE	DRIVER	CAR
Dayton Beach, FL	Marshall Teague	Hudson

Charlotte, NC	Curtis Turner	Nash
Mobile, AL	Tim Flock	Oldsmobile
Gardena, CA	Marshall Teague	Hudson
Hillsboro, NC	Fonty Flock	Oldsmobile
Phoenix, AZ	Marshall Teague	Hudson
N. Wilkesboro, NC	Fonty Flock	Oldsmobile
Martinsville, VA	Curtis Turner	Oldsmobile
Canfield, OH	Marshall Teague	Hudson
Columbus, OH	Tim Flock	Oldsmobile
Columbia, SC	Frank Mundy	Studebaker
Dayton, OH	Curtis Turner	Oldsmobile
Gardena, CA	Lou Figaro	Hudson
Grand Rapids, MI	Marshall Teague	Hudson
Bainbridge, OH	Fonty Flock	Oldsmobile
Heidelberg, PA	Herb Thomas	Oldsmobile
Weaverville, NC	Fonty Flock	Oldsmobile
Rochester, NY	Lee Petty	Plymouth
Altamont, NY	Fonty Flock	Oldsmobile
Detroit, MI	Tommy Thompson	Chrysler
Toledo, OH	Tim Flock	Oldsmobile
Morristown, NJ	Tim Flock	Oldsmobile
Greenville, SC	Bob Flock	Oldsmobile
Darlington, SC	Herb Thomas	Hudson
Columbia, SC	Tim Flock	Oldsmobile
Macon, GA	Herb Thomas	Hudson
Langhorne, PA	Herb Thomas	Hudson
Charlotte, NC	Herb Thomas	Hudson
Dayton, OH	Fonty Flock	Oldsmobile
Wilson, NC	Fonty Flock	Oldsmobile
Hillsboro, NC	Herb Thomas	Hudson
Thompson, CT	Neil Cole	Oldsmobile
Shippenville, PA	Tim Flock	Oldsmobile
Martinsville, VA	Frank Mundy	Oldsmobile
Oakland, CA	Marvin Burke	Mercury
N. Wilkesboro, NC	Fonty Flock	Oldsmobile
Hanford, CA	Danny Weinberg	Studebaker
Jacksonville, FL	Herb Thomas	Hudson
Atlanta, GA	Tim Flock	Hudson
Gardena, CA	Bill Norton	Mercury
Mobile, AL	Frank Mundy	Studebaker

1952

RACE WINNERS

RACE	DRIVER	CAR
W Palm Beach, FL	Tim Flock	Hudson
Daytona Beach, FL	Marshall Teague	Hudson
Jacksonville, FL	Marshall Teague	Hudson
N. Wilkesboro, NC	Herb Thomas	Hudson
Martinsbille, VA	Dick Rathmann	Hudson
Columbia, SC	Buck Baker	Hudson
Atlanta, GA	Bill Blair	Oldsmobile
Macon, GA	Herb Thomas	Hudson
Langhorne, PA	Dick Rathmann	Hudson
Darlington, SC	Dick Rathmann	Hudson
Dayton, OH	Dick Rathmann	Hudson
Canfield, OH	Herb Thomas	Hudson
Augusta, GA	Gober Sosebee	Chrysler
Toledo, OH	Tim Flock	Hudson
Hillsboro, NC	Tim Flock	Hudson
Charlotte, NC	Herb Thomas	Hudson
Detroit, MI	Tim Flock	Hudson
Niagara Falls, ONT	Buddy Shuman	Hudson
Oswego, NY	Tim Flock	Hudson
Monroe, MI	Tim Flock	Hudson
Morristown, NJ	Lee Petty	Plymouth
South Bend, IN	Tim Flock	Hudson
Rochester, NY	Tim Flock	Hudson
Weaverville, NC	Bob Flock	Hudson
Darlington, SC	Fonty Flock	Oldsmobile
Macon, GA	Lee Petty	Plymouth
Langhorne, PA	Lee Petty	Plymouth
Dayton, OH	Dick Rathmann	Hudson
Wilson, NC	Herb Thomas	Hudson
Hillsboro, NC	Fonty Flock	Oldsmobile
Martinsville, VA	Herb Thomas	Hudson
N. Wilkesboro, NC	Herb Thomas	Hudson
Atlanta, GA	Donald Thomas	Hudson
W. Palm Beach, FL	Herb Thomas	Hudson

1953

RACE WINNERS

RACE	DRIVER	CAR
W Palm Beach, FL	Lee Petty	Dodge
Daytona Beach, FL	Bill Blair	Oldsmobile
Spring Lake, NC	Herb Thomas	Hudson
N. Wilkesboro, NC	Herb Thomas	Hudson
Charlotte, NC	Dick Passwater	Oldsmobile
Richmond, VA	Lee Petty	Dodge
Macon, GA	Dick Rathmann	Hudson
Langhorne, PA	Buck Baker	Oldsmobile
Columbia, SC	Buck Baker	Oldsmobile
Hickory, NC	Tim Flock	Hudson
Martinsville, VA	Lee Petty	Dodge
Columbus, OH	Herb Thomas	Hudson
Raleigh, NC	Fonty Flock	Hudson
Shreveport LA	Lee Petty	Dodge
Pensacola, FL	Herb Thomas	Hudson
Langhorne, PA	Dick Rathmann	Hudson
High Point, NC	Herb Thomas	Hudson
Wilson, NC	Fonty Flock	Hudson
Rochester, NY	Herb Thomas	Hudson
Spartanburg, SC	Lee Petty	Dodge
Morrison, NJ	Dick Rathmann	Hudson
Atlanta, GA	Herb Thomas	Hudson
Rapid City, SD	Herb Thomas	Hudson
N Platte NE	Dick Rathmann	Hudson
Davenport, IA	Herb Thomas	Hudson
Hillsboro, NC	Curtis Turner	Oldsmobile
Weaverville, NC	Fonty Flock	Hudson
Norfolk, VA	Herb Thomas	Hudson
Hickory, NC	Fonty Flock	Hudson
Darlington, SC	Buck Baker	Oldsmobile
Macon, GA	Speedy Thompson	Oldsmobile
Langhorne, PA	Dick Rathmann	Hudson
Bloomsburg, PA	Herb Thomas	Hudson
Wilson, NC	Herb Thomas	Hudson
N. Wilkesboro, NC	Speedy Thompson	Oldsmobile
Martinsville, VA	Jim Paschal	Dodge
Atlanta, GA	Buck Baker	Oldsmobile

1954

RACE WINNERS

RACE	DRIVER	CAR
W Palm Beach, FL	Herb Thomas	Hudson
Daytona Beach, FL	Lee Petty	Chrysler
Jacksonville, FL	Herb Thomas	Hudson
Atlanta, GA	Herb Thomas	Hudson
Savannah, GA	Al Keller	Hudson
Oakland, CA	Dick Rathmann	Hudson
N. Wilkesboro, NC	Dick Rathmann	Hudson
Hillsboro, NC	Herb Thomas	Hudson
Macon, GA	Gober Sosebee	Oldsmobile
Langhorne, PA	Herb Thomas	Hudson
Wilson, NC	Buck Baker	Oldsmobile
Martinsville, VA	Jim Paschal	Oldsmobile
Sharon, PA	Lee Petty	Chrysler
Raleigh, NC	Herb Thomas	Hudson
Charlotte, NC	Buck Baker	Oldsmobile
Gardena, CA	John Soares	Dodge
Columbia, SC	Curtis Turner	Oldsmobile
Linden, NJ	Al Keller	Jaguar
Hickory, NC	Herb Thomas	Hudson
Rochester, NY	Lee Petty	Chrysler
Mechanicsburg, PA	Herb Thomas	Hudson
Spartanburg, SC	Herb Thomas	Hudson
Weaverville, NC	Herb Thomas	Hudson
Willow Springs, IL	Dick Rathmann	Hudson
Grand Rapids, MI	Lee Petty	Chrysler
Morristown, NJ	Buck Baker	Oldsmobile
Oakland, CA	Danny Letner	Hudson
Charlotte, NC	Lee Petty	Chrysler

RACE	DRIVER	CAR
San Mateo, CA	Hershel McGriff	Oldsmobile
Corbin KY	Lee Petty	Chrysler
Darlington, SC	Herb Thomas	Hudson
Macon, GA	Hershel McGriff	Oldsmobile
Charlotte, NC	Hershel McGriff	Oldsmobile
Langhorne, PA	Herb Thomas	Hudson
LeHi AR	Buck Baker	Oldsmobile
Martinsville, VA	Lee Petty	Chrysler
N. Wilkesboro, NC	Hershel McGriff	Oldsmobile

1955

RACE WINNERS

RACE	DRIVER	CAR
High Point, NC	Lee Petty	Chrysler
W. Palm Beach, FL	Herb Thomas	Hudson
Jacksonville, FL	Lee Petty	Chrysler
Daytona Beach, FL	Tim Flock	Chrysler
Savannah, GA	Lee Petty	Chrysler
Columbia, SC	Fonty Flock	Chevrolet
Hillsboro, NC	Jim Paschal	Oldsmobile
N. Wilkesboro, NC	Buck Baker	Oldsmobile
Montgomery, AL	Tim Flock	Chrysler
Langhorne, PA	Tim Flock	Chrysler
Charlotte, NC	Buck Baker	Buick
Hickory, NC	Junior Johnson	Oldsmobile
Phoenix, AZ	Tim Flock	Chrysler
Tucson, AZ	Danny Letner	Oldsmobile
Martinsville, VA	Tim Flock	Chrysler
Richmond, VA	Tim Flock	Chrysler
Raleigh, NC	Junior Johnson	Oldsmobile
Winston Salem, NC	Lee Petty	Chrysler
New Oxford, PA	Junior Johnson	Oldsmobile
Rochester, NY	Tim Flock	Chrysler
Fonda, NY	Junior Johnson	Oldsmobile
Plattsburg, NY	Lee Petty	Chrysler
Charlotte, NC	Tim Flock	Chrysler
Spartanburg, SC	Tim Flock	Chrysler
Columbia, SC	Jim Paschal	Oldsmobile
Weaverville, NC	Tim Flock	Chrysler
Morristown, NJ	Tim Flock	Chrysler
Altamont, NY	Junior Johnson	Oldsmobile
Syracuse, NY	Tim Flock	Chrysler
San Mateo, CA	Tim Flock	Chrysler
Charlotte, NC	Jim Paschal	Oldsmobile
Winston-Salem, NC	Lee Petty	Dodge
LeHi AR	Fonty Flock	Chrysler
Raleigh, NC	Herb Thomas	Buick
Darlington, SC	Heb Thomas	Chevrolet
Montgomery, AL	Tim Flock	Chrysler
Langhome, PA	Tim Flock	Chrysler
Raleigh, NC	Fonty Flock	Chrysler
Greenville, SC	Tim Flock	Chrysler
LeHi AR	Speedy Thompson	Ford
Columbia, SC	Tim Flock	Chrysler
Matinsville, VA	Speedy Thompson	Chrysler
Las Vegas NV	Norm Nelson	Chrysler
N. Wilkesboro, NC	Buck Baker	Ford
Hillsboro, NC	Tim Flock	Chrysler

1956

RACE WINNERS

RACE	DRIVER	CAR
Hickory, NC	Tim Flock	Chrysler
Charlotte, NC	Fonty Flock	Chrysler
Lancaster, CA	Chuck Stevenson	Ford
W. Palm Beach, FL	Herb Thomas	Chevrolet
Phoenix, AZ	Buck Baker	Chrysler
Daytona Beach, FL	Tim Flock	Chrysler
W. Palm Beach, FL	Billy Myers	Mercury
Wilson, NC	Herb Thomas	Chevrolet

RACE	DRIVER	CAR
Atlanta, GA	Buck Baker	Chrysler
N. Wilkesboro, NC	Tim Flock	Chrysler
Longhorne, PA	Buck Baker	Chrysler
Richmond, VA	Buck Baker	Dodge
Columbia, SC	Speedy Thompson	Dodge
Concord, NC	Speedy Thompson	Chrysler
Greenville, SC	Buck Baker	Dodge
Hickory, NC	Speedy Thompson	Chrysler
Hillsboro, NC	Buck Baker	Chrysler
Martinsville, VA	Buck Baker	Dodge
Abbottstown, PA	Buck Baker	Dodge
Charlotte, NC	Speedy Thompson	Chrysler
Portland, OR	Herb Thomas	Chrysler
Eureka, CA	Herb Thomas	Chrysler
Syracuse, NY	Buck Baker	Chrysler
Merced, CA	Herb Thomas	Chrysler
LeHi AR	Ralph Moody	Ford
Charlotte, NC	Speedy Thompson	Chrysler
Rochester, NY	Speedy Thompson	Chrysler
Portland, OR	John Kieper	Oldsmobile
Weaverville, NC	Lee Petty	Dodge
Raleigh, NC	Fireball Roberts	Ford
Spartanburg, SC	Lee Petty	Dodge
Sacramento, CA	Lloyd Dane	Mercury
Chicago, IL	Fireball Roberts	Ford
Shelby, NC	Speedy Thompson	Dodge
Montgomery, AL	Marvin Panch	Ford
Oklahoma City, OK	Jim Paschal	Mercury
Elkhart Lake WI	Tim Flock	Mercury
Old Bridge, NJ	Ralph Moody	Ford
San Mateo, CA	Eddie Pagan	Ford
Norfolk, VA	Billy Myers	Mercury
Spartanburg, SC	Ralph Moody	Ford
Myrtle Beach, SC	Fireball Roberts	Ford
Portland, OR	Royce Haggerty	Dodge
Darlington, SC	Curtis Turner	Ford
Montgomery, AL	Buck Baker	Chrysler
Charlotte, NC	Ralph Moody	Ford
Langhorne, PA	Paul Goldsmith	Chevrolet
Portland, OR	Lloyd Dane	Ford
Columbia, SC	Buck Baker	Dodge
Hillsboro, NC	Fireball Roberts	Ford
Newport, TN	Fireball Roberts	Ford
Charlotte, NC	Buck Baker	Chrysler
Shelby, NC	Buck Baker	Chrysler
Martinsville, VA	Jack Smith	Dodge
Hickory, NC	Speedy Thompson	Chrysler
Wilson, NC	Buck Baker	Chrysler

1957

RACE WINNERS

RACE	DRIVER	CAR
Lancaster, CA	Marvin Panch	Ford
Concord, NC	Marvin Panch	Ford
Titusville, FL	Fireball Roberts	Ford
Daytona Beach, FL	Cotton Owens	Pontiac
Concord, NC	Jack Smith	Chevrolet
Wilson, NC	Ralph Moody	Ford
Hillsboro, NC	Buck Baker	Chevrolet
Weaverville, NC	Buck Baker	Chevrolet
N. Wilkesboro, NC	Fireball Roberts	Ford
Langhorne, PA	Fireball Roberts	Ford
Charlotte, NC	Fireball Roberts	Ford
Spartanburg, SC	Marvin Panch	Ford
Greensboro, NC	Paul Goldsmith	Ford
Portland, OR	Art Watts	Ford
Shelby, NC	Fireball Roberts	Ford
Richmond, VA	Paul Goldsmith	Ford
Martinsville, VA	Buck Baker	Chevrolet
Portland, OR	Eddie Pagan	Ford
Eureka, CA	Lloyd Dane	Ford
New Oxford, PA	Buck Baker	Chevrolet
Lancaster, SC	Paul Goldsmith	Ford
Los Angeles, CA	Eddie Pagan	Ford
Newport, TN	Fireball Roberts	Ford
Columbia, SC	Jack Smith	Chevrolet
Sacramento, CA	Bill Amick	Ford
Spartanburg, SC	Lee Petty	Oldsmobile

Jacksonville, NC	Buck Baker	Chevrolet
Raleigh, NC	Paul Goldsmith	Ford
Charlotte, NC	Marvin Panch	Ford
LeHi AR	Marvin Panch	Pontiac
Portland, OR	Eddie Pagan	Ford
Hickory, NC	Jack Smith	Chevrolet
Norfolk, VA	Buck Baker	Chevrolet
Lancaster, SC	Speedy Thompson	Chevrolet
Watkins Glen, NY	Buck Baker	Chevrolet
Bremerton, WA	Parnelli Jones	Ford
New Oxford, PA	Marvin Panch	Ford
Old Bridge, NJ	Lee Petty	Oldsmobile
Myrtle Beach, SC	Gwyn Staley	Chevrolet
Darlington, SC	Speedy Thompson	Chevrolet
Syracuse, NY	Gwyn Staley	Chevrolet
Weaverville, PA	Lee Petty	Oldsmobile
Sacramento, CA	Danny Graves	Chevrolet
San Jose, CA	Marvin Porter	Ford
Langhorne, PA	Gwyn Staley	Chevrolet
Columbia, SC	Buck Baker	Chevrolet
Shelby, NC	Buck Baker	Chevrolet
Charlotte, NC	Lee Petty	Oldsmobile
Martinsville, VA	Bob Welborn	Chevrolet
Newberry, SC	Fireball Roberts	Ford
Concord, NC	Fireball Roberts	Ford
N. Wilkesboro, NC	Jack Smith	Chevrolet
Greensboro, NC	Buck Baker	Chevrolet

1958

RACE WINNERS

RACE	WINNER	CAR
Fayetteville, NC	Rex White	Chevrolet
Daytona Beach, FL	Paul Goldsmith	Pontiac
Charlotte, NC	Lee Petty	Oldsmobile
Fayetteville, NC	Curtis Turner	Ford
Wilson, NC	Lee Petty	Oldsmobile
Hillsborough, NC	Buck Baker	Chevrolet
Fayetteville, NC	Bob Welborn	Chevrolet
Columbia,, SC	Speedy Thompson	Chevrolet
Spartanburg,, SC	Speedy Thompson	Chevrolet
Atlanta,, GA	Curtis Turner	Ford
Charlotte, NC	Curtis Turner	Ford
Martinsville,, VA	Bob Welborn	Chevrolet
Manassas, VA	Frankie Schneider	Chevrolet
Old Bridge, NJ	Jim Reed	Ford
Greenville, SC	Jack Smith	Chevrolet
Greensboro, NC	Bob Welborn	Chevrolet
Roanoke, VA	Jim Reed	Ford
N. Wilkesboro, NC	Junior Johnson	Ford
Winston-Salem, NC	Bob Welborn	Chevrolet
Trenton, NJ	Fireball Roberts	Chevrolet
Riverside, CA	Eddie Gray	Ford
Columbia, SC	Junior Johnson	Ford
Bradford,, PA	Junior Johnson	Ford
Reading,, PA	Junior Johnson	Ford
New Oxford, PA	Lee Petty	Oldsmobile
Hickory, NC	Lee Petty	Oldsmobile
Weaverville, NC	Rex White	Chevrolet
Raleigh, NC	Fireball Roberts	Chevrolet
Asheville, NC	Jim Paschal	Chevrolet
Busti, NY	Shortly Rollins	Ford
Toronto,, CAN	Lee Petty	Oldsmobile
Buffalo, NY	Jim Reed	Ford
Rochester, NY	Cotton Owens	Pontiac
Belmar, NJ	Jim Reed	Chevrolet
Bridgehampton, NY	Jack Smith	Chevrolet
Columbia, SC	Speedy Thompson	Chevrolet
Nashville, TN	Joe Weatherly	Ford
Weaverville, NC	Fireball Roberts	Chevrolet
Winston-Salem, NC	Lee Petty	Oldsmobile
Myrtle Beach, SC	Bob Welborn	Chevrolet
Darlington, SC	Fireball Roberts	Chevrolet
Charlotte, NC	Buck Baker	Chevrolet
Birmingham, AL	Fireball Roberts	Chevrolet
Sacramento, CA	Parnelli Jones	Ford
Gastonia, NC	Buck Baker	Chevrolet
Richmond, VA	Speedy Thompson	Chevrolet
Hillsborough, NC	Joe Eubanks	Pontiac

Sallsbury, NC	Loo Petty	Oldsmobile
Martinsville	Fireball Roberts	Chevrolet
N. Wilkesboro, NC	Junior Johnson	Ford
Atlanta, GA	Junior Johnson	Ford

1959

RACE WINNERS

RACE	WINNER	CAR
Fayetteville, NC	Bob Welborn	Chevrolet
Daytona Beach, FL	Bob Welborn	Chevrolet
Daytona Beach, FL	Lee Petty	Oldsmobile
Hillsborough, NC	Curtis Turner	Ford
Atlanta, GA	Johnny Beauchamp	Ford
Wilson, NC	Junior Johnson	Ford
Winston-Salem, NC	Jim Reed	Ford
Columbia, SC	Jack Smith	Chevrolet
N. Wilkesboro, NC	Lee Petty	Oldsmobile
Reading, PA	Junior Johnson	Ford
Hickory, NC	Junior Johnson	Ford
Martinsville, VA	Lee Petty	Oldsmobile
Trenton, NJ	Tom Pistone	Ford
Charlotte, NC	Lee Petty	Oldsmobile
Nashville, TN	Rex White	Chevrolet
Los Angeles, CA	Parnelli Jones	Ford
Spartanburg, SC	Jack Smith	Chevrolet
Greenville, SC	Junior Johnson	Ford
Atlanta, GA	Lee Petty	Plymouth
Columbia, SC	Lee Petty	Plymouth
Wilson, NC	Junior Johnson	Ford
Richmond, VA	Tom Pistone	Ford
Winston-Salem	Rex White	Chevrolet
Weaverville, NC	Rex White	Chevrolet
Daytona Beach, FL	Fireball Roberts	Pontiac
Pittsburgh, PA	Jim Reed	Chevrolet
Charlotte, CA	Jack Smith	Chevrolet
Myrtle Beach, SC	Ned Jarrett	Ford
Charlotte, NC	Ned Jarrett	Ford
Nashville, TN	Joe Lee Johnson	Chevrolet
Weaverville, NC	Bob Welborn	Chevrolet
Winston-Salem,, NC	Rex White	Chevrolet
Greenville, SC	Buck Baker	Chevrolet
Columbia, SC	Lee Petty	Chevrolet
Darlington, SC	Jim Reed	Chevrolet
Hickory, NC	Lee Petty	Chevrolet
Richmond, VA	Cotton Ownes	Ford
Sacramento, CA	Eddie Gray	Ford
Hillsborough, NC	Lee Petty	Plymouth
Martinsville, VA	Rex White	Chevrolet
Weaverville, NC	Lee Petty	Plymouth
N. Wilkesboro, NC	Lee Petty	Plymouth
Charlotte, NC	Jack Smith	Chevrolet

1960

RACE WINNERS

RACE	WINNER	CAR
Charlotte, NC	Jack Smith	Chevrolet
Columbia, SC	Ned Jarrett	Ford
Daytona Beach, FL	Fireball Roberts	Pontiac
Daytona Beach, FL	Jack Smith	Pontiac
Daytona Beach, FL	Junior Johnson	Chevrolet
Charlotte, NC	Richard Petty	Plymouth
N. Wilkesboro, NC	Lee Petty	Plymouth
Phoenix, AZ	John Rostek	Ford
Columbia, SC	Rex White	Chevrolet
Martinsville, VA	Richard Petty	Plymouth
Hickory, NC	Joe Weatherly	Ford
Wilson, NC	Joe Weatherly	Ford
Winston-Salem,, NC	Glen Wood	Ford
Greenville, SC	Ned Jarrett	Ford
Weaverville, NC	Lee Petty	Plymouth

Darlington, SC	Joe Weatherly	Ford
Spartanburg,, SC	Ned Jarrett	Ford
Hillsborough, NC	Lee Petty	Plymouth
Richmond, VA	Lee Petty	Plymouth
Hanford, CA	Marvin Porter	Ford
Concord, NC	Joe Lee Johnson	Chevrolet
Winston-Salem, NC	Glen Wood	Ford
Daytona Beach, FL	Jack Smith	Pontiac
Pittsburgh,, PA	Lee Petty	Plymouth
Montgomery, NY	Rex White	Chevrolet
Myrtle Beach, SC	Buck Baker	Chevrolet
Hampton, GA	Fireball Roberts	Pontiac
Birmingham, AL	Ned Jarrett	Ford
Nashville, TN	Johnny Beauchamp	Chevrolet
Weaverville,, NC	Rex White	Chevrolet
Spartanburg, SC	Cotton Owens	Pontiac
Columbia, SC	Rex White	Chevrolet
South Boston, VA	Junior Johnson	Chevrolet
Winston-Salem, NC	Glen Wood	Ford
Darlington, SC	Buck Baker	Pontiac
Hickory, NC	Junior Johnson	Chevrolet
Sacramento, CA	Jim Cook	Dodge
Sumter, SC	Ned Jarrett	Ford
Hillsborough, NC	Richard Petty	Plymouth
Martinsville, VA	Rex White	Chevrolet
N. Wilkesboro, NC	Rex White	Chevrolet
Concord, NC	Speedy Thompson	Ford
Richmond, VA	Speedy Thompson	Ford
Hampton, GA	Bobby Johns	Pontiac

1961

RACE WINNERS

RACE	WINNER	CAR
Charlotte, NC	Joe Weatherly	Ford
Jacksonville, FL	Lee Petty	Plymouth
Daytona Beach, FL	Fireball Roberts	Pontiac
Daytona Beach, FL	Joe Weatherly	Pontiac
Daytona Beach, FL	Marvin Panch	Pontiac
Spartanburg, SC	Cotton Owens	Pontiac
Weaverville, NC	Rex White	Chevrolet
Hanford, CA	Fireball Roberts	Pontiac
Hampton, GA	Bob Burdick	Pontiac
Greenville, SC	Emanuel Zervakis	Chevrolet
Hillsborough, NC	Cotton Owens	Pontiac
Winston Salem, NC	Rex White	Chevrolet
Martinsville, VA	Fred Lorenzen	Ford
N. Wilkesboro, NC	Rex White	Chevrolet
Columbia, SC	Cotton Owens	Pontiac
Hickory, NC	Junior Johnson	Pontiac
Richmond, VA	Richard Petty	Plymouth
Martinsville, VA	Junior Johnson	Pontiac
Darlington, SC	Fred Lorenzen	Ford
Concord, NC	Richard Petty	Plymouth
Concord, NC	Joe Weatherly	Pontiac
Riverside, CA	Lloyd Dane	Chevrolet
Los Angeles, CA	Eddie Gray	Ford
Concord, NC	David Pearson	Pontiac
Spartanburg, SC	Jim Paschal	Pontiac
Birmingham, AL	Ned Jarrett	Chevrolet
Greenville, SC	Jack Smith	Pontiac
Winston-Salem, NC	Rex White	Chevrolet
Norwood MA	Emanuel Zervakis	Chevrolet
Hartsville, SC	Buck Baker	Chrysler
Roanoke, VA	Junior Johnson	Pontiac
Daytona Beach, FL	David Pearson	Pontiac
Hampton, GA	Fred Lorenzen	Ford
Columbia, SC	Cotton Owens	Pontiac
Myrtle Beach, SC	Joe Weatherly	Pontiac
Nashville, TN	Jim Paschal	Pontiac
Bristol, TN	Jack Smith	Pontiac
Winston-Salem, NC	Rex White	Chevrolet
Weaverville, NC	Junior Johnson	Pontiac
Richmond, VA	Junior Johnson	Pontiac
South Boston, VA	Junior Johnson	Pontiac
Darlington, SC	Nelson Stacy	Ford
Hickory, NC	Rex White	Chevrolet
Richmond, VA	Joe Weatherly	Pontiac
Sacramento, CA	Eddie Gray	Ford

Hampton, GA	David Pearson	Pontiac
Matinsville, VA	Joe Weatherly	Pontiac
N. Wilkesboro, NC	Rex White	Chevrolet
Concord, NC	Joe Weatherly	Pontiac
Bristol, TN	Joe Weatherly	Pontiac
Greenville,, SC	Junior Johnson	Pontiac
Hillsborough, NC	Joe Weatherly	Pontiac

1962

RACE WINNERS

RACE	WINNER	CAR
Concord, NC	Jack Smith	Pontiac
Weaverville, NC	Rex White	Chevrolet
Daytona Beach, FL	Fireball Roberts	Pontiac
Daytona Beach, FL	Joe Weatherly	Pontiac
Daytona Beach, FL	Fireball Roberts	Pontiac
Concord, NC	Joe Weatherly	Pontiac
Weaverville, NC	Joe Weatherly	Pontiac
Savannah, GA	Jack Smith	Pontiac
Hillsborough, NC	Rex White	Chevrolet
Richmond, VA	Rex White	Chevrolet
Columbia, SC	Ned Jarrett	Chevrolet
N. Wilkesboro, NC	Richard Petty	Plymouth
Greenville, SC	Ned Jarrett	Chevrolet
Myrtle Beach, SC	Jack Smith	Pontiac
Martinsville, VA	Richard Petty	Plymouth
Winston-Salem, NC	Rex White	Chevrolet
Bristol, TN	Bobby Johns	Pontiac
Richmond, VA	Jimmy Pardue	Pontiac
Hickory, NC	Jack Smith	Pontiac
Concord, NC	Joe Weatherly	Pontiac
Darlington, SC	Nelson Stacy	Ford
Spartanburg, NC	Ned Jarrett	Chevrolet
Concord, NC	Nelson Stacy	Ford
Hampton, GA	Fred Lorenzen	Ford
Winston-Salem, NC	Johnny Allen	Pontiac
Augusta, GA	Joe Weatherly	Pontiac
Richmond, VA	Jim Paschal	Pontiac
South Boston, VA	Rex White	Chevrolet
Daytona Beach, FL	Fireball Roberts	Pontiac
Columbia, SC	Rex White	Chevrolet
Asheville, NC	Jack Smith	Pontiac
Greenville, SC	Richard Petty	Plymouth
Augusta, GA	Joe Weatherly	Pontiac
Savannah, GA	Joe Weatherly	Pontiac
Myrtle Beach, SC	Ned Jarrett	Chevrolet
Bristol, TN	Jim Paschal	Plymouth
Chattanooga, TN	Joe Weatherly	Pontiac
Nashville, TN	Jim Paschal	Plymouth
Huntsville,, AL	Richard Petty	Plymouth
Weaverville, NC	Jim Paschal	Plymouth
Roanoke, VA	Richard Petty	Plymouth
Winston-Salem, NC	Richard Petty	Plymouth
Spartanburg, SC	Richard Petty	Plymouth
Valdosta, GA	Ned Jarrett	Chevrolet
Darlington, SC	Larry Frank	Ford
Hickory, NC	Rex White	Chevrolet
Richmond, VA	Joe Weatherly	Pontiac
Moyock, NC	Ned Jerrett	Chevrolet
Augusta, GA	Fred Lorenzen	Ford
Martinsville, VA	Nelson Stacy	Ford
N. Wilkesboro, NC	Richard Petty	Plymouth
Concord, NC	Junior Johnson	Pontiac
Hampton, GA	Rex White	Chevrolet

1963

RACE WINNERS

RACE	WINNER	CAR
Birmingham, AL	Jim Paschal	Plymouth
Tampa, FL	Richard Petty	Plymouth

Randleman, NC	Jim Paschal	Plymouth
Riverside, CA	Dan Gurney	Ford
Daytona Beach, FL	Junior Johnson	Chevrolet
Daytona Beach, FL	Johnny Rutherford	Chevrolet
Daytona Beach, FL	Tiny Lund	Ford
Spartanburg, NC	Richard Petty	Plymouth
Weaverville, NC	Richard Petty	Plymouth
Hillsborough, NC	Junior Johnson	Chevrolet
Hampton, GA	Fred Lorenzen	Ford
Hickory, NC	Junior Johnson	Chevrolet
Bristol, TN	Fireball Roberts	Ford
Augusta, GA	Ned Jarrett	Ford
Richmond, VA	Joe Weatherly	Pontiac
Greenville, SC	Buck Baker	Pontiac
South Boston, VA	Richard Petty	Plymouth
Winston-Salem, NC	Jim Paschal	Plymouth
Martinsville, VA	Richard Petty	Plymouth
N. Wilkesboro, NC	Richard Petty	Plymouth
Columbia, SC	Richard Petty	Plymouth
Randleman, NC	Jim Paschal	Plymouth
Darlington, SC	Joe Weatherly	Pontiac
Manassas, VA	Richard Petty	Plymouth
Richmond, VA	Ned Jarrett	Ford
Concord, NC	Fred Lorenzen	Ford
Birmingham, AL	Richard Petty	Plymouth
Hampton, GA	Junior Johnson	Chevrolet
Daytona Beach, FL	Fireball Roberts	Ford
Myrtle Beach, SC	Ned Jarrett	Ford
Savannah, GA	Ned Jarrett	Ford
Moyock, NC	Jimmy Pardue	Ford
Winston-Salem, NC	Glen Wood	Ford
Asheville, NC	Ned Jarrett	Ford
Old Bridge, NJ	Fireball Roberts	Ford
Bridgehampton, NY	Richard Petty	Plymouth
Bristol, TN	Fred Lorenzen	Ford
Greenville, SC	Richard Petty	Plymouth
Nashville, TN	Jim Paschal	Plymouth
Columbia, SC	Richard Petty	Plymouth
Weaverville, NC	Fred Lorenzen	Ford
Spartanburg, NC	Ned Jarrett	Ford
Winston-Salem, NC	Junior Johnson	Plymouth
Huntington, WV	Fred Lorenzen	Ford
Darlington, SC	Fireball Roberts	Ford
Hickory, NC	Junior Johnson	Chevrolet
Richmond, VA	Ned Jarrett	Ford
Martinsville, VA	Fred Lorenzen	Ford
Moyock, NC	Ned Jarrett	Ford
N. Wilkesboro, NC	Marvin Panch	Ford
Randleman, NC	Richard Petty	Plymouth
Concord, NC	Junior Johnson	Chevrolet
South Boston, VA	Richard Petty	Plymouth
Hillsborough,, NC	Joe Weatherly	Pontiac
Riverside, CA	Darel Dieringer	Mercury

Hampton, VA	Ned Jarrett	Ford
Hickory, NC	Ned Jarrett	Ford
South Boston, VA	Richard Petty	Plymouth
Concord, NC	Jim Paschal	Plymouth
Greenville, SC	LeeRoy Yarbrough	Plymouth
Asheville, NC	Ned Jarrett	Ford
Hampton, GA	Ned Jarrett	Ford
Concord, NC	Richard Petty	Plymouth
Nashville, TN	Richard Petty	Plymouth
Chattanooga	David Pearson	Dodge
Birmingham, AL	Ned Jarrett	Ford
Valdosta, GA	Buck Baker	Dodge
Spartanburg, SC	Richard Petty	Plymouth
Daytona Beach, FL	A.J. Foyt	Dodge
Manassas, VA	Ned Jarrett	Ford
Old Bridge, NJ	Billy Wade	Mercury
Bridgehampton, NY	Billy Wade	Mercury
Islip, NY	Billy Wade	Mercury
Watkins Glen, NY	Billy Wade	Mercury
Oxford, PA	David Pearson	Dodge
Bristol, TN	Fred Lorenzen	Ford
Nashville, TN	Richard Petty	Plymouth
Myrtle Beach, SC	David Pearson	Dodge
Weaverville, NC	Ned Jarrett	Ford
Moyock, NC	Ned Jarrett	Ford
Huntington, WV	Richard Petty	Plymouth
Columbia, SC	David Pearson	Dodge
Winston-Salem, NC	Junior Johnson	Ford
Roanoke, VA	Junior Johnson	Ford
Darlington, SC	Buck Baker	Dodge
Hickory, NC	David Pearson	Dodge
Richmond, VA	Cotton Owens	Dodge
Manassas, VA	Ned Jarrett	Ford
Hillsborough, NC	Ned Jarrett	Ford
Martinsville, VA	Fred Lorenzen	Ford
Savannah, GA	Ned Jarrett	Ford
N. Wilkesboro, NC	Marvin Panch	Ford
Concord, NC	Fred Lorenzen	Ford
Harris, NC	Richard Petty	Plymouth
Augusta, GA	Darel Dieringer	Mercury
Jacksonville, NC	Ned Jarrett	Ford

1965

RACE WINNERS

RACE	WINNER	CAR
Riverside, CA	Dan Gurney	Ford
Daytona Beach, FL	Darel Dieringer	Mercury
Daytona Beach, FL	Junior Johnson	Ford
Daytona Beach, FL	Fred Lorenzen	Ford
Spartanburg, SC	Ned Jarrett	Ford
Weaverville, NC	Ned Jarrett	Ford
Richmond, VA	Junior Johnson	Ford
Hillsborough, NC	Ned Jarrett	Ford
Hampton, GA	Marvin Panch	Ford
Greenville, SC	Dick Hutcherson	Ford
N. Wilkesboro, NC	Junior Johnson	Ford
Matinsville, VA	Fred Lorenzen	Ford
Columbia, SC	Tiny Lund	Ford
Bristol, NC	Junior Johnson	Ford
Darlington, SC	Junior Johnson	Ford
Hampton, VA	Ned Jarrett	Ford
Winston-Salem, NC	Junior Johnson	Ford
Hickory, NC	Junior Johnson	Ford
Concord, NC	Fred Lorenzen	Ford
Shelby, NC	Ned Jarrett	Ford
Ashville, NC	Junior Johnson	Ford
Harris, NC	Ned Jarrett	Ford
Nashville, TN	Dick Hutcherson	Ford
Birmingham, AL	Ned Jarrett	Ford
Hampton, GA	Marvin Panch	Ford
Greenville, SC	Dick Hutcherson	Ford
Myrtle Beach, SC	Dick Hutcherson	Ford
Valdosta, GA	Cale Yarborough	Ford
Daytona Beach, FL	A.J. Foyt	Ford
Manassas, VA	Junior Johnson	Ford
Old Bridge, NJ	Junior Johnson	Ford
Islip, NY	Marvin Panch	Ford

1964

RACE WINNERS

RACE	WINNER	CAR
Concord, NC	Ned Jarrett	Ford
Augusta, GA	Fireball Roberts	Ford
Jacksonville, FL	Wendell Scott	Chevrolet
Savannah, GA	Richard Petty	Plymouth
Riverside, CA	Dan Gurney	Ford
Daytona Beach, FL	Junior Johnson	Dodge
Daytona Beach, FL	Richard Petty	Plymouth
Richmond, VA	David Pearson	Dodge
Bristol, TN	Fred Lorenzen	Ford
Greenville, SC	David Pearson	Dodge
Winston-Salem, NC	Marvin Panch	Ford
Hampton, GA	Fred Lorenzen	Ford
Weaverville, NC	Marvin Panch	Ford
Hillsborough, NC	David Pearson	Dodge
Spartanburgh, SC	Ned Jarrett	Ford
Columbia, SC	Ned Jarrett	Ford
Wilkesboro, NC	Fred Lorenzen	Ford
Martinsville, VA	Fred Lorenzen	Ford
Savannah, GA	LeeRoy Yarbrough	Plymouth
Darlington,, SC	Fred Lorenzen	Ford

Watkins Glen, NY	Marvin Panch	Ford
Bristol, TN	Ned Jarrett	Ford
Nashville, TN	Richard Petty	Plymouth
Shelby, NC	Ned Jarrett	Ford
Weaverville, NC	Richard Petty	Plymouth
Maryville, NJ	Dick Hutcherson	Ford
Spartanburg, SC	Ned Jarrett	Ford
Augusta, GA	Dick Hutcherson	Ford
Columbia, SC	David Pearson	Dodge
Moyock, NC	Dick Hutcherson	Ford
Beltsville, MD	Ned Jarrett	Ford
Winston-Salem, NC	Junior Johnson	Ford
Darlington, SC	Ned Jarrett	Ford
Hickory, NC	Richard Petty	Plymouth
New Oxford, PA	Dick Hutcherson	Ford
Manassas, VA	Richard Petty	Plymouth
Richmond, VA	David Pearson	Dodge
Martinsville, VA	Junior Johnson	Ford
N. Wilkesboro, NC	Junior Johnson	Ford
Concord, NC	Fred Lorenzen	Ford
Hillsborough, NC	Dick Hutcherson	Ford
Rockingham, NC	Curtis Turner	Ford
Moyock, NC	Ned Jarrett	Ford

1966

RACE WINNERS

RACE	WINNER	CAR
Augusta, GA	Richard Petty	Plymouth
Riverside, CA	Dan Gurney	Ford
Daytona Beach, FL	Paul Goldsmith	Plymouth
Daytona Beach, FL	Earl Balmer	Dodge
Daytona Beach, FL	Richard Petty	Plymouth
Rockingham, NC	Paul Goldsmith	Plymouth
Bristol, TN	Dick Hutcherson	Ford
Hampton, GA	Jim Hurtubise	Plymouth
Hickory, NC	David Pearson	Dodge
Columbia, SC	David Pearson	Dodge
Greenville, SC	David Pearson	Dodge
Winston-Salem, NC	David Pearson	Dodge
N. Wilkesboro, NC	Jim Paschal	Plymouth
Martinsville, VA	Jim Paschal	Plymouth
Darlington, SC	Richard Petty	Plymouth
Hampton, VA	Richard Petty	Plymouth
Macon, GA	Richard Petty	Plymouth
Monroe, NC	Darel Dieringer	Ford
Richmond, VA	David Pearson	Dodge
Concord, NC	Marvin Panch	Plymouth
Moyock, NC	David Pearson	Dodge
Ashville, NC	David Pearson	Dodge
Spartanburg, SC	Elmo Langley	Ford
Maryville, TN	David Pearson	Dodge
Weaverville, NC	Richard Petty	Plymouth
Beltsville, MD	Tiny Lund	Ford
Greenville, SC	David Pearson	Dodge
Daytona Bearch, FL	Sam McQuagg	Dodge
Manassas, VA	Elmo Langley	Ford
Bridgehampton, NY	David Pearson	Dodge
Oxford ME	Bobby Allison	Chevrolet
Fonda, NY	David Pearson	Dodge
Islip, NY	Bobby Allison	Chevrolet
Briston, TN	Paul Goldsmith	Plymouth
Maryville, TN	Paul Lewis	Plymouth
Nashville, TN	Richard Petty	Plymouth
Hampton, GA	Richard Petty	Plymouth
Columbia, SC	David Pearson	Dodge
Weaverville,, NC	Darel Dieringer	Mercury
Beltsville, MD	Bobby Allison	Chevrolet
Winston-Salem, NC	David Pearson	Dodge
Darlington, SC	Darel Dieringer	Mercury
Hickory, NC	David Pearson	Dodge
Richmond, VA	David Pearson	Dodge
Hillsborough, NC	Dick Hutcherson	Ford
Martinsville, VA	Fred Lorenzen	Ford
N. Wilkesboro, NC	Dick Hutcherson	Ford
Concord, NC	LeeRoy Yarbrough	Dodge
Rockingham, NC	Fred Lorenzen	Ford

1967

RACE WINNERS

RACE	WINNER	CAR
Augusta, GA	Richard Petty	Plymouth
Riverside, CA	Parnelli Jones	Ford
Daytona Beach, FL	Fred Lorenzen	Ford
Daytona Beach, FL	Mario Andretti	Ford
Weaverville, NC	Richard Petty	Plymouth
Bristol, TN	David Pearson	Dodge
Greenville, SC	David Pearson	Dodge
Winston-Salem, NC	Bobby Allison	Chevrolet
Hampton, GA	Cale Yearborough	Ford
Columbia, SC	Richard Petty	Plymouth
Hickoary, NC	Richard Petty	Plymouth
N. Wilkesboro, NC	Darel Dieringer	Ford
Martinsville, VA	Richard Petty	Plymouth
Savannah, GA	Bobby Allison	Chevrolet
Richmond VA	Richard Petty	Plymouth
Darlington, SC	Richard Petty	Plymouth
Beltsville, MD	Jim Paschal	Plymouth
Hampton, VA	Richard Petty	Plymouth
Concord, NC	Jim Paschal	Plymouth
Asheville, NC	Jim Paschal	Plymouth
Macon, GA	Richard Petty	Plymouth
Maryville, TN	Richard Petty	Plymouth
Birmingham, AL	Bobby Allison	Dodge
Rockingham, NC	Richard Petty	Plymouth
Greenville, SC	Richard Petty	Plymouth
Montgomery, AL	Jim Paschal	Plymouth
Daytona Beach, FL	Cale Yarborough	Ford
Trenton, NJ	Richard Petty	Plymouth
Oxford ME	Bobby Allison	Chevrolet
Fonda, NY	Richard Petty	Plymouth
Islip, NY	Richard Petty	Plymouth
Bristol, NY	Richard Petty	Plymouth
Maryville, TN	Dick Hutcherson	Ford
Nashville, TN	Richard Petty	Plymouth
Hampton, GA	Dick Hutcherson	Ford
Winston-Salem, NC	Richard Petty	Plymouth
Columbia, SC	Richard Petty	Plymouth
Savannah, GA	Richard Petty	Plymouth
Darlington, SC	Richard Petty	Plymouth
Hickory, NC	Richard Petty	Plymouth
Richmond, VA	Richard Petty	Plymouth
Beltsville, MD	Richard Petty	Plymouth
Hillsborough, NC	Richard Petty	Plymouth
Martinsville, VA	Richard Petty	Plymouth
N. Wilkesboro, NC	Richard Petty	Plymouth
Concord, NC	Buddy Baker	Dodge
Rockingham, NC	Bobby Allison	Ford
Weaverville,, NC	Bobby Allison	Ford

1968

RACE WINNERS

RACE	WINNER	CAR
Macon, GA	Bobby Allison	Ford
Montgomery, AL	Richard Petty	Plymouth
Riverside, CA	Dan Gurney	Ford
Daytona Beach, FL	Cale Yarborough	Mercury
Bristol, TN	David Pearson	Ford
Richmond, VA	David Pearson	Ford
Hampton, GA	Cale Yarborough	Mercury
Hickory, NC	Richard Petty	Plymouth
Greenville, SC	Richard Petty	Plymouth
Columbia, SC	Bobby Isaac	Dodge
N. Wilkesboro, NC	David Pearson	Ford
Martinsville, VA	Cale Yarborough	Mercury
Augusta, GA	Bobby Isaac	Dodge
Weaverville, NC	David Pearson	Ford
Darlington, SC	David Pearson	Ford
Beltsville, MD	David Pearson	Ford
Hampton, VA	David Pearson	Ford

Concord, NC	Buddy Baker	Dodge
Asheville, NC	Richard Petty	Plymouth
Macon, GA	David Pearson	Ford
Maryville, TN	Richard Petty	Plymouth
Birmingham, AL	Richard Petty	Plymouth
Rockingham, NC	Donnie Allison	Ford
Greenville, SC	Richard Petty	Plymouth
Daytona Beach, FL	Cale Yarborough	Mercury
Islip, NY	Bobby Allison	Chevrolet
Oxford ME	Richard Petty	Plymouth
Fond, NY	Richard Petty	Plymouth
Trenton, NJ	LeeRoy Yarbrough	Ford
Bristol, TN	David Pearson	Ford
Maryville, TN	Richard Petty	Plymouth
Nashville, TN	David Pearson	Ford
Hampton, GA	LeeRoy Yarbrough	Ford
Columbia, SC	David Pearson	Ford
Winston-Salem, NC	David Pearson	Ford
Weaverville, NC	David Pearson	Ford
Hampton, VA	David Pearson	Ford
South Boston, VA	Richard Petty	Plymouth
Darlington, SC	Cale Yarborough	Mercury
Hickory, NC	David Pearson	Ford
Richmond, VA	Richard Petty	Plymouth
Beltsville, MD	Bobby Isaac	Dodge
Hillsborough, NC	Richard Petty	Plymouth
Martinsville, VA	Richard Petty	Plymouth
N. Wilkesboro, NC	Richard Petty	Plymouth
Augusta, GA	David Pearson	Ford
Concord, NC	Charlie Glotzbach	Dodge
Rockingham, NC	Richard Petty	Plymouth
Jefferson, GA	Cale Yarborough	Mercury

1969

RACE WINNERS

RACE	WINNER	CAR
Macon, GA	Richard Petty	Plymouth
Montgomery, AL	Bobby Allison	Plymouth
Riverside, CA	Richard Petty	Ford
Daytona Beach, FL	David Pearson	Ford
Daytona Beach, FL	Bobby Isaac	Dodge
Daytona Beach, FL	LeeRoy Yarbrough	Ford
Rockingham, NC	David Pearson	Ford
Augusta, GA	David Pearson	Ford
Briston, TN	Bobby Allison	Dodge
Hampton, GA	Cale Yarborough	Mercury
Columbia, SC	Bobby Isaac	Dodge
Hickory, NC	Bobby Isaac	Dodge
Greenville, SC	Bobby Isaac	Dodge
Richmond, VA	David Pearson	Ford
N. Wilkesboro, NC	Bobby Allison	Dodge
Martinsville, VA	Richard Petty	Ford
Weaverville, NC	Bobby Isaac	Dodge
Darlington, SC	LeeRoy Yarbrough	Mercury
Beltsville, MD	Bobby Isaac	Dodge
Hampton, VA	David Pearson	Ford
Concord, NC	LeeRoy Yarbrough	Mercury
Macon, GA	Bobby Isaac	Dodge
Maryville, TN	Bobby Isaac	Dodge
Brooklyn, MI	Cale Yarborough	Mercury
Kingsport, TN	Richard Petty	Ford
Greenville, SC	Bobby Isaac	Dodge
Raleigh, NC	David Pearson	Ford
Daytona Beach, FL	LeeRoy Yarbrough	Ford
Dover, DE	Richard Petty	Ford
Thompson, CT	David Pearson	Ford
Trenton, NJ	David Pearson	Ford
Beltsville, MD	Richard Petty	Ford
Bristol, TN	David Pearson	Ford
Nashville, TN	Richard Petty	Ford
Maryville, TN	Richard Petty	Ford
Hampton, GA	LeeRoy Yarbrough	Ford
Brooklyn, MI	David Pearson	Ford
South Boston, VA	Bobby Isaac	Dodge
Winston-Salem, NC	Richard Petty	Ford
Weaverville Nc	Bobby Isaac	Dodge
Darlington, SC	LeeRoy Yarbrough	Ford
Hickory, NC	Bobby Isaac	Dodge

Richmond, VA	Bobby Allicon	Dodge
Talladega, AL	Richard Brickhouse	Dodge
Columbia, SC	Bobby Isaac	Dodge
Martinsville, VA	Richard Petty	Ford
N. Wilkesboro, NC	David Pearson	Ford
Concord, NC	Donnie Allison	Ford
Savannah, GA	Bobby Isaac	Dodge
Augusta, GA	Bobby Isaac	Dodge
Rockingham, NC	LeeRoy Yarbrough	Ford
Jefferson, GA	Bobby Isaac	Dodge
Macon, GA	Bobby Isaac	Dodge
College Station,, TX	Bobby Isaac	Dodge

1970

RACE WINNERS

RACE	WINNER	CAR
Riverside, CA	A.J. Foyt	Ford
Daytona Beach, FL	Cale Yarborough	Mercury
Daytona Beach, FL	Charlie Glotzbach	Dodge
Datona Beach, FL	Pete Hamilton	Plymouth
Richmond, VA	James Hylton	Ford
Rockingham, NC	Richard Petty	Plymouth
Savannah, GA	Richard Petty	Plymouth
Hampton, GA	Bobby Allison	Dodge
Bristol, TN	Donnie Allison	Ford
Talladega, AL	Pete Hamilton	Plymouth
N. Wilkesboro, NC	Richard Petty	Plymouth
Columbia, SC	Richard Petty	Plymouth
Darlington, SC	David Pearson	Ford
Beltsville, MD	Bobby Isaac	Dodge
Hampton, VA	Bobby Isaac	Dodge
Concord, NC	Donnie Allison	Ford
Maryville, TN	Bobby Issac	Dodge
Martinsville, VA	Bobby Isaac	Dodge
Brooklyn, MI	Cale Yarborough	Mercury
Riverside, CA	Richard Petty	Plymouth
Hickory, NC	Bobby Isaac	Dodge
Kingsport, TN	Richard Petty	Plymouth
Greenville, SC	Bobby Isaac	Dodge
Daytona Beach, FL	Donnie Allison	Ford
Malta, NY	Richard Petty	Plymouth
Thompson, CT	Bobby Isaac	Dodge
Trenton, NJ	Richard Petty	Plymouth
Bristol, TN	Bobby Allison	Dodge
Maryville, TN	Richard Petty	Plymouth
Nashville, TN	Bobby Isaac	Dodge
Hampton, GA	Richard Petty	Plymouth
Columbia, SC	Bobby Isaac	Dodge
Ona, WV	Richard Petty	Plymouth
Brooklyn, MI	Charlie Glotzbach	Dodge
Talladega, AL	Pete Hamilton	Plymouth
Winston-Salem, NC	Richard Petty	Plymouth
South Boston, VA	Richard Petty	Plymouth
Darlington, SC	Buddy Baker	Dodge
Hickory, NC	Bobby Isaac	Dodge
Richmond, VA	Richard Petty	Plymouth
Dover, DE	Richard Petty	Plymouth
Raleigh, NC	Richard Petty	Plymouth
N. Wilkesboro, NC	Bobby Isaac	Dodge
Concord, NC	LeeRoy Yarbrough	Mercury
Martinsville, VA	Richard Petty	Plymouth
Macon, GA	Richard Petty	Plymouth
Rockingham, NC	Cale Yarborough	Mercury
Hampton, VA	Bobby Allison	Dodge

1971

RACE WINNERS

RACE	WINNER	CAR
Riverside, CA	Ray Elder	Dodge
Daytona Beach, FL	Pete Hamilton	Plymouth

Daytona Beach, FL	David Pearson	Mercury
Daytona Beach, FL	Richard Petty	Plymouth
Ontario, CA	A.J. Foyt	Mercury
Richmond, VA	Richard Petty	Plymouth
Rockingham, NC	Richard Petty	Plymouth
Hickory, NC	Richard Petty	Plymouth
Bristol, TN	David Pearson	Ford
Hampton, GA	A.J. Foyt	Mercury
Columbia, SC	Richard Petty	Plymouth
Greenville, SC	Bobby Isaac	Dodge
Maryville, TN	Richard Petty	Plymouth
N. Wilkesboro, NC	Richard Petty	Plymouth
Martinsville, VA	Richard Petty	Plymouth
Darlington, SC	Buddy Baker	Dodge
South Boston, VA	Benny Parsons	Ford
Talladega, AL	Donnie Allison	Mercury
Asheville, NC	Richard Petty	Plymouth
Kinsport, TN	Bobby Isaac	Dodge
Concord, NC	Bobby Allison	Mercury
Dover, DE	Bobby Allison	Mercury
Brooklyn, MI	Bobby Allison	Mercury
Riverside, CA	Bobby Allison	Dodge
Houston, TX	Bobby Allison	Dodge
Greenville, SC	Richard Petty	Plymouth
Daytona Beach, FL	Bobby Isaac	Dodge
Bristol, TN	Charlie Glotzbach	Chevrolet
Malta, NY	Richard Petty	Plymouth
Islip, NY	Richard Petty	Plymouth
Trenton, NJ	Richard Petty	Plymouth
Nashville, TN	Richard Petty	Plymouth
Hampton, GA	Richard Petty	Plymouth
Winston-Salem, NC	Bobby Allison	Ford
Ona, WV	Richard Petty	Plymouth
Brooklyn, MI	Bobby Allison	Mercury
Talladega, AL	Bobby Allison	Mercury
Columbia, SC	Richard Petty	Plymouth
Hickory, SC	Tiny Lund	Chevrolet
Darlington, SC	Bobby Allison	Mercury
Martinsville, VA	Bobby Isaac	Dodge
Concord, NC	Bobby Allison	Mercury
Dover, DE	Richard Petty	Plymouth
Rockingham, NC	Richard Petty	Plymouth
Macon, GA	Bobby Allison	Ford
Richmond, VA	Richard Petty	Plymouth
North Wilkesboro, NC	Tiny Lund	Chevrolet
College Station, TX	Richard Petty	Plymouth

1972

WINSTON WESTERN 500

January 23
Riverside, California
Time of Race: 3 hours, 45 minutes, 11 seconds
Average Speed: 104.018 mph

FINISH	DRIVER	CAR
1.	Richard Petty	Plymouth
2.	Bobby Allison	Chevrolet
3.	Bobby Isaac	Dodge
4.	Ray Elder	Dodge
5.	Hershel McGriff	Plymouth
6.	Kevin Terris	Plymouth
7.	James Hylton	Ford
8.	Elmo Langley	Ford
9.	Friday Hassler	Chevrolet
10.	Cecil Gordon	Mercury
11.	John Soares Jr.	Dodge
12.	Carl Joyner	Chevrolet
13.	Dick Bown	Plymouth
14.	Walter Ballard	Ford
15.	Raymond Williams	Ford
16.	Don Noel	Dodge
17.	Charlie Roberts	Ford
18.	J. D. McDuffie	Chevrolet
19.	Johnny Anderson	Chevrolet
20.	Ivan Baldwin	Chevrolet

21.	Henley Gray	Ford
22.	Jerry Oliver	Olds
23.	Dick Kranzler	Chevrolet
24.	Larry Esau	Chevrolet
25.	Frank James	Chevrolet
26.	David Pearson	Ford
27.	Ed Negre	Ford
28.	A. J. Foyt	Mercury
29.	Frank Warren	Dodge
30.	Jim Danielson	Mercury
31.	David Ray Boggs	Dodge
32.	Chuck Bown	Plymouth
33.	Paul Dority	Dodge
34.	Ron Keselowski	Dodge
35.	Ron Gautsche	Ford
36.	Jack McCoy	Dodge
37.	Neil Castles	Dodge
38.	Joe Frasson	Dodge
39.	Mark Donohue	Matador
40.	Benny Parsons	Ford

DAYTONA 500

February 20
Daytona Beach, Florida
Time of Race: 34 hours, 5 minutes, 42 seconds
Average Speed: 161.650 mph

FINISH	DRIVER	CAR
1.	A. J. Foyt	Mercury
2.	Charlie Glotzbach	Dodge
3.	Jim Vandiver	Dodge
4.	Benny Parsons	Mercury
5.	James Hylton	Ford
6.	Cale Yarborough	Plymouth
7.	David Sisco	Chevrolet
8.	Jabe Thomas	Plymouth
9.	John Sears	Plymouth
10.	Vic Elford	Plymouth
11.	Tommy Gale	Mercury
12.	Elmo Langley	Ford
13.	Richard Brown	Chevrolet
14.	Henley Gray	Ford
15.	George Altheide	Dodge
16.	Bobby Allison	Chevrolet
17.	Ben Arnold	Ford
18.	Frank Warren	Dodge
19.	David Ray Boggs	Dodge
20.	Dr. Ed Hessert	Dodge
21.	Larry Dickson	Ford
22.	Jim Hurtubise	Chevrolet
23.	Bill Dennis	Ford
24.	J. D. McDuffie	Chevrolet
25.	Coo Coo Marlin	Chevrolet
26.	Richard Petty	Plymouth
27.	Dave Marcis	Dodge
28.	Ron Keselowski	Dodge
29.	Bill Seifert	Ford
30.	Red Farmer	Ford
31.	Jimmy Finger	Ford
32.	Buddy Arington	Plymouth
33.	Bobby Isaac	Dodge
34.	Buddy Baker	Dodge
35.	Mark Donohue	Matador
36.	Walter Ballard	Ford
37.	Ramo Stott	Dodge
38.	Bill Champion	Ford
39.	Cecil Gordon	Mercury
40.	Raymond Williams	Ford

RICHMOND 500

February 27
Richmond, Virginia
Time of Race: 3 hours, 32 minutes, 12 seconds
Average Speed: 76.258 mph

FINISH	DRIVER	CAR
1.	Richard Petty	Plymouth
2.	Bobby Allison	Chevrolet
3.	Bobby Isaac	Dodge
4.	Dave Marcis	Dodge
5.	Bill Dennis	Ford
6.	James Hylton	Dodge
7.	Elmo Langley	Ford
8.	Benny Parsons	Ford
9.	Cecil Gordon	Mercury
10.	John Sears	Dodge
11.	Neil Castles	Dodge
12.	J. D. McDuffie	Chevrolet
13.	Eddie Yarboro	Plymouth
14.	Richard Brown	Chevrolet
15.	Frank Warren	Plymouth
16.	Phil Finney	Chevrolet
17.	Jabe Thomas	Plymouth
18.	David Ray Boggs	Dodge
19.	Bill Seifert	Ford
20.	Bill Champion	Ford
21.	Walter Ballard	Plymouth
22.	Bill Shirey	Plymouth
23.	Raymond Williams	Ford
24.	Ron Keselowski	Dodge
25.	Dean Dalton	Mercury
26.	Dub Simpson	Chevrolet
27.	Les Covey	C.
28.	Jim Vandiver	Dodge
29.	Richard Childress	Chevrolet
30.	Ed Negre	Chevrolet

MILLER HIGH LIFE 500

March 5
Ontario, California
Time of Race: 3 hours, 56 minutes, 4 seconds
Average Speed: 127.082 mph

FINISH	DRIVER	CAR
1.	A. J. Foyt	Mercury
2.	Bobby Allison	Chevrolet
3.	Buddy Baker	Dodge
4.	Richard Petty	Plymouth
5.	Ray Elder	Dodge
6.	Hershel McGriff	Plymouth
7.	James Hylton	Ford
8.	Marty Robbins	Dodge
9.	Elmo Langley	Ford
10.	Ramo Stott	Plymouth
11.	Jimmy Finger	Ford
12.	Jack McCoy	Dodge
13.	John Soares Jr.	Dodge
14.	Benny Parsons	Mercury
15.	Bill Burns	Dodge
16.	Cliff Garner	Ford
17.	Johnny Anderson	Chevrolet
18.	Dick Bown	Plymouth
19.	J.C. Danielson	Mercury
20.	Bill Champion	Ford
21.	Ben Arnold	Ford
22.	Kevin Terris	Plymouth
23.	J. D. McDuffie	Chevrolet
24.	Mike James	Chevrolet
25.	Dean Dalton	Mercury
26.	Raymond Williams	Ford
27.	Jim Whitt	Ford
28.	George Altheide	Dodge
29.	Bob Kauf	Chevrolet
30.	Carl Adams	Ford
31.	Henley Gray	Ford
32.	Charlie Roberts	Ford
33.	Chuck Bown	Plymouth
34.	Les Louder	Chevrolet
35.	Ron Gausche	Ford
36.	Cecil Gordon	Mercury
37.	Dick Kranzler	Chevrolet
38.	Don White	Plymouth
39.	Gene Romero	Plymouth
40.	T.T. Tallas	Ford

41.	Red Farmer	Ford
42.	Earle Canavan	Plymouth
43.	Frank Warren	Dodge
44.	Mark Donohue	Matador
45.	Bobby Isaac	Dodge
46.	Bill Osborne	Ford
47.	Walter Ballard	Ford
48.	Don Noel	Ford
49.	George Follmer	Dodge
50.	David Ray Boggs	Dodge
51.	Jim Vandiver	Dodge

CAROLINA 500

March 12
Rockingham, North Carolina
Time of Race: 4 hours, 23 minutes, 50 seconds
Average Speed: 113.895 mph

FINISH	DRIVER	CAR
1.	Bobby Isaac	Dodge
2.	Richard Petty	Plymouth
3.	Jim Vandiver	Dodge
4.	LeeRoy Yarbrough	Ford
5.	Dave Marcis	Dodge
6.	James Hylton	Mercury
7.	Benny Parsons	Ford
8.	Buddy Arrington	Dodge
9.	Elmo Langley	Ford
10.	Neil Castles	Dodge
11.	Larry Smith	Ford
12.	Joe Frasson	Dodge
13.	Jabe Thomas	Plymouth
14.	Ed Negre	Dodge
15.	Ben Arnold	Ford
16.	John Sears	Plymouth
17.	David Ray Boggs	Dodge
18.	Dean Dalton	Mercury
19.	Frank Warren	Dodge
20.	Henley Gray	
21.	H. B. Balley	Ford
22.	George Altheide	Dodge
23.	Richard Brown	Chevrolet
24.	Charlie Roberts	Ford
25.	Ron Keselowski	Dodge
26.	Cecil Gordon	Ford
27.	Bobby Allison	Chevrolet
28.	Johnny Halford	Plymouth
29.	Bill Champion	Ford
30.	G. C. Spencer	Plymouth
31.	Bill Shirey	Plymouth
32.	Walter Ballard	Chevrolet
33.	Les Covey	Chevrolet
34.	Buddy Baker	Dodge
35.	Raymond Williams	Ford
36.	Buck Baker	Chevrolet
37.	Richard Childress	Chevrolet
38.	Dub Simpson	Chevrolet
39.	Bobby Mausgrover	Dodge
40.	Jackie Oliver	Ford

ATLANTA 500

March 26
Atlanta, Georgia
Time of Race: 3 hours, 53 minutes, 37 seconds
Average Speed: 128.214 mph

FINISH	DRIVER	CAR
1.	Bobby Allison	Chevrolet
2.	A. J. Foyt	Mercury
3.	Bobby Isaac	Dodge
4.	David Pearson	Ford
5.	Donnie Allison	Chevrolet
6.	Richard Petty	Plymouth
7.	Benny Parsons	Ford

8.	Buddy Baker	Dodge
9.	LeeRoy Yarbrough	Ford
10.	James Hylton	Ford
11.	Buddy Arrington	Dodge
12.	Coo Coo Marlin	Chevrolet
13.	Richard Brown	Chevrolet
14.	G. C. Spencer	Plymouth
15.	Mark Donohue	Matador
16.	Bill Dennis	Plymouth
17.	Cecil Gordon	Mercury
18.	Ed Negre	Dodge
19.	Jabe Thomas	Plymouth
20.	Charlie Roberts	Ford
21.	John Sears	Plymouth
22.	George Altheide	Dodge
23.	Dave Marcis	Dodge
24.	Henley Gray	Ford
25.	Frank Warren	Dodge
26.	Walter Ballard	Ford
27.	Tommy Gale	Mercury
28.	Dean Dalton	Mercury
29.	Ben Arnold	Ford
30.	Joe Frasson	Dodge
31.	Red Farmer	Ford
32.	Jim Vandiver	Dodge
33.	Raymond Williams	Ford
34.	Elmo Langley	Ford
35.	Dick May	Ford
36.	Ron Keselowski	Dodge
37.	David Sisco	Chevrolet
38.	Larry Smith	Ford
39.	Lem Blankenship	Dodge
40.	Dick Brooks	Ford

SOUTHEASTERN 500

April 9
Bristol, Tennessee
Time of Race: 2 hours, 50 minutes, 18 seconds
Average Speed: 92.826 mph

FINISH	DRIVER	CAR
1.	Bobby Allison	Chevrolet
2.	Bobby Isaac	Dodge
3.	Richard Petty	Plymouth
4.	LeeRoy Yarbrough	Ford
5.	Cecil Gordon	Mercury
6.	Coo Coo Marlin	Chevrolet
7.	Elmo Langley	Ford
8.	James Hylton	Ford
9.	G. C. Spencer	Plymouth
10.	Jabe Thomas	Plymouth
11.	Walter Ballard	Ford
12.	Henley Gray	Ford
13.	Dean Dalton	Mercury
14.	Charlie Roberts	Ford
15.	Frank Warren	Plymouth
16.	Bill Champion	Ford
17.	Jim Vandiver	Dodge
18.	Richard Childress	Chevrolet
19.	J. D. McDuffie	Chevrolet
20.	David Ray Boggs	Dodge
21.	Benny Parsons	Mercury
22.	Ed Negre	Dodge
23.	David Sisco	Chevrolet
24.	Raymond Williams	Ford
25.	John Sears	Plymouth
26.	Dave Marcis	Dodge
27.	Ben Arnold	Ford
28.	George Altheide	Dodge
29.	Ronnie Daniels	Chevrolet
30.	Richard Brown	Chevrolet

REBEL 400

April 16
Darlington, South Carolina

Time of Race: 3 hours, 13 minutes, 0 seconds
Average Speed: 124.406 mph

FINISH	DRIVER	CAR
1.	David Pearson	Mercury
2.	Richard Petty	Plymouth
3.	Joe Frasson	Dodge
4.	Benny Parsons	Mercury
5.	James Hylton	Ford
6.	Buddy Arrington	Dodge
7.	Bobby Allison	Chevrolet
8.	John Sears	Plymouth
9.	Jabe Thomas	Plymouth
10.	Cecil Gordon	Mercury
11.	Bill Champion	Ford
12.	Dean Dalton	Mercury
13.	Elmo Langley	Ford
14.	Raymond Williams	Ford
15.	Charlie Roberts	Ford
16.	Jim Vandiver	Dodge
17.	Ben Arnold	Ford
18.	Walter Ballard	Mercury
19.	J. D. McDuffie	Chevrolet
20.	Buddy Baker	Dodge
21.	Frank Warren	Dodge
22.	Jackie Oliver	Ford
23.	Bill Dennis	Plymouth
24.	Ed Negre	Dodge
25.	Dave Marcis	Dodge
26.	LeeRoy Yarbrough	Ford
27.	Bobby Mausgrover	Dodge
28.	Bobby Isaac	Dodge
29.	Fred Lorenzon	Ford
30.	Buck Baker	Chevrolet
31.	Neil Castles	Dodge
32.	H. B. Bailey	Ford
33.	Larry Smith	Ford
34.	Henley Gray	Ford
35.	Dick Brooks	Pontiac
36.	G. C. Spencer	Plymouth

GWYN STALEY MEMORIAL

April 23
North Wilkesboro, North Carolina
Time of Race: 2 hours, 53 minutes, 19 seconds
Average Speed: 88.381

FINISH	DRIVER	CAR
1.	Richard Petty	Plymouth
2.	Bobby Allison	Chevrolet
3.	Bobby Isaac	Dodge
4.	James Hylton	Ford
5.	Benny Parsons	Mercury
6.	LeeRoy Yarbrough	Dodge
7.	Dave Marcis	Dodge
8.	Larry Smith	Ford
9.	Walter Ballard	Mercury
10.	John Sears	Plymouth
11.	Dub Simpson	Chevrolet
12.	Raymond Williams	Ford
13.	Neil Castles	Dodge
14.	Richard Brown	Chevrolet
15.	Dean Dalton	Mercury
16.	Charlie Roberts	Ford
17.	Henley Gray	Ford
18.	Cecil Gordon	Mercury
19.	Ben Arnold	Ford
20.	Frank Warren	Plymouth
21.	Buck Baker	Chevrolet
22.	Ed Negre	Dodge
23.	Bill Champion	Ford
24.	Elmo Langley	Ford
25.	J. D. McDuffie	Chevrolet
26.	Jim Vandiver	Dodge
27.	Richard Childress	Chevrolet
28.	Jabe Thomas	Plymouth
29.	Eddie Yarboro	Plymouth
30.	Bill Dennis	Plymouth

VIRGINIA 500

April 30
Martinsville, Virginia
Time of Race: 3 hours, 37 minutes, 0 seconds
Average Speed: 72.657 mph

FINISH	DRIVER	CAR
1.	Richard Petty	Plymouth
2.	Bobby Allison	Chevrolet
3.	Dave Marcis	Dodge
4.	Cecil Gordon	Mercury
5.	Richard Brown	Chevrolet
6.	Bill Champion	Ford
7.	James Hylton	Ford
8.	David Pearson	Ford
9.	Walter Ballard	Mercury
10.	Raymond Williams	Ford
11.	Elmo Langley	Ford
12.	Neil Castles	Dodge
13.	J. D. McDuffie	Chevrolet
14.	Dean Dalton	Mercury
15.	Henley Gray	Ford
16.	Wendell Scott	Ford
17.	Eddie Yarboro	Plymouth
18.	Frank Warren	Plymouth
19.	Bobby Isaac	Dodge
20.	Benny Parsons	Mercury
21.	Les Covey	Chevrolet
22.	John Sears	Plymouth
23.	LeeRoy Yarbrough	Mercury
24.	Charlie Roberts	Ford
25.	Bill Dennis	Plymouth
26.	Bill Shirey	Plymouth
27.	Buddy Arrington	Dodge
28.	Charlie Glotzbach	Plymouth
29.	Richard Childress	Chevrolet
30.	Ed Negre	Dodge
31.	Jabe Thomas	Plymouth
32.	Jim Vandiver	Chevrolet
33.	Jimmy Hensley	Ford
34.	Earl Brooks	Ford
35.	Larry Smith	Ford
36.	David Ray Boggs	Dodge

WINSTON 500

May 7
Talladega, Alabama
Time of Race: 3 hours, 43 minutes, 15 seconds
Average Speed: 136.400 mph

FINISH	DRIVER	CAR
1.	David Pearson	Mercury
2.	Bobby Isaac	Dodge
3.	Buddy Baker	Dodge
4.	Fred Lorenzen	Ford
5.	Richard Petty	Dodge
6.	Joe Frasson	Dodge
7.	LeeRoy Yarbrough	Mercury
8.	Dick Brooks	Ford
9.	Frank Warren	Dodge
10.	Benny Parsons	Mercury
11.	Dave Marcis	Dodge
12.	David Ray Boggs	Dodge
13.	Jabe Thomas	Plymouth
14.	Cecil Gordon	Mercury
15.	Ed Negre	Dodge
16.	Jimmy Crawford	Plymouth
17.	Ben Arnold	Ford
18.	Ron Keselowski	Dodge
19.	Walter Ballard	Mercury
20.	Larry Smith	Ford
21.	John Sears	Plymouth
22.	Dean Dalton	Mercury
23.	Bobby Mausgrover	Dodge
24.	Elmo Langley	Ford
25.	Henley Gray	Ford
26.	Raymond Williams	Ford

27.	Richard Brown	Chevrolet
28.	Dennis Allison	Chevrolet
29.	Dub Simpson	Chevrolet
30.	Bill Champion	Mercury
31.	Buddy Arrington	Dodge
32.	Clarence Lovell	Ford
33.	James Hylton	Ford
34.	J. D. McDuffie	Chevrolet
35.	Coo Coo Marlin	Chevrolet
36.	Jim Vandiver	Dodge
37.	David Sisco	Chevrolet
38.	Darrell Waltrip	Mercury
39.	Red Farmer	Ford
40.	Buck Baker	Chevrolet
41.	Wayne Smith	Chevrolet
42.	Roy Mayne	Chevrolet
43.	Charlie Roberts	Ford
44.	Jackie Oliver	Ford
45.	Bobby Allison	Chevrolet
46.	Bill Dennis	Plymouth
47.	Neil Castles	Dodge
48.	Robert Wales	Dodge
49.	Bill Ward	Ford
50.	Marty Robbins	Dodge

WORLD 600

May 28
Charlotte, North Carolina
Time of Race: 4 hours, 13 minutes, 4 seconds
Average Speed: 142.255 mph

FINISH	DRIVER	CAR
1.	Buddy Baker	Dodge
2.	Bobby Allison	Chevrolet
3.	Charlie Glotzbach	Dodge
4.	Benny Parsons	Mercury
5.	LeeRoy Yarbrough	Mercury
6.	Larry Smith	Ford
7.	Buddy Arrington	Dodge
8.	Cecil Gordon	Mercury
9.	Frank WArren	Dodge
10.	Ben Arnold	Ford
11.	Elmo Langley	Mercury
12.	Ron Keselowski	Dodge
13.	Raymond Williams	Ford
14.	Jabe Thomas	Plymouth
15.	Walter Ballard	Mercury
16.	Jim Paschal	Chevrolet
17.	Dean Dalton	Mercury
18.	Fred Lorenzen	Ford
19.	Richard Petty	Dodge
20.	James Hylton	Ford
21.	Joe Frasson	Dodge
22.	Wendell Scott	Chevrolet
23.	Bobby Isaac	Dodge
24.	John Sears	Plymouth
25.	Dave Pearson	Mercury
26.	Bill Champion	Ford
27.	Clarence Lovell	Ford
28.	Coo Coo Marlin	Chevrolet
29.	Ken Rush	Dodge
30.	Richard Brown	Chevrolet
31.	Dave Marcis	Matador
32.	Jackie Oliver	Ford
33.	J. D. McDuffie	Chevrolet
34.	Donnie Allison	Ford
35.	Neil Castles	Dodge
36.	Dick Brooks	Ford
37.	Wayne Smith	Chevrolet
38.	David Ray Boggs	Dodge
39.	G. C.Spencer	Plymouth
40.	Jim Vandiver	Dodge

MASON-DIXON 500

June 4
Dover, Delaware

Time of Race: 4 hours, 12 minutes, 40 seconds
Average Speed: 118.019 mph

FINISH	DRIVER	CAR
1.	Bobby Allison	Chevrolet
2.	Richard Petty	Dodge
3.	LeeRoy Yarbrough	Mercury
4.	Jackie Oliver	Ford
5.	John Sears	Plymouth
6.	Benny Parsons	Ford
7.	James Hylton	Ford
8.	Cecil Gordon	Mercury
9.	Ron Keselowski	Dodge
10.	Paul Tyler	Mercury
11.	J. D. McDuffie	Chevrolet
12.	Charlie Roberts	Ford
13.	Dean Dalton	Mercury
14.	Bobby Isaac	Dodge
15.	Jabe Thomas	Plymouth
16.	Walter Ballard	Mercury
17.	Bill Champion	Ford
18.	Ronnie Daniel	Chevrolet
19.	Frank Warren	Dodge
20.	Wendell Scott	Ford
21.	Richard Brown	Chevrolet
22.	Jim Vandiver	Dodge
23.	Bill Shirey	Plymouth
24.	Coo Coo Marlin	Chevrolet
25.	Elmo Langley	Ford
26.	Ben Arnold	Ford
27.	Dick May	Ford
28.	Les Covey	Chevrolet
29.	Neil Castles	Dodge
30.	Earl Brooks	Ford
31.	Ed Negre	Dodge
32.	James Cox	Plymouth
33.	David Ray Boggs	Dodge
34.	Larry Smith	Ford
35.	Earle Canavan	Plymouth
36.	Dave Marcis	Dodge
37.	Richard Childress	Chevrolet
38.	Raymond Williams	Ford
39.	Henley Gray	Ford
40.	Clarence Lovell	Ford

MOTOR STATE 400

June 11
Brooklyn, Michigan
Time of Race: 2 hours, 43 minutes, 40 seconds
Average Speed: 146.639 mph

FINISH	DRIVER	CAR
1.	David Pearson	Mercury
2.	Bobby Allison	Chevrolet
3.	Richard Petty	Dodge
4.	James Hylton	Ford
5.	Ron Keselowski	Dodge
6.	Larry Smith	Ford
7.	Ben Arnold	Ford
8.	Dean Dalton	Mercury
9.	Buddy Arrington	Dodge
10.	Bill Champion	Mercury
11.	Cecil Gordon	Mercury
12.	Walter Ballard	Mercury
13.	John Sears	Plymouth
14.	Raymond Williams	Ford
15.	David Sisco	Chevrolet
16.	J. D. McDuffie	Chevrolet
17.	Johnny Halford	Plymouth
18.	Dick May	Ford
19.	Richard Childress	Plymouth
20.	Doc Faustine	Plymouth
21.	Ed Negre	Dodge
22.	Pete Hamilton	Plymouth
23.	Les Covey	Chevrolet
24.	Jabe Thomas	Plymouth
25.	Benny Parsons	Mercury

26.	Bobby Isaac	Dodge
27.	Dick Brooks	Ford
28.	LeeRoy Yarbrough	Mercury
29.	Elmo Langley	Ford
30.	Dave Marcis	Mercury
31.	Bill Shirey	Plymouth
32.	Charlie Roberts	Ford
33.	Donnie Allison	Ford
34.	Richard Brown	Chevrolet
35.	Joe Frasson	Dodge
36.	Frank Warren	Dodge
37.	Earl Brooks	Ford
38.	Bobby Mausgrover	Dodge
39.	Bill Siefert	Dodge
40.	Neil Castles	Dodge

GOLDEN STATE 400

June 18
Riverside, California
Time of Race: 4 hours, 3 minutes, 32 seconds
Average Speed: 98.781 mph

FINISH	DRIVER	CAR
1.	Ray Elder	Dodge
2.	Benny Parsons	Mercury
3.	Donnie Allison	Matador
4.	James Hylton	Ford
5.	Carl Joiner	Chevrolet
6.	Bobby Allison	Chrysler
7.	Carl Adams	Ford
8.	Cecil Gordon	Mercury
9.	Frank James	Chevrolet
10.	Dick May	Ford
11.	Charlie Roberts	Ford
12.	Howard McGriff	Plymouth
13.	Dick Bown	Plymouth
14.	Chuck Bown	Plymouth
15.	Hanley Gray	Ford
16.	Dick Kranzler	Chevrolet
17.	Kevin Torrie	Plymouth
18.	Paul Donty	Chevrolet
19.	Jim Insolo	Chevrolet
20.	Bill Butts	Dodge
21.	Bobby Isaac	Dodge
22.	Don Dalton	Mercury
23.	Richard Petty	Plymouth
24.	Bill Champion	Ford
25.	Walter Ballard	Mercury
26.	Ray Johnstone	Oldsmobile
27.	Johnny Anderson	Chevrolet
28.	J. D. McDuffie	Chevrolet
29.	John Hren	Chevrolet
30.	Clem Proctor	Oldsmobile
31.	Sonny Easley	Chevrolet
32.	Dick Gulstrand	Chevrolet
33.	Dick Brooks	Ford
34.	Sam Stanley	Ford
35.	John Soares Jr.	Dodge
36.	Tru Cheek	Ford
37.	Ed Negre	Dodge
38.	Jack McCoy	Dodge
39.	Bob Kauf	Chevrolet
40.	Mike James	Chevrolet

LONE STAR 500

June 25
College Station, Texas
Time of Race: 4 3ours, 26 minutes, 4 seconds
Average Speed: 1442.185 mph

FINISH	DRIVER	CAR
1.	Richard Petty	Plymouth
2.	Bobby Allison	Chevrolet

3.	Coo Coo Marlin	Chevrolet
4.	Benny Parsons	Mercury
5.	Bobby Isaac	Dodge
6.	James Hylton	Ford
7.	Larry Smith	Ford
8.	Ben Arnold	Ford
9.	Dean Dalton	Mercury
10.	Bill Champion	Ford
11.	H. B. Bailey	Pontiac
12.	Tiny Lund	Chevrolet
13.	Dave Marcis	Dodge
14.	Raymond Williams	Ford
15.	Cecil Gordon	Mercury
16.	Jabe Thomas	Plymouth
17.	Charlie Roberts	Ford
18.	Paul Jett	Ford
19.	Clarence Lovell	Ford
20.	Dick May	Ford
21.	John Sears	Plymouth
22.	Les Covey	Chevrolet
23.	Frank Warren	Dodge
24.	Joe Frasson	Dodge
25.	Ronnie Churrley	Chevrolet
26.	Jim White	Ford
27.	J. D. McDuffie	Chevrolet
28.	Ed Negre	Dodge
29.	Elmo Langley	Ford
30.	David Ray Boggs	Dodge
31.	Richard Childress	Chevrolet
32.	Wendell Scott	Ford
33.	Walter Ballard	Mercury
34.	Doc Faustina	Plymouth
35.	Dick Brooks	Ford
36.	Jackie Oliver	Ford
37.	Neil Castles	Dodge
38.	D. K. Ulrich	Ford
39.	Henley Gray	Ford
40.	Marty Robbins	Dodge
41.	LeeRoy Yarbrough	Ford
42.	Johnny Anderson	Chevrolet
43.	Ron Keselowski	Dodge
44.	Bill Shirey	Plymouth

FIRECRACKER 400

July 4
Daytona Beach, Florida
Time of Race: 2 hours, 29minutes, 14seconds
Average Speed: 160.821

FINISH	DRIVER	CAR
1.	David Pearson	Mercury
2.	Richard Petty	Dodge
3.	Bobby Allison	Chevrolet
4.	Coo Coo Marlin	Chevrolet
5.	James Hylton	Ford
6.	LeeRoy Yarbrough	Mercury
7.	Ron Keselowski	Dodge
8.	Donnie Allison	Ford
9.	Wayne Smith	Chevrolet
10.	Johnny Halford	Plymouth
11.	Cecil Gordon	Mercury
12.	Charlie Roberts	Ford
13.	Dave Marcis	Dodge
14.	Richard Brown	Chevrolet
15.	Mel Larson	Plymouth
16.	Ben Arnold	Ford
17.	Buddy Arrington	Dodge
18.	Bill Champion	Mercury
19.	Jabe Thomas	Plymouth
20.	George Altheide	Dodge
21.	Frank Warren	Dodge
22.	Henley Gray	Ford
23.	Walter Ballard	Mercury
24.	Buddy Baker	Dodge
25.	Jackie Oliver	Ford
26.	David Boggs	Dodge
27.	Bobby Isaac	Dodge
28.	J. D. McDuffie	Chevrolet
29.	David Sisco	Chevrolet

30.	Clarence Lovell	Ford
31.	Dean Dalton	Mercury
32.	John Sears	Plymouth
33.	Pete Hamilton	Plymouth
34.	Bill Shirey	Plymouth
35.	Elmo Langley	Ford
36.	Benny Parsons	Mercury
37.	Neil Castles	Dodge
38.	Larry Smith	Ford
39.	Roy Mayne	Chevrolet
40.	Joe Frasson	Dodge

VOLUNTEER 500

July 9
Bristol, Tennessee
Time of Race: 2 hours, 30 minutes, 28 seconds
Average Speed: 92.735 mph

FINISH	DRIVER	CAR
1.	Bobby Allison	Chevrolet
2.	Richard Petty	Plymouth
3.	Dave Marcis	Dodge
4.	Benny Parsons	Mercury
5.	J. D. McDuffie	Dodge
6.	John Sears	Plymouth
7.	Raymond Williams	Ford
8.	Cecil Gordon	Mercury
9.	Walter Ballard	Mercury
10.	Ben Arnold	Ford
11.	Elmo Langley	Ford
12.	James Hylton	Ford
13.	Bill Champion	Ford
14.	Charlie Roberts	Ford
15.	Jabe Thomas	Plymouth
16.	Henley Gray	Ford
17.	Ed Negre	Dodge
18.	Bobby Isaac	Dodge
19.	LeeRoy Yarbrough	Ford
20.	Dean Dalton	Mercury
21.	Bob Brown	Chevrolet
22.	Coo Coo Marlin	Chevrolet
23.	David Ray Boggs	Dodge
24.	David Sisco	Chevrolet
25.	Johnny Halford	Plymouth
26.	Richard Childress	Chevrolet
27.	Ron Keselowski	Dodge
28.	G. C. Spencer	Plymouth
29.	Frank Warren	Dodge
30.	Richard Brown	Chevrolet

NORTHERN 300

July 16
Trenton, New Jersey
Time of Race: 2 hours, 57 minutes, 41 seconds
Average Speed: 114.030 mph

FINISH	DRIVER	CAR
1.	Bobby Allison	Chevrolet
2.	Bobby Isaac	Dodge
3.	Richard Petty	Plymouth
4.	Fred Lorenzen	Ford
5.	Cecil Gordon	Mercury
6.	James Hylton	Ford
7.	Larry Smith	Ford
8.	Benny Parsons	Mercury
9.	Raymond Williams	Ford
10.	Walter Ballard	Mercury
11.	Elmo Langley	Ford
12.	Dean Dalton	Mercury
13.	Bob Greely	Plymouth
14.	Charlie Roberts	Ford
15.	Jabe Thomas	Plymouth
16.	J. D. McDuffie	Chevrolet

17.	Ed Negre	Dodge
18.	Richard Childress	Chevrolet
19.	D. K. Ulrich	Ford
20.	Wendell Scott	Ford
21.	Frank Warren	Dodge
22.	David Ray Boggs	Dodge
23.	Earl Brooks	Ford
24.	Bill Champion	Ford
25.	Dave Marcis	Dodge
26.	Fred Drake	Pontiac
27.	Neil Castles	Dodge
28.	Dr. Ed Hessert	Plymouth
29.	Henley Gray	Ford
30.	Bill Shirey	Plymouth
31.	John Sears	Plymouth
32.	Earle Canavan	Plymouth
33.	A. J. Cox	Dodge

DIXIE 500

July 23
Atlanta, Georgia
Time of Race: 3 hours, 47 minutes, 8 seconds
Average Speed: 131.295 mph

FINISH	DRIVER	CAR
1.	Bobby Allison	Chevrolet
2.	Richard Petty	Dodge
3.	Dave Pearson	Mercury
4.	Benny Parsons	Mercury
5.	LeeRoy Yarbrough	Ford
6.	Fred Lorenzen	Chevrolet
7.	Dave Marcis	Dodge
8.	Darrell Waltrip	Mercury
9.	Cecil Gordon	Mercury
10.	Walter Ballard	Mercury
11.	John Sears	Plymouth
12.	Ben Arnold	Ford
13.	Buddy Arrington	Dodge
14.	Charlie Roberts	Ford
15.	Johnny Halford	Plymouth
16.	Ron Keselowski	Dodge
17.	Bill Champion	Mercury
18.	Raymond Williams	Ford
19.	Bobby Mausgrover	Ford
20.	Elmo Langley	Ford
21.	Eddie Yarboro	Plymouth
22.	Neil Castles	Dodge
23.	Frank Warren	Dodge
24.	Clarence Lovell	Ford
25.	Ed Negre	Dodge
26.	David Ray Boggs	Dodge
27.	Richard Brown	Chevrolet
28.	Joe Frasson	Dodge
29.	Coo Coo Marlin	Chevrolet
30.	Henley Gray	Ford
31.	Bobby Isaac	Dodge
32.	Donnie Allison	Ford
33.	Doc Faustina	Plymouth
34.	Jabe Thomas	Plymouth
35.	James Hylton	Ford
36.	Larry Smith	Ford
37.	Dean Dalton	Mercury
38.	Dick Brooks	Ford
39.	Dub Simpson	Chevrolet
40.	G. C. Spencer	Plymouth

TALLADEGA 500

August 6
Talladega, Alabama
Time of Race: 3 hours, 22 minutes, 9 seconds
Average Speed: 146.728 mph

FINISH	DRIVER	CAR
1.	James Hylton	Mercury
2.	Ramo Stott	Ford
3.	Bobby Allison	Chevrolet
4.	Red Farmer	Ford
5.	Buddy Arrington	Dodge
6.	Ben Arnold	Ford
7.	Richard Petty	Dodge
8.	Henley Gray	Ford
9.	Raymond Williams	Ford
10.	Paul Jett	Ford
11.	John Sears	Plymouth
12.	Dean Dalton	Mercury
13.	David Ray Boggs	Dodge
14.	Elmo Langley	Ford
15.	Walter Ballard	Mercury
16.	Coo Coo Marlin	Chevrolet
17.	David Sisco	Chevrolet
18.	George Altheide	Dodge
19.	Pete Hamilton	Plymouth
20.	Fred Lorenzen	Chevrolet
21.	Bill Champion	Mercury
22.	Buddy Baker	Dodge
23.	Richard Brown	Chevrolet
24.	Clarence Lovell	Ford
25.	Benny Parsons	Mercury
26.	David Pearson	Mercury
27.	Darrell Waltrip	Mercury
28.	Tommy Gale	Mercury
29.	Paul Tyler	Mercury
30.	Mel Larson	Plymouth
31.	Donnie Allison	Plymouth
32.	Charlie Roberts	Ford
33.	LeeRoy Yarbrough	Ford
34.	Frank Warren	Dodge
35.	Jabe Thomas	Plymouth
36.	J. D. McDuffie	Chevrolet
37.	Larry Smith	Ford
38.	Bobby Mausgrover	Ford
39.	Ed Negre	Dodge
40.	Dick Brooks	Ford
41.	Joe Frasson	Dodge
42.	Bobby Isaac	Dodge
43.	Cecil Gordon	Mercury
44.	Ron Keselowski	Dodge
45.	Don Faustine	Plymouth
46.	Dave Marcis	Dodge
47.	Bill Shirey	Plymouth
48.	Neil Castles	Plymouth
49.	Roy Mayne	Chevrolet
50.	Robert Wales	Dodge

YANKEE 400

August 20
Brooklyn, Michigan
Time of race: 2 hours, 58 minutes, 31 seconds
Average speed: 134.416 mph

FINISH	DRIVER	CAR
1.	David Pearson	Mercury
2.	Bobby Allison	Chevrolet
3.	Bobby Isaac	Dodge
4.	Richard Petty	Dodge
5.	Cale Yarborough	Mercury
6.	James Hylton	Ford
7.	Benny Parsons	Mercury
8.	Bill Seifert	Mercury
9.	Dave Marcis	Matador
10.	Larry Smith	Ford
11.	Walter Ballard	Mercury
12.	Elmo Langley	Ford
13.	David Sisco	Chevrolet
14.	Clarence Lovell	Ford
15.	Cecil Gordon	Mercury
16.	John Sears	Plymouth
17.	Mel Larson	Plymouth
18.	Ben Arnold	Ford
19.	Bill Champion	Ford

20.	Raymond Williams	Ford
21.	Jabe Thomas	Plymouth
22.	Ed Negre	Dodge
23.	Dean Dalton	Mercury
24.	Henley Gray	Ford
25.	Dick May	Dodge
26.	Charlie Roberts	Ford
27.	Doc Faustina	Plymouth
28.	Frank Warren	Dodge
29.	J. D. McDuffie	Chevrolet
30.	Joe Frasson	Dodge
31.	David Ray Boggs	Dodge
32.	Ron Keselowski	Dodge
33.	Buddy Arrington	Dodge
34.	Coo Coo Marlin	Chevrolet
35.	George Altheide	Dodge
36.	Jim Vandiver	Dodge
37.	Ron Grana	Chevrolet
38.	G. C. Spencer	Plymouth
39.	Earle Canavan	Plymouth
40.	Dick Brooks	Ford

NASHVILLE 420

August 27
Nashville, Tennessee
Time of Race: 2 hours, 42 minutes, 14 seconds
Average Speed: 92.678 mph

FINISH	DRIVER	CAR
1.	Bobby Allison	Chevrolet
2.	Richard Petty	Plymouth
3.	Darrell Waltrip	Mercury
4.	Benny Parsons	Mercury
5.	Elmo Langley	Ford
6.	Cecil Gordon	Mercury
7.	Henley Gray	Ford
8.	James Hylton	Ford
9.	Walter Ballard	Mercury
10.	J. D. McDuffie	Chevrolet
11.	D. K. Ulrich	Ford
12.	John Sears	Plymouth
13.	Earl Brooks	Ford
14.	Frank Warren	Plymouth
15.	David Ray Boggs	Dodge
16.	Richard Childress	Chevrolet
17.	David Sisco	Chevrolet
18.	Raymond Williams	Ford
19.	Charlie Roberts	Ford
20.	Ben Arnold	Ford
21.	Bob Brown	Chevrolet
22.	Jabe Thomas	Plymouth
23.	Dean Dalton	Mercury
24.	George Altheide	Dodge
25.	Bill Champion	Ford
26.	Coo Coo Marlin	Chevrolet
27.	Bobby Isaac	Dodge
28.	LeeRoy Yarbrough	Ford

SOUTHERN 500

September 4
Darlington, South Carolina
Time of Race: 4 hours, 4 minutes, 14 seconds
Average Speed: 122.655 mph

FINISH	DRIVER	CAR
1.	Bobby Allison	Chevrolet
2.	David Pearson	Mercury
3.	Richard Petty	Dodge
4.	Fred Lorenzen	Chevrolet
5.	H. B. Bailey	Pontiac
6.	Buddy Arrington	Dodge
7.	Dave Marcis	Matador
8.	Jim Vandiver	Dodge

9.	Marty Robbins	Dodge
10.	Coo Coo Marlin	Chevrolet
11.	James Hylton	Mercury
12.	Walter Ballard	Mercury
13.	Bill Champion	Ford
14.	Ed Negre	Dodge
15.	J. D. McDuffie	Dodge
16.	Tommy Gale	Mercury
17.	Frank Warren	Dodge
18.	David Ray Boggs	Dodge
19.	G. C. Spencer	Plymouth
20.	Jabe Thomas	Plymouth
21.	Dean Dalton	Mercury
22.	Elmo Langley	Ford
23.	Neil Castles	Plymouth
24.	Henley Gray	Ford
25.	Larry Smith	Ford
26.	Buck Baker	Chevrolet
27.	Eddie Yarboro	Plymouth
28.	Cecil Gordon	Mercury
29.	Buddy Baker	Dodge
30.	John Sears	Plymouth
31.	Paul Tyler	Mercury
32.	Dick Brooks	Mercury
33.	Clarence Lovell	Ford
34.	Ron Keselowski	Dodge
35.	Benny Parsons	Mercury
36.	Ben Arnold	Ford
37.	Joe Frasson	Dodge
38.	Donnie Allison	Ford
39.	LeeRoy Yarbrough	Ford
40.	Bobby Isaac	Dodge

CAPITAL CITY 500

September 10
Richmond, Virginia
Time of Race: 3 hours, 34 minutes, 14 seconds
Average Speed: 75.899 mph

FINISH	DRIVER	CAR
1.	Richard Petty	Plymouth
2.	Bobby Allison	Chevrolet
3.	Bill Dennis	Chevrolet
4.	James Hylton	Ford
5.	Dave Marcis	Dodge
6.	Bill Champion	Ford
7.	Ben Arnold	Ford
8.	Dean Dalton	Mercury
9.	Jabe Thomas	Plymouth
10.	Buddy Arrington	Dodge
11.	Raymond Williams	Ford
12.	Walter Ballard	Mercury
13.	John Sears	Plymouth
14.	Henley Gray	Ford
15.	Ed Negre	Dodge
16.	Eddie Yarboro	Plymouth
17.	Buddy Baker	Dodge
18.	Frank Warren	Dodge
19.	Larry Smith	Ford
20.	Cecil Gordon	Mercury
21.	Neil Castles	Plymouth
22.	Elmo Langley	Ford
23.	Benny Parsons	Mercury
24.	David Pearson	Ford
25.	Richard Childress	Chevrolet
26.	David Ray Boggs	Dodge
27.	Charlie Roberts	Ford
28.	Ron Keselowski	Dodge
29.	George Altheide	Dodge
30.	J. D. McDuffie	Plymouth

DELAWARE 500

September 17
Dover, Delaware
Time of Race: 4 hours, 8 minutes, 57 seconds
Average Speed: 120.508 mph

FINISH	DRIVER	CAR
1.	David Pearson	Mercury
2.	Richard Petty	Plymouth
3.	Ramo Stott	Ford
4.	James Hylton	Ford
5.	Cecil Gordon	Mercury
6.	Ben Arnold	Ford
7.	Elmo Langley	Ford
8.	Walter Ballard	Mercury
9.	Dean Dalton	Mercury
10.	Charlie Roberts	Ford
11.	Buddy Baker	Dodge
12.	Jabe Thomas	Plymouth
13.	Paul Tyler	Mercury
14.	D. K. Ulrich	Ford
15.	Earle Canavan	Plymouth
16.	Wendell Scott	Ford
17.	Ed Negre	Dodge
18.	Bill Shirey	Plymouth
19.	Henley Gray	Ford
20.	Bobby Allison	Chevrolet
21.	Les Covey	Chevrolet
22.	Raymond Williams	Ford
23.	Ron Keselowski	Dodge
24.	J. D. McDuffie	Chevrolet
25.	Frank Warren	Dodge
26.	Clarence Lovell	Ford
27.	Buddy Arrington	Dodge
28.	John Sears	Plymouth
29.	Earl Brooks	Ford
30.	Larry Smith	Ford
31.	Harry Schilling	Chevrolet
32.	Neil Castles	Plymouth
33.	Richard Childress	Chevrolet
34.	Benny Parsons	Mercury
35.	Bill Champion	Ford
36.	Coo Coo Marlin	Chevrolet
37.	Dave Marcis	Matador
38.	David Ray Boggs	Dodge
39.	Bill Seifert	Mercury
40.	George Altheide	Dodge

OLD DOMINION 500

September 24
Martinsville, Virginia
Time of Race: 3 hours, 45 minutes, 2 seconds
Average Speed: 69.989 mph

FINISH	DRIVER	CAR
1.	Richard Petty	Plymouth
2.	Bobby Allison	Chevrolet
3.	David Pearson	Mercury
4.	Buddy Baker	Dodge
5.	Jimmy Hensley	Ford
6.	Benny Parsons	Mercury
7.	Buddy Arrington	Dodge
8.	James Hylton	Ford
9.	Elmo Langley	Ford
10.	Cecil Gordon	Mercury
11.	Coo Coo Marlin	Chevrolet
12.	Bill Champion	Ford
13.	Raymond Williams	Ford
14.	J. D. McDuffie	Chevrolet
15.	John Sears	Plymouth
16.	Ben Arnold	Ford
17.	Neil Castles	Plymouth
18.	Ed Negre	Dodge
19.	Charlie Roberts	Ford
20.	Walter Ballard	Mercury
21.	Jabe Thomas	Plymouth
22.	James Cox	Plymouth
23.	Henley Gray	Ford
24.	David Ray Boggs	Dodge
25.	Ray Hendrick	Dodge
26.	Tiny Lund	Chevrolet
27.	Fred Lorenzen	Chevrolet
28.	Dean Dalton	Mercury
29.	Dave Marcis	Matador

30.	LeeRoy Yarbrough	Ford
31.	Bill Dennis	Chevrolet
32.	Frank Warren	Dodge
33.	Richard Childress	Chevrolet
34.	Larry Smith	Ford
35.	Bobby Isaac	Ford
36.	Bill Shirey	Plymouth

WILKES 400

October 1
North Wilkesboro
Time of Race: 2 hours, 38 minutes, 33 seconds
Average Speed: 95.818 mph

FINISH	DRIVER	CAR
1.	Richard Petty	Plymouth
2.	Bobby Allison	Chevrolet
3.	Buddy Baker	Dodge
4.	Benny Parsons	Mercury
5.	John Sears	Chevrolet
6.	Dave Marcis	Plymouth
7.	Cecil Gordon	Mercury
8.	Elmo Langley	Ford
9.	Vic Parsons	Ford
10.	Raymond Williams	Ford
11.	Buddy Arrington	Dodge
12.	Jabe Thomas	Plymouth
13.	Ben Arnold	Ford
14.	Bill Champion	Ford
15.	Dean Dalton	Mercury
16.	Frank Warren	Dodge
17.	James Hylton	Ford
18.	Max Berrier	Ford
19.	Walter Ballard	Mercury
20.	Bill Shirey	Plymouth
21.	Charlie Roberts	Ford
22.	Ed Negre	Dodge
23.	J. D. McDuffie	Chevrolet
24.	David Ray Boggs	Dodge
25.	Richard Childress	Chevrolet
26.	Tiny Lund	Chevrolet
27.	Henley Gray	Plymouth
28.	Larry Smith	Ford
29.	Ron Keselowski	Dodge
30.	Coo Coo Marlin	Chevrolet

NATIONAL 500

October 8
Charlotte
Time of Race: 3 hours, 45 minutes, 37 seconds
Average Speed: 133.234 mph

FINISH	DRIVER	CAR
1.	Bobby Allison	Chevrolet
2.	Buddy Baker	Dodge
3.	David Pearson	Mercury
4.	A. J. Foyt	Mercury
5.	Butch Hartman	Ford
6.	Darrell Waltrip	Mercury
7.	James Hylton	Mercury
8.	Buddy Arrington	Dodge
9.	Joe Frasson	Dodge
10.	Richard Petty	Dodge
11.	Larry Smith	Ford
12.	Ron Keselowski	Dodge
13.	Raymond Williams	Ford
14.	Ben Arnold	Ford
15.	Neil Castles	Plymouth
16.	John Sears	Plymouth
17.	Cecil Gordon	Mercury
18.	Bill Champion	Mercury
19.	Walter Ballard	Mercury
20.	David Ray Boggs	Mercury

21.	Frank Warren	Dodge
22.	Henley Gray	Ford
23.	Tommy Gale	Mercury
24.	Dean Dalton	Mercury
25.	Donnie Allison	Ford
26.	Dave Marcis	Matador
27.	Roger McCluskey	Dodge
28.	Bobby Isaac	Chevrolet
29.	Bill Dennis	Chevrolet
30.	Harry Schilling	Chevrolet
31.	Earle Canavan	Plymouth
32.	Pete Hamilton	Plymouth
33.	Jim Vandiver	Dodge
34.	Coo Coo Marlin	Chevrolet
35.	Elmo Langley	Ford
36.	G. C. Spencer	Dodge
37.	Jabe Thomas	Chevrolet
38.	Benny Parsons	Mercury
39.	Cale Yarborough	Chevrolet
40.	Dick Brooks	Mercury
41.	Richard Brown	Ford
42.	Gordon Johncock	Plymouth
43.	Bobby Unser	Chevrolet
44.	Ed Negre	Dodge

AMERICAN 500

October 22
Rockingham
Time of Race: 4 hours, 13 minutes, 49 seconds
Average Speed: 116.275 mph

FINISH	DRIVER	CAR
1.	Bobby Allison	Chevrolet
2.	Richard Petty	Plymouth
3.	Buddy Baker	Dodge
4.	David Pearson	Mercury
5.	Pete Hamilton	Plymouth
6.	Cale Yarborough	Chevrolet
7.	Dave Marcis	Matador
8.	Larry Smith	Ford
9.	David Sisco	Chevrolet
10.	Buddy Arrington	Dodge
11.	John Sears	Plymouth
12.	Clarence Lovell	Ford
13.	Elmo Langley	Ford
14.	Ben Arnold	Ford
15.	Walter Ballard	Mercury
16.	Dean Dalton	Mercury
17.	Ed Negre	Dodge
18.	Charlie Roberts	Ford
19.	James Hylton	Ford
20.	Cecil Gordon	Mercury
21.	Joe Frasson	Dodge
22.	Raymond Williams	Ford
23.	Jabe Thomas	Plymouth
24.	J. D. McDuffie	Chevrolet
25.	Frank Warren	Dodge
26.	Marty Robbins	Dodge
27.	Coo Coo Marlin	Chevrolet
28.	Bill Champion	Mercury
29.	Roy Mayne	Plymouth
30.	Jim Vandiver	Dodge
31.	Neil Castles	Plymouth
32.	Bill Dennis	Chevrolet
33.	Ron Keselowski	Dodge
34.	Dick Brooks	Ford
35.	Benny Parsons	Mercury
36.	Bobby Isaac	Chevrolet
37.	Henley Gray	Mercury
38.	Tiny Lund	Chevrolet
39.	Tommy Gale	Mercury
40.	Ron Hutcherson	Ford

TEXAS 500

November 12
College Station

Time of Race: 3 hours, 24 minutes, 0 seconds
Average Speed: 147.059 mph

FINISH	DRIVER	CAR
1.	Buddy Baker	Dodge
2.	A. J. Foyt	Mercury
3.	Richard Petty	Dodge
4.	Bobby Allison	Chevrolet
5.	Hershel McGriff	Plymouth
6.	Benny Parsons	Mercury
7.	Coo Coo Marlin	Chevrolet
8.	Cecil Gordon	Mercury
9.	Cale Yarborough	Chevrolet
10.	Joe Frasson	Dodge
11.	James Hylton	Mercury
12.	Dave Marcis	Dodge
13.	Ramo Stott	Ford
14.	J. D. McDuffie	Chevrolet
15.	Ben Arnold	Ford
16.	John Sears	Plymouth
17.	Dick Brooks	Ford
18.	Walter Ballard	Mercury
19.	Jim Whitt	Ford
20.	Dean Dalton	Mercury
21.	Raymond Williams	Ford
22.	Dick Newsom	Ford
23.	Harry Schilling	Chevrolet
24.	Elmo Langley	Ford
25.	Ed Negre	Dodge
26.	Johnny Rutherford	Ford
27.	David Sisco	Chevrolet
28.	Charlie Roberts	Ford
29.	Bill Shirey	Dodge
30.	Mel Larson	Plymouth
31.	Larry Smith	Ford
32.	Paul Feldner	Plymouth
33.	Clarence Lowell	Ford
34.	Buddy Arrington	Dodge
35.	Gordon Johncock	Plymouth
36.	H. B. Bailey	Pontiac
37.	Jabe Thomas	Plymouth
38.	Frank Warren	Dodge
39.	Henley Gray	Ford
40.	Bill Hollar	Mercury
41.	Ron Keselowski	Dodge
42.	Earle Canavan	Plymouth
43.	Bill Champion	Ford
44.	Bill Seifert	Mercury

■■■■■

1973

WINSTON WESTERN 500

January 21
Riverside, California
Time of Race: 4 hours, 48 minutes, 33 seconds
Average Speed: 104.055 mph

FINISH	DRIVER	CAR
1.	Mark Donohue	Matador
2.	Bobby Allison	Chevrolet
3.	Ray Elder	Dodge
4.	Bobby Unser	Ford
5.	Jimmy Insolo	Chevrolet
6.	Jack McCoy	Dodge
7.	Elmo Langley	Ford
8.	Richard White	Ford
9.	J. C. Danielson	Mercury
10.	Henley Gray	Mercury
11.	Charlie Roberts	Ford
12.	James Hylton	Mercury
13.	Carl Adams	Ford
14.	Benny Parsons	Chevrolet
15.	Gerald Thompson	Pontiac
16.	Bill Champion	Ford

17.	Dick Bown	Dodge
18.	Jim White	Chevrolet
19.	Walter Ballard	Plymouth
20.	Cecil Gordon	Chevrolet
21.	Richard Petty	Dodge
22.	David Pearson	Mercury
23.	Hershel McGriff	Plymouth
24.	Cale Yarborough	Chevrolet
25.	Sonny Easley	Ford
26.	John Soares Jr.	Dodge
27.	Bobby Isaac	Dodge
28.	Johnny Anderson	Chevrolet
29.	Chuck Bown	Dodge
30.	John Hren	Chevrolet
31.	Glen Francis	Chevrolet
32.	J. D. McDuffie	Chevrolet
33.	Carl Joiner	Chevrolet
34.	Harry Jefferson	Ford
35.	Buddy Baker	Dodge
36.	Hugh Pearson	Chevrolet
37.	Bob Kauf	Chevrolet
38.	Clem Proctor	Ford
39.	Jerry Grant	Chevrolet
40.	Dave Marcis	Dodge

DAYTONA 500

February 18
Daytona Beach, Florida
Time of Race: 3 hours, 10 minutes, 50 seconds
Average Speed: 157.205 mph

FINISH	DRIVER	CAR
1.	Richard Petty	Dodge
2.	Bobby Isaac	Ford
3.	Dick Brooks	Dodge
4.	A. J. Foyt	Chevrolet
5.	Hershel McGriff	Plymouth
6.	Buddy Baker	Dodge
7.	James Hylton	Mercury
8.	Ramo Stott	Mercury
9.	Buddy Arrington	Dodge
10.	Vic Parsons	Mercury
11.	David Sisco	Chevrolet
12.	Darrell Waltrip	Mercury
13.	Joe Frasson	Dodge
14.	Larry Smith	Mercury
15.	Jabe Thomas	Dodge
16.	Frank Warren	Dodge
17.	Ed Negre	Mercury
18.	Ray Elder	Dodge
19.	Walter Ballard	Chevrolet
20.	Ron Keselowski	Dodge
21.	Cecil Gordon	Chevrolet
22.	Cale Yarborough	Chevrolet
23.	Maynard Troyer	Ford
24.	John A. Utsman	Dodge
25.	Bobby Allison	Chevrolet
26.	J. D. McDuffie	Chevrolet
27.	Dave Marcis	Matador
28.	Jim Vandiver	Dodge
29.	Coo Coo Marlin	Chevrolet
30.	Benny Parsons	Chevrolet
31.	John Sears	Dodge
32.	Red Farmer	Ford
33.	David Pearson	Mercury
34.	Marty Robbins	Dodge
35.	Bill Dennis	Chevrolet
36.	Tiny Lund	Chevrolet
37.	Neil Castles	Dodge
38.	Gordon Johncock	Chevrolet
39.	Earl Ross	Chevrolet
40.	Pete Hamilton	Plymouth

RICHMOND 500

February 25
Richmond, Virginia

Time of Race: 3 hours, 37 minutes, 29 seconds
Average Speed: 74.764 mph

FINISH	DRIVER	CAR
1.	Richard Petty	Dodge
2.	Buddy Baker	Dodge
3.	Cale Yarborough	Chevrolet
4.	Bobby Isaac	Ford
5.	Dave Marcis	Dodge
6.	Bill Dennis	Chevrolet
7.	Lennie Pond	Chevrolet
8.	Cecil Gordon	Chevrolet
9.	James Hylton	Mercury
10.	Benny Parsons	Chevrolet
11.	Walter Ballard	Mercury
12.	Elmo Langley	Ford
13.	Jabe Thomas	Dodge
14.	Bill Champion	Ford
15.	Bobby Allison	Chevrolet
16.	Henley Gray	Ford
17.	Buddy Arrington	Dodge
18.	Charlie Roberts	Ford
19.	John Sears	Dodge
20.	Richard Brown	Chevrolet
21.	Sonny Hutchins	Chevrolet
22.	Frank Warren	Dodge
23.	Tiny Lund	Chevrolet
24.	Neil Castles	Dodge
25.	Dennie Allison	Chevrolet
26.	Ray Hendrick	Mercury
27.	Dean Dalton	Mercury
28.	David Sisco	Chevrolet
29.	J. D. McDufle	Chevrolet
30.	Vic Parsons	Mercury

CAROLINA 500

March 18
Rockingham, North Carolina
Time of Race: 4 hours, 13 minutes, 1 second
Average Speed: 157,205 mph

FINISH	DRIVER	CAR
1.	David Pearson	Mercury
2.	Cale Yarborough	Chevrolet
3.	Buddy Baker	Dodge
4.	Bobby Allison	Chevrolet
5.	Dick Brooks	Ford
6.	Darrell Waltrip	Mercury
7.	Jim Vandiver	Dodge
8.	Joe Frasson	Dodge
9.	Richard Childress	Chevrolet
10.	Bill Dennis	Chevrolet
11.	James Hyton	Mercury
12.	Buddy Arrington	Plymouth
13.	Jabe Thomas	Dodge
14.	Coo Coo Marlin	Chevrolet
15.	Frank Warren	Dodge
16.	Ed Negre	Dodge
17.	Charlie Roberts	Ford
18.	Henley Gray	Ford
19.	Larry Smith	Mercury
20.	Lennie Pond	Chevrolet
21.	Elmo Langley	Ford
22.	Cecil Gordon	Chevrolet
23.	Richard Petty	Dodge
24.	David Sisco	Chevrolet
25.	Gordon Johncock	Chevrolet
26.	Dean Dalton	Mercury
27.	Buck Baker	Chevrolet
28.	Eddie Bond	Dodge
29.	J. D. McDuffie	Chevrolet
30.	Bobby Isaac	Ford
31.	Benny Parsons	Chevrolet
32.	Bill Champion	Mercury
33.	John A. Utsman	Dodge
34.	Vic Parsons	Mercury
35.	Raymond Williams	Ford

36.	Neil Castles	Dodge
37.	Dave Marcis	Matador
38.	Clarence Lowell	Chevrolet
39.	Walter Ballard	Mercury
40.	Tiny Lund	Chevrolet

SOUTHEASTERN 500

March 25
Bristol, Tennessee
Time of Race: 2 hours, 57 minutes, 43 seconds
Average Speed: 88.952 mph

FINISH	DRIVER	CAR
1.	Cale Yarborough	Chevrolet
2.	Richard Petty	Dodge
3.	Bobby Allison	Chevrolet
4.	Dave Marcis	Dodge
5.	Benny Parsons	Mercury
6.	Lennie Pond	Chevrolet
7.	Coo Coo Marlin	Chevrolet
8.	James Hylton	Mercury
9.	Vic Parsons	Ford
10.	John A. Utsman	Dodge
11.	David Sisco	Chevrolet
12.	Elmo Langley	Ford
13.	John Sears	Dodge
14.	Buddy Arrington	Plymouth
15.	Bobby Isaac	Ford
16.	Richard Brown	Chevrolet
17.	Walter Ballard	Mercury
18.	Charlie Roberts	Ford
19.	Henley Gray	Ford
20.	Richard Childress	Chevrolet
21.	J. D. McDuffie	Chevrolet
22.	Jabe Thomas	Dodge
23.	Bill Champion	Ford
24.	Donnie Allison	Chevrolet
25.	Buddy Baker	Dodge
26.	Frank Warren	Dodge
27.	Dean Dalton	Mercury
28.	Raymond Williams	Ford
29.	Cecil Gordon	Chevrolet
30.	Darrell Waltrip	Mercury

ATLANTA 500

April 1
Atlanta, Georgia
Time of Race: 3 hours, 34 minutes, 52 seconds
Average Speed: 139.351 mph

FINISH	DRIVER	CAR
1.	David Pearson	Mercury
2.	Bobby Isaac	Ford
3.	Benny Parsons	Chevrolet
4.	Buddy Baker	Dodge
5.	Cale Yarborough	Chevrolet
6.	Coo Coo Marlin	Chevrolet
7.	Dick Brooks	Mercury
8.	Cecil Gordon	Chevrolet
9.	Clarence Lowell	Chevrolet
10.	Jim Vandiver	Dodge
11.	Gordon Johncock	Chevrolet
12.	Dave Marcis	Dodge
13.	Richard Childress	Chevrolet
14.	Walter Ballard	Mercury
15.	Buddy Arrington	Plymouth
16.	Frank Warren	Dodge
17.	Raymond Williams	Ford
18.	Charles Barrett	Ford
19.	Johnny Barnes	Mercury
20.	Larry Smith	Mercury
21.	James Hyton	Mercury
22.	Earle Canavan	Plymouth

23.	Dean Dalton	Mercury
24.	Ed Negre	Mercury
25.	Charlie Roberts	Ford
26.	Elmo Langley	Ford
27.	A. J. Foyt	Chevrolet
28.	Joe Frasson	Dodge
29.	Bill Champion	Mercury
30.	Mark Donahue	Matador
31.	Ron Keselowski	Dodge
32.	Roy Mayne	Dodge
33.	Darrell Waltrip	Mercury
34.	Richard Petty	Dodge
35.	Bobby Allison	Chevrolet
36.	John Sears	Dodge
37.	Bobby Mausgrover	Chevrolet
38.	Tiny Lund	Chevrolet
39.	Pete Hamilton	Plymouth
40.	Tony Bettenhausen Jr.	Dodge

GWYN STALEY MEMORIAL 400

April 8
North Wilkesboro, North Carolina
Time of Race: 2 hours, 34 minutes, 17 seconds
Average Speed: 97.224 mph

FINISH	DRIVER	CAR
1.	Richard Petty	Dodge
2.	Benny Parsons	Chevrolet
3.	Buddy Baker	Dodge
4.	Bobby Allison	Chevrolet
5.	Cecil Gordon	Chevrolet
6.	Cale Yarborough	Chevrolet
7.	Lennie Pond	Chevrolet
8.	James Hylton	Mercury
9.	Donnie Allison	Chevrolet
10.	Yvon DuHamal	Ford
11.	John Sears	Dodge
12.	Vic Parsons	Ford
13.	Elmo Langley	Ford
14.	Bill Champion	Ford
15.	Earl Brooks	Ford
16.	Richard Childress	Chevrolet
17.	Dean Dalton	Mercury
18.	Walter Ballard	Mercury
19.	Ed Negre	Mercury
20.	Dave Marcis	Dodge
21.	Frank Warren	Dodge
22.	Neil Castles	Dodge
23.	J. D. McDuffie	Chevrolet
24.	Henley Gray	Mercury
25.	Buddy Arrington	Dodge
26.	Raymond Williams	Ford
27.	Charlie Roberts	Ford
28.	Bobby Isaac	Ford
29.	Jabe Thomas	Dodge
30.	Rick Newsom	Ford

REBEL 500

April 15
Darlington, South Carolina
Time of Race: 4 hours, 4 minutes, 14 seconds
Average Speed: 122.655 mph

FINISH	DRIVER	CAR
1.	David Pearson	Mercury
2.	Benny Parsons	Chevrolet
3.	Bobby Allison	Chevrolet
4.	Richard Childress	Chevrolet
5.	J. D. McDuffie	Chevrolet
6.	Dean Dalton	Mercury
7.	Richard Petty	Dodge
8.	Buddy Baker	Dodge
9.	Roy Mayne	Dodge
10.	Raymond Williams	Ford

11.	Dick Brooks	Ford
12.	Earle Canavan	Plymouth
13.	Buddy Arrington	Dodge
14.	Wendell Scott	Ford
15.	G. C. Spencer	Dodge
16.	Jabe Thomas	Mercury
17.	Richie Panch	Mercury
18.	Johnny Barnes	Mercury
19.	Cale Yarborough	Chevrolet
20.	Ed Negre	Mercury
21.	Cecil Gordon	Chevrolet
22.	John Sears	Dodge
23.	James Hylton	Mercury
24.	Darrell Waltrip	Mercury
25.	Walter Ballard	Mercury
26.	Charlie Roberts	Ford
27.	Paul Tyler	Mercury
28.	Vic Parsons	Ford
29.	David Ray Boggs	Dodge
30.	Clarence Lovell	Mercury
31.	Charlie Glotzbach	Chevrolet
32.	Frank Warren	Dodge
33.	Bobby Isaac	Ford
34.	Joe Frasson	Dodge
35.	Elmo Langley	Ford
36.	Lennie Pond	Chevrolet
37.	Larry Smith	Mercury
38.	Earl Brooks	Ford
39.	Bill Champion	Mercury
40.	Dave Marcis	Dodge

VIRGINIA 500

April 29
Martinsville, Virginia
Time of Race: 3 hours, 44 minutes, 28 seconds
Average Speed: 70.251 mph

FINISH	DRIVER	CAR
1.	David Pearson	Mercury
2.	Cale Yarborough	Chevrolet
3.	Bobby Isaac	Ford
4.	Buddy Baker	Dodge
5.	Cecil Gordon	Chevrolet
6.	Benny Parsons	Chevrolet
7.	Jimmy Hensley	Mercury
8.	Walter Ballard	Mercury
9.	Vic Parsons	Ford
10.	James Hylton	Ford
11.	Elmo Langley	Ford
12.	Rick Newsom	Ford
13.	J. D. McDuffie	Chevrolet
14.	Henley Gray	Ford
15.	Earl Brooks	Ford
16.	Frank Warren	Ford
17.	Bill Dennis	Chevrolet
18.	Buddy Arrington	Dodge
19.	Lennie Pond	Chevrolet
20.	Charlie Roberts	Ford
21.	Richard Petty	Dodge
22.	Ed Negre	Mercury
23.	Ronnie Daniels	Chevrolet
24.	Richard Childress	Chevrolet
25.	David Sisco	Chevrolet
26.	Dave Marcis	Matador
27.	Donnie Allison	Chevrolet
28.	John Sears	Dodge
29.	Dean Dalton	Mercury
30.	Jabe Thomas	Dodge
31.	Raymond Williams	Ford
32.	Bobby Allison	Chevrolet
33.	Richard Brown	Chevrolet
34.	Bill Champion	Ford

WINSTON 500

May 6
Talladega, Alabama

Time of Race: 3 hours, 47 minutes, 23 seconds
Average Speed: 131.958 mph

FINISH	DRIVER	CAR
1.	David Pearson	Mercury
2.	Donnie Allison	Chevrolet
3.	Benny Parsons	Chevrolet
4.	Clarence Lovell	Chevrolet
5.	Cecil Gordon	Chevrolet
6.	Coo Coo Marlin	Chevrolet
7.	Dick Simon	Dodge
8.	Jim Vandiver	Dodge
9.	Vic Parsons	Mercury
10.	Charles Barrett	Ford
11.	Ed Negre	Dodge
12.	Eddie Bond	Dodge
13.	Tommy Gale	Mercury
14.	Earl Ross	Chevrolet
15.	Jabe Thomas	Dodge
16.	Dean Dalton	Mercury
17.	Dave Marcis	Dodge
18.	J. D. McDuffie	Chevrolet
19.	Elmo Langley	Ford
20.	John Sears	Dodge
21.	Dick May	Mercury
22.	Richard Childress	Chevrolet
23.	Dick Brooks	Plymouth
24.	Frank Warren	Dodge
25.	Paul Tyler	Mercury
26.	Bobby Isaac	Ford
27.	Johnny Barnes	Mercury
28.	Raymond Williams	Ford
29.	Mel Larson	Chevrolet
30.	Tony Bettenhausen Jr.	Chevrolet
31.	Darrell Waltrip	Mercury
32.	Red Farmer	Ford
33.	D. K. Ulrich	Ford
34.	Henley Gray	Mercury
35.	Richard Petty	Dodge
36.	David Sisco	Chevrolet
37.	Bill Champion	Mercury
38.	Gordon Johncock	Chevrolet
39.	Alton Jones	Chevrolet
40.	Buddy Baker	Dodge
41.	Cale Yarborough	Chevrolet
42.	Bobby Allison	Chevrolet
43.	Joe Frasson	Dodge
44.	Ramo Stott	Mercury
45.	James Hylton	Mercury
46.	Lennie Pond	Chevrolet
47.	Slick Gardner	Mercury
48.	Walter Ballard	Mercury
49.	Buddy Arrington	Plymouth
50.	Ron Keselowski	Dodge
51.	Bill Ward	Chevrolet
52.	Ben Arnold	Mercury
53.	Charlie Roberts	Ford
54.	Bobby Mausgrover	Ford
55.	Wendell Scott	Mercury
56.	Earl Brooks	Ford
57.	Ronnie Daniel	Chevrolet
58.	Larry Smith	Mercury
59.	Eddie Yarboro	Dodge
60.	Richard Brown	Chevrolet

MUSIC CITY 420

May 20
Nashville, Tennessee
Time of Race: 2 hours, 34 minutes, 48 seconds
Average Speed: 98.419 mph

FINISH	DRIVER	CAR
1.	Cale Yarborough	Chevrolet
2.	Benny Parsons	Chevrolet
3.	Buddy Baker	Dodge
4.	Cecil Gordon	Chevrolet
5.	Bobby Allison	Chevrolet

6.	Coo Coo Marlin	Chevrolet
7.	Bobby Isaac	Ford
8.	David Sisco	Chevrolet
9.	J. D. McDuffie	Chevrolet
10.	Vic Parsons	Ford
11.	Dave Marcis	Dodge
12.	James Hylton	Mercury
13.	Richard Petty	Dodge
14.	Buddy Arrington	Dodge
15.	Dean Dalton	Mercury
16.	Rick Newsom	Ford
17.	Elmo Langley	Ford
18.	Jabe Thomas	Dodge
19.	Bob Brown	Chevrolet
20.	Frank Warren	Dodge
21.	Charlie Roberts	Ford
22.	Walter Ballard	Mercury
23.	Richard Childress	Chevrolet
24.	Darrell Waltrip	Mercury
25.	Henley Gray	Ford
26.	Alton Jones	Chevrolet
27.	Ed Negre	Mercury
28.	Bobby Poole	Mercury

WORLD 600

May 27
Charlotte, North Carolina
Time of Race: 4 hours, 26 minutes, 53 seconds
Average Speed: 134.890 mph

FINISH	DRIVER	CAR
1.	Buddy Baker	Dodge
2.	David Pearson	Mercury
3.	Cale Yarborough	Chevrolet
4.	Bobby Isaac	Ford
5.	Benny Parsons	Chevrolet
6.	Jim Vandiver	Dodge
7.	Darrell Waltrip	Mercury
8.	Cecil Gordon	Chevrolet
9.	Dick Brooks	Ford
10.	David Sisco	Chevrolet
11.	Richard Childress	Chevrolet
12.	James Hylton	Mercury
13.	Richard Petty	Dodge
14.	Elmo Langley	Ford
15.	Larry Smith	Mercury
16.	Bill Champion	Ford
17.	Raymond Williams	Ford
18.	Walter Ballard	Mercury
19.	Ed Negre	Dodge
20.	Charlie Blanton	Dodge
21.	J. D. McDuffie	Chevrolet
22.	Billy Scott	Chevrolet
23.	Frank Warren	Dodge
24.	Charlie Glotzbach	Chevrolet
25.	Joe Frasson	Dodge
26.	Vic Parsons	Ford
27.	Charles Barrett	Ford
28.	Dave Marcis	Matador
29.	G. C. Spencer	Dodge
30.	Dean Dalton	Mercury
31.	Jabe Thomas	Dodge
32.	Buddy Arrington	Plymouth
33.	Coo Coo Marlin	Chevrolet
34.	Neil Castles	Dodge
35.	Paul Tyler	Mercury
36.	Tiny Lund	Chevrolet
37.	Peter Gregg	Dodge
38.	Lennie Pond	Chevrolet
39.	Richard Brown	Chevrolet
40.	Alton Jones	Chevrolet

MASON-DIXON 500

June 3
Dover, Delaware

Time of Race: 4 hours, 10 minutes, 32 seconds
Average Speed: 119.745 mph

FINISH	DRIVER	CAR
1.	David Pearson	Mercury
2.	Cale Yarborough	Chevrolet
3.	Bobby Allison	Chevrolet
4.	Richard Petty	Dodge
5.	Cecil Gordon	Chevrolet
6.	Benny Parsons	Chevrolet
7.	Buddy Baker	Dodge
8.	Dave Marcis	Matador
9.	Dean Dalton	Mercury
10.	David Sisco	Chevrolet
11.	Jabe Thomas	Dodge
12.	James Hylton	Mercury
13.	Henley Gray	Mercury
14.	Charlie Roberts	Ford
15.	Bill Hollar	Mercury
16.	Jimmy Crawford	Plymouth
17.	Elmo Langley	Ford
18.	Richard Childress	Chevrolet
19.	J. D. McDuffie	Chevrolet
20.	Lennie Pond	Chevrolet
21.	Buddy Arrington	Dodge
22.	John Sears	Dodge
23.	Paul Tyler	Mercury
24.	Frank Warren	Dodge
25.	Raymond Williams	Ford
26.	G. C. Spencer	Dodge
27.	D. K. Ulrich	Ford
28.	Walter Ballard	Mercury
29.	Bobby Isaac	Ford
30.	Vic Parsons	Ford
31.	Bill Champion	Mercury
32.	Mel Larson	Chevrolet
33.	Ed Negre	Dodge
34.	Earle Canavan	Plymouth
35.	Coo Coo Marlin	Chevrolet
36.	Richard Brown	Chevrolet
37.	Neil Castles	Dodge
38.	Donnie Allison	Chevrolet
39.	Rick Newsom	Ford
40.	Eddie Pettyjohn	Mercury

ALAMO 500

June 10
College Station, Texas
Time of Race: 3 hours, 26 minutes, 44 seconds
Average Speed: 142.114 mph

FINISH	DRIVER	CAR
1.	Richard Petty	Dodge
2.	Darrell Waltrip	Chevrolet
3.	Joe Frasson	Dodge
4.	Cale Yarborough	Chevrolet
5.	Cecil Gordon	Chevrolet
6.	Buddy Baker	Dodge
7.	Benny Parsons	Chevrolet
8.	Ramo Stott	Plymouth
9.	David Sisco	Chevrolet
10.	J. D. McDuffie	Chevrolet
11.	H. B. Bailey	Pontiac
12.	Jabe Thomas	Dodge
13.	Frank Warren	Dodge
14.	Bill Champion	Ford
15.	James Hylton	Ford
16.	Walter Ballard	Mercury
17.	Buddy Arrington	Plymouth
18.	Charlie Roberts	Ford
19.	Henley Gray	Mercury
20.	Ed Sczech	Chevrolet
21.	Bob Whitlow	Ford
22.	Dean Dalton	Ford
23.	Tony Bettenhausen	Chevrolet
24.	Lennie Pond	Chevrolet
25.	Raymond Williams	Ford

26.	Bobby Allison	Chevrolet
27.	Elmo Langley	Ford
28.	Coo Coo Marlin	Chevrolet
29.	Marty Robbins	Dodge
30.	Jimmy Crawford	Plymouth
31.	D. K. Ulrich	Ford
32.	Bobby Isaac	Ford
33.	Dave Marcis	Matador
34.	Rick Newsom	Ford
35.	Richard Childress	Chevrolet
36.	Mel Larson	Ford
37.	Ed Negre	Dodge
38.	Richie Panch	Ford

TUBORG 400

June 17
Riverside, California
Time of Race: 4 hours, 0 minutes, 0 seconds
Average Speed: 100.215 mph

FINISH	DRIVER	CAR
1.	Bobby Allison	Chevrolet
2.	Richard Petty	Dodge
3.	Benny Parsons	Chevrolet
4.	Jimmy Insolo	Chevrolet
5.	Cecil Gordon	Chevrolet
6.	Richard White	Ford
7.	Hershel McGriff	Plymouth
8.	James Hylton	Ford
9.	Jack McCoy	Dodge
10.	Chuck Bown	Dodge
11.	Bill Champion	Mercury
12.	J. D. McDuffie	Chevrolet
13.	Larry Smith	Mercury
14.	Leon Fox	Chevrolet
15.	Walter Ballard	Mercury
16.	George Behlman	Chevrolet
17.	Richard Childress	Chevrolet
18.	Glen Francis	Chevrolet
19.	Elmo Langley	Ford
20.	Mike James	Chevrolet
21.	Johnny Anderson	Chevrolet
22.	Carl Adams	Ford
23.	Don Noel	Ford
24.	Cale Yarborough	Chevrolet
25.	Dick Kranzler	Chevrolet
26.	Jack Simpson	Chevrolet
27.	Henley Gray	Mercury
28.	High Pearson	Chevrolet
29.	Sonny Easley	Ford
30.	Ron Hornaday Sr.	Chevrolet
31.	John Soares Jr.	Dodge
32.	Dick Bown	Dodge
33.	Bobby Isaac	Ford
34.	Ronnie Aldeman	Chevrolet
35.	Nels Miller	Chevrolet
36.	Ray Elder	Dodge
37.	Jim Whitt	Chevrolet
38.	Buddy Baker	Dodge
39.	Chuck Wahl	Chevrolet
40.	Dean Dalton	Mercury

MOTOR STATE 400

June 24
Brooklyn, Michigan
Time of Race: 2 hours, 36 minutes, 22 seconds
Average Speed: 163.485 mph

FINISH	DRIVER	CAR
1.	David Pearson	Mercury
2.	Buddy Baker	Dodge
3.	Richard Petty	Dodge
4.	Bobby Allison	Chevrolet

5.	Ron Keselowski	Dodge
6.	Cale Yarborough	Chevrolet
7.	Donnie Allison	Chevrolet
8.	Cecil Gordon	Chevrolet
9.	Benny Parsons	Chevrolet
10.	J. D. McDuffie	Chevrolet
11.	Coo Coo Marlin	Chevrolet
12.	Earle Canavan	Plymouth
13.	Larry Smith	Mercury
14.	Richard Childress	Chevrolet
15.	James Hylton	Ford
16.	Buddy Arrington	Dodge
17.	David Sisco	Chevrolet
18.	Ed Negre	Dodge
19.	Elmo Langley	Ford
20.	Vic Parsons	Chevrolet
21.	Johnny Benson Sr.	Dodge
22.	Frank Warren	Dodge
23.	Dean Dalton	Mercury
24.	Jabe Thomas	Dodge
25.	Tommy Gale	Mercury
26.	D. K. Ulrich	Ford
27.	Charlie Roberts	Ford
28.	Rick Newsom	Ford
29.	Bill Champion	Mercury
30.	Walter Ballard	Mercury
31.	Eddie Bond	Dodge
32.	Tony Bettenhausen	Chevrolet
33.	Earl Ross	Chevrolet
34.	Henley Gray	Mercury
35.	Joe Frasson	Dodge
36.	Dave Marcis	Dodge
37.	Lennie Pond	Chevrolet
38.	John Sears	Dodge
39.	Raymond Williams	Ford
40.	Richard Brown	Chevrolet

FIRECRACKER 400

July 4
Daytona Beach, Florida
Time of Race: 2 hours, 31 minutes, 27 seconds
Average Speed: 168.488 mph

FINISH	DRIVER	CAR
1.	David Pearson	Mercury
2.	Richard Petty	Dodge
3.	Buddy Baker	Dodge
4.	Gordon Johncock	Chevrolet
5.	Benny Parsons	Chevrolet
6.	Dave Marcis	Dodge
7.	Vic Parsons	Ford
8.	Marty Robbins	Dodge
9.	Dick Brooks	Ford
10.	Joe Frasson	Dodge
11.	David Sisco	Chevrolet
12.	James Hylton	Mercury
13.	Cecil Gordon	Chevrolet
14.	G. C. Spencer	Dodge
15.	Roy Mayne	Dodge
16.	Elmo Langley	Ford
17.	Dean Dalton	Mercury
18.	Buddy Arrington	Plymouth
19.	Frank Warren	Dodge
20.	Lennie Pond	Chevrolet
21.	Larry Smith	Mercury
22.	Raymond Williams	Ford
23.	Henley Gray	Mercury
24.	Bill Champion	Mercury
25.	Darrell Waltrip	Mercury
26.	Walter Ballard	Mercury
27.	Richard Childress	Chevrolet
28.	Donnie Allison	Chevrolet
29.	Ed Negre	Dodge
30.	Bobby Allison	Chevrolet
31.	Jabe Thomas	Dodge
32.	Jim Vandiver	Dodge
33.	John Sears	Dodge
34.	Ed Sczech	Chevrolet
35.	Dick Simon	Dodge

36.	Cale Yarborough	Chevrolet
37.	A. J. Foyt	Chevrolet
38.	Coo Coo Marlin	Chevrolet
39.	Bobby Isaac	Ford
40.	J. D. McDuffie	Chevrolet

VOLUNTEER 500

July 8
Bristol, Tennessee
Time of Race: 2 hours, 53 minutes, 4 seconds
Average Speed: 912.342 mph

FINISH	DRIVER	CAR
1.	Benny Parsons	Chevrolet
2.	L. D. Ottinger	Chevrolet
3.	Cecil Gordon	Chevrolet
4.	Lennie Pond	Chevrolet
5.	J. D. McDuffie	Chevrolet
6.	Ed Negre	Dodge
7.	Raymond Williams	Ford
8.	James Hylton	Mercury
9.	Elmo Langley	Ford
10.	Henley Gray	Mercury
11.	David Sisco	Chevrolet
12.	Rick Newsom	Ford
13.	Jabe Thomas	Dodge
14.	Walter Ballard	Mercury
15.	Frank Warren	Dodge
16.	Ronnie Daniel	Chevrolet
17.	Charlie Roberts	Ford
18.	Bill Champion	Mercury
19.	Cale Yarborough	Chevrolet
20.	Bobby Allison	Chevrolet
21.	Richard Petty	Dodge
22.	Bobby Isaac	Ford
23.	Dean Dalton	Mercury
24.	D. K. Ulrich	Ford
25.	Richard Childress	Chevrolet
26.	Richard Brown	Chevrolet
27.	Coo Coo Marlin	Chevrolet
28.	Dave Marcis	Matador
29.	G. C. Spencer	Dodge
30.	Buddy Arrington	Dodge

DIXIE 500

July 22
Atlanta, Georgia
Time of Race: 3 hours, 50 minutes, 1 second
Average Speed: 130.211 mph

FINISH	DRIVER	CAR
1.	David Pearson	Mercury
2.	Cale Yarborough	Chevrolet
3.	Donnie Allison	Chevrolet
4.	Joe Frasson	Dodge
5.	Jody Ridley	Mercury
6.	Lennie Pond	Chevrolet
7.	J. D. McDuffie	Chevrolet
8.	G. C. Spencer	Dodge
9.	Jabe Thomas	Dodge
10.	Larry Smith	Mercury
11.	Buddy Arrington	Dodge
12.	Rick Newsom	Ford
13.	Henley Gray	Ford
14.	Frank Warren	Dodge
15.	Walter Ballard	Mercury
16.	Randy Tissot	Chevrolet
17.	Bill Champion	Mercury
18.	Ed Negre	Dodge
19.	Charlie Robert	Ford
20.	Raymond Williams	Ford
21.	James Hylton	Ford
22.	Dean Dalton	Mercury

23.	Richard Childress	Chevrolet
24.	Cecil Gordon	Chevrolet
25.	Benny Parsons	Chevrolet
26.	David Sisco	Chevrolet
27.	Bobby Allison	Chevrolet
28.	Ed Sczech	Chevrolet
29.	Vic Parsons	Ford
30.	Coo Coo Marlin	Chevrolet
31.	Darrell Waltrip	Mercury
32.	Dave Marcis	Dodge
33.	Richard Petty	Dodge
34.	Buddy Baker	Dodge
35.	Bobby Isaac	Ford
36.	John Sears	Dodge
37.	Tommy Gale	Mercury
38.	Elmo Langley	Ford
39.	H. B. Bailey	Pontiac
40.	Charlie Barrett	Ford

TALLADEGA 500

August 12
Talladega, Alabama
Time of Race: 3 hours, 26 minutes, 17 seconds
Average Speed: 187.084 mph

FINISH	DRIVER	CAR
1.	Dick Brooks	Plymouth
2.	Buddy Baker	Dodge
3.	David Pearson	Mercury
4.	James Hylton	Mercury
5.	David Sisco	Chevrolet
6.	Cale Yarborough	Chevrolet
7.	Darrell Waltrip	Mercury
8.	Cecil Gordon	Mercury
9.	Walter Ballard	Mercury
10.	L. D. Ottinger	Chevrolet
11.	J. D. McDuffie	Chevrolet
12.	Dave Marcis	Dodge
13.	Bobby Isaac	Ford
14.	Richard Petty	Dodge
15.	Frank Warren	Dodge
16.	Jabe Thomas	Dodge
17.	Dean Dalton	Mercury
18.	Bill Ward	Chevrolet
19.	Alton Jones	Chevrolet
20.	Randy Tissot	Chevrolet
21.	Elmo Langley	Ford
22.	Bill Champion	Mercury
23.	Eddie Bond	Dodge
24.	Bobby Mausgrover	Chevrolet
25.	Ed Negre	Dodge
26.	Donnie Allison	Chevrolet
27.	Buddy Arrington	Plymouth
28.	Henley Gray	Mercury
29.	Bobby Allison	Chevrolet
30.	Johnny Barnes	Mercury
31.	Richard Childress	Chevrolet
32.	Red Farmer	Ford
33.	Ed Sczech	Chevrolet
34.	Bob Davis	Dodge
35.	Jim Vandiver	Dodge
36.	Marty Robbins	Dodge
37.	Jody Ridley	Mercury
38.	Benny Parsons	Chevrolet
39.	D. K. Ulrich	Ford
40.	Coo Coo Marlin	Chevrolet
41.	Phil Finney	Chevrolet
42.	Charlie Roberts	Ford
43.	Joe Frasson	Dodge
44.	Mel Larson	Dodge
45.	Ramo Stott	Chevrolet
46.	Raymond Williams	Ford
47.	Lennie Pond	Chevrolet
48.	Tommy Gale	Mercury
49.	Larry Smith	Mercury
50.	Paul Tyler	Mercury

NASHVILLE 420

August 25
Nashville, Tennessee
Time of Race: 2 hours, 48 minutes, 12 seconds
Average Speed: 89.310 mph

FINISH	DRIVER	CAR
1.	Buddy Baker	Dodge
2.	Richard Petty	Dodge
3.	Coo Coo Marlin	Chevrolet
4.	David Sisco	Chevrolet
5.	Ed Negre	Dodge
6.	James Hylton	Mercury
7.	Walter Ballard	Mercury
8.	Cecil Gordon	Chevrolet
9.	Alton Jones	Chevrolet
10.	Bill Champion	Ford
11.	Rick Newsom	Ford
12.	Buddy Arrington	Dodge
13.	Henley Gray	Mercury
14.	Cale Yarborough	Chevrolet
15.	Frank Warren	Ford
16.	Earl Brooks	Ford
17.	Charlie Roberts	Ford
18.	J. D. McDuffie	Chevrolet
19.	Benny Parsons	Chevrolet
20.	Richard Childress	Chevrolet
21.	Elmo Langley	Ford
22.	Bobby Allison	Chevrolet
23.	Lennie Pond	Chevrolet
24.	Darrell Waltrip	Chevrolet
25.	Richard Brown	Chevrolet
26.	Jabe Thomas	Mercury
27.	Dean Dalton	Mercury
28.	Dick May	Ford
29.	Vic Parsons	Ford
30.	Raymond Williams	Ford
31.	Mel Larson	Dodge
32.	Dick Brooks	Mercury
33.	Bob Brown	Chevrolet

SOUTHERN 500

September 3
Darlington, South Carolina
Time of Race: 3 hours, 44 minutes, 25 seconds
Average Speed: 134.033 mph

FINISH	DRIVER	CAR
1.	Cale Yarborough	Chevrolet
2.	David Pearson	Mercury
3.	Buddy Baker	Dodge
4.	Richard Petty	Dodge
5.	Benny Parsons	Chevrolet
6.	Bobby Allison	Chevrolet
7.	Coo Coo Marlin	Chevrolet
8.	Darrell Waltrip	Ford
9.	Dick Brooks	Chevrolet
10.	J. D. McDuffie	Chevrolet
11.	Cecil Gordon	Chevrolet
12.	James Hylton	Mercury
13.	Jabe Thomas	Dodge
14.	Buddy Arrington	Dodge
15.	Randy Tissot	Chevrolet
16.	Charlie Roberts	Chevrolet
17.	Walter Ballard	Mercury
18.	D. K. Ulrich	Ford
19.	Dean Dalton	Mercury
20.	Henley Gray	Mercury
21.	Mel Larson	Dodge
22.	Bill Champion	Mercury
23.	Joe Frasson	Dodge
24.	Frank Warren	Dodge
25.	Raymond Williams	Ford
26.	Ed Negre	Dodge
27.	Jim Vandiver	Dodge

28.	David Sisco	Chevrolet
29.	Bud Moore	Mercury
30.	Charlie Glotzbach	Chevrolet
31.	Elmo Langley	Ford
32.	Dick May	Mercury
33.	Richie Panch	Ford
34.	Vic Parsons	Ford
35.	Johnny Barnes	Mercury
36.	Tommy Gale	Mercury
37.	Lennie Pond	Chevrolet
38.	Richard Brown	Chevrolet
39.	G. C. Spencer	Dodge
40.	Richard Childress	Chevrolet

CAPITAL CITY 500

September 9
Richmond, Virginia
Time of Race: 4 hours, 13 minutes, 17 seconds
Average Speed: 83.215 mph

FINISH	DRIVER	CAR
1.	Richard Petty	Dodge
2.	Cale Yarborough	Chevrolet
3.	Bobby Allison	Chevrolet
4.	Benny Parsons	Chevrolet
5.	Buddy Arrington	Dodge
6.	Walter Ballard	Mercury
7.	Cecil Gordon	Chevrolet
8.	James Hylton	Mercury
9.	Henley Gray	Mercury
10.	Raymond Williams	Ford
11.	Charlie Roberts	Ford
12.	Richard Childress	Chevrolet
13.	Rick Newsom	Ford
14.	Frank Warren	Dodge
15.	Elmo Langley	Ford
16.	David Sisco	Chevrolet
17.	Buddy Baker	Dodge
18.	Jabe Thomas	Dodge
19.	Mel Larson	Dodge
20.	John Sears	Dodge
21.	Ed Negre	Dodge
22.	Earl Brooks	Ford
23.	Ronnie Daniels	Chevrolet
24.	Dick May	Mercury
25.	D. K. Ulrich	Ford
26.	Darrell Waltrip	Ford
27.	Dick Brooks	Mercury
28.	Lennie Pond	Chevrolet
29.	J. D. McDuffie	Chevrolet
30.	Bill Champion	Ford
31.	Dean Dalton	Mercury
32.	Vic Parsons	Ford
33.	Richard Brown	Chevrolet
34.	Baxter Price	Chevrolet

DELAWARE 500

September 16
Dover, Delaware
Time of Race: 4 hours, 25 minutes, 50 seconds
Average Speed: 112.852 mph

FINISH	DRIVER	CAR
1.	David Pearson	Mercury
2.	Bobby Allison	Chevrolet
3.	Buddy Baker	Dodge
4.	Benny Parsons	Chevrolet
5.	J. D. McDuffie	Chevrolet
6.	Coo Coo Marlin	Chevrolet
7.	Richard Petty	Dodge
8.	Elmo Langley	Ford
9.	Lennie Pond	Chevrolet
10.	Eddie Pettyjohn	Mercury

11.	Ed Negre	Dodge
12.	Donnie Allison	Chevrolet
13.	Mel Larson	Dodge
14.	Jabe Thomas	Dodge
15.	Rick Newsom	Ford
16.	Richard Childress	Chevrolet
17.	Walter Ballard	Mercury
18.	Bobby Mausgrover	Chevrolet
19.	James Hylton	Chevrolet
20.	Darrell Waltrip	Chevrolet
21.	Henley Gray	Mercury
22.	Charlie Roberts	Chevrolet
23.	Raymond Williams	Ford
24.	Earle Canavan	Plymouth
25.	Cale Yarborough	Chevrolet
26.	Jimmy Crawford	Plymouth
27.	Cecil Gordon	Chevrolet
28.	Johnny Barnes	Mercury
29.	David Sisco	Chevrolet
30.	G. C. Spencer	Dodge
31.	John Sears	Dodge
32.	Ron Klowski	Dodge
33.	Earl Brooks	Ford
34.	Dean Dalton	Mercury
35.	D. K. Ulrich	Ford
36.	Vic Parsons	Chevrolet
37.	Frank Warren	Dodge
38.	Toby Tooles	Mercury
39.	Bill Champion	Mercury
40.	Buddy Arrington	Dodge

WILKES 400

September 23
North Wilkesboro, North Carolina
Time of Race: 2 hours, 37 minutes, 34 seconds
Average Speed: 95.198 mph

FINISH	DRIVER	CAR
1.	Bobby Allison	Chevrolet
2.	Richard Petty	Dodge
3.	Cale Yarborough	Chevrolet
4.	Buddy Baker	Dodge
5.	Benny Parsons	Chevrolet
6.	Lennie Pond	Chevrolet
7.	Dave Marcis	Dodge
8.	Dick Brooks	Mercury
9.	Cecil Gordon	Chevrolet
10.	J. D. McDuffie	Chevrolet
11.	Coo Coo Marlin	Chevrolet
12.	James Hylton	Mercury
13.	Walter Ballard	Mercury
14.	Elmo Langley	Ford
15.	Henley Gray	Mercury
16.	Jabe Thomas	Dodge
17.	Richard Childress	Chevrolet
18.	Raymond Williams	Ford
19.	Dean Dalton	Ford
20.	Mel Larson	Dodge
21.	Frank Warren	Dodge
22.	Ed Negre	Dodge
23.	D. K. Ulrich	Ford
24.	Earl Brooks	Ford
25.	Buddy Arrington	Dodge
26.	Charlie Roberts	Chevrolet
27.	David Sisco	Chevrolet
28.	John Sears	Dodge
29.	Bill Champion	Mercury
30.	Darrell Waltrip	Ford

OLD DOMINION 500

September 30
Martinsville, Virginia
Time of Race: 3 hours, 48 minutes, 51 seconds
Average Speed: 68.831 mph

FINISH	DRIVER	CAR
1.	Richard Petty	Dodge
2.	Cale Yarborough	Chevrolet
3.	Bobby Allison	Chevrolet
4.	Buddy Baker	Dodge
5.	Jack McCoy	Dodge
6.	Benny Parsons	Chevrolet
7.	Cecil Gordon	Chevrolet
8.	James Hylton	Mercury
9.	Buddy Arrington	Dodge
10.	J. D. McDuffie	Chevrolet
11.	Ray Hendrick	Mercury
12.	John Sears	Dodge
13.	Elmo Langley	Ford
14.	Henley Gray	Mercury
15.	Frank Warren	Dodge
16.	Jabe Thomas	Dodge
17.	Mel Larson	Dodge
18.	Walter Ballard	Mercury
19.	Earl Brooks	Ford
20.	Dean Dalton	Ford
21.	D. K. Ulrich	Ford
22.	Charlie Roberts	Chevrolet
23.	Coo Coo Marlin	Chevrolet
24.	Ronnie Daniel	Chevrolet
25.	Richard Childress	Chevrolet
26.	Ed Negre	Dodge
27.	Pee Wee WEntz	Chevrolet
28.	David Sisco	Chevrolet
29.	Raymond Williams	Ford
30.	Lennie Pond	Chevrolet
31.	David Pearson	Mercury
32.	Rick Newsom	Ford
33.	Dave Marcis	Dodge
34.	Donnie Allison	Chevrolet
35.	Richard Brown	Chevrolet
36.	Bill Champion	Ford

NATIONAL 500

October 7
Charlotte, North Carolina
Time of Race: 3 hours, 26 minutes, 58 seconds
Average Speed: 1452.240 mph

FINISH	DRIVER	CAR
1.	Cale Yarborough	Chevrolet
2.	Richard Petty	Dodge
3.	Bobby Allison	Chevrolet
4.	Benny Parsons	Chevrolet
5.	Dick Trickle	Chevrolet
6.	Lennie Pond	Chevrolet
7.	Buddy Arrington	Plymouth
8.	Elmo Langley	Ford
9.	Cecil Gordon	Chevrolet
10.	Henley Gray	Mercury
11.	Harry Gant	Ford
12.	Wendell Scott	Dodge
13.	James Hylton	Chevrolet
14.	Charlie Roberts	Chevrolet
15.	Johnny Barnes	Mercury
16.	Jimmy Crawford	Plymouth
17.	Jim Vandiver	Dodge
18.	Richard Childress	Chevrolet
19.	Coo Coo Marlin	Chevrolet
20.	Eddie Bond	Dodge
21.	David Sisco	Chevrolet
22.	Joe Frasson	Dodge
23.	Walter Ballard	Mercury
24.	Dave Marcis	Matador
25.	Jabe Thomas	Dodge
26.	Bill Champion	Mercury
27.	Ed Negre	Chevrolet
28.	L. D. Ottinger	Chevrolet
29.	J. D. McDuffie	Chevrolet
30.	Dean Dalton	Mercury
31.	Neil Castles	Dodge
32.	Donnie Allison	Chevrolet
33.	Raymond Williams	Ford
34.	Dick Brooks	Dodge

FINISH	DRIVER	CAR
35.	Frank Warren	Dodge
36.	David Pearson	Mercury
37.	Charlie Glotzbach	Chevrolet
38.	Darrell Waltrip	Ford
39.	G. C. Spencer	Dodge
40.	Wayne Andrews	Mercury
41.	Buddy Baker	Dodge

AMERICAN 500

October 21
Rockingham, North Carolina
Time of Race: 4 hours, 14 minutes, 57 seconds
Average Speed: 117.749 mph

FINISH	DRIVER	CAR
1.	David Pearson	Mercury
2.	Buddy Baker	Dodge
3.	Cale Yarborough	Chevrolet
4.	Bobby Allison	Chevrolet
5.	Dave Marcis	Matador
6.	Donnie Allison	Chevrolet
7.	Richard Brooks	Dodge
8.	Charlie Glotzbach	Mercury
9.	Lennie Pond	Chevrolet
10.	Coo Coo Marlin	Chevrolet
11.	Cecil Gordon	Chevrolet
12.	Elmo Langley	Ford
13.	Johnny Rutherford	Chevrolet
14.	Richard Childress	Chevrolet
15.	David Sisco	Chevrolet
16.	Tony Bellenhausen	Chevrolet
17.	Henley Gray	Mercury
18.	Jabe Thomas	Dodge
19.	James Hylton	Chevrolet
20.	J. D. McDuffie	Chevrolet
21.	Ed Negre	Dodge
22.	Walter Ballard	Mercury
23.	Dean Dalton	Mercury
24.	Buddy Arrington	Plymouth
25.	Gordon Johncock	Chevrolet
26.	PeeWee Wentz	Chevrolet
27.	Darrell Waltrip	Ford
28.	Benny Parsons	Chevrolet
29.	Eddie Bond	Dodge
30.	Bill Champion	Mercury
31.	Jody Ridley	Ford
32.	Jim Vandiver	Dodge
33.	John Sears	Dodge
34.	Charlie Roberts	Chevrolet
35.	Richard Petty	Dodge
36.	Richie Panch	Ford
37.	Paul Tyler	Dodge
38.	Neil Castles	Dodge
39.	Richard Brown	Chevrolet
40.	Joe Frasson	Dodge
41.	G. C. Spencer	Dodge
42.	Johnny Barnes	Mercury
43.	Frank Warren	Ford

1974

WINSTON WESTERN 500

January 26
Riverside, California
Time of Race: 4 hours, 56 minutes, 52 seconds
Average Speed: 101.40 mph

FINISH	DRIVER	CAR
1.	Cale Yarborough	Chevrolet
2.	Richard Petty	Dodge

FINISH	DRIVER	CAR
3.	David Pearson	Mercury
4.	Benny Parsons	Chevrolet
5.	Bobby Allison	Chevrolet
6.	Donnie Allison	Chevrolet
7.	Gary Bettenhausen	Matador
8.	Cecil Gordon	Chevrolet
9.	Richie Panch	Chevrolet
10.	Hershel McGriff	Dodge
11.	J. C. Danielson	Mercury
12.	Sonny Easley	Ford
13.	Carl Adams	Ford
14.	Dick May	Mercury
15.	Elmo Langley	Ford
16.	Charlie Roberts	Ford
17.	Tony Bettenhausen	Chevrolet
18.	George Follmer	Ford
19.	Richard White	Ford
20.	John Anderson	Chevrolet
21.	Jack McCoy	Dodge
22.	J. D. McDuffie	Chevrolet
23.	Jim Insolo	Chevrolet
24.	Odie Robertson	Chevrolet
25.	Jim Gilliam	Chevrolet
26.	Bill Osborne	Chevrolet
27.	Harry Jefferson	Ford
28.	Dave Marcis	Dodge
29.	George Esau	Chevrolet
30.	Jerry Grant	Chevrolet
31.	Dick Bown	Dodge
32.	Don Pruitt	Chevrolet
33.	Ross Surgenor	Chevrolet
34.	Ray Elder	Dodge
35.	Chuck Bown	Dodge

DAYTONA 500

February 17
Daytona Beach, Florida
Time of Race: 3 hours, 11 minutes, 38 seconds
Average Speed: 140.894 mph

FINISH	DRIVER	CAR
1.	Richard Petty	Dodge
2.	Cale Yarborough	Chevrolet
3.	Ramo Scott	Chevrolet
4.	Coo Coo Marlin	Chevrolet
5.	A. J. Foyt	Chevrolet
6.	Donnie Allison	Chevrolet
7.	Darrell Waltrip	Chevrolet
8.	Bobby Isaac	Chevrolet
9.	Dick Brooks	Dodge
10.	Walter Ballard	Chevrolet
11.	Earl Ross	Chevrolet
12.	Gary Bettenhausen	Matador
13.	Cecil Gordon	Chevrolet
14.	Dave Marcis	Dodge
15.	David Sisco	Chevrolet
16.	James Hylton	Chevrolet
17.	Bob Burcham	Chevrolet
18.	Richie Panch	Ford
19.	Jimmy Crawford	Plymouth
20.	George Follmer	Ford
21.	Bill Dennis	Ford
22.	Benny Parsons	Chevrolet
23.	Lennie Pond	Chevrolet
24.	Johnny Rutherford	Chevrolet
25.	Jim Hurtubise	Chevrolet
26.	Joe Frasson	Dodge
27.	Jim Vandiver	Dodge
28.	J. D. McDuffie	Chevrolet
29.	L. D. Ottinger	Chevrolet
30.	Bobby Allison	Chevrolet
31.	Dick Simon	Dodge
32.	Jackie Rogers	Chevrolet
33.	Tony Bettenhausen	Chevrolet
34.	Frank Warren	Dodge
35.	David Pearson	Mercury
36.	Charlie Glotzbach	Chevrolet
37.	Joe Mihalic	Chevrolet
38.	Dan Daughtry	Ford

FINISH	DRIVER	CAR
39.	Hershel McGriff	Dodge
40.	Richard Childress	Chevrolet

RICHMOND 500

February 24
Richmond, Virginia
Time of Race: 3 hours, 2 minutes, 2 seconds
Average Speed: 80.095 mph

FINISH	DRIVER	CAR
1.	Bobby Allison	Chevrolet
2.	Richard Petty	Dodge
3.	Cale Yarborough	Chevrolet
4.	Lennie Pond	Chevrolet
5.	Dave Marcis	Dodge
6.	James Hylton	Chevrolet
7.	J. D. McDuffie	Chevrolet
8.	Bill Dennis	Ford
9.	Elmo Langley	Ford
10.	Buddy Arrington	Plymouth
11.	Cecil Gordon	Chevrolet
12.	Tony Bettenhausen	Chevrolet
13.	Benny Parsons	Chevrolet
14.	Jimmy Hailey	Chevrolet
15.	Neil Castles	Dodge
16.	Richard Childress	Chevrolet
17.	Donnie Allison	Chevrolet
18.	Travis Tiller	Dodge
19.	Walter Ballard	Chevrolet
20.	Frank Warren	Dodge
21.	Richie Panch	Chevrolet
22.	D. K. Ulrich	Chevrolet
23.	David Sisco	Chevrolet
24.	Ed Negre	Dodge
25.	Jerry Hufflin	Chevrolet
26.	Jabe Thomas	Dodge
27.	Bill Champion	Ford
28.	Dean Dalton	Chevrolet

CAROLINA 500

March 3
Rockingham, North Carolina
Time of Race: 3 hours, 42 minutes, 50 seconds
Average Speed: 121.622 mph

FINISH	DRIVER	CAR
1.	Richard Petty	Dodge
2.	Cale Yarborough	Chevrolet
3.	Bobby Allison	Chevrolet
4.	Charlie Glotzbach	Chevrolet
5.	George Follmer	Ford
6.	Walter Ballard	Chevrolet
7.	Bill Dennis	Ford
8.	Dave Marcis	Dodge
9.	Lennie Pond	Chevrolet
10.	James Hylton	Chevrolet
11.	Bob Burcham	Chevrolet
12.	Dick Brooks	Dodge
13.	J. D. McDuffie	Chevrolet
14.	Richie Panch	Chevrolet
15.	Jackie Rogers	Chevrolet
16.	Buddy Arrington	Plymouth
17.	Joe Mihalic	Chevrolet
18.	Grant Adcox	Chevrolet
19.	Tony Bettenhausen Jr.	Chevrolet
20.	Frank Warren	Dodge
21.	Richard Skillen	Chevrolet
22.	Ed Negre	Dodge
23.	Benny Parsons	Chevrolet
24.	Coo Coo Marlin	Chevrolet
25.	Darrell Waltrip	Chevrolet
26.	Jimmy Crawford	Plymouth
27.	Donnie Allison	Chevrolet

FINISH	DRIVER	CAR
28.	Charlie Blanton	Dodge
29.	Cecil Gordon	Chevrolet
30.	Roy Mayne	Dodge
31.	David Sisco	Chevrolet
32.	Hershel McGriff	Dodge
33.	Dean Dalton	Chevrolet
34.	David Pearson	Mercury
35.	Neil Castles	Dodge
36.	Richard Childress	Chevrolet
37.	Joe Frasson	Dodge
38.	Elmo Langley	Ford
39.	G. C. Spencer	Dodge
40.	Charlie Roberts	Ford

SOUTHEASTERN 500

March 17
Bristol, Tennessee
Time of Race: 3 hours, 42 minutes, 50 seconds
Average Speed: 64.533 mph

FINISH	DRIVER	CAR
1.	Cale Yarborough	Chevrolet
2.	Bobby Isaac	Chevrolet
3.	Richard Petty	Dodge
3.	Benny Parsons	Chevrolet
4.	Bobby Allison	Chevrolet
5.	Donnie Allison	Chevrolet
6.	Cecil Gordon	Chevrolet
7.	Joe Mihalic	Chevrolet
8.	James Hylton	Chevrolet
9.	Alton Jones	Chevrolet
10.	Coo Coo Marlin	Chevrolet
11.	Ed Negre	Dodge
12.	J. D. McDuffie	Chevrolet
13.	Frank Warren	Dodge
14.	Walter Ballard	Chevrolet
15.	Bobby Fleming	Chevrolet
16.	Elmo Langley	Ford
17.	David Sisco	Chevrolet
18.	Bill Champion	Ford
19.	Travis Tiller	Dodge
20.	Richard Childress	Chevrolet
21.	Buddy Arrington	Plymouth
22.	Dave Marcis	Dodge
23.	Richard Petty	Dodge
24.	Dean Dalton	Chevrolet
25.	L. D. Ottinger	Chevrolet
26.	Lennie Pond	Chevrolet
27.	Richie Panch	Chevrolet
28.	George Follmer	Ford
29.	Tony Bettenhausen	Chevrolet
30.	Jabe Thomas	Dodge

ATLANTA 500

March 24
Atlanta, Georgia
Time of Race: 3 hours, 1 minute, 26 seconds
Average Speed: 136.910 mph

FINISH	DRIVER	CAR
1.	Cale Yarborough	Chevrolet
2.	David Pearson	Mercury
3.	Buddy Baker	Dodge
4.	George Follmer	Ford
5.	Donnie Allison	Chevrolet
6.	Richard Petty	Dodge
7.	Darrell Waltrip	Chevrolet
8.	Bob Burcham	Chevrolet
9.	Gary Bettenhausen	Matador
10.	Lennie Pond	Chevrolet
11.	Charlie Glotzbach	Chevrolet
12.	James Hylton	Chevrolet
13.	Earl Ross	Chevrolet
14.	David Sisco	Chevrolet

FINISH	DRIVER	CAR
15.	J. D. McDuffie	Chevrolet
16.	Jackie Rogers	Chevrolet
17.	Frank Warren	Dodge
18.	Carl Adams	Ford
19.	Joe Frasson	Dodge
20.	Dave Marcis	Dodge
21.	Roy Mayne	Dodge
22.	Ed Negre	Dodge
23.	Jim Hurtubise	Chevrolet
24.	Richard Brooks	Dodge
25.	Grant Adcox	Chevrolet
26.	Bobby Allison	Chevrolet
27.	Richard Childress	Chevrolet
28.	Coo Coo Marlin	Chevrolet
29.	Benny Parsons	Chevrolet
30.	G. C. Spencer	Dodge
31.	John Martin	Dodge
32.	Dan Daughtry	Ford
33.	Jody Ridley	Ford
34.	Cecil Gordon	Chevrolet
35.	Travis Tiller	Dodge
36.	Richie Panch	Chevrolet

REBEL 500

April 7
Darlington, South Carolina
Time of Race: 3 hours, 50 minutes, 6 seconds
Average Speed: 150.689 mph

FINISH	DRIVER	CAR
1.	David Pearson	Mercury
2.	Bobby Allison	Chevrolet
3.	Buddy Baker	Dodge
4.	Donnie Allison	Chevrolet
5.	Cale Yarborough	Chevrolet
6.	Dave Marcis	Dodge
7.	Sam McQuagg	Chevrolet
8.	Joe Frasson	Dodge
9.	Darrell Waltrip	Chevrolet
10.	Bob Burcham	Chevrolet
11.	Cecil Gordon	Chevrolet
12.	Earl Ross	Chevrolet
13.	David Sisco	Chevrolet
14.	Jackie Rogers	Chevrolet
15.	Roy Mayne	Dodge
16.	Buddy Arrington	Plymouth
17.	Frank Warren	Dodge
18.	Tony Bettenhausen	Chevrolet
19.	Coo Coo Marlin	Chevrolet
20.	Richard Petty	Dodge
21.	Lennie Pond	Chevrolet
22.	George Follmer	Ford
23.	Randy Tissot	Chevrolet
24.	Ed Negre	Dodge
25.	Richard Skillen	Chevrolet
26.	James Hylton	Chevrolet
27.	Johnny Barnes	Dodge
28.	Bill Champion	Ford
29.	Richard Brooks	Dodge
30.	J. D. McDuffie	Chevrolet
31.	Pee Wee Wentz	Chevrolet
32.	Benny Parsons	Chevrolet
33.	Bobby Isaac	Chevrolet
34.	Neil Castles	Dodge
35.	Charlie Roberts	Ford
36.	G. C. Spencer	Dodge
37.	Richie Panch	Chevrolet
38.	Elmo Langley	Ford
39.	Richard Childress	Chevrolet
40.	Walter Ballard	Chevrolet

GWYN STALEY 400

April 21
North Wilkesboro, North Carolina
Time of Race: 2 hours, 20 minutes, 20 seconds
Average Speed: 96.200 mph

FINISH	DRIVER	CAR
1.	Richard Petty	Dodge
2.	Cale Yarborough	Chevrolet
3.	Bobby Allison	Chevrolet
4.	Benny Parsons	Chevrolet
5.	Lennie Pond	Chevrolet
6.	George Follmer	Ford
7.	Donnie Allison	Chevrolet
8.	J. D. McDuffie	Chevrolet
9.	Harry Gant	Ford
10.	Dave Marcis	Dodge
11.	Cecil Gordon	Chevrolet
12.	Walter Ballard	Chevrolet
13.	Elmo Langley	Ford
14.	Tony Bettenhausen	Chevrolet
15.	David Sisco	Chevrolet
16.	Neil Castles	Dodge
17.	Ed Negre	Dodge
18.	Richie Panch	Chevrolet
19.	Frank Warren	Dodge
20.	Jabe Thomas	Dodge
21.	D. K. Ulrich	Chevrolet
22.	Richard Childress	Chevrolet
23.	Jerry Hufflin	Chevrolet
24.	Dick Brooks	Dodge
25.	Bill Champion	Ford
26.	Marv Acton	Chevrolet
27.	Buddy Arrington	Plymouth
28.	James Hylton	Chevrolet
29.	Dean Dalton	Chevrolet
30.	Ronnie Childress	Chevrolet

VIRGINIA 500

April 28
Martinsville, Virginia
Time of Race: 3 hours, 22 minutes, 41 seconds
Average Speed: 70.427 mph

FINISH	DRIVER	CAR
1.	Cale Yarborough	Chevrolet
2.	Richard Petty	Dodge
3.	Bobby Allison	Chevrolet
4.	Benny Parsons	Chevrolet
5.	Lennie Pond	Chevrolet
6.	Jimmie Hensley	Ford
7.	James Hylton	Chevrolet
8.	Dave Marcis	Dodge
9.	J. D. McDuffie	Chevrolet
10.	Richard Childress	Chevrolet
11.	Walter Ballard	Chevrolet
12.	Coo Coo Marlin	Chevrolet
13.	Richie Panch	Chevrolet
14.	Dean Dalton	Chevrolet
15.	Cecil Gordon	Chevrolet
16.	Frank Warren	Dodge
17.	Buddy Arrington	Plymouth
18.	David Sisco	Chevrolet
19.	Jabe Thomas	Dodge
20.	Travis Tiller	Dodge
21.	Ernie Shaw	Chevrolet
22.	George Follmer	Ford
23.	Donnie Allison	Chevrolet
24.	Bill Champion	Ford
25.	Bobby Isaac	Chevrolet
26.	Ed Negre	Dodge
27.	Elmo Langley	Ford
28.	Neil Castles	Dodge
29.	Tony Bettenhausen	Chevrolet
30.	Bobby Fleming	Chevrolet

WINSTON 500

May 5
Talladega, Alabama
Time of Race: 3 hours, 28 minutes, 9 seconds
Average Speed: 130.220 mph

FINISH	DRIVER	CAR
1.	David Pearson	Mercury
2.	Benny Parsons	Chevrolet
3.	Richard Petty	Dodge
4.	Charlie Glotzbach	Chevrolet
5.	Lennie Pond	Chevrolet
6.	Dave Marcis	Dodge
7.	Coo Coo Marlin	Chevrolet
8.	Sam McQuagg	Chevrolet
9.	Cale Yarborough	Chevrolet
10.	Bob Burcham	Chevrolet
11.	Richard Childress	Chevrolet
12.	Hershel McGriff	Dodge
13.	Roy Mayne	Dodge
14.	James Hylton	Chevrolet
15.	Marty Robbins	Dodge
16.	Jim Vandiver	Dodge
17.	Jackie Rogers	Chevrolet
18.	Frank Warren	Dodge
19.	J. D. McDuffie	Chevrolet
20.	Iggy Katona	Chevrolet
21.	Cecil Gordon	Chevrolet
22.	Carl Adams	Ford
23.	Elmo Langley	Ford
24.	Walter Ballard	Chevrolet
25.	Joe Frasson	Dodge
26.	D. K. Ulrich	Chevrolet
27.	Red Farmer	Ford
28.	George Follmer	Ford
29.	Richard Brooks	Dodge
30.	Tony Bettenhausen	Chevrolet
31.	Bobby Allison	Chevrolet
32.	Randy Tissot	Chevrolet
33.	Buddy Baker	Dodge
34.	Ed Negre	Dodge
35.	Travis Tiller	Dodge
36.	Donnie Allison	Chevrolet
37.	Gary Bettenhausen	Matador
38.	Grant Adcox	Chevrolet
39.	David Sisco	Chevrolet
40.	Jerry Schild	Chevrolet
41.	John Ray	Dodge
42.	John Martin	Dodge
43.	Terry Link	Pontiac
44.	Richie Panch	Chevrolet
45.	Neil Bonnett	Chevrolet
46.	Buddy Arrington	Plymouth
47.	Alton Jones	Chevrolet
48.	Dan Daughtry	Ford
49.	Dean Dalton	Chevrolet
50.	Earl Ross	Chevrolet

MUSIC CITY USA 420

May 11
Nashville, Tennessee
Time of Race: 3 hours, 6 minutes, 31 seconds
Average Speed: 84.240 mph

FINISH	DRIVER	CAR
1.	Richard Petty	Dodge
2.	Donnie Allison	Chevrolet
3.	Darrell Waltrip	Chevrolet
4.	Bob Burcham	Chevrolet
5.	Dave Marcis	Dodge
6.	George Follmer	Ford
7.	J. D. McDuffie	Chevrolet
8.	David Sisco	Chevrolet
9.	Coo Coo Marlin	Chevrolet
10.	Buddy Arrington	Plymouth
11.	Lennie Pond	Chevrolet
12.	Elmo Langley	Ford
13.	Henley Gray	Chevrolet
14.	Cale Yarborough	Chevrolet
15.	Dean Dalton	Chevrolet
16.	Benny Parsons	Chevrolet
17.	D. K. Ulrich	Chevrolet
18.	Frank Warren	Dodge
19.	Jack Donahue	Chevrolet

20.	Bobby Allison	Chevrolet
21.	Walter Ballard	Chevrolet
22.	Jerry Sisco	Chevrolet
23.	Tony Bettenhausen	Chevrolet
24.	James Hylton	Chevrolet
25.	Cecil Gordon	Chevrolet
26.	Richard Childress	Chevrolet
27.	Alton Jones	Chevrolet
28.	Richie Panch	Chevrolet

MASON-DIXON 500

May 19
Dover, Delaware
Time of Race: 3 hours, 54 minutes, 40 seconds
Average Speed: 119.99 mph

FINISH	DRIVER	CAR
1.	Cale Yarborough	Chevrolet
2.	David Pearson	Chevrolet
3.	Richard Petty	Dodge
4.	Benny Parsons	Chevrolet
5.	George Follmer	Ford
6.	Lennie Pond	Chevrolet
7.	Dave Marcis	Dodge
8.	Jackie Rogers	Chevrolet
9.	Ramo Scott	Chevrolet
10.	James Hylton	Chevrolet
11.	J. D. McDuffie	Chevrolet
12.	Buddy Arrington	Plymouth
13.	Dean Dalton	Chevrolet
14.	Ed Negre	Dodge
15.	Frank Warren	Dodge
16.	Earl Canavan	Plymouth
17.	D. K. Ulrich	Chevrolet
18.	Elmo Langley	Ford
19.	Bill Champion	Ford
20.	Darrell Waltrip	Chevrolet
21.	Richard Childress	Chevrolet
22.	Walter Ballard	Chevrolet
23.	Travis Tiller	Dodge
24.	Dave Sisco	Chevrolet
25.	Jabe Thomas	Dodge
26.	Ernie Shaw	Chevrolet
27.	Cecil Gordon	Chevrolet
28.	Bobby Allison	Chevrolet
29.	Jack Donoho	Chevrolet
30.	Donnie Allison	Chevrolet
31.	G. C. Spencer	Dodge
32.	Ed Pettyjohn	Ford
33.	Jim Bray	Chevrolet
34.	Tony Bettenhausen	Chevrolet
35.	Richard Brown	Pontiac

WORLD 600

May 26
Charlotte, North Carolina
Time of Race: 3 hours, 58 minutes, 21 seconds
Average Speed: 135.720 mph

FINISH	DRIVER	CAR
1.	David Pearson	Mercury
2.	Richard Petty	Dodge
3.	Bobby Allison	Chevrolet
4.	Darrell Waltrip	Chevrolet
5.	Earl Ross	Chevrolet
6.	Dave Marcis	Dodge
7.	Dick Trickle	Dodge
8.	Jim Vandiver	Dodge
9.	Dave Sisco	Chevrolet
10.	J. D. McDuffie	Chevrolet
11.	Cale Yarborough	Chevrolet
12.	Walter Ballard	Chevrolet
13.	Roy Mayne	Dodge

14.	Harry Gant	Ford
15.	James Hylton	Chevrolet
16.	Neil Castles	Dodge
17.	Frank Warren	Dodge
18.	Richard Skillen	Chevrolet
19.	Buddy Arrington	Plymouth
20.	Lennie Pond	Chevrolet
21.	Tony Bettenhausen	Chevrolet
22.	Buddy Baker	Dodge
23.	Richie Panch	Chevrolet
24.	Billy Scott	Chevrolet
25.	G. C. Spencer	Dodge
26.	Travis Tiller	Dodge
27.	Dick Brooks	Dodge
28.	Cecil Gordon	Chevrolet
29.	Dan Daughtry	Ford
30.	Donnie Allison	Chevrolet
31.	Benny Parsons	Chevrolet
32.	Sam McQuagg	Chevrolet
33.	Bobby Isaac	Chevrolet
34.	Richard Childress	Chevrolet
35.	Randy Tissot	Chevrolet
36.	Bob Burcham	Chevrolet
37.	Charlie Glotzbach	Chevrolet
38.	Coo Coo Marlin	Chevrolet
39.	Jackie Rogers	Chevrolet
40.	Joe Frasson	Dodge

TUBORG 400

June 9
Riverside, California
Time of Race: 3 hours, 31 minutes, 40 seconds
Average Speed: 102.489 mph

FINISH	DRIVER	CAR
1.	Cale Yarborough	Chevrolet
2.	Bobby Allison	Chevrolet
3.	Benny Parsons	Chevrolet
4.	Cecil Gordon	Chevrolet
5.	Frank Warren	Dodge
6.	James Hylton	Chevrolet
7.	Sonny Easley	Ford
8.	Chuck Wahl	Chevrolet
9.	Eddie Bradshaw	Chevrolet
10.	Don Reynolds	Chevrolet
11.	Buck Peralta	Ford
12.	Ross Sergenor	Chevrolet
13.	Glen Frances	Chevrolet
14.	Leon Fox	Chevrolet
15.	Richard Childress	Chevrolet
16.	Jack Simpson	Chevrolet
17.	J. D. McDuffie	Chevrolet
18.	Markey James	Ford
19.	Hugh Pearson	Chevrolet
20.	Chuck Bown	Dodge
21.	Walt Price	Chevrolet
22.	Jim Insolo	Chevrolet
23.	Ed Negre	Dodge
24.	Harry Schelling	Chevrolet
25.	Richard Petty	Dodge
26.	Gary Mathews	Chevrolet
27.	Dave Marcis	Dodge
28.	John Anderson	Chevrolet
29.	George Behlman	Chevrolet
30.	Dick Brown	Dodge
31.	Tony Bettenhausen	Chevrolet
32.	Jim Lee	Chevrolet
33.	George Follmer	Matador
34.	Jack McCoy	Dodge
35.	Hershel McGriff	Chevrolet

MOTORSTATE 400

June 16
Brooklyn, Michigan
Time of Race: 2 hours, 48 minutes, 46 seconds
Average Speed: 127.098 mph

FINISH	DRIVER	CAR
1.	Richard Petty	Dodge
2.	Earl Ross	Chevrolet
3.	David Pearson	Mercury
4.	Gary Bettenhausen	Matador
5.	Marty Robbins	Dodge
6.	Richard Childress	Chevrolet
7.	David Sisco	Chevrolet
8.	Dave Marcis	Dodge
9.	Richie Panch	Chevrolet
10.	Cecil Gordon	Chevrolet
11.	Jackie Rogers	Chevrolet
12.	Buddy Arrington	Plymouth
13.	Coo Coo Marlin	Chevrolet
14.	Frank Warren	Dodge
15.	D. K. Ulrich	Chevrolet
16.	Bob Burcham	Chevrolet
17.	J. D. McDuffie	Chevrolet
18.	Joe Frasson	Dodge
19.	Dick Brooks	Dodge
20.	Donnie Allison	Chevrolet
21.	Dean Dalton	Chevrolet
22.	Henley Gray	Chevrolet
23.	Bobby Allison	Chevrolet
24.	Ron Keselowski	Dodge
25.	Benny Parsons	Chevrolet
26.	Lennie Pond	Chevrolet
27.	Cale Yarborough	Chevrolet
28.	Jabe Thomas	Dodge
29.	Travis Tiller	Dodge
30.	Buddy Baker	Ford
31.	Ed Negre	Dodge
32.	James Hylton	Chevrolet
33.	Bill Champion	Ford
34.	Neil Castles	Dodge
35.	Walter Ballard	Chevrolet
36.	Tony Bettenhausen	Chevrolet

FIRECRACKER 400

July 4
Daytona Beach, Florida
Time of Race: 2 hours, 53 minutes, 32 seconds
Average Speed: 138.301 mph

FINISH	DRIVER	CAR
1.	David Pearson	Mercury
2.	Richard Petty	Dodge
3.	Buddy Baker	Ford
4.	Cale Yarborough	Chevrolet
5.	Bobby Allison	Chevrolet
6.	Bobby Isaac	Chevrolet
7.	Lennie Pond	Chevrolet
8.	Jackie Rogers	Chevrolet
9.	David Sisco	Chevrolet
10.	Cecil Gordon	Chevrolet
11.	J. D. McDuffie	Chevrolet
12.	Dean Dalton	Chevrolet
13.	Earl Ross	Chevrolet
14.	Tony Bettenhausen	Chevrolet
15.	Richard Brooks	Dodge
16.	Frank Warren	Dodge
17.	Joe Frasson	Dodge
18.	Coo Coo Marlin	Chevrolet
19.	Dave Marcis	Dodge
20.	Walter Ballard	Chevrolet
21.	Buddy Arrington	Plymouth
22.	Charles Glotzbach	Ford
23.	Richard Childress	Chevrolet
24.	Darrell Waltrip	Chevrolet
25.	Roy Mayne	Dodge
26.	Ed Negre	Dodge
27.	Benny Parsons	Chevrolet
28.	Ron Keselowski	Dodge
29.	A. J. Foyt	Chevrolet
30.	G. C. Spencer	Dodge
31.	Dan Daughtry	Ford
32.	James Hylton	Chevrolet
33.	Donnie Allison	Chevrolet

FINISH	DRIVER	CAR
34.	Richie Panch	Chevrolet
35.	Jim Vandiver	Dodge
36.	Jim Crawford	Plymouth
37.	L. D. Ottinger	Chevrolet
38.	Bob Burcham	Chevrolet
39.	Johnny Rutherford	Chevrolet
40.	Bill Champion	Ford

VOLUNTEER 500

July 14
Bristol, Tennessee
Time of Race: 3 hours, 31 minutes, 59 seconds
Average Speed: 75.430 mph

FINISH	DRIVER	CAR
1.	Cale Yarborough	Chevrolet
2.	Buddy Baker	Ford
3.	Richard Petty	Dodge
4.	Charles Glotzbach	Ford
5.	Bobby Allison	Chevrolet
6.	Cecil Gordon	Chevrolet
7.	Richard Brooks	Dodge
8.	Buddy Arrington	Plymouth
9.	Dave Marcis	Dodge
10.	Walter Ballard	Chevrolet
11.	J. D. McDuffie	Chevrolet
12.	Coo Coo Marlin	Chevrolet
13.	Ed Negre	Dodge
14.	Bob Burcham	Chevrolet
15.	Richie Panch	Chevrolet
16.	Earl Ross	Chevrolet
17.	Benny Parsons	Chevrolet
18.	Ernie Shaw	Chevrolet
19.	David Sisco	Chevrolet
20.	James Hylton	Chevrolet
21.	Frank Warren	Dodge
22.	Bill Champion	Ford
23.	D. K. Ulrich	Chevrolet
24.	Richard Childress	Chevrolet
25.	L. D. Ottinger	Chevrolet
26.	Tony Bettenhausen	Chevrolet
27.	Elmo Langley	Ford
28.	Dean Dalton	Chevrolet
29.	Roy Mayne	Dodge
30.	Jackie Rogers	Chevrolet

NASHVILLE 420

July 20
Nashville, Tennessee
Time of Race: 3 hours, 10 minutes, 40 seconds
Average Speed: 76.368 mph

FINISH	DRIVER	CAR
1.	Cale Yarborough	Chevrolet
2.	Bobby Allison	Chevrolet
3.	Darrell Waltrip	Chevrolet
4.	David Sisco	Chevrolet
5.	Alton Jones	Chevrolet
6.	Charles Glotzbach	Ford
7.	Benny Parsons	Chevrolet
8.	Earl Ross	Chevrolet
9.	Buddy Arrington	Plymouth
10.	Richie Panch	Chevrolet
11.	Tony Bettenhausen	Chevrolet
12.	D. K. Ulrich	Chevrolet
13.	Richard Petty	Dodge
14.	Henley Gray	Chevrolet
15.	Dean Dalton	Chevrolet
16.	Ernie Shaw	Chevrolet
17.	Bobby Ore	Chevrolet
18.	Elmo Langley	Ford
19.	Dick Simpson	Chevrolet
20.	Cecil Gordon	Chevrolet

FINISH	DRIVER	CAR
21.	Dave Marcis	Dodge
22.	James Hylton	Chevrolet
23.	Richard Childress	Chevrolet
24.	Roy Mayne	Dodge
25.	Buddy Baker	Ford
26.	Walter Ballard	Chevrolet
27.	J. D. McDuffie	Chevrolet
28.	Coo Coo Marlin	Chevrolet
29.	Ed Negre	Dodge
30.	Frank Warren	Dodge

DIXIE 500

July 28
Atlanta, Georgia
Time of Race: 3 hours, 42 minutes, 31 seconds
Average Speed: 131.651 mph

FINISH	DRIVER	CAR
1.	Richard Petty	Dodge
2.	David Pearson	Mercury
3.	Buddy Baker	Ford
4.	Darrell Waltrip	Chevrolet
5.	Lennie Pond	Chevrolet
6.	Dave Marcis	Dodge
7.	Joe Frasson	Dodge
8.	Benny Parsons	Chevrolet
9.	Coo Coo Marlin	Chevrolet
10.	Cecil Gordon	Chevrolet
11.	Richard Childress	Chevrolet
12.	David Sisco	Chevrolet
13.	Walter Ballard	Chevrolet
14.	Cale Yarborough	Chevrolet
15.	Buddy Arrington	Plymouth
16.	Elmo Langley	Ford
17.	Frank Warren	Dodge
18.	Jackie Rogers	Chevrolet
19.	J. D. McDuffie	Chevrolet
20.	Earl Ross	Chevrolet
21.	G. C. Spencer	Dodge
22.	Bob Burcham	Chevrolet
23.	James Hylton	Chevrolet
24.	Tony Bettenhausen	Chevrolet
25.	Ed Negre	Dodge
26.	Charles Glotzbach	Ford
27.	Richie Panch	Chevrolet
28.	Bobby Allison	Chevrolet
29.	Dean Dalton	Chevrolet
30.	Donnie Allison	Chevrolet
31.	Jimmy Crawford	Plymouth
32.	Roy Mayne	Dodge
33.	Bill Champion	Ford
34.	Bobby Isaac	Chevrolet
35.	Neil Castles	Dodge

PUROLATOR 500

August 4
Pocono, Pennsylvania
Time of Race: 4 hours, 9 minutes, 9 seconds
Average Speed: 115.593 mph

FINISH	DRIVER	CAR
1.	Richard Petty	Dodge
2.	Buddy Baker	Ford
3.	Cale Yarborough	Chevrolet
4.	David Pearson	Mercury
5.	Benny Parsons	Chevrolet
6.	Dave Marcis	Dodge
7.	Cecil Gordon	Chevrolet
8.	Jan Opperman	Chevrolet
9.	Jackie Rogers	Chevrolet
10.	Ken Brightbill	Chevrolet
11.	David Sisco	Chevrolet
12.	Richard Childress	Chevrolet

13.	Earl Ross	Chevrolet
14.	Earl Canavan	Plymouth
15.	Bob Burcham	Chevrolet
16.	Buddy Arrington	Plymouth
17.	D. K. Ulrich	Chevrolet
18.	Elmo Langley	Ford
19.	Frank Warren	Dodge
20.	Ed Negre	Dodge
21.	Bobby Allison	Chevrolet
22.	Bill Champion	Ford
23.	John Martin	Dodge
24.	Travis Tiller	Dodge
25.	J. D. McDuffie	Chevrolet
26.	Richie Panch	Chevrolet
27.	Tony Bettenhausen	Chevrolet
28.	Larry Richardson	Chevrolet
29.	Walter Ballard	Chevrolet
30.	Lennie Pond	Chevrolet
31.	Roy Mayne	Dodge
32.	Dean Dalton	Chevrolet
33.	Neil Castles	Dodge
34.	James Hylton	Chevrolet
35.	Jim Bray	Chevrolet

TALLADEGA 500

August 11
Talladega, Alabama
Time of Race: 3 hours, 21 minutes, 52 seconds
Average Speed: 148.637 mph

FINISH	DRIVER	CAR
1.	Richard Petty	Dodge
2.	David Person	Mercury
3.	Bobby Allison	Matador
4.	Cale Yarborough	Chevrolet
5.	Benny Parsons	Chevrolet
6.	Buddy Baker	Ford
7.	Ramo Stott	Chevrolet
8.	Bobby Isaac	Chevrolet
9.	Marty Robbins	Dodge
10.	Earl Ross	Dodge
11.	Dave Marcis	Dodge
12.	James Hylton	Chevrolet
13.	Richard Childress	Chevrolet
14.	Ed Negre	Dodge
15.	Cecil Gordon	Chevrolet
16.	Jerry Schield	Chevrolet
17.	Frank Warren	Dodge
18.	Dick May	Ford
19.	Roy Mayne	Dodge
20.	Elmo Langley	Ford
21.	Jackie Rogers	Chevrolet
22.	John Ray	Dodge
23.	Red Farmer	Ford
24.	J. D. McDuffie	Chevrolet
25.	Jerry Hansen	Chevrolet
26.	Alton Jones	Chevrolet
27.	Bob Burcham	Chevrolet
28.	David Sisco	Chevrolet
29.	Dick Brooks	Dodge
30.	D. K. Ulrich	Chevrolet
31.	Phil Finney	Chevrolet
32.	Tony Bettenhausen	Chevrolet
33.	Jim Vandiver	Dodge
34.	Charlie. Glotzbach	Ford
35.	Coo Coo Marlin	Chevrolet
36.	Bill Champion	Ford
37.	Terry Link	Pontiac
38.	Travis Tiller	Dodge
39.	Neil Bonnett	Chevrolet
40.	Donnie Allison	Chevrolet
41.	Dan Daughtry	Ford
42.	Joe Frasson	Dodge
43.	Richie Panch	Ford
44.	Darrell Waltrip	Chevrolet
45.	A. J. Reno	Chevrolet
46.	Neil Castles	Dodge
47.	Johnny Barnes	Ford
48.	Walter Ballard	Chevrolet

YANKEE 400

August 25
Brooklyn, Michigan
Time of Race: 3 hours, 23 seconds
Average Speed: 133.045 mph

FINISH	DRIVER	CAR
1.	David Pearson	Mercury
2.	Richard Petty	Dodge
3.	Cale Yarborough	Dodge
4.	Buddy Baker	Ford
5.	Bobby Allison	Matador
6.	Earl Ross	Chevrolet
7.	Dave Marcis	Dodge
8.	Richard Brooks	Dodge
9.	David Sisco	Chevrolet
10.	Richie Panch	Chevrolet
11.	Coo Coo Marlin	Chevrolet
12.	Cecil Gordon	Chevrolet
13.	J. D. McDuffie	Chevrolet
14.	Bob Burcham	Chevrolet
15.	Earl Canavan	Plymouth
16.	Elmo Langley	Ford
17.	Travis Tiller	Dodge
18.	Clyde Dagit	Dodge
19.	Bob Whitlow	Dodge
20.	Frank Warren	Dodge
21.	Ed Negre	Chevrolet
22.	Benny Parsons	Chevrolet
23.	Joe Frasson	Dodge
24.	Walter Ballard	Chevrolet
25.	Tony Bettenhausen	Chevrolet
26.	Jerry Hansen	Chevrolet
27.	Richard Childress	Chevrolet
28.	D. K. Ulrich	Dodge
29.	Ron Keselowski	Dodge
30.	Bill Champion	Ford
31.	Jackie Rogers	Chevrolet
32.	Jabe Thomas	Dodge
33.	John Banks	Dodge
34.	Jim Bray	Chevrolet
35.	James Hylton	Chevrolet
36.	Gary Myers	Chevrolet

SOUTHERN 500

September 2
Darlington, South Carolina
Time of Race: 3 hours, 30 minutes, 48 seconds
Average Speed: 111.075 mph

FINISH	DRIVER	CAR
1.	Cale Yarborough	Chevrolet
2.	Darrell Waltrip	Chevrolet
3.	David Sisco	Chevrolet
4.	Dave Marcis	Dodge
5.	James Hylton	Chevrolet
6.	G. C. Spencer	Dodge
7.	Jackie Rogers	Chevrolet
8.	Jerry Schild	Dodge
9.	Joe Frasson	Dodge
10.	PeeWee Wentz	Plymouth
11.	Tony Bettenhausen	Chevrolet
12.	Frank Warren	Dodge
13.	Lennie Pond	Chevrolet
14.	Charlie Glotzbach	Ford
15.	Jim Vandiver	Dodge
16.	Walter Ballard	Dodge
17.	J. D. McDuffie	Chevrolet
18.	Richard Childress	Chevrolet
19.	Cecil Gordon	Chevrolet
20.	Elmo Langley	Ford
21.	Ed Negre	Dodge
22.	Earl Ross	Chevrolet
23.	Earl Canavan	Plymouth
24.	Richie Panch	Chevrolet

FINISH	DRIVER	CAR
25.	David Pearson	Mercury
26.	Benny Parsons	Chevrolet
27.	Bob Burcham	Chevrolet
28.	Ramo Stott	Chevrolet
29.	Coo Coo Marlin	Chevrolet
30.	Bobby Allison	Matador
31.	Bill Champion	Ford
32.	Henley Gray	Chevrolet
33.	Buddy Baker	Ford
34.	Dick Brooks	Dodge
35.	Richard Petty	Dodge
36.	Neil Castles	Dodge
37.	Bobby Isaac	Chevrolet
38.	Jerry Hansen	Chevrolet
39.	Roy Mayne	Dodge
40.	Earl Brooks	Dodge

CAPITAL CITY 500

September 8
Richmond, Virginia
Time of Race: 4 hours, 12 minutes, 22 seconds
Average Speed: 64.430 mph

FINISH	DRIVER	CAR
1.	Richard Petty	Dodge
2.	Benny Parsons	Chevrolet
3.	Richie Panch	Chevrolet
4.	Charlie Glotzbach	Ford
5.	Walter Ballard	Chevrolet
6.	Elmo Langley	Ford
7.	Tony Bettenhausen	Chevrolet
8.	J. D. McDuffie	Chevrolet
9.	Cecil Gordon	Chevrolet
10.	Lennie Pond	Chevrolet
11.	Bill Champion	Ford
12.	Travis Tiller	Dodge
13.	Dave Marcis	Dodge
14.	Bob Burcham	Ford
15.	Earl Ross	Chevrolet
16.	Dick Brooks	Dodge
17.	David Sisco	Chevrolet
18.	Coo Coo Marlin	Chevrolet
19.	Frank Warren	Dodge
20.	Ed Negre	Dodge
21.	Cale Yarborough	Chevrolet
22.	Jackie Rogers	Chevrolet
23.	James Hylton	Chevrolet
24.	Richard Childress	Chevrolet
25.	Johnny Barnes	Chevrolet
26.	George England	Chevrolet
27.	Joey Arrington	Plymouth

DELAWARE 500

September 15
Dover, Delaware
Time of Race: 4 hours, 23 minutes, 59 seconds
Average Speed: 113.64 mph

FINISH	DRIVER	CAR
1.	Richard Petty	Dodge
2.	Buddy Baker	Ford
3.	Earl Ross	Chevrolet
4.	Benny Parsons	Chevrolet
5.	Dave Marcis	Dodge
6.	David Sisco	Dodge
7.	Cecil Gordon	Chevrolet
8.	Kenneth Brightbill	Chevrolet
9.	Henley Gray	Chevrolet
10.	Walter Ballard	Chevrolet
11.	Ed Negre	Dodge
12.	J. D. McDuffie	Chevrolet
13.	Bobby Allison	Matador
14.	Rick Newsom	Ford

FINISH	DRIVER	CAR
15.	Tony Bettenhausen	Chevrolet
16.	Frank Warren	Dodge
17.	Earl Canavan	Plymouth
18.	Richard Childress	Chevrolet
19.	James Hylton	Chevrolet
20.	Richie Panch	Chevrolet
21.	Jim Bray	Chevrolet
22.	Elmo Langley	Ford
23.	Joe Mihalic	Chevrolet
24.	William Pettyjohn	Ford
25.	Coo Coo Marlin	Chevrolet
26.	D. K. Ulrich	Chevrolet
27.	George England	Chevrolet
28.	Cale Yarborough	Chevrolet
29.	Bob Burcham	Chevrolet
30.	David Pearson	Mercury
31.	Donnie Allison	Chevrolet
32.	Lennie Pond	Chevrolet
33.	Jackie Rogers	Chevrolet
34.	Gary Myers	Chevrolet
35.	Darrell Waltrip	Chevrolet
36.	Travis Tiller	Dodge
37.	G. C. Spencer	Dodge
38.	Bill Champion	Ford
39.	Larry Manning	Plymouth
40.	Johnny Barnes	Chevrolet

WILKES 400

September 22
North Wilkesboro, North Carolina
Time of Race: 3 hours, 5 minutes, 41 seconds
Average Speed: 80.782 mph

FINISH	DRIVER	CAR
1.	Cale Yarborough	Chevrolet
2.	Richard Petty	Dodge
3.	Buddy Baker	Ford
4.	Earl Ross	Chevrolet
5.	Dave Marcis	Dodge
6.	Bobby Isaac	Chevrolet
7.	Richard Childress	Chevrolet
8.	Jackie Rogers	Chevrolet
9.	Walter Ballard	Chevrolet
10.	David Sisco	Chevrolet
11.	Coo Coo Marlin	Chevrolet
12.	Joey Arrington	Plymouth
13.	Benny Parsons	Chevrolet
14.	D. K. Ulrich	Chevrolet
15.	Charlie Glotzbach	Ford
16.	Travis Tiller	Dodge
17.	Richie Panch	Chevrolet
18.	Frank Warren	Dodge
19.	Bob Burcham	Chevrolet
20.	Jabe Thomas	Chevrolet
21.	Neil Castles	Dodge
22.	Rick Newsom	Ford
23.	J. D. McDuffie	Chevrolet
24.	James Hylton	Chevrolet
25.	Tony Bettenhausen	Chevrolet
26.	Elmo Langley	Ford
27.	Cecil Gordon	Chevrolet
28.	Bill Champion	Ford
29.	George England	Chevrolet
30.	Ed Negre	Dodge

OLD DOMINION 500

September 29,
Martinsville, Virginia
Time of Race: 3 hours, 58 minutes, 3 seconds
Average Speed: 66.232 mph

FINISH	DRIVER	CAR
1.	Earl Ross	Chevrolet
2.	Buddy Baker	Ford

3.	Donnie Allison	Chevrolet
4.	Dave Marcis	Dodge
5.	Richie Panch	Chevrolet
6.	James Hylton	Chevrolet
7.	Elmo Langley	Ford
8.	Frank Warren	Dodge
9.	Satch Worley	Plymouth
10.	Jabe Thomas	Chevrolet
11.	Cale Yarborough	Chevrolet
12.	Lennie Pond	Chevrolet
13.	D. K. Ulrich	Chevrolet
14.	Tony Bettenhausen	Chevrolet
15.	Benny Pasons	Chevrolet
16.	J. D. McDuffie	Chevrolet
17.	Ed Negre	Dodge
18.	Ray Hendrick	Dodge
19.	Jimmy Hensley	Dodge
20.	Dave Sisco	Chevrolet
21.	Sonny Hutchins	Chevrolet
22.	Coo Coo Marlin	Chevrolet
23.	Pee Wee Wentz	Chevrolet
24.	Richard Childress	Chevrolet
25.	Walter Ballard	Chevrolet
26.	Cecil Gordon	Chevrolet
27.	Randy Hutchison	Ford
28.	Jackie Rogers	Chevrolet
29.	Richard Petty	Dodge
30.	Paul Radford	Ford

NATIONAL 500

October 6
Charlotte, North Carolina
Time of Race: 4 hours, 10 minutes, 41 seconds
Average Speed: 119.912 mph

FINISH	DRIVER	CAR
1.	David Pearson	Mercury
2.	Richard Petty	Dodge
3.	Darrell Waltrip	Chevrolet
4.	Donnie Allison	Chevrolet
5.	Bobby Allison	Matador
6.	Lennie Pond	Chevrolet
7.	Harry Jefferson	Ford
8.	Dick Trickle	Dodge
9.	Bob Burcham	Chevrolet
10.	Dan Daughtry	Ford
11.	James Hylton	Chevrolet
12.	Walter Ballard	Chevrolet
13.	David Sisco	Chevrolet
14.	Richie Panch	Chevrolet
15.	Cecil Gordon	Chevrolet
16.	Ron Keselowski	Dodge
17.	Ed Negre	Dodge
18.	Grant Adcox	Chevrolet
19.	Ramo Stott	Chevrolet
20.	Earl Ross	Chevrolet
21.	J. D. McDuffie	Chevrolet
22.	Coo Coo Marlin	Chevrolet
23.	Cale Yarborough	Chevrolet
24.	Johnny Rutherford	Chevrolet
25.	Frank Warren	Dod ge
26.	A. J. Foyt	Chevrolet
27.	Benny Parsons	Chevrolet
28.	Jackie Rogers	Chevrolet
29.	Wally Dallenbach Sr.	Dodge
30.	Charles Glotzbach	Ford
31.	Dave Marcis	Dodge
32.	Bobby Isaac	Dodge
33.	Elmo Langley	Ford
34.	Jerry Schild	Chevrolet
35.	Harry Gant	Dodge
36.	Richard Brooks	Dodge
37.	Buddy Baker	Ford
38.	Joe Frasson	Dodge
39.	Jim Vandiver	Dodge
40.	Neil Castles	Dodge
41.	Richard Childress	Chevrolet
42.	Marty Robbins	Dodge

AMERICAN 500

October 20
Rockingham, North Carolina
Time of Race: 4 hours, 13 minutes, 21 seconds
Average Speed: 118.493 mph

FINISH	DRIVER	CAR
1.	David Pearson	Mercury
2.	Cale Yarborough	Chevrolet
3.	Richard Petty	Dodge
4.	Bobby Allison	Matador
5.	Darrell Waltrip	Chevrolet
6.	Donnie Allison	Chevrolet
7.	Dick Trickle	Mercury
8.	Earl Ross	Chevrolet
9.	Benny Parsons	Chevrolet
10.	Jackie Rogers	Chevrolet
11.	Lennie Pond	Chevrolet
12.	Coo Coo Marlin	Chevrolet
13.	Jerry Schild	Chevrolet
14.	Bob Burcham	Chevrolet
15.	Walter Ballard	Chevrolet
16.	Joe Mihalic	Chevrolet
17.	Joe Millikan	Plymouth
18.	James Hylton	Chevrolet
19.	J. D. McDuffie	Chevrolet
20.	Tony Bettenhausen	Chevrolet
21.	Cecil Gordon	Chevrolet
22.	Bill Champion	Ford
23.	Frank Warren	Dodge
24.	Richard Childress	Chevrolet
25.	Elmo Langley	Ford
26.	David Sisco	Chevrolet
27.	Richie Panch	Chevrolet
28.	Ed Negre	Dodge
29.	Dave Marcis	Dodge
30.	Jody Ridley	Ford
31.	Dick Brooks	Chevrolet
32.	Harry Jefferson	Ford
33.	Neil Castles	Dodge
34.	Buddy Baker	Ford
35.	G. C. Spencer	Dodge
36.	Joe Frasson	Dodge

TIMES 500

November 24
Ontario, California
Time of Race: 3 hours, 42 minutes, 17 seconds
Average Speed: 134.963 mph

FINISH	DRIVER	CAR
1.	Bobby Allison	Matador
2.	David pearson	Mercury
3.	Cale Yarborough	Chevrolet
4.	A. J. Foyt	Chevrolet
5.	Buddy Baker	Ford
6.	Darrell Waltrip	Chevrolet
7.	Ramo Stott	Chevrolet
8.	Earl Ross	Chevrolet
9.	Richie Panch	Chevrolet
10.	J. D. McDuffie	Chevrolet
11.	David Sisco	Chevrolet
12.	Richard Childress	Chevrolet
13.	Bruce Hill	Chevrolet
14.	James Hylton	Chevrolet
15.	Richard Petty	Dodge
16.	Walter Ballard	Chevrolet
17.	Dave Marcis	Ford
18.	Don Reynolds	Chevrolet
19.	Jim Insolo	Chevrolet
20.	Chuck Wahl	Chevrolet
21.	Frank Warren	Dodge
22.	Glen Francis	Chevrolet
23.	Ed Negre	Dodge
24.	D. K. Ulrich	Chevrolet
25.	Jackie Rogers	Chevrolet

26.	Sonny Easley	Ford
27.	Don Hall	Chevrolet
28.	Bill Osborne	Ford
29.	Cecil Gordon	Chevrolet
30.	Earl Canavan	Plymouth
31.	Walt Price	Chevrolet
32.	George Follmer	Ford
33.	Jack McCoy	Dodge
34.	Harry Jefferson	Ford
35.	Benny Parsons	Ford
36.	Ray Elder	Dodge
37.	Hugh Pearson	Chevrolet
38.	John Martin	Chevrolet
39.	Chuck Bown	Plymouth
40.	Carl Adams	Ford

1975

Winston Western 500

January 19
Riverside, California
Time of Race: 5 hours, 4 minutes, 26 seconds
Average Speed: 98.627 mph

FINISH	DRIVER	CAR
1.	Bobby Allison	Matador
2.	David Pearson	Mercury
3.	Cecil Gordon	Chevrolet
4.	Dave Marcis	Dodge
5.	Elmo Langley	Ford
6.	James Hylton	Chevrolet
7.	Richard Petty	Dodge
8.	Gary Mathews	Chevrolet
9.	Ed Negre	Dodge
10.	Hershell McGriff	Chevrolet
11.	Richard Childress	Chevrolet
12.	Don Puskarich	Chevrolet
13.	Ray Elder	Dodge
14.	J. D. McDuffie	Chevrolet
15.	Larry Esau	Chevrolet
16.	Bill Osborne	Ford
17.	Chuck Wahl	Chevrolet
18.	Bill Schmitt	Chevrolet
19.	Richard White	Chevrolet
20.	Don Reynolds	Chevrolet
21.	Sonny Easley	Ford
22.	Ron Esau	Chevrolet
23.	Hugh Pearson	Chevrolet
24.	Benny Parsons	Chevrolet
25.	Glen Francis	Chevrolet
26.	Pete Torres	Ford
27.	Chuck Bown	Dodge
28.	Chuck Little	Ford
29.	G. T. Tallas	Ford
30.	Dick Bown	Chevrolet
31.	Walter Ballard	Chevrolet
32.	Harry Jefferson	Ford
33.	Jim Insolo	Chevrolet
34.	Carl Adams	Ford
35.	Ivan Baldwin	Dodge

DAYTONA 500

February 16
Daytona Beach, Florida
Time of Race: 3 hours, 15 minutes, 15 seconds
Average Speed: 153.649 mph

FINISH	DRIVER	CAR
1.	Benny Parsons	Chevrolet
2.	Bobby Allison	Matador

3.	Cale Yarborough	Chevrolet
4.	David Pearson	Mercury
5.	Ramo Stott	Chevrolet
6.	Dave Marcis	Dodge
7.	Richard Petty	Dodge
8.	Richie Panch	Chevrolet
9.	G. C. Spencer	Dodge
10.	James Hylton	Chevrolet
11.	A. J. Foyt	Chevrolet
12.	Bruce Jacobii	Chevrolet
13.	Bob Burcham	Ford
14.	Ed Negre	Dodge
15.	Cecil Gordon	Chevrolet
16.	Ferrell Harris	Dodge
17.	Coo Coo Marlin	Chevrolet
18.	Richard Childress	Chevrolet
19.	Lennie Pond	Chevrolet
20.	Buddy Baker	Ford
21.	David Sisco	Chevrolet
22.	Richard Brooks	Ford
23.	Tommy Gale	Ford
24.	George Follmer	Chevrolet
25.	Walter Ballard	Chevrolet
26.	Darrell Waltrip	Chevrolet
27.	Johnny Rutherford	Chevrolet
28.	Donnie Allison	Chevrolet
29.	Randy Tissot	Chevrolet
30.	Hershel McGriff	Chevrolet
31.	Rick Newsom	Ford
32.	Bruce Hill	Chevrolet
33.	J. D. McDuffie	Chevrolet
34.	Joe Mihalic	Chevrolet
35.	Jim Vandiver	Dodge
36.	Dick Trickle	Mercury
37.	Grant Adcox	Chevrolet
38.	Dan Daughtry	Ford
39.	Marty Robbins	Dodge
40.	Warren Tope	Ford

RICHMOND 500

February 23
Richmond, Virginia
Time of Race: 3 hours, 37 minutes, 3 seconds
Average Speed: 74.913 mph

FINISH	DRIVER	CAR
1.	Richard Petty	Dodge
2.	Lennie Pond	Chevrolet
3.	Benny Parsons	Chevrolet
4.	Dick Brooks	Ford
5.	Elmo Langley	Ford
6.	Buddy Arrington	Dodge
7.	Cecil Gordon	Chevrolet
8.	David Sisco	Chevrolet
9.	Richard Childress	Chevrolet
10.	Ed Negre	Dodge
11.	Bruce Hill	Chevrolet
12.	Jabe Thomas	Dodge
13.	Earl Canavan	Dodge
14.	James Hylton	Chevrolet
15.	Darrell Waltrip	Chevrolet
16.	Dave Marcis	Dodge
17.	Frank Warren	Dodge
18.	Neil Castles	Dodge
19.	Walter Ballard	Ford
20.	Dick May	Chevrolet
21.	Bill Champion	Chevrolet
22.	Rick Newsom	Ford

CAROLINA 500

March 2
Rockingham, North Carolina
Time of Race: 4 hours, 15 minutes, 18 seconds
Average Speed: 117.588 mph

FINISH	DRIVER	CAR
1.	Cale Yarborough	Chevrolet
2.	David Pearson	Mercury
3.	Richard Petty	Dodge
4.	Richard Brooks	Ford
5.	Bruce Hill	Chevrolet
6.	Richard Childress	Chevrolet
7.	Ed Negre	Dodge
8.	James Hylton	Chevrolet
9.	Buddy Arrington	Dodge
10.	Dean Dalton	Ford
11.	Ricky Rudd	Ford
12.	Elmo Langley	Ford
13.	Carl Adams	Ford
14.	David Sisco	Chevrolet
15.	Clyde Dagit	Dodge
16.	Travis Tiller	Dodge
17.	Walter Ballard	Chevrolet
18.	Frank Warren	Dodge
19.	Rick Newsom	Ford
20.	Cecil Gordon	Chevrolet
21.	Darrell Waltrip	Chevrolet
22.	Benny Parsons	Chevrolet
23.	Lennie Pond	Chevrolet
24.	Dave Marcis	Dodge
25.	Buddy Baker	Ford
26.	Coo Coo Marlin	Chevrolet
27.	Jabe Thomas	Chevrolet
28.	Donnie Allison	Chevrolet
29.	Bobby Isaac	Chevrolet
30.	Richard Skillen	Chevrolet
31.	Earl Canavan	Dodge

FINISH	DRIVER	CAR
3.	David Pearson	Mercury
4.	Richard Brooks	Ford
5.	Darrell Waltrip	Chevrolet
6.	Donnie Allison	Chevrolet
7.	Coo Coo Marlin	Chevrolet
8.	Cecil Gordon	Chevrolet
9.	Harry Jefferson	Ford
10.	Lennie Pond	Chevrolet
11.	Ferrell Harris	Dodge
12.	Frank Warren	Dodge
13.	James Hylton	Chevrolet
14.	Skip Manning	Chevrolet
15.	Richard Childress	Chevrolet
16.	Carl Adams	Ford
17.	Elmo Langley	Ford
18.	Warren Tope	Ford
19.	Henley Gray	Chevrolet
20.	Rick Newsom	Ford
21.	Grant Adcox	Chevrolet
22.	Cale Yarborough	Chevrolet
23.	Bruce Hill	Chevrolet
24.	Walter Ballard	Chevrolet
25.	Ricky Rudd	Ford
26.	Jim Vandiver	Dodge
27.	Dave Marcis	Dodge
28.	Benny Parsons	Chevrolet
29.	Jody Ridley	Ford
30.	Bobby Allison	Matador
31.	David Sisco	Chevrolet
32.	Johnny Rutherford	Chevrolet
33.	Joe Mihalic	Chevrolet
34.	Richie Panch	Chevrolet
35.	A. J. Foyt	Chevrolet
36.	G. C. Spencer	Dodge

SOUTHEASTERN 500

March 16
Bristol, Tennessee
Time of Race: 2 hours, 43 minutes, 53 seconds
Average Speed: 97.053 mph

FINISH	DRIVER	CAR
1.	Richard Petty	Dodge
2.	Benny Parsons	Chevrolet
3.	Buddy Baker	Ford
4.	Cecil Gordon	Chevrolet
5.	James Hylton	Chevrolet
6.	Darrell Waltrip	Chevrolet
7.	David Sisco	Chevrolet
8.	Dave Marcis	Dodge
9.	Richard Childress	Chevrolet
10.	Ricky Rudd	Ford
11.	D. K. Ulrich	Chevrolet
12.	Frank Warren	Dodge
13.	Ed Negre	Dodge
14.	Jabe Thomas	Chevrolet
15.	Buddy Arrington	Plymouth
16.	Henley Gray	Chevrolet
17.	Elmo Langley	Ford
18.	Walter Ballard	Chevrolet
19.	Richard Brooks	Ford
20.	Cale Yarborough	Chevrolet
21.	Travis Tiller	Dodge
22.	Joe Frasson	Dodge
23.	Earl Canavan	Dodge

ATLANTA 500

March 23
Atlanta, Georgia
Time of Race: 3 hours, 44 minutes, 6 seconds
Average Speed: 133.496 mph

FINISH	DRIVER	CAR
1.	Richard Petty	Dodge
2.	Buddy Baker	Ford

GWYN STALEY 400

April 6
North Wilkesboro, North Carolina
Time of Race: 2 hours, 46 minutes, 39 seconds
Average Speed: 90.009 mph

FINISH	DRIVER	CAR
1.	Richard Petty	Dodge
2.	Cale Yarborough	Chevrolet
3.	Buddy Baker	Ford
4.	Dave Marcis	Dodge
5.	Lennie Pond	Chevrolet
6.	Benny Parsons	Chevrolet
7.	Darrell Waltrip	Chevrolet
8.	Dick Brooks	Ford
9.	Cecil Gordon	Chevrolet
10.	Walter Ballard	Chevrolet
11.	James Hylton	Chevrolet
12.	Frank Warren	Dodge
13.	J. D. McDuffie	Chevrolet
14.	Joe Mihalic	Chevrolet
15.	Jabe Thomas	Chevrolet
16.	Bruce Hill	Chevrolet
17.	Richard Childress	Chevrolet
18.	Carl Adams	Ford
19.	Ed Negre	Dodge
20.	Buddy Arrington	Plymouth
21.	Travis Tiller	Dodge
22.	Neil Castles	Dodge
23.	David Sisco	Chevrolet
24.	Rick Newsom	Ford
25.	Earl Canavan	Dodge
26.	Charlie Griffin	Dodge
27.	Elmo Langley	Ford
28.	Ricky Rudd	Ford

REBEL 500

April 13
Darlington South Carolina
Time of Race: 4 hours, 15 minutes, 41 seconds
Average Speed: 117.597 mph

FINISH	DRIVER	CAR
1.	Bobby Allison	Matador
2.	Darrell Waltrip	Chevrolet
3.	Donnie Allison	Chevrolet
4.	Dave Marcis	Dodge
5.	Coo Coo Marlin	Chevrolet
6.	Benny Parsons	Chevrolet
7.	David Pearson	Mercury
8.	James Hylton	Chevrolet
9.	Bruce Jacobii	Chevrolet
10.	Buddy Arrington	Plymouth
11.	J. D. McDuffie	Chevrolet
12.	Carl Adams	Ford
13.	Joe Mihalic	Chevrolet
14.	Ferrell Harris	Dodge
15.	Bruce Hill	Chevrolet
16.	Frank Warren	Dodge
17.	Earl Canavan	Dodge
18.	Walter Ballard	Chevrolet
19.	Buddy Baker	Ford
20.	Elmo Langley	Ford
21.	Cecil Gordon	Chevrolet
22.	Richard Childress	Chevrolet
23.	Richard Skillen	Chevrolet
24.	G. C. Spencer	Dodge
25.	Richard Brooks	Ford
26.	Richard Petty	Dodge
27.	Lennie Pond	Chevrolet
28.	David Sisco	Chevrolet
29.	Randy Tissot	Chevrolet
30.	Neil Castles	Dodge
31.	Ed Negre	Dodge
32.	Dean Dalton	Ford
33.	Rick Newsom	Ford
34.	Bill Champion	Ford
35.	Jabe Thomas	Chevrolet
36.	Cale Yarborough	Chevrolet

VIRGINIA 500

April 27
Martinsville, Virginia
Time of Race: 3 hours, 47 minutes, 15 seconds
Average Speed: 69.282 mph

FINISH	DRIVER	CAR
1.	Richard Petty	Dodge
2.	Darrell Waltrip	Chevrolet
3.	Cale Yarborough	Chevrolet
4.	Bobby Allison	Matador
5.	Dave Marcis	Dodge
6.	Benny Parsons	Chevrolet
7.	Jimmy Hensley	Chevrolet
8.	Richard Brooks	Ford
9.	Richard Childress	Chevrolet
10.	James Hylton	Chevrolet
11.	Elmo Langley	Ford
12.	Carl Adams	Ford
13.	Ed Negre	Ford
14.	Buddy Arrington	Plymouth
15.	Walter Ballard	Chevrolet
16.	Bill Champion	Ford
17.	Richie Panch	Chevrolet
18.	Frank Warren	Dodge
19.	Buddy Baker	Ford
20.	David Pearson	Mercury
21.	Donnie Allison	Chevrolet
22.	Jabe Thomas	Chevrolet
23.	Cecil Gordon	Chevrolet
24.	Travis Tiller	Dodge
25.	Lennie Pond	Chevrolet
26.	David Sisco	Chevrolet
27.	Joey Arrington	Dodge
28.	J. D. McDuffie	Chevrolet
29.	Richard Brown	Pontiac
30.	Dean Dalton	Dodge

WINSTON 500

May 4
Talladega, Alabama
Time of Race: 3 hours, 26 minutes, 59 seconds
Average Speed: 144.948 mph

FINISH	DRIVER	CAR
1.	Buddy Baker	Ford
2.	David Pearson	Mercury
3.	Dick Brooks	Ford
4.	Darrell Waltrip	Chevrolet
5.	Coo Coo Marlin	Chevrolet
6.	Harry Jefferson	Ford
7.	Grant Adcox	Chevrolet
8.	Bruce Jacobii	Chevrolet
9.	Joe Mihalic	Chevrolet
10.	Richard Childress	Chevrolet
11.	Bill Champion	Ford
12.	Walter Ballard	Chevrolet
13.	Dave Marcis	Dodge
14.	Elmo Langley	Ford
15.	Skip Manning	Chevrolet
16.	David Sisco	Chevrolet
17.	Earl Canavan	Dodge
18.	Joe Frasson	Pontiac
19.	Richard Petty	Dodge
20.	Tom Williams	Chevrolet
21.	Cecil Gordon	Chevrolet
22.	G. C. Spencer	Dodge
23.	Travis Tiller	Dodge
24.	Frank Warren	Dodge
25.	Jabe Thomas	Dodge
26.	Lennie Pond	Chevrolet
27.	Jim Vandiver	Dodge
28.	Randy Tissot	Chevrolet
29.	J. D. McDuffie	Chevrolet
30.	Ramo Stott	Chevrolet
31.	Marty Robbins	Dodge
32.	Ed Negre	Ford
33.	James Hylton	Chevrolet
34.	William Miller	Chevrolet
35.	Bobby Allison	Matador
36.	Gordon Johncock	Chevrolet
37.	Red Farmer	Ford
38.	Buddy Arrington	Plymouth
39.	Dean Dalton	Dodge
40.	Cale Yarborough	Chevrolet
41.	Rick Newsom	Ford
42.	Donnie Allison	Chevrolet
43.	Benny Parsons	Chevrolet
44.	Carl Adams	Ford
45.	Ferrell Harris	Dodge
46.	Dan Daughtry	Ford
47.	Bruce Hill	Chevrolet
48.	John Ray	Chevrolet
49.	Richie Panch	Chevrolet
50.	John Banks	Dodge

MUSIC CITY USA 420

May 10
Nashville, Tennessee
Time of Race: 2 hours, 39 minutes, 45 seconds
Average Speed: 94.107 mph

FINISH	DRIVER	CAR
1.	Darrell Waltrip	Chevrolet
2.	Benny Parsons	Chevrolet
3.	Coo Coo Marlin	Chevrolet
4.	Dave Marcis	Dodge
5.	Cecil Gordon	Chevrolet
6.	Alton Jones	Chevrolet
7.	Richard Petty	Dodge
8.	David Sisco	Chevrolet
9.	James Hylton	Chevrolet
10.	Walter Ballard	Chevrolet

FINISH	DRIVER	CAR
11.	J. D. McDuffie	Chevrolet
12.	Frank Warren	Dodge
13.	Rick Newsom	Ford
14.	Cale Yarborough	Chevrolet
15.	Elmo Langley	Ford
16.	Richard Childress	Chevrolet
17.	Earl Canavan	Dodge
18.	Bill Champion	Ford
19.	Jabe Thomas	Chevrolet
20.	Baxter Price	Chevrolet
21.	Paul Dean Holt	Ford
22.	Earl Brooks	Dodge
23.	Bruce Hill	Chevrolet
24.	Ed Negre	Dodge
25.	Richard Brown	Pontiac
26.	Travis Tiller	Dodge
27.	Joey Arrington	Dodge
28.	Buddy Arrington	Plymouth

MASON-DIXON 500

May 18
Dover, Delaware
Time of Race: 4 hours, 57 minutes, 32 seconds
Average Speed: 100.82 mph

FINISH	DRIVER	CAR
1.	David Pearson	Mercury
2.	Cecil Gordon	Chevrolet
3.	Richard Petty	Dodge
4.	James Hylton	Chevrolet
5.	David Sisco	Chevrolet
6.	Coo Coo Marlin	Chevrolet
7.	Kenneth Brightbill	Ford
8.	Bruce Hill	Chevrolet
9.	Henley Gray	Chevrolet
10.	Jabe Thomas	Chevrolet
11.	Buddy Baker	Ford
12.	Elmo Langley	Ford
13.	Buddy Arrington	Plymouth
14.	Joe Frasson	Dodge
15.	Frank Warren	Dodge
16.	Richard Childress	Chevrolet
17.	Dean Dalton	Ford
18.	J. D. McDuffie	Chevrolet
19.	Bill Champion	Ford
20.	Dave Marcis	Dodge
21.	John Harkins	Dodge
22.	Darrell Waltrip	Chevrolet
23.	Benny Parsons	Chevrolet
24.	Travis Tiller	Dodge
25.	Walter Ballard	Chevrolet
26.	Earl Brooks	Dodge
27.	Cale Yarborough	Chevrolet
28.	Donnie Allison	Chevrolet
29.	Richard Brooks	Ford
30.	D. K. Ulrich	Chevrolet
31.	Ed Negre	Dodge
32.	Joey Arrington	Dodge
33.	Lennie Pond	Chevrolet
34.	Earl Canavan	Dodge
35.	Dick May	Dodge

WORLD 600

May 25
Charlotte, North Carolina
Time of Race: 4 hours, 7 minutes, 42 seconds
Average Speed: 145.327 mph

FINISH	DRIVER	CAR
1.	Richard Petty	Dodge
2.	Cale Yarborough	Chevrolet
3.	David Pearson	Mercury
4.	Darrell Waltrip	Chevrolet

FINISH	DRIVER	CAR
5.	Buddy Baker	Ford
6.	Charlie Glotzbach	Chevrolet
7.	Dick Brooks	Ford
8.	Richie Panch	Chevrolet
9.	Donnie Allison	Chevrolet
10.	Walter Ballard	Chevrolet
11.	J. D. McDuffie	Chevrolet
12.	Darel Dieringer	Chevrolet
13.	Earl Ross	Ford
14.	Jackie Rogers	Chevrolet
15.	Jim Vandiver	Dodge
16.	Bruce Jacobii	Chevrolet
17.	Dean Dalton	Ford
18.	Bruce Hill	Chevrolet
19.	Frank Warren	Dodge
20.	James Hylton	Chevrolet
21.	Harry Jefferson	Ford
22.	Dale Earnhardt	Dodge
23.	Richard Childress	Chevrolet
24.	Elmo Langley	Ford
25.	Richard Skillen	Chevrolet
26.	Buddy Arrington	Plymouth
27.	David Sisco	Chevrolet
28.	Joe Frasson	Chevrolet
29.	Bill Champion	Ford
30.	Travis Tiller	Dodge
31.	Harry Gant	Chevrolet
32.	Ed Negre	Dodge
33.	Randy Bethea	Chevrolet
34.	Dave Marcis	Dodge
35.	Bobby Isaac	Chevrolet
36.	Lennie Pond	Chevrolet
37.	Cecil Gordon	Chevrolet
38.	G. C. Spencer	Dodge
39.	Benny Parsons	Chevrolet
40.	Coo Coo Marlin	Chevrolet

TUBORG 400

June 8
Riverside, California
Time of Race: 3 hours, 58 minutes, 4 seconds
Average Speed: 101.028 mph

FINISH	DRIVER	CAR
1.	Richard Petty	Dodge
2.	Bobby Allison	Matador
3.	Benny Parsons	Chevrolet
4.	Ray Elder	Dodge
5.	Dave Marcis	Dodge
6.	Chuck Wahl	Chevrolet
7.	J. D. McDuffie	Chevrolet
8.	Bill Schmitt	Chevrolet
9.	Richard Childress	Chevrolet
10.	Gene Rinker	Chevrolet
11.	Glen Francis	Chevrolet
12.	Elmo Langley	Ford
13.	James Hylton	Chevrolet
14.	Jim Boyd	Dodge
15.	Gary Mathews	Chevrolet
16.	Pete Torres	Ford
17.	Frank Warren	Dodge
18.	Cecil Gordon	Chevrolet
19.	Hershel McGriff	Chevrolet
20.	John Kieper	Chevrolet
21.	Darrell Waltrip	Chevrolet
22.	Carl Joiner	Chevrolet
23.	Carl Adams	Ford
24.	Walter Ballard	Chevrolet
25.	Ed Bradshaw	Chevrolet
26.	Bill Osborne	Ford
27.	Jim Insolo	Chevrolet
28.	Ed Negre	Dodge
29.	George Follmer	Chevrolet
30.	Sonny Easley	Ford
31.	John Soares	Dodge
32.	Don Puskarich	Chevrolet
33.	Ted Fritz	Chevrolet
34.	Chuck Bown	Dodge
35.	Ivan Baldwin	Dodge

MOTOR STATE 400

June 15
Brooklyn, Michigan
Time of Race: 3 hours, 2 minutes, 39 seconds
Average Speed: 131.398 mph

FINISH	DRIVER	CAR
1.	David Pearson	Mercury
2.	Richard Petty	Dodge
3.	Dave Marcis	Dodge
4.	Cale Yarborough	Chevrolet
5.	Darrell Waltrip	Chevrolet
6.	Richie Panch	Chevrolet
7.	Richard Brooks	Ford
8.	David Sisco	Chevrolet
9.	James Hylton	Chevrolet
10.	Richard Childress	Chevrolet
11.	Walter Ballard	Chevrolet
12.	Coo Coo Marlin	Chevrolet
13.	Ferrell Harris	Dodge
14.	Elmo Langley	Chevrolet
15.	Buddy Arrington	Plymouth
16.	Frank Warren	Dodge
17.	Salt Walther	Chevrolet
18.	J. D. McDuffie	Chevrolet
19.	Dean Dalton	Ford
20.	John Banks	Dodge
21.	Carl Adams	Ford
22.	Bobby Allison	Matador
23.	Travis Tiller	Dodge
24.	John Ray	Chevrolet
25.	Bruce Jacobii	Chevrolet
26.	D. K. Ulrich	Chevrolet
27.	Ed Negre	Dodge
28.	William Miller	Chevrolet
29.	Grant Adcox	Chevrolet
30.	Bruce Hill	Chevrolet
31.	Joe Frasson	Dodge
32.	Mel Larson	Chevrolet
33.	Cecil Gordon	Chevrolet
34.	Benny Parsons	Chevrolet
35.	Donnie Allison	Chevrolet
36.	Rick Newsom	Ford

FIRECRACKER 400

July 4
Daytona Beach, Florida
Time of Race: 2 hours, 31 minutes, 32 seconds
Average Speed: 158.381 mph

FINISH	DRIVER	CAR
1.	Richard Petty	Dodge
2.	Buddy Baker	Ford
3.	Dave Marcis	Dodge
4.	Darrell Waltrip	Chevrolet
5.	Donnie Allison	Chevrolet
6.	Richard Brooks	Ford
7.	Bruce Hill	Chevrolet
8.	Benny Parsons	Chevrolet
9.	Carl Adams	Ford
10.	Darel Dieringer	Ford
11.	James Hylton	Chevrolet
12.	Ed Negre	Dodge
13.	Richard Childress	Chevrolet
14.	Jim Vandiver	Dodge
15.	Skip Manning	Chevrolet
16.	Randy Tissot	Chevrolet
17.	Frank Warren	Dodge
18.	Tommy Gale	Ford
19.	Jackie Rogers	Chevrolet
20.	David Pearson	Mercury
21.	Buddy Arrington	Plymouth
22.	J. D. McDuffie	Chevrolet
23.	Dick May	Chevrolet
24.	A. J. Foyt	Chevrolet

25.	Elmo Langley	Ford
26.	Cale Yarborough	Chevrolet
27.	Joe Mihalic	Chevrolet
28.	Richie Panch	Chevrolet
29.	Cecil Gordon	Chevrolet
30.	John Ray	Chevrolet
31.	Walter Ballard	Chevrolet
32.	Bruce Jacobii	Chevrolet
33.	David Sisco	Chevrolet
34.	Coo Coo Marlin	Chevrolet
35.	Bobby Allison	Matador
36.	Grant Adcox	Chevrolet
37.	Salt Walther	Chevrolet
38.	Lennie Pond	Chevrolet
39.	G. C. Spencer	Dodge
40.	Johnny Rutherford	Chevrolet

NASHVILLE 420

July 20
Nashville, Tennessee
Time of Race: 2 hours, 47 minutes, 16 seconds
Average Speed: 89.792 mph

FINISH	DRIVER	CAR
1.	Cale Yarborough	Chevrolet
2.	Richard Petty	Dodge
3.	Dave Marcis	Dodge
4.	Benny Parsons	Chevrolet
5.	Cecil Gordon	Chevrolet
6.	Richard Childress	Chevrolet
7.	David Sisco	Chevrolet
8.	Carl Adams	Ford
9.	J. D. McDuffie	Chevrolet
10.	Elmo Langley	Ford
11.	James Hylton	Chevrolet
12.	Alton Jones	Chevrolet
13.	Bruce Hill	Chevrolet
14.	Neil Bonnett	Chevrolet
15.	Ed Negre	Dodge
16.	Frank Warren	Dodge
17.	Richard Brown	Pontiac
18.	Walter Ballard	Chevrolet
19.	Bruce Jacobii	Chevrolet
20.	D. K. Ulrich	Chevrolet
21.	Jabe Thomas	Chevrolet
22.	Baxter Price	Chevrolet
23.	Earl Brooks	Dodge
24.	Paul Dean Holt	Ford
25.	Buddy Arrington	Plymouth
26.	Coo Coo Marlin	Chevrolet
27.	Grant Adcox	Chevrolet
28.	Darrell Waltrip	Chevrolet
29.	Neil Castles	Chevrolet
30.	Bill Champion	Ford

PUROLATOR 500

August 3
Pocono, Pennsylvania
Time of Race: 4 hours, 29 minutes, 50 seconds
Average Speed: 111.179 mph

FINISH	DRIVER	CAR
1.	David Pearson	Mercury
2.	Richard Petty	Dodge
3.	Buddy Baker	Ford
4.	Benny Parsons	Chevrolet
5.	Richard Childress	Chevrolet
6.	Carl Adams	Ford
7.	Coo Coo Marlin	Chevrolet
8.	Bruce Hill	Chevrolet
9.	James Hylton	Chevrolet
10.	Cecil Gordon	Chevrolet
11.	Bruce Jacobii	Chevrolet

12.	Buddy Arrington	Plymouth
13.	Walter Ballard	Ford
14.	Ed Negre	Dodge
15.	D. K. Ulrich	Chevrolet
16.	Frank Warren	Dodge
17.	Dick May	Dodge
18.	Baxter Price	Chevrolet
19.	David Sisco	Chevrolet
20.	Jabe Thomas	Chevrolet
21.	Joe Mihalic	Chevrolet
22.	Doc Faustina	Dodge
23.	Carl Van Horn	Chevrolet
24.	Elmo Langley	Ford
25.	Dave Marcis	Dodge
26.	Earl Brooks	Dodge
27.	J. D. McDuffie	Chevrolet
28.	Tommy Gale	Ford
29.	Earl Canavan	Dodge
30.	Jackie Rogers	Chevrolet
31.	Bobby Allison	Matador
32.	George Wiltshire	Dodge
33.	Richie Panch	Chevrolet
34.	Darrell Waltrip	Chevrolet
35.	Cale Yarborough	Chevrolet

TALLADEGA 500

August 17
Talladega, Alabama
Time of Race: 3 hours, 49 minutes, 14 seconds
Average Speed: 130.892 mph

FINISH	DRIVER	CAR
1.	Buddy Baker	Ford
2.	Richard Petty	Dodge
3.	Donnie Allison	Chevrolet
4.	Dave Marcis	Dodge
5.	Coo Coo Marlin	Chevrolet
6.	Benny Parsons	Chevrolet
7.	James Hylton	Chevrolet
8.	Joe Frasson	Chevrolet
9.	Jackie Rogers	Chevrolet
10.	Cecil Gordon	Chevrolet
11.	Dean Dalton	Ford
12.	Bruce Jacobii	Chevrolet
13.	Richard Childress	Chevrolet
14.	Elmo Langley	Ford
15.	Ferrell Harris	Dodge
16.	Jabe Thomas	Chevrolet
17.	Frank Warren	Dodge
18.	Ed Negre	Dodge
19.	Billy Joe Hagan	Chevrolet
20.	Jeff Handy	Chevrolet
21.	A. J. Reno	Ford
22.	Earl Brooks	Chevrolet
23.	Carl Adams	Ford
24.	Buddy Arrington	Plymouth
25.	D. K. Ulrich	Chevrolet
26.	Joe Mihalic	Chevrolet
27.	David Sisco	Chevrolet
28.	Bill Ward	Chevrolet
29.	Bobby Allison	Matador
30.	Bill Champion	Ford
31.	Bruce Hill	Chevrolet
32.	Lennie Pond	Chevrolet
33.	Jim Vandiver	Dodge
34.	Grant Adcox	Chevrolet
35.	Neil Bonnett	Chevrolet
36.	Harold Miller	Chevrolet
37.	Darel Dieringer	Ford
38.	Richard Brooks	Ford
39.	David Pearson	Mercury
40.	John Ray	Chevrolet
41.	Cale Yarborough	Chevrolet
42.	Darrell Waltrip	Chevrolet
43.	Richie Panch	Chevrolet
44.	Red Farmer	Ford
45.	J. D. McDuffie	Chevrolet
46.	Tiny Lund	Dodge
47.	Terry Link	Pontiac
48.	Walter Ballard	Chevrolet
49.	G. C. Spencer	Dodge
50.	Randy Tissot	Chevrolet

CHAMPION SPARK PLUG 400

August 24
Bristol, Tennessee
Time of Race: 3 hours, 43 minutes, 5 seconds
Average Speed: 107.583 mph

FINISH	DRIVER	CAR
1.	Richard Petty	Dodge
2.	David Pearson	Mercury
3.	Cale Yarborough	Chevrolet
4.	Bobby Allison	Matador
5.	Dave Marcis	Dodge
6.	Buddy Baker	Ford
7.	Darrell Waltrip	Chevrolet
8.	Bruce Hill	Chevrolet
9.	Terry Bivens	Chevrolet
10.	Dean Dalton	Ford
11.	Walter Ballard	Chevrolet
12.	David Sisco	Chevrolet
13.	Cecil Gordon	Chevrolet
14.	Grant Adcox	Chevrolet
15.	Bruce Jacobii	Chevrolet
16.	Ferrell Harris	Dodge
17.	James Hylton	Chevrolet
18.	Elmo Langley	Ford
19.	Dick May	Chevrolet
20.	Richard Brooks	Ford
21.	D. K. Ulrich	Chevrolet
22.	Buddy Arrington	Plymouth
23.	Jabe Thomas	Chevrolet
24.	Harold Miller	Chevrolet
25.	Richie Panch	Chevrolet
26.	Frank Warren	Dodge
27.	Henley Gray	Chevrolet
28.	J. D. McDuffie	Chevrolet
29.	Carl Adams	Ford
30.	A. J. Foyt	Chevrolet
31.	Richard Childress	Chevrolet
32.	Earl Canavan	Dodge
33.	Ed Negre	Dodge
34.	Benny Parsons	Chevrolet
35.	Coo Coo Marlin	Chevrolet
36.	Jackie Rogers	Chevrolet

SOUTHERN 500

September 1
Darlington, South Carolina
Time of Race: 4 hours, 17 minutes, 28 seconds
Average Speed: 116.825 mph

FINISH	DRIVER	CAR
1.	Bobby Allison	Matador
2.	Richard Petty	Dodge
3.	David Sisco	Chevrolet
4.	Jim Vandiver	Dodge
5.	Bruce Hill	Chevrolet
6.	Cecil Gordon	Chevrolet
7.	Richard Childress	Chevrolet
8.	Dick May	Chevrolet
9.	Bruce Jacobii	Chevrolet
10.	Elmo Langley	Ford
11.	Skip Manning	Chevrolet
12.	Jabe Thomas	Chevrolet
13.	Grant Adcox	Chevrolet
14.	Frank Warren	Dodge
15.	Randy Tissot	Chevrolet
16.	D. K. Ulrich	Chevrolet
17.	Buddy Arrington	Plymouth
18.	Ferrell Harris	Dodge

FINISH	DRIVER	CAR
19.	Cale Yarborough	Chevrolet
20.	Benny Parsons	Chevrolet
21.	Lennie Pond	Chevrolet
22.	Tommy Gale	Ford
23.	James Hylton	Chevrolet
24.	Dave Marcis	Dodge
25.	Walter Ballard	Chevrolet
26.	Dick Brooks	Ford
27.	David Pearson	Mercury
28.	Buddy Baker	Ford
29.	Bill Champion	Chevrolet
30.	Ed Negre	Chevrolet
31.	G. C. Spencer	Dodge
32.	Dean Dalton	Ford
33.	J. D. McDuffie	Chevrolet
34.	Darrell Waltrip	Chevrolet
35.	Earl Canavan	Dodge
36.	Henley Gray	Chevrolet
37.	Dick Skillen	Chevrolet
38.	Jackie Rogers	Chevrolet
39.	Coo Coo Marlin	Chevrolet
40.	H. B. Bailey	Pontiac

DELAWARE 500

September 14
Dover, Delaware
Time of Race: 4 hours, 29 minutes, 22 seconds
Average Speed: 111.372 mph

FINISH	DRIVER	CAR
1.	Richard Petty	Dodge
2.	Dick Brooks	Ford
3.	Benny Parsons	Chevrolet
4.	Cale Yarborough	Chevrolet
5.	Bruce Hill	Chevrolet
6.	Richard Childress	Chevrolet
7.	James Hylton	Chevrolet
8.	J. D. McDuffie	Chevrolet
9.	Dean Dalton	Ford
10.	D. K. Ulrich	Chevrolet
11.	Ed Negre	Dodge
12.	Rick Newsom	Chevrolet
13.	Jabe Thomas	Chevrolet
14.	Walter Ballard	Chevrolet
15.	Randy Tissott	Chevrolet
16.	Frank Warren	Dodge
17.	David Sisco	Chevrolet
18.	Buddy Arrington	Plymouth
19.	Henley Gray	Chevrolet
20.	Lennie Pond	Chevrolet
21.	Terry Bivens	Chevrolet
22.	Bruce Jacobii	Chevrolet
23.	Bill Hollar	Chevrolet
24.	Elmo Langley	Ford
25.	Earle Canavan	Dodge
26.	David Pearson	Mercury
27.	Darrell Waltrip	Chevrolet
28.	Bobby Allison	Matador
29.	Cecil Gordon	Chevrolet
30.	Dave Marcis	Dodge
31.	Coo Coo Marlin	Chevrolet
32.	Joe Mihalic	Chevrolet
33.	Buddy Baker	Ford
34.	Earl Brooks	Dodge
35.	Tommy Gale	Ford
36.	Joe Frasson	Dodge
37.	Dick May	Ford

FINISH	DRIVER	CAR
1.	Richard Petty	Dodge
2.	Cale Yarborough	Chevrolet
3.	Darrell Waltrip	Chevrolet
4.	Buddy Baker	Ford
5.	Lennie Pond	Chevrolet
6.	Benny Parsons	Chevrolet
7.	J. D. McDuffie	Chevrolet
8.	Richard Childress	Chevrolet
9.	Jim Vandiver	Dodge
10.	Bruce Hill	Chevrolet
11.	Dick Brooks	Ford
12.	Coo Coo Marlin	Chevrolet
13.	James Hylton	Chevrolet
14.	Elmo Langley	Ford
15.	Dean Dalton	Ford
16.	Cecil Gordon	Chevrolet
17.	Ed Negre	Dodge
18.	Buddy Arrington	Plymouth
19.	David Sisco	Chevrolet
20.	Carl Adams	Ford
21.	Bill Champion	Ford
22.	Bill Hollar	Chevrolet
23.	D. K. Ulrich	Chevrolet
24.	Frank Warren	Dodge
25.	Walter Ballard	Chevrolet
26.	Jabe Thomas	Chevrolet
27.	Dave Marcis	Dodge
28.	Charlie Griffith	Dodge
29.	Henley Gray	Chevrolet
30.	Richard Brown	Pontiac

OLD DOMINION 500

September 28
Martinsville, Virginia
Time of Race: 3 hours, 27 minutes, 47 seconds
Average Speed: 75.800 mph

FINISH	DRIVER	CAR
1.	Dave Marcis	Dodge
2.	Benny Parsons	Chevrolet
3.	Bobby Allison	Matador
4.	Richard Childress	Chevrolet
5.	Richie Panch	Chevrolet
6.	Richard Brooks	Ford
7.	Carl Adams	Ford
8.	Jim Vandiver	Dodge
9.	Cecil Gordon	Chevrolet
10.	Elmo Langley	Ford
11.	Buddy Arrington	Plymouth
12.	Frank Warren	Ford
13.	James Hylton	Chevrolet
14.	Walter Ballard	Chevrolet
15.	Jabe Thomas	Chevrolet
16.	Joe Mihalic	Chevrolet
17.	Darrell Waltrip	Chevrolet
18.	Buddy Baker	Ford
19.	Cale Yarborough	Chevrolet
20.	David Sisco	Chevrolet
21.	Ed Negre	Ford
22.	Richard Petty	Dodge
23.	David Pearson	Mercury
24.	Lennie Pond	Chevrolet
25.	Bruce Hill	Chevrolet
26.	Chuck Bown	Chevrolet
27.	Jimmy Hensley	Chevrolet
28.	D. K. Ulrich	Chevrolet
29.	Coo Coo Marlin	Chevrolet
30.	J. D. McDuffie	Chevrolet

WILKES 400

September 21
North Wilkesboro, North Carolina
Time of Race: 2 hours, 48 minutes, 34 seconds
Average Speed: 88.986 mph

NATIONAL 500

October 5
Charlotte, North Carolina
Time of Race: 3 hours, 47 minutes, 22 seconds
Average Speed: 132.209 mph

FINISH	DRIVER	CAR
1.	Richard Petty	Dodge
2.	David Pearson	Mercury
3.	Buddy Baker	Ford
4.	Benny Parsons	Chevrolet
5.	Cecil Gordon	Chevrolet
6.	James Hylton	Chevrolet
7.	Darel Dieringer	Ford
8.	Richard Childress	Chevrolet
9.	J. D. McDuffie	Chevrolet
10.	Elmo Langley	Ford
11.	Hershel McGriff	Dodge
12.	Chuck Bown	Chevrolet
13.	Joe Frasson	Chevrolet
14.	Frank Warren	Dodge
15.	David Sisco	Chevrolet
16.	Grant Adcox	Chevrolet
17.	Buddy Arrington	Chevrolet
18.	Bob Burcham	Chevrolet
19.	Cale Yarborough	Chevrolet
20.	Jabe Thomas	Chevrolet
21.	A. J. Foyt	Chevrolet
22.	Lennie Pond	Chevrolet
23.	Jim Vandiver	Dodge
24.	Darrell Waltrip	Chevrolet
25.	Richie Panch	Chevrolet
26.	Dave Marcis	Dodge
27.	Bruce Hill	Chevrolet
28.	Harry Jefferson	Ford
29.	Jackie Rogers	Chevrolet
30.	Ed Negre	Dodge
31.	Bobby Allison	Matador
32.	G. C. Spencer	Dodge
33.	Donnie Allison	Chevrolet
34.	Johnny Rutherford	Chevrolet
35.	Dick Brooks	Ford
36.	Charlie Glotzbach	Chevrolet
37.	Bobby Isaac	Mercury
38.	Skip Manning	Chevrolet
39.	Jim Insolo	Chevrolet
40.	Neil Castles	Chevrolet
41.	Walter Ballard	Chevrolet
42.	Coo Coo Marlin	Chevrolet

CAPITAL CITY 500

October 12
Richmond, Virginia
Time of Race: 3 hours, 18 minutes, 34 seconds
Average Speed: 81.886 mph

FINISH	DRIVER	CAR
1.	Darrell Waltrip	Chevrolet
2.	Lennie Pond	Chevrolet
3.	Dick Brooks	Ford
4.	Cecil Gordon	Chevrolet
5.	J. D. McDuffie	Chevrolet
6.	James Hylton	Chevrolet
7.	Elmo Langley	Ford
8.	Bruce Hill	Chevrolet
9.	Coo Coo Marlin	Chevrolet
10.	Jabe Thomas	Chevrolet
11.	Carl Adams	Ford
12.	Buddy Arrington	Plymouth
13.	D. K. Ulrich	Chevrolet
14.	Frank Warren	Dodge
15.	Walter Ballard	Chevrolet
16.	Bill Hollar	Chevrolet
17.	Earl Brooks	Dodge
18.	Benny Parsons	Chevrolet
19.	Dean Dalton	Ford
20.	Bruce Jacobii	Chevrolet
21.	Richard Childress	Chevrolet
22.	Ed Negre	Dodge
23.	Dave Marcis	Dodge
24.	David Sisco	Chevrolet
25.	Bill Champion	Ford
26.	Cale Yarborough	Chevrolet
27.	Jim Vandiver	Dodge
28.	Richard Petty	Dodge

AMERICAN 500

October 19
Rockingham, North Carolina
Time of Race: 4 hours, 9 minutes, 54 seconds
Average Speed: 120.135 mph

FINISH	DRIVER	CAR
1.	Cale Yarborough	Chevrolet
2.	Bobby Allison	Matador
3.	Dave Marcis	Dodge
4.	Lennie Pond	Chevrolet
5.	A. J. Foyt	Chevrolet
6.	Bruce Hill	Chevrolet
7.	Bobby Isaac	Chevrolet
8.	Jim Vandiver	Dodge
9.	Donnie Allison	Chevrolet
10.	Coo Coo Marlin	Chevrolet
11.	Walter Ballard	Chevrolet
12.	Ed Negre	Dodge
13.	Buddy Arrington	Plymouth
14.	Frank Warren	Dodge
15.	James Hylton	Chevrolet
16.	Bruce Jacobii	Chevrolet
17.	Dick May	Chevrolet
18.	Jabe Thomas	Chevrolet
19.	Glen McDuffie	Chevrolet
20.	J. D. McDuffie	Chevrolet
21.	Richard Childress	Chevrolet
22.	Ferrell Harris	Dodge
23.	Elmo Langley	Ford
24.	Benny Parsons	Chevrolet
25.	David Pearson	Mercury
26.	David Sisco	Chevrolet
27.	Richard Skillen	Chevrolet
28.	Buddy Baker	Ford
29.	Dick Brooks	Ford
30.	Cecil Gordon	Chevrolet
31.	D. K. Ulrich	Chevrolet
32.	Darrell Waltrip	Chevrolet
33.	Henley Gray	Chevrolet
34.	Neil Castles	Chevrolet
35.	Richard Petty	Dodge
36.	Jackie Rogers	Chevrolet
37.	Joe Frasson	Chevrolet

VOLUNTEER 500

November 2
Bristol, Tennessee
Time of Race: 2 hours, 44 minutes, 49 seconds
Average Speed: 97.016 mph

FINISH	DRIVER	CAR
1.	Richard Petty	Dodge
2.	Lennie Pond	Chevrolet
3.	Darrell Waltrip	Chevrolet
4.	Dave Marcis	Dodge
5.	Benny Parsons	Chevrolet
6.	Dick Brooks	Ford
7.	Coo Coo Marlin	Chevrolet
8.	Cecil Gordon	Chevrolet
9.	James Hylton	Chevrolet
10.	Bruce Hill	Chevrolet
11.	Ed Negre	Dodge
12.	Walter Ballard	Chevrolet
13.	Richard Childress	Chevrolet
14.	Carl Adams	Ford
15.	Buddy Arrington	Plymouth
16.	David Sisco	Chevrolet
17.	Bill Champion	Ford
18.	Jabe Thomas	Chevrolet
19.	Elmo Langley	Ford
20.	Cale Yarborough	Chevrolet
21.	Dick May	Chevrolet
22.	Frank Warren	Dodge
23.	Bobby Isaac	Chevrolet

FINISH	DRIVER	CAR
24.	Buddy Baker	Ford
25.	Grant Adcox	Chevrolet
26.	Joe Frasson	Chevrolet
27.	D. K. Ulrich	Chevrolet
28.	Travis Tiller	Dodge
29.	Dean Dalton	Ford
30.	J. D. McDuffie	Chevrolet

DIXIE 500

November 9
Atlanta, Georgia
Time of Race: 3 hours, 48 minutes, 40 seconds
Average Speed: 130.900 mph

FINISH	DRIVER	CAR
1.	Buddy Baker	Ford
2.	Dave Marcis	Dodge
3.	Richard Petty	Dodge
4.	David Pearson	Mercury
5.	Cale Yarborough	Chevrolet
6.	Lennie Pond	Chevrolet
7.	Dick Brooks	Ford
8.	Coo Coo Marlin	Chevrolet
9.	Cecil Gordon	Chevrolet
10.	Ed Negre	Dodge
11.	Jody Ridley	Ford
12.	Richard Childress	Chevrolet
13.	Bruce Hill	Chevrolet
14.	Bruce Jacobii	Chevrolet
15.	Elmo Langley	Chevrolet
16.	Carl Adams	Ford
17.	Walter Ballard	Chevrolet
18.	J. D. McDuffie	Chevrolet
19.	Benny Parsons	Chevrolet
20.	Buddy Arrington	Plymouth
21.	John Banks	Dodge
22.	James Hylton	Chevrolet
23.	Bob Burcham	Chevrolet
24.	Ferrell Harris	Dodge
25.	Frank Warren	Dodge
26.	Bobby Allison	Matador
27.	Donnie Allison	Chevrolet
28.	Jim Vandiver	Dodge
29.	David Sisco	Chevrolet
30.	Bobby Isaac	Chevrolet
31.	Neil Castles	Chevrolet
32.	Dean Dalton	Ford
33.	D. K. Ulrich	Chevrolet
34.	Harold Miller	Chevrolet
35.	Richie Panch	Mercury
36.	Darrell Waltrip	Chevrolet

L.A. TIMES 500

November 23
Ontario, California
Time of Race: 3 hours, 33 minutes, 12 seconds
Average Speed: 140.712 mph (new record)

FINISH	DRIVER	CAR
1.	Buddy Baker	Ford
2.	David Pearson	Mercury
3.	Dave Marcis	Dodge
4.	Cale Yarborough	Chevrolet
5.	Bobby Allison	Matador
6.	Lennie Pond	Chevrolet
7.	Jim Insolo	Chevrolet
8.	Dick Brooks	Ford
9.	James Hylton	Chevrolet
10.	Richard Childress	Chevrolet
11.	Don Hall	Chevrolet
12.	David Sisco	Chevrolet
13.	D. K. Ulrich	Chevrolet
14.	A. J. Foyt	Chevrolet
15.	Don Hoffman	Chevrolet

FINISH	DRIVER	CAR
16.	Richard Petty	Dodge
17.	Frank Warren	Dodge
18.	Hugh Pearson	Chevrolet
19.	Cecil Gordon	Chevrolet
20.	Walter Ballard	Chevrolet
21.	J. D. McDuffie	Chevrolet
22.	Elmo Langley	Chevrolet
23.	Tom Williams	Chevrolet
24.	John Kieper	Chevrolet
25.	Ray Elder	Dodge
26.	Bruce Hill	Chevrolet
27.	Jim Boyd	Dodge
28.	Carl Adams	Ford
29.	Roy Smith	Chevrolet
30.	John Martin	Dodge
31.	Hershel McGriff	Chevrolet
32.	Jim Thurkettle	Chevrolet
33.	Bill Schmitt	Chevrolet
34.	Benny Parsons	Chevrolet
35.	Chuck Wahl	Chevrolet
36.	Richie Panch	Mercury
37.	Don Puskarich	Dodge
38.	Chuck Bown	Dodge
39.	Sonny Easley	Ford
40.	Ed Negre	Dodge

1976

WINSTON WESTERN 500

January 18
Riverside, California
Time of Race: 5 hours, 2 minutes, 44 seconds
Average Speed: 99.180 mph

FINISH	DRIVER	CAR
1.	David Pearson	Mercury
2.	Cale Yarborough	Chevrolet
3.	Jim Insolo	Chevrolet
4.	Ray Elder	Dodge
5.	Benny Parsons	Chevrolet
6.	Lennie Pond	Chevrolet
7.	Richard Childress	Chevrolet
8.	Dave Marcis	Dodge
9.	James Hylton	Chevrolet
10.	Bill Schmitt	Chevrolet
11.	Frank Warren	Dodge
12.	D. K. Ulrich	Chevrolet
13.	Larry Esau	Chevrolet
14.	Ron Esau	Chevrolet
15.	Bobby Allison	Matador
16.	Chuck Bown	Dodge
17.	Gary Mathews	Dodge
18.	Ed Bradshaw	Chevrolet
19.	J. D. McDuffie	Chevrolet
20.	Carl Joiner	Chevrolet
21.	Darrell Waltrip	Chevrolet
22.	Chuck Wahl	Chevrolet
23.	Cecil Gordon	Chevrolet
24.	Hugh Pearson	Chevrolet
25.	Richard Petty	Dodge
26.	Bill Polich	Chevrolet
27.	Don Puskarich	Chevrolet
28.	Buddy Baker	Ford
29.	Gary Johnson	Dodge
30.	Hershel McGriff	Chevrolet
31.	John Ray	Ford
32.	Sonny Easley	Ford
33.	Richard Brooks	Chevrolet
34.	Sam Beler	Ford
35.	Harry Jefferson	Ford

DAYTONA 500

February 15
Daytona Beach, Florida

Time of Race: 3 hours, 17 minutes, 8 seconds
Average Speed: 152.181 mph

FINISH	DRIVER	CAR
1.	David Pearson	Mercury
2.	Richard Petty	Dodge
3.	Benny Parsons	Chevrolet
4.	Lennie Pond	Chevrolet
5.	Neil Bonnett	Chevrolet
6.	Terry Ryan	Chevrolet
7.	J. D. McDuffie	Chevrolet
8.	Terry Bivins	Chevrolet
9.	Richard Childress	Chevrolet
10.	Frank Warren	Dodge
11.	Buddy Arrington	Dodge
12.	Salt Walther	Chevrolet
13.	Ed Negre	Dodge
14.	Joe Frasson	Chevrolet
15.	Jackie Rogers	Chevrolet
16.	Jim Hurtubise	Chevrolet
17.	Joe Mihalic	Chevrolet
18.	Cecil Gordon	Chevrolet
19.	D. K. Ulrich	Chevrolet
20.	Roy Smith	Chevrolet
21.	Coo Coo Marlin	Chevrolet
22.	A. J. Foyt	Chevrolet
23.	James Hylton	Chevrolet
24.	Jim Lee Capps	Chevrolet
25.	Bobby Allison	Mercury
26.	Ramo Stott	Chevrolet
27.	Dave Marcis	Dodge
28.	John Ray	Chevrolet
29.	David Sisco	Chevrolet
30.	Skip Manning	Dodge
31.	Richard Skillen	Chevrolet
32.	Darrell Waltrip	Chevrolet
33.	Buddy Baker	Ford
34.	David Hobbs	Chevrolet
35.	Tighe Scott	Chevrolet
36.	Bruce Hill	Chevrolet
37.	Tom Williams	Chevrolet
38.	Dick May	Chevrolet
39.	Earl Ross	Chevrolet
40.	Jimmy Means	Chevrolet
41.	Richard Brooks	Ford
42.	Cale Yarborough	Chevrolet

CAROLINA 500

February 29
Rockingham, North Carolina
Time of Race: 4 hours, 24 minutes, 8 seconds
Average Speed: 113.665 mph

FINISH	DRIVER	CAR
1.	Richard Petty	Dodge
2.	Darrell Waltrip	Chevrolet
3.	Cale Yarborough	Chevrolet
4.	Buddy Baker	Ford
5.	Benny Parsons	Chevrolet
6.	Bobby Isaac	Chevrolet
7.	Grant Adcox	Chevrolet
8.	Coo Coo Marlin	Chevrolet
9.	Ed Negre	Dodge
10.	J. D. McDuffie	Chevrolet
11.	Darrell Bryant	Chevrolet
12.	Jackie Rogers	Chevrolet
13.	Terry Bivins	Chevrolet
14.	John Utsman	Dodge
15.	Tommy Gale	Ford
16.	Dick May	Chevrolet
17.	D. K. Ulrich	Chevrolet
18.	Travis Tiller	Dodge
19.	James Hylton	Chevrolet
20.	David Sisco	Chevrolet
21.	Bobby Allison	Mercury
22.	Bruce Hill	Chevrolet
23.	Richard Childress	Chevrolet

24.	Richard Brooks	Ford
25.	Walter Ballard	Chevrolet
26.	Dave Marcis	Dodge
27.	Glen McDuffie	Chevrolet
28.	Frank Warren	Dodge
29.	David Pearson	Mercury
30.	Lennie Pond	Chevrolet
31.	Buddy Arrington	Dodge
32.	A. J. Foyt	Chevrolet
33.	Bill Elliott	Ford
34.	Cecil Gordon	Chevrolet
35.	Skip Manning	Chevrolet
36.	Henley Gray	Chevrolet

RICHMOND 400

March 7
Richmond, Virginia
Time of Race: 2 hours, 58 minutes, 44 seconds
Average Speed: 72.792 mph

FINISH	DRIVER	CAR
1.	Dave Marcis	Dodge
2.	Richard Petty	Dodge
3.	Bobby Allison	Mercury
4.	Cale Yarborough	Chevrolet
5.	Terry Bivins	Chevrolet
6.	Richard Childress	Chevrolet
7.	Cecil Gordon	Chevrolet
8.	David Sisco	Chevrolet
9.	Benny Parsons	Chevrolet
10.	Elmo Langley	Ford
11.	Buddy Arrington	Plymouth
12.	Joe Mihalic	Chevrolet
13.	Ed Negre	Dodge
14.	Walter Ballard	Chevrolet
15.	James Hylton	Chevrolet
16.	Ernie Shaw	Chevrolet
17.	Travis Tiller	Dodge
18.	Earl Canavan	Dodge
19.	Frank Warren	Dodge
20.	D. K. Ulrich	Chevrolet
21.	J. D. McDuffie	Chevrolet
22.	Richard Brown	Pontiac
23.	Lennie Pond	Chevrolet
24.	Darrell Waltrip	Chevrolet
25.	Neil Castles	Chevrolet
26.	Richard Brooks	Ford
27.	Jabe Thomas	Chevrolet
28.	Bill Champion	Ford
29.	Buddy Baker	Ford
30.	Skip Manning	Chevrolet

SOUTHEASTERN 400

March 14
Bristol, Tennessee
Time of Race: 2 hours, 26 minutes, 24 seconds
Average Speed: 87.377 mph

FINISH	DRIVER	CAR
1.	Cale Yarborough	Chevrolet
2.	Darrell Waltrip	Chevrolet
3.	Benny Parsons	Chevrolet
4.	Dave Marcis	Dodge
5.	Bobby Allison	Mercury
6.	Richard Brooks	Ford
7.	James Hylton	Chevrolet
8.	Ed Negre	Dodge
9.	Buddy Arrington	Plymouth
10.	J. D. McDuffie	Chevrolet
11.	Jerry Sisco	Chevrolet
12.	Skip Manning	Chevrolet
13.	Jabe Thomas	Chevrolet
14.	Frank Warren	Dodge

15.	Elmo Langley	Ford
16.	Baxter Price	Chevrolet
17.	Earle Canavan	Dodge
18.	Travis Tiller	Dodge
19.	Walter Ballard	Chevrolet
20.	Richard Childress	Chevrolet
21.	Buddy Baker	Ford
22.	Lennie Pond	Chevrolet
23.	David Sisco	Chevrolet
24.	Terry Bivins	Chevrolet
25.	D. K. Ulrich	Chevrolet
26.	Joe Mihalic	Chevrolet
27.	Richard Petty	Dodge
28.	Cecil Gordon	Chevrolet
29.	Bill Champion	Ford
30.	Henley Gray	Chevrolet

ATLANTA 500

March 21
Atlanta, Georgia
Time of Race: 3 hours, 52 minutes, 16 seconds
Average Speed: 128.904 mph

FINISH	DRIVER	CAR
1.	David Pearson	Mercury
2.	Benny Parsons	Chevrolet
3.	Cale Yarborough	Chevrolet
4.	Lennie Pond	Chevrolet
5.	Darrell Waltrip	Chevrolet
6.	Coo Coo Marlin	Chevrolet
7.	Richard Brooks	Ford
8.	Neil Bonnett	Chevrolet
9.	David Sisco	Chevrolet
10.	Jackie Rogers	Chevrolet
11.	Richard Childress	Chevrolet
12.	Grant Adcox	Chevrolet
13.	Ed Negre	Dodge
14.	Bob Burcham	Chevrolet
15.	Frank Warren	Dodge
16.	Cecil Gordon	Chevrolet
17.	Skip Manning	Chevrolet
18.	Bruce Hill	Chevrolet
19.	John Utsman	Dodge
20.	Darrell Bryant	Chevrolet
21.	D. K. Ulrich	Chevrolet
22.	Jerry Sisco	Chevrolet
23.	Henley Gray	Chevrolet
24.	Walter Ballard	Chevrolet
25.	Buddy Baker	Ford
26.	Terry Bivins	Chevrolet
27.	J. D. McDuffie	Chevrolet
28.	Richard Petty	Dodge
29.	Bobby Allison	Mercury
30.	Buddy Arrington	Dodge
31.	James Hylton	Chevrolet
32.	Dave Marcis	Dodge
33.	Jimmy Capps	Chevrolet
34.	Jimmy Means	Chevrolet
35.	Tommy Gale	Ford
36.	Bill Elliott	Ford

GWYN STALEY 400

April 4
North Wilkesboro, North Carolina
Time of Race: 2 hours, 34 minutes, 52 seconds
Average Speed: 96.858 mph

FINISH	DRIVER	CAR
1.	Cale Yarborough	Chevrolet
2.	Richard Petty	Dodge
3.	Bobby Allison	Mercury
4.	Benny Parsons	Chevrolet
5.	J. D. McDuffie	Chevrolet

6.	Lennie Pond	Chevrolet
7.	Richard Brooks	Ford
8.	Dave Marcis	Dodge
9.	Richard Childress	Chevrolet
10.	Walter Ballard	Chevrolet
11.	Skip Manning	Chevrolet
12.	Cecil Gordon	Chevrolet
13.	James Hylton	Chevrolet
14.	Junior Miller	Chevrolet
15.	Elmo Langley	Ford
16.	Bill Champion	Ford
17.	Ed Negre	Dodge
18.	Buddy Arrington	Plymouth
19.	D. K. Ulrich	Chevrolet
20.	Frank Warren	Dodge
21.	Jabe Thomas	Chevrolet
22.	Darrell Waltrip	Chevrolet
23.	Baxter Price	Chevrolet
24.	Richard Brown	Pontiac
25.	Neil Castles	Dodge
26.	Buddy Baker	Ford
27.	David Sisco	Chevrolet
28.	Jeff Handy	Chevrolet

REBEL 500

April 11
Darlington, South Carolina
Time of Race: 4 hours, 4 minutes, 36 seconds
Average Speed: 122.973 mph

FINISH	DRIVER	CAR
1.	David Pearson	Mercury
2.	Buddy Baker	Ford
3.	Benny Parsons	Chevrolet
4.	Lennie Pond	Chevrolet
5.	Dave Marcis	Dodge
6.	Buck Baker	Ford
7.	Grant Adcox	Chevrolet
8.	Joe Frasson	Chevrolet
9.	Richard Childress	Chevrolet
10.	Bruce Hill	Chevrolet
11.	Cecil Gordon	Chevrolet
12.	John Utsman	Dodge
13.	David Sisco	Chevrolet
14.	Skip Manning	Chevrolet
15.	Dick May	Chevrolet
16.	D. K. Ulrich	Chevrolet
17.	Frank Warren	Dodge
18.	Bobby Allison	Mercury
19.	Earle Canavan	Dodge
20.	Earl Brooks	Chevrolet
21.	Dick Skillen	Chevrolet
22.	Tommy Gale	Ford
23.	Richard Petty	Dodge
24.	Buddy Arrington	Dodge
25.	Cale Yarborough	Chevrolet
26.	Jerry Sisco	Chevrolet
27.	J. D. McDuffie	Chevrolet
28.	Ed Negre	Dodge
29.	Henley Gray	Chevrolet
30.	Neil Bonnett	Chevrolet
31.	Darrell Waltrip	Chevrolet
32.	James Hylton	Chevrolet
33.	Bob Burcham	Chevrolet
34.	Donnie Allison	Chevrolet
35.	Richard Brooks	Ford
36.	Darrell Bryant	Chevrolet

VIRGINIA 500

April 25
Martinsville, Virginia
Time of Race: 3 hours, 39 minutes, 43 seconds
Average Speed: 71.759 mph

FINISH	DRIVER	CAR
1.	Darrell Waltrip	Chevrolet
2.	Cale Yarborough	Chevrolet
3.	David Pearson	Mercury
4.	Richard Petty	Dodge
5.	Richard Brooks	Ford
6.	Bobby Allison	Mercury
7.	Bruce Hill	Chevrolet
8.	Richard Childress	Chevrolet
9.	Walter Ballard	Chevrolet
10.	Cecil Gordon	Chevrolet
11.	Gary Myers	Chevrolet
12.	James Hylton	Chevrolet
13.	Elmo Langley	Ford
14.	Jabe Thomas	Chevrolet
15.	Bruce Blodgett	Dodge
16.	D. K. Ulrich	Chevrolet
17.	Skip Manning	Chevrolet
18.	Rick Newsom	Ford
19.	Neil Bonnett	Chevrolet
20.	Benny Parsons	Chevrolet
21.	Dave Marcis	Dodge
22.	Lennie Pond	Chevrolet
23.	J. D. McDuffie	Chevrolet
24.	David Sisco	Chevrolet
25.	Jimmy Hensley	Chevrolet
26.	Travis Tiller	Dodge
27.	Buddy Baker	Ford
28.	Buddy Arrington	Dodge
29.	Frank Warren	Dodge
30.	Ed Negre	Chevrolet

WINSTON 500

May 2
Talladega, Alabama
Time of Race: 2 hours, 56 minutes, 37 seconds
Average Speed: 169.887 mph

FINISH	DRIVER	CAR
1.	Buddy Baker	Ford
2.	Cale Yarborough	Chevrolet
3.	Bobby Allison	Mercury
4.	Richard Petty	Dodge
5.	Terry Ryan	Chevrolet
6.	Cecil Gordon	Chevrolet
7.	Donnie Allison	Chevrolet
8.	Bruce Hill	Chevrolet
9.	Dave Marcis	Dodge
10.	Frank Warren	Dodge
11.	Lennie Pond	Chevrolet
12.	Richard Brooks	Ford
13.	Jim Vandiver	Dodge
14.	David Sisco	Chevrolet
15.	John Utsman	Dodge
16.	Skip Manning	Chevrolet
17.	Tighe Scott	Chevrolet
18.	Tommy Gale	Ford
19.	Grant Adcox	Chevrolet
20.	D. K. Ulrich	Chevrolet
21.	Dick Skillen	Chevrolet
22.	Buddy Arrington	Dodge
23.	Ricky Rudd	Chevrolet
24.	Richard Childress	Chevrolet
25.	Ferrell Harris	Dodge
26.	Benny Parsons	Chevrolet
27.	J. D. McDuffie	Chevrolet
28.	James Hylton	Chevrolet
29.	Bob Wawak	Chevrolet
30.	Bob Burcham	Chevrolet
31.	Jimmy Means	Chevrolet
32.	Ed Negre	Chevrolet
33.	Darrell Waltrip	Chevrolet
34.	Buck Baker	Chevrolet
35.	Gary Myers	Chevrolet
36.	Joe Frasson	Chevrolet
37.	David Pearson	Mercury
38.	Bill Elliott	Ford
39.	Neil Bonnett	Chevrolet
40.	Darrell Bryant	Chevrolet

MUSIC CITY USA 420

May 8
Nashville, Tennessee
Time of Race: 2 hours, 57 minutes, 43 seconds
Average Speed: 84.512 mph

FINISH	DRIVER	CAR
1.	Cale Yarborough	Chevrolet
2.	Richard Petty	Dodge
3.	Benny Parsons	Chevrolet
4.	Buddy Baker	Ford
5.	Bobby Allison	Mercury
6.	Lennie Pond	Chevrolet
7.	Dave Marcis	Dodge
8.	Walter Ballard	Chevrolet
9.	David Sisco	Chevrolet
10.	Frank Warren	Dodge
11.	D. K. Ulrich	Chevrolet
12.	Darrell Waltrip	Chevrolet
13.	Elmo Langley	Ford
14.	Cecil Gordon	Chevrolet
15.	Jimmy Means	Chevrolet
16.	Buck Baker	Chevrolet
17.	Richard Childress	Chevrolet
18.	James Hylton	Chevrolet
19.	Ed Negre	Dodge
20.	J. D. McDuffie	Chevrolet
21.	Jabe Thomas	Chevrolet
22.	Skip Manning	Chevrolet
23.	Bruce Hill	Chevrolet
24.	Baxter Price	Chevrolet
25.	Henley Gray	Chevrolet
26.	Buddy Arrington	Dodge
27.	Gary Myers	Chevrolet
28.	Walter Wallace	Chevrolet
29.	Sterling Marlin	Chevrolet
30.	Rick Newsom	Ford

MASON-DIXON 500

May 16
Dover, Delaware
Time of Race: 4 hours, 19 minutes, 53 seconds
Average Speed: 115.436 mph

FINISH	DRIVER	CAR
1.	Benny Parsons	Chevrolet
2.	David Pearson	Mercury
3.	Dave Marcis	Dodge
4.	Bobby Allison	Mercury
5.	Buddy Baker	Ford
6.	Richard Petty	Dodge
7.	Richard Brooks	Ford
8.	Lennie Pond	Chevrolet
9.	Darrell Bryant	Chevrolet
10.	Richard Childress	Chevrolet
11.	Skip Manning	Chevrolet
12.	D. K. Ulrich	Chevrolet
13.	Frank Warren	Dodge
14.	Jabe Thomas	Chevrolet
15.	J. D. McDuffie	Chevrolet
16.	Walter Ballard	Chevrolet
17.	James Hylton	Chevrolet
18.	Joe Mihalic	Chevrolet
19.	Budd Hagelin	Dodge
20.	Rick Newsom	Ford
21.	Baxter Price	Chevrolet
22.	David Sisco	Chevrolet
23.	Travis Tiller	Dodge
24.	Doc Faustina	Dodge
25.	Gary Myers	Chevrolet
26.	Bobby Wawak	Chevrolet
27.	Cale Yarborough	Chevrolet
28.	Buck Baker	Chevrolet
29.	Dean Dalton	Chevrolet
30.	Darrell Waltrip	Chevrolet

FINISH	DRIVER	CAR
31.	Buddy Arrington	Dodge
32.	Earl Brooks	Ford
33.	Ricky Rudd	Chevrolet
34.	Ed Negre	Dodge
35.	Donnie Allison	Chevrolet
36.	Cecil Gordon	Chevrolet
37.	Tommy Gale	Ford
38.	Neil Castles	Chevrolet
39.	Bruce Hill	Chevrolet

WORLD 600

May 30
Charlotte, North Carolina
Time of Race: 4 hours, 22 minutes, 6 seconds
Average Speed: 137.352 mph

FINISH	DRIVER	CAR
1.	David Pearson	Mercury
2.	Richard Petty	Dodge
3.	Cale Yarborough	Chevrolet
4.	Bobby Allison	Mercury
5.	Benny Parsons	Chevrolet
6.	Donnie Allison	Chevrolet
7.	Richard Brooks	Ford
8.	Lennie Pond	Chevrolet
9.	Harry Gant	Chevrolet
10.	David Sisco	Chevrolet
11.	Darrell Waltrip	Chevrolet
12.	Grant Adcox	Chevrolet
13.	James Hylton	Chevrolet
14.	Buddy Arrington	Dodge
15.	Janet Guthrie	Chevrolet
16.	D. K. Ulrich	Chevrolet
17.	Richard Childress	Chevrolet
18.	Frank Warren	Dodge
19.	Darrell Bryant	Chevrolet
20.	Cecil Gordon	Chevrolet
21.	Dick May	Chevrolet
22.	Walter Ballard	Chevrolet
23.	Bill Elliott	Ford
24.	Sam Sommers	Chevrolet
25.	J. D. McDuffie	Chevrolet
26.	Bobby Wawak	Chevrolet
27.	Ed Negre	Dodge
28.	Buddy Baker	Ford
29.	Dave Marcis	Dodge
30.	Gary Myers	Chevrolet
31.	Dale Earnhardt	Chevrolet
32.	Dick Trickle	Ford
33.	Skip Manning	Chevrolet
34.	Charlie Glotzbach	Chevrolet
35.	Bob Burcham	Chevrolet
36.	Jackie Rogers	Chevrolet
37.	Bruce Hill	Chevrolet
38.	Bobby Isaac	Chevrolet
39.	Jimmy Means	Chevrolet
40.	Terry Ryan	Chevrolet

RIVERSIDE 400

June 6
Riverside, California
Time of Race: 2 hours, 20 minutes, 31 seconds
Average Speed: 106.279 mph

FINISH	DRIVER	CAR
1.	David Pearson	Mercury
2.	Bobby Allison	Mercury
3.	Benny Parsons	Chevrolet
4.	Ray Elder	Dodge
5.	Buddy Baker	Ford
6.	Darrell Waltrip	Chevrolet
7.	Cale Yarborough	Chevrolet
8.	Jim Insolo	Chevrolet

FINISH	DRIVER	CAR
9.	Richard Petty	Dodge
10.	Dave Marcis	Dodge
11.	Richard Childress	Chevrolet
12.	Cecil Gordon	Chevrolet
13.	Chuck Wahl	Chevrolet
14.	J. D. McDuffie	Chevrolet
15.	Eddie Bradshaw	Chevrolet
16.	James Hylton	Chevrolet
17.	Bill Polich	Chevrolet
18.	Don Reynolds	Chevrolet
19.	Chuck Bown	Chevrolet
20.	Frank Warren	Dodge
21.	Don Puskarich	Chevrolet
22.	John Dineen	Ford
23.	Gary Johnson	Chevrolet
24.	Ed Negre	Dodge
25.	Lennie Pond	Chevrolet
26.	D. K. Ulrich	Chevrolet
27.	Roy Smith	Chevrolet
28.	J. C. Danielson	Dodge
29.	Neil Bonnett	Chevrolet
30.	Hugh Pearson	Chevrolet
31.	Rusty Sanders	Chevrolet
32.	John Hamson	Chevrolet
33.	Ernie Stierly	Chevrolet
34.	Jim Thirkettle	Chevrolet
35.	Ron Esau	Ford

CAM2 MOTOR OIL 400

June 13
Brooklyn, Michigan
Time of Race: 2 hours, 50 minutes, 2 seconds
Average Speed: 141.148 mph

FINISH	DRIVER	CAR
1.	David Pearson	Mercury
2.	Cale Yarborough	Chevrolet
3.	Bobby Allison	Mercury
4.	Richard Petty	Dodge
5.	Buddy Baker	Ford
6.	Richard Brooks	Ford
7.	Lennie Pond	Chevrolet
8.	David Sisco	Chevrolet
9.	Jackie Rogers	Chevrolet
10.	Cecil Gordon	Chevrolet
11.	Buddy Arrington	Dodge
12.	D. K. Ulrich	Chevrolet
13.	Coo Coo Marlin	Chevrolet
14.	Dick May	Chevrolet
15.	Tighe Scott	Chevrolet
16.	J. D. McDuffie	Chevrolet
17.	Ed Negre	Dodge
18.	Richard Childress	Chevrolet
19.	Benny Parsons	Chevrolet
20.	Skip Manning	Chevrolet
21.	Tommy Gale	Ford
22.	Travis Tiller	Dodge
23.	Jimmy Means	Chevrolet
24.	Frank Warren	Dodge
25.	Bruce Hill	Chevrolet
26.	Bobby Wawak	Chevrolet
27.	Gary Myers	Chevrolet
28.	Bill Elliott	Ford
29.	Darrell Waltrip	Chevrolet
30.	Dave Marcis	Dodge
31.	Walter Ballard	Chevrolet
32.	Terry Ryan	Chevrolet
33.	Henley Gray	Chevrolet
34.	Earl Canavan	Dodge
35.	James Hylton	Chevrolet
36.	Joe Frasson	Chevrolet

FIRECRACKER 400

July 4
Daytona Beach, Florida

Time of Race: 2 hours, 29 minutes, 6 seconds
Average Speed: 160.966 mph

FINISH	DRIVER	CAR
1.	Cale Yarborough	Chevrolet
2.	David Pearson	Mercury
3.	Bobby Allison	Mercury
4.	A. J. Foyt	Chevrolet
5.	Dave Marcis	Dodge
6.	Coo Coo Martin	Chevrolet
7.	Benny Parsons	Chevrolet
8.	Richard Brooks	Ford
9.	David Sisco	Chevrolet
10.	Ricky Rudd	Chevrolet
11.	Jimmy Means	Chevrolet
12.	Richard Childress	Chevrolet
13.	Frank Warren	Dodge
14.	Bobby Wawak	Chevrolet
15.	Janet Guthrie	Chevrolet
16.	D. K. Ulrich	Chevrolet
17.	Dick Skillen	Chevrolet
18.	Harold Miller	Chevrolet
19.	Bill Elliott	Ford
20.	John Rutherford	Chevrolet
21.	Jimmy Capps	Chevrolet
22.	Richard Petty	Dodge
23.	Joe Mihalic	Chevrolet
24.	J. D. McDuffie	Chevrolet
25.	Bruce Hill	Chevrolet
26.	James Hylton	Chevrolet
27.	Dick May	Chevrolet
28.	Ferrell Harris	Dodge
29.	Tommy Gale	Chevrolet
30.	Grant Adcox	Chevrolet
31.	Skip Manning	Chevrolet
32.	Lennie Pond	Chevrolet
33.	Neil Bonnett	Chevrolet
34.	Cecil Gordon	Chevrolet
35.	Buddy Baker	Ford
36.	Buck Baker	Chevrolet
37.	Ed Negre	Chevrolet
38.	Jackie Rogers	Chevrolet
39.	Darrell Waltrip	Chevrolet
40.	Buddy Arrington	Dodge

NASHVILLE 420

July 16
Nashville, Tennessee
Time of Race: 2 hours, 52 minutes, 49 seconds
Average Speed: 86.908 mph

FINISH	DRIVER	CAR
1.	Benny Parsons	Chevrolet
2.	Richard Petty	Dodge
3.	Darrell Waltrip	Chevrolet
4.	Lennie Pond	Chevrolet
5.	Cale Yarborough	Chevrolet
6.	Dave Marcis	Dodge
7.	Bobby Allison	Mercury
8.	Coo Coo Marlin	Chevrolet
9.	Skip Manning	Chevrolet
10.	Bobby Wawak	Chevrolet
11.	James Hylton	Chevrolet
12.	Frank Warren	Dodge
13.	J. D. McDuffie	Chevrolet
14.	Bill Elliott	Ford
15.	Cecil Gordon	Chevrolet
16.	David Sisco	Chevrolet
17.	D. K. Ulrich	Chevrolet
18.	Walter Wallace	Chevrolet
19.	Gary Myers	Chevrolet
20.	Walter Ballard	Chevrolet
21.	Dick May	Chevrolet
22.	Terry Bivins	Chevrolet
23.	Buddy Baker	Ford
24.	Jimmy Means	Chevrolet
25.	Ed Negre	Dodge

26.	Buddy Arrington	Dodge
27.	Bruce Hill	Chevrolet
28.	Richard Childress	Chevrolet
29.	Richard Brooks	Ford
30.	Joe Frasson	Chevrolet

PUROLATOR 500

August 1
Pocono, Pennsylvania
Time of Race: 4 hours, 18 minutes, 54 seconds
Average Speed: 115.875 mph

FINISH	DRIVER	CAR
1.	Richard Petty	Dodge
2.	Buddy Baker	Ford
3.	Benny Parsons	Chevrolet
4.	David Pearson	Mercury
5.	Lennie Pond	Chevrolet
6.	Cecil Gordon	Chevrolet
7.	Buddy Arrington	Plymouth
8.	Jackie Rogers	Chevrolet
9.	Richard Childress	Chevrolet
10.	David Sisco	Chevrolet
11.	Ed Negre	Dodge
12.	Skip Manning	Chevrolet
13.	Joe Mihalic	Chevrolet
14.	Bobby Wawak	Chevrolet
15.	Dean Dalton	Chevrolet
16.	Frank Warren	Dodge
17.	James Hylton	Chevrolet
18.	Dick May	Chevrolet
19.	Terry Bivins	Chevrolet
20.	Henley Gray	Chevrolet
21.	J. D. McDuffie	Chevrolet
22.	Dave Marcis	Dodge
23.	Jimmy Means	Chevrolet
24.	Bobby Allison	Mercury
25.	Cale Yarborough	Chevrolet
26.	Darrell Waltrip	Chevrolet
27.	Gary Myers	Chevrolet
28.	Baxter Price	Chevrolet
29.	Bruce Hill	Chevrolet
30.	Tighe Scott	Chevrolet
31.	Richard Brooks	Ford
32.	Bill Elliott	Ford
33.	Travis Tiller	Dodge
34.	Tommy Gale	Ford
35.	Darrell Bryant	Chevrolet
36.	Earle Canavan	Dodge
37.	Walter Ballard	Dodge
38.	D. K. Ulrich	Chevrolet
39.	Bill Hollar	Chevrolet
40.	Joe Frasson	Chevrolet

TALLADEGA 500

August 8
Talladega, Alabama
Time of Race: 3 hours, 10 minutes, 27 seconds
Average Speed: 157.547 mph

FINISH	DRIVER	CAR
1.	Dave Marcis	Dodge
2.	Buddy Baker	Ford
3.	Richard Brooks	Ford
4.	James Hylton	Chevrolet
5.	Lennie Pond	Chevrolet
6.	Tighe Scott	Chevrolet
7.	J. D. McDuffie	Chevrolet
8.	Richard Childress	Chevrolet
9.	Skip Manning	Chevrolet
10.	Jimmy Capps	Chevrolet
11.	Jimmy Means	Chevrolet
12.	Frank Warren	Dodge

FINISH	DRIVER	CAR
13.	Joe Mihalic	Chevrolet
14.	Harold Miller	Chevrolet
15.	Jackie Rogers	Chevrolet
16.	Buck Baker	Chevrolet
17.	Henley Gray	Chevrolet
18.	Grant Adcox	Chevrolet
19.	Dick May	Chevrolet
20.	Richard Petty	Dodge
21.	D. K. Ulrich	Chevrolet
22.	A. J. Foyt	Chevrolet
23.	Bobby Allison	Mercury
24.	Bobby Wawak	Chevrolet
25.	G. C. Spencer	Dodge
26.	Cale Yarborough	Chevrolet
27.	Ed Negre	Dodge
28.	David Pearson	Mercury
29.	Cecil Gordon	Chevrolet
30.	Dick Skillen	Chevrolet
31.	David Sisco	Chevrolet
32.	Bruce Hill	Chevrolet
33.	Buddy Arrington	Dodge
34.	Coo Coo Marlin	Chevrolet
35.	Bob Burcham	Chevrolet
36.	Sam Sommers	Chevrolet
37.	Darrell Waltrip	Chevrolet
38.	Neil Bonnett	Chevrolet
39.	Benny Parsons	Chevrolet
40.	Tommy Gale	Ford

CHAMPION SPARK PLUG 400

August 22
Brooklyn, Michigan
Time of Race: 2 hours, 51 minutes, 20 seconds
Average Speed: 140.078 mph

FINISH	DRIVER	CAR
1.	David Pearson	Mercury
2.	Cale Yarborough	Chevrolet
3.	Richard Petty	Dodge
4.	Bobby Allison	Mercury
5.	Dave Marcis	Dodge
6.	Neil Bonnett	Chevrolet
7.	D. K. Ulrich	Chevrolet
8.	J. D. McDuffie	Chevrolet
9.	Benny Parsons	Chevrolet
10.	Bobby Wawak	Chevrolet
11.	Henley Gray	Chevrolet
12.	Coo Coo Marlin	Chevrolet
13.	Richard Childress	Chevrolet
14.	Skip Manning	Chevrolet
15.	Terry Bivins	Ford
16.	Dick May	Chevrolet
17.	David Hobbs	Ford
18.	Dean Dalton	Chevrolet
19.	Bruce Hill	Chevrolet
20.	Harold Miller	Chevrolet
21.	James Hylton	Chevrolet
22.	Joe Mihalic	Chevrolet
23.	Frank Warren	Dodge
24.	Jimmy Means	Chevrolet
25.	Lennie Pond	Chevrolet
26.	Cecil Gordon	Chevrolet
27.	Darrell Waltrip	Chevrolet
28.	Joe Frasson	Chevrolet
29.	Richard Brooks	Ford
30.	Ed Negre	Dodge
31.	Buddy Baker	Ford
32.	David Sisco	Chevrolet
33.	John Haver	Chevrolet
34.	G. C. Spencer	Dodge
35.	Jackie Rogers	Chevrolet
36.	Tighe Scott	Chevrolet

VOLUNTEER 400

August 29
Bristol, Tennessee

Time of Race: 2 hours, 8 minutes, 59 seconds
Average Speed: 99.175 mph

FINISH	DRIVER	CAR
1.	Cale Yarborough	Chevrolet
2.	Richard Petty	Dodge
3.	Darrell Waltrip	Chevrolet
4.	Benny Parsons	Chevrolet
5.	Buddy Baker	Ford
6.	Bobby Allison	Mercury
7.	Richard Brooks	Ford
8.	Lennie Pond	Chevrolet
9.	Bobby Wawak	Chevrolet
10.	Richard Childress	Chevrolet
11.	D. K. Ulrich	Chevrolet
12.	Terry Bivins	Chevrolet
13.	James Hylton	Chevrolet
14.	David Sisco	Chevrolet
15.	Henley Gray	Chevrolet
16.	Dick May	Chevrolet
17.	Buddy Arrington	Plymouth
18.	Skip Manning	Chevrolet
19.	Jimmy Means	Chevrolet
20.	Frank Warren	Dodge
21.	Cecil Gordon	Chevrolet
22.	Dave Marcis	Dodge
23.	J. D. McDuffie	Chevrolet
24.	Clyde Lynn	Ford
25.	Elmo Langley	Ford
26.	Walter Ballard	Chevrolet
27.	Gary Myers	Chevrolet
28.	Dean Dalton	Chevrolet
29.	Ed Negre	Dodge
30.	Joe Frasson	Chevrolet

SOUTHERN 500

September 6
Darlington, South Carolina
Time of Race: 4 hours, 9 minutes, 33 seconds
Average Speed: 120.534 mph

FINISH	DRIVER	CAR
1.	David Pearson	Mercury
2.	Richard Petty	Dodge
3.	Darrell Waltrip	Chevrolet
4.	Dave Marcis	Dodge
5.	Lennie Pond	Chevrolet
6.	Richard Brooks	Ford
7.	Benny Parsons	Chevrolet
8.	Coo Coo Marlin	Chevrolet
9.	Bobby Allison	Mercury
10.	Bobby Wawak	Chevrolet
11.	Dean Dalton	Chevrolet
12.	Cecil Gordon	Chevrolet
13.	Grant Adcox	Chevrolet
14.	Terry Bivins	Chevrolet
15.	Jackie Rogers	Chevrolet
16.	D. K. Ulrich	Chevrolet
17.	Buck Baker	Chevrolet
18.	Jimmy Means	Chevrolet
19.	Frank Warren	Dodge
20.	James Hylton	Chevrolet
21.	Henley Gray	Chevrolet
22.	Bruce Hill	Chevrolet
23.	Cale Yarborough	Chevrolet
24.	Neil Bonnett	Chevrolet
25.	J. D. McDuffie	Chevrolet
26.	Ed Negre	Dodge
27.	Gary Myers	Chevrolet
28.	Dick May	Dodge
29.	Earle Canavan	Dodge
30.	Sam Sommers	Chevrolet
31.	Buddy Baker	Ford
32.	Skip Manning	Chevrolet
33.	Donnie Allison	Chevrolet
34.	Joe Frasson	Chevrolet
35.	Buddy Arrington	Dodge

36.	Richard Childress	Chevrolet
37.	Bruce Jacobii	Ford
38.	Rick Newsom	Chevrolet
39.	David Sisco	Chevrolet
40.	Darrell Bryant	Chevrolet

CAPITAL CITY 400

September 12
Richmond, Virginia
Time of Race: 2 hours, 46 minutes, 47 seconds
Average Speed: 77.993 mph

FINISH	DRIVER	CAR
1.	Cale Yarborough	Chevrolet
2.	Bobby Allison	Mercury
3.	Richard Petty	Dodge
4.	Darrell Waltrip	Chevrolet
5.	Buddy Baker	Ford
6.	Lennie Pond	Chevrolet
7.	Dave Marcis	Dodge
8.	Richard Brooks	Ford
9.	Terry Bivins	Chevrolet
10.	Bobby Wawak	Chevrolet
11.	J. D. McDuffie	Chevrolet
12.	Henley Gray	Chevrolet
13.	Cecil Gordon	Chevrolet
14.	Dean Dalton	Chevrolet
15.	Elmo Langley	Ford
16.	James Hylton	Chevrolet
17.	D. K. Ulrich	Chevrolet
18.	Buddy Arrington	Dodge
19.	Dick May	Chevrolet
20.	Earl Brooks	Chevrolet
21.	Gary Myers	Chevrolet
22.	Walter Ballard	Chevrolet
23.	David Sisco	Chevrolet
24.	Jimmy Means	Chevrolet
25.	Richard Childress	Chevrolet
26.	Frank Warren	Dodge
27.	Ed Negre	Dodge
28.	Travis Tiller	Dodge
29.	Benny Parsons	Chevrolet
30.	Larry Lamay	Chevrolet

DELAWARE 500

September 19
Dover, Delaware
Time of Race: 4 hours, 19 minutes, 12 seconds
Average Speed: 115.740 mph

FINISH	DRIVER	CAR
1.	Cale Yarborough	Chevrolet
2.	Richard Petty	Dodge
3.	David Pearson	Mercury
4.	Bobby Allison	Mercury
5.	Buddy Baker	Ford
6.	Richard Brooks	Ford
7.	J. D. McDuffie	Chevrolet
8.	D. K. Ulrich	Chevrolet
9.	James Hylton	Chevrolet
10.	Buddy Arrington	Dodge
11.	David Sisco	Chevrolet
12.	Skip Manning	Chevrolet
13.	Henley Gray	Chevrolet
14.	Dave Marcis	Dodge
15.	Ed Negre	Dodge
16.	Walter Ballard	Chevrolet
17.	Dick May	Chevrolet
18.	Joe Mihalic	Chevrolet
19.	Jack Donohue	Chevrolet
20.	Richard Childress	Chevrolet
21.	Tommy Ellis	Ford
22.	Bobby Wawak	Chevrolet

23.	Frank Warren	Dodge
24.	Earle Canavan	Dodge
25.	Tommy Gale	Ford
26.	Benny Parsons	Chevrolet
27.	Jimmy Means	Chevrolet
28.	Bruce Jacobii	Chevrolet
29.	Gary Myers	Chevrolet
30.	Rick Newsom	Ford
31.	Darrell Waltrip	Chevrolet
32.	Terry Bivins	Chevrolet
33.	Janet Guthrie	Chevrolet
34.	Lennie Pond	Chevrolet
35.	Cecil Gordon	Chevrolet
36.	Bruce Hill	Chevrolet

OLD DOMINION 500

September 26
Martinsville, Virginia
Time of Race: 2 hours, 22 minutes, 15 seconds
Average Speed: 75.370 mph

FINISH	DRIVER	CAR
1.	Cale Yarborough	Chevrolet
2.	Darrell Waltrip	Chevrolet
3.	Buddy Baker	Ford
4.	Richard Petty	Dodge
5.	Benny Parsons	Chevrolet
6.	Richard Brooks	Ford
7.	Jimmy Hensley	Chevrolet
8.	Terry Bivins	Chevrolet
9.	Sonny Easley	Ford
10.	Richard Childress	Chevrolet
11.	Buddy Arrington	Dodge
12.	Dave Marcis	Dodge
13.	D. K. Ulrich	Chevrolet
14.	Frank Warren	Chevrolet
15.	Cecil Gordon	Chevrolet
16.	David Sisco	Chevrolet
17.	Dick May	Chevrolet
18.	James Hylton	Chevrolet
19.	David Pearson	Mercury
20.	Jimmy Means	Chevrolet
21.	J. D. McDuffie	Chevrolet
22.	Ed Negre	Ford
23.	Skip Manning	Chevrolet
24.	Rick Newsom	Ford
25.	Bobby Wawak	Chevrolet
26.	Gary Myers	Chevrolet
27.	Bobby Allison	Mercury
28.	Chuck Bown	Chevrolet
29.	Lennie Pond	Chevrolet
30.	Bruce Hill	Chevrolet

WILKES 400

October 3
North Wilkesboro, North Carolina
Time of Race: 2 hours, 35 minutes, 38 seconds
Average Speed: 96.380 mph

FINISH	DRIVER	CAR
1.	Cale Yarborough	Chevrolet
2.	Benny Parsons	Chevrolet
3.	Richard Petty	Dodge
4.	Buddy Baker	Ford
5.	Lennie Pond	Chevrolet
6.	Richard Brooks	Ford
7.	J. D. McDuffie	Chevrolet
8.	Bobby Wawak	Chevrolet
9.	Terry Bivins	Chevrolet
10.	Sonny Easley	Ford
11.	James Hylton	Chevrolet
12.	Buddy Arrington	Plymouth
13.	Cecil Gordon	Chevrolet

14.	David Sisco	Chevrolet
15.	Junior Miller	Chevrolet
16.	Larry Lamay	Chevrolet
17.	Dave Marcis	Dodge
18.	Gary Myers	Chevrolet
19.	Henley Gray	Chevrolet
20.	Dick May	Chevrolet
21.	Skip Manning	Ford
22.	Frank Warren	Dodge
23.	Richard Childress	Chevrolet
24.	Darrell Waltrip	Chevrolet
25.	Ed Negre	Dodge
26.	D. K. Ulrich	Chevrolet
27.	Jimmy Means	Chevrolet
28.	Neil Bonnett	Chevrolet
29.	Bobby Allison	Mercury
30.	Richard Brown	Pontiac

NATIONAL 500

October 10
Charlotte, North Carolina
Time of Race: 3 hours, 32 minutes, 51 seconds
Average Speed: 141.226 mph

FINISH	DRIVER	CAR
1.	Donnie Allison	Chevrolet
2.	Cale Yarborough	Chevrolet
3.	Bobby Allison	Mercury
4.	Buddy Baker	Ford
5.	Benny Parsons	Chevrolet
6.	David Pearson	Mercury
7.	Lennie Pond	Chevrolet
8.	Richard Petty	Dodge
9.	Richard Brooks	Ford
10.	Bobby Wawak	Chevrolet
11.	Darrell Waltrip	Chevrolet
12.	Buddy Arrington	Dodge
13.	Skip Manning	Chevrolet
14.	Grant Adcox	Chevrolet
15.	Richard Childress	Chevrolet
16.	Ricky Rudd	Chevrolet
17.	G. C. Spencer	Dodge
18.	James Hylton	Chevrolet
19.	David Sisco	Chevrolet
20.	Earl Brooks	Chevrolet
21.	Bill Dennis	Chevrolet
22.	Janet Guthrie	Chevrolet
23.	J. D. McDuffie	Chevrolet
24.	Buck Baker	Chevrolet
25.	Terry Bivins	Chevrolet
26.	Frank Warren	Dodge
27.	Bruce Jacobii	Chevrolet
28.	Cecil Gordon	Chevrolet
29.	Dave Marcis	Dodge
30.	D. K. Ulrich	Chevrolet
31.	Johnny Rutherford	Chevrolet
32.	Coo Coo Marlin	Chevrolet
33.	Sonny Easley	Ford
34.	Bruce Hill	Chevrolet
35.	Neil Bonnett	Chevrolet
36.	Sam Sommers	Chevrolet
37.	Ed Negre	Dodge
38.	A. J. Foyt	Chevrolet
39.	Gordon Johncock	Dodge
40.	Al Holbert	Ford

AMERICAN 500

October 24
Rockingham, North Carolina
Time of Race: 4 hours, 15 minutes, 1 second
Average Speed: 117.718 mph

FINISH	DRIVER	CAR
1.	Richard Petty	Dodge

2.	Lennie Pond	Chevrolet
3.	Darrell Waltrip	Chevrolet
4.	Bobby Allison	Mercury
5.	Cale Yarborough	Chevrolet
6.	David Pearson	Mercury
7.	Donnie Allison	Chevrolet
8.	Richard Brooks	Ford
9.	Skip Manning	Chevrolet
10.	Coo Coo Marlin	Chevrolet
11.	Sonny Easley	Ford
12.	Grant Adcox	Chevrolet
13.	Ed Negre	Dodge
14.	D. K. Ulrich	Chevrolet
15.	Cecil Gordon	Chevrolet
16.	Buddy Arrington	Dodge
17.	Terry Bivins	Chevrolet
18.	Rick Newsom	Ford
19.	Jackie Rogers	Chevrolet
20.	David Sisco	Chevrolet
21.	Jack Donohue	Chevrolet
22.	Frank Warren	Chevrolet
23.	Jimmy Means	Chevrolet
24.	Tommy Gale	Ford
25.	Dave Marcis	Dodge
26.	J. D. McDuffie	Chevrolet
27.	Richard Childress	Chevrolet
28.	Buddy Baker	Ford
29.	James Hylton	Dodge
30.	Dick May	Chevrolet
31.	Benny Parsons	Chevrolet
32.	Travis Tiller	Dodge
33.	Bobby Wawak	Chevrolet
34.	Gary Myers	Chevrolet
35.	Bruce Hill	Chevrolet
36.	Henley Gray	Dodge

DIXIE 500

November 7
Atlanta, Georgia
Time of Race: 3 hours, 55 minutes, 7 seconds
Average Speed: 127.396 mph

FINISH	DRIVER	CAR
1.	Dave Marcis	Dodge
2.	David Pearson	Mercury
3.	Donnie Allison	Chevrolet
4.	Cale Yarborough	Chevrolet
5.	Buddy Baker	Ford
6.	Benny Parsons	Chevrolet
7.	Darrell Waltrip	Chevrolet
8.	Neil Bonnett	Chevrolet
9.	Sam Sommers	Chevrolet
10.	Bobby Wawak	Chevrolet
11.	Bruce Hill	Chevrolet
12.	James Hylton	Chevrolet
13.	J. D. McDuffie	Chevrolet
14.	Skip Manning	Chevrolet
15.	Sonny Easley	Ford
16.	Gene Felton	Ford
17.	Jimmy Means	Chevrolet
18.	D. K. Ulrich	Chevrolet
19.	Dale Earnhardt	Chevrolet
20.	Grant Adcox	Chevrolet
21.	Richie Panch	Ford
22.	Terry Bivins	Chevrolet
23.	Cecil Gordon	Chevrolet
24.	Lennie Pond	Chevrolet
25.	Richard Childress	Chevrolet
26.	Bobby Allison	Mercury
27.	Frank Warren	Dodge
28.	Richard Petty	Dodge
29.	Richard Brooks	Ford
30.	Coo Coo Marlin	Chevrolet
31.	Chuck Bown	Chevrolet
32.	Dick May	Chevrolet
33.	David Sisco	Chevrolet
34.	Billy McGinnis	Chevrolet
35.	G. C. Spencer	Dodge
36.	Jack Donohue	Chevrolet

LOS ANGELES TIMES 500

November 21
Ontario, California
Time of Race: 3 hours, 38 minutes, 49 seconds
Average Speed: 137.101 mph

FINISH	DRIVER	CAR
1.	David Pearson	Mercury
2.	Lennie Pond	Chevrolet
3.	Benny Parsons	Chevrolet
4.	Richard Brooks	Ford
5.	James Hylton	Chevrolet
6.	Bobby Wawak	Chevrolet
7.	Terry Bivins	Chevrolet
8.	Skip Manning	Chevrolet
9.	Terry Ryan	Chevrolet
10.	Bruce Hill	Chevrolet
11.	J. D. McDuffie	Chevrolet
12.	Ed Negre	Dodge
13.	Larry Phillips	Ford
14.	Sonny Easley	Ford
15.	Don Puskarich	Chevrolet
16.	Cecil Gordon	Chevrolet
17.	Tommy Gale	Ford
18.	Frank Warren	Dodge
19.	Chuck Bown	Chevrolet
20.	Janet Guthrie	Chevrolet
21.	Jim Insolo	Chevrolet
22.	Mike Hiss	Chevrolet
23.	Cale Yarborough	Chevrolet
24.	Dave Marcis	Dodge
25.	D. K. Ulrich	Chevrolet
26.	Bill Schmitt	Chevrolet
27.	Richard Petty	Dodge
28.	Glen Francis	Chevrolet
29.	Jim Thirkettle	Chevrolet
30.	David Sisco	Chevrolet
31.	Carl Joiner	Chevrolet
32.	Hershel McGriff	Chevrolet
33.	Bobby Allison	Mercury
34.	Donnie Allison	Chevrolet
35.	John Kleper	Chevrolet
36.	Richard Childress	Chevrolet
37.	Dick May	Chevrolet
38.	Roy Smith	Chevrolet
39.	Buddy Baker	Ford
40.	Darrell Waltrip	Chevrolet

1977

WINSTON WESTERN 500

January 16
Riverside, California
Time of Race: 2 hours, 54 minutes, 46 seconds
Average Speed: 107.038 mph

FINISH	DRIVER	CAR
1.	David Pearson	Mercury
2.	Cale Yarborough	Chevrolet
3.	Richard Petty	Dodge
4.	Dave Marcis	Chevrolet
5.	Sonny Easley	Ford
6.	Richard Childress	Chevrolet
7.	Hershel McGriff	Chevrolet
8.	Hugh Pearson	Chevrolet
9.	Darrell Waltrip	Chevrolet
10.	Eddie Bradshaw	Chevrolet
11.	Cecil Gordon	Chevrolet
12.	Buddy Baker	Ford
13.	Chuck Bown	Chevrolet
14.	James Hylton	Chevrolet
15.	D. K. Ulrich	Chevrolet

16.	Jim Thirkettle	Chevrolet
17.	Neil Bonnett	Dodge
18.	Bobby Wawak	Chevrolet
19.	Bill Schmitt	Chevrolet
20.	Gary Johnson	Chevrolet
21.	Benny Parsons	Chevrolet
22.	Roy Smith	Chevrolet
23.	Norm Palmer	Dodge
24.	Gary Mathews	Plymouth
25.	Frank Warren	Dodge
26.	Chuck Wahl	Chevrolet
27.	Ed Negre	Dodge
28.	Bill Baker	Chevrolet
29.	J. D. McDuffie	Chevrolet
30.	Don Puskarich	Chevrolet
31.	Carl Joiner	Chevrolet
32.	Henley Gray	Chevrolet
33.	Glen Francis	Chevrolet
34.	Jim Insolo	Chevrolet
35.	Bobby Allison	Matador

DAYTONA 500

February 20
Daytona Beach, Florida
Time of Race: 3 hours, 15 minutes, 48 seconds
Average Speed: 153.218 mph

FINISH	DRIVER	CAR
1.	Cale Yarborough	Chevrolet
2.	Benny Parsons	Chevrolet
3.	Buddy Baker	Ford
4.	Coo Coo Marlin	Chevrolet
5.	Richard Brooks	Ford
6.	A. J. Foyt	Chevrolet
7.	Darrell Waltrip	Chevrolet
8.	Jimmy Means	Chevrolet
9.	Bob Burcham	Chevrolet
10.	James Hylton	Chevrolet
11.	Frank Warren	Dodge
12.	Janet Guthrie	Chevrolet
13.	J. D. McDuffie	Chevrolet
14.	D. K. Ulrich	Chevrolet
15.	Bobby Allison	Matador
16.	Tighe Scott	Chevrolet
17.	Cecil Gordon	Chevrolet
18.	Terry Ryan	Chevrolet
19.	Walter Ballard	Chevrolet
20.	Jim Vandiver	Dodge
21.	David Pearson	Mercury
22.	Ricky Rudd	Chevrolet
23.	Richard Childress	Chevrolet
24.	Salt Walther	Chevrolet
25.	Bruce Hill	Chevrolet
26.	Richard Petty	Dodge
27.	Ramo Stott	Chevrolet
28.	Dave Marcis	Mercury
29.	Ed Negre	Dodge
30.	Donnie Allison	Chevrolet
31.	Sam Sommers	Chevrolet
32.	Ron Hutcherson	Chevrolet
33.	Jimmy Capps	Chevrolet
34.	Grant Adcox	Chevrolet
35.	Jim Hurtubise	Chevrolet
36.	Skip Manning	Chevrolet
37.	Neil Bonnett	Dodge
38.	Buddy Arrington	Dodge
39.	Roy Smith	Chevrolet
40.	Elliott Forbes-Robinson	Dodge
41.	Johnny Rutherford	Chevrolet
42.	Bobby Wawak	Chevrolet

RICHMOND 400

February 27
Richmond, Virginia
Time of Race: 1 hour, 49 minutes, 1 second
Average Speed: 73.084 mph

FINISH	DRIVER	CAR
1.	Cale Yarborough	Chevrolet
2.	Darrell Waltrip	Chevrolet
3.	Benny Parsons	Chevrolet
4.	Dave Marcis	Chevrolet
5.	Bobby Allison	Matador
6.	Richard Petty	Dodge
7.	Neil Bonnett	Dodge
8.	James Hylton	Chevrolet
9.	Buddy Baker	Ford
10.	Richard Childress	Chevrolet
11.	Tighe Scott	Chevrolet
12.	Janet Guthrie	Chevrolet
13.	Cecil Gordon	Chevrolet
14.	Terry Bivins	Chevrolet
15.	Ed Negre	Dodge
16.	J. D. McDuffie	Chevrolet
17.	Junior Miller	Chevrolet
18.	Skip Manning	Chevrolet
19.	Henley Gray	Chevrolet
20.	Elmo Langley	Ford
21.	Robin Schildknecht	Chevrolet
22.	Walter Ballard	Chevrolet
23.	Rick Newsom	Ford
24.	Buddy Arrington	Dodge
25.	Earl Brooks	Chevrolet
26.	Ricky Rudd	Ford
27.	Richard Brooks	Ford
28.	D. K. Ulrich	Chevrolet
29.	Jimmy Means	Chevrolet
30.	Frank Warren	Dodge

CAROLINA 500

March 13
Rockingham, North Carolina
Time of Race: 5 hours, 6 minutes, 46 seconds
Average Speed: 97.86 mph

FINISH	DRIVER	CAR
1.	Richard Petty	Dodge
2.	Darrell Waltrip	Chevrolet
3.	Donnie Allison	Chevrolet
4.	Buddy Baker	Ford
5.	Neil Bonnett	Dodge
6.	Cale Yarborough	Chevrolet
7.	Sam Sommers	Chevrolet
8.	Skip Manning	Chevrolet
9.	James Hylton	Chevrolet
10.	Cecil Gordon	Chevrolet
11.	Gary Myers	Chevrolet
12.	Benny Parsons	Chevrolet
13.	Ed Negre	Dodge
14.	Buddy Arrington	Dodge
15.	J. D. McDuffie	Chevrolet
16.	Henley Gray	Chevrolet
17.	Richard Childress	Chevrolet
18.	Jimmy Lee Capps	Chevrolet
19.	Ricky Rudd	Chevrolet
20.	Elliott Forbes-Robinson	Dodge
21.	Tommy Gale	Ford
22.	Richard Brooks	Ford
23.	D. K. Ulrich	Chevrolet
24.	Dave Marcis	Chevrolet
25.	Earl Brooks	Chevrolet
26.	Terry Bivins	Chevrolet
27.	Bobby Allison	Matador
28.	Jimmy Means	Chevrolet
29.	Joe Mihalic	Chevrolet
30.	Bill Elliott	Ford
31.	Junior Miller	Chevrolet
32.	David Pearson	Mercury
33.	Tighe Scott	Chevrolet
34.	Lennie Pond	Chevrolet
35.	Frank Warren	Dodge
36.	Bruce Hill	Chevrolet

ATLANTA 500

March 20
Atlanta, Georgia
Time of Race: 3 hours, 27 minutes, 51 seconds
Average Speed: 144.093 mph

FINISH	DRIVER	CAR
1.	Richard Petty	Dodge
2.	David Pearson	Mercury
3.	Cale Yarborough	Chevrolet
4.	Donnie Allison	Chevrolet
5.	Buddy Baker	Ford
6.	Dave Marcis	Chevrolet
7.	Darrell Waltrip	Chevrolet
8.	Coo Coo Marlin	Chevrolet
9.	Lennie Pond	Chevrolet
10.	Bruce Hill	Chevrolet
11.	Buddy Arrington	Dodge
12.	Neil Bonnett	Dodge
13.	Sam Sommers	Chevrolet
14.	Jody Ridley	Mercury
15.	Ramo Stott	Chevrolet
16.	Cecil Gordon	Chevrolet
17.	Harold Miller	Chevrolet
18.	Jimmy Capps	Chevrolet
19.	Richard Childress	Chevrolet
20.	Jimmy Means	Chevrolet
21.	G. C. Spencer	Dodge
22.	Tommy Gale	Ford
23.	Richard Brooks	Ford
24.	Terry Bivins	Chevrolet
25.	Tighe Scott	Chevrolet
26.	Benny Parsons	Chevrolet
27.	Frank Warren	Dodge
28.	Skip Manning	Chevrolet
29.	D. K. Ulrich	Chevrolet
30.	Janet Guthrie	Chevrolet
31.	J. D. McDuffie	Chevrolet
32.	Bill Elliott	Ford
33.	Henley Gray	Chevrolet
34.	A. J. Foyt	Chevrolet
35.	Phil Finney	Chevrolet
36.	Elliott Forbes-Robinson	Dodge
37.	Dean Dalton	Chevrolet
38.	James Hylton	Chevrolet
39.	Ed Negre	Chevrolet
40.	Johnny Rutherford	Chevrolet
41.	Bobby Allison	Matador
42.	Jim Hurtubise	Ford

GWYN STALEY 400

March 27
North Wilkesboro, North Carolina
Time of Race: 2 hours, 48 minutes, 38 seconds
Average Speed: 88.950 mph

FINISH	DRIVER	CAR
1.	Cale Yarborough	Chevrolet
2.	Richard Petty	Dodge
3.	Benny Parsons	Chevrolet
4.	Buddy Baker	Ford
5.	Bobby Allison	Matador
6.	Richard Brooks	Ford
7.	Darrell Waltrip	Chevrolet
8.	Richard Childress	Chevrolet
9.	James Hylton	Chevrolet
10.	Buddy Arrington	Dodge
11.	Gary Myers	Chevrolet
12.	Dave Marcis	Chevrolet
13.	Cecil Gordon	Chevrolet
14.	Henley Gray	Ford
15.	Robin Schildknect	Chevrolet
16.	Frank Warren	Dodge
17.	Terry Bivins	Chevrolet
18.	Junior Miller	Chevrolet

19.	David Sisco	Chevrolet
20.	D. K. Ulrich	Chevrolet
21.	Neil Bonnett	Dodge
22.	J. D. McDuffie	Chevrolet
23.	Tighe Scott	Chevrolet
24.	Larry LaMay	Chevrolet
25.	Earl Brooks	Chevrolet
26.	Skip Manning	Chevrolet
27.	Jimmy Means	Chevrolet
28.	Ed Negre	Dodge
29.	Rick Newsom	Ford

11.	Janet Guthrie	Chevrolet
12.	Skip Manning	Chevrolet
13.	Frank Warren	Dodge
14.	Buddy Arrington	Dodge
15.	Sam Sommers	Chevrolet
16.	Elmo Langley	Ford
17.	Cecil Gordon	Chevrolet
18.	Ferrell Harris	Chevrolet
19.	Darrell Waltrip	Chevrolet
20.	J. D. McDuffie	Chevrolet
21.	Dave Marcis	Chevrolet
22.	David Sisco	Chevrolet
23.	Henley Gray	Chevrolet
24.	Junior Miller	Chevrolet
25.	Ed Negre	Dodge
26.	D. K. Ulrich	Chevrolet
27.	Rick Newsom	Ford
28.	Tighe Scott	Chevrolet
29.	Buddy Baker	Ford
30.	Larry LaMay	Chevrolet

REBEL 500

April 3
Darlington, South Carolina
Time of Race: 3 hours, 53 minutes, 18 seconds
Average Speed: 128.817 mph

FINISH	DRIVER	CAR
1.	Darrell Waltrip	Chevrolet
2.	Donnie Allison	Chevrolet
3.	Richard Petty	Dodge
4.	David Pearson	Mercury
5.	Benny Parsons	Chevrolet
6.	Dave Marcis	Chevrolet
7.	Buddy Baker	Ford
8.	G. C. Spencer	Dodge
9.	Richard Brooks	Ford
10.	Bruce Hill	Chevrolet
11.	Butch Hartman	Chevrolet
12.	Cecil Gordon	Chevrolet
13.	Sam Sommers	Chevrolet
14.	Buddy Arrington	Dodge
15.	Gary Myers	Chevrolet
16.	Cale Yarborough	Chevrolet
17.	Richard Childress	Chevrolet
18.	Ferrell Harris	Chevrolet
19.	J. D. McDuffie	Chevrolet
20.	Jimmy Means	Chevrolet
21.	Tommy Gale	Ford
22.	Ricky Rudd	Chevrolet
23.	Skip Manning	Chevrolet
24.	Ed Negre	Dodge
25.	Joe Mihalic	Chevrolet
26.	Tighe Scott	Chevrolet
27.	Frank Warren	Dodge
28.	Henley Gray	Chevrolet
29.	Bobby Allison	Matador
30.	Terry Bivins	Chevrolet
31.	Lennie Pond	Chevrolet
32.	James Hylton	Chevrolet
33.	Neil Bonnett	Dodge
34.	D. K. Ulrich	Chevrolet
35.	Dean Dalton	Chevrolet
36.	Earle Canavan	Dodge

SOUTHEASTERN 500

April 17
Bristol, Tennessee
Time of Race: 2 hours, 38 minutes, 20 seconds
Average Speed: 100.989 mph

FINISH	DRIVER	CAR
1.	Cale Yarborough	Chevrolet
2.	Richard Brooks	Ford
3.	Richard Petty	Dodge
4.	Neil Bonnett	Dodge
5.	Benny Parsons	Chevrolet
6.	Bobby Allison	Matador
7.	James Hylton	Chevrolet
8.	Richard Childress	Chevrolet
9.	Jimmy Means	Chevrolet
10.	Ricky Rudd	Chevrolet

VIRGINIA 500

April 24
Martinsville, Virginia
Time of Race: 2 hours, 36 minutes, 26 seconds
Average Speed: 77.405 mph

FINISH	DRIVER	CAR
1.	Cale Yarbourough	Chevrolet
2.	Benny Parsons	Chevrolet
3.	Richard Petty	Dodge
4.	Lennie Pond	Chevrolet
5.	David Pearson	Mercury
6.	Richard Brooks	Ford
7.	Bruce Hill	Chevrolet
8.	Jimmy Means	Chevrolet
9.	J. D. McDufie	Chevrolet
10.	Richard Childress	Chevrolet
11.	Terry Bivins	Chevrolet
12.	Neil Bonnett	Dodge
13.	Cecil Gordon	Chevrolet
14.	Tighe Scott	Chevrolet
15.	D. K. Ulrich	Chevrolet
16.	Ferrell Harris	Chevrolet
17.	James Hylton	Chevrolet
18.	Henley Gray	Chevrolet
19.	Bobby Allison	Matador
20.	Dave Marcis	Chevrolet
21.	Darrell Waltrip	Chevrolet
22.	Jimmy Hensley	Chevrolet
23.	Tommy Gale	Ford
24.	Buddy Baker	Ford
25.	Ed Negre	Dodge
26.	Donnie Allison	Chevrolet
27.	Skip Manning	Chevrolet
28.	Sam Sommers	Chevrolet
29.	Gary Myers	Chevrolet
30.	Bobby Wawak	Chevrolet

WINSTON 500

May 1
Talladega, Alabama
Time of Race: 3 hours, 1 minute, 59 seconds
Average Speed: 164.877 mph

FINISH	DRIVER	CAR
1.	Darrell Waltrip	Chevrolet
2.	Cale Yarborough	Chevrolet
3.	Benny Parsons	Chevrolet
4.	Donnie Allison	Chevrolet
5.	Dave Marcis	Mercury
6.	Ron Hutcherson	Chevrolet
7.	Richard Brooks	Ford

8.	Coo Coo Marlin	Chevrolet
9.	Terry Bivins	Chevrolet
10.	Sam Sommers	Chevrolet
11.	Ramo Stott	Chevrolet
12.	Peter Knab	Chevrolet
13.	Frank Warren	Dodge
14.	Ferrell Harris	Chevrolet
15.	Tommy Gale	Ford
16.	Cecil Gordon	Chevrolet
17.	Tighe Scott	Chevrolet
18.	James Hylton	Chevrolet
19.	Buddy Arrington	Dodge
20.	Richard Petty	Dodge
21.	Richard Childress	Chevrolet
22.	David Pearson	Mercury
23.	Skip Manning	Chevrolet
24.	Joe Frasson	Chevrolet
25.	Butch Hartman	Chevrolet
26.	J. D. McDuffie	Chevrolet
27.	Bruce Hill	Chevrolet
28.	Ricky Rudd	Chevrolet
29.	Neil Bonnett	Dodge
30.	David Sisco	Chevrolet
31.	D. K. Ulrich	Chevrolet
32.	Janet Guthrie	Chevrolet
33.	Buddy Baker	Ford
34.	Jimmy Means	Chevrolet
35.	Terry Ryan	Chevrolet
36.	Richard Skillen	Chevrolet
37.	Grant Adcox	Chevrolet
38.	A. J. Foyt	Chevrolet
39.	Henley Gray	Dodge
40.	Bobby Allison	Matador
41.	Ed Negre	Dodge

MUSIC CITY USA 420

May 7
Nashville, Tennessee
Time of Race: 2 hours, 51 minutes, 40 seconds
Average Speed: 87.490 mph

FINISH	DRIVER	CAR
1.	Benny Parsons	Chevrolet
2.	Cale Yarborough	Chevrolet
3.	Darrell Waltrip	Chevrolet
4.	Dave Marcis	Chevrolet
5.	Richard Petty	Dodge
6.	Buddy Baker	Ford
7.	Bobby Allison	Matador
8.	Coo Coo Marlin	Chevrolet
9.	Jimmy Means	Chevrolet
10.	Ricky Rudd	Chevrolet
11.	James Hylton	Chevrolet
12.	Gary Myers	Chevrolet
13.	Cecil Gordon	Chevrolet
14.	D. K. Ulrich	Chevrolet
15.	Buddy Arrington	Dodge
16.	Rick Newsom	Ford
17.	Earl Brooks	Chevrolet
18.	Ralph Jones	Ford
19.	David Sisco	Chevrolet
20.	Ferrell Harris	Chevrolet
21.	Skip Manning	Chevrolet
22.	Richard Brooks	Ford
23.	Elmo Langley	Chevrolet
24.	J. D. McDuffie	Chevrolet
25.	Henley Gray	Chevrolet
26.	Richard Childress	Chevrolet
27.	Terry Ryan	Chevrolet
28.	Paul Dean Holt	Ford
29.	Frank Warren	Dodge
30.	Dean Dalton	Chevrolet

MASON-DIXON 500

May 15
Dover, Delaware

Time of Race: 4 hours, 3 minutes, 26 seconds
Average Speed: 123.327 mph

FINISH	DRIVER	CAR
1.	Cale Yarborough	Chevrolet
2.	David Pearson	Mercury
3.	Richard Petty	Dodge
4.	Darrell Waltrip	Chevrolet
5.	Richard Brooks	Ford
6.	Benny Parsons	Chevrolet
7.	Lennie Pond	Chevrolet
8.	Bobby Allison	Matador
9.	Buddy Baker	Ford
10.	Morgan Shepherd	Mercury
11.	Buddy Arrington	Dodge
12.	Cecil Gordon	Chevrolet
13.	J. D. McDuffie	Chevrolet
14.	Tighe Scott	Chevrolet
15.	Ed Negre	Dodge
16.	Dick May	Ford
17.	Skip Manning	Chevrolet
18.	Tommy Gale	Ford
19.	Ferrell Harris	Chevrolet
20.	D. K. Ulrich	Chevrolet
21.	Richard Childress	Chevrolet
22.	Gary Myers	Chevrolet
23.	Earle Canavan	Dodge
24.	Baxter Price	Chevrolet
25.	Earl Brooks	Chevrolet
26.	Frank Warren	Dodge
27.	Ricky Rudd	Chevrolet
28.	Rick Newsom	Ford
29.	Jimmy Means	Chevrolet
30.	David Sisco	Chevrolet
31.	Elmo Langley	Chevrolet
32.	Henley Gray	Chevrolet
33.	James Hylton	Chevrolet
34.	Dean Dalton	Chevrolet
35.	Bruce Hill	Chevrolet
36.	Raymond Williams	Ford

WORLD 600

May 29
Charlotte, North Carolina
Time of Race: 4 hours, 21 minutes, 29 seconds
Average Speed: 137.676 mph

FINISH	DRIVER	CAR
1.	Richard Petty	Dodge
2.	David Pearson	Mercury
3.	Benny Parsons	Chevrolet
4.	Lennie Pond	Chevrolet
5.	Buddy Baker	Ford
6.	Darrell Waltrip	Chevrolet
7.	Neil Bonnett	Dodge
8.	Richard Brooks	Ford
9.	Sam Sommers	Chevrolet
10.	Skip Manning	Chevrolet
11.	Ron Hutcherson	Chevrolet
12.	Coo Coo Marlin	Chevrolet
13.	Morgan Shepherd	Mercury
14.	Richard Childress	Chevrolet
15.	Bill Elliott	Ford
16.	Tighe Scott	Chevrolet
17.	Ricky Rudd	Chevrolet
18.	Buddy Arrington	Dodge
19.	Jimmy Means	Chevrolet
20.	G. C. Spencer	Dodge
21.	Dick May	Ford
22.	Cecil Gordon	Chevrolet
23.	Butch Hartman	Chevrolet
24.	Cale Yarborough	Chevrolet
25.	J. D. McDuffie	Chevrolet
26.	Frank Warren	Dodge
27.	Harold Miller	Chevrolet
28.	James Hylton	Chevrolet
29.	Terry Ryan	Chevrolet

30.	Harry Gant	Chevrolet
31.	Bruce Hill	Chevrolet
32.	David Sisco	Chevrolet
33.	Donnie Allison	Chevrolet
34.	D. K. Ulrich	Chevrolet
35.	Ed Negre	Dodge
36.	Dave Marcis	Mercury
37.	Tommy Gale	Ford
38.	Henley Gray	Chevrolet
39.	Bobby Allison	Matador
40.	Ramo Stott	Chevrolet

NAPA RIVERSIDE 400

June 12
Riverside, California
Time of Race: 2 hours, 22 minutes, 12 seconds
Average Speed: 105.021 mph

FINISH	DRIVER	CAR
1.	Richard Petty	Dodge
2.	David Pearson	Mercury
3.	Cale Yarborough	Chevrolet
4.	Jim Insolo	Ford
5.	Buddy Baker	Ford
6.	Norm Palmer	Dodge
7.	Sonny Easley	Ford
8.	Richard Childress	Chevrolet
9.	Cecil Gordon	Chevrolet
10.	Skip Manning	Chevrolet
11.	D. K. Ulrich	Chevrolet
12.	Richard Brooks	Ford
13.	John Dineen	Ford
14.	James Hylton	Chevrolet
15.	Frank Warren	Dodge
16.	Bill Baker	Chevrolet
17.	Bobby Allison	Matador
18.	Chuck Wahl	Chevrolet
19.	Buddy Arrington	Dodge
20.	Ernie Stierly	Chevrolet
21.	Harry Goularte	Chevrolet
22.	Richard White	Chevrolet
23.	Roy Smith	Chevrolet
24.	Jim Thirkettle	Chevrolet
25.	Chuck Bown	Chevrolet
26.	Darrell Waltrip	Chevrolet
27.	Benny Parsons	Chevrolet
28.	Don Puskarich	Chevrolet
29.	Gary Johnson	Chevrolet
30.	Bill Schmitt	Chevrolet
31.	Sumner McKnight	Chevrolet
32.	Ray Elder	Plymouth
33.	J. D. McDuffie	Chevrolet
34.	Hershel McGriff	Chevrolet
35.	Don Noel	Chevrolet

CAM 2 MOTOR OIL 400

June 19
Brooklyn, Michigan
Time of Race: 2 hours, 57 minutes, 44 seconds
Average Speed: 135.033 mph

FINISH	DRIVER	CAR
1.	Cale Yarborough	Chevrolet
2.	Richard Petty	Dodge
3.	Benny Parsons	Chevrolet
4.	Dave Marcis	Chevrolet
5.	David Pearson	Mercury
6.	Buddy Baker	Ford
7.	Richard Brooks	Ford
8.	Sam Sommers	Chevrolet
9.	Butch Hartman	Chevrolet
10.	Bobby Allison	Matador
11.	James Hylton	Chevrolet
12.	Bill Elliott	Ford

13.	Marty Robbins	Dodge
14.	Jimmy Means	Chevrolet
15.	Bill Elliott	Ford
16.	D. K. Ulrich	Chevrolet
17.	Terry Ryan	Chevrolet
18.	Bobby Wawak	Chevrolet
19.	Buddy Arrington	Dodge
20.	J. D. McDuffie	Chevrolet
21.	Cecil Gordon	Chevrolet
22.	Henley Gray	Chevrolet
23.	Tommy Gale	Ford
24.	Donnie Allison	Chevrolet
25.	David Sisco	Chevrolet
26.	Janet Guthrie	Chevrolet
27.	Skip Manning	Chevrolet
28.	Ricky Rudd	Chevrolet
29.	Roland Wlodyka	Chevrolet
30.	Frank Warren	Dodge
31.	Tighe Scott	Chevrolet
32.	Bruce Hill	Chevrolet
33.	John Kennedy	Ford
34.	Richard Childress	Chevrolet
35.	Darrell Waltrip	Chevrolet
36.	Ferrell Harris	Chevrolet

FIRECRACKER 400

July 4
Daytona Beach, Florida
Time of Race: 2 hours, 48 minutes, 10 seconds
Average Speed: 142.716 mph

FINISH	DRIVER	CAR
1.	Richard Petty	Dodge
2.	Darrell Waltrip	Chevrolet
3.	Benny Parsons	Chevrolet
4.	David Pearson	Mercury
5.	A. J. Foyt	Chevrolet
6.	Donnie Allison	Chevrolet
7.	Buddy Baker	Ford
8.	Neil Bonnett	Dodge
9.	Richard Brooks	Ford
10.	Sam Sommers	Chevrolet
11.	Cecil Gordon	Chevrolet
12.	Terry Ryan	Chevrolet
13.	Coo Coo Marlin	Chevrolet
14.	G. C. Spencer	Dodge
15.	Jim Hurtubise	Chevrolet
16.	Skip Manning	Chevrolet
17.	Bobby Allison	Matador
18.	Butch Hartman	Chevrolet
19.	Richard Childress	Chevrolet
20.	Jimmy Means	Chevrolet
21.	Frank Warren	Dodge
22.	Buddy Arrington	Dodge
23.	Cale Yarborough	Chevrolet
24.	J. D. McDuffie	Chevrolet
25.	Baxter Price	Chevrolet
26.	Grant Adcox	Chevrolet
27.	Tighe Scott	Chevrolet
28.	Harold Miller	Chevrolet
29.	Ron Hutcherson	Chevrolet
30.	Bruce Hill	Chevrolet
31.	Lella Lombardi	Chevrolet
32.	Ramo Stott	Chevrolet
33.	Lennie Pond	Chevrolet
34.	David Sisco	Chevrolet
35.	Bill Elliott	Ford
36.	Ricky Rudd	Chevrolet
37.	Christine Beckers	Ford
38.	Tommy Gale	Ford
39.	James Hylton	Chevrolet
40.	Janet Guthrie	Chevrolet
41.	D. K. Ulrich	Chevrolet

NASHVILLE 420

July 16
Nashville, Tennessee

Time of Race: 3 hours, 10 minutes, 9 seconds
Average Speed: 78.999 mph

FINISH	DRIVER	CAR
1.	Darrell Waltrip	Chevrolet
2.	Bobby Allison	Matador
3.	Richard Petty	Dodge
4.	Cale Yarborough	Chevrolet
5.	Richard Brooks	Ford
6.	Buddy Baker	Ford
7.	Skip Manning	Chevrolet
8.	J. D. McDuffie	Chevrolet
9.	Buddy Arrington	Dodge
10.	Ricky Rudd	Chevrolet
11.	Coo Coo Marlin	Chevrolet
12.	Frank Warren	Dodge
13.	Tighe Scott	Chevrolet
14.	D. K. Ulrich	Chevrolet
15.	Janet Guthrie	Chevrolet
16.	Baxter Price	Chevrolet
17.	Henley Gray	Chevrolet
18.	Benny Parsons	Chevrolet
19.	James Hylton	Chevrolet
20.	Cecil Gordon	Chevrolet
21.	Neil Bonnett	Dodge
22.	David Sisco	Chevrolet
23.	Ralph Jones	Ford
24.	Sam Sommers	Chevrolet
25.	Grant Adcox	Chevrolet
26.	Gary Myers	Chevrolet
27.	Richard Childress	Chevrolet
28.	Elmo Langley	Ford
29.	Jimmy Means	Chevrolet
30.	Mike Kempton	Chevrolet

COCA-COLA 500

July 31
Pocono, Pennsylvania
Time of Race: 3 hours, 53 minutes, 41 seconds
Average Speed: 128.379 mph

FINISH	DRIVER	CAR
1.	Benny Parsons	Chevrolet
2.	Richard Petty	Dodge
3.	Darrell Waltrip	Chevrolet
4.	Bobby Allison	Matador
5.	Richard Brooks	Ford
6.	Cale Yarborough	Chevrolet
7.	Ricky Rudd	Chevrolet
8.	Skip Manning	Chevrolet
9.	Butch Hartman	Chevrolet
10.	James Hylton	Chevrolet
11.	Janet Guthrie	Chevrolet
12.	Kenny Brightbill	Mercury
13.	Tighe Scott	Chevrolet
14.	J. D. McDuffie	Chevrolet
15.	Buddy Arrington	Dodge
16.	Ed Negre	Dodge
17.	Richard Childress	Chevrolet
18.	Joe Mihalic	Chevrolet
19.	Frank Warren	Dodge
20.	Jimmy Means	Chevrolet
21.	Cecil Gordon	Chevrolet
22.	Baxter Price	Chevrolet
23.	Nestor Peles	Chevrolet
24.	Dick May	Ford
25.	Tommy Gale	Ford
26.	C. Maggiacomo	Matador
27.	Buddy Baker	Ford
28.	David Pearson	Mercury
29.	Greg Heller	Ford
30.	Gary Myers	Chevrolet
31.	Roland Wlodyka	Chevrolet
32.	Sam Sommers	Chevrolet
33.	Ronnie Thomas	Chevrolet
34.	D. K. Ulrich	Chevrolet
35.	Earle Canavan	Dodge

TALLADEGA 500

August 7
Talladega, Alabama
Time of Race: 3 hours, 4 minutes, 37 seconds
Average Speed: 162.524 mph

FINISH	DRIVER	CAR
1.	Donnie Allison	Chevrolet
2.	Cale Yarborough	Chevrolet
3.	Skip Manning	Chevrolet
4.	Ricky Rudd	Chevrolet
5.	Lennie Pond	Chevrolet
6.	Buddy Baker	Ford
7.	Bobby Allison	Matador
8.	J. D. McDuffie	Chevrolet
9.	James Hylton	Chevrolet
10.	Frank Warren	Dodge
11.	Richard Petty	Dodge
12.	Buddy Arrington	Dodge
13.	Harold Miller	Chevrolet
14.	Tommy Gale	Ford
15.	Grant Adcox	Chevrolet
16.	Cecil Gordon	Chevrolet
17.	Dick May	Chevrolet
18.	D. K. Ulrich	Chevrolet
19.	Steve Moore	Chevrolet
20.	Richard Childress	Chevrolet
21.	Johnny Rutherford	Chevrolet
22.	Darrell Waltrip	Chevrolet
23.	Bill Elliott	Mercury
24.	Benny Parsons	Chevrolet
25.	Neil Bonnett	Dodge
26.	Sam Sommers	Chevrolet
27.	Tighe Scott	Chevrolet
28.	David Sisco	Chevrolet
29.	Butch Hartman	Chevrolet
30.	Jim Raptis	Chevrolet
31.	G. C. Spencer	Dodge
32.	Joe Mihalic	Chevrolet
33.	Peter Knab	Chevrolet
34.	Janet Guthrie	Chevrolet
35.	Bruce Hill	Chevrolet
36.	Jimmy Means	Chevrolet
37.	David Pearson	Mercury
38.	Marty Robbins	Dodge
39.	Richard Brooks	Ford
40.	Coo Coo Marlin	Chevrolet

CHAMPION SPARK PLUG 400

August 22
Brooklyn, Michigan
Time of Race: 2 hours, 53 minutes, 59 seconds
Average Speed: 137.944 mph

FINISH	DRIVER	CAR
1.	Darrell Waltrip	Chevrolet
2.	David Pearson	Mercury
3.	Benny Parsons	Chevrolet
4.	Sam Sommers	Chevrolet
5.	Cale Yarborough	Chevrolet
6.	Dick Brooks	Ford
7.	Ricky Rudd	Chevrolet
8.	Richard Petty	Dodge
9.	Terry Ryan	Chevrolet
10.	Janet Guthrie	Chevrolet
11.	Tighe Scott	Chevrolet
12.	Skip Manning	Chevrolet
13.	Bruce Hill	Chevrolet
14.	Buddy Arrington	Dodge
15.	Bobby Wawak	Chevrolet
16.	James Hylton	Chevrolet
17.	Jimmy Means	Chevrolet
18.	D. K. Ulrich	Chevrolet
19.	Cecil Gordon	Chevrolet
20.	J. D. McDuffie	Chevrolet

21.	Dean Dalton	Chevrolet
22.	Dave Marcis	Chevrolet
23.	Frank Warren	Dodge
24.	Joe Mihalic	Chevrolet
25.	Butch Hartman	Chevrolet
26.	Bobby Allison	Matador
27.	C. Maggiacomo	Matador
28.	Harold Miller	Chevrolet
29.	Bill Elliott	Mercury
30.	Buddy Baker	Ford
31.	Ed Negre	Dodge
32.	Tommy Gale	Ford
33.	Richard Childress	Chevrolet
34.	Baxter Price	Chevrolet
35.	Elmo Langley	Dodge
36.	Earle Canavan	Dodge

VOLUNTEER 400

August 28
Bristol, Tennessee
Time of Race: 2 hours, 40 minutes, 27 seconds
Average Speed: 79.726 mph

FINISH	DRIVER	CAR
1.	Cale Yarborough	Chevrolet
2.	Darrell Waltrip	Chevrolet
3.	Benny Parsons	Chevrolet
4.	Richard Brooks	Ford
5.	Tighe Scott	Chevrolet
6.	Janet Guthrie	Chevrolet
7.	Skip Manning	Chevrolet
8.	Richard Childress	Chevrolet
9.	James Hylton	Chevrolet
10.	Buddy Arrington	Dodge
11.	D. K. Ulrich	Chevrolet
12.	Ed Negre	Dodge
13.	Frank Warren	Dodge
14.	Ferrell Harris	Chevrolet
15.	Buddy Baker	Ford
16.	Ricky Rudd	Chevrolet
17.	Neil Bonnett	Dodge
18.	J. D. McDuffie	Chevrolet
19.	Ralph Jones	Ford
20.	Sam Sommers	Chevrolet
21.	Travis Tiller	Dodge
22.	Richard Petty	Dodge
23.	Dean Dalton	Ford
24.	Dick May	Chevrolet
25.	Earl Brooks	Chevrolet
26.	Baxter Price	Chevrolet
27.	Jimmy Means	Chevrolet
28.	Bobby Allison	Matador
29.	Cecil Gordon	Chevrolet

SOUTHERN 500

September 5
Darlington, South Carolina
Time of Race: 4 hours, 41 minutes, 48 seconds
Average Speed: 106.797 mph

FINISH	DRIVER	CAR
1.	David Pearson	Mercury
2.	Donnie Allison	Chevrolet
3.	Buddy Baker	Ford
4.	Richard Petty	Dodge
5.	Cale Yarborough	Chevrolet
6.	Darrell Waltrip	Chevrolet
7.	Ricky Rudd	Chevrolet
8.	Richard Childress	Chevrolet
9.	Bruce Hill	Chevrolet
10.	Bill Elliott	Ford
11.	Ed Negre	Dodge
12.	J. D. McDuffie	Chevrolet

13.	James Hylton	Chevrolet
14.	Buddy Arrington	Dodge
15.	Gary Myers	Chevrolet
16.	Janet Guthrie	Chevrolet
17.	Frank Warren	Dodge
18.	Tommy Gale	Ford
19.	Cecil Gordon	Chevrolet
20.	Mike Kempton	Chevrolet
21.	Baxter Price	Chevrolet
22.	Bobby Wawak	Chevrolet
23.	Earle Canavan	Dodge
24.	Terry Bivins	Chevrolet
25.	Benny Parsons	Chevrolet
26.	Coo Coo Marlin	Chevrolet
27.	D. K. Ulrich	Chevrolet
28.	Lennie Pond	Chevrolet
29.	Sam Sommers	Chevrolet
30.	Ralph Jones	Ford
31.	Dick May	Ford
32.	Tighe Scott	Chevrolet
33.	Ferrell Harris	Chevrolet
34.	Richard Brooks	Ford
35.	Butch Hartman	Chevrolet
36.	Roland Wlodyka	Chevrolet
37.	G. C. Spencer	Dodge
38.	Skip Manning	Chevrolet
39.	Bobby Allison	Matador
40.	Joe Mihalic	Chevrolet

CAPITAL CITY 400

September 11
Richmond, Virginia
Time of Race: 2 hours, 41 minutes, 18 seconds
Average Speed: 80.644 mph

FINISH	DRIVER	CAR
1.	Neil Bonnett	Dodge
2.	Richard Petty	Dodge
3.	Benny Parsons	Chevrolet
4.	Cale Yarborough	Chevrolet
5.	Lennie Pond	Chevrolet
6.	Bobby Allison	Matador
7.	Darrell Waltrip	Chevrolet
8.	Richard Brooks	Ford
9.	James Hylton	Chevrolet
10.	Jimmy Means	Chevrolet
11.	Ricky Rudd	Chevrolet
12.	Janet Guthrie	Chevrolet
13.	J. D. McDuffie	Chevrolet
14.	D. K. Ulrich	Chevrolet
15.	Skip Manning	Chevrolet
16.	Ed Negre	Dodge
17.	Cecil Gordon	Chevrolet
18.	Tighe Scott	Chevrolet
19.	Dick May	Chevrolet
20.	Frank Warren	Dodge
21.	Baxter Price	Chevrolet
22.	Ferrell Harris	Chevrolet
23.	Marv Acton	Chevrolet
24.	Tommy Gale	Ford
25.	Buddy Arrington	Dodge
26.	Richard Childress	Chevrolet
27.	Buddy Baker	Ford
28.	Rick Newsom	Chevrolet

DELAWARE 500

September 18
Dover, Delaware
Time of Race: 4 hours, 21 minutes, 32 seconds
Average Speed: 114.706 mph

FINISH	DRIVER	CAR
1.	Benny Parsons	Chevrolet
2.	David Pearson	Mercury

3.	Cale Yarborough	Chevrolet
4.	Donnie Allison	Chevrolet
5.	Darrell Waltrip	Chevrolet
6.	Buddy Baker	Ford
7.	Richard Childress	Chevrolet
8.	Richard Brooks	Ford
9.	Bobby Allison	Matador
10.	Sam Sommers	Chevrolet
11.	Janet Guthrie	Chevrolet
12.	J. D. McDuffie	Chevrolet
13.	Buddy Arrington	Dodge
14.	Jimmy Means	Chevrolet
15.	Ed Negre	Dodge
16.	James Hylton	Chevrolet
17.	Neil Bonnett	Dodge
18.	Joe Mihalic	Chevrolet
19.	Skip Manning	Chevrolet
20.	Dick May	Chevrolet
21.	Cecil Gordon	Chevrolet
22.	Frank Warren	Dodge
23.	Richard Petty	Dodge
24.	Tighe Scott	Chevrolet
25.	Ronnie Thomas	Chevrolet
26.	Tommy Gale	Ford
27.	Rick Newsom	Chevrolet
28.	C. Maggiacomo	Matador
29.	Dean Dalton	Dodge
30.	Lennie Pond	Chevrolet
31.	D. K. Ulrich	Chevrolet
32.	Ricky Rudd	Chevrolet
33.	Bill Seifert	Chevrolet
34.	Gary Myers	Chevrolet
35.	Nestor Peles	Chevrolet
36.	Steve Stolarek	Chevrolet
37.	Baxter Price	Chevrolet
38.	Marv Acton	Chevrolet
39.	Jim Hurtubise	Ford
40.	Kenny Brightbill	Mercury

OLD DOMINION 500

September 25
Martinsville, Virginia
Time of Race: 3 hours, 34 minutes, 40 seconds
Average Speed: 73.447 mph

FINISH	DRIVER	CAR
1.	Cale Yarborough	Chevrolet
2.	Benny Parsons	Chevrolet
3.	David Pearson	Mercury
4.	Richard Petty	Dodge
5.	Sam Sommers	Chevrolet
6.	Jimmy Hensley	Chevrolet
7.	Buddy Arrington	Dodge
8.	James Hylton	Chevrolet
9.	Jimmy Means	Chevrolet
10.	Darrell Waltrip	Chevrolet
11.	Frank Warren	Dodge
12.	D. K. Ulrich	Chevrolet
13.	Skip Manning	Chevrolet
14.	Dick May	Chevrolet
15.	Richard Childress	Chevrolet
16.	Elmo Langley	Ford
17.	J. D. McDuffie	Chevrolet
18.	Cecil Gordon	Chevrolet
19.	Ronnie Thomas	Chevrolet
20.	Tighe Scott	Chevrolet
21.	Buddy Baker	Ford
22.	Neil Bonnett	Dodge
23.	Bobby Allison	Matador
24.	Ed Negre	Dodge
25.	Lennie Pond	Chevrolet
26.	Richard Brooks	Ford
27.	Ricky Rudd	Chevrolet
28.	Donnie Allison	Chevrolet
29.	Travis Tiller	Dodge
30.	Baxter Price	Chevrolet

WILKES 400

October 2
North Wilkesboro
Time of Race: 2 hours, 52 minutes, 59 seconds
Average Speed: 86.713 mph

FINISH	DRIVER	CAR
1.	Darrell Waltrip	Chevrolet
2.	Cale Yarborough	Chevrolet
3.	Neil Bonnett	Dodge
4.	Bobby Allison	Matador
5.	Benny Parsons	Chevrolet
6.	Richard Childress	Chevrolet
7.	Ricky Rudd	Chevrolet
8.	Richard Brooks	Ford
9.	Buddy Baker	Ford
10.	Buddy Arrington	Dodge
11.	Jimmy Means	Chevrolet
12.	James Hylton	Chevrolet
13.	Skip Manning	Ford
14.	Sam Sommers	Chevrolet
15.	Cecil Gordon	Chevrolet
16.	Walter Ballard	Chevrolet
17.	Ed Negre	Dodge
18.	Baxter Price	Chevrolet
19.	Roger Hamby	Chevrolet
20.	Dick May	Chevrolet
21.	Frank Warren	Dodge
22.	D. K. Ulrich	Chevrolet
23.	J. D. McDuffie	Chevrolet
24.	Richard Petty	Dodge
25.	Ferrell Harris	Chevrolet
26.	Junior Miller	Chevrolet

NAPA NATIONAL 500

October 9
Charlotte, North Carolina
Time of Race: 3 hours, 30 minutes, 32 seconds
Average Speed: 142.780 mph

FINISH	DRIVER	CAR
1.	Benny Parsons	Chevrolet
2.	Cale Yarborough	Chevrolet
3.	David Pearson	Mercury
4.	Buddy Baker	Ford
5.	Darrell Waltrip	Chevrolet
6.	Richard Brooks	Ford
7.	A. J. Foyt	Chevrolet
8.	Neil Bonnett	Dodge
9.	Janet Guthrie	Chevrolet
10.	Bill Elliott	Mercury
11.	Ron Hutcherson	Chevrolet
12.	Coo Coo Marlin	Chevrolet
13.	Dick May	Chevrolet
14.	James Hylton	Chevrolet
15.	J. D. McDuffie	Chevrolet
16.	Richard Childress	Chevrolet
17.	Buddy Arrington	Dodge
18.	G. C. Spencer	Dodge
19.	D. K. Ulrich	Chevrolet
20.	Peter Knab	Chevrolet
21.	Tommy Gale	Ford
22.	Ed Negre	Dodge
23.	Dave Marcis	Chevrolet
24.	Ricky Rudd	Chevrolet
25.	Tighe Scott	Chevrolet
26.	Bobby Allison	Matador
27.	Tom Sneva	Dodge
28.	Jimmy Means	Chevrolet
29.	Dick Trickle	Chevrolet
30.	Lennie Pond	Chevrolet
31.	Butch Hartman	Chevrolet
32.	Richard Petty	Dodge
33.	Frank Warren	Dodge
34.	Sam Sommers	Chevrolet

35.	Skip Manning	Chevrolet
36.	Donnie Allison	Chevrolet
37.	Cecil Gordon	Chevrolet
38.	Dale Earnhardt	Chevrolet
39.	Roland Wlodyka	Chevrolet
40.	Jim Raptis	Chevrolet
41.	Bruce Hill	Chevrolet

AMERICAN 500

October 23
Rockingham, North Carolina
Time of Race: 4 hours, 24 minutes, 18 seconds
Average Speed: 113.584 mph

FINISH	DRIVER	CAR
1.	Donnie Allison	Chevrolet
2.	Richard Petty	Dodge
3.	Darrell Waltrip	Chevrolet
4.	Cale Yarborough	Chevrolet
5.	Richard Brooks	Ford
6.	Bobby Allison	Matador
7.	Benny Parsons	Chevrolet
8.	Skip Manning	Chevrolet
9.	Janet Guthrie	Chevrolet
10.	J. D. McDuffie	Chevrolet
11.	Bobby Wawak	Chevrolet
12.	Buddy Arrington	Dodge
13.	James Hylton	Chevrolet
14.	Dick May	Chevrolet
15.	Tommy Gale	Ford
16.	Baxter Price	Chevrolet
17.	Sam Sommers	Chevrolet
18.	Richard Childress	Chevrolet
19.	Dean Dalton	Ford
20.	Randy Myers	Chevrolet
21.	Joe Mihalic	Chevrolet
22.	Jimmy Means	Chevrolet
23.	Cecil Gordon	Chevrolet
24.	Ed Negre	Dodge
25.	Ricky Rudd	Chevrolet
26.	Bruce Hill	Chevrolet
27.	David Pearson	Mercury
28.	Neil Bonnett	Dodge
29.	Buddy Baker	Ford
30.	Ronnie Thomas	Chevrolet
31.	Dave Marcis	Chevrolet
32.	Travis Tiller	Chevrolet
33.	D. K. Ulrich	Chevrolet
34.	Tighe Scott	Chevrolet
35.	Frank Warren	Dodge
36.	Lennie Pond	Chevrolet

DIXIE 500

November 6
Atlanta, Georgia
Time of Race: 3 hours, 42 minutes, 23 seconds
Average Speed: 110.052 mph

FINISH	DRIVER	CAR
1.	Darrell Waltrip	Chevrolet
2.	David Pearson	Mercury
3.	Benny Parsons	Chevrolet
4.	Donnie Allison	Chevrolet
5.	Cale Yarborough	Chevrolet
6.	Richard Petty	Dodge
7.	Buddy Baker	Ford
8.	Ricky Rudd	Chevrolet
9.	Bobby Allison	Matador
10.	Coo Coo Marlin	Chevrolet
11.	Bill Elliott	Mercury
12.	Butch Hartman	Chevrolet
13.	Skip Manning	Chevrolet
14.	Billy McGinnis	Chevrolet

15.	Bruce Hill	Chevrolet
16.	Janet Guthrie	Chevrolet
17.	Buddy Arrington	Dodge
18.	D. K. Ulrich	Chevrolet
19.	Tighe Scott	Chevrolet
20.	Cecil Gordon	Chevrolet
21.	Richard Childress	Chevrolet
22.	Grant Adcox	Chevrolet
23.	Frank Warren	Dodge
24.	Ervin Wangerin	Mercury
25.	G. C. Spencer	Dodge
26.	James Hylton	Chevrolet
27.	J. D. McDuffie	Chevrolet
28.	Sam Sommers	Chevrolet
29.	Bobby Wawak	Chevrolet
30.	Harold Miller	Chevrolet
31.	Roger Hamby	Chevrolet
32.	Dick May	Chevrolet
33.	Morgan Shepherd	Mercury
34.	Bob Burcham	Chevrolet
35.	Ed Negre	Dodge
36.	Dave Marcis	Chevrolet
37.	Dick Brooks	Ford
38.	Neil Bonnett	Dodge
39.	Jim Raptis	Chevrolet
40.	Jimmy Means	Chevrolet

LOS ANGELES TIMES 500

November 20
Ontario, California
Time of Race: 3 hours, 53 minutes, 50 seconds
Average Speed: 128.296 mph

FINISH	DRIVER	CAR
1.	Neil Bonnett	Dodge
2.	Richard Petty	Dodge
3.	Cale Yarborough	Chevrolet
4.	Buddy Baker	Ford
5.	David Pearson	Mercury
6.	Richard Brooks	Ford
7.	Bobby Allison	Matador
8.	Ricky Rudd	Chevrolet
9.	James Hylton	Chevrolet
10.	Richard Childress	Chevrolet
11.	A. J. Foyt	Chevrolet
12.	Benny Parsons	Chevrolet
13.	Joe Ruttman	Ford
14.	Dave Marcis	Chevrolet
15.	Roland Wlodyka	Chevrolet
16.	Frank Warren	Dodge
17.	Tighe Scott	Chevrolet
18.	Harry Jefferson	Ford
19.	Buddy Arrington	Ford
20.	J. D. McDuffie	Chevrolet
21.	D. K. Ulrich	Chevrolet
22.	Tommy Gale	Ford
23.	Bill Osborne	Chevrolet
24.	Janet Guthrie	Chevrolet
25.	Richard White	Chevrolet
26.	Sonny Easley	Ford
27.	Ed Negre	Dodge
28.	John Borneman	Chevrolet
29.	Darrell Waltrip	Chevrolet
30.	Don Graham	Chevrolet
31.	Ron McGee	Chevrolet
32.	Cecil Gordon	Chevrolet
33.	V. Giamformaggio	Chevrolet
34.	Norm Palmer	Dodge
35.	Ernie Stierly	Chevrolet
36.	John Kieper	Chevrolet
37.	Eddie Bradshaw	Chevrolet
38.	Sam Sommers	Chevrolet
39.	Chuck Bown	Chevrolet
40.	Roger McCluskey	Chevrolet
41.	Bill Schmitt	Chevrolet
42.	Donnie Allison	Chevrolet

1978

WINSTON WESTERN 500

January 22
Riverside, California
Time of Race: 3 hours, 2 minutes, 55 seconds
Average Speed: 102.269 mph

FINISH	DRIVER	CAR
1.	Cale Yarborough	Oldsmobile
2.	Benny Parsons	Chevrolet
3.	David Pearson	Mercury
4.	Neil Bonnett	Dodge
5.	Dave Marcis	Chevrolet
6.	Hershel McGriff	Ford
7.	Jim Insolo	Chevrolet
8.	Al Holbert	Chevrolet
9.	Roy Smith	Chevrolet
10.	D. K. Ulrich	Chevrolet
11.	Buddy Arrington	Ford
12.	Rick McCray	Dodge
13.	Frank Warren	Dodge
14.	Norm Palmer	Dodge
15.	Dick Brooks	Ford
16.	Richard Petty	Dodge
17.	Jim Thirkettle	Buick
18.	Tighe Scott	Chevrolet
19.	Ernie Stierly	Chevrolet
20.	Richard Childress	Chevrolet
21.	Skip Manning	Chevrolet
22.	Jack Simpson	Chevrolet
23.	Darrell Waltrip	Chevrolet
24.	Richard White	Chevrolet
25.	Cecil Gordon	Chevrolet
26.	Rocky Moran	Chevrolet
27.	John Borneman	Chevrolet
28.	J. D. McDuffie	Chevrolet
29.	V. Giamformaggio	Chevrolet
30.	Bobby Allison	Ford
31.	Don Puskarich	Chevrolet
32.	Bill Schmitt	Chevrolet
33.	Eddie Bradshaw	Chevrolet
34.	Ray Elder	Dodge
35.	Gary Johnson	Chevrolet

DAYTONA 500

February 19
Daytona Beach, Florida
Time of Race: 3 hours, 7 minutes, 49 seconds
Average Speed: 159.730 mph

FINISH	DRIVER	CAR
1.	Bobby Allison	Ford
2.	Cale Yarborough	Oldsmobile
3.	Benny Parsons	Oldsmobile
4.	Ron Hutcherson	Buick
5.	Dick Brooks	Mercury
6.	Dave Marcis	Chevrolet
7.	Buddy Baker	Oldsmobile
8.	Bill Elliott	Mercury
9.	Ferrell Harris	Dodge
10.	Lennie Pond	Oldsmobile
11.	Tighe Scott	Oldsmobile
12.	Skip Manning	Buick
13.	Richard Childress	Oldsmobile
14.	Grant Adcox	Chevrolet
15.	Roger Hamby	Chevrolet
16.	Buddy Arrington	Dodge
17.	D. K. Ulrich	Chevrolet
18.	Dick May	Ford
19.	Roland Wlodyka	Buick
20.	Jerry Jolly	Chevrolet
21.	Cecil Gordon	Chevrolet
22.	Claude Ballot-Lena	Dodge
23.	Jimmy Lee Capps	Chevrolet
24.	Frank Warren	Dodge
25.	Tommy Gale	Ford
26.	Coo Coo Marlin	Chevrolet
27.	Neil Bonnet	Dodge
28.	Darrell Waltrip	Chevrolet
29.	Al Holbert	Chevrolet
30.	J. D. McDuffie	Chevrolet
31.	Joe Mihalic	Oldsmobile
32.	A. J. Foyt	Buick
33.	Richard Petty	Dodge
34.	David Pearson	Mercury
35.	Jimmy Means	Chevrolet
36.	Blackie Wangerin	Mercury
37.	Ricky Rudd	Chevrolet
38.	Jim Vandiver	Chevrolet
39.	Donnie Allison	Oldsmobile
40.	Morgan Shepherd	Mercury
41.	Harry Gant	Buick

RICHMOND 400

February 26
Richmond, Virginia
Time of Race: 2 hours, 41 minutes, 59 seconds
Average Speed: 80.304 mph

FINISH	DRIVER	CAR
1.	Benny Parsons	Chevrolet
2.	Lennie Pond	Chevrolet
3.	Cale Yarborough	Oldsmobile
4.	Darrell Waltrip	Chevrolet
5.	Dick Brooks	Ford
6.	Bobby Allison	Ford
7.	Dave Marcis	Chevrolet
8.	Richard Childress	Chevrolet
9.	Neil Bonnett	Dodge
10.	Tighe Scott	Chevrolet
11.	James Hylton	Chevrolet
12.	Jimmy Means	Chevrolet
13.	Skip Manning	Chevrolet
14.	Frank Warren	Dodge
15.	Buddy Arrington	Dodge
16.	D. K. Ulrich	Chevrolet
17.	Cecil Gordon	Chevrolet
18.	Ronnie Thomas	Chevrolet
19.	Jimmy Lee Capps	Chevrolet
20.	Baxter Price	Chevrolet
21.	Ed Negre	Dodge
22.	Richard Petty	Dodge
23.	Tommy Gale	Ford
24.	Earle Canavan	Dodge
25.	Roger Hamby	Chevrolet
26.	Roland Wlodyka	Chevrolet
27.	J. D. McDuffie	Chevrolet
28.	Woody Fisher	Chevrolet
29.	Dick May	Chevrolet
30.	Nelson Oswald	Chevrolet

CAROLINA 500

March 5
Rockingham, North Carolina
Time of Race: 4 hours, 17 minutes, 17 seconds
Average Speed: 116.681 mph

FINISH	DRIVER	CAR
1.	David Pearson	Mercury
2.	Bobby Allison	Ford
3.	Benny Parsons	Chevrolet
4.	Richard Petty	Dodge
5.	Lennie Pond	Chevrolet
6.	Neil Bonnett	Dodge
7.	Skip Manning	Chevrolet

8.	Richard Childress	Chevrolet
9.	Buddy Arrington	Dodge
10.	Jimmy Means	Chevrolet
11.	Dave Marcis	Chevrolet
12.	Frank Warren	Dodge
13.	Ronnie Thomas	Chevrolet
14.	Tommy Gale	Ford
15.	James Hylton	Chevrolet
16.	Joe Frasson	Chevrolet
17.	Dick May	Chevrolet
18.	Cale Yarborough	Oldsmobile
19.	Joe Mihalic	Oldsmobile
20.	Ralph Jones	Ford
21.	Darrell Waltrip	Chevrolet
22.	Cecil Gordon	Chevrolet
23.	Baxter Price	Chevrolet
24.	Earle Canavan	Dodge
25.	J. D. McDuffie	Chevrolet
26.	D. K. Ulrich	Chevrolet
27.	Roger Hamby	Chevrolet
28.	Dick Brooks	Ford
29.	Ed Negre	Dodge
30.	Grant Adcox	Chevrolet
31.	Donnie Allison	Chevrolet
32.	Roland Wlodyka	Chevrolet
33.	Buddy Baker	Chevrolet
34.	Tighe Scott	Chevrolet
35.	Jimmy Lee Capps	Chevrolet
36.	Woody Fisher	Chevrolet

ATLANTA 500

March 19
Atlanta, Georgia
Time of Race: 3 hours, 30 minutes, 10 seconds
Average Speed: 142.520 mph

FINISH	DRIVER	CAR
1.	Bobby Allison	Ford
2.	Dave Marcis	Chevrolet
3.	Donnie Allison	Chevrolet
4.	Cale Yarborough	Oldsmobile
5.	Lennie Pond	Chevrolet
6.	Dick Brooks	Ford
7.	Grant Adcox	Chevrolet
8.	Connie Saylor	Dodge
9.	Bruce Hill	Oldsmobile
10.	Janet Guthrie	Chevrolet
11.	D. K. Ulrich	Chevrolet
12.	Sam Sommers	Chevrolet
13.	Benny Parsons	Chevrolet
14.	Buddy Arrington	Dodge
15.	Richard Childress	Oldsmobile
16.	J. D. McDuffie	Chevrolet
17.	Cecil Gordon	Chevrolet
18.	Roland Wlodyka	Chevrolet
19.	Frank Warren	Dodge
20.	Woody Fisher	Chevrolet
21.	David Pearson	Mercury
22.	Tommy Gale	Ford
23.	Skip Manning	Chevrolet
24.	Ronnie Thomas	Chevrolet
25.	Ed Negre	Dodge
26.	Richard Petty	Dodge
27.	Buddy Baker	Oldsmobile
28.	Billy McGinnis	Chevrolet
29.	Blackie Wangerin	Mercury
30.	Chuck Bown	Chevrolet
31.	Al Holbert	Chevrolet
32.	Jimmy Means	Chevrolet
33.	Neil Bonnett	Dodge
34.	Tighe Scott	Oldsmobile
35.	Darrell Waltrip	Chevrolet
36.	Butch Hartman	Chevrolet
37.	Roger Hamby	Chevrolet
38.	Bill Elliott	Mercury
39.	Coo Coo Marlin	Chevrolet
40.	John Utsman	Chevrolet

SOUTHEASTERN 500

April 2
Bristol, Tennessee
Time of Race: 2 hours, 53 minutes, 3 seconds
Average Speed: 92.401 mph

FINISH	DRIVER	CAR
1.	Darrell Waltrip	Chevrolet
2.	Benny Parsons	Oldsmobile
3.	Dave Marcis	Chevrolet
4.	Cale Yarborough	Oldsmobile
5.	Lennie Pond	Chevrolet
6.	Richard Childress	Oldsmobile
7.	James Hylton	Chevrolet
8.	Buddy Arrington	Dodge
9.	Tighe Scott	Chevrolet
10.	Ed Negre	Dodge
11.	D. K. Ulrich	Chevrolet
12.	Dick May	Chevrolet
13.	Frank Warren	Dodge
14.	Lynn Carroll	Chevrolet
15.	Skip Manning	Chevrolet
16.	Baxter Price	Chevrolet
17.	Roger Hamby	Oldsmobile
18.	Cecil Gordon	Chevrolet
19.	Dick Brooks	Ford
20.	Ronnie Thomas	Chevrolet
21.	Bobby Allison	Ford
22.	Tommy Gale	Ford
23.	Jimmy Means	Chevrolet
24.	Joe Mihalic	Chevrolet
25.	Richard Petty	Dodge
26.	Neil Bonnett	Dodge
27.	Roland Wlodyka	Chevrolet
28.	J. D. McDuffie	Chevrolet
29.	Bobby Wawak	Chevrolet

REBEL 500

April 9
Darlington, South Carolina
Time of Race: 3 hours, 55 minutes, 50 seconds
Average Speed: 127.544 mph

FINISH	DRIVER	CAR
1.	Benny Parsons	Chevrolet
2.	Darrell Waltrip	Chevrolet
3.	Lennie Pond	Oldsmobile
4.	Dave Marcis	Chevrolet
5.	Richard Petty	Dodge
6.	Buddy Baker	Chevrolet
7.	Al Holbert	Chevrolet
8.	Skip Manning	Chevrolet
9.	Bill Elliott	Mercury
10.	Ricky Rudd	Chevrolet
11.	J. D. McDuffie	Chevrolet
12.	Jimmy Means	Chevrolet
13.	Roger Hamby	Chevrolet
14.	Bobby Allison	Ford
15.	Cale Yarborough	Oldsmobile
16.	Baxter Price	Chevrolet
17.	Frank Warren	Dodge
18.	Buddy Arrington	Dodge
19.	Blackie Wangerin	Mercury
20.	D. K. Ulrich	Chevrolet
21.	Tommy Gale	Ford
22.	Earle Canavan	Dodge
23.	Donnie Allison	Chevrolet
24.	Joe Frasson	Chevrolet
25.	Grant Adcox	Chevrolet
26.	Joe Mihalic	Chevrolet
27.	Sam Sommers	Chevrolet
28.	Richard Childress	Oldsmobile
29.	David Pearson	Mercury
30.	Chuck Bown	Chevrolet
31.	Ronnie Thomas	Chevrolet

32.	Neil Bonnett	Dodge
33.	Cecil Gordon	Chevrolet
34.	Tighe Scott	Chevrolet
35.	Dick Brooks	Ford
36.	Dick May	Chevrolet

24.	Chuck Bown	Chevrolet
25.	Tighe Scott	Chevrolet
26.	J. D. McDuffie	Chevrolet
27.	Dick Brooks	Ford
28.	Dick May	Chevrolet
29.	John Kennedy	Ford
30.	Gary Myers	Chevrolet

GWYN STALEY 400

April 16
North Wilkesboro, North Carolina
Time of Race: 2 hours, 42 minutes, 26 seconds
Average Speed: 92.345 mph

FINISH	DRIVER	CAR
1.	Darrell Waltrip	Chevrolet
2.	Richard Petty	Dodge
3.	Benny Parsons	Chevrolet
4.	Lennie Pond	Chevrolet
5.	Dave Marcis	Chevrolet
6.	Bobby Allison	Ford
7.	J. D. McDuffie	Chevrolet
8.	Dick Brooks	Ford
9.	Skip Manning	Chevrolet
10.	Richard Childress	Oldsmobile
11.	Buddy Arrington	Dodge
12.	James Hylton	Chevrolet
13.	D. K. Ulrich	Chevrolet
14.	Jimmy Means	Chevrolet
15.	Ed Negre	Dodge
16.	Joe Booher	Chevrolet
17.	Cecil Gordon	Chevrolet
18.	Dick May	Chevrolet
19.	Baxter Price	Chevrolet
20.	Gary Myers	Chevrolet
21.	Ronnie Thomas	Chevrolet
22.	Frank Warren	Dodge
23.	Roger Hamby	Chevrolet
24.	Neil Bonnett	Dodge
25.	Tighe Scott	Chevrolet
26.	Cale Yarborough	Oldsmobile
27.	Tommy Gale	Ford
28.	Bill Hollar	Chevrolet
29.	John Kennedy	Ford

VIRGINIA 500

April 23
Martinsville, Virginia
Time of Race: 3 hours, 22 minutes
Average Speed: 77.971 mph

FINISH	DRIVER	CAR
1.	Darrell Waltrip	Chevrolet
2.	Neil Bonnett	Dodge
3.	Richard petty	Dodge
4.	Dave Marcis	Chevrolet
5.	Buddy Arrington	Dodge
6.	Bobby Allison	Ford
7.	James Hylton	Chevrolet
8.	Richard Childress	Oldsmobile
9.	Cecil Gordon	Chevrolet
10.	Jimmy Means	Chevrolet
11.	Baxter Price	Chevrolet
12.	Bobby Wawak	Chevrolet
13.	D. K. Ulrich	Chevrolet
14.	Roger Hamby	Chevrolet
15.	Benny Parsons	Chevrolet
16.	Cale Yarborough	Oldsmobile
17.	Tommy Gale	Ford
18.	Lennie Pond	Chevrolet
19.	Ed Negre	Dodge
20.	Ronnie Thomas	Chevrolet
21.	David Pearson	Mercury
22.	Frank Warren	Dodge
23.	Skip Manning	Chevrolet

WINSTON 500

May 14
Talladega, Alabama
Time of Race: 3 hours, 7 minutes, 53 seconds
Average Speed: 159.699 mph

FINISH	DRIVER	CAR
1.	Cale Yarborough	Oldsmobile
2.	Buddy Baker	Oldsmobile
3.	A. J. Foyt	Buick
4.	Skip Manning	Buick
5.	Grant Adcox	Chevrolet
6.	Bill Elliott	Mercury
7.	Ferrell Harris	Dodge
8.	Dave Marcis	Chevrolet
9.	Richard Childress	Oldsmobile
10.	James Hylton	Oldsmobile
11.	Richard Petty	Dodge
12.	Buddy Arrington	Dodge
13.	Tighe Scott	Oldsmobile
14.	Ronnie Thomas	Chevrolet
15.	Dick Brooks	Mercury
16.	Tommy Gale	Ford
17.	D. K. Ulrich	Chevrolet
18.	Claude Ballot-Lena	Dodge
19.	Roger Hamby	Oldsmobile
20.	Baxter Price	Chevrolet
21.	Lennie Pond	Oldsmobile
22.	Darrell Waltrip	Chevrolet
23.	Dick May	Chevrolet
24.	Donnie Allison	Chevrolet
25.	Cecil Gordon	Chevrolet
26.	Jimmy Means	Chevrolet
27.	Ricky Rudd	Buick
28.	Ed Negre	Dodge
29.	Frank Warren	Dodge
30.	Blackie Wangerin	Mercury
31.	Benny Parsons	Oldsmobile
32.	John Utsman	Chevrolet
33.	Chuck Bown	Chervolet
34.	Ron Hutcherson	Buick
35.	David Pearson	Mercury
36.	Bruce Hill	Oldsmobile
37.	Frank Hill	Chrvrolet
38.	Bobby Allison	Ford
39.	Neil Bonnett	Oldsmobile
40.	J. D. McDuffie	Chevrolet
41.	Coo Coo Marlin	Chevrolet

MASON-DIXON 500

May 21
Dover, Delaware
Time of Race: 4 hours, 20 minutes, 12 seconds
Average Speed: 138.355 mph
Margin of Victory: 1 car length (finished under caution)

FINISH	DRIVER	CAR
1.	David Pearson	Mercury
2.	Cale Yarborough	Oldsmobile
3.	Lennie Pond	Chevrolet
4.	Benny Parsons	Chevrolet
5.	Neil Bonnett	Dodge
6.	Darrell Waltrip	Chevrolet
7.	Richard Petty	Dodge

8.	Bobby Allison	Ford
9.	Dick Brooks	Ford
10.	Al Holbert	Chevrolet
11.	Tighe Scott	Chevrolet
12.	Skip Manning	Buick
13.	Buddy Arrington	Dodge
14.	Satch Worley	Chevrolet
15.	Dave Marcis	Chevrolet
16.	D. K. Ulrich	Chevrolet
17.	Jimmy Means	Chevrolet
18.	Tommy Gale	Ford
19.	Bruce Hill	Oldsmobile
20.	Earle Canavan	Dodge
21.	Dick May	Chevrolet
22.	Baxter Price	Chevrolet
23.	Buddy Baker	Chevrolet
24.	Nestor Peles	Chevrolet
25.	Cecil Gordon	Chevrolet
26.	Gary Myers	Chevrolet
27.	Frank Warren	Dodge
28.	Bobby Wawak	Chevrolet
29.	Greg Heller	Ford
30.	Joe Mihalic	Chevrolet
31.	Roger Hamby	Chevrolet
32.	Ronnie Thomas	Chevrolet
33.	Richard Childress	Oldsmobile
34.	J. D. McDuffie	Chevrolet
35.	Ed Negre	Dodge
36.	Bill Hollar	Chevrolet
37.	Elmo Langley	Chevrolet
38.	Nelson Oswald	Chevrolet
39.	Wayne Morgan	Chevrolet
40.	Dave Dion	Ford

WORLD 600

May 28
Charlotte, North Carolina
Time of Race: 4 hours, 20 minutes, 12 seconds
Average Speed: 138.355 mph
Margin of Victory: 1 car length (finished under caution)

FINISH	DRIVER	CAR
1.	Darrell Waltrip	Chevrolet
2.	Donnie Allison	Chevrolet
3.	Bobby Allison	Ford
4.	Cale Yarborough	Oldsmobile
5.	David Pearson	Mercury
6.	Benny Parsons	Oldsmobile
7.	Buddy Baker	Chevrolet
8.	Richard Petty	Dodge
9.	Sterling Marlin	Chevrolet
10.	Bruce Hill	Oldsmobile
11.	Grant Adcox	Chevrolet
12.	Morgan Shepherd	Mercury
13.	Dick May	Ford
14.	Bill Elliott	Mercury
15.	Buddy Arrington	Dodge
16.	John Utsman	Chevrolet
17.	Dale Earnhardt	Ford
18.	Gary Myers	Chevrolet
19.	Dick Brooks	Mercury
20.	Richard Childress	Oldsmobile
21.	Roland Wlodyka	Chevrolet
22.	J. D. McDuffie	Chevrolet
23.	Frank Warren	Chevrolet
24.	Tommy Gale	Ford
25.	Baxter Price	Chevrolet
26.	Skip Manning	Chevrolet
27.	Jim Vandiver	Chevrolet
28.	Ricky Rudd	Chevrolet
29.	D. K. Ulrich	Chevrolet
30.	Ronnie Thomas	Chevrolet
31.	Tighe Scott	Oldsmobile
32.	Dave Marcis	Chevrolet
33.	Lennie Pond	Oldsmobile
34.	Connie Saylor	Dodge
35.	Neil Bonnett	Oldsmobile
36.	Harry Gant	Chevrolet
37.	Jimmy Means	Chevrolet

38.	Al Holbert	Oldsmobile
39.	Ron Hutcherson	Buick
40.	Jerry Jolly	Chevrolet

MUSIC CITY USA 420

June 3
Nashville, Tennessee
Time of Race: 2 hours, 51 minutes, 34 seconds
Average Speed: 87.541 mph

FINISH	DRIVER	CAR
1.	Cale Yarborough	Oldsmobile
2.	Lennie Pond	Chevrolet
3.	Richard Petty	Dodge
4.	Dave Marcis	Chevrolet
5.	Neil Bonnett	Dodge
6.	Grant Adcox	Chevrolet
7.	Tighe Scott	Chevrolet
8.	Richard Childress	Oldsmobile
9.	Buddy Arrington	Dodge
10.	D. K. Ulrich	Chevrolet
11.	James Hylton	Chevrolet
12.	J. D. McDuffie	Chevrolet
13.	Bobby Wawak	Chevrolet
14.	Dick Brooks	Ford
15.	Ronnie Thomas	Chevrolet
16.	Frank Warren	Dodge
17.	Baxter Price	Chevrolet
18.	Dick May	Chevrolet
19.	Cecil Gordon	Chevrolet
20.	Benny Parsons	Chevrolet
21.	Bobby Allison	Ford
22.	Coo Coo Marlin	Chevrolet
23.	Roger Hamby	Oldsmobile
24.	Ralph Jones	Ford
25.	Bruce Hill	Oldsmobile
26.	Darrell Waltrip	Chevrolet
27.	Ed Negre	Dodge
28.	Gary Myers	Chevrolet
29.	Richard Waters	Chevrolet
30.	Jimmy Means	Chevrolet

NAPA RIVERSIDE 400

June 11
Riverside, California
Time of Race: 2 hours, 23 minutes, 10 seconds
Average Speed: 104.311 mph
Margin of Victory: 29 seconds

FINISH	DRIVER	CAR
1.	Benny Parsons	Chevrolet
2.	Richard Petty	Dodge
3.	Bobby Allison	Ford
4.	Dave Marcis	Chevrolet
5.	Cale Yarborough	Oldsmobile
6.	Ray Elder	Dodge
7.	Lennie Pond	Chevrolet
8.	Bill Schmitt	Oldsmobile
9.	Jim Thirkettle	Buick
10.	Neil Bonnett	Dodge
11.	Tighe Scott	Chevrolet
12.	Cecil Gordon	Chevrolet
13.	Rick McCray	Chevrolet
14.	D. K. Ulrich	Chevrolet
15.	Richard Childress	Oldsmobile
16.	Darrell Waltrip	Chevrolet
17.	Hershel McGriff	Chevrolet
18.	Buddy Arrington	Ford
19.	Harry Goularte	Chevrolet
20.	Richard White	Chevrolet
21.	Dick May	Chevrolet
22.	Don Graham	Chevrolet

23.	John Borneman	Chevrolet
24.	J. D. McDuffie	Chevrolet
25.	Ronnie Thomas	Chevrolet
26.	Dick Brooks	Ford
27.	David Pearson	Mercury
28.	Chuck Wahl	Chevrolet
29.	Frank Warren	Dodge
30.	Rocky Moran	Buick
31.	Ernie Stierly	Chevrolet
32.	Jim Insolo	Oldsmobile
33.	Don Noel	Chevrolet
34.	Bill Baker	Buick
35.	Norm Palmer	Dodge

GABRIEL 400

June 18
Brooklyn, Michigan
Time of Race: 2 hours, 40 minutes, 28 seconds
Average Speed: 149.563 mph
Margin of Victory: 12 seconds

FINISH	DRIVER	CAR
1.	Cale Yarborough	Oldsmobile
2.	David Pearson	Mercury
3.	Benny Parsons	Oldsmobile
4.	Dave Marcis	Chevrolet
5.	Donnie Allison	Chevrolet
6.	Richard Petty	Dodge
7.	Dick Brooks	Ford
8.	Buddy Baker	Chevrolet
9.	Ricky Rudd	Chevrolet
10.	Richard Childress	Oldsmobile
11.	Tighe Scott	Oldsmobile
12.	Buddy Arrington	Dodge
13.	J. D. McDuffie	Chevrolet
14.	D. K. Ulrich	Chevrolet
15.	Jimmy Means	Chevrolet
16.	Skip Manning	Chevrolet
17.	Cecil Gordon	Chevrolet
18.	Ronnie Thomas	Chevrolet
19.	Dick May	Chevrolet
20.	Frank Warren	Dodge
21.	Tommy Gale	Chevrolet
22.	Grant Adcox	Chevrolet
23.	Gary Myers	Chevrolet
24.	Bobby Allison	Ford
25.	Lennie Pond	Oldsmobile
26.	Baxter Price	Chevrolet
27.	Roger Hamby	Oldsmobile
28.	Darrell Waltrip	Chevrolet
29.	Bruce Hill	Oldsmobile
30.	John Kennedy	Ford
31.	Al Holbert	Chevrolet
32.	Blackie Wangerin	Mercury
33.	Earle Canavan	Dodge
34.	Joe Booher	Chevrolet
35.	Ed Negre	Dodge
36.	Neil Bonnett	Dodge

FIRECRACKER 400

July 4
Daytona Beach, Florida
Time of Race: 2 hours, 35 minutes, 30 seconds
Average Speed: 154.340 mph
Margin of Victory: 1 car length

FINISH	DRIVER	CAR
1.	David Pearson	Mercury
2.	Cale Yarborough	Oldsmobile
3.	Darrell Waltrip	Chevrolet
4.	Richard Petty	Dodge
5.	Lennie Pond	Chevrolet

6.	Dave Marcis	Chevrolet
7.	Dale Earnhardt	Ford
8.	Ferrell Harris	Chevrolet
9.	Bill Elliott	Mercury
10.	Tighe Scott	Oldsmobile
11.	Janet Guthrie	Chevrolet
12.	J. D. McDuffie	Chevrolet
13.	Jimmy Means	Chevrolet
14.	Joe Frasson	Chevrolet
15.	Tommy Gale	Ford
16.	Dick May	Chevrolet
17.	Frank Warren	Dodge
18.	Satch Worley	Oldsmobile
19.	D. K. Ulrich	Chevrolet
20.	Baxter Price	Chevrolet
21.	Ricky Rudd	Buick
22.	Grant Adcox	Chevrolet
23.	Neil Bonnett	Chevrolet
24.	Richard Childress	Oldsmobile
25.	Ronnie Thomas	Chevrolet
26.	Benny Parsons	Oldsmobile
27.	Bobby Allison	Ford
28.	Paul Fess	Chevrolet
29.	Raymond Williams	Buick
30.	Al Holbert	Oldsmobile
31.	Blackie Wangerin	Mercury
32.	Cecil Gordon	Chevrolet
33.	Donnie Allison	Chevrolet
34.	Buddy Arrington	Dodge
35.	Claude Ballot-Lena	Dodge
36.	Dick Brooks	Mercury
37.	Buddy Baker	Oldsmobile
38.	Coo Coo Marlin	Chevrolet
39.	Skip Manning	Buick
40.	Bruce Hill	Oldsmobile

NASHVILLE 420

July 15
Nashville, Tennessee
Time of Race: 2 hours, 48 minutes, 54 seconds
Average Speed: 88.924 mph
Margin of Victory: 2 laps

FINISH	DRIVER	CAR
1.	Cale Yarborough	Oldsmobile
2.	Darrell Waltrip	Chevrolet
3.	Richard Childress	Oldsmobile
4.	Dave Marcis	Chevrolet
5.	J. D. McDuffie	Chevrolet
6.	Benny Parsons	Chevrolet
7.	Bobby Allison	Ford
8.	Dick Brooks	Ford
9.	Farrel Harris	Chevrolet
10.	Ronnie Thomas	Chevrolet
11.	Grant Adcox	Chevrolet
12.	Buddy Arrington	Dodge
13.	Frank Warren	Dodge
14.	Bruce Hill	Oldsmobile
15.	Gary Myers	Chevrolet
16.	Elmo Langley	Ford
17.	Roger Hamby	Chevrolet
18.	Dick May	Chevrolet
19.	Cecil Gordon	Chevrolet
20.	D. K. Ulrich	Chevrolet
21.	Ralph Jones	Ford
22.	Tighe Scott	Chevrolet
23.	Richard Petty	Dodge
24.	Jimmy Means	Chevrolet
25.	Sterling Marlin	Chevrolet
26.	Lennie Pond	Chevrolet
27.	Baxter Price	Chevrolet
28.	Neil Bonnett	Chevrolet
29.	Bobby Fisher	Chevrolet
30.	Walter Ballard	Chevrolet

COCA-COLA 500

July 30
Pocono, Pennsylvania
Time of Race: 3 hours, 30 minutes, 28 seconds
Average Speed: 142.540 mph
Margin of Victory: half a second

FINISH	DRIVER	CAR
1.	Darrell Waltrip	Chevrolet
2.	David Pearson	Mercury
3.	Bobby Allison	Ford
4.	Dave Marcis	Chevrolet
5.	Buddy Baker	Chevrolet
6.	Ricky Rudd	Chevrolet
7.	Dick Brooks	Mercury
8.	Tighe Scott	Chevrolet
9.	Satch Worley	Oldsmobile
10.	J. D. McDuffie	Chevrolet
11.	Dick May	Ford
12.	Al Holbert	Chevrolet
13.	Jimmy Means	Chevrolet
14.	Buddy Arrington	Dodge
15.	Blackie Wangerin	Mercury
16.	Tommy Gale	Ford
17.	Bruce Hill	Oldsmobile
18.	Frank Warren	Dodge
19.	Gary Myers	Chevrolet
20.	Ferrell Harris	Chevrolet
21.	Nestor Peles	Chevrolet
22.	Joe Booher	Chevrolet
23.	Kenny Brightbill	Mercury
24.	Richard Childress	Oldsmobile
25.	D. K. Ulrich	Chevrolet
26.	Cale Yarborough	Oldsmobile
27.	Roger Hamby	Chevrolet
28.	Baxter Price	Chevrolet
29.	Benny Parsons	Chevrolet
30.	Richard Petty	Dodge
31.	Janet Guthrie	Chevrolet
32.	Joe Mihalic	Chevrolet
33.	Ronnie Thomas	Chevrolet
34.	Bobby Wawak	Ford
35.	Donnie Allison	Oldsmobile
36.	Neil Bonnett	Chevrolet
37.	Jocko Maggiacomo	Matador
38.	Dave Dion	Ford
39.	James Hylton	Chevrolet
40.	Cecil Gordon	Chevrolet

TALLADEGA 500

August 6
Talladega, Alabama
Time of Race: 2 hours, 51 minutes, 43 seconds
Average Speed: 174.700 mph
Margin of Victory: 1 foot

FINISH	DRIVER	CAR
1.	Lennie Pond	Oldsmobile
2.	Donnie Allison	Oldsmobile
3.	Benny Parsons	Oldsmobile
4.	Cale Yarborough	Oldsmobile
5.	David Pearson	Mercury
6.	Bobby Allison	Ford
7.	Richard Petty	Dodge
8.	Neil Bonnett	Chevrolet
9.	Dick Brooks	Mercury
10.	Tighe Scott	Oldsmobile
11.	Ferrell Harris	Chevrolet
12.	Dale Earnhardt	Ford
13.	Bill Elliott	Mercury
14.	Dave Marcis	Oldsmobile
15.	Buddy Arrington	Dodge
16.	Dick May	Chevrolet
17.	J. D. McDuffie	Chevrolet
18.	Marty Robbins	Dodge

FINISH	DRIVER	CAR
19.	D. K. Ulrich	Chevrolet
20.	Tommy Gale	Ford
21.	Gary Myers	Chevrolet
22.	Grant Adcox	Chevrolet
23.	Baxter Price	Chevrolet
24.	Ronnie Thomas	Chevrolet
25.	Richard Childress	Oldsmobile
26.	Coo Coo Marlin	Chevrolet
27.	Steve Moore	Chevrolet
28.	Buddy Baker	Oldsmobile
29.	Janet Guthrie	Buick
30.	Al Holbert	Oldsmobile
31.	Earle Canavan	Dodge
32.	Jimmy Means	Chevrolet
33.	Frank Warren	Dodge
34.	Darrell Waltrip	Chevrolet
35.	Bruce Hill	Oldsmobile
36.	Roger Hamby	Chevrolet
37.	Claude Ballot-Lena	Dodge
38.	Skip Manning	Buick
39.	Ricky Rudd	Chevrolet
40.	Blackie Wangerin	Mercury
41.	James Hylton	Buick

CHAMPION SPARK PLUG 400

August 20
Brooklyn, Michigan
Time of Race: 3 hours, 5 minutes, 14 seconds
Average Speed: 129.566 mph
Margin of Victory: 10 feet

FINISH	DRIVER	CAR
1.	David Pearson	Mercury
2.	Cale Yarborough	Oldsmobile
3.	Darrell Waltrip	Chevrolet
4.	Dave Marcis	Chevrolet
5.	Bobby Allison	Ford
6.	Dick Brooks	Mercury
7.	J. D. McDuffie	Chevrolet
8.	Lennie Pond	Oldsmobile
9.	Neil Bonnett	Oldsmobile
10.	Ferrell Harris	Chevrolet
11.	Dick May	Chevrolet
12.	Buddy Arrington	Dodge
13.	Benny Parsons	Oldsmobile
14.	Richard Petty	Chevrolet
15.	Jimmy Means	Chevrolet
16.	Tommy Gale	Ford
17.	Cecil Gordon	Chevrolet
18.	Ed Negre	Dodge
19.	Tighe Scott	Chevrolet
20.	Gary Myers	Chevrolet
21.	Baxter Price	Chevrolet
22.	Joey Arrington	Dodge
23.	D. K. Ulrich	Chevrolet
24.	Frank Warren	Dodge
25.	Blackie Wangerin	Mercury
26.	Ronnie Thomas	Chevrolet
27.	Janet Guthrie	Buick
28.	Ricky Rudd	Chevrolet
29.	Donnie Allison	Oldsmobile
30.	Roger Hamby	Chevrolet
31.	Richard Childress	Oldsmobile
32.	Earle Canavan	Dodge
33.	Mel Larson	Oldsmobile
34.	Bruce Hill	Oldsmobile
35.	James Hylton	Chevrolet
36.	Buddy Baker	Oldsmobile

VOLUNTEER 500

August 26
Bristol, Tennessee
Time of Race: 3 hours, 25 minutes
Average Speed: 88.628 mph
Margin of Victory: 15 seconds

FINISH	DRIVER	CAR
1.	Cale Yarborough	Oldsmobile
2.	Benny Parsons	Oldsmobile
3.	Darrell Waltrip	Chevrolet
4.	Dick Brooks	Ford
5.	Richard Petty	Chevrolet
6.	Dave Marcis	Chevrolet
7.	Richard Childress	Oldsmobile
8.	J. D. McDuffie	Chevrolet
9.	D. K. Ulrich	Chevrolet
10.	Roger Hamby	Chevrolet
11.	Ronnie Thomas	Chevrolet
12.	Buddy Arrington	Dodge
13.	Cecil Gordon	Chevrolet
14.	Gary Myers	Chevrolet
15.	Frank Warren	Dodge
16.	Baxter Price	Chevrolet
17.	James Hylton	Chevrolet
18.	Ferrell Harris	Chevrolet
19.	Jimmy Means	Chevrolet
20.	Neil Bonnett	Chevrolet
21.	Tommy Gale	Ford
22.	Bobby Allison	Ford
23.	Tighe Scott	Chevrolet
24.	Nelson Oswald	Chevrolet
25.	Dick May	Chevrolet
26.	Lennie Pond	Oldsmobile
27.	Ralph Jones	Ford
28.	Bobby Wawak	Chevrolet
29.	Ed Negre	Dodge
30.	Bil Green	Chevrolet

SOUTHERN 500

September 4
Darlington, South Carolina
Time of Race: 4 hours, 17 minutes, 46 seconds
Average Speed: 116.828 mph
Margin of Victory: .05 seconds

FINISH	DRIVER	CAR
1.	Cale Yarborough	Oldsmobile
2.	Darrell Waltrip	Chevrolet
3.	Richard Petty	Chevrolet
4.	Terry Labonte	Chevrolet
5.	Bobby Allison	Ford
6.	Bill Elliott	Mercury
7.	James Hylton	Chevrolet
8.	Buddy Arrington	Dodge
9.	Ronnie Thomas	Chevrolet
10.	Benny Parsons	Chevrolet
11.	Jimmy Means	Chevrolet
12.	Frank Warren	Dodge
13.	Tommy Gale	Ford
14.	Gary Myers	Chevrolet
15.	Baxter Price	Chevrolet
16.	Dale Earnhardt	Ford
17.	Joe Frasson	Chevrolet
18.	Ralph Jones	Ford
19.	Roger Hamby	Chevrolet
20.	J. D. McDuffie	Chevrolet
21.	Ed Negre	Chrysler
22.	Bob Burcham	Chevrolet
23.	Tighe Scott	Chevrolet
24.	Donnie Allison	Chevrolet
25.	Dick Brooks	Mercury
26.	Lennie Pond	Chevrolet
27.	Richard Childress	Oldsmobile
28.	David Pearson	Mercury
29.	D. K. Ulrich	Chevrolet
30.	Coo Coo Marlin	Chevrolet
31.	Grant Adcox	Chevrolet
32.	Buddy Baker	Chevrolet
33.	Blackie Wangerin	Mercury
34.	Neil Bonnett	Chevrolet
35.	Dave Marcis	Chevrolet
36.	Ricky Rudd	Chevrolet
37.	Bobby Wawak	Chevrolet
38.	Dick May	Ford

| 39. | Earle Canavan | Dodge |
| 40. | Bruce Hill | Oldsmobile |

CAPITAL CITY 400

September 10
Richmond, Virginia
Time of Race: 2 hours, 43 minutes, 19 seconds
Average Speed: 79.568 mph
Margin of Victory: 1 second

FINISH	DRIVER	CAR
1.	Darrell Waltrip	Chevrolet
2.	Bobby Allison	Ford
3.	Neil Bonnett	Chevrolet
4.	Cale Yarborough	Oldsmobile
5.	Dick Brooks	Ford
6.	Benny Parsons	Chevrolet
7.	Terry Labonte	Chevrolet
8.	J. D. McDuffie	Chevrolet
9.	Dave Marcis	Chevrolet
10.	Roger Hamby	Chevrolet
11.	Richard Childress	Oldsmobile
12.	Lennie Pond	Chevrolet
13.	Jimmy Means	Chevrolet
14.	Ronnie Thomas	Chevrolet
15.	Dick May	Dodge
16.	Buddy Arrington	Dodge
17.	Cecil Gordon	Chevrolet
18.	James Hylton	Chevrolet
19.	Joey Arrington	Dodge
20.	Richard Petty	Chevrolet
21.	Gary Myers	Chevrolet
22.	Baxter Price	Chevrolet
23.	Frank Warren	Dodge
24.	Tommy Gale	Ford
25.	Nelson Oswald	Chevrolet
26.	Dave Dion	Ford
27.	Tighe Scott	Chevrolet
28.	Ferrell Harris	Chevrolet
29.	Wayne Morgan	Chevrolet
30.	Ed Negre	Chrysler

DELAWARE 500

September 17
Dover, Delaware
Time of Race: 4 hours, 11 minutes, 20 seconds
Average Speed: 119.323 mph
Margin of Victory: 19.7 seconds

FINISH	DRIVER	CAR
1.	Bobby Allison	Ford
2.	Cale Yarborough	Oldsmobile
3.	Buddy Baker	Chevrolet
4.	David Pearson	Mercury
5.	Darrel Waltrip	Chevrolet
6.	Dick Brooks	Ford
7.	Lennie Pond	Oldsmobile
8.	Dave Marcis	Chevrolet
9.	Donnie Allison	Oldsmobile
10.	Dick May	Chevrolet
11.	Ronnie Thomas	Chevrolet
12.	Richard Childress	Oldsmobile
13.	Al Holbert	Chevrolet
14.	Cecil Gordon	Chevrolet
15.	Ed Negre	Dodge
16.	Earle Canavan	Dodge
17.	Tommy Gale	Ford
18.	Roger Hamby	Oldsmobile
19.	Nestor Peles	Chevrolet
20.	Gary Myers	Chevrolet
21.	Frank Warren	Dodge
22.	Buddy Arrington	Dodge

23.	Baxter Price	Chevrolet
24.	Nelson Oswald	Chevrolet
25.	Tighe Scott	Chevrolet
26.	Benny Parsons	Chevrolet
27.	Richard Petty	Chevrolet
28.	Dave Dion	Ford
29.	Neil Bonnett	Oldsmobile
30.	Ralph Jones	Ford
31.	Joey Arrington	Dodge
32.	Jimmy Means	Chevrolet
33.	J. D. McDuffie	Chevrolet
34.	James Hylton	Chevrolet
35.	Louis Gatto	Chevrolet
36.	Ferrel Haris	Chrysler
37.	Jabe Thomas	Chevrolet

OLD DOMINION 500

September 24
Martinsville, Virginia
Time of Race: 3 hours, 18 minutes, 54 seconds
Average Speed: 79.185 mph
Margin of Victory: half a car length

FINISH	DRIVER	CAR
1.	Cale Yarborough	Oldsmobile
2.	Darrell Waltrip	Chevrolet
3.	Benny Parsons	Chevrolet
4.	Neil Bonnett	Chevrolet
5.	Lennie Pond	Chevrolet
6.	Richard Petty	Chevrolet
7.	Bobby Allison	Ford
8.	Dave Marcis	Chevrolet
9.	Terry Labonte	Chevrolet
10.	Buddy Arrington	Dodge
11.	James Hylton	Chevrolet
12.	Richard Childress	Oldsmobile
13.	Dick Brooks	Ford
14.	Satch Worley	Oldsmobile
15.	Gary Myers	Chevrolet
16.	Ronnie Thomas	Chevrolet
17.	Dick May	Buick
18.	Ed Negre	Dodge
19.	Baxter Price	Chevrolet
20.	Ferrell Harris	Chevrolet
21.	Frank Warren	Dodge
22.	J. D. McDuffie	Chevrolet
23.	Jimmy Means	Chevrolet
24.	Roger Hamby	Chevrolet
25.	David Pearson	Mercury
26.	Buddy Baker	Chevrolet
27.	Tommy Gale	Ford
28.	Harry Gant	Chevrolet
29.	Tighe Scott	Chevrolet
30.	Cecil Gordon	Chevrolet

WILKES 400

October 1
North Wilkesboro, North Carolina
Time of Race: 2 hours, 23 minutes, 18 seconds
Average Speed: 97.847 mph
Margin of Victory: 10 seconds

FINISH	DRIVER	CAR
1.	Cale Yarborough	Oldsmobile
2.	Darrell Waltrip	Chevrolet
3.	Bobby Allison	Ford
4.	Richard Petty	Chevrolet
5.	Neil Bonnett	Chevrolet
6.	Benny Parsons	Chevrolet
7.	Lennie Pond	Chevrolet
8.	Dave Marcis	Chevrolet
9.	Dick Brooks	Ford

10.	Tighe Scott	Chevrolet
11.	J. D. McDuffie	Chevrolet
12.	Roger Hamby	Chevrolet
13.	Buddy Arrington	Dodge
14.	Richard Childress	Oldsmobile
15.	Junior Miller	Chevrolet
16.	James Hylton	Chevrolet
17.	Tommy Gale	Ford
18.	Nelson Oswald	Chevrolet
19.	Ronnie Thomas	Chevrolet
20.	Ed Negre	Dodge
21.	Baxter Price	Chevrolet
22.	Gary Myers	Chevrolet
23.	Jimmy Means	Chevrolet
24.	Frank Warren	Dodge
25.	Dick May	Buick
26.	Cecil Gordon	Chevrolet
27.	John Kennedy	Ford

NAPA NATIONAL 500

October 8
Charlotte, North Carolina
Time of Race: 3 hours, 31 minutes, 57 seconds
Average Speed: 141.826 mph
Margin of Victory: 30.2 seconds

FINISH	DRIVER	CAR
1.	Bobby Allison	Ford
2.	Darrel Waltrip	Chevrolet
3.	Dave Marcis	Chevrolet
4.	Donnie Allison	Chevrolet
5.	David Pearson	Mercury
6.	Lennie Pond	Chevrolet
7.	Coo Coo Marlin	Chevrolet
8.	Dick May	Ford
9.	Richard Childress	Oldsmobile
10.	Dick Brooks	Mercury
11.	J. D. McDuffie	Chevrolet
12.	Tighe Scott	Chevrolet
13.	Bruce Hill	Oldsmobile
14.	Buddy Arrington	Dodge
15.	James Hylton	Chevrolet
16.	Connie Saylor	Dodge
17.	Bill Elliott	Mercury
18.	Roger Hamby	Chervolet
19.	Harry Gant	Chevrolet
20.	Glenn Jarrett	Oldsmobile
21.	Ed Negre	Chrysler
22.	Cale Yarborough	Oldsmobile
23.	Ricky Rudd	Chevrolet
24.	Terry Labonte	Chevrolet
25.	Frank Warren	Dodge
26.	Butch Mock	Chevrolet
27.	Richard Petty	Chevrolet
28.	Benny Parsons	Oldsmobile
29.	Baxter Price	Ford
30.	Neil Bonnett	Chevrolet
31.	Tommy Gale	Ford
32.	John Utsman	Chevrolet
33.	Grant Adcox	Chevrolet
34.	Buddy Baker	Chevrolet
35.	Janet Guthrie	Buick
36.	Jerry Jolly	Buick
37.	Bill Dennis	Chevrolet
38.	Skip Manning	Chevrolet
39.	Dick Trickle	Ford
40.	Bobby Fisher	Chevrolet

AMERICAN 500

October 22
Rockingham, North Carolina
Time of Race: 4 hours, 15 minutes, 58 seconds
Average Speed: 117.288 mph
Margin of Victory: 2 laps & 21 seconds

FINISH	DRIVER	CAR
1.	Cale Yarborough	Oldsmobile
2.	Bobby Allison	Ford
3.	Darrell Waltrip	Chevrolet
4.	Benny Parsons	Chevrolet
5.	Dick Brooks	Ford
6.	Richard Petty	Chevrolet
7.	Lennie Pond	Chevrolet
8.	Dave Marcis	Chevrolet
9.	Buddy Arrington	Dodge
10.	Richard Childress	Oldsmobile
11.	Dick May	Chevrolet
12.	J. D. McDuffie	Chevrolet
13.	Jimmy Means	Chevrolet
14.	James Hylton	Chevrolet
15.	Cecil Gordon	Oldsmobile
16.	Frank Warren	Dodge
17.	Gary Myers	Chevrolet
18.	Tommy Gale	Ford
19.	Baxter Price	Chevrolet
20.	Donnie Allison	Chevrolet
21.	Tighe Scott	Chevrolet
22.	Buddy Baker	Chevrolet
23.	Joe Frasson	Buick
24.	David Pearson	Mercury
25.	Ricky Rudd	Chevrolet
26.	Roger Hamby	Chevrolet
27.	Bobby Wawak	Chevrolet
28.	Junior Miller	Chevrolet
29.	Elmo Langley	Buick
30.	Johnny Halford	Chevrolet
31.	Neil Bonnett	Chevrolet
32.	Charlie Blanton	Chevrolet
33.	Ronnie Thomas	Chevrolet
34.	Ferrell Harris	Chevrolet
35.	Ed Negre	Dodge
36.	Bill Hollar	Chevrolet

DIXIE 500

November 5
Atlanta, Georgia
Time of Race: 4 hours, 43 seconds
Average Speed: 124.312 mph
Margin of Victory: 2 car lengths

FINISH	DRIVER	CAR
1.	Donnie Allison	Chevrolet
2.	Richard Petty	Chevrolet
3.	Dave Marcis	Chevrolet
4.	Dale Earnhardt	Chevrolet
5.	Benny Parsons	Oldsmobile
6.	Bobby Allison	Ford
7.	Harry Gant	Chevrolet
8.	Cale Yarborough	Oldsmobile
9.	Ricky Rudd	Chevrolet
10.	Coo Coo Marlin	Chevrolet
11.	Roger Hamby	Chevrolet
12.	Dick Brooks	Mercury
13.	Terry Labonte	Chevrolet
14.	J. D. McDuffie	Chevrolet
15.	Ronnie Thomas	Chevrolet
16.	Buddy Arrington	Dodge
17.	Dave Watson	Chevrolet
18.	Cecil Gordon	Oldsmobile
19.	Dick May	Chevrolet
20.	Ferrel Harris	Chevrolet
21.	Buddy Baker	Chevrolet
22.	Tighe Scott	Oldsmobile
23.	Jimmy Means	Chevrolet
24.	Butch Mock	Chevrolet
25.	Skip Manning	Mercury
26.	Ed Negre	Chrysler
27.	Gary Myers	Chevrolet
28.	Darrell Waltrip	Chevrolet
29.	Ralph Jones	Ford
30.	Richard Childress	Oldsmobile
31.	Tommy Gale	Chevrolet
32.	David Pearson	Mercury

33.	Frank Warren	Dodge
34.	Neil Bonnett	Chevrolet
35.	Al Holbert	Chevrolet
36.	Bruce Hill	Oldsmobile
37.	Bill Elliott	Oldsmobile
38.	Grant Adcox	Chevrolet
39.	Lennie Pond	Chevrolet
40.	John Kennedy	Ford

LOS ANGELES TIMES 500

November 19
Ontario, California
Time of Race: 3 hours, 37 minutes, 44 seconds
Average Speed: 137.783 mph
Margin of Victory: 1.7 seconds

FINISH	DRIVER	CAR
1.	Bobby Allison	Ford
2.	Cale Yarborough	Oldsmobile
3.	Donnie Allison	Chevrolet
4.	Buddy Baker	Chevrolet
5.	Darrell Waltrip	Chevrolet
6.	Lennie Pond	Chevrolet
7.	Jim Insolo	Chevrolet
8.	Benny Parsons	Chevrolet
9.	Dick Brooks	Mercury
10.	Jim Thirkettle	Buick
11.	Richard Childress	Oldsmobile
12.	Roger Hamby	Chevrolet
13.	Janet Guthrie	Buick
14.	Bill Schmitt	Oldsmobile
15.	Cecil Gordon	Oldsmobile
16.	James Hylton	Oldsmobile
17.	Tommy Gale	Ford
18.	Richard White	Chevrolet
19.	Ferrell Harris	Chevrolet
20.	Rocky Moran	Buick
21.	Ed Negre	Chrysler
22.	Jimmy Means	Chevrolet
23.	Frank Warren	Dodge
24.	Gary Myers	Chevrolet
25.	John Borneman	Chevrolet
26.	J. D. McDuffie	Chevrolet
27.	Dave Marcis	Chevrolet
28.	Don Noel	Chevrolet
29.	Mel Larson	Buick
30.	Ronnie Thomas	Chevrolet
31.	Dick May	Chevrolet
32.	Steve Pfeifer	Chevrolet
33.	Harry Goularte	Chevrolet
34.	Richard Petty	Chevrolet
35.	Buddy Arrington	Ford
36.	Chuck Wahl	Chevrolet
37.	Neil Bonnett	Chevrolet
38.	David Pearson	Mercury
39.	Rick McCray	Chevrolet
40.	Ray Elder	Dodge

1979

WINSTON WESTERN 500

January 14
Riverside, California
Time of Race: 2 hours, 53 minutes, 30 seconds
Average Speed: 107.820 mph
Margin of Victory: 32.9 seconds

FINISH	DRIVER	CAR
1.	Darrell Waltrip	Chevrolet
2.	David Pearson	Mercury

3.	Cale Yarborough	Oldsmobile
4.	Bill Schmitt	Oldsmobile
5.	Donnie Allison	Chevrolet
6.	Joe Millikan	Chevrolet
7.	Buddy Baker	Chevrolet
8.	Jim Thirkettle	Buick
9.	Tim Williamson	Chevrolet
10.	Harry Gant	Chevrolet
11.	James Hylton	Chevrolet
12.	Ronnie Thomas	Chevrolet
13.	Vince Giamformaggio	Chevrolet
14.	D. K. Ulrich	Buick
15.	Richard Childress	Oldsmobile
16.	Jim Insolo	Oldsmobile
17.	J. D. McDuffie	Chevrolet
18.	Buddy Arrington	Ford
19.	Bobby Allison	Ford
20.	Al Holbert	Chevrolet
21.	Dale Earnhardt	Chevrolet
22.	Don Graham	Chevrolet
23.	Harry Goularte	Chevrolet
24.	Dave Marcis	Chevrolet
25.	Cecil Gordon	Oldsmobile
26.	Benny Parsons	Chevrolet
27.	Frank Warren	Dodge
28.	Don Puskarich	Chevrolet
29.	Richard White	Chevrolet
30.	Jim Robinson	Chevrolet
31.	Don Noel	Chevrolet
32.	Richard Petty	Chevrolet
33.	Dick Brooks	Oldsmobile
34.	Neil Bonnett	Chevrolet
35.	Terry Labonte	Chevrolet

DAYTONA 500

February 18
Daytona Beach, Florida
Time of Race: 3 hours, 28 minutes, 22 seconds
Average Speed: 143.977 mph
Margin of Victory: 1 car length

FINISH	DRIVER	CAR
1.	Richard Petty	Oldsmobile
2.	Darrell Waltrip	Oldsmobile
3.	A. J. Foyt	Oldsmobile
4.	Donnie Allison	Oldsmobile
5.	Cale Yarborough	Oldsmobile
6.	Tighe Scott	Buick
7.	Chuck Bown	Buick
8.	Dale Earnhardt	Buick
9.	Coo Coo Marlin	Chevrolet
10.	Frank Warren	Dodge
11.	Bobby Allison	Ford
12.	Buddy Arrington	Dodge
13.	D. K. Ulrich	Buick
14.	Bill Dennis	Chevrolet
15.	Ralph Jones	Ford
16.	Terry Labonte	Buick
17.	Richard Childress	Oldsmobile
18.	Benny Parsons	Oldsmobile
19.	Bruce Hill	Oldsmobile
20.	Blackie Wangerin	Mercury
21.	Bobby Wawak	Oldsmobile
22.	Paul Fess	Oldsmobile
23.	Grant Adcox	Chevrolet
24.	Dave Marcis	Chevrolet
25.	J. D. McDuffie	Oldsmobile
26.	Dave Watson	Chevrolet
27.	Dick Brooks	Oldsmobile
28.	John Utsman	Chevrolet
29.	Geoff Bodine	Oldsmobile
30.	Lennie Pond	Oldsmobile
31.	Ricky Rudd	Mercury
32.	Neil Bonnett	Oldsmobile
33.	Harry Gant	Oldsmobile
34.	Ronnie Thomas	Chevrolet
35.	Gary Balough	Oldsmobile
36.	Joe Millikan	Oldsmobile
37.	David Pearson	Mercury

38.	Skip Manning	Oldsmobile
39.	Butch Mock	Buick
40.	Buddy Baker	Oldsmobile
41.	Jim Vandiver	Oldsmobile

CAROLINA 500

March 4
Rockingham, North Carolina
Time of Race: 4 hours, 6 minutes, 30 seconds
Average Speed: 121.727 mph
Margin of Victory: 52 seconds

FINISH	DRIVER	CAR
1.	Bobby Allison	Ford
2.	Joe Millikan	Chevrolet
3.	Dick Brooks	Oldsmobile
4.	Tighe Scott	Buick
5.	Richard Childress	Chevrolet
6.	D. K. Ulrich	Buick
7.	James Hylton	Chevrolet
8.	Dave Watson	Chevrolet
9.	Frank Warren	Dodge
10.	Benny Parsons	Chevrolet
11.	Cecil Gordon	Oldsmobile
12.	Dale Earnhardt	Chevrolet
13.	Tommy Gale	Ford
14.	Baxter Price	Chevrolet
15.	Terry Labonte	Buick
16.	Dave Marcis	Chevrolet
17.	Darrell Waltrip	Chevrolet
18.	Cale Yarborough	Oldsmobile
19.	Buddy Arrington	Dodge
20.	Dick May	Chevrolet
21.	Roger Hamby	Chevrolet
22.	Geoff Bodine	Oldsmobile
23.	David Pearson	Mercury
24.	Jimmy Means	Chevrolet
25.	J. D. McDuffie	Chevrolet
26.	Harry Gant	Chevrolet
27.	Slick Johnson	Chevrolet
28.	Nelson Oswald	Chevrolet
29.	Ronnie Thomas	Chevrolet
30.	Donnie Allison	Chevrolet
31.	Buddy Baker	Chevrolet
32.	Richard Petty	Chevrolet
33.	Neil Bonnett	Oldsmobile
34.	Ricky Rudd	Ford
35.	Bill Hollar	Chevrolet

RICHMOND 400

March 11
Richmond, Virginia
Time of Race: 2 hours, 35 minutes, 34 seconds
Average Speed: 83.608 mph
Margin of Victory: 6 seconds

FINISH	DRIVER	CAR
1.	Cale Yarborough	Oldsmobile
2.	Bobby Allison	Ford
3.	Darrell Waltrip	Chevrolet
4.	Benny Parsons	Chevrolet
5.	Richard Petty	Chevrolet
6.	Joe Millikan	Chevrolet
7.	J. D. McDuffie	Chevrolet
8.	Terry Labonte	Chevrolet
9.	Donnie Allison	Chevrolet
10.	D. K. Ulrich	Buick
11.	Ricky Rudd	Ford
12.	James Hylton	Chevrolet
13.	Dale Earnhardt	Chevrolet
14.	Lennie Pond	Oldsmobile
15.	Buddy Arrington	Dodge

16.	Dave Marcis	Chevrolet
17.	Ronnie Thomas	Buick
18.	Dave Watson	Chevrolet
19.	Dave Dion	Ford
20.	Joe Fields	Chevrolet
21.	Frank Warren	Dodge
22.	Tommy Gale	Ford
23.	Baxter Price	Chevrolet
24.	Bill Hollar	Chevrolet
25.	Cecil Gordon	Oldsmobile
26.	Richard Childress	Chevrolet
27.	Jimmy Means	Chevrolet
28.	Dick Brooks	Oldsmobile
29.	Buddy Baker	Chevrolet
30.	Roger Hamby	Chevrolet

ATLANTA 500

March 18
Atlanta, Georgia
Time of Race: 3 hours, 41 minutes, 47 seconds
Average Speed: 135.136 mph
Margin of Victory: 6 seconds

FINISH	DRIVER	CAR
1.	Buddy Baker	Oldsmobile
2.	Bobby Allison	Ford
3.	Darrell Waltrip	Chevrolet
4.	Cale Yarborough	Oldsmobile
5.	Benny Parsons	Chevrolet
6.	Dave Marcis	Chevrolet
7.	Donnie Allison	Chevrolet
8.	Joe Millikan	Oldsmobile
9.	Ricky Rudd	Mercury
10.	Dick Brooks	Oldsmobile
11.	Richard Petty	Oldsmobile
12.	Dale Earnhardt	Buick
13.	James Hylton	Chevrolet
14.	D. K. Ulrich	Buick
15.	Bruce Hill	Oldsmobile
16.	Chuck Bown	Buick
17.	J. D. McDuffie	Oldsmobile
18.	David Pearson	Mercury
19.	Baxter Price	Chevrolet
20.	Richard Childress	Oldsmobile
21.	Tommy Gale	Ford
22.	Frank Warren	Dodge
23.	Cecil Gordon	Oldsmobile
24.	Dick May	Chevrolet
25.	Terry Labonte	Chevrolet
26.	Roger Hamby	Chevrolet
27.	Claude Ballot-Lena	Oldsmobile
28.	Grant Adcox	Chevrolet
29.	Buddy Arrington	Dodge
30.	Blackie Wangerin	Mercury
31.	Ralph Jones	Ford
32.	Dave Watson	Chevrolet
33.	Jimmy Means	Chevrolet
34.	Ronnie Thomas	Buick
35.	Geoff Bodine	Oldsmobile
36.	Bill Elliott	Mercury
37.	Tighe Scott	Buick
38.	Coo Coo Marlin	Chevrolet
39.	John Kennedy	Chevrolet
40.	Keith Davis	Chevrolet

NORTHWESTERN BANK 400

March 25
North Wilkesboro, North Carolina
Time of Race: 2 hours, 49 minutes, 41 seconds
Average Speed: 88.400 mph
Margin of Victory: 5 seconds

FINISH	DRIVER	CAR
1.	Bobby Allison	Ford
2.	Richard Petty	Chevrolet
3.	Benny Parsons	Chevrolet
4.	Dale Earnhardt	Chevrolet
5.	Darrell Waltrip	Chevrolet
6.	J. D. McDuffie	Chevrolet
7.	Richard Childress	Chevrolet
8.	Buddy Baker	Chevrolet
9.	Cale Yarborough	Oldsmobile
10.	Joe Millikan	Chevrolet
11.	Donnie Allison	Chevrolet
12.	Dave Marcis	Chevrolet
13.	Dick Brooks	Oldsmobile
14.	Ricky Rudd	Ford
15.	Terry Labonte	Chevrolet
16.	James Hylton	Chevrolet
17.	Frank Warren	Dodge
18.	D. K. Ulrich	Buick
19.	Roger Hamby	Chevrolet
20.	Tommy Gale	Ford
21.	Dick May	Chevrolet
22.	Cecil Gordon	Oldsmobile
23.	Baxter Price	Chevrolet
24.	Slick Johnson	Chevrolet
25.	Buddy Arrington	Dodge
26.	Nelson Oswald	Chevrolet
27.	Earl Brooks	Dodge
28.	Ronnie Thomas	Buick
29.	Bill Hollar	Chevrolet
30.	Jimmy Means	Chevrolet

SOUTHEASTERN 500

April 1
Bristol, Tennessee
Time of Race: 2 hours, 55 minutes, 39 seconds
Average Speed: 91.033 mph
Margin of Victory: 3 seconds

FINISH	DRIVER	CAR
1.	Dale Earnhardt	Chevrolet
2.	Bobby Allison	Ford
3.	Darrell Waltrip	Chevrolet
4.	Richard Petty	Oldsmobile
5.	Benny Parsons	Oldsmobile
6.	Donnie Allison	Chevrolet
7.	Terry Labonte	Chevrolet
8.	Joe Millikan	Chevrolet
9.	James Hylton	Chevrolet
10.	Ricky Rudd	Ford
11.	Richard Childress	Chevrolet
12.	D. K. Ulrich	Chevrolet
13.	Buddy Arrington	Dodge
14.	Roger Hamby	Oldsmobile
15.	Cecil Gordon	Oldsmobile
16.	Mike Potter	Chevrolet
17.	Dave Marcis	Chevrolet
18.	Tommy Gale	Ford
19.	Baxter Price	Chevrolet
20.	Frank Warren	Dodge
21.	Harry Gant	Oldsmobile
22.	Dick Brooks	Oldsmobile
23.	Ronnie Thomas	Chevrolet
24.	Cale Yarborough	Oldsmobile
25.	Buddy Baker	Chevrolet
26.	J. D. McDuffie	Chevrolet
27.	Dick May	Chevrolet
28.	Jimmy Means	Chevrolet
29.	Bobby Wawak	Chevrolet
30.	Ralph Jones	Ford

CRC CHEMICALS REBEL 500

April 8
Darlington, South Carolina

Time of Race: 4 hours, 7 minutes, 7 seconds
Average Speed: 121.721 mph
Margin of Victory: half car length

FINISH	DRIVER	CAR
1.	Darrell Waltrip	Chevrolet
2.	Richard Petty	Chevrolet
3.	Donnie Allison	Chevrolet
4.	Benny Parsons	Chevrolet
5.	Buddy Baker	Chevrolet
6.	Cale Yarborough	Oldsmobile
7.	Bill Elliott	Mercury
8.	Ricky Rudd	Mercury
9.	Dick Brooks	Oldsmobile
10.	Joe Millikan	Chevrolet
11.	Lennie Pond	Chevrolet
12.	D. K. Ulrich	Chevrolet
13.	Neil Bonnett	Oldsmobile
14.	Butch Hartman	Chevrolet
15.	James Hylton	Chevrolet
16.	Richard Childress	Chevrolet
17.	Frank Warren	Dodge
18.	Ed Negre	Chrysler
19.	J. D. McDuffie	Chevrolet
20.	Baxter Price	Chevrolet
21.	Al Holbert	Chevrolet
22.	David Pearson	Mercury
23.	Dale Earnhardt	Chevrolet
24.	Ronnie Thomas	Chevrolet
25.	Buddy Arrington	Dodge
26.	Bobby Allison	Ford
27.	Dave Marcis	Chevrolet
28.	Bobby Wawak	Chevrolet
29.	Terry Labonte	Chevrolet
30.	Jimmy Means	Chevrolet
31.	Cecil Gordon	Oldsmobile
32.	Roger Hamby	Oldsmobile
33.	Dick May	Chevrolet
34.	Tommy Gale	Ford
35.	Earle Canavan	Dodge
36.	Travis Tiller	Dodge

VIRGINIA 500

April 22
Martinsville, Virginia
Time of Race: 3 hours, 25 minutes, 43 seconds
Average Speed: 76.562 mph
Margin of Victory: 4 seconds

FINISH	DRIVER	CAR
1.	Richard Petty	Chevrolet
2.	Buddy Baker	Chevrolet
3.	Darrell Waltrip	Chevrolet
4.	Bobby Allison	Ford
5.	Joe Millikan	Chevrolet
6.	Harry Gant	Chevrolet
7.	James Hylton	Chevrolet
8.	Dale Earnhardt	Chevrolet
9.	Terry Labonte	Chevrolet
10.	J. D. McDuffie	Chevrolet
11.	Cale Yarborough	Oldsmobile
12.	Ricky Rudd	Ford
13.	Tighe Scott	Buick
14.	Richard Childress	Chevrolet
15.	D. K. Ulrich	Chevrolet
16.	Tommy Gale	Ford
17.	Cecil Gordon	Oldsmobile
18.	Frank Warren	Dodge
19.	Benny Parsons	Chevrolet
20.	Ronnie Thomas	Chevrolet
21.	Dick Brooks	Oldsmobile
22.	Buddy Arrington	Dodge
23.	Chuck Bown	Buick
24.	Baxter Price	Chevrolet
25.	Neil Bonnett	Mercury
26.	Dave Marcis	Chevrolet

27.	Donnie Allison	Chevrolet
28.	Jimmy Means	Chevrolet
29.	Lennie Pond	Chevrolet
30.	Dick May	Chevrolet

WINSTON 500

May 12
Talladega, Alabama
Time of Race: 3 hours, 13 minutes, 52 seconds
Average Speed: 154.770 mph
Margin of Victory: 1 lap and 50 seconds

FINISH	DRIVER	CAR
1.	Bobby Allison	Ford
2.	Darrell Waltrip	Oldsmobile
3.	Buddy Arrington	Dodge
4.	Richard Petty	Oldsmobile
5.	Joe Millikan	Oldsmobile
6.	Bill Elliott	Mercury
7.	Tommy Gale	Ford
8.	Frank Warren	Dodge
9.	Terry Labonte	Buick
10.	Coo Coo Marlin	Chevrolet
11.	Cecil Gordon	Oldsmobile
12.	Jimmy Means	Chevrolet
13.	Ed Negre	Chrysler
14.	Dave Marcis	Chevrolet
15.	James Hylton	Oldsmobile
16.	Kevin Housby	Chevrolet
17.	Neil Bonnett	Mercury
18.	Connie Saylor	Oldsmobile
19.	Jimmy Finger	Buick
20.	Dick May	Chevrolet
21.	D. K. Ulrich	Buick
22.	Jerry Jolly	Ford
23.	Donnie Allison	Oldsmobile
24.	Richard Childress	Oldsmobile
25.	Ronnie Thomas	Buick
26.	Baxter Price	Chevrolet
27.	Ricky Rudd	Mercury
28.	Blackie Wangerin	Mercury
29.	Wayne Broome	Oldsmobile
30.	Keith Davis	Oldsmobile
31.	J. D. McDuffie	Chevrolet
32.	Buddy Baker	Oldsmobile
33.	Cale Yarborough	Oldsmobile
34.	Benny Parsons	Oldsmobile
35.	Tighe Scott	Buick
36.	Dale Earnhardt	Buick
37.	Dick Brooks	Oldsmobile
38.	Lennie Pond	Oldsmobile
39.	Harry Gant	Oldsmobile
40.	Travis Tiller	Dodge

SUN-DROP MUSIC CITY USA 420

May 12
Nashville, Tennessee
Time of Race: 2 hours, 49 minutes, 25 seconds
Average Speed: 88.652 mph
Margin of Victory: 3 seconds

FINISH	DRIVER	CAR
1.	Cale Yarborough	Oldsmobile
2.	Richard Petty	Chevrolet
3.	Bobby Allison	Ford
4.	Dale Earnhardt	Chevrolet
5.	J. D. McDuffie	Chevrolet
6.	Richard Childress	Chevrolet
7.	Benny Parsons	Chevrolet
8.	Buddy Baker	Chevrolet
9.	Terry Labonte	Chevrolet
10.	Ricky Rudd	Ford

11.	Jimmy Means	Chevrolet
12.	Steve Spencer	Buick
13.	Tommy Gale	Ford
14.	Bobby Wawak	Chevrolet
15.	Al Elmore	Chevrolet
16.	D. K. Ulrich	Oldsmobile
17.	Ronnie Thomas	Chevrolet
18.	Mike Kempton	Chevrolet
19.	Baxter Price	Chevrolet
20.	Frank Warren	Dodge
21.	Darrell Waltrip	Chevrolet
22.	James Hylton	Chevrolet
23.	Joe Millikan	Chevrolet
24.	Darrell Busham	Mercury
25.	Nelson Oswald	Chevrolet
26.	Buddy Arrington	Dodge
27.	Dick Brooks	Chevrolet
28.	Harry Gant	Chevrolet

MASON-DIXON 500

May 20
Dover, Delaware
Time of Race: 4 hours, 29 minutes, 37 seconds
Average Speed: 111.269 mph
Margin of Victory: 2 car lengths

FINISH	DRIVER	CAR
1.	Neil Bonnett	Mercury
2.	Cale Yarboroough	Chevrolet
3.	Buddy Baker	Chevrolet
4.	Bobby Allison	Ford
5.	Dale Earnhardt	Chevrolet
6.	Terry Labonte	Chevrolet
7.	Benny Parsons	Chevrolet
8.	Joe Millikan	Chevrolet
9.	Lennie Pond	Chevrolet
10.	Buddy Arrington	Dodge
11.	Dick May	Buick
12.	D. K. Ulrich	Chevrolet
13.	J. D. McDuffie	Chevrolet
14.	Ricky Rudd	Ford
15.	Baxter Price	Chevrolet
16.	Ronnie Thomas	Chevrolet
17.	James Hylton	Chevrolet
18.	Darrell Waltrip	Chevrolet
19.	Tommy Gale	Ford
20.	Steve Peles	Chevrolet
21.	Frank Warren	Dodge
22.	Nelson Oswald	Chevrolet
23.	Cecil Gordon	Oldsmobile
24.	Tighe Scott	Bucik
25.	Harry Gant	Chevrolet
26.	Joey Arrington	Dodge
27.	Louis Gatto	Chevrolet
28.	Elmo Langley	Chevrolet
29.	Richard Childress	Chevrolet
30.	Richard Petty	Oldsmobile
31.	Jimmy Means	Chevrolet

WORLD 600

May 27
Charlotte, North Carolina
Time of Race: 4 hours, 23 minutes, 24 seconds
Average Speed: 136.674 mph
Margin of Victory: 7 seconds

FINISH	DRIVER	CAR
1.	Darrell Waltrip	Chevrolet
2.	Richard Petty	Chevrolet
3.	Dale Earnhardt	Chevrolet
4.	Cale Yarborough	Oldsmobile
5.	Benny Parsons	Chevrolet

6.	Ricky Rudd	Mercury
7.	Terry Labonte	Chevrolet
8.	Al Holbert	Chevrolet
9.	Lennie Pond	Chevrolet
10.	Richard Childress	Oldsmobile
11.	Grant Adcox	Oldsmobile
12.	Buddy Arrington	Dodge
13.	J. D. McDuffie	Chevrolet
14.	Ronnie Thomas	Chevrolet
15.	Blackie Wangerin	Mercury
16.	Tighe Scott	Buick
17.	Cecil Gordon	Oldsmobile
18.	D. K. Ulrich	Chevrolet
19.	Jim Vandiver	Oldsmobile
20.	Tommy Gale	Ford
21.	Frank Warren	Dodge
22.	Bobby Allison	Ford
23.	Harry Gant	Chevrolet
24.	Bruce Hill	Buick
25.	Neil Bonnett	Mercury
26.	Dave Marcis	Chevrolet
27.	Joe Millikan	Chevrolet
28.	Bill Dennis	Chevrolet
29.	Glenn Jarrett	Chevrolet
30.	Coo Coo Marlin	Chevrolet
31.	Bobby Fisher	Buick
32.	Skip Manning	Chevrolet
33.	James Hylton	Chevrolet
34.	Connie Saylor	Oldsmobile
35.	Travis Tiller	Dodge
36.	Buddy Baker	Chevrolet
37.	Donnie Allison	Chevrolet
38.	Bill Elliott	Mercury
39.	Dick Brooks	Oldsmobile
40.	Chuck Bown	Buick

TEXAS 400

June 3
College Station, Texas
Time of Race: 2 hours, 33 minutes, 39 seconds
Average Speed: 156.216 mph
Margin of Victory: 1 lap & 1 second

FINISH	DRIVER	CAR
1.	Darrell Waltrip	Chevrolet
2.	Bobby Allison	Ford
3.	Buddy Baker	Chevrolet
4.	Cale Yarborough	Chevrolet
5.	Terry Labonte	Chevrolet
6.	Richard Petty	Chevrolet
7.	Richard Childress	Oldsmobile
8.	Joe Millikan	Chevrolet
9.	Buddy Arrington	Dodge
10.	James Hylton	Chevrolet
11.	John Rezek	Olsmobile
12.	Dale Earnhardt	Chevrolet
13.	Bruce Hill	Buick
14.	J. D. McDuffie	Chevrolet
15.	D. K. Ulrich	Buick
16.	H. B. Bailey	Pontiac
17.	Billy Hagan	Chevrolet
18.	Earle Canavan	Dodge
19.	Frank Warren	Dodge
20.	Tommy Gale	Ford
21.	Cecil Gordon	Oldsmobile
22.	Mike Potter	Chevrolet
23.	Jimmy Means	Chevrolet
24.	Jim Hurlbert	Ford
25.	Benny Parsons	Chevrolet
26.	Ronnie Thomas	Chevrolet
27.	Baxter Price	Chevrolet
28.	Ricky Rudd	Mercury
29.	Mike Kempton	Chevrolet
30.	Dick May	Oldsmobile
31.	Lennie Pond	Chevrolet
32.	Bill Meazell	Chevrolet
33.	John Haver	Chevrolet
34.	Jimmy Finger	Buick

NAPA RIVERSIDE 400

June 10
Riverside, California
Time of Race: 2 hours, 23 minutes, 58 seconds
Average Speed: 103.732 mph
Margin of Victory: 33 seconds

FINISH	DRIVER	CAR
1.	Bobby Allison	Ford
2.	Darrell Waltrip	Chevrolet
3.	Richard Petty	Chevrolet
4.	Cale Yarborough	Chevrolet
5.	Benny Parsons	Chevrolet
6.	Richard Childress	Oldsmobile
7.	J. D. McDuffie	Chevrolet
8.	Norm Palmer	Dodge
9.	Buddy Arrington	Ford
10.	Joe Millikan	Chevrolet
11.	Cecil Gordon	Oldsmobile
12.	Hal Callentine	Oldsmobile
13.	Dale Earnhardt	Chevrolet
14.	James Hylton	Chevrolet
15.	Ed Hale	Chevrolet
16.	Richard White	Chevrolet
17.	Baxter Price	Chevrolet
18.	Terry Labonte	Chevrolet
19.	Dick Whalen	Chevrolet
20.	John Borneman	Chevrolet
21.	Jim Robinson	Chevrolet
22.	Frank Warren	Dodge
23.	Ronnie Thomas	Chevrolet
24.	Robert Tartagila	Chevrolet
25.	Jimmy Insolo	Oldsmobile
26.	Tim Williamson	Chevrolet
27.	Rick McCray	Buick
28.	Neil Bonnett	Mercury
29.	Dick Kranzier	Chevrolet
30.	Bill Schmitt	Oldsmobile
31.	Jimmy Means	Chevrolet
32.	Steve Pfeifer	Chevrolet
33.	D. K. Ulrich	Chevrolet
34.	Chris Monoleos	Chevrolet
35.	Elmo Langley	Ford

GABRIEL 400

June 17
Brooklyn, Michigan
Time of Race: 2 hours, 56 minutes, 44 seconds
Average Speed: 135.798 mph
Margin of Victory: 1 second

FINISH	DRIVER	CAR
1.	Buddy Baker	Chevrolet
2.	Donnie Allison	Chevrolet
3.	Cale Yarborough	Oldsmobile
4.	Neil Bonnett	Mercury
5.	Richard Petty	Chevrolet
6.	Dale Earnhardt	Chevrolet
7.	Bobby Allison	Ford
8.	Ricky Rudd	Mercury
9.	Tighe Scott	Buick
10.	Dick Brooks	Chevrolet
11.	Lennie Pond	Chevrolet
12.	Bill Elliott	Mercury
13.	Darrell Waltrip	Chevrolet
14.	J. D. McDuffie	Chevrolet
15.	Buddy Arrington	Dodge
16.	Jimmy Means	Chevrolet
17.	Harry Gant	Chevrolet
18.	John Kennedy	Chevrolet
19.	Sandy Satullo	Buick
20.	James Hylton	Chevrolet
21.	D. K. Ulrich	Buick
22.	Frank Warren	Dodge
23.	Richard Childress	Oldsmobile

24.	Bob Burcham	Chevrolet
25.	Terry Labonte	Chevrolet
26.	Dave Marcis	Chevrolet
27.	Ronnie Thomas	Chevrolet
28.	David Sosebee	Chevrolet
29.	Roger Hamby	Chevrolet
30.	Joe Millikan	Chevrolet
31.	Benny Parsons	Chevrolet
32.	Paul Fess	Oldsmobile
33.	Tommy Gale	Ford
34.	Bill Green	Chevrolet
35.	Marty Robbins	Dodge
36.	Bill Seifert	Oldsmobile

FIRECRACKER 400

July 4
Daytona Beach, Florida
Time of Race: 2 hours, 18 minutes, 49 seconds
Average Speed: 172.890 mph
Margin of Victory: 1 second

FINISH	DRIVER	CAR
1.	Neil Bonnett	Mercury
2.	Benny Parsons	Oldsmobile
3.	Dale Earnhardt	Oldsmobile
4.	Darrell Waltrip	Oldsmobile
5.	Richard Petty	Oldsmobile
6.	Chuck Bown	Buick
7.	Harry Gant	Oldsmobile
8.	Joe Millikan	Oldsmobile
9.	Dick Brooks	Oldsmobile
10.	A. J. Foyt	Oldsmobile
11.	Bill Elliott	Mercury
12.	Donnie Allison	Chevrolet
13.	Ricky Rudd	Mercury
14.	Tighe Scott	Buick
15.	Buddy Arrington	Dodge
16.	Gary Balough	Oldsmobile
17.	Dave Marcis	Chevrolet
18.	D. K. Ulrich	Buick
19.	James Hylton	Chevrolet
20.	Cale Yarborough	Oldsmobile
21.	J. D. McDuffie	Chevrolet
22.	Jimmy Means	Chevrolet
23.	Rick Newsom	Oldsmobile
24.	Blackie Wangerin	Mercury
25.	Coo Coo Marlin	Chevrolet
26.	Roger Hamby	Oldsmobile
27.	Tommy Gale	Ford
28.	Lennie Pond	Oldsmobile
29.	Terry Labonte	Buick
30.	Bobby Allison	Ford
31.	Claude Ballot-Lena	Oldsmobile
32.	Al Holbert	Chevrolet
33.	Grant Adcox	Oldsmobile
34.	Buddy Baker	Oldsmobile
35.	Cecil Gordon	Oldsmobile
36.	Travis Tiller	Dodge
37.	Richard Childress	Oldsmobile
38.	Sandy Satullo	Buick
39.	Jimmy Finger	Buick
40.	Frank Warren	Dodge
41.	Bruce Hill	Buick

BUSCH NASHVILLE 420

July 14
Nashville, Tennessee
Time of Race: 2 hours, 42 minutes, 51 seconds
Average Speed: 92.227 mph
Margin of Victory: 1 lap & 1 second

FINISH	DRIVER	CAR
1.	Darrell Waltrip	Chevrolet
2.	Cale Yarborough	Chevrolet
3.	Dale Earnhardt	Chevrolet
4.	Benny Parsons	Chevrolet
5.	Richard Petty	Chevrolet
6.	James Hylton	Chevrolet
7.	Richard Childress	Chevrolet
8.	J. D. McDuffie	Chevrolet
9.	Ronnie Thomas	Chevrolet
10.	Jimmy Means	Chevrolet
11.	Cecil Gordon	Oldsmobile
12.	Waye Watercutter	Chevrolet
13.	Roger Hamby	Oldsmobile
14.	Frank Warren	Dodge
15.	Sterling Marlin	Chevrolet
16.	Bobby Allison	Ford
17.	Buddy Arrington	Dodge
18.	Baxter Price	Chevrolet
19.	Dick Brooks	Chevrolet
20.	Steve Spencer	Chevrolet
21.	Joe Millikan	Chevrolet
22.	Harry Gant	Chevrolet
23.	D. K. Ulrich	Chevrolet
24.	Ralph Jones	Ford
25.	Terry Labonte	Chevrolet
26.	Henry Jones	Chevrolet
27.	Nelson Oswald	Chevrolet
28.	Tommy Gale	Ford
29.	Dick May	Chevrolet
30.	Jimmy Hindman	Ford

COCA-COLA 500

July 30
Pocono, Pennsylvania
Time of Race: 4 hours, 20 minutes, 24 seconds
Average Speed: 115.207 mph
Margin of Victory: 1 second

FINISH	DRIVER	CAR
1.	Cale Yarborough	Chevrolet
2.	Richard Petty	Chevrolet
3.	Buddy Baker	Chevrolet
4.	Benny Parsons	Chevrolet
5.	Ricky Rudd	Mercury
6.	Joe Millikan	Chevrolet
7.	Darrell Waltrip	Chevrolet
8.	Neil Bonnett	Mercury
9.	Bobby Allison	Ford
10.	Tighe Scott	Buick
11.	D. K. Ulrich	Chevrolet
12.	Richard Childress	Chevrolet
13.	J. D. McDuffie	Chevrolet
14.	Ronnie Thomas	Chevrolet
15.	Harry Gant	Chevrolet
16.	Jimmy Means	Chevrolet
17.	Tommy Gale	Ford
18.	Cecil Gordon	Oldsmobile
19.	Frank Warren	Dodge
20.	Dick Brooks	Chevrolet
21.	Steve Peles	Chevrolet
22.	Buddy Arrington	Dodge
23.	Terry Labonte	Chevrolet
24.	Jocko Maggiacomo	Oldsmobile
25.	Nelson Oswald	Chevrolet
26.	Rick Newsom	Oldsmobile
27.	Earle Canavan	Dodge
28.	Dick May	Ford
29.	Dale Earnhardt	Chevrolet
30.	Wayne Broome	Oldsmobile
31.	Baxter Price	Chevrolet
32.	Wayne Watercutter	Chevrolet
33.	James Hylton	Chevrolet
34.	Lennie Pond	Oldsmobile
35.	Gary Balough	Oldsmobile
36.	Louis Gatto	Chevrolet
37.	Al Holbert	Chevrolet
38.	Roger Hamby	Oldsmobile
39.	Steve Gray	Chevrolet

TALLADEGA 500

August 5
Talladega, Alabama
Time of Race: 3 hours, 6 minutes, 6 seconds
Average Speed: 161.229 mph
Margin of Victory: 62 seconds

FINISH	DRIVER	CAR
1.	Darrell Waltrip	Oldsmobile
2.	David Pearson	Oldsmobile
3.	Ricky Rudd	Mercury
4.	Richard Petty	Oldsmobile
5.	Jody Ridley	Mercury
6.	Tighe Scott	Buick
7.	Harry Gant	Oldsmobile
8.	Buddy Arrington	Dodge
9.	Kyle Petty	Dodge
10.	Richard Childress	Oldsmobile
11.	Dick Brooks	Oldsmobile
12.	Bill Elliott	Mercury
13.	Jimmy Means	Chevrolet
14.	Bob Burcham	Chevrolet
15.	Rick Newsom	Oldsmobile
16.	Bruce Hill	Oldsmobile
17.	Steve Moore	Chevrolet
18.	J. D. McDuffie	Chevrolet
19.	Grant Adcox	Oldsmobile
20.	James Hylton	Oldsmobile
21.	Benny Parsons	Oldsmobile
22.	Ronnie Thomas	Buick
23.	Frank Warren	Dodge
24.	Cale Yarborough	Oldsmobile
25.	Joe Millikan	Oldsmobile
26.	Baxter Price	Oldsmobile
27.	D. K. Ulrich	Buick
28.	Bobby Allison	Ford
29.	Coo Coo Marlin	Chevrolet
30.	Donnie Allison	Chevrolet
31.	Dave Marcis	Chevrolet
32.	Marty Robbins	Dodge
33.	Terry Labonte	Buick
34.	Neil Bonnett	Mercury
35.	Jack Ingram	Oldsmobile
36.	Tommy Gale	Ford
37.	Blackie Wangerin	Mercury
38.	Al Holbert	Oldsmobile
39.	Buddy Baker	Oldsmobile
40.	Cecil Gordon	Oldsmobile
41.	Dick May	Oldsmobile

CHAMPION SPARK PLUG 400

August 19
Brooklyn, Michigan
Time of Race: 3 hours, 4 minutes, 5 seconds
Average Speed: 130.376 mph
Margin of Victory: 1 second

FINISH	DRIVER	CAR
1.	Richard Petty	Chevrolet
2.	Buddy Baker	Chevrolet
3.	Benny Parsons	Chevrolet
4.	David Pearson	Chevrolet
5.	John Anderson	Chevrolet
6.	Joe Millikan	Chevrolet
7.	Ricky Rudd	Mercury
8.	Tighe Scott	Buick
9.	J. D. McDuffie	Chevrolet
10.	Richard Childress	Oldsmobile
11.	Bill Elliott	Mercury
12.	James Hylton	Chevrolet
13.	Kyle Petty	Dodge
14.	Tommy Gale	Ford
15.	John Kennedy	Chevrolet
16.	Frank Warren	Dodge
17.	Cale Yarborough	Chevrolet

18.	Cecil Gordon	Oldsmobile
19.	Darrell Waltrip	Chevrolet
20.	Buddy Arrington	Dodge
21.	Baxter Price	Oldsmobile
22.	Jimmy Means	Chevrolet
23.	Bobby Allison	Ford
24.	Ronnie Thomas	Chevrolet
25.	Harry Gant	Chevrolet
26.	Terry Labonte	Chevrolet
27.	Marty Robbins	Dodge
28.	D. K. Ulrich	Buick
29.	Dick Brooks	Chevrolet
30.	Dave Marcis	Chevrolet
31.	Lennie Pond	Chevrolet
32.	Al Rudd Jr.	Chevrolet
33.	Neil Bonnett	Mercury
34.	Earle Canavan	Dodge
35.	H. B. Bailey	Pontiac
36.	Blackie Wangerin	Mercury

VOLUNTEER 500

August 25
Bristol, Tennessee
Time of Race: 2 hours, 54 minutes, 46 seconds
Average Speed: 91.493 mph
Margin of Victory: 3 seconds

FINISH	DRIVER	CAR
1.	Darrell Waltrip	Chevrolet
2.	Richard Petty	Chevrolet
3.	Bobby Allison	Ford
4.	Benny Parsons	Chevrolet
5.	Cale Yarborough	Chevrolet
6.	Joe Millikan	Oldsmobile
7.	David Pearson	Chevrolet
8.	Terry Labonte	Chevrolet
9.	Ricky Rudd	Chevrolet
10.	Bill Elliott	Chevrolet
11.	Richard Childress	Chevrolet
12.	D. K. Ulrich	Chevrolet
13.	James Hylton	Chevrolet
14.	Buddy Arrington	Dodge
15.	Tommy Gale	Ford
16.	Harry Gant	Chevrolet
17.	Frank Warren	Dodge
18.	Dave Marcis	Chevrolet
19.	Jimmy Means	Chevrolet
20.	Dick Brooks	Oldsmobile
21.	Dick May	Chevrolet
22.	Cecil Gordon	Oldsmobile
23.	Mike Potter	Chevrolet
24.	Baxter Price	Chevrolet
25.	Jack Ingram	Chevrolet
26.	J. D. McDuffie	Chevrolet
27.	Ronnie Thomas	Chevrolet
28.	Melvin Revis	Chevrolet
29.	Henry Jones	Chevrolet
30.	John Kennedy	Chevrolet

SOUTHERN 500

September 3
Darlington, South Carolina
Time of Race: 3 hours, 58 minutes, 14 seconds
Average Speed: 126.259 mph
Margin of Victory: 2 laps & 4 seconds

FINISH	DRIVER	CAR
1.	David Pearson	Chevrolet
2.	Bill Elliott	Mercury
3.	Terry Labonte	Chevrolet
4.	Buddy Baker	Chevrolet
5.	Benny Parsons	Chevrolet
6.	Dave Marcis	Chevrolet

7.	Dick Brooks	Chevrolet
8.	Ricky Rudd	Mercury
9.	Richard Petty	Chevrolet
10.	Bobby Allison	Ford
11.	Darrell Waltrip	Chevrolet
12.	Harry Gant	Chevrolet
13.	D. K. Ulrich	Buick
14.	Buddy Arrington	Dodge
15.	Joe Millikan	Chevrolet
16.	Jimmy Means	Chevrolet
17.	Chuck Bown	Buick
18.	J. D. McDuffie	Chevrolet
19.	Cale Yarborough	Chevrolet
20.	Ed Negre	Chrysler
21.	Tommy Gale	Ford
22.	Frank Warren	Dodge
23.	Baxter Price	Chevrolet
24.	Ronnie Thomas	Chevrolet
25.	Lennie Pond	Chevrolet
26.	Cecil Gordon	Oldsmobile
27.	H. B. Bailey	Pontiac
28.	Jim Vandiver	Chevrolet
29.	Richard Childress	Chevrolet
30.	Jack Ingram	Oldsmobile
31.	Donnie Allison	Chevrolet
32.	Neil Bonnett	Mercury
33.	Billy Smith	Ford
34.	Dick May	Ford
35.	Tighe Scott	Buick
36.	Coo Coo Marlin	Chevrolet
37.	Ralph Jones	Ford
38.	James Hylton	Chevrolet
39.	Earle Canavan	Dodge
40.	Ferrell Harris	Ford

CAPITAL CITY 400

September 9
Richmond, Virginia
Time of Race: 2 hours, 41 minutes, 23 seconds
Average Speed: 80.604 mph
Margin of Victory: 11 seconds

FINISH	DRIVER	CAR
1.	Bobby Allison	Ford
2.	Darrell Waltrip	Chevrolet
3.	Ricky Rudd	Ford
4.	Dale Earnhardt	Chevrolet
5.	Cale Yarborough	Oldsmobile
6.	Richard Petty	Chevrolet
7.	Dave Marcis	Chevrolet
8.	Benny Parsons	Chevrolet
9.	Harry Gant	Chevrolet
10.	Joe Millikan	Chevrolet
11.	Bill Elliott	Chevrolet
12.	D. K. Ulrich	Chevrolet
13.	Buddy Arrington	Dodge
14.	J. D. McDuffie	Chevrolet
15.	Richard Childress	Chevrolet
16.	Billy Elswick	Oldsmobile
17.	Terry Labonte	Chevrolet
18.	Cecil Gordon	Oldsmobile
19.	Baxter Price	Chevrolet
20.	Jimmy Means	Chevrolet
21.	James Hylton	Chevrolet
22.	Earle Canavan	Dodge
23.	Ronnie Thomas	Chevrolet
24.	Tommy Gale	Ford
25.	Lennie Pond	Chevrolet
26.	Frank Warren	Dodge

CRC CHEMICALS 500

September 16
Dover, Delaware
Time of Race: 4 hours, 22 minutes, 19 seconds
Average Speed: 114.366 mph
Margin of Victory: half a car length

FINISH	DRIVER	CAR
1.	Richard Petty	Chevrolet
2.	Donnie Allison	Chevrolet
3.	Cale Yarborough	Chevrolet
4.	Buddy Baker	Chevrolet
5.	Joe Millikan	Chevrolet
6.	Bobby Allison	Ford
7.	Dave Marcis	Chevrolet
8.	Ricky Rudd	Ford
9.	Dale Earnhardt	Chevrolet
10.	Tighe Scott	Buick
11.	John Anderson	Chevrolet
12.	D. K. Ulrich	Chevrolet
13.	Richard Childress	Chevrolet
14.	James Hylton	Oldsmobile
15.	Tommy Gale	Ford
16.	Jimmy Means	Chevrolet
17.	Roger Hamby	Chevrolet
18.	Frank Warren	Dodge
19.	Nester Peles	Oldsmobile
20.	Cecil Gordon	Oldsmobile
21.	Neil Bonnett	Mercury
22.	Benny Parsons	Chevrolet
23.	Lennie Pond	Chevrolet
24.	Ronnie Thomas	Chevrolet
25.	Terry Labonte	Chevrolet
26.	Dick Brooks	Chevrolet
27.	J. D. McDuffie	Chevrolet
28.	Harry Gant	Chevrolet
29.	Darrell Waltrip	Chevrolet
30.	Bill Hollar	Chevrolet
31.	Baxter Price	Chevrolet
32.	Buddy Arrington	Dodge
33.	Earle Canavan	Dodge
34.	Dick May	Oldsmobile
35.	Rick Newsom	Oldsmobile
36.	Jeff Halverson	Chevrolet

OLD DOMINION 500

September 23
Martinsville, Virginia
Time of Race: 3 hours, 29 minutes, 40 seconds
Average Speed: 75.119 mph
Margin of Victory: 18 seconds

FINISH	DRIVER	CAR
1.	Buddy Baker	Chevrolet
2.	Richard Petty	Chevrolet
3.	Joe Millikan	Chevrolet
4.	Bobby Allison	Ford
5.	Dave Marcis	Chevrolet
6.	Ricky Rudd	Ford
7.	Buddy Arrington	Dodge
8.	Cale Yarborough	Oldsmobile
9.	Terry Labonte	Chevrolet
10.	D. K. Ulrich	Chevrolet
11.	Darrell Waltrip	Chevrolet
12.	Harry Gant	Chevrolet
13.	Richard Childress	Chevrolet
14.	Baxter Price	Chevrolet
15.	Dick Brooks	Chevrolet
16.	Frank Warren	Dodge
17.	Jimmy Means	Chevrolet
18.	Neil Bonnett	Mercury
19.	Roger Hamby	Chevrolet
20.	Ronnie Thomas	Chevrolet
21.	J. D. McDuffie	Chevrolet
22.	Tommy Gale	Ford
23.	James Hylton	Chevrolet
24.	Cecil Gordon	Oldsmobile
25.	Dick May	Chevrolet
26.	Dave Dion	Chevrolet
27.	Benny Parsons	Chevrolet
28.	Butch Lindley	Chevrolet
29.	Dale Earnhardt	Chevrolet
30.	Bill Hollar	Chevrolet

NAPA NATIONAL 500

October 7
North Wilkesboro, North Carolina
Time of Race: 3 hours, 43 minutes, 53 seconds
Average Speed: 134.266 mph
Margin of Victory: 1 lap and 5 seconds

FINISH	DRIVER	CAR
1.	Cale Yarborough	Chevrolet
2.	Bobby Allison	Ford
3.	Darrell Waltrip	Chevrolet
4.	Richard Petty	Chevrolet
5.	Donnie Allison	Chevrolet
6.	Benny Parsons	Chevrolet
7.	Bill Elliott	Mercury
8.	Dick Brooks	Chevrolet
9.	D. K. Ulrich	Buick
10.	Dale Earnhardt	Chevrolet
11.	Ricky Rudd	Mercury
12.	Buddy Arrington	Dodge
13.	Tighe Scott	Buick
14.	Richard Childress	Chevrolet
15.	Terry Labonte	Chevrolet
16.	John Anderson	Chevrolet
17.	Dick May	Ford
18.	Kyle Petty	Dodge
19.	Frank Warren	Pontiac
20.	Harry Gant	Chevrolet
21.	Tommy Gale	Ford
22.	J. D. McDuffie	Chevrolet
23.	James Hylton	Chevrolet
24.	Baxter Price	Oldsmobile
25.	Buddy Baker	Chevrolet
26.	Jody Ridley	Mercury
27.	David Sosebee	Chevrolet
28.	John Rezek	Oldsmobile
29.	Joe Millikan	Chevrolet
30.	Steve Pfeifer	Chevrolet
31.	Neil Bonnett	Mercury
32.	Cecil Gordon	Chevrolet
33.	Chuck Bown	Chevrolet
34.	Jim Vandiver	Oldsmobile
35.	Bobby Brack	Chevrolet
36.	Jack Ingram	Chevrolet
37.	Dave Marcis	Chevrolet
38.	Ronnie Thomas	Chevrolet
39.	Richard Brickhouse	Oldsmobile
40.	Jimmy Means	Chevrolet

HOLLY FARMS 400

October 14
North Wilkesboro, North Carolina
Time of Race: 2 hours, 44 minutes, 1 second
Average Speed: 91.454 mph
Margin of Victory: ¼ car length

FINISH	DRIVER	CAR
1.	Benny Parsons	Chevrolet
2.	Bobby Allison	Ford
3.	Richard Petty	Chevrolet
4.	Dale Earnhardt	Chevrolet
5.	Ricky Rudd	Ford
6.	Terry Labonte	Chevrolet
7.	Ronnie Thomas	Chevrolet
8.	D. K. Ulrich	Chevrolet
9.	Buddy Arrington	Dodge
10.	Richard Childress	Chevrolet
11.	James Hylton	Chevrolet
12.	Roger Hamby	Chevrolet
13.	Darrell Waltrip	Chevrolet
14.	Harry Gant	Chevrolet
15.	Joe Millikan	Chevrolet
16.	Ernie Shaw	Chevrolet
17.	Baxter Price	Chevrolet
18.	Cecil Gordon	Buick

19.	Bill Elswick	Oldsmobile
20.	Cale Yarborough	Oldsmobile
21.	Dave Marcis	Chevrolet
22.	Larry Iseley	Chevrolet
23.	John Kennedy	Chevrolet
24.	Jimmy Means	Chevrolet
25.	Dick May	Oldsmobile
26.	Frank Warren	Dodge
27.	Tommy Gale	Ford
28.	J. D. McDuffie	Chevrolet
29.	Henry Jones	Chevrolet

AMERICAN 500

October 21
Rockingham, North Carolina
Time of Race: 4 hours, 37 minutes, 4 seconds
Average Speed: 108.356 mph
Margin of Victory: 17 seconds

FINISH	DRIVER	CAR
1.	Richard Petty	Chevrolet
2.	Benny Parsons	Chevrolet
3.	Cale Yarborough	Chevrolet
4.	Donnie Allison	Chevrolet
5.	Dale Earnhardt	Chevrolet
6.	Darrell Waltrip	Chevrolet
7.	Richard Childress	Chevrolet
8.	Ronnie Thomas	Chevrolet
9.	Dave Marcis	Chevrolet
10.	Slick Johnson	Chevrolet
11.	James Hylton	Chevrolet
12.	Tommy Gale	Ford
13.	Cecil Gordon	Oldsmobile
14.	Bill Elswick	Oldsmobile
15.	Dick Brooks	Chevrolet
16.	Freddy Smith	Chevrolet
17.	Buddy Arrington	Dodge
18.	Joe Millikan	Chevrolet
19.	Bobby Allison	Ford
20.	Ricky Rudd	Ford
21.	Harry Gant	Chevrolet
22.	Baxter Price	Oldsmobile
23.	Bill Elliott	Chevrolet
24.	Frank Warren	Dodge
25.	J. D. McDuffie	Chevrolet
26.	Dick May	Chevrolet
27.	Terry Labonte	Chevrolet
28.	D. K. Ulrich	Buick
29.	Neil Bonnett	Mercury
30.	Randy Ogden	Chevrolet
31.	Jimmy Means	Chevrolet
32.	Glenn Jarrett	Chevrolet
33.	Buddy Baker	Chevrolet
34.	Travis Tiller	Buick
35.	Mike Potter	Chevrolet
36.	Bub Strickler	Oldsmobile
37.	Tighe Scott	Buick

DIXIE 500

November 4
Atlanta, Georgia
Time of Race: 3 hours, 33 minutes, 46 seconds
Average Speed: 140.120 mph
Margin of Victory: half a car length

FINISH	DRIVER	CAR
1.	Neil Bonnett	Mercury
2.	Dale Earnhardt	Chevrolet
3.	Cale Yarborough	Oldsmobile
4.	Bobby Allison	Ford
5.	Darrell Waltrip	Chevrolet
6.	Richard Petty	Chevrolet

7.	Terry Labonte	Chevrolet
8.	Ricky Rudd	Mercury
9.	Joe Millikan	Chevrolet
10.	Jody Ridley	Mercury
11.	Harry Gant	Oldsmobile
12.	J. D. McDuffie	Chevrolet
13.	Slick Johnson	Chevrolet
14.	Buck Simmons	Chevrolet
15.	Richard Childress	Chevrolet
16.	James Hylton	Chevrolet
17.	Buddy Arrington	Dodge
18.	Freddy Smith	Chevrolet
19.	Jimmy Means	Chevrolet
20.	H. B. Bailey	Pontiac
21.	Frank Warren	Dodge
22.	Tommy Gale	Ford
23.	Dave Marcis	Chevrolet
24.	John Anderson	Chevrolet
25.	D. K. Ulrich	Buick
26.	Wayne Watercutter	Chevrolet
27.	Grant Adcox	Buick
28.	Ronnie Thomas	Chevrolet
29.	Tighe Scott	Buick
30.	Ralph Jones	Ford
31.	Benny Parsons	Chevrolet
32.	Kyle Petty	Dodge
33.	David Sosebee	Chevrolet
34.	Steve Pfeifer	Chevrolet
35.	Donnie Allison	Chevrolet
36.	John Rezek	Oldsmobile
37.	Randy Ogden	Chevrolet
38.	Cecil Gordon	Oldsmobile
39.	Buddy Baker	Chevrolet
40.	Dick Brooks	Chevrolet
41.	Dick May	Chevrolet

LOS ANGELES TIMES 500

November 18
Ontario, California
Time of Race: 3 hours, 45 minutes, 52 seconds
Average Speed: 132.822 mph
Margin of Victory: 42 seconds

FINISH	DRIVER	CAR
1.	Benny Parsons	Chevrolet
2.	Bobby Allison	Ford
3.	Cale Yarborough	Oldsmobile
4.	Buddy Baker	Chevrolet
5.	Richard Petty	Chevrolet
6.	Neil Bonnett	Mercury
7.	Dick Brooks	Chevrolet
8.	Darrell Waltrip	Chevrolet
9.	Dale Earnhardt	Chevrolet
10.	Ricky Rudd	Mercury
11.	Donnie Allison	Chevrolet
12.	Joe Millikan	Chevrolet
13.	Terry Labonte	Oldsmobile
14.	Kyle Petty	Chevrolet
15.	Bruce Hill	Oldsmobile
16.	Richard Childress	Chevrolet
17.	Dave Marcis	Chevrolet
18.	Bill Schmitt	Oldsmobile
19.	Buddy Arrington	Dodge
20.	Harry Gant	Chevrolet
21.	Roy Smith	Oldsmobile
22.	Tim Williamson	Chevrolet
23.	Hal Callantine	Oldsmobile
24.	Cecil Gordon	Oldsmobile
25.	Frank Warren	Dodge
26.	James Hylton	Chevrolet
27.	Ronnie Thomas	Chevrolet
28.	Randy Ogden	Chevrolet
29.	Buck Simmons	Chevrolet
30.	Richard White	Chevrolet
31.	J. D. McDuffie	Chevrolet
32.	Jim Robinson	Chevrolet
33.	D. K. Ulrich	Chevrolet
34.	Tommy Gale	Ford
35.	John Rezek	Buick

| 36. | Jimmy Insolo | Oldsmobile |
| 37. | Vince Giamformaggio | Chevrolet |

1980

WINSTON WESTERN 500

January 19
Riverside, California
Time of Race: 3 hours, 16 minutes, 58 seconds
Average Speed: 94.974 mph
Margin of Victory: 2.97 seconds

FINISH	DRIVER	CAR
1.	Darrell Waltrip	Chevrolet
2.	Dale Earnhardt	Chevrolet
3.	Richard Petty	Chevrolet
4.	Joe Millikan	Chevrolet
5.	Bill Schmitt	Oldsmobile
6.	Richard Childress	Chevrolet
7.	Terry Labonte	Chevrolet
8.	Bill Whittington	Chevrolet
9.	Don Whittington	Chevrolet
10.	Ronnie Thomas	Chevrolet
11.	James Hylton	Chevrolet
12.	Harry Gant	Oldsmobile
13.	Roy Smith	Chevrolet
14.	Buddy Arrington	Dodge
15.	J. D. McDuffie	Chevrolet
16.	Jody Ridley	Ford
17.	Dave Marcis	Chevrolet
18.	Bobby Allison	Ford
19.	Don Puskarich	Chevrolet
20.	Vince Giamformaggio	Chevrolet
21.	Jimmy Means	Chevrolet
22.	Dick Brooks	Chevrolet
23.	Cale Yarborough	Chevrolet
24.	Jim Robinson	Chevrolet
25.	Chuck Wahl	Chevrolet
26.	Hershel McGriff	Dodge
27.	Steve Pfeifer	Chevrolet
28.	Dan Gurney	Chevrolet
29.	Lake Speed	Oldsmobile
30.	Randy Ogden	Chevrolet
31.	John Borneman	Chevrolet
32.	Dick May	Dodge
33.	Benny Parsons	Chevrolet
34.	Neil Bonnett	Mercury
35.	Rick McCray	Buick
36.	Chuck Bown	Chevrolet
37.	Bill Osborne	Chevrolet

DAYTONA 500

February 17
Daytona Beach, Florida
Time of Race: 2 hours, 48 minutes, 55 seconds
Average Speed: 177.602 mph
Margin of Victory: 12 seconds (finished under caution)

FINISH	DRIVER	CAR
1.	Buddy Baker	Oldsmobile
2.	Bobby Allison	Mercury
3.	Neil Bonnett	Mercury
4.	Dale Earnhardt	Oldsmobile
5.	Benny Parsons	Oldsmobile
6.	Terry Labonte	Oldsmobile
7.	Donnie Allison	Oldsmobile
8.	Sterling Marlin	Chevrolet
9.	Lennie Pond	Buick
10.	Jody Ridley	Ford

11.	Janet Guthrie	Chevrolet
12.	Bill Elliott	Mercury
13.	Richard Childress	Oldsmobile
14.	Slick Johnson	Chevrolet
15.	Jimmy Means	Buick
16.	Don Whittington	Chevrolet
17.	Joe Booher	Buick
18.	John Anderson	Oldsmobile
19.	Cale Yarborough	Oldsmobile
20.	Tommy Gale	Ford
21.	Cecil Gordon	Oldsmobile
22.	Dave Marcis	Oldsmobile
23.	Bill Schmitt	Oldsmobile
24.	Bill Elswick	Oldsmobile
25.	Richard Petty	Oldsmobile
26.	James Hylton	Oldsmobile
27.	J. D. McDuffie	Buick
28.	John Utsman	Chevrolet
29.	Ronnie Thomas	Buick
30.	Kevin Housby	Oldsmobile
31.	A. J. Foyt	Oldsmobile
32.	Bill Whittington	Buick
33.	Bruce Hill	Oldsmobile
34.	Joe Millikan	Oldsmobile
35.	Chuck Bown	Oldsmobile
36.	Dick Brooks	Oldsmobile
37.	Jim Vandiver	Oldsmobile
38.	James Hurlbert	Dodge
39.	Tighe Scott	Buick
40.	Darrell Waltrip	Oldsmobile
41.	Buddy Arrington	Dodge
42.	Harry Gant	Oldsmobile

RICHMOND 400

February 24
Richmond, Virginia
Time of Race: 3 hours, 12 minutes, 8 seconds
Average Speed: 67.703 mph
Margin of Victory: 1.2 seconds

FINISH	DRIVER	CAR
1.	Darrell Waltrip	Chevrolet
2.	Bobby Allison	Ford
3.	Richard Petty	Chevrolet
4.	Dave Marcis	Chevrolet
5.	Dale Earnhardt	Chevrolet
6.	Buddy Arrington	Dodge
7.	James Hylton	Chevrolet
8.	Cecil Gordon	Oldsmobile
9.	J. D. McDuffie	Chevrolet
10.	Bobby Wawak	Chevrolet
11.	Joe Booher	Chevrolet
12.	Harry Gant	Chevrolet
13.	Joey Arrington	Dodge
14.	Bud Strickler	Chevrolet
15.	Bill Elswick	Chevrolet
16.	Roger Hamby	Chevrolet
17.	Tommy Houston	Chevrolet
18.	Jody Ridley	Ford
19.	Rick Newsom	Chevrolet
20.	Dick May	Chevrolet
21.	Tommy Gale	Ford
22.	Richard Childress	Oldsmobile
23.	Bill Hollar	Chevrolet
24.	Terry Labonte	Chevrolet
25.	Cale Yarborough	Chevrolet
26.	Ronnie Thomas	Chevrolet
27.	Joe Millikan	Chevrolet
28.	Benny Parsons	Chevrolet
29.	Dick Brooks	Chevrolet
30.	Jimmy Means	Chevrolet
31.	Baxter Price	Chevrolet

CAROLINA 500

March 9
Rockingham, North Carolina

Time of Race: 4 hours, 36 minutes, 6 seconds
Average Speed: 108.735 mph
Margin of Victory: 3 seconds

FINISH	DRIVER	CAR
1.	Cale Yarborough	Oldsmobile
2.	Richard Petty	Chevrolet
3.	Dale Earnhardt	Chevrolet
4.	Darrell Waltrip	Chevrolet
5.	Donnie Allison	Chevrolet
6.	Neil Bonnett	Mercury
7.	Bobby Allison	Ford
8.	Harry Gant	Chevrolet
9.	Dave Marcis	Chevrolet
10.	Terry Labonte	Chevrolet
11.	Ronnie Thomas	Chevrolet
12.	Ricky Rudd	Chevrolet
13.	James Hylton	Chevrolet
14.	Richard Childress	Chevrolet
15.	Buddy Baker	Chevrolet
16.	Dick Brooks	Chevrolet
17.	Bobby Wawak	Chevrolet
18.	Roger Hamby	Chevrolet
19.	Dick May	Dodge
20.	Jimmy Means	Chevrolet
21.	Benny Parsons	Chevrlolet
22.	Buck Simmons	Chevrolet
23.	Bill Elswick	Chevrolet
24.	John Anderson	Chevrolet
25.	Buddy Arrington	Dodge
26.	Tommy Gale	Ford
27.	Baxter Price	Oldsmobile
28.	Joe Millikan	Oldsmobile
29.	Jody Ridley	Ford
30.	Slick Johnson	Chevrolet
31.	Kyle Petty	Chevrolet
32.	J. D. McDuffie	Chevrolet
33.	Cecil Gordon	Oldsmobile
34.	Randy Ogden	Chevrolet
35.	Bill Osborne	Chevrolet
36.	Mike Potter	Chevrolet
37.	Tighe Scott	Buick
38.	Junior Miller	Chevrolet

ATLANTA 500

March 16
Atlanta, Georgia
Time of Race: 3 hours, 42 minutes, 32 seconds
Average Speed: 134.080 mph
Margin of Victory: 9 seconds

FINISH	DRIVER	CAR
1.	Dale Earnhardt	Chevrolet
2.	Rusty Wallace	Chevrolet
3.	Bobby Allison	Ford
4.	Dave Marcis	Oldsmobile
5.	Dick Brooks	Chevrolet
6.	Jody Ridley	Ford
7.	Buddy Baker	Oldsmobile
8.	Cale Yarborough	Chevrolet
9.	J. D. McDuffie	Chevrolet
10.	Slick Johnson	Chevrolet
11.	Lake Speed	Chevrolet
12.	Jimmy Means	Chevrolet
13.	Richard Childress	Oldsmobile
14.	Kyle Petty	Chevrolet
15.	Terry Labonte	Chevrolet
16.	Harry Gant	Chevrolet
17.	Kevin Housby	Oldsmobile
18.	Tommy Gale	Ford
19.	Buddy Arrington	Dodge
20.	Frank Warren	Dodge
21.	Baxter Price	Oldsmobile
22.	Ronnie Thomas	Chevrolet
23.	Lennie Pond	Chevrolet
24.	Cecil Gordon	Oldsmobile

25.	Ralph Jones	Ford
26.	Donnie Allison	Chevrolet
27.	Bruce Hill	Oldsmobile
28.	Darell Waltrip	Chevrolet
29.	Bill Elliott	Mercury
30.	Benny Parsons	Chevrolet
31.	Ricky Rudd	Chevrolet
32.	Tighe Scott	Buick
33.	Richard Petty	Chevrolet
34.	Roger Hamby	Chevrolet
35.	Joe Booher	Buick
36.	Rick Newson	Oldsmobile
37.	Joe Millikan	Chevrolet
38.	Don Whittington	Oldsmobile
39.	James Hylton	Chevrolet
40.	Buck Simmons	Chevrolet
41.	Neil Bonnett	Mercury
42.	Randy Ogden	Chevrolet

VALLEYDALE SOUTHEASTERN 500

March 30
Bristol, Tennessee
Time of Race: 2 hours, 44 minutes, 53 seconds
Average Speed: 96.977 mph
Margin of Victory: 8 seconds

FINISH	DRIVER	CAR
1.	Dale Earnhardt	Chevrolet
2.	Darrell Waltrip	Chevrolet
3.	Bobby Allison	Ford
4.	Benny Parsons	Chevroler
5.	Cale Yarborough	Chevrolet
6.	Joe Millikan	Chevrolet
7.	Harry Gant	Chevrolet
8.	Richard Petty	Chevrolet
9.	Dave Marcis	Chevrolet
10.	Terry Labonte	Chevrolet
11.	Jody Ridley	Ford
12.	Ronnie Thomas	Chevrolet
13.	J. D. McDuffie	Chevrolet
14.	James Hylton	Chevrolet
15.	Tommy Houston	Chevrolet
16.	Dick May	Chevrolet
17.	Tommy Gale	Ford
18.	Roger Hamby	Chevrolet
19.	Bill Elswick	Chevrolet
20.	John Utsman	Chevrolet
21.	Buddy Arrington	Dodge
22.	Cecil Gordon	Oldsmobile
23.	Baxter Price	Chevrolet
24.	Jimmy Means	Chevrolet
25.	Junior Miller	Chevrolet
26.	Slick Johnson	Chevrolet
27.	Dick Brooks	Chevrolet
28.	Travis Tiller	Dodge
29.	Richard Childress	Oldsmobile
30.	Mike Potter	Chevrolet
31.	Bobby Wawak	Chevrolet
32.	Buck Simmons	Chevrolet

CRC CHEMICALS REBEL 500

April 13
Darlington, South Carolina
Time of Race: 2 hours, 23 minutes, 49 seconds
Average Speed: 112.397 mph
Margin of Victory: 3 seconds

FINISH	DRIVER	CAR
1.	David Pearson	Chevrolet
2.	Benny Parsons	Chevrolet
3.	Harry Gant	Chevrolet
4.	Darrell Waltrip	Chevrolet

5.	Dick Brooks	Chevrolet
6.	Lennie Pond	Chevrolet
7.	Joe Millikan	Chevrolet
8.	Lake Speed	Chevrolet
9.	Richard Petty	Chevrolet
10.	Jody Ridley	Ford
11.	Sterling Marlin	Oldsmobile
12.	Cale Yarborough	Chevrolet
13.	Bobby Wawak	Chevrolet
14.	Buddy Arrington	Dodge
15.	Tommy Gale	Ford
16.	Roger Hamby	Chevrolet
17.	John Anderson	Chevrolet
18.	James Hylton	Chevrolet
19.	Ricky Rudd	Chevrolet
20.	Bill Elswick	Chevrolet
21.	Richard Childress	Oldsmobile
22.	J. D. McDuffie	Chevrolet
23.	Dave Marcis	Chevrolet
24.	Dick May	Chevrolet
25.	Slick Johnson	Chevrolet
26.	Ronnie Thomas	Chevrolet
27.	Buck Simmons	Chevrolet
28.	Jimmy Means	Chevrolet
29.	Dale Earnhardt	Chevrolet
30.	Bobby Allison	Ford
31.	Baxter Price	Chevrolet
32.	Terry Labonte	Chevrolet
33.	Melvin Revis	Chevrolet
34.	Cecil Gordon	Chrysler
35.	Buddy Baker	Chevrolet
36.	Neil Bonnett	Mercury

NORTHWESTERN BANK 400

April 20
North Wilkesboro, North Carolina
Time of Race: 2 hours, 37 minutes, 4 seconds
Average Speed: 95.501 mph
Margin of Victory: 5 seconds

FINISH	DRIVER	CAR
1.	Richard Petty	Chevrolet
2.	Harry Gant	Chevrolet
3.	Bobby Allison	Ford
4.	Cale Yarborough	Chevrolet
5.	Benny Parsons	Chevrolet
6.	Dale Earnhardt	Chevrolet
7.	Jody Ridley	Ford
8.	Kyle Petty	Chevrolet
9.	Slick Johnson	Chevrolet
10.	Joe Millikan	Chevrolet
11.	Richard Childress	Chevrolet
12.	Darrell Waltrip	Chevrolet
13.	Buddy Arrington	Dodge
14.	Jimmy Means	Chevrolet
15.	Dick May	Chevrolet
16.	Bobby Wawak	Chevrolet
17.	James Hylton	Chevrolet
18.	Jeff McDuffie	Buick
19.	Baxter Price	Chevrolet
20.	Rick Newsom	Chevrolet
21.	Dave Marcis	Chevrolet
22.	Terry Labonte	Chevrolet
23.	Ronnie Thomas	Chevrolet
24.	Bill Elswick	Chevrolet
25.	Roger Hamby	Chevrolet
26.	D. K. Ulrich	Chevrolet
27.	Dick Brooks	Chevrolet
28.	John Anderson	Chevrolet
29.	Tommy Gale	Ford
30.	J. D. McDuffie	Chevrolet
31.	Tommy Houston	Chevrolet

VIRGINIA 500

April 27
Martinsville, Virginia

Time of Race: 3 hours, 48 minutes, 6 seconds
Average Speed: 69.049 mph
Margin of Victory: 9 seconds (finished under caution)

FINISH	DRIVER	CAR
1.	Darrell Waltrip	Chevrolet
2.	Benny Parsons	Chevrolet
3.	Richard Petty	Chevrolet
4.	Cale Yarborough	Chevrolet
5.	Joe Millikan	Chevrolet
6.	Neil Bonnett	Mercury
7.	Jody Ridley	Ford
8.	Dave Marcis	Chevrolet
9.	Slick Johnson	Chevrolet
10.	Buddy Arrington	Chevrolet
11.	Richard Childress	Chevrolet
12.	Jimmy Means	Chevrolet
13.	Dale Earnhardt	Chevrolet
14.	Junior Miller	Chevrolet
15.	Kyle Petty	Chevrolet
16.	Buck Simmons	Chevrolet
17.	Cecil Gordon	Oldsmobile
18.	James Hylton	Chevrolet
19.	Baxter Price	Chevrolet
20.	Dick May	Chevrolet
21.	Harry Gant	Chevrolet
22.	Ronnie Thomas	Chevrolet
23.	Terry Labonte	Chevrolet
24.	Buddy Baker	Chevrolet
25.	Bobby Allison	Ford
26.	Dick Brooks	Chevrolet
27.	Bill Elswick	Chevrolet
28.	D. K. Ulrich	Chevrolet
29.	Tommy Gale	Ford
30.	J. D. McDuffie	Chevrolet
31.	Bobby Wawak	Chevrolet
32.	Rick Newsom	Oldsmobile

WINSTON 500

May 4
Talladega, Alabama
Time of Race: 2 hours, 56 minutes
Average Speed: 170.481 mph
Margin of Victory: 3 feet

FINISH	DRIVER	CAR
1.	Buddy Baker	Oldsmobile
2.	Dale Earnhardt	Oldsmobile
3.	David Pearson	Oldsmobile
4.	Lennie Pond	Oldsmobile
5.	Tighe Scott	Oldsmobile
6.	Cale Yarborough	Oldsmobile
7.	Lake Speed	Chevrolet
8.	Benny Parsons	Oldsmobile
9.	Dick Brooks	Oldsmobile
10.	Jody Ridley	Mercury
11.	Coo Coo Marlin	Chevrolet
12.	Richard Childress	Oldsmobile
13.	James Hylton	Chevrolet
14.	Steve Moore	Chevrolet
15.	Dick May	Dodge
16.	Tommy Gale	Ford
17.	Roger Hamby	Chevrolet
18.	Buddy Arrington	Dodge
19.	Frank Warren	Dodge
20.	Ronnie Thomas	Buick
21.	Bill Elliott	Mercury
22.	Gary Baker	Chevrolet
23.	Cecil Gordon	Oldsmobile
24.	Buick Simmons	Oldsmobile
25.	Donnie Allison	Oldsmobile
26.	John Anderson	Buick
27.	Neil Bonnett	Mercury
28.	Dick Skillen	Buick
29.	Dave Marcis	Oldsmobile
30.	Bobby Wawak	Dodge

31.	Richard Petty	Oldsmobile
32.	Terry Labonte	Oldsmobile
33.	Marty Robbins	Dodge
34.	Don Whittington	Oldsmobile
35.	Bill Elswick	Oldsmobile
36.	Bruce Hill	Oldsmobile
37.	Harry Gant	Oldsmobile
38.	Phil Finney	Oldsmobile
39.	Jim Vandiver	Oldsmobile
40.	Bobby Allison	Mercury
41.	J. D. McDuffie	Buick
42.	Darrell Waltrip	Oldsmobile

MUSIC CITY 420

May 10
Nashville, Tennessee
Time of Race: 2 hours, 47 minutes, 52 seconds
Average Speed: 89.471 mph
Margin of Victory: 1 car length

FINISH	DRIVER	CAR
1.	Richard Petty	Chevrolet
2.	Benny Parsons	Chevrolet
3.	Cale Yarborough	Chevrolet
4.	Darrell Waltrip	Chevrolet
5.	Bobby Allison	Ford
6.	Dale Earnhardt	Chevrolet
7.	Terry Labonte	Chevrolet
8.	Jody Ridley	Ford
9.	Harry Gant	Chevrolet
10.	Mike Alexander	Chevrolet
11.	Dave Marcis	Chevrolet
12.	Jimmy Means	Chevrolet
13.	James Hylton	Chevrolet
14.	Don Spouse	Chevrolet
15.	Tommy Gale	Ford
16.	Junior Miller	Chevrolet
17.	Dick May	Chevrolet
18.	Bobby Wawak	Chevrolet
19.	Cecil Gordon	Oldsmobile
20.	J. D. McDuffie	Chevrolet
21.	Ronnie Thomas	Chevrolet
22.	Baxter Price	Chevrolet
23.	Roger Hamby	Chevrolet
24.	John Anderson	Chevrolet
25.	Slick Johnson	Chevrolet
26.	Rick Newsom	Oldsmobile
27.	Buddy Arrington	Dodge
28.	Steve Spencer	Chevrolet
29.	Richard Childress	Chevrolet
30.	Dick Brooks	Chevrolet

MASON-DIXON 500

May 18
Dover, Delaware
Time of Race: 4 hours, 23 minutes, 28 seconds
Average Speed: 113.866 mph
Margin of Victory: 26 seconds

FINISH	DRIVER	CAR
1.	Bobby Allison	Ford
2.	Richard Petty	Chevrolet
3.	Buddy Baker	Chevrolet
4.	Harry Gant	Chevrolet
5.	Terry Labonte	Chevrolet
6.	Jody Ridley	Ford
7.	Dick May	Chevrolet
8.	Richard Childress	Chevrolet
9.	Cecil Gordon	Oldsmobile
10.	Dale Earnhardt	Chevrolet
11.	Ronnie Thomas	Buick
12.	Tommy Gale	Ford
13.	Roger Hamby	Chevrolet

14.	Baxter Price	Chevrolet
15.	Jim Ingram	Chevrolet
16.	Cale Yarborough	Chevrolet
17.	Dick Brooks	Chevrolet
18.	Neil Bonnett	Mercury
19.	James Hylton	Chevrolet
20.	Darrell Waltrip	Chevrolet
21.	Kyle Petty	Chevrolet
22.	Benny Parsons	Chevrolet
23.	Tighe Scott	Chevrolet
24.	Jocko Maggiacomo	Oldsmobile
25.	Dave Marcis	Chevrolet
26.	Buddy Arrington	Dodge
27.	Jimmy Means	Chevrolet
28.	Nestor Peles	Oldsmobile
29.	Bobby Wawak	Chevrolet
30.	Bill Elswick	Chevrolet
31.	Junior Miller	Chevrolet
32.	Rick Newsom	Oldsmobile
33.	J. D. McDuffie	Chevrolet
34.	D. K. Ulrich	Chevrolet

WORLD 600

May 25
Charlotte, North Carolina
Time of Race: 5 hours, 1 minute, 51 seconds
Average Speed: 119.265 mph
Margin of Victory: half a car length

FINISH	DRIVER	CAR
1.	Benny Parsons	Chevrolet
2.	Darrell Waltrip	Chevrolet
3.	Terry Labonte	Chevrolet
4.	Richard Petty	Chevrolet
5.	Neil Bonnett	Mercury
6.	David Pearson	Chevrolet
7.	Kyle Petty	Chevrolet
8.	Jim Vandiver	Oldsmobile
9.	Ricky Rudd	Chevrolet
10.	Buddy Arrington	Dodge
11.	Richard Chldress	Oldsmobile
12.	Jody Ridley	Mercury
13.	Blackie Wangerin	Mercury
14.	Jimmy Means	Chevrolet
15.	Dick Brooks	Chevrolet
16.	Sterling Marlin	Oldsmobile
17.	Cale Yarborough	Chevrolet
18.	John Anderson	Chevrolet
19.	Connie Saylor	Chevrolet
20.	Dale Earnhardt	Chevrolet
21.	Baxter Price	Oldsmobile
22.	Ronnie Thomas	Chevrolet
23.	James Hylton	Chevrolet
24.	Tommy Houston	Chevrolet
25.	Bobby Wawak	Buick
26.	Bobby Allison	Mercury
27.	Billy Harvey	Oldsmobile
28.	Harry Gant	Chevrolet
29.	Dave Marcis	Oldsmobile
30.	J. D. McDuffie	Chevrolet
31.	Donnie Allison	Chevrolet
32.	Slick Johnson	Chevrolet
33.	Tommy Gale	Ford
34.	Bill Elswick	Chevrolet
35.	Steve Moore	Chevrolet
36.	Tighe Scott	Oldsmobile
37.	Cecil Gordon	Oldsmobile
38.	Bruce Hill	Oldsmobile
39.	Buddy Baker	Buick
40.	John Greenwood	Chevrolet
41.	Lennie Pond	Chevrolet
42.	Bill Elliott	Mercury

NASCAR 400

June 1
College Station, Texas

Time of Race: 2 hours, 30 minutes, 54 seconds
Average Speed: 159.046 mph
Margin of Victory: 14 seconds

FINISH	DRIVER	CAR
1.	Cale Yarborough	Chevrolet
2.	Richard Petty	Chevrolet
3.	Bobby Allison	Ford
4.	Darrell Waltrip	Chevrolet
5.	Terry Labonte	Chevrolet
6.	Richard Childress	Chevrolet
7.	Dave Marcis	Oldsmobile
8.	Harry Gant	Chevrolet
9.	Dale Earnhardt	Chevrolet
10.	James Hylton	Chevrolet
11.	Ronnie Thomas	Chevrolet
12.	Lake Speed	Chevrolet
13.	Jimmy Finger	Buick
14.	Cecil Gordon	Oldsmobile
15.	D. K. Ulrich	Chevrolet
16.	Dick May	Buick
17.	Frank Warren	Dodge
18.	Baxter Price	Chevrolet
19.	Jimmy Means	Chevrolet
20.	Nelson Oswald	Buick
21.	Henry Jones	Oldsmobile
22.	Roger Hamby	Chevrolet
23.	Benny Parsons	Chevrolet
24.	Bobby Wawak	Buick
25.	Tommy Gale	Ford
26.	Jody Ridley	Ford
27.	Dick Brooks	Chevrolet
28.	Buddy Arrington	Dodge
29.	J. D. McDuffie	Chevrolet
30.	Slick Johnson	Chevrolet
31.	Randy Ogden	Chevrolet

WARNER W. HODGDON 400

June 8
Riverside, California
Time of Race: 2 hours, 26 minutes, 38 seconds
Average Speed: 101.846 mph
Margin of Victory: 1 car length

FINISH	DRIVER	CAR
1.	Darrell Waltrip	Chevrolet
2.	Neil Bonnett	Mercury
3.	Benny Parsons	Chevrolet
4.	Cale Yarborough	Chevrolet
5.	Dale Earnhardt	Chevrolet
6.	Dave Marcis	Chevrolet
7.	Harry Gant	Chevrolet
8.	Richard Petty	Chevrolet
9.	J. D. McDuffie	Chevrolet
10.	Cecil Gordon	Oldsmobile
11.	Jody Ridley	Ford
12.	James Hylton	Chevrolet
13.	Bill Schmitt	Oldsmobile
14.	Buddy Arrington	Dodge
15.	Bobby Allison	Ford
16.	Ronnie Thomas	Chevrolet
17.	Don Puskarich	Chevrolet
18.	Richard Childress	Chevrolet
19.	Joe Booher	Dodge
20.	Jim Robinson	Chevrolet
21.	Steve Pfeifer	Chevrolet
22.	Bobby Wawak	Buick
23.	Roger Hamby	Chevrolet
24.	Hershel McGriff	Chevrolet
25.	Don Waterman	Oldsmobile
26.	Lake Speed	Chevrolet
27.	Jim Hopkinson	Chevrolet
28.	Roy Smith	Oldsmobile
29.	Ed Hale	Chevrolet
30.	Donnie Allison	Chevrolet
31.	Dick Brooks	Chevrolet

32.	Rick McCray	Buick
33.	Terry Labonte	Chevrolet
34.	John Borneman	Chevrolet
35.	Don Whittington	Chevrolet
36.	D. K. Ulrich	Chevrolet

GABRIEL 400

June 15
Brooklyn, Michigan
Time of Race: 3 hours, 2 minutes, 5 seconds
Average Speed: 131.808 mph
Margin of Victory: 1 car length

FINISH	DRIVER	CAR
1.	Benny Parsons	Chevrolet
2.	Cale Yarborough	Chevrolet
3.	Buddy Baker	Chevrolet
4.	Neil Bonnett	Mercury
5.	Richard Petty	Chevrolet
6.	Jody Ridley	Ford
7.	Kyle Petty	Chevrolet
8.	Bobby Allison	Ford
9.	Bill Elliott	Mercury
10.	Tighe Scott	Chevrolet
11.	Terry Labonte	Chevrolet
12.	Dale Earnhardt	Chevrolet
13.	John Anderson	Chevrolet
14.	Richard Childress	Chevrolet
15.	J. D. McDuffie	Chevrolet
16.	Wayne Watercutter	Oldsmobile
17.	Lake Speed	Chevrolet
18.	Mike Potter	Chevrolet
19.	Tommy Gale	Chevrolet
20.	Cecil Gordon	Oldsmobile
21.	Roger Hamby	Chevrolet
22.	Jimmy Means	Chevrolet
23.	Buddy Arrington	Dodge
24.	James Hylton	Chevrolet
25.	David Pearson	Chevrolet
26.	Darrell Waltrip	Chevrolet
27.	Baxter Price	Oldsmobile
28.	Harry Gant	Chevrolet
29.	Bobby Wawak	Buick
30.	Ronnie Thomas	Chevrolet
31.	Chuck Bown	Oldsmobile
32.	Ricky Rudd	Chevrolet
33.	Dick Brooks	Chevrolet
34.	Junior Miller	Chevrolet
35.	Dave Marcis	Chevrolet
36.	Donnie Allison	Chevrolet
37.	Henry Jones	Oldsmobile

FIRECRACKER 400

July 4
Daytona Beach, Florida
Time of Race: 2 hours, 18 minutes, 21 seconds
Average Speed: 173.473 mph
Margin of Victory: 1 second

FINISH	DRIVER	CAR
1.	Bobby Allison	Mercury
2.	David Pearson	Odsmobile
3.	Dale Earnhardt	Oldsmobile
4.	Buddy Baker	Oldsmobile
5.	Richard Petty	Oldsmobile
6.	Benny Parsons	Oldsmobile
7.	Jody Ridley	Mercury
8.	Richard Childress	Oldsmobile
9.	John Anderson	Buick
10.	Buddy Arrington	Dodge
11.	Lennie Pond	Buick
12.	Bill Elliott	Mercury

13.	Ricky Rudd	Oldsmobile
14.	Coo Coo Marlin	Chevrolet
15.	Rick Wilson	Oldsmobile
16.	Harry Gant	Oldsmobile
17.	RonnieThomas	Oldsmobile
18.	Steve Moore	Chevrolet
19.	Donnie Allison	Oldsmobile
20.	Phil Finney	Oldsmobile
21.	John Greenwood	Oldsmobile
22.	Don Whittington	Oldsmobile
23.	J. D. McDuffie	Buick
24.	James Hylton	Oldsmobile
25.	James Vandiver	Oldsmobile
26.	Jimmy Means	Buick
27.	Roger Hamby	Chevrolet
28.	Tommy Gale	Ford
29.	Cecil Gordon	Oldsmobile
30.	Marty Robbins	Dodge
31.	Darrell Waltrip	Oldsmobile
32.	Terry Labonte	Oldsmobile
33.	Dave Marcis	Oldsmobile
34.	Neil Bonnett	Mercury
35.	Bruce Hill	Oldsmobile
36.	Tighe Scott	Oldsmobile
37.	Chuck Bown	Oldsmobile
38.	Lake Speed	Chevrolet
39.	Connie Saylor	Chevrolet
40.	Cale Yarborough	Oldsmobile

BUSCH NASHVILLE 420

July 12
Nashville, Tennessee
Time of Race: 2 hours, 40 minutes, 5 seconds
Average Speed: 93.821 mph
Margin of Victory: 1 second

FINISH	DRIVER	CAR
1.	Dale Earnhardt	Chevrolet
2.	Cale Yarborough	Chevrolet
3.	Benny Parsons	Chevrolet
4.	Darrell Waltrip	Chevrolet
5.	Richard Petty	Chevrolet
6.	Bobby Allison	Ford
7.	Sterling Marlin	Chevrolet
8.	Jody Ridley	Ford
9.	Richard Childress	Chevrolet
10.	Buddy Arrington	Dodge
11.	J. D. McDuffie	Chevrolet
12.	John Anderson	Chevrolet
13.	Slick Johnson	Chevrolet
14.	Dave Marcis	Chevrolet
15.	Roger Hamby	Chevrolet
16.	Jimmy Means	Chevrolet
17.	James Hylton	Chevrolet
18.	Tommy Gale	Ford
19.	Baxter Price	Chevrolet
20.	Junior Miller	Chevrolet
21.	Cecil Gordon	Buick
22.	Terry Labonte	Chevrolet
23.	Bobby Wawak	Buick
24.	Don Sprouse	Chevrolet
25.	Steve Spencer	Chevrolet
26.	Ronnie Thomas	Chevrolet
27.	Donnie Allison	Chevrolet
28.	Ricky Rudd	Chevrolet
29.	Harry Gant	Chevrolet
30.	Dick May	Dodge

COCA-COLA 500

July 19
Pocono, Pennsylvania
Time of Race: 4 hours, 1 minute, 10 seconds
Average Speed: 124.395 mph
Margin of Victory: .5 second

FINISH	DRIVER	CAR
1.	Neil Bonnett	Mercury
2.	Buddy Baker	Buick
3.	Cale Yarborough	Chevrolet
4.	Dale Earnhardt	Chevrolet
5.	Harry Gant	Chevrolet
6.	Terry Labonte	Chevrolet
7.	Kyle Petty	Chevrolet
8.	Dave Marcis	Chevrolet
9.	Richard Childress	Chevrolet
10.	Ricky Rudd	Chevrolet
11.	Billy Harvey	Chevrolet
12.	Tim Richmond	Chevrolet
13.	Buddy Arrington	Dodge
14.	Jimmy Means	Chevrolet
15.	James Hylton	Chevrolet
16.	Cecil Gordon	Oldsmobile
17.	Dave Dion	Ford
18.	Jody Ridley	Ford
19.	Tommy Gale	Ford
20.	Benny Parsons	Chevrolet
21.	Junior Miller	Chevrolet
22.	Baxter Price	Chevrolet
23.	Ronnie Thomas	Chevrolet
24.	Roger Hamby	Chevrolet
25.	Ken Hemphill	Chevrolet
26.	Darrell Waltrip	Chevrolet
27.	Bob Riley	Chevrolet
28.	Janet Guthrie	Ford
29.	Dick May	Chevrolet
30.	Lake Speed	Chevrolet
31.	Slick Johnson	Chevrolet
32.	Tighe Scott	Chevrolet
33.	Richard Petty	Chevrolet
34.	Bobby Allison	Ford
35.	Chuck Bown	Oldsmobile
36.	J. D. McDuffie	Chevrolet
37.	Henry Jones	Oldsmobile
38.	Nelson Oswald	Buick
39.	Jocko Magiacomo	Oldsmobile
40.	Travis Tiller	Oldsmobile

TALLADEGA 500

August 3
Talladega, Alabama
Time of Race: 2 hours, 59 minutes, 47 seconds
Average Speed: 166.894 mph
Margin of Victory: 1 second

FINISH	DRIVER	CAR
1.	Neil Bonnett	Mercury
2.	Cale Yarborough	Oldsmobile
3.	Dale Earnhardt	Oldsmobile
4.	Benny Parsons	Oldsmobile
5.	Harry Gant	Oldsmobile
6.	Richard Childress	Oldsmobile
7.	Bill Elliott	Mercury
8.	Lake Speed	Chevrolet
9.	Kyle Petty	Chevrolet
10.	Dick May	Buick
11.	Darrell Waltrip	Oldsmobi;e
12.	Harry Dinwiddle	Buick
13.	Marty Robbins	Dodge
14.	James Hylton	Oldsmobile
15.	Jimmy Means	Chevrolet
16.	Billy Harvey	Oldsmobile
17.	David Pearson	Oldsmobile
18.	Richard Petty	Oldsmobile
19.	Slick Johnson	Chevrolet
20.	Ricky Rudd	Oldsmobile
21.	Ronnie Thomas	Oldsmobile
22.	Roger Hamby	Chevrolet
23.	Cecil Gordon	Oldsmobile
24.	Bobby Wawak	Buick
25.	J. D. McDuffie	Buick
26.	Donnie Allison	Oldsmobile
27.	Baxter Price	Oldsmobile
28.	Lennie Pond	Oldsmobile

29.	Tommy Gale	Ford		5.	Benny Parsons	Chevrolet
30.	Jody Ridley	Mercury		6.	Bobby Allison	Ford
31.	Terry Labonte	Oldsmobile		7.	Dave Marcis	Chevrolet
32.	Buddy Baker	Oldsmobile		8.	Lennie Pond	Oldsmobile
33.	Frank Warren	Dodge		9.	Richard Childress	Chevrolet
34.	Tighe Scott	Oldsmobile		10.	D. K. Ulrich	Chevrolet
35.	Bobby Allison	Mercury		11.	J. D. McDuffie	Chevrolet
36.	Rick Wilson	Oldsmobile		12.	Jody Ridley	Mercury
37.	Coo Coo Marlin	Chevrolet		13.	Tommy Gale	Ford
38.	Buddy Arrington	Dodge		14.	Harry Gant	Chevrolet
39.	Dave Marcis	Oldsmobile		15.	John Anderson	Chevrolet
40.	Ferrell Harris	Chevrolet		16.	Roger Hamby	Chevrolet
41.	Bruce Hill	Oldsmobile		17.	James Hylton	Chevrolet
				18.	Baxter Price	Chevrolet
				19.	Cecil Gordon	Oldsmobile
				20.	Buddy Arrington	Dodge
				21.	Bub Strickler	Oldsmobile
				22.	Jimmy Means	Chevrolet
				23.	Terry Labonte	Chevrolet
				24.	Stuart Huffman	Buick
				25.	Steve Spencer	Chevrolet
				26.	Dick May	Buick
				27.	Junior Miller	Chevrolet
				28.	Ricky Rudd	Chevrolet
				29.	Ronnie Thomas	Chevrolet
				30.	Bobby Sands	Chevrolet

CHAMPION SPARK PLUG 400

August 17
Brooklyn, Michigan
Time of Race: 2 hours, 45 minutes, 7 seconds
Average Speed: 145.352 mph
Margin of Victory: 1 second

FINISH	DRIVER	CAR
1.	Cale Yarborough	Chevrolet
2.	Neil Bonnett	Mercury
3.	Donnie Allison	Chevrolet
4.	Darrell Waltrip	Chevrolet
5.	Richard Petty	Chevrolet
6.	Buddy Baker	Chevrolet
7.	Bobby Allison	Mercury
8.	Benny Parsons	Chevrolet
9.	Bill Elliott	Mercury
10.	Kenny Hemphill	Chevrolet
11.	Terry Labonte	Chevrolet
12.	Kyle Petty	Chevrolet
13.	Buddy Arrington	Dodge
14.	Jimmy Means	Chevrolet
15.	D. K. Ulrich	Chevrolet
16.	Lake Speed	Chevrolet
17.	Billy Harvey	Chevrolet
18.	Jody Ridley	Mercury
19.	Dick May	Chevrolet
20.	J. D. McDuffie	Chevrolet
21.	Cecil Gordon	Oldsmobile
22.	Tommy Gale	Ford
23.	Bruce Jacobi	Ford
24.	Wayne Watercutter	Oldsmobile
25.	James Hylton	Oldsmobile
26.	Dave Marcis	Chevrolet
27.	Richard Childress	Chevrolet
28.	Stuart Huffman	Buick
29.	Ronnie Thomas	Buicl
30.	Roger Hamby	Chevrolet
31.	Frank Warren	Dodge
32.	Baxter Price	Oldsmobile
33.	Bobby Wawak	Buick
34.	Ricky Rudd	Chevrolet
35.	Dale Earnhardt	Chevrolet
36.	John Anderson	Chevrolet
37.	Harry Gant	Chevrolet

BUSCH VOLUNTEER 500

August 23
Bristol, Tennessee
Time of Race: 3 hours, 3 minutes, 51 seconds
Average Speed: 86.973 mph
Margin of Victory: 1 second

FINISH	DRIVER	CAR
1.	Cale Yarborough	Chevrolet
2.	Dale Earnhardt	Chevrolet
3.	Darrell Waltrip	Chevrolet
4.	Richard Petty	Chevrolet

SOUTHERN 500

September 1
Darlington, South Carolina
Time of Race: 4 hours, 21 minutes, 5 seconds
Average Speed: 115.210 mph
Margin of Victory: under caution

FINISH	DRIVER	CAR
1.	Terry Labonte	Chevrolet
2.	David Pearson	Chevrolet
3.	Harry Gant	Chevrolet
4.	Benny Parsons	Chevrolet
5.	Neil Bonnett	Mercury
6.	Bobby Allison	Ford
7.	Dale Earnhardt	Chevrolet
8.	Dave Marcis	Chevrolet
9.	Richard Petty	Chevrolet
10.	Dick Brooks	Chevrolet
11.	Chuck Bown	Chevrolet
12.	Richard Childress	Chevrolet
13.	D. K. Ulrich	Chevrolet
14.	Connie Saylor	Chevrolet
15.	Slick Johnson	Chevrolet
16.	Jimmy Means	Chevrolet
17.	Buddy Arrington	Dodge
18.	J. D. McDuffie	Chevrolet
19.	Cecil Gordon	Oldsmobile
20.	Ferrell Harris	Dodge
21.	James Hylton	Chevrolet
22.	Ronnie Thomas	Chevrolet
23.	Frank Warren	Dodge
24.	Ralph Jones	Ford
25.	Darrell Waltrip	Chevrolet
26.	Buddy Baker	Chevrolet
27.	Lake Speed	Chevrolet
28.	Dick May	Buick
29.	Cale Yarborough	Chevrolet
30.	Jody Ridley	Ford
31.	Tommy Gale	Ford
32.	Donnie Allison	Chevrolet
33.	Bill Elliott	Mercury
34.	Ricky Rudd	Chevrolet
35.	Roger Hamby	Chevrolet
36.	John Anderson	Chevrolet
37.	Blackie Wangerin	Mercury
38.	Don Whittington	Chevrolet
39.	Bobby Wawak	Buick
40.	Lennie Pond	Chevrolet
41.	Kenny Hemphill	Chevrolet

CAPITAL CITY 400

September 7
Richmond, Virginia
Time of Race: 2 hours, 43 minutes, 10 seconds
Average Speed: 79.722 mph
Margin of Victory: 2 seconds

FINISH	DRIVER	CAR
1.	Bobby Allison	Ford
2.	Richard Petty	Chevrolet
3.	Lennie Pond	Chevrolet
4.	Dale Earnhardt	Chevrolet
5.	Jody Ridley	Ford
6.	Darrell Waltrip	Chevrolet
7.	Dave Marcis	Chevrolet
8.	Terry Labonte	Chevrolet
9.	Dave Dion	Ford
10.	Benny Parsons	Chevrolet
11.	Richard Childress	Chevrolet
12.	Buddy Arrington	Dodge
13.	Jimmy Means	Chevrolet
14.	Bill Elswick	Oldsmobile
15.	Don Sprouse	Chevrolet
16.	Roger Hamby	Chevrolet
17.	James Hylton	Chevrolet
18.	Cecil Gordon	Oldsmobile
19.	Tommy Gale	Ford
20.	Harry Gant	Chevrolet
21.	Eddie Dickerson	Dodge
22.	Ronnie Thomas	Chevrolet
23.	Junior Miller	Chevrolet
24.	Baxter Price	Chevrolet
25.	D. K. Ulrich	Chevrolet
26.	Cale Yarborough	Oldsmobile
27.	Bobby Wawak	Chevrolet
28.	Bub Strickler	Chevrolet
29.	J. D. McDuffie	Chevrolet

CRC CHEMICALS 500

September 14
Dover, Delaware
Time of Race: 4 hours, 18 minutes, 34 seconds
Average Speed: 116.024 mph
Margin of Victory: $^{47}/_{100}$ of a second

FINISH	DRIVER	CAR
1.	Darrell Waltrip	Chevrolet
2.	Harry Gant	Chevrolet
3.	Buddy Baker	Chevrolet
4.	Cale Yarborough	Chevrolet
5.	Benny Parsons	Chevrolet
6.	Neil Bonnett	Mercury
7.	Donnie Allison	Chevrolet
8.	Lennie Pond	Chevrolet
9.	Jody Ridley	Ford
10.	Ronnie Thomas	Chevrolet
11.	Lake Speed	Chevrolet
12.	Dave Marcis	Chevrolet
13.	Buddy Arrington	Dodge
14.	Dave Dion	Ford
15.	Cecil Gordon	Oldsmobile
16.	Joe Booher	Chevrolet
17.	Richard Petty	Chevrolet
18.	Joel Stowe	Chevrolet
19.	James Hylton	Chevrolet
20.	Roger Hamby	Chevrolet
21.	John Callis	Ford
22.	Eddie Dickerson	Dodge
23.	Kyle Petty	Chevrolet
24.	Dick May	Dodge
25.	Frank Warren	Dodge
26.	Travis Tiller	Oldsmobile
27.	Jimmy Means	Chevrolet
28.	Terry Labonte	Chevrolet
29.	Junior Miller	Chevrolet

30.	Bobby Allison	Chevrolet
31.	Tim Richmond	Chevrolet
32.	John Anderson	Chevrolet
33.	Kenny Hemphill	Chevrolet
34.	Dale Earnhardt	Chevrolet
35.	Bub Strickler	Chevrolet
36.	Tommy Gale	Ford
37.	Richard Childress	Chevrolet
38.	J. D. McDuffie	Chevrolet
39.	Bob Riley	Chevrolet
40.	Steve Gray	Buick

HOLLY FARMS 400

September 21
North Wilkesboro, North Carolina
Time of Race: 3 hours, 18 minutes, 39 seconds
Average Speed: 75.510 mph
Margin of Victory: .5 second

FINISH	DRIVER	CAR
1.	Bobby Allison	Ford
2.	Darrell Waltrip	Chevrolet
3.	Dave Marcis	Chevrolet
4.	Harry Gant	Chevrolet
5.	Dale Earnhardt	Chevrolet
6.	Benny Patsons	Chevrolet
7.	Terry Labonte	Chevrolet
8.	Slick Johnson	Chevrolet
9.	Jody Ridley	Ford
10.	Cale Yarborough	Oldsmobile
11.	Bobby Wawak	Chevrolet
12.	Jimmy Means	Chevrolet
13.	Junior Miller	Chevrolet
14.	Cecil Gordon	Oldsmobile
15.	James Hylton	Chevrolet
16.	Joel Stowe	Oldsmobile
17.	Jeff McDuffie	Buick
18.	Richard Petty	Chevrolet
19.	Richard Childress	Chevrolet
20.	Tommy Gale	Ford
21.	Lake Speed	Chevrolet
22.	Roger Hamby	Chevrolet
23.	Bub Strickler	Chevrolet
24.	J. D. McDuffie	Chevrolet
25.	Ronnie Thomas	Chevrolet
26.	Buddy Arrington	Dodge
27.	John Anderson	Chevrolet
28.	Lennie Pond	Chevrolet
29.	Dick May	Chevrolet
30.	D. K. Ulrich	Chevrolet

OLD DOMINION 500

September 28
Martinsville, Virginia
Time of Race: 3 hours, 46 minutes, 7 seconds
Average Speed: 69.654 mph
Margin of Victory: 1 second

FINISH	DRIVER	CAR
1.	Dale Earnhardt	Chevrolet
2.	Buddy Baker	Chevrolet
3.	Cale Yarborough	Oldsmobile
4.	Benny Parsons	Chevrolet
5.	Dave Marcis	Chevrolet
6.	Donnie Allison	Chevrolet
7.	Terry Labonte	Chevrolet
8.	Buddy Arrington	Dodge
9.	Jody Ridley	Ford
10.	James Hylton	Chevrolet
11.	Tommy Gale	Ford
12.	Tim Richmond	Chevrolet
13.	Cecil Gordon	Oldsmobile

14.	Roger Hamby	Chevrolet
15.	Richard Petty	Chevrolet
16.	John Anderson	Buick
17.	Junior Miller	Chevrolet
18.	Ronnie Thomas	Chevrolet
19.	Neil Bonnett	Mercury
20.	Lake Speed	Chevrolet
21.	Darrell Waltrip	Chevrolet
22.	Bobby Allison	Ford
23.	Don Sprouse	Chevrolet
24.	Slick Johnson	Chevrolet
25.	Richard Childress	Chevrolet
26.	J. D. McDuffie	Chevrolet
27.	Kyle Petty	Oldsmobile
28.	Lennie Pond	Chevrolet
29.	Harry Gant	Chevrolet
30.	Jimmy Means	Chevrolet
31.	Dave Dion	Ford

NATIONAL 500

October 5
Charlotte, North Carolina
Time of Race: 3 hours, 42 minutes, 16 seconds
Average Speed: 135.243 mph
Margin of Victory: 1.5 seconds

FINISH	DRIVER	CAR
1.	Dale Earnhardt	Chevrolet
2.	Cale Yarborough	Chevrolet
3.	Buddy Baker	Buick
4.	Ricky Rudd	Chevrolet
5.	Donnie Allison	Chevrolet
6.	Bill Elliott	Mercury
7.	Lake Speed	Chevrolet
8.	Jody Ridley	Mercury
9.	Kyle Petty	Chevrolet
10.	Dick Brooks	Chevrolet
11.	Richard Childress	Chevrolet
12.	Tim Richmond	Chevrolet
13.	Buddy Arrington	Dodge
14.	Rusty Wallace	Chevrolet
15.	Kenny Hemphill	Chevrolet
16.	Harry Gant	Chevrolet
17.	Dick May	Dodge
18.	Darrell Waltrip	Chevrolet
19.	Dave Marcis	Oldsmobile
20.	J. D. McDuffie	Chevrolet
21.	James Hylton	Chevrolet
22.	Tommy Gale	Ford
23.	Connie Saylor	Chevrolet
24.	Cecil Gordon	Oldsmobile
25.	Chuck Bown	Chevrolet
26.	Junior Miller	Chevrolet
27.	Richard Petty	Chevrolet
28.	Roger Hamby	Chevrolet
29.	Bobby Allison	Mercury
30.	Neil Bonnett	Mercury
31.	Terry Labonte	Chevrolet
32.	Marty Robbins	Chevrolet
33.	Benny Parsons	Chevrolet
34.	Lenie Pond	Chevrolet
35.	John Anderson	Chevrolet
36.	Sterling Marlin	Chevrolet
37.	Rick Wilson	Chevrolet
38.	David Pearson	Chevrolet
39.	Mike Miller	Ford
40.	Slick Johnson	Chevrolet
41.	Jim Sauter	Chevrolet

AMERICAN 500

October 12
Rockingham, North Carolina
Time of Race: 4 hours, 22 minutes, 59 seconds
Average Speed: 114.159 mph
Margin of Victory: 3 car lengths

FINISH	DRIVER	CAR
1.	Cale Yarborough	Chevrolet
2.	Harry Gant	Chevrolet
3.	Darrell Waltrip	Chevrolet
4.	Terry Labonte	Chevrolet
5.	Jody Ridley	Ford
6.	Dave Marcis	Chevrolet
7.	Richard Childress	Chevrolet
8.	Slick Johnson	Chevrolet
9.	James Hylton	Chevrolet
10.	Ronnie Thomas	Chevrolet
11.	Stan Barrett	Chevrolet
12.	Buddy Arrington	Dodge
13.	Jimmy Means	Chevrolet
14.	Richard Petty	Chevrolet
15.	Cecil Gordon	Oldsmobile
16.	Dick May	Chevrolet
17.	Roger Hamby	Chevrolet
18.	Dale Earnhardt	Chevrolet
19.	Jeff McDuffie	Buick
20.	Tommy Gale	Ford
21.	J. D. McDuffie	Chevrolet
22.	Donnie Allison	Chevrolet
23.	Benny Parsons	Chevrolet
24.	Joe Millikan	Chevrolet
25.	Neil Bonnett	Mercury
26.	Bobby Allison	Ford
27.	Buddy Baker	Chevrolet
28.	Lake Speed	Chevrolet
29.	Lennie Pond	Chevrolet
30.	Ernie Cline	Chevrolet
31.	Dick Brooks	Chevrolet
32.	John Anderson	Chevrolet
33.	Junior Miller	Chevrolet
34.	Glenn Jarrett	Chevrolet
35.	Kyle Petty	Chevrolet
36.	Bill Elswick	Oldsmobile

ATLANTA JOURNAL 500

November 2
Atlanta, Georgia
Time of Race: 3 hours, 48 minutes, 19 seconds
Average Speed: 131.190 mph
Margin of Victory: 2.01 seconds

FINISH	DRIVER	CAR
1.	Cale Yarborough	Chevrolet
2.	Neil Bonnett	Mercury
3.	Dale Earnhardt	Chevrolet
4.	Buddy Baker	Buick
5.	Terry Labonte	Chevrolet
6.	Jody Ridley	Ford
7.	Lennie Pond	Chevrolet
8.	Ronnie Thomas	Chevrolet
9.	Richard Childress	Chevrolet
10.	Stan Barrett	Chevrolet
11.	Buddy Arrington	Dodge
12.	Roger Hamby	Chevrolet
13.	Steve Moore	Chevrolet
14.	James Hylton	Chevrolet
15.	Tommy Gale	Ford
16.	Charlie Chamblee	Buick
17.	J. D. McDuffie	Chevrolet
18.	Bill Elliott	Mercury
19.	Clay Young	Oldsmobile
20.	Jimmy Means	Chevrolet
21.	Richard Petty	Chevrolet
22.	Dave Marcis	Chevrolet
23.	Joe Millikan	Chevrolet
24.	Lake Speed	Chevrolet
25.	Cecil Gordon	Chevrolet
26.	Darrell Waltrip	Chevrolet
27.	Connie Saylor	Chevrolet
28.	Mike Miller	Ford
29.	Tim Richmond	Chevrolet
30.	Travis Tiller	Oldsmobile
31.	David Pearson	Oldsmobile
32.	Benny Parsons	Chevrolet
33.	John Anderson	Chevrolet

FINISH	DRIVER	CAR
34.	Blackie Wangerin	Mercury
35.	Junior Miller	Chevrolet
36.	Harry Gant	Chevrolet
37.	Donnie Allison	Chevrolet
38.	Bobby Allison	Mercury
39.	Gary Balough	Chevrolet
40.	John Callis	Ford

LOS ANGELES TIMES 500

November 15
Ontario, California
Time of Race: 3 hours, 51 minutes, 46 seconds
Average Speed: 129.441 mph
Margin of Victory: 6 seconds

FINISH	DRIVER	CAR
1.	Benny Parsons	Chevrolet
2.	Neil Bonnett	Mercury
3.	Cale Yarborough	Chevrolet
4.	Bobby Allison	Ford
5.	Dale Earnhardt	Chevrolet
6.	Lake Speed	Chevrolet
7.	Joe Millikan	Chevrolet
8.	Terry Labonte	Chevrolet
9.	John Anderson	Chevrolet
10.	Buddy Arrington	Dodge
11.	Bill Schmitt	Oldsmobile
12.	Glen Jarrett	Chevrolet
13.	Stan Barrett	Chevrolet
14.	J. D. McDuffie	Chevrolet
15.	Dave Marcis	Chevrolet
16.	Tommy Gale	Ford
17.	Cecil Gordon	Oldsmobile
18.	Jody Ridley	Ford
19.	Rick McCray	Buick
20.	Don Waterman	Oldsmobile
21.	Richard Childress	Chevrolet
22.	Henry Jones	Buick
23.	Hershel McGriff	Chevrolet
24.	James Hylton	Chevrolet
25.	Darrell Waltrip	Chevrolet
26.	Kevin Housby	Chevrolet
27.	Chuck Bown	Dodge
28.	Jim Robinson	Chevrolet
29.	Lennie Pond	Chevrolet
30.	Richard Petty	Chevrolet
31.	Jimmy Means	Chevrolet
32.	Glen Francis	Chevrolet
33.	Kyle Petty	Chevrolet
34.	Joe Booher	Dodge
35.	Glen Ward	Chevrolet
36.	Roy Smith	Oldsmobile
37.	D. K. Ulrich	Chevrolet
38.	Ronnie Thomas	Chevrolet
39.	Donnie Allison	Chevrolet
40.	Joe Ruttman	Oldsmobile
41.	Harry Gant	Chevrolet
42.	Don Puskarich	Chevrolet

1981

WINSTON WESTERN 500

January 11
Riverside, California
Time of Race: 3 hours, 16 minutes, 18 seconds
Average Speed: 95.263 mph
Margin of Victory: 173 seconds

FINISH	DRIVER	CAR
1.	Bobby Allison	Chevrolet
2.	Terry Labonte	Chevrolet

FINISH	DRIVER	CAR
3.	Dale Earnhardt	Pontiac
4.	Richard Childress	Chevrolet
5.	Richard Petty	Chevrolet
6.	Jim Robinson	Chevrolet
7.	Jody Ridley	Ford
8.	Elliott Forbes-Robinson	Buick
9.	Buddy Arrington	Dodge
10.	Don Waterman	Oldsmobile
11.	James Hylton	Chevrolet
12.	John Borneman	Chevrolet
13.	Joe Millikan	Chevrolet
14.	Don Whittington	Chevrolet
15.	Harry Gant	Chevrolet
16.	Benny Parsons	Ford
17.	Darrell Waltrip	Chevrolet
18.	Jimmy Means	Chevrolet
19.	Ricky Rudd	Chevrolet
20.	Kyle Petty	Chevrolet
21.	Bob Bondurant	Oldsmobile
22.	Bill Schmitt	Buick
23.	J. D. McDuffie	Chevrolet
24.	Steve Pfeifer	Chevrolet
25.	John Gunn	Chevrolet
26.	Rick McCray	Chevrolet
27.	Neil Bonnett	Ford
28.	Dave Marcis	Chevrolet
29.	Tim Richmond	Chevrolet
30.	Jim Insolo	Buick
31.	Roy Smith	Oldsmobile
32.	Don Puskarich	Chevrolet
33.	Hershel McGriff	Dodge
34.	Lake Speed	Chevrolet
35.	Robert Tartaglia	Chevrolet
36.	Cecil Gordon	Oldsmobile

DAYTONA 500

February 15
Daytona Beach, Florida
Time of Race: 2 hours, 56 minutes, 50 seconds
Average Speed: 169.651 mph
Margin of Victory: 3.5 seconds

FINISH	DRIVER	CAR
1.	Richard Petty	Buick
2.	Bobby Allison	Pontiac
3.	Ricky Rudd	Oldsmobile
4.	Buddy Baker	Oldsmobile
5.	Dale Earnhardt	Pontiac
6.	Bill Elliott	Ford
7.	Jody Ridley	Ford
8.	Cale Yarborough	Oldsmobile
9.	Joe Millikan	Buick
10.	Johnny Rutherford	Pontiac
11.	Bill Elswick	Oldsmobile
12.	Donnie Allison	Oldsmobile
13.	Stan Barrett	Pontiac
14.	Don Whittington	Oldsmobile
15.	Dave Marcis	Oldsmobile
16.	Dick Brooks	Buick
17.	Tommy Gale	Ford
18.	Ronnie Sanders	Buick
19.	Glenn Jarrett	Buick
20.	Don Sprouse	Oldsmobile
21.	Jimmy Means	Pontiac
22.	Geoff Bodine	Pontiac
23.	Harry Gant	Buick
24.	J. D. McDuffie	Pontiac
25.	Elliott Forbes-Robinson	Buick
26.	Buddy Arrington	Dodge
27.	Lennie Pond	Buick
28.	Ronnie Thomas	Pontiac
29.	David Pearson	Chevrolet
30.	Tim Richmond	Buick
31.	Benny Parsons	Ford
32.	Kyle Petty	Buick
33.	Neil Bonnett	Ford
34.	James Hylton	Pontiac
35.	A. J. Foyt	Oldsmobile
36.	Darrell Waltrip	Buick

37.	Cecil Gordon	Buick
38.	Richard Childress	Pontiac
39.	Bruce Hill	Buick
40.	Terry Labonte	Buick
41.	Billy Harvey	Pontiac
42.	Blackie Wangerin	Ford

RICHMOND 500

February 22
Richmond, Virginia
Time of Race: 2 hours, 49 minutes, 53 seconds
Average Speed: 76.570 mph
Margin of Victory: 5 seconds

FINISH	DRIVER	CAR
1.	Darrell Waltrip	Buick
2.	Ricky Rudd	Oldsmobile
3.	Richard Petty	Buick
4.	Morgan Shepherd	Pontiac
5.	Benny Parsons	Ford
6.	Harry Gant	Buick
7.	Dale Earnhardt	Pontiac
8.	Jody Ridley	Ford
9.	Joe Millikan	Buick
10.	J. D. McDuffie	Pontiac
11.	Lennie Pond	Buick
12.	Lake Speed	Oldsmobile
13.	Richard Childress	Pontiac
14.	Jimmy Means	Pontiac
15.	Don Sprouse	Oldsmobile
16.	Buddy Arrington	Dodge
17.	Tim Richmond	Buick
18.	Tommy Gale	Oldsmobile
19.	Cecil Gordon	Buick
20.	Henry Jones	Buick
21.	Ronnie Thomas	Pontiac
22.	Dave Marcis	Dodge
23.	Bobby Allison	Chevrolet
24.	Kyle Petty	Buick
25.	Glenn Jarrett	Chevrolet
26.	Terry Labonte	Buick
27.	Rick Newsom	Chevrolet
28.	Joe Fields	Pontiac
29.	James Hylton	Pontiac
30.	Baxter Price	Buick

CAROLINA 500

March 1
Rockingham, North Carolina
Time of Race: 4 hours, 21 minutes, 59 seconds
Average Speed: 114.594 mph
Margin of Victory: 5.5 seconds

FINISH	DRIVER	CAR
1.	Darrell Waltrip	Buick
2.	Cale Yarborough	Buick
3.	Richard Petty	Buick
4.	Neil Bonnett	Ford
5.	Buddy Baker	Oldsmobile
6.	Bobby Allison	Pontiac
7.	Joe Millikan	Chevrolet
8.	Kyle Petty	Buick
9.	Lake Speed	Buick
10.	Elliott Forbes-Robinson	Buick
11.	Ronnie Thomas	Pontiac
12.	Johnnie Rutherford	Pontiac
13.	Mike Alexander	Oldsmobile
14.	Bobby Wawak	Buick
15.	Dave Marcis	Dodge
16.	Tim Richmond	Buick
17.	Jody Ridley	Oldsmobile
18.	Harry Gant	Buick

19.	Tommy Gale	Ford
20.	James Hylton	Pontiac
21.	Terry Labonte	Buick
22.	Richard Childress	Pontiac
23.	Cecil Gordon	Buick
24.	Benny Parsons	Ford
25.	Slick Johnson	Chevrolet
26.	Dale Earnhardt	Pontiac
27.	Glenn Jarrett	Chevrolet
28.	Morgan Shepherd	Pontiac
29.	Jimmy Means	Pontiac
30.	David Pearson	Chevrolet
31.	Ricky Rudd	Oldsmobile
32.	Rick Newsom	Chevrolet
33.	J. D. McDuffie	Pontiac
34.	Donnie Allison	Oldsmobile
35.	Rick Wilson	Oldsmobile
36.	Stan Barrett	Pontiac
37.	Buddy Arrington	Dodge

COCA-COLA 500

March 15
Atlanta, Georgia
Time of Race: 3 hours, 44 minutes, 10 seconds
Average Speed: 133.619 mph
Margin of Victory: 33 seconds

FINISH	DRIVER	CAR
1.	Cale Yarborough	Buick
2.	Harry Gant	Buick
3.	Dale Earnhardt	Pontiac
4.	Bobby Allison	Pontiac
5.	Benny Parsons	Ford
6.	Jody Ridley	Ford
7.	A. J. Foyt	Oldsmobile
8.	Morgan Shepherd	Pontiac
9.	Bill Elliott	Ford
10.	Joe Ruttman	Buick
11.	J. D. McDuffie	Pontiac
12.	Johnny Rutherford	Pontiac
13.	Bill Elswick	Buick
14.	Buddy Arrington	Dodge
15.	Joe Millikan	Buick
16.	Stan Barrett	Pontiac
17.	Richard Childress	Pontiac
18.	Tommy Gale	Ford
19.	Terry Labonte	Buick
20.	Rick Newsom	Chevrolet
21.	Jimmy Means	Pontiac
22.	Ricky Rudd	Buick
23.	Bruce Hill	Buick
24.	Dick May	Oldsmobile
25.	James Hylton	Pontiac
26.	Tim Richmond	Buick
27.	Dave Marcis	Oldsmobile
28.	Neil Bonnett	Ford
29.	Donnie Allison	Oldsmobile
30.	Steve Spencer	Buick
31.	Ronnie Thomas	Pontiac
32.	David Pearson	Chevrolet
33.	Mike Alexander	Buick
34.	Slick Johnson	Chevrolet
35.	Lake Speed	Buick
36.	Darrell Waltrip	Buick
37.	Cecil Gordon	Buick
38.	Richard Petty	Buick
39.	Elliott Forbes-Robinson	Buick
40.	Buddy Baker	Oldsmobile
41.	Kyle Petty	Buick
42.	Bobby Wawak	Pontiac

VALLEYDALE 500

March 29
Bristol, Tennessee
Time of Race: 2 hours, 58 minutes, 36 seconds

Average Speed: 89.530 mph
Margin of Victory: 25 seconds

FINISH	DRIVER	CAR
1.	Darrell Waltrip	Buick
2.	Ricky Rudd	Oldsmobile
3.	Bobby Allison	Pontiac
4.	Morgan Shepherd	Pontiac
5.	Benny Parsons	Ford
6.	Jody Ridley	Ford
7.	Terry Labonte	Buick
8.	Harry Gant	Pontiac
9.	Lake Speed	Oldsmobile
10.	Tim Richmond	Buick
11.	Kyle Petty	Buick
12.	Mike Alexander	Oldsmobile
13.	Buddy Arrington	Dodge
14.	Jimmy Means	Chevrolet
15.	Tommy Gale	Ford
16.	Richard Childress	Pontiac
17.	Joe Millikan	Buick
18.	Ronnie Thomas	Pontiac
19.	D. K. Ulrich	Buick
20.	Steve Spencer	Chevrolet
21.	Cecil Gordon	Buick
22.	J. D. McDuffie	Pontiac
23.	Rick Newsom	Chevrolet
24.	Ron Bouchard	Buick
25.	Butch Lindley	Chevrolet
26.	Bruce Hill	Buick
27.	Elliott Forbes-Robinson	Oldsmobile
28.	Dale Earnhardt	Pontiac
29.	Richard Petty	Buick
30.	Ernie Cline	Pontiac
31.	Dave Marcis	Chevrolet

NORTHWESTERN BANK 400

April 5
North Wilkesboro, North Carolina
Time of Race: 2 hours, 55 minutes, 41 seconds
Average Speed: 85.381 mph
Margin of Victory: 3 seconds

FINISH	DRIVER	CAR
1.	Richard Petty	Buick
2.	Bobby Allison	Pontiac
3.	Darrell Waltrip	Buick
4.	Dave Marcis	Chevrolet
5.	Harry Gant	Oldsmobile
6.	Ricky Rudd	Buick
7.	Terry Labonte	Buick
8.	Ron Bouchard	Buick
9.	Morgan Shepherd	Pontiac
10.	Dale Earnhardt	Pontiac
11.	Mike Alexander	Oldsmobile
12.	Ronnie Thomas	Pontiac
13.	D. K. Ulrich	Buick
14.	Jimmy Means	Chevrolet
15.	James Hylton	Pontiac
16.	J. D. McDuffie	Pontiac
17.	Richard Childress	Pontiac
18.	Tim Richmond	Buick
19.	Tommy Gale	Ford
20.	Tommy Houston	Buick
21.	Benny Parsons	Ford
22.	Kyle Petty	Buick
23.	Lake Speed	Oldsmobile
24.	Butch Lindley	Chevrolet
25.	Joe Fields	Oldsmobile
26.	Joe Millikan	Chevrolet
27.	Mark Martin	Pontiac
28.	Jody Ridley	Ford
29.	Buddy Arrington	Dodge
30.	Bobby Wawak	Buick
31.	Cecil Gordon	Buick

CRC CHEMICALS REBEL 500

April 12
Darlington, South Carolina
March 1
Rockingham, North Carolina
Time of Race: 3 hours, 57 minutes, 24 seconds
Average Speed: 126.703 mph
Margin of Victory: half a car length

FINISH	DRIVER	CAR
1.	Darrell Waltrip	Buick
2.	Harry Gant	Pontiac
3.	Dave Marcis	Chevrolet
4.	Bill Elliott	Ford
5.	Benny Parsons	Ford
6.	Buddy Baker	Buick
7.	Jody Ridley	Ford
8.	David Pearson	Chevrolet
9.	Bobby Allison	Buick
10.	Joe Millikan	Buick
11.	Ricky Rudd	Buick
12.	Tim Richmond	Buick
13.	Buddy Arrington	Dodge
14.	Terry Labonte	Buick
15.	Dick Brooks	Buick
16.	J. D. McDuffie	Pontiac
17.	Dale Earnhardt	Pontiac
18.	Tommy Gale	Ford
19.	James Hylton	Pontiac
20.	Ronnie Thomas	Buick
21.	Cecil Gordon	Buick
22.	D. K. Ulrich	Buick
23.	Jimmy Means	Pontiac
24.	Bobby Wawak	Buick
25.	Kyle Petty	Buick
26.	Cale Yarborough	Buick
27.	Ron Bouchard	Buick
28.	Johnny Rutherford	Pontiac
29.	Neil Bonnett	Ford
30.	Geoff Bodine	Pontiac
31.	Richard Childress	Pontiac
32.	Slick Johnson	Chevrolet
33.	Richard Petty	Buick
34.	Morgan Shepherd	Pontiac
35.	Mike Potter	Chevrolet
36.	Mike Alexander	Buick

VIRGINIA 500

April 26
Martinsville, Virginia
Time of Race: 3 hours, 30 minutes, 10 seconds
Average Speed: 75.019 mph
Margin of Victory: 15 seconds

FINISH	DRIVER	CAR
1.	Morgan Shepherd	Pontiac
2.	Neil Bonnett	Ford
3.	Ricky Rudd	Buick
4.	Harry Gant	Oldsmobile
5.	Terry Labonte	Buick
6.	Jody Ridley	Ford
7.	Lake Speed	Oldsmobile
8.	Buddy Arrington	Dodge
9.	Ron Bouchard	Pontiac
10.	Mike Alexander	Oldsmobile
11.	Dave Marcis	Chevrolet
12.	Jimmy Means	Pontiac
13.	Bobby Allison	Pontiac
14.	Tim Richmond	Buick
15.	Kyle Petty	Buick
16.	Joe Fields	Buick
17.	James Hylton	Pontiac
18.	Tommy Gale	Buick
19.	Bobby Wawak	Buick

20.	Tommy Houston	Chevrolet
21.	Cale Yarborough	Buick
22.	Richard Childress	Pontiac
23.	Benny Parsons	Ford
24.	Cecil Gordon	Buick
25.	Dale Earnhardt	Pontiac
26.	Darrell Waltrip	Buick
27.	Butch Lindley	Chevrolet
28.	Richard Petty	Buick
29.	Joe Millikan	Buick
30.	J. D. McDuffie	Pontiac
31.	Ronnie Thomas	Pontiac

WINSTON 500

May 3
Talladega, Alabama
Time of Race: 3 hours, 20 minutes, 52 seconds
Average Speed: 149.376 mph
Margin of Victory: 1 foot

FINISH	DRIVER	CAR
1.	Bobby Allison	Buick
2.	Buddy Baker	Buick
3.	Darrell Waltrip	Buick
4.	Ricky Rudd	Oldsmobile
5.	Donnie Allison	Oldsmobile
6.	Tim Richmond	Buick
7.	Terry Labonte	Buick
8.	Dale Earnhardt	Pontiac
9.	Dick May	Dodge
10.	Bobby Wawak	Buick
11.	Tommy Gale	Ford
12.	Tommy Houston	Buick
13.	Richard Childress	Pontiac
14.	Dave Marcis	Buick
15.	Cecil Gordon	Buick
16.	Elliott Forbes-Robinson	Buick
17.	Buddy Arrington	Dodge
18.	Lake Speed	Buick
19.	James Hylton	Pontiac
20.	Ron Bouchard	Buick
21.	Mike Alexander	Buick
22.	J. D. McDuffie	Pontiac
23.	Morgan Shepherd	Pontiac
24.	Cale Yarborough	Buick
25.	Rick Wilson	Oldsmobile
26.	Ronnie Thomas	Buick
27.	Jimmy Means	Pontiac
28.	Bruce Hill	Buick
29.	Joe Ruttman	Buick
30.	Kyle Petty	Buick
31.	Jody Ridley	Ford
32.	Neil Bonnett	Ford
33.	Rick Newsom	Chevrolet
34.	Harry Gant	Pontiac
35.	Stan Barrett	Pontiac
36.	Benny Parsons	Ford
37.	Connie Saylor	Oldsmobile
38.	Joe Millikan	Oldsmobile
39.	Richard Petty	Buick
40.	Bill Elliott	Ford

MELLING TOOL 420

May 9
Nashville, Tennessee
Time of Race: 2 hours, 47 minutes, 2 seconds
Average Speed: 89.756 mph
Margin of Victory: 1 car length

FINISH	DRIVER	CAR
1.	Benny Parsons	Ford
2.	Darrell Waltrip	Buick

3.	Bobby Allison	Pontiac
4.	Richard Petty	Buick
5.	Ricky Rudd	Buick
6.	Terry Labonte	Buick
7.	Kyle Petty	Buick
8.	Morgan Shepherd	Pontiac
9.	Buddy Arrington	Dodge
10.	Dave Marcis	Chevrolet
11.	Mike Alexander	Buick
12.	Tim Richmond	Buick
13.	Richard Childress	Pontiac
14.	Jimmy Means	Chevrolet
15.	Mike Potter	Chevrolet
16.	J. D. McDuffie	Pontiac
17.	Tommy Gale	Ford
18.	Bobby Wawak	Buick
19.	Cecil Gordon	Pontiac
20.	Dale Earnhardt	Pontiac
21.	James Hylton	Pontiac
22.	Harry Gant	Oldsmobile
23.	D. K. Ulrich	Buick
24.	Lake Speed	Pontiac
25.	Jody Ridley	Ford
26.	Charley Chamblee	Pontiac
27.	Mark Martin	Pontiac

MASON-DIXON 500

May 17
Dover, Delaware
Time of Race: 4 hours, 17 minutes, 18 seconds
Average Speed: 116.595 mph
Margin of Victory: 22 seconds

FINISH	DRIVER	CAR
1.	Jody Ridley	Ford
2.	Bobby Allison	Buick
3.	Dale Earnhardt	Pontiac
4.	D. K. Ulrich	Buick
5.	Ricky Rudd	Buick
6.	Morgan Shepherd	Pontiac
7.	Buddy Arrington	Dodge
8.	Terry Labonte	Buick
9.	Jimmy Means	Pontiac
10.	Cale Yarborough	Buick
11.	Donnie Allison	Oldsmobile
12.	Darrell Waltrip	Buick
13.	Neil Bonnett	Ford
14.	Tommy Gale	Buick
15.	Cecil Gordon	Buick
16.	Harry Gant	Chevrolet
17.	Richard Childress	Pontiac
18.	James Hylton	Pontiac
19.	Richard Petty	Buick
20.	Kyle Petty	Buick
21.	Mike Alexander	Oldsmobile
22.	Joe Fields	Buick
23.	J. D. McDuffie	Pontiac
24.	Ronnie Thomas	Pontiac
25.	David Pearson	Oldsmobile
26.	Junior Miller	Oldsmobile
27.	Ron Bouchard	Buick
28.	Lowell Cowell	Chevrolet
29.	Elmo Langley	Oldsmobile
30.	Bob Riley	Buick
31.	Dave Marcis	Chevrolet
32.	Benny Parsons	Ford

WORLD 600

May 24
Charlotte, North Carolina
Time of Race: 4 hours, 38 minutes, 22 seconds
Average Speed: 129.326 mph
Margin of Victory: 9 seconds

FINISH	DRIVER	CAR
1.	Bobby Allison	Buick
2.	Harry Gant	Chevrolet
3.	Cale Yarborough	Buick
4.	Ricky Rudd	Buick
5.	Kyle Petty	Buick
6.	Morgan Shepherd	Pontiac
7.	Joe Ruttman	Buick
8.	Joe Millikan	Chevrolet
9.	Darrell Waltrip	Buick
10.	Elliott Forbes-Robinson	Buick
11.	Lennie Pond	Buick
12.	Connie Saylor	Oldsmobile
13.	J. D. McDuffie	Pontiac
14.	Terry Labonte	Buick
15.	Buddy Arrington	Dodge
16.	James Hylton	Pontiac
17.	Tommy Gale	Ford
18.	Dale Earnhardt	Pontiac
19.	Richard Childress	Pontiac
20.	Jody Ridley	Ford
21.	Bill Dennis	Buick
22.	Ronnie Thomas	Pontiac
23.	Jimmy Means	Pontiac
24.	Richard Petty	Buick
25.	Dick May	Buick
26.	Ron Bouchard	Buick
27.	Mike Alexander	Buick
28.	Lake Speed	Oldsmobile
29.	Neil Bonnett	Ford
30.	Rusty Wallace	Pontiac
31.	Bobby Wawak	Buick
32.	Stan Barrett	Pontiac
33.	Buddy Baker	Oldsmobile
34.	Jack Ingram	Ford
35.	Dave Marcis	Dodge
36.	Dick Brooks	Buick
37.	Benny Parsons	Ford
38.	Donnie Allison	Oldsmobile
39.	Chuck Bown	Buick
40.	Bill Elliott	Ford
41.	Bruce Hill	Buick
42.	Rick Wilson	Oldsmobile

BUDWEISER NASCAR 400

June 7
College Station, Texas
Time of Race: 3 hours, 1 minute, 10 seconds
Average Speed: 132.475 mph
Margin of Victory: 51 seconds

FINISH	DRIVER	CAR
1.	Benny Parsons	Ford
2.	Dale Earnhardt	Pontiac
3.	Bobby Allison	Buick
4.	Richard Petty	Buick
5.	Dave Marcis	Buick
6.	Jody Ridley	Ford
7.	Tim Richmond	Oldsmobile
8.	Lake Speed	Oldsmobile
9.	Joe Ruttman	Buick
10.	Harry Gant	Pontiac
11.	J. D. McDuffie	Pontiac
12.	Tommy Gale	Ford
13.	Buddy Arrington	Dodge
14.	Richard Childress	Pontiac
15.	H. B. Bailey	Pontiac
16.	Dick May	Buick
17.	Lowell Cowell	Oldsmobile
18.	Cecil Gordon	Buick
19.	Jimmy Means	Pontiac
20.	Ronnie Thomas	Pontiac
21.	Rick Baldwin	Buick
22.	Randy Ogden	Oldsmobile
23.	Terry Labonte	Buick
24.	Ricky Rudd	Oldsmobile
25.	James Hylton	Pontiac
26.	Bobby Wawak	Buick

FINISH	DRIVER	CAR
27.	Roger Hamby	Chevrolet
28.	Rick Newsom	Chevrolet
29.	Kyle Petty	Buick
30.	Darrell Waltrip	Buick
31.	Morgan Shepherd	Pontiac
32.	D. K. Ulrich	Buick
33.	Kirk Shelmerdine	Pontiac
34.	Baxter Price	Chevrolet

WARNER W. HODGDON 400

June 14
Riverside, California
Time of Race: 2 hours, 39 minutes, 30 seconds
Average Speed: 93.597 mph
Margin of Victory: 1 car length

FINISH	DRIVER	CAR
1.	Darrell Waltrip	Buick
2.	Dale Earnhardt	Pontiac
3.	Richard Petty	Buick
4.	Neil Bonnett	Ford
5.	Ricky Rudd	Buick
6.	Kyle Petty	Buick
7.	Jody Ridley	Ford
8.	Roy Smith	Buick
9.	Dave Marcis	Chevrolet
10.	Jim Robinson	Oldsmobile
11.	Stan Barrett	Pontiac
12.	J. D. McDuffie	Pontiac
13.	Cecil Gordon	Buick
14.	Steve Pfeifer	Chevrolet
15.	Randy Ogden	Oldsmobile
16.	Rick O'Dell	Buick
17.	Don Puskarich	Oldsmobile
18.	Richard Childress	Pontiac
19.	James Hylton	Pontiac
20.	Benny Parsons	Ford
21.	Morgan Shepherd	Pontiac
22.	Terry Labonte	Buick
23.	Don Waterman	Buick
24.	Bill Schmitt	Buick
25.	Hershel McGriff	Buick
26.	Buddy Arrington	Dodge
27.	D. K. Ulrich	Oldsmobile
28.	Jimmy Means	Pontiac
29.	Bobby Allison	Buick
30.	Tommy Gale	Buick
31.	Harry Gant	Chevrolet
32.	Jim Bown	Oldsmobile
33.	Tim Richmond	Buick
34.	Ronnie Thomas	Pontiac
35.	Elliott Forbes-Robinson	Buick
36.	Jim Insolo	Buick

GABRIEL 400

June 21
Brooklyn, Michigan
Time of Race: 3 hours, 3 minutes, 47 seconds
Average Speed: 130.589 mph
Margin of Victory: 1 car length

FINISH	DRIVER	CAR
1.	Bobby Allison	Buick
2.	Harry Gant	Pontiac
3.	Benny Parsons	Ford
4.	Jody Ridley	Ford
5.	Dale Earnhardt	Pontiac
6.	Richard Petty	Buick
7.	Darrell Waltrip	Buick
8.	Cale Yarborough	Buick
9.	Neil Bonnett	Ford
10.	Ron Bouchard	Buick

11.	Terry Labonte	Buick
12.	Buddy Arrington	Dodge
13.	Buddy Baker	Buick
14.	Tim Richmond	Oldsmobile
15.	Morgan Shepherd	Pontiac
16.	Lake Speed	Buick
17.	Johnny Rutherford	Pontiac
18.	Stan Barrett	Pontiac
19.	Richard Childress	Pontiac
20.	D. K. Ulrich	Oldsmobile
21.	Kyle Petty	Buick
22.	J. D. McDuffie	Pontiac
23.	James Hylton	Pontiac
24.	Joe Booher	Buick
25.	Ronnie Thomas	Pontiac
26.	Mike Potter	Buick
27.	Cecil Gordon	Buick
28.	Jimmy Means	Pontiac
29.	Dave Marcis	Buick
30.	Ricky Rudd	Buick
31.	Joe Millikan	Chevrolet
32.	Mike Alexander	Buick
33.	Bobby Wawak	Buick
34.	Randy Ogden	Oldsmobile
35.	Bill Elliott	Ford
36.	Tommy Gale	Ford
37.	Rick Wilson	Oldsmobile

FIRECRACKER 400

July 4
Daytona Beach, Florida
Time of Race: 2 hours, 48 minutes, 32 seconds
Average Speed: 142.588 mph
Margin of Victory: half a car length

FINISH	DRIVER	CAR
1.	Cale Yarborough	Buick
2.	Harry Gant	Buick
3.	Richard Petty	Buick
4.	Buddy Baker	Oldsmobile
5.	Johnny Rutherford	Pontiac
6.	Kyle Petty	Buick
7.	Mike Alexander	Buick
8.	Terry Labonte	Buick
9.	Ron Bouchard	Buick
10.	Darrell Waltrip	Buick
11.	Lennie Pond	Buick
12.	J. D. McDuffie	Pontiac
13.	Dave Marcis	Buick
14.	Connie Saylor	Oldsmobile
15.	Tim Richmond	Buick
16.	Bruce Hill	Buick
17.	Buddy Arrington	Dodge
18.	Jimmy Means	Pontiac
19.	Tommy Gale	Ford
20.	Morgan Shepherd	Pontiac
21.	Richard Childress	Pontiac
22.	James Hylton	Pontiac
23.	Elliott Forbes-Robinson	Buick
24.	Bill Elswick	Buick
25.	Cecil Gordon	Buick
26.	Stan Barrett	Pontiac
27.	Tommy Houston	Oldsmobile
28.	Bobby Allison	Buick
29.	Joe Ruttman	Buick
30.	Neil Bonnett	Ford
31.	Dick May	Buick
32.	A. J. Foyt	Oldsmobile
33.	Lake Speed	Buick
34.	Bill Elliott	Ford
35.	Dale Earnhardt	Pontiac
36.	Kevin Housby	Oldsmobile
37.	Jack Ingram	Ford
38.	Jody Ridley	Ford
39.	Benny Parsons	Ford
40.	Ricky Rudd	Oldsmobile
41.	Billy Harvey	Pontiac
42.	Rick Wilson	Oldsmobile

BUSCH NASHVILLE 420

July 11
Nashville, Tennessee
Time of Race: 2 hours, 46 minutes, 47 seconds
Average Speed: 90.052 mph
Margin of Victory: half a car length

FINISH	DRIVER	CAR
1.	Darrell Waltrip	Buick
2.	Bobby Allison	Buick
3.	Benny Parsons	Ford
4.	Ricky Rudd	Chevrolet
5.	Terry Labonte	Buick
6.	Kyle Petty	Buick
7.	Dale Earnhardt	Pontiac
8.	Harry Gant	Pontiac
9.	Richard Petty	Buick
10.	Jody Ridley	Ford
11.	Mark Martin	Pontiac
12.	Tim Richmond	Chevrolet
13.	Morgan Shephard	Pontiac
14.	Ronnie Thomas	Pontiac
15.	Jimmy Means	Buick
16.	James Hylton	Pontiac
17.	Richard Childress	Pontiac
18.	Steve Spencer	Buick
19.	Tommy Houston	Chevrolet
20.	J. D. McDuffie	Pontiac
21.	Tommy Gale	Ford
22.	Lake Speed	Oldsmobile
23.	D. K. Ulrich	Buick
24.	Randy Ogden	Oldsmobile
25.	Dave Marcis	Chrysler
26.	Sterling Marlin	Buick
27.	Mike Alexander	Buick
28.	Buddy Arrington	Dodge
29.	Cecil Gordon	Buick
30.	Donald Satterfield	Chevrolet

MOUNTAIN DEW 500

July 26
Pocono, Pennsylvania
Time of Race: 4 hours, 11 minutes, 52 seconds
Average Speed: 119.111 mph
Margin of Victory: 1 car length

FINISH	DRIVER	CAR
1.	Darrell Waltrip	Buick
2.	Richard Petty	Buick
3.	Benny Parsons	Ford
4.	Harry Gant	Pontiac
5.	Cale Yarborough	Buick
6.	Ricky Rudd	Chevrolet
7.	Buddy Baker	Buick
8.	Kyle Petty	Buick
9.	Tim Richmond	Oldsmobile
10.	Ron Bouchard	Buick
11.	Dale Earnhardt	Pontiac
12.	Gary Balough	Chevrolet
13.	Terry Labonte	Buick
14.	Stan Barrett	Pontiac
15.	Jody Ridley	Ford
16.	Buddy Arrington	Dodge
17.	Mike Alexander	Buick
18.	J. D. McDuffie	Pontiac
19.	Jimmy Means	Pontiac
20.	Joe Booher	Buick
21.	Cecil Gordon	Buick
22.	James Hylton	Pontiac
23.	Richard Childress	Pontiac
24.	Al Loquasto	Buick
25.	Bobby Allison	Buick
26.	Rick Newson	Chevrolet
27.	Lake Speed	Oldsmobile
28.	Lowell Cowell	Chevrolet

29.	Morgan Shepherd	Pontiac
30.	Bruce Jacobii	Buick
31.	Tommy Gale	Ford
32.	Bob Riley	Pontiac
33.	Dave Marcis	Buick]
34.	Neil Bonnett	Ford
35.	Ronnie Thomas	Pontiac

TALLADEGA 500

August 2
Talladega, Alabama
Time of Race: 3 hours, 11 minutes, 24 seconds
Average Speed: 156. 737 mph
Margin of Victory: 2 feet

FINISH	DRIVER	CAR
1.	Ron Bouchard	Buick
2.	Darrell Waltrip	Buick
3.	Terry Labonte	Buick
4.	Harry Gant	Buick
5.	Bobby Allison	Buick
6.	Lake Speed	Buick
7.	Kyle Petty	Buick
8.	Jody Ridley	Ford
9.	Stan Barrett	Pontiac
10.	Dave Marcis	Buick
11.	Bill Elliott	Ford
12.	Elliott Forbes-Robinson	Buick
13.	Benny Parsons	Ford
14.	Terry Herman	Buick
15.	Dick May	Buick
16.	Jimmy Means	Pontiac
17.	Cecil Gordon	Buick
18.	Tommy Gale	Ford
19.	Bobby Wawak	Buick
20.	Rick Wilson	Oldsmobile
21.	Rusty Wallace	Pontiac
22.	Joe Ruttman	Buick
23.	Ricky Rudd	Buick
24.	Lennie Pond	Buick
25.	Gary Balough	Buick
26.	Richard Childress	Pontiac
27.	Mike Potter	Buick
28.	Cale Yarborough	Buick
29.	Dale Earnhardt	Pontiac
30.	Bruce Hill	Buick
31.	Sandy Satullo	Buick
32.	Buddy Baker	Buick
33.	Connie Saylor	Oldsmobile
34.	Tim Richmond	Buick
35.	Mike Alexander	Buick
36.	Morgan Shepherd	Pontiac
37.	Neil Bonnett	Ford
38.	Jack Ingram	Ford
39.	James Hylton	Buick
40.	Richard Petty	Buick
41.	Buddy Arrington	Chrysler
42.	Joe Booher	Pontiac

CHAMPION SPARK PLUG 400

August 16
Brooklyn, Michigan
Time of Race: 3 hours, 14 minutes, 24 seconds
Average Speed: 123.457 mph
Margin Of Victory: 1 car length

FINISH	DRIVER	CAR
1.	Richard Petty	Buick
2.	Darrell Waltrip	Buick
3.	Ricky Rudd	Chevrolet
4.	Harry Gant	Pontiac
5.	Buddy Baker	Buick

6.	Joe Ruttman	Pontiac
7.	Bobby Allison	Buick
8.	Bill Elliott	Ford
9.	Dale Earnhardt	Pontiac
10.	Mike Alexander	Buick
11.	Dave Marcis	Buick
12.	Jody Ridley	Ford
13.	Johnny Rutherford	Pontiac
14.	Terry Labonte	Buick
15.	Lake Speed	Buick
16.	J. D. McDuffie	Pontiac
17.	Cale Yarborough	Buick
18.	Gary Balough	Buick
19.	Kyle Petty	Buick
20.	Rick Knoop	Buick
21.	Tommy Gale	Ford
22.	Joe Booher	Buick
23.	Joe Millikan	Pontiac
24.	Cecil Gordon	Buick
25.	Jimmy Means	Pontiac
26.	Benny Parsons	Ford
27.	James Hylton	Pontiac
28.	Neil Bonnett	Ford
29.	Ron Bouchard	Buick
30.	Tim Richmond	Buick
31.	Bobby Wawak	Buick
32.	Bob Schacht	Oldsmobile
33.	Bruce Hill	Buick
34.	Morgan Shepherd	Buick
35.	Buddy Arrington	Dodge
36.	Dick May	Buick

BUSCH 500

August 22
Bristol, Tennessee
Time of Race: 3 hours, 8 minutes, 44 seconds
Average Speed: 84.723 mph
Margin of Victory: 1 lap (finished under caution)

FINISH	DRIVER	CAR
1.	Darrell Waltrip	Buick
2.	Ricky Rudd	Chevrolet
3.	Terry Labonte	Buick
4.	Bobby Allison	Buick
5.	Ron Bouchard	Buick
6.	Benny Parsons	Ford
7.	Lake Speed	Oldsmobile
8.	Tim Richmond	Oldsmobile
9.	Dave Marcis	Buick
10.	Buddy Arrington	Dodge
11.	Harry Gant	Pontiac
12.	Jimmy Means	Pontiac
13.	J. D. McDuffie	Pontiac
14.	Lennie Pond	Buick
15.	James Hylton	Pontiac
16.	Joe Millikan	Pontiac
17.	Ronnie Thomas	Pontiac
18.	Morgan Shepherd	Buick
19.	Jody Ridley	Ford
20.	Joe Ruttman	Pontiac
21.	Rick Newsom	Chevrolet
22.	Elliott Forbes-Robinson	Buick
23.	Richard Petty	Buick
24.	Mike Alexander	Buick
25.	Mike Potter	Chevrolet
26.	Dale Earnhardt	Pontiac
27.	Kyle Petty	Buick
28.	Joel Stowe	Pontiac
29.	Cecil Gordon	Buick

SOUTHERN 500

September 7
Darlington, South Carolina
Time of Race: 3 hours, 57 minutes, 57 seconds

Average Speed: 126.410 mph
Margin of Victory: 1 car length

FINISH	DRIVER	CAR
1.	Neil Bonnett	Ford
2.	Darrell Waltrip	Buick
3.	Dave Marcis	Buick
4.	Terry Labonte	Buick
5.	Buddy Baker	Buick
6.	Dale Earnhardt	Pontiac
7.	Bill Elliott	Ford
8.	David Pearson	Buick
9.	Bobby Allison	Chevrolet
10.	Cale Yarborough	Buick
11.	Ron Bouchard	Buick
12.	Jody Ridley	Ford
13.	Lake Speed	Buick
14.	Harry Gant	Pontiac
15.	Joe Ruttman	Pontiac
16.	Morgan Shepherd	Buick
17.	Lennie Pond	Buick
18.	Joe Millikan	Pontiac
19.	Dick May	Dodge
20.	Mike Alexander	Oldsmobile
21.	J. D. McDuffie	Pontiac
22.	Tim Richmond	Buick
23.	Ricky Rudd	Chevrolet
24.	Bobby Wawak	Buick
25.	Gary Balough`	Buick
26.	James Hylton	Pontiac
27.	Ronnie Thomas	Pontiac
28.	Mike Potter	Buick
29.	Tommy Gale	Ford
30.	Richard Petty	Buick
31.	D. K. Ulrich	Buick
32.	Jack Ingram	Ford
33.	Johnny Rutherford	Pontiac
34.	Kyle Petty	Buick
35.	Slick Johnson	Buick
36.	H. B. Bailey	Pontiac
37.	Buddy Arrington	Dodge
38.	Jimmy Means	Pontiac
39.	Benny Parsons	Ford
40.	Connie Saylor	Oldsmobile

WRANGLER SANFORSET 400

September 13
Richmond, Virginia
Time of Race: 3 hours, 5 minutes, 50 seconds
Average Speed: 69.998 mph
Margin of Victory: 1 car length

FINISH	DRIVER	CAR
1.	Benny Parsons	Ford
2.	Harry Gant	Pontiac
3.	Darrell Waltrip	Buick
4.	Terry Labonte	Buick
5.	Bobby Allison	Buick
6.	Dale Earnhardt	Pontiac
7.	Mark Martin	Pontiac
8.	Joe Millikan	Pontiac
9.	Jody Ridley	Ford
10.	Gary Balough	Buick
11.	Richard Petty	Buick
12.	Ricky Rudd	Chevrolet
13.	Buddy Arrington	Dodge
14.	Tim Richmond	Buick
15.	Joe Fields	Buick
16.	Jimmy Means	Pontiac
17.	Tommy Gale	Ford
18.	James Hylton	Pontiac
19.	Dave Marcis	Chevrolet
20.	Lake Speed	Oldsmobile
21.	D. K. Ulrich	Buick
22.	Kyle Petty	Buick
23.	Cecil Gordon	Buick
24.	Ronnie Thomas	Chevrolet

25.	Ron Bouchard	Buick
26.	Tommy Ellis	Chevrolet
27.	Lennie Pond	Buick
28.	Dave Dion	Ford
29.	Morgan Shepherd	Buick
30.	Joe Ruttman	Pontiac
31.	Johnny Rutherford	Pontiac
32.	Mike Alexander	Buick

CRC CHEMICALS 500

September 20
Dover, Delaware
Time of Race: 4 hours, 10 minutes, 55 seconds
Average Speed: 119.561 mph
Margin of Victory: 1 lap, 15 seconds

FINISH	DRIVER	CAR
1.	Neil Bonnett	Ford
2.	Darrell Waltrip	Buick
3.	Bobby Allison	Buick
4.	Ron Bouchard	Buick
5.	Ricky Rudd	Chevrolet
6.	Joe Ruttman	Pontiac
7.	Kyle Petty	Buick
8.	Dave Marcis	Chevrolet
9.	Tim Richmond	Buick
10.	Richard Petty	Buick
11.	Jody Ridley	Ford
12.	Morgan Shepherd	Buick
13.	Cale Yarborough	Buick
14.	Buddy Arrington	Dodge
15.	Dale Earnhardt	Pontiac
16.	Lennie Pond	Buick
17.	Gary Balough	Buick
18.	D. K. Ulrich	Buick
19.	Jimmy Means	Pontiac
20.	Ronnie Thomas	Pontiac
21.	Joe Millikan	Pontiac
22.	Lowell Cowell	Chevrolet
23.	Harry Gant	Pontiac
24.	Tommy Gale	Ford
25.	Dick May	Buick
26.	Cecil Gordon	Chevrolet
27.	Lake Speed	Buick
28.	J. D. McDuffie	Pontiac
29.	Terry Labonte	Buick
30.	Robert Schacht	Oldsmobile
31.	Jocko Maggiacomo	Oldsmobile
32.	James Hylton	Pontiac
33.	Bob Riley	Pontiac
34.	Benny Parsons	Ford

OLD DOMINION 500

September 27
Martinsville, Virginia
Time of Race: 3 hours, 44 minutes, 57 seconds
Average Speed: 70.089 mph
Margin of Victory: 9 seconds

FINISH	DRIVER	CAR
1.	Darrell Waltrip	Buick
2.	Harry Gant	Pontiac
3.	Mark Martin	Pontiac
4.	Neil Bonnett	Ford
5.	Joe Millikan	Pontiac
6.	Ron Bouchard	Buick
7.	Jimmy Hensley	Buick
8.	Ricky Rudd	Chevrolet
9.	Terry Labonte	Buick
10.	Bobby Allison	Buick
11.	Buddy Arrington	Dodge
12.	Tommy Houston	Chevrolet

13.	Tommy Gale	Ford
14.	Dave Marcis	Chevrolet
15.	Jimmy Means	Pontiac
16.	Bob McElwee	Buick
17.	Joe Ruttman	Buick
18.	Richard Petty	Buick
19.	Kyle Petty	Buick
20.	Tim Richmond	Buick
21.	Jody Ridley	Ford
22.	Lake Speed	Buick
23.	Geoff Bodine	Buick
24.	Benny Parsons	Ford
25.	Lennie Pond	Buick
26.	Dale Earnhardt	Pontiac
27.	Ronnie Thomas	Pontiac
28.	Morgan Shepherd	Pontiac
29.	Buddy Baker	Buick
30.	Tommy Ellis	Chevrolet

HOLLY FARMS 400

October 4
North Wilkesboro, North Carolina
Time of Race: 2 hours, 41 minutes, 8 seconds
Average Speed: 93.091 mph
Margin of Victory: 1 lap, 10 seconds

FINISH	DRIVER	CAR
1.	Darrell Waltrip	Buick
2.	Bobby Allison	Buick
3.	Joe Millikan	Pontiac
4.	Dale Earnhardt	Pontiac
5.	Ron Bouchard	Buick
6.	Morgan Shepherd	Buick
7.	Jody Ridley	Ford
8.	Bob McElwee	Buick
9.	Jimmy Means	Chevrolet
10.	Buddy Arrington	Dodge
11.	Tommy Houston	Oldsmobile
12.	J. D. McDuffie	Pontiac
13.	Tim Richmond	Buick
14.	Tommy Gale	Ford
15.	James Hylton	Pontiac
16.	Dave Marcis	Chevrolet
17.	Ronnie Thomas	Pontiac
18.	Kyle Petty	Buick
19.	Cecil Gordon	Buick
20.	Junior Miller	Oldsmobile
21.	Richard Petty	Buick
22.	Rick Newsom	Chevrolet
23.	Lennie Pond	Buick
24.	Harry Gant	Pontiac
25.	Ricky Rudd	Chevrolet
26.	Joe Ruttman	Pontiac
27.	Lake Speed	Oldsmobile
28.	Dean Combs	Buick
29.	Benny Parsons	Ford
30.	Terry Labonte	Buick

NATIONAL 500

October 11
Charlotte, North Carolina
Time of Race: 4 hours, 15 minutes, 52 seconds
Average Speed: 117.483 mph
Margin of Victory: 32 seconds

FINISH	DRIVER	CAR
1.	Darrell Waltrip	Buick
2.	Bobby Allison	Chevrolet
3.	Ricky Rudd	Chevrolet
4.	Tommy Ellis	Chevrolet
5.	Ron Bouchard	Buick
6.	Rusty Wallace	Buick

7.	Geoff Bodine	Buick
8.	Morgan Shepherd	Buick
9.	Jack Ingram	Ford
10.	Buddy Arrington	Dodge
11.	Connie Saylor	Oldsmobile
12.	Jimmy Means	Dodge
13.	Rick Wilson	Oldsmobile
14.	D. K. Ulrich	Buick
15.	Jody Ridley	Ford
16.	H. B. Bailey	Pontiac
17.	J. D. McDuffie	Pontiac
18.	Tim Richmond	Buick
19.	Joe Ruttman	Buick
20.	Kyle Petty	Buick
21.	Bob Senneker	Pontiac
22.	Tommy Gale	Ford
23.	Terry Labonte	Buick
24.	Gary Balough	Buick
25.	Dale Earnhardt	Pontiac
26.	Charlie Glotzbach	Buick
27.	Johnny Rutherford	Buick
28.	Sterlin Marlin	Chevrolet
29.	Neil Bonnett	Ford
30.	Richard Petty	Buick
31.	Cale Yarborough	Buick
32.	Ronnie Thomas	Buick
33.	Bill Elliott	Ford
34.	Lake Speed	Buick
35.	Joe Millikan	Pontiac
36.	Bobby Wawak	Buick
37.	Buddy Baker	Buick
38.	Benny Parsons	Ford
39.	John Anderson	Buick
40.	Dave Marcis	Buick
41.	Harry Gant	Pontiac

AMERICAN 500

November 1
Rockingham, North Carolina
Time of Race: 4 hours, 39 minutes, 32 seconds
Average Speed: 107.399 mph
Margin of Victory: half car length

FINISH	DRIVER	CAR
1.	Darrell Waltrip	Buick
2.	Bobby Allison	Buick
3.	Harry Gant	Pontiac
4.	Richard Petty	Buick
5.	Joe Ruttman	Pontiac
6.	Benny Parsons	Ford
7.	Terry Labonte	Buick
8.	Bill Elliott	Ford
9.	Dale Earnhardt	Pontiac
10.	Jody Ridley	Ford
11.	Ron Bouchard	Buick
12.	Dave Marcis	Chevrolet
13.	Tommy Gale	Ford
14.	Buddy Arrington	Dodge
15.	Cecil Gordon	Buick
16.	Buddy Baker	Buick
17.	D. K. Ulrich	Buick
18.	Ricky Rudd	Chevrolet
19.	Joe Millikan	Pontiac
20.	Jimmy Means	Pontiac
21.	Dick Brooks	Ford
22.	Tim Richmond	Buick
23.	Joe Fields	Buick
24.	John Anderson	Buick
25.	Cale Yarborough	Buick
26.	James Hylton	Pontiac
27.	Morgan Shepherd	Buick
28.	Chuck Bown	Buick
29.	Johnny Rutherford	Buick
30.	J. D. McDuffie	Pontiac
31.	Lake Speed	Oldsmobile
32.	Gary Balough`	Buick
33.	Don Hume	Buick
34.	Dean Combs	Buick
35.	Neil Bonnett	Ford

| 36. | Lennie Pond | Buick |
| 37. | Kyle Petty | Buick |

ATLANTA JOURNAL 500

November 8
Atlanta, Georgia
Time of Race: 3 hours, 49 minutes, 43 seconds
Average Speed: 130.391 mph
Margin of Victory: half car length

FINISH	DRIVER	CAR
1.	Neil Bonnett	Ford
2.	Darrell Waltrip	Buick
3.	Cale Yarborough	Buick
4.	Bobby Allison	Buick
5.	Jody Ridley	Ford
6.	Bill Elliott	Ford
7.	Terry Labonte	Buick
8.	Kyle Petty	Buick
9.	Buddy Baker	Buick
10.	Joe Millikan	Pontiac
11.	Rick Wilson	Oldsmobile
12.	Connie Saylor	Oldsmobile
13.	Dick Brooks	Ford
14.	Lake Speed	Buick
15.	Chuck Bown	Buick
16.	John Anderson	Buick
17.	Buddy Arrington	Dodge
18.	Delma Cowart	Buick
19.	James Hylton	Buick
20.	Harry Gant	Pontiac
21.	Tim Richmond	Buick
22.	Tommy Gale	Ford
23.	J. D. McDuffie	Pontiac
24.	Dale Earnhardt	Pontiac
25.	Joe Ruttman	Buick
26.	Richard Petty	Buick
27.	D. K. Ulrich	Buick
28.	Dave Marcis	Buick
29.	Rusty Wallace	Buick
30.	Geoff Bodine	Buick
31.	Morgan Shepherd	Buick
32.	Travis Tiller	Chevrolet
33.	Tommy Ellis	Chevrolet
34.	Gary Balough	Buick
35.	Jimmy Means	Pontiac
36.	Benny Parsons	Ford
37.	Johnny Rutherford	Buick
38.	Ricky Rudd	Buick
40.	H. B. Bailey	Pontiac

WINSTON WESTERN 500

November 22
Riverside, California
Time of Race: 3 hours, 16 minutes, 19 seconds
Average Speed: 95.288 mph
Margin of Victory: 2 car lengths

FINISH	DRIVER	CAR
1.	Bobby Allison	Buick
2.	Joe Ruttman	Buick
3.	Terry Labonte	Buick
4.	Dale Earnhardt	Pontiac
5.	Joe Millikan	Pontiac
6.	Darrell Waltrip	Buick
7.	Richard Petty	Buick
8.	Harry Gant	Pontiac
9.	Jody Ridley	Ford
10.	Ron Bouchard	Buick
11.	J. D. McDuffie	Pontiac
12.	Gary Kershaw	Buick
13.	Morgan Shepherd	Buick

14.	Bill Schmitt	Buick
15.	Don Waterman	Buick
16.	Lake Speed	Buick
17.	James Hylton	Buick
18.	Bob Bondurant	Pontiac
19.	Gary Balough	Buick
20.	Tim Richmond	Buick
21.	Don Puskarich	Oldsmobile
22.	Gene Thonesen	Buick
23.	Mark Stahl	Ford
24.	Buddy Arrington	Dodge
25.	Dave Marcis	Pontiac
26.	Tommy Gale	Dodge
27.	Benny Parsons	Ford
28.	Chuck Pittenger	Buick
29.	Scott Miller	Pontiac
30.	Roy Smith	Buick
31.	Terry Herman	Buick
32.	Jim Robinson	Oldsmobile
33.	Neil Bonnett	Ford
34.	Pat Mintey	Chevrolet
35.	Don Whittington	Oldsmobile
36.	Jim Bown	Buick
37.	Kyle Petty	Buick
38.	Hershel McGriff	Buick
39.	Richard Childress	Buick
40.	Ricky Rudd	Buick

1982

DAYTONA 500

February 14
Daytona Beach, Florida
Time of Race: 3 hours, 14 minutes, 49 seconds
Average Speed: 153.991 mph
Margin of Victory: 23 seconds

FINISH	DRIVER	CAR
1.	Bobby Allison	Buick
2.	Cale Yarborough	Buick
3.	Joe Ruttman	Buick
4.	Terry Labonte	Buick
5.	Bill Elliott	Ford
6.	Ron Bouchard	Buick
7.	Harry Gant	Buick
8.	Buddy Baker	Buick
9.	Jody Ridley	Ford
10.	Roy Smith	Pontiac
11.	Gary Balough	Pontiac
12.	James Sauter	Buick
13.	J. D. McDuffie	Pontiac
14.	Lowell Cowell	Buick
15.	Buddy Arrington	Dodge
16.	Tommy Gale	Ford
17.	Jimmy Means	Buick
18.	Rick Wilson	Oldsmobile
19.	Morgan Shepherd	Buick
20.	Darrell Waltrip	Buick
21.	A. J. Foyt	Oldsmobile
22.	Tom Sneva	Buick
23.	Kyle Petty	Pontiac
24.	Dave Marcis	Buick
25.	Neil Bonnett	Ford
26.	Benny Parsons	Pontiac
27.	Richard Petty	Pontiac
28.	Elliott Forbes-Robinson	Buick
29.	Tighe Scott	Buick
30.	Mark Martin	Buick
31.	Stan Barrett	Buick
32.	Bobby Wawak	Buick
33.	Delma Cowart	Buick
34.	Donnie Allison	Buick
35.	Ricky Rudd	Pontiac
36.	Dale Earnhardt	Ford
37.	Rusty Wallace	Buick
38.	Dick Brooks	Ford

39.	Billie Harvey	Buick
40.	Joe Millikan	Pontiac
41.	Lake Speed	Buick
42.	Geoff Bodine	Buick

RICHMOND 400

February 21
Richmond, Virginia
Time of Race: 1 hour, 51 minutes, 30 seconds
Average Speed: 72.914 mph
Margin of Victory: 12 seconds

FINISH	DRIVER	CAR
1.	Dave Marcis	Chevrolet
2.	Richard Petty	Pontiac
3.	Benny Parson	Pontiac
4.	Dale Earnhardt	Ford
5.	Terry Labonte	Chevrolet
6.	Joe Millikan	Pontiac
7.	Neil Bonnett	Ford
8.	Bobby Allison	Chevrolet
9.	Ron Bouchard	Buick
10.	Morgan Shepherd	Buick
11.	Tommy Ellis	Chevrolet
12.	Bill Elliott	Ford
13.	Jody Ridley	Ford
14.	Buddy Arrington	Dodge
15.	Joe Ruttman	Buick
16.	Bob Schacht	Oldsmobile
17.	Slick Johnson	Pontiac
18.	Jimmy Means	Chevrolet
19.	Lake Speed	Buick
20.	Kyle Petty	Pontiac
21.	Tommy Gale	Ford
22.	Ricky Rudd	Pontiac
23.	J. D. McDuffie	Pontiac
24.	Lennie Pond	Buick
25.	Tommy Houston	Buick
26.	Mark Martin	Pontiac
27.	Darrell Waltrip	Buick
28.	Joe Fields	Buick
29.	D. K. Ulrich	Buick
30.	Harry Gant	Buick
31.	Tom Sneva	Buick
32.	Gary Balough	Buick

VALLEYDALE 500

March 14
Bristol, Tennessee
Time of Race: 2 hours, 49 minutes, 52 seconds
Average Speed: 94.025 mph
Margin of Victory: 13 seconds

FINISH	DRIVER	CAR
1.	Darrell Waltrip	Buick
2.	Dale Earnhardt	Ford
3.	Morgan Shepherd	Buick
4.	Terry Labonte	Chevrolet
5.	Bobby Allison	Chevrolet
6.	Harry Gant	Buick
7.	Richard Petty	Pontiac
8.	Ron Bouchard	Buick
9.	Benny Parsons	Pontiac
10.	Dave Marcis	Chevrolet
11.	Kyle Petty	Pontiac
12.	Brad Teague	Chevrolet
13.	Joe Millikan	Pontiac
14.	Mark Martin	Pontiac
15.	Buddy Arrington	Dodge
16.	Jimmy Means	Pontiac
17.	Tommy Gale	Ford
18.	Joe Ruttman	Buick

19.	J. D. McDuffie	Pontiac
20.	Jody Ridley	Ford
21.	Slick Johnson	Pontiac
22.	Neil Bonnett	Buick
23.	Gary Balough	Buick
24.	John McFadden	Buick
25.	Ronnie Thomas	Pontiac
26.	D. K. Ulrich	Buick
27.	Ricky Rudd	Pontiac
28.	Dick Brooks	Ford
29.	Lake Speed	Buick
30.	Dick May	Buick

COCA-COLA 500

March 21
Atlanta, Georgia
Time of Race: 3 hours, 29 minutes, 58 seconds
Average Speed: 124.824 mph
Margin of Victory: 2 inches

FINISH	DRIVER	CAR
1.	Darrell Waltrip	Buick
2.	Richard Petty	Pontiac
3.	Cale Yarborough	Buick
4.	Benny Parsons	Pontiac
5.	Harry Gant	Buick
6.	Morgan Shepherd	Buick
7.	Gary Balough	Buick
8.	Terry Labonte	Buick
9.	Rick Wilson	Oldsmobile
10.	Jim Sauter	Buick
11.	Donnie Allison	Buick
12.	Dave Marcis	Buick
13.	Brad Teague	Chevrolet
14.	Buddy Arrington	Dodge
15.	Tom Sneva	Buick
16.	Jimmy Means	Buick
17.	Jody Ridley	Ford
18.	Steve Moore	Pontiac
19.	Mark Martin	Buick
20.	Dick May	Pontiac
21.	Bill Elliott	Ford
22.	Bobby Allison	Buick
23.	Delma Cowart	Buick
24.	Joe Millikan	Pontiac
25.	Ricky Rudd	Pontiac
26.	Kyle Petty	Pontiac
27.	Neil Bonnett	Ford
28.	Dale Earnhardt	Ford
29.	Joe Ruttman	Buick
30.	Buddy Baker	Buick
31.	Connie Saylor	Oldsmobile
32.	D. K. Ulrich	Buick
33.	Lake Speed	Buick
34.	Dick Brooks	Ford
35.	Rusty Wallace	Buick
36.	Ron Bouchard	Buick
37.	Tommy Gale	Ford
38.	J. D. McDuffie	Pontiac
39.	A. J. Foyt	Oldsmobile
40.	Elliott Forbes-Robinson	Buick

WARNER W. HODGDON CAROLINA 500

March 28
Darlington, South Carolina
Time of Race: 4 hours, 35 minutes, 27 seconds
Average Speed: 108.992 mph
Margin of Victory: 1 lap, 1 car length

FINISH	DRIVER	CAR
1.	Cale Yarborough	Buick
2.	Terry Labonte	Chevrolet

FINISH	DRIVER	CAR
3.	Benny Parsons	Pontiac
4.	Bobby Allison	Chevrolet
5.	Morgan Shepherd	Buick
6.	Joe Millikan	Pontiac
7.	Darrell Waltrip	Buick
8.	Harry Gant	Buick
9.	Buddy Arrington	Dodge
10.	J. D. McDuffie	Pontiac
11.	Tommy Gale	Ford
12.	Gary Balough	Buick
13.	Dick May	Buick
14.	Buddy Baker	Buick
15.	Ricky Rudd	Pontiac
16.	Ron Bouchard	Buick
17.	Jimmy Means	Pontiac
18.	Slick Johnson	Buick
19.	Neil Bonnett	Ford
20.	Ronnie Thomas	Pontiac
21.	Dave Marcis	Chevrolet
22.	Donnie Allison	Buick
23.	Bill Elliott	Ford
24.	Joe Ruttman	Buick
25.	Dale Earnhardt	Ford
26.	D. K. Ulrich	Buick
27.	Kyle Petty	Pontiac
28.	Bobby Wawak	Buick
29.	Ernie Cline	Pontiac
30.	Richard Petty	Pontiac
31.	Tim Richmond	Ford
32.	Mark Martin	Buick
33.	Jody Ridley	Ford
34.	Lake Speed	Buick

CRC CHEMICALS REBEL 500

April 4
Darlington, South Carolina
Time of Race: 4 hours, 3 minutes, 27 seconds
Average Speed: 123.554 mph
Margin of Victory: 1 car length

FINISH	DRIVER	CAR
1.	Dale Earnhardt	Ford
2.	Cale Yarborough	Buick
3.	Bill Elliott	Ford
4.	Benny Parsons	Pontiac
5.	Tim Richmond	Buick
6.	Terry Labonte	Buick
7.	Mark Martin	Buick
8.	Buddy Arrington	Dodge
9.	Donnie Allison	Buick
10.	Lennie Pond	Buick
11.	Jimmy Means	Buick
12.	Tommy Gale	Ford
13.	Ronnie Thomas	Pontiac
14.	Rick Newsom	Chevrolet
15.	D. K. Ulrich	Buick
16.	Joe Millikan	Pontiac
17.	Lake Speed	Buick
18.	Kyle Petty	Pontiac
19.	Harry Gant	Buick
20.	Dick May	Buick
21.	Bobby Wawak	Chevrolet
22.	Jody Ridley	Ford
23.	Darrell Waltrip	Buick
24.	Neil Bonnett	Ford
25.	Bobby Allison	Chevrolet
26.	Slick Johnson	Buick
27.	Dave Marcis	Buick
28.	John Anderson	Buick
29.	Ricky Rudd	Pontiac
30.	Morgan Shepherd	Buick
31.	Richard Petty	Pontiac
32.	Dick Brooks	Ford
33.	James Sauter	Buick
34.	Ron Bouchard	Buick
35.	H. B. Bailey	Pontiac
36.	J. D. McDuffie	Pontiac
37.	Buddy Baker	Buick

NORTHWESTERN BANK 400

April 18
North Wilkesboro, North Carolina
Time of Race: 2 hours, 33 minutes, 37 seconds
Average Speed: 97.646 mph
Margin of Victory: 1 car length

FINISH	DRIVER	CAR
1.	Darrell Waltrip	Buick
2.	Terry Labonte	Chevrolet
3.	Dale Earnhardt	Ford
4.	Benny Parsons	Pontiac
5.	Richard Petty	Pontiac
6.	Harry Gant	Buick
7.	Morgan Shepherd	Buick
8.	Bobby Allison	Chevrolet
9.	Ricky Rudd	Pontiac
10.	Neil Bonnett	Buick
11.	Tim Richmond	Buick
12.	Joe Ruttman	Buick
13.	Ron Bouchard	Buick
14.	Kyle Petty	Pontiac
15.	Geoff Bodine	Pontiac
16.	Buddy Arrington	Dodge
17.	Jody Ridley	Ford
18.	Jimmy Means	Buick
19.	D. K. Ulrich	Buick
20.	J. D. McDuffie	Pontiac
21.	Bobby Hillin Jr.	Buick
22.	Brad Teague	Chevrolet
23.	Ronnie Thomas	Pontiac
24.	Lake Speed	Buick
25.	Mark Martin	Pontiac
26.	Lennie Pond	Buick
27.	Bob Schacht	Oldsmobile
28.	Butch Lindley	Buick
29.	Dave Marcis	Chevrolet
30.	Slick Johnson	Pontiac
31.	D. K. Ulrich	

VIRGINIA NATIONAL BANK 500

April 25
Martinsville, Virginia
Time of Race: 3 hours, 30 minutes, 1 second
Average Speed: 75.073 mph
Margin of Victory: 1 lap, 1 second

FINISH	DRIVER	CAR
1.	Harry Gant	Buick
2.	Butch Lindley	Buick
3.	Neil Bonnett	Ford
4.	Ricky Rudd	Pontiac
5.	Darrell Waltrip	Buick
6.	Dave Marcis	Chevrolet
7.	Mark Martin	Pontiac
8.	Buddy Arrington	Dodge
9.	Jimmy Hensley	Buick
10.	Slick Johnson	Pontiac
11.	Brad Teague	Chevrolet
12.	Jody Ridley	Ford
13.	Jimmy Means	Buick
14.	Joe Ruttman	Buick
15.	Richard Petty	Pontiac
16.	J. D. McDuffie	Pontiac
17.	Bobby Allison	Chevrolet
18.	Tim Richmond	Buick
19.	Ron Bouchard	Buick
20.	Terry Labonte	Chevrolet
21.	Bob Schacht	Oldsmobile
22.	Lennie Pond	Buick
23.	Dale Earnhardt	Ford
24.	Lake Speed	Buick
25.	Geoff Bodine	Pontiac
26.	Morgan Shepherd	Buick
27.	Kyle Petty	Pontiac

FINISH	DRIVER	CAR
28.	Buddy Baker	Buick
29.	Benny Parsons	Pontiac
30.	Donnie Allison	Buick
31.	D. K. Ulrich	Buick

WINSTON 500

May 2
Talladega, Alabama
Time of Race: 3 hours, 11 minutes, 19 seconds
Average Speed: 156.697 mph
Margin of Victory: 1 car length

FINISH	DRIVER	CAR
1.	Darrell Waltrip	Buick
2.	Terry Labonte	Buick
3.	Benny Parsons	Pontiac
4.	Kyle Petty	Pontiac
5.	Morgan Shepherd	Buick
6.	Donnie Allison	Buick
7.	Tim Richmond	Buick
8.	Dale Earnhardt	Ford
9.	Jimmy Means	Buick
10.	Mark Martin	Buick
11.	Buddy Arrington	Dodge
12.	Slick Johnson	Buick
13.	Bobby Allison	Buick
14.	Harry Gant	Buick
15.	D. K. Ulrich	Buick
16.	Tommy Gale	Ford
17.	Philip Duffie	Buick
18.	J. D. McDuffie	Pontiac
19.	Neil Bonnett	Ford
20.	John Anderson	Buick
21.	Lowell Cowell	Buick
22.	Joe Ruttman	Pontiac
23.	Ferrell Harris	Buick
24.	Ricky Rudd	Pontiac
25.	Buddy Baker	Buick
26.	Bill Elliott	Ford
27.	Richard Petty	Pontiac
28.	Bill Scott	Buick
29.	Elliott Forbes-Robinson	Buick
30.	Dave Marcis	Buick
31.	Lennie Pond	Buick
32.	Rick Wilson	Oldsmobile
33.	Geoff Bodine	Pontiac
34.	Lake Speed	Buick
35.	Steve Moore	Pontiac
36.	Ron Bouchard	Buick
37.	Cale Yarborough	Buick
38.	Jody Ridley	Ford
39.	L. W. Wright	Chevrolet
40.	David Simko	Pontiac

CRACKER BARREL 420

May 8
Nashville, Tennessee
Time of Race: 2 hours, 59 minutes, 52 seconds
Average Speed: 83.502 mph
Margin of Victory: one lap, three seconds

FINISH	DRIVER	CAR
1.	Darrell Waltrip	Buick
2.	Terry Labonte	Chevrolet
3.	Ron Bouchard	Buick
4.	Joe Ruttman	Buick
5.	Neil Bonnett	Buick
6.	Bobby Allison	Chevrolet
7.	Tim Richmond	Buick
8.	Dave Marcis	Chevrolet
9.	Richard Petty	Pontiac
10.	Dale Earnhardt	Ford

FINISH	DRIVER	CAR
11.	Bill Elliott	Ford
12.	Mark Martin	Buick
13.	Jody Ridley	Ford
14.	Buddy Arrington	Dodge
15.	Morgan Shepherd	Buick
16.	Tommy Gale	Ford
17.	James Hylton	Pontiac
18.	J. D. McDuffie	Pontiac
19.	Ricky Rudd	Pontiac
20.	Brad Teague	Chevrolet
21.	Geoff Bodine	Pontiac
22.	Benny Parsons	Pontiac
23.	Jimmy Means	Buick
24.	Ronnie Thomas	Pontiac
25.	Slick Johnson	Buick
26.	D. K. Ulrich	Buick
27.	Kyle Petty	Pontiac
28.	Bob Jarvis	Buick
29.	Harry Gant	Buick
30.	Lake Speed	Pontiac

MASON-DIXON 500

May 16
Dover, Delaware
Time of Race: 4 hours, 9 minutes, 43 seconds
Average Speed: 120.136 mph
Margin of Victory: 3 laps, 6 seconds

FINISH	DRIVER	CAR
1.	Bobby Allison	Chevrolet
2.	Dave Marcis	Chevrolet
3.	Dale Earnhardt	Ford
4.	Terry Labonte	Chevrolet
5.	Mark Martin	Buick
6.	Ron Bouchard	Buick
7.	Morgan Shepherd	Buick
8.	Donnie Allison	Buick
9.	Tim Richmond	Buick
10.	Lake Speed	Pontiac
11.	Buddy Arrington	Dodge
12.	James Hylton	Pontiac
13.	Tommy Gale	Ford
14.	D. K. Ulrich	Buick
15.	Darrell Waltrip	Buick
16.	Slick Johnson	Buick
17.	Jody Ridley	Ford
18.	Joe Ruttman	Pontiac
19.	Neil Bonnett	Ford
20.	Benny Parsons	Pontiac
21.	Geoff Bodine	Pontiac
22.	Ricky Rudd	Pontiac
23.	Ronnie Thomas	Buick
24.	Richard Petty	Pontiac
25.	Brad Teague	Pontiac
26.	Jocko Maggiacomo	Oldsmobile
27.	J. D. McDuffie	Pontiac
28.	Jimmy Walker	Ford
29.	Kyle Petty	Pontiac
30.	Harry Gant	Buick
31.	Jimmy Means	Pontiac
32.	John Callis	Pontiac

WORLD 600

May 30
Charlotte, North Carolina
Time of Race: 4 hours, 36 minutes, 48 seconds
Average Speed: 130.058 mph
Margin of Victory: 2 car lengths

FINISH	DRIVER	CAR
1.	Neil Bonnett	Ford
2.	Bill Elliott	Ford

3.	Bobby Allison	Buick
4.	Cale Yarborough	Buick
5.	Buddy Baker	Buick
6.	Jody Ridley	Ford
7.	Ricky Rudd	Pontiac
8.	Richard Petty	Pontiac
9.	Dave Marcis	Buick
10.	Ron Bouchard	Buick
11.	Buddy Arrington	Dodge
12.	Lake Speed	Buick
13.	Harry Gant	Buick
14.	Jimmy Means	Buick
15.	Connie Saylor	Oldsmobile
16.	Bosco Lowe	Buick
17.	Kyle Petty	Pontiac
18.	Slick Johnson	Buick
19.	Morgan Shepherd	Buick
20.	Bobby Wawak	Buick
21.	David Pearson	Buick
22.	Darrell Waltrip	Buick
23.	Tommy Gale	Buick
24.	Brad Teague	Chevrolet
25.	Geoff Bodine	Pontiac
26.	H. B. Bailey	Pontiac
27.	Mark Martin	Pontiac
28.	D. K. Ulrich	Buick
29.	Rusty Wallace	Buick
30.	Dale Earnhardt	Ford
31.	Lennie Pond	Buick
32.	Delma Cowart	Buick
33.	J. D. McDuffie	Pontiac
34.	Terry Labonte	Buick
35.	Steve Moore	Pontiac
36.	Rick Wilson	Buick
37.	Donnie Allison	Buick
38.	Dean Combs	Buick
39.	Benny Parsons	Pontiac
40.	Tim Richmond	Buick
41.	Joe Ruttman	Buick
42.	John Anderson	Buick

VAN SCOY DIAMOND MINE 500

June 6
Pocono, Pennsylvania
Time of Race: 4 hours, 24 minutes, 8 seconds
Average Speed: 113.579 mph
Margin of Victory: 3 seconds

FINISH	DRIVER	CAR
1.	Bobby Allison	Buick
2.	Tim Richmond	Buick
3.	Benny Parsons	Pontiac
4.	Harry Gant	Buick
5.	Terry Labonte	Chevrolet
6.	Ricky Rudd	Pontiac
7.	Richard Petty	Pontiac
8.	Geoff Bodine	Pontiac
9.	Jody Ridley	Ford
10.	Dave Marcis	Chevrolet
11.	Kyle Petty	Pontiac
12.	Buddy Arrington	Dodge
13.	Darrell Waltrip	Buick
14.	Bobby Wawak	Buick
15.	D. K. Ulrich	Buick
16.	Al Loquasto	Buick
17.	Rick Newsom	Chevrolet
18.	Tommy Gale	Ford
19.	Bill Elliott	Ford
20.	Lake Speed	Buick
21.	Lowell Cowell	Buick
22.	Buddy Baker	Buick
23.	Ronnie Thomas	Buick
24.	Jimmy Means	Buick
25.	Brad Teague	Chevrolet
26.	Mark Martin	Buick
27.	Steve Gray	Buick
28.	Cale Yarborough	Buick
29.	Slick Johnson	Buick
30.	Joe Ruttman	Buick
31.	Ron Bouchard	Buick

32.	Jocko Maggiacano	Oldsmobile
33.	J. D. McDuffie	Pontiac
34.	Dale Earnhardt	Ford
35.	Morgan Shepherd	Buick
36.	Bobby Hillin Jr.	Buick
37.	Jimmy Walker	Ford

BUDWEISER 400

June 13
Riverside, California
Time of Race: 2 hours, 23 minutes, 51 seconds
Average Speed: 103.816 mph
Margin of Victory: 4 seconds

FINISH	DRIVER	CAR
1.	Tim Richmond	Buick
2.	Terry Labonte	Buick
3.	Geoff Bodine	Pontiac
4.	Dale Earnhardt	Ford
5.	Neil Bonnett	Ford
6.	Roy Smith	Buick
7.	Jody Ridley	Ford
8.	Mark Martin	Buick
9.	Ron Bouchard	Buick
10.	Jim Reich	Chevrolet
11.	Don Waterman	Buick
12.	Kyle Petty	Pontiac
13.	Scott Miller	Pontiac
14.	Rick McCray	Pontiac
15.	Buddy Arrington	Dodge
16.	D. K. Ulrich	Buick
17.	Jim Bown	Buick
18.	Jimmy Means	Buick
19.	John Krebs	Pontiac
20.	Don Puskarich	Buick
21.	Randy Becker	Dodge
22.	Mark Stahl	Ford
23.	Benny Parsons	Pontiac
24.	Bill Schmitt	Buick
25.	J. D. McDuffie	Pontiac
26.	Joe Ruttman	Pontiac
27.	Bobby Allison	Chevrolet
28.	Jim Robinson	Oldsmobile
29.	Ricky Rudd	Pontiac
30.	Dave Marcis	Pontiac
31.	Lake Speed	Buick
32.	Darrell Waltrip	Buick
33.	Hershel McGriff	Buick
34.	Jimmie Lee	Buick
35.	Harry Gant	Buick
36.	Richard Petty	Pontiac

GABRIEL 400

June 20
Brooklyn, Michigan
Time of Race: 3 hours, 23 minutes, 13 seconds
Average Speed: 118.101 mph
Margin of Victory: 3 car lengths

FINISH	DRIVER	CAR
1.	Cale Yarborough	Buick
2.	Darrell Waltrip	Buick
3.	Bill Elliott	Ford
4.	Bobby Allison	Buick
5.	Ricky Rudd	Pontiac
6.	Kyle Petty	Pontiac
7.	Dale Earnhardt	Ford
8.	Morgan Shepherd	Buick
9.	Geoff Bodine	Pontiac
10.	Harry Gant	Buick
11.	Neil Bonnett	Ford
12.	Ron Bouchard	Buick
13.	Joe Ruttman	Buick
14.	Dave Marcis	Buick

15.	Buddy Arrington	Dodge
16.	Bobby Hillin Jr.	Buick
17.	Dean Combs	Buick
18.	Tommy Gale	Ford
19.	Dick May	Buick
20.	Jimmy Means	Buick
21.	H. B. Bailey	Pontiac
22.	D. K. Ulrich	Buick
23.	James Hylton	Buick
24.	Dennis Devea	Buick
25.	Tim Richmond	Buick
26.	Richard Petty	Pontiac
27.	Jody Ridley	Ford
28.	Terry Labonte	Buick
29.	Robin McCall	Buick
30.	Slick Johnson	Buick
31.	Buddy Baker	Pontiac
32.	Benny Parsons	Buick
33.	Mark Martin	Pontiac
34.	Lake Speed	Buick
35.	Ronnie Thomas	Pontiac
36.	David Pearson	Buick
37.	J. D. McDuffie	Pontiac

FIRECRACKER 400

July 4
Daytona Beach, Florida
Time of Race: 2 hours, 27 minutes, 9 seconds
Average Speed: 163.099
Margin of Victory: half a car length

FINISH	DRIVER	CAR
1.	Bobby Allison	Buick
2.	Bill Elliott	Ford
3.	Ron Bouchard	Buick
4.	Morgan Shepherd	Buick
5.	David Pearson	Buick
6.	Geoff Bodine	Pontiac
7.	Ricky Rudd	Pontiac
8.	Buddy Baker	Pontiac
9.	Lake Speed	Buick
10.	Dave Marcis	Buick
11.	J. D. McDuffie	Pontiac
12.	Buddy Arrington	Dodge
13.	Lowell Cowell	Oldsmobile
14.	Tommy Gale	Ford
15.	Jody Ridley	Ford
16.	Lennie Pond	Buick
17.	Delma Cowart	Buick
18.	Philip Duffie	Buick
19.	James Hylton	Buick
20.	Bobby Hillin Jr.	Buick
21.	Jimmy Means	Buick
22.	Cale Yarborough	Buick
23.	Tim Richmond	Buick
24.	Harry Gant	Buick
25.	Richard Petty	Pontiac
26.	Travis Tiller	Buick
27.	Terry Labonte	Buick
28.	Benny Parsons	Buick
29.	Dale Earnhardt	Ford
30.	Blackie Wangerin	Ford
31.	Mark Martin	Pontiac
32.	Neil Bonnett	Ford
33.	Rick Wilson	Buick
34.	Slick Johnson	Buick
35.	Dr. Bob Jarvis	Buick
36.	Darrell Waltrip	Buick
37.	Marty Robbins	Buick
38.	Kyle Petty	Buick
39.	Connie Saylor	Oldsmobile
40.	Joe Ruttman	Buick

BUSCH NASHVILLE 420

July 10
Nashville, Tennessee

Time of Race: 2 hours, 53 minutes, 35 seconds
Average Speed: 86.524 mph
Margin of Victory: 1 lap

FINISH	DRIVER	CAR
1.	Darrell Waltrip	Buick
2.	Terry Labonte	Chevrolet
3.	Harry Gant	Buick
4.	Ricky Rudd	Pontiac
5.	Tim Richmond	Buick
6.	Geoff Bodine	Pontiac
7.	Richard Petty	Pontiac
8.	Jody Ridley	Ford
9.	Dale Earnhardt	Ford
10.	Ron Bouchard	Buick
11.	Dave Marcis	Chevrolet
12.	Joe Ruttman	Buick
13.	Lake Speed	Buick
14.	Jimmy Means	Chevrolet
15.	Mark Martin	Pontiac
16.	Darryl Sage	Chevrolet
17.	D. K. Ulrich	Buick
18.	Tommy Gale	Ford
19.	Bobby Allison	Chevrolet
20.	James Hylton	Pontiac
21.	Bill Elliott	Ford
22.	Buddy Arrington	Dodge
23.	Kyle Petty	Pontiac
24.	Buddy Baker	Pontiac
25.	J. D. McDuffie	Pontiac
26.	Morgan Shepherd	Buick
27.	Lennie Pond	Buick
28.	Slick Johnson	Buick

MOUNTAIN DEW 500

July 25
Pocono, Pennsylvania
Time of Race: 4 hours, 19 minutes, 45 seconds
Average Speed: 115.496 mph
Margin of Victory: 17 seconds

FINISH	DRIVER	CAR
1.	Bobby Allison	Buick
2.	Richard Petty	Pontiac
3.	Terry Labonte	Buick
4.	Ron Bouchard	Buick
5.	Buddy Baker	Pontiac
6.	Darrell Waltrip	Buick
7.	Joe Ruttman	Buick
8.	Dave Marcis	Buick
9.	Buddy Arrington	Dodge
10.	Mark Martin	Pontiac
11.	Geoff Bodine	Pontiac
12.	James Hylton	Pontiac
13.	Rick Newsom	Chevrolet
14.	Cecil Gordon	Buick
15.	Kyle Petty	Buick
16.	J. D. McDuffie	Pontiac
17.	Jimmy Means	Pontiac
18.	Charlie Baker	Buick
19.	Bobby Wawak	Buick
20.	Mike Potter	Buick
21.	Joe Booher	Buick
22.	Harry Gant	Buick
23.	Tommy Gale	Ford
24.	Tim Richmond	Buick
25.	Dale Earnhardt	Ford
26.	Cale Yarborough	Buick
27.	John Callis	Pontiac
28.	Morgan Shepherd	Buick
29.	Al Loquasto	Buick
30.	Bill Elliott	Ford
31.	Ricky Rudd	Pontiac
32.	Ronnie Thomas	Buick
33.	Lake Speed	Buick
34.	Jocko Maggiacomo	Oldsmobile

FINISH	DRIVER	CAR
35.	Tom Hessert	Pontiac
36.	Jody Ridley	Ford

TALLADEGA 500

August 1
Talladega, Alabama
Time of Race: 2 hours, 58 minutes, 26 seconds
Average Speed: 168.157 mph
Margin of Victory: 1 car length

FINISH	DRIVER	CAR
1.	Darrell Waltrip	Buick
2.	Buddy Baker	Pontiac
3.	Richard Petty	Pontiac
4.	Cale Yarborough	Buick
5.	Terry Labonte	Buick
6.	Bill Elliott	Ford
7.	Tim Richmond	Buick
8.	Morgan Shepherd	Buick
9.	Ricky Rudd	Pontiac
10.	Bobby Allison	Pontiac
11.	Joe Ruttman	Buick
12.	Mark Martin	Pontiac
13.	Dave Marcis	Buick
14.	Jody Ridley	Ford
15.	Geoff Bodine	Pontiac
16.	Neil Bonnett	Ford
17.	Jimmy Means	Buick
18.	Lowell Cowell	Oldsmobile
19.	Bobby Hillin Jr.	Buick
20.	Buddy Arrington	Dodge
21.	Lake Speed	Buick
22.	J. D. McDuffie	Pontiac
23.	Philip Duffie	Buick
24.	Al Loquasto	Buick
25.	James Hylton	Buick
26.	Bobby Wawak	Buick
27.	Rick Wilson	Buick
28.	Travis Tiller	Buick
29.	Tommy Gale	Ford
30.	Delma Cowart	Buick
31.	Charlie Baker	Buick
32.	Slick Johnson	Buick
33.	Bob Slawinski	Buick
34.	Ron Bouchard	Buick
35.	Dale Earnhardt	Ford
36.	Lennie Pond	Buick
37.	Connie Saylor	Oldsmobile
38.	Harry Gant	Buick
39.	Kyle Petty	Buick
40.	Jim Hurlbert	Buick

CHAMPION SPARK PLUG 400

August 22
Brooklyn, Michigan
Time of Race: 2 hours, 45 minutes, 53 seconds
Average Speed: 136.454
Margin of Victory: ¾ car length

FINISH	DRIVER	CAR
1.	Bobby Allison	Buick
2.	Richard Petty	Pontiac
3.	Harry Gant	Buick
4.	Geoff Bodine	Pontiac
5.	Benny Parsons	Buick
6.	Buddy Arrington	Chrysler
7.	Darrell Waltrip	Buick
8.	Dave Marcis	Buick
9.	Neil Bonnett	Ford
10.	Ron Bouchard	Buick
11.	Jimmy Means	Buick
12.	Lake Speed	Buick

13.	Dean Combs	Buick
14.	Ricky Rudd	Pontiac
15.	Kyle Petty	Pontiac
16.	J. D. McDuffie	Pontiac
17.	Ronnie Thomas	Pontiac
18.	Joe Booher	Buick
19.	Charlie Baker	Buick
20.	Tommy Gale	Ford
21.	Terry Labonte	Buick
22.	James Hylton	Chevrolet
23.	Tim Richmond	Buick
24.	Tony Bettenhausen	Buick
25.	Buddy Baker	Pontiac
26.	Jody Ridley	Ford
27.	Bill Elliott	Ford
28.	Cale Yarborough	Buick
29.	Dave Simko	Buick
30.	Dale Earnhardt	Ford
31.	David Pearson	Buick
32.	Morgan Shepherd	Buick
33.	Robin McCall	Buick
34.	Mark Martin	Pontiac
35.	H. B. Bailey	Pontiac
36.	Al Loquasto	Buick
37.	Earle Canavan	Oldsmobile
38.	Joe Ruttman	Buick

BUSCH 500

August 28
Bristol, Tennessee
Time of Race: 2 hours, 49 minutes, 32 seconds
Average Speed: 94.318 mph
Margin of Victory: 3 car lengths

FINISH	DRIVER	CAR
1.	Darrell Waltrip	Buick
2.	Bobby Allison	Chevrolet
3.	Harry Gant	Buick
4.	Terry Labonte	Buick
5.	Morgan Shepherd	Buick
6.	Dale Earnhardt	Ford
7.	Ricky Rudd	Pontiac
8.	Jody Ridley	Ford
9.	Buddy Baker	Pontiac
10.	Geoff Bodine	Pontiac
11.	Mark Martin	Pontiac
12.	Ron Bouchard	Oldsmobile
13.	Lake Speed	Buick
14.	Jimmy Means	Chevrolet
15.	Brad Teague	Chevrolet
16.	Buddy Arrington	Dodge
17.	Darryl Sage	Chevrolet
18.	D. K. Ulrich	Buick
19.	Tommy Gale	Ford
20.	Connie Saylor	Buick
21.	Dave Marcis	Buick
22.	J. D. McDuffie	Pontiac
23.	James Hylton	Pontiac
24.	Joe Ruttman	Buick
25.	Tim Richmond	Buick
26.	Richard Petty	Pontiac
27.	Al Laquasto	Buick
28.	Ronnie Thomas	Pontiac
29.	Rick Newsom	Chevrolet
30.	Kyle Petty	Pontiac

SOUTHERN 500

September 6
Darlington, South Carolina
Time of Race: 4 hours, 21 minutes, 0 seconds
Average Speed: 115.224 mph
Margin of Victory: 1 car length

FINISH	DRIVER	CAR
1.	Cale Yarborough	Buick
2.	Richard Petty	Pontiac
3.	Dale Earnhardt	Ford
4.	Bill Elliott	Ford
5.	Buddy Baker	Pontiac
6.	Lake Speed	Buick
7.	Geoff Bodine	Pontiac
8.	Benny Parsons	Buick
9.	Buddy Arrington	Dodge
10.	Dave Marcis	Chevrolet
11.	Harry Gant	Buick
12.	Connie Saylor	Oldsmobile
13.	Joe Ruttman	Buick
14.	Kyle Petty	Buick
15.	Dick May	Buick
16.	J. D. McDuffie	Pontiac
17.	Philip Duffie	Buick
18.	Joe Millikan	Pontiac
19.	Rick Newsome	Chevrolet
20.	Bobby Allison	Buick
21.	Bobby Wawak	Chevrolet
22.	Mark Martin	Buick
23.	Jimmy Means	Pontiac
24.	Darrell Waltrip	Buick
25.	Tommy Gale	Ford
26.	Ron Bouchard	Buick
27.	D. K. Ulrich	Buick
28.	Jody Ridley	Ford
29.	H. B. Bailey	Pontiac
30.	Tim Richmond	Buick
31.	Ricky Rudd	Pontiac
32.	Slick Johnson	Buick
33.	Mike Potter	Oldsmobile
34.	Neil Bonnett	Ford
35.	Terry Labonte	Chevrolet
36.	Morgan Shepherd	Buick
37.	David Pearson	Buick
38.	Ronnie Thomas	Pontiac
39.	Earl Canavan	Buick
40.	Lennie Pond	Buick

WRANGLER SANFORSET 400

September 12
Richmond, Virginia
Time of Race: 2 hours, 37 minutes, 6 seconds
Average Speed: 82.800 mph
Margin of Victory: 17 seconds

FINISH	DRIVER	CAR
1.	Bobby Allison	Chevrolet
2.	Tim Richmond	Buick
3.	Darrell Waltrip	Buick
4.	Ricky Rudd	Pontiac
5.	Neil Bonnett	Ford
6.	Terry Labonte	Buick
7.	Harry Gant	Buick
8.	Dave Marcis	Chevrolet
9.	Buddy Baker	Pontiac
10.	Lake Speed	Pontiac
11.	Tommy Ellis	Chevrolet
12.	Morgan Shepherd	Buick
13.	Richard Petty	Pontiac
14.	Kyle Petty	Pontiac
15.	Ron Bouchard	Oldsmobile
16.	Buddy Arrington	Dodge
17.	James Hylton	Chevrolet
18.	Darryl Sage	Chevrolet
19.	Jimmy Means	Buick
20.	D. K. Ulrich	Buick
21.	Tommy Gale	Ford
22.	Joe Fields	Buick
23.	Ronnie Thomas	Pontiac
24.	Butch Lindley	Buick
25.	Jody Ridley	Ford
26.	Mark Martin	Buick
27.	Dale Earnhardt	Ford
28.	Geoff Bodine	Pontiac

29.	Jimmy Hensley	Buick
30.	J. D. McDuffie	Pontiac
31.	Joe Ruttman	Buick

CRC CHEMICALS 500

September 19
Dover, Delaware
Time of Race: 4 hours, 38 minutes, 42.5 seconds
Average Speed: 107.642 mph
Margin of Victory: 1 car length

FINISH	DRIVER	CAR
1.	Darrell Waltrip	Buick
2.	Kyle Petty	Pontiac
3.	Bill Elliott	Ford
4.	Geoff Bodine	Pontiac
5.	Benny Parsons	Buick
6.	Dave Marcis	Chevrolet
7.	Buddy Arrington	Dodge
8.	Ron Bouchard	Buick
9.	Tim Richmond	Buick
10.	Bobby Allison	Chevrolet
11.	Ricky Rudd	Pontiac
12.	Harry Gant	Buick
13.	J. D. McDuffie	Pontiac
14.	Tommy Gale	Ford
15.	James Hylton	Chevrolet
16.	Cecil Gordon	Buick
17.	Jimmy Means	Pontiac
18.	Joe Ruttman	Buick
19.	D. K. Ulrich	Buick
20.	Dale Earnhardt	Ford
21.	Neil Bonnett	Ford
22.	Lake Speed	Pontiac
23.	Dick May	Buick
24.	Morgan Shepherd	Buick
25.	Jody Ridley	Ford
26.	John Callis	Pontiac
27.	Terry Labonte	Chevrolet
28.	Jocko Maggiacomo	Oldsmobile
29.	Buddy Baker	Pontiac
30.	Richard Petty	Pontiac
31.	Ronnie Thomas	Pontiac
32.	J. R. Charbonneau	Buick
33.	Mark Martin	Pontiac
34.	Dr. Gil Roth	Oldsmobile
35.	Rick Newsom	Chevrolet

HOLLY FARMS 400

October 3
North Wilkesboro, North Carolina
Time of Race: 2 hours, 32 minutes, 57 seconds
Average Speed: 98.071
Margin of Victory: 14 seconds

FINISH	DRIVER	CAR
1.	Darrell Waltrip	Buick
2.	Harry Gant	Buick
3.	Terry Labonte	Chevrolet
4.	Richard Petty	Pontiac
5.	Geoff Bodine	Pontiac
6.	Joe Ruttman	Buick
7.	Ron Bouchard	Buick
8.	Lake Speed	Pontiac
9.	Jody Ridley	Ford
10.	Kyle Petty	Pontiac
11.	Dave Marcis	Chevrolet
12.	Mark Martin	Buick
13.	Morgan Shepherd	Buick
14.	Jimmy Means	Pontiac
15.	D. K. Ulrich	Buick
16.	Jeff McDuffie	Pontiac
17.	James Hylton	Chevrolet

FINISH	DRIVER	CAR
18.	Cecil Gordon	Buick
19.	Tommy Gale	Ford
20.	Dale Earnhardt	Ford
21.	Buddy Arrington	Dodge
22.	Tim Richmond	Buick
23.	Bobby Allison	Chevrolet
24.	Buddy Baker	Pontiac
25.	Ricky Rudd	Pontiac
26.	Dean Combs	Buick
27.	Joel Stowe	Buick
28.	Jimmy Walker	Ford
29.	Ronnie Thomas	Pontiac
30.	J. D. McDuffie	Pontiac

NATIONAL 500

October 10
Charlotte, North Carolina
Time of Race: 3 hours, 39 minutes, 5 seconds
Average Speed: 137.208 mph
Margin of Victory: 2 seconds

FINISH	DRIVER	CAR
1.	Harry Gant	Buick
2.	Bill Elliott	Ford
3.	David Pearson	Buick
4.	Joe Ruttman	Buick
5.	Benny Parsons	Buick
6.	Buddy Baker	Pontiac
7.	Jody Ridley	Ford
8.	Richard Petty	Pontiac
9.	Bobby Allison	Buick
10.	Rick Wilson	Dodge
11.	Jimmy Means	Buick
12.	Rick Baldwin	Dodge
13.	Geoff Bodine	Pontiac
14.	Darrell Waltrip	Buick
15.	D. K. Ulrich	Buick
16.	Terry Labonte	Buick
17.	John Anderson	Buick
18.	J. D. McDuffie	Pontiac
19.	Tim Richmond	Buick
20.	Lennie Pond	Buick
21.	Lake Speed	Buick
22.	Buddy Arrington	Chrysler
23.	Sterling Marlin	Oldsmobile
24.	Dick Brooks	Pontiac
25.	Dale Earnhardt	Ford
26.	H. B. Bailey	Pontiac
27.	Richard Brickhouse	Pontiac
28.	Neil Bonnett	Ford
29.	Kyle Petty	Buick
30.	Morgan Shepherd	Buick
31.	Ricky Rudd	Pontiac
32.	Dave Marcis	Buick
33.	Cale Yarborough	Buick
34.	Dean Combs	Buick
35.	Ron Bouchard	Oldsmobile
36.	Tommy Gale	Ford
37.	Ronnie Thomas	Pontiac
38.	Mark Martin	Buick
39.	Connie Saylor	Oldsmobile
40.	Travis Tiller	Buick

OLD DOMINION 500

October 17
Martinsville, Virginia
Time of Race: 3 hours, 41 minutes, 5 seconds
Average Speed: 71.315 mph
Margin of Victory: 2 seconds

FINISH	DRIVER	CAR
1.	Darrell Waltrip	Buick
2.	Ricky Rudd	Pontiac

FINISH	DRIVER	CAR
3.	Richard Petty	Pontiac
4.	Terry Labonte	Chevrolet
5.	Joe Ruttman	Buick
6.	Buddy Baker	Pontiac
7.	Jody Ridley	Ford
8.	Harry Gant	Buick
9.	Jimmy Means	Chevrolet
10.	Buddy Arrington	Dodge
11.	Geoff Bodine	Pontiac
12.	D. K. Ulrich	Buick
13.	Tim Richmond	Buick
14.	Ron Bouchard	Buick
15.	J. D. McDuffie	Buick
16.	James Hylton	Chevrolet
17.	Tommy Gale	Ford
18.	Morgan Shepherd	Buick
19.	Bobby Allison	Chevrolet
20.	Mark Martin	Buick
21.	Kyle Petty	Pontiac
22.	Neil Bonnett	Ford
23.	Jimmy Hensley	Buick
24.	Joe Fields	Buick
25.	Ronnie Thomas	Pontiac
26.	Butch Lindley	Buick
27.	Dale Earnhardt	Ford
28.	Dave Marcis	Chevrolet
29.	Lake Speed	Pontiac
30.	Darryl Sage	Chevrolet
31.	Rick Newsom	Chevrolet

WARNER W. HODGDON AMERICAN 500

October 31
Rockingham, North Carolina
Time of Race: 4 hours, 20 minutes, 47 seconds
Average Speed: 115.122 mph
Margin of Victory: 9.5 seconds

FINISH	DRIVER	CAR
1.	Darrell Waltrip	Buick
2.	Bobby Allison	Chevrolet
3.	Neil Bonnett	Ford
4.	Terry Labonte	Buick
5.	Morgan Shepherd	Buick
6.	Richard Petty	Pontiac
7.	Buddy Baker	Pontiac
8.	Ron Bouchard	Buick
9.	Lennie Pond	Chevrolet
10.	D. K. Ulrich	Buick
11.	Dave Marcis	Chevrolet
12.	Bill Elliott	Ford
13.	Bobby Wawak	Buick
14.	Dale Earnhardt	Ford
15.	Jimmy Means	Chevrolet
16.	Tommy Gale	Ford
17.	Tim Richmond	Buick
18.	Joe Ruttman	Buick
19.	Slick Johnson	Buick
20.	Randy Baker	Pontiac
21.	Richard Brickhouse	Pontiac
22.	J. D. McDuffie	Pontiac
23.	Buddy Arrington	Dodge
24.	Mark Martin	Buick
25.	Cale Yarborough	Buick
26.	Joe Millikan	Buick
27.	Geoff Bodine	Pontiac
28.	Ricky Rudd	Pontiac
29.	Kyle Petty	Pontiac
30.	Ronnie Thomas	Pontiac
31.	Jody Ridley	Ford
32.	Harry Gant	Buick
33.	Lake Speed	Pontiac
34.	Benny Parsons	Buick
35.	Rick Newsom	Chevrolet

ATLANTA JOURNAL 500

November 7
Atlanta, Georgia

Time of Race: 3 hours, 48 minutes, 451 seconds
Average Speed: 130.884 mph
Margin of Victory: .5 seconds

FINISH	DRIVER	CAR
1.	Bobby Allison	Buick
2.	Harry Gant	Buick
3.	Darrell Waltrip	Buick
4.	Tim Richmond	Buick
5.	Joe Ruttman	Buick
6.	Dave Marcis	Buick
7.	Ricky Rudd	Pontiac
8.	Terry Labonte	Buick
9.	Rodney Combs	Buick
10.	Mark Martin	Buick
11.	Neil Bonnett	Ford
12.	Lennie Pond	Chevrolet
13.	Jimmy Means	Chevrolet
14.	Buddy Arrington	Chrysler
15.	Richard Petty	Pontiac
16.	Philip Duffie	Buick
17.	Bobby Wawak	Chevrolet
18.	Travis Tiller	Buick
19.	Geoff Bodine	Pontiac
20.	Benny Parsons	Buick
21.	Buddy Baker	Pontiac
22.	Darryl Sage	Chevrolet
23.	D. K. Ulrich	Buick
24.	Bill Elliott	Ford
25.	Morgan Shepherd	Buick
26.	Tommy Gale	Ford
27.	Rick Wilson	Oldsmobile
28.	Jody Ridley	Ford
29.	Lake Speed	Pontiac
30.	J. D. McDuffie	Pontiac
31.	Kyle Petty	Pontiac
32.	Ron Bouchard	Buick
33.	Marty Robbins	Buick
34.	Dale Earnhardt	Ford
35.	Cale Yarborough	Buick
36.	Jerry Bowman	Oldsmobile
37.	Dick May	Buick
38.	Donnie Allison	Oldsmobile
39.	Glenn Jarrett	Ford
40.	Steve Moore	Pontiac

WINSTON WESTERN 500

November 21
Riverside, California
Time of Race: 3 hours, 7 minutes, 24 seconds
Average Speed: 99.823 mph
Margin of Victory: 7 seconds

FINISH	DRIVER	CAR
1.	Tim Richmond	Buick
2.	Ricky Rudd	Pontiac
3.	Darrell Waltrip	Buick
4.	Neil Bonnett	Ford
5.	Mark Martin	Buick
6.	Ron Bouchard	Buick
7.	Benny Parsons	Buick
8.	Morgan Shepherd	Buick
9.	Jody Ridley	Ford
10.	Jim Bown	Buick
11.	Geoff Bodine	Pontiac
12.	Jimmy Means	Pontiac
13.	Terry Herman	Buick
14.	Glen Francis	Pontiac
15.	D. K. Ulrich	Buick
16.	Bobby Allison	Pontiac
17.	Cecil Gordon	Buick
18.	J. D. McDuffie	Buick
19.	Jim Reich	Chevrolet
20.	Jim Robinson	Oldsmobile
21.	Bill Schmitt	Buick
22.	Trevor Boys	Pontiac

23.	Jimmie Lee	Buick
24.	Roy Smith	Buick
25.	Bill Elliott	Ford
26.	Harry Gant	Buick
27.	Terry Labonte	Buick
28.	Hershel McGriff	Buick
29.	Dave Marcis	Pontiac
30.	Jimmy Insolo	Pontiac
31.	Richard Petty	Pontiac
32.	Lake Speed	Pontiac
33.	Don Waterman	Buick
34.	Rick McCray	Pontiac
35.	Buddy Arrington	Chrysler
36.	Derrike Cope	Ford
37.	John Krebs	Pontiac
38.	Randy Baker	Chrysler
39.	Mark Stahl	Ford
40.	Joe Ruttman	Pontiac
41.	Kevin Terris	Buick
42.	Dale Earnhardt	Ford

1983

DAYTONA 500

February 20
Daytona Beach, Florida
Time of Race: 3 hours, 12 minutes, 20 seconds
Average Speed: 155.979 mph
Margin of Victory: 1 car length

FINISH	DRIVER	CAR
1.	Cale Yarborough	Pontiac
2.	Bill Elliott	Ford
3.	Buddy Baker	Ford
4.	Joe Ruttman	Chevrolet
5.	Dick Brooks	Ford
6.	Terry Labonte	Chevrolet
7.	Tom Sneva	Chevrolet
8.	David Pearson	Chevrolet
9.	Bobby Allison	Chevrolet
10.	Jody Ridley	Buick
11.	A. J. Foyt	Chevrolet
12.	Lennie Pond	Buick
13.	Phil Parsons	Buick
14.	Jimmy Means	Buick
15.	Dean Roper	Pontiac
16.	Buddy Arrington	Chrysler
17.	Ronnie Thomas	Pontiac
18.	Jim Sauter	Chevrolet
19.	Ronnie Hopkins	Buick
20.	Rick Baldwin	Dodge
21.	Clark Dwyer	Chevrolet
22.	Neil Bonnett	Chevrolet
23.	James Hylton	Chevrolet
24.	Ricky Rudd	Chevrolet
25.	Lake Speed	Chevrolet
26.	Ron Bouchard	Buick
27.	Tommy Gale	Ford
28.	Mark Martin	Buick
29.	J. D. McDuffie	Pontiac
30.	Geoff Bodine	Pontiac
31.	Delma Cowart	Buick
32.	Dave Marcis	Chevrolet
33.	Kyle Petty	Pontiac
34.	Sterling Marlin	Chevrolet
35.	Dale Earnhardt	Ford
36.	Darrell Waltrip	Chevrolet
37.	Harry Gant	Buick
38.	Richard Petty	Pontiac
39.	Bosco Lowe	Buick
40.	Elliott Forbes-Robinson	Buick
41.	Tim Richmond	Pontiac
42.	Benny Parsons	Buick

RICHMOND 400

February 27
Richmond, Virginia
Time of Race: 2 hours, 43 minutes, 45 seconds
Average Speed: 79.584 mph
Margin of Victory: 4 car lengths

FINISH	DRIVER	CAR
1.	Bobby Allison	Chevrolet
2.	Dale Earnhardt	Ford
3.	Neil Bonnett	Chevrolet
4.	Geoff Bodine	Pontiac
5.	Harry Gant	Buick
6.	Bill Elliott	Ford
7.	Joe Ruttman	Buick
8.	Richard Petty	Pontiac
9.	Dave Marcis	Chevrolet
10.	Buddy Baker	Ford
11.	Butch Lindley	Buick
12.	Ron Bouchard	Buick
13.	Dick Brooks	Ford
14.	Kyle Petty	Pontiac
15.	Lake Speed	Chevrolet
16.	Jimmy Means	Chevrolet
17.	Tim Richmond	Pontiac
18.	Sterling Marlin	Pontiac
19.	Jim Sauter	Buick
20.	Buddy Arrington	Dodge
21.	James Hylton	Chevrolet
22.	Terry Labonte	Chevrolet
23.	Ronnie Thomas	Pontiac
24.	Mark Martin	Buick
25.	J. D. McDuffie	Pontiac
26.	Joe Fields	Buick
27.	Slick Johnson	Buick
28.	Ricky Rudd	Chevrolet
29.	Darrell Waltrip	Chevrolet
30.	Dave Dion	Ford
31.	Morgan Shephard	Ford
32.	Tommy Gale	Buick

WARNER W. HODGDON CAROLINA 500

March 13
Rockingham, North Carolina
Time of Race: 4 hours, 25 minutes, 30 seconds
Average Speed: 113.055 mph
Margin of Victory: half a car length

FINISH	DRIVER	CAR
1.	Richard Petty	Pontiac
2.	Bill Elliott	Ford
3.	Darrell Waltrip	Chevrolet
4.	Lake Speed	Chevrolet
5.	Harry Gant	Buick
6.	Ricky Rudd	Chevrolet
7.	Tim Richmond	Pontiac
8.	Dick Brooks	Ford
9.	Cale Yarborough	Chevrolet
10.	Bobby Allison	Chevrolet
11.	Mark Martin	Buick
12.	Neil Bonnett	Chevrolet
13.	Sterling Marlin	Pontiac
14.	Jimmy Means	Pontiac
15.	Kyle Petty	Pontiac
16.	Bobby Wawak	Buick
17.	Ronnie Hopkins	Buick
18.	D. K. Ulrich	Buick
19.	Geoff Bodine	Pontiac
20.	Ron Bouchard	Buick
21.	Tommy Gale	Ford
22.	Buddy Arrington	Chrysler
23.	Slick Johnson	Buick
24.	Terry Labonte	Chevrolet
25.	Bobby Hillin Jr.	Buick
26.	Jim Sauter	Buick

27.	Ronnie Thomas	Pontiac
28.	Rick Newsom	Chevrolet
29.	Joo Ruttman	Buick
30.	J. D. McDuffie	Pontiac
31.	Lennie Pond	Pontiac
32.	Buddy Baker	Ford
33.	Dale Earnhardt	Ford
34.	Dave Marcis	Chevrolet
35.	Ernie Cline	Pontiac

COCA-COLA 500

March 27
Atlanta, Georgia
Time of Race: 4 hours, 1 minute, 27 seconds
Average Speed: 124.055 mph
Margin of Victory: 2.5 seconds

FINISH	DRIVER	CAR
1.	Cale Yarborough	Chevrolet
2.	Neil Bonnett	Chevrolet
3.	Buddy Baker	Ford
4.	Joe Ruttman	Buick
5.	Richard Petty	Pontiac
6.	Dick Brooks	Ford
7.	Mark Martin	Buick
8.	Terry Labonte	Chevrolet
9.	Tim Richmond	Pontiac
10.	Ricky Rudd	Chevrolet
11.	Hary Gant	Buick
12.	Ron Bouchard	Buick
13.	Dave Marcis	Chevrolet
14.	Benny Parsons	Buick
15.	Lake Speed	Chevrolet
16.	Buddy Arrington	Dodge
17.	Jody Ridley	Buick
18.	Bobby Wawak	Buick
19.	Bobby Hillin Jr.	Buick
20.	Darryl Sage	Chevrolet
21.	Ronnie Hopkins	Buick
22.	H. B. Bailey	Pontiac
23.	Tommy Gale	Ford
24.	Ronnie Thomas	Pontiac
25.	Bobby Allison	Buick
26.	Eddie Bierschwale	Buick
27.	Ken Ragan	Buick
28.	Bob Senneker	Pontiac
29.	Jim Sauter	Chevrolet
30.	Bill Elliott	Ford
31.	Sterling Marlin	Chevrolet
32.	Jimmy Means	Buick
33.	Dale Earnhardt	Ford
34.	Slick Johnson	Buick
35.	Kyle Petty	Pontiac
36.	J. D. McDuffie	Buick
37.	David Simko	Oldsmobile
38.	A. J. Foyt	Chevrolet
39.	Jim Vandiver	Chrysler
40.	Darrell Waltrip	Chevrolet
41.	Geoff Bodine	Pontiac

TRANSOUTH 500

April 10
Darlington, South Carolina
Time of Race: 3 hours, 50 minutes, 5 seconds
Average Speed: 130.406 mph
Margin of Victory: .5 seconds

FINISH	DRIVER	CAR
1.	Harry Gant	Buick
2.	Darrell Waltrip	Chevrolet
3.	Mark Martin	Buick
4.	Ricky Rudd	Chevrolet

5.	Bill Elliott	Ford
6.	Cale Yarborough	Chevrolet
7.	Neil Bonnett	Chevrolet
8.	Bobby Allison	Buick
9.	Geoff Bodine	Pontiac
10.	D. K. Ulrich	Buick
11.	Sterling Marlin	Chevrolet
12.	Jimmy Means	Pontiac
13.	Dale Earnhardt	Ford
14.	Tommy Gale	Ford
15.	Travis Tiller	Buick
16.	Bobby Wawak	Buick
17.	J. D. McDuffie	Pontiac
18.	Ron Bouchard	Buick
19.	Dick Brooks	Ford
20.	Joe Ruttman	Buick
21.	Dick May	Buick
22.	David Pearson	Chevrolet
23.	Buddy Arrington	Dodge
24.	Ronnie Thomas	Pontiac
25.	Richard Petty	Pontiac
26.	Cecil Gordon	Chrysler
27.	Jody Ridley	Buick
28.	Lake Speed	Chevrolet
29.	Slick Johnson	Buick
30.	Ronnie Hopkins	Chevrolet
31.	Kyle Petty	Pontiac
32.	Buddy Baker	Ford
33.	Dave Marcis	Chevrolet
34.	Benny Parsons	Buick
35.	Tim Richmond	Pontiac
36.	Terry Labonte	Chevrolet

NORTHWESTERN BANK 400

April 17
North Wilkesboro, North Carolina
Time of Race: 2 hours, 44 minutes, 3 seconds
Average Speed: 91.436 mph
Margin of Victory: 8 seconds

FINISH	DRIVER	CAR
1.	Darrell Waltrip	Chevrolet
2.	Bobby Allison	Buick
3.	Harry Gant	Buick
4.	Neil Bonnett	Chevrolet
5.	Geoff Bodine	Pontiac
6.	Terry Labonte	Chevrolet
7.	Joe Ruttman	Buick
8.	Lake Speed	Chevrolet
9.	Dave Marcis	Chevrolet
10.	Richard Petty	Pontiac
11.	Ron Bouchard	Buick
12.	Lennie Pond	Chevrolet
13.	D. K. Ulrich	Buick
14.	Jimmy Means	Chevrolet
15.	Buddy Arrington	Chrysler
16.	Bobby Hillin Jr.	Buick
17.	Ronnie Thomas	Pontiac
18.	Joe Millikan	Ford
19.	Tommy Gale	Ford
20.	Dick Brooks	Ford
21.	Bill Elliott	Ford
22.	Sterling Marlin	Pontiac
23.	Rick McCray	Pontiac
24.	Ronnie Hopkins	Chevrolet
25.	Slick Johnson	Buick
26.	Mark Martin	Buick
27.	Ricky Rudd	Chevrolet
28.	Tim Richmond	Pontiac
29.	Dale Earnhardt	Ford
30.	Kyle Petty	Pontiac

VIRGINIA NATIONAL BANK 500

April 24
Martinsville, Virginia

Time of Race: 3 hours, 57 minutes, 14 seconds
Average Speed: 66.460 mph
Margin of Victory: .5 seconds

FINISH	DRIVER	CAR
1.	Darrell Waltrip	Chevrolet
2.	Harry Gant	Buick
3.	Bobby Allison	Buick
4.	Joe Ruttman	Buick
5.	Ricky Rudd	Chevrolet
6.	Terry Labonte	Chevrolet
7.	Ron Bouchard	Buick
8.	Dick Brooks	Ford
9.	Buddy Arrington	Dodge
10.	Jimmy Means	Chevrolet
11.	Kyle Petty	Pontiac
12.	Sterling Marlin	Pontiac
13.	D. K. Ulrich	Ford
14.	Lennie Pond	Chevrolet
15.	Tim Richmond	Pontiac
16.	Neil Bonnett	Chevrolet
17.	Richard Petty	Pontiac
18.	Ronnie Thomas	Pontiac
19.	Dave Marcis	Chevrolet
20.	Rick Newsom	Buick
21.	Bill Elliott	Ford
22.	Tommy Gale	Buick
23.	Lake Speed	Chevrolet
24.	Rick McCray	Pontiac
25.	Geoff Bodine	Pontiac
26.	Dale Earnhardt	Ford
27.	Mark Martin	Buick
28.	Slick Johnson	Buick
29.	Trevor Boys	Chevrolet
30.	Ronnie Hopkins	Buick
31.	Buddy Baker	Ford
32.	Morgan Shepherd	Buick

WINSTON 500

May 1
Talladega, Alabama
Time of Race: 3 hours, 14 minutes, 55 seconds
Average Speed: 153.936 mph
Margin of Victory: 1 car length

FINISH	DRIVER	CAR
1.	Richard Petty	Pontiac
2.	Benny Parsons	Buick
3.	Lake Speed	Chevrolet
4.	Harry Gant	Buick
5.	Bill Elliott	Ford
6.	Terry Labonte	Chevrolet
7.	Jimmy Means	Buick
8.	Ricky Rudd	Chevrolet
9.	Dave Marcis	Chevrolet
10.	Bobby Allison	Buick
11.	Joe Ruttman	Chevrolet
12.	Ken Ragan	Buick
13.	Tommy Gale	Ford
14.	Dick Brooks	Ford
15.	Neil Bonnett	Chevrolet
16.	Cecil Gordon	Chrysler
17.	Morgan Shepherd	Buick
18.	Dean Roper	Pontiac
19.	Lennie Pond	Chevrolet
20.	Ron Bouchard	Buick
21.	Geoff Bodine	Pontiac
22.	Steve Moore	Pontiac
23.	Buddy Arrington	Chrysler
24.	Dale Earnhardt	Ford
25.	Buddy Baker	Ford
26.	Lowell Cowell	Oldsmobile
27.	Tim Richmond	Pontiac
28.	Phil Parsons	Pontiac
29.	Cale Yarborough	Chevrolet
30.	Kyle Petty	Pontiac

31.	David Pearson	Chevrolet
32.	Jody Ridley	Buick
33.	Darrell Waltrip	Chevrolet
34.	A. J. Foyt	Chevrolet
35.	Ronnie Thomas	Pontiac
36.	Mark Martin	Chevrolet
37.	Rick Wilson	Buick
38.	Philip Duffie	Buick
39.	Clark Dwyer	Chevrolet
40.	Connie Saylor	Oldsmobile
41.	Sterling Marlin	Chevrolet
42.	Rick Baldwin	Buick

MARTY ROBBINS 420

May 7
Nashville, Tennessee
Time of Race: 3 hours, 32 minutes, 23 seconds
Average Speed: 70.717 mph
Margin of Victory: 1 lap, 4 seconds

FINISH	DRIVER	CAR
1.	Darrell Warltrip	Chevrolet
2.	Bobby Allison	Buick
3.	Harry Gant	Buick
4.	Morgan Shepherd	Buick
5.	Bill Elliott	Ford
6.	Richard Petty	Pontiac
7.	Joe Ruttman	Buick
8.	Terry Labonte	Chevrolet
9.	Ron Bouchard	Buick
10.	Tim Richmond	Pontiac
11.	Sterling Marlin	Pontiac
12.	Jimmy Means	Chevrolet
13.	Neil Bonnett	Chevrolet
14.	Ricky Rudd	Chevrolet
15.	Ronnie Thomas	Pontiac
16.	Buddy Arrington	Chrysler
17.	Kyle Petty	Pontiac
18.	J. D. McDuffie	Pontiac
19.	Trevor Boys	Chevrolet
20.	Geoff Bodine	Pontiac
21.	Mark Martin	Buick
22.	Steve Gray	Buick
23.	Rick Newsom	Buick
24.	Dale Earnhardt	Ford
25.	Dick Brooks	Ford
26.	Darryl Sage	Chevrolet
27.	Dave Marcis	Chevrolet
28.	Tommy Gale	Ford
29.	Ronnie Hopkins	Chevrolet

MASON-DIXON 500

May 15
Dover, Delaware
Time of Race: 4 hours, 21 minutes, 13 seconds
Average Speed: 114.847 mph
Margin of Victory: 2 seconds

FINISH	DRIVER	CAR
1.	Bobby Allison	Buick
2.	Darrell Waltrip	Chevrolet
3.	Joe Ruttman	Buick
4.	Bill Elliott	Ford
5.	Buddy Baker	Ford
6.	Morgan Shepherd	Buick
7.	Richard Petty	Pontiac
8.	Dale Earnhardt	Ford
9.	Harry Gant	Buick
10.	Sterling Marlin	Pontiac
11.	Kyle Petty	Pontiac
12.	Jimmy Means	Pontiac
13.	Jerry Bowman	Ford

14.	Rick Newsom	Chevrolet
15.	Dick Brooks	Ford
16.	Dave Marcis	Chevrolet
17.	Jimmy Ingle	Buick
18.	D. K. Ulrich	Buick
19.	Buddy Arrington	Chrysler
20.	John Callis	Ford
21.	Cecil Gordon	Chrysler
22.	Cale Yarborough	Chevrolet
23.	J. D. McDuffie	Pontiac
24.	Ricky Rudd	Chevrolet
25.	Ronnie Thomas	Pontiac
26.	Ronnie Hopkins	Chevrolet
27.	Tommy Gale	Ford
28.	Neil Bonnett	Chevrolet
29.	Benny Parsons	Buick
30.	Tim Richmond	Pontiac
31.	Terry Labonte	Chevrolet
32.	Trevor Boys	Chevrolet
33.	Dick May	Ford
34.	Ron Bouchard	Buick
35.	Geoff Bodine	Pontiac
36.	Jocko Maggiacomo	Oldsmobile

VALLEYDALE 500

May 21
Bristol, Tennessee
Time of Race: 2 hours, 51 minutes, 7 seconds
Average Speed: 93.445 mph
Margin of Victory: 2 seconds

FINISH	DRIVER	CAR
1.	Darrell Waltrip	Chevrolet
2.	Bobby Allison	Buick
3.	Morgan Shepherd	Buick
4.	Neil Bonnett	Chevrolet
5.	Richard Petty	Pontiac
6.	Terry Labonte	Chevrolet
7.	Ron Bouchard	Buick
8.	Bill Elliott	Ford
9.	Dale Earnhardt	Ford
10.	Tim Richmond	Pontiac
11.	Kyle Petty	Pontiac
12.	Dave Marcis	Chevrolet
13.	D. K. Ulrich	Buick
14.	Jimmy Means	Chevrolet
15.	Ronnie Thomas	Pontiac
16.	Buddy Arrington	Chrysler
17.	Ronnie Hopkins	Buick
18.	Sterling Marlin	Pontiac
19.	Rick Newsom	Buick
20.	Tommy Gale	Ford
21.	Dick Brooks	Ford
22.	Trevor Boys	Chevrolet
23.	Joe Ruttman	Pontiac
24.	J. D. McDuffie	Pontiac
25.	Geoff Bodine	Pontiac
26.	Ricky Rudd	Chevrolet
27.	Harry Gant	Buick
28.	Mike Potter	Buick

WORLD 600

May 29
Charlotte, North Carolina
Time of Race: 4 hours, 15 minutes, 51 seconds
Average Speed: 140.707 mph
Margin of Victory: 1 second

FINISH	DRIVER	CAR
1.	Neil Bonnett	Chevrolet
2.	Richard Petty	Pontiac
3.	Bobby Allison	Buick

4.	Darrell Waltrip	Chevrolet
5.	Dale Earnhardt	Ford
6.	Lake Speed	Chevrolet
7.	Buddy Baker	Ford
8.	Kyle Petty	Pontiac
9.	Morgan Shepherd	Buick
10.	Dave Marcis	Chevrolet
11.	Bobby Hillin Jr.	Buick
12.	Buddy Arrington	Chrysler
13.	Dean Combs	Buick
14.	Joe Ruttman	Chevrolet
15.	Tommy Ellis	Buick
16.	Bill Elliott	Ford
17.	Ken Ragan	Buick
18.	Bobby Wawak	Chevrolet
19.	Sterling Marlin	Chevrolet
20.	Trevor Boys	Chevrolet
21.	Jim Vandiver	Chrysler
22.	H. B. Bailey	Pontiac
23.	D. K. Ulrich	Chevrolet
24.	Slick Johnson	Buick
25.	Harry Gant	Buick
26.	J. D. McDuffie	Pontiac
27.	Bob Senneker	Pontiac
28.	Cale Yarborough	Chevrolet
29.	Mark Martin	Chevrolet
30.	Philip Duffie	Buick
31.	Rick Newsom	Chevrolet
32.	Ricky Rudd	Chevrolet
33.	Terry Labonte	Chevrolet
34.	Benny Parsons	Buick
35.	Tommy Gale	Ford
36.	Geoff Bodine	Pontiac
37.	Dick Brooks	Ford
38.	Jimmy Means	Buick
39.	David Pearson	Chevrolet
40.	Tim Richmond	Pontiac
41.	Ron Bouchard	Buick

BUDWEISER 400

June 5
Riverside, California
Time of Race: 2 hours, 49 minutes, 35 seconds
Average Speed: 88.063 mph
Margin of Victory: 7 seconds

FINISH	DRIVER	CAR
1.	Ricky Budd	Chevrolet
2.	Bill Elliott	Ford
3.	Harry Gant	Buick
4.	Dale Earnhardt	Ford
5.	Dick Brooks	Ford
6.	Kyle Petty	Pontiac
7.	Darrell Waltrip	Chevrolet
8.	Morgan Shepherd	Buick
9.	Bill Schmitt	Chevrolet
10.	Richard Petty	Pontiac
11.	Jim Robinson	Oldsmobile
12.	Dave Marcis	Pontiac
13.	Neil Bonnett	Chevrolet
14.	Glen Fancis	Pontiac
15.	Summer McKnight	Chevrolet
16.	D. K. Ulrich	Buick
17.	Buddy Arrington	Chrysler
18.	Jimmy Means	Chevrolet
19.	Bob Kennedy	Chevrolet
20.	Don Waterman	Buick
21.	Stephen Wheeler	Buick
22.	Bobby Allison	Buick
23.	Jim Bown	Buick
24.	J. D. McDuffie	Pontiac
25.	Sterling Marlin	Pontiac
26.	Hershel McGriff	Buick
27.	Rick McCray	Pontiac
28.	Tim Richmond	Pontiac
29.	Geoff Bodine	Pontiac
30.	Scott Miller	Pontiac
31.	Terry Labonte	Chevrolet
32.	Trevor Boys	Chevrolet

33.	Ronnie Thomas	Pontiac
34.	Joe Ruttman	Buick
35.	Ron Esau	Buick
36.	Randy Becker	Buick
37.	Pat Mintey	Pontiac

VAN SCOY DIAMOND MINE 500

June 12
Pocono, Pennsylvania
Time of Race: 3 hours, 53 minutes, 13 seconds
Average Speed: 128.636 mph
Margin of Victory: 9.56 seconds

FINISH	DRIVER	CAR
1.	Bobby Allison	Buick
2.	Darrell Waltrip	Chevrolet
3.	Richard Petty	Pontiac
4.	Tim Richmond	Pontiac
5.	Benny Parsons	Buick
6.	Bill Elliott	Chevrolet
7.	Neil Bonnett	Ford
8.	Dale Earnhardt	Ford
9.	Terry Labonte	Chevrolet
10.	Joe Ruttman	Pontiac
11.	Dave Marcis	Chevrolet
12.	Lake Speed	Chevrolet
13.	Kyle Petty	Pontiac
14.	Trevor Boys	Chevrolet
15.	Morgan Shepherd	Buick
16.	D. K. Ulrich	Buick
17.	Buddy Arrington	Dodge
18.	Harry Gant	Buick
19.	J. D. McDuffie	Pontiac
20.	Jimmy Means	Chevrolet
21.	Ronnie Thomas	Pontiac
22.	Mike Potter	Buick
23.	Cecil Gordon	Chrysler
24.	Steve Gra;y	Buick
25.	Tommy Gale	Ford
26.	Ronnie Hopkins	Chevrolet
27.	Cale Yarborough	Chevrolet
28.	Dick Brooks	Ford
29.	Sterling Marlin	Pontiac
30.	Geoff Bodine	Pontiac
31.	Ricky Rudd	Chevrolet
32.	Bob Riley	Pontiac
33.	John Callis	Chevrolet
34.	Ron Bouchard	Buick
35.	Jocko Maggiacomo	Buick
36.	Jerry Bowman	Ford
37.	Bobby Hillin Jr.	Buick
38.	Bobby Gerhart	Buick

GABRIEL 400

June 19
Brooklyn, Michigan
Time of Race: 2 hours, 53 minutes, 0 seconds
Average Speed: 138.728 mph
Margin of Victory: 1.01 seconds

FINISH	DRIVER	CAR
1.	Cale Yarborough	Chevrolet
2.	Bobby Allison	Buick
3.	Tim Richmond	Pontiac
4.	Darrell Waltrip	Chevrolet
5.	Terry Labonte	Chevrolet
6.	Ricky Rudd	Chevrolet
7.	Buddy Baker	Ford
8.	Harry Gant	Buick
9.	Geoff Bodine	Buick
10.	Morgan Shepherd	Buick
11.	Richard Petty	Pontiac

12.	Dick Brooks	Ford
13.	Benny Parson	Buick
14.	Bob Senneker	Pontiac
15.	Dale Earnhardt	Ford
16.	Kyle Petty	Pontiac
17.	Ronnie Hopkins	Chevrolet
18.	Trevor Boys	Chevrolet
19.	Lake Speed	Chevrolet
20.	Sterling Marlin	Pontiac
21.	Jimmy Means	Buick
22.	D. K. Ulrich	Chevrolet
23.	Steve Moore	Pontiac
24.	Ronnie Thomas	Pontiac
25.	Bill Elliott	Ford
26.	Tommy Gale	Ford
27.	Mark Martin	Oldsmobile
28.	Ron Bouchard	Buick
29.	Buddy Arrington	Chrysler
30.	Dave Marcis	Chevrolet
31.	Neil Bonnett	Chevrolet
32.	Tom Sneva	Chevrolet
33.	Joe Ruttman	Buick
34.	J. D. McDuffie	Pontiac
35.	David Pearson	Chevrolet
36.	Rick Baldwin	Chrysler
37.	Bobby Wawak	Buick

FIRECRACKER 400

July 4
Daytona Beach, Florida
Time of Race: 2 hours, 23 minutes, 20 seconds
Average Speed: 167.442 mph
Margin of Victory: 29 seconds

FINISH	DRIVER	CAR
1.	Buddy Baker	Ford
2.	Morgan Shepherd	Buick
3.	David Pearson	Chevrolet
4.	Ron Bouchard	Buick
5.	Terry Labonte	Chevrolet
6.	Geoff Bodine	Pontiac
7.	Bill Elliott	Ford
8.	Jody Ridley	Buick
9.	Dale Earnhardt	Ford
10.	Lennie Pond	Buick
11.	Harry Gant	Buick
12.	Ken Ragan	Chevrolet
13.	Dave Marcis	Chevrolet
14.	Bobby Allison	Buick
15.	Bobby Hillin Jr.	Buick
16.	Sterling Marlin	Chevrolet
17.	Trevor Boys	Chevrolet
18.	Connie Saylor	Chevrolet
19.	Mark Martin	Oldsmobile
20.	Darrell Waltrip	Chevrolet
21.	Ricky Rudd	Chevrolet
22.	Cecil Gordon	Chrysler
23.	Tommy Gale	Ford
24.	Ronnie Thomas	Pontiac
25.	Clark Dwyer	Chevrolet
26.	Benny Parsons	Chevrolet
27.	Bobby Wawak	Chevrolet
28.	Neil Bonnett	Chevrolet
29.	Lake Speed	Chevrolet
30.	Kyle Petty	Pontiac
31.	Tim Richmond	Pontiac
32.	Dick Brooks	Ford
33.	Richard Petty	Pontiac
34.	Buddy Arrington	Chrysler
35.	Delma Cowart	Buick
36.	Jimmy Means	Buick
37.	Joe Ruttman	Chevrolet
38.	Greg Sacks	Chevrolet
39.	Blackie Wangerin	Ford
40.	Cale Yarborough	Chevrolet

BUSCH NASHVILLE 420

July 16
Nashville, Tennessee
Time of Race: 2 hours, 55 minutes, 12 seconds
Average Speed: 85.726 mph
Margin of Victory: 11 seconds

FINISH	DRIVER	CAR
1.	Dale Earnhardt	Ford
2.	Darrell Waltrip	Chevrolet
3.	Tim Richmond	Pontiac
4.	Bobby Allison	Buick
5.	Ricky Rudd	Chevrolet
6.	Neil Bonnett	Chevrolet
7.	Bill Elliott	Ford
8.	Harry Gant	Buick
9.	Dave Marcis	Chevrolet
10.	Morgan Shepherd	Buick
11.	Terry Labonte	Chevrolet
12.	Jimmy Means	Chevrolet
13.	Trevor Boys	Chevrolet
14.	Dick Brooks	Ford
15.	Sterling Marlin	Pontiac
16.	Geoff Bodine	Pontiac
17.	J. D. McDuffie	Pontiac
18.	Al Elmore	Buick
19.	Richard Petty	Pontiac
20.	Kyle Petty	Pontiac
21.	Steve Gray	Buick
22.	Joe Ruttman	Pontiac
23.	Ronnie Thomas	Pontiac
24.	Buddy Arrington	Chrysler
25.	Don Satterfield	Buick
26.	Darryl Sage	Chevrolet
27.	Ron Bouchard	Buick
28.	Tommy Gale	Ford
29.	James Walker	Ford
30.	D. K. Ulrich	Buick

LIKE COLA 500

July 24
Pocono, Pennsylvania
Time of Race: 4 hours, 21 minutes, 17 seconds
Average Speed: 114.818 mph
Margin of Victory: 2 seconds

FINISH	DRIVER	CAR
1.	Tim Richmond	Pontiac
2.	Darrell Waltrip	Chevrolet
3.	Bobby Allison	Buick
4.	Neil Bonnett	Chevrolet
5.	Harry Gant	Buick
6.	Bill Elliott	Ford
7.	Ricky Rudd	Chevrolet
8.	Dave Marcis	Chevrolet
9.	Joe Ruttman	Buick
10.	Richard Petty	Pontiac
11.	Kyle Petty	Pontiac
12.	Terry Labonte	Chevrolet
13.	Ron Bouchard	Buick
14.	Trevor Boys	Chevrolet
15.	Dick Brooks	Ford
16.	Bobby Hillin Jr.	Buick
17.	D. K. Ulrich	Pontiac
18.	Sterling Marlin	Pontiac
19.	Morgan Shepherd	Buick
20.	Ronnie Thomas	Pontiac
21.	Mike Potter	Oldsmobile
22.	Al Elmore	Buick
23.	Cecil Gordon	Chrysler
24.	Tommy Gale	Ford
25.	J. D. McDuffie	Pontiac
26.	Jocko Maggiacomo	Oldsmobile
27.	Bobby Wawak	Buick
28.	Jerry Bowman	Ford

29.	Greg Sacks	Chevrolet
30.	Dale Earnhardt	Ford
31.	Benny Parsons	Chevrolet
32.	Buddy Arrington	Dodge
33.	Dick May	Buick
34.	Bobby Gerhart	Buick
35.	Jimmy Means	Pontiac
36.	Glenn Jarrett	Ford
37.	Slick Johnson	Buick
38.	Bob Riley	Pontiac
39.	Geoff Bodine	Pontiac
40.	Clark Dwyer	Chevrolet

TALLADEGA 500

July 31
Talladega, Alabama
Time of Race: 2 hours, 55 minutes, 52 seconds
Average Speed: 170.611 mph
Margin of Victory: half a car length

FINISH	DRIVER	CAR
1.	Dale Earnhardt	Ford
2.	Darrell Waltrip	Chevrolet
3.	Tim Richmond	Pontiac
4.	Richard Petty	Pontiac
5.	Harry Gant	Buick
6.	Geoff Bodine	Pontiac
7.	Dick Brooks	Ford
8.	Bill Elliott	Ford
9.	Bobby Allison	Chevrolet
10.	Mark Martin	Chevrolet
11.	Kyle Petty	Pontiac
12.	Ron Bouchard	Buick
13.	Bobby Hillin Jr.	Buick
14.	Ken Ragan	Chevrolet
15.	Joe Ruttman	Chevrolet
16.	Ricky Rudd	Chevrolet
17.	Trevor Boys	Chevrolet
18.	Buddy Arrington	Dodge
19.	Al Elmore	Chevrolet
20.	Ronnie Thomas	Pontiac
21.	Sterling Marlin	Chevrolet
22.	Benny Parsons	Chevrolet
23.	J. D. McDuffie	Pontiac
24.	Cale Yarborough	Chevrolet
25.	David Pearson	Chevrolet
26.	Lake Speed	Chevrolet
27.	Morgan Shepherd	Buick
28.	Buddy Baker	Ford
29.	Terry Labonte	Chevrolet
30.	Mike Potter	Oldsmobile
31.	Jody Ridley	Chevrolet
32.	Dave Marcis	Chevrolet
33.	Cecil Gordon	Chrysler
34.	Bobby Wawak	Chevrolet
35.	Neil Bonnett	Chevrolet
36.	Grant Adcox	Chevrolet
37.	Billie Harvey	Buick
38.	Tommy Gale	Ford
39.	Travis Tiller	Chevrolet
40.	Richard Skillen	Pontiac

CHAMPION SPARK PLUG 400

August 21
Brooklyn, Michigan
Time of Race: 2 hours, 42 minutes, 42 seconds
Average Speed: 147.511 mph
Margin of Victory: .5 seconds

FINISH	DRIVER	CAR
1.	Cale Yarborough	Chevrolet
2.	Darrell Waltrip	Chevrolet
3.	Bill Elliott	Ford
4.	Terry Labonte	Chevrolet
5.	Tim Richmond	Pontiac
6.	Richard Petty	Pontiac
7.	Dale Earnhardt	Ford
8.	Lake Speed	Chevrolet
9.	David Pearson	Chevrolet
10.	Buddy Baker	Ford
11.	Dave Marcis	Chevrolet
12.	Ron Bouchard	Buick
13.	Benny Parsons	Chevrolet
14.	Kyle Petty	Pontiac
15.	Jody Ridley	Chevrolet
16.	Bob Senneker	Pontiac
17.	Greg Sacks	Chevrolet
18.	Mark Martin	Oldsmobile
19.	Trevor Boys	Chevrolet
20.	Dean Combs	Buick
21.	Dick Brooks	Ford
22.	Lennie Pond	Chevrolet
23.	Buddy Arrington	Dodge
24.	Joe Ruttman	Chevrolet
25.	Bobby Hillin Jr.	Buick
26.	Eddie Bierschwale	Buick
27.	Ricky Rudd	Chevrolet
28.	Tommy Gale	Ford
29.	Sterling Marlin	Chevrolet
30.	Harry Gant	Buick
31.	Phil Parsons	Chevrolet
32.	J. D. McDuffie	Pontiac
33.	D. K. Ulrich	Pontiac
34.	Bobby Allison	Buick
35.	Neil Bonnett	Chevrolet
36.	Geoff Bodine	Pontiac
37.	Morgan Shepherd	Buick

BUSCH 500

August 27
Bristol, Tennessee
Time of Race: 2 hours, 29 minutes, 50 seconds
Average Speed: 89.430 mph
Margin of Victory: 1 car length

FINISH	DRIVER	CAR
1.	Darrell Waltrip	Chevrolet
2.	Dale Earnhardt	Ford
3.	Bobby Allison	Buick
4.	Geoff Bodine	Pontiac
5.	Terry Labonte	Chevrolet
6.	Harry Gant	Buick
7.	Ron Bouchard	Buick
8.	Morgan Shepherd	Buick
9.	Richard Petty	Pontiac
10.	Neil Bonnett	Chevrolet
11.	Kyle Petty	Pontiac
12.	Ronnie Thomas	Pontiac
13.	Buddy Arrington	Chrysler
14.	Ricky Rudd	Chevrolet
15.	Sterling Marlin	Pontiac
16.	Al Elmore	Buick
17.	Trevor Boys	Chevrolet
18.	Joe Ruttman	Pontiac
19.	Don Satterfield	Buick
20.	Dave Marcis	Chevrolet
21.	Dick Brooks	Ford
22.	Tim Richmond	Pontiac
23.	Tommy Gale	Ford
24.	Mike Potter	Pontiac
25.	J. D. McDuffie	Pontiac
26.	Jimmy Means	Chevrolet
27.	Bill Elliott	Ford
28.	Ronnie Hopkins	Chevrolet
29.	John McFadden	Buick

SOUTHERN 500

September 5
Darlington, South Carolina
Time of Race: 4 hours, 3 minutes, 52 seconds
Average Speed: 123.343 mph
Margin of Victory: 7 seconds

FINISH	DRIVER	CAR
1.	Bobby Allison	Buick
2.	Bill Elliott	Ford
3.	Darrell Waltrip	Chevrolet
4.	Neil Bonnett	Chevrolet
5.	Terry Labonte	Chevrolet
6.	Buddy Baker	Ford
7.	Cale Yarborough	Chevrolet
8.	Benny Parsons	Chevrolet
9.	Morgan Shepherd	Buick
10.	David Pearson	Chevrolet
11.	Dale Earnhardt	Ford
12.	Richard Petty	Pontiac
13.	Geoff Bodine	Pontiac
14.	Dave Marcis	Chevrolet
15.	Lake Speed	Chevrolet
16.	D. K. Ulrich	Buick
17.	Mark Martin	Oldsmobile
18.	Buddy Arrington	Dodge
19.	Ken Ragan	Chevrolet
20.	Jimmy Means	Chevrolet
21.	Bobby Wawak	Chevrolet
22.	Harry Gant	Buick
23.	Dick May	Ford
24.	Sterling Marlin	Pontiac
25.	Ricky Rudd	Chevrolet
26.	Tim Richmond	Pontiac
27.	Slick Johnson	Buick
28.	Trevor Boys	Chevrolet
29.	Tommy Gale	Ford
30.	Ronnie Thomas	Pontiac
31.	Dick Brooks	Ford
32.	Ron Bouchard	Buick
33.	Jody Ridley	Chevrolet
34.	Philip Duffie	Buick
35.	Kyle Petty	Pontiac
36.	Mike Potter	Oldsmobile
37.	J. D. McDuffie	Pontiac
38.	Joe Ruttman	Pontiac
39.	Lennie Pond	Buick
40.	Ronnie Hopkins	Chevrolet
41.	Bobby Hillin Jr.	Buick

WRANGLER SANFORSET 400

September 11
Richmond, Virginia
Time of Race: 2 hours, 43 minutes, 8 seconds
Average Speed: 79.381 mph
Margin of Victory: 2 seconds

FINISH	DRIVER	CAR
1.	Bobby Allison	Buick
2.	Ricky Rudd	Chevrolet
3.	Darrell Waltrip	Chevrolet
4.	Bill Elliott	Ford
5.	Terry Labonte	Chevrolet
6.	Richard Petty	Pontiac
7.	Buddy Baker	Ford
8.	Neil Bonnett	Chevrolet
9.	Trevor Boys	Chevrolet
10.	D. K. Ulrich	Buick
11.	J. D. McDuffie	Pontiac
12.	Kyle Petty	Pontiac
13.	Dick Brooks	Ford
14.	Buddy Arrington	Dodge
15.	Joe Fields	Buick
16.	Morgan Shepherd	Buick
17.	Ronnie Thomas	Pontiac

18.	Dave Marcis	Chevrolet
19.	Mike Potter	Pontiac
20.	Harry Gant	Buick
21.	Geoff Bodine	Pontiac
22.	Dale Earnhardt	Ford
23.	Tim Richmond	Pontiac
24.	Jimmy Means	Chevrolet
25.	Ron Bouchard	Buick
26.	Sterling Marlin	Pontiac
27.	Joe Ruttman	Pontiac
28.	Lennie Pond	Buick
29.	Don Satterfield	Buick
30.	Tommy Gale	Ford

BUDWEISER 500

September 18
Dover, Delaware
Time of Race: 4 hours, 18 minutes, 45 seconds
Average Speed: 116.077 mph
Margin of Victory: 1 car length

FINISH	DRIVER	CAR
1.	Bobby Allison	Buick
2.	Geoff Bodine	Pontiac
3.	Tim Richmond	Pontiac
4.	Terry Labonte	Chevrolet
5.	Darrell Waltrip	Chevrolet
6.	Morgan Shepherd	Buick
7.	Neil Bonnett	Chevrolet
8.	Bill Elliott	Ford
9.	Richard Petty	Pontiac
10.	Clark Dwyer	Chevrolet
11.	Bobby Hillin Jr.	Buick
12.	D. K. Ulrich	Buick
13.	Ricky Rudd	Chevrolet
14.	Joe Fields	Buick
15.	Cecil Gordon	Chrysler
16.	Ron Bouchard	Buick
17.	Harry Gant	Buick
18.	Jimmy Ingalls	Buick
19.	Laurent Rioux	Chevrolet
20.	Joe Ruttman	Pontiac
21.	Jimmy Means	Chevrolet
22.	Dave Marcis	Chevrolet
23.	Buddy Arrington	Dodge
24.	Ronnie Thomas	Pontiac
25.	Buddy Baker	Ford
26.	Kyle Petty	Pontiac
27.	Sterling Marlin	Pontiac
28.	Tommy Gale	Pontiac
29.	Bob Riley	Pontiac
30.	Jerry Bowman	Ford
31.	Trevor Boys	Chevrolet
32.	Dick Brooks	Ford
33.	Dean Combs	Buick
34.	Natz Peters	Buick
35.	Dale Earnhardt	Ford
36.	J. D. McDuffie	Pontiac

GOODY'S 500

September 29
Martinsville, Virginia
Time of Race: 3 hours, 27 minutes, 16 seconds
Average Speed: 76.134 mph
Margin of Victory: 4.5 seconds

FINISH	DRIVER	CAR
1.	Ricky Rudd	Chevrolet
2.	Bobby Allison	Buick
3.	Darrell Waltrip	Chevrolet
4.	Dale Earnhardt	Ford
5.	Geoff Bodine	Pontiac
6.	Neil Bonnett	Chevrolet

7.	Joe Ruttman	Buick
8.	Harry Gant	Buick
9.	Richard Petty	Pontiac
10.	Buddy Arrington	Dodge
11.	Trevor Boys	Chevrolet
12.	Kyle Petty	Pontiac
13.	J. D. McDuffie	Pontiac
14.	Bill Elliott	Ford
15.	Jimmy Means	Chevrolet
16.	Dick Brooks	Ford
17.	Laurent Rioux	Chevrolet
18.	D. K. Ulrich	Buick
19.	Tommy Gale	Ford
20.	Mike Potter	Pontiac
21.	Ronnie Thomas	Pontiac
22.	Buddy Baker	Ford
23.	Mark Stahl	Ford
24.	Terry Labonte	Chevrolet
25.	Butch Lindley	Buick
26.	Tim Richmond	Pontiac
27.	Sterling Marlin	Pontiac
28.	Dave Marcis	Chevrolet
29.	Morgan Shepherd	Buick

HOLLY FARMS 400

October 2
North Wilkeboro, North Carolina
Time of Race: 2 hours, 28 minutes, 56 seconds
Average Speed: 100.716 mph
Margin of Victory: 3 seconds

FINISH	DRIVER	CAR
1.	Darrell Waltrip	Chevrolet
2.	Dale Earnhardt	Ford
3.	Bobby Allison	Buick
4.	Bill Elliott	Ford
5.	Terry Labonte	Chevrolet
6.	Ricky Rudd	Chevrolet
7.	Ron Bouchard	Buick
8.	Morgan Shepherd	Buick
9.	Harry Gant	Buick
10.	Tim Richmond	Pontiac
11.	Geoff Bodine	Pontiac
12.	Richard Petty	Pontiac
13.	Neil Bonnett	Chevrolet
14.	Joe Ruttman	Buick
15.	Dick Brooks	Ford
16.	Kyle Petty	Pontiac
17.	Sterling Marlin	Pontiac
18.	Buddy Arrington	Chrysler
19.	Trevor Boys	Chevrolet
20.	D. K. Ulrich	Buick
21.	Ronnie Thomas	Pontiac
22.	Jimmy Means	Chevrolet
23.	Mark Stahl	Ford
24.	Tommy Gale	Ford
25.	Dave Marcis	Chevrolet
26.	J. D. McDuffie	Pontiac
27.	Jimmy Walker	Ford
28.	John McFadden	Buick
29.	Mike Potter	Pontiac
30.	Ed Baugess	Chevrolet

MILLER HIGH LIFE 500

October 9
Charlotte, North Carolina
Time of Race: 3 hours, 34 minutes, 43 seconds
Average Speed: 139.998 mph
Margin of Victory: 4 seconds

FINISH	DRIVER	CAR
1.	Richard Petty	Pontiac
2.	Darrell Waltrip	Chevrolet

3.	Benny Parsons	Chevrolet
4.	Terry Labonte	Chevrolet
5.	Tim Richmond	Pontiac
6.	Buddy Baker	Ford
7.	Bobby Allison	Buick
8.	Bill Elliott	Ford
9.	Ricky Rudd	Chevrolet
10.	Cale Yarborough	Chevrolet
11.	Lake Speed	Chevrolet
12.	Jody Ridley	Chevrolet
13.	Joe Ruttman	Chevrolet
14.	Dale Earnhardt	Ford
15.	Ron Bouchard	Buick
16.	Trevor Boys	Chevrolet
17.	Dave Marcis	Oldsmobile
18.	Kyle Petty	Pontiac
19.	Phil Parsons	Chevrolet
20.	D. K. Ulrich	Chevrolet
21.	Jim Sauter	Chevrolet
22.	Rodney Combs	Buick
23.	Jimmy Means	Chevrolet
24.	John Anderson	Chevrolet
25.	Morgan Shepherd	Buick
26.	Neil Bonnett	Chevrolet
27.	Phil Duffie	Buick
28.	Geoff Bodine	Pontiac
29.	Harry Gant	Buick
30.	Greg Sacks	Chevrolet
31.	Tommy Gale	Ford
32.	Dean Combs	Oldsmobile
33.	Mark Martin	Chevrolet
34.	Buddy Arrington	Chrysler
35.	Delma Cowart	Chevrolet
36.	Bobby Hillin Jr.	Buick
37.	Dick Brooks	Ford
38.	Ken Ragan	Chevrolet
39.	David Pearson	Chevrolet
40.	Sterling Marlin	Chevrolet

WARNER W. HODGDON AMERICAN 500

October 30
Rockingham, North Carolina
Time of Race: 4 hours, 11 minutes, 36 seconds
Average Speed: 119.324 mph
Margin of Victory: 1 second

FINISH	DRIVER	CAR
1.	Terry Labonte	Chevrolet
2.	Tim Richmond	Pontiac
3.	Ricky Rudd	Chevrolet
4.	Neil Bonnett	Chevrolet
5.	Darrell Waltrip	Chevrolet
6.	Ron Bouchard	Buick
7.	Dave Marcis	Chevrolet
8.	Lennie Pond	Buick
9.	Jimmy Means	Chevrolet
10.	Tommy Gale	Ford
11.	D. K. Ulrich	Chevrolet
12.	Buddy Arrington	Dodge
13.	Rick Baldwin	Chrysler
14.	J. D. McDuffie	Pontiac
15.	Sterling Marlin	Pontiac
16.	Bobby Allison	Buick
17.	Dale Earnhardt	Ford
18.	Dick Brooks	Ford
19.	Ronnie Thomas	Pontiac
20.	Slick Johnson	Chevrolet
21.	Bill Elliott	Ford
22.	Dick May	Ford
23.	Harry Gant	Buick
24.	Kyle Petty	Pontiac
25.	Jerry Bowman	Ford
26.	Richard Petty	Pontiac
27.	Morgan Shepherd	Buick
28.	Lake Speed	Chevrolet
29.	Buddy Baker	Ford
30.	Joe Ruttman	Pontiac
31.	Mike Potter	Pontiac
32.	Trevor Boys	Chevrolet

33.	Geoff Bodine	Pontiac
34.	Blackie Wangerin	Ford
35.	John McFadden	Buick
36.	Cale Yarborough	Chevrolet

ATLANTA JOURNAL 500

November 6
Atlanta, Georgia
Time of Race: 3 hours, 37 minutes, 37 seconds
Average Speed: 137.643 mph
Margin of Victory: .5 second

FINISH	DRIVER	CAR
1.	Neil Bonnett	Chevrolet
2.	Buddy Baker	Ford
3.	Bobby Allison	Buick
4.	Terry Labonte	Chevrolet
5.	Richard Petty	Pontiac
6.	Bill Elliott	Ford
7.	Morgan Shepherd	Buick
8.	Dean Combs	Oldsmobile
9.	Darrell Waltrip	Chevrolet
10.	Jody Ridley	Chevrolet
11.	Trevor Boys	Chevrolet
12.	Lake Speed	Chevrolet
13.	Dave Marcis	Oldsmobile
14.	Buddy Arrington	Chrysler
15.	Bob Senneker	Pontiac
16.	Sterling Marlin	Chevrolet
17.	Ken Ragan	Chevrolet
18.	Jimmy Means	Chevrolet
19.	Tommy Gale	Ford
20.	Kyle Petty	Pontiac
21.	D. K. Ulrich	Chevrolet
22.	Mike Potter	Pontiac
23.	Cale Yarborough	Chevrolet
24.	Delma Cowart	Buick
25.	Benny Parsons	Chevrolet
26.	Ricky Rudd	Chevrolet
27.	Rick Baldwin	Chrysler
28.	Phil Parsons	Chevrolet
29.	Tim Richmond	Pontiac
30.	Joe Ruttman	Pontiac
31.	Dick Brooks	Ford
32.	J. D. McDuffie	Pontiac
33.	Dale Earnhardt	Ford
34.	Eddie Bierschwale	Buick
35.	Ron Bouchard	Buick
36.	Donnie Allison	Pontiac
37.	Harry Gant	Buick
38.	Greg Sacks	Chevrolet
39.	Joe Booher	Buick

WINSTON WESTERN 500

November 20
Riverside, California
Time of Race: 3 hours, 15 minutes, 9 seconds
Average Speed: 95.859 mph
Margin of Victory: 3 seconds

FINISH	DRIVER	CAR
1.	Bill Elliott	Ford
2.	Benny Parsons	Chevrolet
3.	Neil Bonnett	Chevrolet
4.	Dale Earnhardt	Ford
5.	Tim Richmond	Pontiac
6.	Darrell Waltrip	Chevrolet
7.	Terry Labonte	Chevrolet
8.	Hershel McGriff	Buick
9.	Bobby Allison	Buick
10.	Richard Petty	Pontiac
11.	Ron Bouchard	Buick

12.	Dave Marcis	Oldsmobile
13.	Kyle Petty	Pontiac
14.	Donnie Allison	Pontiac
15.	Randy Becker	Buick
16.	Jimmy Means	Chevrolet
17.	Sterling Marlin	Pontiac
18.	Doug Wheller	Buick
19.	Sumner McNight	Chevrolet
20.	Buddy Baker	Ford
21.	Jim Robinson	Oldsmobile
22.	Scott Miller	Pontiac
23.	Buddy Arrington	Dodge
24.	Trevor Boys	Chevrolet
25.	Don Waterman	Buick
26.	D. K. Ulrich	Ford
27.	Ronnie Thomas	Pontiac
28.	Glen Francis	Pontiac
29.	Pat Mintey	Chevrolet
30.	J. D. McDuffie	Pontiac
31.	Harry Gant	Buick
32.	John Krebs	Oldsmobile
33.	Morgan Shepherd	Buick
34.	Dick Brooks	Ford
35.	Jim Bown	Buick
36.	Roy Smith	Buick
37.	Ricky Rudd	Chevrolet
38.	Ron Esau	Buick
39.	Rick McCay	Pontiac
40.	Bill Schmitt	Chevrolet
41.	Joe Ruttman	Pontiac
42.	Jimmy Insolo	Buick

1984

DAYTONA 500

February 19
Daytona Beach, Florida
Time of Race: 3 hours, 18 minutes, 41 seconds
Average Speed: 15.994 mph
Margin of Victory: 8 car lengths

FINISH	DRIVER	CAR
1.	Cale Yarborough	Chevrolet
2.	Dale Earnhardt	Chevrolet
3.	Darrell Waltrip	Chevrolet
4.	Neil Bonnett	Chevrolet
5.	Bill Elliott	Ford
6.	Harry Gant	Chevrolet
7.	Ricky Rudd	Ford
8.	Geoff Bodine	Chevrolet
9.	David Pearson	Chevrolet
10.	Jody Ridley	Chevrolet
11.	Phil Parson	Chevrolet
12.	Terry Labonte	Chevrolet
13.	Lennie Pond	Chevrolet
14.	Ken Ragan	Chevrolet
15.	Sterling Marlin	Chevrolet
16.	Dean Roper	Pontiac
17.	Jimmy Means	Chevrolet
18.	Greg Sacks	Chevrolet
19.	Dean Combs	Oldsmobile
20.	Clark Dwyer	Chevrolet
21.	Mike Alexander	Oldsmobile
22.	Connie Saylor	Chevrolet
23.	Doug Heveron	Chevrolet
24.	Ronnie Thomas	Chevrolet
25.	Buddy Arrington	Chrysler
26.	Dick Brooks	Ford
27.	Ron Bouchard	Buick
28.	Joe Ruttman	Chevrolet
29.	Benny Parsons	Chevrolet
30.	Rusty Wallace	Pontiac
31.	Richard Petty	Pontiac
32.	Tommy Gale	Ford
33.	Tim Richmond	Pontiac
34.	Bobby Allison	Buick

35.	Bobby Hillin Jr.	Chevrolet
36.	Dick Trickle	Chevrolet
37.	Lake Speed	Chevrolet
38.	Buddy Baker	Ford
39.	A. J. Foyt	Oldsmobile
40.	Kyle Petty	Ford
41.	Trevor Boys	Chevrolet
42.	Dave Marcis	Pontiac

MILLER HIGH LIFE 400

February 26
Richmond, Virginia
Time of Race: 2 hours, 9 minutes, 31 seconds
Average Speed: 76.736 mph
Margin of Victory: 1 second

FINISH	DRIVER	CAR
1.	Ricky Rudd	Ford
2.	Darrell Waltrip	Chevrolet
3.	Terry Labonte	Chevrolet
4.	Bill Elliott	Ford
5.	Neil Bonnett	Chevrolet
6.	Dale Earnhardt	Chevrolet
7.	Tim Richmond	Pontiac
8.	Harry Gant	Chevrolet
9.	Geoff Bodine	Chevrolet
10.	Joe Ruttman	Chevrolet
11.	Dave Marcis	Chevrolet
12.	Lake Speed	Chevrolet
13.	Morgan Shepherd	Buick
14.	Cale Yarborough	Chevrolet
15.	Richard Petty	Ford
16.	Rusty Wallace	Pontiac
17.	Kyle Petty	Ford
18.	Phil Parsons	Chevrolet
19.	Dick Brooks	Ford
20.	Lennie Pond	Chevrolet
21.	Mike Alexander	Oldsmobile
22.	Jimmy Hensley	Ford
23.	J. D. McDuffie	Pontiac
24.	Greg Sacks	Chevrolet
25.	Dean Combs	Oldsmobile
26.	Trevor Boys	Chevrolet
27.	Clark Dwyer	Pontiac
28.	Jimmy Means	Chevrolet
29.	Ron Bouchard	Buick
30.	Bobby Allison	Buick
31.	Ronnie Thomas	Chevrolet
32.	David Pearson	Chevrolet

WARNER W. HODGDON CAROLINA 500

March 4
Rockingham, North Carolina
Time of Race: 4 hours, 3 minutes, 55 seconds
Average Speed: 122.931 mph
Margin of Victory: half a car length

FINISH	DRIVER	CAR
1.	Bobby Allison	Buick
2.	Terry Labonte	Chevrolet
3.	Lake Speed	Chevrolet
4.	Richard Petty	Pontiac
5.	Buddy Baker	Ford
6.	Geoff Bodine	Chevrolet
7.	Ricky Rudd	Ford
8.	Bill Elliott	Ford
9.	Dave Marcis	Pontiac
10.	Darrell Waltrip	Chevrolet
11.	Mike Alexander	Oldsmobile
12.	Clark Dwyer	Chevrolet
13.	Jimmy Means	Pontiac
14.	Dale Earnhardt	Chevrolet

15.	Buddy Arrington	Chrysler
16.	J. D. McDuffie	Pontiac
17.	Joe Ruttman	Chevrolet
18.	Mark Stahl	Ford
19.	Trevor Boys	Chevrolet
20.	Laurent Rioux	Chevrolet
21.	Ron Bouchard	Buick
22.	D. K. Ulrich	Chevrolet
23.	Dick Brooks	Ford
24.	Harry Gant	Chevrolet
25.	Lennie Pond	Chevrolet
26.	Rusty Wallace	Pontiac
27.	Tim Richmond	Pontiac
28.	Neil Bonnett	Chevrolet
29.	Rick Newsom	Buick
30.	Tommy Gale	Ford
31.	Kyle Petty	Ford
32.	Ronnie Thomas	Chevrolet
33.	Connie Saylor	Pontiac
34.	Greg Sacks	Chevrolet
35.	Sterling Marlin	Buick
36.	Blackie Wangerin	Ford

COCA-COLA 500

March 18
Atlanta, Georgia
Time of Race: 3 hours, 26 minutes, 39 seconds
Average Speed: 144.945 mph
Margin of Victory: .5 second

FINISH	DRIVER	CAR
1.	Benny Parsons	Chevrolet
2.	Dale Earnhardt	Chevrolet
3.	Cale Yarborough	Chevrolet
4.	Richard Petty	Pontiac
5.	Bobby Allison	Buick
6.	Harry Gant	Chevrolet
7.	Terry Labonte	Chevrolet
8.	Ricky Rudd	Ford
9.	Lake Speed	Chevrolet
10.	Darrell Waltrip	Chevrolet
11.	Bill Elliott	Ford
12.	Ron Bouchard	Buick
13.	Geoff Bodine	Chevrolet
14.	Dick Brooks	Ford
15.	Trevor Boys	Chevrolet
16.	Greg Sacks	Chevrolet
17.	Jim Sauter	Chevrolet
18.	Dave Marcis	Pontiac
19.	Rusty Wallace	Pontiac
20.	Buddy Arrington	Dodge
21.	Ken Ragan	Chevrolet
22.	H. B. Bailey	Pontiac
23.	Buddy Baker	Ford
24.	Tommy Gale	Ford
25.	Ronnie Thomas	Chevrolet
26.	Don Hume	Oldsmobile
27.	Jody Ridley	Chevrolet
28.	Joe Ruttman	Chevrolet
29.	Phil Parsons	Chevrolet
30.	Doug Heveron	Chevrolet
31.	Mike Anderson	Oldsmobile
32.	Dean Combs	Oldsmobile
33.	Neil Bonnett	Chevrolet
34.	Tim Richmond	Pontiac
35.	A. J. Foyt	Oldsmobile
36.	Delma Cowart	Buick
37.	Bobby Hillin Jr.	Chevrolet
38.	Kyle Petty	Ford
39.	Lennie Pond	Chevrolet
40.	Clark Dwyer	Pontiac

VALLEYDALE 500

April 1
Bristol, Tennessee

Time of Race: 2 hours, 50 minutes, 10 seconds
Average Speed: 93.967 mph
Margin of Victory: 2 seconds

FINISH	DRIVER	CAR
1.	Darrell Waltrip	Chevrolet
2.	Terry Labonte	Chevrolet
3.	Ron Bouchard	Buick
4.	Dave Marcis	Pontiac
5.	Tim Richmond	Pontiac
6.	Ricky Rudd	Ford
7.	Dale Earnhardt	Ford
8.	Richard Petty	Pontiac
9.	Bill Elliott	Ford
10.	Joe Ruttman	Chevrolet
11.	Neil Bonnett	Chevrolet
12.	Rusty Wallace	Pontiac
13.	Phil Parsons	Chevrolet
14.	Doug Heveron	Chevrolet
15.	Ronnie Thomas	Chevrolet
16.	Trevor Boys	Chevrolet
17.	Jimmy Means	Pontiac
18.	Clark Dwyer	Chevrolet
19.	Bobby Allison	Buick
20.	Tommy Gale	Ford
21.	J. D. McDuffie	Pontiac
22.	Buddy Arrington	Dodge
23.	Harry Gant	Chevrolet
24.	D. K. Ulrich	Chevrolet
25.	Geoff Bodine	Chevrolet
26.	Kyle Petty	Ford
27.	Morgan Shepherd	Buick
28.	Tommy Ellis	Chevrolet
29.	Mike Alexander	Oldsmobile
30.	Dick Brooks	Ford

NORTHWESTERN BANK 400

April 8
North Wilkesboro, North Carolina
Time of Race: 2 hours, 33 minutes, 19 seconds
Average Speed: 97.83 mph
Margin of Victory: .5 second

FINISH	DRIVER	CAR
1.	Tim Richmond	Pontiac
2.	Harry Gant	Chevrolet
3.	Ricky Rudd	Ford
4.	Terry Labonte	Chevrolet
5.	Kyle Petty	Ford
6.	Darrell Waltrip	Chevrolet
7.	Ron Bouchard	Buick
8.	Dale Earnhardt	Chevrolet
9.	Neil Bonnett	Chevrolet
10.	Bill Elliott	Ford
11.	Dick Brooks	Ford
12.	Richard Petty	Pontiac
13.	Dave Marcis	Pontiac
14.	Geoff Bodine	Chevrolet
15.	Phil Parsons	Chrysler
16.	Clark Dwyer	Pontiac
17.	Trevor Boys	Chevrolet
18.	Greg Sacks	Chevrolet
19.	D. K. Ulrich	Buick
20.	Buddy Arrington	Chrysler
21.	Mike Alexander	Oldsmobile
22.	Bobby Allison	Buick
23.	Tommy Gale	Ford
24.	J. D. McDuffie	Pontiac
25.	Jimmy Means	Chevrolet
26.	Ronnie Thomas	Chevrolet
27.	Brent Elliott	Buick
28.	Rusty Wallace	Pontiac
29.	Tommy Ellis	Chevrolet
30.	Joe Ruttman	Chevrolet
31.	Dean Combs	Oldsmobile

TRANSOUTH 500

April 15
Darlington, South Carolina
Time of Race: 4 hours, 18 minutes, 16 seconds
Average Speed: 119.925 mph
Margin of Victory: 2 seconds

FINISH	DRIVER	CAR
1.	Darrell Waltrip	Chevrolet
2.	Terry Labonte	Chevrolet
3.	Bill Elliott	Ford
4.	Cale Yarborough	Chevrolet
5.	Dale Earnhardt	Chevrolet
6.	Harry Gant	Chevrolet
7.	Richard Petty	Pontiac
8.	Phil Parsons	Chevrolet
9.	Ricky Rudd	Ford
10.	Neil Bonnett	Chevrolet
11.	Buddy Arrington	Dodge
12.	Bobby Hillin Jr.	Buick
13.	Dave Marcis	Pontiac
14.	Jimmy Means	Pontiac
15.	Clark Dwyer	Pontiac
16.	Trevor Boys	Chevrolet
17.	Ron Bouchard	Buick
18.	Tommy Gale	Ford
19.	Joe Ruttman	Chevrolet
20.	Bobby Allison	Buick
21.	Greg Sacks	Chevrolet
22.	Lake Speed	Chevrolet
23.	Tommy Ellis	Chevrolet
24.	Kyle Petty	Ford
25.	Connie Saylor	Pontiac
26.	Morgan Shepherd	Chevrolet
27.	Benny Parsons	Chevrolet
28.	Ronnie Thomas	Chevrolet
29.	D. K. Ulrich	Buick
30.	Rusty Wallace	Pontiac
31.	Dick Brooks	Ford
32.	Mike Alexander	Oldsmobile
33.	Buddy Baker	Ford
34.	Tim Richmond	Pontiac
35.	Geoff Bodine	Chevrolet
36.	Jody Ridley	Chevrolet
37.	David Pearson	Chevrolet
38.	Lennie Pond	Buick

SOVRAN BANK 500

April 29
Martinsville, Virginia
Time of Race: 3 hours, 35 minutes, 23 seconds
Average Speed: 73.264 mph
Margin of Victory: 6 seconds

FINISH	DRIVER	CAR
1.	Geoff Bodine	Chevrolet
2.	Ron Bouchard	Buick
3.	Darrell Waltrip	Chevrolet
4.	Bobby Allison	Buick
5.	Neil Bonnett	Chevrolet
6.	Joe Ruttman	Chevrolet
7.	Bill Elliott	Ford
8.	Kyle Petty	Ford
9.	Dale Earnhardt	Chevrolet
10.	Buddy Baker	Ford
11.	Dick Brooks	Ford
12.	Richard Petty	Pontiac
13.	Harry Gant	Chevrolet
14.	Dale Jarrett	Chevrolet
15.	Rusty Wallace	Pontiac
16.	Phil Parsons	Chevrolet
17.	Greg Sacks	Chevrolet
18.	Ricky Rudd	Ford
19.	Dave Marcis	Pontiac
20.	Jimmy Hensley	Ford

21.	Clark Dwyer	Pontiac
22.	Trevor Boys	Chevrolet
23.	Tim Richmond	Pontiac
24.	Terry Labonte	Chevrolet
25.	Buddy Arrington	Chrysler
26.	Morgan Shepherd	Buick
27.	Dean Combs	Oldsmobile
28.	Doug Heveron	Chevrolet
29.	Tommy Ellis	Chevrolet
30.	Ronnie Thomas	Chevrolet
31.	Mike Alexander	Oldsmobile

WINSTON 500

May 6
Talladega, Alabama
Time of Race: 2 hours, 53 minutes, 27 seconds
Average Speed: 172.988 mph
Margin of Victory: 1 car length

FINISH	DRIVER	CAR
1.	Cale Yarborough	Chevrolet
2.	Harry Gant	Chevrolet
3.	Buddy Baker	Ford
4.	Bobby Allison	Buick
5.	Benny Parsons	Chevrolet
6.	Richard Petty	Pontiac
7.	Phil Parsons	Chevrolet
8.	Dave Marcis	Pontiac
9.	Bill Elliott	Ford
10.	Ron Bouchard	Buick
11.	Bobby Hillin Jr.	Chevrolet
12.	Sterling Marlin	Chevrolet
13.	Tommy Ellis	Chevrolet
14.	Greg Sacks	Chevrolet
15.	Kyle Petty	Ford
16.	Jody Ridley	Chevrolet
17.	Mike Alexander	Oldsmobile
18.	Trevor Boys	Chevrolet
19.	Tommy Gale	Chevrolet
20.	Ronnie Thomas	Chevrolet
21.	Joe Ruttman	Chevrolet
22.	Ricky Rudd	Ford
23.	Neil Bonnett	Chevrolet
24.	Buddy Arrington	Chrysler
25.	Terry Labonte	Chevrolet
26.	Tim Richmond	Pontiac
27.	Dale Earnhardt	Chevrolet
28.	Dean Roper	Pontiac
29.	Clark Dwyer	Chevrolet
30.	Dick Brooks	Ford
31.	Rusty Wallace	Pontiac
32.	David Pearson	Chevrolet
33.	Lake Speed	Chevrolet
34.	Geoff Bodine	Chevrolet
35.	Phil Barkdoll	Chevrolet
36.	Doug Heveron	Chevrolet
37.	Jim Sauter	Chevrolet
38.	Darrell Waltrip	Chevrolet
39.	Elliott Forbes-Robinson	Buick
40.	Jimmy Means	Chevrolet

COORS 400

May 12
Nashville, Tennessee
Time of Race: 2 hours, 55 minutes, 15 seconds
Average Speed: 85.702 mph
Margin of Victory: 1 car length

FINISH	DRIVER	CAR
1.	Darrell Waltrip	Chevrolet
2.	Neil Bonnett	Chevrolet
3.	Geoff Bodine	Chevrolet

4.	Ricky Rudd	Ford
5.	Ron Bouchard	Buick
6.	Rusty Wallace	Pontiac
7.	Richard Petty	Pontiac
8.	Terry Labonte	Chevrolet
9.	Dick Brooks	Ford
10.	Dave Marcis	Pontiac
11.	Kyle Petty	Pontiac
12.	Bobby Allison	Buick
13.	Mike Alexander	Oldsmobile
14.	Tommy Ellis	Chevrolet
15.	Joe Ruttman	Buick
16.	Harry Gant	Chevrolet
17.	Trevor Boys	Chevrolet
18.	Sterling Marlin	Chevrolet
19.	Dale Earnhardt	Chevrolet
20.	Bill Elliott	Ford
21.	Buddy Arrington	Dodge
22.	Jimmy Means	Chevrolet
23.	Ronnie Thomas	Chevrolet
24.	D. K. Ulrich	Chevrolet
25.	Clark Dwyer	Pontiac
26.	J. D. McDuffie	Pontiac
27.	Tommy Gale	Ford
28.	Tim Richmond	Pontiac
29.	Greg Sacks	Chevrolet
30.	Maurice Randall	Chrysler

BUDWEISER 500

May 20
Dover, Delaware
Time of Race: 4 hours, 12 minutes, 42 seconds
Average Speed: 118.717 mph
Margin of Victory: 4 seconds

FINISH	DRIVER	CAR
1.	Richard Petty	Pontiac
2.	Tim Richmond	Pontiac
3.	Terry Labonte	Chevrolet
4.	Bill Elliott	Ford
5.	Dale Earnhardt	Chevrolet
7.	Buddy Baker	Ford
8.	Ricky Rudd	Ford
9.	Ron Bouchard	Buick
10.	Geoff Bodine	Chevrolet
11.	Rusty Wallace	Pontiac
12.	Bobby Allison	Buick
13.	Kyle Petty	Ford
14.	Joe Ruttman	Pontiac
15.	Neil Bonnett	Chevrolet
16.	Jimmy Means	Pontiac
17.	D. K. Ulrich	Buick
18.	Jerry Bowman	Ford
19.	Trevor Boys	Chevrolet
20.	Dave Marcis	Pontiac
21.	Lake Speed	Chevrolet
22.	Clark Dwyer	Chevrolet
23.	Tommy Gale	Ford
24.	Greg Sacks	Chevrolet
25.	Bobby Hillin Jr.	Buick
26.	Joe Fields	Buick
27.	Harry Gant	Chevrolet
28.	Dick May	Ford
29.	Dean Combs	Oldsmobile
30.	Ronnie Thomas	Chevrolet
31.	Jim Southard	Buick
32.	Buddy Arrington	Chrysler
33.	J. D. McDuffie	Pontiac
34.	Jerry Churchill	Chevrolet
35.	Dick Brooks	Ford
36.	Morgan Shepherd	Chevrolet

WORLD 600

May 27
Charlotte, North Carolina

Time of Race: 4 hours, 38 minutes, 34 seconds
Average Speed: 129.233 mph
Margin of Victory: 17 seconds

FINISH	DRIVER	CAR
1.	Bobby Allison	Buick
2.	Dale Earnhardt	Chevrolet
3.	Ron Bouchard	Buick
4.	Harry Gant	Chevrolet
5.	Geoff Bodine	Chevrolet
6.	Lake Speed	Chevrolet
7.	Buddy Baker	Ford
8.	Jody Ridley	Chevrolet
9.	David Pearson	Chevrolet
10.	Tim Richmond	Pontiac
11.	Ricky Rudd	Ford
12.	Neil Bonnett	Chevrolet
13.	Dick Brooks	Ford
14.	Tommy Ellis	Chevrolet
15.	Rusty Wallace	Pontiac
16.	Mike Alexander	Oldsmobile
17.	Morgan Shepherd	Chevrolet
18.	Dean Combs	Oldsmobile
19.	Ken Ragan	Chevrolet
20.	Jim Sauter	Chevrolet
21.	Cale Yarborough	Chevrolet
22.	Delma Cowart	Buick
23.	Clark Dwyer	Chevrolet
24.	Randy Baker	Buick
25.	Tommy Gale	Ford
26.	Darrell Waltrip	Chevrolet
27.	Jimmy Means	Pontiac
28.	Bill Elliott	Ford
29.	Sterling Marlin	Chevrolet
30.	Terry Labonte	Chevrolet
31.	Phil Parsons	Chevrolet
32.	Buddy Arrington	Dodge
33.	Bobby Hillin Jr.	Chevrolet
34.	Richard Petty	Pontiac
35.	Trevor Boys	Chevrolet
36.	Dave Marcis	Pontiac
37.	Kyle Petty	Ford
38.	Greg Sacks	Chevrolet
39.	Connie Saylor	Pontiac
40.	Doug Heveron	Chevrolet
41.	Joe Ruttman	Chevrolet
42.	Benny Parsons	Chevrolet

BUDWEISER 400

June 3
Riverside, California
Time of Race: 2 hours, 25 minutes, 7 seconds
Average Speed: 102.910 mph
Margin of Victory: 9 seconds

FINISH	DRIVER	CAR
1.	Terry Labonte	Chevrolet
2.	Neil Bonnett	Chevrolet
3.	Bobby Allison	Buick
4.	Geoff Bodine	Chevrolet
5.	Dale Earnhardt	Chevrolet
6.	Tim Richmond	Pontiac
7.	Joe Ruttman	Chevrolet
8.	Kyle Petty	Ford
9.	Ricky Rudd	Ford
10.	Bill Elliott	Ford
11.	Darrell Waltrip	Chevrolet
12.	Dick Brooks	Ford
13.	Trevor Boys	Chevrolet
14.	Jim Robinson	Oldsmobile
15.	Derrike Cope	Ford
16.	Glen Francis	Pontiac
17.	Clark Dwyer	Pontiac
18.	D. K. Ulrich	Buick
19.	Ron Rouchard	Buick
20.	Rusty Wallace	Pontiac

21.	Buddy Arrington	Chrysler
22.	Harry Goularte	Buick
23.	Richard Petty	Pontiac
24.	Kevin Terris	Buick
25.	Sumner McKnight	Chevrolet
26.	Roy Smith	Pontiac
27.	Ron Esau	Buick
28.	Jim Bown	Buick
29.	Harry Gant	Chevrolet
30.	Rick McCray	Pontiac
31.	Mike Alexander	Oldsmobile
32.	Greg Sacks	Chevrolet
33.	Ruben Garcia	Buick
34.	Dave Marcis	Pontiac
35.	Hershel McGriff	Pontiac
36.	Scott Miller	Pontiac
37.	Gary Mayeda	Ford
38.	Jerry Jolly	Chevrolet
39.	Bill Schmitt	Chevrolet
40.	John Krebs	Oldsmobile

VAN SCOY DIAMOND MINES 500

June 10
Pocono, Pennsylvania
Time of Race: 3 hours, 37 minutes, 8 seconds
Average Speed: 138.164 mph
Margin of Victory: 3.75 seconds

FINISH	DRIVER	CAR
1.	Cale Yarborough	Chevrolet
2.	Harry Gant	Chevrolet
3.	Terry Labonte	Chevrolet
4.	Bill Elliott	Ford
5.	Tim Richmond	Pontiac
6.	Darrell Waltrip	Chevrolet
7.	Bobby Allison	Buick
8.	Dale Earnhardt	Chevrolet
9.	Benny Parsons	Chevrolet
10.	Lake Speed	Chevrolet
11.	Joe Ruttman	Chevrolet
12.	Kyle Petty	Ford
13.	Richard Petty	Pontiac
14.	Neil Bonnett	Chevrolet
15.	Dave Marcis	Pontiac
16.	Bobby Hillin Jr.	Buick
17.	Rusty Wallace	Pontiac
18.	Ricky Rudd	Ford
19.	Ron Bouchard	Buick
20.	Dick Brooks	Ford
21.	Phil Parsons	Chevrolet
22.	Greg Sacks	Chevrolet
23.	Buddy Arrington	Chrysler
24.	Ronnie Thomas	Chevrolet
25.	Clark Dwyer	Pontiac
26.	Doug Heveron	Chevrolet
27.	Tommy Gale	Ford
28.	Bobby Wawak	Pontiac
29.	Bob Riley	Pontiac
30.	Steve Gray	Chevrolet
31.	Jim Southard	Chevrolet
32.	Trevor Boys	Chevrolet
33.	Sterling Marlin	Chevrolet
34.	Bobby Gerhart	Chevrolet
35.	Buddy Baker	Ford
36.	Geoff Bodine	Chevrolet
37.	D. K. Ulrich	Buick
38.	Jerry Bowman	Ford
39.	J. D. McDuffie	Pontiac

MILLER HIGH LIFE 400

June 17
Brooklyn, Michigan
Time of Race: 2 hours, 58 minutes, 10 seconds
Average Speed: 134.705 mph
Margin of Victory: 2 seconds

FINISH	DRIVER	CAR
1.	Bill Elliott	Ford
2.	Dale Earnhardt	Chevrolet
3.	Darrell Waltrip	Chevrolet
4.	Harry Gant	Chevrolet
5.	Lake Speed	Chevrolet
6.	Bobby Allison	Buick
7.	Geoff Bodine	Buick
8.	Joe Ruttman	Chevrolet
9.	David Pearson	Chevrolet
10.	Buddy Baker	Ford
11.	Dick Brooks	Ford
12.	Kyle Petty	Ford
13.	Cale Yarborough	Chevrolet
14.	Rusty Wallace	Pontiac
15.	Phil Parsons	Chevrolet
16.	Tim Richmond	Pontiac
17.	Neil Bonnett	Chevrolet
18.	Buddy Arrington	Chevrolet
19.	Bobby Hillin Jr.	Buick
20.	Ron Bouchard	Buick
21.	Dave Marcis	Pontiac
22.	Morgan Shepherd	Chevrolet
23.	Mike Alexander	Oldsmobile
24.	Elliott Forbes-Robinson	Buick
25.	Ronnie Thomas	Chevrolet
26.	Ken Ragan	Chevrolet
27.	David Simko	Buick
28.	Benny Parsons	Chevrolet
29.	D. K. Ulrich	Buick
30.	Doug Heveron	Chevrolet
31.	Terry Labonte	Chevrolet
32.	Greg Sacks	Chevrolet
33.	Joe Ruttman	Buick
34.	Tommy Gale	Ford
35.	Richard Petty	Pontiac
36.	Jody Ridley	Chevrolet
37.	Trevor Boys	Chevrolet
38.	Tommy Ellis	Chevrolet
39.	Clark Dwyer	Chevrolet
40.	Ricky Rudd	Ford

PEPSI FIRECRACKER 400

July 4
Daytona Beach, Florida
Time of Race: 2 hours, 19 minutes, 59 seconds
Average Speed: 171.204 mph
Margin of Victory: under caution

FINISH	DRIVER	CAR
1.	Richard Petty	Pontiac
2.	Harry Gant	Chevrolet
3.	Cale Yarborough	Chevrolet
4.	Bobby Allison	Buick
5.	Benny Parsons	Chevrolet
6.	Bill Elliott	Ford
7.	Terry Labonte	Chevrolet
8.	Dale Earnhardt	Chevrolet
9.	Neil Bonnett	Chevrolet
10.	Joe Ruttman	Chevrolet
11.	Tim Richmond	Pontiac
12.	Geoff Bodine	Chevrolet
13.	Phil Parsons	Chevrolet
14.	Tommy Ellis	Chevrolet
15.	Ricky Rudd	Ford
16.	Trevor Boys	Chevrolet
17.	David Pearson	Chevrolet
18.	Dave Marcis	Pontiac
19.	Jody Ridley	Chevrolet
20.	Rusty Wallace	Pontiac
21.	Dean Roper	Pontiac
22.	Mike Alexander	Oldsmobile
23.	Dale Jarrett	Pontiac
24.	Tommy Gale	Ford
25.	Clark Dwyer	Chevrolet
26.	Ken Ragan	Chevrolet
27.	Connie Saylor	Chevrolet
28.	Doug Heveron	Chevrolet

FINISH	DRIVER	CAR
29.	Ronnie Thomas	Chevrolet
30.	Kyle Petty	Ford
31.	Darrell Waltrip	Chevrolet
32.	Dean Combs	Chevrolet
33.	Sterling Marlin	Chevrolet
34.	Ron Bouchard	Buick
35.	Steve Moore	Chevrolet
36.	Buddy Arrington	Chrysler
37.	Bobby Hillin Jr.	Chevrolet
38.	Dick Brooks	Ford
39.	Greg Sacks	Chevrolet
40.	Morgan Shepherd	Chevrolet
41.	Buddy Baker	Ford
42.	Lake Speed	Chevrolet

PEPSI 420

July 14
Nashville, Tennessee
Time of Race: 3 hours, 5 minutes, 38 seconds
Average Speed: 80.908 mph
Margin of Victory: 1 car length

FINISH	DRIVER	CAR
1.	Geoff Bodine	Chevrolet
2.	Darrell Waltrip	Chevrolet
3.	Dale Earnhardt	Chevrolet
4.	Ron Bouchard	Buick
5.	Bobby Allison	Buick
6.	Terry Labonte	Chevrolet
7.	Bill Elliott	Ford
8.	Joe Ruttman	Chevrolet
9.	Harry Gant	Chevrolet
10.	Neil Bonnett	Chevrolet
11.	Tommy Ellis	Chevrolet
12.	Mike Alexander	Oldsmobile
13.	Phil Parsons	Chevrolet
14.	Tim Richmond	Pontiac
15.	Kyle Petty	Ford
16.	Ricky Rudd	Ford
17.	Buddy Arrington	Chrysler
18.	Rusty Wallace	Pontiac
19.	Ken Schrader	Ford
20.	Jeff Hooker	Pontiac
21.	Ronnie Thomas	Chevrolet
22.	Trevor Boys	Chevrolet
23.	Dave Marcis	Pontiac
24.	Clark Dwyer	Chevrolet
25.	Richard Petty	Pontiac
26.	Morgan Shepherd	Buick
27.	Dick Brooks	Ford
28.	Jody Ridley	Chevrolet
29.	Greg Sacks	Chevrolet
30.	Sterling Marlin	Pontiac

LIKE COLA 500

July 22
Pocono, Pennsylvania
Time of Race: 4 hours, 7 minutes, 21 seconds
Average Speed: 121.351 mph
Margin of Victory: 2 car lengths

FINISH	DRIVER	CAR
1.	Harry Gant	Chevrolet
2.	Cale Yarborough	Chevrolet
3.	Bill Elliott	Ford
4.	Terry Labonte	Chevrolet
5.	Benny Parsons	Chevrolet
6.	Rusty Wallace	Pontiac
7.	Ron Bouchard	Buick
8.	Kyle Petty	Ford
9.	Tim Richmond	Pontiac
10.	Dale Earnhardt	Chevrolet

11.	Dick Brooks	Ford
12.	Geoff Bodine	Chevrolet
13.	Trevor Boys	Chovrolet
14.	Joe Ruttman	Chevrolet
15.	Clark Dwyer	Pontiac
16.	Buddy Arrington	Chrysler
17.	Phil Parsons	Chevrolet
18.	Gene Coyle	Chevrolet
19.	Neil Bonnett	Chevrolet
20.	Jim Southard	Buick
21.	Doug Heveron	Chevrolet
22.	Darrell Waltrip	Chevrolet
23.	Charles Poalillo	Chevrolet
24.	Greg Sacks	Chevrolet
25.	Jimmy Means	Pontiac
26.	Dave Marcis	Pontiac
27.	Richard Petty	Pontiac
28.	Bobby Allison	Buick
29.	Connie Saylor	Pontiac
30.	Jerry Bowman	Ford
31.	J. D. McDuffie	Pontiac
32.	Bobby Wawak	Buick
33.	Bobby Hillin	Chevrolet
34.	Tommy Ellis	Chevrolet
35.	Ken Ragan	Chevrolet
36.	Tommy Gale	Ford
37.	Jim Ingalls	Buick
38.	Bobby Gerhart	Chevrolet
39.	Ricky Rudd	Ford
40.	Ronnie Thomas	Chevrolet

TALLADEGA 500

July 29
Talladega, Alabama
Time of Race: 3 hours, 12 minutes, 4 seconds
Average Speed: 155.485 mph
Margin of Victory: 1.66 seconds

FINISH	DRIVER	CAR
1.	Dale Earnhardt	Chevrolet
2.	Buddy Baker	Ford
3.	Terry Labonte	Chevrolet
4.	Bobby Allison	Buick
5.	Cale Yarborough	Chevrolet
6.	Darrell Waltrip	Chevrolet
7.	Harry Gant	Chevrolet
8.	Lake Speed	Chevrolet
9.	Tommy Ellis	Chevrolet
10.	Bill Elliott	Ford
11.	Ken Ragan	Chevrolet
12.	Rusty Wallace	Pontiac
13.	Dave Marcis	Pontiac
14.	Ricky Rudd	Ford
15.	Bobby Hillin Jr.	Chevrolet
16.	Ron Bouchard	Buick
17.	Mike Alexander	Oldsmobile
18.	Steve Moore	Chevrolet
19.	Neil Bonnett	Chevrolet
20.	Phil Parson	Chevrolet
21.	Buddy Arrington	Chrysler
22.	Kyle Petty	Ford
23.	Richard Petty	Pontiac
24.	Trevor Boys	Chevrolet
25.	Phil Barkdoll	Chevrolet
26.	Geoff Bodine	Chevrolet
27.	Ronnie Thomas	Chevrolet
28.	Clark Dwyer	Chevrolet
29.	Greg Sacks	Chevrolet
30.	Morgan Shepherd	Chevrolet
31.	Eddie Bierschwale	Chevrolet
32.	Sterling Marlin	Chevrolet
33.	Tim Richmond	Pontiac
34.	Jody Ridley	Chevrolet
35.	Dick Brooks	Ford
36.	A. J. Foyt	Oldsmobile
37.	Joe Ruttman	Chevrolet
38.	Elliott Forges-Robinson	Chevrolet
39.	Randy Baker	Buick
40.	Grant Adcox	Chevrolet

CHAMPION SPARK PLUG 400

August 12
Brooklyn, Michigan
Time of Race: 2 hours, 35 minutes, 59 seconds
Average Speed: 153.863 mph
Margin of Victory: 1 second

FINISH	DRIVER	CAR
1.	Darrell Waltrip	Chevrolet
2.	Terry Labonte	Chevrolet
3.	Bill Elliott	Ford
4.	Harry Gant	Chevrolet
5.	Cale Yarborough	Chevrolet
6.	Benny Parsons	Chevrolet
7.	Dale Earnhardt	Chevrolet
8.	Buddy Baker	Ford
9.	Richard Petty	Pontiac
10.	Bobby Allison	Buick
11.	Ron Bouchard	Buick
12.	Ricky Rudd	Ford
13.	Neil Bonnett	Chevrolet
14.	Jody Ridley	Chevrolet
15.	Tim Richmond	Pontiac
16.	Lake Speed	Chevrolet
17.	Kyle Petty	Ford
18.	Dick Brooks	Ford
19.	Dave Marcis	Pontiac
20.	Joe Ruttman	Chevrolet
21.	Bobby Hillin Jr.	Chevrolet
24.	Mike Alexander	Oldsmobile
25.	Rodney Combs	Buick
26.	Jimmy Means	Chevrolet
27.	Trevor Boys	Chevrolet
28.	Morgan Shepard	Chevrolet
29.	Phil Parsons	Chevrolet
30.	Jeff Hooker	Pontiac
31.	Buddy Arrington	Chrysler
32.	Sterling Marlin	Chevrolet
33.	Ken Schrader	Ford
34.	Geoff Bodine	Chevrolet
35.	Rusty Wallace	Pontiac
36.	Tommy Ellis	Chevrolet
37.	Doug Heveron	Chevrolet
38.	Dean Combs	Chevrolet
39.	David Pearson	Chevrolet
40.	Clark Dwyer	Chevrolet

BUSCH 500

August 25
Bristol, Tennessee
Time of Race: 3 hours, 7 minutes, 19 seconds
Average Speed: 85.365 mph
Margin of Victory: 1.44 seconds

FINISH	DRIVER	CAR
1.	Terry Labonte	Chevrolet
2.	Bobby Allison	Buick
3.	Dick Brooks	Ford
4.	Dave Marcis	Pontiac
5.	Harry Gant	Chevrolet
6.	Bill Elliott	Ford
7.	Mike Alexander	Oldsmobile
8.	Sterling Marlin	Oldsmobile
9.	Greg Sacks	Chevrolet
10.	Dale Earnhardt	Chevrolet
11.	Tommy Gale	Ford
12.	J. D. McDuffie	Pontiac
13.	Buddy Arrington	Chrysler
14.	Ron Bouchard	Buick
15.	Clark Dwyer	Buick
16.	Ricky Rudd	Ford
17.	Richard Petty	Pontiac
18.	Trevor Boys	Chevrolet
19.	Morgan Shepherd	Chevrolet
20.	Rusty Wallace	Pontiac

21.	Darrell Waltrip	Chevrolet
22.	Geoff Bodine	Chevrolet
23.	Neil Bonnett	Chevrolet
24.	Kyle Petty	Ford
25.	Tim Richmond	Pontiac
26.	Phil Parsons	Chevrolet
27.	Ronnie Thomas	Chevrolet
28.	Tommy Ellis	Chevrolet
29.	Joe Ruttman	Chevrolet
30.	Jimmy Means	Pontiac

SOUTHERN 500

September 2
Darlington, South Carolina
Time of Race: 3 hours, 54 minutes, 2 seconds
Average Speed: 128.270 mph
Margin of Victory: 2 seconds

FINISH	DRIVER	CAR
1.	Harry Gant	Chevrolet
2.	Tim Richmond	Pontiac
3.	Buddy Baker	Ford
4.	Rusty Wallace	Pontiac
5.	Ricky Rudd	Ford
6.	Dick Brooks	Ford
7.	Phil Parsons	Chevrolet
8.	Terry Labonte	Chevrolet
9.	Benny Parsons	Chevrolet
10.	Bobby Allison	Buick
11.	Trevor Boys	Chevrolet
12.	Geoff Bodine	Chevrolet
13.	Joe Ruttman	Chevrolet
14.	Lake Speed	Chevrolet
15.	Bill Elliott	Ford
16.	Jody Ridley	Chevrolet
17.	Cale Yarborough	Chevrolet
18.	Jimmy Means	Pontiac
19.	Tommy Ellis	Chevrolet
20.	Clark Dwyer	Chevrolet
21.	Dave Marcis	Pontiac
22.	Tommy Gale	Ford
23.	Bobby Hillin Jr.	Chevrolet
24.	J. D. McDuffie	Pontiac
25.	H.B Bailey	Pontiac
26.	Ken Ragan	Chevrolet
27.	Randy Baker	Buick
28.	Buddy Arrington	Chrysler
29.	Richard Petty	Pontiac
30.	Neil Bonnet	Chevrolet
31.	Connie Saylor	Chevrolet
32.	Kyle Petty	Ford
33.	Ron Bouchard	Buick
34.	Mike Alexander	Oldsmobile
35.	Morgan Shepherd	Chevrolet
36.	Slick Johnson	Chevrolet
37.	Greg Sacks	Chevrolet
38.	Dale Earnhardt	Chevrolet
39.	Sterling Marlin	Chevrolet
40.	Darrell Waltrip	Chevrolet
41.	David Pearson	Chevrolet

WRANGLER SANFOREST 400

September 9
Richmond, Virginia
Time of Race: 2 hours, 53 minutes, 57 seconds
Average Speed: 74.780 mph
Margin of Victory: 3 seconds

FINISH	DRIVER	CAR
1.	Darrell Waltrip	Chevrolet
2.	Ricky Rudd	Ford
3.	Dale Earnhardt	Chevrolet

4.	Geoff Bodine	Chevrolet
5.	Richard Petty	Pontiac
6.	Kyle Petty	Ford
7.	Neil Bonnett	Chevrolet
8.	Terry Labonte	Chevrolet
9.	Harry Gant	Chevrolet
10.	Dick Brooks	Ford
11.	Rusty Wallace	Pontiac
12.	Morgan Shepherd	Pontiac
13.	Ron Bouchard	Buick
14.	Cale Yarborough	Chevrolet
15.	Tommy Ellis	Chevrolet
16.	Dave Marcis	Pontiac
17.	Lennie Pond	Oldsmobile
18.	Jimmy Means	Chevrolet
19.	Buddy Baker	Ford
20.	Tim Richmond	Pontiac
21.	Greg Sacks	Pontiac
22.	Jimmy Hensley	Ford
23.	Buddy Arrington	Chrysler
24.	Bill Elliott	Ford
25.	Bobby Allison	Buick
26.	Clark Dwyer	Chevrolet
27.	Trevor Boys	Chevrolet
28.	J. D. McDuffie	Pontiac
29.	Derrike Cope	Ford
30.	Joe Ruttman	Chevrolet

DELAWARE 500

September 16
Dover, Delaware
Time of Race: 4 hours, 28 minutes, 12 seconds
Average Speed: 111.856 mph
Margin of Victory: under caution

FINISH	DRIVER	CAR
1.	Harry Gant	Chevrolet
2.	Terry Labonte	Chevrolet
3.	Ricky Rudd	Ford
4.	Dave Marcis	Pontiac
5.	Dale Earnhardt	Chevrolet
6.	Neil Bonnett	Chevrolet
7.	Dick Brooks	Ford
8.	Ron Bouchard	Buick
9.	Geoff Bodine	Chevrolet
10.	Trevor Boys	Chevrolet
11.	Darrell Waltrip	Chevrolet
12.	Lennie Pond	Oldsmobile
13.	Doug Heveron	Chevrolet
14.	Kyle Petty	Ford
15.	Jimmy Means	Chevrolet
16.	J. D. McDuffie	Pontiac
17.	Buddy Arrington	Chrysler
18.	Clark Dwyer	Ford
19.	Dick May	Ford
20.	Jim Southard	Buick
21.	Gene Coyle	Chevrolet
22.	Morgan Shepherd	Chevrolet
23.	Johnny Coy	Buick
24.	Phil Good	Chrysler
25.	Greg Sacks	Chevrolet
26.	Buddy Baker	Ford
27.	Tommie Crozier	Pontiac
28.	Tim Richmond	Pontiac
29.	Jody Ridley	Chevrolet
30.	Rusty Wallace	Pontiac
31.	Joe Fields	Buick
32.	Bill Elliott	Ford
33.	Joe Ruttman	Chevrolet
34.	Tommy Ellis	Chevrolet
35.	Ronnie Thomas	Chevrolet
36.	Bobby Allison	Buick
37.	Richard Petty	Pontiac
38.	Jerry Bowman	Ford
39.	Bobby Gerhart	Chevrolet
40.	Jim Ingalls	Chevrolet

GOODY'S 500

September 23
Martinsville, Virginia
Time of Race: 3 hours, 28 minutes, 55 seconds
Average Speed: 75.532 mph
Margin of Victory: 1 lap & 3 seconds

FINISH	DRIVER	CAR
1.	Darrell Waltrip	Chevrolet
2.	Terry Labonte	Chevrolet
3.	Bill Elliott	Ford
4.	Harry Gant	Chevrolet
5.	Neil Bonnett	Chevrolet
6.	Buddy Baker	Ford
7.	Dave Marcis	Pontiac
8.	Richard Petty	Pontiac
9.	Lennie Pond	Oldsmobile
10.	Kyle Petty	Ford
11.	Dick Brooks	Ford
12.	Dale Earnhardt	Chevrolet
13.	Rusty Wallace	Pontiac
14.	Doug Heveron	Buick
15.	Jimmy Means	Pontiac
16.	Ronnie Thomas	Chevrolet
17.	Tommy Ellis	Chevrolet
18.	Buddy Arrington	Dodge
19.	Ron Bouchard	Buick
20.	Phil Parsons	Chevrolet
21.	Tim Richmond	Pontiac
22.	Jimmy Hensley	Ford
23.	Bobby Allison	Buick
24.	Morgan Shepherd	Pontiac
25.	J. D. McDuffie	Pontiac
26.	Trevor Boys	Chevrolet
27.	Ricky Rudd	Ford
28.	Geoff Bodine	Chevrolet
29.	Joe Ruttman	Chevrolet
30.	Greg Sacks	Chevrolet
31.	Sam Ard	Chevrolet

MILLER HIGH LIFE 500

October 7
Charlotte, North Carolina
Time of Race: 3 hours, 24 minutes, 41 seconds
Average Speed: 146.861 mph
Margin of Victory: 14.5 seconds

FINISH	DRIVER	CAR
1.	Bill Elliott	Ford
2.	Benny Parsons	Chevrolet
3.	Cale Yarborough	Chevrolet
4.	Harry Gant	Chevrolet
5.	Terry Labonte	Chevrolet
6.	Geoff Bodine	Chevrolet
7.	Jody Ridley	Chevrolet
8.	Ricky Rudd	Ford
9.	Richard Petty	Pontiac
10.	Bobby Allison	Buick
11.	Ron Bouchard	Buick
12.	Trevor Boys	Chevrolet
13.	Dick Brooks	Ford
14.	Rusty Wallace	Pontiac
15.	Bobby Hillin Jr.	Chevrolet
16.	Neil Bonnett	Chevrolet
17.	Kyle Petty	Ford
18.	Greg Sacks	Chevrolet
19.	Jimmy Means	Pontiac
20.	Elliott Forbes-Robinson	Buick
21.	L. D. Ottinger	Chevrolet
22.	Bobby Wawak	Buick
23.	Morgan Shepherd	Chevrolet
24.	Dave Marcis	Pontiac
25.	Lennie Pond	Oldsmobile
26.	Ken Schrader	Ford
27.	Darrell Waltrip	Chevrolet

FINISH	DRIVER	CAR
28.	Dean Combs	Chevrolet
29.	Buddy Baker	Ford
30.	Tim Richmond	Pontiac
31.	Phil Parsons	Chevrolet
32.	Lake Speed	Chevrolet
33.	Tommy Ellis	Chevrolet
34.	Connie Saylor	Chevrolet
35.	Sterling Marlin	Chevrolet
36.	Ken Ragan	Chevrolet
37.	Doug Heveron	Chevrolet
38.	David Pearson	Chevrolet
39.	Dale Earnhardt	Chevrolet
40.	Joe Ruttman	Chevrolet
41.	Don Paul	Chevrolet

HOLLY FARMS 400

October 14
North Wilkesboro, North Carolina
Time of Race: 2 hours, 45 minutes, 42 seconds
Average Speed: 90.525 mph
Margin of Victory: .5 second

FINISH	DRIVER	CAR
1.	Darrell Waltrip	Chevrolet
2.	Harry Gant	Chevrolet
3.	Bobby Allison	Buick
4.	Neil Bonnett	Chevrolet
5.	Rusty Wallace	Pontiac
6.	Ricky Rudd	Ford
7.	Dale Earnhardt	Chevrolet
8.	Bill Elliott	Ford
9.	Terry Labonte	Chevrolet
10.	Buddy Baker	Ford
11.	Dick Brooks	Ford
12.	Lennie Pond	Oldsmobile
13.	Tim Richmond	Pontiac
14.	Tommy Ellis	Chevrolet
15.	Phil Parsons	Chevrolet
16.	Jimmy Means	Pontiac
17.	Ken Schrader	Ford
18.	Richard Petty	Pontiac
19.	Bobby Gerhart	Chevrolet
20.	Kyle Petty	Ford
21.	Jeff Hooker	Pontiac
22.	L. D. Ottinger	Chevrolet
23.	Geoff Bodine	Chevrolet
24.	Greg Sacks	Chevrolet
25.	Lake Speed	Pontiac
26.	Dave Marcis	Pontiac
27.	Trevor Boys	Chevrolet
28.	Ron Bouchard	Buick
29.	Buddy Arrington	Chevrolet
30.	J. D. McDuffie	Pontiac

WARNER W. HODGDON AMERICAN 500

October 21
Rockingham, North Carolina
Time of Race: 4 hours, 26 minutes, 35 seconds
Average Speed: 112.617 mph
Margin of Victory: 1 foot

FINISH	DRIVER	CAR
1.	Bill Elliott	Ford
2.	Harry Gant	Chevrolet
3.	Terry Labonte	Chevrolet
4.	Darrell Waltrip	Chevrolet
5.	Bobby Allison	Buick
6.	Morgan Shepherd	Chevrolet
7.	Buddy Baker	Ford
8.	Tim Richmond	Pontiac
9.	Dave Marcis	Pontiac
10.	Lennie Pond	Oldsmobile

11.	Trevor Boys	Chevrolet
12.	Bobby Hillin Jr.	Buick
13.	Dale Earnhardt	Chevrolet
14.	Ron Bouchard	Buick
15.	Richard Petty	Pontiac
16.	Dick May	Ford
17.	Joe Millikan	Ford
18.	Jimmy Means	Pontiac
19.	Geoff Bodine	Chevrolet
20.	Buddy Arrington	Dodge
21.	Terry Schoonover	Chrysler
22.	Jim Ingalls	Chevrolet
23.	Ricky Rudd	Ford
24.	Kyle Petty	Ford
25.	Bobby Fox	Chevrolet
26.	Rusty Wallace	Pontiac
27.	Mark Stahl	Ford
28.	Bobby Wawak	Buick
29.	Lake Speed	Chevrolet
30.	Dick Brooks	Ford
31.	Buddy Boys	Buick
32.	Jerry Bowman	Ford
33.	Neil Bonnett	Chevrolet
34.	Joe Ruttman	Chevrolet
35.	Greg Sacks	Chevrolet
36.	J. D. McDuffie	Pontiac
37.	Dale Jarrett	nc>Chevrolet
38.	Clark Dwyer	Pontiac
39.	Jeff Hooker	Pontiac
40.	Mike Potter	Ford

ATLANTA JOURNAL 500

November 11
Atlanta, Georgia
Time of Race: 3 hours, 42 minutes, 31 seconds
Average Speed: 134.610 mph
Margin of Victory: .56 seconds

FINISH	DRIVER	CAR
1.	Dale Earnhardt	Chevrolet
2.	Bill Elliott	Ford
3.	Ricky Rudd	Ford
4.	Benny Parsons	Chevrolet
5.	Bobby Allison	Buick
6.	Darrell Waltrip	Chevrolet
7.	Lake Speed	Chevrolet
8.	Richard Petty	Pontiac
9.	Sterling Marlin	Chevrolet
10.	Dave Marcis	Pontiac
11.	Cale Yarborough	Chevrolet
12.	Ron Bouchard	Buick
13.	Tim Richmond	Pontiac
14.	Morgan Shepherd	Chevrolet
15.	Rusty Wallace	Pontiac
16.	Jimmy Means	Pontiac
17.	Dick Brooks	Ford
18.	Doug Heveron	Chevrolet
19.	Elliott Forbes-Robinson	Buick
20.	Buddy Baker	Ford
21.	Neil Bonnett	Chevrolet
22.	Kyle Petty	Ford
23.	Trevor Boys	Chevrolet
24.	Geoff Bodine	Chevrolet
25.	David Pearson	Chevrolet
26.	Harry Gant	Chevrolet
27.	Ken Schrader	Ford
28.	Phil Parsons	Chevrolet
29.	Eddie Bierschwale	Buick
30.	Terry Labonte	Chevrolet
31.	Greg Sacks	Chevrolet
32.	Jody Ridley	Chevrolet
33.	Bobby Hillin Jr.	Chevrolet
34.	Terry Schoonover	Chevrolet
35.	Joe Ruttman	Chevrolet
36.	Dean Combs	Chevrolet
37.	Lennie Pond	Oldsmobile
38.	Mark Stahl	Ford
39.	Bob Penrod	Chevrolet
40.	Ken Ragan	Chevrolet

WINSTON WESTERN 500

November 18
Riverside, California
Time of Race: 3 hours, 10 minutes, 1 second
Average Speed: 98.448 mph
Margin of Victory: 5 seconds

FINISH	DRIVER	CAR
1.	Geoff Bodine	Chevrolet
2.	Tim Richmond	Pontiac
3.	Terry Labonte	Chevrolet
4.	Bill Elliott	Ford
5.	Benny Parsons	Chevrolet
6.	Neil Bonnett	Chevrolet
7.	Bobby Allison	Buick
8.	Harry Gant	Chevrolet
9.	Hershel McGriff	Pontiac
10.	Joe Ruttman	Chevrolet
11.	Dale Earnhardt	Chevrolet
12.	Trevor Boys	Chevrolet
13.	Bill Schmitt	Buick
14.	Richard Petty	Pontiac
15.	Ricky Rudd	Ford
16.	Greg Sacks	Chevrolet
17.	Lake Speed	Chevrolet
18.	Derrike Cope	Ford
19.	Sumner McKnight	Chevrolet
20.	Dave Marcis	Pontiac
21.	Jimmy Means	Pontiac
22.	Morgan Shepherd	Chevrolet
23.	Doug Heveron	Chevrolet
24.	Dick Brooks	Ford
25.	Clark Dwyer	Pontiac
26.	Rusty Wallace	Pontiac
27.	Ron Esau	Buick
28.	Kyle Petty	Ford
29.	Jim Robinson	Oldsmobile
30.	J. D. McDuffie	Pontiac
31.	Harry Goularte	Buick
32.	Ruben Garcia	Buick
33.	Scott Miller	Pontiac
34.	Darrell Waltrip	Chevrolet
35.	Ron Bouchard	Buick
36.	Jim Bown	Buick
37.	Rick McCray	Buick
38.	Joe Millikan	Chevrolet
39.	John Krebs	Oldsmobile
40.	Bobby Rahal	Ford
41.	Phil Parsons	Chevrolet

1985

DAYTONA 500

February 17
Daytona Beach, Florida
Time of Race: 2 hours, 54 minutes, 9 seconds
Average Speed: 172.265 mph
Margin of Victory: .94 seconds

FINISH	DRIVER	CAR
1.	Bill Elliott	Ford
2.	Lake Speed	Pontiac
3.	Darrell Waltrip	Chevrolet
4.	Buddy Baker	Oldsmobile
5.	Ricky Rudd	Ford
6.	Greg Sacks	Chevrolet
7.	Geoff Bodine	Chevrolet
8.	Rusty Wallace	Pontiac
9.	Bobby Hillin Jr.	Chevrolet
10.	Neil Bonnett	Chevrolet
11.	Ken Schrader	Ford
12.	Mike Alexander	Chevrolet

13.	Bobby Wawak	Chevrolet
14.	Jimmy Means	Chevrolet
15.	Morgan Shepherd	Chrysler
16.	Sterling Marlin	Chevrolet
17.	Joe Ruttman	Chevrolet
18.	Clark Dwyer	Ford
19.	Lennie Pond	Chevrolet
20.	Slick Johnson	Chevrolet
21.	Ken Ragan	Chevrolet
22.	Dick Brooks	Ford
23.	Jim Sauter	Pontiac
24.	Dave Marcis	Chevrolet
25.	Terry Labonte	Chevrolet
26.	Harry Gant	Chevrolet
27.	Trevor Boys	Chevrolet
28.	David Pearson	Chevrolet
29.	Phil Parsons	Chevrolet
30.	A. J. Foyt	Oldsmobile
31.	Benny Parsons	Chevrolet
32.	Dale Earnhardt	Chevrolet
33.	Bobby Allison	Buick
34.	Richard Petty	Pontiac
35.	Tim Richmond	Pontiac
36.	Cale Yarborough	Ford
37.	Kyle Petty	Ford
38.	Ron Bouchard	Buick
39.	Doug Heveron	Chevrolet
40.	Delma Cowart	Chevrolet

MILLER HIGH LIFE 400

February 24
Richmond, Virginia
Time of Race: 3 hours, 11 minutes, 27 seconds
Average Speed: 67.945 mph
Margin of Victory: .3 seconds

FINISH	DRIVER	CAR
1.	Dale Earnhardt	Chevrolet
2.	Geoff Bodine	Chevrolet
3.	Darrell Waltrip	Chevrolet
4.	Ron Bouchard	Buick
5.	Harry Gant	Chevrolet
6.	Terry Labonte	Chevrolet
7.	Kyle Petty	Ford
8.	Dave Marcis	Oldsmobile
9.	Tim Richmond	Pontiac
10.	Lake Speed	Pontiac
11.	Bobby Hillin Jr.	Chevrolet
12.	Ronnie Thomas	Chevrolet
13.	Lennie Pond	Chevrolet
14.	Ken Schrader	Ford
15.	Phil Parsons	Chevrolet
16.	Bobby Allison	Buick
17.	Phil Good	Dodge
18.	Clark Dwyer	Ford
19.	Butch Lindley	Chevrolet
20.	J. D. McDuffie	Pontiac
21.	Jimmy Means	Chevrolet
22.	Bill Elliott	Ford
23.	Neil Bonnett	Chevrolet
24.	Trevor Boys	Chevrolet
25.	Ricky Rudd	Ford
26.	Richard Petty	Pontiac
27.	Rusty Wallace	Pontiac
28.	Rick Newsom	Chevrolet
29.	Buddy Baker	Oldsmobile
30.	Cecil Gordon	Chevrolet

CAROLINA 500

March 3
Rockingham, North Carolina
Time of Race: 4 hours, 21 minutes, 10 seconds
Average Speed: 114.953 mph
Margin of Victory: 8 inches

FINISH	DRIVER	CAR
1.	Neil Bonnett	Chevrolet
2.	Harry Gant	Chevrolet
3.	Terry Labonte	Chevrolet
4.	Lake Speed	Pontiac
5.	Kyle Petty	Ford
6.	Joe Ruttman	Chevrolet
7.	Cale Yarborough	Ford
8.	Richard Petty	Pontiac
9.	Rusty Wallace	Pontiac
10.	Dale Earnhardt	Chevrolet
11.	Tim Richmond	Pontiac
12.	Geoff Bodine	Chevrolet
13.	Greg Sacks	Chevrolet
14.	Lennie Pond	Chevrolet
15.	Slick Johnson	Ford
16.	Buddy Arrington	Dodge
18.	Darrell Waltrip	Chevrolet
19.	Phil Parsons	Chevrolet
20.	Dick Brooks	Ford
21.	Jonathan Edwards	Buick
22.	Jim Southard	Buick
23.	Eddie Bierschwale	Chevrolet
24.	Bobby Hillin Jr.	Chevrolet
25.	Buddy Baker	Oldsmobile
26.	Dave Marcis	Oldsmobile
27.	Bobby Wawak	Buick
28.	J. D. McDuffie	Pontiac
29.	Bill Elliott	Ford
30.	Jimmy Means	Pontiac
31.	Bobby Allison	Buick
32.	Ricky Rudd	Ford
33.	Ron Bouchard	Buick
34.	Ronnie Thomas	Chevrolet
35.	Maurice Randall	Chrysler
36.	Rick Newsome	Buick
37.	Clark Dwyer	Ford
38.	Morgan Shepherd	Chevrolet
39.	Trevor Boys	Chevrolet
40.	Ken Schrader	Ford

COCA-COLA 500

March 17
Atlanta, Georgia
Time of Race: 3 hours, 33 minutes, 32 seconds
Average Speed: 140.273 mph
Margin of Victory: 2.64 seconds

FINISH	DRIVER	CAR
1.	Bill Elliott	Ford
2.	Geoff Bodine	Chevrolet
3.	Neil Bonnett	Chevrolet
4.	Ricky Rudd	Ford
5.	Bobby Allison	Buick
6.	Terry Labonte	Chevrolet
7.	Ron Bouchard	Buick
8.	Benny Parsons	Chevrolet
9.	Dale Earnhardt	Chevrolet
10.	Greg Sacks	Chevrolet
11.	Kyle Petty	Ford
12.	Bobby Hillin Jr.	Chevrolet
13.	Richard Petty	Pontiac
14.	Randy LaJoie	Chevrolet
15.	Eddie Bierschwale	Chevrolet
16.	Ken Schrader	Ford
17.	Darrell Waltrip	Chevrolet
18.	Buddy Arrington	Chrysler
19.	Don Hume	Chevrolet
20.	Clark Dwyer	Ford
21.	Slick Johnson	Ford
22.	Cale Yarborough	Ford
23.	J. D. McDuffie	Chevrolet
24.	Harry Gant	Chevrolet
25.	Sterling Marlin	Chevrolet
26.	Joe Ruttman	Chevrolet
27.	Rusty Wallace	Pontiac
28.	Jimmy Means	Chevrolet
29.	David Pearson	Chevrolet

30.	Tim Richmond	Pontiac
31.	Lennie Pond	Chevrolet
32.	Tom Sneva	Pontiac
33.	Ken Ragan	Chevrolet
34.	Mike Alexander	Chevrolet
35.	H. B. Bailey	Pontiac
36.	A. J. Foyt	Oldsmobile
37.	Dave Marcis	Chevrolet
38.	Dick Brooks	Ford
39.	Buddy Baker	Oldsmobile
40.	Lake Speed	Pontiac
41.	Phil Parsons	Chevrolet

VALLEYDALE 500

April 6
Bristol, Tennessee
Time of Race: 3 hours, 15 minutes, 42 seconds
Average Speed: 81.790 mph
Margin of Victory: 1 second

FINISH	DRIVER	CAR
1.	Dale Earnhardt	Chevrolet
2.	Ricky Rudd	Ford
3.	Terry Labonte	Chevrolet
4.	Buddy Baker	Oldsmobile
5.	Rusty Wallace	Pontiac
6.	Kyle Petty	Ford
7.	Lake Speed	Pontiac
8.	Richard Petty	Pontiac
9.	Bobby Hillin Jr.	Chevrolet
10.	Ken Schrader	Ford
11.	Bill Elliott	Ford
12.	Jimmy Means	Chevrolet
13.	Bobby Allison	Buick
14.	Clark Dwyer	Ford
15.	Eddie Bierschwale	Chevrolet
16.	Don Hume	Chevrolet
17.	Ron Bouchard	Buick
18.	Geoff Bodine	Chevrolet
19.	Neil Bonnett	Chevrolet
20.	Harry Gant	Chevrolet
21.	Ronnie Thomas	Chevrolet
22.	Sterling Marlin	Chevrolet
23.	Darrell Waltrip	Chevrolet
24.	Dave Marcis	Oldsmobile
25.	Buddy Arrington	Chrysler
26.	Mike Potter	Ford
27.	J. D. McDuffie	Pontiac
28.	Phil Parsons	Chevrolet
29.	Joe Ruttman	Chevrolet
30.	Tim Richmond	Pontiac

TRANSOUTH 500

April 14
Darlington, South Carolina
Time of Race: 3 hours, 58 minutes, 8 seconds
Average Speed: 126.295 mph
Margin of Victory: 2.5 seconds

FINISH	DRIVER	CAR
1.	Bill Elliott	Ford
2.	Darrell Waltrip	Chevrolet
3.	Tim Richmond	Pontiac
4.	Terry Labonte	Chevrolet
5.	Rusty Wallace	Pontiac
6.	Neil Bonnett	Chevrolet
7.	Geoff Bodine	Chevrolet
8.	Phil Parsons	Chevrolet
9.	Lake Speed	Pontiac
10.	Bobby Allison	Buick
11.	Joe Ruttman	Chevrolet
12.	Kyle Petty	Ford

13.	Ken Schrader	Ford
14.	Harry Gant	Chevrolet
15.	Jimmy Means	Pontiac
16.	Ron Bouchard	Buick
17.	Buddy Arrington	Ford
18.	Morgan Shepherd	Ford
19.	Eddie Bierschwale	Chevrolet
20.	Bobby Hillin Jr.	Chevrolet
21.	Don Hume	Chevrolet
22.	Dick May	Ford
23.	Mike Alexander	Chevrolet
24.	Dale Earnhardt	Chevrolet
25.	Ricky Rudd	Ford
26.	Clark Dwyer	Ford
27.	Buddy Baker	Oldsmobile
28.	David Pearson	Chevrolet
29.	Trevor Boys	Chevrolet
30.	Cale Yarborough	Ford
31.	Dave Marcis	Oldsmobile
32.	Benny Parsons	Chevrolet
33.	Richard Petty	Pontiac
34.	Bobby Wawak	Chevrolet
35.	Connie Saylor	Chevrolet
36.	Slick Johnson	Ford
37.	Ken Ragan	Chevrolet
38.	Elton Dotson	Chevrolet
39.	J. D. McDuffie	Pontiac
40.	Jeff Hooker	Oldsmobile

NORTHWESTERN BANK 400

April 21
North Wilkesboro, North Carolina
Time of Race: 2 hours, 39 minutes, 53 seconds
Average Speed: 93.818 mph
Margin of Victory: 1 car length

FINISH	DRIVER	CAR
1.	Neil Bonnett	Chevrolet
2.	Darrell Waltrip	Chevrolet
3.	Bobby Allison	Buick
4.	Ricky Rudd	Ford
5.	Geoff Bodine	Chevrolet
6.	Bill Elliott	Ford
7.	Terry Labonte	Chevrolet
8.	Dale Earnhardt	Chevrolet
9.	Lake Speed	Pontiac
10.	Harry Gant	Chevrolet
11.	Tim Richmond	Pontiac
12.	Kyle Petty	Ford
13.	Ron Bouchard	Buick
14.	Ken Schrader	Ford
15.	Phil Parsons	Chevrolet
16.	Dave Marcis	Oldsmobile
17.	Jimmy Means	Pontiac
18.	Clark Dwyer	Ford
19.	Bobby Hillin Jr.	Chevrolet
20.	Buddy Arrington	Ford
21.	Richard Petty	Pontiac
22.	Rusty Wallace	Pontiac
23.	Don Hume	Chevrolet
24.	J. D. McDuffie	Pontiac
25.	Dick May	Buick
26.	Ed Sanger	Chevrolet
27.	Bobby Gerhart	Chevrolet
28.	Brent Elliott	Buick
29.	Eddie Bierschwale	Chevrolet
30.	Buddy Baker	Oldsmobile

SOVRAN BANK 500

April 28
Martinsville, Virginia
Time of Race: 3 hours, 36 minutes, 6 seconds
Average Speed: 73.022 mph
Margin of Victory: 3 seconds

FINISH	DRIVER	CAR
1.	Harry Gant	Chevrolet
2.	Ricky Rudd	Ford
3.	Geoff Bodine	Chevrolet
4.	Bobby Allison	Buick
5.	Neil Bonnett	Chevrolet
6.	Terry Labonte	Chevrolet
7.	Richard Petty	Pontiac
8.	Lake Speed	Pontiac
9.	Phil Parsons	Chevrolet
10.	Rusty Wallace	Pontiac
11.	Kyle Petty	Ford
12.	Buddy Baker	Oldsmobile
13.	Bill Elliott	Ford
14.	Jimmy Means	Pontiac
15.	Buddy Arrington	Ford
16.	Ken Schrader	Ford
17.	Clark Dwyer	Ford
18.	Bobby Hillin Jr.	Chevrolet
19.	Don Hume	Chevrolet
20.	Eddie Bierschwale	Chevrolet
21.	Tim Richmond	Pontiac
22.	Brent Elliott	Buick
23.	Darrell Waltrip	Chevrolet
24.	J. D. McDuffie	Pontiac
25.	Dale Earnhardt	Chevrolet
26.	Dave Marcis	Oldsmobile
27.	Morgan Shepherd	Chevrolet
28.	Ron Bouchard	Buick
29.	Mike Alexander	Chevrolet
30.	Ronnie Thomas	Chevrolet

WINSTON 500

May 5
Talladega, Alabama
Time of Race: 2 hours, 41 minutes, 4 seconds
Average Speed: 186.288 mph
Margin of Victory: 2 seconds

FINISH	DRIVER	CAR
1.	Bill Elliott	Ford
2.	Kyle Petty	Ford
3.	Cale Yarborough	Ford
4.	Bobby Allison	Buick
5.	Ricky Rudd	Ford
6.	Buddy Baker	Oldsmobile
7.	Terry Labonte	Chevrolet
8.	Dave Marcis	Chevrolet
9.	Bobby Hillin Jr.	Chevrolet
10.	Lake Speed	Pontiac
11.	Geoff Bodine	Chevrolet
12.	Jimmy Means	Chevrolet
13.	Morgan Shepherd	Chevrolet
14.	Buddy Arrington	Ford
15.	J. D. McDuffie	Pontiac
16.	Tim Richmond	Pontiac
17.	Bosco Lowe	Chevrolet
18.	Dick Skillen	Chevrolet
19.	Eddie Bierschwale	Chevrolet
20.	Ken Schrader	Ford
21.	Dale Earnhardt	Chevrolet
22.	Connie Saylor	Chevrolet
23.	Clark Dwyer	Ford
24.	Darrell Waltrip	Chevrolet
25.	Sterling Marlin	Chevrolet
26.	Neil Bonnett	Chevrolet
27.	Richard Petty	Pontiac
28.	Ron Bouchard	Buick
29.	Benny Parsons	Chevrolet
30.	Joe Ruttman	Chevrolet
31.	Mike Alexander	Chevrolet
32.	Bobby Wawak	Chevrolet
33.	Don Hume	Chevrolet
34.	Phil Parsons	Chevrolet
35.	Phil Barkdoll	Chevrolet
36.	David Pearson	Chevrolet
37.	Rusty Wallace	Pontiac
38.	Harry Gant	Chevrolet
39.	Trevor Boys	Chevrolet

BUDWEISER 500

May 19
Dover, Delaware
Time of Race: 4 hours, 3 minutes, 43 seconds
Average Speed: 123.094 mph
Margin of Victory: 29 seconds

FINISH	DRIVER	CAR
1.	Bill Elliott	Ford
2.	Harry Gant	Chevrolet
3.	Kyle Petty	Ford
4.	Ricky Rudd	Ford
5.	Darrell Waltrip	Chevrolet
6.	Tim Richmond	Pontiac
7.	Richard Petty	Pontiac
8.	Neil Bonnett	Chevrolet
9.	Dave Marcis	Oldsmobile
10.	Ken Schrader	Ford
11.	Geoff Bodine	Chevrolet
12.	Bobby Hillin Jr.	Chevrolet
13.	Bobby Allison	Buick
14.	Bob Riley	Pontiac
15.	Tommie Crozier	Pontiac
16.	Terry Labonte	Chevrolet
17.	Phil Good	Chrysler
18.	Rusty Wallace	Pontiac
19.	Jerry Bowman	Ford
20.	Ron Bouchard	Buick
21.	Rick Newsom	Chevrolet
22.	Buddy Baker	Oldsmobile
23.	Buddy Arrington	Ford
24.	Lake Speed	Pontiac
25.	Dale Earnhardt	Chevrolet
26.	James Hylton	Chevrolet
27.	Jimmy Walker	Ford
28.	Clark Dwyer	Ford
29.	Phil Parsons	Chevrolet
30.	Jimmy Means	Pontiac
31.	J. D. McDuffie	Ford
32.	Eddie Bierschwale	Chevrolet

COCA-COLA WORLD 600

May 26
Charlotte, North Carolina
Time of Race: 4 hours, 13 minutes, 52 seconds
Average Speed: 141.807 mph
Margin of Victory: 14 seconds

FINISH	DRIVER	CAR
1.	Darrell Waltrip	Chevrolet
2.	Harry Gant	Chevrolet
3.	Bobby Allison	Buick
4.	Dale Earnhardt	Chevrolet
5.	Terry Labonte	Chevrolet
6.	Lake Speed	Pontiac
7.	Joe Ruttman	Chevrolet
8.	Rusty Wallace	Pontiac
9.	Tim Richmond	Pontiac
10.	Dick Brooks	Chevrolet
11.	Dave Marcis	Oldsmobile
12.	Bobby Hillin Jr.	Chevrolet
13.	Ricky Rudd	Ford
14.	Kyle Petty	Ford
15.	Neil Bonnett	Chevrolet
16.	Geoff Bodine	Chevrolet
17.	Slick Johnson	Ford
18.	Bill Elliott	Ford
19.	Eddie Bierschwale	Chevrolet
20.	Tommy Ellis	Chevrolet
21.	Mark Stahl	Ford
22.	Buddy Arrington	Ford
23.	Clark Dwyer	Ford
24.	Mike Alexander	Chevrolet
25.	Morgan Shepherd	Chevrolet
26.	Richard Petty	Pontiac

27.	David Pearson	Chevrolet
28.	Michael Waltrip	Chevrolet
29.	Ron Bouchard	Buick
30.	Lennie Pond	Chevrolet
31.	Jim Sauter	Pontiac
32.	Jimmy Means	Pontiac
33.	Phil Parsons	Chevrolet
34.	Sterling Marlin	Chevrolet
35.	Greg Sacks	Chevrolet
36.	Dick Trickle	Chevrolet
37.	Buddy Baker	Oldsmobile
38.	Ken Schrader	Ford
39.	J. D. McDuffie	Pontiac
40.	Cale Yarborough	Ford
41.	Trevor Boys	Chevrolet
42.	Benny Parsons	Chevrolet

BUDWEISER 400

June 2
Riverside, California
Time of Race: 2 hours, 23 minutes, 13 seconds
Average Speed: 104.276 mph
Margin of Victory: 5 seconds

FINISH	DRIVER	CAR
1.	Terry Labonte	Chevrolet
2.	Harry Gant	Chevrolet
3.	Bobby Allison	Buick
4.	Ricky Rudd	Ford
5.	Kyle Petty	Chevrolet
6.	Bill Elliott	Ford
7.	Richard Petty	Pontiac
8.	Darrell Waltrip	Chevrolet
9.	Tim Richmond	Pontiac
10.	Ken Schrader	Ford
11.	Glen Steurer	Chevrolet
12.	Dave Marcis	Oldsmobile
13.	Jim Robinson	Oldsmobile
14.	Sumner McKnight	Ford
15.	Derrike Cope	Ford
16.	Clark Dwyer	Ford
17.	Bobby Hillin Jr.	Chevrolet
18.	Eddie Bierschwale	Chevrolet
19.	John Soares	Pontiac
20.	Glen Francis	Pontiac
21.	Bill Osborne	Buick
22.	Geoff Bodine	Chevrolet
23.	Ruben Garcia	Chevrolet
24.	Rusty Wallace	Pontiac
25.	Lake Speed	Pontiac
26.	John Krebs	Oldsmobile
27.	Neil Bonnett	Chevrolet
28.	Jim Bown	Buick
29.	Hershel McGriff	Pontiac
30.	Dale Perry	Buick
31.	Buddy Arrington	Chrysler
32.	Ron Bouchard	Buick
33.	Phil Parsons	Chevrolet
34.	Bill Schmitt	Chevrolet
35.	Buddy Baker	Oldsmobile
36.	Greg Sacks	Chevrolet
37.	Jimmy Means	Chevrolet
38.	Blair Aiken	Chevrolet
39.	Norm Palmer	Chevrolet
40.	Dale Earnhardt	Chevrolet
41.	Rick McCray	Chevrolet
42.	J. D. McDuffie	Pontiac

VAN SCOY DIAMOND MINE 500

June 9
Pocono, Pennsylvania
Time of Race: 3 hours, 35 minutes, 48 seconds
Average Speed: 138.974 mph
Margin of Victory: .02 seconds

FINISH	DRIVER	CAR
1.	Bill Elliott	Ford
2.	Harry Gant	Chevrolet
3.	Darrell Waltrip	Chevrolet
4.	Geoff Bodine	Chevrolet
5.	Neil Bonnett	Chevrolet
6.	Benny Parsons	Chevrolet
7.	Ricky Rudd	Ford
8.	Buddy Baker	Oldsmobile
9.	Bobby Allison	Buick
10.	Tim Richmond	Pontiac
11.	Phil Parsons	Chevrolet
12.	Lake Speed	Pontiac
13.	Rusty Wallace	Pontiac
14.	Kyle Petty	Chevrolet
15.	Ken Schrader	Ford
16.	Greg Sacks	Chevrolet
17.	Lennie Pond	Chevrolet
18.	Bobby Hillin Jr.	Chevrolet
19.	Buddy Arrington	Ford
20.	Clark Dwyer	Ford
21.	Mike Potter	Ford
22.	Jimmy Means	Pontiac
23.	Bobby Wawak	Chevrolet
24.	Cale Yarborough	Ford
25.	J. D. McDuffie	Pontiac
26.	Steve Gray	Chevrolet
27.	Dave Marcis	Chevrolet
28.	Terry Labonte	Chevrolet
29.	Ron Bouchard	Buick
30.	Phil Good	Dodge
31.	Bobby Gerhart	Chevrolet
32.	Bill Scott	Chevrolet
33.	Richard Petty	Pontiac
34.	Eddie Bierschwale	Chevrolet
35.	Joe Ruttman	Chevrolet
36.	Charlie Poalillo	Chevrolet
37.	Jerry Bowman	Ford
38.	Rick Newsom	Buick
39.	Dale Earnhardt	Chevrolet
40.	Ronnie Thomas	Chevrolet

MILLER 400

June 16
Brooklyn, Michigan
Time of Race: 2 hours, 45 minutes, 48 seconds
Average Speed: 144.724 mph
Margin of Victory: 13 seconds

FINISH	DRIVER	CAR
1.	Bill Elliott	Ford
2.	Darrell Waltrip	Chevrolet
3.	Cale Yarborough	Ford
4.	Tim Richmond	Pontiac
5.	Dale Earnhardt	Chevrolet
6.	Bobby Allison	Buick
7.	Ricky Rudd	Ford
8.	Neil Bonnett	Chevrolet
9.	Dave Marcis	Chevrolet
10.	Benny Parsons	Chevrolet
11.	Geoff Bodine	Chevrolet
12.	Kyle Petty	Chevrolet
13.	Ron Bouchard	Buick
14.	Lake Speed	Pontiac
15.	Buddy Baker	Oldsmobile
16.	Harry Gant	Chevrolet
17.	David Pearson	Chevrolet
18.	Lennie Pond	Chevrolet
19.	Phil Parsons	Chevrolet
20.	Jim Sauter	Pontiac
21.	Tommy Ellis	Chevrolet
22.	Terry Labonte	Chevrolet
23.	Buddy Arrington	Ford
24.	Trevor Boys	Chevrolet
25.	Clark Dwyer	Ford
26.	Rusty Wallace	Pontiac
27.	Bobby Wawak	Buick
28.	Bobby Hillin Jr.	Chevrolet

29.	Eddie Bierschwale	Chevrolet
30.	Richard Petty	Pontiac
31.	J. D. McDuffie	Pontiac
32.	Jim Hull	Chevrolet
33.	Tommie Crozier	Pontiac
34.	Ken Schrader	Ford
35.	Jimmy Means	Pontiac
36.	Edward Cooper	Buick
37.	Maurice Randall	Chrysler

PEPSI FIRECRACKER 400

July 4
Daytona Beach, Florida
Time of Race: 2 hours, 31 minutes, 12 seconds
Average Speed: 158.730 mph
Margin of Victory: 23.5 seconds

FINISH	DRIVER	CAR
1.	Greg Sacks	Chevrolet
2.	Bill Elliott	Ford
3.	Darrell Waltrip	Chevrolet
4.	Ron Bouchard	Buick
5.	Kyle Petty	Chevrolet
6.	Buddy Baker	Oldsmobile
7.	Ricky Rudd	Ford
8.	Terry Labonte	Chevrolet
9.	Dale Earnhardt	Chevrolet
10.	David Pearson	Chevrolet
11.	Benny Parsons	Chevrolet
12.	Neil Bonnett	Chevrolet
13.	Mike Alexander	Chevrolet
14.	Geoff Bodine	Chevrolet
15.	Bobby Hillin Jr.	Chevrolet
16.	Buddy Arrington	Ford
17.	Tommy Ellis	Chevrolet
18.	Bobby Allison	Buick
19.	Lennie Pond	Chevrolet
20.	J. D. McDuffie	Chevrolet
21.	Ken Schrader	Ford
22.	Grant Adcox	Chevrolet
23.	Dave Marcis	Chevrolet
24.	Harry Gant	Chevrolet
25.	Clark Dwyer	Ford
26.	Trevor Boys	Chevrolet
27.	Phil Parsons	Chevrolet
28.	Tim Richmond	Pontiac
29.	Richard Petty	Pontiac
30.	A. J. Foyt	Oldsmobile
31.	Eddie Bierschwale	Chevrolet
32.	Jimmy Means	Chevrolet
33.	Sterling Marlin	Chevrolet
34.	Lake Speed	Pontiac
35.	Joe Ruttman	Chevrolet
36.	Cale Yarborough	Ford
37.	Bobby Wawak	Chevrolet
38.	Eldon Dotson	Chevrolet
39.	Morgan Shepherd	Chevrolet
40.	Connie Saylor	Chevrolet
41.	Rusty Wallace	Pontiac

SUMMER 500

July 21
Pocono, Pennsylvania
Time of Race: 3 hours, 43 minutes, 52 seconds
Average Speed: 134.008 mph
Margin of Victory: 5 seconds

FINISH	DRIVER	CAR
1.	Bill Elliott	Ford
2.	Neil Bonnett	Chevrolet
3.	Darrell Waltrip	Chevrolet
4.	Geoff Bodine	Chevrolet
5.	Harry Gant	Chevrolet

6.	Benny Parsons	Chevrolet
7.	Kyle Petty	Chevrolet
8.	Phil Parsons	Chevrolet
9.	Ron Bouchard	Buick
10.	Buddy Baker	Oldsmobile
11.	Lake Speed	Pontiac
12.	Bobby Allison	Buick
13.	Lennie Pond	Chevrolet
14.	Ricky Rudd	Ford
15.	Ken Schrader	Ford
16.	Clark Dwyer	Ford
17.	Eddie Bierschwale	Chevrolet
18.	Buddy Arrington	Ford
19.	Doug Heveron	Ford
20.	Trevor Boys	Chevrolet
21.	Rick Newsom	Buick
22.	Jerry Bowman	Ford
23.	Jimmy Means	Pontiac
24.	Bobby Gerhart	Chevrolet
25.	Bobby Wawak	Buick
26.	Terry Labonte	Chevrolet
27.	Richard Petty	Pontiac
28.	Joe Booher	Buick
29.	Bobby Hillin Jr.	Chevrolet
30.	Tim Richmond	Pontiac
31.	Cale Yarborough	Ford
32.	Mike Stolarcyk	Buick
33.	Rusty Wallace	Pontiac
34.	Greg Sacks	Buick
35.	David Pearson	Chevrolet
36.	Tommy Ellis	Chevrolet
37.	Don Hume	Chevrolet
38.	Dave Marcis	Chevrolet
39.	Dale Earnhardt	Chevrolet
40.	J. D. McDuffie	Ford

TALLADEGA 500

July 28
Talladega, Alabama
Time of Race: 3 hours, 21 minutes, 41 seconds
Average Speed: 148.772 mph
Margin of Victory: 1 second

FINISH	DRIVER	CAR
1.	Cale Yarborough	Ford
2.	Neil Bonnett	Chevrolet
3.	Ron Bouchard	Buick
4.	Bill Elliott	Ford
5.	A. J. Foyt	Oldsmobile
6.	Richard Petty	Pontiac
7.	Harry Gant	Chevrolet
8.	Lake Speed	Pontiac
9.	Darrell Waltrip	Chevrolet
10.	Davey Allison	Chevrolet
11.	Ken Schrader	Ford
12.	Sterling Marlin	Chevrolet
13.	Tim Richmond	Pontiac
14.	Buddy Baker	Oldsmobile
15.	Greg Sacks	Buick
16.	Buddy Arrington	Ford
17.	Rusty Wallace	Pontiac
18.	Ricky Rudd	Ford
19.	Lennie Pond	Ford
20.	Clark Dwyer	Ford
21.	Bobby Wawak	Chevrolet
22.	Phil Barkdoll	Chevrolet
23.	Geoff Bodine	Chevrolet
24.	Dale Earnhardt	Chevrolet
25.	Kyle Petty	Chevrolet
26.	Dave Marcis	Chevrolet
27.	Bobby Allison	Chevrolet
28.	J. D. McDuffie	Chevrolet
29.	Rick Wilson	Chevrolet
30.	Tommy Ellis	Chevrolet
31.	Phil Parsons	Chevrolet
32.	Trevor Boys	Chevrolet
33.	Joe Ruttman	Chevrolet
34.	Eddie Bierschwale	Chevrolet
35.	David Pearson	Ford
36.	Benny Parsons	Chevrolet

37.	Delma Cowart	Chevrolet
38.	Bobby Hillin Jr.	Chevrolet
39.	Terry Labonte	Chevrolet
40.	Grant Adcox	Chevrolet
41.	Connie Saylor	Chevrolet
42.	Jimmy Means	Pontiac

CHAMPION SPARK PLUG 400

August 11
Brooklyn, Michigan
Time of Race: 2 hours, 54 minutes, 38 seconds
Average Speed: 137.430 mph
Margin of Victory: 4 seconds

FINISH	DRIVER	CAR
1.	Bill Elliott	Ford
2.	Darrell Waltrip	Chevrolet
3.	Harry Gant	Chevrolet
4.	Kyle Petty	Chevrolet
5.	Benny Parsons	Chevrolet
6.	Phil Parsons	Chevrolet
7.	Rusty Wallace	Pontiac
8.	Dick Trickle	Pontiac
9.	Terry Labonte	Chevrolet
10.	Buddy Arrington	Ford
11.	Neil Bonnett	Chevrolet
12.	Dave Marcis	Chevrolet
13.	Mike Alexander	Chevrolet
14.	Buddy Baker	Oldsmobile
15.	Jimmy Means	Pontiac
16.	Lake Speed	Pontiac
17.	Ken Ragan	Chevrolet
18.	Michael Waltrip	Chevrolet
19.	Ronnie Thomas	Chevrolet
20.	Ken Schrader	Ford
21.	Eddie Bierschwale	Chevrolet
22.	Dale Earnhardt	Chevrolet
23.	Geoff Bodine	Chevrolet
24.	Joe Booher	Chevrolet
25.	Bobby Gerhart	Chevrolet
26.	Bobby Hillin Jr.	Chevrolet
27.	Bobby Wawak	Buick
28.	Rick Baldwin	Chrysler
29.	J. D. McDuffie	Pontiac
30.	Trevor Boys	Chevrolet
31.	Ricky Rudd	Ford
32.	Cale Yarborough	Ford
33.	Greg Sacks	Buick
34.	Clark Dwyer	Ford
35.	Morgan Shepherd	Chevrolet
36.	Bobby Allison	Ford
37.	Richard Petty	Pontiac
38.	Ron Bouchard	Buick
39.	David Pearson	Ford
40.	Tim Richmond	Pontiac

BUSCH 500

August 24
Bristol, Tennessee
Time of Race: 3 hours, 27 minutes, 44 seconds
Average Speed: 81.388 mph
Margin of Victory: 3 car lengths

FINISH	DRIVER	CAR
1.	Dale Earnhardt	Chevrolet
2.	Tim Richmond	Pontiac
3.	Neil Bonnett	Chevrolet
4.	Darrell Waltrip	Chevrolet
5.	Bill Elliott	Ford
6.	Harry Gant	Chevrolet
7.	Ron Bouchard	Buick
8.	Richard Petty	Pontiac
9.	Ricky Rudd	Ford

10.	Lake Speed	Pontiac
11.	Buddy Baker	Oldsmobile
12.	Rusty Wallace	Pontiac
13.	Joe Ruttman	Chevrolet
14.	Ronnie Thomas	Chevrolet
15.	Buddy Arrington	Ford
16.	Kyle Petty	Chevrolet
17.	Trevor Boys	Chevrolet
18.	Clark Dwyer	Ford
19.	Ken Schrader	Ford
20.	Eddie Bierschwale	Chevrolet
21.	Phil Parsons	Chevrolet
22.	Bobby Allison	Buick
23.	Dave Marcis	Oldsmobile
24.	Bobby Hillin Jr.	Chevrolet
25.	Geoff Bodine	Chevrolet
26.	Mike Alexander	Chevrolet
27.	Jimmy Means	Chevrolet
28.	Greg Sacks	Buick
29.	Terry Labonte	Chevrolet
30.	Tommy Ellis	Chevrolet
31.	Mike Potter	Ford

SOUTHERN 500

September 1
Darlington, South Carolina
Time of Race: 4 hours, 8 minutes, 2 seconds
Average Speed: 121.254 mph
Margin of Victory: 2 seconds

FINISH	DRIVER	CAR
1.	Bill Elliott	Ford
2.	Cale Yarborough	Ford
3.	Geoff Bodine	Chevrolet
4.	Neil Bonnett	Chevrolet
5.	Ron Bouchard	Buick
6.	Ricky Rudd	Ford
7.	Terry Labonte	Chevrolet
8.	Benny Parsons	Chevrolet
9.	Joe Ruttman	Chevrolet
10.	Kyle Petty	Chevrolet
11.	Tim Richmond	Pontiac
12.	Richard Petty	Pontiac
13.	Bobby Hillin Jr.	Chevrolet
14.	Ken Schrader	Ford
15.	Buddy Baker	Oldsmobile
16.	Lake Speed	Pontiac
17.	Darrell Waltrip	Chevrolet
18.	Buddy Arrington	Ford
19.	Dale Earnhardt	Chevrolet
20.	Ken Ragan	Chevrolet
21.	Harry Gant	Chevrolet
22.	Pancho Carter	Chevrolet
23.	Dave Marcis	Chevrolet
24.	Michael Waltrip	Chevrolet
25.	A. J. Foyt	Oldsmobile
26.	Clark Dwyer	Ford
27.	Jimmy Means	Chevrolet
28.	Mike Potter	Buick
29.	Slick Johnson	Ford
30.	Bobby Allison	Ford
31.	Trevor Boys	Chevrolet
32.	Eddie Bierschwale	Chevrolet
33.	Tommy Ellis	Chevrolet
34.	H. B. Bailey	Pontiac
35.	Greg Sacks	Buick
36.	Tommy Houston	Chevrolet
37.	Morgan Shepherd	Chevrolet
38.	Rusty Wallace	Pontiac
39.	Phil Parsons	Chevrolet
40.	David Pearson	Ford

WRANGLER SANFORSET 400

September 8
Richmond, Virginia

Time of Race: 2 hours, 58 minutes, 54 seconds
Average Speed: 72.508 mph
Margin of Victory: 1 car length

FINISH	DRIVER	CAR
1.	Darrell Waltrip	Chevrolet
2.	Terry Labonte	Chevrolet
3.	Richard Petty	Pontiac
4.	Dale Earnhardt	Chevrolet
5.	Ricky Rudd	Ford
6.	Harry Gant	Chevrolet
7.	Geoff Bodine	Chevrolet
8.	Kyle Petty	Chevrolet
9.	Neil Bonnett	Chevrolet
10.	Tommy Ellis	Chevrolet
11.	Lake Speed	Pontiac
12.	Bill Elliott	Ford
13.	Rusty Wallace	Pontiac
14.	Tim Richmond	Pontiac
15.	Ken Schrader	Ford
16.	Buddy Baker	Oldsmobile
17.	Dave Marcis	Chevrolet
18.	Ron Bouchard	Buick
19.	Alan Kulwicki	Ford
20.	Greg Sacks	Buick
21.	Bobby Hillin Jr.	Chevrolet
22.	Buddy Arrington	Ford
23.	Jimmy Means	Pontiac
24.	Clark Dwyer	Ford
25.	Lennie Pond	Chevrolet
26.	J. D. McDuffie	Pontiac
27.	Phil Parsons	Chevrolet
28.	Bobby Allison	Buick
29.	Eddie Bierschwale	Chevrolet
30.	Morgan Shepherd	Chevrolet

DELAWARE 500

September 15
Dover, Delaware
Time of Race: 4 hours, 8 minutes, 52 seconds
Average Speed: 120.538 mph
Margin of Victory: 28 seconds

FINISH	DRIVER	CAR
1.	Harry Gant	Chevrolet
2.	Darrell Waltrip	Chevrolet
3.	Ricky Rudd	Ford
4.	Bobby Allison	Ford
5.	Neil Bonnett	Chevrolet
6.	Tim Richmond	Pontiac
7.	Dale Earnhardt	Chevrolet
8.	Ron Bouchard	Buick
9.	Richard Petty	Pontiac
10.	Lake Speed	Pontiac
11.	Buddy Arrington	Ford
12.	Phil Parsons	Chevrolet
13.	Jimmy Means	Pontiac
14.	Jerry Bowman	Ford
15.	Kyle Petty	Ford
16.	Ken Schrader	Ford
17.	Bobby Wawak	Buick
18.	Phil Good	Chrysler
19.	Dave Marcis	Chevrolet
20.	Bill Elliott	Ford
21.	Alan Kulwicki	Ford
22.	Morgan Shepherd	Chevrolet
23.	Bobby Hillin Jr.	Chevrolet
24.	Terry Labonte	Chevrolet
25.	Geoff Bodine	Chevrolet
26.	Tommy Ellis	Chevrolet
27.	Eddie Bierschwale	Chevrolet
28.	J. D. McDuffie	Ford
29.	Greg Sacks	Buick
30.	Clark Dwyer	Ford
31.	Rusty Wallace	Pontiac
32.	Rick Newsom	Buick

33.	Joe Ruttman	Chevrolet
34.	Trevor Boys	Chevrolet
35.	Buddy Baker	Oldsmobile
36.	Earle Canavan	Oldsmobile
37.	Tommie Crozier	Pontiac
38.	Chuck Walton	Chevrolet
39.	Maurice Randall	Chrysler

GOODY'S 500

Setember 22
Martinsville, Virginia
Time of Race: 3 hours, 43 minutes, 13 seconds
Average Speed: 70.694 mph
Margin of Victory: 2 car lengths

FINISH	DRIVER	CAR
1.	Dale Earnhardt	Chevrolet
2.	Darrell Waltrip	Chevrolet
3.	Harry Gant	Chevrolet
4.	Ricky Rudd	Ford
5.	Kyle Petty	Ford
6.	Ron Bouchard	Buick
7.	Tim Richmond	Pontiac
8.	Bobby Hillin Jr.	Chevrolet
9.	Neil Bonnett	Chevrolet
10.	Bobby Allison	Buick
11.	Lake Speed	Pontiac
12.	Trevor Boys	Chevrolet
13.	Jimmy Means	Pontiac
14.	Greg Sacks	Buick
15.	J. D. McDuffie	Pontiac
16.	Bobby Wawak	Buick
17.	Bill Elliott	Ford
18.	Eddie Bierschwale	Chevrolet
19.	Clark Dwyer	Ford
20.	Phil Parsons	Chevrolet
21.	Buddy Arrington	Ford
22.	Richard Petty	Pontiac
23.	Dave Marcis	Chevrolet
24.	Geoff Bodine	Chevrolet
25.	Rusty Wallace	Pontiac
26.	Ken Schrader	Ford
27.	Terry Labonte	Chevrolet
28.	Brent Elliott	Buick
29.	Morgan Shepherd	Chevrolet
30.	Tommy Ellis	Chevrolet
31.	Buddy Baker	Oldsmobile

HOLLY FARMS 400

September 29
North Wilkesboro, North Carolina
Time of Race: 2 hours, 37 minutes, 44 seconds
Average Speed: 95.077 mph
Margin of Victory: 14 seconds

FINISH	DRIVER	CAR
1.	Harry Gant	Chevrolet
2.	Geoff Bodine	Chevrolet
3.	Terry Labonte	Chevrolet
4.	Dale Earnhardt	Chevrolet
5.	Ricky Rudd	Ford
6.	Ron Bouchard	Buick
7.	Tim Richmond	Pontiac
8.	Richard Petty	Pontiac
9.	Dave Marcis	Chevrolet
10.	Neil Bonnett	Chevrolet
11.	Tommy Ellis	Chevrolet
12.	Lake Speed	Pontiac
13.	Phil Parsons	Chevrolet
14.	Darrell Waltrip	Chevrolet
15.	Ken Schrader	Ford
16.	Greg Sacks	Buick

17.	Bobby Hillin Jr.	Chevrolet
18.	Clark Dwyer	Ford
19.	Eddie Bierschwale	Chevrolet
20.	Bobby Wawak	Buick
21.	Jimmy Means	Pontiac
22.	Trevor Boys	Chevrolet
23.	Buddy Arrington	Ford
24.	Bobby Gerhart	Chevrolet
25.	Rusty Wallace	Pontiac
26.	Mike Alexander	Chevrolet
27.	Morgan Shepherd	Chevrolet
28.	Kyle Petty	Ford
29.	Buddy Baker	Oldsmobile
30.	Bill Elliott	Ford
31.	Bobby Allison	Buick

MILLER 500

October 6
Charlotte, North Carolina
Time of Race: 3 hours, 39 minutes, 48 seconds
Average Speed: 136.761 mph
Margin of Victory: 1 second

FINISH	DRIVER	CAR
1.	Cale Yarborough	Ford
2.	Bill Elliott	Ford
3.	Geoff Bodine	Chevrolet
4.	Darrell Waltrip	Chevrolet
5.	Joe Ruttman	Chevrolet
6.	Tim Richmond	Pontiac
7.	Morgan Shepherd	Chevrolet
8.	Buddy Baker	Oldsmobile
9.	Bobby Hillin Jr.	Chevrolet
10.	Richard Petty	Pontiac
11.	Greg Sacks	Buick
12.	Lake Speed	Pontiac
13.	Alan Kulwicki	Ford
14.	Bobby Allison	Ford
15.	Ricky Rudd	Ford
16.	Clark Dwyer	Ford
17.	Buddy Arrington	Ford
18.	Mike Alexander	Chevrolet
19.	Davey Allison	Chevrolet
20.	Dale Earnhardt	Chevrolet
21.	Eddie Bierschwale	Chevrolet
22.	Kyle Petty	Ford
23.	Trevor Boys	Chevrolet
24.	Harry Gant	Chevrolet
25.	Ken Schrader	Ford
26.	Ron Bouchard	Buick
27.	Phil Parsons	Chevrolet
28.	Ken Ragan	Ford
29.	Sterling Marlin	Chevrolet
30.	Rusty Wallace	Pontiac
31.	Michael Waltrip	Chevrolet
32.	A. J. Foyt	Oldsmobile
33.	Terry Labonte	Chevrolet
34.	Dave Marcis	Chevrolet
35.	Don Paul	Chevrolet
36.	Dick Trickle	Chevrolet
37.	David Pearson	Ford
38.	Jimmy Means	Pontiac
39.	Lennie Pond	Chevrolet
40.	Tommy Ellis	Chevrolet
41.	Bennie Parsons	Chevrolet
42.	Neil Bonnett	Chevrolet

NATIONWIDE 500

October 20
Rockingham, North Carolina
Time of Race: 4 hours, 13 minutes, 40 seconds
Average Speed: 118.344 mph
Margin of Victory: 1 second

FINISH	DRIVER	CAR
1.	Darrell Waltrip	Chevrolet
2.	Ron Bouchard	Buick
3.	Harry Gant	Chevrolet
4.	Bill Elliott	Ford
5.	Geoff Bodine	Chevrolet
6.	Tim Richmond	Pontiac
7.	Ricky Rudd	Ford
8.	Dale Earnhardt	Chevrolet
9.	Rusty Wallace	Pontiac
10.	Greg Sacks	Buick
11.	Buddy Baker	Oldsmobile
12.	Terry Labonte	Chevrolet
13.	Phil Parsons	Chevrolet
14.	Dave Marcis	Chevrolet
15.	Neil Bonnett	Chevrolet
16.	Buddy Arrington	Ford
17.	Eddie Bierschwale	Chevrolet
18.	Jimmy Means	Pontiac
19.	Ken Schrader	Ford
20.	Trevor Boys	Chevrolet
21.	Randy Baker	Buick
22.	Mike Potter	Ford
23.	Jeff McDuffie	Chevrolet
24.	Clark Dwyer	Ford
25.	Bobby Hillin Jr.	Chevrolet
26.	J. D. McDuffie	Pontiac
27.	Alan Kulwicki	Ford
28.	Cale Yarborough	Ford
29.	Lake Speed	Pontiac
30.	Tommy Ellis	Chevrolet
31.	Kyle Petty	Ford
32.	D. K. Ulrich	Buick
33.	Richard Petty	Pontiac
34.	Bobby Wawak	Buick
35.	Jerry Bowman	Ford
36.	Jonathan Edwards	Buick
37.	Craig Spetman	Chevrolet
38.	Bobby Allison	Buick
39.	Morgan Shepherd	Ford
40.	Joe Ruttman	Chevrolet

ATLANTA JOURNAL 500

November 3
Atlanta, Georgia
Time of Race: 3 hours, 34 minutes, 34 seconds
Average Speed: 139.597 mph
Margin of Victory: 4.25 seconds

FINISH	DRIVER	CAR
1.	Bill Elliott	Ford
2.	Cale Yarborough	Ford
3.	Darrell Waltrip	Chevrolet
4.	Dale Earnhardt	Chevrolet
5.	Morgan Shepherd	Chevrolet
6.	Terry Labonte	Chevrolet
7.	Lake Speed	Pontiac
8.	Harry Gant	Chevrolet
9.	Greg Sacks	Buick
10.	Richard Petty	Pontiac
11.	Geoff Bodine	Chevrolet
12.	Neil Bonnett	Chevrolet
13.	Buddy Baker	Oldsmobile
14.	Phil Parsons	Chevrolet
15.	Ken Schrader	Ford
16.	Ron Bouchard	Buick
17.	Tim Richmond	Pontiac
18.	Rick Wilson	Chevrolet
19.	Bobby Hillin Jr.	Chevrolet
20.	Buddy Arrington	Ford
21.	Rusty Wallace	Pontiac
22.	Alan Kulwicki	Ford
23.	Rick Baldwin	Pontiac
24.	Eddie Bierschwale	Chevrolet
25.	Chet Fillip	Ford
26.	Bobby Allison	Buick
27.	J. D. McDuffie	Pontiac
28.	Dave Marcis	Chevrolet

29.	Kyle Petty	Chevrolet
30.	Sammy Swindell	Chevrolet
31.	Ricky Rudd	Ford
32.	Joe Ruttman	Chevrolet
33.	Benny Parsons	Chevrolet
34.	Ken Ragan	Chevrolet
35.	Connie Saylor	Chevrolet
36.	Tommy Ellis	Chevrolet
37.	Trevor Boys	Chevrolet
38.	A. J. Foyt	Oldsmobile
39.	Michael Waltrip	Chevrolet
40.	Clark Dwyer	Ford
41.	Jimmy Means	Pontiac
42.	Davey Allison	Chevrolet

WINSTON WESTERN 500

November 17
Riverside, California
Time of Race: 2 hours, 58 minutes, 3 seconds
Average Speed: 105.065 mph
Margin of Victory: 2 car lengths

FINISH	DRIVER	CAR
1.	Ricky Rudd	Ford
2.	Terry Labonte	Chevrolet
3.	Neil Bonnett	Chevrolet
4.	Harry Gant	Chevrolet
5.	Dale Earnhardt	Chevrolet
6.	Geoff Bodine	Chevrolet
7.	Darrell Waltrip	Chevrolet
8.	Richard Petty	Pontiac
9.	Lake Speed	Pontiac
10.	Ron Bouchard	Buick
11.	Glen Steurer	Chevrolet
12.	Jim Robinson	Oldsmobile
13.	Bobby Hillin Jr.	Chevrolet
14.	Ruben Garcia	Chevrolet
15.	Bill Schmitt	Chevrolet
16.	Jim Bown	Chevrolet
17.	Bobby Allison	Buick
18.	Dave Marcis	Chevrolet
19.	Derrike Cope	Ford
20.	Jimmy Means	Pontiac
21.	Greg Sacks	Buick
22.	Buddy Arrington	Ford
23.	Ken Schrader	Ford
24.	Bill Osborne	Buick
25.	J. D. McDuffie	Pontiac
26.	Hershel McGriff	Pontiac
27.	Kyle Petty	Ford
28.	Clark Dwyer	Ford
29.	Blair Aiken	Chevrolet
30.	John Soares	Pontiac
31.	Bill Elliott	Ford
32.	Eddie Bierschwale	Chevrolet
33.	Phil Parsons	Chevrolet
34.	Scott Autrey	Oldsmobile
35.	Buddy Baker	Oldsmobile
36.	Rusty Wallace	Pontiac
37.	Tim Richmond	Pontiac
38.	Bud Hickey	Chevrolet
39.	Rick McCray	Chevrolet
40.	Trevor Boys	Chevrolet
41.	Ron Esau	Chevrolet

1986

DAYTONA 500

February 16
Daytona Beach, Florida
Time of Race: 3 hours, 22 minutes, 32 seconds

Average Speed of Race: 148.124 mph
Margin of Victory: 11.26 seconds

FINISH	DRIVER	CAR
1.	Geoff Bodine	Chevrolet
2.	Terry Labonte	Oldsmobile
3.	Darrell Waltrip	Chevrolet
4.	Bobby Hillin Jr.	Chevrolet
5.	Benny Parsons	Oldsmobile
6.	Ron Bouchard	Pontiac
7.	Rick Wilson	Oldsmobile
8.	Rusty Wallace	Pontiac
9.	Sterling Marlin	Chevrolet
10.	Lake Speed	Pontiac
11.	Ricky Rudd	Ford
12.	Jody Ridley	Ford
13.	Bill Elliott	Ford
14.	Dale Earnhardt	Chevrolet
15.	Doug Heveron	Chevrolet
16.	Kyle Petty	Ford
17.	Dick Trickle	Chevrolet
18.	Trevor Boys	Chevrolet
19.	Tommy Ellis	Chevrolet
20.	Tim Richmond	Chevrolet
21.	Ken Ragan	Chevrolet
22.	Morgan Shepherd	Chevrolet
23.	Buddy Arrington	Ford
24.	Phil Parsons	Oldsmobile
25.	Jim Sauter	Pontiac
26.	Buddy Baker	Oldsmobile
27.	Cale Yarborough	Ford
28.	Joe Ruttman	Buick
29.	A. J. Foyt	Oldsmobile
30.	Harry Gant	Chevrolet
31.	Eddie Bierschwale	Chevrolet
32.	Neil Bonnett	Chevrolet
33.	Ken Schrader	Ford
34.	Pancho Carter	Ford
35.	Greg Sacks	Pontiac
36.	Richard Petty	Pontiac
37.	Mark Martin	Ford
38.	Dave Marcis	Pontiac
39.	Jimmy Means	Pontiac
40.	Larry Pearson	Chevrolet
41.	Kirk Bryant	Pontiac
42.	Bobby Allison	Buick

MILLER HIGH LIFE 400

February 23
Richmond, Virginia
Time of Race: 3 hours, 2 minutes, 54 seconds
Average Speed: 71.078 mph
Margin of Victory: 4 seconds

FINISH	DRIVER	CAR
1.	Kyle Petty	Ford
2.	Joe Ruttman	Buick
3.	Dale Earnhardt	Chevrolet
4.	Bobby Allison	Buick
5.	Darrell Waltrip	Chevrolet
6.	Bobby Hillin Jr.	Buick
7.	Neil Bonnett	Chevrolet
8.	Geoff Bodine	Chevrolet
9.	Dave Marcis	Chevrolet
10.	Rusty Wallace	Pontiac
11.	Jimmy Means	Pontiac
12.	Davey Allison	Chevrolet
13.	Doug Heveron	Ford
14.	Buddy Arrington	Ford
15.	Terry Labonte	Oldsmobile
16.	J. D. McDuffie	Pontiac
17.	Lake Speed	Pontiac
18.	Ron Bouchard	Pontiac
19.	Greg Sacks	Pontiac
20.	Richard Petty	Pontiac
21.	Bill Elliott	Chevrolet
22.	Tim Richmond	Chevrolet

23.	Ken Schrader	Ford
24.	Tommy Ellis	Chevrolet
25.	Michael Waltrip	Pontiac
26.	Trevor Boys	Chevrolet
27.	Kirk Bryant	Pontiac
28.	Harry Gant	Chevrolet
29.	Phil Parsons	Oldsmobile
30.	Ricky Rudd	Ford
31.	Eddie Bierschwale	Chevrolet

GOODWRENCH 500

March 2
Rockingham, North Carolina
Time of Race: 4 hours, 9 minutes, 10 seconds
Average Speed: 120.488 mph
Margin of Victory: 1 second

FINISH	DRIVER	CAR
1.	Terry Labonte	Oldsmobile
2.	Harry Gant	Chevrolet
3.	Richard Petty	Pontiac
4.	Morgan Shepherd	Buick
5.	Darrell Waltrip	Chevrolet
6.	Cale Yarborough	Ford
7.	Bill Elliott	Ford
8.	Dale Earnhardt	Chevrolet
9.	Neil Bonnett	Chevrolet
10.	Lake Speed	Pontiac
11.	Kyle Petty	Ford
12.	Rusty Wallace	Pontiac
13.	Ron Bouchard	Buick
14.	Tommy Ellis	Chevrolet
15.	Alan Kulwicki	Ford
16.	Tim Richmond	Chevrolet
17.	Buddy Arrington	Ford
18.	Kirk Bryant	Pontiac
19.	Jimmy Means	Pontiac
20.	Geoff Bodine	Chevrolet
21.	Michael Waltrip	Pontiac
22.	Ken Schrader	Ford
23.	Pancho Carter	Ford
24.	Jonathan Edwards	Chevrolet
25.	Davey Allison	Chevrolet
26.	Ronnie Thomas	Chevrolet
27.	Dave Marcis	Chevrolet
28.	Ricky Rudd	Ford
29.	Eddie Bierschwale	Pontiac
30.	Phil Parsons	Oldsmobile
31.	J. D. McDuffie	Pontiac
32.	Earle Canavan	Pontiac
33.	Joe Ruttman	Buick
34.	Bobby Allison	Buick
35.	Trevor Boys	Chevrolet
36.	Wayne Slark	Chevrolet
37.	Greg Sacks	Pontiac
38.	Bobby Wawak	Chevrolet
39.	Bobby Hillin Jr.	Buick
40.	Rick Newsom	Buick

MOTORCRAFT 500

March 16
Atlanta, Georgia
Time of Race: 3 hours, 46 minutes, 41 seconds
Average Speed: 132.126 mph
Margin of Victory: 1 second

FINISH	DRIVER	CAR
1.	Morgan Shephered	Buick
2.	Dale Earnhardt	Chevrolet
3.	Terry Labonte	Oldsmobile
4.	Darrell Waltrip	Chevrolet
5.	Bill Elliott	Ford

6.	Benny Parsons	Oldsmobile
7.	Tim Richmond	Chevrolet
8.	Rusty Wallace	Pontiac
9.	Bobby Allison	Buick
10.	Geoff Bodine	Chevrolet
11.	Richard Petty	Pontiac
12.	Harry Gant	Chevrolet
13.	Tommy Ellis	Chevrolet
14.	Alan Kulwicki	Ford
15.	Buddy Baker	Oldsmobile
16.	Bobby Hillin Jr.	Buick
17.	A. J. Foyt	Oldsmobile
18.	Phil Parsons	Oldsmobile
19.	Michael Waltrip	Pontiac
20.	Buddy Arrington	Ford
21.	Ken Schrader	Ford
22.	Lake Speed	Pontiac
23.	Bobby Wawak	Chevrolet
24.	Trevor Boys	Chevrolet
25.	Greg Sacks	Chevrolet
26.	Ricky Rudd	Ford
27.	CaleYarborough	Ford
28.	Kyle Petty	Ford
29.	Jody Ridley	Ford
30.	Eddie Bierschwale	Chevrolet
31.	Kirk Bryant	Pontiac
32.	Sterling Marlin	Chevrolet
33.	Dave Marcis	Pontiac
34.	Neil Bonnett	Chevrolet
35.	Doug Heveron	Chevrolet
36.	Chet Fillip	Ford
37.	H. B. Bailey	Pontiac
38.	Pancho Carter	Ford
39.	Rick Wilson	Oldsmobile
40.	Ron Bouchard	Pontiac
41.	Jimmy Means	Pontiac
42.	Joe Ruttman	Buick

VALLEYDALE MEATS 500

April 6
Bristol, Tennessee
Time of Race: 2 hours, 58 minutes, 14 seconds
Average Speed: 89.747 mph
Margin of Victory: 10.69 seconds

FINISH	DRIVER	CAR
1.	Rusty Wallace	Pontiac
2.	Ricky Rudd	Ford
3.	Darrell Waltrip	Chevrolet
4.	Harry Gant	Chevrolet
5.	Bill Elliott	Ford
6.	Bobby Allison	Buick
7.	Terry Labonte	Oldsmobile
8.	Tim Richmond	Chevrolet
9.	Kyle Petty	Ford
10.	Dale Earnhardt	Chevrolet
11.	Tommy Ellis	Chevrolet
12.	Rick Wilson	Oldsmobile
13.	Ken Schrader	Ford
14.	Richard Petty	Pontiac
15.	Alan Kulwicki	Ford
16.	Butch Miller	Buick
17.	Buddy Arrington	Ford
18.	Trevor Boys	Chevrolet
19.	Joe Ruttman	Buick
20.	Davey Allison	Chevrolet
21.	Doug Heveron	Chevrolet
22.	Chet Fillip	Ford
23.	Jody Ridley	Pontiac
24.	Geoff Bodine	Chevrolet
25.	Ron Bouchard	Pontiac
26.	Ronnie Thomas	Chevrolet
27.	Dave Marcis	Chevrolet
28.	Bobby Hillin Jr.	Buick
29.	Eddie Bierschwale	Pontiac
30.	Neil Bonnett	Chevrolet
31.	Morgan Shepherd	Ford
32.	Michael Waltrip	Buick

TRANSOUTH 500

April 13
Darlington, South Carolina
Time of Race: 3 hours, 53 minutes, 11 seconds
Average Speed: 128.994 mph
Margin of Victory: 3 car lengths

FINISH	DRIVER	CAR
1.	Dale Earnhardt	Chevrolet
2.	Darrell Waltrip	Chevrolet
3.	Bobby Allison	Buick
4.	Neil Bonnett	Chevrolet
5.	Tim Richmond	Chevrolet
6.	Rusty Wallace	Pontiac
7.	Richard Petty	Pontiac
8.	Bill Elliott	Ford
9.	Kyle Petty	Ford
10.	Ken Schrader	Ford
11.	Alan Kulwicki	Ford
12.	H. B. Bailey	Pontiac
13.	Michael Waltrip	Pontiac
14.	Harry Gant	Chevrolet
15.	Rick Wilson	Oldsmobile
16.	Mark Stahl	Ford
17.	J. D. McDuffie	Pontiac
18.	Connie Saylor	Ford
19.	Bobby Wawak	Buick
20.	Jody Ridley	Pontiac
21.	Joe Ruttman	Buick
22.	Cale Yarborough	Ford
23.	Morgan Shepherd	Buick
24.	Trevor Boys	Chevrolet
25.	Jimmy Means	Pontiac
26.	Ricky Rudd	Ford
27.	Dave Marcis	Chevrolet
28.	Benny Parsons	Oldsmobile
29.	Tommy Ellis	Chevrolet
30.	Buddy Baker	Oldsmobile
31.	Phil Parsons	Oldsmobile
32.	Terry Labonte	Oldsmobile
33.	Sterling Marlin	Chevrolet
34.	Eddie Bierschwale	Pontiac
35.	Doug Heveron	Oldsmobile
36.	Ronnie Thomas	Chevrolet
37.	Ron Bouchard	Pontiac
38.	Bobby Hillin Jr.	Buick
39.	Davey Allison	Chevrolet
40.	Geoff Bodine	Chevrolet

FIRST UNION 400

April 20
North Wilkesboro, North Carolina
Time of Race: 2 hours, 49 minutes, 40 seconds
Average Speed: 88.408 mph
Margin of Victory: 1 second

FINISH	DRIVER	CAR
1.	Dale Earnhardt	Chevrolet
2.	Ricky Rudd	Ford
3.	Geoff Bodine	Chevrolet
4.	Darrell Waltrip	Chevrolet
5.	Joe Ruttman	Buick
6.	Bobby Allison	Buick
7.	Harry Gant	Chevrolet
8.	Kyle Petty	Ford
9.	Bill Elliott	Ford
10.	Rusty Wallace	Pontiac
11.	Neil Bonnett	Chevrolet
12.	Tim Richmond	Chevrolet
13.	Bobby Hillin Jr.	Buick
14.	Ken Schrader	Ford
15.	Jody Ridley	Pontiac
16.	Doug Heveron	Oldsmobile
17.	Ron Bouchard	Pontiac
18.	Alan Kulwicki	Ford

19.	Morgan Shepherd	Chevrolet
20.	Jimmy Means	Pontiac
21.	Buddy Arrington	Ford
22.	Willy T. Ribbs	Pontiac
23.	Chet Fillip	Ford
24.	Rick Baldwin	Ford
25.	Dave Marcis	Chevrolet
26.	Michael Waltrip	Pontiac
27.	Terry Labonte	Oldsmobile
28.	J. D. McDuffie	Pontiac
29.	Richard Petty	Pontiac
30.	Trevor Boys	Chevrolet

SOVRAN BANK 500

April 27
Martinsville, Virginia
Time of Race: 3 hours, 25 minutes, 15 seconds
Average Speed: 76.882 mph
Margin of Victory: 24 seconds

FINISH	DRIVER	CAR
1.	Ricky Rudd	Ford
2.	Joe Ruttman	Buick
3.	Terry Labonte	Oldsmobile
4.	Alan Kulwicki	Ford
5.	Kyle Petty	Ford
6.	Bobby Hillin Jr.	Buick
7.	Ken Schrader	Ford
8.	Bobby Allison	Buick
9.	Derrike Cope	Ford
10.	Jody Ridley	Pontiac
11.	Michael Waltrip	Pontiac
12.	Jimmy Means	Pontiac
13.	Jerry Cranmer	Chevrolet
14.	Trevor Boys	Chevrolet
15.	Buddy Arrington	Ford
16.	Dave Marcis	Chevrolet
17.	Geoff Bodine	Chevrolet
18.	J. D. McDuffie	Pontiac
19.	Morgan Shepherd	Pontiac
20.	Tim Richmond	Chevrolet
21.	Dale Earnhardt	Chevrolet
22.	Mike Skinner	Pontiac
23.	Jimmy Hinsley	Ford
24.	Tommy Ellis	Chevrolet
25.	Harry Gant	Chevrolet
26.	Neil Bonnett	Chevrolet
27.	Darrell Waltrip	Chevrolet
28.	Richard Petty	Pontiac
29.	Doug Heveron	Chevrolet
30.	Rusty Wallace	Pontiac
31.	Bill Elliott	Ford

WINSTON 500

May 4
Talladega, Alabama
Time of Race: 3 hours, 10 minutes, 16 seconds
Average Speed: 157.698 mph
Margin of Victory: 1 car length

FINISH	DRIVER	CAR
1.	Bobby Allison	Buick
2.	Dale Earnhardt	Chevrolet
3.	Buddy Baker	Oldsmobile
4.	Bobby Hillin Jr.	Buick
5.	Phil Parsons	Oldsmobile
6.	Morgan Shepherd	Buick
7.	Richard Petty	Pontiac
8.	Rick Wilson	Chevrolet
9.	Ron Bouchard	Pontiac
10.	Greg Sacks	Pontiac
11.	Dave Marcis	Pontiac
12.	Tim Richmond	Chevrolet

13.	Rusty Wallace	Pontiac
14.	Ronnie Thomas	Chevrolet
15.	Doug Heveron	Pontiac
16.	Jimmy Means	Chevrolet
17.	Joe Ruttman	Buick
18.	Pancho Carter	Chevrolet
19.	Delma Cowart	Chevrolet
20.	Benny Parsons	Oldsmobile
21.	Harry Gant	Chevrolet
22.	Buddy Arrington	Ford
23.	Chet Fillip	Ford
24.	Bill Elliott	Ford
25.	Tommy Gale	Ford
26.	Ken Schrader	Ford
27.	Geoff Bodine	Chevrolet
28.	Phil Barkdoll	Ford
29.	Terry Labonte	Oldsmobile
30.	Eddie Birerschwale	Chevrolet
31.	Kyle Petty	Ford
32.	Tommy Ellis	Chevrolet
33.	Connie Saylor	Chevrolet
34.	Darrell Waltrip	Chevrolet
35.	Michael Waltrip	Pontiac
36.	Ricky Rudd	Ford
37.	Cale Yarborough	Ford
38.	Trevor Boys	Chevrolet
39.	Sterling Marlin	Chevrolet
40.	Neil Bonnett	Chevrolet
41.	Jim Sauter	Chevrolet
42.	Jody Ridley	Pontiac

BUDWEISER 500

May 18
Dover, Delaware
Time of Race: 4 hours, 20 minutes, 51 seconds
Average Speed: 115.009 mph
Margin of Victory: 3 seconds

FINISH	DRIVER	CAR
1.	Geoff Bodine	Chevrolet
2.	Bobby Allison	Buick
3.	Dale Earnhardt	Chevrolet
4.	Ricky Rudd	Ford
5.	Darrell Waltrip	Chevrolet
6.	Richard Petty	Pontiac
7.	Bill Elliott	Ford
8.	Bobby Hillin Jr.	Buick
9.	Tommy Ellis	Chevrolet
10.	Ken Schrader	Ford
11.	Joe Ruttman	Buick
12.	Michael Waltrip	Pontiac
13.	Trevor Boys	Pontiac
14.	Harry Gant	Chevrolet
15.	Buddy Arrington	Ford
16.	Jerry Cranmer	Chevrolet
17.	Terry Labonte	Oldsmobile
18.	Jody Ridley	Pontiac
19.	Kyle Petty	Ford
20.	J. D. McDuffie	Pontiac
21.	Dave Marcis	Chevrolet
22.	Gary Fedewa	Chevrolet
23.	Alan Kulwicki	Ford
24.	Jimmy Means	Pontiac
25.	Rick Newsom	Buick
26.	Rusty Wallace	Pontiac
27.	Ron Bouchard	Pontiac
28.	Neil Bonnett	Chevrolet
29.	Jerry Bowman	Ford
30.	Jerry Holden	Ford
31.	Joe Booher	Chevrolet
32.	Tim Richmond	Chevrolet
33.	Mike Porter	Ford
34.	Rick Baldwin	Ford
35.	Doug Heveron	Chevrolet
36.	Howard Mark	Chevrolet
37.	Joe Fields	Ford

COCA-COLA 600

May 25
Charlotte, North Carolina
Time of Race: 4 hours, 16 minutes, 24 seconds
Average Speed: 140.406 mph
Margin of Victory: 5 seconds

FINISH	DRIVER	CAR
1.	Dale Earnhardt	Chevrolet
2.	Tim Richmond	Chevrolet
3.	Cale Yarborough	Ford
4.	Harry Gant	Chevrolet
5.	Darrell Waltrip	Chevrolet
6.	Bill Elliott	Ford
7.	Sterling Marlin	Chevrolet
8.	Ricky Rudd	Ford
9.	Morgan Shepherd	Buick
10.	Rusty Wallace	Pontiac
11.	Terry Labonte	Oldsmobile
12.	Bobby Allison	Buick
13.	Neil Bonnett	Chevrolet
14.	Lake Speed	Oldsmobile
15.	Bobby Hillin Jr.	Buick
16.	Dave Marcis	Ford
17.	Buddy Baker	Oldsmobile
18.	Brett Bodine	Chevrolet
19.	Ron Bouchard	Pontiac
20.	Kyle Petty	Ford
21.	Jody Ridley	Pontiac
22.	Mark Martin	Ford
23.	Ken Schrader	Ford
24.	Phil Parsons	Oldsmobile
25.	Trevor Boys	Pontiac
26.	Michael Waltrip	Pontiac
27.	Alan Kulwicki	Ford
28.	Connie Saylor	Ford
29.	Eddie Bierschwale	Chevrolet
30.	Derrike Cope	Ford
31.	Geoff Bodine	Chevrolet
32.	Joe Ruttman	Buick
33.	Doug Heveron	Chevrolet
34.	Benny Parsons	Oldsmobile
35.	Tommy Ellis	Chevrolet
36.	David Pearson	Chevrolet
37.	Chet Fillip	Ford
38.	Richard Petty	Chevrolet
39.	Greg Sacks	Chevrolet
40.	Brad Teague	Chevrolet
41.	Ken Ragan	Pontiac

BUDWEISER 400

June 1
Riverside, California
Time of Race: 2 hours, 22 minutes, 7 seconds
Average Speed: 105.083 mph
Margin of Victory: 4 feet

FINISH	DRIVER	CAR
1.	Darrell Waltrip	Chevrolet
2.	Tim Richmond	Chevrolet
3.	Ricky Rudd	Ford
4.	Rusty Wallace	Pontiac
5.	Dale Earnhardt	Chevrolet
6.	Richard Petty	Pontiac
7.	Bobby Allison	Buick
8.	Neil Bonnett	Chevrolet
9.	Harry Gant	Chevrolet
10.	Glen Steurer	Chevrolet
11.	Bill Elliott	Ford
12.	Terry Labonte	Oldsmobile
13.	Chad Little	Ford
14.	J. D. McDuffie	Pontiac
15.	Jim Robinson	Oldsmobile
16.	Ron Esau	Chevrolet
17.	Ken Schrader	Ford

18.	Bill Schmitt	Chevrolet
19.	Buddy Arrington	Ford
20.	Doug Heveron	Chevrolet
21.	Clay Young	Buick
22.	Jimmy Means	Pontiac
23.	Ted Kennedy	Chevrolet
24.	Terrry Petris	Chevrolet
25.	Michael Waltrip	Pontiac
26.	John Krebs	Oldsmobile
27.	Morgan Shepherd	Pontiac
28.	Hershel McGriff	Pontiac
29.	Willy T. Ribbs	Chevrolet
30.	Ruben Garcia	Chevrolet
31.	Derrike Cope	Ford
32.	Bobby Hillin Jr.	Buick
33.	D. K. Ulrich	Chevrolet
34.	Trevor Boys	Pontiac
35.	Bill Osborn	Buick
36.	Ray Kelly	Pontiac
37.	Rick McCray	Buick
38.	Dave Marcis	Pontiac
39.	Geoff Bodine	Chevrolet
40.	Rick Lach	Buick
41.	Kyle Petty	Ford
42.	Joe Ruttman	Buick

MILLER HIGH LIFE 500

June 8
Pocono, Pennsylvania
Time of Race: 4 hours, 24 minutes, 50 seconds
Average Speed: 113.279 mph
Margin of Victory: under caution

FINISH	DRIVER	CAR
1.	Tim Richmond	Chevrolet
2.	Dale Earnhardt	Chevrolet
3.	Cale Yarborough	Ford
4.	Ricky Rudd	Ford
5.	Bill Elliott	Ford
6.	Rusty Wallace	Pontiac
7.	Joe Ruttman	Buick
8.	Kyle Petty	Ford
9.	Geoff Bodine	Chevrolet
10.	Bobby Hillin Jr.	Buick
11.	Jody Ridley	Pontiac
12.	Ron Bouchard	Pontiac
13.	Bobby Allison	Buick
14.	Dave Marcis	Pontiac
15.	Tommy Ellis	Chevrolet
16.	J. D. McDuffie	Pontiac
17.	D. K. Ulrich	Chevrolet
18.	Morgan Shepherd	Buick
19.	Richard Petty	Pontiac
20.	Chet Fillip	Ford
21.	Buddy Arrington	Ford
22.	Jimmy Means	Pontiac
23.	Neil Bonnett	Chevrolet
24.	Jerry Cranmer	Chevrolet
25.	Jack Ely	Chevrolet
26.	Harry Gant	Chevrolet
27.	Ken Schrader	Ford
28.	Pancho Carter	Chevrolet
29.	Randy LaJoie	Chevrolet
30.	Jonathan Edwards	Buick
31.	Phil Parsons	Oldsmobile
32.	Eddie Bierschwale	Ford
33.	Benny Parsons	Oldsmobile
34.	Bobby Gerhart	Chevrolet
35.	Terry Labonte	Oldsmobile
36.	Buddy Baker	Oldsmobile
37.	Rick Newsom	Buick
38.	Buddie Boys	Pontiac
39.	Michael Waltrip	Pontiac
40.	Darrell Waltrip	Chevrolet

MILLER AMERICAN 400

June 15
Brooklyn, Michigan
Time of Race: 2 hours, 53 minutes, 21 seconds
Average Speed: 138.851 mph
Margin of Victory: 2 car lengths

FINISH	DRIVER	CAR
1.	Bill Elliott	Ford
2.	Harry Gant	Chevrolet
3.	Geoff Bodine	Chevrolet
4.	Buddy Baker	Oldsmobile
5.	Darrell Waltrip	Chevrolet
6.	Dale Earnhardt	Chevrolet
7.	Bobby Hillin Jr.	Buick
8.	Rick Wilson	Oldsmobile
9.	Joe Ruttman	Buick
10.	Ricky Rudd	Ford
11.	Bobby Allison	Buick
12.	Terry Labonte	Oldsmobile
13.	Richard Petty	Pontiac
14.	Tommy Ellis	Chevrolet
15.	Tim Richmond	Chevrolet
16.	Alan Kulwicki	Ford
17.	Pancho Carter	Chevrolet
18.	Jim Sauter	Pontiac
19.	Rusty Wallace	Pontiac
20.	Ken Schrader	Ford
21.	Butch Miller	Chevrolet
22.	Michael Waltrip	Pontiac
23.	Gary Fedewa	Chevrolet
24.	Bobby Wawak	Chevrolet
25.	Neil Bonnett	Chevrolet
26.	Chet Fillip	Ford
27.	Eddie Bierschwale	Ford
28.	Derrike Cope	Ford
29.	Morgan Shepherd	Buick
30.	Cale Yarborough	Ford
31.	Mike Laws	Chevrolet
32.	Kyle Petty	Ford
33.	Phil Parsons	Oldsmobile
34.	Jody Ridley	Pontiac
35.	J. D. McDuffie	Pontiac
36.	Ron Bouchard	Pontiac
37.	Dave Marcis	Pontiac
38.	James Hylton	Chevrolet
39.	Willy T. Ribbs	Chevrolet
40.	D. K. Ulrich	Chevrolet
41.	Benny Parsons	Oldsmobile

PEPSI FIRECRACKER 400

July 4
Daytona Beach, Florida
Time of Race: 3 hours, 1 minute, 56 seconds
Average Speed: 131.916 mph
Margin of Victory: 1.35 seconds

FINISH	DRIVER	CAR
1.	Tim Richmond	Chevrolet
2.	Sterling Marlin	Chevrolet
3.	Bobby Hillin Jr.	Buick
4.	Darrell Waltrip	Chevrolet
5.	Kyle Petty	Ford
6.	Ricky Rudd	Ford
7.	Joe Ruttman	Buick
8.	Rusty Wallace	Pontiac
9.	Phil Parsons	Oldsmobile
10.	Alan Kulwicki	Ford
11.	Neil Bonnett	Chevrolet
12.	Ken Schrader	Ford
13.	Jody Ridley	Pontiac
14.	Buddy Baker	Oldsmobile
15.	Bobby Allison	Buick
16.	Bill Elliott	Ford
17.	Cale Yarborough	Ford

18.	Michael Waltrip	Pontiac
19.	Terry Labonte	Oldsmobile
20.	Dave Marcis	Pontiac
21.	Rick Wilson	Oldsmobile
22.	Richard Petty	Pontiac
23.	Jim Sauter	Chevrolet
24.	Jimmy Means	Pontiac
25.	Buddy Arrington	Ford
26.	Grant Adcox	Chevrolet
27.	Dale Earnhardt	Chevrolet
28.	Pancho Carter	Chevrolet
29.	Geoff Bodine	Chevrolet
30.	Connie Saylor	Ford
31.	Harry Gant	Chevrolet
32.	Rodney Combs	Chevrolet
33.	Doug Heveron	Chevrolet
34.	Ken Ragen	Chevrolet
35.	Eddie Bierschwale	Chevrolet
36.	Benny Parsons	Oldsmobile
37.	Morgan Shepherd	Buick
38.	Tommy Ellis	Chevrolet
39.	Greg Sacks	Chevrolet
40.	Chet Fillip	Ford
41.	Ron Bouchard	Pontiac
42.	A. J. Foyt	Oldsmobile

SUMMER 500

July 20
Pocono, Pennsylvania
Time of Race: 2 hours, 41 minutes, 8 seconds
Average Speed: 124,218 mph
Margin of Victory: .05 seconds

FINISH	DRIVER	CAR
1.	Tim Richmond	Chevrolet
2.	Ricky Rudd	Ford
3.	Geoff Bodine	Chevrolet
4.	Darrell Waltrip	Chevrolet
5.	Bobby Allison	Buick
6.	Terry Labonte	Oldsmobile
7.	Dale Earnhardt	Chevrolet
8.	Kyle Petty	Ford
9.	Tommy Ellis	Chevrolet
10.	Rick Wilson	Oldsmobile
11.	Michael Waltrip	Pontiac
12.	Chet Filip	Ford
13.	Jimmy Means	Pontiac
14.	Jim Sauter	Pontiac
15.	Eddie Bierschwale	Ford
16.	Doug Heveron	Chevrolet
17.	Buddy Arrington	Ford
18.	D. K. Ulrich	Chevrolet
19.	J. D. McDuffie	Pontiac
20.	Jack Ely	Chevrolet
21.	Gary Fedewa	Chevrolet
22.	Alan Kulwicki	Ford
23.	Ken Schrader	Ford
24.	Dave Marcis	Pontiac
25.	Cale Yarborough	Ford
26.	Jerry Cranmer	Chevrolet
27.	Rusty Wallace	Pontiac
28.	Bobby Gerhart	Chevrolet
29.	Benny Parsons	Oldsmobile
30.	Harry Gant	Chevrolet
31.	Neil Bonnett	Chevrolet
32.	Morgan Shepherd	Buick
33.	Bobby Hillin Jr.	Buick
34.	Richard Petty	Pontiac
35.	Bill Elliott	Ford
36.	Buddy Baker	Oldsmobile
37.	Phil Parsons	Oldsmobile
38.	Joe Ruttman	Buick
39.	Jocko Maggiacomo	Oldsmobile
40.	Cliff Hucul	Pontiac

TALLADEGA 500

July 27
Talladega, Alabama
Time of Race: 3 hours, 17 minutes, 59 seconds
Average Speed: 151.552 mph
Margin of Victory: 3 car lengths

FINISH	DRIVER	CAR
1.	Bobby Hillin Jr.	Buick
2.	Tim Richmond	Chevrolet
3.	Ricky Rudd	Ford
4.	Sterling Marlin	Chevrolet
5.	Benny Parsons	Oldsmobile
6.	Morgan Shepherd	Buick
7.	Davey Allison	Chevrolet
8.	Joe Ruttman	Buick
9.	Kyle Petty	Ford
10.	Bobby Allison	Buick
11.	Rick Wilson	Oldsmobile
12.	Jim Sauter	Pontiac
13.	Phil Parsons	Oldsmobile
14.	Michael Waltrip	Pontiac
15.	Jimmy Means	Pontiac
16.	Ronnie Thomas	Chevrolet
17.	Ron Bouchard	Pontiac
18.	Ken Ragan	Chevrolet
19.	Rodney Combs	Chevrolet
20.	Buddy Baker	Oldsmobile
21.	Buddy Arrington	Ford
22.	Harry Gant	Chevrolet
23.	Geoff Bodine	Chevrolet
24.	Cale Yarborough	Ford
25.	Darrell Waltrip	Chevrolet
26.	Dale Earnhardt	Chevrolet
27.	Bill Elliott	Ford
28.	Chet Fillip	Ford
29.	Delma Cowart	Chevrolet
30.	A. J. Foyt	Oldsmobile
31.	Ken Schrader	Ford
32.	Alan Kulwicki	Ford
33.	Phil Barkdoll	Ford
34.	Tommy Ellis	Chevrolet
35.	Rusty Wallace	Pontiac
36.	Dave Marcis	Pontiac
37.	Richard Petty	Pontiac
38.	Terry Labonte	Oldsmobile
39.	Eddie Bierschwale	Chevrolet
40.	Pancho Carter	Chevrolet

THE BUDWEISER AT THE GLEN

August 10
Watkins Glen, New York
Time of Race: 2 hours, 12 minutes, 56 seconds
Average Speed: 90.463 mph
Margin of Victory: 1.45 seconds

FINISH	DRIVER	CAR
1.	Tim Richmond	Chevrolet
2.	Darrell Waltrip	Chevrolet
3.	Dale Earnhardt	Chevrolet
4.	Bill Elliott	Ford
5.	Neil Bonnett	Chevrolet
6.	Rusty Wallace	Pontiac
7.	Ricky Rudd	Ford
8.	Benny Parsons	Oldsmobile
9.	Kyle Petty	Ford
10.	Richard Petty	Pontiac
11.	Morgan Shepherd	Pontiac
12.	Bobby Allison	Buick
13.	Dave Marcis	Chevrolet
14.	Phil Parsons	Oldsmobile
15.	Tommy Riggins	Pontiac
16.	Ken Schrader	Ford
17.	Michael Waltrip	Pontiac
18.	George Follmer	Chevrolet

19.	Geoff Bodine	Chevrolet
20.	Rick Knoop	Chevrolet
21.	Jimmy Means	Pontiac
22.	Chet Fillip	Ford
23.	Rick Wilson	Oldsmobile
24.	Buddy Arrington	Ford
25.	J. D. McDuffie	Pontiac
26.	Tom Rotsell	Ford
27.	James Hylton	Chevrolet
28.	Bobby Hillin Jr.	Buick
29.	Al Unser, Sr.	Oldsmobile
30.	Eddie Bierschwale	Ford
31.	Pancho Carter	Chevrolet
32.	Terry Labonte	Oldsmobile
33.	Joe Ruttman	Buick
34.	Harry Gant	Chevrolet
35.	Phil Good	Ford
36.	Jocko Maggiacomo	Buick

CHAMPION SPARK PLUG 400

August 17
Brooklyn, Michigan
Time of Race: 2 hours, 57 minutes, 28 seconds
Average Speed: 135.376 mph
Margin of Victory: 1.45 seconds

FINISH	DRIVER	CAR
1.	Bill Elliott	Ford
2.	Tim Richmond	Chevrolet
3.	Darrell Waltrip	Chevrolet
4.	Geoff Bodine	Chevrolet
5.	Dale Earnhardt	Chevrolet
6.	Rusty Wallace	Pontiac
7.	Cale Yarborough	Ford
8.	Harry Gant	Chevrolet
9.	Phil Parsons	Oldsmobile
10.	David Pearson	Chevrolet
11.	Ken Schrader	Ford
12.	Terry Labonte	Oldsmobile
13.	Bobby Hillin Jr.	Buick
14.	Alan Kulwicki	Ford
15.	Chet Fillip	Ford
16.	Eddie Bierschwale	Ford
17.	Ken Ragan	Chevrolet
18.	Richard Petty	Pontiac
19.	Buddy Arrington	Ford
20.	D. K. Ulrich	Chevrolet
21.	Ricky Rudd	Ford
22.	Bobby Gerhart	Chevrolet
23.	Jim Hull	Oldsmobile
24.	Bobby Allison	Buick
25.	Jimmy Means	Pontiac
26.	Benny Parsons	Oldsmobile
27.	David Simko	Chevrolet
28.	Kyle Petty	Ford
29.	Rodney Combs	Pontiac
30.	Joe Ruttman	Buick
31.	J. D. McDuffie	Pontiac
32.	Michael Waltrip	Pontiac
33.	Butch Miller	Chevrolet
34.	Neil Bonnett	Chevrolet
35.	Dave Marcis	Chevrolet
36.	Morgan Shepherd	Buick
37.	Jim Sauter	Pontiac
38.	Greg Sacks	Chevrolet
39.	Tommy Ellis	Chevrolet
40.	Rick Wilson	Oldsmobile
41.	Buddy Baker	Oldsmobile

BUSCH 500

August 23
Bristol, Tennessee
Time of Race: 3 hours, 3 minutes, 55 seconds
Average Speed: 86.934 mph
Margin of Victory: 8.55 seconds

FINISH	DRIVER	CAR
1.	Darrell Waltrip	Chevrolet
2.	Terry Labonte	Chevrolet
3.	Geoff Bodine	Chevrolet
4.	Dale Earnhardt	Chevrolet
5.	Harry Gant	Chevrolet
6.	Tim Richmond	Chevrolet
7.	Richard Petty	Pontiac
8.	Bobby Allison	Buick
9.	Bobby Hillin Jr.	Buick
10.	Alan Kulwicki	Ford
11.	Neil Bonnett	Chevrolet
12.	Tommy Ellis	Chevrolet
13.	Michael Waltrip	Pontiac
14.	Rusty Wallace	Pontiac
15.	Dave Marcis	Chevrolet
16.	Buddy Arrington	Ford
17.	Joe Ruttman	Buick
18.	Eddie Bierschwale	Oldsmobile
19.	Bill Elliott	Ford
20.	D. K. Ulrich	Chevrolet
21.	Brad Teague	Chevrolet
22.	Morgan Shepherd	Pontiac
23.	Ricky Rudd	Ford
24.	J. D. McDuffie	Pontiac
25.	Chet Fillip	Ford
26.	Rick Wilson	Oldsmobile
27.	Jimmy Means	Pontiac
28.	Ken Schrader	Ford
29.	Dale Jarrett	Pontiac
30.	Kyle Petty	Ford

SOUTHERN 500

August 31
Darlington, South Carolina
Time of Race: 4 hours, 8 minutes, 45 seconds
Average Speed: 121.068 mph
Margin of Victory: 2 seconds

FINISH	DRIVER	CAR
1.	Tim Richmond	Chevrolet
2.	Bobby Allison	Buick
3.	Bill Elliott	Ford
4.	Morgan Shepherd	Buick
5.	Darrell Waltrip	Chevrolet
6.	Ricky Rudd	Ford
7.	Bobby Hillin Jr.	Buick
8.	Geoff Bodine	Chevrolet
9.	Dale Earnhardt	Chevrolet
10.	Cale Yarborough	Ford
11.	Dave Marcis	Chevrolet
12.	Alan Kulwicki	Ford
13.	Jim Sauter	Pontiac
14.	Kyle Petty	Ford
15.	Jimmy Means	Pontiac
16.	Michael Waltrip	Pontiac
17.	H. B. Bailey	Pontiac
18.	D. K. Ulrich	Chevrolet
19.	Buddy Baker	Oldsmobile
20.	Buddy Arrington	Ford
21.	Terry Labonte	Chevrolet
22.	Phil Parsons	Oldsmobile
23.	Rusty Wallace	Pontiac
24.	Neil Bonnett	Chevrolet
25.	Eddie Bierschwale	Chevrolet
26.	Connie Saylor	Ford
27.	Harry Gant	Chevrolet
28.	Rick Wilson	Oldsmobile
29.	Jonathan Edwards	Chevrolet
30.	Ron Bouchard	Pontiac
31.	Benny Parsons	Oldsmobile
32.	Mark Stahl	Ford
33.	Donnie Allison	Chevrolet
34.	J. D. McDuffie	Pontiac
35.	Chet Fillip	Ford
36.	Ken Schrader	Ford
37.	Sterling Marlin	Chevrolet
38.	Joe Ruttman	Buick

39.	James Hylton	Chevrolet
40.	Richard Petty	Pontiac

WRANGLER JEANS INDIGO 400

September 7
Richmond, Virginia
Time of Race: 3 hours, 5 minutes, 24 seconds
Average Speed: 70.161 mph
Margin of Victory: 2 car lengths

FINISH	DRIVER	CAR
1.	Tim Richmond	Chevrolet
2.	Dale Earnhardt	Chevrolet
3.	Morgan Shepherd	Pontiac
4.	Richard Petty	Pontiac
5.	Neil Bonnett	Chevrolet
6.	Joe Ruttman	Buick
7.	Harry Gant	Chevrolet
8.	Bobby Allison	Buick
9.	Bill Elliott	Ford
10.	Bobby Hillin Jr.	Buick
11.	Eddie Bierschwale	Chevrolet
12.	Buddy Arrington	Ford
13.	Geoff Bodine	Chevrolet
14.	Michael Waltrip	Pontiac
15.	Alan Kulwicki	Ford
16.	Jimmy Hensley	Ford
17.	D. K. Ulrich	Chevrolet
18.	Terry Labonte	Oldsmobile
19.	Rusty Wallace	Pontiac
20.	Kyle Petty	Ford
21.	Tommy Ellis	Chevrolet
22.	James Hylton	Chevrolet
23.	Dave Marcis	Chevrolet
24.	Ricky Rudd	Ford
25.	Ken Schrader	Ford
26.	Jimmy Means	Pontiac
27.	Ron Shepherd	Oldsmobile
28.	J. D. McDuffie	Pontiac
29.	Darrell Waltrip	Chevrolet

DELAWARE 500

September 14
Dover, Delaware
Time of Race: 4 hours, 22 minutes, 24 seconds
Average Speed: 114.329 mph
Margin of Victory: 6 seconds

FINISH	DRIVER	CAR
1.	Ricky Rudd	Ford
2.	Neil Bonnett	Chevrolet
3.	Kyle Petty	Ford
4.	Buddy Baker	Oldsmobile
5.	Dave Marcis	Chevrolet
6.	Joe Ruttman	Buick
7.	Alan Kulwicki	Ford
8.	Tommy Ellis	Chevrolet
9.	Bobby Hillin Jr.	Buick
10.	Morgan Shepherd	Pontiac
11.	Mark Martin	Ford
12.	Richard Petty	Pontiac
13.	Rusty Wallace	Pontiac
14.	Darrell Waltrip	Chevrolet
15.	Buddy Arrington	Ford
16.	Michael Waltrip	Pontiac
17.	Johnny Coy Jr.	Chevrolet
18.	Joe Booher	Chevrolet
19.	Terry Labonte	Oldsmobile
20.	Bobby Allison	Buick
21.	Dale Earnhardt	Chevrolet
22.	Ken Schrader	Ford
23.	Chet Fillip	Ford
24.	Jimmy Means	Pontiac
25.	Ed Bierschwale	Chevrolet

26.	Tim Richmond	Chevrolet
27.	Bill Elliott	Ford
28.	Geoff Bodine	Chevrolet
29.	Brian Baker	Ford
30.	Howard Rose	Pontiac
31.	Cliff Hucul	Pontiac
32.	Rick Wilson	Oldsmobile
33.	Bobby Wawak	Chevrolet
34.	Gary Fedewa	Chevrolet
35.	Harry Gant	Chevrolet
36.	Jerry Bowman	Ford
37.	J. D. McDuffie	Pontiac
38.	Roy Lee Hendrick	Ford
39.	Tommie Crozier	Pontiac
40.	Mike Potter	Ford

GOODY'S 500

September 21
Martinsville, Virginia
Time of Race: 3 hours, 35 minutes, 32 seconds
Average Speed: 73.191 mph
Margin of Victory: 2 car lengths

FINISH	DRIVER	CAR
1.	Rusty Wallace	Pontiac
2.	Geoff Bodine	Chevrolet
3.	Harry Gant	Chevrolet
4.	Darrell Waltrip	Chevrolet
5.	Joe Ruttman	Chevrolet
6.	Kyle Petty	Ford
7.	Ken Schrader	Ford
8.	Neil Bonnett	Chevrolet
9.	Dave Marcis	Chevrolet
10.	Tim Richmond	Chevrolet
11.	Bill Elliott	Ford
12.	Dale Earnhardt	Chevrolet
13.	Alan Kulwicki	Ford
14.	Michael Waltrip	Pontiac
15.	Terry Labonte	Oldsmobile
16.	Richard Petty	Pontiac
17.	Bobby Hillin Jr.	Buick
18.	Jimmy Hensley	Ford
19.	Buddy Arrington	Ford
20.	J. D. McDuffie	Pontiac
21.	Bobby Allison	Buick
22.	Jimmy Means	Pontiac
23.	Jerry Cranmer	Chevrolet
24.	Eddie Bierschwale	Chevrolet
25.	Phil Good	Ford
26.	Tommy Ellis	Chevrolet
27.	D. K. Ulrich	Chevrolet
28.	Ricky Rudd	Ford
29.	Morgan Shepherd	Pontiac
30.	Mike Skinner	Pontiac

HOLLY FARMS 400

September 28
North Wilkesboro, North Carolina
Time of Race: 2 hours, 36 minutes, 53 seconds
Average Speed: 95.612 mph
Magin of Victory: 1.21 second

FINISH	DRIVER	CAR
1.	Darrell Waltrip	Chevrolet
2.	Geoff Bodine	Chevrolet
3.	Richard Petty	Pontiac
4.	Rusty Wallace	Pontiac
5.	Harry Gant	Chevrolet
6.	Joe Ruttman	Buick
7.	Ricky Rudd	Ford
8.	Dave Marcis	Chevrolet
9.	Dale Earnhardt	Chevrolet
10.	Terry Labonte	Oldsmobile

11.	Tim Richmond	Chevrolet
12.	Neil Bonnett	Chevrolet
13.	Tommy Ellis	Chevrolet
14.	Kyle Petty	Ford
15.	Bobby Hillin Jr.	Buick
16.	Bill Elliott	Ford
17.	Alan Kulwicki	Ford
18.	Ken Schrader	Ford
19.	Buddy Arrington	Ford
20.	Eddie Bierschwale	Chevrolet
21.	Chet Fillip	Ford
22.	Bobby Allison	Buick
23.	Michael Waltrip	Pontiac
24.	Brent Elliott	Buick
25.	Morgan Shepherd	Pontiac
26.	J. D. McDuffie	Pontiac
27.	Jimmy Means	Pontiac
28.	D. K. Ulrich	Chevrolet
29.	Trevor Boys	Chevrolet
30.	Joe Millikan	Ford

OAKWOOD HOMES 500

October 5
Charlotte, North Carolina
Time of Race: 3 hours, 47 minutes, 2 seconds
Average Speed: 132.403 mph
Margin of Victory: 1.9 seconds

FINISH	DRIVER	CAR
1.	Dale Earnhardt	Chevrolet
2.	Harry Gant	Chevrolet
3.	Neil Bonnett	Chevrolet
4.	Ricky Rudd	Ford
5.	Buddy Baker	Oldsmobile
6.	Geoff Bodine	Chevrolet
7.	Bill Elliott	Ford
8.	Rusty Wallace	Pontiac
9.	Darrell Waltrip	Chevrolet
10.	Phil Parsons	Oldsmobile
11.	Dave Marcis	Chevrolet
12.	Larry Pearson	Chevrolet
13.	Kyle Petty	Ford
14.	Alan Kulwicki	Ford
15.	Terry Labonte	Oldsmobile
16.	Rodney Combs	Pontiac
17.	Connie Saylor	Ford
18.	Jimmy Means	Pontiac
19.	Michael Waltrip	Pontiac
20.	J. D. McDuffie	Pontiac
21.	Ron Bouchard	Pontiac
22.	Buddy Arrington	Ford
23.	Ken Ragan	Chevrolet
24.	Eddie Bierschwale	Oldsmobile
25.	Joe Ruttman	Buick
26.	Bobby Hillin Jr.	Buick
27.	Tim Richmond	Chevrolet
28.	Ken Schrader	Ford
29.	Rick Wilson	Oldsmobile
30.	Benny Parsons	Oldsmobile
31.	Tommy Ellis	Chevrolet
32.	Morgan Shepherd	Pontiac
33.	Sterling Marlin	Chevrolet
34.	David Sosobee	Chevrolet
35.	Richard Petty	Pontiac
36.	Cale Yarborough	Ford
37.	A. J. Foyt	Oldsmobile
38.	Chet Fillip	Ford
39.	Delma Cowart	Chevrolet
40.	Brad Teague	Chevrolet
41.	Bobby Allison	Buick
42.	Randy Baker	Chevrolet

NATIONWIDE 500

October 19
Charlotte, North Carolina
Time of Race: 3 hours, 57 minutes, 33 seconds

Average Speed: 126.381 mph
Margin of Victory: 2.53 seconds

FINISH	DRIVER	CAR
1.	Neil Bonnett	Chevrolet
2.	Ricky Rudd	Ford
3.	Darrell Waltrip	Chevrolet
4.	Harry Gant	Chevrolet
5.	Buddy Baker	Oldsmobile
6.	Dale Earnhardt	Chevrolet
7.	Bill Elliott	Ford
8.	Richard Petty	Pontiac
9.	Joe Ruttman	Buick
10.	Kyle Petty	Ford
11.	Bobby Hillin Jr.	Buick
12.	Alan Kulwicki	Ford
13.	Michael Waltrip	Pontiac
14.	Ken Schrader	Ford
15.	Dick Trickle	Chevrolet
16.	Eddie Bierschwale	Oldsmobile
17.	Buddy Arrington	Ford
18.	Charlie Baker	Chevrolet
19.	Rusty Wallace	Pontiac
20.	Tim Richmond	Chevrolet
21.	J. D. McDuffie	Pontiac
22.	Jimmy Means	Pontiac
23.	Mike Skinner	Pontiac
24.	Morgan Shepherd	Pontiac
25.	Bobby Allison	Buick
26.	Mike Potter	Ford
27.	Jonathan Edwards	Buick
28.	Tommie Crozier	Pontiac
29.	Bobby Wawak	Chevrolet
30.	Mark Stahl	Ford
31.	Terry Labonte	Oldsmobile
32.	Geoff Bodine	Chevrolet
33.	Cale Yarborough	Ford
34.	Dave Marcis	Chevrolet
35.	Tommy Ellis	Chevrolet
36.	Johnny Coy Jr.	Chevrolet
37.	Trevor Boys	Chevrolet
38.	Joe Milliken	Ford
39.	Buddy Boys	Chevrolet
40.	Ronnie Thomas	Pontiac

ATLANTA JOURNAL 500

November 2
Atlanta, Georgia
Time of Race: 3 hours, 15 minutes, 22 seconds
Average Speed: 152.523 mph
Margin of Victory: 1 lap, 3 seconds

FINISH	DRIVER	CAR
1.	Dale Earnhardt	Chevrolet
2.	Richard Petty	Pontiac
3.	Bill Elliott	Ford
4.	Tim Richmond	Chevrolet
5.	Buddy Baker	Oldsmobile
6.	Neil Bonnett	Chevrolet
7.	Kyle Petty	Ford
8.	Terry Labonte	Oldsmobile
9.	Joe Ruttman	Buick
10.	Phil Parsons	Oldsmobile
11.	Benny Parsons	Oldsmobile
12.	Tommy Ellis	Chevrolet
13.	Rusty Wallace	Pontiac
14.	Rick Wilson	Oldsmobile
15.	Bobby Hillin Jr.	Buick
16.	Bobby Allison	Buick
17.	Ken Schrader	Ford
18.	Alan Kulwicki	Ford
19.	Ken Ragan	Chevrolet
20.	Michael Waltrip	Pontiac
21.	Buddy Arrington	Ford
22.	Randy Baker	Chevrolet
23.	Eddie Bierschwale	Oldsmobile
24.	Mike Laws	Chevrolet
25.	Ricky Rudd	Ford

26.	Mark Martin	Ford
27.	Morgan Shepherd	Pontiac
28.	Harry Gant	Chevrolet
29.	Jimmy Means	Pontiac
30.	Connie Saylor	Ford
31.	Jeff Swindell	Chevrolet
32.	Sterling Marlin	Chevrolet
33.	Dave Marcis	Chevrolet
34.	Cale Yarborough	Ford
35.	Bobby Gerhart	Chevrolet
36.	David Sosebee	Chevrolet
37.	Rodney Combs	Chevrolet
38.	Geoff Bodine	Chevrolet
39.	Darrell Waltrip	Chevrolet
40.	Tom Bigelow	Chevrolet
41.	H. B. Bailey	Chevrolet
42.	Ron Bouchard	Pontiac

WINSTON WESTERN 500

November 16
Riverside, California
Time of Race: 3 hours, 4 minutes, 46 seconds
Average Speed: 101.246 mph
Margin of Victory: 1 second

FINISH	DRIVER	CAR
1.	Tim Richmond	Chevrolet
2.	Dale Earnhardt	Chevrolet
3.	Geoff Bodine	Chevrolet
4.	Darrell Waltrip	Chevrolet
5.	Joe Ruttman	Buick
6.	Bobby Hillin Jr.	Buick
7.	Bobby Allison	Buick
8.	Rusty Wallace	Pontiac
9.	Neil Bonnett	Chevrolet
10.	Terry Labonte	Oldsmobile
11.	Ken Schrader	Ford
12.	Dave Marcis	Chevrolet
13.	Mark Martin	Ford
14.	Bill Schmitt	Chevrolet
15.	Kyle Petty	Ford
16.	Glen Steurer	Chevrolet
17.	Jimmy Means	Pontiac
18.	Buddy Arrington	Ford
19.	Ricky Rudd	Ford
20.	Al Unser, Sr.	Pontiac
21.	Richard Petty	Pontiac
22.	Ruben Garcia	Chevrolet
23.	Bill Elliott	Ford
24.	Alan Kulwicki	Ford
25.	Jim Robinson	Oldsmobile
26.	Hershel McGriff	Pontiac
27.	Benny Parsons	Oldsmobile
28.	Rick McCray	Ford
29.	Buddy Baker	Oldsmobile
30.	Ted Kennedy	Chevrolet
31.	Michael Waltrip	Pontiac
32.	Jim Bown	Chevrolet
33.	Ron Esau	Oldsmobile
34.	Terry Petris	Chevrolet
35.	Chad Little	Ford
36.	George Follmer	Chevrolet
37.	Harry Gant	Chevrolet
38.	Morgan Shepherd	Pontiac
39.	Jim Fitzgerald	Chevrolet
40.	Rick Wilson	Oldsmobile
41.	Derrike Cope	Ford
42.	John Krebs	Oldsmobile

1987

DAYTONA 500

February 15
Daytona Beach, Florida

Time of Race: 2 hours, 50 minutes, 12 seconds
Average Speed: 176.263 mph
Margin of Victory: 3 car lengths

FINISH	DRIVER	CAR
1.	Bill Elliott	Ford
2.	Benny Parsons	Chevrolet
3.	Richard Petty	Pontiac
4.	Buddy Baker	Oldsmobile
5.	Dale Earnhardt	Chevrolet
6.	Bobby Allison	Buick
7.	Ken Schrader	Ford
8.	Darrell Waltrip	Chevrolet
9.	Ricky Rudd	Ford
10.	Cale Yarborough	Oldsmobile
11.	Phil Parsons	Oldsmobile
12.	Neil Bonnett	Pontiac
13.	Bobby Hillin Jr.	Buick
14.	Geoff Bodine	Chevrolet
15.	Alan Kulwicki	Ford
16.	Morgan Shepherd	Buick
17.	Ken Ragan	Ford
18.	Terry Labonte	Chevrolet
19.	Rodney Combs	Oldsmobile
20.	Greg Sacks	Pontiac
21.	Ronnie Sanders	Ford
22.	Michael Waltrip	Chevrolet
23.	Trevor Boys	Chevrolet
24.	Jimmy Means	Pontiac
25.	J. D. McDuffie	Pontiac
26.	Lake Speed	Oldsmobile
27.	Davey Allison	Ford
28.	David Sosebee	Chevrolet
29.	Tom Sneva	Oldsmobile
30.	Sterling Marlin	Oldsmobile
31.	Harry Gant	Chevrolet
32.	Ron Bouchard	Chevrolet
33.	Derrike Cope	Ford
34.	Dave Marcis	Chevrolet
35.	Kyle Petty	Ford
36.	Eddie Bierschwale	Ford
37.	Rick Wilson	Oldsmobile
38.	Mark Stahl	Ford
39.	Chet Fillip	Ford
40.	Connie Saylor	Ford
41.	Rusty Wallace	Pontiac
42.	A. J. Foyt	Oldsmobile

GOODWRENCH 500

March 1
Rockingham, North Carolina
Time of Race: 4 hours, 15 minutes, 23 seconds
Average Speed: 117.556 mph
Margin of Victory: 11 seconds

FINISH	DRIVER	CAR
1.	Dale Earnhardt	Chevrolet
2.	Ricky Rudd	Ford
3.	Neil Bonnett	Pontiac
4.	Bill Elliott	Ford
5.	Morgan Shepherd	Buick
6.	Rusty Wallace	Pontiac
7.	Darrell Waltrip	Chevrolet
8.	Terry Labonte	Chevrolet
9.	Davey Allison	Ford
10.	Ken Schrader	Ford
11.	Phil Parsons	Oldsmobile
12.	Lake Speed	Oldsmobile
13.	Bobby Allison	Buick
14.	Bobby Hillin Jr.	Buick
15.	Richard Petty	Pontiac
16.	Kyle Petty	Ford
17.	Michael Waltrip	Chevrolet
18.	Eddie Bierschwale	Ford
19.	Sterling Marlin	Oldsmobile
20.	J. D. McDuffie	Pontiac

21.	Charlie Baker	Chevrolet
22.	Jimmy Means	Pontiac
23.	Jerry Cranmer	Ford
24.	Chet Fillip	Ford
25.	Alan Kulwicki	Ford
26.	D. K. Ulrich	Chevrolet
27.	Bobby Wawak	Chevrolet
28.	Cale Yarborough	Oldsmobile
29.	Harry Gant	Chevrolet
30.	Greg Sacks	Pontiac
31.	Buddy Baker	Oldsmobile
32.	Geoff Bodine	Chevrolet
33.	Mark Stahl	Ford
34.	Benny Parsons	Chevrolet
35.	Dave Marcis	Chevrolet
36.	Ron Bouchard	Chevrolet
37.	James Hylton	Chevrolet
38.	Tommy Ellis	Chevrolet
39.	David Sosebee	Chevrolet
40.	Patrick Latimer	Chevrolet
41.	Jesse Samples Jr.	Chevrolet
42.	Jerry Holden	Chevrolet

MILLER HIGH LIFE 400

March 8
Richmond, Virginia
Time of Race: 2 hours, 39 minutes, 34 seconds
Average Speed: 81.520 mph
Margin of Victory: 46 seconds

FINISH	DRIVER	CAR
1.	Dale Earnhardt	Chevrolet
2.	Geoff Bodine	Chevrolet
3.	Rusty Wallace	Pontiac
4.	Bill Elliott	Ford
5.	Terry Labonte	Chevrolet
6.	Alan Kulwicki	Ford
7.	Kyle Petty	Ford
8.	Dave Marcis	Chevrolet
9.	Bobby Allison	Buick
10.	Benny Parsons	Chevrolet
11.	Bobby Hillin Jr.	Buick
12.	Michael Waltrip	Chevrolet
13.	Ken Schrader	Ford
14.	Jimmy Means	Pontiac
15.	Phil Parsons	Oldsmobile
16.	J. D. McDuffie	Pontiac
17.	Buddy Arrington	Ford
18.	Eddie Bierschwale	Ford
19.	Slick Johnson	Oldsmobile
20.	Darrell Waltrip	Chevrolet
21.	Sterling Marlin	Oldsmobile
22.	Neil Bonnett	Pontiac
23.	Richard Petty	Pontiac
24.	Jerry Cranmer	Ford
25.	Harry Gant	Chevrolet
26.	Davey Allison	Ford
27.	Tommy Ellis	Chevrolet
28.	Ricky Rudd	Ford
29.	Steve Christman	Pontiac
30.	D. K. Ulrich	Chevrolet
31.	Morgan Shepherd	Buick
32.	Bobby Wawak	Chevrolet

MOTORCRAFT QUALITY PARTS 500

March 15
Atlanta, Georgia
Time of Race: 3 hours, 44 minutes, 2 seconds
Average Speed: 133.689 mph
Margin of Victory: 41 seconds

FINISH	DRIVER	CAR
1.	Ricky Rudd	Ford
2.	Benny Parsons	Chevrolet
3.	Rusty Wallace	Pontiac
4.	Terry Labonte	Chevrolet
5.	Davey Allison	Ford
6.	Darrell Waltrip	Chevrolet
7.	Neil Bonnett	Pontiac
8.	Cale Yarborough	Oldsmobile
9.	Kyle Petty	Ford
10.	Morgan Shepherd	Buick
11.	Rick Wilson	Oldsmobile
12.	Ron Bouchard	Chevrolet
13.	Sterling Marlin	Oldsmobile
14.	Richard Petty	Pontiac
15.	Geoff Bodine	Chevrolet
16.	Dale Earnhardt	Chevrolet
17.	Tommy Ellis	Chevrolet
18.	H. B. Bailey	Pontiac
19.	Bobby Allison	Buick
20.	A. J. Foyt	Oldsmobile
21.	David Sosebee	Oldsmobile
22.	Steve Christman	Pontiac
23.	D. K. Ulrich	Chevrolet
24.	Bobby Hillin Jr.	Buick
25.	Mike Potter	Chevrolet
26.	Ken Ragan	Ford
27.	Phil Parsons	Oldsmobile
28.	Bill Elliott	Ford
29.	Ken Schrader	Ford
30.	Mark Stahl	Ford
31.	Dave Marcis	Chevrolet
32.	Jimmy Means	Pontiac
33.	Alan Kulwicki	Ford
34.	Harry Gant	Chevrolet
35.	Lake Speed	Oldsmobile
36.	Derrike Cope	Ford
37.	Greg Sacks	Pontiac
38.	Buddy Baker	Oldsmobile
39.	Michael Waltrip	Chevrolet
40.	J. D. McDuffie	Pontiac
41.	Connie Saylor	Ford

VALLEYDALE MEATS 500

March 29
Darlington, South Carolina
Time of Race: 3 hours, 31 minutes, 27 seconds
Average Speed: 75.621 mph
Margin of Victory: .78 seconds

FINISH	DRIVER	CAR
1.	Dale Earnhardt	Chevrolet
2.	Richard Petty	Pontiac
3.	Ricky Rudd	Ford
4.	Bill Elliott	Ford
5.	Alan Kulwicki	Ford
6.	Harry Gant	Chevrolet
7.	Kyle Petty	Ford
8.	Morgan Shepherd	Buick
9.	Terry Labonte	Chevrolet
10.	Dale Jarrett	Chevrolet
11.	Neil Bonnett	Pontiac
12.	Darrell Waltrip	Chevrolet
13.	Michael Waltrip	Pontiac
14.	Slick Johnson	Chevrolet
15.	D. K. Ulrich	Chevrolet
16.	Rusty Wallace	Pontiac
17.	Ken Schrader	Ford
18.	Mike Potter	Ford
19.	Geoff Bodine	Chevrolet
20.	Phil Parsons	Oldsmobile
21.	J. D. McDuffie	Pontiac
22.	Jerry Cranmer	Ford
23.	Bobby Allison	Buick
24.	Sterling Marlin	Oldsmobile
25.	Eddie Bierschwale	Ford
26.	Bobby Hillin Jr.	Buick
27.	Dave Marcis	Chevrolet

28.	Benny Parsons	Chevrolet
29.	Jimmy Means	Pontiac
30.	Ronnie Thomas	Chevrolet

SOVRAN BANK 500

April 5
North Wilkesboro, North Carolina
Time of Race: 3 hours, 36 minutes, 44 seconds
Average Speed: 72.808 mph
Margin of Victory: 2.73 seconds

FINISH	DRIVER	CAR
1.	Dale Earnhardt	Chevrolet
2.	Rusty Wallace	Pontiac
3.	Geoff Bodine	Chevrolet
4.	Phil Parsons	Oldsmobile
5.	Terry Labonte	Chevrolet
6.	Bill Elliott	Ford
7.	Ken Schrader	Ford
8.	Bobby Allison	Buick
9.	Neil Bonnett	Pontiac
10.	Michael Waltrip	Chevrolet
11.	Buddy Arrington	Ford
12.	Kyle Petty	Ford
13.	Derrike Cope	Chevrolet
14.	Jimmy Means	Pontiac
15.	Bobby Hillin Jr.	Buick
16.	Ricky Rudd	Ford
17.	Morgan Shepherd	Buick
18.	Tony Spanos	Chevrolet
19.	Sterling Marlin	Oldsmobile
20.	Jerry Cranmer	Ford
21.	Darrell Waltrip	Chevrolet
22.	Richard Petty	Pontiac
23.	Dave Marcis	Chevrolet
24.	Eddie Bierschwale	Ford
25.	Steve Christman	Pontiac
26.	Benny Parsons	Chevrolet
27.	Harry Gant	Chevrolet
28.	Alan Kulwicki	Ford
29.	Dale Jarrett	Chevrolet
30.	Slick Johnson	Oldsmobile
31.	J. D. McDuffie	Pontiac

TRANSOUTH 500

April 12
Bristol, Tennessee
Time of Race: 4 hours, 5 minutes, 28 seconds
Average Speed: 122.540 mph
Margin of Victory: 3 seconds

FINISH	DRIVER	CAR
1.	Dale Earnhardt	Chevrolet
2.	Bill Elliott	Ford
3.	Richard Petty	Pontiac
4.	Sterling Marlin	Oldsmobile
5.	Ken Schrader	Ford
6.	Neil Bonnett	Pontiac
7.	Harry Gant	Chevrolet
8.	Ron Bouchard	Chevrolet
9.	Phil Parsons	Oldsmobile
10.	Darrell Waltrip	Chevrolet
11.	Geoff Bodine	Chevrolet
12.	Slick Johnson	Chevrolet
13.	Kyle Petty	Ford
14.	Alan Kulwicki	Ford
15.	Cale Yarborough	Oldsmobile
16.	Eddie Bierschwale	Ford
17.	H. B. Bailey	Pontiac
18.	D. K. Ulrich	Chevrolet
19.	Michael Waltrip	Chevrolet
20.	Rusty Wallace	Pontiac

21.	Benny Parsons	Chevrolet
22.	Morgan Shepherd	Buick
23.	Bobby Hillin Jr.	Buick
24.	Connie Saylor	Ford
25.	Buddy Baker	Oldsmobile
26.	Greg Sacks	Pontiac
27.	Davey Allison	Ford
28.	Bobby Allison	Buick
29.	Bobby Wawak	Chevrolet
30.	Ricky Rudd	Ford
31.	Lake Speed	Oldsmobile
32.	Terry Labonte	Chevrolet
33.	Dave Marcis	Chevrolet
34.	Rick Wilson	Oldsmobile
35.	Jonathan Edwards	Chevrolet
36.	Jimmy Means	Pontiac
37.	Rodney Combs	Chevrolet
38.	James Hylton	Chevrolet
39.	Steve Christman	Pontiac
40.	Tommy Ellis	Chevrolet
41.	J. D. McDuffie	Pontiac

FIRST UNION 400

April 26
Martinsville, Virginia
Time of Race: 2 hours, 39 minutes, 24 seconds
Average Speed: 94.103 mph
Margin of Victory: 1.2 seconds

FINISH	DRIVER	CAR
1.	Dale Earnhardt	Chevrolet
2.	Kyle Petty	Ford
3.	Neil Bonnett	Pontiac
4.	Alan Kulwicki	Ford
5.	Ricky Rudd	Ford
6.	Richard Petty	Pontiac
7.	Phil Parsons	Oldsmobile
8.	Terry Labonte	Chevrolet
9.	Rusty Wallace	Pontiac
10.	Bill Elliott	Ford
11.	Harry Gant	Chevrolet
12.	Dale Jarrett	Chevrolet
13.	Bobby Hillin Jr.	Buick
14.	Bobby Allison	Buick
15.	Benny Parsons	Chevrolet
16.	Ken Schrader	Ford
17.	Sterling Marlin	Oldsmobile
18.	Eddie Bierschwale	Ford
19.	Slick Johnson	Oldsmobile
20.	Rodney Combs	Chevrolet
21.	Darrell Waltrip	Chevrolet
22.	Jerry Cranmer	Ford
23.	Bobby Baker	Chevrolet
24.	Michael Waltrip	Chevrolet
25.	Larry Pearson	Chevrolet
26.	Dave Marcis	Chevrolet
27.	Morgan Shepherd	Buick
28.	Geoff Bodine	Chevrolet
29.	Jesse Samples Jr.	Chevrolet
30.	Jimmy Means	Pontiac
31.	Steve Christman	Pontiac
32.	J. D. McDuffie	Pontiac

WINSTON 500

May 3
Talladega, Alabama
Time of Race: 3 hours, 4 minutes, 12 seconds
Average Speed: 154.228 mph
Margin of Victory: .78 seconds

FINISH	DRIVER	CAR
1.	Davey Allison	Ford
2.	Terry Labonte	Chevrolet

3.	Kyle Petty	Ford
4.	Dale Earnhardt	Chevrolet
5.	Bobby Hillin Jr.	Buick
6.	Rusty Wallace	Pontiac
7.	Neil Bonnett	Pontiac
8.	Ken Schrader	Ford
9.	Lake Speed	Oldsmobile
10.	Morgan Shepherd	Buick
11.	Darrell Waltrip	Chevrolet
12.	Benny Parsons	Chevrolet
13.	Dave Marcis	Chevrolet
14.	Sterling Marlin	Oldsmobile
15.	Slick Johnson	Chevrolet
16.	Richard Petty	Pontiac
17.	Mark Stahl	Ford
18.	Eddie Bierschwale	Ford
19.	Steve Christman	Pontiac
20.	Rick Wilson	Oldsmobile
21.	Ken Ragan	Ford
22.	Bill Elliott	Ford
23.	Connie Saylor	Ford
24.	Rick Knoop	Chevrolet
25.	Michael Waltrip	Chevrolet
26.	Greg Sacks	Pontiac
27.	Ed Pimm	Buick
28.	Dale Jarrett	Chevrolet
29.	Harry Gant	Chevrolet
30.	Ricky Rudd	Ford
31.	Phil Parsons	Oldsmobile
32.	Buddy Baker	Oldsmobile
33.	Jimmy Means	Pontiac
34.	Alan Kulwicki	Ford
35.	Phil Barkdoll	Chevrolet
36.	Joe Ruttman	Chevrolet
37.	Cale Yarborough	Oldsmobile
38.	Ron Bouchard	Buick
39.	Bobby Allison	Buick
40.	Geoff Bodine	Chevrolet
41.	Chet Fillip	Ford

32.	Sterling Marlin	Oldsmobile
33.	Connie Saylor	Chevrolet
34.	Bobby Hillin Jr.	Buick
35.	Allan Grice	Oldsmobile
36.	Greg Sacks	Pontiac
37.	Derrike Cope	Ford
38.	Dale Jarrett	Chevrolet
39.	Mark Martin	Oldsmobile
40.	Brad Teague	Chevrolet
41.	Steve Christman	Pontiac
42.	Cale Yarborough	Oldsmobile

BUDWEISER 500

May 31
Dover, Delaware
Time of Race: 4 hours, 25 minutes, 35 seconds
Average Speed: 112.958 mph
Margin of Victory: 7 seconds

FINISH	DRIVER	CAR
1.	Davey Allison	Ford
2.	Bill Elliott	Ford
3.	Terry Labonte	Chevrolet
4.	Dale Earnhardt	Chevrolet
5.	Benny Parsons	Chevrolet
6.	Ken Schrader	Ford
7.	Darrell Waltrip	Chevrolet
8.	Dave Marcis	Chevrolet
9.	Neil Bonnett	Pontiac
10.	Sterling Marlin	Oldsmobile
11.	Buddy Baker	Oldsmobile
12.	Ricky Rudd	Ford
13.	Jimmy Means	Pontiac
14.	Brett Bodine	Chevrolet
15.	Alan Kulwicki	Ford
16.	Larry Pollard	Chevrolet
17.	Rusty Wallace	Pontiac
18.	Buddy Arrington	Ford
19.	Charles Rudolph	Chevrolet
20.	Rodney Combs	Ford
21.	Michael Waltrip	Chevrolet
22.	Phil Parsons	Oldsmobile
23.	J. D. McDuffie	Pontiac
24.	Kyle Petty	Ford
25.	Bobby Allison	Buick
26.	Bobby Hillin Jr.	Buick
27.	Gary Fedewa	Chevrolet
28.	Geoff Bodine	Chevrolet
29.	Rick Wilson	Oldsmobile
30.	Harry Gant	Chevrolet
31.	Jerry Bowman	Ford
32.	Morgan Shepherd	Buick
33.	Mike Potter	Ford
34.	D. K. Ulrich	Chevrolet
35.	Dale Jarrett	Chevrolet
36.	Richard Petty	Pontiac
37.	Steve Christman	Pontiac
38.	Curtis Markham	Ford
39.	Ron Shepard	Chevrolet

COCA-COLA 600

May 24
Charlotte, North Carolina
Time of Race: 4 hours, 33 minutes, 48 seconds
Average Speed: 131.483 mph
Margin of Victory: 33.53 seconds

FINISH	DRIVER	CAR
1.	Kyle Petty	Ford
2.	Morgan Shepherd	Buick
3.	Lake Speed	Oldsmobile
4.	Richard Petty	Pontiac
5.	Darrell Waltrip	Chevrolet
6.	Terry Labonte	Chevrolet
7.	Buddy Baker	Oldsmobile
8.	Phil Parsons	Oldsmobile
9.	Jim Sauter	Pontiac
10.	Rusty Wallace	Pontiac
11.	Michael Waltrip	Chevrolet
12.	Buddy Arrington	Ford
13.	Neil Bonnett	Pontiac
14.	Dave Marcis	Chevrolet
15.	Jimmy Means	Pontiac
16.	Davey Allison	Ford
17.	Randy Baker	Chevrolet
18.	Geoff Bodine	Chevrolet
19.	Bobby Wawak	Chevrolet
20.	Dale Earnhardt	Chevrolet
21.	Brett Bodine	Chevrolet
22.	Bobby Allison	Buick
23.	Bill Elliott	Ford
24.	Harry Gant	Chevrolet
25.	Ricky Rudd	Ford
26.	Benny Parsons	Chevrolet
27.	Alan Kulwicki	Ford
28.	Eddie Bierschwale	Ford
29.	Ken Schrader	Ford
30.	Rick Wilson	Oldsmobile
31.	Larry Pearson	Chevrolet

MILLER HIGH LIFE 500

June 14
Pocono, Pennsylvania
Time of Race: 4 hours, 5 minutes, 57 seconds
Average Speed: 122.166 mph
Margin of Victory: 1 second

FINISH	DRIVER	CAR
1.	Tim Richmond	Chevrolet
2.	Bill Elliott	Ford
3.	Kyle Petty	Ford
4.	Cale Yarborough	Oldsmobile

5.	Dale Earnhardt	Chevrolet
6.	Bobby Allison	Buick
7.	Ricky Rudd	Ford
8.	Neil Bonnett	Pontiac
9.	Geoff Bodine	Chevrolet
10.	Buddy Baker	Oldsmobile
11.	Phil Parsons	Oldsmobile
12.	Davey Allison	Ford
13.	Darrell Waltrip	Chevrolet
14.	Bobby Hillin Jr.	Buick
15.	Sterling Marlin	Oldsmobile
16.	Michael Waltrip	Chevrolet
17.	Ken Schrader	Ford
18.	Trevor Boys	Chevrolet
19.	Jimmy Means	Pontiac
20.	Rodney Combs	Ford
21.	Jimmy Horton	Ford
22.	Charles Rudolph	Chevrolet
23.	Jim Bown	Chevrolet
24.	Bobby Wawak	Chevrolet
25.	Buddy Arrington	Ford
26.	Steve Christman	Pontiac
27.	Dave Marcis	Chevrolet
28.	J. D. McDuffie	Pontiac
29.	Richard Petty	Pontiac
30.	Alan Kulwicki	Ford
31.	Morgan Shepherd	Buick
32.	Harry Gant	Chevrolet
33.	Benny Parsons	Chevrolet
34.	Brett Bodine	Chevrolet
35.	Dale Jarrett	Chevrolet
36.	Greg Sacks	Pontiac
37.	Terry Labonte	Chevrolet
38.	Derrike Cope	Chevrolet
39.	Bobby Gerhart	Chevrolet
40.	Rusty Wallace	Pontiac

BUDWEISER 400

June 21
Riverside, California
Time of Race: 2 hours, 26 minutes, 9 seconds
Average Speed: 102.183 mph
Margin of Victory: 1.5 seconds

FINISH	DRIVER	CAR
1.	Tim Richmond	Chevrolet
2.	Ricky Rudd	Ford
3.	Neil Bonnett	Pontiac
4.	Terry Labonte	Chevrolet
5.	Bill Elliott	Ford
6.	Richard Petty	Pontiac
7.	Dale Earnhardt	Chevrolet
8.	Bobby Allison	Buick
9.	Sterling Marlin	Oldsmobile
10.	Ken Schrader	Ford
11.	Phil Parsons	Oldsmobile
12.	Hershel McGriff	Pontiac
13.	Bobby Hillin Jr.	Buick
14.	Rick Wilson	Oldsmobile
15.	Chad Little	Ford
16.	Dave Marcis	Chevrolet
17.	Jim Fitzgerald	Chevrolet
18.	Dale Jarrett	Chevrolet
19.	Ruben Garcia	Chevrolet
20.	Harry Goularte	Chevrolet
21.	Chet Fillip	Ford
22.	Ron Esau	Chevrolet
23.	Jimmy Means	Pontiac
24.	Kyle Petty	Ford
25.	Harry Gant	Chevrolet
26.	Rick McCray	Ford
27.	Geoff Bodine	Chevrolet
28.	Alan Kulwicki	Ford
29.	John Krebs	Oldsmobile
30.	Darrell Waltrip	Chevrolet
31.	Jim Bown	Oldsmobile
32.	Michael Waltrip	Chevrolet
33.	Bill Schmitt	Chevrolet
34.	Benny Parsons	Chevrolet

35.	Morgan Shepherd	Buick
36.	Jim Robinson	Oldsmobile
37.	J. D. McDuffie	Pontiac
38.	Brett Bodine	Chevrolet
39.	Roy Smith	Ford
40.	George Follmer	Chevrolet
41.	Rusty Wallace	Pontiac

MILLER AMERICAN 400

June 28
Brooklyn, Michigan
Time of Race: 2 hours, 41 minutes, 40 seconds
Average Speed: 148.454 mph
Margin of Victory: 1 second

FINISH	DRIVER	CAR
1.	Dale Earnhardt	Chevrolet
2.	Davey Allison	Ford
3.	Kyle Petty	Ford
4.	Tim Richmond	Chevrolet
5.	Rusty Wallace	Pontiac
6.	Bobby Hillin Jr.	Buick
7.	Darrell Waltrip	Chevrolet
8.	Ken Schrader	Ford
9.	Benny Parsons	Chevrolet
10.	Lake Speed	Oldsmobile
11.	Geoff Bodine	Chevrolet
12.	Richard Petty	Pontiac
13.	Harry Gant	Chevrolet
14.	Ricky Rudd	Ford
15.	Dave Marcis	Chevrolet
16.	Buddy Baker	Oldsmobile
17.	Neil Bonnett	Chevrolet
18.	Sterling Marlin	Chevrolet
19.	Eddie Bierschwale	Ford
20.	Dale Jarrett	Chevrolet
21.	Phil Parsons	Oldsmobile
22.	Brett Bodine	Chevrolet
23.	Rodney Combs	Ford
24.	Jim Sauter	Pontiac
25.	Morgan Shepherd	Buick
26.	Dave Simko	Chevrolet
27.	Bobby Allison	Buick
28.	Terry Labonte	Chevrolet
29.	Greg Sacks	Pontiac
30.	Rick Wilson	Oldsmobile
31.	Alan Kulwicki	Ford
32.	Ken Bouchard	Chevrolet
33.	Cale Yarborough	Oldsmobile
34.	Bill Elliott	Ford
35.	Don Paul	Chevrolet
36.	Butch Miller	Chevrolet
37.	Buddy Arrington	Ford
38.	Connie Saylor	Chevrolet
39.	Michael Waltrip	Chevrolet
40.	H. B. Bailey	Pontiac

PEPSI FIRECRACKER 400

July 4
Daytona Beach, Florida
Time of Race: 2 hours, 29 minutes, 0 seconds
Average Speed: 161.074 mph
Margin of Victory: 4 seconds

FINISH	DRIVER	CAR
1.	Bobby Allison	Buick
2.	Buddy Baker	Oldsmobile
3.	Dave Marcis	Chevrolet
4.	Darrell Waltrip	Chevrolet
5.	Morgan Shepherd	Buick
6.	Dale Earnhardt	Chevrolet
7.	Ken Schrader	Ford

8.	Rusty Wallace	Pontiac
9.	Harry Gant	Chevrolet
10.	Terry Labonte	Chevrolet
11.	Brett Bodine	Buick
12.	Bill Elliott	Ford
13.	Bobby Hillin Jr.	Buick
14.	Ricky Rudd	Ford
15.	Phil Parsons	Oldsmobile
16.	Sterling Marlin	Oldsmobile
17.	Kyle Petty	Ford
18.	Neil Bonnett	Pontiac
19.	Michael Waltrip	Chevrolet
20.	Davey Allison	Ford
21.	Chet Fillip	Ford
22.	Tim Richmond	Chevrolet
23.	Dale Jarrett	Chevrolet
24.	Cale Yarborough	Oldsmobile
25.	Greg Sacks	Pontiac
26.	Richard Petty	Pontiac
27.	Larry Pollard	Chevrolet
28.	Buddy Arrington	Ford
29.	Jimmy Means	Chevrolet
30.	Rick Wilson	Oldsmobile
31.	Rodney Combs	Ford
32.	Alan Kulwicki	Ford
33.	Eddie Bierschwale	Ford
34.	Ed Pimm	Buick
35.	Benny Parsons	Chevrolet
36.	Dave Pletcher	Ford
37.	Mark Stahl	Ford
38.	A. J. Foyt	Oldsmobile
39.	Geoff Bodine	Chevrolet
40.	Lake Speed	Oldsmobile
41.	Brad Teague	Chevrolet

SUMMER 500

July 19
Pocono, Pennsylvania
Time of Race: 4 hours, 6 minutes, 25 seconds
Average Speed: 121.745 mph
Margin of Victory: 1 second

FINISH	DRIVER	CAR
1.	Dale Earnhardt	Chevrolet
2.	Alan Kulwicki	Ford
3.	Buddy Baker	Oldsmobile
4.	Benny Parsons	Chevrolet
5.	Davey Allison	Ford
6.	Terry Labonte	Chevrolet
7.	Neil Bonnett	Pontiac
8.	Richard Petty	Pontiac
9.	Dave Marcis	Chevrolet
10.	Ken Schrader	Ford
11.	Trevor Boys	Chevrolet
12.	Dale Jarrett	Chevrolet
13.	Charles Rudolph	Chevrolet
14.	Rusty Wallace	Pontiac
15.	Bobby Hillin Jr.	Buick
16.	Rodney Combs	Ford
17.	Buddy Arrington	Ford
18.	Connie Saylor	Chevrolet
19.	Darrell Waltrip	Chevrolet
20.	Kyle Petty	Ford
21.	Ronnie Shephard	Chevrolet
22.	Brett Bodine	Chevrolet
23.	Steve Christman	Pontiac
24.	Jocko Maggiacomo	Chevrolet
25.	Sterling Marlin	Oldsmobile
26.	Ricky Rudd	Ford
27.	Bobby Allison	Buick
28.	Bobby Gerhart	Chevrolet
29.	Tim Richmond	Chevrolet
30.	Harry Gant	Chevrolet
31.	Derrike Cope	Chevrolet
32.	Bill Elliott	Ford
33.	Jimmy Horton	Ford
34.	Geoff Bodine	Chevrolet
35.	Greg Sacks	Pontiac
36.	Morgan Shepherd	Buick

37.	Michael Waltrip	Chevrolet
38.	Jimmy Means	Chevrolet
39.	Phil Parsons	Oldsmobile
40.	Rick Wilson	Oldsmobile

TALLADEGA 500

July 26
Talladega, Alabama
Time of Race: 2 hours, 55 minutes, 10 seconds
Average Speed: 171.293 mph
Margin of Victory: 15 seconds

FINISH	DRIVER	CAR
1.	Bill Elliott	Ford
2.	Davey Allison	Ford
3.	Dale Earnhardt	Chevrolet
4.	Darrell Waltrip	Chevrolet
5.	Cale Yarborough	Oldsmobile
6.	Terry Labonte	Chevrolet
7.	Lake Speed	Oldsmobile
8.	Rusty Wallace	Pontiac
9.	Kyle Petty	Ford
10.	Buddy Baker	Oldsmobile
11.	Tim Richmond	Chevrolet
12.	Bobby Allison	Buick
13.	Geoff Bodine	Chevrolet
14.	Sterling Marlin	Oldsmobile
15.	Ricky Rudd	Ford
16.	Rick Wilson	Oldsmobile
17.	Michael Waltrip	Chevrolet
18.	Ken Schrader	Ford
19.	Rodney Combs	Ford
20.	Chet Fillip	Ford
21.	Dale Jarrett	Chevrolet
22.	Dave Marcis	Chevrolet
23.	Alan Kulwicki	Ford
24.	Delma Cowart	Chevrolet
25.	J. D. McDuffie	Pontiac
26.	Steve Christman	Pontiac
27.	Dave Pletcher	Ford
28.	Jerry Holden	Chevrolet
29.	Phil Parsons	Oldsmobile
30.	Benny Parsons	Oldsmobile
31.	Harry Gant	Chevrolet
32.	Neil Bonnett	Pontiac
33.	Mark Stahl	Ford
34.	Jeff Swindell	Chevrolet
35.	A. J. Foyt	Oldsmobile
36.	Jimmy Means	Chevrolet
37.	Richard Petty	Pontiac
38.	Brett Bodine	Chevrolet
39.	Morgan Shepherd	Buick
40.	Bobby Hillin Jr.	Buick

THE BUDWEISER AT THE GLEN

August 10
Watkins Glen, New York
Time of Race: 2 hours, 24 minutes, 36 seconds
Average Speed: 90.682 mph
Margin of Victory: 12 seconds

FINISH	DRIVER	CAR
1.	Rusty Wallace	Pontiac
2.	Terry Labonte	Chevrolet
3.	Dave Marcis	Chevrolet
4.	Ricky Rudd	Ford
5.	Benny Parsons	Chevrolet
6.	Alan Kulwicki	Ford
7.	Phil Parsons	Oldsmobile
8.	Dale Earnhardt	Chevrolet
9.	Bobby Allison	Buick
10.	Tim Richmond	Chevrolet

11.	Darrell Waltrip	Chevrolet
12.	Kyle Petty	Ford
13.	Buddy Baker	Oldsmobile
14.	Richard Petty	Pontiac
15.	Geoff Bodine	Chevrolet
16.	Michael Waltrip	Chevrolet
17.	Davey Allison	Ford
18.	Harry Gant	Chevrolet
19.	Jimmy Means	Pontiac
20.	Buddy Arrington	Ford
21.	Rick Wilson	Oldsmobile
22.	Morgan Shepherd	Buick
23.	Rodney Combs	Ford
24.	J. D. McDuffie	Pontiac
25.	Rick Knoop	Chevrolet
26.	Tom Rotsell	Ford
27.	Ken Schrader	Ford
28.	Bill Elliott	Ford
29.	Bobby Hillin Jr.	Buick
30.	Mike Potter	Ford
31.	Derrike Cope	Chevrolet
32.	Sterling Marlin	Oldsmobile
33.	Patty Moise	Chevrolet
34.	Steve Christman	Pontiac
35.	Jocko Maggiacomo	Chevrolet
36.	Dale Jarrett	Chevrolet
37.	Neil Bonnett	Pontiac
38.	Trevor Boys	Chevrolet
39.	Phil Good	Ford
40.	Chuck Schroedel	Pontiac

CHAMPION SPARK PLUG 400

August 16
Brooklyn, Michigan
Time of Race: 2 hours, 53 minutes, 6 seconds
Average Speed: 138.648 mph
Margin of Victory: 76 seconds

FINISH	DRIVER	CAR
1.	Bill Elliott	Ford
2.	Dale Earnhardt	Chevrolet
3.	Morgan Shepherd	Buick
4.	Rusty Wallace	Pontiac
5.	Davey Allison	Ford
6.	Alan Kulwicki	Ford
7.	Bobby Allison	Buick
8.	Buddy Baker	Oldsmobile
9.	Neil Bonnett	Pontiac
10.	Geoff Bodine	Chevrolet
11.	Richard Petty	Pontiac
12.	Rick Wilson	Oldsmobile
13.	Bobby Hillin Jr.	Buick
14.	Phil Parsons	Oldsmobile
15.	Sterling Marlin	Oldsmobile
16.	Lake Speed	Oldsmobile
17.	Darrell Waltrip	Chevrolet
18.	Benny Parsons	Chevrolet
19.	Greg Sacks	Pontiac
20.	Michael Waltrip	Chevrolet
21.	Brett Bodine	Chevrolet
22.	J. D. McDuffie	Pontiac
23.	Buddy Arrington	Ford
24.	Jim Sauter	Pontiac
25.	Ricky Rudd	Ford
26.	Harry Gant	Chevrolet
27.	Kyle Petty	Ford
28.	Dave Simko	Chevrolet
29.	Tim Richmond	Chevrolet
30.	Ken Ragan	Ford
31.	Rodney Combs	Ford
32.	Bobby Wawak	Chevrolet
33.	Terry Labonte	Chevrolet
34.	Ken Schrader	Ford
35.	Dave Marcis	Chevrolet
36.	Charlie Rudolph	Chevrolet
37.	Jimmy Means	Chevrolet
38.	Derrike Cope	Ford
39.	Dale Jarrett	Chevrolet
40.	Cale Yarborough	Oldsmobile

BUSCH 500

August 22
Bristol, Tennessee
Time of Race: 2 hours, 56 minutes, 56 seconds
Average Speed: 90.373 mph
Margin of Victory: 5.50 seconds

FINISH	DRIVER	CAR
1.	Dale Earnhardt	Chevrolet
2.	Rusty Wallace	Pontiac
3.	Ricky Rudd	Ford
4.	Terry Labonte	Chevrolet
5.	Richard Petty	Pontiac
6.	Geoff Bodine	Chevrolet
7.	Rick Wilson	Oldsmobile
8.	Harry Gant	Chevrolet
9.	Bill Elliott	Ford
10.	Neil Bonnett	Pontiac
11.	Alan Kulwicki	Ford
12.	Dale Jarrett	Chevrolet
13.	Jimmy Means	Pontiac
14.	Michael Waltrip	Chevrolet
15.	Steve Christman	Pontiac
16.	Derrike Cope	Ford
17.	Buddy Arrington	Ford
18.	Dave Marcis	Chevrolet
19.	Phil Parsons	Oldsmobile
20.	Sterling Marlin	Oldsmobile
21.	Darrell Waltrip	Chevrolet
22.	Bobby Allison	Buick
23.	Rodney Combs	Ford
24.	Morgan Shepherd	Buick
25.	Brad Teague	Oldsmobile
26.	Benny Parsons	Chevrolet
27.	Ken Schrader	Ford
28.	Kyle Petty	Ford
29.	Bobby Hillin Jr.	Buick
30.	Ronnie Thomas	Chevrolet

SOUTHERN 500

September 6
Darlington, South Carolina
Time of Race: 2 hours, 23 minutes, 19 seconds
Average Speed: 115.520 mph
Margin of Victory: 5 seconds

FINISH	DRIVER	CAR
1.	Dale Earnhardt	Chevrolet
2.	Rusty Wallace	Pontiac
3.	Richard Petty	Pontiac
4.	Sterling Marlin	Oldsmobile
5.	Terry Labonte	Chevrolet
6.	Bobby Hillin Jr.	Buick
7.	Ricky Rudd	Ford
8.	Bill Elliott	Ford
9.	Morgan Shepherd	Buick
10.	Darrell Waltrip	Chevrolet
11.	Ken Schrader	Ford
12.	Phil Parsons	Oldsmobile
13.	Cale Yarborough	Oldsmobile
14.	Kyle Petty	Ford
15.	Dale Jarrett	Chevrolet
16.	Dave Marcis	Chevrolet
17.	Buddy Baker	Oldsmobile
18.	Geoff Bodine	Chevrolet
19.	Michael Waltrip	Chevrolet
20.	Brett Bodine	Chevrolet
21.	Steve Christman	Pontiac
22.	Jimmy Means	Chevrolet
23.	Bobby Wawak	Chevrolet
24.	Buddy Arrington	Ford
25.	Eddie Bierschwale	Chevrolet
26.	Bobby Allison	Buick
27.	Rodney Combs	Ford
28.	Rick Wilson	Oldsmobile

29.	Davey Allison	Ford
30.	Lake Speed	Oldsmobile
31.	Denny Parsons	Chevrolet
32.	Neil Bonnett	Pontiac
33.	Mike Potter	Ford
34.	Connie Saylor	Oldsmobile
35.	H. B. Bailey	Pontiac
36.	Trevor Boys	Oldsmobile
37.	Jonathan Edwards	Chevrolet
38.	Greg Sacks	Pontiac
39.	Harry Gant	Chevrolet
40.	Alan Kulwicki	Ford

WRANGLER JEANS INDIGO 400

September 13
Richmond, Virginia
Time of Race: 3 hours, 3 minutes, 56 seconds
Average Speed: 67.074 mph
Margin of Victory: 2.5 seconds

FINISH	DRIVER	CAR
1.	Dale Earnhardt	Chevrolet
2.	Darrell Waltrip	Chevrolet
3.	Ricky Rudd	Ford
4.	Bill Elliott	Ford
5.	Richard Petty	Pontiac
6.	Geoff Bodine	Chevrolet
7.	Dave Marcis	Chevrolet
8.	Terry Labonte	Chevrolet
9.	Jimmy Means	Pontiac
10.	Neil Bonnett	Pontiac
11.	Steve Christman	Pontiac
12.	Bobby Allison	Buick
13.	Larry Pollard	Oldsmobile
14.	Buddy Arrington	Ford
15.	Bobby Hillin	Buick
16.	Benny Parsons	Chevrolet
17.	Rusty Wallace	Pontiac
18.	Kyle Petty	Ford
19.	Michael Waltrip	Chevrolet
20.	Phil Parsons	Oldsmobile
21.	Ken Schrader	Ford
22.	Sterling Marlin	Oldsmobile
23.	Alan Kulwicki	Ford
24.	Trevor Boys	Ford
25.	Harry Gant	Chevrolet
26.	D. K. Ulrich	Chevrolet
27.	Dale Jarrett	Chevrolet
28.	Doug French	Buick
29.	Ernie Irvan	Chevrolet
30.	Morgan Shepherd	Buick

DELAWARE 500

September 20
Dover, Delaware
Time of Race: 4 hours, 0 minutes, 34 seconds
Average Speed: 124.706 mph
Margin of Victory: 2 seconds

FINISH	DRIVER	CAR
1.	Ricky Rudd	Ford
2.	Davey Allison	Ford
3.	Neil Bonnett	Pontiac
4.	Bill Elliott	Ford
5.	Sterling Marlin	Oldsmobile
6.	Geoff Bodine	Chevrolet
7.	Bobby Allison	Buick
8.	Buddy Baker	Oldsmobile
9.	Richard Petty	Pontiac
10.	Darrell Waltrip	Chevrolet
11.	Ken Schrader	Ford
12.	Rusty Wallace	Pontiac

13.	Brett Bodine	Chevrolet
14.	Alan Kulwicki	Ford
15.	Dave Marcis	Chevrolet
16.	Benny Parsons	Chevrolet
17.	Steve Christman	Pontiac
18.	Michael Waltrip	Chevrolet
19.	Buddy Arrington	Ford
20.	Rick Knoop	Chevrolet
21.	Larry Caudill	Oldsmobile
22.	Jimmy Means	Pontiac
23.	Kyle Petty	Ford
24.	Rick Jeffrey	Chevrolet
25.	Harry Gant	Chevrolet
26.	Wayne Strout	Oldsmobile
27.	Rick Wilson	Oldsmobile
28.	J. D. McDuffie	Pontiac
29.	Phil Parsons	Oldsmobile
30.	David Simko	Chevrolet
31.	Dale Earnhardt	Chevrolet
32.	Terry Labonte	Chevrolet
33.	Trevor Boys	Ford
34.	Mark Gibson	Pontiac
35.	Mike Potter	Ford
36.	Cale Yarborough	Oldsmobile
37.	Eddie Bierschwale	Chevrolet
38.	Dale Jarrett	Chevrolet
39.	Bobby Hillin	Buick
40.	Morgan Shepherd	Buick

GOODY'S 500

September 27
Martinsville, Virginia
Time of Race: 3 hours, 26 minutes, 31 seconds
Average Speed: 76.410 mph
Margin of Victory: 1 second

FINISH	DRIVER	CAR
1.	Darrell Waltrip	Chevrolet
2.	Dale Earnhardt	Chevrolet
3.	Terry Labonte	Chevrolet
4.	Neil Bonnett	Pontiac
5.	Morgan Shepherd	Buick
6.	Alan Kulwicki	Ford
7.	Sterling Marlin	Oldsmobile
8.	Bobby Allison	Buick
9.	Kyle Petty	Ford
10.	Dale Jarrett	Chevrolet
11.	Bill Elliott	Ford
12.	Ken Schrader	Ford
13.	Richard Petty	Pontiac
14.	Harry Gant	Chevrolet
15.	Ernie Irvan	Chevrolet
16.	Phil Parsons	Oldsmobile
17.	J. D. McDuffie	Pontiac
18.	Michael Waltrip	Chevrolet
19.	Steve Christman	Pontiac
20.	Geoff Bodine	Chevrolet
21.	Ricky Rudd	Ford
22.	Bobby Hillin	Buick
23.	Benny Parsons	Chevrolet
24.	Greg Sacks	Pontiac
25.	Slick Johnson	Oldsmobile
26.	Curtis Markham	Ford
27.	Dave Marcis	Chevrolet
28.	Rusty Wallace	Pontiac
29.	Buddy Arrington	Ford
30.	Jimmy Means	Pontiac
31.	Buddy Baker	Oldsmobile

HOLLY FARMS 400

October 4
North Wilkesboro, North Carolina
Time of Race: 2 hours, 36 minutes, 9 seconds
Average Speed: 96.051 mph
Margin of Victory: 5.31 seconds

FINISH	DRIVER	CAR
1.	Terry Labonte	Chevrolet
2.	Dale Earnhardt	Chevrolet
3.	Bill Elliott	Ford
4.	Morgan Shepherd	Buick
5.	Geoff Bodine	Chevrolet
6.	Kyle Petty	Ford
7.	Alan Kulwicki	Ford
8.	Bobby Hillin	Buick
9.	Richard Petty	Pontiac
10.	Rusty Wallace	Pontiac
11.	Neil Bonnett	Pontiac
12.	Darrell Waltrip	Chevrolet
13.	Ricky Rudd	Ford
14.	Phil Parsons	Oldsmobile
15.	Ken Schrader	Ford
16.	Michael Waltrip	Chevrolet
17.	Bobby Allison	Buick
18.	Dale Jarrett	Chevrolet
19.	Benny Parsons	Chevrolet
20.	Sterling Marlin	Oldsmobile
21.	Jimmy Means	Pontiac
22.	Ernie Irvan	Chevrolet
23.	Larry Pollard	Chevrolet
24.	Trevor Boys	Ford
25.	Ronnie Thomas	Chevrolet
26.	Davey Allison	Ford
27.	Buddy Arrington	Ford
28.	Hut Stricklin	Oldsmobile
29.	Steve Christman	Pontiac
30.	Dave Marcis	Chevrolet
31.	Harry Gant	Chevrolet
32.	Slick Johnson	Ford

OAKWOOD HOMES 500

October 11
Charlotte, North Carolina
Time of Race: 3 hours, 54 minutes, 2 seconds
Average Speed: 128.443 mph
Margin of Victory: 1.5 seconds

FINISH	DRIVER	CAR
1.	Bill Elliott	Ford
2.	Bobby Allison	Buick
3.	Sterling Marlin	Oldsmobile
4.	Terry Labonte	Chevrolet
5.	Richard Petty	Pontiac
6.	Larry Pearson	Chevrolet
7.	Lake Speed	Oldsmobile
8.	Ernie Irvan	Chevrolet
9.	Darrell Waltrip	Chevrolet
10.	Kyle Petty	Ford
11.	Ricky Rudd	Ford
12.	Dale Earnhardt	Chevrolet
13.	Brad Teague	Oldsmobile
14.	Buddy Arrington	Ford
15.	Steve Christman	Pontiac
16.	Connie Saylor	Chevrolet
17.	Ken Schrader	Ford
18.	Dave Marcis	Chevrolet
19.	Davey Allison	Ford
20.	Morgan Shepherd	Buick
21.	A. J. Foyt	Oldsmobile
22.	Rusty Wallace	Pontiac
23.	Mark Stahl	Ford
24.	Cale Yarborough	Oldsmobile
25.	Trevor Boys	Ford
26.	Ken Ragan	Ford
27.	Phil Parsons	Oldsmobile
28.	Bobby Hillin	Buick
29.	Alan Kulwicki	Ford
30.	Rick Wilson	Oldsmobile
31.	Geoff Bodine	Chevrolet
32.	Brett Bodine	Chevrolet
33.	Harry Gant	Chevrolet
34.	Dale Jarrett	Chevrolet
35.	Michael Waltrip	Chevrolet
36.	Neil Bonnett	Pontiac

37.	Rodney Combs	Chevrolet
38.	Benny Parsons	Chevrolet
39.	Derrike Cope	Ford
40.	Jimmy Means	Chevrolet
41.	Buddy Baker	Oldsmobile
42.	Greg Sacks	Pontiac

AC DELCO 500

October 25
Rockingham, North Carolina
Time of Race: 4 hours, 13 minutes, 52 seconds
Average Speed: 118.258 mph
Margin of Victory: 2 seconds

FINISH	DRIVER	CAR
1.	Bill Elliott	Ford
2.	Dale Earnhardt	Chevrolet
3.	Darrell Waltrip	Chevrolet
4.	Terry Labonte	Chevrolet
5.	Morgan Shepherd	Buick
6.	Kyle Petty	Ford
7.	Buddy Baker	Oldsmobile
8.	Geoff Bodine	Chevrolet
9.	Phil Parsons	Oldsmobile
10.	Joe Ruttman	Pontiac
11.	Sterling Marlin	Oldsmobile
12.	Rusty Wallace	Pontiac
13.	Harry Gant	Chevrolet
14.	Ken Schrader	Ford
15.	Benny Parsons	Chevrolet
16.	Dale Jarrett	Chevrolet
17.	Richard Petty	Pontiac
18.	Alan Kulwicki	Ford
19.	Michael Waltrip	Chevrolet
20.	Jimmy Means	Pontiac
21.	Trevor Boys	Oldsmobile
22.	Dave Marcis	Chevrolet
23.	Eddie Bierschwale	Chevrolet
24.	Buddy Arrington	Ford
25.	Connie Saylor	Chevrolet
26.	Ronnie Thomas	Chevrolet
27.	Greg Sacks	Pontiac
28.	Mark Stahl	Ford
29.	Hut Stricklin	Oldsmobile
30.	Curtis Markham	Ford
31.	Ricky Rudd	Ford
32.	Steve Christman	Pontiac
33.	Bobby Hillin	Buick
34.	Kirk Bryant	Pontiac
35.	Dave Simko	Chevrolet
36.	Bobby Wawak	Chevrolet
37.	Cale Yarborough	Oldsmobile
38.	Bobby Allison	Buick
39.	Butch Miller	Chevrolet
40.	J. D. McDuffie	Pontiac
41.	Brett Bodine	Chevrolet
42.	Davey Allison	Ford

WINSTON WESTERN 500

November 8
Riverside, California
Time of Race: 3 hours, 10 minutes, 49 seconds
Average Speed: 98.035 mph
Margin of Victory: 1 second

FINISH	DRIVER	CAR
1.	Rusty Wallace	Pontiac
2.	Benny Parsons	Chevrolet
3.	Kyle Petty	Ford
4.	Richard Petty	Pontiac
5.	Bobby Allison	Buick
6.	Darrell Waltrip	Chevrolet

7.	Joe Ruttman	Pontiac
8.	Terry Labonte	Chevrolet
9.	Dave Marcis	Chevrolet
10.	Geoff Bodine	Chevrolet
11.	Alan Kulwicki	Ford
12.	Jim Robinson	Oldsmobile
13.	Phil Parsons	Oldsmobile
14.	Davey Allison	Ford
15.	Chad Little	Ford
16.	George Follmer	Chevrolet
17.	Dale Jarrett	Chevrolet
18.	Rick Wilson	Oldsmobile
19.	Ernie Irvan	Chevrolet
20.	Derrike Cope	Chevrolet
21.	Buddy Arrington	Ford
22.	Irv Hoerr	Oldsmobile
23.	Bill Elliott	Ford
24.	Sterling Marlin	Oldsmobile
25.	Morgan Shepherd	Buick
26.	Michael Waltrip	Chevrolet
27.	Jimmy Means	Pontiac
28.	Harry Gant	Chevrolet
29.	Ken Schrader	Ford
30.	Dale Earnhardt	Chevrolet
31.	Ricky Rudd	Ford
32.	Harry Goularte	Chevrolet
33.	Rick Hendrick	Chevrolet
34.	Bobby Hillin	Buick
35.	Rick McCray	Chevrolet
36.	Bill Schmitt	Chevrolet
37.	Jocko Maggiacomo	Chevrolet
38.	Tom Kendall	Buick
39.	Ruben Garcia	Chevrolet
40.	Roy Smith	Ford
41.	Glen Steurer	Chevrolet
42.	Hershel McGriff	Pontiac

ATLANTA JOURNAL 500

November 22
Atlanta, Georgia
Time of Race: 3 hours, 35 minutes, 25 seconds
Average Speed: 139.047 mph
Margin of Victory: 12.94 seconds

FINISH	DRIVER	CAR
1.	Bill Elliott	Ford
2.	Dale Earnhardt	Chevrolet
3.	Ricky Rudd	Ford
4.	Bobby Allison	Buick
5.	Davey Allison	Ford
6.	Alan Kulwicki	Ford
7.	Benny Parsons	Chevrolet
8.	Phil Parsons	Oldsmobile
9.	Sterling Marlin	Oldsmobile
10.	Buddy Baker	Oldsmobile
11.	Joe Ruttman	Pontiac
12.	Rusty Wallace	Pontiac
13.	Kyle Petty	Ford
14.	Bobby Hillin	Buick
15.	Brett Bodine	Chevrolet
16.	Hut Stricklin	Oldsmobile
17.	Brad Teague	Oldsmobile
18.	Darrell Waltrip	Chevrolet
19.	H. B. Bailey	Pontiac
20.	Randy Baker	Chevrolet
21.	Mark Stahl	Ford
22.	Buddy Arrington	Ford
23.	Ken Ragan	Ford
24.	Harry Gant	Chevrolet
25.	Larry Pearson	Chevrolet
26.	Greg Sacks	Pontiac
27.	Rick Wilson	Oldsmobile
28.	Terry Labonte	Chevrolet
29.	Jimmy Means	Pontiac
30.	Richard Petty	Pontiac
31.	Geoff Bodine	Chevrolet
32.	Dave Marcis	Chevrolet
33.	Charlie Baker	Chevrolet
34.	Curtis Markham	Ford
35.	Ken Schrader	Ford

36.	Dale Jarrett	Chevrolet
37.	A. J. Foyt	Oldsmobile
38.	Michael Waltrip	Chevrolet
39.	Morgan Shepherd	Buick
40.	Cale Yarborough	Oldsmobile
41.	Lake Speed	Oldsmobile
42.	Ed Pimm	Buick

1988

DAYTONA 500

February 14
Daytona Beach, Florida
Time of Race: 3 hours, 38 minutes, 8 seconds
Average Speed: 137.531 mph
Margin of Victory: 2 car lengths

FINISH	DRIVER	CAR
1.	Bobby Allison	Buick
2.	Davey Allison	Ford
3.	Phil Parsons	Oldsmobile
4.	Neil Bonnett	Pontiac
5.	Terry Labonte	Chevrolet
6.	Ken Schrader	Chevrolet
7.	Rusty Wallace	Pontiac
8.	Sterling Marlin	Oldsmobile
9.	Buddy Baker	Oldsmobile
10.	Dale Earnhardt	Chevrolet
11.	Darrell Waltrip	Chevrolet
12.	Bill Elliott	Ford
13.	Bobby Hillin	Buick
14.	Geoff Bodine	Chevrolet
15.	Rick Wilson	Oldsmobile
16.	Dale Jarrett	Buick
17.	Ricky Rudd	Buick
18.	Kyle Petty	Ford
19.	Trevor Boys	Chevrolet
20.	Dave Marcis	Chevrolet
21.	Brad Teague	Oldsmobile
22.	Michael Waltrip	Pontiac
23.	Steve Moore	Chevrolet
24.	Ed Pimm	Buick
25.	Jimmy Means	Ford
26.	Ralph Jones	Ford
27.	Derrike Cope	Ford
28.	Eddie Bierschwale	Oldsmobile
29.	Harry Gant	Chevrolet
30.	Rick Jeffrey	Chevrolet
31.	Benny Parsons	Ford
32.	Alan Kulwicki	Ford
33.	A. J. Foyt	Oldsmobile
34.	Richard Petty	Pontiac
35.	Brett Bodine	Ford
36.	Phil Barkdoll	Ford
37.	Lake Speed	Oldsmobile
38.	Cale Yarborough	Oldsmobile
39.	Connie Saylor	Chevrolet
40.	Greg Sacks	Pontiac
41.	Mark Martin	Ford
42.	Morgan Shepherd	Buick

PONTIAC EXCITEMENT 400

February 21
Richmond, Virginia
Time of Race: 3 hours, 15 minutes, 54 seconds
Average Speed: 66.401 mph
Margin of Victory: 1 second

FINISH	DRIVER	CAR
1.	Neil Bonnett	Pontiac
2.	Ricky Rudd	Buick

3.	Richard Petty	Pontiac
4.	Darrell Waltrip	Chevrolet
5.	Sterling Marlin	Oldsmobile
6.	Lake Speed	Oldsmobile
7.	Rusty Wallace	Pontiac
8.	Bobby Hillin	Buick
9.	Terry Labonte	Chevrolet
10.	Dale Earnhardt	Chevrolet
11.	Bobby Allison	Buick
12.	Bill Elliott	Ford
13.	Geoff Bodine	Chevrolet
14.	Benny Parsons	Ford
15.	Buddy Baker	Oldsmobile
16.	Morgan Shepherd	Buick
17.	Dave Marcis	Chevrolet
18.	Kyle Petty	Ford
19.	Brad Teague	Oldsmobile
20.	Ken Schrader	Ford
21.	Alan Kulwicki	Ford
22.	Lennie Pond	Chevrolet
23.	Ken Bouchard	Ford
24.	Jimmy Means	Chevrolet
25.	Mark Martin	Ford
26.	Dale Jarrett	Oldsmobile
27.	Brett Bodine	Ford
28.	Harry Gant	Chevrolet
29.	Davey Allison	Ford
30.	Phil Parsons	Oldsmobile
31.	Michael Waltrip	Pontiac
32.	Derrike Cope	Ford

GOODWRENCH 500

March 6
Rockingham, North Carolina
Time of Race: 4 hours, 9 minutes, 51 seconds
Average Speed: 120.159 mph
Margin of Victory: 3 car lengths

FINISH	DRIVER	CAR
1.	Neil Bonnett	Pontiac
2.	Lake Speed	Oldsmobile
3.	Sterling Marlin	Oldsmobile
4.	Alan Kulwicki	Ford
5.	Dale Earnhardt	Chevrolet
6.	Bill Elliott	Ford
7.	Morgan Shephard	Buick
8.	Ken Bouchard	Ford
9.	Davey Allison	Ford
10.	Ken Schrader	Chevrolet
11.	Buddy Baker	Oldsmobile
12.	Mark Martin	Ford
13.	Michael Waltrip	Chevrolet
14.	Rusty Wallace	Pontiac
15.	Phil Parsons	Oldsmobile
16.	Dale Jarrett	Oldsmobile
17.	Ricky Rudd	Buick
18.	Geoff Bodine	Chevrolet
19.	Kyle Petty	Ford
20.	Derrike Cope	Ford
21.	Bobby Hillin	Buick
22.	Bobby Allison	Buick
23.	Dave Marcis	Chevrolet
24.	Darrell Waltrip	Chevrolet
25.	Ernie Irvan	Chevrolet
26.	Rick Jeffrey	Ford
27.	Brett Bodine	Ford
28.	Harry Gant	Chevrolet
29.	Dave Pletcher	Ford
30.	Steve Moore	Chevrolet
31.	Terry Labonte	Chevrolet
32.	Eddie Bierschwale	Chevrolet
33.	Benny Parsons	Ford
34.	Ed Pimm	Buick
35.	Mickey Gibbs	Ford
36.	Rick Wilson	Oldsmobile
37.	Mark Stahl	Ford
38.	Charlie Baker	Chevrolet
39.	Brad Teague	Oldsmobile
40.	Jimmy Means	Pontiac
41.	Richard Petty	Pontiac

MOTORCRAFT QUALITY PARIS 500

March 20
Atlanta, Georgia
Time of Race: 3 hours, 37 minutes, 42 seconds
Average Speed: 137.588 mph
Margin of Victory: 1.5 seconds

FINISH	DRIVER	CAR
1.	Dale Earnhardt	Chevrolet
2.	Rusty Wallace	Pontiac
3.	Darrell Waltrip	Chevrolet
4.	Terry Labonte	Chevrolet
5.	Kyle Petty	Ford
6.	Bobby Hillin	Buick
7.	Buddy Baker	Oldsmobile
8.	Ken Schrader	Chevrolet
9.	Brett Bodine	Ford
10.	Rick Wilson	Oldsmobile
11.	Bobby Allison	Buick
12.	Michael Waltrip	Chevrolet
13.	Benny Parsons	Ford
14.	Brad Noffsinger	Buick
15.	Dave Marcis	Chevrolet
16.	Ken Bouchard	Ford
17.	Eddie Bierschwale	Chevrolet
18.	Ernie Irvan	Chevrolet
19.	Bill Elliott	Ford
20.	Sterling Marlin	Oldsmobile
21.	Harry Gant	Chevrolet
22.	Neil Bonnett	Pontiac
23.	Richard Petty	Pontiac
24.	Ricky Rudd	Buick
25.	Jim Sauter	Pontiac
26.	Derrike Cope	Ford
27.	Rodney Combs	Buick
28.	David Sosebee	Ford
29.	Dale Jarrett	Chevrolet
30.	Morgan Shepherd	Buick
31.	Mark Martin	Ford
32.	Cale Yarborough	Oldsmobile
33.	Geoff Bodine	Chevrolet
34.	A. J. Foyt	Oldsmobile
35.	Ken Ragan	Ford
36.	Brad Teague	Oldsmobile
37.	Phil Parsons	Oldsmobile
38.	Lake Speed	Oldsmobile
39.	Alan Kulwicki	Ford
40.	Davey Allison	Ford
41.	H. B. Bailey	Pontiac
42.	Jimmy Means	Pontiac

TRANSOUTH 500

March 27
Darlington, South Carolina
Time of Race: 3 hours, 49 minutes, 7 seconds
Average Speed: 131.284 mph
Margin of Victory: 18.80 seconds

FINISH	DRIVER	CAR
1.	Lake Speed	Oldsmobile
2.	Alan Kulwicki	Ford
3.	Davey Allison	Ford
4.	Bill Elliott	Ford
5.	Sterling Marlin	Oldsmobile
6.	Mark Martin	Ford
7.	Geoff Bodine	Chevrolet
8.	Phil Parsons	Oldsmobile
9.	Bobby Allison	Buick
10.	Buddy Baker	Oldsmobile
11.	Dale Earnhardt	Chevrolet
12.	Dale Jarrett	Oldsmobile
13.	Ken Bouchard	Ford
14.	Eddie Bierschwale	Oldsmobile
15.	Brett Bodine	Ford
16.	H. B. Bailey	Pontiac

17.	Bobby Hillin	Buick
18.	Jimmy Horton	Ford
19.	Noil Bonnett	Pontiac
20.	Brad Teague	Chevrolet
21.	Michael Waltrip	Pontiac
22.	Ernie Irvan	Chevrolet
23.	Terry Labonte	Chevrolet
24.	Darrell Waltrip	Chevrolet
25.	Rusty Wallace	Pontiac
26.	Derrike Cope	Ford
27.	Rick Wilson	Oldsmobile
28.	Buddy Arrington	Ford
29.	Ken Schrader	Chevrolet
30.	Ricky Rudd	Buick
31.	Greg Sacks	Pontiac
32.	Rodney Combs	Buick
33.	Steve Moore	Chevrolet
34.	Benny Parsons	Ford
35.	Jimmy Means	Pontiac
36.	Brad Noffsinger	Buick
37.	Dave Marcis	Chevrolet
38.	Harry Gant	Chevrolet
39.	Morgan Shepherd	Buick
40.	Kyle Petty	Ford
41.	Richard Petty	Pontiac

VALLEYDALE MEATS 500

April 10
Bristol, Tennessee
Time of Race: 3 hours, 12 minutes, 23 seconds
Average Speed: 83.115 mph
Margin of Victory: 2 car lengths

FINISH	DRIVER	CAR
1.	Bill Elliott	Ford
2.	Mark Martin	Ford
3.	Geoff Bodine	Chevrolet
4.	Rusty Wallace	Pontiac
5.	Bobby Allison	Buick
6.	Richard Petty	Pontiac
7.	Kyle Petty	Ford
8.	Sterling Marlin	Oldsmobile
9.	Dave Marcis	Chevrolet
10.	Ken Schrader	Chevrolet
11.	Neil Bonnett	Pontiac
12.	Michael Waltrip	Pontiac
13.	Benny Parsons	Ford
14.	Dale Earnhardt	Chevrolet
15.	Bobby Hillin	Buick
16.	Terry Labonte	Chevrolet
17.	Brett Bodine	Ford
18.	Harry Gant	Chevrolet
19.	Alan Kulwicki	Ford
20.	Ricky Rudd	Buick
21.	Ken Bouchard	Ford
22.	Phil Pharsons	Oldsmobile
23.	Darrell Waltrip	Chevrolet
24.	Derrike Cope	Ford
25.	Rick Wilson	Oldsmobile
26.	Ernie Irvan	Chevrolet
27.	Brad Teague	Oldsmobile
28.	Dale Jarrett	Oldsmobile
29.	Davey Allison	Ford
30.	Lake Speed	Oldsmobile
31.	Buddy Baker	Oldsmobile
32.	Jimmy Means	Pontiac

FIRST UNION 400

April 17
North Wilkesboro, North Carolina
Time of Race: 2 hours, 31 minutes, 24 seconds
Average Speed: 99.075 mph
Margin of Victory: 1.51seconds

FINISH	DRIVER	CAR
1.	Terry Labonte	Chevrolet
2.	Ricky Rudd	Buick
3.	Dale Earnhardt	Chevrolet
4.	Rusty Wallace	Pontiac
5.	Kyle Petty	Ford
6.	Richard Petty	Pontiac
7.	Phil Parsons	Oldsmobile
8.	Davey Allison	Ford
9.	Geoff Bodine	Chevrolet
10.	Bill Elliott	Ford
11.	Ken Schrader	Chevrolet
12.	Harry Gant	Chevrolet
13.	Brett Bodine	Ford
14.	Darrell Waltrip	Chevrolet
15.	Alan Kulwicki	Ford
16.	Sterling Marlin	Oldsmobile
17.	Benny Parsons	Ford
18.	Bobby Hillin	Buick
19.	Neil Bonnett	Pontiac
20.	Bobby Allison	Buick
21.	Dale Jarrett	Oldsmobile
22.	Derrike Cope	Ford
23.	Rodney Combs	Buick
24.	Ernie Irvan	Pontiac
25.	Dave Marcis	Chevrolet
26.	Lake Speed	Oldsmobile
27.	Ken Bouchard	Chevrolet
28.	Rick Wilson	Oldsmobile
29.	Mark Martin	Ford
30.	Jimmy Means	Pontiac
31.	Buddy Baker	Oldsmobile
32.	Michael Waltrip	Pontiac

PANNILL SWEATSHIRTS 500

April 24
Martinsville, Virginia
Time of Race: 3 hours, 31 minutes, 8 seconds
Average Speed: 74.740 mph
Margin of Victory: 1.99 seconds

FINISH	DRIVER	CAR
1.	Dale Earnhardt	Chevrolet
2.	Sterling Marlin	Oldsmobile
3.	Bobby Hillin	Buick
4.	Terry Labonte	Chevrolet
5.	Darrell Waltrip	Chevrolet
6.	Davey Allison	Ford
7.	Buddy Baker	Oldsmobile
8.	Bobby Allison	Buick
9.	Phil Pharsons	Oldsmobile
10.	Ken Schrader	Chevrolet
11.	Bill Elliott	Ford
12.	Dave Marcis	Chevrolet
13.	Dale Jarrett	Oldsmobile
14.	Benny Parsons	Ford
15.	Geoff Bodine	Chevrolet
16.	Rusty Wallace	Pontiac
17.	Kyle Petty	Ford
18.	Ricky Rudd	Buick
19.	Brad Teague	Oldsmobile
20.	Alan Kulwicki	Ford
21.	Brad Noffsinger	Buick
22.	Michael Waltrip	Pontiac
23.	Mark Martin	Ford
24.	Jimmy Hensley	Ford
25.	Rick Wilson	Oldsmobile
26.	Harry Gant	Chevrolet
27.	Brett Bodine	Ford
28.	Lake Speed	Oldsmobile
29.	Derrike Cope	Ford
30.	Neil Bonnett	Pontiac
31.	Ken Bouchard	Buick
32.	Richard Petty	Pontiac

WINSTON 500

May 1, Talladega, Alabama
Time of Race: 3 hours, 11 minutes, 40 seconds
Average Speed: 156.547 mph
Margin of Victory: .21 seconds

FINISH	DRIVER	CAR
1.	Phil Pharsons	Oldsmobile
2.	Bobby Allison	Buick
3.	Geoff Bodine	Chevrolet
4.	Terry Labonte	Chevrolet
5.	Ken Schrader	Chevrolet
6.	Sterling Marlin	Oldsmobile
7.	Bill Elliott	Ford
8.	Kyle Petty	Ford
9.	Dale Earnhardt	Chevrolet
10.	Rusty Wallace	Pontiac
11.	Dale Jarrett	Buick
12.	Mark Martin	Ford
13.	Bobby Hillin	Buick
14.	Neil Bonnett	Pontiac
15.	Lake Speed	Oldsmobile
16.	Buddy Baker	Oldsmobile
17.	Greg Sacks	Pontiac
18.	Cale Yarborough	Oldsmobile
19.	Brett Bodine	Ford
20.	Richard Petty	Pontiac
21.	Brad Teague	Oldsmobile
22.	Alan Kulwicki	Ford
23.	Jimmy Means	Pontiac
24.	Benny Parsons	Ford
25.	Brad Noffsinger	Buick
26.	Derrike Cope	Ford
27.	Dave Marcis	Chevrolet
28.	A. J. Foyt	Oldsmobile
29.	Ricky Rudd	Buick
30.	Rick Jeffrey	Chevrolet
31.	Phil Barkdoll	Chevrolet
32.	Ernie Irvan	Chevrolet
33.	Michael Waltrip	Pontiac
34.	Davey Allison	Ford
35.	Rick Wilson	Oldsmobile
36.	Harry Gant	Chevrolet
37.	Darrell Waltrip	Chevrolet
38.	Rodney Combs	Buick
39.	Eddie Bierschwale	Oldsmobile
40.	Mickey Gibbs	Chevrolet
41.	Ken Ragan	Ford

COCA-COLA 600

May 29
Charlotte, North Carolina
Time of Race: 4 hours, 49 minutes, 15 seconds
Average Speed: 124.460 mph
Margin of Victory: .24 seconds

FINISH	DRIVER	CAR
1.	Darrell Waltrip	Chevrolet
2.	Rusty Wallace	Pontiac
3.	Alan Kulwicki	Ford
4.	Brett Bodine	Ford
5.	Davey Allison	Ford
6.	Ken Schrader	Chevrolet
7.	Ricky Rudd	Buick
8.	Phil Parsons	Oldsmobile
9.	Terry Labonte	Chevrolet
10.	Greg Sacks	Pontiac
11.	Ken Bouchard	Ford
12.	Jimmy Means	Pontiac
13.	Dale Earnhardt	Chevrolet
14.	Bobby Hillin	Buick
15.	Richard Petty	Pontiac
16.	Kyle Petty	Ford
17.	Bobby Allison	Buick
18.	Rick Wilson	Oldsmobile

19.	Bill Elliott	Ford
20.	Joe Ruttman	Oldsmobile
21.	Lake Speed	Oldsmobile
22.	Ernie Irvan	Chevrolet
23.	Michael Waltrip	Pontiac
24.	Geoff Bodine	Chevrolet
25.	Benny Parsons	Ford
26.	Morgan Shepherd	Buick
27.	Sterling Marlin	Oldsmobile
28.	Eddie Bierschwale	Oldsmobile
29.	Buddy Baker	Oldsmobile
30.	Harry Gant	Chevrolet
31.	Jimmy Horton	Ford
32.	Rodney Combs	Buick
33.	Brad Noffsinger	Buick
34.	Dave Marcis	Chevrolet
35.	H. B. Bailey	Pontiac
36.	Neil Bonnett	Pontiac
37.	Mark Martin	Ford
38.	Cale Yarborough	Oldsmobile
39.	Jim Sauter	Pontiac
40.	Derrike Cope	Ford
41.	Dale Jarrett	Chevrolet

BUDWEISER 500

June 5
Dover, Delaware
Time of Race: 4 hours, 12 minutes, 41 seconds
Average Speed: 118.726 mph
Margin of Victory: 21 seconds

FINISH	DRIVER	CAR
1.	Bill Elliott	Ford
2.	Morgan Shepherd	Chevrolet
3.	Rusty Wallace	Pontiac
4.	Lake Speed	Oldsmobile
5.	Davey Allison	Ford
6.	Alan Kulwicki	Ford
7.	Rick Wilson	Oldsmobile
8.	Geoff Bodine	Chevrolet
9.	Mark Martin	Ford
10.	Bobby Allison	Buick
11.	Sterling Marlin	Oldsmobile
12.	Terry Labonte	Chevrolet
13.	Buddy Baker	Oldsmobile
14.	Ken Bouchard	Ford
15.	Richard Petty	Pontiac
16.	Dale Earnhardt	Chevrolet
17.	Bobby Hillin	Buick
18.	Derrike Cope	Ford
19.	Ricky Rudd	Buick
20.	Dale Jarrett	Oldsmobile
21.	Ken Schrader	Chevrolet
22.	Benny Parsons	Ford
23.	Darrell Waltrip	Chevrolet
24.	Brad Noffsinger	Buick
25.	J. D. McDuffie	Pontiac
26.	Ernie Irvan	Chevrolet
27.	Jimmy Means	Pontiac
28.	Dana Patten	Buick
29.	Rodney Combs	Buick
30.	Joe Ruttman	Oldsmobile
31.	Brett Bodine	Ford
32.	Dave Marcis	Chevrolet
33.	Kyle Petty	Ford
34.	Jimmy Horton	Ford
35.	Neil Bonnett	Pontiac
36.	Michael Waltrip	Pontiac
37.	Jay Sommers	Chevrolet
38.	Joe Booher	Chevrolet
39.	Phil Parsons	Oldsmobile
40.	Eddie Bierschwale	Oldsmobile

BUDWEISER 400

June 12
Riverside, California

Time of Race: 2 hours, 43 minutes, 3 seconds
Average Speed: 88.341 mph
Margin of Victory: .34 seconds

FINISH	DRIVER	CAR
1.	Rusty Wallace	Pontiac
2.	Terry Labonte	Chevrolet
3.	Ricky Rudd	Buick
4.	Dale Earnhardt	Chevrolet
5.	Phil Parsons	Oldsmobile
6.	Richard Petty	Pontiac
7.	Mark Martin	Ford
8.	Dale Jarrett	Oldsmobile
9.	Sterling Marlin	Oldsmobile
10.	Neil Bonnett	Pontiac
11.	Michael Waltrip	Pontiac
12.	Bill Schmitt	Chevrolet
13.	Benny Parsons	Ford
14.	Kyle Petty	Ford
15.	Rick Hendrick	Chevrolet
16.	Bill Elliott	Ford
17.	Derrike Cope	Chevrolet
18.	Tom Kendall	Buick
19.	Buddy Baker	Oldsmobile
20.	Ken Schrader	Chevrolet
21.	Dave Marcis	Chevrolet
22.	Bobby Allison	Buick
23.	Chad Little	Ford
24.	Bobby Hillin	Buick
25.	John Krebs	Oldsmobile
26.	Lake Speed	Oldsmobile
27.	Roy Smith	Ford
28.	Darrell Waltrip	Chevrolet
29.	Joe Ruttman	Oldsmobile
30.	Jocko Maggiacomo	Chevrolet
31.	Ernie Irvan	Chevrolet
32.	Davey Allison	Ford
33.	Rick Wilson	Oldsmobile
34.	Geoff Bodine	Chevrolet
35.	Terry Petris	Chevrolet
36.	Hershel McGriff	Pontiac
37.	Rick McCray	Pontiac
38.	Alan Kulwicki	Ford
39.	Ruben Garcia	Chevrolet
40.	Brett Bodine	Ford
41.	Jim Bown	Chevrolet
42.	Morgan Shepherd	Chevrolet
43.	Jimmy Means	Pontiac

MILLER HIGH LIFE 500

June 19
Pocono, Pennsylvania
Time of Race: 3 hours, 58 minutes, 21 seconds
Average Speed: 126.147 mph
Margin of Victory: 8.18 seconds

FINISH	DRIVER	CAR
1.	Geoff Bodine	Chevrolet
2.	Michael Waltrip	Pontiac
3.	Rusty Wallace	Pontiac
4.	Mark Martin	Ford
5.	Davey Allison	Ford
6.	Darrell Waltrip	Chevrolet
7.	Buddy Baker	Oldsmobile
8.	Phil Parsons	Oldsmobile
9.	Ken Schrader	Chevrolet
10.	Bill Elliott	Ford
11.	Neil Bonnett	Pontiac
12.	Kyle Petty	Ford
13.	Dale Jarrett	Oldsmobile
14.	Ken Bouchard	Ford
15.	Bobby Hillin	Buick
16.	Morgan Shepherd	Chevrolet
17.	Joe Ruttman	Oldsmobile
18.	Jimmy Horton	Ford
19.	Brad Noffsinger	Buick

20.	Jimmy Means	Pontiac
21.	Buddy Arrington	Ford
22.	Bobby Gerhart	Chevrolet
23.	Lake Spped	Oldsmobile
24.	Derrike Cope	Ford
25.	Rick Wilson	Oldsmobile
26.	Richard Petty	Pontiac
27.	Alan Kulwicki	Ford
28.	Sterling Marlin	Oldsmobile
29.	Eddie Bierschwale	Oldsmobile
30.	Ricky Rudd	Buick
31.	Benny Parsons	Ford
32.	Terry Labonte	Chevrolet
33.	Dale Earnhardt	Chevrolet
34.	Rodney Combs	Buick
35.	Brett Bodine	Ford
36.	Bob Schacht	Ford
37.	Ernie Irvan	Chevrolet
38.	Dave Marcis	Chevrolet
39.	Bobby Allison	Buick
40.	Jocko Maggiacomo	Chevrolet

MILLER HIGH LIFE 400

June 26
Brooklyn, Michigan
Time of Race: 2 hours, 36 minutes, 18 seconds
Average Speed: 153.551 mph
Margin of Victory: .28 seconds

FINISH	DRIVER	CAR
1.	Rusty Wallace	Pontiac
2.	Bill Elliott	Ford
3.	Terry Labonte	Chevrolet
4.	Dale Earnhardt	Chevrolet
5.	Geoff Bodine	Chevrolet
6.	Ken Schrader	Chevrolet
7.	Phil Parsons	Oldsmobile
8.	Darrell Waltrip	Chevrolet
9.	Cale Yarborough	Oldsmobile
10.	Mike Alexander	Buick
11.	Ricky Rudd	Buick
12.	Bobby Hillin	Buick
13.	Buddy Baker	Oldsmobile
14.	Mark Martin	Ford
15.	Ernie Irvan	Chevrolet
16.	Joe Ruttman	Oldsmobile
17.	Ken Bouchard	Ford
18.	Dave Marcis	Chevrolet
19.	Neil Bonnett	Pontiac
20.	Brad Noffsinger	Buick
21.	Alan Kulwicki	Ford
22.	Dana Patten	Buick
23.	Buddy Arrington	Ford
24.	Richard Petty	Pontiac
25.	Dale Jarrett	Buick
26.	Eddie Bierschwale	Oldsmobile
27.	Brett Bodine	Ford
28.	Michael Waltrip	Pontiac
29.	Lake Speed	Oldsmobile
30.	Rodney Combs	Buick
31.	David Sosebee	Ford
32.	Derrike Cope	Ford
33.	Kyle Petty	Ford
34.	Morgan Shepherd	Chevrolet
35.	Davey Allison	Ford
36.	Jimmy Means	Pontiac
37.	Sterling Marlin	Oldsmobile
38.	Benny Parsons	Ford
39.	H. B. Bailey	Pontiac
40.	Dave Simko	Pontiac
41.	Rick Wilson	Oldsmobile

PEPSI FIRECRACKER 400

July 2
Daytona Beach, Florida

Time of Race: 2 hours, 36 minutes, 18 seconds
Average Speed: 163.302 mph
Margin of Victory: 18 inches

FINISH	DRIVER	CAR
1.	Bill Elliott	Ford
2.	Rick Wilson	Oldsmobile
3.	Phil Parsons	Oldsmobile
4.	Dale Earnhardt	Chevrolet
5.	Darrell Waltrip	Chevrolet
6.	Buddy Baker	Oldsmobile
7.	Morgan Shepherd	Chevrolet
8.	Ken Schrader	Chevrolet
9.	Lake Speed	Oldsmobile
10.	Greg Sacks	Pontiac
11.	Joe Ruttman	Oldsmobile
12.	Rusty Wallace	Pontiac
13.	Bobby Hillin	Buick
14.	Dale Jarrett	Buick
15.	Mike Alexander	Buick
16.	Geoff Bodine	Chevrolet
17.	Mark Martin	Ford
18.	Neil Bonnett	Pontiac
19.	Terry Labonte	Chevrolet
20.	Richard Petty	Pontiac
21.	Michael Waltrip	Pontiac
22.	Ricky Rudd	Buick
23.	Dave Marcis	Chevrolet
24.	Kyle Petty	Ford
25.	Ernie Irvan	Chevrolet
26.	Patty Moise	Buick
27.	Jimmy Means	Pontiac
28.	Buddy Arrington	Chevrolet
29.	Rick Jeffrey	Chevrolet
30.	Ken Ragan	Ford
31.	Eddie Bierschwale	Oldsmobile
32.	Larry Moyer	Pontiac
33.	Rodney Combs	Buick
34.	Sterling Marlin	Oldsmobile
35.	Benny Parsons	Ford
36.	Ken Bouchard	Ford
37.	A. J. Foyt	Oldsmobile
38.	Davey Allison	Ford
39.	Derrike Cope	Ford
40.	Alan Kulwicki	Ford
41.	Cale Yarborough	Oldsmobile
42.	Brett Bodine	Ford

AC SPARK PLUG 500

July 24
Pocono, Pennsylvania
Time of Race: 4 hours, 4 minutes, 10 seconds
Average Speed: 122.866 mph
Margin of Victory: 8.27 seconds

FINISH	DRIVER	CAR
1.	Bill Elliott	Ford
2.	Ken Schrader	Chevrolet
3.	Davey Allison	Ford
4.	Geoff Bodine	Chevrolet
5.	Darrell Waltrip	Chevrolet
6.	Morgan Shepherd	Pontiac
7.	Mark Martin	Ford
8.	Alan Kulwicki	Ford
9.	Terry Labonte	Chevrolet
10.	Harry Gant	Chevrolet
11.	Dale Earnhardt	Chevrolet
12.	Ricky Rudd	Buick
13.	Rick Wilson	Oldsmobile
14.	Sterling Marlin	Oldsmobile
15.	Mike Alexander	Buick
16.	Ken Bouchard	Ford
17.	Michael Waltrip	Pontiac
18.	Kyle Petty	Ford
19.	Brad Noffsinger	Buick
20.	Brett Bodine	Ford

FINISH	DRIVER	CAR
21.	Bobby Hillin	Buick
22.	Ernie Irvan	Chevrolet
23.	Buddy Baker	Oldsmobile
24.	Rusty Wallace	Pontiac
25.	Dale Jarrett	Oldsmobile
26.	Bobby Gerhardt	Chevrolet
27.	Joe Ruttman	Oldsmobile
28.	Richard Petty	Pontiac
29.	Jimmy Horton	Ford
30.	Dave Marcis	Chevrolet
31.	Phil Parsons	Oldsmobile
32.	Lake Speed	Oldsmobile
33.	Derrike Cope	Ford
34.	Greg Sacks	Pontiac
35.	Benny Parsons	Ford
36.	Rodney Combs	Buick
37.	Mike Potter	Chevrolet
38.	Eddie Bierschwale	Oldsmobile
39.	Jimmy Means	Pontiac
40.	Bob Schact	Ford

TALLEDEGA DIEHARD 500

July 31
Talladega, Alabama
Time of Race: 3 hours, 14 minutes, 12 seconds
Average Speed: 154.505 mph
Margin of Victory: 1 car length

FINISH	DRIVER	CAR
1.	Ken Schrader	Chevrolet
2.	Geoff Bodine	Chevrolet
3.	Dale Earnhardt	Chevrolet
4.	Rick Wilson	Oldsmobile
5.	Rusty Wallace	Pontiac
6.	Sterling Marlin	Oldsmobile
7.	Mark Martin	Ford
8.	Bill Elliott	Ford
9.	Cale Yarborough	Oldsmobile
10.	Buddy Baker	Oldsmobile
11.	Phil Parsons	Oldsmobile
12.	A. J. Foyt	Oldsmobile
13.	Lake Speed	Oldsmobile
14.	Terry Labonte	Chevrolet
15.	Kyle Petty	Ford
16.	Harry Gant	Chevrolet
17.	Bobby Hillin	Buick
18.	Dave Marcis	Chevrolet
19.	Alan Kulwicki	Ford
20.	Michael Waltrip	Pontiac
21.	Richard Petty	Pontiac
22.	Brad Noffsinger	Buick
23.	Jimmy Means	Pontiac
24.	Derrike Cope	Ford
25.	Mike Alexander	Buick
26.	Phil Barkdoll	Chevrolet
27.	Benny Parsons	Ford
28.	Brett Bodine	Ford
29.	Rodney Combs	Buick
30.	Ken Ragan	Ford
31.	Eddie Bierschwale	Oldsmobile
32.	Ernie Irvan	Chevrolet
33.	Darrell Waltrip	Chevrolet
34.	Mickey Gibbs	Ford
35.	Ken Bouchard	Ford
36.	Ron Esau	Chevrolet
37.	Dale Jarrett	Buick
38.	Greg Sacks	Pontiac
39.	Davey Allison	Ford
40.	Morgan Shepherd	Pontiac
41.	Ricky Rudd	Buick
42.	Joe Ruttman	Oldsmobile

THE BUDWEISER AT THE GLEN

August 14
Watkins Glen, New York

Time of Race: 2 hours, 56 minutes, 58 seconds
Average Speed: 74.096 mph
Margin of Victory: 1.5 car lengths

FINISH	DRIVER	CAR
1.	Ricky Rudd	Buick
2.	Rusty Wallace	Pontiac
3.	Bill Elliott	Ford
4.	Phil Parsons	Oldsmobile
5.	Mike Alexander	Buick
6.	Dale Earnhardt	Chevrolet
7.	Morgan Shepherd	Ford
8.	Sterling Marlin	Oldsmobile
9.	Joe Ruttman	Oldsmobile
10.	Ken Schrader	Chevrolet
11.	Dale Jarrett	Oldsmobile
12.	Rick Wilson	Oldsmobile
13.	Bobby Hillin	Buick
14.	Jimmy Means	Pontiac
15.	Brad Noffsinger	Buick
16.	Davey Allison	Ford
17.	Richard Petty	Pontiac
18.	Terry Labonte	Chevrolet
19.	Alan Kulwicki	Ford
20.	Darrell Waltrip	Chevrolet
21.	Ron Esau	Oldsmobile
22.	Tom Rotsell	Ford
23.	Brett Bodine	Ford
24.	Rodney Combs	Buick
25.	Hershel McGriff	Pontiac
26.	Dave Marcis	Chevrolet
27.	Ken Bouchard	Ford
28.	Mark Martin	Ford
29.	Ernie Irvan	Pontiac
30.	Patty Moise	Buick
31.	Harry Gant	Chevrolet
32.	Geoff Bodine	Chevrolet
33.	Michael Waltrip	Pontiac
34.	Kyle Petty	Ford
35.	Jocko Maggiacomo	Chevrolet
36.	J. D. McDuffie	Pontiac
37.	Lake Speed	Oldsmobile
38.	Neil Bonnett	Pontiac
39.	Benny Parsons	Ford
40.	Derrike Cope	Ford

CHAMPION SPARK PLUG 400

August 21
Brooklyn, Michigan
Time of Race: 2 hours, 33 minutes, 0 seconds
Average Speed: 156.863 mph
Margin of Victory: 4 seconds

FINISH	DRIVER	CAR
1.	Davey Allison	Ford
2.	Rusty Wallace	Pontiac
3.	Bill Elliott	Ford
4.	Morgan Shepherd	Oldsmobile
5.	Lake Speed	Oldsmobile
6.	Brett Bodine	Ford
7.	Michael Waltrip	Pontiac
8.	Kyle Petty	Ford
9.	Rick Wilson	Oldsmobile
10.	Geoff Bodine	Chevrolet
11.	Sterling Marlin	Oldsmobile
12.	Ken Schrader	Chevrolet
13.	Terry Labonte	Chevrolet
14.	Rodney Combs	Buick
15.	Benny Parsons	Ford
16.	Ricky Rudd	Buick
17.	Darrell Waltrip	Chevrolet
18.	Cale Yarborough	Oldsmobile
19.	Jim Sauter	Pontiac
20.	Phil Parsons	Oldsmobile
21.	Harry Gant	Chevrolet
22.	Dave Marcis	Chevrolet

23.	Mike Alexander	Buick
24.	Eddie Bierschwale	Oldsmobile
25.	Ken Bouchard	Ford
26.	Brad Noffsinger	Buick
27.	Chad Little	Ford
28.	H. B. Bailey	Pontiac
29.	Dale Earnhardt	Chevrolet
30.	Dana Patten	Buick
31.	Mickey Gibbs	Ford
32.	Mark Martin	Ford
33.	Ernie Irvan	Pontiac
34.	Derrike Cope	Ford
35.	Donnie Allison	Oldsmobile
36.	Alan Kulwicki	Ford
37.	Bobby Hillin	Buick
38.	Jimmy Means	Pontiac
39.	Richard Petty	Pontiac
40.	Neil Bonnett	Pontiac
41.	Dale Jarrett	Buick
42.	Greg Sacks	Pontiac

BUSCH 500

August 27
Bristol, Tennessee
Time of Race: 3 hours, 22 minutes, 59 seconds
Average Speed: 78.775 mph
Margin of Victory: 1 car length

FINISH	DRIVER	CAR
1.	Dale Earnhardt	Chevrolet
2.	Bill Elliott	Ford
3.	Geoff Bodine	Chevrolet
4.	Davey Allison	Ford
5.	Alan Kulwicki	Ford
6.	Harry Gant	Chevrolet
7.	Darrell Waltrip	Chevrolet
8.	Richard Petty	Pontiac
9.	Rusty Wallace	Pontiac
10.	Bobby Hillin	Buick
11.	Rodney Combs	Buick
12.	Sterling Marlin	Oldsmobile
13.	Kyle Petty	Ford
14.	Neil Bonnett	Pontiac
15.	Ernie Irvan	Pontiac
16.	Ricky Rudd	Buick
17.	Butch Miller	Oldsmobile
18.	Mike Alexander	Buick
19.	Phil Parsons	Oldsmobile
20.	Lake Speed	Oldsmobile
21.	Ken Schrader	Chevrolet
22.	Terry Labonte	Chevrolet
23.	Rick Wilson	Oldsmobile
24.	Dave Mader III	Pontiac
25.	Brett Bodine	Ford
26.	Dale Jarrett	Oldsmobile
27.	Mark Martin	Ford
28.	Rick Mast	Oldsmobile
29.	Dave Marcis	Chevrolet
30.	Derrike Cope	Ford
31.	Michael Waltrip	Pontiac
32.	Brad Noffsinger	Buick

SOUTHERN 500

September 4
Darlington, South Carolina
Time of Race: 3 hours, 54 minutes, 27 seconds
Average Speed: 128.297 mph
Margin of Victory: .24 seconds

FINISH	DRIVER	CAR
1.	Bill Elliott	Ford
2.	Rusty Wallace	Pontiac

3.	Dale Earnhardt	Chevrolet
4.	Darrell Waltrip	Chevrolet
5.	Sterling Marlin	Oldsmobile
6.	Phil Parsons	Oldsmobile
7.	Geoff Bodine	Chevrolet
8.	Terry Labonte	Chevrolet
9.	Davey Allison	Ford
10.	Ricky Rudd	Buick
11.	Ken Schrader	Chevrolet
12.	Lake Speed	Oldsmobile
13.	Benny Parsons	Ford
14.	Mike Alexander	Buick
15.	Alan Kulwicki	Ford
16.	Neil Bonnett	Pontiac
17.	Brett Bodine	Ford
18.	Ken Bouchard	Ford
19.	Mark Martin	Ford
20.	Ernie Irvan	Chevrolet
21.	Rodney Combs	Buick
22.	Dave Marcis	Chevrolet
23.	Jim Sauter	Oldsmobile
24.	Jimmy Means	Pontiac
25.	Michael Waltrip	Pontiac
26.	Eddie Bierschwale	Oldsmobile
27.	H. B. Bailey	Pontiac
28.	Kyle Petty	Ford
29.	Phillip Duffie	Buick
30.	Bobby Hillin	Buick
31.	Ken Ragan	Ford
32.	Rick Mast	Oldsmobile
33.	Richard Petty	Pontiac
34.	Dale Jarrett	Oldsmobile
35.	Derrike Cope	Ford
36.	Randy Baker	Oldsmobile
37.	Jimmy Horton	Ford
38.	Rick Wilson	Oldsmobile
39.	Morgan Shepherd	Buick
40.	Harry Gant	Chevrolet

MILLER HIGH LIFE 400

September 11
Richmond, Virginia
Time of Race: 3 hours, 7 minutes, 57 seconds
Average Speed: 95.770 mph
Margin of Victory: 3.37 seconds

FINISH	DRIVER	CAR
1.	Davey Allison	Ford
2.	Dale Earnhardt	Chevrolet
3.	Terry Labonte	Chevrolet
4.	Mark Martin	Ford
5.	Alan Kulwicki	Ford
6.	Kyle Petty	Ford
7.	Bill Elliott	Ford
8.	Darrell Waltrip	Chevrolet
9.	Neil Bonnett	Pontiac
10.	Dave Marcis	Chevrolet
11.	Brett Bodine	Ford
12.	Michael Waltrip	Pontiac
13.	Greg Sacks	Oldsmobile
14.	Bobby Hillin	Buick
15.	Dale Jarrett	Oldsmobile
16.	Sterling Marlin	Oldsmobile
17.	Mike Alexander	Buick
18.	Ken Schrader	Chevrolet
19.	Ken Bouchard	Ford
20.	Benny Parsons	Ford
21.	Rodney Combs	Buick
22.	Geoff Bodine	Chevrolet
23.	Lee Faulk	Oldsmobile
24.	Phil Parsons	Oldsmobile
25.	Butch Miller	Oldsmobile
26.	Ricky Rudd	Buick
27.	Eddie Bierschwale	Oldsmobile
28.	Ernie Irvan	Pontiac
29.	Jimmy Means	Pontiac
30.	Bob Schacht	Buick
31.	Morgan Shepherd	Buick
32.	Harry Gant	Chevrolet
33.	Rick Wilson	Oldsmobile

34.	Richard Petty	Pontiac
35.	Rusty Wallace	Pontiac
36.	Lake Speed	Oldsmobile

DELWARE 500

September 18
Dover, Delaware
Time of Race: 4 hours, 34 minutes, 21 seconds
Average Speed: 109.349 mph
Margin of Victory: 1.48 seconds

FINISH	DRIVER	CAR
1.	Bill Elliott	Ford
2.	Dale Earnhardt	Chevrolet
3.	Rusty Wallace	Pontiac
4.	Davey Allison	Ford
5.	Geoff Bodine	Chevrolet
6.	Kyle Petty	Ford
7.	Mike Alexander	Buick
8.	Neil Bonnett	Pontiac
9.	Lake Speed	Oldsmobile
10.	Ricky Rudd	Buick
11.	Harry Gant	Chevrolet
12.	Michael Waltrip	Pontiac
13.	Ernie Irvan	Chevrolet
14.	Phil Parsons	Oldsmobile
15.	Chad Little	Ford
16.	Dave Marcis	Chevrolet
17.	Darrell Waltrip	Chevrolet
18.	Terry Labonte	Chevrolet
19.	Jimmy Means	Pontiac
20.	Jimmy Horton	Ford
21.	Bobby Hillin	Buick
22.	Brett Bodine	Ford
23.	Sterling Marlin	Oldsmobile
24.	Rick Wilson	Oldsmobile
25.	Ken Bouchard	Ford
26.	Eddie Bierschwale	Oldsmobile
27.	Benny Parsons	Ford
28.	Dale Jarrett	Oldsmobile
29.	Morgan Shepherd	Oldsmobile
30.	Brad Teague	Ford
31.	Alan Kulwicki	Ford
32.	Jim Sauter	Oldsmobile
33.	Dana Pattton	Buick
34.	Brad Noffsinger	Buick
35.	Ken Schrader	Chevrolet
36.	Derrike Cope	Ford
37.	Randy LaJoie	Chevrolet
38.	Richard Petty	Pontiac
39.	Mark Martin	Ford
40.	Rodney Combs	Buick

GOODY'S 500

September 25
Martinsville, Virginia
Time of Race: 3 hours, 30 minutes, 26 seconds
Average Speed: 74.988 mph
Margin of Victory: 5.27 seconds

FINISH	DRIVER	CAR
1.	Darrell Waltrip	Chevrolet
2.	Alan Kulwicki	Ford
3.	Rusty Wallace	Pontiac
4.	Ken Schrader	Chevrolet
5.	Geoff Bodine	Chevrolet
6.	Bill Elliott	Ford
7.	Terry Labonte	Chevrolet
8.	Dale Earnhardt	Chevrolet
9.	Mark Martin	Ford
10.	Brett Bodine	Ford
11.	Ernie Irvan	Pontiac
12.	Greg Sacks	Oldsmobile

13.	Dave Marcis	Chevrolet
14.	Bobby Hillin	Buick
15.	Brad Teague	Ford
16.	Rick Wilson	Oldsmobile
17.	Ken Bouchard	Ford
18.	Davey Allison	Ford
19.	Neil Bonnett	Pontiac
20.	Benny Parsons	Ford
21.	Phil Parsons	Oldsmobile
22.	Kyle Petty	Ford
23.	Jimmy Means	Pontiac
24.	Ricky Rudd	Buick
25.	Michael Waltrip	Pontiac
26.	Sterling Marlin	Oldsmobile
27.	Richard Petty	Pontiac
28.	Lake Speed	Oldsmobile
29.	Mike Alexander	Buick
30.	Harry Gant	Chevrolet
31.	Morgan Shepherd	Buick
32.	Dale Jarrett	Oldsmobile

OAKWOOD HOMES 500

October 9
Charlotte, North Carolina
Time of Race: 3 hours, 50 minutes, 2 seconds
Average Speed: 130.677 mph
Margin of Victory: 1 car length

FINISH	DRIVER	CAR
1.	Rusty Wallace	Pontiac
2.	Darrell Waltrip	Chevrolet
3.	Brett Bodine	Ford
4.	Bill Elliott	Ford
5.	Sterling Marlin	Oldsmobile
6.	Bobby Hillin	Buick
7.	Ken Schrader	Chevrolet
8.	Ricky Rudd	Buick
9.	Mark Martin	Ford
10.	Terry Labonte	Chevrolet
11.	Kyle Petty	Ford
12.	Benny Parsons	Ford
13.	Jim Sauter	Pontiac
14.	Rob Moroso	Chevrolet
15.	Brad Teague	Chevrolet
16.	Morgan Shepherd	Buick
17.	Dale Earnhardt	Chevrolet
18.	Neil Bonnett	Pontiac
19.	Davey Allison	Ford
20.	Lee Faulk	Oldsmobile
21.	Mike Alexander	Buick
22.	Cale Yarborough	Oldsmobile
23.	Michael Waltrip	Pontiac
24.	Harry Gant	Chevrolet
25.	Rick Wilson	Oldsmobile
26.	Dave Marcis	Chevrolet
27.	Phil Parsons	Oldsmobile
28.	Alan Kulwicki	Ford
29.	Greg Sacks	Oldsmobile
30.	Tommy Ellis	Buick
31.	Geoff Bodine	Chevrolet
32.	Derrike Cope	Ford
33.	Ken Bouchard	Ford
34.	Lake Speed	Oldsmobile
35.	Joe Ruttman	Chevrolet
36.	A. J. Foyt	Oldsmobile
37.	Dale Jarrett	Buick
38.	Richard Petty	Pontiac
39.	Mickey Gibbs	Ford
40.	Eddie Bierschwale	Oldsmobile
41.	Larry Pearson	Chevrolet
42.	Jimmy Means	Pontiac

HOLLY FARMS 400

October 16
North Wilkesboro, North Carolina

Time of Race: 2 hours, 39 minutes, 15 seconds
Average Speed: 94.192 mph
Margin of Victory: 1 car length

FINISH	DRIVER	CAR
1.	Rusty Wallace	Pontiac
2.	Phil Parsons	Oldsmobile
3.	Geoff Bodine	Chevrolet
4.	Terry Labonte	Chevrolet
5.	Bill Elliott	Ford
6.	Dale Earnhardt	Chevrolet
7.	Ricky Rudd	Buick
8.	Ken Schrader	Chevrolet
9.	Mike Alexander	Buick
10.	Greg Sacks	Oldsmobile
11.	Davey Allison	Ford
12.	Darrell Waltrip	Chevrolet
13.	Bobby Hillin	Buick
14.	Sterling Marlin	Oldsmobile
15.	Lake Speed	Oldsmobile
16.	Kyle Petty	Ford
17.	Brett Bodine	Ford
18.	Richard Petty	Pontiac
19.	Mark Matin	Ford
20.	Rick Wilson	Oldsmobile
21.	Dave Marcis	Chevrolet
22.	Morgan Shepherd	Buick
23.	Dale Jarrettt	Oldsmobile
24.	Jimmy Means	Ford
25.	Michael Waltrip	Pontiac
26.	Ernie Irvan	Pontiac
27.	Ken Bouchard	Ford
28.	Neil Bonnett	Pontiac
29.	Alan Kulwicki	Ford
30.	Harry Gant	Chevrolet
31.	Rob Moroso	Oldsmobile
32.	Lee Faulk	Oldsmobile

AC DELCO 500

October 23
Rockingham, North Carolina
Time of Race: 4 hours, 29 minutes, 7 seconds
Average Speed: 111.557 mph
Margin of Victory: 13.50 seconds

FINISH	DRIVER	CAR
1.	Rusty Wallace	Pontiac
2.	Ricky Rudd	Buick
3.	Terry Labonte	Chevrolet
4.	Bill Elliott	Ford
5.	Dale Earnhardt	Chevrolet
6.	Mike Alexander	Buick
7.	Harry Gant	Chevrolet
8.	Phil Parsons	Oldsmobile
9.	Kyle Petty	Ford
10.	Neil Bonnett	Pontiac
11.	Ken Schrader	Chevrolet
12.	Greg Sacks	Oldsmobile
13.	Benny Parsons	Ford
14.	Morgan Shepherd	Buick
15.	Ernie Irvan	Pontiac
16.	Dave Marcis	Chevrolet
17.	Jim Sauter	Oldsmobile
18.	Ken Bouchard	Pontiac
19.	Michael Waltrip	Pontiac
20.	Ben Hess	Oldsmobile
21.	Connie Saylor	Buick
22.	Rick Wilson	Oldsmobile
23.	Bobby Hillin	Buick
24.	Lake Speed	Oldsmobile
25.	Richard Petty	Pontiac
26.	Alan Kulwicki	Ford
27.	Davey Allison	Ford
28.	Mark Martin	Ford
29.	Brett Bodine	Ford
30.	Geoff Bodine	Chevrolet

FINISH	DRIVER	CAR
31.	Darrell Waltrip	Chevrolet
32.	Dale Jarrett	Oldsmobile
33.	Eddie Bierschwale	Oldsmobile
34.	Sterling Marlin	Oldsmobile
35.	Brad Teague	Ford
36.	Derrike Cope	Ford
37.	Brad Noffsinger	Buick
38.	Joe Ruttman	Buick
39.	Jimmy Means	Pontiac
40.	Rodney Combs	Chevrolet

CHECKER 500

November 6
Phoenix, Arizona
Time of Race: 3 hours, 26 minutes, 57 seconds
Average Speed: 90.457 mph
Margin of Victory: 18.5 seconds

FINISH	DRIVER	CAR
1.	Alan Kulwicki	Ford
2.	Terry Labonte	Chevrolet
3.	Davey Allison	Ford
4.	Bill Elliott	Ford
5.	Rusty Wallace	Pontiac
6.	Geoff Bodine	Chevrolet
7.	Bobby Hillin	Buikc
8.	Benny Parsons	Ford
9.	Phil Parsons	Oldsmobile
10.	Sterling Marlin	Oldsmobile
11.	Dale Earnhardt	Chevrolet
12.	Harry Gant	Chevrolet
13.	Darrell Waltrip	Chevrolet
14.	Ken Schrader	Chevrolet
15.	Lake Speed	Oldsmobile
16.	Derrike Cope	Ford
17.	Kyle Petty	Ford
18.	Dave Marcis	Chevrolet
19.	Chad Little	Ford
20.	Trevor Boys	Oldsmobile
21.	Neil Bonnett	Pontiac
22.	Ernie Irvan	Pontiac
23.	Ken Bouchard	Pontiac
24.	Jimmy Means	Pontiac
25.	Brad Noffsinger	Buick
26.	Ricky Rudd	Buick
27.	Mike Alexander	Buick
28.	Michael Waltrip	Pontiac
29.	Rick Wilson	Oldsmobile
30.	Roy Smith	Ford
31.	Dale Jarrett	Oldsmobile
32.	Jim Sauter	Pontiac
33.	Gary Collins	Oldsmobile
34.	Hershel McGriff	Pontiac
35.	Richard Petty	Pontiac
36.	Mark Martin	Ford
37.	Bill Schmitt	Chevrolet
38.	Gerg Sacks	Oldsmobile
39.	Johnny Rutherford	Oldsmobile
40.	Eddie Bierschwale	Oldsmobile
41.	Joe Ruttman	Ford
42.	Jim Bown	Chevrolet
43.	Brett Bodine	Ford

ATLANTA JOURNAL 500

November 20
Atlanta, Georgia
Time of Race: 3 hours, 52 minutes, 9 seconds
Average Speed: 129.024 mph
Margin of Victory: 4.25 seconds

FINISH	DRIVER	CAR
1.	Rusty Wallace	Pontiac
2.	Davey Allison	Ford

FINISH	DRIVER	CAR
3.	Mike Alexander	Buick
4.	Ricky Rudd	Buick
5.	Darrell Waltrip	Chevrolet
6.	Ken Schrader	Chevrolet
7.	Michael Waltrip	Pontiac
8.	Terry Labonte	Chevrolet
9.	Bobby Hillin	Buick
10.	Cale Yarborough	Oldsmobile
11.	Bill Elliott	Ford
12.	Sterling Marlin	Oldsmobile
13.	Neil Bonnett	Pontiac
14.	Dale Earnhardt	Chevrolet
15.	Geoff Bodine	Chevrolet
16.	Phil Parsons	Oldsmobile
17.	Rick Wilson	Oldsmobile
18.	Ernie Irvan	Pontiac
19.	Dave Marcis	Chevrolet
20.	Mark Martin	Ford
21.	Larry Pearson	Chevrolet
22.	Kyle Petty	Ford
23.	Jim Sauter	Oldsmobile
24.	Eddie Bierschwale	Oldsmobile
25.	Alan Kulwicki	Ford
26.	Brad Noffsinger	Buick
27.	Brett Bodine	Ford
28.	Greg Sacks	Oldsmobile
29.	Rodney Combs	Buick
30.	Harry Gant	Chevrolet
31.	A. J. Foyt	Oldsmobile
32.	Jimmy Horton	Ford
33.	Derrike Cope	Ford
34.	Benny Parsons	Ford
35.	H. B. Bailey	Pontiac
36.	Richard Petty	Pontiac
37.	Lake Speed	Oldsmobile
38.	Jimmy Means	Pontiac
39.	Brad Teague	Chevrolet
40.	Morgan Shepherd	Pontiac
41.	Dale Jarrett	Buick
42.	Tommy Ellis	Buick

1989

DAYTONA 500

February 19
Daytona Beach, Florida
Time of Race: 3 hours, 22 minutes, 4 seconds
Average Speed: 148.466 mph
Margin of Victory: 6 seconds

FINISH	DRIVER	CAR
1.	Darrell Waltrip	Chevrolet
2.	Ken Schrader	Chevrolet
3.	Dale Earnhardt	Chevrolet
4.	Geoff Bodine	Chevrolet
5.	Phil Parsons	Oldsmobile
6.	Rick Mast	Chevrolet
7.	Alan Kulwicki	Ford
8.	Rick Wilson	Oldsmobile
9.	Terry Labonte	Ford
10.	Eddie Bierschwale	Oldsmobile
11.	Sterling Marlin	Oldsmobile
12.	Harry Gant	Oldsmobile
13.	Joe Ruttman	Pontiac
14.	Larry Pearson	Buick
15.	Morgan Shepherd	Pontiac
16.	Ken Bouchard	Pontiac
17.	Richard Petty	Pontiac
18.	Rusty Wallace	Pontiac
19.	Ricky Rudd	Buick
20.	Dave Marcis	Chevrolet
21.	Michael Waltrip	Pontiac
22.	Ben Hess	Oldsmobile
23.	Greg Sacks	Pontiac
24.	J. D. McDuffie	Pontiac
25.	Davey Allison	Ford

26.	Lee Raymond	Ford
27.	Mike Alexander	Buick
28.	Ronnie Sandora	Chevrolet
29.	Brett Bodine	Ford
30.	Lake Speed	Oldsmobile
31.	Phil Barkdoll	Oldsmobile
32.	Dale Jarrett	Pontiac
33.	Mark Martin	Ford
34.	Mickey Gibbs	Pontiac
35.	Bill Elliott	Ford
36.	Chad Little	Ford
37.	Rodney Combs	Pontiac
38.	A. J. Foyt	Oldsmobile
39.	Bobby Hillin	Buick
40.	Charlie Baker	Chevrolet
41.	Ernie Irvan	Pontiac
42.	Neil Bonnett	Ford

GOODWRENCH 500

March 5
Rockingham, North Carolina
Time of Race: 4 hours, 20 minutes, 47 seconds
Average Speed: 115.122 mph
Margin of Victory: 1.6 seconds

FINISH	DRIVER	CAR
1.	Rusty Wallace	Pontiac
2.	Alan Kulwicki	Ford
3.	Dale Earnhardt	Chevrolet
4.	Geoff Bodine	Chevrolet
5.	Mark Martin	Ford
6.	Davey Allison	Ford
7.	Sterling Marlin	Oldsmobile
8.	Lake Speed	Oldsmobile
9.	Greg Sacks	Pontiac
10.	Jim Sauter	Pontiac
11.	Dale Jarrett	Pontiac
12.	Michael Waltrip	Pontiac
13.	Dick Trickle	Buick
14.	Neil Bonnett	Ford
15.	Bobby Hillin	Buick
16.	Richard Petty	Pontiac
17.	Rick Wilson	Oldsmobile
18.	Terry Labonte	Ford
19.	Bill Elliott	Ford
20.	Mickey Gibbs	Pontiac
21.	Rick Mast	Chevrolet
22.	Ben Hess	Oldsmobile
23.	Ernie Irvan	Pontiac
24.	Dave Mader III	Pontiac
25.	Ken Schrader	Chevrolet
26.	Eddie Bierschwale	Oldsmobile
27.	Morgan Shepherd	Pontiac
28.	Jerry O'Neil	Chevrolet
29.	Darrell Waltrip	Chevrolet
30.	Larry Pearson	Buick
31.	Harry Gant	Oldsmobile
32.	Ricky Rudd	Buick
33.	Jimmy Means	Pontiac
34.	Brett Bodine	Ford
35.	Dave Marcis	Chevrolet
36.	Jim Bown	Chevrolet
37.	J. D. McDuffie	Pontiac
38.	Ken Bouchard	Pontiac
39.	Phil Parsons	Oldsmobile
40.	Rodney Combs	Buick
41.	Hut Stricklin	Pontiac
42.	Butch Miller	Chevrolet

MOTORCRAFT QUALITY PARTS 500

March 19
Atlanta, Georgia
Time of Race: 3 hours, 34 minutes, 26 seconds
Average Speed: 139.684 mph
Margin of Victory: .65 second

FINISH	DRIVER	CAR
1.	Darrell Waltrip	Chevrolet
2.	Dale Earnhardt	Chevrolet
3.	Dick Tricke	Buick
4.	Kyle Petty	Pontiac
5.	Sterling Marlin	Oldsmobile
6.	Rick Wilson	Oldsmobile
7.	Neil Bonnett	Ford
8.	Hut Stricklin	Pontiac
9.	Dale Jarrett	Pontiac
10.	Morgan Shepherd	Pontiac
11.	Bill Elliott	Ford
12.	Ernie Irvan	Pontiac
13.	Jimmy Horton	Pontiac
14.	Phil Parsons	Oldsmobile
15.	Ken Schrader	Chevrolet
16.	Alan Kulwicki	Ford
17.	Ben Hess	Oldsmobile
18.	Jimmy Means	Pontiac
19.	Geoff Bodine	Chevrolet
20.	Michael Waltrip	Pontiac
21.	Lake Speed	Oldsmobile
22.	Larry Pearson	Buick
23.	Eddie Bierschwale	Oldsmobile
24.	Ricky Rudd	Buick
25.	Rick Mast	Chevrolet
26.	Greg Sacks	Pontiac
27.	Richard Petty	Pontiac
28.	A. J. Foyt	Oldsmobile
29.	Harry Gant	Oldsmobile
30.	Bobby Hillin	Buick
31.	Rusty Wallace	Pontiac
32.	Jim Sauter	Pontiac
33.	Brett Bodine	Ford
34.	Derrike Cope	Pontiac
35.	Chad Little	Ford
36.	Terry Labonte	Ford
37.	Ken Bouchard	Pontiac
38.	Mark Martin	Ford
39.	Mickey Gibbs	Pontiac
40.	Davey Allison	Ford
41.	Jimmy Bown	Chevrolet
42.	Dave Marcis	Chevrolet

PONTIAC EXCITEMENT 400

March 26
Richmond, Vriginia
Time of Race: 3 hours, 20 minutes, 51 seconds
Average Speed: 89.619 mph
Margin of Victory: 2.8 seconds

FINISH	DRIVER	CAR
1.	Rusty Wallace	Pontiac
2.	Alan Kulwicki	Ford
3.	Dale Earnhardt	Chevrolet
4.	Ricky Rudd	Buick
5.	Davey Allison	Ford
6.	Larry Pearson	Buick
7.	Darrell Waltrip	Chevrolet
8.	Sterling Marlin	Oldsmobile
9.	Ernie Irvan	Pontiac
10.	Bill Elliott	Ford
11.	Mark Martin	Ford
12.	Lake Speed	Ford
13.	Michael Waltrip	Pontiac
14.	Harry Gant	Oldsmobile
15.	Bobby Hillin	Buick
16.	Rick Mast	Chevrolet
17.	Rick Wilson	Oldsmobile
18.	Geoff Bodine	Chevrolet
19.	Ken Schrader	Chevrolet
20.	Dave Marcis	Chevrolet
21.	Neil Bonnett	Ford
22.	Chad Little	Ford
23.	Dale Jarrett	Pontiac
24.	Ben Hess	Oldsmobile
25.	Dick Trickle	Buick
26.	Butch Miller	Chevrolet

27.	Phil Parsons	Oldsmobile
28.	Brett Bodine	Ford
29.	Mickey Gibbs	Pontiac
30.	Terry Labonte	Chevrolet
31.	Eddie Bierschwale	Oldsmobile
32.	Rodney Combs	Buick
33.	Morgan Shepherd	Pontiac
34.	Greg Sacks	Pontiac
35.	Derrike Cope	Pontiac
36.	Jim Sauter	Oldsmobile

TRANSOUTH 500

April 2
Darlington, South Carolina
Time of Race: 4 hours, 20 minutes, 29 seconds
Average Speed: 115.475 mph
Margin of Victory: 1.05 second

FINISH	DRIVER	CAR
1.	Harry Gant	Oldsmobile
2.	Davey Allison	Ford
3.	Geoff Bodine	Chevrolet
4.	Mark Martin	Ford
5.	Sterling Marlin	Oldsmobile
6.	Bill Elliott	Ford
7.	Alan Kulwicki	Ford
8.	Rusty Wallace	Pontiac
9.	Michael Waltrip	Pontiac
10.	Lake Speed	Oldsmobile
11.	Rick Wilson	Oldsmobile
12.	Ricky Rudd	Buick
13.	Dick Trickle	Buick
14.	Brett Bodine	Ford
15.	Richard Petty	Pontiac
16.	Morgan Shepherd	Pontiac
17.	Dave Marcis	Chevrolet
18.	Terry Labonte	Ford
19.	Jim Sauter	Pontiac
20.	Larry Pearson	Buick
21.	Eddie Bierschwale	Oldsmobile
22.	Ken Bouchard	Pontiac
23.	Ben Hess	Oldsmobile
24.	Ernie Irvan	Pontiac
25.	Greg Sacks	Pontiac
26.	Bobby Hillin	Buick
27.	Ken Schrader	Chevrolet
28.	Kyle Petty	Pontiac
29.	Rodney Combs	Pontiac
30.	Hut Stricklin	Pontiac
31.	J. D. McDuffie	Pontiac
32.	Jimmy Horton	Pontiac
33.	Dale Earnhardt	Chevrolet
34.	Rick Mast	Chevrolet
35.	Derrke Cope	Pontiac
36.	Darrell Waltrip	Chevrolet
37.	Chad Little	Ford
38.	Jimmy Means	Pontiac
39.	Neil Bonnett	Ford
40.	Dale Jarrett	Pontiac
41.	Phil Parsons	Oldsmobile

VALLEYDALE MEATS 500

April 9
Bristol, Tennessee
Time of Race: 3 hours, 30 minutes, 18 seconds
Average Speed: 76.034 mph
Margin of Victory: .26 second

FINISH	DRIVER	CAR
1.	Rusty Wallace	Pontiac
2.	Darrell Waltrip	Chevrolet
3.	Geoff Bodine	Chevrolet

4.	Davey Allison	Ford
5.	Dick Trickle	Buick
6.	Mark Martin	Ford
7.	Greg Sacks	Pontiac
8.	Ricky Rudd	Buick
9.	Bill Elliott	Ford
10.	Harry Gant	Oldsmobile
11.	Michael Waltrip	Pontiac
12.	Neil Bonnett	Ford
13.	Jim Sauter	Pontiac
14.	Rick Mast	Chevrolet
15.	Sterling Marlin	Oldsmobile
16.	Dale Earnhardt	Chevrolet
17.	Brad Teague	Pontiac
18.	Larry Pearson	Buick
19.	Eddie Bierschwale	Oldsmobile
20.	Alan Kulwicki	Ford
21.	Rick Wilson	Oldsmobile
22.	Dale Jarrett	Pontiac
23.	Phil Parsons	Oldsmobile
24.	Terry Labonte	Ford
25.	Lake Speed	Oldsmobile
26.	Morgan Shepherd	Pontiac
27.	Bobby Hillin	Buick
28.	Hut Stricklin	Pontiac
29.	Ernie Irvan	Pontiac
30.	Brett Bodine	Ford
31.	Butch Miller	Chevrolet
32.	Ken Schrader	Chevrolet

FIRST UNION 400

April 16
North Wilkesboro, North Carolina
Time of Race: 2 hours, 46 minutes, 47 seconds
Average Speed: 89.937 mph
Margin of Victory: 3 seconds

FINISH	DRIVER	CAR
1.	Dale Earnhardt	Chevrolet
2.	Alan Kulwicki	Ford
3.	Mark Martin	Ford
4.	Dick Trickle	Buick
5.	Terry Labonte	Ford
6.	Ricky Rudd	Buick
7.	Geoff Bodine	Chevrolet
8.	Darrell Waltrip	Chevrolet
9.	Rusty Wallace	Pontiac
10.	Ernie Irvan	Pontiac
11.	Davey Allison	Ford
12.	Phil Parsons	Chevrolet
13.	Neil Bonnett	Ford
14.	Ken Schrader	Chevrolet
15.	Ben Hess	Oldsmobile
16.	Hut Stricklin	Pontiac
17.	Morgan Shepherd	Pontiac
18.	Eddie Bierschwale	Oldsmobile
19.	Dale Jarrett	Pontiac
20.	Dave Marcis	Chevrolet
21.	Greg Sacks	Pontiac
22.	Bill Elliott	Ford
23.	Harry Gant	Oldsmobile
24.	Larry Pearson	Buick
25.	Rick Mast	Chevrolet
26.	Sterling Marlin	Oldsmobile
27.	Lake Speed	Oldsmobile
28.	Brett Bodine	Ford
29.	Michael Waltrip	Pontiac
30.	Rick Wilson	Oldsmobile
31.	Jim Sauter	Oldsmobile
32.	Jimmy Means	Pontiac

PANNILL SWEATSHIRTS 500

April 23
Martinsville, Virginia
Time of Race: 3 hours, 19 minutes, 41 seconds

Average Speed: 79.025 mph
Margin of Victory: 6.79 seconds

FINISH	DRIVER	CAR
1.	Darrell Waltrip	Chevrolet
2.	Dale Earnhardt	Chevrolet
3.	Dick Trickle	Buick
4.	Rick Wilson	Oldsmobile
5.	Terry Labonte	Ford
6.	Mark Martin	Ford
7.	Ken Schrader	Chevrolet
8.	Sterling Marlin	Oldsmobile
9.	Dave Marcis	Chevrolet
10.	Neil Bonnett	Ford
11.	Lake Speed	Oldsmobile
12.	Harry Gant	Oldsmobile
13.	Phil Parsons	Oldsmobile
14.	Davey Allison	Ford
15.	Dale Jarrett	Pontiac
16.	Geoff Bodine	Chevrolet
17.	Ben Hess	Oldsmobile
18.	Morgan Shepherd	Pontiac
19.	Ernie Irvan	Pontiac
20.	Bill Elliott	Ford
21.	Bobby Hillin	Buick
22.	Alan Kulwicki	Ford
23.	Ricky Rudd	Buick
24.	Richard Petty	Pontiac
25.	Michael Waltrip	Pontiac
26.	Chad Little	Ford
27.	Brett Bodine	Ford
28.	Greg Sacks	Pontiac
29.	Larry Pearson	Buick
30.	Hut Stricklin	Pontiac
31.	Rusty Wallace	Pontiac
32.	Rick Mast	Chevrolet

WINSTON 500

May 7
Talladega, Alabama
Time of Race: 3 hours, 12 minutes, 30 seconds
Average Speed: 155.869 mph
Margin of Victory: 1 car length

FINISH	DRIVER	CAR
1.	Davey Allison	Ford
2.	Terry Labonte	Ford
3.	Mark Martin	Ford
4.	Morgan Shepherd	Pontiac
5.	Darrell Waltrip	Chevrolet
6.	Ken Schrader	Chevrolet
7.	Harry Gant	Oldsmobile
8.	Dale Earnhardt	Chevrolet
9.	Neil Bonnett	Ford
10.	Rusty Wallace	Pontiac
11.	Bill Elliott	Ford
12.	Geoff Bodine	Chevrolet
13.	Alan Kulwicki	Ford
14.	Sterling Marlin	Oldsmobile
15.	Rick Wilson	Oldsmobile
16.	A. J. Foyt	Oldsmobile
17.	Phil Parsons	Oldsmobile
18.	Lake Speed	Oldsmobile
19.	Brett Bodine	Ford
20.	Dave Marcis	Chevrolet
21.	Michael Waltrip	Pontiac
22.	Ben Hess	Oldsmobile
23.	Richard Petty	Pontiac
24.	Grant Adcox	Chevrolet
25.	Ernie Irvan	Pontiac
26.	Charlie Baker	Buick
27.	Dick Trickle	Buick
28.	Kyle Petty	Pontiac
29.	Larry Pearson	Buick
30.	Derrike Cope	Pontiac
31.	Ricky Rudd	Buick
32.	Phil Barkdoll	Oldsmobile

33.	Hut Stricklin	Pontiac
34.	Chad Little	Ford
35.	Bobby Hillin Jr.	Buick
36.	Jim Sauter	Pontiac
37.	Greg Sacks	Pontiac
38.	Ron Esau	Pontiac
39.	Eddie Bierschwale	Oldsmobile
40.	Dale Jarrett	Pontiac
41.	Jimmy Means	Pontiac

COCA-COLA 600

May 28
Charlotte, North Carolina
Time of Race: 4 hours, 9 minutes, 52 seconds
Average Speed: 144.077 mph
Margin of Victory: .99 second

FINISH	DRIVER	CAR
1.	Darrell Waltrip	Chevrolet
2.	Sterling Marlin	Oldsmobile
3.	Ken Schrader	Chevrolet
4.	Geoff Bodine	Chevrolet
5.	Bill Elliott	Ford
6.	Mark Martin	Ford
7.	Neil Bonnett	Ford
8.	Brett Bodine	Ford
9.	Bobby Hillin	Buick
10.	Ricky Rudd	Buick
11.	Rick Mast	Chevrolet
12.	Derrike Cope	Pontiac
13.	Phil Parsons	Oldsmobile
14.	Hut Stricklin	Pontiac
15.	Ernie Irvan	Pontiac
16.	Dave Marcis	Chevrolet
17.	Kyle Petty	Chevrolet
18.	Chad Little	Ford
19.	Richard Petty	Pontiac
20.	Ben Hess	Oldsmobile
21.	Terry Byers	Chevrolet
22.	Larry Pearson	Buick
23.	Alan Kulwicki	Ford
24.	Lake Speed	Oldsmobile
25.	Tracy Leslie	Oldsmobile
26.	Jerry O'Neil	Chevrolet
27.	Michael Waltrip	Pontiac
28.	Dale Jarrett	Pontiac
29.	Dick Trickle	Buick
30.	Greg Sacks	Pontiac
31.	Rusty Wallace	Pontiac
32.	Morgan Shepherd	Pontiac
33.	Davey Allison	Ford
34.	Allan Grice	Pontiac
35.	Rick Wilson	Oldsmobile
36.	Eddie Bierschwale	Oldsmobile
37.	Jim Sauter	Pontiac
38.	Dale Earnhardt	Chevrolet
39.	Terry Labonte	Ford
40.	Harry Gant	Oldsmobile
41.	Jimmy Means	Pontiac
42.	Butch Miller	Chevrolet

BUDWEISER 500

June 4
Dover, Delaware
Time of Race: 4 hours, 6 minutes, 34 seconds
Average Speed: 121.670 mph
Margin of Victory: .51 second

FINISH	DRIVER	CAR
1.	Dale Earnhardt	Chevrolet
2.	Mark Martin	Ford
3.	Ken Schrader	Chevrolet

4.	Terry Labonte	Ford
5.	Rusty Wallace	Pontiac
6.	Ricky Rudd	Buick
7.	Neil Bonnett	Ford
8.	Bill Elliott	Ford
9.	Darrell Waltrip	Chevrolet
10.	Phil Parsons	Oldsmobile
11.	Dale Jarrett	Pontiac
12.	Hut Stricklin	Pontiac
13.	Bobby Hillin	Buick
14.	Rick Wilson	Oldsmobile
15.	Brett Bodine	Ford
16.	Dave Marcis	Chevrolet
17.	Ernie Irvan	Pontiac
18.	Lake Speed	Oldsmobile
19.	Larry Pearson	Buick
20.	Richard Petty	Pontiac
21.	Dick Trickle	Buick
22.	Michael Waltrip	Pontiac
23.	Harry Gant	Oldsmobile
24.	Jimmy Means	Pontiac
25.	Alan Kulwicki	Ford
26.	Sterling Marlin	Oldsmobile
27.	Eddie Bierschwale	Oldsmobile
28.	Derrike Cope	Pontiac
29.	Geoff Bodine	Chevrolet
30.	Norm Benning	Chevrolet
31.	Jimmy Horton	Pontiac
32.	Davey Allison	Ford
33.	Morgan Shepherd	Pontiac
34.	Jimmy Spencer	Pontiac
35.	Bill Flowers	Buick

BANQUET FROZEN FOODS 300

June 11
Sonoma, California
Time of Race: 2 hours, 27 minutes, 3 seconds
Average Speed: 76.088 mph
Margin of Victory: .05 second

FINISH	DRIVER	CAR
1.	Ricky Rudd	Buick
2.	Rusty Wallace	Pontiac
3.	Bill Elliott	Ford
4.	Dale Earnhardt	Chevrolet
5.	Lake Speed	Oldsmobile
6.	Joe Ruttman	Pontiac
7.	Morgan Shepherd	Pontiac
8.	Rick Wilson	Oldsmobile
9.	Davey Allison	Ford
10.	Michael Waltrip	Pontiac
11.	Neil Bonnett	Ford
12.	Harry Gant	Oldsmobile
13.	Bobby Hillin	Buick
14.	Hershel McGriff	Pontiac
15.	Terry Labonte	Ford
16.	Dave Marcis	Chevrolet
17.	Bill Schmitt	Chevrolet
18.	Phil Parsons	Oldsmobile
19.	Larry Pearson	Buick
20.	Geoff Bodine	Chevrolet
21.	Hut Stricklin	Pontiac
22.	Darin Brassfield	Chevrolet
23.	Ernie Irvan	Pontiac
24.	Troy Beebe	Buick
25.	Terry Fisher	Chevrolet
26.	Richard Petty	Pontiac
27.	Brett Bodine	Ford
28.	Rick McCray	Pontiac
29.	Jim Bown	Chevrolet
30.	Dick Trickle	Buick
31.	Mark Martin	Ford
32.	Dick Johnson	Ford
33.	John Krebs	Pontiac
34.	Eddie Bierschwale	Oldsmobile
35.	Bill Cooper	Ford
36.	Alan Kulwicki	Ford
37.	Ken Schrader	Chevrolet
38.	Darrell Waltrip	Chevrolet

39.	Roy Smith	Ford
40.	Sterling Marlin	Oldsmobile
41.	Ron Esau	Oldsmobile
42.	Dale Jarrett	Pontiac

MILLER HIGH LIFE 500

June 18
Pocono, Pennsylvania
Time of Race: 3 hours, 48 minutes, 27 seconds
Average Speed: 131.320 mph
Margin of Victory: 2 seconds

FINISH	DRIVER	CAR
1.	Terry Labonte	Ford
2.	Harry Gant	Oldsmobile
3.	Dale Earnhardt	Chevrolet
4.	Ken Schrader	Chevrolet
5.	Morgan Shepherd	Pontiac
6.	Sterling Marlin	Oldsmobile
7.	Dale Jarrett	Pontiac
8.	Neil Bonnett	Ford
9.	Larry Pearson	Buick
10.	Brett Bodine	Ford
11.	Lake Speed	Oldsmobile
12.	Phil Parsons	Oldsmobile
13.	Bobby Hillin	Buick
14.	Michael Waltrip	Pontiac
15.	Mark Martin	Ford
16.	Davey Allison	Ford
17.	Hut Stricklin	Pontiac
18.	Dave Marcis	Chevrolet
19.	Terry Byers	Chevrolet
20.	Ricky Rudd	Buick
21.	Bill Elliott	Ford
22.	Rusty Wallace	Pontiac
23.	Bobby Gerhart	Oldsmobile
24.	Dick Trickle	Buick
25.	Richard Petty	Pontiac
26.	Ernie Irvan	Pontiac
27.	Rick Wilson	Oldsmobile
28.	Randy LaJoie	Chevrolet
29.	Jimmy Means	Pontiac
30.	Norm Benning	Chevrolet
31.	Trevor Boys	Buick
32.	Darrell Waltrip	Chevrolet
33.	Jimmy Spencer	Pontiac
34.	Alan Kulwicki	Ford
35.	Geoff Bodine	Chevrolet
36.	Derrike Cope	Pontiac
37.	Jimmy Horton	Pontiac
38.	Tommie Crozier	Chevrolet

MILLER HIGH LIFE 400

June 25
Brooklyn, Michigan
Time of Race: 2 hours, 52 minutes, 38 seconds
Average Speed: 139.023 mph
Margin of Victory: 2.09 seconds

FINISH	DRIVER	CAR
1.	Bill Elliott	Ford
2.	Rusty Wallace	Pontiac
3.	Darrell Waltrip	Chevrolet
4.	Ricky Rudd	Buick
5.	Brett Bodine	Ford
6.	Rick Wilson	Oldsmobile
7.	Lake Speed	Oldsmobile
8.	Sterling Marlin	Oldsmobile
9.	Derrike Cope	Pontiac
10.	Kyle Petty	Pontiac
11.	Ken Schrader	Chevrolet
12.	Mark Martin	Ford

13.	Jimmy Spencer	Pontiac
14.	Terry Labonte	Ford
15.	Phil Parsons	Oldsmobile
16.	Michael Waltrip	Pontiac
17.	Dale Earnhardt	Chevrolet
18.	Ernie Irvan	Pontiac
19.	Larry Pearson	Buick
20.	Bobby Hillin	Buick
21.	Dave Marcis	Chevrolet
22.	Dale Jarrett	Pontiac
23.	Ronnie Thomas	Ford
24.	Neil Bonnett	Ford
25.	Dick Trickle	Buick
26.	H. B. Bailey	Pontiac
27.	Geoff Bodine	Chevrolet
28.	Jimmy Means	Pontiac
29.	Eddie Bierschwale	Oldsmobile
30.	Richard Petty	Pontiac
31.	Davey Allison	Ford
32.	Harry Gant	Oldsmobile
33.	Hut Stricklin	Pontiac
34.	Mike Miller	Chevrolet
35.	Morgan Shepherd	Pontiac
36.	Alan Kulwicki	Ford
37.	Bill Venturini	Chevrolet
38.	Butch Miller	Chevrolet
39.	Greg Sacks	Pontiac
40.	Rodney Combs	Pontiac

PEPSI 400

July 1
Daytona Beach, Florida
Time of Race: 3 hours, 1 minute, 32 seconds
Average Speed: 132.207 mph
Margin of Victory: .18 second

FINISH	DRIVER	CAR
1.	Davey Allison	Ford
2.	Morgan Shepherd	Pontiac
3.	Phil Parsons	Oldsmobile
4.	Bill Elliott	Ford
5.	Alan Kulwicki	Ford
6.	Terry Labonte	Ford
7.	Sterling Marlin	Oldsmobile
8.	Dick Trickle	Buick
9.	Ricky Rudd	Buick
10.	Hut Stricklin	Pontiac
11.	Brett Bodine	Ford
12.	Jimmy Means	Pontiac
13.	Grant Adcox	Chevrolet
14.	Kyle Petty	Pontiac
15.	Phil Barkdoll	Oldsmobile
16.	Mark Martin	Ford
17.	Rusty Wallace	Pontiac
18.	Dale Earnhardt	Chevrolet
19.	Darrell Waltrip	Chevrolet
20.	Richard Petty	Pontiac
21.	Neil Bonnett	Ford
22.	Geoff Bodine	Chevrolet
23.	Ernie Irvan	Pontiac
24.	Lake Speed	Oldsmobile
25.	Dave Marcis	Chevrolet
26.	Derrike Cope	Pontiac
27.	Jimmy Spencer	Pontiac
28.	Bobby Hillin	Buick
29.	Rick Wilson	Oldsmobile
30.	Larry Pearson	Buick
31.	Dale Jarrett	Pontiac
32.	Harry Gant	Oldsmobile
33.	Mark Gibson	Pontiac
34.	Michael Waltrip	Pontiac
35.	A. J. Foyt	Oldsmobile
36.	Ken Schrader	Chevrolet
37.	Stan Barrett	Ford
38.	Jim Sauter	Pontiac
39.	Patty Moise	Buick
40.	John McFadden	Pontiac

AC SPARK PLUG 500

July 23
Pocono, Pennsylvania
Time of Race: 4 hours, 14 minutes, 34 seconds
Average Speed: 117.847 mph
Margin of Victory: 2.21 seconds

FINISH	DRIVER	CAR
1.	Bill Elliott	Ford
2.	Rusty Wallace	Pontiac
3.	Mark Martin	Ford
4.	Darrell Waltrip	Chevrolet
5.	Harry Gant	Oldsmobile
6.	Davey Allison	Ford
7.	Ken Schrader	Chevrolet
8.	Morgan Shepherd	Pontiac
9.	Dale Earnhardt	Chevrolet
10.	Bertt Bodine	Ford
11.	Bobby Hillin	Buick
12.	Phil Parsons	Oldsmobile
13.	Terry Labonte	Ford
14.	Kyle Petty	Pontiac
15.	Jimmy Spencer	Pontiac
16.	Jim Sauter	Pontiac
17.	Geoff Bodine	Chevrolet
18.	Dale Jarrett	Pontiac
19.	Dave Marcis	Chevrolet
20.	Dick Trickle	Buick
21.	Terry Byers	Chevrolet
22.	Dick Johnson	Ford
23.	Neil Bonnett	Ford
24.	Jimmy Means	Pontiac
25.	Rick Wilson	Oldsmobile
26.	Ernie Irvan	Pontiac
27.	Bob Schacht	Ford
28.	Michael Waltrip	Pontiac
29.	Lake Speed	Oldsmobile
30.	Gerg Sacks	Pontiac
31.	Ricky Rudd	Buick
32.	Eddie Bierschwale	Chevrolet
33.	Jimmy Horton	Pontiac
34.	Joe Ruttman	Oldsmobile
35.	Derrike Cope	Pontiac
36.	Sterling Marlin	Oldsmobile
37.	Hut Stricklin	Pontiac
38.	Richard Petty	Pontiac
39.	Alan Kulwicki	Ford
40.	Larry Pearson	Buick

TALLADEGA DIEHARD 500

July 30
Talladega, Alabama
Time of Race: 3 hours, 10 minutes, 441 seconds
Average Speed: 157.354 mph
Margin of Victory: .2 second

FINISH	DRIVER	CAR
1.	Terry Labonte	Ford
2.	Darrell Waltrip	Chevrolet
3.	Mark Martin	Ford
4.	Ken Schrader	Chevrolet
5.	Rick Wilson	Oldsmobile
6.	Morgan Shepherd	Pontiac
7.	Kyle Petty	Pontiac
8.	Harry Gant	Oldsmobile
9.	Davey Allison	Ford
10.	Neil Bonnett	Ford
11.	Dale Earnhardt	Chevrolet
12.	Bill Elliott	Ford
13.	Hut Stricklin	Pontiac
14.	Brett Bodine	Ford
15.	Phil Barkdoll	Oldsmobile
16.	Dick Trickle	Buick
17.	Ricky Rudd	Buick
18.	A. J. Foyt	Oldsmobile

19.	Dave Marcis	Chevrolet
20.	Ernie Irvan	Pontiac
21.	Richard Petty	Pontiac
22.	Larry Pearson	Buick
23.	Dale Jarrett	Pontiac
24.	Dick Johnson	Ford
25.	Mickey Gibbs	Pontiac
26.	Bill Ingram	Oldsmobile
27.	Mark Stahl	Ford
28.	Sterling Marlin	Oldsmobile
29.	Bobby Hillin	Buick
30.	Alan Kulwicki	Ford
31.	Joe Ruttman	Oldsmobile
32.	Rick Mast	Chevrolet
33.	Patty Moise	Buick
34.	Stan Barrett	Ford
35.	Geoff Bodine	Chevrolet
36.	Michael Waltrip	Pontiac
37.	Rusty Wallace	Pontiac
38.	Derrike Cope	Pontiac
39.	Jimmy Means	Pontiac
40.	Jimmy Spencer	Pontiac
41.	Phil Parsons	Oldsmobile

BUDWEISER AT THE GLEN

August 13
Watkins Glen, New York
Time of Race: 2 hours, 26 minutes, 55 seconds
Average Speed: 87.242 mph
Margin of Victory: 1.06 seconds

FINISH	DRIVER	CAR
1.	Rusty Wallace	Pontiac
2.	Mark Martin	Ford
3.	Dale Earnhardt	Chevrolet
4.	Davey Allison	Ford
5.	Bobby Hillin	Buick
6.	Morgan Shepherd	Pontiac
7.	Sterling Marlin	Oldsmobile
8.	Rick Wilson	Oldsmobile
9.	Jim Sauter	Pontiac
10.	Michael Waltrip	Pontiac
11.	Larry Pearson	Buick
12.	Darin Brassfield	Chevrolet
13.	Richard Petty	Pontiac
14.	Terry Labonte	Ford
15.	Brett Bodine	Ford
16.	Darrell Waltrip	Chevrolet
17.	Phil Parsons	Oldsmobile
18.	Bill Elliott	Ford
19.	Harry Gant	Oldsmobile
20.	Ken Schrader	Chevrolet
21.	Geoff Bodine	Chevrolet
22.	Hut Stricklin	Pontiac
23.	Dale Jarrett	Pontiac
24.	Ernie Irvan	Pontiac
25.	Dave Marcis	Chevrolet
26.	Stan Barrett	Ford
27.	Tom Kendall	Chevrolet
28.	Jimmy Spencer	Pontiac
29.	Ricky Rudd	Buick
30.	Oma Kimbrough	Chevrolet
31.	Ted Thomas	Ford
32.	Dick Johnson	Ford
33.	Jimmy Means	Pontiac
34.	Dick Trickle	Buick
35.	J. D. McDuffie	Pontiac
36.	Neil Bonnett	Ford
37.	A. J. Foyt	Oldsmobile
38.	Eddie Bierschwale	Oldsmobile
39.	Alan Kulwicki	Ford
40.	Derrike Cope	Pontiac

CHAMPION SPARK PLUG 400

August 20
Brooklyn, Michigan

Time of Race: 2 hours, 32 minutes, 11 seconds
Average Speed: 157.704 mph
Margin of Victory: 15.71 seconds

FINISH	DRIVER	CAR
1.	Rusty Wallace	Pontiac
2.	Morgan Shepherd	Pontiac
3.	Harry Gant	Oldsmobile
4.	Hut Stricklin	Pontiac
5.	Geoff Bodine	Chevrolet
6.	Derrike Cope	Pontiac
7.	Davey Allison	Ford
8.	Ricky Rudd	Buick
9.	Mark Martin	Ford
10.	Alan Kulwicki	Ford
11.	Ken Schrader	Chevrolet
12.	Jimmy Spencer	Pontiac
13.	Kyle Petty	Pontiac
14.	Bobby Hillin	Buick
15.	Neil Bonnett	Ford
16.	Larry Pearson	Buick
17.	Dale Earnhardt	Chevrolet
18.	Richard Petty	Pontiac
19.	Dick Trickle	Buick
20.	Tracy Leslie	Oldsmobile
21.	Joe Ruttman	Oldsmobile
22.	Butch Miller	Chevrolet
23.	Jim Sauter	Pontiac
24.	Dave Marcis	Chevrolet
25.	Ernie Irvan	Pontiac
26.	Chad Little	Ford
27.	Jimmy Means	Pontiac
28.	Eddie Bierschwale	Oldsmobile
29.	Ken Ragan	Ford
30.	Rick Jeffrey	Pontiac
31.	Michael Waltrip	Pontiac
32.	Rick Wilson	Oldsmobile
33.	Phil Parsons	Oldsmobile
34.	Sterling Marlin	Oldsmobile
35.	Greg Sacks	Pontiac
36.	Brett Bodine	Ford
37.	Darrell Waltrip	Chevrolet
38.	Dale Jarrett	Pontiac
39.	Bill Elliott	Ford
40.	Terry Labonte	Ford

BUSCH 500

August 26
Bristol, Tennessee
Time of Race: 3 hours, 4 minutes, 14 seconds
Average Speed: 85.554 mph
Margin of Victory: 5.04 seconds

FINISH	DRIVER	CAR
1.	Darrell Waltrip	Chevrolet
2.	Alan Kulwicki	Ford
3.	Ricky Rudd	Buick
4.	Harry Gant	Oldsmobile
5.	Terry Labonte	Ford
6.	Rusty Wallace	Pontiac
7.	Bobby Hillin	Buick
8.	Jimmy Spencer	Pontiac
9.	Neil Bonnett	Ford
10.	Dale Jarrett	Pontiac
11.	Phil Parsons	Oldsmobile
12.	Dave Marcis	Chevrolet
13.	Rick Mast	Chevrolet
14.	Dale Earnhardt	Chevrolet
15.	Ernie Irvan	Pontiac
16.	Geoff Bodine	Chevrolet
17.	Brett Bodine	Ford
18.	Sterling Marlin	Oldsmobile
19.	Hut Stricklin	Pontiac
20.	Mark Martin	Ford
21.	Larry Pearson	Buick
22.	Kyle Petty	Pontiac

23.	Ken Schrader	Chevrolet
24.	Bill Elliott	Ford
25.	Davey Allison	Ford
26.	Morgan Shepherd	Pontiac
27.	Rick Wilson	Oldsmobile
28.	Dick Trickle	Buick
29.	Derrike Cope	Pontiac
30.	Greg Sacks	Pontiac
31.	Joe Ruttman	Oldsmobile
32.	Michael Waltrip	Pontiac

HEINZ SOUTHERN 500

September 3
Darlington, South Carolina
Time of Race: 3 hours, 42 minutes, 3 seconds
Average Speed: 135.462 mph
Margin of Victory: 1.5 seconds

FINISH	DRIVER	CAR
1.	Dale Earnhardt	Chevrolet
2.	Mark Martin	Ford
3.	Ricky Rudd	Buick
4.	Rusty Wallace	Pontiac
5.	Ken Schrader	Chevrolet
6.	Harry Gant	Chevrolet
7.	Bill Elliott	Ford
8.	Bobby Hillin	Buick
9.	Morgan Shepherd	Pontiac
10.	Sterling Marlin	Oldsmobile
11.	Rick Wilson	Oldsmobile
12.	Geoff Bodine	Chevrolet
13.	Michael Waltrip	Pontiac
14.	Kyle Petty	Pontiac
15.	Neil Bonnett	Ford
16.	Brett Bodine	Ford
17.	Dick Trickle	Buick
18.	Davey Allison	Ford
19.	Hut Stricklin	Pontiac
20.	Dale Jarrett	Pontiac
21.	Phil Parsons	Oldsmobile
22.	Darrell Waltrip	Chevrolet
23.	Rodney Combs	Oldsmobile
24.	Ernie Irvan	Pontiac
25.	Derrike Cope	Pontiac
26.	Jimmy Means	Pontiac
27.	H. B. Bailey	Pontiac
28.	Dave Marcis	Chevrolet
29.	Larry Pearson	Buick
30.	Joe Ruttman	Oldsmobile
31.	John McFadden	Chevrolet
32.	Alan Kulwicki	Ford
33.	Terry Labonte	Ford
34.	Mike Potter	Ford
35.	Richard Petty	Pontiac
36.	J. D. McDuffie	Pontiac
37.	Jimmy Spencer	Oldsmobile
38.	Greg Sacks	Pontiac
39.	James Hylton	Buick

MILLER HIGH LIFE 400

September 10
Richmond, Virginia
Time of Race: 3 hours, 23 minutes, 40 seconds
Average Speed: 88.380 mph
Margin of Victory: 7.41 seconds

FINISH	DRIVER	CAR
1.	Rusty Wallace	Pontiac
2.	Dale Earnhardt	Chevrolet
3.	Geoff Bodine	Chevrolet
4.	Ricky Rudd	Buick
5.	Harry Gant	Oldsmobile

6.	Darrell Waltrip	Chevrolet
7.	Neil Bonnett	Ford
8.	Dick Trickle	Buick
9.	Hut Stricklin	Pontiac
10.	Davey Allison	Ford
11.	Lennie Pond	Ford
12.	Terry Labonte	Ford
13.	Bobby Hillin	Buick
14.	Lake Speed	Oldsmobile
15.	Alan Kulwicki	Ford
16.	Dave Marcis	Chevrolet
17.	Mark Martin	Ford
18.	Bill Elliott	Ford
19.	Jimmy Means	Pontiac
20.	Larry Pearson	Buick
21.	Butch Miller	Chevrolet
22.	Rick Wilson	Oldsmobile
23.	Michael Waltrip	Pontiac
24.	Ken Schrader	Chevrolet
25.	Derrike Cope	Pontiac
26.	Ernie Irvan	Pontiac
27.	Morgan Shepherd	Pontiac
28.	Sterling Marlin	Oldsmobile
29.	Jimmy Spencer	Pontiac
30.	Darin Brassfield	Chevrolet
31.	J. D. McDuffie	Pontiac
32.	Kyle Petty	Pontiac
33.	Richard Petty	Pontiac
34.	Brett Bodine	Ford
35.	Dale Jarrett	Pontiac
36.	Phil Parsons	Oldsmobile

PEAK PERFORMANCE 500

September 17
Dover, Delaware
Time of Race: 4 hours, 4 minutes, 5 seconds
Average Speed: 122.909 mph
Margin of Victory: .28 second

FINISH	DRIVER	CAR
1.	Dale Earnhardt	Chevrolet
2.	Mark Martin	Ford
3.	Ken Schrader	Chevrolet
4.	Bill Elliott	Ford
5.	Ricky Rudd	Buick
6.	Michael Waltrip	Pontiac
7.	Rusty Wallace	Pontiac
8.	Derrike Cope	Pontiac
9.	Brett Bodine	Ford
10.	Jimmy Spencer	Pontiac
11.	Kyle Petty	Pontiac
12.	Jim Sauter	Pontiac
13.	Phil Parsons	Oldsmobile
14.	Terry Labonte	Ford
15.	Bobby Hillin	Buick
16.	Morgan Shepherd	Pontiac
17.	Sterling Marlin	Oldsmobile
18.	Darrell Waltrip	Chevrolet
19.	Rick Wilson	Oldsmobile
20.	Hut Striklin	Pontiac
21.	Jimmy Means	Pontiac
22.	Dave Marcis	Chevrolet
23.	Dale Jarrett	Pontiac
24.	Davey Allison	Ford
25.	Dick Trickle	Buick
26.	Neil Bonnett	Ford
27.	Geoff Bodine	Chevrolet
28.	Rob Moroso	Oldsmobile
29.	Andy Belmont	Ford
30.	Richard Petty	Pontiac
31.	Norm Benning	Chevrolet
32.	Alan Kulwicki	Ford
33.	Ernie Irvan	Pontiac
34.	J. D. McDuffie	Pontiac
35.	Jack Ely	Buick
36.	Lake Speed	Oldsmobile
37.	Tommie Crozier	Chevrolet
38.	Harry Gant	Oldsmobile
39.	James Hylton	Buick
40.	Larry Pearson	Buick

GOODY'S 500

September 24
Martinsville, Virginia
Time of Race: 3 hours, 26 minutes, 15 seconds
Average Speed: 76.571 mph
Margin of Victory: under caution

FINISH	DRIVER	CAR
1.	Darrel Waltrip	Chevrolet
2.	Harry Gant	Oldsmobile
3.	Dick Trickle	Buick
4.	Rusty Wallace	Pontiac
5.	Dale Jarrett	Pontiac
6.	Ernie Irvan	Pontiac
7.	Brett Bodine	Ford
8.	Ricky Rudd	Buick
9.	Dale Earnhardt	Chevrolet
10.	Ken Schrader	Chevrolet
11.	Terry Labonte	Ford
12.	Michael Waltrip	Pontiac
13.	Derrike Cope	Pontiac
14.	Phil Parsons	Oldsmobile
15.	Bill Elliott	Ford
16.	Geoff Bodine	Chevrolet
17.	Hut Stricklin	Pontiac
18.	Rick Wilson	Oldsmobile
19.	Greg Sacks	Pontiac
20.	Sterling Marlin	Oldsmobile
21.	Davey Allison	Ford
22.	Lake Speed	Oldsmobile
23.	Mark Martin	Ford
24.	Richard Petty	Pontiac
25.	Larry Pearson	Buick
26.	Alan Kulwicki	Ford
27.	Bobby Hillin	Buick
28.	Morgan Shepherd	Pontiac
29.	Tommy Ellis	Ford
30.	Kyle Petty	Pontiac
31.	Jimmy Means	Pontiac
32.	Butch Miller	Chevrolet

ALL PRO AUTO PARTS 500

October 8
Charlotte, North Carolina
Time of Race: 3 hours, 20 minutes, 35 seconds
Average Speed: 149.863 mph
Margin of Victory: 4 seconds

FINISH	DRIVER	CAR
1.	Ken Schrader	Chervrolet
2.	Harry Gant	Oldsmobile
3.	Mark Martin	Ford
4.	Bill Elliott	Ford
5.	Davey Allison	Ford
6.	Derrike Cope	Pontiac
7.	Sterling Marlin	Oldsmobile
8.	Rusty Wallace	Pontiac
9.	Bobby Hillin	Buick
10.	Morgan Shepherd	Pontiac
11.	Terry Labonte	Ford
12.	Brett Bodine	Ford
13.	Rick Mast	Chevrolet
14.	Darrell Waltrip	Chevrolet
15.	Larry Pearson	Buick
16.	Jimmy Spencer	Pontiac
17.	Michael Waltrip	Pontiac
18.	Tommy Ellis	Ford
19.	Dave Marcis	Chevrolet
20.	Phil Parsons	Oldsmobile
21.	Ricky Rudd	Buick
22.	Geoff Bodine	Chevrolet
23.	Hut Stricklin	Pontiac
24.	Dale Jarrett	Pontiac
25.	Eddie Bierschwale	Oldsmobile
26.	Mickey Gibbs	Pontiac

27.	Ken Ragan	Ford
28.	Alan Kulwicki	Ford
29.	Kyle Petty	Pontiac
30.	Dick Trickle	Buick
31.	Brad Teague	Pontiac
32.	Rodney Combs	Pontiac
33.	Ernie Irvan	Pontiac
34.	Richard Petty	Pontiac
35.	Greg Sacks	Pontiac
36.	Jerry O'Neil	Oldsmobile
37.	Jimmy Means	Pontiac
38.	Lake Speed	Oldsmobile
39.	Rich Bickle	Buick
40.	Jim Sauter	Pontiac
41.	Rick Wilson	Oldsmobile
42.	Dale Earnhardt	Chevrolet

HOLLY FARMS 400

October 15
North Wilkesboro, North Carolina
Time of Race: 2 hours, 46 minutes, 8 seconds
Average Speed: 90.289 mph
Margin of Victory: 3 seconds

FINISH	DRIVER	CAR
1.	Geoff Bodine	Chevrolet
2.	Mark Martin	Ford
3.	Terry Labonte	Ford
4.	Harry Gant	Oldsmobile
5.	Morgan Shepherd	Pontiac
6.	Bill Elliott	Ford
7.	Rusty Wallace	Pontiac
8.	Ernie Irvan	Pontiac
9.	Ricky Rudd	Buick
10.	Dale Earnhardt	Chevrolet
11.	Alan Kulwicki	Ford
12.	Dick Trickle	Buick
13.	Ken Schrader	Chevrolet
14.	Dave Marcis	Chevrolet
15.	Bobby Hillin	Buick
16.	Tommy Ellis	Ford
17.	Brett Bodine	Ford
18.	Jimmy Spencer	Pontiac
19.	Sterling Marlin	Oldsmobile
20.	Darrell Waltrip	Chevrolet
21.	Davey Allison	Ford
22.	Jimmy Means	Pontiac
23.	Michael Waltrip	Pontiac
24.	Larry Pearson	Buick
25.	Lake Speed	Oldsmobile
26.	Derrike Cope	Ford
27.	Dale Jarrett	Pontiac
28.	Phil Parsons	Oldsmobile
29.	Rick Wilson	Oldsmobile
30.	Hut Stricklin	Pontiac
31.	Kyle Petty	Pontiac
32.	Richard Petty	Pontiac

AC DELCO 500

October 22
Rockingham, North Carolina
Time of Race: 4 hours, 23 minutes, 10 seconds
Average Speed: 114.079 mph
Margin of Victory: 2.98 seconds

FINISH	DRIVER	CAR
1.	Mark Martin	Ford
2.	Rusty Wallace	Pontiac
3.	Darrell Waltrip	Chevrolet
4.	Ken Schrader	Chevrolet
5.	Dick Trickle	Buick
6.	Neil Bonnett	Ford
7.	Geoff Bodine	Chevrolet

8.	Bobby Hillin	Buick
9.	Alan Kulwicki	Ford
10.	Kyle Petty	Pontiac
11.	Derrike Cope	Pontiac
12.	Larry Pearson	Chevrolet
13.	Rick Wilson	Oldsmobile
14.	Terry Labonte	Ford
15.	Bill Elliott	Ford
16.	Ernie Irvan	Pontiac
17.	Michael Waltrip	Pontiac
18.	Greg Sacks	Pontiac
19.	Lake Speed	Oldsmobile
20.	Dale Earnhardt	Chevrolet
21.	Brett Bodine	Ford
22.	Hut Stricklin	Pontiac
23.	Sterling Marlin	Oldsmobile
24.	Phil Parsons	Oldsmobile
25.	Bob Schact	Buick
26.	Davey Allison	Ford
27.	Joe Ruttman	Oldsmobile
28.	Ricky Rudd	Buick
29.	Harry Gant	Oldsmobile
30.	Dave Marcis	Chevrolet
31.	Jimmy Means	Pontiac
32.	Jack Pennington	Chevrolet
33.	Jim Sauter	Pontiac
34.	Richard Petty	Pontiac
35.	Jimmy Spencer	Oldsmobile
36.	Morgan Shepherd	Pontiac
37.	Jimmy Bown	Buick
38.	Jerry O'Neil	Oldsmobile
39.	Dale Jarrett	Pontiac
40.	Charlie Baker	Buick

AUTOWORKS 500

November 5
Phoeniz, Arizona
Time of Race: 2 hours, 57 minutes, 8 seconds
Average Speed: 105.683 mph
Margin of Victory: 2 car lengths

FINISH	DRIVER	CAR
1.	Bill Elliott	Ford
2.	Terry Labonte	Ford
3.	Mark Martin	Ford
4.	Darrell Waltrip	Chevrolet
5.	Dale Jarrett	Pontiac
6.	Dale Earnhardt	Chevrolet
7.	Dick Trickle	Buick
8.	Harry Gant	Oldsmobile
9.	Michael Waltrip	Pontiac
10.	Jimmy Spencer	Pontiac
11.	Alan Kulwicki	Ford
12.	Morgan Shepherd	Pontiac
13.	Ken Schrader	Chevrolet
14.	Derrike Cope	Pontiac
15.	Dave Marcis	Chevrolet
16.	Rusty Wallace	Pontiac
17.	Jim Sauter	Pontiac
18.	Bobby Hillin	Buick
19.	Brett Bodine	Ford
20.	Joe Ruttman	Chevrolet
21.	Kyle Petty	Pontiac
22.	Lake Speed	Oldsmobile
23.	Hut Stricklin	Pontiac
24.	Larry Pearson	Buick
25.	Jimmy Means	Pontiac
26.	Bill Schmitt	Chevrolet
27.	Rodney Combs	Pontiac
28.	Geoff Bodine	Chevrolet
29.	Ricky Rudd	Buick
30.	Sterling Marlin	Oldsmobile
31.	Stan Barrett	Ford
32.	Bobby Hamilton	Chevrolet
33.	Ernie Irvan	Pontiac
34.	Neil Bonnett	Ford
35.	Ron Esau	Oldsmobile
36.	Bill Sedgwick	Buick
37.	Phil Parsons	Oldsmobile

38.	Greg Sacks	Chevrolet
39.	Davey Allison	Ford
40.	Rick Wilson	Oldsmobile
41.	Roy Smith	Pontiac
42.	Richard Petty	Pontiac
43.	Butch Miller	Chevrolet

ATLANTA JOURNAL 500

November 18
Atlanta, Georgia
Time of Race: 3 hours, 33 minutes, 36 seconds
Average Speed: 140.229 mph
Margin of Victory: 25.71 seconds

FINISH	DRIVER	CAR
1.	Dale Earnhardt	Chevrolet
2.	Geoff Bodine	Chevrolet
3.	Sterling Marlin	Oldsmobile
4.	Ken Schrader	Chevrolet
5.	Darrell Waltrip	Chevrolet
6.	Kyle Petty	Pontiac
7.	Bobby Hillin	Buick
8.	Morgan Shepherd	Pontiac
9.	Neil Bonnett	Ford
10.	Lake Speed	Oldsmobile
11.	Ernie Irvan	Pontiac
12.	Derrike Cope	Pontiac
13.	Alan Kulwicki	Ford
14.	Ricky Rudd	Buick
15.	Rusty Wallace	Pontiac
16.	Dale Jarrett	Pontiac
17.	Harry Gant	Oldsmobile
18.	Rick Wilson	Oldsmobile
19.	Larry Pearson	Buick
20.	Hut Stricklin	Pontiac
21.	Jim Sauter	Pontiac
22.	Rich Bickle	Buick
23.	Brett Bodine	Ford
24.	Jack Pennington	Oldsmobile
25.	Davey Allison	Ford
26.	Michael Waltrip	Pontiac
27.	Bill Elliott	Ford
28.	Richard Petty	Pontiac
29.	Greg Sacks	Pontiac
30.	Mark Martin	Ford
31.	Rick Mast	Chevrolet
32.	Grant Adcox	Oldsmobile
33.	Dave Marcis	Chevrolet
34.	Rob Moroso	Oldsmobile
35.	Dick Trickle	Buick
36.	A. J. Foyt	Oldsmobile
37.	Jimmy Spencer	Pontiac
38.	Mickey Gibbs	Ford
39.	Ken Ragan	Ford
40.	Terry Labonte	Ford
41.	Rodney Combs	Pontiac
42.	Phil Parsons	Oldsmobile

1990

DAYTONA 500

February 18
Daytona Beach, Florida
Time of Race: 3 hours, 0 minutes, 59 seconds
Average Speed: 165.761 mph
Margin of Victory: 1.5 car lengths

FINISH	DRIVER	CAR
1.	Derrike Cope	Chevrolet
2.	Terry Labonte	Oldsmobile

3.	Bill Elliott	Ford
4.	Ricky Rudd	Chevrolet
5.	Dale Earnhardt	Chevrolet
6.	Bobby Hillin	Buick
7.	Rusty Wallace	Pontiac
8.	Michael Waltrip	Pontiac
9.	Geoff Bodine	Ford
10.	Morgan Shepherd	Ford
11.	Neil Bonnett	Ford
12.	Dick Trickle	Pontiac
13.	Ernie Irvan	Ford
14.	Darrell Waltrip	Chevrolet
15.	Jimmy Spencer	Pontiac
16.	Lake Speed	Oldsmobile
17.	Brett Bodine	Buick
18.	Harry Gant	Oldsmobile
19.	Sterling Marlin	Oldsmobile
20.	Davey Allison	Ford
21.	Mark Martin	Ford
22.	Butch Miller	Chevrolet
23.	Dave Marcis	Chevrolet
24.	Kyle Petty	Pontiac
25.	Jack Pennington	Oldsmobile
26.	Joe Ruttman	Pontiac
27.	Larry Pearson	Buick
28.	Rich Bickle	Oldsmobile
29.	Jimmy Means	Pontiac
30.	Rick Wilson	Oldsmobile
31.	Jerry O'Neil	Oldsmobile
32.	Eddie Bierschwale	Oldsmobile
33.	Hut Stricklin	Chevrolet
34.	Richard Petty	Pontiac
35.	Alan Kulwicki	Ford
36.	A. J. Foyt	Oldsmobile
37.	Jimmy Horton	Oldsmobile
38.	Rob Moroso	Oldsmobile
39.	Phil Barkdoll	Oldsmobile
40.	Ken Schrader	Chevrolet
41.	Mike Alexander	Buick
42.	Phil Parsons	Oldsmobile

PONTIAC EXCITEMENT 400

February 25
Richmond, Virginia
Time of Race: 3 hours, 15 minutes, 18 seconds
Average Speed: 92.158 mph
Margin of Victory: 3 seconds

FINISH	DRIVER	CAR
1.	Mark Martin	Ford
2.	Dale Earnhardt	Chevrolet
3.	Ricky Rudd	Chevrolet
4.	Bill Elliott	Ford
5.	Dick Trickle	Pontiac
6.	Rusty Wallace	Pontiac
7.	Morgan Shepherd	Ford
8.	Brett Bodine	Buick
9.	Jimmy Spencer	Pontiac
10.	Ken Schrader	Chevrolet
11.	Kyle Petty	Pontiac
12.	Darrell Waltrip	Chevrolet
13.	Sterling Marlin	Oldsmobile
14.	Mike Alexander	Buick
15.	Rob Moroso	Oldsmobile
16.	Chad Little	Ford
17.	Dave Marcis	Chevrolet
18.	Jimmy Means	Pontiac
19.	Mickey Gibbs	Ford
20.	Davey Allison	Ford
21.	Rick Mast	Pontiac
22.	Ernie Irvan	Ford
23.	Larry Pearson	Buick
24.	Alan Kulwicki	Ford
25.	Neil Bonnett	Ford
26.	Phil Parsons	Oldsmobile
27.	Michael Waltrip	Pontiac
28.	Butch Miller	Chevrolet
29.	Derrike Cope	Chevrolet
30.	Rick Wilson	Oldsmobile

31.	Bobby Hillin	Buick
32.	Terry Labonte	Oldsmobile
33.	Geoff Bodine	Ford
34.	Bill Meacham	Oldsmobile
35.	Richard Petty	Pontiac
36.	Harry Gant	Oldsmobile

GOODWRENCH 500

March 4
Rockingham, North Carolina
Time of Race: 4 hours, 4 minutes, 21 seconds
Average Speed: 122.864 mph
Margin of Victory: 26 seconds

FINISH	DRIVER	CAR
1.	Kyle Petty	Pontiac
2.	Geoff Bodine	Ford
3.	Ken Schrader	Chevrolet
4.	Sterling Marlin	Oldsmobile
5.	Rusty Wallace	Pontiac
6.	Darrell Waltrip	Chevrolet
7.	Morgan Shepherd	Ford
8.	Jimmy Spencer	Pontiac
9.	Terry Labonte	Oldsmobile
10.	Dale Earnhardt	Chevrolet
11.	Harry Gant	Oldsmobile
12.	Derrike Cope	Chevrolet
13.	Butch Miller	Chevrolet
14.	Phil Parsons	Oldsmobile
15.	Mickey Gibbs	Ford
16.	Mike Alexander	Buick
17.	Bobby Hillin	Buick
18.	Rick Wilson	Oldsmobile
19.	Rick Mast	Pontiac
20.	Larry Pearson	Buick
21.	Jimmy Means	Pontiac
22.	Dave Marcis	Chevrolet
23.	Dick Trickle	Pontiac
24.	Mark Stahl	Ford
25.	Brett Bodine	Buick
26.	Mark Martin	Ford
27.	Alan Kulwicki	Ford
28.	Michael Waltrip	Pontiac
29.	Ernie Irvan	Ford
30.	Rob Moroso	Oldsmobile
31.	Ricky Rudd	Chevrolet
32.	Richard Petty	Pontiac
33.	Bill Elliott	Ford
34.	Davey Allison	Ford
35.	J. D. McDuffie	Pontiac
36.	Neil Bonnett	Ford
37.	Charlie Baker	Buick
38.	J. T. Hayes	Ford

MOTORCRAFT QUALITY PARTS 500

March 18
Atlanta, Georgia
Time of Race: 3 hours, 10 minutes, 58 seconds
Average Speed: 156.849 mph
Margin of Victory: 32 seconds

FINISH	DRIVER	CAR
1.	Dale Earnhardt	Chevrolet
2.	Morgan Shepherd	Ford
3.	Ernie Irvan	Oldsmobile
4.	Ken Schrader	Chevrolet
5.	Mark Martin	Ford
6.	Kyle Petty	Pontiac
7.	Geoff Bodine	Ford
8.	Alan Kulwicki	Ford
9.	Harry Gant	Oldsmobile
10.	Sterling Marlin	Oldsmobile

11.	Brett Bodine	Buick
12.	Bill Elliott	Ford
13.	Davey Allison	Ford
14.	Dick Trickle	Pontiac
15.	Jimmy Spencer	Pontiac
16.	Bobby Hillin	Buick
17.	Rick Wilson	Oldsmobile
18.	Neil Bonnett	Ford
19.	Chad Little	Ford
20.	Butch Miller	Chevrolet
21.	Buddy Baker	Ford
22.	Dave Marcis	Chevrolet
23.	Mike Alexander	Buick
24.	Rusty Wallace	Pontiac
25.	Richard Petty	Pontiac
26.	Darrell Waltrip	Chevrolet
27.	Ricky Rudd	Chevrolet
28.	Mark Stahl	Ford
29.	Derrike Cope	Chevrolet
30.	Jack Pennington	Oldsmobile
31.	Jimmy Means	Pontiac
32.	H. B. Bailey	Pontiac
33.	Rob Moroso	Oldsmobile
34.	Larry Pearson	Buick
35.	Rick Mast	Pontiac
36.	Ken Ragan	Ford
37.	Hut Stricklin	Pontiac
38.	Michael Waltrip	Pontiac
39.	Mickey Gibbs	Ford
40.	Terry Labonte	Oldsmobile

TRANSOUTH 500

April 1
Darlington, South Carolina
Time of Race: 4 hours, 20 minutes, 26 seconds
Average Speed: 124.073 mph
Margin of Victory: 25 seconds

FINISH	DRIVER	CAR
1.	Dale Earnhardt	Chevrolet
2.	Mark Martin	Ford
3.	Davey Allison	Ford
4.	Geoff Bodine	Ford
5.	Morgan Shepherd	Ford
6.	Harry Gant	Oldsmobile
7.	Bill Elliott	Ford
8.	Brett Bodine	Buick
9.	Michael Waltrip	Pontiac
10.	Ken Schrader	Chevrolet
11.	Darrell Waltrip	Chevrolet
12.	Bobby Hillin	Buick
13.	Kyle Petty	Pontiac
14.	Terry Labonte	Oldsmobile
15.	Dave Marcis	Chevrolet
16.	Chad Liffle	Ford
17.	Butch Miller	Chevrolet
18.	Rusty Wallace	Pontiac
19.	Mike Alexander	Buick
20.	Jack Pennington	Oldsmobile
21.	Richard Petty	Pontiac
22.	Dick Trickle	Pontiac
23.	Alan Kulwicki	Ford
24.	Ricky Rudd	Chevrolet
25.	Jimmy Spencer	Pontiac
26.	Ron Moroso	Oldsmobile
27.	Derrike Cope	Chevrolet
28.	Sterling Marlin	Oldsmobile
29.	Rick Wilson	Oldsmobile
30.	Neil Bonnett	Ford
31.	Jimmy Means	Pontiac
32.	Ernie Irvan	Oldsmobile
33.	H. B. Bailey	Pontiac
34.	Dick Johnson	Ford
35.	J. D. McDuffie	Pontiac
36.	Hut Stricklin	Chevrolet
37.	Greg Sacks	Chevrolet
38.	Mickey Gibbs	Chevrolet
39.	Rick Mast	Pontiac
40.	Buddy Baker	Ford

VALLEYDALE MEATS 500

April 8
Brisol, Tennessee
Time of Race: 3 hours, 3 minutes, 15 seconds
Average Speed: 87.258 mph
Margin of Victory: 8 inches

FINISH	DRIVER	CAR
1.	Davey Allison	Ford
2.	Mark Martin	Ford
3.	Ricky Rudd	Chevrolet
4.	Terry Labonte	Oldsmobile
5.	Rick Wilson	Oldsmobile
6.	Ken Schrader	Chevrolet
7.	Sterling Marlin	Oldsmobile
8.	Morgan Shepherd	Ford
9.	Darrell Waltrip	Chevrolet
10.	Kyle Petty	Pontiac
11.	Dale Jarrett	Ford
12.	Rick Mast	Pontiac
13.	Dick Trickle	Pontiac
14.	Butch Miller	Chevrolet
15.	Dave Marcis	Chevrolet
16.	Ernie Irvan	Oldsmobile
17.	Bill Elliott	Ford
18.	Jimmy Spencer	Pontiac
19.	Dale Earnhardt	Chevrolet
20.	Michael Waltrip	Pontiac
21.	Bobby Hillin	Buick
22.	Brett Bodine	Buick
23.	Mike Alexander	Buick
24.	Geoff Bodine	Ford
25.	Phil Parsons	Oldsmobile
26.	Richard Petty	Pontiac
27.	J. D. McDuffie	Pontiac
28.	Rusty Wallace	Pontiac
29.	Jimmy Means	Pontiac
30.	Rob Moroso	Oldsmobile
31.	Alan Kulwicki	Ford
32.	Derrike Cope	Chevrolet

FIRST UNION 400

April 22
North Wilkesboro, North Carolina
Time of Race: 2 hours, 58 minutes, 46 seconds
Average Speed: 83.908 mph
Margin of Victory: 95 seconds

FINISH	DRIVER	CAR
1.	Brett Bodine	Buick
2.	Darrell Waltrip	Chevrolet
3.	Dale Earnhardt	Chevrolet
4.	Ricky Rudd	Chevrolet
5.	Morgan Shepherd	Ford
6.	Mark Martin	Ford
7.	Rusty Wallace	Pontiac
8.	Geoff Bodine	Ford
9.	Davey Allison	Ford
10.	Kyle Petty	Pontiac
11.	Alan Kulwicki	Ford
12.	Dave Marcis	Chevrolet
13.	Harry Gant	Oldsmobile
14.	Dale Jarrett	Ford
15.	Terry Labonte	Oldsmobile
16.	Ernie Irvan	Oldsmobile
17.	Mike Alexander	Buick
18.	Bill Elliott	Ford
19.	Ken Schrader	Chevrolet
20.	Jimmy Spencer	Pontiac
21.	Derrike Cope	Chevrolet
22.	Rick Wilson	Oldsmobile
23.	Rick Mast	Chevrolet
24.	Dick Trickle	Pontiac
25.	Butch Miller	Chevrolet
26.	Kenny Wallace	Pontiac

27.	Michael Waltrip	Pontiac
28.	Jimmy Means	Pontiac
29.	Richard Petty	Pontiac
30.	Bobby Hillin	Buick
31.	Sterling Marlin	Oldsmobile
32.	Rob Moroso	Oldsmobile

HANES ACTIVEWEAR 500

April 29
Martinsville, Virginia
Time of Race: 3 hours, 23 minutes, 49 seconds
Average Speed: 77.423 mph
Margin of Victory: 4.50 seconds

FINISH	DRIVER	CAR
1.	Geoff Bodine	Ford
2.	Rusty Wallace	Pontiac
3.	Morgan Shepherd	Ford
4.	Darrell Waltrip	Chevrolet
5.	Dale Earnhardt	Chevrolet
6.	Ken Schrader	Chevrolet
7.	Mark Martin	Chevrolet
8.	Michael Waltrip	Pontiac
9.	Dick Trickle	Pontiac
10.	Bill Elliott	Ford
11.	Jimmy Spencer	Pontiac
12.	Brett Bodine	Buick
13.	Rob Moroso	Oldsmobile
14.	Dave Marcis	Chevrolet
15.	Ernie Irvan	Oldsmobile
16.	Kyle Petty	Pontiac
17.	Derrike Cope	Chevrolet
18.	Butch Miller	Chevrolet
19.	Jimmy Means	Pontiac
20.	Richard Petty	Pontiac
21.	Bobby Hillin	Buick
22.	Davey Allison	Ford
23.	Ricky Rudd	Chevrolet
24.	Bill Sedgwick	Chevrolet
25.	Alan Kulwicki	Ford
26.	Harry Gant	Oldsmobile
27.	Rick Wilson	Oldsmobile
28.	Jeff Purvis	Buick
29.	Rick Mast	Pontiac
30.	Dale Jarrett	Ford
31.	Terry Labonte	Oldsmobile
32.	Sterling Marlin	Oldsmobile

WINSTON 500

May 6
Talladega, Alabama
Time of Race: 3 hours, 8 minutes, 2 seconds
Average Speed: 159.571 mph
Margin of Victory: 2 car lengths

FINISH	DRIVER	CAR
1.	Dale Earnhardt	Chevrolet
2.	Greg Sacks	Chevrolet
3.	Mark Martin	Ford
4.	Ernie Irvan	Oldsmobile
5.	Michael Waltrip	Pontiac
6.	Terry Labonte	Oldsmobile
7.	Kyle Petty	Pontiac
8.	Morgan Shepherd	Ford
9.	Hut Stricklin	Buick
10.	Darrell Waltrip	Chevrolet
11.	Jack Pennington	Oldsmobile
12.	Brett Bodine	Buick
13.	AlanKulwicki	Ford
14.	Dave Marcis	Chevrolet
15.	Chad Little	Ford
16.	Butch Miller	Chevrolet

17.	Rick Mast	Pontiac
18.	Bill Venturini	Chevrolet
19.	Mickey Gibbs	Ford
20.	Rusty Wallace	Pontiac
21.	Jimmy Means	Pontiac
22.	Bill Elliott	Ford
23.	Bobby Hillin	Buick
24.	Geoff Bodine	Ford
25.	Davey Allison	Ford
26.	Sterling Marlin	Oldsmobile
27.	Dick Trickle	Pontiac
28.	Ken Schrader	Chevrolet
29.	Richard Petty	Pontiac
30.	Phil Barkdoll	Oldsmobile
31.	Buddy Baker	Ford
32.	Jimmy Spencer	Pontiac
33.	Ricky Rudd	Chevrolet
34.	Dale Jarrett	Ford
35.	Phil Parsons	Oldsmobile
36.	Harry Gant	Oldsmobile
37.	Rob Moroso	Oldsmobile
38.	Lake Speed	Oldsmobile
39.	Rick Wilson	Oldsmobile
40.	Derrike Cope	Chevrolet

COCA-COLA 600

May 27
Charlotte, North Carolina
Time of Race: 4 hours, 21 minutes, 32 seconds
Average Speed: 137.650 mph
Margin of Victory: 2 car lengths

FINISH	DRIVER	CAR
1.	Rusty Wallace	Pontiac
2.	Bill Elliott	Ford
3.	Mark Martin	Ford
4.	Michael Waltrip	Pontiac
5.	Ernie Irvan	Oldsmobile
6.	Alan Kulwicki	Ford
7.	Davey Allison	Ford
8.	Morgan Shepherd	Ford
9.	Derrike Cope	Chevrolet
10.	Geoff Bodine	Ford
11.	Ken Schrader	Chevrolet
12.	Dick Trickle	Pontiac
13.	Terry Labonte	Oldsmobile
14.	Greg Sacks	Chevrolet
15.	Buddy Baker	Ford
16.	Dave Marcis	Chevrolet
17.	Kyle Petty	Pontiac
18.	Butch Miller	Chevrolet
19.	Rick Wilson	Oldsmobile
20.	Jack Pennington	Oldsmobile
21.	Jimmy Spencer	Pontiac
22.	Darrell Waltrip	Chevrolet
23.	Jimmy Horton	Ford
24.	Chad Little	Ford
25.	Harry Gant	Oldsmobile
26.	Rob Moroso	Oldsmobile
27.	Richard Petty	Pontiac
28.	Ricky Rudd	Chevrolet
29.	Brett Bodine	Buick
30.	Dale Earnhardt	Chevrolet
31.	Rick Mast	Pontiac
32.	Dale Jarrett	Ford
33.	Rodney Combs	Pontiac
34.	Bobby Hillin	Buick
35.	Sterling Marlin	Oldsmobile
36.	Tracy Leslie	Oldsmobile
37.	Hut Stricklin	Buick
38.	Lake Speed	Oldsmobile
39.	Bobby Hamilton	Pontiac
40.	Terry Byers	Pontiac
41.	Ken Ragan	Ford
42.	Larry Pearson	Pontiac

BUDWEISER 500

June 3
Dover, Delaware
Time of Race: 4 hours, 2 minutes, 1 second
Average Speed: 123.960 mph
Margin of Victory: 1.24 seconds

FINISH	DRIVER	CAR
1.	Derrike Cope	Chevrolet
2.	Ken Schrader	Chevrolet
3.	Dick Trickle	Pontiac
4.	Mark Martin	Ford
5.	Sterling Marlin	Oldsmobile
6.	Morgan Shepherd	Ford
7.	Ernie Irvan	Oldsmobile
8.	Bill Elliott	Ford
9.	Kyle Petty	Pontiac
10.	Rusty Wallace	Pontiac
11.	Ricky Rudd	Chevrolet
12.	Dale Jarrett	Ford
13.	Terry Labonte	Oldsmobile
14.	Butch Miller	Chevrolet
15.	Geoff Bodine	Ford
16.	Bobby Hillin	Buick
17.	Davey Allison	Ford
18.	Brett Bodine	Buick
19.	Darrell Waltrip	Chevrolet
20.	Jimmy Horton	Ford
21.	Richard Petty	Pontiac
22.	Jimmy Means	Pontiac
23.	Rick Wilson	Pontiac
24.	Alan Kulwicki	Ford
25.	J. D. McDuffie	Pontiac
26.	Michael Waltrip	Pontiac
27.	Hut Stricklin	Buick
28.	Rick Mast	Chevrolet
29.	Rob Moroso	Oldsmobile
30.	Mike Potter	Pontiac
31.	Dale Earnhardt	Chevrolet
32.	Jimmy Spencer	Pontiac
33.	Bobby Gerhart	Chevrolet
34.	Harry Gant	Oldsmobile
35.	Dave Marcis	Chevrolet
36.	Freddie Crawford	Chevrolet

BANQUET FROZEN FOODS 300

June 10
Sonoma, California
Time of Race: 2 hours, 41 minutes, 35 seconds
Average Speed: 69.245 mph
Margin of Victory: under caution

FINISH	DRIVER	CAR
1.	Rusty Wallace	Pontiac
2.	Mark Martin	Ford
3.	Ricky Rudd	Chevrolet
4.	Geoff Bodine	Ford
5.	Bobby Hillin	Buick
6.	Sterling Marlin	Oldsmobile
7.	Ernie Irvan	Oldsmobile
8.	Irv Hoerr	Oldsmobile
9.	Michael Waltrip	Pontiac
10.	Rick Wilson	Oldsmobile
11.	Alan Kulwicki	Ford
12.	Hut Stricklin	Buick
13.	Derrike Cope	Chevrolet
14.	Dale Jarrett	Ford
15.	Terry Fisher	Pontiac
16.	Kyle Petty	Pontiac
17.	Stan Barrett	Chevrolet
18.	Ken Schrader	Chevrolet
19.	Harry Gant	Oldsmobile
20.	Bill Schmitt	Chevrolet
21.	Bill Elliott	Ford
22.	Jim Bown	Chevrolet

23.	John Krebs	Pontiac
24.	Davey Allison	Ford
25.	Mike Chase	Buick
26.	Richard Petty	Pontiac
27.	Jimmy Spencer	Pontiac
28.	Butch Gilliland	Chevrolet
29.	Morgan Shepherd	Ford
30.	Troy Beebe	Buick
31.	Butch Miller	Chevrolet
32.	Dave Marcis	Chevrolet
33.	Darrell Waltrip	Chevrolet
34.	Dale Earnhardt	Chevrolet
35.	Terry Labonte	Oldsmobile
36.	Bill Sedgwick	Chevrolet
37.	Chad Little	Ford
38.	Tom Kendall	Chevrolet
39.	Dick Trickle	Pontiac
40.	Jack Sellers	Buick
41.	Brett Bodine	Buick
42.	Rob Moroso	Oldsmobile
43.	Ted Kennedy	Oldsmobile
44.	Hershel McGriff	Pontiac

MILLER GENUINE DRAFT 500

June 17
Pocono, Pennsylvania
Time of Race: 4 hours, 8 minutes, 25 seconds
Average Speed: 120.60 mph
Margin of Victory: 2 seconds

FINISH	DRIVER	CAR
1.	Harry Gant	Oldsmobile
2.	Rusty Wallace	Pontiac
3.	Geoff Bodine	Ford
4.	Brett Bodine	Buick
5.	Davey Allison	Ford
6.	Hut Stricklin	Buick
7.	Greg Sacks	Chevrolet
8.	Darrell Waltrip	Chevrolet
9.	Sterling Marlin	Oldsmobile
10.	Kyle Petty	Pontiac
11.	Morgan Shepherd	Ford
12.	Derrike Cope	Chevrolet
13.	Dale Earnhardt	Chevrolet
14.	Mark Martin	Ford
15.	Ken Schrader	Chevrolet
16.	Bill Elliott	Ford
17.	Ernie Irvan	Oldsmobile
18.	Chad Little	Ford
19.	Michael Waltrip	Pontiac
20.	Terry Labonte	Oldsmobile
21.	Jack Pennington	Oldsmobile
22.	Dave Marcis	Chevrolet
23.	Butch Miller	Chevrolet
24.	Jim Sauter	Ford
25.	Dick Trickle	Pontiac
26.	Tommy Riggins	Oldsmobile
27.	Jimmy Means	Pontiac
28.	J. D. McDuffie	Pontiac
29.	Bobby Hillin	Buick
30.	Jimmy Spencer	Pontiac
31.	Dale Jarrett	Ford
32.	Ricky Rudd	Chevrolet
33.	Randy LaJoie	Buick
34.	Alan Kulwicki	Ford
35.	Rick Wilson	Oldsmobile
36.	Rob Moroso	Oldsmobile
37.	Troy Beebe	Pontiac
38.	Richard Petty	Pontiac
39.	Jimmy Horton	Ford
40.	Jerry O'Neil	Oldsmobile

MILLER GENUINE DRAFT 400

June 24
Brooklyn, Michigan
Time of Race: 2 hours, 39 minutes, 46 seconds

Average Speed: 150.219 mph
Margin of Victory: 22 seconds

FINISH	DRIVER	CAR
1.	Dale Earnhardt	Chevrolet
2.	Ernie Irvan	Oldsmobile
3.	Geoff Bodine	Ford
4.	Mark Martin	Ford
5.	Harry Gant	Oldsmobile
6.	Alan Kulwicki	Ford
7.	Terry Labonte	Oldsmobile
8.	Kyle Petty	Pontiac
9.	Ricky Rudd	Chevrolet
10.	Rick Wilson	Oldsmobile
11.	Richard Petty	Pontiac
12.	Derrike Cope	Chevrolet
13.	Morgan Shepherd	Ford
14.	Brett Bodine	Buick
15.	Darrell Waltrip	Chevrolet
16.	Rob Moroso	Oldsmobile
17.	Rusty Wallace	Pontiac
18.	Sterling Marlin	Oldsmobile
19.	Dave Marcis	Chevrolet
20.	Jimmy Spencer	Pontiac
21.	Michael Waltrip	Pontiac
22.	Phil Parsons	Pontiac
23.	Butch Miller	Chevrolet
24.	Dick Trickle	Pontiac
25.	Bill Elliott	Ford
26.	Greg Sacks	Chevrolet
27.	Ken Schrader	Chevrolet
28.	Bobby Hillin	Buick
29.	Eddie Bierschwale	Oldsmobile
30.	Bill Venturini	Chevrolet
31.	Troy Beebe	Pontiac
32.	Hut Stricklin	Buick
33.	Lake Speed	Oldsmobile
34.	Dale Jarrett	Ford
35.	Ed Cooper	Oldsmobile
36.	Davey Allison	Ford
37.	J. D. McDuffie	Pontiac
38.	Jack Pennington	Oldsmobile
39.	Jimmy Means	Pontiac
40.	Rodney Combs	Pontiac

PEPSI 400

July 7
Daytona Beach, Florida
Time of Race: 2 hours, 29 minutes, 10 seconds
Average Speed: 160.894 mph
Margin of Victory: 1.47 seconds

FINISH	DRIVER	CAR
1.	Dale Earnhardt	Chevrolet
2.	Alan Kulwicki	Ford
3.	Ken Schrader	Chevrolet
4.	Terry Labonte	Oldsmobile
5.	Sterling Marlin	Oldsmobile
6.	Bobby Hillin	Buick
7.	Harry Gant	Oldsmobile
8.	Dale Jarrett	Ford
9.	Rob Moroso	Oldsmobile
10.	Kyle Petty	Pontiac
11.	Mark Martin	Ford
12.	Jimmy Means	Pontiac
13.	Ricky Rudd	Chevrolet
14.	Rusty Wallace	Pontiac
15.	Jimmy Spencer	Pontiac
16.	Michael Waltrip	Pontiac
17.	Jimmy Horton	Chevrolet
18.	Jack Pennington	Oldsmobile
19.	Dick Trickle	Pontiac
20.	Dave Marcis	Chevrolet
21.	Philip Duffie	Buick
22.	Brett Bodine	Buick
23.	Butch Miller	Chevrolet
24.	Davey Allison	Ford
25.	Geoff Bodine	Ford
26.	Hut Stricklin	Buick
27.	Chad Little	Ford
28.	Derrike Cope	Chevrolet
29.	Bill Elliott	Ford
30.	Buddy Baker	Ford
31.	Phil Barkdoll	Oldsmobile
32.	Mickey Gibbs	Ford
33.	Ernie Irvan	Oldsmobile
34.	Morgan Shepherd	Ford
35.	Charlie Glotzbach	Pontiac
36.	Richard Petty	Pontiac
37.	Greg Sacks	Chevrolet
38.	A. J. Foyt	Oldsmobile
39.	Rick Wilson	Oldsmobile
40.	Terry Byers	Pontiac

AC SPARK PLUG 500

July 22
Poconoo, Pennsylvania
Time of Race: 4 hours, 1 minute, 48 seconds
Average Speed: 124.07 mph
Margin of Victory: 1.22 seconds

FINISH	DRIVER	CAR
1.	Geoff Bodine	Ford
2.	Bill Elliott	Ford
3.	Rusty Wallace	Pontiac
4.	Dale Earnhardt	Chevrolet
5.	Davey Allison	Ford
6.	Mark Martin	Ford
7.	Ricky Rudd	Chevrolet
8.	Butch Miller	Chevrolet
9.	Richard Petty	Pontiac
10.	Terry Labonte	Oldsmobile
11.	Ken Schrader	Chevrolet
12.	Bobby Hillin	Buick
13.	Derrike Cope	Chevrolet
14.	Harry Gant	Oldsmobile
15.	Dick Trickle	Pontiac
16.	Brett Bodine	Buick
17.	Alan Kulwicki	Ford
18.	Dale Jarrett	Ford
19.	Jimmy Spencer	Pontiac
20.	Darrell Waltrip	Chevrolet
21.	Jimmy Means	Pontiac
22.	Rick Mast	Pontiac
23.	Michael Waltrip	Pontiac
24.	Ken Ragan	Ford
25.	Mike Potter	Pontiac
26.	Ernie Irvan	Oldsmobile
27.	Brian Ross	Pontiac
28.	Dave Marcis	Chevrolet
29.	Hut Stricklin	Buick
30.	Sterling Marlin	Oldsmobile
31.	Rick Wilson	Oldsmobile
32.	Rob Moroso	Oldsmobile
33.	Greg Sacks	Chevrolet
34.	Jerry O'Neil	Oldsmobile
35.	Kyle Petty	Pontiac
36.	Morgan Shepherd	Ford
37.	Tommy Riggins	Oldsmobile
38.	Randy LaJoie	Buick
39.	Dick Johnson	Ford

TALLADEGA DIEHARD 500

July 29
Talladega, Alabama
Time of Race: 2 hours, 52 minutes, 1 second
Average Speed: 174.430 mph
Margin of Victory: 26 seconds

FINISH	DRIVER	CAR
1.	Dale Earnhardt	Chevrolet
2.	Bill Elliott	Ford
3.	Sterling Marlin	Oldsmobile
4.	Alan Kulwicki	Ford
5.	Ricky Rudd	Chevrolet
6.	Ernie Irvan	Chevrolet
7.	Derrike Cope	Chevrolet
8.	Kyle Petty	Pontiac
9.	Mark Martin	Ford
10.	Bobby Hillin	Buick
11.	Lake Speed	Oldsmobile
12.	Rob Moroso	Oldsmobile
13.	Jimmy Horton	Chevrolet
14.	Hut Stricklin	Buick
15.	Harry Gant	Oldsmobile
16.	Ken Schrader	Chevrolet
17.	Geoff Bodine	Ford
18.	Greg Sacks	Chevrolet
19.	Chad Little	Ford
20.	Davey Allison	Ford
21.	Michael Waltrip	Pontiac
22.	Mickey Gibbs	Ford
23.	Jack Pennington	Oldsmobile
24.	Jimmy Spencer	Pontiac
25.	Bill Venturini	Chevrolet
26.	Morgan Shepherd	Ford
27.	A. J. Foyt	Oldsmobile
28.	Dave Marcis	Chevrolet
29.	Richard Petty	Pontiac
30.	Jimmy Means	Pontiac
31.	Mark Stahl	Ford
32.	Rusty Wallace	Pontiac
33.	Brett Bodine	Buick
34.	Butch Miller	Chevrolet
35.	Rick Wilson	Oldsmobile
36.	Dick Trickle	Pontiac
37.	Stan Smith	Pontiac
38.	Tracy Leslie	Oldsmobile
39.	Dale Jarrett	Ford
40.	Buddy Baker	Ford
41.	Phil Parsons	Pontiac
42.	Terry Labonte	Oldsmobile

FINISH	DRIVER	CAR
27.	Dick Johnson	Ford
28.	Ernie Irvan	Chevrolet
29.	Jimmy Spencer	Pontiac
30.	Dick Trickle	Pontiac
31.	Dave Marcis	Chevrolet
32.	Rick Wilson	Oldsmobile
33.	Tommy Riggins	Oldsmobile
34.	Rusty Wallace	Pontiac
35.	Derrike Cope	Chevrolet
36.	Rick Ware	Pontiac
37.	Oma Kimbrough	Buick
38.	John Alexander	Ford
39.	Jimmy Means	Pontiac
40.	Greg Sacks	Chevrolet

CHAMPION SPARK PLUG 400

August 19
Brooklyn, Michigan
Time of Race: 2 hours, 52 minutes, 53 seconds
Average Speed: 138.822 mph
Margin of Victory: 1.70 seconds

FINISH	DRIVER	CAR
1.	Mark Martin	Ford
2.	Greg Sacks	Chevrolet
3.	Rusty Wallace	Pontiac
4.	Bill Elliott	Ford
5.	Ricky Rudd	Chevrolet
6.	Davey Allison	Ford
7.	Geoff Bodine	Ford
8.	Dale Earnhardt	Chevrolet
9.	Morgan Shepherd	Ford
10.	Dale Jarrett	Ford
11.	Alan Kulwicki	Ford
12.	Butch Miller	Chevrolet
13.	Harry Gant	Oldsmobile
14.	Terry Labonte	Oldsmobile
15.	Hut Stricklin	Buick
16.	Kyle Petty	Pontiac
17.	Brett Bodine	Buick
18.	Dave Marcis	Chevrolet
19.	Derrike Cope	Chevrolet
20.	Sterling Marlin	Oldsmobile
21.	Bobby Hillin	Buick
22.	Chad Little	Ford
23.	Buddy Baker	Ford
24.	Mike Chase	Pontiac
25.	Jimmy Spencer	Pontiac
26.	Rob Moroso	Oldsmobile
27.	Jimmy Means	Pontiac
28.	Bill Venturini	Chevrolet
29.	Rick Wilson	Oldsmobile
30.	Michael Waltrip	Pontiac
31.	Ben Hess	Pontiac
32.	Dick Trickle	Pontiac
33.	Richard Petty	Pontiac
34.	Rodney Combs	Pontiac
35.	Ernie Irvan	Chevrolet
36.	Rick Mast	Pontiac
37.	Ken Ragan	Ford
38.	Jack Pennington	Pontiac
39.	Ted Musgrave	Chevrolet
40.	Ken Schrader	Chevrolet
41.	Ed Cooper	Oldsmobile

BUDWEISER AT THE GLEN

August 12
Watkins Glen, New York
Time of Race: 2 hours, 21 minutes, 49 seconds
Average Speed: 92.452 mph
Margin of Victory: 6 seconds

FINISH	DRIVER	CAR
1.	Ricky Rudd	Chevrolet
2.	Geoff Bodine	Ford
3.	Brett Bodine	Buick
4.	Michael Waltrip	Pontiac
5.	Mark Martin	Ford
6.	Morgan Shepherd	Ford
7.	Dale Earnhardt	Chevrolet
8.	Tom Kendall	Chevrolet
9.	Ken Schrader	Chevrolet
10.	Irv Hoerr	Oldsmobile
11.	Alan Kulwicki	Ford
12.	Bill Elliott	Ford
13.	Rob Moroso	Oldsmobile
14.	Terry Labonte	Oldsmobile
15.	Sterling Marlin	Oldsmobile
16.	Bobby Hillin	Buick
17.	Kyle Petty	Pontiac
18.	Richard Petty	Pontiac
19.	Davey Allison	Ford
20.	Dale Jarrett	Ford
21.	Harry Gant	Oldsmobile
22.	J. D. McDuffie	Pontiac
23.	Hut Stricklin	Buick
24.	Sarel van der Merwe	Chevrolet
25.	Butch Miller	Chevrolet
26.	Jerry O'Neil	Pontiac

BUSCH 500

August 25
Bristol, Tennessee
Time of Race: 2 hours, 54 minutes, 13 seconds
Average Speed: 91.782 mph
Margin of Victory: 21 seconds

FINISH	DRIVER	CAR
1.	Ernie Irvan	Chevrolet
2.	Rusty Wallace	Pontiac
3.	Mark Martin	Ford
4.	Terry Labonte	Oldsmobile
5.	Sterling Marlin	Oldsmobile
6.	Alan Kulwicki	Ford
7.	Dale Jarrett	Ford
8.	Dale Earnhardt	Chevrolet
9.	Michael Waltrip	Pontiac
10.	Ricky Rudd	Chevrolet
11.	Geoff Bodine	Ford
12.	Ken Schrader	Chevrolet
13.	Bill Elliott	Ford
14.	Larry Pearson	Chevrolet
15.	Bobby Hillin	Buick
16.	Butch Miller	Chevrolet
17.	Dick Trickle	Pontiac
18.	Jimmy Spencer	Pontiac
19.	Dave Marcis	Chevrolet
20.	Greg Sacks	Chevrolet
21.	Hut Stricklin	Buick
22.	Jimmy Means	Pontiac
23.	Davey Allison	Ford
24.	Rick Mast	Pontiac
25.	Brett Bodine	Buick
26.	Harry Gant	Oldsmobile
27.	Derrike Cope	Chevrolet
28.	Kyle Petty	Pontiac
29.	Richard Petty	Pontiac
30.	Rob Moroso	Oldsmobile
31.	Morgan Shepherd	Ford
32.	Rick Wilson	Oldsmobile

HEINZ SOUTHERN 500

September 2
Darlington, South Carolina
Time of Race: 4 hours, 4 minutes, 16 seconds
Average Speed: 1223.141 mph
Margin of Victory: 4.19 seconds

FINISH	DRIVER	CAR
1.	Dale Earnhardt	Chevrolet
2.	Ernie Irvan	Chevrolet
3.	Alan Kulwicki	Ford
4.	Bill Elliott	Ford
5.	Harry Gant	Oldsmobile
6.	Mark Martin	Ford
7.	Ricky Rudd	Chevrolet
8.	Geoff Bodine	Ford
9.	Derrike Cope	Chevrolet
10.	Brett Bodine	Buick
11.	Dick Trickle	Pontiac
12.	Rick Wilson	Oldsmobile
13.	Rob Moroso	Oldsmobile
14.	Terry Labonte	Oldsmobile
15.	Davey Allison	Ford
16.	Dave Marcis	Chevrolet
17.	Larry Pearson	Chevrolet
18.	Sterling Marlin	Oldsmobile
19.	Phil Parsons	Pontiac
20.	Hut Stricklin	Buick
21.	Morgan Shepherd	Ford
22.	Jack Pennington	Oldsmobile
23.	Jimmy Spencer	Pontiac
24.	Rick Mast	Pontiac
25.	Kyle Petty	Pontiac
26.	Michael Waltrip	Pontiac
27.	Charlie Glotzbach	Pontiac
28.	Dale Jarrett	Ford
29.	Butch Miller	Chevrolet
30.	Greg Sacks	Chevrolet
31.	Bobby Hillin	Buick
32.	Lake Speed	Oldsmobile
33.	Mark Stahl	Ford
34.	Richard Petty	Pontiac
35.	Chad Little	Ford
36.	Jimmy Means	Pontiac

FINISH	DRIVER	CAR
37.	Philip Duffie	Buick
38.	H. B. Bailey	Pontiac
39.	Ken Schrader	Chevrolet
40.	Rusty Wallace	Pontiac

MILLER GENUINE DRAFT 400

September 9
Richmond, Virginia
Time of Race: 3 hours, 8 minutes, 21 seconds
Average Speed: 95.567 mph
Margin of Victory: 1 second

FINISH	DRIVER	CAR
1.	Dale Earnhardt	Chevrolet
2.	Mark Martin	Ford
3.	Darrell Waltrip	Chevrolet
4.	Bill Elliott	Ford
5.	Rusty Wallace	Pontiac
6.	Kyle Petty	Pontiac
7.	Dick Trickle	Pontiac
8.	Ricky Rudd	Chevrolet
9.	Geoff Bodine	Ford
10.	Ken Schrader	Chevrolet
11.	Bobby Hillin	Buick
12.	Ernie Irvan	Chevrolet
13.	Hut Stricklin	Buick
14.	Michael Waltrip	Pontiac
15.	Dave Marcis	Chevrolet
16.	Davey Allison	Ford
17.	Terry Labonte	Oldsmobile
18.	Jimmy Means	Pontiac
19.	Butch Miller	Chevrolet
20.	Rick Wilson	Oldsmobile
21.	Richard Petty	Pontiac
22.	Charlie Glotzbach	Ford
23.	Greg Sacks	Chevrolet
24.	Sterling Marlin	Oldsmobile
25.	Ron Esau	Chevrolet
26.	Alan Kulwicki	Ford
27.	Jimmy Spencer	Pontiac
28.	Rob Moroso	Oldsmobile
29.	Dale Jarrett	Ford
30.	Morgan Shepherd	Ford
31.	Brett Bodine	Buick
32.	Chad Little	Ford
33.	D. K. Ulrich	Pontiac
34.	Mickey Gibbs	Ford
35.	Derrike Cope	Chevrolet
36.	Harry Gant	Oldsmobile

PEAK ANTIFREEZE 500

September 16
Dover, Delaware
Time of Race: 3 hours, 58 minutes, 0 seconds
Average Speed: 125.945 mph
Margin of Victory: 1.38 seconds

FINISH	DRIVER	CAR
1.	Bill Elliott	Ford
2.	Mark Martin	Ford
3.	Dale Earnhardt	Chevrolet
4.	Harry Gant	Oldsmobile
5.	Michael Waltrip	Pontiac
6.	Dale Jarrett	Ford
7.	Rusty Wallace	Pontiac
8.	Kyle Petty	Pontiac
9.	Davey Allison	Ford
10.	Ken Schrader	Chevrolet
11.	Hut Stricklin	Buick
12.	Sterling Marlin	Oldsmobile
13.	Derrike Cope	Chevrolet
14.	Bobby Hillin	Buick

15.	Terry Labonte	Oldsmobile
16.	Richard Petty	Pontiac
17.	Butch Miller	Chevrolet
18.	Jimmy Spencer	Pontiac
19.	Darrell Waltrip	Chevrolet
20.	Brett Bodine	Buick
21.	Greg Sacks	Chevrolet
22.	Dave Marcis	Chevrolet
23.	Dick Trickle	Pontiac
24.	Jimmy Means	Pontiac
25.	Morgan Shepherd	Ford
26.	Ernie Irvan	Chevrolet
27.	Rick Wilson	Oldsmobile
28.	Rob Moroso	Oldsmobile
29.	Alan Kulwicki	Ford
30.	Jimmy Horton	Pontiac
31.	Tommy Ellis	Oldsmobile
32.	Ricky Rudd	Chevrolet
33.	Jeff Purvis	Chevrolet
34.	Jim Sauter	Pontiac
35.	James Hylton	Buick
36.	Geoff Bodine	Ford
37.	Jerry Hufflin	Pontiac
38.	Mike Potter	Pontiac
39.	Tommy Riggins	Oldsmobile
40.	J. D. McDuffie	Pontiac

GOODY'S 500

September 23
Martinsville, Virginia
Time of Race: 3 hours, 26 minutes, 35 seconds
Average Speed: 76.386 mph
Margin of Victory: 2.16 seconds

FINISH	DRIVER	CAR
1.	Geoff Bodine	Ford
2.	Dale Earnhardt	Chevrolet
3.	Mark Martin	Ford
4.	Brett Bodine	Buick
5.	Harry Gant	Oldsmobile
6.	Alan Kulwicki	Ford
7.	Davey Allison	Ford
8.	Bill Elliott	Ford
9.	Terry Labonte	Oldsmobile
10.	Dale Jarrett	Ford
11.	Ernie Irvan	Oldsmobile
12.	Sterling Marlin	Oldsmobile
13.	Hut Stricklin	Buick
14.	Dave Marcis	Chevrolet
15.	Rusty Wallace	Pontiac
16.	Jimmy Means	Pontiac
17.	Chad Little	Ford
18.	Jimmy Spencer	Pontiac
19.	Darrell Waltrip	Chevrolet
20.	Rick Wilson	Oldsmobile
21.	Rob Moroso	Oldsmobile
22.	Dick Trickle	Pontiac
23.	Kyle Petty	Pontiac
24.	Derrike Cope	Chevrolet
25.	Morgan Shepherd	Ford
26.	Bobby Hillin	Buick
27.	Ken Schrader	Chevrolet
28.	Ricky Rudd	Chevrolet
29.	Richard Petty	Pontiac
30.	Michael Waltrip	Pontiac
31.	Rick Mast	Chevrolet

TYSON HOLLY FARMS 400

September 30
North Wilkesboro, North Carolina
Time of Race: 2 hours, 39 minutes, 53 seconds
Average Speed: 93.818 mph
Margin of Victory: 3.63 seconds

FINISH	DRIVER	CAR
1.	Mark Martin	Ford
2.	Dale Earnhardt	Chevrolet
3.	Brett Bodine	Buick
4.	Bill Elliott	Ford
5.	Ken Schrader	Chevrolet
6.	Ernie Irvan	Oldsmobile
7.	Darrell Waltrip	Chevrolet
8.	Rusty Wallace	Pontiac
9.	Alan Kulwicki	Ford
10.	Kyle Petty	Pontiac
11.	Ricky Rudd	Chevrolet
12.	Morgan Shepherd	Ford
13.	Sterling Marlin	Oldsmobile
14.	Bobby Hillin	Buick
15.	Michael Waltrip	Pontiac
16.	Geoff Bodine	Ford
17.	Richard Petty	Pontiac
18.	Rick Wilson	Pontiac
19.	Dale Jarrett	Ford
20.	Hut Stricklin	Buick
21.	Rob Moroso	Oldsmobile
22.	Derrike Cope	Chevrolet
23.	Jimmy Spencer	Pontiac
24.	Chad Little	Ford
25.	Dave Marcis	Chevrolet
26.	Davey Allison	Ford
27.	Terry Labonte	Oldsmobile
28.	Harry Gant	Oldsmobile
29.	Dick Trickle	Pontiac
30.	Jimmy Means	Pontiac
31.	Jeff Purvis	Chevrolet
32.	Rick Mast	Chevrolet

MELLO YELLO 500

October 6
Charlotte, North Carolina
Time of Race: 3 hours, 38 minutes, 44 seconds
Average Speed: 137.428 mph
Margin of Victory: 2.59 seconds

FINISH	DRIVER	CAR
1.	Davey Allison	Ford
2.	Morgan Shepherd	Ford
3.	Michael Waltrip	Pontiac
4.	Kyle Petty	Pontiac
5.	Alan Kulwicki	Ford
6.	Ricky Rudd	Chevrolet
7.	Derrike Cope	Chevrolet
8.	Brett Bodine	Buick
9.	Darrell Waltrip	Chevrolet
10.	Dale Jarrett	Ford
11.	Rick Wilson	Pontiac
12.	Jack Pennington	Oldsmobile
13.	Dave Marcis	Chevrolet
14.	Mark Martin	Ford
15.	Bill Elliott	Ford
16.	Sterling Marlin	Oldsmobile
17.	Terry Labonte	Oldsmobile
18.	Phil Parsons	Oldsmobile
19.	Larrry Pearson	Chevrolet
20.	Richard Petty	Pontiac
21.	Mickey Gibbs	Ford
22.	Eddie Bierschwale	Oldsmobile
23.	Jimmy Horton	Pontiac
24.	Chuck Bown	Chevrolet
25.	Dale Earnhardt	Chevrolet
26.	Harry Gant	Oldsmobile
27.	Ernie Irvan	Chevrolet
28.	Bobby Hamilton	Pontiac
29.	Hut Stricklin	Buick
30.	Dick Trickle	Pontiac
31.	Bobby Hillin	Buick
32.	Mark Stahl	Ford
33.	Jimmy Hensley	Oldsmobile
34.	Rick Mast	Chevrolet
35.	Ken Schrader	Chevrolet
36.	Geoff Bodine	Ford

37.	Buddy Baker	Ford
38.	Rusty Wallace	Pontiac
39.	Jimmy Means	Pontiac
40.	Chad Little	Ford
41.	Jimmy Spencer	Pontiac

AC DELCO 500

October 21
Rockingham, North Carolina
Time of Race: 3 hours, 57 minutes, 25 seconds
Average Speed: 126.452 mph
Margin of Victory: under caution

FINISH	DRIVER	CAR
1.	Alan Kulwicki	Ford
2.	Bill Elliott	Ford
3.	Harry Gant	Oldsmobile
4.	Geoff Bodine	Ford
5.	Ken Schrader	Chevrolet
6.	Sterling Marlin	Oldsmobile
7.	Ricky Rudd	Chevrolet
8.	Darrell Waltrip	Chevrolet
9.	Ernie Irvan	Chevrolet
10.	Dale Earnhardt	Chevrolet
11.	Mark Martin	Ford
12.	Morgan Shepherd	Ford
13.	Terry Labonte	Oldsmobile
14.	Bobby Hillin	Buick
15.	Michael Waltrip	Pontiac
16.	Dale Jarrett	Ford
17.	Brett Bodine	Buick
18.	Rick Wilson	Pontiac
19.	Larry Pearson	Chevrolet
20.	Kyle Petty	Pontiac
21.	Richard Petty	Pontiac
22.	Rick Mast	Chevrolet
23.	Dave Marcis	Chevrolet
24.	Jack Pennington	Oldsmobile
25.	Chad Little	Ford
26.	Tom Kendall	Chevrolet
27.	Jim Bown	Pontiac
28.	Jimmy Means	Pontiac
29.	Davey Allison	Ford
30.	Rick Jeffrey	Chevrolet
31.	Jimmy Hensley	Oldsmobile
32.	Rusty Wallace	Pontiac
33.	Derrike Cope	Chevrolet
34.	Hut Stricklin	Buick
35.	Mike Skinner	Buick
36.	Dick Trickle	Pontiac
37.	Ted Musgrave	Chevrolet
38.	Jeff Purvis	Chevrolet
39.	Tracy Leslie	Oldsmobile
40.	Charlie Baker	Buick

CHECKER 500

November 4
Phoenix, Arizona
Time of Race: 3 hours, 13 minutes, 25 seconds
Average Speed: 96.786 mph
Margin of Victory: 53 seconds

FINISH	DRIVER	CAR
1.	Dale Earnhardt	Chevrolet
2.	Ken Schrader	Chevrolet
3.	Morgan Shepherd	Ford
4.	Darrell Waltrip	Chevrolet
5.	Bill Elliott	Ford
6.	Alan Kulwicki	Ford
7.	Rick Mast	Chevrolet
8.	Geoff Bodine	Ford
9.	Ernie Irvan	Chevrolet

10.	Mark Martin	Ford
11.	Davey Allison	Ford
12.	Greg Sacks	Chevrolet
13.	Terry Labonte	Oldsmobile
14.	Derrike Cope	Chevrolet
15.	Brett Bodine	Buick
16.	Sterling Marlin	Oldsmobile
17.	Dave Marcis	Chevrolet
18.	Bill Schmitt	Chevrolet
19.	Rick Wilson	Oldsmobile
20.	Bill Sedgwick	Chevrolet
21.	Chad Little	Oldsmobile
22.	Ted Musgrave	Pontiac
23.	Richard Petty	Pontiac
24.	Chuck Bown	Oldsmobile
25.	Jimmy Means	Pontiac
26.	Hut Stricklin	Buick
27.	Rodney Combs	Pontiac
28.	Jim Bown	Pontiac
29.	Brent Kaeding	Chevrolet
30.	Dale Jarrett	Ford
31.	John Krebs	Pontiac
32.	Ricky Rudd	Chevrolet
33.	Gary Collins	Oldsmobile
34.	Mark Reed	Chevrolet
35.	Troy Beebe	Buick
36.	Jeff Purvis	Chevrolet
37.	Harry Gant	Oldsmobile
38.	Rusty Wallace	Pontiac
39.	Mike Chase	Buick
40.	Dick Trickle	Pontiac
41.	Kyle Petty	Pontiac
42.	Bobby Hillin	Buick
43.	Michael Waltrip	Pontiac

ATLANTA JOURNAL 500

November 18
Atlanta, Georgia
Time of Race: 3 hours, 32 minutes, 34 seconds
Average Speed: 140.911 mph
Margin of Victory: 2.47 seconds

FINISH	DRIVER	CAR
1.	Morgan Shepherd	Ford
2.	Geoff Bodine	Ford
3.	Dale Earnhardt	Chevrolet
4.	Dale Jarrett	Ford
5.	Darrell Waltrip	Chevrolet
6.	Mark Martin	Ford
7.	Ernie Irvan	Chevrolet
8.	Alan Kulwicki	Ford
9.	Rusty Wallace	Pontiac
10.	Greg Sacks	Chevrolet
11.	Ken Schrader	Chevrolet
12.	Derrike Cope	Chevrolet
13.	Hut Stricklin	Buick
14.	Michael Waltrip	Pontiac
15.	Bill Elliott	Ford
16.	Ricky Rudd	Chevrolet
17.	Richard Petty	Pontiac
18.	Brett Bodine	Buick
19.	Harry Gant	Oldsmobile
20.	Dave Mader III	Pontiac
21.	Terry Labonte	Oldsmobile
22.	Bobby Hillin	Buick
23.	Chuck Bown	Chevrolet
24.	Steve Grissom	Oldsmobile
25.	Davey Allison	Ford
26.	Ted Musgrave	Pontiac
27.	Chad Little	Ford
28.	Jimmy Means	Pontiac
29.	Rick Mast	Chevrolet
30.	Rodney Combs	Pontiac
31.	Jim Sauter	Ford
32.	Pancho Carter	Ford
33.	Rick Wilson	Oldsmobile
34.	Dave Marcis	Chevrolet
35.	Jimmy Horton	Chevrolet
36.	Jack Pennington	Oldsmobile

37.	Dick Trickle	Pontiac
38.	Sterling Marlin	Oldsmobile
30.	Jim Bown	Pontiac
40.	Bobby Hamilton	Pontiac
41.	Kyle Petty	Pontiac

1991

DAYTONA 500

Febrary 17
Daytona Beach, Florida
Time of Race: 3 hours, 22 minutes, 30 seconds
Average Speed: 148.148 mph
Margin of Victory: under caution

FINISH	DRIVER	CAR
1.	Ernie Irvan	Chevrolet
2.	Sterling Marlin	Ford
3.	Joe Ruttman	Oldsmobile
4.	Rick Mast	Oldsmobile
5.	Dale Earnhardt	Chevrolet
6.	Dale Jarrett	Ford
7.	Bobby Hillin	Oldsmobile
8.	Alan Kulwicki	Ford
9.	Ricky Rudd	Chevrolet
10.	Bobby Hamilton	Oldsmobile
11.	Dick Trickle	Pontiac
12.	Eddie Bierschwale	Oldsmobile
13.	Terry Labonte	Oldsmobile
14.	Chad Little	Ford
15.	Davey Allison	Ford
16.	Kyle Petty	Pontiac
17.	Mickey Gibbs	Pontiac
18.	Robby Gordon	Ford
19.	Richard Petty	Pontiac
20.	Phil Barkdoll	Oldsmobile
21.	Mark Martin	Ford
22.	Brett Bodine	Buick
23.	Jim Sauter	Pontiac
24.	Darrell Waltrip	Chevrolet
25.	Harry Gant	Oldsmobile
26.	Derrike Cope	Chevrolet
27.	Rusty Wallace	Pontiac
28.	Bill Elliott	Ford
29.	Hut Stricklin	Buick
30.	Ted Musgrave	Pontiac
31.	Ken Schrader	Chevrolet
32.	Geoff Bodine	Ford
33.	Rick Wilson	Buick
34.	Morgan Shepherd	Ford
35.	Dave Marcis	Chevrolet
36.	Jeff Purvis	Oldsmobile
37.	Buddy Baker	Pontiac
38.	Michael Waltrip	Pontiac
39.	Jimmy Means	Pontiac
40.	Jimmy Spencer	Chevrolet
41.	Sammy Swindell	Oldsmobile
42.	Greg Sacks	Chevrolet

PONTIAC EXCITEMENT 400

February 24
Richmond, Virginia
Time of Race: 2 hours, 50 minutes, 47 seconds
Average Speed: 105.397 mph
Margin of Victory: 1.5 car lengths

FINISH	DRIVER	CAR
1.	Dale Earnhardt	Chevrolet
2.	Ricky Rudd	Chevrolet

3.	Harry Gant	Oldsmobile
4.	Rusty Wallace	Pontiac
5.	Alan Kulwicki	Ford
6.	Mark Martin	Ford
7.	Darrell Waltrip	Chevrolet
8.	Morgan Shepherd	Ford
9.	Sterling Marlin	Ford
10.	Ken Schrader	Chevrolet
11.	Richard Petty	Pontiac
12.	Davey Allison	Ford
13.	Geoff Bodine	Ford
14.	Terry Labonte	Oldsmobile
15.	Dick Trickle	Pontiac
16.	Chad Little	Ford
17.	Michael Waltrip	Pontiac
18.	Rick Wilson	Buick
19.	Ted Musgrave	Pontiac
20.	Bobby Hillin	Oldsmobile
21.	Dale Jarrett	Ford
22.	Hut Stricklin	Buick
23.	Mickey Gibbs	Pontiac
24.	Brett Bodine	Buick
25.	Kyle Petty	Pontiac
26.	Robby Gordon	Ford
27.	Ernie Irvan	Chevrolet
28.	Bobby Hamilton	Oldsmobile
29.	Joe Ruttman	Oldsmobile
30.	Bill Elliott	Ford
31.	Jimmy Means	Pontiac
32.	Derrike Cope	Chevrolet
33.	Dave Marcis	Chevrolet
34.	Jimmy Spencer	Chevrolet
35.	Rick Mast	Oldsmobile

GOODWRENCH 500

March 3
Rockingham, North Carolina
Time of Race: 4 hours, 1 minute, 57 seconds
Average Speed: 124.083 mph
Margin of Victory: 1.1 seconds

FINISH	DRIVER	CAR
1.	Kyle Petty	Pontiac
2.	Ken Schrader	Chevrolet
3.	Harry Gant	Oldsmobile
4.	Ricky Rudd	Chevrolet
5.	Bill Elliott	Ford
6.	Ernie Irvan	Chevrolet
7.	Michael Waltrip	Pontiac
8.	Dale Earnhardt	Chevrolet
9.	Darrell Waltrip	Chevrolet
10.	Morgan Shepherd	Ford
11.	Dale Jarrett	Ford
12.	Geoff Bodine	Ford
13.	Brett Bodine	Buick
14.	Mark Martin	Ford
15.	Richard Petty	Pontiac
16.	Davey Allison	Ford
17.	Alan Kulwicki	Ford
18.	Bobby Hillin	Oldsmobile
19.	Rick Wilson	Buick
20.	Mickey Gibbs	Pontiac
21.	Bobby Hamilton	Oldsmobile
22.	Chad Little	Ford
23.	Dave Marcis	Chevrolet
24.	Joe Ruttrman	Oldsmobile
25.	Ted Musgrave	Pontiac
26.	Rich Bickle	Oldsmobile
27.	Jimmy Means	Pontiac
28.	Rusty Wallace	Pontiac
29.	Dick Trickle	Pontiac
30.	Rick Mast	Oldsmobile
31.	Hut Stricklin	Buick
32.	Mike Skinner	Chevrolet
33.	Sterling Marlin	Ford
34.	Derrike Cope	Chevrolet
35.	Jeff Purvis	Oldsmobile
36.	Bill Meacham	Oldsmobile
37.	Stanley Smith	Buick

38.	Jimmy Spencer	Chevrolet
39.	Terry Labonte	Oldsmobile
40.	Andy Hillenburg	Buick

MOTORCRAFT QUALITY PARTS 500

March 18
Atlanta, Georgia
Time of Race: 3 hours, 33 minutes, 14 seconds
Average Speed: 140.470 mph
Margin of Victory: 3.02 seconds

FINISH	DRIVER	CAR
1.	Ken Schrader	Chevrolet
2.	Bill Elliott	Ford
3.	Dale Earnhardt	Chevrolet
4.	Morgan Shepherd	Ford
5.	Michael Waltrip	Pontiac
6.	Ricky Rudd	Chevrolet
7.	Sterling Marlin	Ford
8.	Alan Kulwicki	Ford
9.	Darrell Waltrip	Chevrolet
10.	Rusty Wallace	Pontiac
11.	Derrike Cope	Chevrolet
12.	Rick Wilson	Buick
13.	Hut Stricklin	Buick
14.	Ernie Irvan	Chevrolet
15.	Brett Bodine	Buick
16.	Jimmy Spencer	Chevrolet
17.	Mark Martin	Ford
18.	Chad Little	Ford
19.	Harry Gant	Oldsmobile
20.	Dale Jarrett	Ford
21.	Bobby Hillin	Oldsmobile
22.	Jimmy Sauter	Pontiac
23.	Geoff Bodine	Ford
24.	Jeff Purvis	Oldsmobile
25.	Mickey Gibbs	Pontiac
26.	Wally Dallenbach Jr.	Ford
27.	Joe Ruttman	Oldsmobile
28.	Dick Trickle	Pontiac
29.	Rick Mast	Oldsmobile
30.	Dave Mader III	Pontiac
31.	Jimmy Means	Pontiac
32.	Andy Hillenburg	Buick
33.	Bobby Hamilton	Oldsmobile
34.	Rich Bickle	Oldsmobile
35.	Terry Labonte	Oldsmobile
36.	Dave Marcis	Chevrolet
37.	Ted Musgrave	Pontiac
38.	Richard Petty	Pontiac
39.	Kyle Petty	Pontiac
40.	Davey Allison	Ford

TRANSOUTH 500

April 7
Darlington, South Carolina
Time of Race: 3 hours, 41 minutes, 50 seconds
Average Speed: 135.594 mph
Margin of Victory: 11.32 seconds

FINISH	DRIVER	CAR
1.	Ricky Rudd	Chevrolet
2.	Davey Allison	Ford
3.	Michael Waltrip	Pontiac
4.	Mark Martin	Ford
5.	Rusty Wallace	Pontiac
6.	Kyle Petty	Pontiac
7.	Ernie Irvan	Chevrolet
8.	Morgan Shepherd	Ford
9.	Geoff Bodine	Ford
10.	Sterling Marlin	Ford
11.	Jimmy Spencer	Chevrolet

12.	Bill Elliott	Ford
13.	Rick Mast	Oldsmobile
14.	Rick Wilson	Buick
15.	Terry Labonte	Oldsmobile
16.	Brett Bodine	Buick
17.	Bobby Hillin	Oldsmobile
18.	Dave Marcis	Chevrolet
19.	Ken Schrader	Chevrolet
20.	Bobby Hamilton	Oldsmobile
21.	Ted Musgrave	Pontiac
22.	Mickey Gibbs	Pontiac
23.	Jimmy Means	Pontiac
24.	Rich Bickle	Oldsmobile
25.	Darrell Waltrip	Chevrolet
26.	Joe Ruttman	Oldsmobile
27.	Harry Gant	Oldsmobile
28.	Randy Baker	Chevrolet
29.	Dale Earnhardt	Chevrolet
30.	J. D. McDuffie	Pontiac
31.	Derrike Cope	Chevrolet
32.	Hut Stricklin	Buick
33.	Dave Mader III	Pontiac
34.	Alan Kulwicki	Ford
35.	H. B. Bailey	Pontiac
36.	Chad Little	Ford
37.	Richard Petty	Pontiac
38.	Bill Meacham	Oldsmobile
39.	Dale Jarrett	Ford
40.	Lake Speed	Pontiac

VALLEYDALE MEATS 500

April 14
Bristol, Tennessee
Time of Race: 3 hours, 39 minutes, 37 seconds
Average Speed: 72.809 mph
Margin of Victory: half a car length

FINISH	DRIVER	CAR
1.	Rusty Wallace	Pontiac
2.	Ernie Irvan	Chevrolet
3.	Davey Allison	Ford
4.	Mark Martin	Ford
5.	Ricky Rudd	Chevrolet
6.	Darrell Waltrip	Chevrolet
7.	Dale Jarrett	Ford
8.	Jimmy Spencer	Chevrolet
9.	Terry Labonte	Oldsmobile
10.	Morgan Shepherd	Ford
11.	Harry Gant	Oldsmobile
12.	Ted Musgrave	Pontiac
13.	Joe Ruttman	Oldsmobile
14.	Chad Little	Ford
15.	Bobby Hillin	Oldsmobile
16.	Hut Stricklin	Buick
17.	Richard Petty	Pontiac
18.	Rick Mast	Oldsmobile
19.	Mickey Gibbs	Pontiac
20.	Dale Earnhardt	Chevrolet
21.	Kyle Petty	Pontiac
22.	Brett Bodine	Buick
23.	Michael Waltrip	Pontiac
24.	Geoff Bodine	Ford
25.	Lake Speed	Pontiac
26.	Alan Kulwicki	Ford
27.	Sterling Marlin	Ford
28.	Bill Elliott	Ford
29.	Ken Schrader	Chevrolet
30.	Dick Trickle	Buick
31.	Bobby Hamilton	Oldsmobile
32.	Derrike Cope	Chevrolet
33.	Rick Wilson	Buick

FIRST UNION 400

April 21
North Wilkesboro, North Carolina

Time of Race: 3 hours, 8 minutes, 26 seconds
Average Speed: 79.604 mph
Margin of Victory: .81 second

FINISH	DRIVER	CAR
1.	Darrell Waltrip	Chevrolet
2.	Dale Earnhardt	Chevrolet
3.	Jimmy Spencer	Chevrolet
4.	Morgan Shepherd	Ford
5.	Ken Schrader	Chevrolet
6.	Davey Allison	Ford
7.	Michael Waltrip	Pontiac
8.	Bill Elliott	Ford
9.	Mark Martin	Ford
10.	Ernie Irvan	Chevrolet
11.	Ricky Rudd	Chevrolet
12.	Rick Mast	Oldsmobile
13.	Lake Speed	Pontiac
14.	Hut Stricklin	Buick
15.	Derrike Cope	Chevrolet
16.	Richard Petty	Pontiac
17.	Ted Musgrave	Pontiac
18.	Kyle Petty	Pontiac
19.	Dave Marcis	Chevrolet
20.	Bobby Hillin	Oldsmobile
21.	Bobby Hamilton	Pontiac
22.	Sterling Marlin	Ford
23.	Harry Gant	Oldsmobile
24.	Joe Ruttman	Oldsmobile
25.	Dale Jarrett	Ford
26.	Dick Trickle	Buick
27.	Rick Wilson	Buick
28.	Geoff Bodine	Ford
29.	Alan Kulwicki	Ford
30.	Brett Bodine	Buick
31.	Terry Labonte	Oldsmobile
32.	Rusty Wallace	Pontiac
33.	Mickey Gibbs	Pontiac

HANES 500

April 28
Martinsville, Virginia
Time of Race: 3 hours, 26 minutes, 41 seconds
Average Speed: 75.139 mph
Margin of Victory: 3.34 seconds

FINISH	DRIVER	CAR
1.	Dale Earnhardt	Chevrolet
2.	Kyle Petty	Pontiac
3.	Darrell Waltrip	Chevrolet
4.	Brett Bodine	Buick
5.	Harry Gant	Oldsmobile
6.	Jimmy Spencer	Chevrolet
7.	Michael Waltrip	Pontiac
8.	Davey Allison	Ford
9.	Alan Kulwicki	Ford
10.	Hut Stricklin	Buick
11.	Ricky Rudd	Chevrolet
12.	Dale Jarrett	Ford
13.	Rick Mast	Oldsmobile
14.	Richard Petty	Pontiac
15.	Ernie Irvan	Chevrolet
16.	Joe Ruttman	Oldsmobile
17.	Bobby Hillin	Oldsmobile
18.	Lake Speed	Pontiac
19.	Bill Sedgwick	Chevrolet
20.	Geoff Bodine	Ford
21.	Rusty Wallace	Pontiac
22.	Rick Wilson	Buick
23.	Ken Schrader	Chevrolet
24.	Ted Musgrave	Pontiac
25.	Mickey Gibbs	Pontiac
26.	Bill Elliott	Ford
27.	Chad Little	Ford
28.	Sterling Marlin	Ford
29.	Mark Martin	Ford
30.	Morgan Shepherd	Ford

31.	Terry Labonte	Oldsmobile
32.	Dick Trickle	Buick

WINSTON 500

May 6
Talladega, Alabama
Time of Race: 3 hours, 1 minute, 10 seconds
Average Speed: 165.620 mph
Margin of Victory: 11 seconds

FINISH	DRIVER	CAR
1.	Harry Gant	Oldsmobile
2.	Darrell Waltrip	Chevrolet
3.	Dale Earnhardt	Chevrolet
4.	Sterling Marlin	Ford
5.	Michael Waltrip	Pontiac
6.	Geoff Bodine	Ford
7.	Ken Schrader	Chevrolet
8.	Bill Elliott	Ford
9.	Jimmy Spencer	Chevrolet
10.	Rick Mast	Oldsmobile
11.	Brett Bodine	Buick
12.	Bobby Hamilton	Oldsmobile
13.	Ricky Rudd	Chevrolet
14.	Morgan Shepherd	Ford
15.	Mickey Gibbs	Pontiac
16.	Ted Musgrave	Pontiac
17.	Bobby Hillin	Oldsmobile
18.	Dave Marcis	Chevrolet
19.	Phil Barkdoll	Oldsmobile
20.	Jimmy Means	Pontiac
21.	Stanley Smith	Buick
22.	Davey Allison	Ford
23.	Hut Stricklin	Buick
24.	Mark Martin	Ford
25.	Rick Wilson	Buick
26.	Rusty Wallace	Pontiac
27.	Alan Kulwicki	Ford
28.	Derrike Cope	Chevrolet
29.	Joe Ruttman	Oldsmobile
30.	Jeff Purvis	Oldsmobile
31.	Lake Speed	Pontiac
32.	Ernie Irvan	Chevrolet
33.	Kyle Petty	Pontiac
34.	Wally Dallenbach Jr.	Ford
35.	Dale Jarrett	Ford
36.	Buddy Baker	Oldsmobile
37.	Terry Labonte	Oldsmobile
38.	Chad Little	Ford
39.	Greg Sacks	Oldsmobile
40.	Richard Petty	Pontiac
41.	Larry Pearson	Chevrolet

COCA-COLA 600

May 26
Charlotte, North Carolina
Time of Race: 4 hours, 19 minutes, 5 seconds
Average Speed: 138.951 mph
Margin of Victory: 1.28 seconds

FINISH	DRIVER	CAR
1.	Davey Allison	Ford
2.	Ken Schrader	Chevrolet
3.	Dale Earnhardt	Chevrolet
4.	Harry Gant	Oldsmobile
5.	Dale Jarrett	Ford
6.	Hut Stricklin	Buick
7.	Ernie Irvan	Chevrolet
8.	Darrell Waltrip	Chevrolet
9.	Ricky Rudd	Chevrolet
10.	Terry Labonte	Oldsmobile
11.	Sterling Marlin	Ford
12.	Derrike Cope	Chevrolet

13.	Kenny Wallace	Pontiac
14.	Morgan Shepherd	Ford
15.	Michael Waltrip	Pontiac
16.	Tommy Ellis	Ford
17.	Ted Musgrave	Pontiac
18.	Rick Wilson	Buick
19.	Bobby Hillin	Oldsmobile
20.	Richard Petty	Pontiac
21.	Joe Ruttman	Oldsmobile
22.	Rusty Wallace	Pontiac
23.	Mark Martin	Ford
24.	Eddie Bierschwale	Oldsmobile
25.	Chad Little	Ford
26.	Bill Elliott	Ford
27.	Bobby Hamilton	Oldsmobile
28.	Brett Bodine	Buick
29.	Lake Speed	Pontiac
30.	Rick Mast	Oldsmobile
31.	Jimmy Spencer	Chevrolet
32.	Dave Marcis	Chevrolet
33.	Wally Dallenbach	Ford
34.	Mickey Gibbs	Pontiac
35.	Alan Kulwicki	Ford
36.	Stanley Smith	Buick
37.	Jim Sauter	Pontiac
38.	Jimmy Means	Pontiac
39.	Greg Sacks	Oldsmobile
40.	Dick Trickle	Buick
41.	Larry Pearson	Chevrolet

BUDWEISER 500

June 2
Dover, Delaware
Time of Race: 4 hours, 9 minutes, 41 seconds
Average Speed: 120.152 mph
Margin of Victory: 1.18 seconds

FINISH	DRIVER	CAR
1.	Ken Schrader	Chevrolet
2.	Dale Earnhardt	Chevrolet
3.	Harry Gant	Chevrolet
4.	Ernie Irvan	Chevrolet
5.	Mark Martin	Ford
6.	Hut Stricklin	Buick
7.	Darrell Waltrip	Chevrolet
8.	Morgan Shepherd	Ford
9.	Rusty Wallace	Pontiac
10.	Ricky Rudd	Chevrolet
11.	Bobby Hamilton	Oldsmobile
12.	Joe Ruttman	Oldsmobile
13.	Bill Elliott	Ford
14.	Alan Kulwicki	Ford
15.	Sterling Marlin	Ford
16.	Davey Allison	Ford
17.	Richard Petty	Pontiac
18.	Ted Musgrave	Pontiac
19.	Bobby Hillin	Pontiac
20.	Rick Mast	Oldsmobile
21.	Tommy Ellis	Ford
22.	Lake Speed	Pontiac
23.	Dave Marcis	Chevrolet
24.	Terry Labonte	Oldsmobile
25.	Rick Wilson	Buick
26.	Kenny Wallace	Pontiac
27.	Derrike Cope	Chevrolet
28.	Jimmy Spencer	Chevrolet
29.	Chad Little	Ford
30.	Mickey Gibbs	Pontiac
31.	J. D. McDuffie	Pontiac
32.	Michael Waltrip	Pontiac
33.	Brett Bodine	Buick
34.	Bobby Labonte	Oldsmobile
35.	Dale Jarrett	Ford

BANQUET FROZEN FOODS 300

June 9
Sonoma, California

Time of Race: 2 hours, 33 minutes, 20 seconds
Average Speed: 72.970 mph
Margin of Victory: 1 second

FINISH	DRIVER	CAR
1.	Davey Allison	Ford
2.	Ricky Rudd	Chevrolet
3.	Rusty Wallace	Pontiac
4.	Ernie Irvan	Chevrolet
5.	Ken Schrader	Chevrolet
6.	Terry Labonte	Oldsmobile
7.	Dale Earnhardt	Chevrolet
8.	Geoff Bodine	Ford
9.	Mark Martin	Ford
10.	Michael Waltrip	Pontiac
11.	Brett Bodine	Buick
12.	Lake Speed	Pontiac
13.	Bill Schmitt	Ford
14.	Mickey Gibbs	Pontiac
15.	Bill Sedgwick	Chevrolet
16.	Rick Wilson	Buick
17.	Alan Kulwicki	Ford
18.	Tom Kendall	Pontiac
19.	Rick Mast	Oldsmobile
20.	Bill Elliott	Ford
21.	Bobby Hillin	Pontiac
22.	Bobby Hamilton	Oldsmobile
23.	Stanley Smith	Buick
24.	Dave Marcis	Chevrolet
25.	Darrell Waltrip	Chevrolet
26.	Sterling Marlin	Ford
27.	Harry Gant	Oldsmobile
28.	Chad Little	Ford
29.	Jimmy Spencer	Chevrolet
30.	Derrike Cope	Chevrolet
31.	Joe Ruttman	Oldsmobile
32.	Hershel McGriff	Pontiac
33.	Scott Gaylord	Oldsmobile
34.	Richard Petty	Pontiac
35.	Hut Stricklin	Buick
36.	Irv Hoerr	Oldsmobile
37.	Ted Musgrave	Pontiac
38.	John Krebs	Pontiac
39.	Robert Sprague	Ford
40.	Mike Chase	Ford
41.	Dale Jarrett	Ford
42.	Morgan Shepherd	Ford
43.	R. K. Smith	Pontiac

CHAMPION SPARK PLUG 500

June 16
Pocono, Pennsylvania
Time of Race: 4 hours, 4 minutes, 34 seconds
Average Speed: 122.666 mph
Margin of Victory: 1.8 seconds

FINISH	DRIVER	CAR
1.	Darrell Waltrip	Chevrolet
2.	Dale Earnhardt	Chevrolet
3.	Mark Martin	Ford
4.	Harry Gant	Oldsmobile
5.	Geoff Bodine	Ford
6.	Ernie Irvan	Chevrolet
7.	Ken Schrader	Chevrolet
8.	Sterling Marlin	Ford
9.	Morgan Shepherd	Ford
10.	Derrike Cope	Chevrolet
11.	Richard Petty	Pontiac
12.	Davey Allison	Ford
13.	Rick Wilson	Buick
14.	Jimmy Spencer	Chevrolet
15.	Bobby Hillin	Pontiac
16.	Alan Kulwicki	Ford
17.	Lake Speed	Pontiac
18.	Michael Waltrip	Pontiac
19.	Dale Jarrett	Ford

20.	Ricky Rudd	Chevrolet
21.	Terry Labonte	Oldsmobile
22.	Joe Ruttman	Oldsmobile
23.	Chad Little	Ford
24.	Dave Marcis	Chevrolet
25.	Rick Mast	Oldsmobile
26.	Jimmy Means	Pontiac
27.	Ted Musgrave	Pontiac
28.	Hut Stricklin	Buick
29.	Randy LaJoie	Buick
30.	Mickey Gibbs	Pontiac
31.	Rusty Wallace	Pontiac
32.	Larry Pearson	Chevrolet
33.	Brett Bodine	Buick
34.	J. D. McDuffe	Pontiac
35.	Bobby Hamilton	Oldsmobile
36.	Bill Elliott	Ford
37.	James Hylton	Chevrolet

MILLER GENUINE DRAFT 400

June 23
Brooklyn, Michigan
Time of Race: 2 hours, 29 minutes, 9 seconds
Average Speed: 160.912 mph
Margin of Victory: 11.72 seconds

FINISH	DRIVER	CAR
1.	Davey Allison	Ford
2.	Hut Stricklin	Buick
3.	Mark Martin	Ford
4.	Dale Earnhardt	Chevrolet
5.	Ernie Irvan	Chevrolet
6.	Ken Schrader	Chevrolet
7.	Darrell Waltrip	Chevrolet
8.	Ricky Rudd	Chevrolet
9.	Morgan Shepherd	Ford
10.	Harry Gant	Oldsmobile
11.	Bill Elliott	Ford
12.	Dale Jarrett	Ford
13.	Sterling Marlin	Ford
14.	Mickey Gibbs	Pontiac
15.	Bobby Hillin	Pontiac
16.	Dave Marcis	Pontiac
17.	Rusty Wallace	Pontiac
18.	Lake Speed	Pontiac
19.	Joe Ruttman	Oldsmobile
20.	Larry Pearson	Chevrolet
21.	Ted Musgrave	Pontiac
22.	Bobby Hamilton	Chevrolet
23.	Stanley Smith	Buick
24.	Alan Kulwicki	Ford
25.	Terry Labonte	Oldsmobile
26.	Chad Little	Ford
27.	Jimmy Means	Pontiac
28.	Wally Dallenbach Jr.	Ford
29.	Rick Mast	Oldsmobile
30.	Buddy Baker	Oldsmobile
31.	Rick Wilson	Buick
32.	Jimmy Spencer	Chevrolet
33.	H. B. Bailey	Pontiac
34.	Michael Waltrip	Pontiac
35.	Richard Petty	Pontiac
36.	Brett Bodine	Buick
37.	Jim Sauter	Pontiac
38.	Eddie Bierschwale	Oldsmobile
39.	Geoff Bodine	Ford
40.	Bill Venturini	Chevrolet
41.	Derrike Cope	Chevrolet

PEPSI 400

July 6
Daytona Beach, Florida
Time of Race: 2 hours, 30 minutes, 50 seconds
Average Speed: 159.116 mph
Margin of Victory: .18 second

FINISH	DRIVER	CAR
1.	Bill Elliott	Ford
2.	Geoff Bodine	Ford
3.	Davey Allison	Ford
4.	Ken Schrader	Chevrolet
5.	Ernie Irvan	Chevrolet
6.	Michael Waltrip	Pontiac
7.	Dale Earnhardt	Chevrolet
8.	Sterling Marlin	Ford
9.	Ricky Rudd	Chevrolet
10.	Jimmy Spencer	Chevrolet
11.	Mark Martin	Ford
12.	Rusty Wallace	Pontiac
13.	Buddy Baker	Oldsmobile
14.	Alan Kulwicki	Ford
15.	Bobby Hillin	Pontiac
16.	Hut Stricklin	Buick
17.	Derrike Cope	Chevrolet
18.	Dale Jarrett	Ford
19.	Rick Mast	Oldsmobile
20.	Morgan Shepherd	Ford
21.	Larry Pearson	Chevrolet
22.	Richard Petty	Pontiac
23.	Harry Gant	Oldsmobile
24.	Rick Wilson	Buick
25.	Dave Marcis	Chevrolet
26.	Jimmy Means	Pontiac
27.	Mickey Gibbs	Pontiac
28.	Bobby Hamilton	Oldsmobile
29.	Chad Little	Ford
30.	Jeff Purvis	Oldsmobile
31.	Joe Ruttman	Oldsmobile
32.	Darrell Waltrip	Chevrolet
33.	Mike Chase	Oldsmobile
34.	Wally Dallenbach Jr.	Ford
35.	Phil Barkdoll	Oldsmobile
36.	Brett Bodine	Buick
37.	Ted Musgrave	Pontiac
38.	Lake Speed	Pontiac
39.	Greg Sacks	Oldsmobile
40.	Stanley Smith	Buick
41.	Terry Labonte	Oldsmobile

MILLER GENUINE DRAFT 500

July 21
Pocono, Pennsylvania
Time of Race: 3 hours, 52 minutes, 33 seconds
Average Speed: 115.459 mph
Margin of Victory: under caution

FINISH	DRIVER	CAR
1.	Rusty Wallace	Pontiac
2.	Mark Martin	Ford
3.	Geoff Bodine	Ford
4.	Hut Stricklin	Buick
5.	Sterling Marlin	Ford
6.	Dale Jarrett	Ford
7.	Ernie Irvan	Chevrolet
8.	Brett Bodine	Buick
9.	Bill Elliott	Ford
10.	Joe Ruttman	Oldsmobile
11.	Bobby Hamilton	Oldsmobile
12.	Chad Little	Ford
13.	Ted Musgrave	Pontiac
14.	Davey Allison	Ford
15.	Terry Labonte	Oldsmobile
16.	Alan Kulwicki	Ford
17.	Greg Sacks	Oldsmobile
18.	Dave Marcis	Chevrolet
19.	Irv Hoerr	Oldsmobile
20.	Ricky Rudd	Chevrolet
21.	Jimmy Means	Pontiac
22.	Dale Earnhardt	Chevrolet
23.	Ken Schrader	Chevrolet
24.	Rick Wilson	Buick
25.	J. D. McDuffe	Pontiac
26.	Harry Gant	Oldsmobile
27.	Rick Mast	Oldsmobile

FINISH	DRIVER	CAR
28.	Bobby Hillin	Pontiac
29.	Darrell Waltrip	Chevrolet
30.	Lake Speed	Pontiac
31.	Richard Petty	Pontiac
32.	John Paul Jr.	Chevrolet
33.	Gary Wright	Chevrolet
34.	Morgan Shepherd	Ford
35.	Dick Trickle	Pontiac
36.	Derrike Cope	Chevrolet
37.	Jimmy Spencer	Chevrolet
38.	Michael Waltrip	Pontiac
39.	Bill Venturini	Chevrolet
40.	Gary Balough	Buick

DIEHARD 500

July 28
Talladega, Alabama
Time of Race: 3 hours, 23 minutes, 35 seconds
Average Speed: 147.3836 mph
Margin of Victory: half a car length

FINISH	DRIVER	CAR
1.	Dale Earnhardt	Chevrolet
2.	Bill Elliott	Ford
3.	Mark Martin	Ford
4.	Ricky Rudd	Chevrolet
5.	Sterling Marlin	Ford
6.	Rusty Wallace	Pontiac
7.	Michael Waltrip	Pontiac
8.	Dale Jarrett	Ford
9.	Davey Allison	Ford
10.	Joe Ruttman	Oldsmobile
11.	Bobby Hillin	Pontiac
12.	Chad Little	Ford
13.	Buddy Baker	Oldsmobile
14.	Morgan Shepherd	Ford
15.	Darrell Waltrip	Chevrolet
16.	Alan Kulwicki	Ford
17.	Larry Pearson	Chevrolet
18.	Richard Petty	Pontiac
19.	Greg Sacks	Oldsmobile
20.	Dick Trickle	Pontiac
21.	Dave Marcis	Chevrolet
22.	Phil Barkdoll	Oldsmobile
23.	Jimmy Means	Pontiac
24.	Terry Labonte	Oldsmobile
25.	Mikes Chase	Oldsmobile
26.	Ted Musgrave	Pontiac
27.	Eddie Bierschwale	Chevrolet
28.	Rick Mast	Oldsmobile
29.	Hut Stricklin	Buick
30.	Geoff Bodine	Ford
31.	Stanley Smith	Buick
32.	Brett Bodine	Buick
33.	Ernie Irvan	Chevrolet
34.	Bobby Hamilton	Oldsmobile
35.	Derrike Cope	Chevrolet
36.	Lake Speed	Pontiac
37.	Jimmy Spencer	Chevrolet
38.	Rick Wilson	Buick
39.	Harry Gant	Oldsmobile
40.	Ken Schrader	Chevrolet
41.	Wally Dallenbach Jr.	Ford

BUDWEISER AT THE GLEN

August 11
Watkins Glen, New York
Time of Race: 2 hours, 12 minutes, 28 seconds
Average Speed: 98.977 mph
Margin of Victory: 7 seconds

FINISH	DRIVER	CAR
1.	Ernie Irvan	Chevrolet
2.	Ricky Rudd	Chevrolet
3.	Mark Martin	Ford
4.	Rusty Wallace	Pontiac
5.	Dale Jarrett	Ford
6.	Darrell Waltrip	Chevrolet
7.	Bill Elliott	Ford
8.	Hut Stricklin	Buick
9.	Richard Petty	Pontiac
10.	Dave Allison	Ford
11.	Chad Little	Ford
12.	Sterling Marlin	Ford
13.	Derrike Cope	Chevrolet
14.	Joe Ruttman	Oldsmobile
15.	Dale Earnhardt	Chevrolet
16.	John Paul Jr.	Chevrolet
17.	Dorsey Schroeder	Pontiac
18.	Bobby Hillin	Pontiac
19.	Rick Wilson	Buick
20.	Jim Derhaag	Oldsmobile
21.	Michael Waltrip	Pontiac
22.	Geoff Bodine	Ford
23.	Alan Kulwicki	Ford
24.	Oma Kimbrough	Buick
25.	Brett Bodine	Buick
26.	Ted Musgrave	Pontiac
27.	Jimmy Spencer	Chevrolet
28.	Harry Gant	Oldsmobile
29.	Bobby Hamilton	Oldsmobile
30.	Ken Schrader	Chevrolet
31.	Kim Campbell	Oldsmobile
32.	Wally Dallenbach Jr.	Ford
33.	Lake Speed	Pontiac
34.	Terry Labonte	Oldsmobile
35.	Rick Mast	Oldsmobile
36.	Morgan Shepherd	Ford
37.	Dave Marcis	Chevrolet
38.	Irv Hoerr	Oldsmobile
39.	Jimmy Means	Pontiac
40.	J. D. McDuffie	Pontiac

CHAMPION SPARK PLUG 400

August 18
Brooklyn, Michigan
Time of Race: 2 hours, 51 minutes, 34 seconds
Average Speed: 142.972 mph
Margin of Victory: 10 inches

FINISH	DRIVER	CAR
1.	Dale Jarrett	Ford
2.	Davey Allison	Ford
3.	Rusty Wallace	Pontiac
4.	Mark Martin	Ford
5.	Bill Elliott	Ford
6.	Harry Gant	Oldsmobile
7.	Ernie Irvan	Chevrolet
8.	Alan Kulwicki	Ford
9.	Michael Waltrip	Pontiac
10.	Ken Schrader	Chevrolet
11.	Ricky Rudd	Chevrolet
12.	Sterling Marlin	Ford
13.	Buddy Baker	Oldsmobile
14.	Hut Stricklin	Buick
15.	Lake Speed	Pontiac
16.	Terry Labonte	Oldsmobile
17.	Ted Musgrave	Pontiac
18.	Rick Mast	Oldsmobile
19.	Bobby Hamilton	Oldsmobile
20.	Dave Marcis	Chevrolet
21.	Dick Trickle	Pontiac
22.	Wally Dallenbach Jr.	Ford
23.	Richard Petty	Pontiac
24.	Dale Earnhardt	Chevrolet
25.	Chad Little	Ford
26.	Morgan Shepherd	Ford
27.	Jimmy Means	Pontiac
28.	H. B. Bailey	Pontiac

FINISH	DRIVER	CAR
29.	Mike Chase	Oldsmobile
30.	Joe Ruttman	Chevrolet
31.	Jim Sauter	Pontiac
32.	Darrell Waltrip	Chevrolet
33.	Bobby Hillin	Pontiac
34.	Derrike Cope	Chevrolet
35.	Geoff Bodine	Ford
36.	Jimmy Spencer	Chevrolet
37.	Brett Bodine	Buick
38.	Bobby Labonte	Oldsmobile
39.	Rick Wilson	Buick
40.	Stanley Smith	Buick

BUD 500

August 24
Bristol, Tennessee
Time of Race: 3 hours, 14 minutes, 56 seconds
Average Speed: 82.028 mph
Margin of Victory: 9 seconds

FINISH	DRIVER	CAR
1.	Alan Kulwicki	Ford
2.	Sterling Marlin	Ford
3.	Ken Schrader	Chevrolet
4.	Mark Martin	Ford
5.	Ricky Rudd	Chevrolet
6.	Morgan Shepherd	Ford
7.	Dale Earnhardt	Chevrolet
8.	Darrell Waltrip	Chevrolet
9.	Terry Labonte	Oldsmobile
10.	Brett Bodine	Buick
11.	Lake Speed	Pontiac
12.	Richard Petty	Pontiac
13.	Bobby Hamilton	Oldsmobile
14.	Chad Little	Ford
15.	Jimmy Spencer	Chevrolet
16.	Ted Musgrave	Pontiac
17.	Joe Ruttman	Oldsmobile
18.	Ernie Irvan	Chevrolet
19.	Harry Gant	Oldsmobile
20.	Rick Wilson	Buick
21.	Bill Elliott	Ford
22.	Hut Stricklin	Buick
23.	Dave Marcis	Chevrolet
24.	Davey Allison	Ford
25.	Michael Waltrip	Pontiac
26.	Rick Mast	Oldsmobile
27.	Dick Trickle	Pontiac
28.	Dale Jarrett	Ford
29.	Derrike Cope	Chevrolet
30.	Bobby Hillin	Pontiac
31.	Geoff Bodine	Ford
32.	Rusty Wallace	Pontiac

HEINZ SOUTHERN 500

September 1
Darlington, South Carolina
Time of Race: 3 hours, 45 minutes, 18 seconds
Average Speed: 133.508 mph
Margin of Victory: 10.97 seconds

FINISH	DRIVER	CAR
1.	Hary Gant	Oldsmobile
2.	Ernie Irvan	Chevrolet
3.	Ken Schrader	Chevrolet
4.	Derrike Cope	Chevrolet
5.	Terry Labonte	Oldsmobile
6.	Sterling Marlin	Ford
7.	Geoff Bodine	Ford
8.	Dale Earnhardt	Chevrolet
9.	Joe Ruttman	Chevrolet
10.	Bobby Hamilton	Oldsmobile
11.	Rick Mast	Oldsmobile

FINISH	DRIVER	CAR
12.	Davey Allison	Ford
13.	Rick Wilson	Buick
14.	Brett Bodine	Buick
15.	Ricky Rudd	Chevrolet
16.	Richard Petty	Pontiac
17.	Hut Stricklin	Buick
18.	Bill Elliott	Ford
19.	Morgan Shepherd	Ford
20.	Ted Musgrave	Pontiac
21.	Greg Sacks	Oldsmobile
22.	Kyle Petty	Pontiac
23.	Dick Trickle	Pontiac
24.	Darrell Waltrip	Chevrolet
25.	Dale Jarrett	Ford
26.	Randy Baker	Chevrolet
27.	Michael Waltrip	Pontiac
28.	Jimmy Means	Pontiac
29.	Mark Martin	Ford
30.	Larry Pearson	Chevrolet
31.	Jimmy Spencer	Chevrolet
32.	Rusty Wallace	Pontiac
33.	Dave Marcis	Chevrolet
34.	Lake Speed	Pontiac
35.	Alan Kulwicki	Ford
36.	Chad Little	Ford
37.	Mark Stahl	Ford
38.	James Hylton	Buick

MILLER GENUINE DRAFT 400

September 7
Richmond, Virginia
Time of Race: 2 hours, 57 minutes, 35 seconds
Average Speed: 101.361 mph
Margin of Victory: 4 car lengths

FINISH	DRIVER	CAR
1.	Harry Gant	Oldsmobile
2.	Davey Allison	Ford
3.	Rusty Wallace	Pontiac
4.	Ernie Irvan	Chevrolet
5.	Ricky Rudd	Chevrolet
6.	Alan Kulwicki	Ford
7.	Darrell Waltrip	Chevrolet
8.	Ken Schrader	Chevrolet
9.	Bill Elliott	Ford
10.	Sterling Marlin	Ford
11.	Dale Earnhardt	Chevrolet
12.	Bobby Hamilton	Oldsmobile
13.	Rick Wilson	Buick
14.	Geoff Bodine	Ford
15.	Jimmy Spencer	Chevrolet
16.	Derrike Cope	Chevrolet
17.	Lake Speed	Pontiac
18.	Brett Bodine	Buick
19.	Terry Labonte	Oldsmobile
20.	Dale Jarrett	Ford
21.	Hut Stricklin	Buick
22.	Ted Musgrave	Pontiac
23.	Morgan Shepherd	Ford
24.	Richard Petty	Pontiac
25.	Wally Dallenbach Jr.	Ford
26.	Kyle Petty	Pontiac
27.	Rick Mast	Oldsmobile
28.	Joe Ruttman	Oldsmobile
29.	Dave Marcis	Chevrolet
30.	Michael Waltrip	Pontiac
31.	Kenny Wallace	Pontiac
32.	Greg Sacks	Oldsmobile
33.	Mark Martin	Ford
34.	Chad Little	Ford
35.	Jimmy Means	Pontiac
36.	Larry Pearson	Chevrolet

PEAK ANTIFREEZE 500

September 15
Dover, Delaware

Time of Race: 4 hours, 32 minutes, 17 seconds
Average Speed: 110.179 mph
Margin of Victory: 1 lap and 2.75 seconds

FINISH	DRIVER	CAR
1.	Harry Gant	Oldsmobile
2.	Geoff Bodine	Ford
3.	Morgan Shepherd	Ford
4.	Hut Stricklin	Buick
5.	Michael Waltrip	Pontiac
6.	Dick Trickle	Pontiac
7.	Ricky Rudd	Chevrolet
8.	Bobby Hamilton	Oldsmobile
9.	Rick Mast	Oldsmobile
10.	Dave Marcis	Chevrolet
11.	Bill Elliott	Ford
12.	Kyle Petty	Pontiac
13.	Joe Ruttman	Oldsmobile
14.	Ted Musgrave	Pontiac
15.	Dale Earnhardt	Chevrolet
16.	Chad Little	Ford
17.	Sterling Marlin	Ford
18.	Jimmy Spencer	Chevrolet
19.	Darrell Waltrip	Chevrolet
20.	Richard Petty	Pontiac
21.	Mark Martin	Ford
22.	Stanley Smith	Buick
23.	Jimmy Means	Pontiac
24.	Alan Kulwicki	Ford
25.	Rusty Wallace	Pontiac
26.	Terry Labonte	Oldsmobile
27.	Steve Perry	Ford
28.	Ernie Irvan	Chevrolet
29.	Rick Wilson	Buick
30.	Larry Pearson	Chevrolet
31.	Davey Allison	Ford
32.	Brett Bodine	Buick
33.	Ken Schrader	Chevrolet
34.	Dale Jarrett	Ford
35.	Lake Speed	Pontiac
36.	Derrike Cope	Chevrolet
37.	James Hylton	Buick
38.	Jerry Hill	Pontiac
39.	Brian Ross	Chevrolet
40.	Andy Belmont	Ford

GOODY'S 500

September 22
Martinsville, Virginia
Time of Race: 3 hours, 31 minutes, 42 seconds
Average Speed: 74.535 mph
Margin of Victory: 1 second

FINISH	DRIVER	CAR
1.	Harry Gant	Oldsmobile
2.	Brett Bodine	Buick
3.	Dale Earnhardt	Chevrolet
4.	Ernie Irvan	Chevrolet
5.	Mark Martin	Ford
6.	Terry Labonte	Oldsmobile
7.	Rusty Wallace	Pontiac
8.	Ricky Rudd	Chevrolet
9.	Ken Schrader	Chevrolet
10.	Jimmy Hensley	Pontiac
11.	Morgan Shepherd	Ford
12.	Kyle Petty	Pontiac
13.	Rick Mast	Oldsmobile
14.	Sterling Marlin	Ford
15.	Darrell Waltrip	Chevrolet
16.	Hut Stricklin	Buick
17.	Bobby Hamilton	Oldsmobile
18.	Dale Jarrett	Ford
19.	Derrike Cope	Chevrolet
20.	Ted Musgrave	Pontiac
21.	Dave Marcis	Chevrolet
22.	Alan Kulwicki	Ford

FINISH	DRIVER	CAR
23.	Geoff Bodine	Ford
24.	Chad Little	Ford
25.	Michael Waltrip	Pontiac
26.	Rick Wilson	Buick
27.	Bill Elliott	Ford
28.	Jimmy Spencer	Chevrolet
29.	Davey Allison	Ford
30.	Richard Petty	Pontiac
31.	Joe Ruttman	Oldsmobile
32.	Lake Speed	Pontiac

TYSON HOLLY FARMS 400

September 29
North Wilkesboro, North Carolina
Time of Race: 2 hours, 39 minutes, 23 seconds
Average Speed: 94.113 mph
Margin of Victory: 1.47 seconds

FINISH	DRIVER	CAR
1.	Dale Earnhardt	Chevrolet
2.	Harry Gant	Oldsmobile
3.	Morgan Shepherd	Ford
4.	Davey Allison	Ford
5.	Mark Martin	Ford
6.	Rusty Wallace	Pontiac
7.	Brett Bodine	Buick
8.	Ken Schrader	Chevrolet
9.	Dale Jarrett	Ford
10.	Alan Kulwicki	Ford
11.	Jimmy Hensley	Pontiac
12.	Ricky Rudd	Chevrolet
13.	Sterling Marlin	Ford
14.	Terry Labonte	Oldsmobile
15.	Geoff Bodine	Ford
16.	Kyle Petty	Pontiac
17.	Hut Stricklin	Buick
18.	Bobby Hamilton	Oldsmobile
19.	Richard Petty	Pontiac
20.	Darrell Waltrip	Chevrolet
21.	Chad Little	Ford
22.	Ted Musgrave	Pontiac
23.	Jimmy Spencer	Chevrolet
24.	Bill Elliott	Ford
25.	Rick Mast	Oldsmobile
26.	Chuck Bown	Pontiac
27.	Michael Waltrip	Pontiac
28.	Jimmy Means	Oldsmobile
29.	Joe Ruttman	Chevrolet
30.	Derrike Cope	Chevrolet
31.	Dave Marcis	Chevrolet
32.	Rick Wilson	Buick
33.	Ernie Irvan	Chevrolet

MELLO YELLO 500

October 6
Charlotte, North Carolina
Time of Race: 3 hours, 36 minutes, 17 seconds
Average Speed: 138.984 mph
Margin of Victory: 11.28 seconds

FINISH	DRIVER	CAR
1.	Geoff Bodine	Ford
2.	Davey Allison	Ford
3.	Alan Kulwicki	Ford
4.	Harry Gant	Oldsmobile
5.	Sterling Marlin	Ford
6.	Terry Labonte	Oldsmobile
7.	Michael Waltrip	Pontiac
8.	Brett Bodine	Buick
9.	Darrell Waltrip	Chevrolet
10.	Chad Little	Ford
11.	Bill Elliott	Ford

12.	Richard Petty	Pontiac
13.	Rick Mast	Oldsmobile
14.	Ted Musgrave	Pontiac
15.	Kyle Petty	Pontiac
16.	Joe Ruttman	Oldsmobile
17.	Rick Wilson	Buick
18.	Bobby Hillin	Chevrolet
19.	Wally Dallenbach Jr.	Ford
20.	Jimmy Hensley	Pontiac
21.	Brad Teague	Chevrolet
22.	Stanley Smith	Chevrolet
23.	Jimmy Spencer	Chevrolet
24.	Jimmy Means	Pontiac
25.	Dale Earnhardt	Chevrolet
26.	Dale Jarrett	Ford
27.	Rusty Wallace	Pontiac
28.	Morgan Shepherd	Ford
29.	Bobby Hamilton	Oldsmobile
30.	Ernie Irvan	Chevrolet
31.	Greg Sacks	Oldsmobile
32.	Ricky Rudd	Chevrolet
33.	Derrike Cope	Chevrolet
34.	Dave Marcis	Chevrolet
35.	Mark Martin	Ford
36.	Hut Stricklin	Buick
37.	Kerry Teague	Chevrolet
38.	Ken Schrader	Chevrolet
39.	Gary Balough	Pontiac
40.	Mike Skinner	Chevrolet
41.	Dorsey Schroeder	Pontiac

AC DELCO 500

October 20
Rockingham, North Carolina
Time of Race: 3 hours, 55 minutes, 51 seconds
Average Speed: 127.292 mph
Margin of Victory: .91 second

FINISH	DRIVER	CAR
1.	Davey Allison	Ford
2.	Harry Gant	Oldsmobile
3.	Mark Martin	Ford
4.	Geoff Bodine	Ford
5.	Ken Schrader	Chevrolet
6.	Bobby Hamilton	Oldsmobile
7.	Dale Earnhardt	Chevrolet
8.	Sterling Marlin	Ford
9.	Kyle Petty	Pontiac
10.	Bill Elliott	Ford
11.	Rusty Wallace	Pontiac
12.	Ricky Rudd	Chevrolet
13.	Hut Stricklin	Buick
14.	Jimmy Hensley	Pontiac
15.	Derrike Cope	Chevrolet
16.	Richard Petty	Pontiac
17.	Morgan Shepherd	Ford
18.	Rick Mast	Oldsmobile
19.	Michael Waltrip	Pontiac
20.	Rick Wilson	Buick
21.	Ted Musgrave	Pontiac
22.	Jimmy Spencer	Chevrolet
23.	Chad Little	Ford
24.	Randy LaJoie	Pontiac
25.	Dale Jarrett	Ford
26.	Dave Marcis	Chevrolet
27.	Joe Ruttman	Chevrolet
28.	Terry Labonte	Oldsmobile
29.	Greg Sacks	Oldsmobile
30.	Brett Bodine	Buick
31.	Ernie Irvan	Chevrolet
32.	Darrell Waltrip	Chevrolet
33.	Alan Kulwicki	Ford
34.	Ricky Craven	Oldsmobile
35.	Jimmy Means	Pontiac
36.	Mark Stahl	Ford
37.	Keith VanHouten	Pontiac
38.	Jerry Hill	Pontiac
39.	Gary Brooks	Oldsmobile
40.	James Hylton	Buick

PYROIL 500

November 3
Phoenix, Arizona
Time of Race: 3 hours, 15 minutes, 31 seconds
Average Speed: 95.746 mph
Margin of Victory: 11.44 seconds

FINISH	DRIVER	CAR
1.	Davey Allison	Ford
2.	Darrell Waltrip	Chevrolet
3.	Sterling Marlin	Ford
4.	Alan Kulwicki	Ford
5.	Rusty Wallace	Pontiac
6.	Ernie Irvan	Chevrolet
7.	Jimmy Spencer	Chevrolet
8.	Geoff Bodine	Ford
9.	Dale Earnhardt	Chevrolet
10.	Morgan Shepherd	Ford
11.	Ricky Rudd	Chevrolet
12.	Terry Labonte	Oldsmobile
13.	Bobby Hamilton	Oldsmobile
14.	Brett Bodine	Buick
15.	Rick Wilson	Buick
16.	Derrike Cope	Chevrolet
17.	Ken Schrader	Chevrolet
18.	Ted Musgrave	Pontiac
19.	Mark Martin	Ford
20.	Kyle Petty	Pontiac
21.	Bill Sedgwick	Chevrolet
22.	Joe Ruttman	Oldsmobile
23.	Harry Gant	Oldsmobile
24.	Michael Waltrip	Pontiac
25.	Bill Elliott	Ford
26.	Mike Chase	Chevrolet
27.	Hershel McGriff	Pontiac
28.	Rick Mast	Oldsmobile
29.	Butch Gilliland	Pontiac
30.	Chad Little	Ford
31.	Mike Wallace	Pontiac
32.	Randy LaJoie	Pontiac
33.	Larry Pearson	Chevrolet
34.	Mark Reed	Chevrolet
35.	Dale Jarrett	Ford
36.	Stanley Smith	Buick
37.	Bill Schmitt	Ford
38.	Jeff Purvis	Chevrolet
39.	Hut Stricklin	Buick
40.	Dave Marcis	Chevrolet
41.	Richard Petty	Pontiac
42.	Gary Collins	Oldsmobile
43.	Kenny Wallace	Pontiac

HARDEE'S 500

November 17
Atlanta, Georgia
Time of Race: 3 hours, 37 minutes, 6 seconds
Average Speed: 137.968 mph
Margin of Victory: 10.44 seconds

FINISH	DRIVER	CAR
1.	Mark Martin	Ford
2.	Ernie Irvan	Chevrolet
3.	Bill Elliott	Ford
4.	Harry Gant	Oldsmobile
5.	Dale Eanhardt	Chevrolet
6.	Morgan Shepherd	Ford
7.	Sterling Marlin	Ford
8.	Geoff Bodine	Ford
9.	Alan Kulwicki	Ford
10.	Darrell Waltrip	Chevrolet
11.	Ricky Rudd	Chevrolet
12.	Dave Marcis	Chevrolet
13.	Hut Stricklin	Buick
14.	Larry Pearson	Chevrolet
15.	Terry Labonte	Oldsmobile

16.	Dale Jarrett	Ford
17.	Davey Allison	Ford
18.	Bobby Hamilton	Oldsmobile
19.	Kyle Petty	Pontiac
20.	Joe Ruttman	Chevrolet
21.	Chad Little	Ford
22.	Richard Petty	Pontiac
23.	Kenny Wallace	Pontiac
24.	Derrike Cope	Chevrolet
25.	Stanley Smith	Buick
26.	Greg Sacks	Oldsmobile
27.	Eddie Bierschwale	Chevrolet
28.	Rick Mast	Oldsmobile
29.	Brett Bodine	Buick
30.	Ted Musgrave	Pontiac
31.	Randy LaJoie	Pontiac
32.	Bobby Hillin	Chevrolet
33.	Rick Wilson	Buick
34.	Rusty Wallace	Pontiac
35.	Jim Sauter	Pontiac
36.	Wally Dallenbach	Ford
37.	Ken Schrader	Chevrolet
38.	Jimmy Spencer	Chevrolet
39.	Mike Wallace	Oldsmobile
40.	Michael Waltrip	Pontiac

1992

DAYTONA 500

February 16
Daytona Beach, Florida
Time of Race: 3 hours, 7 minutes, 12 seconds
Average Speed: 160.256 mph
Margin of Victory: 2 car lengths

FINISH	DRIVER	CAR
1.	Davey Allison	Ford
2.	Morgan Shepherd	Ford
3.	Geoff Bodine	Ford
4.	Alan Kulwicki	Ford
5.	Dick Trickle	Oldsmobile
6.	Kyle Petty	Pontiac
7.	Terry Labonte	Chevrolet
8.	Ted Musgrave	Chevrolet
9.	Dale Earnhardt	Chevrolet
10.	Phil Parsons	Ford
11.	Buddy Baker	Oldsmobile
12.	Harry Gant	Oldsmobile
13.	Rick Mast	Oldsmobile
14.	Greg Sacks	Chevrolet
15.	Wally Dallenbach Jr.	Ford
16.	Richard Petty	Pontiac
17.	Phil Barkdoll	Oldsmobile
18.	Michael Waltrip	Pontiac
19.	Dorsey Schroeder	Ford
20.	Dave Marcis	Chevrolet
21.	A. J. Foyt	Oldsmobile
22.	Stanley Smith	Chevrolet
23.	Rick Wilson	Ford
24.	Hut Stricklin	Chevrolet
25.	Delma Cowart	Ford
26.	Darrell Waltrip	Chevrolet
27.	Bill Elliott	Ford
28.	Ernie Irvan	Chevrolet
29.	Mark Martin	Ford
30.	Mike Potter	Chevrolet
31.	Rusty Wallace	Pontiac
32.	Bobby Hamilton	Oldsmobile
33.	Kerry Teague	Oldsmobile
34.	Derrike Cope	Chevrolet
35.	Sterling Marlin	Ford
36.	Dale Jarrett	Chevrolet
37.	Ken Schrader	Chevrolet
38.	Bobby Hillin Jr.	Chevrolet
39.	Chad Little	Ford
40.	Ricky Rudd	Chevrolet

| 41. | Brett Bodine | Ford |
| 42. | Bob Schacht | Oldsmobile |

GOODWRENCH 500

March 1
Rockingham, North Carolina
Time of Race: 3 hours, 58 minutes, 2 seconds
Average Speed: 126.125 mph
Margin of Victory: 14 seconds

FINISH	DRIVER	CAR
1.	Bill Elliott	Ford
2.	Davey Allison	Ford
3.	Harry Gant	Oldsmobile
4.	Michael Waltrip	Pontiac
5.	Ken Schrader	Chevrolet
6.	Mark Martin	Ford
7.	Terry Labonte	Oldsmobile
8.	Brett Bodine	Ford
9.	Hut Stricklin	Chevrolet
10.	Darrell Waltrip	Chevrolet
11.	Ernie Irvan	Chevrolet
12.	Rick Mast	Oldsmobile
13.	Morgan Shepherd	Ford
14.	Geoff Bodine	Ford
15.	Sterling Marlin	Ford
16.	Richard Petty	Pontiac
17.	Ted Musgrave	Oldsmobile
18.	Bobby Hamilton	Oldsmobile
19.	Derrike Cope	Chevrolet
20.	Jimmy Spencer	Chevrolet
21.	Wally Dallenbach Jr.	Ford
22.	Chad Little	Ford
23.	Mike Skinner	Chevrolet
24.	Dale Earnhardt	Chevrolet
25.	Randy Baker	Chevrolet
26.	Rusty Wallace	Pontiac
27.	Jerry Hill	Pontiac
28.	Ricky Rudd	Chevrolet
29.	Kyle Petty	Pontiac
30.	Phil Parsons	Ford
31.	Alan Kulwicki	Ford
32.	Stanley Smith	Chevrolet
33.	Jimmy Means	Pontiac
34.	Greg Sacks	Chevrolet
35.	Delma Cowart	Ford
36.	Dick Trickle	Ford
37.	Dale Jarrett	Chevrolet
38.	Andy Belmont	Ford
39.	Dave Marcis	Chevrolet
40.	Johnny McFadden	Chevrolet

PONTIAC EXCITEMENT 400

March 8
Richmond, Virginia
Time of Race: 2 hours, 52 minutes, 27 seconds
Average Speed: 104.378 mph
Margin of Victory: 18 inches

FINISH	DRIVER	CAR
1.	Bill Elliott	Ford
2.	Alan Kulwicki	Ford
3.	Harry Gant	Oldsmobile
4.	Davey Allison	Ford
5.	Darrell Waltrip	Chevrolet
6.	Ricky Rudd	Chevrolet
7.	Sterling Marlin	Ford
8.	Terry Labonte	Chevrolet
9.	Hut Stricklin	Chevrolet
10.	Morgan Shepherd	Ford
11.	Dale Earnhardt	Chevrolet
12.	Jimmy Spencer	Chevrolet
13.	Dale Jarrett	Chevrolet

FINISH	DRIVER	CAR
14.	Ken Schrader	Chevrolet
15.	Ernie Irvan	Chevrolet
16.	Geoff Bodine	Ford
17.	Rusty Wallace	Pontiac
18.	Rick Mast	Oldsmobile
19.	Derrike Cope	Chevrolet
20.	Kyle Petty	Pontiac
21.	Richard Petty	Pontiac
22.	Dick Trickle	Ford
23.	Chad Little	Ford
24.	Wally Dallenbach Jr.	Ford
25.	Ted Musgrave	Oldsmobile
26.	Charlie Glotzbach	Ford
27.	Stanley Smith	Chevrolet
28.	Dave Marcis	Chevrolet
29.	Jeff Fuller	Pontiac
30.	Mark Martin	Ford
31.	Bobby Hamilton	Oldsmobile
32.	Greg Sacks	Chevrolet
33.	Brett Bodine	Ford
34.	Michael Waltrip	Pontiac
35.	Jimmy Means	Pontiac

MOTORCRAFT QUALITY PARTS 500

March 15
Atlanta, Georgia
Time of Race: 3 hours, 22 minutes, 44 seconds
Average Speed: 147,746 mph
Margin of Victory: 18.25 seconds

FINISH	DRIVER	CAR
1.	Bill Elliott	Ford
2.	Harry Gant	Oldsmobile
3.	Dale Earnhardt	Chevrolet
4.	Davey Allison	Ford
5.	Dick Trickle	Ford
6.	Geoff Bodine	Ford
7.	Alan Kulwicki	Ford
8.	Kyle Petty	Pontiac
9.	Terry Labonte	Oldsmobile
10.	Morgan Shepherd	Ford
11.	Dale Jarrett	Chevrolet
12.	Ricky Rudd	Chevrolet
13.	Mark Martin	Ford
14.	Derrike Cope	Chevrolet
15.	Rusty Wallace	Pontiac
16.	Richard Petty	Pontiac
17.	Sterling Marlin	Ford
18.	Charlie Glotzbach	Ford
19.	Ted Musgrave	Chevrolet
20.	Brett Bodine	Ford
21.	Bobby Hillin Jr.	Chevrolet
22.	Rick Mast	Oldsmobile
23.	Chad Little	Ford
24.	Bobby Hamilton	Oldsmobile
25.	Ernie Irvan	Chevrolet
26.	Jimmy Horton	Chevrolet
27.	Wally Dallenbach Jr.	Ford
28.	Michael Waltrip	Pontiac
29.	Hut Stricklin	Chevrolet
30.	Dave Marcis	Chevrolet
31.	Greg Sacks	Chevrolet
32.	Stanley Smith	Chevrolet
33.	Mike Wallace	Oldsmobile
34.	Lake Speed	Chevrolet
35.	Dorsey Schroeder	Ford
36.	Buddy Baker	Oldsmobile
37.	Jimmy Spencer	Chevrolet
38.	Jimmy Means	Pontiac
39.	Darrell Waltrip	Chevrolet
40.	Eddie Bierschwale	Oldsmobile
41.	Ken Schrader	Chevrolet
42.	Bob Schacht	Chevrolet

TRANSOUTH 500

March 29
Darlington, South Carolina

Time of Race: 3 hours, 35 minutes, 50 seconds
Average Speed: 139.364 mph
Margin of Victory: 8.8 seconds

FINISH	DRIVER	CAR
1.	Bill Elliott	Ford
2.	Harry Gant	Oldsmobile
3.	Mark Martin	Ford
4.	Davey Allison	Ford
5.	Ricky Rudd	Chevrolet
6.	Brett Bodine	Ford
7.	Dick Trickle	Ford
8.	Geoff Bodine	Ford
9.	Terry Labonte	Oldsmobile
10.	Dale Earnhardt	Chevrolet
11.	Rusty Wallace	Pontiac
12.	Ken Schrader	Chevrolet
13.	Morgan Shepherd	Ford
14.	Michael Waltrip	Pontiac
15.	Ted Musgrave	Pontiac
16.	Derrike Cope	Chevrolet
17.	Rick Mast	Oldsmobile
18.	Alan Kulwicki	Ford
19.	Bob Schacht	Oldsmobile
20.	Jimmy Means	Pontiac
21.	Dale Jarrett	Chevrolet
22.	Sterling Marlin	Ford
23.	Bobby Hamilton	Oldsmobile
24.	Darrell Waltrip	Chevrolet
25.	Dave Marcis	Chevrolet
26.	Ernie Irvan	Chevrolet
27.	Kyle Petty	Pontiac
28.	Greg Sacks	Chevrolet
29.	Hut Stricklin	Chevrolet
30.	Wally Dallenbach Jr.	Ford
31.	Mike Potter	Chevrolet
32.	Richard Petty	Pontiac
33.	Chad Little	Ford
34.	Dave Mader III	Ford
35.	Jerry Hill	Pontiac
36.	Jimmy Spencer	Chevrolet
37.	Johnny McFadden	Pontiac
38.	Kerry Teague	Ford
39.	James Hylton	Pontiac

FOOD CITY 500

April 5
Bristol, Tennessee
Time of Race: 3 hours, 5 minutes, 15 seconds
Average Speed: 86.316 mph
Margin of Victory: .72 second

FINISH	DRIVER	CAR
1.	Alan Kulwicki	Ford
2.	Dale Jarrett	Chevrolet
3.	Ken Schrader	Chevrolet
4.	Terry Labonte	Oldsmobile
5.	Dick Trickle	Ford
6.	Ricky Rudd	Chevrolet
7.	Morgan Shepherd	Ford
8.	Hut Stricklin	Chevrolet
9.	Rusty Wallace	Pontiac
10.	Derrike Cope	Chevrolet
11.	Brett Bodine	Ford
12.	Geoff Bodine	Ford
13.	Greg Sacks	Chevrolet
14.	Ted Musgrave	Oldsmobile
15.	Mark Martin	Ford
16.	Dave Mader III	Ford
17.	Michael Waltrip	Pontiac
18.	Dale Earnhardt	Chevrolet
19.	Kyle Petty	Pontiac
20.	Bill Elliott	Ford
21.	Brad Teague	Pontiac
22.	Wally Dallenbach Jr.	Ford
23.	Chad Little	Ford

24.	Ernie Irvan	Chevrolet
25.	Darrell Waltrip	Chevrolet
26.	Bobby Hamilton	Oldsmobile
27.	Richard Petty	Pontiac
28.	Davey Allison	Ford
29.	Harry Gant	Oldsmobile
30.	Rick Mast	Oldsmobile
31.	Dave Marcis	Chevrolet
32.	Sterling Marlin	Ford

FIRST UNION 400

April 12
North Wilkesboron, North Carolina
Time of Race: 2 hours, 45 minutes, 28 seconds
Average Speed: 90.653 mph.
Margin of Victory: .15 second

FINISH	DRIVER	CAR
1.	Davey Allison	Ford
2.	Rusty Wallace	Pontiac
3.	Ricky Rudd	Chevrolet
4.	Geoff Bodine	Ford
5.	Harry Gant	Oldsmobile
6.	Dale Earnhardt	Chevrolet
7.	Alan Kulwicki	Ford
8.	Sterling Marlin	Ford
9.	Terry Labonte	Oldsmobile
10.	Brett Bodine	Ford
11.	Dick Trickle	Ford
12.	Morgan Shepherd	Ford
13.	Ernie Irvan	Chevrolet
14.	Derrike Cope	Chevrolet
15.	Darrell Waltrip	Chevrolet
16.	Mark Martin	Ford
17.	Dale Jarrett	Chevrolet
18.	Hut Stricklin	Chevrolet
19.	Ted Musgrave	Oldsmobile
20.	Bill Elliott	Ford
21.	Greg Sacks	Chevrolet
22.	Ken Schrader	Chevrolet
23.	Rick Mast	Oldsmobile
24.	Dave Marcis	Chevrolet
25.	Bobby Hillin Jr.	Ford
26.	Jimmy Spencer	Chevrolet
27.	Bobby Hamilton	Oldsmobile
28.	Kyle Petty	Pontiac
29.	Michael Waltrip	Pontiac
30.	Wally Dallenbach Jr.	Ford
31.	Richard Petty	Pontiac
32.	Jimmy Means	Pontiac

HANES 500

April 26
Martinsville, Virginia
Time of Race: 3 hours, 22 minutes, 5 seconds
Average Speed: 78.086 mph
Margin of Victory: 12.125 seconds

FINISH	DRIVER	CAR
1.	Mark Martin	Ford
2.	Sterling Marlin	Ford
3.	Darrell Waltrip	Chevrolet
4.	Terry Labonte	Oldsmobile
5.	Harry Gant	Oldsmobile
6.	Morgan Shepherd	Ford
7.	Ken Schrader	Chevrolet
8.	Brett Bodine	Ford
9.	Dale Earnhardt	Chevrolet
10.	Bill Elliott	Ford
11.	Hut Stricklin	Chevrolet
12.	Greg Sacks	Chevrolet
13.	Bobby Hamilton	Oldsmobile

14.	Rick Mast	Oldsmobile
15.	Jimmy Hensley	Ford
16.	Alan Kulwicki	Ford
17.	Dick Trickle	Ford
18.	Kyle Petty	Pontiac
19.	Wally Dallenbach Jr.	Ford
20.	Ted Musgrave	Oldsmobile
21.	Dave Mader III	Ford
22.	Derrike Cope	Chevrolet
23.	Ricky Rudd	Chevrolet
24.	Dave Marcis	Chevrolet
25.	Ernie Irvan	Chevrolet
26.	Dave Allison	Ford
27.	Michael Waltrip	Pontiac
28.	Dale Jarrett	Chevrolet
29.	Richard Petty	Pontiac
30.	Jimmy Means	Pontiac
31.	Rusty Wallace	Pontiac
32.	Geoff Bodine	Ford

WINSTON 500

May 3
Talladega, Alabama
Time of Race: 2 hours, 59 minutes, 1 second
Average Speed: 167.609 mph
Margin of Victory: 2 car lengths

FINISH	DRIVER	CAR
1.	Davey Allison	Ford
2.	Bill Elliott	Ford
3.	Dale Earnhardt	Chevrolet
4.	Sterling Marlin	Ford
5.	Ernie Irvan	Chevrolet
6.	Alan Kulwicki	Ford
7.	Dale Jarrett	Chevrolet
8.	Mark Martin	Ford
9.	Morgan Shepherd	Ford
10.	Kyle Petty	Pontiac
11.	Rusty Wallace	Pontiac
12.	Derrike Cope	Chevrolet
13.	Geoff Bodine	Ford
14.	Wally Dallenbach Jr.	Ford
15.	Richard Petty	Pontiac
16.	Brett Bodine	Ford
17.	Rick Mast	Oldsmobile
18.	Dave Mader III	Ford
19.	Dick Trickle	Ford
20.	Bobby Hamilton	Oldsmobile
21.	Ted Musgrave	Chevrolet
22.	Hut Stricklin	Chevrolet
23.	Ken Schrader	Chevrolet
24.	Harry Gant	Oldsmobile
25.	Jimmy Hensley	Ford
26.	Ricky Rudd	Chevrolet
27.	Dave Marcis	Chevrolet
28.	Bobby Hillin Jr.	Chevrolet
29.	Darrell Waltrip	Chevrolet
30.	Bob Schacht	Oldsmobile
31.	Buddy Baker	Chevrolet
32.	Jimmy Spencer	Chevrolet
33.	Stanley Smith	Chevrolet
34.	Jimmy Means	Pontiac
35.	Greg Sacks	Chevrolet
36.	Terry Labonte	Ford
37.	Charlie Glotzbach	Ford
38.	Michael Waltrip	Pontiac
39.	Clay Young	Pontiac
40.	John McFadden	Pontiac

COCA COLA 600

May 24
Charlotte, North Carolina
Time of Race: 4 hours, 30 minutes, 43 seconds
Average Speed: 132.980 mph
Margin of Victory: .41 seconds

FINISH	DRIVER	CAR
1.	Dale Earnhardt	Chevrolet
2.	Ernie Irvan	Chevrolet
3.	Kyle Petty	Pontiac
4.	Davey Allison	Ford
5.	Harry Gant	Oldsmobile
6.	Terry Labonte	Oldsmobile
7.	Alan Kulwicki	Ford
8.	Ted Musgrave	Ford
9.	Ricky Rudd	Chevrolet
10.	Dick Trickle	Ford
11.	Jimmy Hensley	Ford
12.	Dale Jarrett	Chevrolet
13.	Bobby Hillin Jr.	Chevrolet
14.	Bill Elliott	Ford
15.	Dave Marcis	Chevrolet
16.	Greg Sacks	Chevrolet
17.	Derrike Cope	Chevrolet
18.	Rusty Wallace	Pontiac
19.	Lake Speed	Ford
20.	Brett Bodine	Ford
21.	Bobby Hamilton	Oldsmobile
22.	Sterling Marlin	Ford
23.	Rick Mast	Oldsmobile
24.	Randy Porter	Pontiac
25.	Michael Waltrip	Pontiac
26.	Ken Schrader	Chevrolet
27.	Jimmy Spencer	Chevrolet
28.	Wally Dallenbach Jr.	Ford
29.	Morgan Shepherd	Ford
30.	Stanley Smith	Chevrolet
31.	Bob Schacht	Chevrolet
32.	Geoff Bodine	Ford
33.	Mark Martin	Ford
34.	Hut Stricklin	Chevrolet
35.	Joe Ruttman	Oldsmobile
36.	Charlie Glotzbach	Ford
37.	Jim Sauter	Pontiac
38.	Darrell Waltrip	Chevrolet
39.	Dave Mader III	Ford
40.	Gary Balough	Chevrolet
41.	Richard Petty	Pontiac
42.	Jimmy Means	Pontiac

BUDWEISER 500

May 31
Dover, Delaware
Time of Race: 4 hours, 34 minutes, 5 seconds
Average Speed: 109.456 mph
Margin of Victory: 26 seconds

FINISH	DRIVER	CAR
1.	Harry Gant	Oldsmobile
2.	Dale Earnhardt	Chevrolet
3.	Rusty Wallace	Pontiac
4.	Ernie Irvan	Chevrolet
5.	Darrell Waltrip	Chevrolet
6.	Ricky Rudd	Chevrolet
7.	Hut Stricklin	Chevrolet
8.	Jimmy Hensley	Ford
9.	Dick Trickle	Ford
10.	Morgan Shepherd	Ford
11.	Davey Allison	Ford
12.	Alan Kulwicki	Ford
13.	Bill Elliott	Ford
14.	Sterling Marlin	Ford
15.	Michael Waltrip	Pontiac
16.	Ted Musgrave	Ford
17.	Geoff Bodine	Ford
18.	Bobby Hamilton	Oldsmobile
19.	Greg Sacks	Chevrolet
20.	Richard Petty	Pontiac
21.	Terry Labonte	Oldsmobile
22.	Jimmy Horton	Chevrolet
23.	Ken Schrader	Chevrolet
24.	Mark Martin	Ford
25.	David Marcis	Chevrolet
26.	Chad Little	Ford

FINISH	DRIVER	CAR
27.	Dale Jarrett	Chevrolet
28.	Mike Potter	Chevrolet
29.	Kyle Petty	Pontiac
30.	Brett Bodine	Ford
31.	Jimmy Means	Pontiac
32.	Rick Mast	Oldsmobile
33.	Derrike Cope	Chevrolet
34.	Wally Dallenbach Jr.	Ford
35.	James Hylton	Pontiac
36.	Jerry O'Neil	Oldsmobile
37.	Andy Belmont	Ford
38.	Jerry Hill	Pontiac
39.	D. K. Ulrich	Oldsmobile
40.	Graham Taylor	Pontiac

SAVE MART 300

June 7
Sonoma, California
Time of Race: 2 hours, 17 minutes, 26 seconds
Average Speed: 81.4126 mph
Margin of Victory: 3.60 seconds

FINISH	DRIVER	CAR
1.	Ernie Irvan	Chevrolet
2.	Terry Labonte	Oldsmobile
3.	Mark Martin	Ford
4.	Ricky Rudd	Chevrolet
5.	Bill Elliott	Ford
6.	Dale Earnhardt	Chevrolet
7.	Rusty Wallace	Pontiac
8.	Darrell Waltrip	Chevrolet
9.	Ken Schrader	Chevrolet
10.	Geoff Bodine	Ford
11.	Rick Mast	Oldsmobile
12.	Kyle Petty	Pontiac
13.	Tommy Kendall	Pontiac
14.	Alan Kulwicki	Ford
15.	Brett Bodine	Ford
16.	Sterling Marlin	Ford
17.	Harry Gant	Oldsmobile
18.	Derrike Cope	Chevrolet
19.	Bill Sedgwick	Chevrolet
20.	Michael Waltrip	Pontiac
21.	Richard Petty	Pontiac
22.	Ted Musgrave	Oldsmobile
23.	Dave Marcis	Chevrolet
24.	Bill Schmitt	Ford
25.	Wally Dallenbach Jr.	Ford
26.	Dick Trickle	Ford
27.	Hut Stricklin	Chevrolet
28.	Davey Allison	Ford
29.	Morgan Shepherd	Ford
30.	Jimmy Hensley	Ford
31.	John Krebs	Pontiac
32.	Ron Hornaday Jr.	Chevrolet
33.	R. K. Smith	Pontiac
34.	Bobby Hamilton	Oldsmobile
35.	Mike Chase	Pontiac
36.	Rick Scribner	Chevrolet
37.	Rick Carelli	Chevrolet
38.	Butch Gilliland	Pontiac
39.	Dale Jarrett	Chevrolet
40.	Jack Sellers	Buick
41.	Irv Hoerr	Oldsmobile
42.	Hershel McGriff	Chevrolet
43.	Greg Sacks	Chevrolet

CHAMPION SPARK PLUG 500

June 14
Pocono, Pennsylvania
Time of Race: 3 hours, 3 minutes, 18 seconds
Average Speed: 144.023 mph
Margin of Victory: 2.34 seconds

FINISH	DRIVER	CAR
1.	Alan Kulwicki	Ford
2.	Mark Martin	Ford
3.	Bill Elliott	Ford
4.	Ken Schrader	Chevrolet
5.	Davey Allison	Ford
6.	Kyle Petty	Pontiac
7.	Sterling Marlin	Ford
8.	Brett Bodine	Ford
9.	Jimmy Hensley	Ford
10.	Terry Labonte	Oldsmobile
11.	Greg Sacks	Chevrolet
12.	Derrike Cope	Chevrolet
13.	Darrell Waltrip	Chevrolet
14.	Geoff Bodine	Ford
15.	Michael Waltrip	Pontiac
16.	Richard Petty	Pontiac
17.	Bobby Hamilton	Oldsmobile
18.	Dave Marcis	Chevrolet
19.	Ernie Irvan	Chevrolet
20.	Mike Potter	Buick
21.	Jerry O'Neil	Buick
22.	Dale Jarrett	Chevrolet
23.	Harry Gant	Oldsmobile
24.	Rusty Wallace	Pontiac
25.	Morgan Shepherd	Ford
26.	James Hylton	Pontiac
27.	Wally Dallenbach Jr.	Ford
28.	Dale Earnhardt	Chevrolet
29.	Dick Trickle	Ford
30.	Rick Mast	Oldsmobile
31.	Hut Stricklin	Chevrolet
32.	Bobby Gerhart	Chevrolet
33.	Ted Musgrave	Ford
34.	Jimmy Horton	Chevrolet
35.	Jimmy Means	Pontiac
36.	Ricky Rudd	Chevrolet
37.	Chad Little	Ford
38.	Jerry Hill	Pontiac
39.	Mark Thompson	Ford
40.	Andy Belmont	Ford

MILLER GENUINE DRAFT 400

June 21
Brooklyn, Michigan
Time of Race: 2 hours, 37 minutes, 12 seconds
Average Speed: 152.672 mph
Margin of Victory: 3.31 seconds

FINISH	DRIVER	CAR
1.	Davey Allison	Ford
2.	Darrell Waltrip	Chevrolet
3.	Alan Kulwicki	Ford
4.	Kyle Petty	Pontiac
5.	Ricky Rudd	Chevrolet
6.	Mark Martin	Ford
7.	Harry Gant	Oldsmobile
8.	Ted Musgrave	Ford
9.	Dale Earnhardt	Chevrolet
10.	Bill Elliott	Ford
11.	Geoff Bodine	Ford
12.	Morgan Shepherd	Ford
13.	Ken Schrader	Chevrolet
14.	Greg Sacks	Chevrolet
15.	Richard Petty	Pontiac
16.	Charlie Glotzbach	Ford
17.	Bobby Hillin Jr.	Chevrolet
18.	Wally Dallenbach Jr.	Ford
19.	Brett Bodine	Ford
20.	Dick Trickle	Ford
21.	Chad Little	Ford
22.	Derrike Cope	Chevrolet
23.	Jimmy Means	Pontiac
24.	Dale Jarrett	Chevrolet
25.	James Hylton	Chevrolet
26.	Jimmy Horton	Chevrolet
27.	Michael Waltrip	Pontiac
28.	Rick Mast	Oldsmobile

FINISH	DRIVER	CAR
29.	Jimmy Hensley	Ford
30.	Ernie Irvan	Chevrolet
31.	Bobby Hamilton	Oldsmobile
32.	Sterling Marlin	Ford
33.	Mike Potter	Chevrolet
34.	Andy Belmont	Ford
35.	Hut Stricklin	Chevrolet
36.	Dave Marcis	Chevrolet
37.	Rusty Wallace	Pontiac
38.	Terry Labonte	Oldsmobile
39.	Jim Sauter	Pontiac
40.	Stanley Smith	Chevrolet
41.	H. B. Bailey	Pontiac

PEPSI 400

July 4
Daytona Beach, Florida
Time of Race: 2 hours, 20 minutes, 47 seconds
Average Speed: 170.457 mph
Margin of Victory: 2 car lengths

FINISH	DRIVER	CAR
1.	Ernie Irvan	Chevrolet
2.	Sterling Marlin	Ford
3.	Dale Jarrett	Chevrolet
4.	Geoff Bodine	Ford
5.	Bill Elliott	Ford
6.	Ken Schrader	Chevrolet
7.	Ricky Rudd	Chevrolet
8.	Mark Martin	Ford
9.	Rusty Wallace	Pontiac
10.	Davey Allison	Ford
11.	Wally Dallenbach Jr.	Ford
12.	Brett Bodine	Ford
13.	Darrell Waltrip	Chevrolet
14.	Kyle Petty	Pontiac
15.	Jimmy Hensley	Ford
16.	Ted Musgrave	Chevrolet
17.	Rick Mast	Oldsmobile
18.	Hut Stricklin	Chevrolet
19.	Morgan Shepherd	Ford
20.	Charlie Glotzbach	Ford
21.	Terry Labonte	Ford
22.	Stanley Smith	Chevrolet
23.	Harry Gant	Oldsmobile
24.	Chad Little	Ford
25.	Bobby Hillin Jr.	Chevrolet
26.	Greg Sacks	Chevrolet
27.	Michael Waltrip	Pontiac
28.	Phil Barkdoll	Oldsmobile
29.	Brad Teague	Chevrolet
30.	Alan Kulwicki	Ford
31.	Andy Belmont	Ford
32.	Dave Marcis	Chevrolet
33.	Bobby Hamilton	Chevrolet
34.	Derrike Cope	Chevrolet
35.	Dick Trickle	Ford
36.	Richard Petty	Pontiac
37.	Bobby Gerhart	Chevrolet
38.	Eddie Bierschwale	Oldsmobile
39.	Jimmy Means	Pontiac
40.	Dale Earnhardt	Chevrolet

MILLER GENUINE DRAFT 500

July 19
Pocono, Pennsylvania
Time of Race: 3 hours, 43 minutes, 47 seconds
Average Speed: 134.058 mph
Margin of Victory: 1.31 seconds

FINISH	DRIVER	CAR
1.	Darrell Waltrip	Chevrolet
2.	Harry Gant	Oldsmobile

3.	Alan Kulwicki	Ford
4.	Ricky Rudd	Chevrolet
5.	Ted Musgrave	Ford
6.	Mark Martin	Ford
7.	Kyle Petty	Pontiac
8.	Brett Bodine	Ford
9.	Dick Trickle	Ford
10.	Dale Jarrett	Chevrolet
11.	Sterling Marlin	Ford
12.	Ken Schrader	Chevrolet
13.	Bill Elliott	Ford
14.	Jimmy Hensley	Ford
15.	Morgan Shepherd	Ford
16.	Terry Labonte	Oldsmobile
17.	Chad Little	Ford
18.	Rusty Wallace	Pontiac
19.	Derrike Cope	Chevrolet
20.	Richard Petty	Pontiac
21.	Hut Stricklin	Chevrolet
22.	Bobby Hamilton	Oldsmobile
23.	Dale Earnhardt	Chevrolet
24.	Rick Mast	Oldsmobile
25.	Bobby Hillin Jr.	Chevrolet
26.	Michael Waltrip	Pontiac
27.	Mike Potter	Chevrolet
28.	Andy Belmont	Ford
29.	Greg Sacks	Chevrolet
30.	Geoff Bodine	Ford
31.	Dave Marcis	Chevrolet
32.	Wally Dallenbach Jr.	Ford
33.	Davey Allison	Ford
34.	Jimmy Horton	Chevrolet
35.	Jerry O'Neil	Oldsmobile
36.	Lake Speed	Ford
37.	Ernie Irvan	Chevrolet
38.	Bob Schacht	Chevrolet
39.	Jimmy Means	Pontiac
40.	James Hylton	Pontiac

DIEHARD 500

July 26
Talladega, Alabama
Time of Race: 2 hours, 5 minutes, 11 seconds
Average Speed: 176.309 mph
Margin of Victory: .19 second

FINISH	DRIVER	CAR
1.	Ernie Irvan	Chevrolet
2.	Sterling Marlin	Ford
3.	Davey Allison	Ford
4.	Ricky Rudd	Chevrolet
5.	Bill Elliott	Ford
6.	Kyle Petty	Pontiac
7.	Michael Waltrip	Pontiac
8.	Chad Little	Ford
9.	Ken Schrader	Chevrolet
10.	Brett Bodine	Ford
11.	Rusty Wallace	Pontiac
12.	Ted Musgrave	Chevrolet
13.	Morgan Shepherd	Ford
14.	Wally Dallenbach Jr.	Ford
15.	Richard Petty	Pontiac
16.	Hut Stricklin	Chevrolet
17.	Harry Gant	Oldsmobile
18.	Terry Labonte	Ford
19.	Greg Sacks	Chevrolet
20.	Mark Martin	Ford
21.	Dale Jarrett	Chevrolet
22.	Derrike Cope	Chevrolet
23.	Darrell Waltrip	Chevrolet
24.	Bobby Hamilton	Chevrolet
25.	Alan Kulwicki	Ford
26.	Rick Mast	Oldsmobile
27.	Stanley Smith	Chevrolet
28.	Dick Trickle	Ford
29.	Dave Marcis	Chevrolet
30.	Charlie Glotzbach	Ford
31.	Jimmy Hensley	Ford
32.	Jimmy Means	Pontiac
33.	Randy Porter	Pontiac

34.	Bobby Gerhart	Chevrolet
35.	T. W. Taylor	Pontiac
36.	Stan Fox	Chevrolet
37.	Delma Cowart	Ford
38.	Geoff Bodine	Ford
39.	Andy Belmont	Ford
40.	Dale Earnhardt	Chevrolet

BUDWEISER AT THE GLEN

August 9
Watkins Glen, New York
Time of Race: 1 hour, 27 minutes, 21 seconds
Average Speed: 88.980 mph
Margin of Victory: under caution

FINISH	DRIVER	CAR
1.	Kyle Petty	Pontiac
2.	Morgan Shepherd	Ford
3.	Ernie Irvan	Chevrolet
4.	Mark Martin	Ford
5.	Wally Dallenbach Jr.	Ford
6.	Rusty Wallace	Pontiac
7.	Alan Kulwicki	Ford
8.	Terry Labonte	Oldsmobile
9.	Dale Earnhardt	Chevrolet
10.	Brett Bodine	Ford
11.	Ted Musgrave	Ford
12.	Darrell Waltrip	Chevrolet
13.	Ricky Rudd	Chevrolet
14.	Bill Elliott	Ford
15.	Dale Jarrett	Chevrolet
16.	Sterling Marlin	Ford
17.	Dave Marcis	Chevrolet
18.	Harry Gant	Oldsmobile
19.	Scott Sharp	Chevrolet
20.	Davey Allison	Ford
21.	Ken Schrader	Chevrolet
22.	Bobby Hamilton	Oldsmobile
23.	Bobby Hillin Jr.	Chevrolet
24.	Dick Trickle	Ford
25.	Jerry O'Neil	Oldsmobile
26.	Jimmy Hensley	Ford
27.	Geoff Bodine	Ford
28.	Richard Petty	Pontiac
29.	Ed Ferree	Chevrolet
30.	Bob Schacht	Oldsmobile
31.	Greg Sacks	Chevrolet
32.	Rick Mast	Oldsmobile
33.	Mike Potter	Buick
34.	Derrike Cope	Chevrolet
35.	Michael Waltrip	Pontiac
36.	Hut Stricklin	Chevrolet
37.	Todd Bodine	Ford
38.	Denny Wilson	Pontiac
39.	James Hylton	Pontiac

CHAMPION SPARK PLUG 400

August 16
Brooklyn, Michigan
Time of Race: 2 hours, 47 minutes, 46 seconds
Average Speed: 146.056 mph
Margin of Victory: 4.94 seconds

FINISH	DRIVER	CAR
1.	Harry Gant	Oldsmobile
2.	Darrell Waltrip	Chevrolet
3.	Bill Elliott	Ford
4.	Ernie Irvan	Chevrolet
5.	Davey Allison	Ford
6.	Kyle Petty	Pontiac
7.	Sterling Marlin	Ford
8.	Dale Jarrett	Chevrolet
9.	Mark Martin	Ford

FINISH	DRIVER	CAR
10.	Morgan Shepherd	Ford
11.	Ken Schrader	Chevrolet
12.	Brett Bodine	Ford
13.	Rick Mast	Olds
14.	Alan Kulwicki	Ford
15.	Bobby Hamilton	Ford
16.	Dale Earnhardt	Chevrolet
17.	Chad Little	Ford
18.	Richard Petty	Pontiac
19.	Dick Trickle	Ford
20.	Wally Dallenbach Jr.	Ford
21.	Rusty Wallace	Pontiac
22.	Michael Waltrip	Pontiac
23.	Terry Labonte	Oldsmobile
24.	Hut Stricklin	Ford
25.	Ted Musgrave	Ford
26.	Bobby Hillin Jr.	Chevrolet
27.	Jeff Purvis	Chevrolet
28.	Eddie Bierschwale	Oldsmobile
29.	Jimmy Hensley	Ford
30.	Mike Potter	Chevrolet
31.	Jeff McClure	Chevrolet
32.	Dave Marcis	Chevrolet
33.	Derrike Cope	Chevrolet
34.	Lake Speed	Ford
35.	Stanley Smith	Chevrolet
36.	Ricky Rudd	Chevrolet
37.	Stan Fox	Chevrolet
38.	Jimmy Horton	Chevrolet
39.	Jimmy Means	Chevrolet
40.	Geoff Bodine	Ford
41.	Greg Sacks	Chevrolet

BUD 500

August 29
Bristol, Tennessee
Time of Race: 2 hours, 55 minutes, 20 seconds
Average Speed: 91.198 mph
Margin of Victory: 9.28 seconds

FINISH	DRIVER	CAR
1.	Darrell Waltrip	Chevrolet
2.	Dale Earnhardt	Chevrolet
3.	Ken Schrader	Chevrolet
4.	Kyle Petty	Pontiac
5.	Alan Kulwicki	Ford
6.	Bill Elliott	Ford
7.	Jimmy Hensley	Ford
8.	Ricky Rudd	Chevrolet
9.	Brett Bodine	Ford
10.	Rusty Wallace	Pontiac
11.	Geoff Bodine	Ford
12.	Derrike Cope	Chevrolet
13.	Morgan Shepherd	Ford
14.	Michael Waltrip	Pontiac
15.	Sterling Marlin	Ford
16.	Richard Petty	Pontiac
17.	Dale Jarrett	Chevrolet
18.	Jim Sauter	Chevrolet
19.	Wally Dallenbach Jr.	Ford
20.	Jimmy Spencer	Ford
21.	Bobby Hamilton	Oldsmobile
22.	Ted Musgrave	Ford
23.	Dick Trickle	Ford
24.	Jimmy Means	Pontiac
25.	Mark Martin	Ford
26.	Harry Gant	Oldsmobile
27.	Hut Strickin	Chevrolet
28.	Ernie Irvan	Chevrolet
29.	Rick Mast	Oldsmobile
30.	Davey Allison	Ford
31.	Terry Labonte	Oldsmobile
32.	Dave Marcis	Chevrolet

MOUNTAIN DEW SOUTHERN 500

September 6
Darlington, South Carolina

Time of Race: 3 hours, 9 minutes, 10 seconds
Average Speed: 129.114 mph
Margin of Victory: under caution

FINISH	DRIVER	CAR
1.	Darrell Waltrip	Chevrolet
2.	Mark Martin	Ford
3.	Bill Elliott	Ford
4.	Brett Bodine	Ford
5.	Davey Allison	Ford
6.	Dale Jarrett	Chevrolet
7.	Kyle Petty	Pontiac
8.	Alan Kulwicki	Ford
9.	Rusty Wallace	Pontiac
10.	Ricky Rudd	Chevrolet
11.	Hut Stricklin	Ford
12.	Derrike Cope	Chevrolet
13.	Ken Schrader	Chevrolet
14.	Terry Labonte	Oldsmobile
15.	Jimmy Hensley	Ford
16.	Harry Gant	Oldsmobile
17.	Bobby Hillin Jr.	Chevrolet
18.	Dave Marcis	Chevrolet
19.	Geoff Bodine	Ford
20.	Richard Petty	Pontiac
21.	Bobby Hamilton	Ford
22.	Jimmy Means	Pontiac
23.	Rick Mast	Oldsmobile
24.	Wally Dallenbach Jr.	Ford
25.	Ernie Irvan	Chevrolet
26.	Lake Speed	Ford
27.	Dick Trickle	Ford
28.	Sterling Marlin	Ford
29.	Dale Earnhardt	Chevrolet
30.	Ted Musgrave	Ford
31.	Morgan Shepherd	Ford
32.	Andy Belmont	Ford
33.	Mike Potter	Buick
34.	Chad Little	Ford
35.	Michael Waltrip	Pontiac
36.	Jim Sauter	Chevrolet
37.	James Hylton	Pontiac
38.	John McFadden	Pontiac

MILLER GENUINE DRAFT 400

September 12
Richmond, Virginia
Time of Race: 2 hours, 31 minutes, 59 seconds
Average Speed: 104.6613 mph
Margin of Victory: 3.59 seconds

FINISH	DRIVER	CAR
1.	Rusty Wallace	Pontiac
2.	Mark Martin	Ford
3.	Darrell Waltrip	Chevrolet
4.	Dale Earnhardt	Chevrolet
5.	Geoff Bodine	Ford
6.	Ricky Rudd	Chevrolet
7.	Morgan Shepherd	Ford
8.	Harry Gant	Oldsmobile
9.	Ken Schrader	Chevrolet
10.	Ted Musgrave	Ford
11.	Ernie Irvan	Chevrolet
12.	Kyle Petty	Pontiac
13.	Terry Labonte	Oldsmobile
14.	Bill Elliott	Ford
15.	Alan Kulwicki	Ford
16.	Richard Petty	Pontiac
17.	Jimmy Hensley	Ford
18.	Brett Bodine	Buick
19.	Davey Allison	Ford
20.	Dick Trickle	Ford
21.	Sterling Marlin	Ford
22.	Jeff Purvis	Chevrolet
23.	Wally Dallenbach	Ford
24.	Dave Marcis	Chevrolet

25.	Dale Jarrett	Chevrolet
26.	Jim Sauter	Chevrolet
27.	Chad Little	Ford
28.	Rick Mast	Oldsmobile
29.	Jimmy Means	Pontiac
30.	Hut Stricklin	Ford
31.	Jimmy Horton	Chevrolet
32.	Bobby Hamilton	Ford
33.	Michael Waltrip	Pontiac
34.	Stanley Smith	Chevrolet
35.	Derrike Cope	Chevrolet

PEAK ANTIFREEZE 500

September 20
Dover, Delaware
Time of Race: 4 hours, 20 minutes, 13 seconds
Average Speed: 115.289 mph
Margin of Victory: .47 second

FINISH	DRIVER	CAR
1.	Ricky Rudd	Chevrolet
2.	Bill Elliott	Ford
3.	Kyle Petty	Pontiac
4.	Davey Allison	Ford
5.	Morgan Shepherd	Ford
6.	Harry Gant	Oldsmobile
7.	Terry Labonte	Oldsmobile
8.	Ted Musgrave	Ford
9.	Derrike Cope	Chevrolet
10.	Bobby Hamilton	Ford
11.	Ernie Irvan	Chevrolet
12.	Dale Jarrett	Chevrolet
13.	Jimmy Hensley	Ford
14.	Geoff Bodine	Ford
15.	Hut Stricklin	Ford
16.	Rusty Wallace	Pontiac
17.	Michael Waltrip	Pontiac
18.	Jim Sauter	Chevrolet
19.	Mark Martin	Ford
20.	Darrell Waltrip	Chevrolet
21.	Dale Earnhardt	Chevrolet
22.	Brett Bodine	Ford
23.	Jimmy Means	Pontiac
24.	Rick Mast	Oldsmobile
25.	Mike Potter	Buick
26.	Dave Marcis	Chevrolet
27.	Dick Trickle	Ford
28.	Richard Petty	Pontiac
29.	Chad Little	Ford
30.	Ken Schrader	Chevrolet
31.	Wally Dallenbach Jr.	Ford
32.	Jeff Purvis	Chevrolet
33.	Sterling Marlin	Ford
34.	Alan Kulwicki	Ford
35.	James Hylton	Pontiac
36.	Graham Taylor	Chevrolet

GOODY'S 500

September 27
Martinsville, Virginia
Time of Race: 3 hours, 29 minutes, 13 seconds
Average Speed: 75.424 mph
Margin of Victory: .19 second

FINISH	DRIVER	CAR
1.	Geoff Bodine	Ford
2.	Rusty Wallace	Pontiac
3.	Brett Bodine	Ford
4.	Kyle Petty	Pontiac
5.	Alan Kulwicki	Ford
6.	Dick Trickle	Ford
7.	Sterling Marlin	Ford

8.	Mark Martin	Ford
9.	Rick Mast	Oldsmobile
10.	Ricky Rudd	Chevrolet
11.	Terry Labonte	Oldsmobile
12.	Ted Musgrave	Ford
13.	Ken Schrader	Chevrolet
14.	Wally Dallenbach Jr.	Ford
15.	Darrell Waltrip	Chevrolet
16.	Davey Allison	Ford
17.	Jimmy Hensley	Ford
18.	Richard Petty	Pontiac
19.	Harry Gant	Oldsmobile
20.	Derrike Cope	Chevrolet
21.	Morgan Shepherd	Ford
22.	Jim Sauter	Chevrolet
23.	Dale Jarrett	Chevrolet
24.	Hut Stricklin	Ford
25.	Dave Marcis	Chevrolet
26.	Jeff Purvis	Chevrolet
27.	Ernie Irvan	Chevrolet
28.	Bobby Hamilton	Ford
29.	Michael Waltrip	Pontiac
30.	Bill Elliott	Ford
31.	Dale Earnhardt	Chevrolet

TYSON HOLLY FARMS 400

October 5
North Wilkesboro, North Carolina
Time of Race: 2 hours, 19 minutes, 43 seconds
Average Speed: 107.360 mph
Margin of Victory: 5.34 seconds

FINISH	DRIVER	CAR
1.	Geoff Bodine	Ford
2.	Mark Martin	Ford
3.	Kyle Petty	Pontiac
4.	Rusty Wallace	Pontiac
5.	Sterling Marlin	Ford
6.	Ernie Irvan	Chevrolet
7.	Brett Bodine	Ford
8.	Terry Labonte	Oldsmobile
9.	Darrell Waltrip	Chevrolet
10.	Dale Jarrett	Chevrolet
11.	Davey Allison	Ford
12.	Alan Kulwicki	Ford
13.	Harry Gant	Oldsmobile
14.	Ted Musgrave	Ford
15.	Ricky Rudd	Chevrolet
16.	Michael Waltrip	Pontiac
17.	Morgan Shepherd	Ford
18.	Dick Trickle	Ford
19.	Dale Earnhardt	Chevrolet
20.	Rich Bickle	Ford
21.	Rick Mast	Oldsmobile
22.	Derrike Cope	Chevrolet
23.	Ken Schrader	Chevrolet
24.	Wally Dallenbach Jr.	Ford
25.	Jimmy Hensley	Ford
26.	Bill Elliott	Ford
27.	Richard Petty	Pontiac
28.	Dave Marcis	Chevrolet
29.	Jim Sauter	Chevrolet
30.	Hut Stricklin	Ford
31.	Bobby Hamilton	Ford
32.	Jeff Purvis	Chevrolet

MELLO YELLO 500

October 12
Charlotte, North Carolina
Time of Race: 3 hours, 15 minutes, 47 seconds
Average Speed: 153.537 mph
Margin of Victory: 1.88 seconds

FINISH	DRIVER	CAR
1.	Mark Martin	Ford
2.	Alan Kulwicki	Ford
3.	Kyle Petty	Pontiac
4.	Jimmy Spencer	Ford
5.	Ricky Rudd	Chevrolet
6.	Ernie Irvan	Chevrolet
7.	Ken Schrader	Chevrolet
8.	Harry Gant	Oldsmobile
9.	Dick Trickle	Ford
10.	Geoff Bodine	Ford
11.	Ted Musgrave	Ford
12.	Terry Labonte	Chevrolet
13.	Morgan Shepherd	Ford
14.	Dale Earnhardt	Chevrolet
15.	Bobby Hamilton	Ford
16.	Sterling Marlin	Ford
17.	Derrike Cope	Chevrolet
18.	Jimmy Hensley	Ford
19.	Davey Allison	Ford
20.	Wally Dallenbach Jr.	Ford
21.	Jim Sauter	Chevrolet
22.	Bob Schacht	Oldsmobile
23.	Michael Waltrip	Pontiac
24.	Dale Jarrett	Chevrolet
25.	Rich Bickle	Ford
26.	Lake Speed	Ford
27.	Richard Petty	Pontiac
28.	Brett Bodine	Ford
29.	Jerry O'Neil	Oldsmobile
30.	Bill Elliott	Ford
31.	Hut Stricklin	Ford
32.	Poncho Carter	Ford
33.	Chad Little	Ford
34.	Darrell Waltrip	Chevrolet
35.	Rick Mast	Oldsmobile
36.	Stanley Smith	Chevrolet
37.	Rusty Wallace	Pontiac
38.	Jimmy Means	Pontiac
39.	Dave Marcis	Chevrolet
40.	Bobby Hillin Jr.	Chevrolet

AC DELCO 500

October 25
Rockingham, North Carolina
Time of Race: 3 hours, 49 minutes, 37 seconds
Average Speed: 130.748 mph
Margin of Victory: .91 second

FINISH	DRIVER	CAR
1.	Kyle Petty	Pontiac
2.	Ernie Irvan	Chevrolet
3.	Ricky Rudd	Chevrolet
4.	Bill Eilliott	Ford
5.	Sterling Marlin	Ford
6.	Harry Gant	Oldsmobile
7.	Brett Bodine	Ford
8.	Dale Earnhardt	Chevrolet
9.	Terry Labonte	Oldsmobile
10.	Davey Allison	Ford
11.	Jimmy Spencer	Chevrolet
12.	Alan Kulwicki	Ford
13.	Morgan Shepherd	Ford
14.	Derrike Cope	Chevrolet
15.	Dale Jarrett	Chevrolet
16.	Dick Trickle	Ford
17.	Rick Mast	Oldsmobile
18.	Jimmy Hensley	Ford
19.	Bobby Hamilton	Ford
20.	Michael Waltrip	Pontiac
21.	Rusty Wallace	Pontiac
22.	Darrell Waltrip	Chevrolet
23.	Wally Dallenbach Jr.	Ford
24.	Chad Little	Ford
25.	Richard Petty	Pontiac
26.	Jimmy Means	Pontiac
27.	Mike Wallace	Ford
28.	Mike Skinner	Chevrolet
29.	Ted Musgrave	Ford

FINISH	DRIVER	CAR
30.	Mark Martin	Ford
31.	Dave Blaney	Pontiac
32.	Ken Schrader	Chevrolet
33.	Greg Sacks	Chevrolet
34.	Jimmy Horton	Chevrolet
35.	Geoff Bodine	Ford
36.	Lake Speed	Ford
37.	Jerry O'Neil	Oldsmobile
38.	Dave Marcis	Chevrolet
39.	Mike Potter	Pontiac
40.	Johnny McFadden	Chevrolet

PYROIL 500

November 1
Phoenix, Arizona
Time of Race: 3 hours, 0 minutes, 12 seconds
Average Speed: 103.885 mph
Margin of Victory: 3.22 seconds

FINISH	DRIVER	CAR
1.	Davey Allison	Ford
2.	Mark Martin	Ford
3.	Darrell Waltrip	Chevrolet
4.	Alan Kulwicki	Ford
5.	Jimmy Spencer	Ford
6.	Ken Schrader	Chevrolet
7.	Derrike Cope	Chevrolet
8.	Bobby Hamilton	Ford
9.	Sterling Marlin	Ford
10.	Dale Earnhardt	Chevrolet
11.	Michael Waltrip	Pontiac
12.	Brett Bodine	Ford
13.	Wally Dallenbach Jr.	Ford
14.	Harry Gant	Oldsmobile
15.	Hut Stricklin	Chevrolet
16.	Terry Labonte	Oldsmobile
17.	Rick Mast	Oldsmobile
18.	Lake Speed	Ford
19.	Kyle Petty	Pontiac
20.	Dale Jarrett	Chevrolet
21.	Jimmy Hensley	Ford
22.	Richard Petty	Pontiac
23.	John Krebs	Chevrolet
24.	Ted Musgrave	Ford
25.	Ron Hornaday Jr.	Chevrolet
26.	Jeff Davis	Ford
27.	Bill Sedgwick	Chevrolet
28.	Rusty Wallace	Pontiac
29.	Butch Gilliland	Pontiac
30.	Ricky Rudd	Chevrolet
31.	Bill Elliott	Ford
32.	Stanley Smith	Chevrolet
33.	Bill Schmitt	Ford
34.	Ernie Irvan	Chevrolet
35.	Dave Marcis	Chevrolet
36.	Jeff Purvis	Chevrolet
37.	Scott Gaylord	Pontiac
38.	Morgan Shepherd	Ford
39.	Geoff Bodine	Ford
40.	Dick Trickle	Ford
41.	Rick Scribner	Chevrolet
42.	Rick Carelli	Chevrolet

HOOTERS 500

November 15
Atlanta, Georgia
Time of Race: 3 hours, 44 minutes, 20 seconds
Average Speed: 133.322 mph
Margin of Victory: 8.06 seconds

FINISH	DRIVER	CAR
1.	Bill Elliott	Ford
2.	Alan Kulwicki	Ford

3.	Geoff Bodine	Ford
4.	Jimmy Spencer	Ford
5.	Terry Labonte	Chevrolet
6.	Rusty Wallace	Pontiac
7.	Sterling Marlin	Ford
8.	Jimmy Hensley	Ford
9.	Ted Musgrave	Ford
10.	Dale Jarrett	Chevrolet
11.	Morgan Shepherd	Ford
12.	Bobby Hamilton	Ford
13.	Harry Gant	Oldsmobile
14.	Michael Waltrip	Pontiac
15.	Derrike Cope	Chevrolet
16.	Kyle Petty	Pontiac
17.	Chad Little	Ford
18.	Lake Speed	Ford
19.	Eddie Bierschwale	Oldsmobile
20.	Mike Wallace	Pontiac
21.	Jimmy Means	Ford
22.	Dave Marcis	Chevrolet
23.	Darrell Waltrip	Chevrolet
24.	Jimmy Horton	Chevrolet
25.	Ricky Rudd	Chevrolet
26.	Dale Earnhardt	Chevrolet
27.	Davey Allison	Ford
28.	Rick Mast	Oldsmobile
29.	Ernie Irvan	Chevrolet
30.	Bobby Hillin Jr.	Ford
31.	Jeff Gordon	Chevrolet
32.	Mark Martin	Ford
33.	Bob Schacht	Oldsmobile
34.	Rich Bickle	Ford
35.	Richard Petty	Pontiac
36.	Ken Schrader	Chevrolet
37.	Dick Trickle	Ford
38.	Wally Dallenbach Jr.	Ford
39.	Stanley Smith	Chevrolet
40.	Brett Bodine	Ford
41.	Hut Stricklin	Ford

27.	Bobby Hamilton	Ford
28.	Davey Allison	Ford
29.	Derrike Cope	Ford
30.	Ricky Rudd	Chevrolet
31.	Kyle Petty	Pontiac
32.	Rusty Wallace	Pontiac
33.	Dave Marcis	Chevrolet
34.	Rick Wilson	Pontiac
35.	Bobby Hillin	Ford
36.	Al Unser Jr.	Chevrolet
37.	Ernie Irvan	Chevrolet
38.	Joe Ruttman	Ford
39.	Bill Elliott	Ford
40.	Jimmy Hensley	Ford
41.	Dick Trickle	Ford

1993

DAYTONA 500

February 14
Daytona Beach, Florida
Time of Race: 3 hours, 13 minutes, 35 seconds
Average Speed: 154.972 mph
Margin of Victory: .16 second

FINISH	DRIVER	CAR
1.	Dale Jarrett	Chevrolet
2.	Dale Earnhardt	Chevrolet
3.	Geoff Bodine	Ford
4.	Hut Stricklin	Ford
5.	Jeff Gordon	Chevrolet
6.	Mark Martin	Ford
7.	Morgan Shepherd	Ford
8.	Ken Schrader	Chevrolet
9.	Sterling Marlin	Ford
10.	Wally Dallenbach Jr.	Ford
11.	Terry Labonte	Chevrolet
12.	Rick Mast	Ford
13.	Jimmy Spencer	Ford
14.	Lake Speed	Ford
15.	Ted Musgrave	Ford
16.	Michael Waltrip	Pontiac
17.	Brett Bodine	Ford
18.	Darrell Waltrip	Chevrolet
19.	Jim Sauter	Ford
20.	Bobby Labonte	Ford
21.	Harry Gant	Chevrolet
22.	Phil Parsons	Chevrolet
23.	Kenny Wallace	Pontiac
24.	Chad Little	Ford
25.	Jimmy Horton	Chevrolet
26.	Alan Kulwicki	Ford

GOODWRENCH 500

February 28
Rockingham, North Carolina
Time of Race: 4 hours, 1 minute, 10 seconds
Average Speed: 124.486 mph
Margin of Victory: .5 second

FINISH	DRIVER	CAR
1.	Rusty Wallace	Pontiac
2.	Dale Earnhardt	Chevrolet
3.	Ernie Irvan	Chevrolet
4.	Alan Kulwicki	Ford
5.	Mark Martin	Ford
6.	Dale Jarrett	Chevrolet
7.	Ted Musgrave	Ford
8.	Phil Parsons	Chevrolet
9.	Geoff Bodine	Ford
10.	Terry Labonte	Chevrolet
11.	Bill Elliott	Ford
12.	Ricky Rudd	Chevrolet
13.	Hut Stricklin	Ford
14.	Davey Allison	Ford
15.	Bobby Hamilton	Ford
16.	Jimmy Spencer	Ford
17.	Rick Wilson	Pontiac
18.	Derrike Cope	Ford
19.	Bobby Hillin Jr.	Ford
20.	Wally Dallenbach Jr.	Ford
21.	Dave Marcis	Chevrolet
22.	Brett Bodine	Ford
23.	Kenny Wallace	Pontiac
24.	Ken Schrader	Chevrolet
25.	Jimmy Hensley	Ford
26.	Michael Waltrip	Pontiac
27.	Ed Ferree	Chevrolet
28.	Sterling Marlin	Ford
29.	Dick Trickle	Ford
30.	Darrell Waltrip	Chevrolet
31.	Harry Gant	Chevrolet
32.	Kyle Petty	Pontiac
33.	Bobby Labonte	Ford
34.	Jeff Gordon	Chevrolet
35.	Morgan Shepherd	Ford
36.	John Chapman	Pontiac
37.	Mike Potter	Ford
38.	Jerry Hill	Chevrolet
39.	Rick Mast	Ford
40.	James Hylton	Pontiac

PONTIAC EXCITEMENT 400

March 7
Richmond, Virginia
Time of Race: 2 hours, 47 minutes, 7 seconds
Average Speed: 107.709 mph
Margin of Victory: 4.38 seconds

FINISH	DRIVER	CAR
1.	Davey Allison	Ford
2.	Rusty Wallace	Pontiac
3.	Alan Kulwicki	Ford
4.	Dale Jarrett	Chevrolet
5.	Kyle Petty	Pontiac
6.	Jeff Gordon	Chevrolet
7.	Mark Martin	Ford
8.	Darrell Waltrip	Chevrolet
9.	Harry Gant	Chevrolet
10.	Dale Earnhardt	Chevrolet
11.	Ernie Irvan	Chevrolet
12.	Geoff Bodine	Ford
13.	Jimmy Spencer	Ford
14.	Morgan Shepherd	Ford
15.	Ricky Rudd	Chevrolet
16.	Phil Parsons	Chevrolet
17.	Ted Musgrave	Ford
18.	Hut Stricklin	Ford
19.	Derrike Cope	Ford
20.	Ken Schrader	Chevrolet
21.	Dick Trickle	Ford
22.	Bobby Hamilton	Ford
23.	Michael Waltrip	Pontiac
24.	Terry Labonte	Chevrolet
25.	Rick Wilson	Pontiac
26.	Kenny Wallace	Pontiac
27.	Wally Dallenbach Jr.	Ford
28.	Bobby Hillin Jr.	Ford
29.	Bobby Labonte	Ford
30.	Lake Speed	Ford
31.	Sterling Marlin	Ford
32.	Brett Bodine	Ford
33.	Bill Elliott	Ford
34.	Jimmy Hensley	Ford
35.	Rick Mast	Ford
36.	Dave Marcis	Chevrolet

MOTORCRAFT 500

March 20
Atlanta, Georgia
Time of Race: 3 hours, 17 minutes, 26 seconds
Average Speed: 150.442 mph
Margin of Victory: 18 seconds

FINISH	DRIVER	CAR
1.	Morgan Shepherd	Ford
2.	Ernie Irvan	Chevrolet
3.	Rusty Wallace	Pontiac
4.	Jeff Gordon	Chevrolet
5.	Ricky Rudd	Chevrolet
6.	Geoff Bodine	Ford
7.	Kyle Petty	Pontiac
8.	Brett Bodine	Ford
9.	Bill Elliott	Ford
10.	Jimmy Spencer	Ford
11.	Dale Earnhardt	Chevrolet
12.	Sterling Marlin	Ford
13.	Davey Allison	Ford
14.	Michael Waltrip	Pontiac
15.	Bobby Hillin	Ford
16.	Kenney Wallace	Pontiac
17.	Derrike Cope	Ford
18.	Bobby Labonte	Ford
19.	Ted Musgrave	Ford
20.	Hut Stricklin	Ford
21.	Harry Gant	Chevrolet
22.	Jimmy Means	Ford
23.	Greg Sacks	Ford
24.	Rick Wilson	Pontiac
25.	Wally Dallenbach	Ford
26.	Bobby Hamilton	Ford
27.	Jimmy Horton	Chevrolet
28.	Lake Speed	Ford
29.	Ken Schrader	Chevrolet
30.	Rick Mast	Ford
31.	Dale Jarrett	Chevrolet
32.	Mark Martin	Ford

FINISH	DRIVER	CAR
33.	Terry Labonte	Chevrolet
34.	Dave Marcis	Chevrolet
35.	Darrell Waltrip	Chevrolet
36.	Alan Kulwicki	Ford
37.	Dick Trickle	Ford
38.	Joe Ruttman	Ford
39.	Phil Parsons	Chevrolet
40.	Bob Schacht	Oldsmobile

TRANSOUTH 500

March 28
Darlington, South Carolina
Time of Race: 3 hours, 33 minutes, 29 seconds
Average Speed: 139.958 mph
Margin of Victory: 1.63 seconds

FINISH	DRIVER	CAR
1.	Dale Earnhardt	Chevrolet
2.	Mark Martin	Ford
3.	Dale Jarrett	Chevrolet
4.	Ken Schrader	Chevrolet
5.	Rusty Wallace	Pontiac
6.	Alan Kulwicki	Ford
7.	Kyle Petty	Pontiac
8.	Geoff Bodine	Ford
9.	Terry Labonte	Chevrolet
10.	Morgan Shepherd	Ford
11.	Davey Allison	Ford
12.	Brett Bodine	Ford
13.	Wally Dallenbach	Ford
14.	Bill Elliott	Ford
15.	Rick Mast	Ford
16.	Darrell Waltrip	Chevrolet
17.	Derrike Cope	Ford
18.	Bobby Labonte	Ford
19.	Ricky Rudd	Chevrolet
20.	Dick Trickle	Ford
21.	Sterling Marlin	Ford
22.	Ernie Irvan	Chevrolet
23.	Bobby Hamilton	Ford
24.	Jeff Gordon	Chevrolet
25.	Dave Marcis	Chevrolet
26.	Rick Wilson	Oldsmobile
27.	Bob Schacht	Oldsmobile
28.	Hut Stricklin	Ford
29.	Jimmy Spencer	Ford
30.	Ted Musgrave	Ford
31.	Jimmy Means	Ford
32.	Kenny Wallace	Pontiac
33.	Michael Waltrip	Pontiac
34.	James Hylton	Pontiac
35.	Bobby Hillin	Ford
36.	Phil Parsons	Chevrolet
37.	Harry Gant	Chevrolet
38.	Mike Potter	Ford
39.	Norm Benning	Oldsmobile

FOOD CITY 500

April 4
Bristol, Tennessee
Time of Race: 3 hours, 8 minutes, 43 seconds
Average Speed: 84.730 mph
Margin of Victory: .82 seconds

FINISH	DRIVER	CAR
1.	Rusty Wallace	Pontiac
2.	Dale Earnhardt	Chevrolet
3.	Kyle Petty	Pontiac
4.	Jimmy Spencer	Ford
5.	Davey Allison	Ford
6.	Darrell Waltrip	Chevrolet
7.	Morgan Shepherd	Ford

8.	Mark Martin	Ford
9.	Brett Bodine	Ford
10.	Rick Mast	Ford
11.	Wally Dallenbach	Ford
12.	Derrike Cope	Ford
13.	Kenny Wallace	Pontiac
14.	Michael Waltrip	Pontiac
15.	Ted Musgrave	Ford
16.	Jimmy Means	Ford
17.	Jeff Gordon	Chevrolet
18.	Geoff Bodine	Ford
19.	Joe Ruttman	Ford
20.	Sterling Marlin	Ford
21.	Terry Labonte	Chevrolet
22.	Dick Trickle	Ford
23.	Ernie Irvan	Chevrolet
24.	Bobby Labonte	Ford
25.	Rick Wilson	Pontiac
26.	Ricky Rudd	Chevrolet
27.	Hut Stricklin	Ford
28.	Harry Gant	Chevrolet
29.	Lake Speed	Ford
30.	Bill Elliott	Ford
31.	Phil Parsons	Chevrolet
32.	Dale Jarrett	Chevrolet
33.	Bobby Hillin	Ford
34.	Ken Schrader	Chevrolet
35.	Bobby Hamilton	Ford

FIRST UNION 400

April 18
North Wilkesboro, North Carolina
Time of Race: 2 hours, 41 minutes, 59 seconds
Average Speed: 92.602 mph
Margin of Victory: 1.66 seconds

FINISH	DRIVER	CAR
1.	Rusty Wallace	Pontiac
2.	Kyle Petty	Pontiac
3.	Ken Schrader	Chevrolet
4.	Davey Allison	Ford
5.	Darrell Waltrip	Chevrolet
6.	Terry Labonte	Chevrolet
7.	Ricky Rudd	Chevrolet
8.	Morgan Shepherd	Ford
9.	Sterling Marlin	Ford
10.	Bill Elliott	Ford
11.	Ernie Irvan	Chevrolet
12.	Jimmy Hensley	Ford
13.	Harry Gant	Chevrolet
14.	Jimmy Spencer	Ford
15.	Kenny Wallace	Pontiac
16.	Dale Earnhardt	Chevrolet
17.	Brett Bodine	Ford
18.	Phil Parsons	Chevrolet
19.	Rick Mast	Ford
20.	Michael Waltrip	Pontiac
21.	Wally Dallenbach	Ford
22.	Hut Stricklin	Ford
23.	Rick Wilson	Pontiac
24.	Ted Musgrave	Ford
25.	Bobby Labonte	Ford
26.	Bobby Hillin	Ford
27.	Jimmy Means	Ford
28.	Geoff Bodine	Ford
29.	Bobby Hamilton	Ford
30.	Derrike Cope	Ford
31.	Mark Martin	Ford
32.	Dale Jarrett	Chevrolet
33.	Dick Trickle	Ford
34.	Jeff Gordon	Chevrolet

HANES 500

April 25
Martinsville, Virginia

Time of Race: 3 hours, 18 minutes, 33 seconds
Average Speed: 79.078 mph
Margin of Victory: under caution

FINISH	DRIVER	CAR
1.	Rusty Wallace	Pontiac
2.	Davey Allison	Ford
3.	Dale Jarrett	Chevrolet
4.	Darrell Waltrip	Chevrolet
5.	Kyle Petty	Pontiac
6.	Geoff Bodine	Ford
7.	Brett Bodine	Ford
8.	Jeff Gordon	Chevrolet
9.	Terry Labonte	Chevrolet
10.	Mark Martin	Ford
11.	Rick Mast	Ford
12.	Bobby Labonte	Ford
13.	Jimmy Hensley	Ford
14.	Dick Trickle	Ford
15.	Dave Marcis	Chevrolet
16.	Michael Waltrip	Pontiac
17.	Rick Wilson	Ford
18.	Ken Schrader	Chevrolet
19.	Morgan Shepherd	Ford
20.	Phil Parsons	Chevrolet
21.	Sterling Marlin	Ford
22.	Dale Earnhardt	Chevrolet
23.	Bobby Hillin	Ford
24.	Kenny Wallace	Pontiac
25.	Derrike Cope	Ford
26.	Hut Stricklin	Ford
27.	Bill Elliott	Ford
28.	Ted Musgrave	Ford
29.	Ricky Rudd	Chevrolet
30.	Jimmy Spencer	Ford
31.	Harry Gant	Chevrolet
32.	Ernie Irvan	Chevrolet
33.	Bobby Hamilton	Ford
34.	Wally Dallenbach	Ford

WINSTON 500

May 2
Talladega, Alabama
Time of Race: 3 hours, 13 minutes, 4 seconds
Average Speed: 155.412 mph
Margin of Victory: 1 car length

FINISH	DRIVER	CAR
1.	Ernie Irvan	Chevrolet
2.	Jimmy Spencer	Ford
3.	Dale Jarrett	Chevrolet
4.	Dale Earnhardt	Chevrolet
5.	Joe Ruttman	Ford
6.	Rusty Wallace	Pontiac
7.	Davey Allison	Ford
8.	Derrike Cope	Ford
9.	Jimmy Hensley	Ford
10.	Michael Waltrip	Pontiac
11.	Jeff Gordon	Chevrolet
12.	Mark Martin	Ford
13.	Rick Mast	Ford
14.	Kenny Wallace	Pontiac
15.	Morgan Shepherd	Ford
16.	Rick Wilson	Pontiac
17.	Bobby Hillin	Ford
18.	Kyle Petty	Pontiac
19.	Phil Parsons	Chevrolet
20.	Hut Stricklin	Ford
21.	Ken Schrader	Chevrolet
22.	Bill Elliott	Ford
23.	Harry Gant	Chevrolet
24.	Sterling Marlin	Ford
25.	Ritchie Petty	Ford
26.	Darrell Waltrip	Chevrolet
27.	Geoff Bodine	Ford
28.	Ted Musgrave	Ford

29.	Wally Dallenbach	Ford
30.	Brett Bodine	Ford
31.	Dick Trickle	Ford
32.	Jimmy Means	Ford
33.	Greg Sacks	Ford
34.	Lake Speed	Ford
35.	Bobby Labonte	Ford
36.	Jimmy Horton	Chevrolet
37.	Terry Labonte	Chevrolet
38.	Rich Bickle	Ford
39.	Jeff Purvis	Chevrolet
40.	Ken Bouchard	Ford
41.	Ricky Rudd	Chevrolet

SAVE MART SUPERMARKETS 300

May 16
Sonoma, California
Time of Race: 2 hours, 25 minutes, 17 seconds
Average Speed: 77.013 mph
Margin of Victory: .53 second

FINISH	DRIVER	CAR
1.	Geoff Bodine	Ford
2.	Ernie Irvan	Chevrolet
3.	Ricky Rudd	Chevrolet
4.	Ken Schrader	Chevrolet
5.	Kyle Petty	Pontiac
6.	Dale Earnhardt	Chevrolet
7.	Wally Dallenbach	Ford
8.	Rick Wilson	Pontiac
9.	Terry Labonte	Chevrolet
10.	Hut Stricklin	Ford
11.	Jeff Gordon	Chevrolet
12.	Sterling Marlin	Ford
13.	Dale Jarrett	Chevrolet
14.	Morgan Shepherd	Ford
15.	Davey Allison	Ford
16.	Bobby Labonte	Ford
17.	Bill Elliott	Ford
18.	Derrike Cope	Ford
19.	Harry Gant	Chevrolet
20.	Dick Trickle	Ford
21.	Rick Carelli	Chevrolet
22.	Tommy Kendall	Ford
23.	Michael Waltrip	Pontiac
24.	Brett Bodine	Ford
25.	P. J. Jones	Ford
26.	Bill Sedgwick	Chevrolet
27.	Jimmy Spencer	Ford
28.	Dave Marcis	Chevrolet
29.	Rick Mast	Ford
30.	Dirk Stephens	Ford
31.	Bill Schmitt	Ford
32.	Butch Gilliland	Chevrolet
33.	Dorsey Schroeder	Ford
34.	John Krebs	Chevrolet
35.	Darrell Waltrip	Chevrolet
36.	Kenny Wallace	Pontiac
37.	Phil Parsons	Chevrolet
38.	Rusty Wallace	Pontiac
39.	Ted Musgrave	Ford
40.	Mark Martin	Ford
41.	Bobby Hillin	Ford
42.	Jeff Davis	Ford
43.	Hershel McGriff	Chevrolet

COCA COLA 600

May 30
Charlotte, North Carolina
Time of Race: 4 hours, 7 minutes, 25 seconds
Average Speed: 145.504 mph
Margin of Victory: 3.73 seconds

FINISH	DRIVER	CAR
1.	Dale Earnhardt	Chevrolet
2.	Jeff Gordon	Chevrolet
3.	Dale Jarrett	Chevrolet
4.	Ken Schrader	Chevrolet
5.	Ernie Irvan	Chevrolet
6.	Bill Elliott	Ford
7.	Jimmy Spencer	Ford
8.	Bobby Labonte	Ford
9.	Morgan Shepherd	Ford
10.	Geoff Bodine	Ford
11.	Darrell Waltrip	Chevrolet
12.	Phil Parsons	Chevrolet
13.	Michael Waltrip	Pontiac
14.	Kyle Petty	Pontiac
15.	Jimmy Hensley	Ford
16.	Bobby Hillin	Ford
17.	Greg Sacks	Ford
18.	Harry Gant	Chevrolet
19.	Dick Trickle	Ford
20.	Hut Stricklin	Ford
21.	Rich Bickle	Ford
22.	Mike Wallace	Pontiac
23.	Kenny Wallace	Pontiac
24.	Sterling Marlin	Ford
25.	Jimmy Horton	Chevrolet
26.	Ted Musgrave	Ford
27.	Lake Speed	Ford
28.	Mark Martin	Ford
29.	Rusty Wallace	Pontiac
30.	Davey Allison	Ford
31.	Rick Mast	Ford
32.	Rick Wilson	Pontiac
33.	Terry Labonte	Chevrolet
34.	Chad Little	Ford
35.	Joe Ruttman	Ford
36.	Derrike Cope	Ford
37.	Ricky Rudd	Chevrolet
38.	Jimmy Means	Ford
39.	Dave Marcis	Chevrolet
40.	Wally Dallenbach	Ford
41.	Brett Bodine	Ford

BUDWEISER 500

June 6
Dover, Delaware
Time of Race: 4 hours, 44 minutes, 6 seconds
Average Speed: 105.600 mph
Margin of Victory: .38 second

FINISH	DRIVER	CAR
1.	Dale Earnhardt	Chevrolet
2.	Dale Jarrett	Chevrolet
3.	Davey Allison	Ford
4.	Mark Martin	Ford
5.	Ken Schrader	Chevrolet
6.	Rick Mast	Ford
7.	Harry Gant	Chevrolet
8.	Jimmy Spencer	Ford
9.	Morgan Shepherd	Ford
10.	Bobby Hamilton	Ford
11.	Rick Wilson	Pontiac
12.	Wally Dallenbach	Ford
13.	Kenny Wallace	Pontiac
14.	Ted Musgrave	Ford
15.	Hut Stricklin	Ford
16.	Brett Bodine	Ford
17.	Bill Elliott	Ford
18.	Jeff Gordon	Chevrolet
19.	Bobby Labonte	Ford
20.	Terry Labonte	Chevrolet
21.	Rusty Wallace	Pontiac
22.	Jimmy Hensley	Ford
23.	Geoff Bodine	Ford
24.	Darrell Waltrip	Chevrolet
25.	Bobby Hillin	Ford
26.	Jimmy Means	Ford
27.	Michael Waltrip	Pontiac

28.	Dick Trickle	Ford
29.	Kyle Petty	Pontiac
30.	Lake Speed	Ford
31.	Derrike Cope	Ford
32.	Ernie Irvan	Chevrolet
33.	Sterling Marlin	Ford
34.	P. J. Jones	Ford
35.	Ricky Rudd	Chevrolet
36.	Dave Marcis	Chevrolet
37.	Phil Parsons	Chevrolet
38.	Greg Sacks	Ford

CHAMPION SPARK PLUG 500

June 13
Pocono, Pennsylvania
Time of Race: 3 hours, 37 minutes, 23 seconds
Average Speed: 138.005 mph
Margin of Victory: 5.08 seconds

FINISH	DRIVER	CAR
1.	Kyle Petty	Pontiac
2.	Ken Schrader	Chevrolet
3.	Harry Gant	Chevrolet
4.	Jimmy Spencer	Ford
5.	Ted Musgrave	Ford
6.	Davey Allison	Ford
7.	Morgan Shepherd	Ford
8.	Sterling Marlin	Ford
9.	Ricky Rudd	Chevrolet
10.	Bill Elliott	Ford
11.	Dale Earnhardt	Chevrolet
12.	Rick Wilson	Pontiac
13.	Hut Stricklin	Ford
14.	Phil Parsons	Chevrolet
15.	Kenny Wallace	Pontiac
16.	Rick Mast	Ford
17.	Jimmy Hensley	Ford
18.	Greg Sacks	Ford
19.	Dale Jarrett	Chevrolet
20.	Bobby Labonte	Ford
21.	Michael Waltrip	Pontiac
22.	Jimmy Means	Ford
23.	Dave Marcis	Chevrolet
24.	Geoff Bodine	Ford
25.	Wally Dallenbach	Ford
26.	Kerry Teague	Chevrolet
27.	Lake Speed	Ford
28.	Jeff Gordon	Chevrolet
29.	Brett Bodine	Ford
30.	Darrell Waltrip	Chevrolet
31.	Mark Martin	Ford
32.	Terry Labonte	Chevrolet
33.	Derrike Cope	Ford
34.	Ernie Irvan	Chevrolet
35.	Trevor Boys	Pontiac
36.	Dick Trickle	Ford
37.	Jimmy Horton	Chevrolet
38.	Bobby Hillin	Ford
39.	Rusty Wallace	Pontiac
40.	Graham Taylor	Ford

MILLER GENUINE DRAFT 400

June 20
Brooklyn, Michigan
Time of Race: 2 hours, 41 minutes, 38 seconds
Average Speed: 148.484 mph
Margin of Victory: 1.74 seconds

FINISH	DRIVER	CAR
1.	Ricky Rudd	Chevrolet
2.	Jeff Gordon	Chevrolet
3.	Ernie Irvan	Chevrolet

4.	Dale Jarrett	Chevrolet
5.	Rusty Wallace	Pontiac
6.	Mark Martin	Ford
7.	Morgan Shepherd	Ford
8.	Sterling Marlin	Ford
9.	Bill Elliott	Ford
10.	Harry Gant	Chevrolet
11.	Rick Mast	Ford
12.	Kyle Petty	Pontiac
13.	Phil Parsons	Chevrolet
14.	Dale Earnhardt	Chevrolet
15.	Ted Musgrave	Ford
16.	Ken Schrader	Chevrolet
17.	Geoff Bodine	Ford
18.	Jimmy Spencer	Ford
19.	Darrell Waltrip	Chevrolet
20.	Terry Labonte	Chevrolet
21.	Hut Stricklin	Ford
22.	Greg Sacks	Ford
23.	Jimmy Hensley	Ford
24.	Dave Marcis	Chevrolet
25.	Wally Dallenbach	Ford
26.	Jim Sauter	Chevrolet
27.	Derrike Cope	Ford
28.	Jimmy Means	Ford
29.	Kenny Wallace	Pontiac
30.	Lake Speed	Ford
31.	Dick Trickle	Ford
32.	H. B. Bailey	Pontiac
33.	Bobby Hillin	Ford
34.	Rick Wilson	Pontiac
35.	Davey Allison	Ford
36.	Bobby Labonte	Ford
37.	Michael Waltrip	Pontiac
38.	P. J. Jones	Ford
39.	Brett Bodine	Ford
40.	Clay Young	Ford
41.	Jimmy Horton	Chevrolet

PEPSI 400

July 3
Daytona Beach, Florida
Time of Race: 2 hours, 38 minutes, 9 seconds
Average Speed: 151.755
Margin of Victory: .16 seconds

FINISH	DRIVER	CAR
1.	Dale Earnhardt	Chevrolet
2.	Sterling Marlin	Ford
3.	Ken Schrader	Chevrolet
4.	Ricky Rudd	Chevrolet
5.	Jeff Gordon	Chevrolet
6.	Mark Martin	Ford
7.	Ernie Irvan	Chevrolet
8.	Dale Jarrett	Chevrolet
9.	Terry Labonte	Chevrolet
10.	Ted Musgrave	Ford
11.	Rick Wilson	Pontiac
12.	Bobby Hillin	Ford
13.	Darrell Waltrip	Chevrolet
14.	Morgan Shepherd	Ford
15.	Greg Sacks	Ford
16.	Rick Mast	Ford
17.	Bobby Hamilton	Ford
18.	Rusty Wallace	Pontiac
19.	Brett Bodine	Ford
20.	Bill Elliott	Ford
21.	Harry Gant	Chevrolet
22.	Michael Waltrip	Pontiac
23.	Jeff Purvis	Chevrolet
24.	Derrike Cope	Ford
25.	Phil Parsons	Chevrolet
26.	Dick Trickle	Ford
27.	Dave Marcis	Chevrolet
28.	Kenny Wallace	Pontiac
29.	Loy Allen	Ford
30.	P. J. Jones	Ford
31.	Davey Allison	Ford
32.	Ritchie Petty	Ford

33.	Kyle Petty	Pontiac
34.	Jimmy Hensley	Ford
35.	Wally Dallenbach	Ford
36.	Jimmy Means	Ford
37.	Geoff Bodine	Ford
38.	Jimmy Horton	Chevrolet
39.	Jimmy Spencer	Ford
40.	Hut Stricklin	Ford
41.	Bobby Labonte	Ford

SLICK 50 300

July 11
Loudon, New Hampshire
Time of Race: 2 hours, 59 minutes, 45 seconds
Average Speed: 105.947 mph
Margin of Victory: 1.31 seconds

FINISH	DRIVER	CAR
1.	Rusty Wallace	Pontiac
2.	Mark Martin	Ford
3.	Davey Allison	Ford
4.	Dale Jarrett	Chevrolet
5.	Ricky Rudd	Chevrolet
6.	Sterling Marlin	Ford
7.	Jeff Gordon	Chevrolet
8.	Kyle Petty	Pontiac
9.	Bill Elliott	Ford
10.	Bobby Labonte	Ford
11.	Jimmy Hensley	Ford
12.	Geoff Bodine	Ford
13.	Brett Bodine	Ford
14.	Morgan Shepherd	Ford
15.	Ernie Irvan	Chevrolet
16.	Rick Mast	Ford
17.	Harry Gant	Chevrolet
18.	Jimmy Spencer	Ford
19.	Darrell Waltrip	Chevrolet
20.	Bobby Hillin	Ford
21.	Kenny Wallace	Pontiac
22.	Derrike Cope	Ford
23.	Michael Waltrip	Pontiac
24.	Ted Musgrave	Ford
25.	Hut Stricklin	Ford
26.	Dale Earnhardt	Chevrolet
27.	Wally Dallenbach	Ford
28.	Rick Wilson	Pontiac
29.	Ken Bouchard	Ford
30.	Dave Marcis	Chevrolet
31.	Terry Labonte	Chevrolet
32.	Greg Sacks	Ford
33.	Dick Trickle	Ford
34.	Jimmy Means	Ford
35.	Lake Speed	Ford
36.	Joe Neemechek	Chevrolet
37.	Jeff Burton	Ford
38.	Ken Schrader	Chevrolet
39.	Phil Parsons	Chevrolet
40.	Jerry O'Neil	Chevrolet

MILLER GENUINE DRAFT 500

July 18
Pocono, Pennsylvania
Time of Race: 3 hours, 44 minutes, 59 seconds
Average Speed: 133.343 mph
Margin of Victory: .78 second

FINISH	DRIVER	CAR
1.	Dale Earnhardt	Chevrolet
2.	Rusty Wallace	Pontiac
3.	Bill Elliott	Ford
4.	Morgan Shepherd	Ford
5.	Brett Bodine	Ford
6.	Ken Schrader	Chevrolet

7.	Sterling Marlin	Ford
8.	Dale Jarrett	Chevrolet
9.	Harry Gant	Chevrolet
10.	Darrell Waltrip	Chevrolet
11.	Ricky Rudd	Chevrolet
12.	Geoff Bodine	Ford
13.	Mark Martin	Ford
14.	Michael Waltrip	Pontiac
15.	Bobby Labonte	Ford
16.	Terry Labonte	Chevrolet
17.	Wally Dallenbach	Ford
18.	Phil Parsons	Chevrolet
19.	Bobby Hamiltion	Ford
20.	Bobby Hillin	Ford
21.	Rick Wilson	Pontiac
22.	Dave Marcis	Chevrolet
23.	Kenny Wallace	Pontiac
24.	Jimmy Spencer	Ford
25.	Ken Bouchard	Ford
26.	Jimmy Horton	Chevrolet
27.	Kyle Petty	Pontiac
28.	Hut Stricklin	Ford
29.	Derrike Cope	Ford
30.	Dick Trickle	Ford
31.	Ernie Irvan	Chevrolet
32.	Greg Sacks	Ford
33.	Ted Musgrave	Ford
34.	Kerry Teague	Chevrolet
35.	John Krebs	Chevrolet
36.	Rick Mast	Ford
37.	Jeff Gordon	Chevrolet
38.	Clay Young	Ford
39.	Jimmy Hensley	Ford
40.	T. W. Taylor	Ford

DIEHARD 500

July 25
Talladega, Alabama
Time of Race: 3 hours, 15 minutes, 1 second
Average Speed: 153.858 mph
Margin of Victory: .005 second

FINISH	DRIVER	CAR
1.	Dale Earnhardt	Chevrolet
2.	Ernie Irvan	Chevrolet
3.	Mark Martin	Ford
4.	Kyle Petty	Pontiac
5.	Dale Jarrett	Chevrolet
6.	Greg Sacks	Ford
7.	Morgan Shepherd	Ford
8.	Harry Gant	Chevrolet
9.	Brett Bodine	Ford
10.	Wally Dallenbach	Ford
11.	Bill Elliott	Ford
12.	Hut Stricklin	Ford
13.	Bobby Hillin	Ford
14.	Terry Labonte	Chevrolet
15.	Bobby Labonte	Ford
16.	Geoff Bodine	Ford
17.	Rusty Wallace	Pontiac
18.	Lake Speed	Ford
19.	Dick Trickle	Ford
20.	Michael Waltrip	Pontiac
21.	Jeff Purvis	Chevrolet
22.	Phil Parsons	Chevrolet
23.	Rick Wilson	Pontiac
24.	Ricky Rudd	Chevrolet
25.	Jimmy Means	Ford
26.	Loy Allen	Ford
27.	Sterling Marlin	Ford
28.	Jimmy Hensley	Ford
29.	Dave Marcis	Chevrolet
30.	Jimmy Spencer	Ford
31.	Jeff Gordon	Chevrolet
32.	Ken Schrader	Chevrolet
33.	Ted Musgrave	Ford
34.	Neil Bonnett	Chevrolet
35.	Kenny Wallace	Pontiac
36.	Derrike Cope	Ford
37.	Darrell Waltrip	Chevrolet

38.	Rick Mast	Ford
39.	Jimmy Horton	Chevrolet
40.	Stanley Smith	Chevrolet
41.	Ritchie Petty	Ford
42.	Robby Gordon	Ford

BUDWEISER AT THE GLEN

August 8
Watkins Glen, New York
Time of Race: 2 hours, 36 minutes, 4 seconds
Average Speed: 84.771 mph
Margin of Victory: 3.84 seconds

FINISH	DRIVER	CAR
1.	Mark Martin	Ford
2.	Wally Dallenbach	Ford
3.	Jimmy Spencer	Ford
4.	Bill Elliott	Ford
5.	Ken Schrader	Chevrolet
6.	Sterling Marlin	Ford
7.	Bobby Labonte	Ford
8.	P. J. Jones	Ford
9.	Kenny Wallace	Pontiac
10.	Harry Gant	Chevrolet
11.	Derrike Cope	Ford
12.	Michael Waltrip	Pontiac
13.	Scott Lagasse	Chevrolet
14.	Darrell Waltrip	Chevrolet
15.	Ernie Irvan	Chevrolet
16.	Geoff Bodine	Ford
17.	Hut Stricklin	Ford
18.	Dale Earnhardt	Chevrolet
19.	Rusty Wallace	Pontiac
20.	Brett Bodine	Ford
21.	Joe Nemechek	Chevrolet
22.	Rick Wilson	Pontiac
23.	Terry Labonte	Chevrolet
24.	Ricky Rudd	Chevrolet
25.	Tommy Kendall	Ford
26.	Kyle Petty	Pontiac
27.	Lake Speed	Ford
28.	Morgan Shepherd	Ford
29.	Scott Gaylord	Oldsmobile
30.	Todd Bodine	Ford
31.	Jeff Gordon	Chevrolet
32.	Dale Jarrett	Chevrolet
33.	Phil Parsons	Chevrolet
34.	Ted Musgrave	Ford
35.	Bobby Hillin	Ford
36.	Ed Ferree	Chevrolet
37.	Rick Mast	Ford
38.	Dorsey Schroeder	Ford

CHAMPION SPARK PLUG 400

August 15
Brooklyn, Michigan
Time of Race: 2 hours, 46 minutes, 1 second
Average Speed: 144.564 mph
Margin of Victory: 1.28 seconds

FINISH	DRIVER	CAR
1.	Mark Martin	Ford
2.	Morgan Shepherd	Ford
3.	Jeff Gordon	Chevrolet
4.	Dale Jarrett	Chevrolet
5.	Ted Musgrave	Ford
6.	Rusty Wallace	Pontiac
7.	Lake Speed	Ford
8.	Bobby Labonte	Ford
9.	Dale Earnhardt	Chevrolet
10.	Bill Elliott	Ford
11.	Bobby Hillin	Ford
12.	Greg Sacks	Ford

13.	Darrell Waltrip	Chevrolet
14.	Brett Bodine	Ford
15.	Jimmy Hensley	Ford
16.	Michael Waltrip	Pontiac
17.	Sterling Marlin	Ford
18.	Kyle Petty	Pontiac
19.	Phil Parsons	Chevrolet
20.	Jimmy Spencer	Ford
21.	Derrike Cope	Ford
22.	Dave Marcis	Chevrolet
23.	Kenny Wallace	Pontiac
24.	Geoff Bodine	Ford
25.	Jimmy Means	Ford
26.	P. J. Jones	Ford
27.	Ken Schrader	Chevrolet
28.	Rick Wilson	Pontiac
29.	Terry Labonte	Chevrolet
30.	Harry Gant	Chevrolet
31.	Wally Dallenbach	Ford
32.	Ernie Irvan	Chevrolet
33.	Rick Mast	Ford
34.	Hut Stricklin	Ford
35.	Ricky Rudd	Chevrolet
36.	Jim Sauter	Ford
37.	Joe Nemechek	Chevrolet
38.	Jimmy Horton	Chevrolet
39.	Dick Trickle	Chevrolet
40.	Todd Bodine	Ford
41.	Rich Bickle	Ford

BUD 500

August 28
Bristol, Tennessee
Time of Race: 3 hours, 1 minute, 21 seconds
Average Speed: 88.172 mph
Margin of Victory: .14 second

FINISH	DRIVER	CAR
1.	Mark Martin	Ford
2.	Rusty Wallace	Pontiac
3.	Dale Earnhardt	Chevrolet
4.	Harry Gant	Chevrolet
5.	Rick Mast	Ford
6.	Jimmy Hensley	Ford
7.	Brett Bodine	Ford
8.	Geoff Bodine	Ford
9.	Kenny Wallace	Pontiac
10.	Michael Waltrip	Pontiac
11.	Bill Elliott	Ford
12.	Bobby Hillin	Ford
13.	Morgan Shepherd	Ford
14.	Phil Parsons	Chevrolet
15.	Bobby Labonte	Ford
16.	Lake Speed	Ford
17.	Dave Marcis	Chevrolet
18.	Jimmy Means	Ford
19.	Greg Sacks	Ford
20.	Jeff Gordon	Chevrolet
21.	Wally Dallenbach	Ford
22.	Ricky Rudd	Chevrolet
23.	Sterling Marlin	Ford
24.	Ken Schrader	Chevrolet
25.	Jimmy Spencer	Ford
26.	Ernie Irvan	Chevrolet
27.	Derrike Cope	Ford
28.	Rick Wilson	Pontiac
29.	Dale Jarrett	Chevrolet
30.	Kyle Petty	Pontiac
31.	Dale Jarrett	Chevrolet
32.	Hut Stricklin	Ford
33.	Bobby Hamilton	Ford
34.	Terry Labonte	Chevrolet

MOUNTAIN DEW SOUTHERN 500

September 5
Darlington, South Carolina

Time of Race: 3 hours, 28 minutes, 34 seconds
Average Speed: 137.932 mph
Margin of Victory: 1.51 seconds

FINISH	DRIVER	CAR
1.	Mark Martin	Ford
2.	Brett Bodine	Ford
3.	Rusty Wallace	Pontiac
4.	Dale Earnhardt	Chevrolet
5.	Ernie Irvan	Ford
6.	Ricky Rudd	Chevrolet
7.	Harry Gant	Chevrolet
8.	Morgan Shepherd	Ford
9.	Ken Schrader	Chevrolet
10.	Kenny Wallace	Pontiac
11.	Wally Dallenbach	Ford
12.	Dale Jarrett	Chevrolet
13.	Michael Waltrip	Pontiac
14.	Bobby Labonte	Ford
15.	Jimmy Spencer	Ford
16.	Kyle Petty	Pontiac
17.	Derrike Cope	Ford
18.	Bill Elliott	Ford
19.	Bobby Hamilton	Ford
20.	Geoff Bodine	Ford
21.	Phil Parsons	Chevrolet
22.	Jeff Gordon	Chevrolet
23.	Jimmy Hensley	Ford
24.	Bobby Hillin	Ford
25.	Greg Sacks	Ford
26.	Jeff Purvis	Chevrolet
27.	Todd Bodines	Ford
28.	Darrell Waltrip	Chevrolet
29.	Dave Marcis	Chevrolet
30.	Rick Wilson	Pontiac
31.	Sterling Marlin	Ford
32.	Rick Mast	Ford
33.	Terry Labonte	Chevrolet
34.	Ted Musgrave	Ford
35.	Mike Skinner	Ford
36.	Hut Stricklin	Ford
37.	H. B. Bailey	Pontiac
38.	Brad Teague	Chevrolet
39.	Jimmy Means	Ford

MILLER GENUINE DRAFT 400

September 11
Richmond, Virginia
Time of Race: 3 hours, 9 seconds
Average Speed: 99.917 mph
Margin of Victory: .57 second

FINISH	DRIVER	CAR
1.	Rusty Wallace	Pontiac
2.	Bill Elliott	Ford
3.	Dale Earnhardt	Chevrolet
4.	Ricky Rudd	Chevrolet
5.	Brett Bodine	Ford
6.	Mark Martin	Ford
7.	Darrell Waltrip	Chevrolet
8.	Terry Labonte	Chevrolet
9.	Kyle Petty	Pontiac
10.	Jeff Gordon	Chevrolet
11.	Harry Gant	Chevrolet
12.	Ken Schrader	Chevrolet
13.	Bobby Labonte	Ford
14.	Dale Jarrett	Chevrolet
15.	Wally Dallenbach	Ford
16.	Jeff Purvis	Chevrolet
17.	Hut Stricklin	Ford
18.	Rick Mast	Ford
19.	Michael Waltrip	Pontiac
20.	Phil Parsons	Chevrolet
21.	Jimmy Hensley	Ford
22.	Ted Musgrave	Ford
23.	Dave Marcis	Chevrolet

FINISH	DRIVER	CAR
24.	Sterling Marlin	Ford
25.	Dick Trickle	Chevrolet
26.	Jimmy Means	Ford
27.	Bobby Hillin	Ford
28.	Derrike Cope	Ford
29.	Rick Wilson	Pontiac
30.	Morgan Shepherd	Ford
31.	Greg Sacks	Ford
32.	Kenny Wallace	Pontiac
33.	Todd Bodine	Ford
34.	Geoff Bodine	Ford
35.	Jimmy Spencer	Ford
36.	Ernie Irvan	Ford

SPLITFIRE SPARK PLUG 500

September 19
Dover, Delaware
Time of Race: 4 hours, 59 minutes
Average Speed: 100.334 mph
Margin of Victory: .41 second

FINISH	DRIVER	CAR
1.	Rusty Wallace	Pontiac
2.	Ken Schrader	Chevrolet
3.	Darrell Waltrip	Chevrolet
4.	Dale Jarrett	Chevrolet
5.	Harry Gant	Chevrolet
6.	Jimmy Spencer	Ford
7.	Bobby Labonte	Ford
8.	Terry Labonte	Chevrolet
9.	Morgan Shepherd	Ford
10.	Bill Elliott	Ford
11.	Sterling Marlin	Ford
12.	Bobby Hillin	Ford
13.	Jeff Purvis	Chevrolet
14.	Kyle Petty	Pontiac
15.	Wally Dallenbach	Ford
16.	Kenny Wallace	Pontiac
17.	Jimmy Means	Ford
18.	Rick Mast	Ford
19.	Dave Marcis	Chevrolet
20.	Greg Sacks	Ford
21.	Ricky Rudd	Chevrolet
22.	Jimmy Horton	Chevrolet
23.	Michael Waltrip	Pontiac
24.	Jeff Gordon	Chevrolet
25.	Dick Trickle	Ford
26.	Ernie Irvan	Ford
27.	Dale Earnhardt	Chevrolet
28.	Ted Musgrave	Ford
29.	Hut Stricklin	Ford
30.	Geoff Bodine	Ford
31.	Mark Martin	Ford
32.	Derrike Cope	Ford
33.	Lake Speed	Ford
34.	Rick Wilson	Pontiac
35.	Todd Bodine	Ford
36.	Bob Schacht	Chevrolet
37.	Phil Parsons	Chevrolet

GOODY'S 500

September 26
Martinsville, Virginia
Time of Race: 3 hours, 32 minutes, 57 seconds
Average Speed: 74.101 mph
Margin of Victory: 2.77 seconds

FINISH	DRIVER	CAR
1.	Ernie Irvan	Ford
2.	Rusty Wallace	Pontiac
3.	Jimmy Spencer	Ford
4.	Ricky Rudd	Chevrolet

5.	Dale Jarrett	Chevrolet
6.	Brett Bodine	Ford
7.	Terry Labonte	Chevrolet
8.	Michael Waltrip	Pontiac
9.	Morgan Shepherd	Ford
10.	Kyle Petty	Pontiac
11.	Jeff Gordon	Chevrolet
12.	Bill Elliott	Ford
13.	Ken Schrader	Chevrolet
14.	Geoff Bodine	Ford
15.	Kenny Wallace	Pontiac
16.	Mark Martin	Ford
17.	Jeff Purvis	Chevrolet
18.	Darrell Waltrip	Chevrolet
19.	Phil Parsons	Chevrolet
20.	Derrike Cope	Ford
21.	Dave Marcis	Chevrolet
22.	Bobby Hillin	Ford
23.	Hut Stricklin	Ford
24.	Lake Speed	Ford
25.	Todd Bodine	Ford
26.	Rick Mast	Ford
27.	Wally Dallenbach	Ford
28.	Greg Sacks	Ford
29.	Dale Earnhardt	Chevrolet
30.	Sterling Marlin	Ford
31.	Ted Musgrave	Ford
32.	Bobby Labonte	Ford
33.	Harry Gant	Chevrolet
34.	Jimmy Hensley	Pontiac

TYSONS HOLLY FARMS 400

October 3
North Wilkesboro, North Carolina
Time of Race: 2 hours, 34 minutes, 46 seconds
Average Speed: 96.920 mph
Margin of Victory: 1.64 seconds

FINISH	DRIVER	CAR
1.	Rusty Wallace	Pontiac
2.	Dale Earnhardt	Chevrolet
3.	Ernie Irvan	Ford
4.	Kyle Petty	Pontiac
5.	Ricky Rudd	Chevrolet
6.	Harry Gant	Chevrolet
7.	Terry Labonte	Chevrolet
8.	Rick Mast	Ford
9.	Dale Jarrett	Chevrolet
10.	Ken Schrader	Chevrolet
11.	Darrell Waltrip	Chevrolet
12.	Bobby Labonte	Ford
13.	Jimmy Spencer	Ford
14.	Michael Waltrip	Pontiac
15.	Wally Dallenbach	Ford
16.	Mark Martin	Ford
17.	Lake Speed	Ford
18.	Bill Elliott	Ford
19.	Sterling Marlin	Ford
20.	Derrike Cope	Ford
21.	Brett Bodine	Ford
22.	Bobby Hillin	Ford
23.	Todd Bodine	Ford
24.	John Andretti	Chevrolet
25.	Jeff Purvis	Chevrolet
26.	Jay Hedgecock	Ford
27.	Kenny Wallace	Pontiac
28.	Hut Stricklin	Ford
29.	Ted Musgrave	Ford
30.	Dick Trickle	Chevrolet
31.	Geoff Bodine	Ford
32.	Morgan Shepherd	Ford
33.	Rick Wilson	Pontiac
34.	Jeff Gordon	Chevrolet

MELLO YELLO 500

October 10
Charlotte, North Carolina

Time of Race: 3 hours, 14 minutes, 31 seconds
Average Speed: 154.357 mph
Margin of Victory: 1.83 seconds

FINISH	DRIVER	CAR
1.	Ernie Irvan	Ford
2.	Mark Martin	Ford
3.	Dale Earnhardt	Chevrolet
4.	Rusty Wallace	Pontiac
5.	Jeff Gordon	Chevrolet
6.	Jimmy Spencer	Ford
7.	Kyle Petty	Pontiac
8.	Ricky Rudd	Chevrolet
9.	Ken Schrader	Chevrolet
10.	Bill Elliott	Ford
11.	Lake Speed	Ford
12.	Harry Gant	Chevrolet
13.	Geoff Bodine	Ford
14.	Morgan Shepherd	Ford
15.	Brett Bodine	Ford
16.	Terry Labonte	Chevrolet
17.	Sterling Marlin	Ford
18.	Rick Mast	Ford
19.	Darrell Waltrip	Chevrolet
20.	Bobby Hillin	Ford
21.	Ted Musgrave	Ford
22.	Dick Trickle	Chevrolet
23.	Hut Stricklin	Ford
24.	Wally Dallenbach	Ford
25.	Joe Nemechek	Chevrolet
26.	Dale Jarrett	Chevrolet
27.	Michael Waltrip	Pontiac
28.	Bobby Labonte	Ford
29.	Jeremy Mayfield	Ford
30.	Mike Wallace	Ford
31.	John Andretti	Chevrolet
32.	Greg Sacks	Ford
33.	Chad Little	Ford
34.	Jerry O'Neil	Chevrolet
35.	Kenny Wallace	Pontiac
36.	Rick Wilson	Pontiac
37.	Bobby Hamilton	Ford
38.	Jim Sauter	Ford
39.	Derrike Cope	Ford
40.	Rich Bickle	Ford
41.	Andy Hillenburg	Chevrolet
42.	Todd Bodine	Ford

AC-DELCO 500

October 24
Rockingham, North Carolina
Time of Race: 4 hours, 23 minutes, 16 seconds
Average Speed: 114.036 mph
Margin of Victory: 3.23 seconds

FINISH	DRIVER	CAR
1.	Rusty Wallace	Pontiac
2.	Dale Earnhardt	Chevrolet
3.	Bill Elliott	Ford
4.	Harry Gant	Chevrolet
5.	Mark Martin	Ford
6.	Ernie Irvan	Ford
7.	Darrell Waltrip	Chevrolet
8.	Ken Schrader	Chevrolet
9.	Dick Trickle	Chevrolet
10.	Geoff Bodine	Ford
11.	Morgan Shepherd	Ford
12.	Sterling Marlin	Ford
13.	Kyle Petty	Pontiac
14.	Ricky Rudd	Chevrolet
15.	Terry Labonte	Chevrolet
16.	Lake Speed	Ford
17.	Rick Mast	Ford
18.	Michael Waltrip	Pontiac
19.	Derrike Cope	Ford
20.	Jimmy Spencer	Ford
21.	Jeff Gordon	Chevrolet

22.	Bobby Labonte	Ford
23.	Joe Nemechek	Chevrolet
24.	Hut Stricklin	Ford
25.	Todd Bodine	Ford
26.	Rick Wilson	Pontiac
27.	Dave Marcis	Chevrolet
28.	Ted Musgrave	Ford
29.	Jimmy Means	Ford
30.	Dale Jarrett	Chevrolet
31.	Wally Dallenbach	Ford
32.	Greg Sacks	Ford
33.	Bobby Hillin	Ford
34.	Jimmy Horton	Chevrolet
35.	Brett Bodine	Ford
36.	Mike Wallace	Ford
37.	Kenny Wallace	Pontiac
38.	Jerry Hill	Chevrolet
39.	John Andretti	Chevrolet
40.	T. W. Taylor	Ford
41.	Loy Allen	Ford

SLICK 50 500

October 31
Phoenix, Arizona
Time of Race: 3 hours, 6 minutes, 30 seconds
Average Speed: 100.375 mph
Margin of Victory: .17 second

FINISH	DRIVER	CAR
1.	Mark Martin	Ford
2.	Ernie Irvan	Ford
3.	Kyle Petty	Pontiac
4.	Dale Earnhardt	Chevrolet
5.	Bill Elliott	Ford
6.	Ricky Rudd	Chevrolet
7.	Darrell Waltrip	Chevrolet
8.	Bobby Labonte	Ford
9.	Michael Waltrip	Pontiac
10.	Rick Mast	Ford
11.	Morgan Shepherd	Ford
12.	Harry Gant	Chevrolet
13.	Lake Speed	Ford
14.	Terry Labonte	Chevrolet
15.	Ted Musgrave	Ford
16.	Dale Jarrett	Chevrolet
17.	Kenny Wallace	Pontiac
18.	Bobby Hillin	Ford
19.	Rusty Wallace	Pontiac
20.	Rick Wilson	Pontiac
21.	Rick Carelli	Chevrolet
22.	Ron Hornaday	Chevrolet
23.	Derrike Cope	Ford
24.	Chuck Bown	Chevrolet
25.	Todd Bodine	Ford
26.	Loy Allen	Ford
27.	Jimmy Spencer	Ford
28.	Brett Bodine	Ford
29.	Steve Grissom	Chevrolet
30.	Sterling Marlin	Ford
31.	Dick Trickle	Chevrolet
32.	Jimmy Hensley	Chevrolet
33.	Ken Schrader	Chevrolet
34.	Wally Dallenbach	Ford
35.	Jeff Gordon	Chevrolet
36.	Hut Stricklin	Ford
37.	Terry Fisher	Pontiac
38.	Rich Wookland	Oldsmobile
39.	Mike Chase	Chevrolet
40.	John Andretti	Chevrolet
41.	Wayne Jacks	Pontiac
42.	Dirk Stephens	Ford
43.	Geoff Bodine	Ford

HOOTERS 500

November 24
Atlanta, Georgia

Time of Race: 3 hours, 59 minutes, 12 seconds
Average Speed: 125.221 mph
Margin of Victory: 5.66 seconds

FINISH	DRIVER	CAR
1.	Rusty Wallace	Pontiac
2.	Ricky Rudd	Chevrolet
3.	Darrell Waltrip	Chevrolet
4.	Bill Elliott	Ford
5.	Dick Trickle	Chevrolet
6.	Michael Waltrip	Pontiac
7.	Dale Jarrett	Chevrolet
8.	Ted Musgrave	Ford
9.	Phil Parsons	Ford
10.	Dale Earnhardt	Chevrolet
11.	Kyle Petty	Pontiac
12.	Ernie Irvan	Ford
13.	Terry Labonte	Chevrolet
14.	Bobby Labonte	Ford
15.	Mike Wallace	Pontiac
16.	Jimmy Spencer	Ford
17.	Sterling Marlin	Ford
18.	Dave Marcis	Chevrolet
19.	Derrike Cope	Ford
20.	Mark Martin	Ford
21.	Bobby Hamilton	Ford
22.	Hut Stricklin	Ford
23.	Rick Wilson	Pontiac
24.	Greg Sacks	Ford
25.	Jimmy Hensley	Chevrolet
26.	Lake Speed	Ford
27.	Ken Schrader	Chevrolet
28.	Harry Gant	Chevrolet
29.	Loy Allen	Ford
30.	Kenny Wallace	Pontiac
31.	Jeff Gordon	Chevrolet
32.	Morgan Shepherd	Ford
33.	Wally Dallenbach	Ford
34.	T. W. Taylor	Ford
35.	Rick Carelli	Chevrolet
36.	Rich Bickle	Ford
37.	Rick Mast	Ford
38.	Jimmy Horton	Chevrolet
39.	Geoff Bodine	Ford
40.	Brett Bodine	Ford
41.	Bobby Hillin	Ford
42.	Neil Bonnett	Chevrolet

1994

DAYTONA 500

February 20
Daytona Beach, Florida
Time of Race: 3 hours, 11 minutes, 10 seconds
Average Speed: 156.931 mph

FINISH	DRIVER	CAR
1.	Sterling Marlin	Chevrolet
2.	Ernie Irvan	Ford
3.	Terry Labonte	Chevrolet
4.	Jeff Gordon	Chevrolet
5.	Morgan Shepherd	Ford
6.	Greg Sacks	Ford
7.	Dale Earnhardt	Chevrolet
8.	Ricky Rudd	Ford
9.	Bill Elliott	Ford
10.	Ken Schrader	Chevrolet
11.	Geoff Bodine	Ford
12.	Bobby Hamilton	Pontiac
13.	Mark Martin	Ford
14.	Lake Speed	Ford
15.	Jimmy Hensley	Ford
16.	Bobby Labonte	Pontiac
17.	Wally Dallenbach	Pontiac

18.	Joe Ruttman	Ford
19.	Jimmy Horton	Ford
20.	Dick Trickle	Chevrolet
21.	Derrike Cope	Ford
22.	Loy Allen	Ford
23.	Chuck Bown	Ford
24.	Bobby Hillin	Ford
25.	Dave Marcis	Chevrolet
26.	Jeff Burton	Ford
27.	Rick Mast	Ford
28.	Darrell Waltrip	Chevrolet
29.	Chad Little	Ford
30.	Jeremy Mayfield	Ford
31.	Michael Waltrip	Pontiac
32.	Brett Bodine	Ford
33.	Hut Stricklin	Ford
34.	Harry Gant	Chevrolet
35.	Dale Jarrett	Chevrolet
36.	Todd Bodine	Ford
37.	Jimmy Spencer	Ford
38.	Ted Musgrave	Ford
39.	Kyle Petty	Pontiac
40.	Robert Pressley	Chevrolet
41.	Rusty Wallace	Ford
42.	John Andretti	Chevrolet

GOODWRENCH 500

February 27
Rockingham, North Carolina
Time of Race: 3 hours, 59 minutes, 43 seconds
Average Speed: 125.239 mph

FINISH	DRIVER	CAR
1.	Rusty Wallace	Ford
2.	Sterling Marlin	Chevrolet
3.	Rick Mast	Ford
4.	Mark Martin	Ford
5.	Ernie Irvan	Ford
6.	Brett Bodine	Ford
7.	Dale Earnhardt	Chevrolet
8.	Kyle Petty	Pontiac
9.	Ken Schrader	Chevrolet
10.	Michael Waltrip	Pontiac
11.	Ricky Rudd	Ford
12.	Jimmy Spencer	Ford
13.	Ted Musgrave	Ford
14.	Dick Trickle	Chevrolet
15.	Geoff Bodine	Ford
16.	Morgan Shepherd	Ford
17.	Terry Labonte	Chevrolet
18.	Dale Jarrett	Chevrolet
19.	Bobby Labonte	Pontiac
20.	Jeff Burton	Ford
21.	Lake Speed	Ford
22.	Jimmy Hensley	Ford
23.	Darrell Waltrip	Chevrolet
24.	John Andretti	Chevrolet
25.	Chuck Bown	Ford
26.	Hut Stricklin	Ford
27.	Wally Dallenbach	Pontiac
28.	Greg Sacks	Ford
29.	Derrike Cope	Ford
30.	Steve Grissom	Chevrolet
31.	Mike Skinner	Ford
32.	Jeff Gordon	Chevrolet
33.	Bobby Hillin	Ford
34.	Todd Bodine	Ford
35.	Dave Marcis	Chevrolet
36.	Joe Nemechek	Chevrolet
37.	Harry Gant	Chevrolet
38.	Bobby Hamilton	Pontiac
39.	Bill Elliott	Ford
40.	Loy Allen	Ford
41.	Rich Bickle	Ford
42.	Billy Standridge	Ford

PONTIAC EXCITEMENT 400

March 6
Richmond, Virginia
Time of Race: 3 hours, 3 minutes, 3 seconds
Average Speed: 98.334 mph

FINISH	DRIVER	CAR
1.	Ernie Irvan	Ford
2.	Rusty Wallace	Ford
3.	Jeff Gordon	Chevrolet
4.	Dale Earnhardt	Chevrolet
5.	Kyle Petty	Pontiac
6.	Mark Martin	Ford
7.	Rick Mast	Ford
8.	Brett Bodine	Ford
9.	Terry Labonte	Chevrolet
10.	Dale Jarrett	Chevrolet
11.	Ken Schrader	Chevrolet
12.	Bill Elliott	Ford
13.	Ted Musgrave	Ford
14.	Lake Speed	Ford
15.	Morgan Shepherd	Ford
16.	Darrell Waltrip	Chevrolet
17.	Chuck Bown	Ford
18.	Ricky Rudd	Ford
19.	Sterling Marlin	Chevrolet
20.	Jeff Burton	Ford
21.	Joe Nemechek	Chevrolet
22.	Jimmy Spencer	Ford
23.	Steve Grissom	Chevrolet
24.	Bobby Labonte	Pontiac
25.	Todd Bodine	Ford
26.	Bobby Hillin	Ford
27.	Jeremy Mayfield	Ford
28.	Greg Sacks	Ford
29.	Derrike Cope	Ford
30.	John Andretti	Chevrolet
31.	Michael Waltrip	Pontiac
32.	Geoff Bodine	Ford
33.	Bobby Hamilton	Pontiac
34.	Harry Gant	Chevrolet
35.	Ward Burton	Chevrolet
36.	Jimmy Hensley	Ford
37.	Dick Trickle	Chevrolet

PUROLATOR 500

March 13
Atlanta, Georgia
Time of Race: 3 hours, 24 minutes, 58 seconds
Average Speed: 146.136 mph

FINISH	DRIVER	CAR
1.	Ernie Irvan	Ford
2.	Morgan Shepherd	Ford
3.	Darrell Waltrip	Chevrolet
4.	Jeff Burton	Ford
5.	Mark Martin	Ford
6.	Lake Speed	Ford
7.	Greg Sacks	Ford
8.	Jeff Gordon	Chevrolet
9.	Ricky Rudd	Ford
10.	Jimmy Spencer	Ford
11.	Ted Musgrave	Ford
12.	Dale Earnhardt	Chevrolet
13.	Kyle Petty	Pontiac
14.	Terry Labonte	Chevrolet
15.	Bobby Labonte	Pontiac
16.	Ken Schrader	Chevrolet
17.	Hut Stricklin	Ford
18.	Joe Nemechek	Chevrolet
19.	Bobby Hamilton	Pontiac
20.	Steve Grissom	Chevrolet
21.	Jeff Purvis	Chevrolet
22.	Loy Allen	Ford
23.	Michael Waltrip	Pontiac
24.	Rusty Wallace	Ford
25.	Sterling Marlin	Chevrolet

26.	Rick Mast	Ford
27.	Mike Wallace	Ford
28.	Dick Trickle	Chevrolet
29.	Jimmy Hensley	Ford
30.	Harry Gant	Chevrolet
31.	Brett Bodine	Ford
32.	Bill Elliott	Ford
33.	Todd Bodine	Ford
34.	Derrike Cope	Ford
35.	Dale Jarrett	Chevrolet
36.	Dave Marcis	Chevrolet
37.	Rich Bickle	Ford
38.	Geoff Bodine	Ford
39.	Curtis Markham	Ford
40.	Ward Burton	Chevrolet
41.	Chuck Bown	Ford
42.	John Andretti	Chevrolet

TRANSOUTH FINANCIAL 400

March 27
Darlington, South Carolina
Time of Race: 3 hours, 1 minute, 20 seconds
Average Speed: 132.432 mph

FINISH	DRIVER	CAR
1.	Dale Earnhardt	Chevrolet
2.	Mark Martin	Ford
3.	Bill Elliott	Ford
4.	Dale Jarrett	Chevrolet
5.	Lake Speed	Ford
6.	Ernie Irvan	Ford
7.	Ken Schrader	Chevrolet
8.	Harry Gant	Chevrolet
9.	Ricky Rudd	Ford
10.	Ted Musgrave	Ford
11.	Kyle Petty	Pontiac
12.	Chuck Bown	Ford
13.	Jimmy Hensley	Ford
14.	Steve Grissom	Chevrolet
15.	Michael Waltrip	Pontiac
16.	Derrike Cope	Ford
17.	Hut Stricklin	Ford
18.	Mike Wallace	Ford
19.	Joe Nemechek	Chevrolet
20.	Jeff Burton	Ford
21.	Ward Burton	Chevrolet
22.	Todd Bodine	Ford
23.	Rich Bickle	Ford
24.	Brad Teague	Ford
25.	Bobby Hamilton	Pontiac
26.	Darrell Waltrip	Chevrolet
27.	Jimmy Spencer	Ford
28.	Dave Marcis	Chevrolet
29.	Dick Trickle	Chevrolet
30.	Greg Sacks	Ford
31.	Jeff Gordon	Chevrolet
32.	Morgan Shepherd	Ford
33.	Rusty Wallace	Ford
34.	Sterling Marlin	Chevrolet
35.	Terry Labonte	Chevrolet
36.	Brett Bodine	Ford
37.	Rick Mast	Ford
38.	John Andretti	Chevrolet
39.	Bobby Labonte	Pontiac
40.	Geoff Bodine	Ford
41.	Wally Dallenbach	Pontiac

FOOD CITY 500

April 10
Bristol, Tennessee
Time of Race: 2 hours, 58 minutes, 22 seconds
Average Speed: 89.647

FINISH	DRIVER	CAR
1.	Dale Earnhardt	Chevrolet
2.	Ken Schrader	Chevrolet

3.	Lake Speed	Ford
4.	Geoff Bodine	Ford
5.	Michael Waltrip	Pontiac
6.	Bobby Labonte	Pontiac
7.	Rusty Wallace	Ford
8.	Sterling Marlin	Chevrolet
9.	Bobby Hamilton	Pontiac
10.	Dave Marcis	Chevrolet
11.	Greg Sacks	Ford
12.	Steve Grissom	Chevrolet
13.	Brett Bodine	Ford
14.	Hut Stricklin	Ford
15.	Darrell Waltrip	Chevrolet
16.	Joe Nemechek	Chevrolet
17.	Wally Dallenbach	Pontiac
18.	Morgan Shepherd	Ford
19.	Ted Musgrave	Ford
20.	Kyle Petty	Pontiac
21.	Mark Martin	Ford
22.	Jeff Gordon	Chevrolet
23.	Chuck Bown	Ford
24.	Terry Labonte	Chevrolet
25.	Ward Burton	Chevrolet
26.	Todd Bodine	Ford
27.	Derrike Cope	Ford
28.	Mike Wallace	Ford
29.	Rick Mast	Ford
30.	Bill Elliott	Ford
31.	Jeff Burton	Ford
32.	Ricky Rudd	Ford
33.	Ernie Irvan	Ford
34.	Dick Trickle	Chevrolet
35.	Jimmy Spencer	Ford
36.	Dale Jarrett	Chevrolet
37.	Harry Gant	Chevrolet

FIRST UNION 400

April 17
North Wilkesboro, North Carolina
Time of Race: 2 hours, 36 minutes, 33 seconds
Average Speed: 95.816 mph

FINISH	DRIVER	CAR
1.	Terry Labonte	Chevrolet
2.	Rusty Wallace	Ford
3.	Ernie Irvan	Ford
4.	Kyle Petty	Pontiac
5.	Dale Earnhardt	Chevrolet
6.	Ricky Rudd	Ford
7.	Geoff Bodine	Ford
8.	Harry Gant	Chevrolet
9.	Ken Schrader	Chevrolet
10.	Rick Mast	Ford
11.	Michael Waltrip	Pontiac
12.	Lake Speed	Ford
13.	Mark Martin	Ford
14.	Bobby Hamilton	Pontiac
15.	Jeff Gordon	Chevrolet
16.	Wally Dallenbach	Pontiac
17.	Sterling Marlin	Chevrolet
18.	Bill Elliott	Ford
19.	Todd Bodine	Ford
20.	Hut Stricklin	Ford
21.	Ted Musgrave	Ford
22.	Morgan Shepherd	Ford
23.	Brett Bodine	Ford
24.	Dick Trickle	Chevrolet
25.	Dale Jarrett	Chevrolet
26.	Bobby Labonte	Pontiac
27.	Derrike Cope	Ford
28.	Darrell Waltrip	Chevrolet
29.	Dave Marcis	Chevrolet
30.	Jeremy Mayfield	Ford
31.	John Andretti	Chevrolet
32.	Jimmy Spencer	Ford
33.	Jeff Burton	Ford
34.	Greg Sacks	Ford
35.	Chuck Bown	Ford
36.	Jay Hedgecock	Ford

HANES 500

April 24
Martinsville, Virginia
Time of Race: 3 hours, 25 minutes, 43 seconds
Average Speed: 76.700 mph

FINISH	DRIVER	CAR
1.	Rusty Wallace	Ford
2.	Ernie Irvan	Ford
3.	Mark Martin	Ford
4.	Darrell Waltrip	Chevrolet
5.	Morgan Shepherd	Ford
6.	Todd Bodine	Ford
7.	Chuck Bown	Ford
8.	Rick Mast	Ford
9.	Bill Elliott	Ford
10.	Ted Musgrave	Ford
11.	Dale Earnhardt	Chevrolet
12.	Ricky Rudd	Ford
13.	Bobby Hamilton	Pontiac
14.	Steve Grissom	Chevrolet
15.	Terry Labonte	Chevrolet
16.	Ward Burton	Chevrolet
17.	Michael Waltrip	Pontiac
18.	Jimmy Spencer	Ford
19.	Bobby Labonte	Pontiac
20.	Hut Stricklin	Ford
21.	Dale Jarrett	Chevrolet
22.	Joe Nemecheck	Chevrolet
23.	Jimmy Hensley	Ford
24.	Brett Bodine	Ford
25.	Jay Hedgecock	Ford
26.	Kyle Petty	Pontiac
27.	Sterling Marlin	Chevrolet
28.	Derrike Cope	Ford
29.	Greg Sacks	Ford
30.	Lake Speed	Ford
31.	Ken Schrader	Chevrolet
32.	Dick Trickle	Chevrolet
33.	Jeff Gordon	Chevrolet
34.	Geoff Bodine	Ford
35.	John Andretti	Chevrolet
36.	Jeff Burton	Ford

WINSTON SELECT 500

May 1
Talladega, Alabama
Time of Race: 3 hours, 10 minutes, 32 seconds
Average Speed: 157.478 mph

FINISH	DRIVER	CAR
1.	Dale Earnhardt	Chevrolet
2.	Ernie Irvan	Ford
3.	Michael Waltrip	Pontiac
4.	Jimmy Spencer	Ford
5.	Ken Schrader	Chevrolet
6.	Greg Sacks	Ford
7.	Lake Speed	Ford
8.	Sterling Marlin	Chevrolet
9.	Sterling Marlin	Chevrolet
10.	Morgan Shepherd	Ford
11.	Steve Grissom	Chevrolet
12.	Ted Musgrave	Ford
13.	Bobby Hamilton	Pontiac
14.	Kyle Petty	Pontiac
15.	Darrell Waltrip	Chevrolet
16.	Dave Marcis	Chevrolet
17.	Brett Bodine	Ford
18.	Hut Stricklin	Ford
19.	Bill Elliott	Ford
20.	Rick Mast	Ford
21.	Dale Jarrett	Chevrolet
22.	Bobby Labonte	Pontiac
23.	Harry Gant	Chevrolet
24.	Jeff Gordon	Chevrolet

FINISH	DRIVER	CAR
25.	Ricky Rudd	Ford
26.	Kirk Shelmerdine	Ford
27.	Chuck Bown	Ford
28.	Todd Bodine	Ford
29.	John Andretti	Chevrolet
30.	Jimmy Hensley	Ford
31.	Errike Cope	Ford
32.	Terry Labonte	Chevrolet
33.	Rusty Wallace	Ford
34.	Wally Dallenbach	Pontiac
35.	Jeff Purvis	Chevrolet
36.	Dick Trickle	Chevrolet
37.	Jeremy Mayfield	Ford
38.	Mark Martin	Ford
39.	Jeff Burton	Ford
40.	Loy Allen	Ford
41.	Geoff Bodine	Ford
42.	Joe Nemechek	Chevrolet

SAVE MART SUPERMARKETS 300

May 15
Sonoma, California
Time of Race: 2 hours, 24 minutes, 27 seconds
Average Speed: 77.458 mph

FINISH	DRIVER	CAR
1.	Ernie Irvan	Ford
2.	Geoff Bodine	Ford
3.	Dale Earnhardt	Chevrolet
4.	Wally Dallenbach	Pontiac
5.	Rusty Wallace	Ford
6.	Ted Musgrave	Ford
7.	Morgan Shepherd	Ford
8.	Mark Martin	Ford
9.	Ken Schrader	Chevrolet
10.	Harry Gant	Chevrolet
11.	Kyle Petty	Pontiac
12.	Dale Jarrett	Chevrolet
13.	Brett Bodine	Ford
14.	Ricky Rudd	Ford
15.	Jeff Burton	Ford
16.	Michael Waltrip	Pontiac
17.	Bobby Labonte	Pontiac
18.	Darrell Waltrip	Chevrolet
19.	John Andretti	Chevrolet
20.	Hut Stricklin	Ford
21.	Chuck Bown	Ford
22.	Joe Nemechek	Chevrolet
23.	Mike Wallace	Ford
24.	Greg Sacks	Ford
25.	Dave Marcis	Chevrolet
26.	Jimmy Spencer	Ford
27.	Butch Gilliland	Chevrolet
28.	Terry Labonte	Chevrolet
29.	Sterling Marlin	Chevrolet
30.	Bill Elliott	Ford
31.	Mike Chase	Chevrolet
32.	Lake Speed	Ford
33.	Bobby Hamilton	Pontiac
34.	Rick Mast	Ford
35.	Steve Grissom	Chevrolet
36.	Ward Burton	Chevrolet
37.	Jeff Gordon	Chevrolet
38.	Todd Bodine	Ford
39.	Ron Hornaday	Chevrolet
40.	Gary Collins	Ford
41.	Rick Carelli	Chevrolet
42.	John Krebs	Chevrolet
43.	Derrike Cope	Ford

COCA-COLA 600

May 19
Charlotte, North Carolina
Time of Race: 4 hours, 18 minutes, 10 seconds
Average Speed: 139.445 mph

FINISH	DRIVER	CAR
1.	Jeff Gordon	Chevrolet
2.	Rusty Wallace	Ford
3.	Geoff Bodine	Ford
4.	Dale Jarrett	Chevrolet
5.	Ernie Irvan	Ford
6.	Ricky Rudd	Ford
7.	Harry Gant	Chevrolet
8.	Todd Bodine	Ford
9.	Dale Earnhardt	Chevrolet
10.	Michael Waltrip	Pontiac
11.	Loy Allen	Ford
12.	Hut Stricklin	Ford
13.	Chuck Bown	Ford
14.	Lake Speed	Ford
15.	Sterling Marlin	Chevrolet
16.	Ted Musgrave	Ford
17.	Bobby Hamilton	Pontiac
18.	Derrike Cope	Ford
19.	Jimmy Spencer	Ford
20.	Randy LaJoie	Ford
21.	Jeremy Mayfield	Ford
22.	Bill Elliott	Ford
23.	Mike Wallace	Ford
24.	Ken Schrader	Chevrolet
25.	Wally Dallenbach	Pontiac
26.	Kyle Petty	Pontiac
27.	Greg Sacks	Ford
28.	Morgan Shepherd	Ford
29.	Jeff Burton	Ford
30.	Darrell Waltrip	Chevrolet
31.	Rick Mast	Ford
32.	Mark Martin	Ford
33.	Joe Nemechek	Chevrolet
34.	Richie Bickle	Ford
35.	Terry Labonte	Chevrolet
36.	John Andretti	Chevrolet
37.	Ward Burton	Chevrolet
38.	Dick Trickle	Chevrolet
39.	Steve Grissom	Chevrolet
40.	Bobby Labonte	Pontiac
41.	Brad Teague	Ford
42.	Brett Bodine	Ford
43.	Billy Standridge	Ford

BUDWEISER 500

June 5
Dover, Delaware
Time of Race: 4 hours, 52 minutes, 36 seconds
Average Speed: 102.529 mph

FINISH	DRIVER	CAR
1.	Rusty Wallace	Ford
2.	Ernie Irvan	Ford
3.	Ken Schrader	Chevrolet
4.	Mark Martin	Ford
5.	Jeff Gordon	Chevrolet
6.	Darrell Waltrip	Chevrolet
7.	Michael Waltrip	Pontiac
8.	Sterling Marlin	Chevrolet
9.	Hut Stricklin	Ford
10.	Wally Dallenbach	Pontiac
11.	Kyle Petty	Pontiac
12.	Lake Speed	Ford
13.	Mike Wallace	Ford
14.	Joe Nemechek	Chevrolet
15.	Loy Allen	Ford
16.	Todd Bodine	Ford
17.	Jimmy Hensley	Ford
18.	Dave Marcis	Chevrolet
19.	Ricky Rudd	Ford
20.	Bobby Labonte	Pontiac
21.	Chuck Bown	Ford
22.	John Andretti	Chevrolet
23.	Derrike Cope	Ford
24.	Greg Sacks	Ford
25.	Morgan Shepherd	Ford
26.	Terry Labonte	Chevrolet

FINISH	DRIVER	CAR
27.	Steve Grissom	Chevrolet
28.	Dale Earnhardt	Chevrolet
29.	Dale Jarrett	Chevrolet
30.	Rick Mast	Ford
31.	Bill Elliott	Ford
32.	Brett Bodine	Ford
33.	Jeff Burton	Ford
34.	Bobby Hamilton	Pontiac
35.	Ted Musgrave	Ford
36.	Billy Standridge	Ford
37.	Ward Burton	Chevrolet
38.	Dick Trickle	Chevrolet
39.	Jimmy Spencer	Ford
40.	Brad Teague	Ford
41.	Geoff Bodine	Ford
42.	Harry Gant	Chevrolet

UAW-GM TEAMWORK 500

June 12
Pocono, Pennsylvania
Time of Race: 3 hours, 52 minutes, 55 seconds
Average Speed: 128.801 mph

FINISH	DRIVER	CAR
1.	Rusty Wallace	Ford
2.	Dale EArnhardt	Chevrolet
3.	Ken Schrader	Chevrolet
4.	Morgan Shepherd	Ford
5.	Mark Martin	Ford
6.	Jeff Gordon	Chevrolet
7.	Ernie Irvan	Ford
8.	Brett Bodine	Ford
9.	Rick Mast	Ford
10.	Bill Elliott	Ford
11.	Michael Waltrip	Pontiac
12.	Kyle Petty	Pontiac
13.	Hut Stricklin	Ford
14.	Todd Bodine	Ford
15.	Ted Musgrave	Ford
16.	Harry Gant	Chevrolet
17.	Wally Dallenbach	Pontiac
18.	Terry Labonte	Chevrolet
19.	Geoff Bodine	Ford
20.	Dale Jarrett	Chevrolet
21.	Ricky Rudd	Ford
22.	Jeff Burton	Ford
23.	Lake Speed	Ford
24.	Greg Sacks	Ford
25.	Bobby Labonte	Pontiac
26.	Steve Grissom	Chevrolet
27.	Bobby Hamilton	Pontiac
28.	Rich Bickle	Ford
29.	Jimmy Hensley	Ford
30.	Darrell Waltrip	Chevrolet
31.	Loy Allen	Ford
32.	Joe Nemechek	Chevrolet
33.	Dave Marcis	Chevrolet
34.	Dick Trickle	Chevrolet
35.	John Andretti	Chevrolet
36.	Mike Wallace	Ford
37.	Jimmy Spencer	Ford
38.	Sterling Marlin	Chevrolet
39.	Chuck Bown	Ford
40.	Derrike Cope	Ford
41.	Bob Keselowski	Ford
42.	Ward Burton	Chevrolet

MILLER GENUINE DRAFT 400

June 19
Brooklyn, Michigan
Time of Race: 3 hours, 11 minutes, 58 seconds
Average Speed: 125.022 mph

FINISH	DRIVER	CAR
1.	Rusty Wallace	Ford
2.	Dale Earnhardt	Chevrolet
3.	Mark Martin	Ford
4.	Ricky Rudd	Ford
5.	Morgan Shepherd	Ford
6.	Ken Schrader	Chevrolet
7.	Joe Nemechek	Chevrolet
8.	Michael Waltrip	Pontiac
9.	Ted Musgrave	Ford
10.	Darrell Waltrip	Chevrolet
11.	Bill Elliott	Ford
12.	Jeff Gordon	Chevrolet
13.	Rick Mast	Ford
14.	Dale Jarrett	Chevrolet
15.	Bobby Labonte	Pontiac
16.	Bobby Hillin	Ford
17.	Kyle Petty	Pontiac
18.	Ernie Irvan	Ford
19.	Kenny Wallace	Ford
20.	Terry Labonte	Chevrolet
21.	Jeff Burton	Ford
22.	Hut Stricklin	Ford
23.	Jimmy Spencer	Ford
24.	Loy Allen	Ford
25.	Jeremy Mayfield	Ford
26.	Steve Grissom	Chevrolet
27.	Jeff Purvis	Chevrolet
28.	Geoff Bodine	Ford
29.	Ward Burton	Chevrolet
30.	Rich Bickle	Ford
31.	Todd Bodine	Ford
32.	Brett Bodine	Ford
33.	Greg Sacks	Ford
34.	Sterling Marlin	Chevrolet
35.	Harry Gant	Chevrolet
36.	John Andretti	Chevrolet
37.	Derrike Cope	Ford
38.	Robby Gordon	Ford
39.	Tim Steele	Ford
40.	Lake Speed	Ford
41.	Bobby Hamilton	Pontiac
42.	Jimmy Hensley	Ford

FINISH	DRIVER	CAR
28.	Sterling Marlin	Chevrolet
29.	Rick Mast	Ford
30.	Jeremy Mayfield	Ford
31.	Harry Gant	Chevrolet
32.	Jimmy Hensley	Ford
33.	Steve Grissom	Chevrolet
34.	Kyle Petty	Pontiac
35.	John Andretti	Chevrolet
36.	Ward Burton	Chevrolet
37.	Greg Sacks	Ford
38.	Jeff Purvis	Chevrolet
39.	Joe Nemechek	Chevrolet
40.	Loy Allen	Ford
41.	Ritchie Petty	Ford
42.	Hut Stricklin	Ford
43.	Tim Steele	Ford

PEPSI 400

July 2
Daytona Beach, Florida
Time of Race: 2 hours, 34 minutes, 17 seconds
Average Speed: 155.558 mph

FINISH	DRIVER	CAR
1.	Jimmy Spencer	Ford
2.	Ernie Irvan	Ford
3.	Dale Earnhardt	Chevrolet
4.	Mark Martin	Ford
5.	Ken Schrader	Chevrolet
6.	Geoff Bodine	Ford
7.	Todd Bodine	Ford
8.	Jeff Gordon	Chevrolet
9.	Morgan Shepherd	Ford
10.	Lake Speed	Ford
11.	Dale Jarrett	Chevrolet
12.	Mike Wallace	Ford
13.	Michael Waltrip	Pontiac
14.	Ted Musgrave	Ford
15.	Terry Labonte	Chevrolet
16.	Brett Bodine	Ford
17.	Ricky Rudd	Ford
18.	Jeff Burton	Ford
19.	Bill Elliott	Ford
20.	Rich Bickle	Ford
21.	Dick Trickle	Chevrolet
22.	Bobby Labonte	Pontiac
23.	Derrike Cope	Ford
24.	Bobby Hamilton	Pontiac
25.	Darrell Waltrip	Chevrolet
26.	Rusty Wallace	Ford
27.	Dave Marcis	Chevrolet

SLICK 50 300

July 10
Loudon, New Hampshire
Time of Race: 3 hours, 37 minutes, 24 seconds
Average Speed: 87.599 mph

FINISH	DRIVER	CAR
1.	Ricky Rudd	Ford
2.	Dale Earnhardt	Chevrolet
3.	Rusty Wallace	Ford
4.	Mark Martin	Ford
5.	Todd Bodine	Ford
6.	Morgan Shepherd	Ford
7.	Ted Musgrave	Ford
8.	Kyle Petty	Pontiac
9.	Rick Mast	Ford
10.	Sterling Marlin	Chevrolet
11.	Terry Labonte	Chevrolet
12.	Brett Bodine	Ford
13.	Bobby Labonte	Pontiac
14.	Dale Jarrett	Chevrolet
15.	Lake Speed	Ford
16.	Bill Elliott	Ford
17.	Harry Gant	Chevrolet
18.	Dave Marcis	Chevrolet
19.	Joe Nemechek	Chevrolet
20.	Randy LaJoie	Ford
21.	Rich Bickle	Ford
22.	Mike McLaughlin	Chevrolet
23.	Darrell Waltrip	Chevrolet
24.	Ken Schrader	Chevrolet
25.	Greg Sacks	Ford
26.	Jeremy Mayfield	Ford
27.	John Andretti	Chevrolet
28.	Mike Wallace	Ford
29.	Jimmy Hensley	Ford
30.	Ernie Irvan	Ford
31.	Geoff Bodine	Ford
32.	Jimmy Spencer	Ford
33.	Steve Grissom	Chevrolet
34.	Dick Trickle	Chevrolet
35.	Derrike Cope	Ford
36.	Hut Stricklin	Ford
37.	Michael Waltrip	Pontiac
38.	Jeff Burton	Ford
39.	Jeff Gordon	Chevrolet
40.	Bobby Hamilton	Pontiac
41.	Tim Steele	Ford
42.	Ward Burton	Chevrolet

MILLER GENUINE DRAFT 500

July 17
Pocono, Pennsylvania
Time of Race: 3 hours, 40 minutes, 28 seconds
Average Speed: 136.075 mph

FINISH	DRIVER	CAR
1.	Geoff Bodine	Ford
2.	Ward Burton	Chevrolet
3.	Joe Nemechek	Chevrolet
4.	Jeff Burton	Ford
5.	Morgan Shepherd	Ford
6.	Ricky Rudd	Ford
7.	Dale Earnhardt	Chevrolet
8.	Jeff Gordon	Chevrolet
9.	Rusty Wallace	Ford
10.	Dale Jarrett	Chevrolet
11.	Todd Bodine	Ford
12.	Sterling Marlin	Chevrolet
13.	Bobby Labonte	Pontiac
14.	Michael Waltrip	Pontiac
15.	Terry Labonte	Chevrolet
16.	Wally Dallenbach	Pontiac
17.	Bill Elliott	Ford
18.	Loy Allen	Ford
19.	Derrike Cope	Ford
20.	Lake Speed	Ford
21.	Jeremy Mayfield	Ford
22.	Hut Sticklin	Ford
23.	Bobby Hamilton	Pontiac
24.	Jimmy Spencer	Ford
25.	John Andretti	Chevrolet
26.	Dave Marcis	Chevrolet
27.	Kyle Petty	Pontiac
28.	Darrell Waltrip	Chevrolet
29.	Steve Grissom	Chevrolet
30.	Mike Wallace	Ford
31.	Mark Martin	Ford
32.	Ted Musgrave	Ford
33.	Tim Steele	Ford
34.	Richie Bickle	Ford
35.	Brett Bodine	Ford
36.	Greg Sacks	Ford
37.	Ernie Irvan	Ford
38.	Harry Gant	Chevrolet
39.	Ken Schrader	Chevrolet
40.	Rick Mast	Ford
41.	Billy Standridge	Ford
42.	Bob Schacht	Ford

DIEHARD 500

July 24
Talladega, Alabama
Time of Race: 3 hours, 3 minutes, 50 seconds
Average Speed: 163.217 mph

FINISH	DRIVER	CAR
1.	Jimmy Spencer	Ford
2.	Bill Elliott	Ford
3.	Ernie Irvan	Ford
4.	Ken Schrader	Chevrolet
5.	Sterling Marlin	Chevrolet
6.	Mark Martin	Ford
7.	Ricky Rudd	Ford
8.	Wally Dallenbach	Pontiac
9.	Kenny Wallace	Ford
10.	Terry Labonte	Chevrolet
11.	Michael Waltrip	Pontiac
12.	Bobby Labonte	Pontiac
13.	Mike Wallace	Ford
14.	Lake Speed	Ford
15.	Morgan Shepherd	Ford
16.	Todd Bodine	Ford
17.	Brett Bodine	Ford
18.	Steve Grissom	Chevrolet
19.	Kyle Petty	Pontiac
20.	Rick Mast	Ford
21.	Harry Gant	Chevrolet
22.	Bobby Hamilton	Pontiac
23.	Bobby Hillin	Ford
24.	Darrell Waltrip	Chevrolet
25.	Hut Sticklin	Ford
26.	Jeff Burton	Ford
27.	Dave Marcis	Chevrolet

FINISH	DRIVER	CAR
28.	Brad Teague	Ford
29.	Greg Sacks	Ford
30.	Jimmy Hensley	Ford
31.	Jeff Gordon	Chevrolet
32.	Jeremy Mayfield	Ford
33.	Geoff Bodine	Ford
34.	Dale Earnhardt	Chevrolet
35.	Joe Nemechek	Chevrolet
36.	Jeff Purvis	Chevrolet
37.	Loy Allen	Ford
38.	Tim Steele	Ford
39.	Dale Jarrett	Chevrolet
40.	John Andretti	Chevrolet
41.	Ted Musgrave	Ford
42.	Rusty Wallace	Ford

BRICKYARD 400

August 6
Indianapolis, Indiana
Time of Race: 3 hours, 1 minute, 51 seconds
Average Speed: 131.977 mph

FINISH	DRIVER	CAR
1.	Jeff Gordon	Chevrolet
2.	Brett Bodine	Ford
3.	Bill Elliott	Ford
4.	Rusty Wallace	Ford
5.	Dale Earnhardt	Chevrolet
6.	Darrell Waltrip	Chevrolet
7.	Ken Schrader	Chevrolet
8.	Michael Waltrip	Pontiac
9.	Todd Bodine	Ford
10.	Morgan Shepherd	Ford
11.	Ricky Rudd	Ford
12.	Terry Labonte	Chevrolet
13.	Ted Musgrave	Ford
14.	Sterling Marlin	Chevrolet
15.	Lake Speed	Ford
16.	Bobby Labonte	Pontiac
17.	Ernie Irvan	Ford
18.	Greg Sacks	Ford
19.	Jeff Burton	Ford
20.	Joe Nemechek	Chevrolet
21.	Bobby Hillin	Ford
22.	Rick Mast	Ford
23.	Wally Dallenbach Jr.	Pontiac
24.	Bobby Hamilton	Pontiac
25.	Kyle Petty	Pontiac
26.	Jeremy Mayfield	Ford
27.	Derrike Cope	Ford
28.	John Andretti	Chevrolet
29.	Rich Bickle	Ford
30.	A. J. Foyt	Ford
31.	Ward Burton	Chevrolet
32.	Jimmy Hensley	Ford
33.	Danny Sullivan	Chevrolet
34.	Jeff Purvis	Chevrolet
35.	Mark Martin	Ford
36.	Hut Stricklin	Ford
37.	Harry Gant	Chevrolet
38.	Geoff Brabham	Ford
39.	Geoff Bodine	Ford
40.	Dale Jarrett	Chevrolet
41.	Dave Marcis	Chevrolet
42.	Mike Chase	Chevrolet
43.	Jimmy Spencer	Ford

THE BUD AT THE GLEN

August 14
Watkins Glen, New York
Time of Race: 2 hours, 21 minutes, 7 seconds
Average Speed: 93.752 mph

FINISH	DRIVER	CAR
1.	Mark Martin	Ford
2.	Ernie Irvan	Ford
3.	Dale Earnhardt	Chevrolet
4.	Ken Schrader	Chevrolet
5.	Ricky Rudd	Ford
6.	Terry Labonte	Chevrolet
7.	Darrell Waltrip	Chevrolet
8.	Joe Nemechek	Chevrolet
9.	Jeff Gordon	Chevrolet
10.	Harry Gant	Chevrolet
11.	Dale Jarrett	Chevrolet
12.	Bill Elliott	Ford
13.	Lake Speed	Ford
14.	Wally Dallenbach	Pontiac
15.	Todd Bodine	Ford
16.	Morgan Shepherd	Ford
17.	Rusty Wallace	Ford
18.	Bobby Labonte	Pontiac
19.	Ted Musgrave	Ford
20.	Michael Waltrip	Pontiac
21.	Dave Marcis	Chevrolet
22.	Tom Kendall	Ford
23.	Steve Grissom	Chevrolet
24.	Ward Burton	Chevrolet
25.	Jeff Burton	Ford
26.	Sterling Marlin	Chevrolet
27.	Mike McLaughlin	Chevrolet
28.	Brett Bodine	Ford
29.	Geoff Bodine	Ford
30.	Hut Stricklin	Ford
31.	Butch Leitzinger	Chevrolet
32.	Dick Trickle	Chevrolet
33.	Jimmy Hensley	Ford
34.	Bobby Hamilton	Pontiac
35.	PontiacJ. Jones	Ford
36.	Scott Lagasse	Chevrolet
37.	Kyle Petty	Pontiac
38.	Rick Mast	Ford
39.	Greg Sacks	Ford
40.	Derrike Cope	Ford

GM GOODWRENCH DEALER 400

August 21
Brooklyn, Michigan
Time of Race: 2 hours, 51 minutes, 32 seconds
Average Speed: 139.914 mph

FINISH	DRIVER	CAR
1.	Geoff Bodine	Ford
2.	Mark Martin	Ford
3.	Rick Mast	Ford
4.	Rusty Wallace	Ford
5.	Bobby Labonte	Pontiac
6.	Kyle Petty	Pontiac
7.	Bill Elliott	Ford
8.	Terry Labonte	Chevrolet
9.	Darrell Waltrip	Chevrolet
10.	Ricky Rudd	Ford
11.	Ken Schrader	Chevrolet
12.	Brett Bodine	Ford
13.	Lake Speed	Ford
14.	Michael Waltrip	Pontiac
15.	Jeff Gordon	Chevrolet
16.	Mike Wallace	Ford
17.	John Andretti	Pontiac
18.	Derrike Cope	Ford
19.	Steve Grissom	Chevrolet
20.	Jimmy Spencer	Ford
21.	Joe Nemechek	Chevrolet
22.	Loy Allen	Ford
23.	Jeremy Mayfield	Ford
24.	Ted Musgrave	Ford
25.	Harry Gant	Chevrolet
26.	Morgan Shepherd	Ford
27.	Rick Carelli	Chevrolet
28.	Jeff Purvis	Ford
29.	Ward Burton	Chevrolet

FINISH	DRIVER	CAR
30.	Dale Jarrett	Chevrolet
31.	Phil Parsons	Ford
32.	Greg Sacks	Ford
33.	Jeff Burton	Ford
34.	Sterling Marlin	Chevrolet
35.	Rich Bickle	Ford
36.	Dave Marcis	Chevrolet
37.	Dale Earnhardt	Chevrolet
38.	Todd Bodine	Ford
39.	Billy Standridge	Ford
40.	Bobby Hillin	Ford
41.	Dick Trickle	Chevrolet

GOODY'S 500

August 27
Bristol, Tennessee
Time of Race: 2 hours, 55 minutes, 1 second
Average Speed: 91.363 mph

FINISH	DRIVER	CAR
1.	Rusty Wallace	Ford
2.	Mark Martin	Ford
3.	Dale Earnhardt	Chevrolet
4.	Darrell Waltrip	Chevrolet
5.	Bill Elliott	Ford
6.	Sterling Marlin	Chevrolet
7.	Michael Waltrip	Pontiac
8.	Todd Bodine	Ford
9.	Harry Gant	Chevrolet
10.	Rick Mast	Ford
11.	Ted Musgrave	Ford
12.	Ricky Rudd	Ford
13.	Kenny Wallace	Ford
14.	Brett Bodine	Ford
15.	Kyle Petty	Pontiac
16.	Derrike Cope	Ford
17.	Dick Trickle	Chevrolet
18.	Morgan Shepherd	Ford
19.	Ken Schrader	Chevrolet
20.	Jeff Burton	Ford
21.	Jeremy Mayfield	Ford
22.	Brad Teague	Ford
23.	Geoff Bodine	Ford
24.	Mike Wallace	Ford
25.	Lake Speed	Ford
26.	Dale Jarrett	Chevrolet
27.	Greg Sacks	Ford
28.	Bobby Hamilton	Pontiac
29.	Joe Nemechek	Chevrolet
30.	John Andretti	Pontiac
31.	Bobby Labonte	Pontiac
32.	Jeff Gordon	Chevrolet
33.	Terry Labonte	Chevrolet
34.	Steve Grissom	Chevrolet
35.	Hut Stricklin	Ford
36.	Ward Burton	Chevrolet

MOUNTAIN DEW SOUTHERN 500

September 4
Darlington, South Carolina
Time of Race: 3 hours, 55 minutes, 5 seconds
Average Speed: 127.952 mph

FINISH	DRIVER	CAR
1.	Bill Elliott	Ford
2.	Dale Earnhardt	Chevrolet
3.	Morgan Shepherd	Ford
4.	Ricky Rudd	Ford
5.	Sterling Marlin	Chevrolet
6.	Jeff Gordon	Chevrolet
7.	Rusty Wallace	Ford
8.	Jeff Burton	Ford
9.	Dale Jarrett	Chevrolet

10.	Terry Labonte	Chevrolet
11.	Kenny Wallace	Ford
12.	Kyle Petty	Pontiac
13.	Darrell Waltrip	Chevrolet
14.	Hut Stricklin	Ford
15.	Phil Parsons	Ford
16.	John Andretti	Pontiac
17.	Mike Wallace	Ford
18.	Butch Miller	Ford
19.	Greg Sacks	Ford
20.	Rick Mast	Ford
21.	Loy Allen	Ford
22.	Bobby Hamilton	Pontiac
23.	Steve Grissom	Chevrolet
24.	Billy Standridge	Ford
25.	Mark Martin	Ford
26.	Todd Bodine	Ford
27.	Geoff Bodine	Ford
28.	Dave Marcis	Chevrolet
29.	Brett Bodine	Ford
30.	Brad Teague	Ford
31.	Michael Waltrip	Pontiac
32.	Ken Schrader	Chevrolet
33.	Jeremy Mayfield	Ford
34.	Ward Burton	Chevrolet
35.	Derrike Cope	Ford
36.	Bobby Labonte	Pontiac
37.	Jimmy Spencer	Ford
38.	Dick Trickle	Chevrolet
39.	Ted Musgrave	Ford
40.	Lake Speed	Ford
41.	Harry Gant	Chevrolet
42.	Joe Nemechek	Chevrolet

MILLER GENUINE DRAFT 400

September 10
Richmond, Virginia
Time of Race: 2 hours, 52 minutes, 59 seconds
Average Speed: 104.156 mph

FINISH	DRIVER	CAR
1.	Terry Labonte	Chevrolet
2.	Jeff Gordon	Chevrolet
3.	Dale Earnhardt	Chevrolet
4.	Rusty Wallace	Ford
5.	Ricky Rudd	Ford
6.	Mark Martin	Ford
7.	Steve Grissom	Chevrolet
8.	Brett Bodine	Ford
9.	Ken Schrader	Chevrolet
10.	Darrell Waltrip	Chevrolet
11.	John Andretti	Pontiac
12.	Dick Trickle	Chevrolet
13.	Sterling Marlin	Chevrolet
14.	Morgan Shepherd	Ford
15.	Bill Elliott	Ford
16.	Dale Jarrett	Chevrolet
17.	Ted Musgrave	Ford
18.	Geoff Bodine	Ford
19.	Derrike Cope	Ford
20.	Todd Bodine	Ford
21.	Lake Speed	Ford
22.	Harry Gant	Chevrolet
23.	Mike Wallace	Ford
24.	Bobby Labonte	Pontiac
25.	Ward Burton	Chevrolet
26.	Michael Waltrip	Pontiac
27.	Greg Sacks	Ford
28.	Joe Nemechek	Chevrolet
29.	Dave Marcis	Chevrolet
30.	Hut Stricklin	Ford
31.	Loy Allen	Ford
32.	Kenny Wallace	Ford
33.	Rick Mast	Ford
34.	Bobby Hamilton	Pontiac
35.	Jimmy Spencer	Ford
36.	Jeff Green	Ford
37.	Jeremy Mayfield	Ford
38.	Kyle Petty	Pontiac

SPLITFIRE SPARK PLUG 500

September 18
Dover, Delaware
Time of Race: 4 hours, 26 minutes, 32 seconds
Average Speed: 112.556 mph

FINISH	DRIVER	CAR
1.	Rusty Wallace	Ford
2.	Dale Earnhardt	Chevrolet
3.	Darrell Waltrip	Chevrolet
4.	Ken Schrader	Chevrolet
5.	Geoff Bodine	Ford
6.	Kyle Petty	Pontiac
7.	Terry Labonte	Chevrolet
8.	Steve Grissom	Chevrolet
9.	Lake Speed	Ford
10.	Morgan Shepherd	Ford
11.	Jeff Gordon	Chevrolet
12.	Derrike Cope	Ford
13.	Harry Gant	Chevrolet
14.	Ted Musgrave	Ford
15.	Rick Mast	Ford
16.	Todd Bodine	Ford
17.	Bobby Labonte	Pontiac
18.	Ricky Rudd	Ford
19.	Mark Martin	Ford
20.	Kenny Wallace	Ford
21.	Dick Trickle	Chevrolet
22.	Loy Allen	Ford
23.	Tim Fedewa	Ford
24.	Jeremy Mayfield	Ford
25.	John Andretti	Pontiac
26.	Brett Bodine	Ford
27.	Ward Burton	Chevrolet
28.	Bill Elliott	Ford
29.	Mike Wallace	Ford
30.	Sterling Marlin	Chevrolet
31.	Bobby Hamilton	Pontiac
32.	Hut Stricklin	Ford
33.	Michael Waltrip	Pontiac
34.	Dale Jarrett	Chevrolet
35.	Dave Marcis	Chevrolet
36.	Joe Nemechek	Chevrolet
37.	Jeff Burton	Ford
38.	Greg Sacks	Ford
39.	Jimmy Spencer	Ford
40.	Brad Teague	Ford

GOODY'S 500

September 25
Martinsville, Virginia
Time of Race: 3 hours, 24 minutes, 34 seconds
Average Speed: 77.139 mph

FINISH	DRIVER	CAR
1.	Rusty Wallace	Ford
2.	Dale Earnhardt	Chevrolet
3.	Bill Elliott	Ford
4.	Kenny Wallace	Ford
5.	Dale Jarrett	Chevrolet
6.	Ken Schrader	Chevrolet
7.	Sterling Marlin	Chevrolet
8.	Harry Gant	Chevrolet
9.	Ted Musgrave	Ford
10.	Darrell Waltrip	Chevrolet
11.	Jeff Gordon	Chevrolet
12.	Steve Grissom	Chevrolet
13.	Bobby Hamilton	Pontiac
14.	Terry Labonte	Chevrolet
15.	Morgan Shepehrd	Ford
16.	Mark Martin	Ford
17.	Derrike Cope	Ford
18.	Geoff Bodine	Ford
19.	Michael Waltrip	Pontiac
20.	Jimmy Spencer	Ford

21.	John Andretti	Pontiac
22.	Joe Nemechek	Chevrolet
23.	Hut Stricklin	Ford
24.	Kyle Petty	Pontiac
25.	Ricky Rudd	Ford
26.	Greg Sacks	Ford
27.	Brad Teague	Ford
28.	Mike Wallace	Ford
29.	Rick Mast	Ford
30.	Brett Bodine	Ford
31.	Bobby Labonte	Pontiac
32.	Dick Trickle	Ford
33.	Todd Bodine	Ford
34.	Lake Speed	Ford
35.	Ward Burton	Chevrolet
36.	Jeff Burton	Ford

TYSON HOLLY FARMS 400

October 2
North Wilkesboro, North Carolina
Time of Race: 2 hours, 32 minutes, 15 seconds
Average Speed: 98.522 mph

FINISH	DRIVER	CAR
1.	Geoff Bodine	Ford
2.	Terry Labonte	Chevrolet
3.	Rick Mast	Ford
4.	Rusty Wallace	Ford
5.	Mark Martin	Ford
6.	Bill Elliott	Ford
7.	Dale Earnhardt	Chevrolet
8.	Jeff Gordon	Chevrolet
9.	Ted Musgrave	Ford
10.	Kenny Wallace	Ford
11.	Ricky Rudd	Ford
12.	Bobby Hamilton	Pontiac
13.	Darrell Waltrip	Chevrolet
14.	Ken Schrader	Chevrolet
15.	Bobby Labonte	Pontiac
16.	Dick Trickle	Chevrolet
17.	John Andretti	Pontiac
18.	Ward Burton	Chevrolet
19.	Derrike Cope	Ford
20.	Steve Grissom	Chevrolet
21.	Michael Waltrip	Pontiac
22.	Hut Stricklin	Ford
23.	Jimmy Spencer	Ford
24.	Dave Marcis	Chevrolet
25.	Lake Speed	Ford
26.	Kyle Petty	Pontiac
27.	Jeremy Mayfield	Ford
28.	Jeff Burton	Ford
29.	Jeff Green	Ford
30.	Morgan Shepherd	Ford
31.	Sterling Marlin	Chevrolet
32.	Harry Gant	Chevrolet
33.	Brett Bodine	Ford
34.	Joe Nemechek	Chevrolet
35.	Greg Sacks	Ford
36.	Phil Parsons	Ford

MELLO YELLO 500

October 9
Charlotte, North Carolina
Time of Race: 3 hours, 26 minutes, 0 seconds
Average Speed: 145.922 mph

FINISH	DRIVER	CAR
1.	Dale Jarrett	Chevrolet
2.	Morgan Shepherd	Ford
3.	Dale Earnhardt	Chevrolet
4.	Ken Schrader	Chevrolet
5.	Lake Speed	Ford

6.	Brett Bodine	Ford
7.	Terry Labonte	Chevrolet
8.	Derrike Cope	Ford
9.	Darrell Waltrip	Chevrolet
10.	Michael Waltrip	Pontiac
11.	Joe Nemechek	Chevrolet
12.	Rick Mast	Ford
13.	Dick Trickle	Chevrolet
14.	Kenny Wallace	Ford
15.	Bobby Hillin	Ford
16.	Jimmy Spencer	Ford
17.	Mike Wallace	Ford
18.	Ted Musgrave	Ford
19.	Bobby Hamilton	Pontiac
20.	Jeremy Mayfield	Ford
21.	Hut Stricklin	Ford
22.	Harry Gant	Chevrolet
23.	Joe Ruttman	Ford
24.	John Andretti	Pontiac
25.	Jeff Burton	Ford
26.	Steve Grissom	Chevrolet
27.	Loy Allen	Ford
28.	Jeff Gordon	Chevrolet
29.	Ricky Rudd	Ford
30.	Kyle Petty	Pontiac
31.	Robert Pressley	Chevrolet
32.	Geoff Bodine	Ford
33.	Bill Elliott	Ford
34.	Billy Standridge	Ford
35.	Greg Sacks	Ford
36.	Sterling Marlin	Chevrolet
37.	Rusty Wallace	Ford
38.	Todd Bodine	Ford
39.	Mark Martin	Ford
40.	Jimmy Hensley	Ford
41.	Ward Burton	Chevrolet
42.	Bobby Labonte	Pontiac

AC DELCO 500

October 23
Rockingham, North Carolina
Time of Race: 3 hours, 57 minutes, 30 seconds
Average Speed: 126.408 mph

FINISH	DRIVER	CAR
1.	Dale Earnhardt	Chevrolet
2.	Rick Mast	Ford
3.	Morgan Shepherd	Ford
4.	Ricky Rudd	Ford
5.	Terry Labonte	Chevrolet
6.	Bill Elliott	Ford
7.	Mark Martin	Ford
8.	Dick Trickle	Chevrolet
9.	Ward Burton	Chevrolet
10.	Lake Speed	Ford
11.	Jeff Burton	Ford
12.	Dale Jarrett	Chevrolet
13.	Ted Musgrave	Ford
14.	Sterling Marlin	Chevrolet
15.	Kenny Wallace	Ford
16.	Mike Wallace	Ford
17.	Joe Nemechek	Chevrolet
18.	Brett Bodine	Ford
19.	Jeremy Mayfield	Ford
20.	Butch Miller	Ford
21.	Todd Bodine	Ford
22.	Rick Carelli	Chevrolet
23.	Darrell Waltrip	Chevrolet
24.	Randy McDonald	Chevrolet
25.	John Andretti	Pontiac
26.	Michael Waltrip	Pontiac
27.	Hut Stricklin	Ford
28.	Bobby Labonte	Pontiac
29.	Jeff Gordon	Chevrolet
30.	Steve Grissom	Chevrolet
31.	Harry Gant	Chevrolet
32.	Ken Schrader	Chevrolet
33.	Bobby Hamilton	Pontiac
34.	Dave Marcis	Chevrolet

FINISH	DRIVER	CAR
35.	Rusty Wallace	Ford
36.	Kyle Petty	Pontiac
37.	Derrike Cope	Ford
38.	Jimmy Spencer	Ford
39.	Greg Sacks	Ford
40.	Geoff Bodine	Ford
41.	Billy Standridge	Ford
42.	Loy Allen	Ford

SLICK 50 500

October 30
Phoenix, Arizona
Time of Race: 2 hours, 54 minutes, 12 seconds
Average Speed: 107.463 mph

FINISH	DRIVER	CAR
1.	Terry Labonte	Chevrolet
2.	Mark Martin	Ford
3.	Sterling Marlin	Chevrolet
4.	Jeff Gordon	Chevrolet
5.	Ted Musgrave	Ford
6.	Kyle Petty	Pontiac
7.	Ricky Rudd	Ford
8.	Geoff Bodine	Ford
9.	Dale Jarrett	Chevrolet
10.	Darrell Waltrip	Chevrolet
11.	Bobby Hamilton	Pontiac
12.	Morgan Shepherd	Ford
13.	Brett Bodine	Ford
14.	Lake Speed	Ford
15.	Ken Schrader	Chevrolet
16.	Bobby Labonte	Pontiac
17.	Rusty Wallace	Ford
18.	Kenny Wallace	Ford
19.	Dave Marcis	Chevrolet
20.	Jeremy Mayfield	Ford
21.	Ward Burton	Chevrolet
22.	Steve Grissom	Chevrolet
23.	Harry Gant	Chevrolet
24.	Hut Stricklin	Ford
25.	Joe Nemechek	Chevrolet
26.	Greg Sacks	Ford
27.	Jeff Burton	Ford
28.	Mike Wallace	Ford
29.	Pontiac J. Jones	Ford
30.	Derrike Cope	Ford
31.	Mike Chase	Chevrolet
32.	Todd Bodine	Ford
33.	Rick Carelli	Chevrolet
34.	Ron Hornaday Jr.	Chevrolet
35.	Bill Elliott	Ford
36.	Michael Waltrip	Pontiac
37.	Rich Bickle	Chevrolet
38.	Jimmy Spencer	Ford
39.	Dick Trickle	Chevrolet
40.	Dale Earnhardt	Chevrolet
41.	Loy Allen	Ford
42.	Rick Mast	Ford
43.	John Andretti	Pontiac

HOOTERS 500

November 13
Atlanta, Georgia
Time of Race: 3 hours, 21 minutes, 3 seconds
Average Speed: 148.982 mph

FINISH	DRIVER	CAR
1.	Mark Martin	Ford
2.	Dale Earnhardt	Chevrolet
3.	Todd Bodine	Ford
4.	Lake Speed	Ford
5.	Mike Wallace	Ford
6.	Morgan Shepherd	Ford

7.	Derrike Cope	Ford
8.	Terry Labonte	Chevrolet
9.	Dale Jarrett	Chevrolet
10.	Michael Waltrip	Pontiac
11.	Ken Schrader	Chevrolet
12.	Jimmy Hensley	Ford
13.	John Andretti	Pontiac
14.	Ricky Rudd	Ford
15.	Jeff Gordon	Chevrolet
16.	Hut Stricklin	Ford
17.	Pancho Carter	Ford
18.	Jeff Green	Ford
19.	Randy LaJoie	Ford
20.	Jimmy Spencer	Ford
21.	Darrell Waltrip	Chevrolet
22.	Kyle Petty	Pontiac
23.	Joe Nemechek	Chevrolet
24.	Bobby Hamilton	Pontiac
25.	Kenny Wallace	Ford
26.	Steve Grissom	Chevrolet
27.	Rick Mast	Ford
28.	Ted Musgrave	Ford
29.	Ken Bouchard	Ford
30.	Gary Bradberry	Ford
31.	Jeff Burton	Ford
32.	Rusty Wallace	Ford
33.	Harry Gant	Chevrolet
34.	Geoff Bodine	Ford
35.	Robert Pressley	Chevrolet
36.	Brett Bodine	Ford
37.	Bobby Labonte	Pontiac
38.	Bill Elliott	Ford
39.	Greg Sacks	Ford
40.	Sterling Marlin	Chevrolet
41.	Ward Burton	Chevrolet
42.	Loy Allen	Ford
43.	Bobby Hillin	Ford

1995

DAYTONA 500

February 19
Daytona Beach, Florida
Time of Race: 3 hours, 31 minutes, 42 seconds
Average Speed: 141.710 mph
Margin of Victory: .61 second

FINISH	DRIVER	CAR
1.	Sterling Marlin	Chevrolet
2.	Dale Earnhardt	Chevrolet
3.	Mark Martin	Ford
4.	Ted Musgrave	Ford
5.	Dale Jarrett	Ford
6.	Michael Waltrip	Pontiac
7.	Steve Grissom	Chevrolet
8.	Terry Labonte	Chevrolet
9.	Ken Schrader	Chevrolet
10.	Morgan Shepherd	Ford
11.	Dick Trickle	Ford
12.	Kyle Petty	Pontiac
13.	Ricky Rudd	Ford
14.	Lake Speed	Ford
15.	Ward Burton	Chevrolet
16.	Ricky Craven	Chevrolet
17.	Loy Allen	Ford
18.	Bobby Hamilton	Pontiac
19.	Joe Ruttman	Ford
20.	Geoff Bodine	Ford
21.	Rick Mast	Ford
22.	Jeff Gordon	Chevrolet
23.	Bill Elliott	Ford
24.	Jeff Burton	Ford
25.	Brett Bodine	Ford
26.	Robert Pressley	Chevrolet
27.	John Andretti	Ford
28.	Ben Hess	Ford

29.	Randy LaJoie	Pontiac
30.	Bobby Labonte	Chevrolet
31.	Derrike Cope	Ford
32.	Darrell Waltrip	Chevrolet
33.	Davy Jones	Ford
34.	Rusty Wallace	Ford
35.	Jeremy Mayfield	Ford
36.	Dave Marcis	Chevrolet
37.	Todd Bodine	Ford
38.	Jeff Purvis	Chevrolet
39.	Mike Wallace	Ford
40.	Steve Kinser	Ford
41.	Phil Parsons	Ford
42.	Joe Nemechek	Chevrolet

GOODWRENCH 500

February 26
Rockingham, North Carolina
Time of Race: 3 hours, 59 minutes, 15 seconds
Average Speed: 125.305 mph
Margin of Victory: 1.19 seconds

FINISH	DRIVER	CAR
1.	Jeff Gordon	Chevrolet
2.	Bobby Labonte	Chevrolet
3.	Dale Earnhardt	Chevrolet
4.	Ricky Rudd	Ford
5.	Dale Jarrett	Ford
6.	Steve Grissom	Chevrolet
7.	Mark Martin	Ford
8.	Derrike Cope	Ford
9.	Ward Burton	Chevrolet
10.	Kyle Petty	Pontiac
11.	Bill Elliott	Ford
12.	Sterling Marlin	Chevrolet
13.	John Andretti	Ford
14.	Brett Bodine	Ford
15.	Mike Wallace	Ford
16.	Ricky Craven	Chevrolet
17.	Michael Waltrip	Pontiac
18.	Jeremy Mayfield	Ford
19.	Jeff Burton	Ford
20.	Kenny Wallace	Ford
21.	Geoff Bodine	Ford
22.	Dick Trickle	Ford
23.	Dave Marcis	Chevrolet
24.	Rusty Wallace	Ford
25.	Randy LaJoie	Pontiac
26.	Terry Labonte	Chevrolet
27.	Steve Kinser	Ford
28.	Loy Allen	Ford
29.	Joe Nemechek	Chevrolet
30.	Jimmy Spencer	Ford
31.	Todd Bodine	Ford
32.	Lake Speed	Ford
33.	Ted Musgrave	Ford
34.	Morgan Shepherd	Ford
35.	Rick Mast	Ford
36.	Bobby Hamilton	Pontiac
37.	Davy Jones	Ford
38.	Darrell Waltrip	Chevrolet
39.	Ken Schrader	Chevrolet
40.	Jimmy Hensley	Chevrolet
41.	Greg Sacks	Pontiac
42.	Robert Pressley	Chevrolet

PONTIAC EXCITEMENT 400

March 5
Richmond, Virginia
Time of Race: 2 hours, 49 minutes, 8 seconds
Average Speed: 106.425 mph
Margin of Victory: 1.25 seconds

FINISH	DRIVER	CAR
1.	Terry Labonte	Chevrolet
2.	Dale Earnhardt	Chevrolet
3.	Rusty Wallace	Ford
4.	Ken Schrader	Chevrolet
5.	Sterling Marlin	Chevrolet
6.	Derrike Cope	Ford
7.	Darrell Waltrip	Chevrolet
8.	Mark Martin	Ford
9.	Bobby Hamilton	Pontiac
10.	John Andretti	Ford
11.	Geoff Bodine	Ford
12.	Dick Trickle	Ford
13.	Ted Musgrave	Ford
14.	Lake Speed	Ford
15.	Morgan Shepherd	Ford
16.	Bill Elliott	Ford
17.	Jeremy Mayfield	Ford
18.	Brett Bodine	Ford
19.	Greg Sacks	Pontiac
20.	Dave Marcis	Chevrolet
21.	Ricky Rudd	Ford
22.	Ward Burton	Chevrolet
23.	Michael Waltrip	Pontiac
24.	Jimmy Spencer	Ford
25.	Dale Jarrett	Ford
26.	Mike Wallace	Ford
27.	Randy LaJoie	Pontiac
28.	Steve Kinser	Ford
29.	Loy Allen	Ford
30.	Bobby Labonte	Chevrolet
31.	Jeff Burton	Ford
32.	Joe Nemechek	Chevrolet
33.	Kyle Petty	Pontiac
34.	Rick Mast	Ford
35.	Robert Pressley	Chevrolet
36.	Jeff Gordon	Chevrolet
37.	Todd Bodine	Ford
38.	Ricky Craven	Chevrolet

PUROLATOR 500

March 12
Atlanta, Georgia
Time of Race: 3 hours, 19 minutes, 32 seconds
Average Speed: 150.115 mph
Margin of Victory: .19 second

FINISH	DRIVER	CAR
1.	Jeff Gordon	Chevrolet
2.	Bobby Labonte	Chevrolet
3.	Terry Labonte	Chevrolet
4.	Dale Earnhardt	Chevrolet
5.	Dale Jarrett	Ford
6.	Morgan Shepherd	Ford
7.	Sterling Marlin	Chevrolet
8.	Ricky Rudd	Ford
9.	Mark Martin	Ford
10.	Rusty Wallace	Ford
11.	Rick Mast	Ford
12.	Ricky Craven	Chevrolet
13.	Derrike Cope	Ford
14.	Kyle Petty	Pontiac
15.	Lake Speed	Ford
16.	Joe Nemechek	Chevrolet
17.	Bobby Hamilton	Pontiac
18.	Steve Grissom	Chevrolet
19.	Ted Musgrave	Ford
20.	John Andretti	Ford
21.	Todd Bodine	Ford
22.	Dick Trickle	Ford
23.	Brett Bodine	Ford
24.	Davy Jones	Ford
25.	Billy Standridge	Ford
26.	Bill Elliott	Ford
27.	Ken Schrader	Chevrolet
28.	Dave Marcis	Chevrolet
29.	Greg Sacks	Pontiac
30.	Geoff Bodine	Ford

31.	Robert Pressley	Chevrolet
32.	Jimmy Spencer	Ford
33.	Jeff Burton	Ford
34.	Darrell Waltrip	Chevrolet
35.	Michael Waltrip	Pontiac
36.	Jeremy Mayfield	Ford
37.	Jeff Purvis	Chevrolet
38.	Jimmy Hensley	Chevrolet
39.	Randy LaJoie	Pontiac
40.	Mike Wallace	Ford
41.	Steve Kinser	Ford
42.	Phil Parsons	Ford

TRANSOUTH FINANCIAL 400

March 26
Darlington, South Carolina
Time of Race: 3 hours, 35 minutes, 35 seconds
Average Speed: 111.392 mph
Margin of Victory: 1.05 seconds

FINISH	DRIVER	CAR
1.	Sterling Marlin	Chevrolet
2.	Dale Earnhardt	Chevrolet
3.	Ted Musgrave	Ford
4.	Todd Bodine	Ford
5.	Derrike Cope	Ford
6.	Steve Grissom	Chevrolet
7.	Michael Waltrip	Pontiac
8.	Morgan Shepherd	Ford
9.	Bobby Hamilton	Pontiac
10.	John Andretti	Ford
11.	Ken Schrader	Chevrolet
12.	Brett Bodine	Ford
13.	Geoff Bodine	Ford
14.	Billy Standridge	Ford
15.	Mike Wallace	Ford
16.	Randy LaJoie	Pontiac
17.	Bill Elliott	Ford
18.	Loy Allen	Ford
19.	Jeff Burton	Ford
20.	Davy Jones	Ford
21.	Darrell Waltrip	Chevrolet
22.	Greg Sacks	Pontiac
23.	Rusty Wallace	Ford
24.	Dave Marcis	Chevrolet
25.	Ward Burton	Chevrolet
26.	Rick Mast	Ford
27.	Bobby Labonte	Chevrolet
28.	Dick Trickle	Ford
29.	Lake Speed	Ford
30.	Robert Pressley	Chevrolet
31.	Jeremy Mayfield	Ford
32.	Jeff Gordon	Chevrolet
33.	Joe Nemechek	Chevrolet
34.	Terry Labonte	Chevrolet
35.	Kyle Petty	Pontiac
36.	Jimmy Spencer	Ford
37.	Mark Martin	Ford
38.	Dale Jarrett	Ford
39.	Chuck Bown	Chevrolet
40.	Steve Kinser	Ford
41.	Ricky Rudd	Ford
42.	Ricky Craven	Chevrolet

FOOD CITY 500

April 2
Bristol, Tennessee
Time of Race: 2 hours, 53 minutes, 47 seconds
Average Speed: 92.011 mph
Margin of Victory: 5.74 seconds

FINISH	DRIVER	CAR
1.	Jeff Gordon	Chevrolet
2.	Rusty Wallace	Ford
3.	Darrell Waltrip	Chevrolet
4.	Bobby Hamilton	Pontiac
5.	Ricky Rudd	Ford
6.	Dale Jarrett	Ford
7.	Terry Labonte	Chevrolet
8.	Mark Martin	Ford
9.	Sterling Marlin	Chevrolet
10.	Robert Pressley	Chevrolet
11.	Steve Grissom	Chevrolet
12.	Randy LaJoie	Pontiac
13.	Derrike Cope	Ford
14.	Bill Elliott	Ford
15.	Rick Mast	Ford
16.	Jimmy Spencer	Ford
17.	Lake Speed	Ford
18.	Ted Musgrave	Ford
19.	John Andretti	Ford
20.	Morgan Shepherd	Ford
21.	Ward Burton	Chevrolet
22.	Michael Waltrip	Pontiac
23.	Geoff Bodine	Ford
24.	Davy Jones	Ford
25.	Dale Earnhardt	Chevrolet
26.	Ken Schrader	Chevrolet
27.	Brett Bodine	Ford
28.	Jeff Burton	Ford
29.	Ricky Craven	Chevrolet
30.	Dick Trickle	Ford
31.	Chuck Bown	Chevrolet
32.	Bobby Labonte	Chevrolet
33.	Todd Bodine	Ford
34.	Dave Marcis	Chevrolet
35.	Kyle Petty	Pontiac
36.	Greg Sacks	Pontiac

FIRST UNION 400

April 9
North Wilkesboro, North Carolina
Time of Race: 2 hours, 26 minutes, 27 seconds
Average Speed: 102.424 mph (Race Record)
Margin of Victory: 13.48 seconds

FINISH	DRIVER	CAR
1.	Dale Earnhardt	Chevrolet
2.	Jeff Gordon	Chevrolet
3.	Mark Martin	Ford
4.	Rusty Wallace	Ford
5.	Steve Grissom	Chevrolet
6.	Ted Musgrave	Ford
7.	Sterling Marlin	Chevrolet
8.	Rick Mast	Ford
9.	Brett Bodine	Ford
10.	Darrell Waltrip	Chevrolet
11.	Dale Jarrett	Ford
12.	Ken Schrader	Chevrolet
13.	Bobby Hamilton	Pontiac
14.	Geoff Bodine	Ford
15.	Bobby Labonte	Chevrolet
16.	Terry Labonte	Chevrolet
17.	John Andretti	Ford
18.	Robert Pressley	Chevrolet
19.	Morgan Shepherd	Ford
20.	Joe Nemechek	Chevrolet
21.	Todd Bodine	Ford
22.	Michael Waltrip	Pontiac
23.	Randy LaJoie	Pontiac
24.	Ward Burton	Chevrolet
25.	Lake Speed	Ford
26.	Jeff Burton	Ford
27.	Jimmy Spencer	Ford
28.	Bill Elliott	Ford
29.	Ricky Rudd	Ford
30.	Derrike Cope	Ford
31.	Kyle Petty	Pontiac
32.	Dick Trickle	Ford

FINISH	DRIVER	CAR
33.	Ricky Craven	Chevrolet
34.	Dave Marcis	Chevrolet
35.	Greg Sacks	Pontiac
36.	Mike Wallace	Ford

HANES 500

April 23
Martinsville, Virginia
Time of Race: 2 hours, 35 minutes, 44 seconds
Average Speed: 72.145 mph
Margin of Victory: 81 seconds

FINISH	DRIVER	CAR
1.	Rusty Wallace	Ford
2.	Ted Musgrave	Ford
3.	Jeff Gordon	Chevrolet
4.	Darrell Waltrip	Chevrolet
5.	Mark Martin	Ford
6.	Ken Schrader	Chevrolet
7.	Dale Jarrett	Ford
8.	Bobby Hamilton	Pontiac
9.	Kyle Petty	Pontiac
10.	Bobby Labonte	Chevrolet
11.	Brett Bodine	Ford
12.	Bill Elliott	Ford
13.	Sterling Marlin	Chevrolet
14.	Joe Nemechek	Chevrolet
15.	Michael Waltrip	Pontiac
16.	Jeremy Mayfield	Ford
17.	Robert Pressley	Chevrolet
18.	Ricky Craven	Chevrolet
19.	Steve Grissom	Chevrolet
20.	Elton Sawyer	Ford
21.	Kenny Wallace	Ford
22.	Greg Sacks	Pontiac
23.	Dave Marcis	Chevrolet
24.	Dick Trickle	Ford
25.	Ward Burton	Chevrolet
26.	Lake Speed	Ford
27.	Mike Wallace	Ford
28.	Derrike Cope	Ford
29.	Dale Earnhardt	Chevrolet
30.	Ricky Rudd	Ford
31.	Morgan Shepherd	Ford
32.	John Andretti	Ford
33.	Hut Stricklin	Ford
34.	Rick Mast	Ford
35.	Geoff Bodine	Ford
36.	Terry Labonte	Chevrolet

WINSTON SELECT 500

April 30
Talladega, Alabama
Time of Race: 2 hours, 47 minutes, 43 seconds
Average Speed: 178.902 mph
Margin of Victory: .18 second

FINISH	DRIVER	CAR
1.	Mark Martin	Ford
2.	Jeff Gordon	Chevrolet
3.	Morgan Shepherd	Ford
4.	Darrell Waltrip	Chevrolet
5.	Bobby Labonte	Chevrolet
6.	Bill Elliott	Ford
7.	Geoff Bodine	Ford
8.	Todd Bodine	Ford
9.	Jimmy Spencer	Ford
10.	Loy Allen	Ford
11.	Ted Musgrave	Ford
12.	Michael Waltrip	Pontiac
13.	Randy LaJoie	Pontiac
14.	Jeremy Mayfield	Ford

15.	Bobby Hamilton	Pontiac
16.	Lake Speed	Ford
17.	Ricky Craven	Chevrolet
18.	Robert Pressley	Chevrolet
19.	Dale Jarrett	Ford
20.	Rusty Wallace	Ford
21.	Dale Earnhardt	Chevrolet
22.	Ricky Rudd	Ford
23.	Mike Wallace	Ford
24.	Hut Stricklin	Ford
25.	Jeff Burton	Ford
26.	Terry Labonte	Chevrolet
27.	Elton Sawyer	Ford
28.	Rick Mast	Ford
29.	Jeff Purvis	Chevrolet
30.	Brett Bodine	Ford
31.	Kyle Petty	Pontiac
32.	Ward Burton	Chevrolet
33.	Davy Jones	Ford
34.	Dave Marcis	Chevrolet
35.	Greg Sacks	Pontiac
36.	Kenny Wallace	Ford
37.	Steve Grissom	Chevrolet
38.	Dick Trickle	Ford
39.	Sterling Marlin	Chevrolet
40.	Ken Schrader	Chevrolet
41.	John Andretti	Ford
42.	Derrike Cope	Ford

SAVEMART SUPERMARKETS 300

May 7
Sears Point, California
Time of Race: 2 hours, 38 minutes, 18 seconds
Average Speed: 70.681mph
Margin of Victory: .32 seconds

FINISH	DRIVER	CAR
1.	Dale Earnhardt	Chevrolet
2.	Mark Martin	Ford
3.	Jeff Gordon	Chevrolet
4.	Ricky Rudd	Ford
5.	Terry Labonte	Chevrolet
6.	Ted Musgrave	Ford
7.	Sterling Marlin	Chevrolet
8.	Todd Bodine	Ford
9.	Ken Schrader	Chevrolet
10.	Michael Waltrip	Pontiac
11.	John Andretti	Ford
12.	Derrike Cope	Ford
13.	Bobby Labonte	Chevrolet
14.	Bobby Hamilton	Pontiac
15.	Morgan Shepherd	Ford
16.	Rick Mast	Ford
17.	Jimmy Spencer	Ford
18.	Jeff Burton	Ford
19.	Bill Elliott	Ford
20.	Rusty Wallace	Ford
21.	Ward Burton	Chevrolet
22.	Geoff Bodine	Ford
23.	Dale Jarrett	Ford
24.	Dick Trickle	Ford
25.	Ricky Craven	Chevrolet
26.	Steve Grissom	Chevrolet
27.	Dave Marcis	Chevrolet
28.	Kyle Petty	Pontiac
29.	Brett Bodine	Ford
30.	Robert Pressley	Chevrolet
31.	Doug George	Ford
32.	Randy LaJoie	Pontiac
33.	Hut Stricklin	Ford
34.	Mike Wallace	Ford
35.	Darrell Waltrip	Chevrolet
36.	Davy Jones	Ford
37.	Joe Nemechek	Chevrolet
38.	Terry Fisher	Pontiac
39.	Wally Dallenbach	Chevrolet
40.	Lake Speed	Ford
41.	Ken Pedersen	Ford
42.	Butch Gilliland	Ford
43.	Dan Obrist	Chevrolet

COCA-COLA 600

May 28
Charlotte, North Carolina
Time of Race: 3 hours, 56 minutes, 55 seconds
Average Speed: 151.952 mph
Margin of Victory: 6.28 seconds

FINISH	DRIVER	CAR
1.	Bobby Labonte	Chevrolet
2.	Terry Labonte	Chevrolet
3.	Michael Waltrip	Pontiac
4.	Sterling Marlin	Chevrolet
5.	Ricky Rudd	Ford
6.	Dale Earnhardt	Chevrolet
7.	Hut Stricklin	Ford
8.	Lake Speed	Ford
9.	Bobby Hamilton	Pontiac
10.	Ricky Craven	Chevrolet
11.	Morgan Shepherd	Ford
12.	Mike Wallace	Ford
13.	Steve Grissom	Chevrolet
14.	Rick Mast	Ford
15.	Ted Musgrave	Ford
16.	Dick Trickle	Ford
17.	John Andretti	Ford
18.	Darrell Waltrip	Chevrolet
19.	Derrike Cope	Ford
20.	Joe Nemechek	Chevrolet
21.	Chuck Bown	Chevrolet
22.	Jeremy Mayfield	Ford
23.	Randy LaJoie	Pontiac
24.	Robert Pressley	Chevrolet
25.	Elton Sawyer	Ford
26.	Geoff Bodine	Ford
27.	Jimmy Spencer	Ford
28.	Mark Martin	Ford
29.	Kyle Petty	Pontiac
30.	Ken Schrader	Chevrolet
31.	Kenny Wallace	Ford
32.	Dale Jarrett	Ford
33.	Jeff Gordon	Chevrolet
34.	Rusty Wallace	Ford
35.	Brett Bodine	Ford
36.	Loy Allen	Ford
37.	Dave Marcis	Chevrolet
38.	Todd Bodine	Ford
39.	Bill Elliott	Ford
40.	Jeff Burton	Ford
41.	Ward Burton	Chevrolet
42.	Chad Little	Ford

MILLER GENUINE DRAFT 500

June 4
Dover, Delaware
Time of Race: 4 hours, 10 minutes, 15 seconds
Average Speed: 119.880 mph
Margin of Victory: 22 seconds

FINISH	DRIVER	CAR
1.	Kyle Petty	Pontiac
2.	Bobby Labonte	Chevrolet
3.	Ted Musgrave	Ford
4.	Hut Stricklin	Ford
5.	Dale Earnhardt	Chevrolet
6.	Jeff Gordon	Chevrolet
7.	Sterling Marlin	Chevrolet
8.	Michael Waltrip	Pontiac
9.	Rusty Wallace	Ford
10.	Joe Nemechek	Chevrolet
11.	Ken Schrader	Chevrolet
12.	Derrike Cope	Ford
13.	Rick Mast	Ford
14.	Mike Wallace	Ford
15.	Bill Elliott	Ford
16.	Steve Grissom	Chevrolet

17.	Jeremy Mayfield	Ford
18.	Kenny Wallace	Ford
19.	Robert Pressley	Chevrolet
20.	Darrell Waltrip	Chevrolet
21.	Brett Bodine	Ford
22.	Ricky Craven	Chevrolet
23.	Randy LaJoie	Pontiac
24.	Bobby Hamilton	Pontiac
25.	Jeff Burton	Ford
26.	Morgan Shepherd	Ford
27.	Geoff Bodine	Ford
28.	Greg Sacks	Pontiac
29.	Jimmy Spencer	Ford
30.	Todd Bodine	Ford
31.	Ricky Rudd	Ford
32.	Dick Trickle	Ford
33.	Chuck Bown	Chevrolet
34.	Lake Speed	Ford
35.	Mark Martin	Ford
36.	Dave Marcis	Chevrolet
37.	Terry Labonte	Chevrolet
38.	Ward Burton	Chevrolet
39.	John Andretti	Ford
40.	Dale Jarrett	Ford
41.	Elton Sawyer	Ford
42.	Bobbly Hillin	Ford

UAW-GM TEAMWORK 500

June 11
Pocono, Pennsylvania
Time of Race: 3 hours, 37 minutes, 50 seconds
Average Speed: 137.720 mph
Margin of Victory: 1.64 seconds

FINISH	DRIVER	CAR
1.	Terry Labonte	Chevrolet
2.	Ted Musgrave	Ford
3.	Ken Schrader	Chevrolet
4.	Sterling Marlin	Chevrolet
5.	Hut Stricklin	Ford
6.	Bill Elliott	Ford
7.	Morgan Shepherd	Ford
8.	Dale Earnhardt	Chevrolet
9.	Michael Waltrip	Pontiac
10.	Brett Bodine	Ford
11.	Mark Martin	Ford
12.	Joe Nemechek	Chevrolet
13.	Ricky Rudd	Ford
14.	Geoff Bodine	Ford
15.	Bobby Hamilton	Pontiac
16.	Jeff Gordon	Chevrolet
17.	Rusty Wallace	Ford
18.	Steve Grissom	Chevrolet
19.	Ward Burton	Chevrolet
20.	Derrike Cope	Ford
21.	Rick Mast	Ford
22.	Dick Trickle	Ford
23.	Bobby Hillin	Ford
24.	Todd Bodine	Ford
25.	Jeremy Mayfield	Ford
26.	Ricky Craven	Chevrolet
27.	Bobby Labonte	Chevrolet
28.	Lake Speed	Ford
29.	Chuck Bown	Chevrolet
30.	John Andretti	Ford
31.	Dave Marcis	Chevrolet
32.	Mike Wallace	Ford
33.	Greg Sacks	Pontiac
34.	Jimmy Horton	Ford
35.	Pancho Carter	Ford
36.	Jeff Burton	Ford
37.	Robert Pressley	Chevrolet
38.	Dale Jarrett	Ford
39.	Kyle Petty	Pontiac
40.	Randy LaJoie	Pontiac
41.	Jimmy Spencer	Ford
42.	Darrell Waltrip	Chevrolet

MILLER GENUINE DRAFT 400

June 18
Brooklyn, Michigan
Time of Race: 2 hours, 58 minutes, 58 seconds
Average Speed: 134.141 mph
Margin of Victory: 0.270 second

FINISH	DRIVER	CAR
1.	Bobby Labonte	Chevrolet
2.	Jeff Gordon	Chevrolet
3.	Rusty Wallace	Ford
4.	John Andretti	Ford
5.	Morgan Shepherd	Ford
6.	Dale Jarrett	Ford
7.	Sterling Marlin	Chevrolet
8.	Mark Martin	Ford
9.	Terry Labonte	Chevrolet
10.	Ted Musgrave	Ford
11.	Lake Speed	Ford
12.	Michael Waltrip	Pontiac
13.	Bobby Hillin	Ford
14.	Bill Elliott	Ford
15.	Dave Marcis	Chevrolet
16.	Dick Trickle	Ford
17.	Robert Pressley	Chevrolet
18.	Ward Burton	Chevrolet
19.	Derrike Cope	Ford
20.	Steve Grissom	Chevrolet
21.	Geoff Bodine	Ford
22.	Jeremy Mayfield	Ford
23.	Elton Sawyer	Ford
24.	Chuck Bown	Chevrolet
25.	Bobby Hamilton	Pontiac
26.	Darrell Waltrip	Chevrolet
27.	Ken Schrader	Chevrolet
28.	Joe Nemechek	Chevrolet
29.	Todd Bodine	Ford
30.	Jimmy Spencer	Ford
31.	Jeff Burton	Ford
32.	Mike Wallace	Ford
33.	Ricky Craven	Chevrolet
34.	Rick Mast	Ford
35.	Dale Earnhardt	Chevrolet
36.	Kenny Wallace	Ford
37.	Hut Stricklin	Ford
38.	Ricky Rudd	Ford
39.	Jeff Purvis	Chevrolet
40.	Brett Bodine	Ford
41.	Randy LaJoie	Pontiac
42.	Kyle Petty	Pontiac

PEPSI 400

July 1
Daytona Beach, Florida
Time of Race: 2 hours, 23 minutes, 44 seconds
Average Speed: 166.976 mph
Margin of Victory: .21 second

FINISH	DRIVER	CAR
1.	Jeff Gordon	Chevrolet
2.	Sterling Marlin	Chevrolet
3.	Dale Earnhardt	Chevrolet
4.	Mark Martin	Ford
5.	Ted Musgrave	Ford
6.	Ken Schrader	Chevrolet
7.	Kyle Petty	Pontiac
8.	Ricky Rudd	Ford
9.	Jimmy Spencer	Ford
10.	Bill Elliott	Ford
11.	Robert Pressley	Chevrolet
12.	Dick Trickle	Ford
13.	Derrike Cope	Ford
14.	Geoff Bodine	Ford
15.	Michael Waltrip	Pontiac
16.	Hut Stricklin	Ford

FINISH	DRIVER	CAR
17.	Greg Sacks	Ford
18.	Jeff Burton	Ford
19.	Terry Labonte	Chevrolet
20.	Brett Bodine	Ford
21.	Lake Speed	Ford
22.	Ricky Craven	Chevrolet
23.	Todd Bodine	Ford
24.	Morgan Shepherd	Ford
25.	Dave Marcis	Chevrolet
26.	Rick Mast	Ford
27.	Rusty Wallace	Ford
28.	Bobby Hillin	Ford
29.	Chuck Bown	Chevrolet
30.	Jimmy Hensley	Pontiac
31.	Loy Allen	Ford
32.	Jeremy Mayfield	Ford
33.	John Andretti	Ford
34.	Darrell Waltrip	Chevrolet
35.	Ward Burton	Chevrolet
36.	Andy Hillenburg	Pontiac
37.	Mike Wallace	Ford
38.	Joe Nemechek	Chevrolet
39.	Jeff Purvis	Chevrolet
40.	Bobby Hamilton	Pontiac
41.	Bobby Labonte	Chevrolet
42.	Dale Jarrett	Ford
43.	Steve Grissom	Chevrolet

SLICK 50 300

July 9
Loudon, New Hampshire
Time of Race: 2 hours, 57 minutes, 56 seconds
Average Speed: 107.029 mph
Margin of Victory: 1.23 seconds

FINISH	DRIVER	CAR
1.	Jeff Gordon	Chevrolet
2.	Morgan Shepherd	Ford
3.	Mark Martin	Ford
4.	Terry Labonte	Chevrolet
5.	Ricky Rudd	Ford
6.	Rusty Wallace	Ford
7.	Derrike Cope	Ford
8.	Ted Musgrave	Ford
9.	Sterling Marlin	Chevrolet
10.	Ken Schrader	Chevrolet
11.	Rick Mast	Ford
12.	Jimmy Spencer	Ford
13.	Robert Pressley	Chevrolet
14.	Michael Waltrip	Pontiac
15.	Bobby Labonte	Chevrolet
16.	Bobby Hamilton	Pontiac
17.	Darrell Waltrip	Chevrolet
18.	Bill Elliott	Ford
19.	Joe Nemechek	Chevrolet
20.	Bobby Hillin	Ford
21.	Brett Bodine	Ford
22.	Dale Earnhardt	Chevrolet
23.	Elton Sawyer	Ford
24.	Lake Speed	Ford
25.	Jeff Burton	Ford
26.	Jeremy Mayfield	Ford
27.	Hut Stricklin	Ford
28.	Steve Grissom	Chevrolet
29.	Dave Marcis	Chevrolet
30.	Dale Jarrett	Ford
31.	Ricky Craven	Chevrolet
32.	Mike Wallace	Ford
33.	John Andretti	Ford
34.	Dick Trickle	Ford
35.	Geoff Bodine	Ford
36.	Todd Bodine	Ford
37.	Kyle Petty	Pontiac
38.	Rick Bickle	Pontiac
39.	Ward Burton	Chevrolet
40.	Chuck Bown	Chevrolet
41.	Jimmy Hensley	Pontiac

MILLER GENUINE DRAFT 500

July 16
Pocono, Pennsylvania
Time of Race: 3 hours, 43 minutes, 49 seconds
Average Speed: 134.038 mph
Margin of Victory: .19 second

FINISH	DRIVER	CAR
1.	Dale Jarrett	Ford
2.	Jeff Gordon	Chevrolet
3.	Ricky Rudd	Ford
4.	Ted Musgrave	Ford
5.	Bill Elliott	Ford
6.	Geoff Bodine	Ford
7.	Mark Martin	Ford
8.	Jeremy Mayfield	Ford
9.	Joe Nemechek	Chevrolet
10.	Dick Trickle	Ford
11.	Ward Burton	Chevrolet
12.	Bobby Hillin	Ford
13.	Rick Mast	Ford
14.	Terry Labonte	Chevrolet
15.	Brett Bodine	Ford
16.	Rusty Wallace	Ford
17.	Jimmy Spencer	Ford
18.	Sterling Marlin	Chevrolet
19.	Bobby Hamilton	Pontiac
20.	Dale Earnhardt	Chevrolet
21.	Michael Waltrip	Pontiac
22.	Lake Speed	Ford
23.	Todd Bodine	Ford
24.	Morgan Shepherd	Ford
25.	Ricky Craven	Chevrolet
26.	Mike Wallace	Ford
27.	Jeff Burton	Ford
28.	Kyle Petty	Pontiac
29.	Elton Sawyer	Ford
30.	Rich Bickle	Pontiac
31.	Steve Grissom	Chevrolet
32.	Jimmy Hensley	Pontiac
33.	Dave Marcis	Chevrolet
34.	Robert Pressley	Chevrolet
35.	Bobby Labonte	Chevrolet
36.	Darrell Waltrip	Chevrolet
37.	Kenny Wallace	Ford
38.	John Andretti	Ford
39.	Derrike Cope	Ford
40.	Ken Schrader	Chevrolet
41.	Hut Stricklin	Ford

DIEHARD 500

July 23
Talladega, Alabama
Time of Race: 2 hours, 53 minutes, 15 seconds
Average Speed: 173.188 mph
Margin of Victory: .05 second

FINISH	DRIVER	CAR
1.	Sterling Marlin	Chevrolet
2.	Dale Jarrett	Ford
3.	Dale Earnhardt	Chevrolet
4.	Morgan Shepherd	Ford
5.	Bill Elliott	Ford
6.	Kyle Petty	Pontiac
7.	Mark Martin	Ford
8.	Jeff Gordon	Chevrolet
9.	Michael Waltrip	Pontiac
10.	Jimmy Spencer	Ford
11.	Ted Mustgrave	Ford
12.	Mike Wallace	Ford
13.	Jeremy Mayfield	Ford
14.	Elton Sawyer	Ford
15.	Derrike Cope	Ford
16.	Bobby Hillin	Ford
17.	Rick Mast	Ford

FINISH	DRIVER	CAR
18.	Chad Little	Ford
19.	Dave Marcis	Chevrolet
20.	Ward Burton	Chevrolet
21.	Bobby Hamilton	Pontiac
22.	Jeff Burton	Ford
23.	Joe Nemechek	Chevrolet
24.	Geoff Bodine	Ford
25.	Steve Grissom	Chevrolet
26.	Ricky Craven	Chevrolet
27.	Robert Presley	Chevrolet
28.	Brett Bodine	Ford
29.	Todd Bodine	Ford
30.	Rusty Wallace	Ford
31.	Bobby Labonte	Chevrolet
32.	Ken Schrader	Chevrolet
33.	Terry Labonte	Chevrolet
34.	John Andretti	Ford
35.	Lake Speed	Ford
36.	Hut Stricklin	Ford
37.	Chuck Bown	Chevrolet
38.	Dick Trickle	Ford
39.	Loy Allen	Ford
40.	Randy LaJoie	Pontiac
41.	Ricky Rudd	Ford
42.	Jeff Purvis	Chevrolet
43.	Darrell Waltrip	Chevrolet

BRICKYARD 400

August 5
Indianapolis, Indiana
Time of Race: 2 hours, 34 minutes, 38 seconds
Average Speed: 155.206 mph
Margin of Victory: .37 second

FINISH	DRIVER	CAR
1.	Dale Earnhardt	Chevrolet
2.	Rusty Wallace	Ford
3.	Dale Jarrett	Ford
4.	Bill Elliott	Ford
5.	Mark Martin	Ford
6.	Jeff Gordon	Chevrolet
7.	Sterling Marlin	Chevrolet
8.	Rick Mast	Ford
9.	Bobby Labonte	Chevrolet
10.	Morgan Shepherd	Ford
11.	Bobby Hamilton	Pontiac
12.	John Andretti	Ford
13.	Terry Labonte	Chevrolet
14.	Michael Waltrip	Pontiac
15.	Geoff Bodine	Ford
16.	Ted Musgrave	Ford
17.	Darrell Waltrip	Chevrolet
18.	Dick Trickle	Ford
19.	Ken Schrader	Chevrolet
20.	Ricky Rudd	Ford
21.	Todd Bodine	Ford
22.	Hut Stricklin	Ford
23.	Jimmy Spencer	Ford
24.	Brett Bodine	Ford
25.	Kyle Petty	Pontiac
26.	Mike Wallace	Ford
27.	Joe Nemechek	Chevrolet
28.	Robert Pressley	Chevrolet
29.	Jeremy Mayfield	Ford
30.	Steve Grissom	Chevrolet
31.	Ricky Craven	Chevrolet
32.	Jimmy Hensley	Pontiac
33.	Greg Sacks	Chevrolet
34.	Lake Speed	Ford
35.	Ward Burton	Chevrolet
36.	Kenny Wallace	Ford
37.	Rich Bickle	Pontiac
38.	Jeff Burton	Ford
39.	Bobby Hillin	Ford
40.	Derrike Cope	Ford
41.	Elton Sawyer	Ford

THE BUD AT THE GLEN

August 13
Watkins Glen, New York
Time of Race: 2 hours, 11 minutes, 54 seconds
Average Speed: 103.030 mph
Margin of Victory: 1.01 seconds

FINISH	DRIVER	CAR
1.	Mark Martin	Ford
2.	Wallay Dallenbach	Pontiac
3.	Jeff Gordon	Chevrolet
4.	Ricky Rudd	Ford
5.	Terry Labonte	Chevrolet
6.	Bobby Labonte	Chevrolet
7.	John Andretti	Ford
8.	Darrell Waltrip	Chevrolet
9.	Geoff Bodine	Ford
10.	Ricky Craven	Chevrolet
11.	Bill Elliott	Ford
12.	Butch Leitzinger	Pontiac
13.	Ted Musgrave	Ford
14.	Michael Waltrip	Pontiac
15.	Derrike Cope	Ford
16.	Brett Bodine	Ford
17.	Dale Jarrett	Ford
18.	Jimmy Spencer	Ford
19.	Ward Burton	Chevrolet
20.	Lake Speed	Ford
21.	Sterling Marlin	Chevrolet
22.	Steve Grissom	Chevrolet
23.	Dale Earnhardt	Chevrolet
24.	Dave Marcis	Chevrolet
25.	Jeremy Mayfield	Ford
26.	Rusty Wallace	Ford
27.	Bobby Hillin	Ford
28.	Dick Trickle	Ford
29.	Elton Sawyer	Ford
30.	Morgan Shepherd	Ford
31.	Joe Nemechek	Chevrolet
32.	Todd Bodine	Ford
33.	Bobby Hamilton	Pontiac
34.	Robert Pressley	Chevrolet
35.	Ron Fellows	Chevrolet
36.	Ken Schrader	Chevrolet
37.	Rick Mast	Ford
38.	Jeff Burton	Ford
39.	Kyle Petty	Pontiac
40.	Hut Stricklin	Ford

GM GOODWRENCH DEALER 400

August 20
Brooklyn, Michigan
Time of Race: 2 hours, 32 minutes, 9 seconds
Average Speed: 157.739 mph
Margin of Victory: 6.80 seconds

FINISH	DRIVER	CAR
1.	Bobby Labonte	Chevrolet
2.	Terry Labonte	Chevrolet
3.	Jeff Gordon	Chevrolet
4.	Sterling Marlin	Chevrolet
5.	Rusty Wallace	Ford
6.	Ward Burton	Chevrolet
7.	Ricky Craven	Chevrolet
8.	Bobby Hamilton	Pontiac
9.	Bill Elliott	Ford
10.	Hut Stricklin	Ford
11.	Michael Waltrip	Pontiac
12.	Jeremy Mayfield	Ford
13.	Dick Trickle	Ford
14.	Jimmy Spencer	Ford
15.	Darrell Waltrip	Chevrolet
16.	Morgan Shepherd	Ford
17.	Lake Speed	Ford
18.	Robert Pressley	Chevrolet

19.	Todd Bodine	Ford
20.	Mike Wallace	Ford
21.	Elton Sawyer	Ford
22.	Jimmy Hensley	Pontiac
23.	Jeff Burton	Ford
24.	Kenny Wallace	Ford
25.	Dave Marcis	Chevrolet
26.	Ken Schrader	Chevrolet
27.	Geoff Bodine	Ford
28.	Ted Musgrave	Ford
29.	Steve Grissom	Chevrolet
30.	Ricky Rudd	Ford
31.	Rick Mast	Ford
32.	Joe Nemechek	Chevrolet
33.	Dale Jarrett	Ford
34.	Derrike Cope	Ford
35.	Dale Earnhardt	Chevrolet
36.	Brett Bodine	Ford
37.	John Andretti	Ford
38.	Mark Martin	Ford
39.	Bobby Hillin	Ford
40.	Greg Sacks	Chevrolet
41.	Gary Bradberry	Chevrolet
42.	Kyle Petty	Pontiac

GOODY'S 500

August 26
Bristol, Tennessee
Time of Race: 3 hours, 15 minutes, .03 second
Average Speed: 81.979 mph
Margin of Victory: 10 seconds

FINISH	DRIVER	CAR
1.	Terry Labonte	Chevrolet
2.	Dale Earnhardt	Chevrolet
3.	Dale Jarrett	Ford
4.	Darrell Waltrip	Chevrolet
5.	Mark Martin	Ford
6.	Jeff Gordon	Chevrolet
7.	Sterlin Marlin	Chevrolet
8.	Mike Wallace	Ford
9.	Jeff Burton	Ford
10.	Derrike Cope	Ford
11.	Bobby Labonte	Chevrolet
12.	Geoff Bodine	Ford
13.	Ted Musgrave	Ford
14.	Ken Schrader	Chevrolet
15.	Michael Waltrip	Pontiac
16.	Joe Nemechek	Chevrolet
17.	Morgan Shepherd	Ford
18.	Jimmy Spencer	Ford
19.	John Andretti	Ford
20.	Bobby Hamilton	Pontiac
21.	Rusty Wallace	Ford
22.	Steve Grissom	Chevrolet
23.	Bill Elliott	Ford
24.	Robert Pressley	Chevrolet
25.	Greg Sacks	Chevrolet
26.	Rick Mast	Ford
27.	Dave Marcis	Chevrolet
28.	Brett Bodine	Ford
29.	Lake Speed	Ford
30.	Jeremy Mayfield	Ford
31.	Rich Bickle	Pontiac
32.	Ricky Craven	Chevrolet
33.	Hut Stricklin	Ford
34.	Ward Burton	Pontiac
35.	Dick Trickle	Ford
36.	Ricky Rudd	Ford

MOUNTAIN DEW SOUTHERN 500

September 3
Darlington, South Carolina
Time of Race: 4 hours, 8 minutes, 7 seconds

Average Speed: 121.231 mph
Margin of Victory: .66 second

FINISH	DRIVER	CAR
1.	Jeff Gordon	Chevrolet
2.	Dale Earnhardt	Chevrolet
3.	Rusty Wallace	Ford
4.	Ward Burton	Pontiac
5.	Michael Waltrip	Pontiac
6.	Ricky Rudd	Ford
7.	Hut Stricklin	Ford
8.	Bobby Labonte	Chevrolet
9.	Lake Speed	Ford
10.	Sterling Marlin	Chevrolet
11.	Morgan Shepherd	Ford
12.	John Andretti	Ford
13.	Bobby Hillin	Ford
14.	Bobby Hamilton	Pontiac
15.	Derrike Cope	Ford
16.	Jeff Burton	Ford
17.	Robert Pressley	Chevrolet
18.	Ricky Craven	Chevrolet
19.	Terry Labonte	Chevrolet
20.	Ed Berrier	Chevrolet
21.	Rich Bickle	Pontiac
22.	Ted Musgrave	Ford
23.	Ken Schrader	Chevrolet
24.	Kyle Petty	Pontiac
25.	Joe Nemechek	Chevrolet
26.	Rick Mast	Ford
27.	Steve Grissom	Chevrolet
28.	Dale Jarrett	Ford
29.	Jimmy Spencer	Ford
30.	Jeremy Mayfield	Ford
31.	Brett Bodine	Ford
32.	Elton Sawyer	Ford
33.	Mark Martin	Ford
34.	Loy Allen	Ford
35.	Geoff Bodine	Ford
36.	Dick Trickle	Ford
37.	Dave Marcis	Chevrolet
38.	Greg Sacks	Chevrolet
39.	Mike Wallace	Ford
40.	Darrell Waltrip	Chevrolet
41.	Bill Elliott	Ford
42.	Todd Bodine	Ford

MILLER GENUINE DRAFT 400

September 9
Richmond, Virginia
Time of Race: 2 hours, 52 minutes, 19 seconds
Average Speed: 104.459 mph
Margin of Victory: 5.6 seconds

FINISH	DRIVER	CAR
1.	Rusty Wallace	Ford
2.	Terry Labonte	Chevrolet
3.	Dale Earnhardt	Chevrolet
4.	Dale Jarrett	Ford
5.	Bobby Hamilton	Pontiac
6.	Jeff Gordon	Chevrolet
7.	John Andretti	Ford
8.	Ricky Rudd	Ford
9.	Ken Schrader	Chevrolet
10.	Ted Musgrave	Ford
11.	Ward Burton	Pontiac
12.	Rick Mast	Ford
13.	Jeff Burton	Ford
14.	Bill Elliott	Ford
15.	Mark Martin	Ford
16.	Brett Bodine	Ford
17.	Bobby Labonte	Chevrolet
18.	Dick Trickle	Ford
19.	Geoff Bodine	Ford
20.	Kenny Wallace	Ford
21.	Lake Speed	Ford
22.	Darrell Waltrip	Chevrolet

23.	Jeremy Mayfield	Ford
24.	Todd Bodine	Ford
25.	Kyle Petty	Pontiac
26.	Joe Nemechek	Chevrolet
27.	Morgan Shepherd	Ford
28.	Michael Waltrip	Pontiac
29.	Ricky Craven	Chevrolet
30.	Robert Pressley	Chevrolet
31.	Jimmy Spencer	Ford
32.	Hut Stricklin	Ford
33.	Sterling Marlin	Chevrolet
34.	Derrike Cope	Ford
35.	Dave Marcis	Chevrolet
36.	Bobby Hillin	Ford
37.	Greg Sacks	Chevrolet
38.	Elton Sawyer	Ford

MBNA 500

September 17
Dover, Delaware
Time of Race: 4 hours, 0 minutes, 30 seconds
Average Speed: 124.740 mph
Margin of Victory: 2.34 seconds

FINISH	DRIVER	CAR
1.	Jeff Gordon	Chevrolet
2.	Bobby Hamilton	Pontiac
3.	Rusty Wallace	Ford
4.	Joe Nemechek	Chevrolet
5.	Dale Earnhardt	Chevrolet
6.	Sterling Marlin	Chevrolet
7.	Derrike Cope	Ford
8.	Mark Martin	Ford
9.	Bobby Labonte	Chevrolet
10.	Ricky Rudd	Ford
11.	Ted Musgrave	Ford
12.	Ken Schrader	Chevrolet
13.	Bobby Hillin	Ford
14.	Robert Pressley	Chevrolet
15.	Terry Labonte	Chevrolet
16.	Jimmy Spencer	Ford
17.	Brett Bodine	Ford
18.	Bill Elliott	Ford
19.	Jeremy Mayfield	Ford
20.	Jeff Burton	Ford
21.	Ward Burton	Pontiac
22.	Ricky Craven	Chevrolet
23.	Dick Trickle	Ford
24.	Geoff Bodine	Ford
25.	Steve Grissom	Chevrolet
26.	Kyle Petty	Pontiac
27.	Dave Marcis	Chevrolet
28.	Rick Mast	Ford
29.	Michael Waltrip	Pontiac
30.	Dale Jarrett	Ford
31.	Mike Wallace	Ford
32.	Lake Speed	Ford
33.	Morgan Shepherd	Ford
34.	Michael Ritch	Chevrolet
35.	Rich Bickle	Pontiac
36.	Darrell Waltrip	Chevrolet
37.	Todd Bodine	Ford
38.	Hut Stricklin	Ford
39.	John Andretti	Ford
40.	Elton Sawyer	Ford

GOODY'S 500

September 24
Martinsville, Virginia
Time of Race: 3 hours, 33 minutes, 24 seconds
Average Speed: 73.946 mph
Margin of Victory: 1.3 seconds

FINISH	DRIVER	CAR
1.	Dale Earnhardt	Chevrolet
2.	Terry Labonte	Chevrolet
3.	Rusty Wallace	Ford
4.	Bobby Hamilton	Pontiac
5.	Geoff Bodine	Ford
6.	Bill Elliott	Ford
7.	Jeff Gordon	Chevrolet
8.	Darrell Waltrip	Chevrolet
9.	Derrike Cope	Ford
10.	Dale Jarrett	Ford
11.	Kyle Petty	Pontiac
12.	Mark Martin	Ford
13.	John Andretti	Ford
14.	Bobby Labonte	Chevrolet
15.	Dick Trickle	Ford
16.	Jeremy Mayfield	Ford
17.	Mike Wallace	Ford
18.	Jimmy Spencer	Ford
19.	Morgan Shepherd	Ford
20.	Lake Speed	Ford
21.	Ward Burton	Pontiac
22.	Brett Bodine	Ford
23.	Sterling Marlin	Chevrolet
24.	Todd Bodine	Ford
25.	Michael Waltrip	Pontiac
26.	Steve Grissom	Chevrolet
27.	Ricky Rudd	Ford
28.	Rick Mast	Ford
29.	Ted Musgrave	Ford
30.	Joe Nemechek	Chevrolet
31.	Jeff Burton	Ford
32.	Ken Schrader	Chevrolet
33.	Elton Sawyer	Ford
34.	Robert Pressley	Chevrolet
35.	Ricky Craven	Chevrolet
36.	Hut Stricklin	Ford

TYSON HOLLY FARMS 400

October 1
North Wilkesboro, North Carolina
Time of Race: 2 hours, 25 minutes, 38 seconds
Average Speed: 102.998 mph
Margin of Victory: 0.860 seconds

FINISH	DRIVER	CAR
1.	Mark Martin	Ford
2.	Rusty Wallace	Ford
3.	Jeff Gordon	Chevrolet
4.	Terry Labonte	Chevrolet
5.	Ricky Rudd	Ford
6.	Ernie Irvan	Ford
7.	Dale Jarrett	Ford
8.	Ken Schrader	Chevrolet
9.	Dale Earnhardt	Chevrolet
10.	Bill Elliott	Ford
11.	Geoff Bodine	Ford
12.	Michael Waltrip	Pontiac
13.	Derrike Cope	Ford
14.	Darrell Waltrip	Chevrolet
15.	Sterling Marlin	Chevrolet
16.	Bobby Hamilton	Pontiac
17.	John Andretti	Ford
18.	Bobby Labonte	Chevrolet
19.	Dick Trickle	Ford
20.	Ted Musgrave	Ford
21.	Ricky Craven	Chevrolet
22.	Brett Bodine	Ford
23.	Morgan Shepherd	Ford
24.	Bobby Hillin	Ford
25.	Hut Stricklin	Ford
26.	Rick Mast	Ford
27.	Rich Bickle	Pontiac
28.	Dave Marcis	Chevrolet
29.	Jimmy Hensley	Chevrolet
30.	Kyle Petty	Pontiac
31.	Steve Grissom	Chevrolet
32.	Joe Nemechek	Chevrolet

33.	Robert Pressley	Chevrolet
34.	Elton Sawyer	Ford
35.	Lake Speed	Ford
36.	Jimmy Spencer	Ford

UAW-GM QUALITY 500

October 8
Charlotte, North Carolina
Time of Race: 3 hours, 26 minutes, 48 seconds
Average Speed: 145.358 mph
Margin of Victory: .97 second

FINISH	DRIVER	CAR
1.	Mark Martin	Ford
2.	Dale Earnhardt	Chevrolet
3.	Terry Labonte	Chevrolet
4.	Ricky Rudd	Ford
5.	Dale Jarrett	Ford
6.	Sterling Marlin	Chevrolet
7.	Ward Burton	Pontiac
8.	Bobby Labonte	Chevrolet
9.	Rusty Wallace	Ford
10.	Bobby Hamilton	Pontiac
11.	Derrike Cope	Ford
12.	Jimmy Spencer	Ford
13.	John Andretti	Ford
14.	Morgan Shepherd	Ford
15.	Kyle Petty	Pontiac
16.	Geoff Bodine	Ford
17.	Michael Waltrip	Pontiac
18.	Hut Stricklin	Ford
19.	Ted Musgrave	Ford
20.	Bill Elliott	Ford
21.	Lake Speed	Ford
22.	Joe Nemechek	Chevrolet
23.	Mike Wallace	Ford
24.	Bobby Hillin	Ford
25.	Ricky Craven	Chevrolet
26.	Todd Bodine	Ford
27.	Brett Bodine	Ford
28.	Elton Sawyer	Ford
29.	Jeremy Mayfield	Ford
30.	Jeff Gordon	Chevrolet
31.	Jeff Burton	Ford
32.	Dick Trickle	Ford
33.	Greg Sacks	Chevrolet
34.	Darrell Waltrip	Chevrolet
35.	Ken Schrader	Chevrolet
36.	Rick Mast	Ford
37.	Loy Allen	Ford
38.	Rich Bickle	Pontiac
39.	Jimmy Hensley	Chevrolet
40.	Dave Marcis	Chevrolet
41.	Steve Grissom	Chevrolet
42.	Robert Pressley	Chevrolet
43.	Gary Bradberry	Chevrolet

AC-DELCO 400

October 22
Rockingham, North Carolina
Time of Race: 3 hours, 28 minutes, 56 seconds
Average Speed: 114.778 mph
Margin of Victory: 1.9 seconds

FINISH	DRIVER	CAR
1.	Ward Burton	Pontiac
2.	Rusty Wallace	Ford
3.	Mark Martin	Ford
4.	Terry Labonte	Chevrolet
5.	Jeff Burton	Ford
6.	Sterling Marlin	Chevrolet
7.	Dale Earnhardt	Chevrolet

FINISH	DRIVER	CAR
8.	Ricky Craven	Chevrolet
9.	Joe Nemechek	Chevrolet
10.	Bill Elliott	Ford
11.	Jeremy Mayfield	Ford
12.	Darrell Waltrip	Chevrolet
13.	Ricky Rudd	Ford
14.	Steve Grissom	Chevrolet
15.	Geoff Bodine	Ford
16.	Dick Trickle	Ford
17.	Todd Bodine	Ford
18.	Morgan Shepherd	Ford
19.	Derrike Cope	Ford
20.	Jeff Gordon	Chevrolet
21.	Bobby Hillin	Ford
22.	Ted Musgrave	Ford
23.	Dale Jarrett	Ford
24.	Lake Speed	Ford
25.	John Andretti	Ford
26.	Jimmy Spencer	Ford
27.	Brett Bodine	Ford
28.	Hut Stricklin	Ford
29.	Robert Pressley	Chevrolet
30.	Bobby Hamilton	Pontiac
31.	Elton Sawyer	Ford
32.	Kyle Petty	Pontiac
33.	Ken Schrader	Chevrolet
34.	Rick Mast	Ford
35.	Gary Bradberry	Chevrolet
36.	Shane Hall	Pontiac
37.	Greg Sacks	Chevrolet
38.	Michael Waltrip	Pontiac
39.	Mike Wallace	Ford
40.	Bobby Labonte	Chevrolet

DURA LUBE 500

October 29
Phoenix, Arizona
Time of Race: 3 hours, 3 minutes, 15 seconds
Average Speed: 102.128 mph
Margin of Victory: .53 seconds

FINISH	DRIVER	CAR
1.	Ricky Rudd	Ford
2.	Derrike Cope	Ford
3.	Dale Earnhardt	Chevrolet
4.	Rusty Wallace	Ford
5.	Jeff Gordon	Chevrolet
6.	Ted Musgrave	Ford
7.	Morgan Shepherd	Ford
8.	Mark Martin	Ford
9.	Rick Mast	Ford
10.	Ken Schrader	Chevrolet
11.	Dale Jarrett	Ford
12.	Sterling Marlin	Chevrolet
13.	Terry Labonte	Chevrolet
14.	Bill Elliott	Ford
15.	John Andretti	Ford
16.	Geoff Bodine	Ford
17.	Brett Bodine	Ford
18.	Joe Nemechek	Chevrolet
19.	Robert Pressley	Chevrolet
20.	Jeremy Mayfield	Ford
21.	Bobby Hillin	Ford
22.	Lake Speed	Ford
23.	Jeff Burton	Ford
24.	Ricky Craven	Chevrolet
25.	Todd Bodine	Ford
26.	Kenny Wallace	Ford
27.	Ron Hornaday	Chevrolet
28.	Dave Marcis	Chevrolet
29.	Dick Trickle	Ford
30.	Elton Sawyer	Ford
31.	Bobby Hamilton	Pontiac
32.	Steve Grisssom	Chevrolet
33.	Jimmy Spencer	Ford
34.	Michael Waltrip	Pontiac
35.	Hut Stricklin	Ford
36.	Mike Wallace	Ford
37.	Bobby Labonte	Chevrolet

FINISH	DRIVER	CAR
38.	Darrell Waltrip	Chevrolet
39.	Kyle Petty	Pontiac
40.	Ernie Irvan	Ford
41.	Doug George	Ford
42.	Ward Burton	Pontiac
43.	Greg Sacks	Chevrolet
44.	Ernie Cope	Chevrolet

NAPA 500

November 12
Atlanta, Georgia
Time of Race: 3 hours, 3 minutes, 3 seconds
Average Speed: 163.633 mph
Margin of Victory: 3.74 seconds

FINISH	DRIVER	CAR
1.	Dale Earnhardt	Chevrolet
2.	Sterling Marlin	Chevrolet
3.	Rusty Wallace	Ford
4.	Bill Elliott	Ford
5.	Ward Burton	Pontiac
6.	Jimmy Spencer	Ford
7.	Ernie Irvan	Ford
8.	Bobby Labonte	Chevrolet
9.	Bobby Hillin	Ford
10.	Ricky Rudd	Ford
11.	Geoff Bodine	Ford
12.	Michael Waltrip	Pontiac
13.	Terry Labonte	Chevrolet
14.	Joe Nemechek	Chevrolet
15.	John Andretti	Ford
16.	Darrell Waltrip	Chevrolet
17.	Mark Martin	Ford
18.	Jeremy Mayfield	Ford
19.	Lake Speed	Ford
20.	Brett Bodine	Ford
21.	Rick Mast	Ford
22.	Morgan Shepherd	Ford
23.	Dick Trickle	Ford
24.	Loy Allen	Ford
25.	Bobby Hamilton	Pontiac
26.	Jeff Purvis	Chevrolet
27.	Ted Musgrave	Ford
28.	Elton Sawyer	Ford
29.	Gary Bradberry	Chevrolet
30.	Ricky Craven	Chevrolet
31.	Dale Jarrett	Ford
32.	Jeff Gordon	Chevrolet
33.	Kyle Petty	Pontiac
34.	Greg Sacks	Chevrolet
35.	Derrike Cope	Ford
36.	Jeff Burton	Ford
37.	Dave Marcis	Chevrolet
38.	Hut Stricklin	Ford
39.	Steve Grissom	Chevrolet
40.	Todd Bodine	Ford
41.	Robert Pressley	Chevrolet
42.	Ken Schrader	Chevrolet

1996

DAYTONA 500

February 18
Daytona Beach, Florida
Time of Race: 3 hours, 14 minutes, 25 seconds
Average Speed: 154.308 mph
Margin of Victory: .12 second

FINISH	DRIVER	CAR
1.	Dale Jarrett	Ford
2.	Dale Earnhardt	Chevrolet

FINISH	DRIVER	CAR
3.	Ken Schrader	Chevrolet
4.	Mark Martin	Ford
5.	Jeff Burton	Ford
6.	Wally Dallenbach	Ford
7.	Ted Musgrave	Ford
8.	Bill Elliott	Ford
9.	Ricky Rudd	Ford
10.	Michael Waltrip	Ford
11.	Jimmy Spencer	Ford
12.	Jeff Purvis	Chevrolet
13.	Ricky Craven	Chevrolet
14.	Lake Speed	Ford
15.	Dave Marcis	Chevrolet
16.	Rusty Wallace	Ford
17.	Bobby Labonte	Chevrolet
18.	Kyle Petty	Pontiac
19.	Jeremy Mayfield	Ford
20.	Bobby Hamilton	Pontiac
21.	Kenny Wallace	Ford
22.	Hut Stricklin	Ford
23.	Johnny Benson	Pontiac
24.	Terry Labonte	Chevrolet
25.	Elton Sawyer	Ford
26.	Ward Burton	Pontiac
27.	Steve Grissom	Chevrolet
28.	Rick Mast	Pontiac
29.	Darrell Waltrip	Chevrolet
30.	Robert Pressley	Chevrolet
31.	Morgan Shepherd	Ford
32.	Brett Bodine	Ford
33.	Chad Little	Pontiac
34.	Geoff Bodine	Ford
35.	Ernie Irvan	Ford
36.	Loy Allen	Ford
37.	Mike Wallace	Ford
38.	John Andretti	Ford
39.	Joe Nemechek	Chevrolet
40.	Sterling Marlin	Chevrolet
41.	Derrike Cope	Ford
42.	Jeff Gordon	Chevrolet
43.	Dick Trickle	Ford

GOODWRENCH 400

February 25
Rockingham, North Carolina
Time of Race: 3 hours, 30 minutes, 26 seconds
Average Speed: 113.959 mph
Margin of Victory: under caution

FINISH	DRIVER	CAR
1.	Dale Earnhardt	Chevrolet
2.	Dale Jarrett	Ford
3.	Ricky Craven	Chevrolet
4.	Ricky Rudd	Ford
5.	Steve Grissom	Chevrolet
6.	Sterling Marlin	Chevrolet
7.	Kenny Wallace	Ford
8.	Derrike Cope	Ford
9.	Joe Nemechek	Chevrolet
10.	Rick Mast	Pontiac
11.	Kyle Petty	Pontiac
12.	Mike Skinner	Chevrolet
13.	Jeff Burton	Ford
14.	Ernie Irvan	Ford
15.	Bill Elliott	Ford
16.	Darrell Waltrip	Chevrolet
17.	Mike Wallace	Ford
18.	Bobby Hillin	Ford
19.	Jeremy Mayfield	Ford
20.	Johnny Benson	Pontiac
21.	Dave Marcis	Chevrolet
22.	Rusty Wallace	Ford
23.	Wally Dallenbach Jr.	Ford
24.	Bobby Hamilton	Pontiac
25.	Lake Speed	Ford
26.	Robert Pressley	Chevrolet
27.	Jimmy Spencer	Ford
28.	Brett Bodine	Ford
29.	Ken Schrader	Chevrolet

FINISH	DRIVER	CAR
30.	Hut Stricklin	Ford
31.	Ted Musgrave	Ford
32.	Mark Martin	Ford
33.	Bobby Labonte	Chevrolet
34.	Terry Labonte	Chevrolet
35.	Michael Waltrip	Ford
36.	Loy Allen	Ford
37.	Morgan Shepherd	Ford
38.	John Andretti	Ford
39.	Geoff Bodine	Ford
40.	Jeff Gordon	Chevrolet
41.	Ward Burton	Pontiac

PONTIAC EXCITEMENT 400

March 3
Richmond, Virginia
Time of Race: 2 hours, 55 minutes, 11 seconds
Average Speed: 102.750 mph
Margin of Victory: .56 seconds

FINISH	DRIVER	CAR
1.	Jeff Gordon	Chevrolet
2.	Dale Jarrett	Ford
3.	Ted Musgrave	Ford
4.	Jeff Burton	Ford
5.	Mark Martin	Ford
6.	Bobby Hamilton	Pontiac
7.	Rusty Wallace	Ford
8.	Terry Labonte	Chevrolet
9.	Ricky Rudd	Ford
10.	Bill Elliott	Ford
11.	Sterling Marlin	Chevrolet
12.	John Andretti	Ford
13.	Ward Burton	Pontiac
14.	Ken Schrader	Chevrolet
15.	Kenny Wallace	Ford
16.	Robert Pressley	Chevrolet
17.	Ricky Craven	Chevrolet
18.	Lake Speed	Ford
19.	Rick Mast	Pontiac
20.	Kyle Petty	Pontiac
21.	Steve Grissom	Chevrolet
22.	Derrike Cope	Ford
23.	Bobby Labonte	Chevrolet
24.	Mike Wallace	Ford
25.	Brett Bodine	Ford
26.	Bobby Hillin	Ford
27.	Darrell Waltrip	Chevrolet
28.	Jeremy Mayfield	Ford
29.	Jimmy Spencer	Ford
30.	Elton Sawyer	Ford
31.	Dale Earnhardt	Chevrolet
32.	Morgan Shepherd	Ford
33.	Geoff Bodine	Ford
34.	Joe Nemechek	Chevrolet
35.	Dave Marcis	Chevrolet
36.	Michael Waltrip	Ford
37.	Johnny Benson	Pontiac
38.	Ernie Irvan	Ford
39.	Hut Stricklin	Ford
40.	Wally Dallenbach	Ford

PUROLATOR 500

March 10
Atlanta, Georgia
Time of Race: 3 hours, 5 minutes, 42 seconds
Average Speed: 161.298 mph
Margin of Victory: 4.28 seconds

FINISH	DRIVER	CAR
1.	Dale Earnhardt	Chevrolet
2.	Terry Labonte	Chevrolet

3.	Jeff Gordon	Chevrolet
4.	Ernie Irvan	Ford
5.	Jeremy Mayfield	Ford
6.	Ken Schrader	Chevrolet
7.	Jimmy Spencer	Ford
8.	Ricky Rudd	Ford
9.	Michael Waltrip	Ford
10.	Bill Elliott	Ford
11.	Dale Jarrett	Ford
12.	Ricky Craven	Chevrolet
13.	Sterling Marlin	Chevrolet
14.	Dick Trickle	Ford
15.	Ward Burton	Pontiac
16.	Bobby Hamilton	Pontiac
17.	Joe Nemechek	Chevrolet
18.	Ted Musgrave	Ford
19.	Elton Sawyer	Ford
20.	Wally Dallenbach	Ford
21.	John Andretti	Ford
22.	Kyle Petty	Pontiac
23.	Geoff Bodine	Ford
24.	Brett Bodine	Ford
25.	Hut Stricklin	Ford
26.	Mark Martin	Ford
27.	Robert Pressley	Chevrolet
28.	Bobby Hillin	Ford
29.	Dave Marcis	Chevrolet
30.	Morgan Shepherd	Ford
31.	Bobby Labonte	Chevrolet
32.	Darrell Waltrip	Chevrolet
33.	Mike Wallace	Ford
34.	Rick Mast	Pontiac
35.	Derrike Cope	Ford
36.	Rusty Wallace	Ford
37.	Kenny Walkace	Ford
38.	Johnny Benson	Pontiac
39.	Steve Grissom	Chevrolet
40.	Chuck Bown	Ford
41.	Lake Speed	Ford

TRANSOUTH FINANCIAL 400

March 24
Darlington, South Carolina
Time of Race: 3 hours, 12 minutes, 26 seconds
Average Speed: 124.792 mph
Margin of Victory: 1.4 seconds

FINISH	DRIVER	CAR
1.	Jeff Gordon	Chevrolet
2.	Bobby Labonte	Chevrolet
3.	Ricky Craven	Chevrolet
4.	Rusty Wallace	Ford
5.	Terry Labonte	Chevrolet
6.	Mark Martin	Ford
7.	Ted Musgrave	Ford
8.	Morgan Shepherd	Ford
9.	Ricky Rudd	Ford
10.	Jeff Burton	Ford
11.	Sterling Marlin	Chevrolet
12.	Kyle Petty	Pontiac
13.	Bill Elliott	Ford
14.	Dale Earnhardt	Ford
15.	Dale Jarrett	Ford
16.	Bobby Hamilton	Pontiac
17.	Kenny Wallace	Ford
18.	Jeremy Mayfield	Ford
19.	Rick Mast	Pontiac
20.	Hut Stricklin	Ford
21.	Mike Wallace	Ford
22.	Geoff Bodine	Ford
23.	Dave Marcis	Chevrolet
24.	Johnny Benson	Pontiac
25.	Lake Speed	Ford
26.	Steve Grissom	Chevrolet
27.	Brett Bodine	Ford
28.	Ken Schrader	Chevrolet
29.	Michael Waltrip	Ford
30.	Elton Sawyer	Ford
31.	Joe Nemechek	Ford
32.	Jimmy Spencer	Ford

33.	Ernie Irvan	Ford
34.	Darrell Waltrip	Chevrolet
35.	Dick Trickle	Ford
36.	Robert Pressley	Chevrolet
37.	Wally Dallenbach	Ford
38.	Ward Burton	Pontiac
39.	Derrike Cope	Ford
40.	John Andretti	Ford
41.	Bobby Hillin	Ford

FOOD CITY 500

March 31
Bristol, Tennessee
Time of Race: 1 hour, 59 minutes, 47 seconds
Average Speed: 91.308 mph
Margin of Victory: under caution

FINISH	DRIVER	CAR
1.	Jeff Gordon	Chevrolet
2.	Terry Labonte	Chevrolet
3.	Mark Martin	Chevrolet
4.	Dale Earnhardt	Chevrolet
5.	Rusty Wallace	Ford
6.	Dale Jarrett	Ford
7.	Bobby Labonte	Chevrolet
8.	Dick Trickle	Ford
9.	Ricky Craven	Chevrolet
10.	Michael Waltrip	Ford
11.	Hut Stricklin	Ford
12.	Rick Mast	Pontiac
13.	Jimmy Spencer	Ford
14.	Ricky Rudd	Ford
15.	Kyle Petty	Pontiac
16.	Ernie Irvan	Ford
17.	Robert Pressley	Chevrolet
18.	Sterling Marlin	Chevrolet
19.	Geoff Bodine	Ford
20.	Brett Bodine	Ford
21.	Jeremy Mayfield	Ford
22.	Derrike Cope	Ford
23.	Jeff Burton	Ford
24.	Wally Dallenbach	Ford
25.	Ted Musgrave	Ford
26.	Darrell Waltrip	Chevrolet
27.	Steve Grissom	Chevrolet
28.	Bill Elliott	Ford
29.	Ken Schrader	Chevrolet
30.	Morgan Shepherd	Ford
31.	Joe Nemechek	Chevrolet
32.	Bobby Hamilton	Pontiac
33.	Ward Burton	Pontiac
34.	Kenny Wallace	Ford
35.	Lake Speed	Ford
36.	Mike Skinner	Chevrolet
37.	Elton Sawyer	Ford

FIRST UNION 400

April 14
North Wilkesboro, North Carolina
Time of Race: 2 hours, 35 minutes, 39 seconds
Average Speed: 96.370 mph
Margin of Victory: .239 second

FINISH	DRIVER	CAR
1.	Terry Labonte	Chevrolet
2.	Jeff Gordon	Chevrolet
3.	Dale Earnhardt	Chevrolet
4.	Robert Pressley	Chevrolet
5.	Sterling Marlin	Chevrolet
6.	Ernie Irvan	Ford
7.	Ricky Craven	Chevrolet
8.	Bobby Hamilton	Pontiac
9.	Ken Schrader	Chevrolet

10.	Bobby Labonte	Chevrolet
11.	Dale Jarrett	Ford
12.	Ted Musgrave	Ford
13.	Derrike Cope	Ford
14.	Rick Mast	Pontiac
15.	Ricky Rudd	Ford
16.	Hut Stricklin	Ford
17.	Michael Waltrip	Ford
18.	Kenny Wallace	Ford
19.	Geoff Bodine	Ford
20.	Jeremy Mayfield	Ford
21.	Bill Elliott	Ford
22.	Dick Trickle	Ford
23.	Brett Bodine	Ford
24.	Johnny Benson	Pontiac
25.	Darrell Waltrip	Chevrolet
26.	Steve Grissom	Chevrolet
27.	Morgan Shepherd	Ford
28.	Wally Dallenbach	Ford
29.	Jeff Burton	Ford
30.	Kyle Petty	Pontiac
31.	Jimmy Spencer	Ford
32.	Elton Sawyer	Ford
33.	Rusty Wallace	Ford
34.	John Andretti	Ford
35.	Lake Speed	Ford
36.	Joe Nemechek	Chevrolet
37.	Mark Martin	Ford

GOODY'S HEADACHE POWDER 500

April 21
Martinsville, Virginia
Time of Race: 3 hours, 13 minutes, 50 secinds
Average Speed: 81.410 mph
Margin of Victory: 2.526 seconds

FINISH	DRIVER	CAR
1.	Rusty Wallace	Ford
2.	Ernie Irvan	Ford
3.	Jeff Gordon	Chevrolet
4.	Jeremy Mayfield	Ford
5.	Dale Earnhardt	Chevrolet
6.	Bobby Hamilton	Pontiac
7.	Ken Schrader	Chevrolet
8.	Bobby Labonte	Chevrolet
9.	Ted Musgrave	Ford
10.	Sterling Marlin	Chevrolet
11.	Lake Speed	Ford
12.	Ricky Craven	Chevrolet
13.	Bill Elliott	Ford
14.	Kenny Wallace	Ford
15.	Rick Mast	Pontiac
16.	Darrell Waltrip	Chevrolet
17.	Michael Waltrip	Ford
18.	Brett Bodine	Ford
19.	Jimmy Spencer	Ford
20.	Morgan Shepherd	Ford
21.	Mark Martin	Ford
22.	Jeff Burton	Ford
23.	Ricky Rudd	Ford
24.	Terry Labonte	Chevrolet
25.	Johnny Benson	Pontiac
26.	Joe Nemechek	Chevrolet
27.	Geoff Bodine	Ford
28.	Derrike Cope	Ford
29.	Dale Jarrett	Ford
30.	Kyle Petty	Pontiac
31.	Hut Stricklin	Ford
32.	Mike Wallace	Ford
33.	Stacy Compton	Chevrolet
34.	Robert Pressley	Chevrolet
35.	Dave Marcis	Chevrolet
36.	John Andretti	Ford

WINSTON SELECT 500

April 28

Talladega, Alabama
Time of Race: 3 hours, 20 minutes, 2 seconds
Average Speed: 149.999 mph
Margin of Victory: .22 second

FINISH	DRIVER	CAR
1.	Sterling Marlin	Chevrolet
2.	Dale Jarrett	Ford
3.	Dale Earnhardt	Chevrolet
4.	Terry Labonte	Chevrolet
5.	Michael Waltrip	Ford
6.	Steve Grissom	Chevrolet
7.	Robert Pressley	Chevrolet
8.	Ted Musgrave	Ford
9.	John Andretti	Ford
10.	Johnny Benson	Pontiac
11.	Bobby Hamilton	Pontiac
12.	Wally Dallenbach	Ford
13.	Joe Nemechek	Chevrolet
14.	Kenny Wallace	Ford
15.	Rick Mast	Pontiac
16.	Jeff Burton	Ford
17.	Mike Skinner	Chevrolet
18.	Kyle Petty	Pontiac
19.	Dick Trickle	Ford
20.	Ken Schrader	Chevrolet
21.	Darrell Waltrip	Chevrolet
22.	Hut Stricklin	Ford
23.	Brett Bodine	Ford
24.	Bobby Labonte	Chevrolet
25.	Chuck Bown	Ford
26.	Geoff Bodine	Ford
27.	Ward Burton	Pontiac
28.	Ricky Rudd	Ford
29.	Derrike Cope	Ford
30.	Rusty Wallace	Ford
31.	Ernie Irvan	Ford
32.	Jeremy Mayfield	Ford
33.	Jeff Gordon	Chevrolet
34.	Mark Martin	Ford
35.	Jeff Purvis	Chevrolet
36.	Ricky Craven	Chevrolet
37.	Elton Sawyer	Ford
38.	Mike Wallace	Ford
39.	Dave Marcis	Chevrolet
40.	Jimmy Spencer	Ford
41.	Bill Elliott	Ford
42.	Lake Speed	Ford
43.	Morgan Shepherd	Ford

SAVE MART SUPERMARKETS 300

May 5
Sonoma, California
Time of Race: 2 hours, 24 minutes, 3 seconds
Average Speed: 77.673 mph
Margin of Victory: .46 second

FINISH	DRIVER	CAR
1.	Rusty Wallace	Ford
2.	Mark Martin	Ford
3.	Wally Dallenbach	Ford
4.	Dale Earnhardt	Chevrolet
5.	Terry Labonte	Chevrolet
6.	Jeff Gordon	Chevrolet
7.	Ricky Rudd	Ford
8.	Ken Schrader	Chevrolet
9.	Bobby Labonte	Chevrolet
10.	Ward Burton	Pontiac
11.	John Andretti	Ford
12.	Dale Jarrett	Ford
13.	Hut Stricklin	Ford
14.	Darrell Waltrip	Chevrolet
15.	Sterling Marlin	Chevrolet
16.	Lake Speed	Ford
17.	Bobby Hamilton	Pontiac
18.	Johnny Benson	Pontiac

19.	Rick Mast	Pontiac
20.	Brett Bodine	Ford
21.	Jimmy Spencer	Ford
22.	Michael Waltrip	Ford
23.	Ted Musgrave	Ford
24.	Morgan Shepherd	Ford
25.	Steve Grissom	Chevrolet
26.	Jeff Burton	Ford
27.	Kenny Wallace	Ford
28.	Tommy Kendall	Ford
29.	Dick Trickle	Ford
30.	Kyle Petty	Pontiac
31.	Ricky Craven	Chevrolet
32.	Jeremy Mayfield	Ford
33.	Dave Marcis	Chevrolet
34.	Robert Pressley	Chevrolet
35.	Jeffrey Krogh	Chevrolet
36.	Larry Gunselman	Ford
37.	Rich Woodland	Chevrolet
38.	Scott Gaylord	Chevrolet
39.	Derrike Cope	Ford
40.	Geoff Bodine	Ford
41.	Joe Nemechek	Chevrolet
42.	Ernie Irvan	Ford
43.	Bobby Hillin	Ford
44.	Mike Wallace	Ford

COCA-COLA 600

May 25
Charlotte, North Carolina
Time of Race: 4 hours, 3 minutes, 56 seconds
Average Speed: 147.581 mph
Margin of Victory: 11.982 seconds

FINISH	DRIVER	CAR
1.	Dale Jarrett	Ford
2.	Dale Earnhardt	Chevrolet
3.	Terry Labonte	Chevrolet
4.	Jeff Gordon	Chevrolet
5.	Ken Schrader	Chevrolet
6.	Sterling Marlin	Chevrolet
7.	Mark Martin	Ford
8.	Michael Waltrip	Ford
9.	Ernie Irvan	Ford
10.	Geoff Bodine	Ford
11.	Ward Burton	Pontiac
12.	Rick Mast	Pontiac
13.	Darrell Waltrip	Chevrolet
14.	Derrike Cope	Ford
15.	Ricky Rudd	Ford
16.	Steve Grissom	Chevrolet
17.	Jimmy Spencer	Ford
18.	Jeff Burton	Ford
19.	Wally Dallenbach Jr.	Ford
20.	Dick Trickle	Ford
21.	Elton Sawyer	Ford
22.	Bobby Labonte	Chevrolet
23.	Kyle Petty	Pontiac
24.	Brett Bodine	Ford
25.	Joe Nemechek	Chevrolet
26.	Bobby Hillin	Ford
27.	John Andretti	Ford
28.	Hut Stricklin	Ford
29.	Morgan Shepherd	Ford
30.	Ted Musgrave	Ford
31.	Bobby Hamilton	Pontiac
32.	Kenny Wallace	Ford
33.	Robert Pressley	Chevrolet
34.	Rusty Wallace	Ford
35.	Lake Speed	Ford
36.	Todd Bodine	Ford
37.	Ricky Craven	Chevrolet
38.	Johnny Benson	Pontiac
39.	Mike Wallace	Ford
40.	Dave Marcis	Chevrolet
41.	Jeremy Mayfield	Ford
42.	Chuck Bown	Ford
43.	Chad Little	Pontiac

MILLER GENUINE DRAFT 500

June 2
Dover, Delaware
Time of Race: 4 hours, 4 minutes, 25 seconds
Average Speed: 122.741 mph
Margin of Victory: 3.90 seconds

FINISH	DRIVER	CAR
1.	Jeff Gordon	Chevrolet
2.	Terry Labonte	Chevrolet
3.	Dale Earnhardt	Chevrolet
4.	Ernie Irvan	Ford
5.	Bobby Labonte	Chevrolet
6.	Jimmy Spencer	Ford
7.	Rusty Wallace	Ford
8.	Ricky Rudd	Ford
9.	Jeff Burton	Ford
10.	Ken Schrader	Chevrolet
11.	Michael Waltrip	Ford
12.	Jeremy Mayfield	Ford
13.	Ted Musgrave	Ford
14.	Ricky Craven	Chevrolet
15.	Todd Bodine	Ford
16.	Ward Burton	Pontiac
17.	Johnny Benson	Pontiac
18.	Kyle Petty	Pontiac
19.	Mike Wallace	Ford
20.	Kenny Wallace	Ford
21.	Bobby Hamilton	Pontiac
22.	Wally Dallenbach	Ford
23.	Derrike Cope	Ford
24.	Brett Bodine	Ford
25.	Joe Nemechek	Chevrolet
26.	Lake Speed	Ford
27.	Greg Sacks	Chevrolet
28.	Dick Trickle	Ford
29.	Bobby Hillin	Ford
30.	Geoff Bodine	Ford
31.	Dave Marcis	Chevrolet
32.	Morgan Shepherd	Ford
33.	John Andretti	Ford
34.	Hut Stricklin	Ford
35.	Rick Mast	Pontiac
36.	Dale Jarrett	Ford
37.	Hermie Sadler	Chevrolet
38.	Gary Bradberry	Ford
39.	Darrell Waltrip	Chevrolet
40.	Mark Martin	Ford
41.	Sterling Marlin	Chevrolet
42.	Steve Grissom	Chevrolet

UAW-GM TEAMWORK 500

June 16
Pocono, Pennsylvania
Time of Race: 3 hours, 35 minutes, 40 seconds
Average Speed: 139.104 mph
Margin of Victory: 3.688 seconds

FINISH	DRIVER	CAR
1.	Jeff Gordon	Chevrolet
2.	Ricky Rudd	Ford
3.	Geoff Bodine	Ford
4.	Mark Martin	Ford
5.	Bobby Hamilton	Pontiac
6.	Morgan Shepherd	Ford
7.	Terry Labonte	Chevrolet
8.	Jimmy Spencer	Ford
9.	Jeff Burton	Ford
10.	Todd Bodine	Ford
11.	Sterling Marlin	Chevrolet
12.	Wally Dallenbach	Ford
13.	Bobby Hillin	Ford
14.	Michael Waltrip	Ford
15.	Jeremy Mayfield	Ford
16.	John Andretti	Ford

17.	Ricky Craven	Chevrolet
18.	Ken Schrader	Chevrolet
19.	Ted Musgrave	Ford
20.	Kyle Petty	Pontiac
21.	Joe Nemechek	Chevrolet
22.	Steve Grissom	Chevrolet
23.	Loy Allen	Ford
24.	Randy MacDonald	Ford
25.	Johnny Benson	Pontiac
26.	Dick Trickle	Ford
27.	Derrike Cope	Ford
28.	Rick Mast	Pontiac
29.	Hut Stricklin	Ford
30.	Darrell Waltrip	Chevrolet
31.	Rusty Wallace	Ford
32.	Dale Earnhardt	Chevrolet
33.	Robert Pressley	Chevrolet
34.	Lake Speed	Ford
35.	Ward Burton	Pontiac
36.	Jeff Green	Chevrolet
37.	Kenny Wallace	Ford
38.	Dale Jarrett	Ford
39.	Ernie Irvan	Ford
40.	Brett Bodine	Ford
41.	Bobby Labonte	Chevrolet

MILLER GENINE DRAFT 400

June 23
Brooklyn, Michigan
Time of Race: 2 hours, 24 minutes, 23 seconds
Average Speed: 166.033 mph
Margin of Victory: 1.10 seconds

FINISH	DRIVER	CAR
1.	Rusty Wallace	Ford
2.	Terry Labonte	Chevrolet
3.	Sterling Marlin	Chevrolet
4.	Jimmy Spencer	Ford
5.	Ernie Irvan	Ford
6.	Jeff Gordon	Chevrolet
7.	Mark Martin	Ford
8.	Ted Musgrave	Ford
9.	Dale Earnhardt	Chevrolet
10.	Dale Jarrett	Ford
11.	Morgan Shepherd	Ford
12.	Bobby Labonte	Chevrolet
13.	Wally Dallenbach	Ford
14.	Bobby Hillin	Ford
15.	Bobby Hamilton	Pontiac
16.	Ken Schrader	Chevrolet
17.	Jeff Burton	Ford
18.	Rick Mast	Pontiac
19.	Lake Speed	Ford
20.	Todd Bodine	Ford
21.	Geoff Bodine	Ford
22.	Brett Bodine	Ford
23.	Robert Pressley	Chevrolet
24.	John Andretti	Ford
25.	Darrell Waltrip	Chevrolet
26.	Dave Marcis	Chevrolet
27.	Hut Stricklin	Ford
28.	Loy Allen	Ford
29.	Ricky Craven	Chevrolet
30.	Jeremy Mayfield	Ford
31.	Ricky Rudd	Ford
32.	Michael Waltrip	Ford
33.	Kenny Wallace	Ford
34.	Steve Grissom	Chevrolet
35.	Ward Burton	Pontiac
36.	Joe Nemechek	Chevrolet
37.	Johnny Benson	Pontiac
38.	Kyle Petty	Pontiac
39.	Dick Trickle	Ford
40.	Derrike Cope	Ford

PEPSI 400

July 6
Daytona Beach, Florida
Time of Race: 1 hour, 48 minutes, 36 seconds
Average Speed: 161.602 mph
Margin of Victory: .104 second

FINISH	DRIVER	CAR
1.	Sterling Marlin	Chevrolet
2.	Terry Labonte	Chevrolet
3.	Jeff Gordon	Chevrolet
4.	Dale Earnhardt	Chevrolet
5.	Ernie Irvan	Chevrolet
6.	Dale Jarrett	Ford
7.	Michael Waltrip	Ford
8.	Ken Schrader	Chevrolet
9.	Brett Bodine	Ford
10.	Jimmy Spencer	Ford
11.	Mark Martin	Ford
12.	Wally Dallenbach	Ford
13.	Ted Musgrave	Ford
14.	Jeff Burton	Ford
15.	Morgan Shepherd	Ford
16.	Bobby Hamilton	Pontiac
17.	Robert Pressley	Chevrolet
18.	Joe Nemechek	Chevrolet
19.	Hut Stricklin	Ford
20.	Rick Mast	Pontiac
21.	Jeff Purvis	Chevrolet
22.	Ricky Craven	Chevrolet
23.	John Andretti	Ford
24.	Kyle Petty	Pontiac
25.	Johnny Benson	Pontiac
26.	Darrell Waltrip	Chevrolet
27.	Jeremy Mayfield	Ford
28.	Dick Trickle	Ford
29.	Lake Speed	Ford
30.	Loy Allen	Ford
31.	Rusty Wallace	Ford
32.	Bobby Hillin	Ford
33.	Ricky Rudd	Ford
34.	Geoff Bodine	Ford
35.	Gary Bradberry	Ford
36.	Dave Marcis	Chevrolet
37.	Bill Elliott	Ford
38.	Kenny Wallace	Ford
39.	Greg Sacks	Chevrolet
40.	Bobby Labonte	Chevrolet
41.	Ward Burton	Pontiac
42.	Derrike Cope	Ford

JIFFY LUBE 300

July 14
Loudon, New Hampshire
Time of Race: 3 hours, 12 minutes, 30 seconds
Average Speed: 98.930 mph
Margin of Victory: 5.470 seconds

FINISH	DRIVER	CAR
1.	Ernie Irvan	Ford
2.	Dale Jarrett	Ford
3.	Ricky Rudd	Ford
4.	Jeff Burton	Ford
5.	Robert Pressley	Chevrolet
6.	Terry Labonte	Chevrolet
7.	Rusty Wallace	Ford
8.	Ken Schrader	Chevrolet
9.	Johnny Benson	Pontiac
10.	Michael Waltrip	Ford
11.	Ted Musgrave	Ford
12.	Dale Earnhardt	Chevrolet
13.	Rick Mast	Pontiac
14.	Bill Elliott	Ford
15.	Geoff Bodine	Ford
16.	Brett Bodine	Ford

17.	Jimmy Spencer	Ford
18.	Wally Dallenbach	Ford
19.	Kenny Wallace	Ford
20.	Bobby Hamilton	Pontiac
21.	Bobby Hillin	Ford
22.	Morgan Shepherd	Ford
23.	Hut Stricklin	Ford
24.	Lake Speed	Ford
25.	Ward Burton	Pontiac
26.	Ricky Craven	Chevrolet
27.	Dick Trickle	Ford
28.	Kyle Petty	Pontiac
29.	Sterling Marlin	Chevrolet
30.	Greg Sacks	Chevrolet
31.	Bobby Labonte	Chevrolet
32.	Randy MacDonald	Ford
33.	Mark Martin	Ford
34.	Jeff Gordon	Chevrolet
35.	Joe Nemechek	Chevrolet
36.	Jeremy Mayfield	Ford
37.	Darrell Waltrip	Chevrolet
38.	Derrike Cope	Ford
39.	Dave Marcis	Chevrolet
40.	John Andretti	Ford

MILLER GENUINE DRAFT 500

July 21
Pocono, Pennsylvania
Time of Race: 3 hours, 27 minutes, 3 seconds
Aversge Speed: 144.892 mph
Margin of Victory: .300 second

FINISH	DRIVER	CAR
1.	Rusty Wallace	Ford
2.	Ricky Rudd	Ford
3.	Dale Jarrett	Ford
4.	Ernie Irvan	Ford
5.	Johnny Benson	Pontiac
6.	Sterling Marlin	Chevrolet
7.	Jeff Gordon	Chevrolet
8.	Lake Speed	Ford
9.	Mark Martin	Ford
10.	Derrike Cope	Ford
11.	Geoff Bodine	Ford
12.	Jeremy Mayfield	Ford
13.	Michael Waltrip	Ford
14.	Dale Earnhardt	Chevrolet
15.	Ken Schrader	Chevrolet
16.	Terry Labonte	Chevrolet
17.	Morgan Shepherd	Ford
18.	Dick Trickle	Ford
19.	Ted Musgrave	Ford
20.	Ricky Craven	Chevrolet
21.	Bill Elliott	Ford
22.	Ward Burton	Pontiac
23.	John Andretti	Ford
24.	Jimmy Spencer	Ford
25.	Robert Pressley	Chevrolet
26.	Kyle Petty	Pontiac
27.	Brett Bodine	Ford
28.	Dave Marcis	Chevrolet
29.	Greg Sacks	Chevrolet
30.	Rick Mast	Pontiac
31.	Randy McDonald	Ford
32.	Hut Stricklin	Ford
33.	Wally Dallenbach	Ford
34.	Joe Nemechek	Chevrolet
35.	Jeff Burton	Ford
36.	Kenny Wallace	Ford
37.	Bobby Labonte	Ford
38.	Bobby Hillin	Ford
39.	Bobby Hamilton	Pontiac
40.	Darrell Waltrip	Chevrolet
41.	Jeff Green	Chevrolet

DIEHARD 500

July 28
Talladega, Alabama
Time of Race: 2 hours, 34 minutes, 21 seconds
Average Speed: 133.387 mph
Margin of Victory: .146 second

FINISH	DRIVER	CAR
1.	Jeff Gordon	Chevrolet
2.	Dale Jarrett	Ford
3.	Mark Martin	Ford
4.	Ernie Irvan	Ford
5.	Jimmy Spencer	Ford
6.	Geoff Bodine	Ford
7.	Jeff Burton	Ford
8.	Bobby Labonte	Chevrolet
9.	Darrell Waltrip	Chevrolet
10.	Rusty Wallace	Ford
11.	Dave Marcis	Chevrolet
12.	Kyle Petty	Pontiac
13.	Bill Elliott	Ford
14.	Morgan Shepherd	Ford
15.	Joe Nemechek	Chevrolet
16.	Jeremy Mayfield	Ford
17.	Bobby Hamilton	Pontiac
18.	Johnny Benson	Pontiac
19.	Ricky Craven	Chevrolet
20.	Kenny Wallace	Ford
21.	Loy Allen	Ford
22.	Brett Bodine	Ford
23.	Gary Bradberry	Ford
24.	Terry Labonte	Chevrolet
25.	Greg Sacks	Chevrolet
26.	Ken Schrader	Chevrolet
27.	Derrike Cope	Ford
28.	Dale Earnhardt	Chevrolet
29.	Sterling Marlin	Chevrolet
30.	Lake Speed	Ford
31.	Robert Pressley	Chevrolet
32.	Wally Dallenbach	Ford
33.	Ward Burton	Pontiac
34.	Hut Stricklin	Ford
35.	Bobby Hillin	Ford
36.	Ted Musgrave	Ford
37.	Ricky Rudd	Ford
38.	Dick Trickle	Ford
39.	John Andretti	Ford
40.	Jeff Purvis	Chevrolet
41.	Rick Mast	Pontiac
42.	Michael Waltrip	Ford

BRICKYARD 400

August 3
Indianapolis, Indiana
Time of Race: 2 hours, 52 minutes, 2 seconds
Average Speed: 139.508 mph
Margin of Victory: under caution

FINISH	DRIVER	CAR
1.	Dale Jarrett	Ford
2.	Ernie Irvan	Ford
3.	Terry Labonte	Chevrolet
4.	Mark Martin	Ford
5.	Morgan Shepherd	Ford
6.	Ricky Rudd	Ford
7.	Rusty Wallace	Ford
8.	Johnny Benson	Pontiac
9.	Rick Mast	Pontiac
10.	Bill Elliott	Ford
11.	Jeff Burton	Ford
12.	Jimmy Spencer	Ford
13.	Lake Speed	Ford
14.	Derrike Cope	Ford
15.	Dale Earnhardt	Chevrolet
16.	Ken Schrader	Chevrolet

17.	Wally Dallenbach	Ford
18.	Hut Stricklin	Ford
19.	John Andretti	Ford
20.	Geoff Bodine	Ford
21.	Ted Musgrave	Ford
22.	Brett Bodine	Ford
23.	Dick Trickle	Ford
24.	Bobby Labonte	Chevrolet
25.	Jeremy Mayfield	Ford
26.	Bobby Hillin	Ford
27.	Joe Nemechek	Chevrolet
28.	Michael Waltrip	Ford
29.	Gary Bradberry	Ford
30.	Robert Pressley	Chevrolet
31.	Bobby Hamilton	Pontiac
32.	Greg Sacks	Chevrolet
33.	Kenny Wallace	Ford
34.	Ricky Craven	Chevrolet
35.	Dave Marcis	Chevrolet
36.	Ward Burton	Pontiac
37.	Jeff Gordon	Chevrolet
38.	Kyle Petty	Pontiac
39.	Sterling Marlin	Chevrolet
40.	Darrell Waltrip	Chevrolet

THE BUD AT THE GLEN

August 11
Watkins Glen, New York
Time of Race: 2 hours, 23 minutes, 17 seconds
Average Speed: 92.334 mph
Margin of Victory: .440 seconds

FINISH	DRIVER	CAR
1.	Geoff Bodine	Ford
2.	Terry Labonte	Chevrolet
3.	Mark Martin	Ford
4.	Jeff Gordon	Chevrolet
5.	Bobby Labonte	Chevrolet
6.	Dale Earnhardt	Chevrolet
7.	Michael Waltrip	Ford
8.	Joe Nemechek	Chevrolet
9.	Morgan Shepherd	Ford
10.	Wally Dallenbach	Ford
11.	Sterling Marlin	Chevrolet
12.	Ted Musgrave	Ford
13.	Dorsey Schroeder	Ford
14.	Brett Bodine	Ford
15.	Johnny Benson	Pontiac
16.	Derrike Cope	Ford
17.	Lake Speed	Ford
18.	Darrell Waltrip	Chevrolet
19.	Jimmy Spencer	Ford
20.	Butch Leitzinger	Chevrolet
21.	Jeff Burton	Ford
22.	Jeremy Mayfield	Ford
23.	Kyle Petty	Pontiac
24.	Dale Jarrett	Ford
25.	Ken Schrader	Chevrolet
26.	John Andretti	Ford
27.	Rick Mast	Pontiac
28.	Dave Marcis	Chevrolet
29.	Bobby Hillin	Ford
30.	Robert Pressley	Chevrolet
31.	Kenny Wallace	Ford
32.	Ward Burton	Pontiac
33.	Rusty Wallace	Ford
34.	Ricky Rudd	Ford
35.	Ernie Irvan	Ford
36.	Ricky Craven	Chevrolet
37.	Hut Stricklin	Ford
38.	Bobby Hamilton	Pontiac
39.	Dick Trickle	Ford

GM GOODWRENCH DEALER 400

August 18
Brooklyn, Michigan

Time of Race: 2 hours, 51 minutes, 41 seconds
Average Speed: 139.792 mph
Margin of Victory: .168 second

FINISH	DRIVER	CAR
1.	Dale Jarrett	Ford
2.	Mark Martin	Ford
3.	Terry Labonte	Chevrolet
4.	Ernie Irvan	Ford
5.	Jeff Gordon	Chevrolet
6.	Bobby Labonte	Chevrolet
7.	Johnny Benson	Pontiac
8.	Ricky Rudd	Ford
9.	Jeff Burton	Ford
10.	Jimmy Spencer	Ford
11.	Morgan Shepherd	Ford
12.	Geoff Bodine	Ford
13.	Bobby Hamilton	Pontiac
14.	Bill Elliott	Ford
15.	Ken Schrader	Chevrolet
16.	Rick Mast	Pontiac
17.	Dale Earnhardt	Chevrolet
18.	Ricky Craven	Chevrolet
19.	Bobby Hillin	Ford
20.	Jeremy Mayfield	Ford
21.	Jim Sauter	Pontiac
22.	Darrell Waltrip	Chevrolet
23.	Ted Musgrave	Ford
24.	Derrike Cope	Ford
25.	Michael Waltrip	Ford
26.	Hut Stricklin	Ford
27.	Joe Nemechek	Chevrolet
28.	Brett Bodine	Ford
29.	Mike Wallace	Ford
30.	Greg Sacks	Chevrolet
31.	John Andretti	Ford
32.	Lake Speed	Ford
33.	Sterling Marlin	Chevrolet
34.	Wally Dallenbach	Ford
35.	Ward Burton	Pontiac
36.	Chad Little	Pontiac
37.	Kenny Wallace	Ford
38.	Dick Trickle	Ford
39.	Rusty Wallace	Ford
40.	Dave Marcis	Chevrolet
41.	Robert Pressley	Chevrolet

GOODY'S HEADACHE POWDER 500

August 24
Bristol, Tennessee
Time of Race: 2 hours, 55 minutes, 12 seconds
Average Speed: 91.267 mph
Margin of Victory: .630 second

FINISH	DRIVER	CAR
1.	Rusty Wallace	Ford
2.	Jeff Gordon	Chevrolet
3.	Mark Martin	Ford
4.	Dale Jarrett	Ford
5.	Terry Labonte	Chevrolet
6.	Michael Waltrip	Ford
7.	Jimmy Spencer	Ford
8.	Ward Burton	Pontiac
9.	Ricky Rudd	Ford
10.	Bobby Hamilton	Pontiac
11.	Darrell Waltrip	Chevrolet
12.	Ted Musgrave	Ford
13.	Ken Schrader	Chevrolet
14.	Brett Bodine	Ford
15.	Kenny Wallace	Ford
16.	Lake Speed	Ford
17.	Jeremy Mayfield	Ford
18.	Sterling Marlin	Ford
19.	Morgan Shepherd	Ford
20.	Hut Stricklin	Ford
21.	Ricky Craven	Chevrolet

FINISH	DRIVER	CAR
22.	Bobby Hillin	Ford
23.	Chad Little	Chevrolet
24.	Dale Earnhardt	Chevrolet
25.	Wally Dallenbach	Ford
26.	Dick Trickle	Ford
27.	Dave Marcis	Chevrolet
28.	Johnny Benson	Pontiac
29.	Derrike Cope	Ford
30.	Gary Bradberry	Ford
31.	Jim Sauter	Pontiac
32.	Bobby Labonte	Chevrolet
33.	Robert Pressley	Chevrolet
34.	Joe Nemechek	Chevrolet
35.	Rick Mast	Pontiac
36.	Ernie Irvan	Ford
37.	Jeff Burton	Ford
38.	John Andretti	Ford
39.	Geoff Bodine	Ford

MOUNTAIN DEW SOUTHERN 500

September 1
Darlington, South Carolina
Time of Race: 3 hours, 41 minutes, 34 seconds
Average Speed: 135.757 mph
Margin of Victory: 0.100 seconds

FINISH	DRIVER	CAR
1.	Jeff Gordon	Chevrolet
2.	Hut Stricklin	Ford
3.	Mark Martin	Ford
4.	Ken Schrader	Chevrolet
5.	John Andretti	Ford
6.	Bobby Labonte	Chevrolet
7.	Ernie Irvan	Ford
8.	Sterling Marlin	Chevrolet
9.	Bill Elliott	Ford
10.	Lake Speed	Ford
11.	Johnny Benson	Pontiac
12.	Dale Earnhardt	Chevrolet
13.	Kenny Wallace	Ford
14.	Dale Jarrett	Ford
15.	Todd Bodine	Ford
16.	Ricky Rudd	Ford
17.	Kyle Petty	Pontiac
18.	Bobby Hillin	Ford
19.	Bobby Hamilton	Pontiac
20.	Chad Little	Chevrolet
21.	Geoff Bodine	Ford
22.	Rick Mast	Pontiac
23.	Jimmy Spencer	Ford
24.	Morgan Shepherd	Ford
25.	Wally Dallenbach	Ford
26.	Terry Labonte	Chevrolet
27.	Robert Presley	Chevrolet
28.	Brett Bodine	Ford
29.	Ted Musgrave	Ford
30.	Dave Marcis	Chevrolet
31.	Jeff Burton	Ford
32.	Darrell Waltrip	Chevrolet
33.	Michael Waltrip	Ford
34.	Derrike Cope	Ford
35.	Gary Bradberry	Ford
36.	Dick Trickle	Ford
37.	Jeremy Mayfield	Ford
38.	Rusty Wallace	Ford
39.	Ed Berrier	Ford
40.	Ward Burton	Pontiac
41.	Loy Allen	Ford
42.	Ricky Craven	Chevrolet

MILLER 400

September 7
Richmond, Virginia
Time of Race: 2 hours, 50 minutes, 40 seconds

Average Speed: 105.469 mph
Margin of Victory: 10 seconds

FINISH	DRIVER	CAR
1.	Ernie Irvan	Ford
2.	Jeff Gordon	Chevrolet
3.	Jeff Burton	Ford
4.	Dale Jarrett	Ford
5.	Terry Labonte	Chevrolet
6.	Rusty Wallace	Ford
7.	Bobby Hamilton	Pontiac
8.	Derrike Cope	Ford
9.	Mark Martin	Ford
10.	Johnny Benson	Pontiac
11.	Bobby Labonte	Chevrolet
12.	Ricky Rudd	Ford
13.	Ken Schrader	Chevrolet
14.	Michael Waltrip	Ford
15.	Ted Musgrave	Ford
16.	Bill Elliott	Ford
17.	Geoff Bodine	Ford
18.	Kyle Petty	Pontiac
19.	Rick Mast	Pontiac
20.	Dale Earnhardt	Chevrolet
21.	Sterling Marlin	Chevrolet
22.	Darrell Waltrip	Chevrolet
23.	Morgan Shepherd	Ford
24.	Hut Stricklin	Ford
25.	Brett Bodine	Ford
26.	Robert Pressley	Chevrolet
27.	Dick Trickle	Ford
28.	Ricky Craven	Chevrolet
29.	Jeremy Mayfield	Ford
30.	Jimmy Spencer	Ford
31.	Lake Speed	Ford
32.	Bobby Hillin	Ford
33.	Wally Dallenbach	Ford
34.	Dave Marcis	Chevrolet
35.	Todd Bodine	Ford
36.	John Andretti	Ford
37.	Ward Burton	Pontiac
38.	Kenny Wallace	Ford
39.	Joe Nemechek	Chevrolet
40.	Chad Little	Chevrolet

MBNA 500

September 15
Dover, Delaware
Time of Race: 4 hours, 43 minutes, 58 seconds
Average Speed: 105.646 mph
Margin of Victory: .441 second

FINISH	DRIVER	CAR
1.	Jeff Gordon	Chevrolet
2.	Rusty Wallace	Ford
3.	Dale Jarrett	Ford
4.	Bobby Labonte	Chevrolet
5.	Mark Martin	Ford
6.	Rick Mast	Pontiac
7.	Ward Burton	Pontiac
8.	Kyle Petty	Pontiac
9.	Michael Waltrip	Ford
10.	Bobby Hamilton	Pontiac
11.	Geoff Bodine	Ford
12.	Bobby Hillin	Ford
13.	Lake Speed	Ford
14.	John Andretti	Ford
15.	Jeremy Mayfield	Ford
16.	Dale Earnhardt	Chevrolet
17.	Sterling Marlin	Chevrolet
18.	Morgan Shepherd	Ford
19.	Mike Skinner	Chevrolet
20.	Kenny Wallace	Ford
21.	Terry Labonte	Chevrolet
22.	Ken Schrader	Chevrolet
23.	Dick Trickle	Ford
24.	Johnny Benson	Pontiac

25.	Joe Nemechek	Chevrolet
26.	Dave Marcis	Chevrolet
27.	Brett Bodine	Ford
28.	Bill Elliott	Ford
29.	Wally Dallenbach	Ford
30.	Jimmy Spencer	Ford
31.	Derrike Cope	Ford
32.	Robert Pressley	Chevrolet
33.	Ted Musgrave	Ford
34.	Ricky Rudd	Ford
35.	Ricky Craven	Ford
36.	Ernie Irvan	Ford
37.	Gary Bradberry	Ford
38.	Hut Stricklin	Ford
39.	Darrell Waltrip	Chevrolet
40.	Jeff Burton	Ford
41.	Chad Little	Chevrolet

HANES 500

September 22
Martinsville, Virginia
Time of Race: 3 hours, 11 minutes, 54 seconds
Average Speed: 82.223 mph
Margin of Victory: .490 seconds

FINISH	DRIVER	CAR
1.	Jeff Gordon	Chevrolet
2.	Terry Labonte	Chevrolet
3.	Bobby Hamilton	Pontiac
4.	Rick Mast	Pontiac
5.	John Andretti	Ford
6.	Morgan Shepherd	Ford
7.	Geoff Bodine	Ford
8.	Kyle Petty	Pontiac
9.	Mark Martin	Ford
10.	Kenny Wallace	Ford
11.	Jeff Burton	Ford
12.	Ernie Irvan	Ford
13.	Dick Trickle	Ford
14.	Michael Waltrip	Ford
15.	Dale Earnhardt	Chevrolet
16.	Dale Jarrett	Ford
17.	Johnny Benson	Pontiac
18.	Bill Elliott	Ford
19.	Jimmy Spencer	Ford
20.	Ted Musgrave	Ford
21.	Bobby Labonte	Chevrolet
22.	Wally Dallenbach	Ford
23.	Darrell Waltrip	Chevrolet
24.	Bobby Hillin	Ford
25.	Hut Stricklin	Ford
26.	Ricky Craven	Chevrolet
27.	Joe Nemechek	Chevrolet
28.	Lake Speed	Ford
29.	Dave Marcis	Chevrolet
30.	Ken Schrader	Chevrolet
31.	Sterling Marlin	Chevrolet
32.	Robert Pressley	Chevrolet
33.	Stacy Compton	Chevrolet
34.	Jeremy Mayfield	Ford
35.	Ricky Rudd	Ford
36.	Rusty Wallace	Ford

TYSON HOLLY FARMS 400

September 29
North Wilkesboro, North Carolina
Time of Race: 2 hours, 34 minutes, 54 seconds
Average Speed: 96.837 mph
Margin of Victory: 1.73 seconds

FINISH	DRIVER	CAR
1.	Jeff Gordon	Chevrolet
2.	Dale Earnhardt	Chevrolet

3.	Dale Jarrett	Ford
4.	Jeff Burton	Ford
5.	Terry Labonte	Chevrolet
6.	Rick Mast	Pontiac
7.	Ricky Rudd	Ford
8.	Bobby Hamilton	Pontiac
9.	Mark Martin	Ford
10.	Rusty Wallace	Ford
11.	Sterling Marlin	Chevrolet
12.	Michael Waltrip	Ford
13.	Bobby Labonte	Chevrolet
14.	Morgan Shepherd	Ford
15.	Kenny Wallace	Ford
16.	Hut Stricklin	Ford
17.	Johnny Benson	Pontiac
18.	Ken Schrader	Chevrolet
19.	Ted Musgrave	Ford
20.	Jimmy Spencer	Ford
21.	Bill Elliott	Ford
22.	Ricky Craven	Chevrolet
23.	Brett Bodine	Ford
24.	John Andretti	Ford
25.	Lake Speed	Ford
26.	Joe Nemechek	Chevrolet
27.	Darrell Waltrip	Chevrolet
28.	Jeremy Mayfield	Ford
29.	Dave Marcis	Chevrolet
30.	Geoff Bodine	Ford
31.	Kyle Petty	Pontiac
32.	Jeff Green	Chevrolet
33.	Robert Pressley	Chevrolet
34.	Wally Dallenbach	Ford
35.	Bobby Hillin	Ford
36.	Ernie Irvan	Ford
37.	Derrike Cope	Ford

UAW-GM QUALITY 500

October 6
Charlotte, North Carolina
Time of Race: 3 hours, 30 minutes, 0 seconds
Average Speed: 143.143 mph
Margin of Victory: 3.84 seconds

FINISH	DRIVER	CAR
1.	Terry Labonte	Chevrolet
2.	Mark Martin	Ford
3.	Dale Jarrett	Ford
4.	Sterling Marlin	Chevrolet
5.	Ricky Craven	Chevrolet
6.	Dale Earnhardt	Chevrolet
7.	Ward Burton	Pontiac
8.	Rusty Wallace	Ford
9.	Michael Waltrip	Ford
10.	Bill Elliott	Ford
11.	Jeff Burton	Ford
12.	Lake Speed	Ford
13.	Ricky Rudd	Ford
14.	Johnny Benson	Pontiac
15.	Rick Mast	Pontiac
16.	Jimmy Spencer	Ford
17.	Ted Musgrave	Ford
18.	Derrike Cope	Ford
19.	Bobby Hamilton	Pontiac
20.	Geoff Bodine	Ford
21.	Todd Bodine	Ford
22.	Chad Little	Pontiac
23.	Morgan Shepherd	Ford
24.	Greg Sacks	Chevrolet
25.	Hut Stricklin	Ford
26.	Jeff Green	Chevrolet
27.	Billy Standridge	Ford
28.	Brett Bodine	Ford
29.	Ken Schrader	Chevrolet
30.	Kenny Wallace	Ford
31.	Jeff Gordon	Chevrolet
32.	Robert Pressley	Chevrolet
33.	Wally Dallenbach	Ford
34.	Loy Allen	Ford
35.	Dick Trickle	Ford

FINISH	DRIVER	CAR
36.	Bobby Hillin	Ford
37.	Ernie Irvan	Ford
38.	Robby Gordon	Chevrolet
39.	John Andretti	Ford
40.	Bobby Labonte	Chevrolet
41.	Kyle Petty	Pontiac
42.	Darrell Waltrip	Chevrolet
43.	Jeremy Mayfield	Ford

AC-DELCO 400

October 20
Rockingham, North Carolina
Time of Race: 3 hours, 16 minutes, 3 seconds
Average Speed: 122.320 mph
Margin of Victory: 3.397 seconds

FINISH	DRIVER	CAR
1.	Ricky Rudd	Ford
2.	Dale Jarrett	Ford
3.	Terry Labonte	Chevrolet
4.	Ernie Irvan	Ford
5.	Jeff Burton	Ford
6.	Bobby Labonte	Chevrolet
7.	Mark Martin	Ford
8.	Rusty Wallace	Ford
9.	Dale Earnhardt	Chevrolet
10.	Jimmy Spencer	Ford
11.	Hut Stricklin	Ford
12.	Jeff Gordon	Chevrolet
13.	Sterling Marlin	Chevrolet
14.	Michael Waltrip	Ford
15.	Geoff Bodine	Ford
16.	Brett Bodine	Ford
17.	Ward Burton	Pontiac
18.	Ted Musgrave	Ford
19.	Kenny Wallace	Ford
20.	Todd Bodine	Chevrolet
21.	Darrell Waltrip	Chevrolet
22.	Ricky Craven	Chevrolet
23.	Ken Schrader	Chevrolet
24.	Joe Nemechek	Chevrolet
25.	Kyle Petty	Pontiac
26.	John Andretti	Ford
27.	Gary Bradberry	Ford
28.	Bobby Hamilton	Pontiac
29.	Morgan Shepherd	Ford
30.	Dave Marcis	Chevrolet
31.	Dick Trickle	Ford
32.	Bill Elliott	Ford
33.	Bobby Hillin	Ford
34.	Jeremy Mayfield	Ford
35.	Lake Speed	Ford
36.	Wally Dallenbach	Ford
37.	Robert Presley	Chevrolet
38.	Rick Mast	Pontiac
39.	Derrike Cope	Ford
40.	Johnny Benson	Pontiac
41.	Billy Standridge	Ford
42.	Robby Gordon	Chevrolet

DURA LUBE 500

October 27
Phoenix, Arizona
Time of Race: 2 hours, 50 minutes, 38 seconds
Average Speed: 109.709 mph
Margin of Victory: 1.23 seconds

FINISH	DRIVER	CAR
1.	Bobby Hamilton	Pontiac
2.	Mark Martin	Ford
3.	Terry Labonte	Chevrolet
4.	Ted Musgrave	Ford

5.	Jeff Gordon	Chevrolet
6.	Geoff Bodine	Ford
7.	Ernie Irvan	Ford
8.	Dale Jarrett	Ford
9.	Bobby Labonte	Chevrolet
10.	Darrell Waltrip	Chevrolet
11.	Todd Bodine	Chevrolet
12.	Dale Earnhardt	Chevrolet
13.	Mike Skinner	Chevrolet
14.	Ricky Rudd	Ford
15.	Wally Dallenbach	Ford
16.	Michael Waltrip	Ford
17.	Morgan Shepherd	Ford
18.	Jimmy Spencer	Ford
19.	John Andretti	Ford
20.	Dick Trickle	Ford
21.	Bill Elliott	Ford
22.	Ward Burton	Pontiac
23.	Jack Sprague	Pontiac
24.	Dave Marcis	Chevrolet
25.	Joe Nemechek	Chevrolet
26.	Brett Bodine	Ford
27.	Sterling Marlin	Chevrolet
28.	Lake Speed	Ford
29.	Kyle Petty	Pontiac
30.	Hut Stricklin	Ford
31.	Jeff Burton	Ford
32.	Johnny Benson	Pontiac
33.	Lance Hooper	Pontiac
34.	Ricky Craven	Chevrolet
35.	Ken Schrader	Chevrolet
36.	Robert Pressley	Chevrolet
37.	Kenny Wallace	Ford
38.	Rick Mast	Pontiac
39.	Bobby Hillin	Ford
40.	Rusty Wallace	Ford
41.	Jeffrey Krogh	Ford
42.	Robby Gordon	Chevrolet
43.	Derrike Cope	Ford
44.	Jeremy Mayfield	Ford

NAPA 500

November 10
Atlanta, Georgia
Time of Race: 3 hours, 39 minutes, 13 seconds
Average Speed: 134.661 mph
Margin of Victory: .41 seconds

FINISH	DRIVER	CAR
1.	Bobby Labonte	Chevrolet
2.	Dale Jarrett	Ford
3.	Jeff Gordon	Chevrolet
4.	Dale Earnhardt	Chevrolet
5.	Terry Labonte	Chevrolet
6.	Bobby Hamilton	Pontiac
7.	Mark Martin	Fotd
8.	Ricky Rudd	Ford
9.	Jeff Burton	Ford
10.	Rusty Wallace	Ford
11.	Michael Waltrip	Ford
12.	Ward Burton	Pontiac
13.	Rick Mast	Pontiac
14.	Jimmy Spencer	Ford
15.	Sterling Marlin	Chevrolet
16.	Bobby Hillin	Ford
17.	Hut Stricklin	Ford
18.	Greg Sacks	Pontiac
19.	Lake Speed	Ford
20.	Bill Elliott	Ford
21.	Brett Bodine	Ford
22.	Chad Little	Pontiac
23.	Elton Sawyer	Ford
24.	John Andretti	Ford
25.	Dave Marcis	Chevrolet
26.	Geoff Bodine	Ford
27.	Johnny Benson	Pontiac
28.	Morgan Shepherd	Ford
29.	Billy Standridge	Ford
30.	Ken Schrader	Chevrolet

31.	Ted Musgrave	Ford
32.	Todd Bodine	Chevrolet
33.	Robert Pressley	Chevrolet
34.	Joe Nemechek	Chevrolet
35.	Ricky Craven	Chevrolet
36.	Ernie Irvan	Ford
37.	Darrell Waltrip	Chevrolet
38.	Gary Bradberry	Ford
39.	Loy Allen	Ford
40.	Wally Dallenbach	Ford
41.	Randy Baker	Chevrolet
42.	Jack Sprague	Pontiac

1997

DAYTONA 500

February 16
Daytona Beach, Florida
Time of Race: 3 hours, 22 minutes, 18 seconds
Average Speed: 148.295 mph
Margin of Victory: under caution

FINISH	DRIVER	CAR
1.	Jeff Gordon	Chevrolet
2.	Terry Labonte	Chevrolet
3.	Ricky Craven	Chevrolet
4.	Bill Elliott	Ford
5.	Sterling Marlin	Chevrolet
6.	Jeremy Mayfield	Ford
7.	Mark Martin	Ford
8.	Ward Burton	Pontiac
9.	Ricky Rudd	Ford
10.	Darrell Waltrip	Chevrolet
11.	Jeff Burton	Ford
12.	Mike Skinner	Chevrolet
13.	Ted Musgrave	Ford
14.	Kyle Petty	Pontiac
15.	Bobby Hamilton	Pontiac
16.	Robby Gordon	Chevrolet
17.	Dave Marcis	Chevrolet
18.	Brett Bodine	Ford
19.	Hut Stricklin	Ford
20.	Ernie Irvan	Ford
21.	Bobby Labonte	Pontiac
22.	Kenny Wallace	Ford
23.	Dale Jarrett	Ford
24.	Lake Speed	Ford
25.	John Andretti	Ford
26.	Loy Allen	Ford
27.	Joe Nemechek	Chevrolet
28.	Johnny Benson	Pontiac
29.	Morgan Shepherd	Pontiac
30.	Dick Trickle	Ford
31.	Dale Earnhardt	Chevrolet
32.	Michael Waltrip	Ford
33.	Ken Schrader	Chevrolet
34.	Geoff Bodine	Ford
35.	Jimmy Spencer	Ford
36.	Derrike Cope	Pontiac
37.	Greg Sacks	Ford
38.	Bobby Hillin	Ford
39.	Robert Pressley	Chevrolet
40.	Steve Grissom	Chevrolet
41.	Rusty Wallace	Ford
42.	Wally Dallenbach	Chevrolet

GM GOODWRENCH 400

February 23
Rockingham, North Carolina
Time of Race: 3 hours, 17 minutes, 35 seconds
Average Speed: 125.927 mph
Margin of Victory: 2.43 seconds

FINISH	DRIVER	CAR
1.	Jeff Gordon	Chevrolet
2.	Dale Jarrett	Ford
3.	Jeff Burton	Ford
4.	Ricky Rudd	Ford
5.	Ricky Craven	Chevrolet
6.	Rusty Wallace	Ford
7.	Terry Labonte	Chevrolet
8.	Geoff Bodine	Ford
9.	Ernie Irvan	Ford
10.	Morgan Shepherd	Pontiac
11.	Dale Earnhardt	Chevrolet
12.	Ted Musgrave	Ford
13.	Mark Martin	Ford
14.	Bobby Labonte	Pontiac
15.	Lake Speed	Ford
16.	Jeremy Mayfield	Ford
17.	Brett Bodine	Ford
18.	Ken Schrader	Chevrolet
19.	Dick Trickle	Ford
20.	Sterling Marlin	Chevrolet
21.	Rick Mast	Ford
22.	Bill Elliott	Ford
23.	Ward Burton	Pontiac
24.	Steve Grissom	Chevrolet
25.	Mike Skinner	Chevrolet
26.	Michael Waltrip	Ford
27.	Johnny Benson	Pontiac
28.	Bobby Hamilton	Pontiac
29.	Kyle Petty	Pontiac
30.	Dave Marcis	Chevrolet
31.	Derrike Cope	Pontiac
32.	Darrell Waltrip	Chevrolet
33.	Robby Gordon	Chevrolet
34.	John Andretti	Ford
35.	Joe Nemechek	Chevrolet
36.	Hut Stricklin	Ford
37.	Robert Pressley	Chevrolet
38.	David Green	Chevrolet
39.	Greg Sacks	Ford
40.	Jimmy Spencer	Ford
41.	Kenny Wallace	Ford
42.	Bobby Hillin	Ford
43.	Loy Allen	Ford

PONTIAC EXCITEMENT 400

March 2
Richmond, Virginia
Time of Race: 2 hours, 45 minutes, 54 seconds
Average Speed: 108.499 miles per hour
Margin of Victory: .441 seconds

FINISH	DRIVER	CAR
1.	Rusty Wallace	Ford
2.	Geoff Bodine	Ford
3.	Dale Jarrett	Ford
4.	Jeff Gordon	Chevrolet
5.	Bobby Hamilton	Pontiac
6.	Ricky Rudd	Ford
7.	Terry Labonte	Chevrolet
8.	Bobby Labonte	Pontiac
9.	Johnny Benson	Pontiac
10.	Kyle Petty	Pontiac
11.	Steve Grissom	Chevrolet
12.	Lake Speed	Ford
13.	Mark Martin	Ford
14.	Ricky Craven	Chevrolet
15.	Bill Elliott	Ford
16.	Darrell Waltrip	Chevrolet
17.	JeremyMayfield	Ford
18.	Rick Mast	Ford
19.	Sterling Marlin	Chevrolet
20.	Ted Musgrave	Ford
21.	Robert Pressley	Chevrolet
22.	Jimmy Spencer	Ford
23.	Brett Bodine	Ford
24.	Ward Burton	Pontiac
25.	Dale Earnhardt	Chevrolet
26.	Mike Skinner	Chevrolet

27.	Michael Waltrip	Ford
28.	Robby Gordon	Chevrolet
29.	Dick Trickle	Ford
30.	Derrike Cope	Pontiac
31.	John Andretti	Ford
32.	Hut Stricklin	Ford
33.	David Green	Chevrolet
34.	Chad Little	Pontiac
35.	Ken Schrader	Chevrolet
36.	Ernie Irvan	Ford
36.	Dave Marcis	Chevrolet
38.	Gary Bradberry	Ford
39.	Joe Nemechek	Chevrolet
40.	Kenny Wallace	Ford
41.	Bobby Hillin	Ford
42.	Jeff Burton	Ford
43.	Morgan Shepherd	Pontiac

PRIMESTAR 500

March 9
Atlanta, Georgia
Time of Race: 3 hours, 45 minutes, 7 seconds
Average Speed: 132.730 mph
Margin of Victory: 1.38 seconds

FINISH	DRIVER	CAR
1.	Dale Jarrett	Ford
2.	Ernie Irvan	Ford
3.	Morgan Shepherd	Pontiac
4.	Bobby Labonte	Pontiac
5.	Jeff Burton	Ford
6.	Mark Martin	Ford
7.	Michael Waltrip	Ford
8.	Dale Earnhardt	Chevrolet
9.	Terry Labonte	Chevrolet
10.	Bobby Hamilton	Pontiac
11.	Johnny Benson	Pontiac
12.	Ward Burton	Pontiac
13.	Kyle Petty	Pontiac
14.	Robby Gordon	Chevrolet
15.	John Andretti	Ford
16.	Darrell Waltrip	Chevrolet
17.	Rick Mast	Ford
18.	Brett Bodine	Ford
19.	Chad Little	Pontiac
20.	Geoff Bodine	Ford
21.	Mike Skinner	Chevrolet
22.	Lake Speed	Ford
23.	Sterling Marlin	Chevrolet
24.	David Green	Chevrolet
25.	Ken Schrader	Chevrolet
26.	Mike Wallace	Chevrolet
27.	Greg Sacks	Ford
28.	Dick Trickle	Ford
29.	Kenny Wallace	Ford
30.	Ricky Rudd	Ford
31.	Rusty Wallace	Ford
32.	Jimmy Spencer	Ford
33.	Steve Grissom	Chevrolet
34.	Ted Musgrave	Ford
35.	Ricky Craven	Chevrolet
36.	Billy Standridge	Ford
37.	Jeremy Mayfield	Ford
38.	Bill Elliott	Ford
39.	Joe Nemechek	Chevrolet
40.	Gary Bradberry	Ford
41.	Hut Stricklin	Ford
42.	Jeff Gordon	Chevrolet

TRANSOUTH FINANCIAL 400

March 23
Darlington, South Carolina
Time of Race: 3 hours, 18 minutes, 12 seconds
Average Speed: 141.410 mph
Margin of Victory: 0.169 seconds

FINISH	DRIVER	CAR
1.	Dale Jarrett	Ford
2.	Ted Musgrave	Ford
3.	Jeff Gordon	Chevrolet
4.	Jeff Burton	Ford
5.	Bobby Labonte	Pontiac
6.	Rusty Wallace	Ford
7.	Michael Waltrip	Ford
8.	Ken Schrader	Chevrolet
9.	Geoff Bodine	Ford
10.	Johnny Benson	Pontiac
11.	Darrell Waltrip	Chevrolet
12.	Morgan Shepherd	Pontiac
13.	Terry Labonte	Chevrolet
14.	Kenny Wallace	Ford
15.	Dale Earnhardt	Chevrolet
16.	Bill Elliott	Ford
17.	Jeremy Mayfield	Ford
18.	Ward Burton	Pontiac
19.	Rick Mast	Ford
20.	Derrike Cope	Pontiac
21.	Ernie Irvan	Ford
22.	Jimmy Spencer	Ford
23.	Ricky Rudd	Ford
24.	Mark Martin	Ford
25.	John Andretti	Ford
26.	Hut Stricklin	Ford
27.	Chad Little	Pontiac
28.	Dave Marcis	Chevrolet
29.	Greg Sacks	Ford
30.	Mike Skinner	Chevrolet
31.	Phil Parsons	Chevrolet
32.	Sterling Marlin	Chevrolet
33.	Kyle Petty	Pontiac
34.	Robby Gordon	Chevrolet
35.	Brett Bodine	Ford
36.	Lake Speed	Ford
37.	Bobby Hamilton	Pontiac
38.	Gary Bradberry	Ford
39.	Robert Pressley	Chevrolet
40.	Ricky Craven	Chevrolet
41.	David Green	Chevrolet
42.	Bobby Hillin	Ford
43.	Mike Wallace	Chevrolet

INTERSTATE BATTERIES 500

April 6
Fort Worth, Texas
Time of Race: 4 hours, 17 seconds
Average Speed: 125.105 mph
Margin of Victory: 4.067 seconds

FINISH	DRIVER	CAR
1.	Jeff Burton	Ford
2.	Dale Jarrett	Ford
3.	Bobby Labonte	Pontiac
4.	Terry Labonte	Chevrolet
5.	Ricky Rudd	Ford
6.	Dale Earnhardt	Chevrolet
7.	Ward Burton	Pontiac
8.	Sterling Marlin	Chevrolet
9.	Michael Waltrip	Ford
10.	Steve Grissom	Chevrolet
11.	Bill Elliott	Ford
12.	John Andretti	Ford
13.	Kenny Wallace	Ford
14.	Geoff Bodine	Ford
15.	Dave Marcis	Chevrolet
16.	Lake Speed	Ford
17.	Mike Wallace	Chevrolet
18.	Ken Schrader	Chevrolet
19.	Brett Bodine	Ford
20.	Bobby Hamilton	Pontiac
21.	Billy Standridge	Ford
22.	Mike Skinner	Chevrolet
23.	Dick Trickle	Ford
24.	Morgan Shepherd	Pontiac
25.	Todd Bodine	Chevrolet

26.	Chad Little	Pontiac
27.	Kyle Petty	Pontiac
28.	Johnny Benson	Pontiac
29.	Joe Nemechek	Chevrolet
30.	Jeff Gordon	Chevrolet
31.	Rick Mast	Ford
32.	Jeremy Mayfield	Ford
33.	Hut Stricklin	Ford
34.	Robby Gordon	Chevrolet
35.	Ted Musgrave	Ford
36.	Ernie Irvan	Ford
37.	Rusty Wallace	Ford
38.	Mark Martin	Ford
39.	Jimmy Spencer	Ford
40.	Greg Sacks	Ford
41.	Derrike Cope	Pontiac
42.	Bobby Hillin Jr.	Ford
43.	Darrell Waltrip	Chevrolet

FOOD CITY 500

April 13
Bristol, Tennessee
Time of Race: 3 hours, 33 minutes, 6 seconds
Average Speed: 75.035 mph
Margin of Victory: 0.499 seconds

FINISH	DRIVER	CAR
1.	Jeff Gordon	Chevrolet
2.	Rusty Wallace	Ford
3.	Terry Labonte	Chevrolet
4.	Dale Jarrett	Ford
5.	Mark Martin	Ford
6.	Dale Earnhardt	Chevrolet
7.	Bill Elliott	Ford
8.	Chad Little	Pontiac
9.	Jeremy Mayfield	Ford
10.	Brett Bodine	Ford
11.	Dick Trickle	Ford
12.	Ken Schrader	Chevrolet
13.	Bobby Hamilton	Pontiac
14.	Robert Pressley	Chevrolet
15.	Jimmy Spencer	Ford
16.	Derrike Cope	Pontiac
17.	Rick Mast	Ford
18.	Ward Burton	Pontiac
19.	Joe Nemechek	Chevrolet
20.	Sterling Marlin	Chevrolet
21.	Michael Waltrip	Ford
22.	David Green	Chevrolet
23.	Ed Berrier	Chevrolet
24.	John Andretti	Ford
25.	Darrell Waltrip	Chevrolet
26.	Hut Stricklin	Ford
27.	Ricky Rudd	Ford
28.	Morgan Shepherd	Pontiac
29.	Kyle Petty	Pontiac
30.	Dave Marcis	Chevrolet
31.	Johnny Benson	Pontiac
32.	Steve Grissom	Chevrolet
33.	Geoff Bodine	Ford
34.	Bobby Labonte	Pontiac
35.	Mike Skinner	Chevrolet
36.	Lake Speed	Ford
37.	Gary Bradberry	Ford
38.	Ted Musgrave	Ford
39.	Ernie Irvan	Ford
40.	Jack Sprague	Chevrolet
41.	Kenny Wallace	Ford
42.	Jeff Burton	Ford
43.	Robby Gordon	Pontiac

GOODY'S 500

April 20
Martinsville, Virginia
Time of Race: 3 hours, 44 minutes, 30 seconds

Average Speed: 70.920 mph
Margin of Victory: 1.047 seconds

FINISH	DRIVER	CAR
1.	Jeff Gordon	Chevrolet
2.	Bobby Hamilton	Pontiac
3.	Mark Martin	Ford
4.	Terry Labonte	Chevrolet
5.	Rusty Wallace	Ford
6.	Kenny Wallace	Ford
7.	Jeremy Mayfield	Ford
8.	Bobby Labonte	Pontiac
9.	Darrell Waltrip	Chevrolet
10.	Ken Schrader	Chevrolet
11.	Jimmy Spencer	Ford
12.	Dale Earnhardt	Chevrolet
13.	Ricky Rudd	Ford
14.	Hut Stricklin	Ford
15.	Jeff Burton	Ford
16.	Dale Jarrett	Ford
17.	Johnny Benson	Pontiac
18.	Ward Burton	Pontiac
19.	Joe Nemechek	Chevrolet
20.	Steve Grissom	Chevrolet
21.	Sterling Marlin	Chevrolet
22.	Ricky Craven	Chevrolet
23.	Robert Pressley	Chevrolet
24.	Ted Musgrave	Ford
25.	Lake Speed	Ford
26.	Michael Waltrip	Ford
27.	Brett Bodine	Ford
28.	John Andretti	Ford
29.	Geoff Bodine	Ford
30.	Dick Trickle	Ford
31.	Ernie Irvan	Ford
32.	Mike Skinner	Chevrolet
33.	Bobby Hillin	Ford
34.	Derrike Cope	Pontiac
35.	Morgan Shepherd	Pontiac
36.	Rick Mast	Ford
37.	Bill Elliott	Ford
38.	Dave Marcis	Chevrolet
39.	Mike Wallace	Ford
40.	Kyle Petty	Pontiac
41.	Robby Gordon	Pontiac
42.	Chad Little	Pontiac

SAVE MART SUPERMARKETS 300

May 4
Sonoma, California
Time of Race: 2 hours, 27 minutes, 38 seconds
Average Speed: 75.788 mph
Margin of Victory: 0.536 seconds

FINISH	DRIVER	CAR
1.	Mark Martin	Ford
2.	Jeff Gordon	Chevrolet
3.	Terry Labonte	Chevrolet
4.	Dale Jarrett	Ford
5.	Darrell Waltrip	Chevrolet
6.	Brett Bodine	Ford
7.	Michael Waltrip	Ford
8.	Ernie Irvan	Ford
9.	Jeff Burton	Ford
10.	Ward Burton	Pontiac
11.	Ted Musgrave	Ford
12.	Dale Earnhardt	Chevrolet
13.	Kyle Petty	Pontiac
14.	Jimmy Spencer	Ford
15.	Wally Dallenbach	Chevrolet
16.	Mike Skinner	Chevrolet
17.	Steve Grissom	Chevrolet
18.	Derrike Cope	Pontiac
19.	Bobby Hamilton	Pontiac
20.	Bobby Labonte	Pontiac
21.	Johnny Benson	Pontiac
22.	Mike Wallace	Chevrolet

23.	Morgan Shepherd	Pontiac
24.	Butch Gilliland	Ford
25.	Dave Marcis	Chevrolet
26.	Sterling Marlin	Chevrolet
27.	Jeremy Mayfield	Ford
28.	Tom Hubert	Ford
29.	Hut Stricklin	Ford
30.	John Andretti	Ford
31.	Ken Schrader	Chevrolet
32.	Bill Elliott	Ford
33.	Sean Woodside	Pontiac
34.	Ricky Rudd	Ford
35.	Bobby Hillin	Ford
36.	Kenny Wallace	Ford
37.	Jeff Davis	Ford
38.	Larry Gunselman	Ford
39.	Ricky Craven	Chevrolet
40.	Rusty Wallace	Ford
41.	Robby Gordon	Chevrolet
42.	Lance Hooper	Ford
43.	Gary Bradberry	Ford
44.	Geoff Bodine	Ford

WINSTON 500

May 10
Talladega, Alabama
Time of Race: 2 hours, 39 minutes, 18 seconds
Average Speed: 188.354 mph
Margin of Victory: .146 seconds

FINISH	DRIVER	CAR
1.	Mark Martin	Ford
2.	Dale Earnhardt	Chevrolet
3.	Bobby Labonte	Pontiac
4.	John Andretti	Ford
5.	Jeff Gordon	Chevrolet
6.	Terry Labonte	Chevrolet
7.	Jimmy Spencer	Ford
8.	Jeff Burton	Ford
9.	Johnny Benson	Pontiac
10.	Ernie Irvan	Ford
11.	Ricky Rudd	Ford
12.	Ken Schrader	Chevrolet
13.	Derrike Cope	Pontiac
14.	Michael Waltrip	Ford
15.	Dick Trickle	Ford
16.	Mike Skinner	Chevrolet
17.	Wally Dallenbach	Chevrolet
18.	Bill Elliott	Ford
19.	Joe Nemechek	Pontiac
20.	Bobby Hillin	Ford
21.	Lake Speed	Ford
22.	Rick Mast	Ford
23.	Jeremy Mayfield	Ford
24.	Ted Musgrave	Ford
25.	Greg Sacks	Ford
26.	Kenny Wallace	Ford
27.	Ricky Craven	Chevrolet
28.	Morgan Shepherd	Pontiac
29.	Robert Pressley	Chevrolet
30.	Dave Marcis	Chevrolet
31.	Bobby Hamilton	Pontiac
32.	Darrell Waltrip	Chevrolet
33.	Brett Bodine	Ford
34.	Chad Little	Pontiac
35.	Dale Jarrett	Ford
36.	Hut Stricklin	Ford
37.	Rusty Wallace	Ford
38.	David Green	Chevrolet
39.	Sterling Marlin	Chevrolet
40.	Kyle Petty	Pontiac
41.	Steve Grissom	Chevrolet
42.	Ward Burton	Pontiac
43.	Geoff Bodine	Ford

COCA-COLA 600

May 25
Charlotte, North Carolina
Time of Race: 3 hours, 34 minutes, 2 seconds
Average Speed: 136.745 mph
Margin of Victory: .468 seconds

FINISH	DRIVER	CAR
1.	Jeff Gordon	Chevrolet
2.	Rusty Wallace	Ford
3.	Mark Martin	Ford
4.	Bill Elliott	Ford
5.	Jeff Burton	Ford
6.	Bobby Labonte	Pontiac
7.	Dale Earnhardt	Chevrolet
8.	Terry Labonte	Chevrolet
9.	Morgan Shepherd	Pontiac
10.	Ricky Rudd	Ford
11.	Steve Grissom	Chevrolet
12.	Derrike Cope	Pontiac
13.	Ernie Irvan	Ford
14.	Kyle Petty	Pontiac
15.	Johnny Benson	Pontiac
16.	David Green	Chevrolet
17.	Michael Waltrip	Ford
18.	Jimmy Spencer	Ford
19.	Joe Nemechek	Chevrolet
20.	Rick Mast	Ford
21.	Darrell Waltrip	Chevrolet
22.	Jeff Green	Chevrolet
23.	Ted Musgrave	Ford
24.	Lake Speed	Ford
25.	Hut Stricklin	Ford
26.	Brett Bodine	Ford
27.	Dale Jarrett	Ford
28.	Jeremy Mayfield	Ford
29.	Bobby Hamilton	Pontiac
30.	John Andretti	Ford
31.	Gary Bradberry	Ford
32.	Billy Standridge	Ford
33.	Dick Trickle	Ford
34.	Mike Skinner	Chevrolet
35.	Wally Dallenbach	Chevrolet
36.	Ward Burton	Pontiac
37.	Ricky Craven	Chevrolet
38.	Ken Schrader	Chevrolet
38.	Kenny Wallace	Ford
40.	Sterling Marlin	Chevrolet
41.	Robby Gordon	Chevrolet
42.	Todd Bodine	Ford

MILLER 500

June 1
Dover, Delaware
Time of Race: 4 hours, 21 minutes, 42 seconds
Average Speed: 114.635 mph
Margin of Victory: .091 seconds

FINISH	DRIVER	CAR
1.	Ricky Rudd	Ford
2.	Mark Martin	Ford
3.	Jeff Burton	Ford
4.	Jeremy Mayfield	Ford
5.	Kyle Petty	Pontiac
6.	Ken Schrader	Chevrolet
7.	Michael Waltrip	Ford
8.	Bill Elliott	Ford
9.	Mike Skinner	Chevrolet
10.	Sterling Marlin	Chevrolet
11.	Ted Musgrave	Ford
12.	Rick Mast	Ford
13.	Ricky Craven	Chevrolet
14.	Terry Labonte	Chevrolet
15.	Joe Nemechek	Chevrolet
16.	Dale Earnhardt	Chevrolet

17.	Bobby Hamilton	Pontiac
18.	David Green	Chevrolet
19.	Hut Stricklin	Ford
20.	Derrike Cope	Pontiac
21.	Johnny Benson	Pontiac
22.	Jimmy Spencer	Ford
23.	Mike Wallace	Chevrolet
24.	Steve Grissom	Chevrolet
25.	Dave Marcis	Chevrolet
26.	Jeff Gordon	Chevrolet
27.	Kenny Wallace	Ford
28.	Darrell Waltrip	Chevrolet
29.	John Andretti	Ford
30.	Ernie Irvan	Ford
31.	Chad Little	Pontiac
32.	Dale Jarrett	Ford
33.	Brett Bodine	Ford
34.	Ward Burton	Pontiac
35.	Gary Bradberry	Ford
36.	Wally Dallenbach	Chevrolet
37.	Jeff Green	Chevrolet
38.	Morgan Shepherd	Pontiac
39.	Rusty Wallace	Ford
40.	Bobby Labonte	Pontiac
41.	Dick Trickle	Ford
42.	Geoff Bodine	Ford
43.	Bobby Hillin	Ford

POCONO 500

June 8
Pocono, Pennsylvania
Time of Race: 3 hours, 24 minutes, 33 seconds
Average Speed: 139.828 mph
Margin of Victory: 1.415 seconds

FINISH	DRIVER	CAR
1.	Jeff Gordon	Chevrolet
2.	Jeff Burton	Ford
3.	Dale Jarrett	Ford
4.	Mark Martin	Ford
5.	Jeremy Mayfield	Ford
6.	Ted Musgrave	Ford
7.	Darrell Waltrip	Chevrolet
8.	Geoff Bodine	Ford
9.	Terry Labonte	Chevrolet
10.	Dale Earnhardt	Chevrolet
11.	Derrike Cope	Pontiac
12.	Morgan Shepherd	Pontiac
13.	Michael Waltrip	Ford
14.	Kyle Petty	Pontiac
15.	Sterling Marlin	Chevrolet
16.	Ricky Craven	Chevrolet
17.	Wally Dallenbach	Chevrolet
18.	Steve Grissom	Chevrolet
19.	Jimmy Spencer	Ford
20.	Rick Mast	Ford
21.	Ricky Rudd	Ford
22.	Rusty Wallace	Ford
23.	Ken Schrader	Chevrolet
24.	Hut Stricklin	Ford
25.	Brett Bodine	Ford
26.	Dick Trickle	Ford
27.	Johnny Benson	Pontiac
28.	David Green	Chevrolet
29.	Ernie Irvan	Ford
30.	Mike Wallace	Chevrolet
31.	Bobby Labonte	Pontiac
32.	Bill Elliott	Ford
33.	Gary Bradberry	Ford
34.	Kenny Wallace	Ford
35.	Jeff Green	Chevrolet
36.	Joe Nemechek	Chevrolet
37.	Bobby Hillin	Ford
38.	Ward Burton	Pontiac
39.	Bobby Hamilton	Pontiac
40.	John Andretti	Ford
41.	Mike Skinner	Chevrolet
42.	Greg Sacks	Chevrolet

MILLER 400

June 15
Brooklyn, Michigan
Time of Race: 2 hours, 36 minutes
Average Speed: 153.338 mph
Margin of Victory: 2.964 seconds

FINISH	DRIVER	CAR
1.	Ernie Irvan	Ford
2.	Bill Elliott	Ford
3.	Mark Martin	Ford
4.	Ted Musgrave	Ford
5.	Jeff Gordon	Chevrolet
6.	Dale Jarrett	Ford
7.	Dale Earnhardt	Chevrolet
8.	Derrike Cope	Pontiac
9.	Bobby Labonte	Pontiac
10.	Johnny Benson	Pontiac
11.	Lake Speed	Ford
12.	Jeremy Mayfield	Ford
13.	Ricky Rudd	Ford
14.	Jeff Burton	Ford
15.	Jimmy Spencer	Ford
16.	Michael Waltrip	Ford
17.	Sterling Marlin	Chevrolet
18.	Ricky Craven	Chevrolet
19.	Brett Bodine	Ford
20.	Wally Dallenbach	Chevrolet
21.	Rick Wilson	Ford
22.	Hut Stricklin	Ford
23.	Dick Trickle	Ford
24.	Darrell Waltrip	Chevrolet
25.	Chad Little	Pontiac
26.	Kyle Petty	Pontiac
27.	Ken Schrader	Chevrolet
28.	David Green	Chevrolet
29.	Rusty Wallace	Ford
30.	Rick Mast	Ford
31.	Jeff Green	Chevrolet
32.	Bobby Hamilton	Pontiac
33.	Billy Standridge	Ford
34.	Dave Marcis	Chevrolet
35.	Ward Burton	Pontiac
36.	Jerry Nadeau	Pontiac
37.	John Andretti	Ford
38.	Steve Grissom	Chevrolet
39.	Terry Labonte	Chevrolet
40.	Geoff Bodine	Ford
41.	Joe Nemechek	Chevrolet
42.	Mike Skinner	Chevrolet
43.	Kenny Wallace	Ford

CALIFORNIA 500 BY NAPA

June 22
Fontana, California
Time of Race: 3 hours, 13 minutes, 31 seconds
Average Speed: 155.025 mph
Margin of Victory: 1.074 seconds

FINISH	DRIVER	CAR
1.	Jeff Gordon	Chevrolet
2.	Terry Labonte	Chevrolet
3.	Ricky Rudd	Ford
4.	Ted Musgrave	Ford
5.	Jimmy Spencer	Ford
6.	Bobby Labonte	Pontiac
7.	Jeff Green	Chevrolet
8.	Dale Jarrett	Ford
9.	Ricky Craven	Chevrolet
10.	Mark Martin	Ford
11.	Michael Waltrip	Ford
12.	Jeremy Mayfield	Ford
13.	Johnny Benson	Pontiac
14.	Rusty Wallace	Ford
15.	Darrell Waltrip	Chevrolet

16.	Dale Earnhardt	Chevrolet
17.	Steve Grissom	Chevrolet
18.	Joe Nemechek	Chevrolet
19.	Chad Little	Pontiac
20.	Lake Speed	Ford
21.	John Andretti	Ford
22.	Dick Trickle	Ford
23.	Bobby Hamilton	Pontiac
24.	Morgan Shepherd	Ford
25.	David Green	Chevrolet
26.	Brett Bodine	Ford
27.	Greg Sacks	Chevrolet
28.	Ward Burton	Pontiac
29.	Derrike Cope	Pontiac
30.	Jeff Burton	Ford
31.	Kyle Petty	Pontiac
32.	Bill Elliott	Ford
33.	Mike Skinner	Chevrolet
34.	Ken Schrader	Chevrolet
35.	Geoff Bodine	Ford
36.	Sterling Marlin	Chevrolet
37.	Ernie Irvan	Ford
38.	Jerry Nadeau	Pontiac
39.	Wally Dallenbach	Chevrolet
40.	Dave Marcis	Chevrolet
41.	Rick Mast	Ford
42.	Hut Stricklin	Ford

PEPSI 400

July 5
Daytona Beach, Florida
Time of Race: 2 hours, 32 minutes, 6 seconds
Average Speed: 157.791 mph
Margin of Victory: .029 seconds

FINISH	DRIVER	CAR
1.	John Andretti	Ford
2.	Terry Labonte	Chevrolet
3.	Sterling Marlin	Chevrolet
4.	Dale Earnhardt	Chevrolet
5.	Dale Jarrett	Ford
6.	Rusty Wallace	Ford
7.	Kyle Petty	Pontiac
8.	Jeff Burton	Ford
9.	Ernie Irvan	Ford
10.	Bobby Labonte	Pontiac
11.	Kenny Wallace	Ford
12.	Ted Musgrave	Ford
13.	Jeremy Mayfield	Ford
14.	Darrell Waltrip	Chevrolet
15.	Ken Schrader	Chevrolet
16.	Johnny Benson	Pontiac
17.	Dave Marcis	Chevrolet
18.	Rick Mast	Ford
19.	David Green	Chevrolet
20.	Bobby Hamilton	Pontiac
21.	Jeff Gordon	Chevrolet
22.	Robby Gordon	Chevrolet
23.	Brett Bodine	Ford
24.	Joe Nemechek	Chevrolet
25.	Dick Trickle	Ford
26.	Ward Burton	Pontiac
27.	Mark Martin	Ford
28.	Derrike Cope	Pontiac
29.	Lake Speed	Ford
30.	Jerry Nadeau	Pontiac
31.	Jimmy Spencer	Ford
32.	Morgan Shepherd	Ford
33.	Bill Elliott	Ford
34.	Ricky Rudd	Ford
35.	Michael Waltrip	Ford
36.	Hut Stricklin	Ford
37.	Ricky Craven	Chevrolet
38.	Steve Grissom	Chevrolet
39.	Wally Dallenbach	Chevrolet
40.	Billy Standridge	Ford
41.	Mike Skinner	Chevrolet
42.	Chad Little	Pontiac

JIFFY LUBE 300

July 13
Loudon, New Hampshire
Time of Race: 2 hours, 42 minutes, 35 seconds
Average Speed: 117.194 mph
Margin of Victory: 5.392 seconds

FINISH	DRIVER	CAR
1.	Jeff Burton	Ford
2.	Dale Earnhardt	Chevrolet
3.	Rusty Wallace	Ford
4.	Steve Grissom	Chevrolet
5.	Mark Martin	Ford
6.	Bill Elliott	Ford
7.	Terry Labonte	Chevrolet
8.	Ernie Irvan	Ford
9.	Ricky Rudd	Ford
10.	Geoff Bodine	Ford
11.	Ken Schrader	Chevrolet
12.	Jimmy Spencer	Ford
13.	Kyle Petty	Pontiac
14.	John Andretti	Ford
15.	Hut Stricklin	Ford
16.	Ricky Craven	Chevrolet
17.	Jeremy Mayfield	Ford
18.	Johnny Benson	Pontiac
19.	Kenny Wallace	Ford
20.	Derrike Cope	Pontiac
21.	Mike Skinner	Chevrolet
22.	Sterling Marlin	Chevrolet
23.	Jeff Gordon	Chevrolet
24.	David Green	Chevrolet
25.	Dick Trickle	Ford
26.	Ted Musgrave	Ford
27.	Bobby Labonte	Pontiac
28.	Rick Mast	Ford
29.	Michael Waltrip	Ford
30.	Chad Little	Pontiac
31.	Bobby Hamilton	Pontiac
32.	Jeff Green	Chevrolet
33.	Darrell Waltrip	Chevrolet
34.	Robby Gordon	Chevrolet
35.	Dave Marcis	Chevrolet
36.	Ward Burton	Pontiac
37.	Morgan Shepherd	Ford
38.	Dale Jarrett	Ford
39.	Jerry Nadeau	Pontiac
40.	Joe Nemechek	Chevrolet
41.	Randy MacDonald	Chevrolet
42.	Brett Bodine	Ford

PENNSYLVANIA 500

July 20
Pocono, Pennsylvania
Time of Race: 3 hours, 31 minutes, 10 seconds
Average Speed: 142.068 mph
Margin of Victory: 2.99 seconds

FINISH	DRIVER	CAR
1.	Dale Jarrett	Ford
2.	Jeff Gordon	Chevrolet
3.	Jeff Burton	Ford
4.	Ted Musgrave	Ford
5.	Mark Martin	Ford
6.	Mike Skinner	Chevrolet
7.	Jimmy Spencer	Ford
8.	Kyle Petty	Pontiac
9.	JeremyMayfield	Ford
10.	Bill Elliott	Ford
11.	Bobby Labonte	Pontiac
12.	Dale Earnhardt	Chevrolet
13.	Johnny Benson	Pontiac
14.	Ken Schrader	Chevrolet
15.	Ward Burton	Pontiac
16.	Derrike Cope	Pontiac

17.	Geoff Bodine	Ford
18.	Ricky Craven	Chevrolet
19.	Dick Trickle	Ford
20.	Sterling Marlin	Chevrolet
21.	Joe Nemechek	Chevrolet
22.	Michael Waltrip	Ford
23.	Hut Stricklin	Ford
24.	John Andretti	Ford
25.	Rick Mast	Ford
26.	Darrell Waltrip	Chevrolet
27.	Morgan Shepherd	Ford
28.	Chad Little	Pontiac
29.	Brett Bodine	Ford
30.	Steve Grissom	Chevrolet
31.	Jeff Green	Chevrolet
32.	Bobby Hamilton	Pontiac
33.	Jerry Nadeau	Pontiac
34.	Kenny Wallace	Ford
35.	Terry Labonte	Chevrolet
36.	Ricky Rudd	Ford
37.	Rusty Wallace	Ford
38.	Wally Dallenbach	Chevrolet
39.	David Green	Chevrolet
40.	Ernie Irvan	Ford
41.	Dave Marcis	Chevrolet
42.	Robby Gordon	Chevrolet

BRICKYARD 400

August 2
Indianapolis, Indiana
Time of Race: 3 hours, 3 minutes, 41 seconds
Average Speed: 130.828 mph
Margin of Victory: 0.18 seconds

FINISH	DRIVER	CAR
1.	Ricky Rudd	Ford
2.	Bobby Labonte	Pontiac
3.	Dale Jarrett	Ford
4.	Jeff Gordon	Chevrolet
5.	Jeremy Mayfield	Ford
6.	Mark Martin	Ford
7.	Johnny Benson	Pontiac
8.	Bill Elliott	Ford
9.	Mike Skinner	Chevrolet
10.	Ernie Irvan	Ford
11.	Ken Schrader	Chevrolet
12.	Lake Speed	Ford
13.	Kyle Petty	Pontiac
14.	Darrell Waltrip	Chevrolet
15.	Jeff Burton	Ford
16.	Ricky Craven	Chevrolet
17.	John Andretti	Ford
18.	Brett Bodine	Ford
19.	Ward Burton	Pontiac
20.	Bobby Hamilton	Pontiac
21.	Rick Wilson	Ford
22.	Ron Barfield	Ford
23.	Rick Mast	Ford
24.	Jimmy Spencer	Ford
25.	Jeff Green	Chevrolet
26.	Steve Grissom	Chevrolet
27.	Ed Berrier	Chevrolet
28.	Robby Gordon	Chevrolet
29.	Dale Earnhardt	Chevrolet
30.	Kenny Wallace	Ford
31.	Greg Sacks	Chevrolet
32.	Joe Nemechek	Chevrolet
33.	Ted Musgrave	Ford
34.	Rich Bickle	Chevrolet
35.	David Green	Chevrolet
36.	Wally Dallenbach	Chevrolet
37.	Jeff Purvis	Chevrolet
38.	Rusty Wallace	Ford
39.	Michael Waltrip	Ford
40.	Terry Labonte	Chevrolet
41.	Derrike Cope	Pontiac
42.	Chad Little	Pontiac
43.	Sterling Marlin	Chevrolet

BUD AT THE GLEN

August 10
Watkins Glen, New York
Time of Race: 2 hours, 24 minutes, 55 seconds
Average Speed: 91.294 mph
Margin of Victory: 1.35 seconds

FINISH	DRIVER	CAR
1.	Jeff Gordon	Chevrolet
2.	Geoff Bodine	Ford
3.	Rusty Wallace	Ford
4.	Robby Gordon	Chevrolet
5.	Mark Martin	Ford
6.	Ted Musgrave	Ford
7.	Bill Elliott	Ford
8.	Terry Labonte	Chevrolet
9.	Steve Grissom	Chevrolet
10.	Wally Dallenbach	Chevrolet
11.	Johnny Benson	Pontiac
12.	Joe Nemechek	Chevrolet
13.	Sterling Marlin	Chevrolet
14.	Ken Schrader	Chevrolet
15.	Jeremy Mayfield	Ford
16.	Dale Earnhardt	Chevrolet
17.	Ricky Craven	Chevrolet
18.	Darrell Waltrip	Chevrolet
19.	Mike Skinner	Chevrolet
20.	John Andretti	Ford
21.	Ernie Irvan	Ford
22.	David Green	Chevrolet
23.	Rick Mast	Ford
24.	Lance Hooper	Pontiac
25.	Michael Waltrip	Ford
26.	Kyle Petty	Pontiac
27.	Kenny Wallace	Ford
28.	Bobby Hamilton	Pontiac
29.	Jeff Burton	Ford
30.	Jeff Green	Chevrolet
31.	Dorsey Schroeder	Ford
32.	Dale Jarrett	Ford
33.	Steve Park	Chevrolet
34.	Jimmy Spencer	Ford
35.	Todd Bodine	Chevrolet
36.	Hut Stricklin	Ford
37.	Bobby Labonte	Pontiac
38.	Derrike Cope	Pontiac
39.	Brett Bodine	Ford
40.	Ricky Rudd	Ford
41.	Ward Burton	Pontiac
42.	Chad Little	Pontiac

DEVILBISS 400

August 17
Brooklyn, Michigan
Time of Race: 3 hours, 9 minutes, 9 seconds
Average Speed: 126.88 mph
Margin of Victory: 2.009 seconds

FINISH	DRIVER	CAR
1.	Mark Martin	Ford
2.	Jeff Gordon	Chevrolet
3.	Ted Musgrave	Ford
4.	Ernie Irvan	Ford
5.	Dale Jarrett	Ford
6.	Bobby Labonte	Pontiac
7.	Bill Elliott	Ford
8.	Jeff Burton	Ford
9.	Dale Earnhardt	Chevrolet
10.	Terry Labonte	Chevrolet
11.	Geoff Bodine	Ford
12.	Ricky Craven	Chevrolet
13.	Rusty Wallace	Ford
14.	Ken Schrader	Chevrolet
15.	Darrell Waltrip	Chevrolet
16.	Derrike Cope	Pontiac

17.	Robby Gordon	Chevrolet
18.	Jeff Green	Chevrolet
19.	Jimmy Spencer	Ford
20.	David Green	Chevrolet
21.	Lake Speed	Ford
22.	Michael Waltrip	Ford
23.	Kyle Petty	Pontiac
24.	Johnny Benson	Pontiac
25.	Steve Grissom	Chevrolet
26.	Bobby Hamilton	Pontiac
27.	Joe Nemechek	Chevrolet
28.	Ward Burton	Pontiac
29.	Ricky Rudd	Ford
30.	Mike Skinner	Chevrolet
31.	Brett Bodine	Ford
32.	Kenny Wallace	Ford
33.	Jeremy Mayfield	Ford
34.	Lance Hooper	Pontiac
35.	John Andretti	Ford
36.	Hut Stricklin	Ford
37.	Gary Bradberry	Ford
38.	Rick Mast	Ford
39.	Dick Trickle	Ford
40.	Morgan Shepherd	Ford
41.	Wally Dallenbach	Chevrolet
42.	Chad Little	Pontiac
43.	Sterling Marlin	Chevrolet

GOODY'S 500

August 23
Bristol, Tennessee
Time of Race: 3 hours, 19 minutes, 51 seconds
Average Speed: 80.010 mph
Margin of Victory: 0.102 seconds

FINISH	DRIVER	CAR
1.	Dale Jarrett	Ford
2.	Mark Martin	Ford
3.	Dick Trickle	Ford
4.	Jeff Burton	Ford
5.	Steve Grissom	Chevrolet
6.	Ken Schrader	Chevrolet
7.	Terry Labonte	Chevrolet
8.	Bobby Labonte	Pontiac
9.	Geoff Bodine	Ford
10.	Sterling Marlin	Chevrolet
11.	John Andretti	Ford
12.	Rusty Wallace	Ford
13.	Ricky Craven	Chevrolet
14.	Dale Earnhardt	Chevrolet
15.	Ted Musgrave	Ford
16.	Bill Elliott	Ford
17.	Ward Burton	Pontiac
18.	Johnny Benson	Pontiac
19.	Ricky Rudd	Ford
20.	Chad Little	Pontiac
21.	Jeff Green	Chevrolet
22.	Bobby Hamilton	Pontiac
23.	Hut Stricklin	Ford
24.	Lance Hooper	Pontiac
25.	Michael Waltrip	Ford
26.	Wally Dallenbach	Chevrolet
27.	Jimmy Spencer	Ford
28.	Ed Berrier	Chevrolet
29.	Lake Speed	Ford
30.	Jeremy Mayfield	Ford
31.	Brett Bodine	Ford
32.	Derrike Cope	Pontiac
33.	Rick Mast	Ford
34.	Mike Skinner	Chevrolet
35.	Jeff Gordon	Chevrolet
36.	Kyle Petty	Pontiac
37.	Gary Bradberry	Ford
38.	Joe Nemechek	Chevrolet
39.	Kenny Wallace	Ford
40.	David Green	Chevrolet
41.	Ernie Irvan	Ford
42.	Darrell Waltrip	Chevrolet

MOUNTAIN DEW SOUTHERN 500

August 31
Darlington, South Carolina
Time of Race: 4 hours, 8 minutes, 17 seconds
Average Speed: 121.149 mph
Margin of Victory: 0.144 seconds

FINISH	DRIVER	CAR
1.	Jeff Gordon	Chevrolet
2.	Jeff Burton	Ford
3.	Dale Jarrett	Ford
4.	Bill Elliott	Ford
5.	Ricky Rudd	Ford
6.	Terry Labonte	Chevrolet
7.	Bobby Labonte	Pontiac
8.	Mark Martin	Ford
9.	Michael Waltrip	Ford
10.	Ken Schrader	Chevrolet
11.	Chad Little	Pontiac
12.	Geoff Bodine	Ford
13.	Dick Trickle	Ford
14.	Derrike Cope	Pontiac
15.	Brett Bodine	Ford
16.	Jeremy Mayfield	Ford
17.	Hut Stricklin	Ford
18.	Lake Speed	Ford
19.	Johnny Benson	Pontiac
20.	Bobby Hamilton	Pontiac
21.	Steve Grissom	Chevrolet
22.	Robby Gordon	Chevrolet
23.	Joe Nemechek	Chevrolet
24.	Kenny Wallace	Ford
25.	Gary Bradberry	Ford
26.	Darrell Waltrip	Chevrolet
27.	Ward Burton	Pontiac
28.	Jimmy Spencer	Ford
29.	Ted Musgrave	Ford
30.	Dale Earnhardt	Chevrolet
31.	Ricky Craven	Chevrolet
32.	Kyle Petty	Pontiac
33.	Ernie Irvan	Ford
34.	Rick Mast	Ford
35.	Lance Hooper	Pontiac
36.	Mike Skinner	Chevrolet
37.	John Andretti	Ford
38.	Jeff Purvis	Chevrolet
39.	Jeff Green	Chevrolet
40.	Sterling Marlin	Chevrolet
41.	Wally Dallenbach	Chevrolet
42.	Todd Bodine	Chevrolet
43.	Rusty Wallace	Ford

EXIDE 400

September 6
Richmond, Virginia
Time of Race: 3 hours, 9 minutes, 44 seconds
Average Speed: 100.376 mph
Margin of Victory: 0.209 seconds

FINISH	DRIVER	CAR
1.	Jeff Gordon	Chevrolet
2.	Ernie Irvan	Ford
3.	Bobby Hamilton	Pontiac
4.	Steve Grissom	Chevrolet
5.	Ricky Craven	Chevrolet
6.	Dale Jarrett	Ford
7.	Jimmy Spencer	Ford
8.	Dale Earnhardt	Chevrolet
9.	Mark Martin	Ford
10.	Hut Stricklin	Ford
11.	Bill Elliott	Ford
12.	Kyle Petty	Pontiac
13.	Joe Nemechek	Chevrolet
14.	Jeff Burton	Ford
15.	Bobby Labonte	Pontiac

16.	Geoff Bodine	Ford
17.	John Andretti	Ford
18.	Lake Speed	Ford
19.	Johnny Benson	Pontiac
20.	Rick Mast	Ford
21.	Rusty Wallace	Ford
22.	Derrike Cope	Pontiac
23.	Dick Trickle	Ford
24.	Ward Burton	Pontiac
25.	Robby Gordon	Chevrolet
26.	Jeremy Mayfield	Ford
27.	Kenny Wallace	Ford
28.	Chad Little	Pontiac
29.	Dave Marcis	Chevrolet
30.	Ted Musgrave	Ford
31.	Wally Dallenbach	Chevrolet
32.	Darrell Waltrip	Chevrolet
33.	Brett Bodine	Ford
34.	Gary Bradberry	Ford
35.	Mike Skinner	Chevrolet
36.	Michael Waltrip	Ford
37.	Ken Schrader	Chevrolet
38.	Jeff Green	Chevrolet
39.	Sterling Marlin	Chevrolet
40.	David Green	Chevrolet
41.	Terry Labonte	Chevrolet
42.	Ricky Rudd	Ford
43.	Robert Pressley	Ford

CMT 300

September 14
Loudon, New Hampshire
Time of Race: 3 hours, 9 minutes, 44 seconds
Average Speed: 100.376 mph
Margin of Victory: 0.209 seconds

FINISH	DRIVER	CAR
1.	Jeff Gordon	Chevrolet
2.	Ernie Irvan	Ford
3.	Bobby Hamilton	Pontiac
4.	Steve Grissom	Chevrolet
5.	Ricky Craven	Chevrolet
6.	Dale Jarrett	Ford
7.	Jimmy Spencer	Ford
8.	Dale Earnhardt	Chevrolet
9.	Mark Martin	Ford
10.	Hut Stricklin	Ford
11.	Bill Elliott	Ford
12.	Kyle Petty	Pontiac
13.	Joe Nemechek	Chevrolet
14.	Jeff Burton	Ford
15.	Bobby Labonte	Pontiac
16.	Geoff Bodine	Ford
17.	John Andretti	Ford
18.	Lake Speed	Ford
19.	Johnny Benson	Pontiac
20.	Rick Mast	Ford
21.	Rusty Wallace	Ford
22.	Dick Trickle	Ford
23.	Ward Burton	Pontiac
24.	Robby Gordon	Chevrolet
25.	Jeremy Mayfield	Ford
26.	Derrike Cope	Pontiac
27.	Kenny Wallace	Ford
28.	Chad Little	Pontiac
29.	Dave Marcis	Chevrolet
30.	Ted Musgrave	Ford
31.	Wally Dallenbach	Chevrolet
32.	Darrell Waltrip	Chevrolet
33.	Brett Bodine	Ford
34.	Gary Bradberry	Ford
35.	Mike Skinner	Chevrolet
36.	Michael Waltrip	Ford
37.	Ken Schrader	Chevrolet
38.	Jeff Green	Chevrolet
39.	Sterling	Chevrolet
40.	David Green	Chevrolet
41.	Terry Labonte	Chevrolet
42.	Ricky Rudd	Ford
43.	Robert Pressley	Ford

MBNA 400

September 21
Dover, Delaware
Time of Race: 3. hours, 50 seconds
Average Speed: 142.719 mph
Margin of Victory: 10.334 seconds

FINISH	DRIVER	CAR
1.	Mark Martin	Ford
2.	Dale Earnhardt	Chevrolet
3.	Kyle Petty	Pontiac
4.	Bobby Labonte	Pontiac
5.	Dale Jarrett	Ford
6.	Ricky Rudd	Ford
7.	Jeff Gordon	Chevrolet
8.	Bill Elliott	Ford
9.	Ernie Irvan	Ford
10.	Rick Mast	Ford
11.	Jeff Burton	Ford
12.	Ken Schrader	Chevrolet
13.	Bobby Hamilton	Pontiac
14.	Geoff Bodine	Ford
15.	John Andretti	Ford
16.	Rusty Wallace	Ford
17.	Hut Stricklin	Ford
18.	Dick Trickle	Ford
19.	Mike Skinner	Chevrolet
20.	Joe Nemechek	Chevrolet
21.	Steve Grissom	Chevrolet
22.	Ward Burton	Pontiac
23.	Jeremy Mayfield	Ford
24.	Ted Musgrave	Ford
25.	David Green	Chevrolet
26.	Brett Bodine	Ford
27.	Sterling Marlin	Chevrolet
28.	Johnny Benson	Pontiac
29.	Chad Little	Pontiac
30.	Derrike Cope	Pontiac
31.	Morgan Shepherd	Pontiac
32.	Darrell Waltrip	Chevrolet
33.	Robby Gordon	Chevrolet
34.	Dave Marcis	Chevrolet
35.	Gary Bradberry	Ford
36.	Jimmy Spencer	Ford
37.	Terry Labonte	Chevrolet
38.	Kenny Wallace	Ford
39.	Robert Pressley	Ford
40.	Jeff Green	Chevrolet
41.	Ricky Craven	Chevrolet
42.	Michael Waltrip	Ford

HANES 500

September 29
Martinsville, Virginia
Time of Race: 3 hours, 35 minutes, 56 seconds
Average Speed: 73.078 mph
Margin of Victory: 0.778 seconds

FINISH	DRIVER	CAR
1.	Jeff Burton	Ford
2.	Dale Earnhardt	Chevrolet
3.	Bobby Hamilton	Pontiac
4.	Jeff Gordon	Chevrolet
5.	Bill Elliott	Ford
6.	Kenny Wallace	Ford
7.	Ward Burton	Pontiac
8.	Ricky Craven	Chevrolet
9.	Ken Schrader	Chevrolet
10.	Ernie Irvan	Ford
11.	Mark Martin	Ford
12.	Dale Jarrett	Ford
13.	Ricky Rudd	Ford
14.	Lake Speed	Ford
15.	Rusty Wallace	Ford
16.	Hut Stricklin	Ford

17.	Brett Bodine	Ford
18.	Jeremy Mayfield	Ford
19.	Johnny Benson	Pontiac
20.	David Green	Chevrolet
21.	Ted Musgrave	Ford
22.	Terry Labonte	Chevrolet
23.	Rick Mast	Ford
24.	Darrell Waltrip	Chevrolet
25.	Joe Nemechek	Chevrolet
26.	Kyle Petty	Pontiac
27.	Bobby Labonte	Pontiac
28.	Geoff Bodine	Ford
29.	John Andretti	Ford
30.	Jeff Green	Chevrolet
31.	Mike Skinner	Chevrolet
32.	Michael Waltrip	Ford
33.	Jimmy Spencer	Ford
34.	Wally Dallenbach	Chevrolet
35.	Chad Little	Pontiac
36.	Derrike Cope	Pontiac
37.	Kenny Irwin	Ford
38.	Robert Pressley	Ford
39.	Sterling Marlin	Chevrolet
40.	Steve Grissom	Chevrolet
41.	Steve Park	Chevrolet
42.	Dick Trickle	Ford

GM/UAW TEAMWORK 500

October 5
Charlotte, North Carolina
Time of Race: 3 hour, 28 minutes, 17 seconds
Average Speed: 144.323 mph
Margin of Victory: 4.142 seconds

FINISH	DRIVER	CAR
1.	Dale Jarrett	Ford
2.	Bobby Labonte	Pontiac
3.	Dale Earnhardt	Chevrolet
4.	Mark Martin	Ford
5.	Jeff Gordon	Chevrolet
6.	Jeff Burton	Ford
7.	Bill Elliott	Ford
8.	Ward Burton	Pontiac
9.	Kyle Petty	Pontiac
10.	Johnny Benson	Pontiac
11.	Terry Labonte	Ford
12.	Rusty Wallace	Ford
13.	Steve Grissom	Chevrolet
14.	Dick Trickle	Ford
15.	Ken Schrader	Chevrolet
16.	Joe Nemechek	Chevrolet
17.	Ted Musgrave	Ford
18.	Ernie Irvan	Ford
19.	Rick Wilson	Ford
20.	Sterling Marlin	Chevrolet
21.	Bobby Hamilton	Pontiac
22.	Morgan Shepherd	Pontiac
23.	Chad Little	Pontiac
24.	Michael Waltrip	Ford
25.	Ricky Craven	Chevrolet
26.	Todd Bodine	Chevrolet
27.	Jeremy Mayfield	Ford
28.	Kenny Wallace	Ford
29.	Jeff Green	Chevrolet
30.	Brett Bodine	Ford
31.	David Green	Chevrolet
32.	John Andretti	Ford
33.	Derrike Cope	Pontiac
34.	Gary Bradberry	Chevrolet
35.	Hut Stricklin	Ford
36.	Robert Pressley	Ford
37.	Wally Dallenbach	Chevrolet
38.	Lake Speed	Ford
39.	Jeff Purvis	Chevrolet
40.	Kevin Lepage	Chevrolet
41.	Ricky Rudd	Ford
42.	Jimmy Spencer	Ford
43.	Geoff Bodine	Ford

DIEHARD 500

October 12
Talladega, Alabama
Time of Race: 3 hours, 11 minutes, 36 seconds
Average Speed: 156.601 mph
Margin of Victory: .146 of a second

FINISH	DRIVER	CAR
1.	Terry Labonte	Chevrolet
2.	Bobby Labonte	Pontiac
3.	John Andretti	Ford
4.	Ken Schrader	Chevrolet
5.	Ernie Irvan	Ford
6.	Ricky Craven	Chevrolet
7.	Kyle Petty	Pontiac
8.	Geoff Bodine	Ford
9.	Rick Mast	Ford
10.	Rusty Wallace	Ford
11.	Ted Musgrave	Ford
12.	Morgan Shepherd	Pontiac
13.	Bill Elliott	Ford
14.	Jeff Burton	Ford
15.	Kenny Wallace	Ford
16.	David Green	Chevrolet
17.	Kevin Lepage	Chevrolet
18.	Derrike Cope	Pontiac
19.	Johnny Benson	Pontiac
20.	Bobby Hamilton	Pontiac
21.	Dale Jarrett	Ford
22.	Brett Bodine	Ford
23.	Dick Trickle	Ford
24.	Jimmy Spencer	Ford
25.	Dave Marcis	Chevrolet
26.	Jeremy Mayfield	Ford
27.	Robert Pressley	Ford
28.	Michael Waltrip	Ford
29.	Dale Earnhardt	Chevrolet
30.	Mark Martin	Ford
31.	Joe Nemechek	Chevrolet
32.	Steve Grissom	Chevrolet
33.	Mike Skinner	Chevrolet
34.	Ricky Rudd	Ford
35.	Jeff Gordon	Chevrolet
36.	Lake Speed	Ford
37.	Darrell Waltrip	Chevrolet
38.	Sterling Marlin	Chevrolet
39.	Greg Sacks	Chevrolet
40.	Chad Little	Pontiac
41.	Wally Dallenbach	Chevrolet
42.	Billy Standridge	Ford

AC DELCO 400

October 27
Rockingham, North Carolina
Time of Race: 3 hours, 17 minutes, 0 seconds
Average Speed: 121.730 mph
Margin of Victory: .941 second

FINISH	DRIVER	CAR
1.	Bobby Hamilton	Pontiac
2.	Dale Jarrett	Ford
3.	Ricky Craven	Chevrolet
4.	Jeff Gordon	Chevrolet
5.	Dick Trickle	Ford
6.	Mark Martin	Ford
7.	Terry Labonte	Chevrolet
8.	Dale Earnhardt	Chevrolet
9.	Sterling Marlin	Chevrolet
10.	Joe Nemechek	Chevrolet
11.	Bobby Labonte	Pontiac
12.	Bill Elliott	Ford
13.	Robert Pressley	Ford
14.	Michael Waltrip	Ford
15.	Jeremy Mayfield	Ford
16.	Chad Little	Pontiac

17.	Lake Speed	Ford
18.	Rusty Wallace	Ford
19.	Geoff Bodine	Ford
20.	Derrike Cope	Pontiac
21.	Jeff Green	Chevrolet
22.	Kyle Petty	Pontiac
23.	Mike Skinner	Chevrolet
24.	Steve Grissom	Chevrolet
25.	Hut Stricklin	Ford
26.	Ward Burton	Pontiac
27.	David Green	Chevrolet
28.	Ernie Irvan	Ford
29.	Darrell Waltrip	Chevrolet
30.	Ken Schrader	Chevrolet
31.	John Andretti	Ford
32.	Ted Musgrave	Ford
33.	Steve Park	Chevrolet
34.	Morgan Shepherd	Pontiac
35.	Wally Dallenbach	Chevrolet
36.	Johnny Benson	Pontiac
37.	Kenny Wallace	Ford
38.	Jeff Burton	Ford
39.	Greg Sacks	Chevrolet
40.	Ricky Rudd	Ford
41.	Gary Bradberry	Ford
42.	Rick Mast	Ford
43.	Jimmy Spencer	Ford

DURA LUBE 500

November 2
Phoenix, Arizona
Time of Race: 2 hours, 48 minutes, 54 seconds
Average Speed: 110.824 mph
Margin of Victory: 2.105 seconds

FINISH	DRIVER	CAR
1.	Dale Jarrett	Ford
2.	Rusty Wallace	Ford
3.	Bobby Hamilton	Pontiac
4.	Ken Schrader	Chevrolet
5.	Dale Earnhardt	Chevrolet
6.	Mark Martin	Ford
7.	Johnny Benson	Pontiac
8.	Steve Grissom	Chevrolet
9.	Kyle Petty	Pontiac
10.	Geoff Bodine	Ford
11.	Terry Labonte	Chevrolet
12.	Darrell Waltrip	Chevrolet
13.	Jeff Burton	Ford
14.	Jimmy Spencer	Ford
15.	Bill Elliott	Ford
16.	Derrike Cope	Pontiac
17.	Jeff Gordon	Chevrolet
18.	Ernie Irvan	Ford
19.	Jeremy Mayfield	Ford
20.	Kenny Irwin	Ford
21.	Greg Sacks	Chevrolet
22.	Ted Musgrave	Ford
23.	Bobby Labonte	Pontiac
24.	Joe Nemechek	Chevrolet
25.	Chad Little	Pontiac
26.	Michael Waltrip	Ford
27.	Sterling Marlin	Chevrolet
28.	Mike Skinner	Chevrolet
29.	David Green	Chevrolet
30.	Hut Stricklin	Ford
31.	Rick Mast	Ford
32.	Jeff Green	Chevrolet
33.	Brett Bodine	Ford
34.	Dave Marcis	Chevrolet
35.	Kenny Wallace	Ford
36.	Ricky Rudd	Ford
37.	Lake Speed	Ford
38.	Robert Pressley	Ford
39.	John Andretti	Ford
40.	Dick Trickle	Ford
41.	Steve Park	Chevrolet
42.	Ward Burton	Pontiac
43.	Ricky Craven	Chevrolet

NAPA 500

November 16
Atlanta, Georgia
Time of Race: 3 hours, 7 minutes, 48 seconds
Average Speed: 159.904 mph
Margin of Victory: 3.801 seconds

FINISH	DRIVER	CAR
1.	Bobby Labonte	Pontiac
2.	Dale Jarrett	Ford
3.	Mark Martin	Ford
4.	Jeff Green	Chevrolet
5.	Derrike Cope	Pontiac
6.	Kyle Petty	Pontiac
7.	Bobby Hamilton	Pontiac
8.	Joe Nemechek	Chevrolet
9.	Ward Burton	Pontiac
10.	Johnny Benson	Pontiac
11.	Sterling Marlin	Chevrolet
12.	Ernie Irvan	Ford
13.	Michael Waltrip	Ford
14.	Dick Trickle	Ford
15.	Steve Park	Chevrolet
16.	Dale Earnhardt	Chevrolet
17.	Jeff Gordon	Chevrolet
18.	Chad Little	Pontiac
19.	Jeremy Mayfield	Ford
20.	Ken Schrader	Chevrolet
21.	Terry Labonte	Chevrolet
22.	John Andretti	Ford
23.	Mike Skinner	Chevrolet
24.	Jimmy Spencer	Ford
25.	Kenny Irwin	Ford
26.	Lake Speed	Ford
27.	Morgan Shepherd	Pontiac
28.	Steve Grissom	Chevrolet
29.	Kevin Lepage	Chevrolet
30.	Kenny Wallace	Ford
31.	Ted Musgrave	Ford
32.	Rusty Wallace	Ford
33.	Geoff Bodine	Ford
34.	Jeff Burton	Ford
35.	Rick Mast	Ford
36.	Bill Elliott	Ford
37.	Ricky Rudd	Ford
38.	Wally Dallenbach	Chevrolet
39.	Ricky Craven	Chevrolet
40.	Darrell Waltrip	Chevrolet
41.	Brett Bodine	Ford
42.	Gary Bradberry	Ford
43.	Buckshot Jones	Pontiac

——————

1998

DAYTONA 500

February 15, 1998
Daytona International Speedway
Time of Race: 2 hours, 53 minutes, 42 seconds
Average Speed: 172.712 mph
Margin of Victory: under caution

FINISH	DRIVER	CAR
1.	Dale Earnhardt	Chevrolet
2.	Bobby Labonte	Pontiac
3.	Jeremy Mayfield	Ford
4.	Ken Schrader	Chevrolet
5.	Rusty Wallace	Ford
6.	Ernie Irvan	Pontiac
7.	Chad Little	Ford
8.	Mike Skinner	Chevrolet
9.	Michael Waltrip	Ford
10.	Bill Elliott	Ford

11.	Kyle Petty	Pontiac
12.	Bobby Hamilton	Chevrolet
13.	Terry Labonte	Chevrolet
14.	Ricky Craven	Chevrolet
15.	Jimmy Spencer	Ford
16.	Jeff Gordon	Chevrolet
17.	Lake Speed	Ford
18.	John Andretti	Pontiac
19.	Kenny Irwin	Ford
20	Ted Musgrave	Ford
21	Jerry Nadeau	Ford
22.	Sterling Marlin	Chevrolet
23.	Mike Wallace	Chevrolet
24.	Brett Bodine	Ford
25.	Ward Burton	Pontiac
26.	Joe Nemechek	Chevrolet
27.	Dick Trickle	Ford
28.	Steve Grissom	Chevrolet
29.	Andy Hillenburg	Chevrolet
30.	Rick Mast	Ford
31	Geoff Bodine	Ford
32.	Robert Pressley	Ford
33.	Darrell Waltrip	Chevrolet
34.	Dale Jarrett	Ford
35.	Billy Standridge	Ford
36.	Dave Marcis	Chevrolet
37.	Derrike Cope	Pontiac
38.	Mark Martin	Ford
39.	Greg Sacks	Ford
40	Jeff Burton	Ford
41	Steve Park	Chevrolet
42.	Ricky Rudd	Ford
43.	Kevin Lepage	Chevrolet

GOODWRENCH 400

February 22, 1998
North Carolina Motor Speedway
Time of Race: 3 hours, 24 minutes, 51 seconds
Average Speed: 117.065 mph
Margin of Victory: 1.281 seconds

FINISH	DRIVER	CAR
1.	Jeff Gordon	Chevrolet
2.	Rusty Wallace	Ford
3.	Mark Martin	Ford
4.	Jimmy Spencer	Ford
5.	Geoff Bodine	Ford
6.	Bill Elliott	Ford
7.	Dale Jarrett	Ford
8.	Terry Labonte	Chevrolet
9.	Bobby Hamilton	Chevrolet
10.	Ricky Craven	Chevrolet
11.	Ward Burton	Pontiac
12.	Rick Mast	Ford
13.	John Andretti	Pontiac
14.	Jeremy Mayfield	Ford
15.	Derrike Cope	Pontiac
16.	Brett Bodine	Ford
17.	Dale Earnhardt	Chevrolet
18.	Jeff Burton	Ford
19.	Ernie Irvan	Pontiac
20	Steve Grissom	Chevrolet
21	Chad Little	Ford
22.	Jeff Green	Chevrolet
23.	Ken Schrader	Chevrolet
24.	Kyle Petty	Pontiac
25.	Sterling Marlin	Chevrolet
26.	Kenny Irwin	Ford
27.	Lake Speed	Ford
28.	Jerry Nadeau	Ford
29.	Hut Stricklin	Chevrolet
30	Johnny Benson	Ford
31	Steve Park	Chevrolet
32.	Mike Skinner	Chevrolet
33.	Bobby Labonte	Pontiac
34.	Michael Waltrip	Ford
35.	Ted Musgrave	Ford
36.	Greg Sacks	Ford
37.	Dick Trickle	Ford

38.	Kenny Wallace	Ford
39.	Joe Nemechek	Chevrolet
40	Robert Pressley	Ford
41.	Darrell Waltrip	Chevrolet
42.	David Green	Chevrolet
43.	Ricky Rudd	Ford

LAS VEGAS 400

March 1
Las Vegas Motor Speedway
Time of Race: 2 hours, 44 minutes, 53 seconds
Average Speed: 146.530 mph
Margin of Victory: 1.605 seconds

FINISH	DRIVER	CAR
1.	Mark Martin	Ford
2.	Jeff Burton	Ford
3.	Rusty Wallace	Ford
4.	Johnny Benson	Ford
5.	Jeremy Mayfield	Ford
6.	Ted Musgrave	Ford
7.	Jimmy Spencer	Ford
8.	Dale Earnhardt	Chevrolet
9.	Bill Elliott	Ford
10.	Chad Little	Ford
11.	Rick Mast	Ford
12.	Ricky Rudd	Ford
13.	Geoff Bodine	Ford
14.	Michael Waltrip	Ford
15.	Terry Labonte	Chevrolet
16.	Dick Trickle	Ford
17.	Jeff Gordon	Chevrolet
18.	Ward Burton	Pontiac
19.	Bobby Labonte	Pontiac
20	Bobby Hamilton	Chevrolet
21	Ken Schrader	Chevrolet
22.	Kyle Petty	Pontiac
23.	Robert Pressley	Ford
24.	Sterling Marlin	Chevrolet
25.	Greg Sacks	Ford
26.	Brett Bodine	Ford
27.	Ricky Craven	Chevrolet
28.	Kevin Lepage	Chevrolet
29.	Mike Skinner	Chevrolet
30	Ernie Irvan	Pontiac
31	Derrike Cope	Pontiac
32.	Lake Speed	Ford
33.	Jeff Green	Chevrolet
34.	David Green	Chevrolet
35.	Darrell Waltrip	Chevrolet
36.	Kenny Irwin	Ford
37.	Joe Nemechek	Chevrolet
38.	Wally Dallenbach	Ford
39.	Steve Grissom	Chevrolet
40	Dale Jarrett	Ford
41	John Andretti	Pontiac
42.	Kenny Wallace	Ford
43.	Hut Stricklin	Chevrolet

PRIMESTAR 500

March 9
Atlanta Motor Speedway
Time of Race: 3 hours, 46 minutes, 12 seconds
Average Speed: 139.501 mph
Margin of Victory: under caution

FINISH	DRIVER	CAR
1.	Bobby Labonte	Pontiac
2.	Dale Jarrett	Ford
3.	Jeremy Mayfield	Ford
4.	Rusty Wallace	Ford
5.	Kenny Irwin	Ford

6.	Dick Trickle	Ford
7.	Kenny Wallace	Ford
8.	Jeff Burton	Ford
9.	Johnny Benson	Ford
10.	Todd Bodine	Pontiac
11.	Bill Elliott	Ford
12.	Terry Labonte	Chevrolet
13.	Dale Earnhardt	Chevrolet
14.	Kevin Lepage	Chevrolet
15.	Ernie Irvan	Pontiac
16.	Steve Grissom	Chevrolet
17.	Ken Schrader	Chevrolet
18.	Michael Waltrip	Ford
19.	Jeff Gordon	Chevrolet
20	John Andretti	Pontiac
21	Bobby Hamilton	Chevrolet
22.	Geoff Bodine	Ford
23.	Ricky Rudd	Ford
24.	Ward Burton	Pontiac
25.	Mark Martin	Ford
26.	Brett Bodine	Ford
27.	Robert Pressley	Ford
28.	Lake Speed	Ford
29.	Ted Musgrave	Ford
30	David Green	Chevrolet
31	Greg Sacks	Ford
32.	Jerry Nadeau	Ford
33.	Rick Mast	Ford
34.	Ricky Craven	Chevrolet
35.	Joe Nemechek	Chevrolet
36.	Kyle Petty	Pontiac
37.	Hut Stricklin	Chevrolet
38.	Derrike Cope	Pontiac
39.	Wally Dallenbach	Ford
40	Darrell Waltrip	Chevrolet
41	Jimmy Spencer	Ford
42.	Mike Skinner	Chevrolet
43.	Gary Bradberry	Ford

TRANSOUTH FINANCIAL 400

March 22
Darlington Raceway
Time of Race: 3 hours, 7 minutes, 56 seconds
Average Speed: 127.962 mph
Margin of Victory: 0.228 seconds

FINISH	DRIVER	CAR
1.	Dale Jarrett	Ford
2.	Jeff Gordon	Chevrolet
3.	Rusty Wallace	Ford
4.	Jeremy Mayfield	Ford
5.	Jeff Burton	Ford
6.	Terry Labonte	Chevrolet
7.	Mark Martin	Ford
8.	Johnny Benson	Ford
9.	Kenny Wallace	Ford
10.	Ted Musgrave	Ford
11.	Ward Burton	Pontiac
12.	Dale Earnhardt	Chevrolet
13.	John Andretti	Pontiac
14.	Sterling Marlin	Chevrolet
15.	Bill Elliott	Ford
16.	Michael Waltrip	Ford
17.	Chad Little	Pontiac
18.	Ken Schrader	Chevrolet
19.	Steve Grissom	Chevrolet
20	Robert Pressley	Ford
21	Jimmy Spencer	Ford
22.	Brett Bodine	Ford
23.	Bobby Labonte	Pontiac
24.	Dick Trickle	Ford
25.	Lake Speed	Ford
26.	David Green	Chevrolet
27.	Todd Bodine	Pontiac
28.	Mike Skinner	Chevrolet
29.	Kyle Petty	Pontiac
30	Darrell Waltrip	Chevrolet
31	Jerry Nadeau	Ford
32.	Jeff Green	Chevrolet

33.	Ricky Rudd	Ford
34.	Kevin Lepage	Chevrolet
35.	Bobby Hamilton	Chevrolet
36.	Ernie Irvan	Pontiac
37.	Joe Nemechek	Chevrolet
38	Randy LaJoie	Chevrolet
39.	Kenny Irwin	Ford
40	Derrike Cope	Pontiac
41	Geoff Bodine	Ford
42.	Greg Sacks	Ford
43.	Rick Mast	Ford

FOOD CITY 500

March 29
Bristol Motor Speedway
Time of Race: 3 hours, 13 minutes
Average Speed: 82.850 mph
Margin of Victory: 0.583 seconds

FINISH	DRIVER	CAR
1.	Jeff Gordon	Chevrolet
2.	Terry Labonte	Chevrolet
3.	Dale Jarrett	Ford
4.	Jeff Burton	Ford
5.	Johnny Benson	Ford
6.	Ken Schrader	Chevrolet
7.	Mark Martin	Ford
8.	Ted Musgrave	Ford
9.	Michael Waltrip	Ford
10.	Randy LaJoie	Chevrolet
11.	Brett Bodine	Ford
12.	Jeremy Mayfield	Ford
13.	Dick Trickle	Ford
14.	Jimmy Spencer	Ford
15.	Bill Elliott	Ford
16.	Steve Grissom	Chevrolet
17.	Ward Burton	Pontiac
18.	Bobby Hamilton	Chevrolet
19.	John Andretti	Pontiac
20	Ernie Irvan	Pontiac
21	David Green	Chevrolet
22.	Dale Earnhardt	Chevrolet
23.	Darrell Waltrip	Chevrolet
24.	Morgan Shepherd	Chevrolet
25.	Rick Mast	Ford
26.	Derrike Cope	Pontiac
27.	Kevin Lepage	Chevrolet
28.	Robert Pressley	Ford
29.	Todd Bodine	Pontiac
30	Ricky Rudd	Ford
31	Lake Speed	Ford
32.	Mike Skinner	Chevrolet
33.	Rusty Wallace	Ford
34.	Bobby Labonte	Pontiac
35.	Chad Little	Ford
36.	Greg Sacks	Ford
37.	Jerry Nadeau	Ford
38.	Kyle Petty	Pontiac
39.	Geoff Bodine	Ford
40	Sterling Marlin	Chevrolet
41	Hut Stricklin	Chevrolet
42.	Kenny Wallace	Ford
43.	Kenny Irwin	Ford

TEXAS 500

April 5
Texas Motor Speedway
Time of Race: 3 hours, 39 minutes
Average Speed: 136.771 mph
Margin of Victory: 0.573 seconds

FINISH	DRIVER	CAR
1.	Mark Martin	Ford
2.	Chad Little	Ford
3.	Robert Pressley	Ford
4.	Joe Nemechek	Chevrolet
5.	Johnny Benson	Ford
6.	Terry Labonte	Chevrolet
7.	Jimmy Spencer	Ford
8.	Bobby Labonte	Pontiac
9.	Michael Waltrip	Ford
10.	Steve Grissom	Chevrolet
11.	Dale Jarrett	Ford
12.	Rusty Wallace	Ford
13.	Bill Elliott	Ford
14.	Sterling Marlin	Chevrolet
15.	Ward Burton	Pontiac
16.	Brett Bodine	Ford
17.	Kyle Petty	Pontiac
18.	David Green	Chevrolet
19.	Wally Dallenbach	Ford
20.	Lake Speed	Ford
21.	Ken Schrader	Chevrolet
22.	Dick Trickle	Ford
23.	Jeremy Mayfield	Ford
24.	Gary Bradberry	Ford
25.	Randy LaJoie	Chevrolet
26.	Bobby Hamilton	Chevrolet
27.	Ricky Rudd	Ford
28.	Dave Marcis	Chevrolet
29.	Jeff Burton	Ford
30.	Ted Musgrave	Ford
31.	Jeff Gordon	Chevrolet
32.	Geoff Bodine	Ford
33.	Mike Skinner	Chevrolet
34.	Kenny Wallace	Ford
35.	Dale Earnhardt	Chevrolet
36.	Darrell Waltrip	Chevrolet.
37.	Kevin Lepage	Chevrolet
38.	Greg Sacks	Ford
39.	Kenny Irwin	Ford
40	Hut Stricklin	Chevrolet
41.	Rick Mast	Ford
42.	John Andretti	Pontiac
43.	Ernie Irvan	Pontiac

26.	Terry Labonte	Chevrolet
27.	Jerry Nadeau	Ford
28.	Ward Burton	Pontiac
29.	Mark Martin	Ford
30.	Jimmy Spencer	Ford
31	Hut Stricklin	Chevrolet
32.	Jeff Burton	Ford
33.	Rick Mast	Ford
34.	Kyle Petty	Pontiac
35.	Geoff Bodine	Ford
36.	Sterling Marlin	Chevrolet
37.	Dick Trickle	Ford
38.	Johnny Benson	Ford
39.	Todd Bodine	Pontiac
40	Darrell Waltrip	Chevrolet
41	Rich Bickle	Ford
42.	Kevin Lepage	Chevrolet
43.	David Green	Chevrolet

DIEHARD 500

April 26
Talladega Superspeedway
Time of Race: 3 hours, 3 minutes, 35 seconds
Average Speed: 163.439 mph
Margin of Victory: .167 seconds

FINISH	DRIVER	CAR
1.	Bobby Labonte	Pontiac
2.	Jimmy Spencer	Ford
3.	Dale Jarrett	Ford
4.	Terry Labonte	Chevrolet
5.	Jeff Gordon	Chevrolet
6.	Ernie Irvan	Pontiac
7.	Kenny Wallace	Ford
8.	Ward Burton	Pontiac
9.	Sterling Marlin	Chevrolet
10.	RAndy Lajoie	Chevrolet
11.	Brett Bodine	Ford
12.	Rusty Wallace	Ford
13.	Jeremy Mayfield	Ford
14.	Kevin Lepage	Chevrolet
15.	Darrell Waltrip	Chevrolet
16.	Steve Grissom	Chevrolet
17.	David Green	Chevrolet
18.	Rick Mast	Ford
19.	Dennis Setzer	Ford
20	Dick Trickle	Ford
21.	Michael Waltrip	Ford
22.	Derrike Cope	Pontiac
23.	Mark Martin	Ford
24.	Ricky Rudd	Ford
25.	Lake Speed	Ford
26.	Wally Dallenbach	Ford
27.	Dave Marcis	Chevrolet
28.	Billy Standridge	Ford
29.	Ken Schrader	Chevrolet
30	Bobby Hamilton	Chevrolet
31.	Robert Pressley	Ford
32.	Joe Nemechek	Chevrolet
33.	John Andretti	Pontiac
34.	Chad Little	Ford
35.	Morgan Shepherd	Chevrolet
36.	Dale Earnhardt	Chevrolet
37.	Jerry Nadeau	Ford
38.	Kyle Petty	Pontiac
39.	Bill Elliott	Ford
40	Kenny Irwin	Ford
41	Johnny Benson	Ford
42	Ted Musgrave	Ford
43.	Jeff Burton	Ford

GOODY'S 500

April 20
Martinsville Speedway
Time of Race: 3 hours, 43 minutes, 10 seconds
Average Speed: 70.709 mph
Margin of Victory: 6.376 seconds

FINISH	DRIVER	CAR
1.	Bobby Hamilton	Chevrolet
2.	Ted Musgrave	Ford
3.	Dale Jarrett	Ford
4.	Dale Earnhardt	Chevrolet
5.	Randy Lajoie	Chevrolet
6.	Rusty Wallace	Ford
7.	Jeremy Mayfield	Ford
8.	Jeff Gordon	Chevrolet
9.	Ernie Irvan	Pontiac
10.	Ken Schrader	Chevrolet
11.	Morgan Shepherd	Chevrolet
12.	Bill Elliott	Ford
13.	Brett Bodine	Ford
14.	Ricky Rudd	Ford
15.	Bobby Labonte	Pontiac
16.	Chad Little	Ford
17.	Jeff Green	Pontiac
18.	John Andretti	Pontiac
19.	Kenny Irwin	Ford
20.	Lake Speed	Ford
21.	Michael Waltrip	Ford
22.	Kenny Wallace	Ford
23.	Robert Pressley	Ford
24.	Joe Nemechek	Chevrolet
25.	Steve Grissom	Chevrolet

CALIFORNIA 500

May 3
California Speedway
Time of Race: 3 hours, 33 minutes, 57 seconds

Average Speed: 140.220 mph
Margin of Victory: 1.287 seconds

FINISH	DRIVER	CAR
1.	Mark Martin	Ford
2.	Jeremy Mayfield	Ford
3.	Terry Labonte	Chevrolet
4.	Jeff Gordon	Chevrolet
5.	Darrell Waltrip	Chevrolet
6.	Chad Little	Ford
7.	Geoff Bodine	Ford
8.	Johnny Benson	Ford
9.	Dale Earnhardt	Chevrolet
10.	Jeff Burton	Ford
11.	Ricky Rudd	Ford
12.	Ward Burton	Pontiac
13.	Ernie Irvan	Pontiac
14.	Sterling Marlin	Chevrolet
15.	Ken Schrader	Chevrolet
16.	Kenny Irwin	Ford
17.	Robert Pressley	Ford
18.	David Green	Chevrolet
19.	Kenny Wallace	Ford
20	Michael Waltrip	Ford
21	Jimmy Spencer	Ford
22.	Joe Nemechek	Chevrolet
23.	Gary Bradberry	Ford
24.	Morgan Shepherd	Chevrolet
25.	Rick Mast	Ford
26.	Jerry Nadeau	Ford
27.	Bobby Hamilton	Chevrolet
28.	Brett Bodine	Ford
29.	Wally Dallenbach	Pontiac
30.	Steve Grissom	Chevrolet
31.	John Andretti	Pontiac
32.	Lake Speed	Ford
33.	Ted Musgrave	Ford
34.	Rusty Wallace	Ford
35.	Mike Dillon	Chevrolet
36	Randy LaJoie	Chevrolet
37.	Dick Trickle	Ford
38.	Bobby Labonte	Pontiac
39.	Derrike Cope	Pontiac
40	Kevin Lepage	Chevrolet
41	Dale Jarrett	Ford
42.	Kyle Petty	Pontiac
43.	Bill Elliott	Ford

COCA-COLA 600

May 24
Charlotte Motor Speedway
Time of Race: 4 hours, 23 minutes, 53 seconds
Average Speed: 136.424 mph
Margin of Victory: 0.41 seconds

FINISH	DRIVER	CAR
1.	Jeff Gordon	Chevrolet
2.	Rusty Wallace	Ford
3.	Bobby Labonte	Pontiac
4.	Mark Martin	Ford
5.	Dale Jarrett	Ford
6.	Joe Nemechek	Chevrolet
7.	John Andretti	Pontiac
8.	Jeff Burton	Ford
9.	Johnny Benson	Ford
10.	Ken Schrader	Chevrolet
11.	Ernie Irvan	Pontiac
12.	Ted Musgrave	Ford
13.	Jimmy Spencer	Ford
14.	Bill Elliott	Ford
15.	Sterling Marlin	Chevrolet
16.	Robert Pressley	Ford
17.	Darrell Waltrip	Chevrolet
18.	Michael Waltrip	Ford
19.	Jeremy Mayfield	Ford
20	Bobby Hamilton	Chevrolet
21	Dick Trickle	Ford

22.	Brett Bodine	Ford
23.	Geoff Bodine	Ford
24.	Rich Bickle	Ford
25	Kenny Wallace	Ford
26.	Rick Mast	Ford85
27.	Lake Speed	Ford82
28.	Todd Bodine	Pontiac
29.	Mike Skinner	Chevrolet
30	Kyle Petty	Pontiac
31	Ricky Rudd	Ford
32.	Steve Grissom	Chevrolet
33.	Derrike Cope	Pontiac
34.	Ward Burton	Pontiac
35.	Chad Little	Ford
36.	Kevin Lepage	Chevrolet
37.	Gary Bradberry	Ford
38	Randy LaJoie	Chevrolet
39.	Dale Earnhardt	Chevrolet
40.	Jerry Nadeau	Ford
41.	Terry Labonte	Chevrolet
42	Elliott Sadler	Chevrolet
43.	David Green	Chevrolet

MBNA 400

May 31
Dover Downs International Speedway
Time of Race: 3 hour, 20 minutes, 48 seconds
Average Speed: 119.522 mph
Margin of Victory: 13.117 seconds

FINISH	DRIVER	CAR
1.	Dale Jarrett	Ford
2.	Jeff Burton	Ford
3.	Jeff Gordon	Chevrolet
4.	Bobby Labonte	Pontiac
5.	Jeremy Mayfield	Ford
6.	Ricky Rudd	Ford
7.	Mark Martin	Ford
8.	Buckshot Jones	Chevrolet
9.	Ernie Irvan	Pontiac
10.	Terry Labonte	Chevrolet
11.	Rick Mast	Ford
12.	John Andretti	Pontiac
13.	Bill Elliott	Ford
14.	Michael Waltrip	Ford
15.	Ken Schrader	Chevrolet
16.	Brett Bodine	Ford
17.	Bobby Hamilton	Chevrolet
18.	Rusty Wallace	Ford
19.	Sterling Marlin	Chevrolet
20	Darrell Waltrip	Chevrolet
21	Dick Trickle	Ford
22.	Ted Musgrave	Ford
23.	Geoff Bodine	Ford
24.	Jimmy Spencer	Ford
25.	Dale Earnhardt	Chevrolet
26.	Joe Nemechek	Chevrolet
27.	Mike Skinner	Chevrolet
28.	Kevin Lepage	Chevrolet
29.	Ward Burton	Pontiac
30.	Dave Marcis	Chevrolet
31	Rich Bickle	Ford
32.	Steve Grissom	Chevrolet
33.	Kenny Irwin	Ford
34.	Gary Bradberry	Ford
35.	Derrike Cope	Pontiac
36.	Lake Speed	Ford
37.	Chad Little	Ford
38.	David Green	Chevrolet
39.	Robert Pressley	Ford
40	Kenny Wallace	Ford
41	Johnny Benson	Ford
42.	Kyle Petty	Pontiac
43	Randy LaJoie	Chevrolet

PONTIAC EXCITEMENT 400

June 6
Richmond International Raceway
Time of Race: 3 hours, 5 minutes, 29 seconds
Average Speed: 97.044 mph
Margin of Victory: under caution

FINISH	DRIVER	CAR
1.	Terry Labonte	Chevrolet
2.	Dale Jarrett	Ford
3.	Rusty Wallace	Ford
4.	Ken Schrader	Chevrolet
5.	Mark Martin	Ford
6.	Jeremy Mayfield	Ford
7.	Jeff Burton	Ford
8.	Bobby Labonte	Pontiac
9.	Kenny Irwin	Ford
10.	Sterling Marlin	Chevrolet
11.	Ricky Rudd	Ford
12.	Joe Nemechek	Chevrolet
13.	Chad Little	Ford
14.	Jimmy Spencer	Ford
15.	Ted Musgrave	Ford
16.	Bobby Hamilton	Chevrolet
17.	Dick Trickle	Ford
18.	Johnny Benson	Ford
19.	Ward Burton	Pontiac
20	Brett Bodine	Ford
21	Dale Earnhardt	Chevrolet
22.	John Andretti	Pontiac
23.	Kenny Wallace	Ford
24.	Kyle Petty	Pontiac
25.	Bill Elliott	Ford
26.	Lake Speed	Ford
27.	Rich Bickle	Ford
28.	Geoff Bodine	Ford
29.	Ernie Irvan	Pontiac
30	Mike Skinner	Chevrolet
31	Randy LaJoie	Chevrolet
32.	Darrell Waltrip	Chevrolet
33.	Kevin Lepage	Chevrolet
34.	Derrike Cope	Pontiac
35.	Todd Bodine	Pontiac
36.	Dave Marcis	Chevrolet
37.	Jeff Gordon	Chevrolet
38.	Jerry Nadeau	Ford
39.	Steve Grissom	Chevrolet
40	Michael Waltrip	Ford1
41	Robert Pressley	Ford
42.	Jeff Green	Ford
43.	Rick Mast	Ford

MILLER LITE 400

June 14
Michigan International Speedway
Time of Race: 2 hours, 31 minutes, 14 seconds
Average Speed: 158.695 mph
Margin of Victory: 2.03 seconds

FINISH	DRIVER	CAR
1.	Mark Martin	Ford
2.	Dale Jarrett	Ford
3.	Jeff Gordon	Chevrolet
4.	Jeff Burton	Ford
5.	Jeremy Mayfield	Ford
6.	Bill Elliott	Ford
7.	Bobby Labonte	Pontiac
8.	Ward Burton	Pontiac
9.	Joe Nemechek	Chevrolet
10.	Wally Dallenbach	Chevrolet
11.	Jimmy Spencer	Ford
12.	Darrell Waltrip	Chevrolet
13.	Kenny Irwin	Ford
14.	Ernie Irvan	Pontiac
15.	Dale Earnhardt	Chevrolet

16.	Chad Little	Ford
17.	Rusty Wallace	Ford
18.	Sterling Marlin	Chevrolet
19.	Terry Labonte	Chevrolet
20	John Andretti	Pontiac
21	Michael Waltrip	Ford
22.	Johnny Benson	Ford
23.	Geoff Bodine	Ford
24.	Dick Trickle	Ford
25.	Lake Speed	Ford
26.	Ted Musgrave	Ford
27.	Rich Bickle	Ford
28.	Ken Schrader	Chevrolet
29.	Mike Skinner	Chevrolet
30	Jeff Green	Ford
31.	Rick Mast	Ford
32.	Robert Pressley	Ford
33.	Brett Bodine	Ford
34.	Gary Bradberry	Ford
35.	Jerry Nadeau	Ford
36.	Kyle Petty	Pontiac
37.	Ricky Rudd	Ford
38.	Bobby Hamilton	Chevrolet
39.	Kenny Wallace	Ford
40	Kevin Lepage	Chevrolet
41	Steve Grissom	Chevrolet
42.	Hut Stricklin	Chevrolet
43.	Morgan Shepherd	Chevrolet

POCONO 500

June 21
Pocono Raceway
Time of Race: 4 hours, 14 minutes, 40 seconds
Average Speed: 117.801 mph
Margin of Victory: .341 seconds

FINISH	DRIVER	CAR
1.	Jeremy Mayfield	Ford
2.	Jeff Gordon	Chevrolet
3.	Dale Jarrett	Ford
4.	Jeff Burton	Ford
5.	Mark Martin	Ford
6.	Darrell Waltrip	Chevrolet
7.	Wally Dallenbach	Chevrolet
8.	Dale Earnhardt	Chevrolet
9.	Sterling Marlin	Chevrolet
10.	Jimmy Spencer	Ford
11.	Kenny Irwin	Ford
12.	Terry Labonte	Chevrolet
13.	John Andretti	Pontiac
14.	Michael Waltrip	Ford
15.	Bobby Labonte	Pontiac
16.	Robert Pressley	Ford
17.	Ted Musgrave	Ford
18.	Brett Bodine	Ford
19.	Kevin Lepage	Chevrolet
20.	Bobby Hamilton	Chevrolet
21.	Jerry Nadeau	Ford
22.	Todd Bodine	Pontiac
23.	Steve Grissom	Chevrolet
24.	Ward Burton	Pontiac
25.	Lake Speed	Ford
26.	Derrike Cope	Pontiac
27.	Dick Trickle	Ford
28.	Hut Stricklin	Chevrolet
29.	Mike Skinner	Chevrolet
30.	Chad Little	Ford
31.	Kyle Petty	Pontiac
32.	Rich Bickle	Ford
33.	Jeff Green	Ford
34.	Ernie Irvan	Pontiac
35.	Joe Nemechek	Chevrolet
36.	Johnny Benson	Ford
37.	Bill Elliott	Ford
38.	Rick Mast	Ford
39.	Kenny Wallace	Ford
40.	Geoff Bodine	Ford
41.	Ricky Rudd	Ford
42.	Rusty Wallace	Ford
43.	Ken Schrader	Chevrolet

SAVE MART/KRAGEN 350

June 28
Sonoma, California
Time of Race: 3 hours, 56 minutes, 29 seconds
Average Speed: 72.387 mph
Margin of Victory: 2.748 seconds

FINISH	DRIVER	CAR
1	Jeff Gordon	Chevrolet
2.	Bobby Hamilton	Chevrolet
3.	John Andretti	Pontiac
4.	Bobby Labonte	Pontiac
5.	Rusty Wallace	Ford
6.	Mark Martin	Ford
7.	Sterling Marlin	Chevrolet
8.	Rick Mast	Ford
9.	Kenny Irwin	Ford
10.	Steve Grissom	Chevrolet
11.	Dale Earnhardt	Chevrolet
12.	Bill Elliott	Ford
13.	Darrell Waltrip	Chevrolet
14.	Ron Hornaday	Chevrolet
15.	Dale Jarrett	Ford
16.	Tom Kendall	Chevrolet
17.	Mike Skinner	Chevrolet
18.	Jeremy Mayfield	Ford
19.	Ted Musgrave	Ford
20.	Ken Schrader	Chevrolet
21.	Johnny Benson	Ford
22.	Kenny Wallace	Ford
23.	Chad Little	Ford
24.	Butch Gilliland	Ford
25.	Joe Nemechek	Chevrolet
26.	Kyle Petty	Pontiac
27.	Wally Dallenbach	Chevrolet
28.	Ricky Rudd	Ford
29.	Jimmy Spencer	Ford
30.	Robert Pressley	Ford
31.	Rich Bickle	Ford
32.	Brett Bodine	Ford
33.	Dick Trickle	Ford
34.	Michael Waltrip	Ford
35.	Geoff Bodine	Ford
36.	Ernie Irvan	Pontiac
37.	Robby Gordon	Chevrolet
38.	Derrike Cope	Pontiac
39.	Jeff Burton	Ford
40.	Ward Burton	Pontiac
41.	Tom Hubert	Ford
42.	Terry Labonte	Chevrolet
43.	Jerry Nadeau	Ford

JIFFY LUBE 300

July 12
Loudon, New Hampshire
Time of Race: 3 hours, 4 minutes, 54 seconds
Average Speed: 102.996 mph
Margin of Victory 7.439 seconds

FINISH	DRIVER	CAR
1.	Jeff Burton	Ford
2.	Mark Martin	Ford
3.	Jeff Gordon	Chevrolet
4.	Rusty Wallace	Ford
5.	Mike Skinner	Chevrolet
6.	John Andretti	Pontiac
7.	Dale Jarrett	Ford
8.	Kyle Petty	Pontiac
9.	Ken Schrader	Chevrolet
10.	Kenny Wallace	Ford
11.	Bobby Labonte	Pontiac
12.	Jeff Green	Chevrolet
13.	Darrell Waltrip	Chevrolet
14.	Terry Labonte	Chevrolet
15.	Bobby Hamilton	Chevrolet

16.	Derrike Cope	Pontiac
17.	Dick Trickle	Ford
18.	Dale Earnhardt	Chevrolet
19.	Ricky Rudd	Ford
20.	Ernie Irvan	Pontiac
21.	Johnny Benson	Ford
22.	Chad Little	Ford
23.	Ward Burton	Pontiac
24.	Michael Waltrip	Ford
25.	Jimmy Spencer	Ford
26.	Bill Elliott	Ford
27.	Jerry Nadeau	Ford
28.	Brett Bodine	Ford
29.	Ricky Craven	Chevrolet
30.	Jeremy Mayfield	Ford
31.	Andy Hillenburg	Chevrolet
32.	Rick Mast	Ford
33.	Kenny Irwin	Ford
34.	Robert Pressley	Ford
35.	Sterling Marlin	Chevrolet
36.	Joe Nemechek	Chevrolet
37.	Geoff Bodine	Ford
38.	Rich Bickle	Ford
39.	Ted Musgrave	Ford
40.	Gary Bradberry	Pontiac
41.	Lake Speed	Ford
42.	Hut Stricklin	Chevrolet
43.	Steve Grissom	Chevrolet

PENNSYLVANIA 500

July 26
Long Pond, Pennsylvania
Time of Race: 3 hours, 42 minutes, 48 seconds
Average Speed: 134.650 mph
Margin of Victory: 1.153 seconds

FINISH	DRIVER	CAR
1.	Jeff Gordon	Chevrolet
2.	Mark Martin	Ford
3.	Jeff Burton	Ford
4.	Bobby Labonte	Pontiac
5.	Dale Jarrett	Ford
6.	Rusty Wallace	Ford
7.	Dale Earnhardt	Chevrolet
8.	Ken Schrader	Chevrolet
9.	Ernie Irvan	Pontiac
10.	Michael Waltrip	Ford
11.	Sterling Marlin	Chevrolet
12.	John Andretti	Pontiac
13.	Darrell Waltrip	Chevrolet
14.	Geoff Bodine	Ford
15.	Ted Musgrave	Ford
16.	Chad Little	Ford
17.	Joe Nemechek	Chevrolet
18.	Jeremy Mayfield	Ford
19.	Jimmy Spencer	Ford
20.	Bobby Hamilton	Chevrolet
21.	Kyle Petty	Pontiac
22.	Kenny Irwin	Ford
23.	Derrike Cope	Pontiac
24.	Jeff Green	Chevrolet
25.	Wally Dallenbach	Ford
26.	Jerry Nadeau	Ford
27.	Hut Stricklin	Chevrolet
28.	Rich Bickle	Ford
29.	Dick Trickle	Ford
30.	Mike Skinner	Chevrolet
31.	Terry Labonte	Chevrolet
32.	Robert Pressley	Ford
33.	Johnny Benson	Ford
34.	Ward Burton	Pontiac
35.	Kenny Wallace	Ford
36.	Bill Elliott	Ford
37.	Rick Mast	Ford
38.	Brett Bodine	Ford
39.	Steve Grissom	Chevrolet
40.	Morgan Shepherd	Chevrolet
41.	Ricky Craven	Chevrolet
42.	Ricky Rudd	Ford
43.	Dave Marcis	Chevrolet

BRICKYARD 400

August 1
Indianapolis Motor Speedway
Time of Race: 3 hours, 9 minutes, 19 seconds
Average Speed: 126.770 mph
Margin of Victory: under caution

FINISH	DRIVER	CAR
1.	Jeff Gordon	Chevrolet
2.	Mark Martin	Ford
3.	Bobby Labonte	Pontiac
4.	Mike Skinner	Chevrolet
5.	Dale Earnhardt	Chevrolet
6.	Ernie Irvan	Pontiac
7.	John Andretti	Pontiac
8.	Rusty Wallace	Ford
9.	Terry Labonte	Chevrolet
10.	Ken Schrader	Chevrolet
11.	Sterling Marlin	Chevrolet
12.	Bill Elliott	Ford
13.	Darrell Waltrip	Chevrolet
14.	Kyle Petty	Pontiac
15.	Morgan Shepherd	Chevrolet
16.	Dale Jarrett	Ford
17.	Ricky Craven	Chevrolet
18.	Dick Trickle	Ford
19.	Ted Musgrave	Ford
20.	Bobby Hamilton	Chevrolet
21.	Michael Waltrip	Ford
22.	Rick Mast	Ford
23.	Steve Grissom	Chevrolet
24.	Joe Nemechek	Chevrolet
25.	Johnny Benson	Ford
26.	Jerry Nadeau	Ford
27	Buckshot Jones	Chevrolet
28.	Chad Little	Chevrolet
29.	Robert Pressley	Ford
30	Jeff Green	Ford
31	Ricky Rudd	Ford
32.	Jimmy Spencer	Ford
33.	Brett Bodine	Ford
34.	Ward Burton	Pontiac
35.	Steve Park	Chevrolet
36.	Jeff Burton	Chevrolet
37.	Geoff Bodine	Ford
38.	Kenny Irwin	Ford
39.	Rich Bickle	Chevrolet
40	Wally Dallenbach	Ford
41	Dave Marcis	Chevrolet
42.	Jeremy Mayfield	Ford
43.	Kenny Wallace	Ford

BUD AT THE GLEN

August 9
Watkins Glen International
Time of Race: 2 hours, 20 minutes, 3 seconds
Average Speed: 94.446 mph
Margin of Victory: 3.437 seconds

FINISH	DRIVER	CAR
1.	Jeff Gordon	Chevrolet
2.	Mark Martin	Ford
3.	Mike Skinner	Chevrolet
4.	Rusty Wallace	Ford
5.	Dale Jarrett	Ford
6.	Kyle Petty	Pontiac
7.	Sterling Marlin	Chevrolet
8.	John Andretti	Pontiac
9.	Johnny Benson	Ford
10.	Bobby Labonte	Pontiac
11.	Dale Earnhardt	Chevrolet
12.	Joe Nemechek	Chevrolet
13.	Bobby Hamilton	Chevrolet
14.	Ricky Rudd	Ford
15.	Jerry Nadeau	Ford

16.	Chad Little	Chevrolet
17	Tommy Kendall	Ford
18.	Steve Park	Chevrolet
19.	Ted Musgrave	Ford
20	Jimmy Spencer	Ford
21	Ward Burton	Pontiac
22.	Rich Bickle	Chevrolet
23.	Jeff Burton	Chevrolet
24.	Ken Schrader	Chevrolet
25.	Darrell Waltrip	Chevrolet
26.	Kenny Wallace	Ford
27.	Bill Elliott	Ford
28.	Michael Waltrip	Ford
29.	Robert Pressley	Ford
30	Rick Mast	Ford
31	Jeremy Mayfield	Ford
32.	Geoff Bodine	Ford
33.	Ernie Irvan	Pontiac
34.	Brett Bodine	Ford
35.	Ricky Craven	Chevrolet
36	Tom Hubert	Ford
37.	Kenny Irwin	Ford
38.	Steve Grissom	Chevrolet
39.	Derrike Cope	Pontiac
40.	Terry Labonte	Chevrolet
41	Dick Trickle	Ford
42.	Ron Fellows	Chevrolet
43.	Morgan Shepherd	Chevrolet

PEPSI 400

August 16
Michigan Speedway
Time of Race: 2 hours, 37 minutes, 54 seconds
Average Speed: 151.995 mph
Margin of Victory: 1.826 seconds

FINISH	DRIVER	CAR
1.	Jeff Gordon	Chevrolet
2.	Bobby Labonte	Pontiac
3.	Dale Jarrett	Ford
4.	Mark Martin	Ford
5.	Jeff Burton	Chevrolet
6.	Ernie Irvan	Pontiac
7.	Jeremy Mayfield	Ford
8.	W. Dallenbach	Chevrolet
9.	John Andretti	Pontiac
10.	Chad Little	Chevrolet
11.	Steve Park	Chevrolet
12.	Joe Nemechek	Chevrolet
13.	Ricky Rudd	Ford
14.	Ken Schrader	Chevrolet
15.	Sterling Marlin	Chevrolet
16.	Kenny Irwin	Ford
17.	Kevin Lepage	Ford
18.	Dale Earnhardt	Chevrolet
19.	Mike Skinner	Chevrolet
20.	Bobby Hamilton	Chevrolet
21.	Geoff Bodine	Ford
22.	Michael Waltrip	Ford
23.	Rusty Wallace	Ford
24.	Robert Pressley	Ford
25.	Darrell Waltrip	Chevrolet
26.	Rick Mast	Ford
27	Buckshot Jones	Chevrolet
28.	Rich Bickle	Chevrolet
29.	Kyle Petty	Pontiac
30.	Jerry Nadeau	Ford
31	Frank Kimmel	Ford
32.	Brett Bodine	Ford
33.	Steve Grissom	Chevrolet
34.	Johnny Benson	Ford
35.	Dennis Setzer	Ford
36.	Terry Labonte	Chevrolet
37.	Ward Burton	Pontiac
38.	Dick Trickle	Ford
39.	Ted Musgrave	Ford
40	Bill Elliott	Ford
41	Jeff Green	Ford
42.	Morgan Shepherd	Chevrolet
43.	Derrike Cope	Pontiac

GOODY'S 500

August 22
Bristol, Tennessee
Time of Race: 3 hours, 3 minutes, 58 seconds
Average Speed: 86.918 mph
Margin of Victory: 2.185 seconds

FINISH	DRIVER	CAR
1.	Mark Martin	Ford
2.	Jeff Burton	Ford
3.	Rusty Wallace	Ford
4.	Dale Jarrett	Ford
5.	Jeff Gordon	Chevrolet
6.	Dale Earnhardt	Chevrolet
7.	Mike Skinner	Chevrolet
8.	Jeremy Mayfield	Ford
9.	Ricky Rudd	Ford
10.	Kevin Lepage	Ford
11.	Bobby Hamilton	Chevrolet
12.	Kyle Petty	Pontiac
13.	Terry Labonte	Chevrolet
14.	Ken Schrader	Chevrolet
15.	Kenny Irwin	Ford
16.	Michael Waltrip	Ford
17.	Jeff Green	Chevrolet
18.	Rich Bickle	Ford
19.	Bill Elliott	Ford
20	Ted Musgrave	Ford
21.	Sterling Marlin	Chevrolet
22.	Ernie Irvan	Pontiac
23.	Chad Little	Ford
24.	Elliott Sadler	Chevrolet
25.	Bobby Labonte	Pontiac
26.	Brett Bodine	Ford
27.	Darrell Waltrip	Pontiac
28.	Wally Dallenbach	Chevrolet
29.	Morgan Shepherd	Chevrolet
30.	Geoff Bodine	Ford
31.	Joe Nemechek	Chevrolet
32.	Jerry Nadeau	Ford
33.	Johnny Benson	Ford
34.	Steve Park	Chevrolet
35.	Rick Mast	Ford
36.	Derrike Cope	Pontiac
37.	Ward Burton	Pontiac
38.	John Andretti	Pontiac
39.	Dennis Setzer	Ford
40.	Robert Pressley	Ford
41.	Hut Stricklin	Chevrolet
42.	Kenny Wallace	Ford
43.	Dick Trickle	Ford

CMT 300

August 30
Loudon, New Hampshire
Time of Race: 2 hours, 49 minutes, 55 seconds
Average Speed: 112.078 mph
Margin of Victory: 0.664 seconds

FINISH	DRIVER	CAR
1	Jeff Gordon	Chevrolet
2.	Mark Martin	Ford
3.	John Andretti	Pontiac
4.	Dale Jarrett	Ford
5.	Jeff Burton	Ford
6.	Kenny Wallace	Ford
7.	Bobby Labonte	Pontiac
8.	Rusty Wallace	Ford
9.	Dale Earnhardt	Chevrolet
10.	Ricky Rudd	Ford
11.	Kenny Irwin	Ford
12.	Robert Pressley	Ford
13.	Jimmy Spencer	Ford
14.	Chad Little	Ford
15.	Mike Skinner	Chevrolet

FINISH	DRIVER	CAR
16.	Kevin Lepage	Ford
17.	Sterling Marlin	Chevrolet
18.	Joe Nemechek	Chevrolet
19.	Dick Trickle	Ford
20	Jeremy Mayfield	Ford
21	Johnny Benson	Ford
22.	Rick Mast	Ford
23.	Geoff Bodine	Ford
24.	Dennis Setzer	Ford
25.	Steve Grissom	Chevrolet
26.	Morgan Shepherd	Chevrolet
27.	Michael Waltrip	Ford
28.	Ernie Irvan	Pontiac
29.	Jerry Nadeau	Ford
30	Brett Bodine	Ford
31	Ward Burton	Pontiac
32.	Darrell Waltrip	Pontiac
33.	Kyle Petty	Pontiac
34.	Bobby Hamilton	Chevrolet
35.	Dave Marcis	Chevrolet
36.	Ron Fellows	Chevrolet
37.	Bill Elliott	Ford
38.	Jeff Green	Chevrolet
39.	Terry Labonte	Chevrolet
40	Rich Bickle	Ford
41	Steve Park	Chevrolet
42.	Ken Schrader	Chevrolet
43.	Wally Dallenbach	Chevrolet

SOUTHERN 500

September 6
Darlington, South Carolina
Time of Race: 3 hours, 36 minutes, 21 seconds
Average Speed: 139.031 mph
Margin of Victory: 3.361 seconds

FINISH	DRIVER	CAR
1.	Jeff Gordon	Chevrolet
2.	Jeff Burton	Ford
3.	Dale Jarrett	Ford
4.	Dale Earnhardt	Chevrolet
5.	Jeremy Mayfield	Ford
6.	Ernie Irvan	Pontiac
7.	Rusty Wallace	Ford
8.	Sterling Marlin	Chevrolet
9.	Geoff Bodine	Ford
10.	Kenny Wallace	Ford
11.	Bill Elliott	Ford
12.	Ward Burton	Pontiac
13.	Ken Schrader	Chevrolet
14.	John Andretti	Pontiac
15.	Bobby Labonte	Pontiac
16.	Jeff Green	Chevrolet
17.	Michael Waltrip	Ford
18.	Chad Little	Ford
19.	Rich Bickle	Ford
20.	Steve Grissom	Chevrolet
21.	Johnny Benson	Ford
22.	Ricky Rudd	Ford
23.	Bobby Hamilton	Chevrolet
24.	Steve Park	Chevrolet
25.	Terry Labonte	Chevrolet
26.	Mike Skinner	Chevrolet
27.	Derrike Cope	Pontiac
28.	Kyle Petty	Pontiac
29.	Dennis Setzer	Ford
30.	Robert Pressley	Ford
31.	Wally Dallenbach	Chevrolet
32.	Jerry Nadeau	Ford
33.	Dick Trickle	Ford
34.	Jimmy Spencer	Ford
35.	Joe Nemechek	Chevrolet
36.	Rick Mast	Ford
37.	Gary Bradberry	Ford
38.	Darrell Waltrip	Pontiac
39.	Kevin Lepage	Ford
40.	Mark Martin	Ford
41.	Kenny Irwin	Ford
42.	Brett Bodine	Ford
43.	Ted Musgrave	Ford

EXIDE 400

September 12
Richmond, Virginia
Time of Race: 3 hours, 15 minutes, 41 seconds
Average Speed: 91.985 mph
Margin of Victory: .051 seconds

FINISH	DRIVER	CAR
1.	Jeff Burton	Ford
2.	Jeff Gordon	Chevrolet
3.	Mark Martin	Ford
4.	Ken Schrader	Chevrolet
5.	John Andretti	Pontiac
6.	Bobby Hamilton	Chevrolet
7.	Rusty Wallace	Ford
8.	Mike Skinner	Chevrolet
9.	Jimmy Spencer	Ford
10.	Kenny Irwin	Ford
11.	Kenny Wallace	Ford
12.	Chad Little	Ford
13.	Geoff Bodine	Ford
14.	Ernie Irvan	Pontiac
15.	Sterling Marlin	Chevrolet
16.	Dale Jarrett	Ford
17.	Steve Grissom	Chevrolet
18.	Darrell Waltrip	Pontiac
19.	Brett Bodine	Ford
20.	Jeff Green	Chevrolet
21.	Terry Labonte	Chevrolet
22.	Jeremy Mayfield	Ford
23.	Jerry Nadeau	Ford
24.	Derrike Cope	Pontiac
25.	Ted Musgrave	Chevrolet
26.	Michael Waltrip	Ford
27.	Steve Park	Chevrolet
28.	Ward Burton	Pontiac
29.	Dennis Setzer	Ford
30.	Wally Dallenbach	Chevrolet
31.	Rick Mast	Ford
32.	Todd Bodine	Chevrolet
33.	Dave Marcis	Chevrolet
34.	Ricky Rudd	Ford
35.	Bobby Labonte	Pontiac
36.	Kevin Lepage	Ford
37.	Joe Nemechek	Chevrolet
38.	Dale Earnhardt	Chevrolet
39.	Kyle Petty	Pontiac
40.	Bill Elliott	Ford
41.	Johnny Benson	Ford
42.	Dick Trickle	Ford
43.	Robert Pressley	Ford

MBNA GOLD 400

September 20
Dover, Delaware
Time of Race: 3 hours, 30 minutes, 50 seconds
Average Speed: 113.834 mph
Margin of Victory: 2.036 seconds

FINISH	DRIVER	CAR
1.	Mark Martin	Ford
2.	Jeff Gordon	Chevrolet
3.	Jeremy Mayfield	Ford
4.	Bobby Labonte	Pontiac
5.	Rusty Wallace	Ford
6.	Matt Kenseth	Ford
7.	Dale Jarrett	Ford
8.	Ernie Irvan	Pontiac
9.	John Andretti	Pontiac
10.	Bobby Hamilton	Chevrolet
11.	Steve Park	Chevrolet
12.	Kevin Lepage	Ford
13.	Ricky Rudd	Ford
14.	Geoff Bodine	Ford
15.	Johnny Benson	Ford

FINISH	DRIVER	CAR
16.	Sterling Marlin	Chevrolet
17.	Chad Little	Ford
18.	Terry Labonte	Chevrolet
19.	Rich Bickle	Ford
20.	Michael Waltrip	Ford
21.	Darrell Waltrip	Pontiac
22.	Brett Bodine	Ford
23.	Dale Earnhardt	Chevrolet
24.	Rick Mast	Ford
25.	Wally Dallenbach	Chevrolet
26.	Ted Musgrave	Ford
27.	Jimmy Spencer	Ford
28.	Gary Bradberry	Ford
29.	Joe Nemechek	Chevrolet
30.	Hut Stricklin	Ford
31	Dick Trickle	Ford
32.	Mike Skinner	Chevrolet
33.	Ward Burton	Pontiac
34.	Jeff Green	Chevrolet
35.	Derrike Cope	Pontiac
36.	Jerry Nadeau	Ford
37.	Todd Bodine	Chevrolet
38.	Jeff Burton	Ford
39.	Ken Schrader	Chevrolet
40.	Kenny Irwin	Ford
41.	Kyle Petty	Pontiac
42.	Buckshot Jones	Chevrolet
43.	Kenny Wallace	Ford

NAPA AUTOCARE 500

September 27
Martinsville, Virgina
Time of Race: 3 hours, 35 minutes, 8 seconds
Average Speed: 73.350 mph
Margin of Victory: .533 seconds

FINISH	DRIVER	CAR
1.	Ricky Rudd	Ford
2.	Jeff Gordon	Chevrolet
3.	Mark Martin	Ford
4.	Rich Bickle	Ford
5.	Jeff Burton	Ford
6.	Terry Labonte	Chevrolet
7.	Bill Elliott	Ford
8.	Ernie Irvan	Pontiac
9.	Johnny Benson	Ford
10.	Bobby Labonte	Pontiac
11.	Ward Burton	Pontiac
12.	Todd Bodine	Pontiac
13.	Ken Schrader	Chevrolet
14.	Bobby Hamilton	Chevrolet
15.	Ted Musgrave	Ford
16.	Mike Skinner	Chevrolet
17.	Kevin Lepage	Ford
18.	Sterling Marlin	Chevrolet
19.	Jimmy Spencer	Ford
20.	Michael Waltrip	Ford
21.	Darrell Waltrip	Pontiac
22.	Dale Earnhardt	Chevrolet
23.	Jeremy Mayfield	Ford
24.	Steve Park	Chevrolet
25.	Mike Bliss	Chevrolet
26.	Dave Marcis	Chevrolet
27.	Kenny Irwin	Ford
28.	Rusty Wallace	Ford
29.	Kyle Petty	Pontiac
30.	Derrike Cope	Pontiac
31.	Jeff Green	Chevrolet
32.	Wally Dallenbach	Chevrolet
33.	Dick Trickle	Ford
34.	Brett Bodine	Ford
35.	Jerry Nadeau	Ford
36.	Chad Little	Ford
37.	John Andretti	Pontiac
38.	Dennis Setzer	Ford
39.	Geoff Bodine	Ford
40.	Joe Nemechek	Chevrolet
41.	Rick Mast	Ford
42.	Dale Jarrett	Ford
43.	Kenny Wallace	Ford

UAW-GM 500

October 4
Charlotte, North Carolina
Time of Race: 4 hours, 4 minutes, 1 second
Average Speed: 123.188 mph
Margin of Victory: 1.110 seconds

FINISH	DRIVER	CAR
1.	Mark Martin	Ford
2.	Ward Burton	Pontiac
3.	Jeff Burton	Ford
4.	Bobby Hamilton	Chevrolet
5.	Jeff Gordon	Chevrolet
6.	Kevin Lepage	Ford
7.	Joe Nemechek	Chevrolet
8.	Chad Little	Ford
9.	Geoff Bodine	Ford
10.	Jimmy Spencer	Ford
11.	Bill Elliott	Ford
12.	John Andretti	Pontiac
13.	Michael Waltrip	Ford
14.	Derrike Cope	Pontiac
15.	Todd Bodine	Chevrolet
16.	Kenny Wallace	Ford
17.	Rich Bickle	Ford
18.	Kyle Petty	Pontiac
19.	Brett Bodine	Ford
20.	Kenny Irwin	Ford
21.	Mike Skinner	Chevrolet
22.	Darrell Waltrip	Pontiac
23.	Wally Dallenbach	Chevrolet
24.	Dale Jarrett	Ford
25.	Jeremy Mayfield	Ford
26.	Rusty Wallace	Ford
27.	Ted Musgrave	Ford
28.	Johnny Benson	Ford
29.	Dale Earnhardt	Chevrolet
30.	Sterling Marlin	Chevrolet
31.	Ernie Irvan	Pontiac
32.	Steve Grissom	Chevrolet
33.	Dick Trickle	Ford
34.	Rick Mast	Ford
35.	Jerry Nadeau	Ford
36.	Steve Park	Chevrolet
37.	Ricky Rudd	Ford
38.	Terry Labonte	Chevrolet
39.	Bobby Labonte	Pontiac
40.	Ken Schrader	Chevrolet
41.	Robert Pressley	Ford
42.	Gary Bradberry	Ford
43.	David Green	Chevrolet

WINSTON 500

October 11
Talladega
Time of Race: 3 hours, 8 minutes, 20 seconds
Average Speed: 159.317 mph
Margin of Victory: 0.14 seconds

FINISH	DRIVER	CAR
1.	Dale Jarrett	Ford
2.	Jeff Gordon	Chevrolet
3.	Terry Labonte	Chevrolet
4.	Jimmy Spencer	Ford
5.	Jeremy Mayfield	Ford
6.	Bobby Labonte	Pontiac
7.	Mike Skinner	Chevrolet
8.	Chad Little	Ford
9.	Michael Waltrip	Ford
10.	Jeff Burton	Ford
11.	Derrike Cope	Pontiac
12.	Dave Marcis	Chevrolet
13.	Brett Bodine	Ford
14.	Sterling Marlin	Chevrolet
15.	Bobby Hamilton	Chevrolet
16.	Buckshot Jones	Chevrolet

FINISH	DRIVER	CAR
17.	Ted Musgrave	Ford
18.	Ricky Rudd	Ford
19.	Bill Elliott	Ford
20.	Kyle Petty	Pontiac
21.	John Andretti	Pontiac
22.	Andy Hillenburg	Chevrolet
23.	Darrell Waltrip	Pontiac
24.	Ken Schrader	Chevrolet
25.	Geoff Bodine	Ford
26.	Robert Pressley	Ford
27.	Rusty Wallace	Ford
28.	Billy Standridge	Ford
29.	Joe Nemechek	Chevrolet
30.	Ward Burton	Pontiac
31.	Johnny Benson	Ford
32.	Dale Earnhardt	Chevrolet
33.	Jeff Green	Chevrolet
34.	Mark Martin	Ford
35.	Kevin Lepage	Ford
36.	Steve Grissom	Chevrolet
37.	Ernie Irvan	Pontiac
38.	Dick Trickle	Ford
39.	Wally Dallenbach	Chevrolet
40.	Kenny Wallace	Ford
41.	Steve Park	Chevrolet
42.	Jerry Nadeau	Ford
43.	Kenny Irwin	Ford

PEPSI 400

October 17
Daytona Beach, Florida
Time of Race: 2 hours, 46 minutes, 2 seconds
Average Speed: 144.549 mph
Margin of Victory: 0.176 seconds

FINISH	DRIVER	CAR
1.	Jeff Gordon	Chevrolet
2.	Bobby Labonte	Pontiac
3.	Mike Skinner	Chevrolet
4.	Jeremy Mayfield	Ford
5.	Rusty Wallace	Ford
6.	Terry Labonte,	Chevrolet
7.	Ward Burton	Pontiac
8.	Ernie Irvan	Pontiac
9.	Ken Schrader	Chevrolet
10.	Dale Earnhardt,	Chevrolet
11.	Bobby Hamilton	Chevrolet
12.	Jimmy Spencer	Ford
13.	Jeff Burton	Ford
14.	John Andretti	Pontiac
15.	Bill Elliott	Ford
16.	Mark Martin	Ford
17.	Joe Nemechek	Chevrolet
18.	Sterling Marlin	Chevrolet
19.	Jerry Nadeau	Ford
20	Chad Little	Ford
21	Dave Marcis	Chevrolet
22.	Kyle Petty	Pontiac
23.	Dale Jarrett,	Ford
24.	Andy Hillenburg,	Chevrolet
25.	Brett Bodine	Ford
26.	Johnny Benson	Ford
27.	Ricky Rudd	Ford
28.	Darrell Waltrip	Pontiac
29.	Steve Grissom	Chevrolet
30	Wally Dallenbach	Chevrolet
31	Michael Waltrip	Ford
32.	Kenny Irwin	Ford
33.	Steve Park	Chevrolet
34.	Ted Musgrave	Ford
35.	Kenny Wallace	Ford
36.	Dan Pardus	Chevrolet
37.	Jeff Green	Chevrolet
38.	Derrike Cope	Pontiac
39.	Rich Bickle,	Ford
40.	Kevin Lepage	Ford
41	Geoff Bodine	Ford
42.	Hut Stricklin	Chevrolet
43.	Billy Standridge	Ford

DURA LUBE 500

October 25
Phoenix, Arizona
Time of Race: 2 hours, 22 minutes, 30 seconds
Average Speed: 108.211 mph
Margin of Victory: under caution

FINISH	DRIVER	CAR
1.	Rusty Wallace	Ford
2.	Mark Martin	Ford
3.	Dale Earnhardt	Chevrolet
4.	Jeff Burton	Ford
5.	Ted Musgrave	Ford
6.	John Andretti	Pontiac
7.	Jeff Gordon	Chevrolet
8.	Kenny Wallace	Ford
9.	Johnny Benson	Ford
10.	Terry Labonte	Chevrolet
11.	Rich Bickle	Ford
12.	Sterling Marlin	Chevrolet
13.	Kevin Lepage	Ford
14.	Ward Burton	Pontiac
15.	Todd Bodine	Chevrolet
16.	Mike Skinner	Chevrolet
17.	Robert Pressley	Ford
18.	Joe Nemechek	Chevrolet
19.	Dick Trickle	Ford
20.	Chad Little	Ford
21.	Bobby Hamilton	Chevrolet
22.	Ken Schrader	Chevrolet
23.	Bobby Labonte	Pontiac
24.	Steve Park	Chevrolet
25.	Wally Dallenbach	Chevrolet
26.	Jimmy Spencer	Ford
27.	Ricky Rudd	Ford
28.	Jeff Green	Chevrolet
29.	Rick Mast	Ford
30.	Ricky Craven	Pontiac
31.	Darrell Waltrip	Pontiac
32.	Dale Jarrett	Ford
33.	Derrike Cope	Pontiac
34.	Geoff Bodine	Ford
35.	Mike Bliss	Chevrolet
36.	Kyle Petty	Pontiac
37.	David Green	Chevrolet
38.	Bill Elliott	Ford
39.	Jerry Nadeau	Ford
40.	Kenny Irwin	Ford
41.	Gary Bradberry	Ford
42.	Jeremy Mayfield	Ford
43.	Brett Bodine	Ford

AC DELCO 400

November 1
Rockingham, North Carolina
Time of Race: 3 hours, 6 minutes, 44 seconds
Average Speed: 128.423 mph
Margin of Victory: .520 seconds

FINISH	DRIVER	CAR
1.	Jeff Gordon	Chevrolet
2.	Dale Jarrett	Ford
3.	Rusty Wallace	Ford
4.	Mark Martin	Ford
5.	Jeff Burton	Ford
6.	Bobby Hamilton	Chevrolet
7.	Ward Burton	Pontiac
8.	Terry Labonte	Chevrolet
9.	Dale Earnhardt	Chevrolet
10.	Ricky Rudd	Ford
11.	Geoff Bodine	Ford
12.	Bill Elliott	Ford
13.	Sterling Marlin	Chevrolet
14.	Ken Schrader	Chevrolet
15.	Bobby Labonte	Pontiac

FINISH	DRIVER	CAR
16.	Kenny Wallace	Ford
17.	Joe Nemechek	Chevrolet
18.	Rich Bickle	Ford
19.	Ted Musgrave	Ford
20.	Todd Bodine	Chevrolet
21.	Mike Skinner	Chevrolet
22.	Michael Waltrip	Ford
23.	Dick Trickle	Ford
24.	Jerry Nadeau	Ford
25.	Derrike Cope	Pontiac
26.	David Green	Chevrolet
27.	Jeff Green	Chevrolet
28.	Gary Bradberry	Ford
29.	Jeremy Mayfield	Ford
30.	Jimmy Spencer	Ford
31.	Brett Bodine	Ford
32.	Darrell Waltrip	Pontiac
33.	Kenny Irwin	Ford
34.	John Andretti	Pontiac
35.	Steve Park	Chevrolet
36.	Wally Dallenbach	Chevrolet
37.	Ricky Craven	Pontiac
38.	Robert Pressley	Ford
39.	Kyle Petty	Pontiac
40.	Chad Little	Ford
41.	Johnny Benson	Ford
42.	Rick Mast	Ford
43.	Kevin Lepage	Ford

NAPA 500

November 8
Hampton, Georgia
Time of Race: 2 hours, 57 minutes, 42 seconds
Average Speed: 114.915 mph
Margin of Victory: 0.739 seconds

FINISH	DRIVER	CAR
1.	Jeff Gordon	Chevrolet
2.	Dale Jarrett	Ford
3.	Mark Martin	Ford
4.	Jeff Burton	Ford
5.	Todd Bodine	Chevrolet
6.	Bobby Hamilton	Chevrolet
7.	Ken Schrader	Chevrolet
8.	Terry Labonte	Chevrolet
9.	Mike Skinner	Chevrolet
10.	Geoff Bodine	Ford
11.	Chad Little	Ford
12.	Dick Trickle	Ford
13.	Dale Earnhardt	Chevrolet
14.	Ward Burton	Pontiac
15.	Jeremy Mayfield	Ford
16.	Kenny Irwin	Ford
17.	Steve Park	Chevrolet
18.	Kevin Lepage	Ford
19.	Ted Musgrave	Ford
20.	Rusty Wallace	Ford
21.	Jimmy Spencer	Ford
22.	Michael Waltrip	Ford
23.	Johnny Benson	Ford
24.	Ricky Rudd	Ford
25.	Ricky Craven	Pontiac
26.	Bill Elliott	Ford
27.	Dave Marcis	Chevrolet
28.	Robert Pressley	Ford
29.	Kyle Petty	Pontiac
30.	Derrike Cope	Pontiac
31.	Brett Bodine	Ford
32.	John Andretti	Pontiac
33.	Gary Bradberry	Ford
34.	Kenny Wallace	Ford
35.	Wally Dallenbach	Chevrolet
36.	Jeff Green	Chevrolet
37.	Jerry Nadeau	Ford
38.	Darrell Waltrip	Pontiac
39.	Morgan Shepherd	Chevrolet
40.	Joe Nemechek	Chevrolet
41.	David Green	Chevrolet
42.	Sterling Marlin	Chevrolet
43.	Bobby Labonte	Pontiac

1999

DAYTONA 500

February 14
Daytona Beach, Florida
Time of Race: 3 hours, 5 minutes, 42 seconds
Average Speed: 161.551 mph
Margin of Victory: 0.128 second

FINISH	DRIVER	CAR
1.	Jeff Gordon	Chevrolet
2.	Dale Earnhardt	Chevrolet
3.	Kenny Irwin	Ford
4.	Mike Skinner	Chevrolet
5.	Michael Waltrip	Chevrolet
6.	Ken Schrader	Chevrolet
7.	Kyle Petty	Pontiac
8.	Rusty Wallace	Ford
9.	Chad Little	Ford
10.	Rick Mast	Ford
11.	Jerry Nadeau	Ford
12.	Wally Dallenbach	Chevrolet
13.	Kevin Lepage	Ford
14.	Ernie Irvan	Pontiac
15.	Ted Musgrave	Ford
16.	Dave Marcis	Chevrolet
17.	Johnny Benson	Ford
18.	Derrike Cope	Pontiac
19.	Robert Pressley	Ford
20.	Jeremy Mayfield	Ford
21.	Darrell Waltrip	Ford
22.	Brett Bodine	Ford
23.	Mike Wallace	Ford
24.	Ward Burton	Pontiac
25.	Bobby Labonte	Pontiac
26.	Ricky Craven	Ford
27.	Bill Elliott	Ford
28.	Tony Stewart	Pontiac
29.	Bobby Hamilton	Chevrolet
30.	Ricky Rudd	Ford
31.	Mark Martin	Ford
32.	Sterling Marlin	Chevrolet
33.	Rich Bickle	Pontiac
34.	Steve Park	Chevrolet
35.	Jeff Burton	Ford
36.	Joe Nemechek	Chevrolet
37.	Dale Jarrett	Ford
38.	Terry Labonte	Chevrolet
39.	Geoffrey Bodine	Chevrolet
40.	Elliott Sadler	Ford
41.	Jimmy Spencer	Ford
42.	Kenny Wallace	Chevrolet
43.	John Andretti	Pontiac

DURA LUBE/BIG K 400

February 21
Rockingham, North Carolina
Time of Race: 3 hours, 18 minutes, 36 seconds
Average Speed: 120.750 mph
Margin of Victory: 1.397 seconds

FINISH	DRIVER	CAR
1.	Mark Martin	Ford
2.	Dale Jarrett	Ford
3.	Bobby Labonte	Pontiac
4.	Jeff Burton	Ford
5.	Jeremy Mayfield	Ford
6.	Mike Skinner	Chevrolet
7.	Terry Labonte	Chevrolet
8.	Geoffrey Bodine	Chevrolet
9.	Bobby Hamilton	Chevrolet
10.	Rusty Wallace	Ford

11.	Ken Schrader	Chevrolet
12.	Tony Stewart	Pontiac
13.	Kenny Wallace	Chevrolet
14.	Robert Pressley	Ford
15.	Bill Elliott	Ford
16.	Johnny Benson	Ford
17.	Wally Dallenbach	Chevrolet
18.	David Green	Chevrolet
19.	John Andretti	Pontiac
20.	Michael Waltrip	Chevrolet
21.	Chad Little	Ford
22.	Ricky Craven	Ford
23.	Kenny Irwin	Ford
24.	Joe Nemechek	Chevrolet
25.	Jimmy Spencer	Ford
26.	Steve Park	Chevrolet
27.	Darrell Waltrip	Ford
28.	Ward Burton	Pontiac
29.	Ernie Irvan	Pontiac
30.	Ricky Rudd	Ford
31.	Jerry Nadeau	Ford
32.	Morgan Shepherd	Ford
33.	Brett Bodine	Ford
34.	Dave Marcis	Chevrolet
35.	Rick Mast	Ford
36.	Steve Grissom	Chevrolet
37.	Sterling Marlin	Chevrolet
38.	Elliott Sadler	Ford
39.	Jeff Gordon	Chevrolet
40.	Ted Musgrave	Ford
41.	Dale Earnhardt	Chevrolet
42.	Kevin Lepage	Ford
43.	Kyle Petty	Pontiac

LAS VEGAS 400

March 7
Las Vegas, Nevada
Time of Race: 2 hours, 54 minutes, 43 seconds
Average Speed: 137.537 mph
Margin of Victory: 1.074 seconds

FINISH	DRIVER	CAR
1.	Jeff Burton	Ford
2.	Ward Burton	Pontiac
3.	Jeff Gordon	Chevrolet
4.	Mike Skinner	Chevrolet
5.	Bobby Labonte	Pontiac
6.	Ernie Irvan	Pontiac
7.	Dale Earnhardt	Chevrolet
8.	Terry Labonte	Chevrolet
9.	Rusty Wallace	Ford
10.	Mark Martin	Ford
11.	Dale Jarrett	Ford
12.	John Andretti	Pontiac
13.	Wally Dallenbach	Chevrolet
14.	Chad Little	Ford
15.	Sterling Marlin	Chevrolet
16.	Steve Park	Chevrolet
17.	Jeremy Mayfield	Ford
18.	Ken Schrader	Chevrolet
19.	Rick Mast	Ford
20.	Brett Bodine	Ford
21.	Kevin Lepage	Ford
22.	Michael Waltrip	Chevrolet
23.	Rich Bickle	Pontiac
24.	Bobby Hamilton	Chevrolet
25.	Darrell Waltrip	Ford
26.	Jimmy Spencer	Ford
27.	David Green	Chevrolet
28	Tom Hubert	Ford
29.	Buckshot Jones	Pontiac
30.	Stanton Barrett	Ford
31.	Jerry Nadeau	Ford
32.	Geoffrey Bodine	Chevrolet
33.	Elliott Sadler	Ford
34.	Derrike Cope	Pontiac
35.	Joe Nemechek	Chevrolet
36.	Tony Stewart	Pontiac
37.	Bill Elliott	Ford

38.	Johnny Benson	Ford
39.	Ricky Craven	Ford
40.	Kenny Wallace	Chevrolet
41.	Kenny Irwin	Ford
42.	Steve Grissom	Chevrolet
43.	Ricky Rudd	Ford

CRACKER BARREL 500

March 14
Hampton, Georgia
Time of Race: 3 hours, 29 minutes, 35 seconds
Average Speed: 143.284 mph
Margin of Victory: 2.537 seconds

FINISH	DRIVER	CAR
1.	Jeff Gordon	Chevrolet
2.	Bobby Labonte	Pontiac
3.	Mark Martin	Ford
4.	Jeff Burton	Ford
5.	Dale Jarrett	Ford
6.	Mike Skinner	Chevrolet
7.	Ernie Irvan	Pontiac
8.	Ward Burton	Pontiac
9.	Chad Little	Ford
10.	Michael Waltrip	Chevrolet
11.	Tony Stewart	Pontiac
12.	Bobby Hamilton	Chevrolet
13.	Terry Labonte	Chevrolet
14.	Joe Nemechek	Chevrolet
15.	Bill Elliott	Ford
16.	Rick Mast	Ford
17.	Jimmy Spencer	Ford
18.	Sterling Marlin	Chevrolet
19.	Kevin Lepage	Ford
20.	Darrell Waltrip	Ford
21.	David Green	Chevrolet
22.	Johnny Benson	Ford
23.	Kenny Irwin	Ford
24	Ted Musgrave	Ford
25.	Ricky Rudd	Ford
26.	Ken Schrader	Chevrolet
27.	Jerry Nadeau	Ford
28.	John Andretti	Pontiac
29.	Kenny Wallace	Chevrolet
30.	Rich Bickle	Pontiac
31.	Elliott Sadler	Ford
32.	Steve Park	Chevrolet
33.	Brett Bodine	Ford
34.	Dave Marcis	Chevrolet
35.	Rusty Wallace	Ford
36.	Jeremy Mayfield	Ford
37.	Buckshot Jones	Pontiac
38.	Geoffrey Bodine	Chevrolet
39.	Wally Dallenbach	Chevrolet
40.	Dale Earnhardt	Chevrolet
41.	Derrike Cope	Pontiac
42.	Ricky Craven	Ford
43.	Kyle Petty	Pontiac

TRANSOUTH 400

March 21
Darlington, South Carolina
Time of Race: 1 hour, 50 minutes, 49 seconds
Average Speed: 121.294 mph
Margin of Victory: under caution

FINISH	DRIVER	CAR
1.	Jeff Burton	Ford
2.	Jeremy Mayfield	Ford
3.	Jeff Gordon	Chevrolet
4.	Dale Jarrett	Ford
5.	Mark Martin	Ford
6.	Tony Stewart	Pontiac

7.	Bobby Hamilton	Chevrolet
8.	Ward Burton	Pontiac
9.	John Andretti	Pontiac
10.	Bobby Labonte	Pontiac
11.	Terry Labonte	Chevrolet
12.	Steve Park	Chevrolet
13.	Rick Mast	Ford
14.	Bill Elliott	Ford
15.	Robert Pressley	Ford
16.	Sterling Marlin	Chevrolet
17.	Geoffrey Bodine	Chevrolet
18.	Johnny Benson	Ford
19.	Joe Nemechek	Chevrolet
20.	Jimmy Spencer	Ford
21.	Michael Waltrip	Chevrolet
22.	Kevin Lepage	Ford
23.	Kenny Wallace	Chevrolet
24.	Ernie Irvan	Pontiac
25.	Dale Earnhardt	Chevrolet
26.	Dick Trickle	Ford
27.	Ricky Rudd	Ford
28.	Chad Little	Ford
29.	Ted Musgrave	Ford
30.	Brett Bodine	Ford
31.	Kyle Petty	Pontiac
32.	Mike Skinner	Chevrolet
33.	Rusty Wallace	Ford
34.	Buckshot Jones	Pontiac
35.	Kenny Irwin	Ford
36.	Elliott Sadler	Ford
37.	Ricky Craven	Ford
38.	Wally Dallenbach	Chevrolet
39.	Ed Berrier	Ford
40.	Jerry Nadeau	Ford
41.	Darrell Waltrip	Ford
42.	David Green	Chevrolet
43	Ken Schrader	Chevrolet

PRIMESTAR 500

March 28
Fort Worth, Texas
Time of Race: 3 hours, 28 minutes, 21 seconds
Average Speed: 144.276 mph
Margin of Victory: under caution

FINISH	DRIVER	CAR
1.	Terry Labonte	Chevrolet
2.	Dale Jarrett	Ford
3.	Bobby Labonte	Chevrolet
4.	Rusty Wallace	Ford
5.	Jeremy Mayfield	Ford
6.	Tony Stewart	Pontiac
7.	Jeff Burton	Ford
8.	Dale Earnhardt	Chevrolet
9.	Sterling Marlin	Chevrolet
10.	Elliott Sadler	Ford
11.	Johnny Benson	Ford
12.	Rich Bickle	Pontiac
13.	Chad Little	Ford
14.	Michael Waltrip	Chevrolet
15.	Kenny Irwin	Ford
16.	Ward Burton	Pontiac
17.	Ken Schrader	Chevrolet
18.	Brett Bodine	Ford
19.	Ricky Rudd	Ford
20.	Robert Pressley	Ford
21.	Bill Elliott	Ford
22.	Derrike Cope	Pontiac
23.	Wally Dallenbach	Chevrolet
24.	Jerry Nadeau	Ford
25.	Darrell Waltrip	Ford
26.	David Green	Chevrolet
27.	Ricky Craven	Ford
28.	Jimmy Spencer	Ford
29.	Bobby Hamilton	Chevrolet
30.	Rick Mast	Ford
31.	Ted Musgrave	Ford
32.	Steve Park	Chevrolet
33.	Joe Nemechek	Chevrolet

FINISH	DRIVER	CAR
34.	Mark Martin	Ford
35.	Buckshot Jones	Pontiac
36.	Geoffrey Bodine	Chevrolet
37.	Ernie Irvan	Pontiac
38.	John Andretti	Pontiac
39.	Kenny Wallace	Chevrolet
40.	Randy LaJoie	Ford
41.	Kevin Lepage	Ford
42.	Mike Skinner	Chevrolet
43.	Jeff Gordon	Chevrolet

FOOD CITY 500

April 11
Bristol, Tennessee
Time of Race: 2 hours, 51 minutes, 16 seconds
Average Speed: 93.363 mph
Margin of Victory: 0.223 second

FINISH	DRIVER	CAR
1.	Rusty Wallace	Ford
2.	Mark Martin	Ford
3.	Dale Jarrett	Ford
4.	John Andretti	Pontiac
5.	Jeff Burton	Ford
6.	Jeff Gordon	Chevrolet
7.	Ted Musgrave	Ford
8.	Kyle Petty	Pontiac
9.	Bobby Labonte	Pontiac
10.	Dale Earnhardt	Chevrolet
11.	Kenny Irwin	Ford
12.	Michael Waltrip	Chevrolet
13.	Terry Labonte	Chevrolet
14.	Sterling Marlin	Chevrolet
15.	Tony Stewart	Pontiac
16	Kenny Wallace	Chevrolet
17.	Jimmy Spencer	Ford
18.	Bobby Hamilton	Chevrolet
19.	Rick Mast	Ford
20.	Ken Schrader	Chevrolet
21.	Mike Skinner	Chevrolet
22	Brett Bodine	Ford
23.	Steve Park	Chevrolet
24.	Chad Little	Ford
25.	Bill Elliott	Ford
26.	Elliott Sadler	Ford
27.	Jeremy Mayfield	Ford
28.	Geoffrey Bodine	Chevrolet
29.	Johnny Benson	Ford
30.	Wally Dallenbach	Chevrolet
31.	Dick Trickle	Chevrolet
32.	Darrell Waltrip	Ford
33.	David Green	Chevrolet
34	Dave Marcis	Chevrolet
35.	Kevin Lepage	Ford
36.	Joe Nemechek	Chevrolet
37.	Bobby Labonte	Pontiac
38.	Ricky Rudd	Ford
39.	Buckshot Jones	Pontiac
40.	Robert Pressley	Ford
41.	Ricky Craven	Ford
42.	Jerry Nadeau	Ford
43.	Ernie Irvan	Pontiac

GOODY'S 500

April 18
Martinsville, Virginia
Time of Race: 3 hours, 28 minutes, 35 seconds
Average Speed: 75.653 mph
Margin of Victory: 1.066 seconds

FINISH	DRIVER	CAR
1.	John Andretti	Pontiac
2.	Jeff Burton	Ford
3.	Jeff Gordon	Chevrolet

4.	Mike Skinner	Chevrolet
5.	Mark Martin	Ford
6.	Kenny Wallace	Chevrolet
7.	Rusty Wallace	Ford
8.	Dale Jarrett	Ford
9.	Ken Schrader	Chevrolet
10.	Kyle Petty	Pontiac
11.	Rich Bickle	Pontiac
12.	Darrell Waltrip	Ford
13.	Sterling Marlin	Chevrolet
14.	Brett Bodine	Ford
15.	Terry Labonte	Chevrolet
16.	Jimmy Spencer	Ford
17.	Chad Little	Ford
18.	Wally Dallenbach	Chevrolet
19.	Dale Earnhardt	Chevrolet
20.	Tony Stewart	Pontiac
21.	Kevin Lepage	Ford
22.	Ernie Irvan	Pontiac
23.	Robert Pressley	Ford
24.	Bobby Labonte	Pontiac
25.	Steve Park	Chevrolet
26	David Green	Chevrolet
27.	Ward Burton	Pontiac
28.	Elliott Sadler	Ford
29.	Ricky Rudd	Ford
30.	Bill Elliott	Ford
31.	Dick Trickle	Chevrolet
32.	Jerry Nadeau	Ford
33.	Bobby Hamilton	Chevrolet
34.	Derrike Cope	Pontiac
35.	Johnny Benson	Ford
36.	Kenny Irwin	Ford
37.	Joe Nemechek	Chevrolet
38.	Geoffrey Bodine	Chevrolet
39	Michael Waltrip	Chevrolet
40.	Ted Musgrave	Ford
41.	Jeremy Mayfield	Ford
42.	Rick Mast	Ford
43	Ricky Craven	Ford

DIEHARD 500

April 24
Talladega, Alabama
Time of Race: 3 hours, 3 minutes, 38 seconds
Average Speed: 163.395 mph
Margin of Victory: 0.137 second

FINISH	DRIVER	CAR
1.	Dale Earnhardt	Chevrolet
2.	Dale Jarrett	Ford
3.	Mark Martin	Ford
4.	Bobby Labonte	Pontiac
5.	Tony Stewart	Pontiac
6.	Ken Schrader	Chevrolet
7.	Kenny Wallace	Chevrolet
8.	Jerry Nadeau	Ford
9.	John Andretti	Pontiac
10.	Bill Elliott	Ford
11.	Jeff Burton	Ford
12.	Kevin Lepage	Ford
13.	Kyle Petty	Pontiac
14.	Rich Bickle	Pontiac
15.	Jeremy Mayfield	Ford
16.	Jimmy Spencer	Ford
17.	Geoffrey Bodine	Chevrolet
18.	Michael Waltrip	Chevrolet
19.	Ricky Rudd	Ford
20.	Wally Dallenbach	Chevrolet
21.	Buckshot Jones	Pontiac
22.	Robert Pressley	Ford
23.	Dave Marcis	Chevrolet
24.	Rick Mast	Ford
25.	Sterling Marlin	Chevrolet
26.	Darrell Waltrip	Ford
27.	Ricky Craven	Chevrolet
28.	Ted Musgrave	Ford
29.	Elliott Sadler	Ford
30.	Johnny Benson	Chevrolet
31.	Bobby Hamilton	Chevrolet

32.	Ward Burton	Pontiac
33.	David Green	Chevrolet
34.	Joe Nemechek	Chevrolet
35.	Kenny Irwin	Ford
36.	Mike Skinner	Chevrolet
37.	Steve Park	Chevrolet
38.	Jeff Gordon	Chevrolet
39.	Terry Labonte	Chevrolet
40.	Ernie Irvan	Pontiac
41.	Rusty Wallace	Ford
42.	Chad Little	Ford
43.	Brett Bodine	Ford

CALIFORNIA 500 BY NAPA

May 2
Fontana, California
Time of Race: 3 hours, 19 minutes, 38 seconds
Average Speed: 150.276 mph
Margin of Victory: 4.492 seconds

FINISH	DRIVER	CAR
1.	Jeff Gordon	Chevrolet
2.	Jeff Burton	Ford
3.	Bobby Labonte	Pontiac
4.	Tony Stewart	Pontiac
5.	Dale Jarrett	Ford
6.	Ward Burton	Pontiac
7.	Jeremy Mayfield	Ford
8.	Wally Dallenbach	Chevrolet
9.	Terry Labonte	Chevrolet
10.	Mike Skinner	Chevrolet
11.	Rusty Wallace	Ford
12.	Dale Earnhardt	Chevrolet
13.	Kenny Irwin	Ford
14.	Ken Schrader	Chevrolet
15.	Darrell Waltrip	Ford
16.	Sterling Marlin	Chevrolet
17.	John Andretti	Pontiac
18.	Kevin Lepage	Ford
19.	Bill Elliott	Ford
20.	Jerry Nadeau	Ford
21.	Elliott Sadler	Ford
22.	Chad Little	Ford
23.	Michael Waltrip	Chevrolet
24.	Steve Park	Chevrolet
25.	David Green	Chevrolet
26.	Kyle Petty	Pontiac
27.	Kenny Wallace	Chevrolet
28.	Brett Bodine	Ford
29.	Ted Musgrave	Ford
30.	Bobby Hamilton	Chevrolet
31.	Rick Mast	Ford
32.	Rich Bickle	Pontiac
33.	Dave Marcis	Chevrolet
34	Ricky Craven	Ford
35.	Ernie Irvan	Pontiac
36.	Jimmy Spencer	Ford
37.	Geoffrey Bodine	Chevrolet
38.	Mark Martin	Ford
39.	Robert Pressley	Ford
40.	Joe Nemechek	Chevrolet
41.	Ricky Rudd	Ford
42.	Derrike Cope	Pontiac
43.	Johnny Benson	Ford

PONTIAC EXCITEMENT 400

May 15
Richmond, Virginia
Time of Race: 2 hours, 59 minutes, 49 seconds
Average Speed: 100.102 mph
Margin of Victory: 0.616 second

FINISH	DRIVER	CAR
1.	Dale Jarrett	Ford
2.	Mark Martin	Ford

3.	Bobby Labonte	Pontiac
4.	Bobby Hamilton	Chevrolet
5.	Rusty Wallace	Ford
6.	Joe Nemechek	Chevrolet
7.	Kyle Petty	Pontiac
8.	Dale Earnhardt	Chevrolet
9.	Ward Burton	Pontiac
10	Rich Bickle	Pontiac
11.	Ted Musgrave	Ford
12.	Bill Elliott	Ford
13.	Kevin Lepage	Ford
14.	Ken Schrader	Chevrolet
15.	Tony Stewart	Pontiac
16.	Rick Mast	Ford
17.	Geoffrey Bodine	Chevrolet
18.	Sterling Marlin	Chevrolet
19.	Ricky Craven	Ford
20.	Wally Dallenbach	Chevrolet
21.	Jerry Nadeau	Ford
22	Michael Waltrip	Chevrolet
23.	Elliott Sadler	Ford
24.	Jeremy Mayfield	Ford
25.	Darrell Waltrip	Ford
26.	Terry Labonte	Chevrolet
27.	Robert Pressley	Ford
28.	Johnny Benson	Ford
29.	Jimmy Spencer	Ford
30.	Mike Skinner	Chevrolet
31.	Jeff Gordon	Chevrolet
32.	Dick Trickle	Chevrolet
33.	Ernie Irvan	Pontiac
34.	Steve Park	Chevrolet
35.	Chad Little	Ford
36.	Ricky Rudd	Ford
37.	Jeff Burton	Ford
38	Brett Bodine	Ford
39.	John Andretti	Pontiac
40.	Kenny Irwin	Ford
41.	Kenny Wallace	Chevrolet
42.	Derrike Cope	Pontiac
43.	David Green	Chevrolet

COCA-COLA 600

May 30
Concord, North Carolina
Time of Race: 3 hours, 57 minutes, 50 seconds
Average Speed: 151.637 mph
Margin of Victory: .574 second

FINISH	DRIVER	CAR
1.	Jeff Burton	Ford
2.	Bobby Labonte	Pontiac
3.	Mark Martin	Ford
4.	Tony Stewart	Pontiac
5.	Dale Jarrett	Ford
6.	Dale Earnhardt	Chevrolet
7.	Ken Schrader	Chevrolet
8.	Ward Burton	Pontiac
9.	Mike Skinner	Chevrolet
10.	Jeremy Mayfield	Ford
11.	Terry Labonte	Chevrolet
12.	Kenny Wallace	Chevrolet
13.	Bobby Hamilton	Chevrolet
14.	Bill Elliott	Ford
15.	Kenny Irwin	Ford
16.	Dale Earnhardt Jr.	Chevrolet
17.	Elliott Sadler	Ford
18.	Johnny Benson	Ford
19.	John Andretti	Pontiac
20.	Jerry Nadeau	Ford
21.	Wally Dallenbach	Chevrolet
22.	Brett Bodine	Ford
23.	Ted Musgrave	Ford
24.	Chad Little	Ford
25.	Rich Bickle	Pontiac
26.	Kevin Lepage	Ford
27.	David Green	Chevrolet
28.	Ricky Rudd	Ford
29.	Buckshot Jones	Pontiac

FINISH	DRIVER	CAR
30.	Kyle Petty	Pontiac
31.	Rusty Wallace	Ford
32.	Joe Nemechek	Chevrolet
33.	Hut Stricklin	Ford
34.	Rick Mast	Ford
35.	Robert Pressley	Ford
36.	Ernie Irvan	Pontiac
37.	Michael Waltrip	Chevrolet
38.	Jimmy Spencer	Ford
39.	Jeff Gordon	Chevrolet
40.	Sterling Marlin	Chevrolet
41.	Geoffrey Bodine	Chevrolet
42.	Steve Park	Chevrolet
43.	Darrell Waltrip	Ford

MBNA PLATINUM 400

June 6
Dover, Delaware
Time of Race: 3 hours, 19 minutes, 0 seconds
Average Speed: 120.603 mph
Margin of Victory: 22.071 seconds

FINISH	DRIVER	CAR
1.	Bobby Labonte	Pontiac
2.	Jeff Gordon	Chevrolet
3.	Mark Martin	Ford
4.	Tony Stewart	Pontiac
5.	Dale Jarrett	Ford
6.	Rusty Wallace	Ford
7.	Johnny Benson	Ford
8.	Jeff Burton	Ford
9.	Jeremy Mayfield	Ford
10.	Kenny Irwin	Ford
11.	Dale Earnhardt	Chevrolet
12.	Bill Elliott	Ford
13.	John Andretti	Pontiac
14.	Ricky Rudd	Ford
15.	Geoffrey Bodine	Chevrolet
16.	Steve Park	Chevrolet
17.	Terry Labonte	Chevrolet
18.	David Green	Chevrolet
19.	Mike Skinner	Chevrolet
20.	Wally Dallenbach	Chevrolet
21.	Bobby Hamilton	Chevrolet
22.	Ward Burton	Pontiac
23.	Jimmy Spencer	Ford
24.	Ted Musgrave	Ford
25.	Joe Nemechek	Chevrolet
26.	Kevin Lepage	Ford
27.	Elliott Sadler	Ford
28.	Chad Little	Ford
29.	Sterling Marlin	Chevrolet
30.	Jerry Nadeau	Ford
31.	Ricky Craven	Ford
32.	Kyle Petty	Pontiac
33.	Rich Bickle	Pontiac
34.	Rick Mast	Ford
35.	Ernie Irvan	Pontiac
36.	Derrike Cope	Pontiac
37.	Brett Bodine	Ford
38.	Dave Marcis	Chevrolet
39.	Kenny Wallace	Chevrolet
40.	Robert Pressley	Ford
41.	Ken Schrader	Chevrolet
42.	Michael Waltrip	Chevrolet
43.	Dick Trickle	Chevrolet

KMART 400

June 13
Brooklyn, Michigan
Time of Race: 2 hours, 17 minutes, 56 seconds
Average Speed: 173.997 mph
Margin of Victory: 0.505 second

FINISH	DRIVER	CAR
1.	Dale Jarrett	Ford
2.	Jeff Gordon	Chevrolet
3.	Jeff Burton	Ford
4.	Ward Burton	Pontiac
5.	Bobby Labonte	Pontiac
6.	Steve Park	Chevrolet
7.	Ernie Irvan	Pontiac
8.	John Andretti	Pontiac
9.	Tony Stewart	Pontiac
10.	Mark Martin	Ford
11.	Kenny Irwin	Ford
12.	Rusty Wallace	Ford
13.	Ken Schrader	Chevrolet
14.	Wally Dallenbach	Chevrolet
15.	Michael Waltrip	Chevrolet
16.	Dale Earnhardt	Chevrolet
17.	Jeremy Mayfield	Ford
18.	Mike Skinner	Chevrolet
19.	Johnny Benson	Ford
20.	Geoffrey Bodine	Chevrolet
21.	Kenny Wallace	Chevrolet
22.	Sterling Marlin	Chevrolet
23.	Terry Labonte	Chevrolet
24.	Rich Bickle	Pontiac
25.	Ted Musgrave	Ford
26.	Jerry Nadeau	Ford
27.	Kyle Petty	Pontiac
28.	Chad Little	Ford
29.	Kevin Lepage	Ford
30.	Brett Bodine	Ford
31.	Bobby Hamilton	Chevrolet
32.	Derrike Cope	Pontiac
33.	Dave Blaney	Pontiac
34.	Joe Nemechek	Chevrolet
35.	David Green	Chevrolet
36.	Elliott Sadler	Ford
37.	Rick Mast	Ford
38.	Ricky Rudd	Ford
39.	Darrell Waltrip	Ford
40.	Loy Allen	Ford
41.	Bill Elliott	Ford
42.	Robert Pressley	Ford
43.	Jimmy Spencer	Ford

POCONO 500

June 20
Pocono, Pennsylvania
Time of Race: 4 hours, 12 minutes, 19 seconds
Average Speed: 118.898 mph
Margin of Victory: 0.304 second

FINISH	DRIVER	CAR
1.	Bobby Labonte	Pontiac
2.	Jeff Gordon	Chevrolet
3.	Dale Jarrett	Ford
4.	Sterling Marlin	Chevrolet
5.	Mark Martin	Ford
6.	Tony Stewart	Pontiac
7.	Dale Earnhardt	Chevrolet
8.	Ernie Irvan	Pontiac
9.	Jeremy Mayfield	Ford
10.	Bobby Hamilton	Chevrolet
11.	Ted Musgrave	Ford
12.	Rick Mast	Ford
13.	Steve Park	Chevrolet
14.	Jimmy Spencer	Ford
15.	Ricky Rudd	Ford
16.	Terry Labonte	Chevrolet
17.	Kevin Lepage	Ford
18.	Kenny Irwin	Ford
19.	Kyle Petty	Pontiac
20.	Elliott Sadler	Ford
21.	Jeff Green	Chevrolet
22.	Mike Skinner	Chevrolet
23.	Jerry Nadeau	Ford
24.	Rich Bickle	Pontiac
25.	Kenny Wallace	Chevrolet
26	Brett Bodine	Ford

FINISH	DRIVER	CAR
27.	Ken Schrader	Chevrolet
28.	John Andretti	Pontiac
29.	Ward Burton	Pontiac
30.	Johnny Benson	Ford
31.	Bill Elliott	Ford
32.	Chad Little	Ford
33.	Geoffrey Bodine	Chevrolet
34.	Darrell Waltrip	Ford
35.	Robert Pressley	Ford
36.	Jeff Burton	Ford
37.	Michael Waltrip	Chevrolet
38.	David Green	Chevrolet
39.	Wally Dallenbach	Chevrolet
40.	Dick Trickle	Chevrolet
41.	Dave Marcis	Chevrolet
42.	Joe Nemechek	Chevrolet
43.	Rusty Wallace	Ford

SAVE MART/KRAGEN 350

June 27
Sears Point, California
Time of Race: 3 hours, 6 minutes, 6 seconds
Average Speed: 70.378 mph
Margin of Victory: 0.453 second

FINISH	DRIVER	CAR
1.	Jeff Gordon	Chevrolet
2.	Mark Martin	Ford
3.	John Andretti	Pontiac
4.	Rusty Wallace	Ford
5.	Jimmy Spencer	Ford
6.	Dale Jarrett	Ford
7.	Jeremy Mayfield	Ford
8.	Kyle Petty	Pontiac
9.	Dale Earnhardt	Chevrolet
10.	Michael Waltrip	Chevrolet
11.	Bobby Hamilton	Chevrolet
12.	Darrell Waltrip	Ford
13.	Bill Elliott	Ford
14.	Kenny Wallace	Chevrolet
15.	Tony Stewart	Pontiac
16.	Chad Little	Ford
17.	Mike Skinner	Chevrolet
18.	Elliott Sadler	Ford
19.	Joe Nemechek	Chevrolet
20.	Ted Musgrave	Ford
21.	Rich Bickle	Pontiac
22.	Kenny Irwin	Ford
23.	Rick Mast	Ford
24.	Jeff Burton	Ford
25.	Sterling Marlin	Chevrolet
26.	Johnny Benson	Ford
27.	Bobby Labonte	Pontiac
28.	Geoffrey Bodine	Chevrolet
29.	Terry Labonte	Chevrolet
30.	Ernie Irvan	Pontiac
31.	Brett Bodine	Ford
32.	Kevin Lepage	Ford
33.	Tom Hubert	Pontiac
34.	Jerry Nadeau	Ford
35.	Ward Burton	Pontiac
36.	David Green	Chevrolet
37.	Derrike Cope	Pontiac
38.	Ricky Rudd	Ford
39.	Ken Schrader	Chevrolet
40.	Robert Pressley	Ford
41.	Wally Dallenbach	Chevrolet
42.	Steve Park	Chevrolet
43.	Butch Gilliland	Ford

PEPSI 400

July 3
Daytona Beach, California
Time of Race: 2 hours, 21 minutes, 50 seconds
Average Speed: 169.213 mph
Margin of Victory: under caution

FINISH	DRIVER	CAR
1.	Dale Jarrett	Ford
2.	Dale Earnhardt	Chevrolet
3.	Jeff Burton	Ford
4.	Mike Skinner	Chevrolet
5.	Bobby Labonte	Pontiac
6.	Tony Stewart	Pontiac
7.	Ward Burton	Pontiac
8.	Bobby Hamilton	Chevrolet
9.	Ernie Irvan	Pontiac
10.	Terry Labonte	Chevrolet
11.	Rusty Wallace	Ford
12.	Sterling Marlin	Chevrolet
13.	Ricky Rudd	Ford
14.	Kenny Irwin	Ford
15.	Kenny Wallace	Chevrolet
16.	Joe Nemechek	Chevrolet
17.	Mark Martin	Ford
18.	Rich Bickle	Pontiac
19.	John Andretti	Pontiac
20.	Ken Schrader	Chevrolet
21.	Jeff Gordon	Chevrolet
22.	Elliott Sadler	Ford
23.	Bill Elliott	Ford
24.	Johnny Benson	Ford
25.	Jeremy Mayfield	Ford
26.	Wally Dallenbach	Chevrolet
27.	Jimmy Spencer	Ford
28.	Geoffrey Bodine	Chevrolet
29.	Chad Little	Ford
30.	Kevin Lepage	Ford
31.	Dave Marcis	Chevrolet
32.	Rick Mast	Ford
33.	David Green	Chevrolet
34.	Brett Bodine	Ford
35.	Ted Musgrave	Ford
36.	Kyle Petty	Pontiac
37.	Jerry Nadeau	Ford
38.	Darrell Waltrip	Ford
39.	Michael Waltrip	Chevrolet
40.	Loy Allen	Ford
41.	Buckshot Jones	Pontiac
42.	Steve Park	Chevrolet
43.	Ricky Craven	Chevrolet

JIFFY LUBE 300

July 11
Loudon, New Hampshire
Time of Race: 3 hours, 6 minutes, 56 seconds
Average Speed: 101.876 mph
Margin of Victory: 1.347 seconds

FINISH	DRIVER	CAR
1.	Jeff Burton	Ford
2.	Kenny Wallace	Chevrolet
3.	Jeff Gordon	Chevrolet
4.	Dale Jarrett	Ford
5.	Bill Elliott	Ford
6.	Mark Martin	Ford
7.	Wally Dallenbach	Chevrolet
8.	Dale Earnhardt	Chevrolet
9.	Jimmy Spencer	Ford
10.	Tony Stewart	Pontiac
11.	Terry Labonte	Chevrolet
12.	Steve Park	Chevrolet
13.	Ricky Craven	Chevrolet
14.	Rich Bickle	Pontiac
15.	Ward Burton	Pontiac
16.	Bobby Hamilton	Chevrolet
17.	Johnny Benson	Ford
18	John Andretti	Pontiac
19.	Michael Waltrip	Chevrolet
20.	Elliott Sadler	Ford
21.	Ernie Irvan	Pontiac
22	Kevin Lepage	Ford
23.	Mike Skinner	Chevrolet
24.	Chad Little	Ford
25.	Ted Musgrave	Ford
26.	Kenny Irwin	Ford

27.	Ricky Rudd	Ford
28.	Jeremy Mayfield	Ford
29.	Dick Trickle	Chevrolet
30.	Rick Mast	Ford
31.	Brett Bodine	Ford
32.	Geoffrey Bodine	Chevrolet
33	Darrell Waltrip	Ford
34.	Sterling Marlin	Chevrolet
35.	Ken Schrader	Chevrolet
36.	Jerry Nadeau	Ford
37.	Joe Nemechek	Chevrolet
38.	Bobby Labonte	Pontiac
39.	Hut Stricklin	Ford
40.	Dave Blaney	Pontiac
41.	Kyle Petty	Pontiac
42.	Rusty Wallace	Ford
43.	Dale Earnhardt Jr.	Chevrolet

PENNSYLVANIA 500

July 25
Pocono, Pennsylvania
Time of Race: 4 hours, 16 minutes, 27 seconds
Average Speed: 116.982 mph
Margin of Victory: 8.653 seconds

FINISH	DRIVER	CAR
1.	Bobby Labonte	Pontiac
2.	Dale Jarrett	Ford
3.	Mark Martin	Ford
4.	Tony Stewart	Pontiac
5.	Wally Dallenbach	Chevrolet
6.	Terry Labonte	Chevrolet
7.	Rich Bickle	Pontiac
8.	Steve Park	Chevrolet
9.	Dale Earnhardt	Chevrolet
10.	Mike Skinner	Chevrolet
11.	Ernie Irvan	Pontiac
12.	Michael Waltrip	Chevrolet
13.	Geoffrey Bodine	Chevrolet
14.	Johnny Benson	Ford
15.	Hut Stricklin	Ford
16.	Kyle Petty	Pontiac
17.	Bobby Hamilton	Chevrolet
18.	Rusty Wallace	Ford
19.	Rick Mast	Ford
20.	Jimmy Spencer	Ford
21.	Elliott Spencer	Ford
22.	Chad Little	Ford
23.	Robert Pressley	Ford
24.	Kevin Lepage	Ford
25.	Darrell Waltrip	Ford
26.	Brett Bodine	Ford
27.	Ricky Rudd	Ford
28.	Sterling Marlin	Chevrolet
29.	Joe Nemechek	Chevrolet
30.	Dave Marcis	Chevrolet
31.	Stanton Barrett	Ford
32.	Jeff Gordon	Chevrolet
33.	Ted Musgrave	Ford
34.	Ken Schrader	Chevrolet
35.	Jeremy Mayfield	Ford
36.	Jeff Burton	Ford
37.	Kenny Wallace	Chevrolet
38.	Jerry Nadeau	Ford
39.	Bill Elliott	Ford
40.	Ward Burton	Pontiac
41.	David Green	Chevrolet
42.	John Andretti	Pontiac
43.	Kenny Irwin	Ford

BRICKYARD 400

August 7
Indianapolis, Indiana
Time of Race: 2 hours, 41 minutes, 55 seconds
Average Speed: 148.194 mph
Margin of Victory: 3.351 seconds

FINISH	DRIVER	CAR
1.	Dale Jarrett	Ford
2.	Bobby Labonte	Pontiac
3.	Jeff Gordon	Chevrolet
4.	Mark Martin	Ford
5.	Jeff Burton	Ford
6.	Ward Burton	Pontiac
7.	Tony Stewart	Pontiac
8.	Rusty Wallace	Ford
9.	Ricky Rudd	Ford
10.	Dale Earnhardt	Chevrolet
11.	Terry Labonte	Chevrolet
12.	Mike Skinner	Chevrolet
13.	Kenny Irwin	Ford
14.	Wally Dallenbach	Chevrolet
15.	Steve Park	Chevrolet
16.	Sterling Marlin	Chevrolet
17.	Robert Pressley	Ford
18.	Ken Schrader	Chevrolet
19.	Johnny Benson	Ford
20.	David Green	Chevrolet
21.	Elliott Sadler	Ford
22.	Joe Nemechek	Chevrolet
23.	Bill Elliott	Ford
24.	Ernie Irvan	Pontiac
25.	Geoffrey Bodine	Chevrolet
26.	Jimmy Spencer	Ford
27.	Michael Waltrip	Chevrolet
28.	Dave Blaney	Pontiac
29.	Jeremy Mayfield	Ford
30.	Kevin Lepage	Ford
31.	Jerry Nadeau	Ford
32.	Derrike Cope	Pontiac
33.	Hut Stricklin	Ford
34.	Ricky Craven	Chevrolet
35.	Ted Musgrave	Ford
36.	Rick Mast	Ford
37.	John Andretti	Pontiac
38.	Bobby Hamilton	Chevrolet
39.	Kenny Wallace	Chevrolet
40.	Dave Marcis	Chevrolet
41.	Kyle Petty	Pontiac
42.	Darrell Waltrip	Ford
43.	Chad Little	Ford

FRONTIER AT THE GLEN

August 15
Watkins Glen, New York
Time of Race: 2 hours, 30 minutes, 49 seconds
Average Speed: 87.722 mph
Margin of Victory: 0.763 second

FINISH	DRIVER	CAR
1.	Jeff Gordon	Chevrolet
2.	Ron Fellows	Chevrolet
3.	Rusty Wallace	Ford
4.	Dale Jarrett	Ford
5.	Jerry Nadeau	Ford
6.	Tony Stewart	Pontiac
7.	Wally Dallenbach Jr.	Chevrolet
8.	Kyle Petty	Pontiac
9.	Mike Skinner	Chevrolet
10.	Mark Martin	Ford
11.	Terry Labonte	Chevrolet
12.	Steve Park	Chevrolet
13.	Jeff Burton	Ford
14.	Chad Little	Ford
15.	Darrell Waltrip	Ford
16.	Jimmy Spencer	Ford
17.	Ken Schrader	Chevrolet
18.	Elliott Sadler	Ford
19.	Kenny Wallace	Chevrolet
20.	Dale Earnhardt	Chevrolet
21.	Michael Waltrip	Chevrolet
22.	Bobby Hamilton	Chevrolet
23.	Rick Mast	Ford
24.	Bobby Labonte	Pontiac
25.	Kevin Lepage	Ford
26.	Kenny Irwin	Ford

27.	Ted Musgrave	Ford
28.	Bill Elliott	Ford
29.	John Andretti	Pontiac
30.	Joe Nemechek	Chevrolet
31.	Ted Christopher	Chevrolet
32.	Ricky Rudd	Ford
33.	Sterling Marlin	Chevrolet
34	Jeremy Mayfield	Ford
35.	Geoffrey Bodine	Chevrolet
36.	Rich Bickle	Pontiac
37.	David Green	Chevrolet
38.	Johnny Benson	Ford
39.	Dave Marcis	Chevrolet
40.	Brett Bodine	Ford
41.	Ernie Irvan	Pontiac
42.	Boris Said	Pontiac
43.	Ward Burton	Pontiac

PEPSI 400 BY MEIJER

August 22
Brooklyn, Michigan
Time of Race: 2 hours, 46 minutes, 17 seconds
Average Speed: 144.332 mph
Margin of Victory: 0.865 second

FINISH	DRIVER	CAR
1.	Bobby Labonte	Pontiac
2.	Jeff Gordon	Chevrolet
3.	Tony Stewart	Pontiac
4.	Dale Jarrett	Ford
5.	Dale Earnhardt	Chevrolet
6.	Chad Little	Ford
7.	Mark Martin	Ford
8.	Jimmy Spencer	Ford
9.	Hut Stricklin	Ford
10.	John Andretti	Pontiac
11.	Elliott Sadler	Ford
12.	Rick Mast	Ford
13.	Michael Waltrip	Chevrolet
14.	Matt Kenseth	Ford
15.	Sterling Marlin	Chevrolet
16.	Rusty Wallace	Ford
17.	Geoffrey Bodine	Chevrolet
18.	Jeremy Mayfield	Ford
19.	Bill Elliott	Ford
20.	Steve Park	Chevrolet
21.	Johnny Benson	Ford
22.	Joe Nemechek	Chevrolet
23.	Wally Dallenbach Jr.	Chevrolet
24.	Dale Earnhardt Jr.	Chevrolet
25.	Ken Schrader	Chevrolet
26.	Terry Labonte	Chevrolet
27.	Kenny Wallace	Chevrolet
28.	Rich Bickle	Pontiac
29.	Jerry Nadeau	Ford
30.	Ricky Craven	Chevrolet
31.	Kyle Petty	Pontiac
32.	David Green	Chevrolet
33.	Dave Marcis	Chevrolet
34.	Kenny Irwin	Ford
35.	Bobby Hamilton	Chevrolet
36.	Mike Skinner	Chevrolet
37.	Jeff Burton	Ford
38.	Ricky Rudd	Ford
39.	Kevin Lepage	Ford
40.	Dick Trickle	Pontiac
41.	Ted Musgrave	Ford
42.	Robert Pressley	Ford
43.	Ward Burton	Pontiac

GOODY'S POWDER 500

August 28
Bristol, Tennessee
Time of Race: 2 hours, 55 minutes, 11 seconds
Average Speed: 91.276 mph
Margin of Victory: 0.189 second

FINISH	DRIVER	CAR
1.	Dale Earnhardt	Chevrolet
2.	Jimmy Spencer	Ford
3.	Ricky Rudd	Ford
4.	Jeff Gordon	Chevrolet
5.	Tony Stewart	Pontiac
6.	Mark Martin	Ford
7.	Sterling Marlin	Chevrolet
8.	Terry Labonte	Chevrolet
9.	Ward Burton	Pontiac
10.	Ken Schrader	Chevrolet
11.	Kenny Wallace	Chevrolet
12.	Brett Bodine	Ford
13.	Geoffrey Bodine	Chevrolet
14.	Darrell Waltrip	Ford
15.	Todd Bodine	Pontiac
16.	Ted Musgrave	Ford
17.	Jeff Burton	Ford
18.	Rusty Wallace	Ford
19.	Joe Nemechek	Chevrolet
20.	Jerry Nadeau	Pontiac
21.	Rick Mast	Ford
22.	Kevin Lepage	Ford
23.	Mike Skinner	Chevrolet
24.	Kenny Irwin	Ford
25.	David Green	Chevrolet
26.	Bobby Labonte	Pontiac
27.	Hut Stricklin	Ford
28.	Wally Dallenbach Jr.	Chevrolet
29.	Kyle Petty	Pontiac
30.	Chad Little	Ford
31.	Steve Park	Chevrolet
32.	Jeremy Mayfield	Ford
33.	Johnny Benson	Ford
34.	Dave Marcis	Chevrolet
35.	Elliott Sadler	Ford
36.	Bill Elliott	Ford
37.	Michael Waltrip	Chevrolet
38.	Dale Jarrett	Ford
39.	Steve Grissom	Ford
40.	John Andretti	Pontiac
41.	Bobby Hamilton	Chevrolet
42.	Ricky Craven	Chevrolet
43.	Robert Pressley	Ford

PEPSI SOUTHERN 500

September 5
Darlington, South Carolina
Time of Race: 3 hours, 25 minutes, 15 seconds
Average Speed: 107.816 mph
Margin of Victory: under caution

FINISH	DRIVER	CAR
1.	Jeff Burton	Ford
2.	Ward Burton	Pontiac
3.	Jeremy Mayfield	Ford
4.	Mark Martin	Ford
5.	Kevin Lepage	Ford
6.	Joe Nemechek	Chevrolet
7.	Bobby Hamilton	Chevrolet
8.	Rusty Wallace	Ford
9	Ken Schrader	Chevrolet
10.	Steve Park	Chevrolet
11.	Bill Elliott	Ford
12.	Tony Stewart	Pontiac
13.	Jeff Gordon	Chevrolet
14.	Elliott Sadler	Ford
15.	Jimmy Spencer	Ford
16.	Dale Jarrett	Ford
17.	Terry Labonte	Chevrolet
18.	John Andretti	Pontiac
19.	Bobby Labonte	Pontiac
20.	Chad Little	Ford
21.	Wally Dallenbach Jr.	Chevrolet
22.	Dale Earnhardt	Chevrolet
23.	Rich Bickle	Pontiac
24.	Geoffrey Bodine	Chevrolet
25.	Robert Pressley	Ford
26.	Brett Bodine	Ford

FINISH	DRIVER	CAR
27.	Hut Stricklin	Ford
28.	Kyle Petty	Pontiac
29.	Darrell Waltrip	Ford
30.	Rick Mast	Ford
31.	Kenny Irwin	Ford
32.	Johnny Benson	Ford
33.	Dave Marcis	Chevrolet
34	Ricky Rudd	Ford
35.	Kenny Wallace	Chevrolet
36.	Mike Skinner	Chevrolet
37.	Matt Kenseth	Ford
38.	Ted Musgrave	Ford
39.	Steve Grissom	Ford
40.	Sterling Marlin	Chevrolet
41.	Michael Waltrip	Chevrolet
42.	David Green	Chevrolet
43.	Jerry Nadeau	Pontiac

EXIDE 400

September 11
Richmond, Virginia
Time of Race: 2 hours, 53 minutes, 4 seconds
Average Speed: 104.006 mph
Margin of Victory: 1.115 seconds

FINISH	DRIVER	CAR
1.	Tony Stewart	Pontiac
2.	Bobby Labonte	Pontiac
3.	Dale Jarrett	Ford
4.	Sterling Marlin	Chevrolet
5.	Kenny Irwin	Ford
6.	Dale Earnhardt	Chevrolet
7.	Bobby Hamilton	Chevrolet
8.	Ted Musgrave	Ford
9.	John Andretti	Pontiac
10.	Dale Earnhardt Jr.	Chevrolet
11.	Mike Skinner	Chevrolet
12.	Kenny Wallace	Chevrolet
13.	Jeff Burton	Ford
14.	Rusty Wallace	Ford
15.	Kyle Petty	Pontiac
16.	Steve Park	Chevrolet
17.	Elliott Sadler	Ford
18.	Jerry Nadeau	Pontiac
19.	Todd Bodine	Pontiac
20.	Joe Nemechek	Chevrolet
21.	Ken Schrader	Chevrolet
22.	Johnny Benson	Ford
23.	Geoffrey Bodine	Chevrolet
24.	Mike Wallace	Ford
25.	Jeremy Mayfield	Ford
26.	Kevin Lepage	Ford
27.	Ricky Rudd	Ford
28.	Wally Dallenbach Jr.	Chevrolet
29.	Ron Hornaday	Chevrolet
30.	Steve Grissom	Ford
31.	Brett Bodine	Ford
32.	Darrell Waltrip	Ford
33.	David Green	Chevrolet
34.	Ward Burton	Pontiac
35.	Mark Martin	Ford
36.	Bill Elliott	Ford
37.	Jimmy Spencer	Ford
38.	Michael Waltrip	Chevrolet
39.	Robert Pressley	Ford
40.	Jeff Gordon	Chevrolet
41.	Rick Mast	Ford
42.	Chad Little	Ford
43.	Terry Labonte	Chevrolet

DURA-LUBE/KMART 300

September 19
Loudon, New Hampshire
Time of Race: 3 hours, 9 minutes, 10 seconds
Average Speed: 100.673 mph
Margin of Victory: under caution

FINISH	DRIVER	CAR
1.	Joe Nemechek	Chevrolet
2.	Tony Stewart	Pontiac
3.	Bobby Labonte	Pontiac
4.	Jeff Burton	Ford
5.	Jeff Gordon	Chevrolet
6.	Rusty Wallace	Ford
7.	Johnny Benson	Ford
8.	Ward Burton	Pontiac
9.	Rick Mast	Ford
10.	Kenny Irwin	Ford
11.	Bobby Hamilton	Chevrolet
12.	Ken Schrader	Chevrolet
13.	Dale Earnhardt	Chevrolet
14.	Elliott Sadler	Ford
15.	Steve Park	Chevrolet
16.	Hut Stricklin	Ford
17.	Mark Martin	Ford
18.	Dale Jarrett	Ford
19.	Bill Elliott	Ford
20.	Rich Bickle	Ford
21.	Sterling Marlin	Chevrolet
22.	Wally Dallenbach Jr.	Chevrolet
23.	Ted Musgrave	Ford
24.	Jimmy Spencer	Ford
25.	Dave Marcis	Chevrolet
26.	Kevin Lepage	Ford
27.	Mike Skinner	Chevrolet
28.	Chad Little	Ford
29.	Brett Bodine	Ford
30.	Robert Pressley	Ford
31.	Terry Labonte	Chevrolet
32.	Jerry Nadeau	Pontiac
33.	Kyle Petty	Pontiac
34.	Kenny Wallace	Chevrolet
35.	Geoffrey Bodine	Chevrolet
36.	Jeremy Mayfield	Ford
37.	Randy LaJoie	Ford
38.	Michael Waltrip	Chevrolet
39.	Todd Bodine	Pontiac
40.	David Green	Pontiac
41.	John Andretti	Pontiac
42.	Ricky Rudd	Ford
43.	Ricky Craven	Chevrolet

MBNA GOLD 400

September 26
Dover, Delaware
Time of Race: 3 hours, 8 minutes, 20 seconds
Average Speed: 127.434 mph
Margin of Victory: 1.145 seconds

FINISH	DRIVER	CAR
1.	Mark Martin	Ford
2.	Tony Stewart	Pontiac
3.	Dale Jarrett	Ford
4.	Matt Kenseth	Ford
5.	Bobby Labonte	Pontiac
6.	Jeff Burton	Ford
7.	Chad Little	Ford
8.	Dale Earnhardt	Chevrolet
9.	Steve Park	Chevrolet
10.	Kenny Irwin	Ford
11.	Ward Burton	Pontiac
12.	Elliott Sadler	Ford
13.	Kevin Lepage	Ford
14.	Jimmy Spencer	Ford
15.	Wally Dallenbach Jr.	Chevrolet
16.	Jerry Nadeau	Pontiac
17.	Jeff Gordon	Chevrolet
18.	Johnny Benson	Ford
19.	Michael Waltrip	Chevrolet
20.	Kyle Petty	Pontiac
21.	Mike Skinner	Chevrolet
22.	Jeremy Mayfield	Ford
23.	Robert Pressley	Ford
24.	Geoffrey Bodine	Chevrolet
25.	Hut Stricklin	Ford
26.	Ken Schrader	Chevrolet

27.	Terry Labonte	Chevrolet
28.	Ted Musgrave	Ford
29.	Brett Bodine	Ford
30.	Bobby Hamilton	Chevrolet
31.	Ed Berrier	Ford
32.	Rusty Wallace	Ford
33.	Bill Elliott	Ford
34.	Rick Mast	Ford
35.	Joe Nemechek	Chevrolet
36.	Rich Bickle	Ford
37.	Ricky Rudd	Ford
38.	Sterling Marlin	Chevrolet
39.	Dave Marcis	Chevrolet
40.	Ricky Craven	Chevrolet
41.	John Andretti	Pontiac
42.	David Green	Chevrolet
43.	Kenny Wallace	Chevrolet

NAPA AUTOCARE 500

October 3
Martinsville, Virginia
Time of Race: 3 hours, 37 minutes, 17 seconds
Average Speed: 72.624 mph
Margin of Victory: 0.198 seconds

FINISH	DRIVER	CAR
1.	Jeff Gordon	Chevrolet
2.	Dale Earnhardt	Chevrolet
3.	Geoffrey Bodine	Chevrolet
4.	Rusty Wallace	Ford
5.	Kenny Wallace	Chevrolet
6.	Mike Skinner	Chevrolet
7.	Kyle Petty	Pontiac
8.	Bobby Labonte	Pontiac
9.	Jeff Burton	Ford
10.	Dale Jarrett	Ford
11.	Sterling Marlin	Chevrolet
12.	Steve Park	Chevrolet
13.	Ward Burton	Pontiac
14.	Hut Stricklin	Ford
15.	Jeremy Mayfield	Ford
16.	Mark Martin	Ford
17.	Jimmy Spencer	Ford
18.	Ricky Rudd	Ford
19.	Ted Musgrave	Ford
20.	Bill Elliott	Ford
21.	Ken Schrader	Chevrolet
22.	Wally Dallenbach	Chevrolet
23.	Darrell Waltrip	Chevrolet
24.	Ricky Craven	Chevrolet
25.	Elliott Sadler	Ford
26.	Jerry Nadeau	Pontiac
27.	Kevin Lepage	Ford
28.	Johnny Benson	Ford
29.	Rick Mast	Ford
30.	Bobby Hamilton	Chevrolet
31.	Chad Little	Ford
32.	Mike Bliss	Pontiac
33.	Michael Waltrip	Chevrolet
34.	Dave Marcis	Chevrolet
35.	Robert Pressley	Ford
36.	David Green	Pontiac
37.	Rich Bickle	Ford
38.	Joe Nemechek	Chevrolet
39.	Kenny Irwin	Ford
40.	Terry Labonte	Chevrolet
41.	Tony Stewart	Pontiac
42.	Brett Bodine	Ford
43.	John Andretti	Pontiac

UAW-GM TEAMWORK 500

October 10
Concord, North Carolina
Time of Race: 3 hours, 7 minutes, 31 seconds
Average Speed: 160.306 mph
Margin of Victory: 0.851 seconds

FINISH	DRIVER	CAR
1.	Jeff Gordon	Chevrolet
2.	Bobby Labonte	Pontiac
3.	Mike Skinner	Chevrolet
4.	Mark Martin	Ford
5.	Ward Burton	Pontiac
6.	Jeremy Mayfield	Chevrolet
7.	Dale Jarrett	Ford
8.	Rusty Wallace	Ford
9.	Kevin Lepage	Ford
10.	Steve Park	Chevrolet
11.	Bill Elliott	Ford
12.	Dale Earnhardt	Chevrolet
13.	Joe Nemechek	Chevrolet
14.	Michael Waltrip	Chevrolet
15.	Kenny Irwin	Ford
16.	Johnny Benson	Ford
17.	John Andretti	Pontiac
18	Chad Little	Ford
19.	Tony Stewart	Pontiac
20.	Geoffrey Bodine	Chevrolet
21.	Terry Labonte	Chevrolet
22.	Bobby Hamilton	Chevrolet
23.	Ken Schrader	Chevrolet
24.	Robert Pressley	Ford
25.	Rick Mast	Ford
26.	Elliott Sadler	Ford
27.	Brett Bodine	Ford
28.	Jimmy Spencer	Ford
29.	Sterling Marlin	Chevrolet
30.	Kenny Wallace	Chevrolet
31.	Ted Musgrave	Ford
32.	Kyle Petty	Pontiac
33.	Wally Dallenbach	Chevrolet
34.	Jerry Nadeau	Pontiac
35.	Derrike Cope	Ford
36.	Todd Bodine	Pontiac
37.	Jeff Burton	Ford
38.	Ricky Rudd	Ford
39.	Rich Bickle	Ford
40.	Matt Kenseth	Ford
41.	Dick Trickle	Chevrolet
42.	David Green	Pontiac
43.	Ricky Craven	Chevrolet

WINSTON 500

October 17
Talladega, Alabama
Time of Race: 3 hours, 0 minutes, 4 seconds
Average Speed: 166.632 mph
Margin of Victory: 0.114 seconds

FINISH	DRIVER	CAR
1.	Dale Earnhardt	Chevrolet
2.	Dale Jarrett	Ford
3.	Ricky Rudd	Ford
4.	Ward Burton	Pontiac
5.	Kenny Wallace	Chevrolet
6.	Tony Stewart	Pontiac
7.	Bobby Labonte	Pontiac
8.	Jeff Burton	Ford
9.	Bobby Hamilton	Chevrolet
10.	Kenny Irwin	Ford
11.	Rusty Wallace	Ford
12.	Jeff Gordon	Chevrolet
13.	Mike Skinner	Chevrolet
14.	Steve Park	Chevrolet
15.	Mark Martin	Ford
16.	Jeremy Mayfield	Ford
17.	David Green	Pontiac
18.	Kevin Lepage	Ford
19.	Kyle Petty	Pontiac
20.	Bill Elliott	Ford
21.	Elliott Sadler	Ford
22.	Sterling Marlin	Chevrolet
23.	Geoffrey Bodine	Chevrolet
24.	Jimmy Spencer	Ford
25.	Ken Schrader	Chevrolet

26.	Rick Mast	Ford
27.	Buckshot Jones	Pontiac
28.	Steve Grissom	Chevrolet
29.	Ted Musgrave	Ford
30.	Joe Nemechek	Chevrolet
31.	Brett Bodine	Ford
32.	John Andretti	Pontiac
33.	Ed Berrier	Ford
34.	Terry Labonte	Chevrolet
35.	Wally Dallenbach Jr.	Chevrolet
36.	Chad Little	Ford
37.	Derrike Cope	Chevrolet
38.	Dave Marcis	Chevrolet
39.	Michael Waltrip	Chevrolet
40.	Jerry Nadeau	Pontiac
41.	Rick Bickle	Ford
42.	Johnny Benson	Ford
43.	Andy Hillenburg	Chevrolet

POP SECRET 400

October 24
Rockingham, North Carolina
Time of Race: 3 hours, 2 minutes, 55 seconds
Average Speed: 131.103 mph
Margin of Victory: 0.337 seconds

FINISH	DRIVER	CAR
1.	Jeff Burton	Ford
2.	Ward Burton	Pontiac
3.	Bobby Labonte	Pontiac
4.	Dale Jarrett	Ford
5.	Rusty Wallace	Ford
6.	Mark Martin	Ford
7.	John Andretti	Pontiac
8.	Sterling Marlin	Chevrolet
9.	Jeremy Mayfield	Ford
10.	Bobby Hamilton	Chevrolet
11.	Jeff Gordon	Chevrolet
12.	Tony Stewart	Pontiac
13.	Kenny Irwin	Ford
14.	Terry Labonte	Chevrolet
15	Steve Park	Chevrolet
16.	Kenny Wallace	Chevrolet
17.	Mike Skinner	Chevrolet
18.	Elliott Sadler	Ford
19.	Ricky Rudd	Ford
20.	Jimmy Spencer	Ford
21.	Chad Little	Ford
22.	Kevin Lepage	Ford
23.	Kyle Petty	Pontiac
24.	David Green	Pontiac
25.	Derrike Cope	Chevrolet
26.	Joe Nemechek	Chevrolet
27.	Michael Waltrip	Chevrolet
28.	Johnny Benson	Ford
29.	Robert Pressley	Ford
30.	Ken Schrader	Chevrolet
31.	Geoffrey Bodine	Chevrolet
32.	Ted Musgrave	Ford
33.	Bill Elliott	Ford
34.	Darrell Waltrip	Ford
35.	Matt Kenseth	Ford
36.	Stacy Compton	Ford
37.	Jerry Nadeau	Pontiac
38.	Rick Mast	Ford
39.	Wally Dallenbach Jr.	Chevrolet
40.	Dale Earnhardt	Chevrolet
41.	Ricky Craven	Chevrolet
42.	Mike Bliss	Pontiac
43.	Brett Bodine	Ford

DURA LUBE 300

November 7
Phoenix, Arizona
Time of Race: 2 hours, 38 minutes, 27 seconds
Average Speed: 118.141 mph
Margin of Victory: 2.081 seconds

FINISH	DRIVER	CAR
1.	Tony Stewart	Pontiac
2.	Mark Martin	Ford
3.	Bobby Labonte	Pontiac
4.	Jeff Burton	Ford
5.	Ricky Rudd	Ford
6.	Dale Jarrett	Ford
7.	Kyle Petty	Pontiac
8.	John Andretti	Pontiac
9.	Wally Dallenbach Jr.	Chevrolet
10.	Jeff Gordon	Chevrolet
11.	Dale Earnhardt	Chevrolet
12.	David Green	Pontiac
13.	Ward Burton	Pontiac
14.	Ken Schrader	Chevrolet
15.	Steve Park	Chevrolet
16.	Chad Little	Ford
17.	Jimmy Spencer	Ford
18.	Kenny Wallace	Chevrolet
19.	Joe Nemechek	Chevrolet
20.	Mike Skinner	Chevrolet
21.	Kenny Irwin	Ford
22.	Geoffrey Bodine	Chevrolet
23.	Bobby Hamilton	Chevrolet
24.	Kevin Lepage	Ford
25.	Todd	BodinePontiac
26.	Darrell Waltrip	Ford
27.	Elliott Sadler	Ford
28.	Terry Labonte	Chevrolet
29.	Ted Musgrave	Ford
30.	Ricky Craven	Chevrolet
31.	Johnny Benson	Ford
32	Rusty Wallace	Ford
33.	Michael Waltrip	Chevrolet
34.	Dave Marcis	Chevrolet
35.	Bill Elliott	Ford
36.	Rick Mast	Ford
37.	Jerry Nadeau	Pontiac
38.	Robert Pressley	Ford
39.	Stacy Compton	Ford
40.	Sterling Marlin	Chevrolet
41.	Jeremy Mayfield	Ford
42.	Brett Bodine	Ford
43.	Derrike Cope	Chevrolet

PENNZOIL 400

November 14
Homestead, Florida
Time of Race: 2 hours, 51 minutes, 14 seconds
Average Speed: 140.335 mph
Margin of Victory: 5.289 seconds

FINISH	DRIVER	CAR
1.	Tony Stewart	Pontiac
2.	Bobby Labonte	Pontiac
3.	Jeff Burton	Ford
4.	Mark Martin	Ford
5.	Dale Jarrett	Ford
6.	Mike Skinner	Chevrolet
7.	Kyle Petty	Pontiac
8.	Dale Earnhardt	Chevrolet
9.	Wally Dallenbach Jr.	Chevrolet
10.	Jeff Gordon	Chevrolet
11.	Geoffrey Bodine	Chevrolet
12.	Rusty Wallace	Ford
13.	Jeremy Mayfield	Ford
14.	Ward Burton	Pontiac
15.	Kenny Wallace	Chevrolet
16.	John Andretti	Pontiac
17.	Sterling Marlin	Chevrolet
18.	Elliott Sadler	Ford
19.	Steve Park	Chevrolet
20.	Jimmy Spencer	Ford
21.	Joe Nemechek	Chevrolet
22.	David Green	Pontiac
23.	Dave Blaney	Pontiac
24.	Bill Elliott	Ford
25.	Bobby Hamilton	Chevrolet
26.	Kevin Lepage	Ford
27.	Todd Bodine	Pontiac

28.	Rick Mast	Ford
29.	Ken Schrader	Chevrolet
30.	Stacy Compton	Ford
31.	Terry Labonte	Chevrolet
32.	Ricky Craven	Chevrolet
33.	Kenny Irwin	Ford
34.	Boris Said	Ford
35.	Johnny Benson	Ford
36.	Michael Waltrip	Chevrolet
37.	Robert Pressley	Ford
38.	Jerry Nadeau	Pontiac
39.	Chad Little	Ford
40.	Brett Bodine	Ford
41.	Ricky Rudd	Ford
42.	Ted Musgrave	Ford
43.	Darrell Waltrip	Ford

NAPA 500

November 7
Hampton, Georgia
Time of Race: 3 hours, 37 minutes, 42 seconds
Average Speed: 137.942 mph
Margin of Victory: 2.428 seconds

FINISH	DRIVER	CAR
1.	Bobby Labonte	Pontiac
2.	Dale Jarrett	Ford
3.	Jeremy Mayfield	Ford
4.	Mark Martin	Ford
5.	Jeff Burton	Ford
6.	Chad Little	Ford
7.	Ricky Rudd	Ford
8.	Mike Skinner	Chevrolet
9.	Dale Earnhardt	Chevrolet
10.	Bobby Hamilton	Chevrolet
11.	Ward Burton	Pontiac
12.	Steve Park	Chevrolet
13.	Rusty Wallace	Ford
14.	Dale Earnhardt Jr.	Chevrolet
15.	Tony Stewart	Pontiac
16.	Elliott Sadler	Ford
17.	Kevin Lepage	Ford
18.	Geoffrey Bodine	Chevrolet
19.	Ken Schrader	Chevrolet
20.	Jerry Nadeau	Pontiac
21.	David Green	Pontiac
22.	Bill Elliott	Ford
23.	Wally Dallenbach Jr.	Chevrolet
24.	Kyle Petty	Pontiac
25.	Ed Berrier	Ford
26.	Buckshot Jones	Pontiac
27.	Robert Pressley	Ford
28.	Dave Marcis	Chevrolet
29.	Kenny Irwin	Ford
30.	Brett Bodine	Ford
31.	Sterling Marlin	Chevrolet
32.	Joe Nemechek	Chevrolet
33.	John Andretti	Pontiac
34.	Kenny Wallace	Chevrolet
35.	Gary Bradberry	Chevrolet
36.	Michael Waltrip	Chevrolet
37.	Dave Blaney	Pontiac
38.	Jeff Gordon	Chevrolet
39.	Johnny Benson	Ford
40.	Terry Labonte	Chevrolet
41.	Rick Mast	Ford
42.	Jimmy Spencer	Ford
43.	Todd Bodine	Pontiac

2000

DAYTONA 500

February 20
Daytona Beach, Florida

Time of Race: 3 hours, 12 minutes, 43 seconds
Average Speed: 155.660 mph
Margin of Victory: under caution

FINISH	DRIVER	CAR
1.	Dale Jarrett	Ford
2.	Jeff Burton	Ford
3.	Bill Elliott	Ford
4.	Rusty Wallace	Ford
5.	Mark Martin	Ford
6.	Bobby Labonte	Pontiac
7.	Terry Labonte	Chevrolet
8.	Ward Burton	Pontiac
9.	Ken Schrader	Pontiac
10.	Matt Kenseth	Ford
11.	Jeremy Mayfield	Ford
12.	Johnny Benson	Pontiac
13.	Dale Earnhardt Jr.	Chevrolet
14.	Kenny Irwin	Chevrolet
15.	Ricky Rudd	Ford
16.	Mike Skinner	Chevrolet
17.	Tony Stewart	Pontiac
18.	Robby Gordon	Ford
19.	Scott Pruett	Ford
20.	Robert Pressley	Ford
21.	Dale Earnhardt	Chevrolet
22.	John Andretti	Pontiac
23.	Chad Little	Ford
24.	Sterling Marlin	Chevrolet
25.	Kyle Petty	Pontiac
26.	Stacy Compton	Ford
27.	Dave Blaney	Pontiac
28.	Rick Mast	Chevrolet
29.	Kenny Wallace	Chevrolet
30.	Jimmy Spencer	Ford
31.	Steve Park	Chevrolet
32.	Darrell Waltrip	Ford
33.	Mike Bliss	Pontiac
34.	Jeff Gordon	Chevrolet
35.	Jerry Nadeau	Chevrolet
36.	Kevin Lepage	Ford
37.	Ed Berrier	Ford
38.	Elliott Sadler	Ford
39.	Michael Waltrip	Chevrolet
40.	Wally Dallenbach	Ford
41.	Derrike Cope	Ford
42.	Joe Nemechek	Chevrolet
43.	Bobby Hamilton	Chevrolet

DURA LUBE/KMART 400

February 27
Rockingham, North Carolina
Time of Race: 3 hours, 7 minutes, 32 seconds
Average Speed: 127.875 mph
Margin of Victory: 1.068 seconds

FINISH	DRIVER	CAR
1.	Bobby Labonte	Pontiac
2.	Dale Earnhardt	Chevrolet
3.	Ward Burton	Pontiac
4.	Tony Stewart	Pontiac
5.	Dale Jarrett	Ford
6.	Ricky Rudd	Ford
7.	Jeremy Mayfield	Ford
8.	Mark Martin	Ford
9.	Steve Park	Chevrolet
10.	Jeff Gordon	Chevrolet
11.	Rusty Wallace	Ford
12.	John Andretti	Pontiac
13.	Ken Schrader	Pontiac
14.	Johnny Benson	Pontiac
15.	Sterling Marlin	Chevrolet
16.	Ted Musgrave	Chevrolet
17.	Terry Labonte	Chevrolet
18.	Chad Little	Ford
19.	Dale Earnhardt Jr.	Chevrolet

20.	Wally Dallenbach	Ford
21.	Mike Skinner	Chevrolet
22.	Kenny Irwin	Chevrolet
23.	Michael Waltrip	Chevrolet
24.	Kenny Wallace	Chevrolet
25.	Bill Elliott	Ford
26.	Jimmy Spencer	Ford
27.	Kevin Lepage	Ford
28.	Elliott Sadler	Ford
29.	Jerry Nadeau	Chevrolet
30.	Joe Nemechek	Chevrolet
31.	Kyle Petty	Pontiac
32.	Jeff Burton	Ford
33.	Rick Mast	Chevrolet
34.	Stacy Compton	Ford
35.	Brett Bodine	Ford
36.	Ed Berrier	Ford
37.	Matt Kenseth	Ford
38.	Robby Gordon	Ford
39.	Darrell Waltrip	Ford
40.	Bobby Hamilton	Chevrolet
41.	Dave Marcis	Chevrolet
42.	Jeff Fuller	Ford
43.	Robert Pressley	Ford

CARSDIRECT.COM 400

March 5
Las Vegas, Nevada
Time of Race: 1 hour, 51 minutes, 1 second
Average Speed: 119.982 mph
Margin of Victory: under caution

FINISH	DRIVER	CAR
1.	Jeff Burton	Ford
2.	Tony Stewart	Pontiac
3.	Mark Martin	Ford
4.	Bill Elliott	Ford
5.	Bobby Labonte	Pontiac
6.	Johnny Benson	Pontiac
7.	Dale Jarrett	Ford
8.	Dale Earnhardt	Chevrolet
9.	Joe Nemechek	Chevrolet
10.	Dale Earnhardt Jr.	Chevrolet
11.	Kevin Irwin	Chevrolet
12.	Ricky Rudd	Ford
13.	Robby Gordon	Ford
14.	Matt Kenseth	Ford
15.	Rusty Wallace	Ford
16.	Ken Schrader	Pontiac
17.	Jeremy Mayfield	Ford
18.	Sterling Marlin	Chevrolet
19.	Chad Little	Ford
20.	Jerry Nadeau	Chevrolet
21.	Robert Pressley	Ford
22.	Dave Blaney	Pontiac
23.	Ward Burton	Pontiac
24.	Kenny Irwin	Chevrolet
25.	John Andretti	Pontiac
26.	Ted Musgrave	Chevrolet
27.	Mike Skinner	Chevrolet
28.	Jeff Gordon	Chevrolet
29.	Kyle Petty	Pontiac
30.	Jimmy Spencer	Ford
31.	Terry Labonte	Chevrolet
32.	Stacy Compton	Ford
33.	Michael Waltrip	Chevrolet
34.	Bobby Hamilton	Chevrolet
35.	Wally Dallenbach	Ford
36.	Jeff Fuller	Pontiac
37.	Derrike Cope	Ford
38.	Darrell Waltrip	Ford
39.	Kenny Wallace	Chevrolet
40.	Ricky Craven	Chevrolet
41.	Elliott Sadler	Ford
42.	Scott Pruett	Ford
43.	Steve Park	Chevrolet

CRACKER BARREL 500

March 12
Hampton, Georgia
Time of Race: 3 hours, 47 minutes, 55 seconds
Average Speed: 131.759 mph
Margin of Victory: 0.010 seconds

FINISH	DRIVER	CAR
1.	Dale Earnhardt	Chevrolet
2.	Bobby Labonte	Pontiac
3.	Mark Martin	Ford
4.	Steve Park	Chevrolet
5.	Joe Nemechek	Chevrolet
6.	Chad Little	Ford
7.	Todd Bodine	Chevrolet
8.	Ward Burton	Pontiac
9.	Jeff Gordon	Chevrolet
10.	Bill Elliott	Ford
11.	Ricky Rudd	Ford
12.	Sterling Marlin	Chevrolet
13.	Bobby Hamilton	Chevrolet
14.	Elliott Sadler	Ford
15.	Terry Labonte	Chevrolet
16.	Brett Bodine	Ford
17.	Jimmy Spencer	Ford
18.	John Andretti	Pontiac
19.	Derrike Cope	Ford
20.	Dave Blaney	Pontiac
21.	Rick Mast	Chevrolet
22.	Jeff Fuller	Pontiac
23.	Ken Schrader	Pontiac
24.	Kenny Irwin	Chevrolet
25.	Michael Waltrip	Chevrolet
26.	Kyle Petty	Pontiac
27.	Ted Musgrave	Chevrolet
28.	Jeremy Mayfield	Ford
29.	Dale Earnhardt Jr.	Chevrolet
30.	Mike Skinner	Chevrolet
31.	Darrell Waltrip	Ford
32.	Rusty Wallace	Ford
33.	Robert Pressley	Ford
34.	Tony Stewart	Pontiac
35.	Stacy Compton	Ford
36.	Dale Jarrett	Ford
37.	Kenny Wallace	Chevrolet
38.	Kevin Lepage	Ford
39.	Wally Dallenbach	Ford
40.	Matt Kenseth	Ford
41.	Scott Pruett	Ford
42.	Jerry Nadeau	Chevrolet
43.	Jeff Fuller	Pontiac

MALL.COM 400

March 19
Darlington, South Carolina
Time of Race: 3 hours, 7 minutes, 30 seconds
Average Speed: 120.076 mph
Margin of Victory: 1.420 seconds

FINISH	DRIVER	CAR
1.	Ward Burton	Pontiac
2.	Dale Jarrett	Ford
3.	Dale Earnhardt	Chevrolet
4.	Tony Stewart	Pontiac
5.	Jeff Burton	Ford
6.	Matt Kenseth	Ford
7.	Bobby Hamilton	Chevrolet
8.	Jeff Gordon	Chevrolet
9.	Mark Martin	Ford
10.	Kevin Lepage	Ford
11.	Terry Labonte	Chevrolet
12.	Elliott Sadler	Ford
13.	Bobby Labonte	Pontiac
14.	Mike Skinner	Chevrolet
15.	Chad Little	Ford

16.	Rusty Wallace	Ford
17.	Ricky Rudd	Ford
18.	Robert Pressley	Ford
19.	Bill Elliott	Ford
20.	John Andretti	Pontiac
21.	Sterling Marlin	Chevrolet
22.	Ken Schrader	Pontiac
23.	Jimmy Spencer	Ford
24.	Johnny Benson	Pontiac
25.	Kyle Petty	Pontiac
26.	Dave Blaney	Pontiac
27.	Brett Bodine	Ford
28.	Robby Gordon	Ford
29.	Stacy Compton	Ford
30.	Rick Mast	Chevrolet
31.	Dick Trickle	Pontiac
32.	Michael Waltrip	Chevrolet
33.	Dave Marcis	Chevrolet
34.	Jeremy Mayfield	Ford
35.	Kenny Wallace	Chevrolet
36.	Jeff Fuller	Pontiac
37.	Jerry Nadeau	Chevrolet
38.	Kenny Irwin	Chevrolet
39.	Steve Park	Chevrolet
40.	Dale Earnhardt Jr.	Chevrolet
41.	Joe Nemechek	Chevrolet
42.	Ted Musgrave	Chevrolet
43.	Darrell Waltrip	Ford

FOOD CITY 500

March 26
Bristol, Tennessee
Time of Race: 3 hours, 1 minute, 40 seconds
Average Speed: 88.018 mph
Margin of Victory: 2.662 seconds

FINISH	DRIVER	CAR
1.	Rusty Wallace	Ford
2.	Johnny Benson	Pontiac
3.	Ward Burton	Pontiac
4.	Jeremy Mayfield	Ford
5.	Terry Labonte	Chevrolet
6.	Bobby Labonte	Pontiac
7.	Steve Park	Chevrolet
8.	Jeff Gordon	Chevrolet
9.	Jeff Burton	Ford
10.	Sterling Marlin	Chevrolet
11.	Michael Waltrip	Chevrolet
12.	Matt Kenseth	Ford
13.	Mike Skinner	Chevrolet
14.	Ricky Rudd	Ford
15.	Bobby Hamilton	Chevrolet
16.	Mark Martin	Ford
17.	Robert Pressley	Ford
18.	Jimmy Spencer	Ford
19.	Jerry Nadeau	Chevrolet
20.	Kenny Wallace	Chevrolet
21.	Dale Jarrett	Ford
22.	Brett Bodine	Ford
23.	Chad Little	Ford
24.	Kyle Petty	Pontiac
25.	Joe Nemechek	Chevrolet
26.	Ken Schrader	Pontiac
27.	Dick Trickle	Pontiac
28.	Stacy Compton	Ford
29.	Wally Dallenbach	Ford
30.	Kevin Lepage	Ford
31.	Darrell Waltrip	Ford
32.	Robby Gordon	Ford
33.	John Andretti	Pontiac
34.	Rick Mast	Chevrolet
35.	Dave Blaney	Pontiac
36.	Bill Elliott	Ford
37.	Jeff Fuller	Pontiac
38.	Dale Earnhardt Jr.	Chevrolet
39.	Dale Earnhardt	Chevrolet
40.	Kenny Irwin	Chevrolet
41.	Elliott Sadler	Ford
42.	Tony Stewart	Pontiac
43.	Ted Musgrave	Chevrolet

DIRECTV 500

April 2
Fort Worth, Texas
Time of Race: 3 hours, 49 minutes, 12 seconds
Average Speed: 131.152 mph
Margin of Victory: 5.920 seconds

FINISH	DRIVER	CAR
1.	Dale Earnhardt Jr.	Chevrolet
2.	Jeff Burton	Ford
3.	Bobby Labonte	Pontiac
4.	Rusty Wallace	Ford
5.	Kevin Lepage	Ford
6.	Jeremy Mayfield	Ford
7.	Dale Earnhardt	Chevrolet
8.	Terry Labonte	Chevrolet
9.	Tony Stewart	Pontiac
10.	Ricky Rudd	Ford
11.	Mark Martin	Ford
12.	Mike Skinner	Chevrolet
13.	Chad Little	Ford
14.	Ward Burton	Pontiac
15.	Jimmy Spencer	Ford
16.	Bobby Hamilton	Chevrolet
17.	Kenny Irwin	Chevrolet
18.	Ken Schrader	Pontiac
19.	Steve Park	Chevrolet
20.	Rick Mast	Chevrolet
21.	Kenny Wallace	Chevrolet
22.	Dave Blaney	Pontiac
23.	Brett Bodine	Ford
24.	Darrell Waltrip	Ford
25.	Jeff Gordon	Chevrolet
26.	Robert Pressley	Ford
27.	Scott Pruett	Ford
28.	Dick Trickle	Pontiac
29.	Michael Waltrip	Chevrolet
30.	Bill Elliott	Ford
31.	Matt Kenseth	Ford
32.	John Andretti	Pontiac
33.	Dale Jarrett	Ford
34.	Sterling Marlin	Chevrolet
35.	Ed Berrier	Ford
36.	Stacy Compton	Ford
37.	Joe Nemechek	Chevrolet
38.	Jeff Fuller	Pontiac
39.	Elliott Sadler	Ford
40.	Adam Petty	Pontiac
41.	Gary Bradberry	Chevrolet
42.	Johnny Benson	Pontiac
43.	Jerry Nadeau	Chevrolet

GOODY'S BODY PAIN 500

April 9
Martinsville, Virginia
Time of Race: 3 hours, 41 minutes, 45 seconds
Average Speed: 71.161 mph
Margin of Victory: 1.505 seconds

FINISH	DRIVER	CAR
1.	Mark Martin	Ford
2.	Jeff Burton	Ford
3.	Michael Waltrip	Chevrolet
4.	Jeff Gordon	Chevrolet
5.	Dale Jarrett	Ford
6.	Tony Stewart	Pontiac
7.	Jeremy Mayfield	Ford
8.	Bill Elliott	Ford
9.	Dale Earnhardt	Chevrolet
10.	Rusty Wallace	Ford
11.	Ward Burton	Pontiac
12.	Bobby Labonte	Pontiac
13.	Ken Schrader	Pontiac
14.	John Andretti	Pontiac
15.	Robert Pressley	Ford

16.	Johnny Benson	Pontiac
17.	Joe Nemechek	Chevrolet
18.	Bobby Hamilton	Chevrolet
19.	Mike Skinner	Chevrolet
20.	Jerry Nadeau	Chevrolet
21.	Matt Kenseth	Ford
22.	Ricky Rudd	Ford
23.	Terry Labonte	Chevrolet
24.	Sterling Marlin	Chevrolet
25.	Steve Park	Chevrolet
26.	Dale Earnhardt Jr.	Chevrolet
27.	Chad Little	Ford
28.	Jimmy Spencer	Ford
29.	Elliott Sadler	Ford
30.	Rich Bickle	Chevrolet
31.	Ricky Craven	Chevrolet
32.	Scott Pruett	Ford
33.	Gary Bradberry	Chevrolet
34.	Kevin Lepage	Ford
35.	Mike Bliss	Pontiac
36.	Brett Bodine	Ford
37.	Kenny Irwin	Chevrolet
38.	Kyle Petty	Pontiac
39.	Stacy Compton	Ford
40.	Robby Gordon	Ford
41.	Dave Blaney	Pontiac
42.	Kenny Wallace	Chevrolet
43.	Darrell Waltrip	Ford

DIEHARD 500

April 16
Talladega, Alabama
Time of Race: 3 hours, 6 minutes, 11 seconds
Average Speed: 161.157 mph
Margin of Victory: 0.189 seconds

FINISH	DRIVER	CAR
1.	Jeff Gordon	Chevrolet
2.	Mike Skinner	Chevrolet
3.	Dale Earnhardt	Chevrolet
4.	Kenny Irwin	Chevrolet
5.	Jimmy Spencer	Ford
6.	Mark Martin	Ford
7.	Terry Labonte	Chevrolet
8.	Sterling Marlin	Chevrolet
9.	Kyle Petty	Pontiac
10.	Ward Burton	Pontiac
11.	John Andretti	Pontiac
12.	Jeff Burton	Ford
13.	Johnny Benson	Pontiac
14.	Jeremy Mayfield	Ford
15.	Bill Elliott	Ford
16.	Wally Dallenbach	Ford
17.	Dale Jarrett	Ford
18.	Matt Kenseth	Ford
19.	Jerry Nadeau	Chevrolet
20.	Scott Pruett	Ford
21.	Bobby Labonte	Pontiac
22.	Joe Nemechek	Chevrolet
23.	Robert Pressley	Ford
24.	Mike Bliss	Pontiac
25.	Chad Little	Ford
26.	Darrell Waltrip	Ford
27.	Ricky Rudd	Ford
28.	Ed Berrier	Ford
29.	Ricky Craven	Chevrolet
30.	Dave Blaney	Pontiac
31.	Michael Waltrip	Chevrolet
32.	Steve Park	Chevrolet
33.	Stacy Compton	Ford
34.	Tony Stewart	Pontiac
35.	Ted Musgrave	Chevrolet
36.	Ken Schrader	Pontiac
37.	Robby Gordon	Ford
38.	Dave Marcis	Chevrolet
39.	Dick Trickle	Pontiac
40.	Kenny Wallace	Chevrolet
41.	Rusty Wallace	Ford
42.	Dale Earnhardt Jr.	Chevrolet
43.	Bobby Hamilton	Chevrolet

NAPA AUTO PARTS 500

April 30
Fontana, California
Time of Race: 3 hours, 20 minutes, 50 seconds
Average Speed: 149.378 mph
Margin of Victory: 0.300 seconds

FINISH	DRIVER	CAR
1.	Jeremy Mayfield	Ford
2.	Bobby Labonte	Pontiac
3.	Matt Kenseth	Ford
4.	Ricky Rudd	Ford
5.	Jeff Burton	Ford
6.	Ward Burton	Pontiac
7.	Mike Skinner	Chevrolet
8.	Rusty Wallace	Ford
9.	Dale Jarrett	Ford
10.	Tony Stewart	Pontiac
11.	Jeff Gordon	Chevrolet
12.	Dale Earnhardt Jr	Chevrolet
13.	Jerry Nadeau	Chevrolet
14.	Mark Martin	Ford
15.	Chad Little	Ford
16.	Steve Park	Chevrolet
17.	Dale Earnhardt	Chevrolet
18.	Bobby Hamilton	Chevrolet
19.	Bill Elliott	Ford
20.	Joe Nemechek	Chevrolet
21.	Robert Pressley	Ford
22.	Kevin Lepage	Ford
23.	Johnny Benson	Pontiac
24.	Ken Schrader	Pontiac
25.	John Andretti	Pontiac
26.	Kyle Petty	Pontiac
27.	Wally Dallenbach	Ford
28.	Stacy Compton	Ford
29.	Darrell Waltrip	Ford
30.	Michael Waltrip	Chevrolet
31.	Robby Gordon	Ford
32.	Sterling Marlin	Chevrolet
33.	Terry Labonte	Chevrolet
34.	Scott Pruett	Ford
35.	Mike Bliss	Pontiac
36.	Kenny Wallace	Chevrolet
37.	Dick Trickle	Pontiac
38.	Dave Blaney	Pontiac
39.	Rick Mast	Chevrolet
40.	Jimmy Spencer	Ford
41.	Brett Bodine	Ford
42.	Kenny Irwin	Chevrolet
43.	Elliott Sadler	Ford

PONTIAC EXCITEMENT 400

May 6
Richmond, Virginia
Time of Race: 3 hours, 1 minute, 8 seconds
Average Speed: 99.374 mph
Margin of Victory: 0.159 seconds

FINISH	DRIVER	CAR
1.	Dale Earnhardt Jr.	Chevrolet
2.	Terry Labonte	Chevrolet
3.	Dale Jarrett	Ford
4.	Ricky Rudd	Ford
5.	Rusty Wallace	Ford
5.	Mark Martin	Ford
6.	Ward Burton	Pontiac
7.	Jeff Burton	Ford
8.	Tony Stewart	Pontiac
9.	Bill Elliott	Ford
10.	Dale Earnhardt	Chevrolet
11.	Steve Park	Chevrolet
12.	Ken Schrader	Pontiac
13.	Geoffrey Bodine	Chevrolet
14.	Jeff Gordon	Chevrolet

15.	Matt Kenseth	Ford
16.	Wally Dallenbach	Ford
17.	Jimmy Spencer	Ford
18.	John Andretti	Pontiac
19.	Michael Waltrip	Chevrolet
20.	Kenny Wallace	Chevrolet
21.	Kevin Lepage	Ford
22.	Stacy Compton	Ford
23.	Joe Nemechek	Chevrolet
24.	Elliott Sadler	Ford
25.	Johnny Benson	Pontiac
26.	Bobby Labonte	Pontiac
27.	Scott Pruett	Ford
28.	Kyle Petty	Pontiac
29.	Sterling Marlin	Chevrolet
30.	Jerry Nadeau	Chevrolet
31.	Bobby Hamilton	Chevrolet
32.	Mark Martin	Ford
33.	Mike Skinner	Chevrolet
34.	Dave Blaney	Pontiac
35.	Robert Pressley	Ford
36.	Jeremy Mayfield	Ford
37.	Robby Gordon	Ford
38.	Brett Bodine	Ford
39.	Chad Little	Ford
40.	Ricky Craven	Chevrolet
41.	Mike Bliss	Pontiac
42.	Kenny Irwin	Chevrolet
43.	Todd Bodine	Chevrolet

COCA-COLA 600

May 28
Concord, North Carolina
Time of Race: 4 hours, 12 minutes, 23 seconds
Average Speed: 142.640 mph
Margin of Victory: 0.573 seconds

FINISH	DRIVER	CAR
1.	Matt Kenseth	Ford
2.	Bobby Labonte	Pontiac
3.	Dale Earnhardt	Chevrolet
4.	Dale Earnhardt Jr.	Chevrolet
5.	Dale Jarrett	Ford
6.	Jeremy Mayfield	Ford
7.	Mike Skinner	Chevrolet
8.	Rusty Wallace	Ford
9.	Steve Park	Chevrolet
10.	Jeff Gordon	Chevrolet
11.	Jeff Burton	Ford
12.	Mark Martin	Ford
13.	Ward Burton	Pontiac
14.	Tony Stewart	Pontiac
15.	Kevin Lepage	Ford
16.	Johnny Benson	Pontiac
17.	Ricky Rudd	Ford
18.	Michael Waltrip	Chevrolet
19.	Sterling Marlin	Chevrolet
20.	Chad Little	Ford
21.	Elliott Sadler	Ford
22.	Terry Labonte	Chevrolet
23.	Joe Nemechek	Chevrolet
24.	Kenny Irwin	Chevrolet
25.	Jimmy Spencer	Ford
26.	Robert Pressley	Ford
27.	Kenny Wallace	Chevrolet
28.	Wally Dallenbach	Ford
29.	Geoffrey Bodine	Chevrolet
30.	Brett Bodine	Ford
31.	John Andretti	Pontiac
32.	Mike Bliss	Pontiac
33.	Stacy Compton	Ford
34.	Bobby Hamilton	Chevrolet
35.	P.J. Jones	Ford
36.	Darrell Waltrip	Ford
37.	Ken Schrader	Pontiac
38.	Jerry Nadeau	Chevrolet
39.	Rick Mast	Chevrolet
40.	Dave Blaney	Pontiac
41.	Scott Pruett	Ford

42.	Ricky Craven	Chevrolet
43.	Bill Elliott	Ford

MBNA PLATINUM 400

June 4
Dover, Delaware
Time of Race: 3 hours, 39 minutes, 9 seconds
Average Speed: 109.514 mph
Margin of Victory: 1.215 seconds

FINISH	DRIVER	CAR
1.	Tony Stewart	Pontiac
2.	Matt Kenseth	Ford
3.	Bobby Labonte	Pontiac
4.	Dale Jarrett	Ford
5.	Ricky Rudd	Ford
6.	Dale Earnhardt	Chevrolet
7.	Joe Nemechek	Chevrolet
8.	Ward Burton	Pontiac
9.	Mike Skinner	Chevrolet
10.	Dale Earnhardt Jr.	Chevrolet
11.	Terry Labonte	Chevrolet
12.	Bill Elliott	Ford
13.	John Andretti	Pontiac
14.	Rusty Wallace	Ford
15.	Johnny Benson	Pontiac
16.	Elliott Sadler	Ford
17.	Kenny Irwin	Chevrolet
18.	Kenny Wallace	Chevrolet
19.	Steve Park	Chevrolet
20.	Chad Little	Ford
21.	Kevin Lepage	Ford
22.	Jimmy Spencer	Ford
23.	Ken Schrader	Pontiac
24.	Wally Dallenbach	Ford
25.	Dave Blaney	Pontiac
26.	Robert Pressley	Ford
27.	Bobby Hamilton	Chevrolet
28.	Brett Bodine	Ford
29.	Dave Marcis	Chevrolet
30.	Stacy Compton	Ford
31.	Sterling Marlin	Chevrolet
32.	Jeff Gordon	Chevrolet
33.	Darrell Waltrip	Ford
34.	Jeff Burton	Ford
35.	Mike Bliss	Pontiac
36.	Mark Martin	Ford
37.	Jeremy Mayfield	Ford
38.	Scott Pruett	Ford
39.	Michael Waltrip	Chevrolet
40.	Geoffrey Bodine	Chevrolet
41.	Ed Berrier	Ford
27.	Jerry Nadeau	Chevrolet
43.	Rick Mast	Chevrolet

KMART 400

June 11
Brooklyn, Michigan
Time of Race: 2 hours, 41 minutes, 45 seconds
Average Speed: 143.926 mph
Margin of Victory: under caution

FINISH	DRIVER	CAR
1.	Tony Stewart	Pontiac
2.	Dale Earnhardt	Chevrolet
3.	Bobby Labonte	Pontiac
4.	Dale Jarrett	Ford
5.	Robert Pressley	Ford
6.	Ward Burton	Pontiac
7.	Rusty Wallace	Ford
8.	Bill Elliott	Ford
9.	John Andretti	Pontiac

FINISH	DRIVER	CAR
10.	Sterling Marlin	Chevrolet
11.	Jeff Burton	Ford
12.	Ricky Rudd	Ford
13.	Dale Earnhardt Jr.	Chevrolet
14.	Jeff Gordon	Chevrolet
15.	Jimmy Spencer	Ford
16.	Ken Schrader	Pontiac
17.	Matt Kenseth	Ford
18.	Joe Nemechek	Chevrolet
19.	Scott Pruett	Ford
20.	Mike Skinner	Chevrolet
21.	Kevin Lepage	Ford
22.	Michael Waltrip	Chevrolet
23.	Jerry Nadeau	Chevrolet
24.	Johnny Benson	Pontiac
25.	Dave Blaney	Pontiac
26.	Terry Labonte	Chevrolet
27.	Elliott Sadler	Ford
28.	Robby Gordon	Ford
29.	Steve Park	Chevrolet
30.	Rick Mast	Pontiac
31.	Kenny Wallace	Chevrolet
32.	Chad Little	Ford
33.	Ed Berrier	Ford
34.	Wally Dallenbach	Ford
35.	Kenny Irwin	Chevrolet
36.	Brett Bodine	Ford
37.	Mike Bliss	Pontiac
38.	Geoffrey Bodine	Chevrolet
39.	Kyle Petty	Pontiac
40.	Mark Martin	Ford
41.	Jeremy Mayfield	Ford
42.	Stacy Compton	Ford
43.	Bobby Hamilton	Chevrolet

POCONO 500

June 19
Pocono, Pennsylvania
Time of Race: 3 hours, 34 minutes, 17 seconds
Average Speed: 139.741 mph
Margin of Victory: 0.581 seconds

FINISH	DRIVER	CAR
1.	Jeremy Mayfield	Ford
2.	Dale Jarrett	Ford
3.	Ricky Rudd	Ford
4.	Dale Earnhardt	Chevrolet
5.	Mark Martin	Ford
6.	Tony Stewart	Pontiac
7.	Jeff Burton	Ford
8.	Jeff Gordon	Chevrolet
9.	Mike Skinner	Chevrolet
10.	Rusty Wallace	Ford
11.	Robert Pressley	Ford
12.	Terry Labonte	Chevrolet
13.	Bobby Labonte	Pontiac
14.	Matt Kenseth	Ford
15.	Steve Park	Chevrolet
16.	Elliott Sadler	Ford
17.	Chad Little	Ford
18.	Ken Schrader	Pontiac
19.	Dale Earnhardt Jr.	Chevrolet
20.	Jerry Nadeau	Chevrolet
21.	John Andretti	Pontiac
22.	Sterling Marlin	Chevrolet
23.	Kenny Wallace	Chevrolet
24.	Geoffrey Bodine	Chevrolet
25.	Kenny Irwin	Chevrolet
26.	Kevin Lepage	Ford
27.	Ward Burton	Pontiac
28.	Ed Berrier	Ford
29.	Dave Marcis	Chevrolet
30.	Dave Blaney	Pontiac
31.	Scott Pruett	Ford
32.	Brett Bodine	Ford
33.	Mike Bliss	Pontiac
34.	Johnny Benson	Pontiac
35.	Rick Mast	Pontiac
36.	Jimmy Spencer	Ford

FINISH	DRIVER	CAR
37.	Stacy Compton	Ford
38.	Bill Elliott	Ford
39.	Wally Dallenbach	Ford
40.	Bobby Hamilton	Chevrolet
41.	Kyle Petty	Pontiac
42.	Joe Nemechek	Chevrolet
43.	Michael Waltrip	Chevrolet

SAVE MART/KRAGEN 350

June 25
Sonoma, California
Time of Race: 2 hours, 46 minutes, 14 seconds
Average Speed: 78.789 mph
Margin of Victory: 4.101 seconds

FINISH	DRIVER	CAR
1.	Jeff Gordon	Chevrolet
2.	Sterling Marlin	Chevrolet
3.	Mark Martin	Ford
4.	Bobby Labonte	Pontiac
5.	Ricky Rudd	Ford
6.	Dale Earnhardt	Chevrolet
7.	Dale Jarrett	Ford
8.	Jerry Nadeau	Chevrolet
9.	Robby Gordon	Ford
10.	Tony Stewart	Pontiac
11.	Joe Nemechek	Chevrolet
12.	Michael Waltrip	Chevrolet
13.	Kenny Wallace	Chevrolet
14.	Bobby Hamilton	Ford
15.	Ken Schrader	Pontiac
16.	Jeff Burton	Ford
17.	Steve Park	Chevrolet
18.	Johnny Benson	Pontiac
19.	Kyle Petty	Pontiac
20.	Mike Skinner	Chevrolet
21.	Ward Burton	Pontiac
22.	Mike Bliss	Pontiac
23.	Kenny Irwin	Chevrolet
24.	Dale Earnhardt Jr.	Chevrolet
25.	Chad Little	Ford
26.	Rusty Wallace	Ford
27.	Terry Labonte	Chevrolet
28.	Darrell Waltrip	Ford
29.	Dave Blaney	Pontiac
30.	Brett Bodine	Ford
31.	Stacy Compton	Ford
32.	Matt Kenseth	Ford
33.	Jeremy Mayfield	Ford
34.	Jimmy Spencer	Ford
35.	Bill Elliott	Ford
36.	Brian Simo	Ford
37.	Robert Pressley	Ford
38.	Elliott Sadler	Ford
39.	Scott Pruett	Ford
40.	Wally Dallenbach	Ford
41.	Kevin Lepage	Ford
42.	Boris Said	Ford
43.	John Andretti	Pontiac

PEPSI 400

July 1
Daytona Beach, Florida
Time of Race: 2 hours, 41 minutes, 32 seconds
Average Speed: 148.576 mph
Margin of Victory: 0.149 seconds

FINISH	DRIVER	CAR
1.	Jeff Burton	Ford
2.	Dale Jarrett	Ford
3.	Rusty Wallace	Ford
4.	Mark Martin	Ford

5.	Ricky Rudd	Ford
6.	Tony Stewart	Pontiac
7.	Ward Burton	Pontiac
8.	Dale Earnhardt	Chevrolet
9.	Mike Skinner	Chevrolet
10.	Jeff Gordon	Chevrolet
11.	Joe Nemechek	Chevrolet
12.	Bobby Labonte	Pontiac
13.	Johnny Benson	Pontiac
14.	John Andretti	Pontiac
15.	Jerry Nadeau	Chevrolet
16.	Chad Little	Ford
17.	Robert Pressley	Ford
18.	Elliott Sadler	Ford
19.	Kenny Wallace	Chevrolet
20.	Matt Kenseth	Ford
21.	Wally Dallenbach	Ford
22.	Kenny Irwin	Chevrolet
23.	Ken Schrader	Pontiac
24.	Dave Blaney	Pontiac
25.	Sterling Marlin	Chevrolet
26.	Ed Berrier	Ford
27.	Darrell Waltrip	Ford
28.	Mike Bliss	Pontiac
29.	Ricky Craven	Ford
30.	Kyle Petty	Pontiac
31.	Rick Mast	Pontiac
32.	Jimmy Spencer	Ford
33.	Steve Park	Chevrolet
34.	Geoffrey Bodine	Chevrolet
35.	Dale Earnhardt Jr.	Chevrolet
36.	Bobby Hamilton	Chevrolet
37.	Kevin Lepage	Ford
38.	Bill Elliott	Ford
39.	Stacy Compton	Ford
40.	Scott Pruett	Ford
41.	Terry Labonte	Chevrolet
42.	Michael Waltrip	Chevrolet
43.	Jeremy Mayfield	Ford

THATLOOK.COM 400

July 9
Loudon, New Hampshire
Time of Race: 2 hours, 48 minutes, 1 second
Average Speed: 103.145 mph
Margin of Victory: under caution

FINISH	DRIVER	CAR
1.	Tony Stewart	Pontiac
2.	Joe Nemechek	Chevrolet
3.	Mark Martin	Ford
4.	Jerry Nadeau	Chevrolet
5.	Jeff Gordon	Chevrolet
6.	Dale Earnhardt	Chevrolet
7.	Dale Jarrett	Ford
8.	Jeremy Mayfield	Ford
9.	Bobby Labonte	Pontiac
10.	Ricky Rudd	Ford
11.	Jeff Burton	Ford
12.	Rick Mast	Pontiac
13.	Geoffrey Bodine	Chevrolet
14.	Johnny Benson	Pontiac
15.	Rusty Wallace	Ford
16.	Elliott Sadler	Ford
17.	Ricky Craven	Chevrolet
18.	Ward Burton	Pontiac
19.	Matt Kenseth	Ford
20.	Brett Bodine	Ford
21.	Dale Earnhardt Jr.	Chevrolet
22.	Bobby Hamilton	Chevrolet
23.	Ken Schrader	Pontiac
24.	Bill Elliott	Ford
25.	Sterling Marlin	Chevrolet
26.	Kenny Wallace	Chevrolet
27.	Wally Dallenbach	Ford
28.	Steve Park	Chevrolet
29.	Stacy Compton	Ford
30.	Scott Pruett	Ford
31.	Kevin Lepage	Ford

32.	Mike Bliss	Pontiac
33.	Darrell Waltrip	Ford
34.	Dave Blaney	Pontiac
35.	Michael Waltrip	Chevrolet
36.	Steve Grissom	Pontiac
37.	Ed Berrier	Ford
38.	Robert Pressley	Ford
39.	Mike Skinner	Chevrolet
40.	John Andretti	Pontiac
41.	Jimmy Spencer	Ford
42.	Chad Little	Ford
43.	Terry Labonte	Chevrolet

PENNSYLVANIA 500

July 23
Pocono, Pennsylvania
Time of Race: 3 hours, 49 minutes, 36 seconds
Average Speed: 130.662 mph
Margin of Victory: 0.126 seconds

FINISH	DRIVER	CAR
1.	Rusty Wallace	Ford
2.	Jeff Burton	Ford
3.	Jeff Gordon	Chevrolet
4.	Dale Jarrett	Ford
5.	Matt Kenseth	Ford
6.	Bobby Labonte	Pontiac
7.	Mike Skinner	Chevrolet
8.	Rick Mast	Pontiac
9.	Jimmy Spencer	Ford
10.	Jeremy Mayfield	Ford
11.	Terry Labonte	Chevrolet
12.	Johnny Benson	Pontiac
13.	Dale Earnhardt Jr.	Chevrolet
14.	Robert Pressley	Ford
15.	Steve Park	Chevrolet
16.	Ted Musgrave	Chevrolet
17.	Michael Waltrip	Chevrolet
18.	Dave Blaney	Pontiac
19.	Ken Schrader	Pontiac
20.	Chad Little	Ford
21.	Kenny Wallace	Chevrolet
22.	Darrell Waltrip	Ford
23.	Kevin Lepage	Ford
24.	Mike Bliss	Pontiac
25.	Dale Earnhardt	Chevrolet
26.	Tony Stewart	Pontiac
27.	Jerry Nadeau	Chevrolet
28.	Ward Burton	Pontiac
29.	Elliott Sadler	Ford
30.	Brett Bodine	Ford
31.	Wally Dallenbach	Ford
32.	Bill Elliott	Ford
33.	Ed Berrier	Ford
34.	Joe Nemechek	Chevrolet
35.	Stacy Compton	Ford
36.	Scott Pruett	Ford
37.	Dave Marcis	Chevrolet
38.	Ricky Rudd	Ford
39.	Bobby Hamilton	Chevrolet
40.	Kyle Petty	Pontiac
41.	John Andretti	Pontiac
42.	Sterling Marlin	Chevrolet
43.	Mark Martin	Ford

BRICKYARD 400

August 5
Indianapolis, Indiana
Time of Race: 2 hours, 33 minutes, 56 seconds
Average Speed: 155.912 mph
Margin of Victory: 4.299 seconds

FINISH	DRIVER	CAR
1.	Bobby Labonte	Pontiac
2.	Rusty Wallace	Ford
3.	Bill Elliott	Ford
4.	Jerry Nadeau	Chevrolet
5.	Tony Stewart	Pontiac
6.	Jeff Burton	Ford
7.	Dale Jarrett	Ford
8.	Dale Earnhardt	Chevrolet
9.	Mike Skinner	Chevrolet
10.	Scott Pruett	Ford
11.	Darrell Waltrip	Ford
12.	Geoffrey Bodine	Chevrolet
13.	Dale Earnhardt Jr.	Chevrolet
14.	Hut Stricklin	Ford
15.	Todd Bodine	Chevrolet
16.	Steve Park	Chevrolet
17.	Jimmy Spencer	Ford
18.	Joe Nemechek	Chevrolet
19.	Chad Little	Ford
20.	Michael Waltrip	Chevrolet
21.	Ricky Rudd	Ford
22.	Ken Schrader	Pontiac
23.	Dave Blaney	Pontiac
24.	Ted Musgrave	Chevrolet
25.	Johnny Benson	Pontiac
26.	Matt Kenseth	Ford
27.	Robert Pressley	Ford
28.	Ward Burton	Pontiac
29.	Kenny Wallace	Chevrolet
30.	Sterling Marlin	Chevrolet
31.	Mike Bliss	Pontiac
32.	Kyle Petty	Pontiac
33.	Jeff Gordon	Chevrolet
34.	Elliott Sadler	Ford
35.	Wally Dallenbach	Ford
36.	Kevin Lepage	Ford
37.	Stacy Compton	Ford
38.	Rick Mast	Pontiac
39.	Brett Bodine	Ford
40.	Bobby Hamilton	Chevrolet
41.	Ricky Craven	Chevrolet
42.	John Andretti	Pontiac
43.	Mark Martin	Ford

27.	Johnny Benson	Pontiac
28.	Elliott Sadler	Ford
29.	Stacy Compton	Ford
30.	Sterling Marlin	Chevrolet
31.	Jimmy Spencer	Ford
32.	Kevin Lepage	Ford
33.	Tom Hubert	Ford
34.	Rusty Wallace	Ford
35.	Dave Blaney	Pontiac
36.	Mike Skinner	Chevrolet
37.	John Andretti	Pontiac
38.	Jerry Nadeau	Chevrolet
39.	Mike Bliss	Pontiac
40.	Dale Earnhardt Jr.	Chevrolet
41.	Kyle Petty	Pontiac
42.	Todd Bodine	Chevrolet
43.	Ron Fellows	Chevrolet

PEPSI 400 BY MEIJER

August 20
Brooklyn, Michigan
Time of Race: 3 hours, 1 minute, 0 seconds
Average Speed: 132.597 mph
Margin of Victory: 2.971 seconds

FINISH	DRIVER	CAR
1.	Rusty Wallace	Ford
2.	Ricky Rudd	Ford
3.	Bobby Labonte	Pontiac
4.	Dale Jarrett	Ford
5.	Johnny Benson	Pontiac
6.	Dale Earnhardt	Chevrolet
7.	Jimmy Spencer	Ford
8.	Matt Kenseth	Ford
9.	Ward Burton	Pontiac
10.	Jeff Burton	Ford
11.	Mark Martin	Ford
12.	Jerry Nadeau	Chevrolet
13.	Jeremy Mayfield	Ford
14.	Bobby Hamilton	Chevrolet
15.	Sterling Marlin	Chevrolet
16.	Mike Skinner	Chevrolet
17.	Scott Pruett	Ford
18.	Kevin Lepage	Ford
19.	Ken Schrader	Pontiac
20.	Terry Labonte	Chevrolet
21.	Michael Waltrip	Chevrolet
22.	Chad Little	Ford
23.	Joe Nemechek	Chevrolet
24.	Dave Blaney	Pontiac
25.	Wally Dallenbach	Ford
26.	Ted Musgrave	Chevrolet
27.	John Andretti	Pontiac
28.	Mike Bliss	Pontiac
29.	Rick Mast	Pontiac
30.	Kenny Wallace	Chevrolet
31.	Dale Earnhardt Jr.	Chevrolet
32.	Robert Pressley	Ford
33.	Steve Park	Chevrolet
34.	Robby Gordon	Ford
35.	Andy Houston	Ford
36.	Jeff Gordon	Chevrolet
37.	Ricky Craven	Chevrolet
38.	Bill Elliott	Ford
39.	Hut Stricklin	Ford
40.	Elliott Sadler	Ford
41.	Tony Stewart	Pontiac
42.	Brett Bodine	Ford
43.	Kerry Earnhardt	Chevrolet

GLOBAL CROSSING AT THE GLEN

August 13
Watkins Glen, New York
Time of Race: 2 hours, 29 minutes, 51 seconds
Average Speed: 91.336 mph
Margin of Victory: 0.384 seconds

FINISH	DRIVER	CAR
1.	Steve Park	Chevrolet
2.	Mark Martin	Ford
3.	Jeff Burton	Ford
4.	Robby Gordon	Ford
5.	Bobby Labonte	Pontiac
6.	Tony Stewart	Pontiac
7.	Dale Jarrett	Ford
8.	Joe Nemechek	Chevrolet
9.	Wally Dallenbach	Ford
10.	Matt Kenseth	Ford
11.	Ricky Rudd	Ford
12.	Chad Little	Ford
13.	Bill Elliott	Ford
14.	Kenny Wallace	Chevrolet
15.	Ron Hornaday	Chevrolet
16.	Bobby Hamilton	Chevrolet
17.	Michael Waltrip	Chevrolet
18.	Ken Schrader	Pontiac
19.	Rick Mast	Pontiac
20.	Darrell Waltrip	Ford
21.	P.J. Jones	Chevrolet
22.	Ward Burton	Pontiac
23.	Jeff Gordon	Chevrolet
24.	Geoffrey Bodine	Chevrolet
25.	Dale Earnhardt	Chevrolet
26.	Robert Pressley	Ford

GORACING.COM 500

August 26
Bristol, Tennessee
Time of Race: 3 hours, 7 minutes, 15 seconds
Average Speed: 85.292 mph
Margin of Victory: 0.501 seconds

FINISH	DRIVER	CAR
1.	Rusty Wallace	Ford
2.	Tony Stewart	Pontiac
3.	Mark Martin	Ford
4.	Dale Earnhardt	Chevrolet
5.	Steve Park	Chevrolet
6.	Jeff Burton	Ford
7.	Elliott Sadler	Ford
8.	Sterling Marlin	Chevrolet
9.	Dale Jarrett	Ford
10.	Ricky Rudd	Ford
11.	Ward Burton	Pontiac
12.	Ken Schrader	Pontiac
13.	Johnny Benson	Pontiac
14.	Mike Skinner	Chevrolet
15.	Bobby Labonte	Pontiac
16.	Terry Labonte	Chevrolet
17.	Ted Musgrave	Chevrolet
18.	Kevin Lepage	Ford
19.	Michael Waltrip	Chevrolet
20.	John Andretti	Pontiac
21.	Dale Earnhardt Jr.	Chevrolet
22.	Kyle Petty	Pontiac
23.	Jeff Gordon	Chevrolet
24.	Jimmy Spencer	Ford
25.	Geoffrey Bodine	Chevrolet
26.	Kenny Wallace	Chevrolet
27.	Joe Nemechek	Chevrolet
28.	Brett Bodine	Ford
29.	Rick Mast	Pontiac
30.	Chad Little	Ford
31.	Dave Marcis	Chevrolet
32.	Jerry Nadeau	Chevrolet
33.	Wally Dallenbach	Ford
34.	Bobby Hamilton	Chevrolet
35.	Jeremy Mayfield	Ford
36.	David Green	Ford
37.	Robert Pressley	Ford
38.	Scott Pruett	Ford
39.	Matt Kenseth	Ford
40.	Bobby Hillin	Ford
41.	Robby Gordon	Ford
42.	Darrell Waltrip	Ford
43.	Dave Blaney	Pontiac

PEPSI SOUTHERN 500

September 3
Darlington, South Carolina
Time of Race: 4 hours, 8 minutes, 20 seconds
Average Speed: 108.273mph
Margin of Victory: under caution

FINISH	DRIVER	CAR
1.	Bobby Labonte	Pontiac
2.	Jeff Burton	Ford
3.	Dale Earnhardt	Chevrolet
4.	Jeff Gordon	Chevrolet
5.	Dale Jarrett	Ford
6.	Ward Burton	Pontiac
7.	Kevin Lepage	Ford
8.	Ricky Rudd	Ford
9.	Tony Stewart	Pontiac
10.	Steve Park	Chevrolet
11.	Dale Earnhardt Jr.	Chevrolet
12.	Rick Mast	Pontiac
13.	Ted Musgrave	Chevrolet
14.	Mark Martin	Ford
15.	Terry Labonte	Chevrolet
16.	Ken Schrader	Pontiac
17.	Sterling Marlin	Chevrolet
18.	Elliott Sadler	Ford
19.	Wally Dallenbach	Ford
20.	Dave Blaney	Pontiac
21.	Chad Little	Ford
22.	Bobby Hamilton	Chevrolet
23.	Dave Marcis	Chevrolet
24.	Scott Pruett	Ford
25.	David Green	Ford

FINISH	DRIVER	CAR
26.	Steve Grissom	Pontiac
27.	Brett Bodine	Ford
28.	Mike Bliss	Pontiac
29.	Jerry Nadeau	Chevrolet
30.	Rusty Wallace	Ford
31.	Joe Nemechek	Chevrolet
32.	Jimmy Spencer	Ford
33.	Matt Kenseth	Ford
34.	Hut Stricklin	Ford
35.	Kenny Wallace	Chevrolet
36.	Robert Pressley	Ford
37.	John Andretti	Pontiac
38.	Johnny Benson	Pontiac
39.	Geoffrey Bodine	Chevrolet
40.	Michael Waltrip	Chevrolet
41.	Jeremy Mayfield	Ford
42.	Darrell Waltrip	Ford
43.	Mike Skinner	Chevrolet

CHEVROLET MONTE CARLO 400

September 9
Richmond, Virginia
Time of Race: 3 hours, 0 minutes, 14 seconds
Average Speed: 99.871 mph
Margin of Victory: 0.744 seconds

FINISH	DRIVER	CAR
1.	Jeff Gordon	Chevrolet
2.	Dale Earnhardt	Chevrolet
3.	Mark Martin	Ford
4.	Steve Park	Chevrolet
5.	Jeff Burton	Ford
6.	Tony Stewart	Pontiac
7.	Johnny Benson	Pontiac
8.	Ward Burton	Pontiac
9.	Ricky Rudd	Ford
10.	Jerry Nadeau	Chevrolet
11.	John Andretti	Pontiac
12.	Bill Elliott	Ford
13.	Dale Earnhardt Jr.	Chevrolet
14.	Kenny Wallace	Chevrolet
15.	Bobby Labonte	Pontiac
16.	Scott Pruett	Ford
17.	Ken Schrader	Pontiac
18.	Dave Blaney	Pontiac
19.	Casey Atwood	Ford
20.	Sterling Marlin	Chevrolet
21.	Ted Musgrave	Chevrolet
22.	Kevin Lepage	Ford
23.	Wally Dallenbach	Ford
24.	Stacy Compton	Ford
25.	Terry Labonte	Chevrolet
26.	Ricky Craven	Chevrolet
27.	Steve Grissom	Pontiac
28.	Rick Mast	Pontiac
29.	Chad Little	Ford
30.	Mike Skinner	Chevrolet
31.	Dale Jarrett	Ford
32.	Matt Kenseth	Ford
33.	Jimmy Spencer	Ford
34.	Rusty Wallace	Ford
35.	Brett Bodine	Ford
36.	Hut Stricklin	Ford
37.	Robert Pressley	Ford
38.	Bobby Hamilton	Chevrolet
39.	Jeremy Mayfield	Ford
40.	Joe Nemechek	Chevrolet
41.	Geoffrey Bodine	Chevrolet
42.	Elliott Sadler	Ford
43.	Michael Waltrip	Chevrolet

DURA-LUBE 300 BY KMART

September 17
Loudon, New Hampshire
Time of Race: 3 hours, 6 minutes, 42 seconds

Average Speed: 102.003 mph
Margin of Victory: under caution

FINISH	DRIVER	CAR
1.	Jeff Burton	Ford
2.	Bobby Labonte	Pontiac
3.	Ricky Rudd	Ford
4.	Dale Jarrett	Ford
5.	Rusty Wallace	Ford
6.	Jeff Gordon	Chevrolet
7.	John Andretti	Pontiac
8.	Mark Martin	Ford
9.	Joe Nemechek	Chevrolet
10.	Ken Schrader	Pontiac
11.	Johnny Benson	Pontiac
12.	Dale Earnhardt	Chevrolet
13.	Elliott Sadler	Ford
14.	Ted Musgrave	Chevrolet
15.	Jimmy Spencer	Ford
16.	Stacy Compton	Ford
17.	Matt Kenseth	Ford
18.	Robert Pressley	Ford
19.	Mike Bliss	Pontiac
20.	Michael Waltrip	Chevrolet
21.	Jerry Nadeau	Chevrolet
22.	Sterling Marlin	Chevrolet
23.	Tony Stewart	Pontiac
24.	Mike Skinner	Chevrolet
25.	Terry Labonte	Chevrolet
26.	Dave Blaney	Pontiac
27.	Joe Bessey	Chevrolet
28.	Hut Stricklin	Ford
29.	Darrell Waltrip	Ford
30.	Ward Burton	Pontiac
31.	Dale Earnhardt Jr.	Chevrolet
32.	Rick Mast	Pontiac
33.	Chad Little	Ford
34.	Steve Park	Chevrolet
35.	Bobby Hamilton	Chevrolet
36.	Ricky Craven	Chevrolet
37.	Bill Elliott	Ford
38.	Kevin Lepage	Ford
39.	Wally Dallenbach	Ford
40.	Jeremy Mayfield	Ford
41.	Scott Pruett	Ford
42.	Brett Bodine	Ford
43.	Kenny Wallace	Chevrolet

MBNA.COM 400

September 24
Dover, Delaware
Time of Race: 3 hours, 28 minutes, 21 seconds
Average Speed: 115.191 mph
Margin of Victory: 6.752 seconds

FINISH	DRIVER	CAR
1.	Tony Stewart	Pontiac
2.	Johnny Benson	Pontiac
3.	Ricky Rudd	Ford
4.	Steve Park	Chevrolet
5.	Jeff Burton	Ford
6.	Mark Martin	Ford
7.	Joe Nemechek	Chevrolet
8.	Rusty Wallace	Ford
9.	Jeff Gordon	Chevrolet
10.	Rick Mast	Pontiac
11.	Mike Skinner	Chevrolet
12.	Matt Kenseth	Ford
13.	Terry Labonte	Chevrolet
14.	Robert Pressley	Ford
15.	Kenny Wallace	Chevrolot
16.	Dale Earnhardt Jr.	Chevrolet
17.	Dale Earnhardt	Chevrolet
18.	Kurt Busch	Ford
19.	Bill Elliott	Ford
20.	Brett Bodine	Ford
21.	Wally Dallenbach	Chevrolet
22.	John Andretti	Pontiac

23.	Ted Musgrave	Chevrolet
24.	Michael Waltrip	Chevrolet
25.	Bobby Hamilton	Chevrolet
26.	Elliott Sadler	Ford
27.	Steve Grissom	Pontiac
28.	Dave Marcis	Chevrolet
29.	Stacy Compton	Ford
30.	Ken Schrader	Pontiac
31.	Darrell Waltrip	Ford
32.	Dale Jarrett	Ford
33.	Jerry Nadeau	Chevrolet
34.	Jimmy Spencer	Ford
35.	Jeremy Mayfield	Ford
36.	Jeff Burton	Ford
37.	Sterling Marlin	Chevrolet
38.	Kevin Lepage	Ford
39.	Dave Blaney	Pontiac
40.	Ward Burton	Pontiac
41.	Carl Long	Ford
42.	Scott Pruett	Ford
43.	Mike Bliss	Pontiac

NAPA AUTOCARE 500

October 1
Martinsville, Virginia
Time of Race: 3 hours, 33 minutes, 39 seconds
Average Speed: 73.859 mph
Margin of Victory: 0.672 seconds

FINISH	DRIVER	CAR
1.	Tony Stewart	Pontiac
2.	Dale Earnhardt	Chevrolet
3.	Jeff Burton	Ford
4.	Ricky Rudd	Ford
5.	Jeff Gordon	Chevrolet
6.	Dale Jarrett	Ford
7.	Jimmy Spencer	Ford
8.	Mike Skinner	Chevrolet
9.	Sterling Marlin	Chevrolet
10.	Bobby Labonte	Pontiac
11.	Steve Park	Chevrolet
12.	Jerry Nadeau	Chevrolet
13.	John Andretti	Pontiac
14.	Joe Nemechek	Chevrolet
15.	Bill Elliott	Ford
16.	Ken Schrader	Pontiac
17.	Terry Labonte	Chevrolet
18.	Mark Martin	Ford
19.	Johnny Benson	Pontiac
20.	Ricky Craven	Chevrolet
21.	Ted Musgrave	Chevrolet
22.	Kenny Wallace	Chevrolet
23.	Rusty Wallace	Ford
24.	Michael Waltrip	Chevrolet
25.	Casey Atwood	Ford
26.	Rick Mast	Pontiac
27.	Darrell Waltrip	Ford
28.	Mike Bliss	Pontiac
29.	Kevin Lepage	Ford
30.	Dave Blaney	Pontiac
31.	Kyle Petty	Pontiac
32.	Elliott Sadler	Ford
33.	Robert Pressley	Ford
34.	Matt Kenseth	Ford
35.	Bobby Hamilton	Chevrolet
36.	Dale Earnhardt Jr.	Chevrolet
37.	Kurt Busch	Ford
38.	Jeremy Mayfield	Ford
39.	Stacy Compton	Ford
40.	Wally Dallenbach	Ford
41.	Brett Bodine	Ford
42.	Hut Stricklin	Ford
43.	Ward Burton	Pontiac

UAW-GM QUALITY 500

October 8
Concord, North Carolina

Time of Race: 3 hours, 44 minutes, 57 seconds
Average Speed: 133.630 mph
Margin of Victory: 1.166 seconds

FINISH	DRIVER	CAR
1.	Bobby Labonte	Pontiac
2.	Jeremy Mayfield	Ford
3.	Ricky Rudd	Ford
4.	Tony Stewart	Pontiac
5.	Mark Martin	Ford
6.	Jeff Burton	Ford
7.	Steve Park	Chevrolet
8.	Johnny Benson	Pontiac
9.	Matt Kenseth	Ford
10.	Ward Burton	Pontiac
11.	Dale Earnhardt	Chevrolet
12.	Kevin Lepage	Ford
13.	Kurt Busch	Ford
14.	Joe Nemechek	Chevrolet
15.	Jimmy Spencer	Ford
16.	Elliott Sadler	Ford
17.	Rick Mast	Pontiac
18.	John Andretti	Pontiac
19.	Dale Earnhardt Jr.	Chevrolet
20.	Mike Skinner	Chevrolet
21.	Rusty Wallace	Ford
22.	Michael Waltrip	Chevrolet
23.	Dick Trickle	Chevrolet
24.	Bobby Hamilton	Chevrolet
25.	Ken Schrader	Pontiac
26.	Andy Houston	Ford
27.	Terry Labonte	Chevrolet
28.	Dave Blaney	Pontiac
29.	Ted Musgrave	Chevrolet
30.	Darrell Waltrip	Ford
31.	Sterling Marlin	Chevrolet
32.	Brett Bodine	Ford
33.	Wally Dallenbach	Ford
34.	Bill Elliott	Ford
35.	Robert Pressley	Ford
36.	Jerry Nadeau	Chevrolet
37.	Kenny Wallace	Chevrolet
38.	Robby Gordon	Ford
39.	Jeff Gordon	Chevrolet
40.	Dale Jarrett	Ford
41.	Jeff Fuller	Ford
42.	Hut Stricklin	Ford
43.	Mike Bliss	Pontiac

FINISH	DRIVER	CAR
20.	John Andretti	Pontiac
21.	Rich Bickle	Chevrolet
22.	Ward Burton	Pontiac
23.	Stacy Compton	Ford
24.	Bill Elliott	Ford
25.	Robert Pressley	Ford
26.	Brett Bodine	Ford
27.	Tony Stewart	Pontiac
28.	Dave Blaney	Pontiac
29.	Jeff Burton	Ford
30.	Ricky Craven	Chevrolet
31.	Rick Mast	Pontiac
32.	Ted Musgrave	Chevrolet
33.	Johnny Benson	Pontiac
34.	Michael Waltrip	Chevrolet
35.	Darrell Waltrip	Ford
36.	Bobby Hamilton	Chevrolet
37.	Ken Schrader	Pontiac
38.	Jimmy Spencer	Ford
39.	Scott Pruett	Ford
40.	Dave Marcis	Chevrolet
41.	Sterling Marlin	Chevrolet
42.	Jeremy Mayfield	Ford
43.	Kevin Lepage	Ford

WINSTON 500

October 15
Talladega, Alabama
Time of Race: 3 hours, 1 minute, 6 seconds
Average Speed: 165.681 mph
Margin of Victory: 0.119 seconds

FINISH	DRIVER	CAR
1.	Dale Earnhardt	Chevrolet
2.	Kenny Wallace	Chevrolet
3.	Joe Nemechek	Chevrolet
4.	Jeff Gordon	Chevrolet
5.	Terry Labonte	Chevrolet
6.	Mike Skinner	Chevrolet
7.	Mark Martin	Ford
8.	Rusty Wallace	Ford
9.	Mike Bliss	Pontiac
10.	Matt Kenseth	Ford
11.	Ricky Rudd	Ford
12.	Bobby Labonte	Pontiac
13.	Jerry Nadeau	Chevrolet
14.	Dale Earnhardt Jr.	Chevrolet
15.	Dale Jarrett	Ford
16.	Steve Grissom	Pontiac
17.	Elliott Sadler	Ford
18.	Chad Little	Ford
19.	Steve Park	Chevrolet

POP SECRET 400

October 22
Rockingham, North Carolina
Time of Race: 3 hours, 37 minutes, 11 seconds
Average Speed: 110.418 mph
Margin of Victory: 2.197 seconds

FINISH	DRIVER	CAR
1.	Dale Jarrett	Ford
2.	Jeff Gordon	Chevrolet
3.	Ricky Rudd	Ford
4.	Jeff Burton	Ford
5.	Rusty Wallace	Ford
6.	Steve Park	Chevrolet
7.	Tony Stewart	Pontiac
8.	Ward Burton	Pontiac
9.	Bobby Hamilton	Chevrolet
10.	Joe Nemechek	Chevrolet
11.	Johnny Benson	Pontiac
12.	Robert Pressley	Ford
13.	Rick Mast	Pontiac
14.	Mike Skinner	Chevrolet
15.	Ricky Craven	Chevrolet
16.	Bill Elliott	Ford
17.	Dale Earnhardt	Chevrolet
18.	Ken Schrader	Pontiac
19.	Elliott Sadler	Ford
20.	Bobby Labonte	Pontiac
21.	Mike Bliss	Pontiac
22.	Wally Dallenbach	Ford
23.	John Andretti	Pontiac
24.	Kurt Busch	Ford
25.	Matt Kenseth	Ford
26.	Brett Bodine	Ford
27.	Jerry Nadeau	Chevrolet
28.	Andy Houston	Ford
29.	Jeremy Mayfield	Ford
30.	Scott Pruett	Ford
31.	Dave Marcis	Chevrolet
32.	Carl Long	Ford
33.	Sterling Marlin	Chevrolet
34.	Dale Earnhardt Jr.	Chevrolet
35.	Michael Waltrip	Chevrolet
36.	Kevin Lepage	Ford
37.	Darrell Waltrip	Ford
38.	Terry Labonte	Chevrolet
39.	Jimmy Spencer	Ford
40.	Mark Martin	Ford
41.	Robby Gordon	Ford
42.	Dave Blaney	Pontiac
43.	Kenny Wallace	Chevrolet

CHECKER AUTO PARTS 400

November 5
Phoenix, Arizona
Time of Race: 2 hours, 58 minutes, 13 seconds
Average Speed: 105.041 mph
Margin of Victory: 0.854 seconds

FINISH	DRIVER	CAR
1.	Jeff Burton	Ford
2.	Jeremy Mayfield	Ford
3.	Steve Park	Chevrolet
4.	Rusty Wallace	Ford
5.	Bobby Labonte	Pontiac
6.	Mark Martin	Ford
7.	Jeff Gordon	Chevrolet
8.	Dave Blaney	Pontiac
9.	Dale Earnhardt	Chevrolet
10.	Dale Jarrett	Ford
11.	Mike Skinner	Chevrolet
12.	Ward Burton	Pontiac
13.	Jimmy Spencer	Ford
14.	Tony Stewart	Pontiac
15.	Sterling Marlin	Chevrolet
16.	Johnny Benson	Pontiac
17.	Terry Labonte	Chevrolet
18.	Ricky Craven	Chevrolet
19.	Kenny Wallace	Chevrolet
20.	Brett Bodine	Ford
21.	Kevin Lepage	Ford
22.	Wally Dallenbach	Ford
23.	Jerry Nadeau	Chevrolet
24.	Joe Nemechek	Chevrolet
25.	Ted Musgrave	Chevrolet
26.	Bill Elliott	Ford
27.	Dale Earnhardt Jr.	Chevrolet
28.	John Andretti	Pontiac
29.	Kurt Busch	Ford
30.	Elliott Sadler	Ford
31.	Robert Pressley	Ford
32.	Michael Waltrip	Chevrolet
33.	Darrell Waltrip	Ford
34.	Scott Pruett	Ford
35.	Rich Bickle	Chevrolet
36.	Andy Houston	Ford
37.	Ricky Rudd	Ford
38.	Mike Bliss	Pontiac
39.	Rick Mast	Pontiac
40.	Ken Schrader	Pontiac
41.	Ryan Newman	Ford
42.	Matt Kenseth	Ford
43.	Bobby Hamilton	Chevrolet

PENNZOIL 400

November 12
Homestead, Florida
Time of Race: 3 hours, 6 minutes, 30 seconds
Average Speed: 127.480 mph
Margin of Victory: 4.561 seconds

FINISH	DRIVER	CAR
1.	Tony Stewart	Pontiac
2.	Jeremy Mayfield	Ford
3.	Mark Martin	Ford
4.	Bobby Labonte	Pontiac
5.	Jimmy Spencer	Ford
6.	Ricky Rudd	Ford
7.	Jeff Gordon	Chevrolet
8.	Steve Park	Chevrolet
9.	Dave Blaney	Pontiac
10.	Casey Atwood	Ford
11.	Jeff Burton	Ford
12.	Jerry Nadeau	Chevrolet
13.	Dale Earnhardt Jr.	Chevrolet
14.	Brett Bodine	Ford
15.	Rusty Wallace	Ford

NAPA 500

November 20
Hampton, Georgia
Time of Race: 3 hours, 32 minutes, 32 seconds
Average Speed: 141.296 mph
Margin of Victory: 1.338 seconds

FINISH	DRIVER	CAR
16.	Robert Pressley	Ford
17.	Dale Jarrett	Ford
18.	Joe Nemechek	Chevrolet
19.	Kurt Busch	Ford
20.	Dale Earnhardt	Chevrolet
21.	Matt Kenseth	Ford
22.	Bill Elliott	Ford
23.	Mike Skinner	Chevrolet
24.	Kenny Wallace	Chevrolet
25.	Terry Labonte	Chevrolet
26.	Sterling Marlin	Chevrolet
27.	Kevin Lepage	Ford
28.	Elliott Sadler	Ford
29.	Rick Mast	Pontiac
30.	Johnny Benson	Pontiac
31.	Bobby Hamilton	Chevrolet
32.	Ken Schrader	Pontiac
33.	Bobby Hamilton Jr.	Chevrolet
34.	Michael Waltrip	Chevrolet
35.	Wally Dallenbach	Ford
36.	Darrell Waltrip	Ford
37.	John Andretti	Pontiac
38.	Stacy Compton	Ford
39.	Ward Burton	Pontiac
40.	Mike Bliss	Pontiac
41.	Geoffrey Bodine	Ford
42.	Andy Houston	Ford
43.	Scott Pruett	Ford

FINISH	DRIVER	CAR
1.	Jerry Nadeau	Chevrolet
2.	Dale Earnhardt	Chevrolet
3.	Ward Burton	Pontiac
4.	Jeff Gordon	Chevrolet
5.	Bobby Labonte	Pontiac
6.	Mike Skinner	Chevrolet
7.	Rusty Wallace	Ford
8.	Sterling Marlin	Chevrolet
9.	Matt Kenseth	Ford
10.	Johnny Benson	Pontiac
11.	Bill Elliott	Ford
12.	Jeff Burton	Ford
13.	Robert Pressley	Ford
14.	Todd Bodine	Ford
15.	Dale Jarrett	Ford
16.	Bobby Hamilton	Chevrolet
17.	Terry Labonte	Chevrolet
18.	Dave Blaney	Pontiac
19.	John Andretti	Pontiac
20.	Dale Earnhardt Jr.	Chevrolet
21.	Steve Park	Chevrolet
22.	Scott Wimmer	Pontiac
23.	Kenny Wallace	Chevrolet
24.	Ricky Rudd	Ford
25.	Joe Nemechek	Chevrolet
26.	Ken Schrader	Pontiac
27.	Robby Gordon	Ford
28.	Brett Bodine	Ford
29.	Wally Dallenbach	Ford
30.	Ricky Craven	Chevrolet
31.	Bobby Hamilton Jr.	Chevrolet
32.	Scott Pruett	Ford
33.	Jimmy Spencer	Ford
34.	Darrell Waltrip	Ford
35.	Rick Mast	Pontiac
36.	Kurt Busch	Ford
37.	Buckshot Jones	Pontiac
38.	Tony Stewart	Pontiac
39.	Michael Waltrip	Chevrolet
40.	Mark Martin	Ford
41.	Jeremy Mayfield	Ford
42.	Elliott Sadler	Ford
43.	Geoffrey Bodine	Chevrolet

2001

DAYTONA 500

February 18
Daytona Beach, Florida
Time of Race: 3 hours, 5 minutes, 26 seconds
Average Speed: 161.783 mph
Margin of Victory: 0.124 seconds

FINISH	DRIVER	CAR
1.	Michael Waltrip	Chevrolet
2.	Dale Earnhardt Jr.	Chevrolet
3.	Rusty Wallace	Ford
4.	Ricky Rudd	Ford
5.	Bill Elliott	Dodge
6.	Mike Wallace	Ford
7.	Sterling Marlin	Dodge
8.	Bobby Hamilton	Chevrolet
9.	Jeremy Mayfield	Ford
10.	Stacy Compton	Dodge
11.	Joe Nemechek	Chevrolet
12.	Dale Earnhardt	Chevrolet
13.	Ken Schrader	Pontiac
14.	Robert Pressley	Ford
15.	Brett Bodine	Ford
16.	Kyle Petty	Dodge
17.	Ron Hornaday	Pontiac
18.	Elliott Sadler	Ford
19.	Jeff Burton	Ford
20.	Casey Atwood	Dodge
21.	Matt Kenseth	Ford
22.	Dale Jarrett	Ford
23.	Ricky Craven	Ford
24.	Terry Labonte	Chevrolet
25.	Kenny Wallace	Pontiac
26.	Mike Skinner	Chevrolet
27.	Jimmy Spencer	Ford
28.	Johnny Benson	Pontiac
29.	Buckshot Jones	Dodge
30.	Jeff Gordon	Chevrolet
31.	Steve Park	Chevrolet
32.	Jerry Nadeau	Chevrolet
33.	Mark Martin	Ford
34.	Jason Leffler	Dodge
35.	Ward Burton	Dodge
36.	Tony Stewart	Pontiac
37.	Robby Gordon	Chevrolet
38.	Andy Houston	Ford
39.	John Andretti	Dodge
40.	Bobby Labonte	Pontiac
41.	Kurt Busch	Ford
42.	Dave Blaney	Dodge
43.	Jeff Purvis	Ford

DURA LUBE 400

February 25
Rockingham, North Carolina
Time of Race: 3 hours, 33 minutes, 21 seconds
Average Speed: 111.877 mph
Margin of Victory: 0.138 seconds

FINISH	DRIVER	CAR
1.	Steve Park	Chevrolet
2.	Bobby Labonte	Pontiac
3.	Jeff Gordon	Chevrolet
4.	Tony Stewart	Pontiac
5.	Ricky Craven	Ford
6.	Johnny Benson	Pontiac
7.	Rusty Wallace	Ford
8.	Sterling Marlin	Dodge
9.	Dave Blaney	Dodge
10.	Dale Jarrett	Ford
11.	Elliott Sadler	Ford

12.	Robert Pressley	Ford
13.	Bobby Hamilton	Chevrolet
14.	Kevin Harvick	Chevrolet
15.	Jerry Nadeau	Chevrolet
16.	Ward Burton	Dodge
17.	Joe Nemechek	Chevrolet
18.	Casey Atwood	Dodge
19.	Michael Waltrip	Chevrolet
20.	Mark Martin	Ford
21.	John Andretti	Dodge
22.	Ken Schrader	Pontiac
23.	Bill Elliott	Dodge
24.	Mike Skinner	Chevrolet
25.	Ron Hornaday	Pontiac
26.	Robby Gordon	Chevrolet
27.	Brett Bodine	Ford
28.	Matt Kenseth	Ford
29.	Terry Labonte	Chevrolet
30.	Jimmy Spencer	Ford
31.	Hut Stricklin	Ford
32.	Rick Mast	Chevrolet
33.	Jason Leffler	Dodge
34.	Todd Bodine	Ford
35.	Buckshot Jones	Dodge
36.	Kurt Busch	Ford
37.	Jeff Burton	Ford
38.	Jeremy Mayfield	Ford
39.	Ricky Rudd	Ford
40.	Mike Wallace	Ford
41.	Stacy Compton	Dodge
42.	Kenny Wallace	Pontiac
43.	Dale Earnhardt Jr.	Chevrolet

UAW-DAIMLER CHRYSLER 400

March 4
Las Vegas, Nevada
Time of Race: 2 hours, 57 minutes, 17 seconds
Average Speed: 135.546 mph
Margin of Victory: 1.477 seconds

FINISH	DRIVER	CAR
1.	Jeff Gordon	Chevrolet
2.	Dale Jarrett	Ford
3.	Sterling Marlin	Dodge
4.	Johnny Benson	Pontiac
5.	Todd Bodine	Ford
6.	Mark Martin	Ford
7.	Steve Park	Chevrolet
8.	Kevin Harvick	Chevrolet
9.	Ron Hornaday	Pontiac
10.	Jimmy Spencer	Ford
11.	Kurt Busch	Ford
12.	Tony Stewart	Pontiac
13.	Michael Waltrip	Chevrolet
14.	Bill Elliott	Dodge
15.	Jerry Nadeau	Chevrolet
16.	Robert Pressley	Ford
17.	Matt Kenseth	Ford
18.	Mike Skinner	Chevrolet
19.	Ricky Rudd	Ford
20.	Elliott Sadler	Ford
21.	Ward Burton	Dodge
22.	Terry Labonte	Chevrolet
23.	Dale Earnhardt Jr.	Chevrolet
24.	Casey Atwood	Dodge
25.	Ken Schrader	Pontiac
26.	Dave Blaney	Dodge
27.	Stacy Compton	Dodge
28.	Jason Leffler	Dodge
29.	Bobby Labonte	Pontiac
30.	Bobby Hamilton	Chevrolet
31.	Kenny Wallace	Pontiac
32.	Mike Skinner	Chevrolet
33.	Ryan Newman	Ford
34.	Robby Gordon	Chevrolet
35.	Joe Nemechek	Chevrolet
36.	Buckshot Jones	Dodge
37.	John Andretti	Dodge
38.	Brett Bodine	Ford
39.	Jeff Burton	Ford

40.	Hut Stricklin	Ford
41.	Ricky Craven	Ford
42.	Jeremy Mayfield	Ford
43.	Rusty Wallace	Ford

CRACKER BARREL OLD COUNTRY STORE 500

March 11
Hampton, Georgia
Time of Race: 3 hours, 29 minutes, 36 seconds
Average Speed: 143.273 mph
Margin of Victory: 0.006 seconds

FINISH	DRIVER	CAR
1.	Kevin Harvick	Chevrolet
2.	Jeff Gordon	Chevrolet
3.	Jerry Nadeau	Chevrolet
4.	Dale Jarrett	Ford
5.	Terry Labonte	Chevrolet
6.	Ricky Rudd	Ford
7.	Johnny Benson	Pontiac
8.	Ken Schrader	Pontiac
9.	Mike Skinner	Chevrolet
10.	Kurt Busch	Ford
11.	Ward Burton	Dodge
12.	Rusty Wallace	Ford
13.	Ricky Craven	Ford
14.	John Andretti	Dodge
15.	Dale Earnhardt Jr.	Chevrolet
16.	Bill Elliott	Dodge
17.	Joe Nemechek	Chevrolet
18.	Todd Bodine	Ford
19.	Buckshot Jones	Dodge
20.	Robby Gordon	Chevrolet
21.	Andy Houston	Ford
22.	Bobby Hamilton	Chevrolet
23.	Michael Waltrip	Chevrolet
24.	Stacy Compton	Dodge
25.	Jimmy Spencer	Ford
26.	Brett Bodine	Ford
27.	Tony Stewart	Pontiac
28.	Hut Stricklin	Ford
29.	Kenny Wallace	Pontiac
30.	Jeff Burton	Ford
31.	Elliott Sadler	Ford
32.	Jason Leffler	Dodge
33.	Bobby Labonte	Pontiac
34.	Dave Blaney	Dodge
35.	Sterling Marlin	Dodge
36.	Robert Pressley	Ford
37.	Matt Kenseth	Ford
38.	Jeremy Mayfield	Ford
39.	Ron Hornaday	Pontiac
40.	Mike Wallace	Ford
41.	Mark Martin	Ford
42.	Kyle Petty	Dodge
43.	Steve Park	Chevrolet

CAROLINA DODGE DEALERS 400

March 18
Darlington, South Carolina
Time of Race: 3 hours, 9 minutes, 45 seconds
Average Speed: 126.557 mph
Margin of Victory: 0.527 seconds

FINISH	DRIVER	CAR
1.	Dale Jarrett	Ford
2.	Steve Park	Chevrolet
3.	Jeremy Mayfield	Ford
4.	Jimmy Spencer	Ford
5.	Sterling Marlin	Dodge
6.	John Andretti	Dodge
7.	Johnny Benson	Pontiac
8.	Ricky Rudd	Ford

9.	Bobby Hamilton	Chevrolet
10.	Rusty Wallace	Ford
11.	Bobby Labonte	Pontiac
12.	Ward Burton	Dodge
13.	Ken Schrader	Pontiac
14.	Kevin Harvick	Chevrolet
15.	Robert Pressley	Ford
16.	Elliott Sadler	Ford
17.	Tony Stewart	Pontiac
18.	Jeff Burton	Ford
19.	Matt Kenseth	Ford
20.	Jerry Nadeau	Chevrolet
21.	Mark Martin	Ford
22.	Dave Blaney	Dodge
23.	Bill Elliott	Dodge
24.	Joe Nemechek	Chevrolet
25.	Michael Waltrip	Chevrolet
26.	Casey Atwood	Dodge
27.	Ricky Craven	Ford
28.	Hut Stricklin	Ford
29.	Robby Gordon	Chevrolet
30.	Kurt Busch	Ford
31.	Kenny Wallace	Pontiac
32.	Mike Wallace	Ford
33.	Todd Bodine	Ford
34.	Dale Earnhardt Jr.	Chevrolet
35.	Kyle Petty	Dodge
36.	Brett Bodine	Ford
37.	Mike Skinner	Chevrolet
38.	Terry Labonte	Chevrolet
39.	Jason Leffler	Dodge
40.	Jeff Gordon	Chevrolet
41.	Buckshot Jones	Dodge
42.	Ron Hornaday	Pontiac
43.	Stacy Compton	Dodge

FOOD CITY 500

March 25
Bristol, Tennessee
Time of Race: 3 hours, 3 minutes, 54 seconds
Average Speed: 86.949 mph
Margin of Victory: 0.426 seconds

FINISH	DRIVER	CAR
1.	Elliott Sadler	Ford
2.	John Andretti	Dodge
3.	Jeremy Mayfield	Ford
4.	Jeff Gordon	Chevrolet
5.	Ward Burton	Dodge
6.	Terry Labonte	Chevrolet
7.	Rusty Wallace	Ford
8.	Bobby Hamilton	Chevrolet
9.	Steve Park	Chevrolet
10.	Ricky Rudd	Ford
11.	Stacy Compton	Dodge
12.	Sterling Marlin	Dodge
13.	Bobby Labonte	Pontiac
14.	Matt Kenseth	Ford
15.	Kevin LePage	Chevrolet
16.	Dale Jarrett	Ford
17.	Bill Elliott	Dodge
18.	Mike Skinner	Chevrolet
19.	Jimmy Spencer	Ford
20.	Casey Atwood	Dodge
21.	Ron Hornaday	Pontiac
22.	Michael Waltrip	Chevrolet
23.	Ricky Craven	Ford
24.	Kevin Harvick	Chevrolet
25.	Tony Stewart	Pontiac
26.	Johnny Benson	Pontiac
27.	Brett Bodine	Ford
28.	Robert Pressley	Ford
29.	Dave Blaney	Dodge
30.	Jerry Nadeau	Chevrolet
31.	Dale Earnhardt Jr.	Chevrolet
32.	Todd Bodine	Ford
33.	Buckshot Jones	Dodge
34.	Mark Martin	Ford
35.	Ken Schrader	Pontiac
36.	Rick Mast	Chevrolet

37.	Mike Wallace	Ford
38.	Kenny Wallace	Pontiac
39.	Andy Houston	Ford
40.	Jeff Burton	Ford
41.	Kyle Petty	Dodge
42.	Kurt Busch	Ford
43.	Joe Nemechek	Chevrolet

HARRAH'S 500

April 1
Fort Worth, Texas
Time of Race: 3 hours, 31 minutes, 59 seconds
Average Speed: 141.804 mph
Margin of Victory: 0.703 seconds

FINISH	DRIVER	CAR
1.	Dale Jarrett	Ford
2.	Steve Park	Chevrolet
3.	Johnny Benson	Pontiac
4.	Kurt Busch	Ford
5.	Jeff Gordon	Chevrolet
6.	Dave Blaney	Dodge
7.	Kevin Harvick	Chevrolet
8.	Dale Earnhardt Jr.	Chevrolet
9.	Mark Martin	Ford
10.	Ken Schrader	Pontiac
11.	Kevin LePage	Chevrolet
12.	Rusty Wallace	Ford
13.	Terry Labonte	Chevrolet
14.	Bill Elliott	Dodge
15.	Stacy Compton	Dodge
16.	Elliott Sadler	Ford
17.	Jason Leffler	Dodge
18.	Bobby Hamilton	Chevrolet
19.	Jeff Burton	Ford
20.	Matt Kenseth	Ford
21.	Ward Burton	Dodge
22.	Jeremy Mayfield	Ford
23.	Tony Stewart	Pontiac
24.	Mike Wallace	Ford
25.	Kenny Wallace	Pontiac
26.	Hut Stricklin	Ford
27.	Ricky Craven	Ford
28.	Brett Bodine	Ford
29.	Jerry Nadeau	Chevrolet
30.	Mike Skinner	Chevrolet
31.	John Andretti	Dodge
32.	Andy Houston	Ford
33.	Buckshot Jones	Dodge
34.	Sterling Marlin	Dodge
35.	Todd Bodine	Ford
36.	Casey Atwood	Dodge
37.	Ricky Rudd	Ford
38.	Jimmy Spencer	Ford
39.	Michael Waltrip	Chevrolet
40.	Ron Hornaday	Pontiac
41.	Joe Nemechek	Chevrolet
42.	Bobby Labonte	Pontiac
43.	Robert Pressley	Ford

VIRGINIA 500

April 8
Martinsville, Virginia
Time of Race: 3 hours, 42 minutes, 53 seconds
Average Speed: 70.799 mph
Margin of Victory: 1.388 seconds

FINISH	DRIVER	CAR
1.	Dale Jarrett	Ford
2.	Ricky Rudd	Ford
3.	Jeff Burton	Ford
4.	Bobby Hamilton	Chevrolet
5.	Sterling Marlin	Dodge
6.	Matt Kenseth	Ford

7.	Tony Stewart	Pontiac
8.	Bobby Labonte	Pontiac
9.	Jimmy Spencer	Ford
10.	Jerry Nadeau	Chevrolet
11.	Dale Earnhardt Jr.	Chevrolet
12.	Jeff Gordon	Chevrolet
13.	Rusty Wallace	Ford
14.	Bill Elliott	Dodge
15.	Stacy Compton	Dodge
16.	Joe Nemechek	Chevrolet
17.	Andy Houston	Ford
18.	Kevin LePage	Chevrolet
19.	Steve Park	Chevrolet
20.	Johnny Benson	Pontiac
21.	Elliott Sadler	Ford
22.	Ward Burton	Dodge
23.	Terry Labonte	Chevrolet
24.	Michael Waltrip	Chevrolet
25.	Ken Schrader	Pontiac
26.	Casey Atwood	Dodge
27.	Ron Hornaday	Pontiac
28.	Ricky Craven	Ford
29.	Dave Blaney	Dodge
30.	Jeremy Mayfield	Ford
31.	Mike Wallace	Ford
32.	Mike Skinner	Chevrolet
33.	Kurt Busch	Ford
34.	Kevin Harvick	Chevrolet
35.	John Andretti	Dodge
36.	Brett Bodine	Ford
37.	Kenny Wallace	Pontiac
38.	Buckshot Jones	Dodge
39.	Mark Martin	Ford
40.	Robert Pressley	Ford
41.	Rick Mast	Chevrolet
42.	Kyle Petty	Dodge
43.	Todd Bodine	Ford

TALLADEGA 500

April 22
Talladega, Alabama
Time of Race: 2 hours, 43 minutes, 4 seconds
Average Speed: 184.003 mph
Margin of Victory: 0.163 seconds

FINISH	DRIVER	CAR
1.	Bobby Hamilton	Chevrolet
2.	Tony Stewart	Pontiac
3.	Kurt Busch	Ford
4.	Mark Martin	Ford
5.	Bobby Labonte	Pontiac
6.	Joe Nemechek	Chevrolet
7.	Johnny Benson	Pontiac
8.	Dale Earnhardt Jr.	Chevrolet
9.	Mike Wallace	Ford
10.	Jeff Burton	Ford
11.	Terry Labonte	Chevrolet
12.	Kevin Harvick	Chevrolet
13.	Rusty Wallace	Ford
14.	Ricky Rudd	Ford
15.	Ricky Craven	Ford
16.	Buckshot Jones	Dodge
17.	Dave Blaney	Dodge
18.	Dale Jarrett	Ford
19.	Matt Kenseth	Ford
20.	Jason Leffler	Dodge
21.	Andy Houston	Ford
22.	Ron Hornaday	Pontiac
23.	Sterling Marlin	Dodge
24.	Robert Pressley	Ford
25.	Jeff Nadeau	Chevrolet
26.	Brett Bodine	Ford
27.	Jeff Gordon	Chevrolet
28.	Michael Waltrip	Chevrolet
29.	Mike Skinner	Chevrolet
30.	Casey Atwood	Dodge
31.	Steve Park	Chevrolet
32.	Bill Elliott	Dodge
33.	Ward Burton	Dodge
34.	Jeff Purvis	Ford

35.	Jeremy Mayfield	Ford
36.	Jimmy Spencer	Ford
37.	John Andretti	Dodge
38.	Dave Marcis	Chevrolet
39.	Elliott Sadler	Ford
40.	Ken Schrader	Pontiac
41.	Todd Bodine	Ford
42.	Kevin LePage	Chevrolet
43.	Stacy Compton	Dodge

NAPA AUTO PARTS 500

April 29
Fontana, California
Time of Race: 3 hours, 29 minutes, 37 seconds
Average Speed: 143.118 mph
Margin of Victory: 0.270 seconds

FINISH	DRIVER	CAR
1.	Rusty Wallace	Ford
2.	Jeff Gordon	Chevrolet
3.	Dale Earnhardt Jr.	Chevrolet
4.	Tony Stewart	Pontiac
5.	Jeremy Mayfield	Ford
6.	Ricky Rudd	Ford
7.	Jimmy Spencer	Ford
8.	Jerry Nadeau	Chevrolet
9.	Sterling Marlin	Dodge
10.	Robert Pressley	Ford
11.	Johnny Benson	Pontiac
12.	Hut Stricklin	Ford
13.	Kurt Busch	Ford
14.	Bill Elliott	Dodge
15.	Steve Park	Chevrolet
16.	Mike Wallace	Ford
17.	Matt Kenseth	Ford
18.	Jason Leffler	Dodge
19.	Andy Houston	Ford
20.	Joe Nemechek	Chevrolet
21.	Jeff Green	Chevrolet
22.	Bobby Labonte	Pontiac
23.	Elliott Sadler	Ford
24.	Dale Jarrett	Ford
25.	Kevin Harvick	Chevrolet
26.	John Andretti	Dodge
27.	Brett Bodine	Ford
28.	Todd Bodine	Ford
29.	Dave Blaney	Dodge
30.	Terry Labonte	Chevrolet
31.	Jeff Burton	Ford
32.	Mike Skinner	Chevrolet
33.	Ken Schrader	Pontiac
34.	Ron Hornaday	Pontiac
35.	Kyle Petty	Dodge
36.	Bobby Hamilton	Chevrolet
37.	Kenny Wallace	Pontiac
38.	Stacy Atwood	Dodge
39.	Casey Atwood	Dodge
40.	Mark Martin	Ford
41.	Ricky Craven	Ford
42.	Ward Burton	Dodge
43.	Michael Waltrip	Chevrolet

PONTIAC EXCITEMENT 400

May 5
Richmond, Virginia
Time of Race: 3 hours, 7 minutes, 45 seconds
Average Speed: 95.872 mph
Margin of Victory: 0.372 seconds

FINISH	DRIVER	CAR
1.	Tony Stewart	Pontiac
2.	Jeff Gordon	Chevrolet
3.	Rusty Wallace	Ford

4.	Steve Park	Chevrolet
5.	Ricky Rudd	Ford
6.	Johnny Benson	Pontiac
7.	Dale Earnhardt Jr.	Chevrolet
8.	Matt Kenseth	Ford
9.	Ken Schrader	Pontiac
10.	Bobby Labonte	Pontiac
11.	Sterling Marlin	Dodge
12.	Casey Atwood	Dodge
13.	Mark Martin	Ford
14.	Jeff Burton	Ford
15.	Dale Jarrett	Ford
16.	Jimmy Spencer	Ford
17.	Kevin Harvick	Chevrolet
18.	Kurt Busch	Ford
19.	Joe Nemechek	Chevrolet
20.	Rick Mast	Chevrolet
21.	Ward Burton	Dodge
22.	Kyle Petty	Dodge
23.	Elliott Sadler	Ford
24.	Mike Skinner	Chevrolet
25.	Mike Wallace	Ford
26.	Jason Leffler	Dodge
27.	Kevin LePage	Chevrolet
28.	Bobby Hamilton	Chevrolet
29.	Stacy Compton	Dodge
30.	Todd Bodine	Ford
31.	Ron Hornaday	Pontiac
32.	Robert Pressley	Ford
33.	Dave Blaney	Dodge
34.	John Andretti	Dodge
35.	Michael Waltrip	Chevrolet
36.	Jeremy Mayfield	Ford
37.	Bill Elliott	Dodge
38.	Terry Labonte	Chevrolet
39.	Brett Bodine	Ford
40.	Kenny Wallace	Pontiac
41.	Jerry Nadeau	Chevrolet
42.	Andy Houston	Ford
43.	Ricky Craven	Ford

COCA-COLA 600

May 27
Concord, North Carolina
Time of Race: 4 hours, 20 minutes, 40 seconds
Average Speed: 138.107 mph
Margin of Victory: 3.190 seconds

FINISH	DRIVER	CAR
1.	Jeff Burton	Ford
2.	Kevin Harvick	Chevrolet
3.	Tony Stewart	Pontiac
4.	Mark Martin	Ford
5.	Bobby Labonte	Pontiac
6.	Jimmy Spencer	Ford
7.	Ricky Rudd	Ford
8.	Dale Jarrett	Ford
9.	Ward Burton	Dodge
10.	Jeremy Mayfield	Ford
11.	Mike Skinner	Chevrolet
12.	Kurt Busch	Ford
13.	Jerry Nadeau	Chevrolet
14.	Rusty Wallace	Ford
15.	Sterling Marlin	Dodge
16.	Hut Stricklin	Ford
17.	Brett Bodine	Ford
18.	Matt Kenseth	Ford
19.	Elliott Sadler	Ford
20.	Johnny Benson	Pontiac
21.	Ken Schrader	Pontiac
22.	Steve Park	Chevrolet
23.	Terry Labonte	Chevrolet
24.	Bobby Hamilton	Chevrolet
25.	Dale Earnhardt Jr.	Chevrolet
26.	Bill Elliott	Dodge
27.	Buckshot Jones	Dodge
28.	Michael Waltrip	Chevrolet
29.	Jeff Gordon	Chevrolet
30.	Jason Leffler	Dodge
31.	Ricky Craven	Ford

32.	Rick Mast	Chevrolet
33.	Dave Blaney	Dodge
34.	Stacy Compton	Dodge
35.	Kevin LePage	Chevrolet
36.	Ron Hornaday	Pontiac
37.	Todd Bodine	Ford
38.	Robert Pressley	Ford
39.	Bobby Hamilton Jr.	Chevrolet
40.	Kenny Wallace	Pontiac
41.	Andy Houston	Ford
42.	Casey Atwood	Dodge
43.	Ryan Newman	Ford

MBNA PLATINUM 400

June 3
Dover, Delaware
Time of Race: 3 hours, 19 minutes, 24 seconds
Average Speed: 120.361 mph
Margin of Victory: 0.828 seconds

FINISH	DRIVER	CAR
1.	Jeff Gordon	Chevrolet
2.	Steve Park	Chevrolet
3.	Dale Earnhardt Jr.	Chevrolet
4.	Ricky Craven	Ford
5.	Dale Jarrett	Ford
6.	Sterling Marlin	Dodge
7.	Tony Stewart	Pontiac
8.	Kevin Harvick	Chevrolet
9.	Mark Martin	Ford
10.	Ricky Rudd	Ford
11.	Mike Skinner	Chevrolet
12.	Bobby Labonte	Pontiac
13.	Jason Leffler	Dodge
14.	Ward Burton	Dodge
15.	Todd Bodine	Ford
16.	Matt Kenseth	Ford
17.	Terry Labonte	Chevrolet
18.	Elliott Sadler	Ford
19.	John Andretti	Dodge
20.	Bobby Hamilton	Chevrolet
21.	Rusty Wallace	Ford
22.	Robert Pressley	Ford
23.	Andy Houston	Ford
24.	Kevin LePage	Chevrolet
25.	Brett Bodine	Ford
26.	Buckshot Jones	Dodge
27.	Kenny Wallace	Pontiac
28.	Mike Wallace	Ford
29.	Casey Atwood	Dodge
30.	Hut Stricklin	Ford
31.	Jeff Burton	Ford
32.	Stacy Compton	Dodge
33.	Dave Blaney	Dodge
34.	Jeremy Mayfield	Ford
35.	Ron Hornaday	Pontiac
36.	Ken Schrader	Pontiac
37.	Jimmy Spencer	Ford
38.	Jerry Nadeau	Chevrolet
39.	Kurt Busch	Ford
40.	Bill Elliott	Dodge
41.	Johnny Benson	Pontiac
42.	Bobby Hamilton Jr.	Chevrolet
43.	Michael Waltrip	Chevrolet

KMART 400

June 10
Brooklyn, Michigan
Time of Race: 2 hours, 58 minutes, 50 seconds
Average Speed: 134.203 mph
Margin of Victory: 0.085 seconds

FINISH	DRIVER	CAR
1.	Jeff Gordon	Chevrolet
2.	Ricky Rudd	Ford
3.	Sterling Marlin	Dodge
4.	Jeremy Mayfield	Ford
5.	Ryan Newman	Ford
6.	Hut Stricklin	Ford
7.	Jeff Burton	Ford
8.	Dave Blaney	Dodge
9.	Bill Elliott	Dodge
10.	Kevin Harvick	Chevrolet
11.	Jimmy Spencer	Ford
12.	Johnny Benson	Pontiac
13.	Bobby Labonte	Pontiac
14.	Ken Schrader	Pontiac
15.	Matt Kenseth	Ford
16.	Mark Martin	Ford
17.	Jeff Green	Chevrolet
18.	Dale Jarrett	Ford
19.	Jason Leffler	Dodge
20.	Mike Skinner	Chevrolet
21.	Robert Pressley	Ford
22.	Bobby Hamilton	Chevrolet
23.	Steve Park	Chevrolet
24.	Bobby Hamilton Jr.	Chevrolet
25.	Tony Stewart	Pontiac
26.	Terry Labonte	Chevrolet
27.	Kyle Petty	Dodge
28.	Jerry Nadeau	Chevrolet
29.	Michael Waltrip	Chevrolet
30.	Casey Atwood	Dodge
31.	Kevin LePage	Chevrolet
32.	Ron Hornaday	Pontiac
33.	Brett Bodine	Ford
34.	Shawna Robinson	Ford
35.	Ricky Craven	Ford
36.	Buckshot Jones	Dodge
37.	John Andretti	Dodge
38.	Ward Burton	Dodge
39.	Dale Earnhardt Jr.	Chevrolet
40.	Elliott Sadler	Ford
41.	Rusty Wallace	Ford
42.	Todd Bodine	Ford
43.	Kurt Busch	Ford

POCONO 500

June 17
Pocono, Pennsylvania
Time of Race: 3 hours, 43 minutes, 14 seconds
Average Speed: 134.389 mph
Margin of Victory: 1.119 seconds

FINISH	DRIVER	CAR
1.	Ricky Rudd	Ford
2.	Jeff Gordon	Chevrolet
3.	Dale Jarrett	Ford
4.	Sterling Marlin	Dodge
5.	Mark Martin	Ford
6.	Matt Kenseth	Ford
7.	Tony Stewart	Pontiac
8.	Bobby Labonte	Chevrolet
9.	Ken Schrader	Pontiac
10.	Jeff Burton	Ford
11.	Dave Blaney	Dodge
12.	Mike Skinner	Chevrolet
13.	Kurt Busch	Ford
14.	Robert Pressley	Ford
15.	Kevin Harvick	Chevrolet
16.	Rusty Wallace	Ford
17.	Jimmy Spencer	Ford
18.	Elliott Sadler	Ford
19.	Jerry Nadeau	Chevrolet
20.	Dale Earnhardt Jr.	Chevrolet
21.	Kevin Lepage	Chevrolet
22.	Rick Mast	Chevrolet
23.	Stacy Compton	Dodge
24.	Johnny Benson	Pontiac
25.	Todd Bodine	Ford
26.	Wally Dallenbach Jr.	Chevrolet

FINISH	DRIVER	CAR
27.	Bill Elliott	Dodge
28.	Hut Stricklin	Ford
29.	Ted Musgrave	Ford
30.	Michael Waltrip	Chevrolet
31.	Terry Labonte	Chevrolet
32.	Steve Park	Chevrolet
33.	Bobby Hamilton Jr.	Chevrolet
34.	Kyle Petty	Dodge
35.	Ron Hornaday	Pontiac
36.	Jeremy Mayfield	Ford
37.	Brett Bodine	Ford
38.	Casey Atwood	Dodge
39.	John Andretti	Dodge
40.	Ward Burton	Dodge
41.	Jason Leffler	Dodge
42.	Buckshot Jones	Dodge
43.	Ricky Craven	Ford

DODGE/SAVE MART 350

June 24
Sonoma, California
Time of Race: 2 hours, 57 minutes, 6 seconds
Average Speed: 75.889 mph
Margin of Victory: 1.746 seconds

FINISH	DRIVER	CAR
1.	Tony Stewart	Pontiac
2.	Robby Gordon	Ford
3.	Jeff Gordon	Chevrolet
4.	Ricky Rudd	Ford
5.	Rusty Wallace	Ford
6.	Ward Burton	Dodge
7.	Bobby Labonte	Chevrolet
8.	Jeff Burton	Ford
9.	Bill Elliott	Dodge
10.	Mark Martin	Ford
11.	Boris Said	Pontiac
12.	Scott Pruett	Chevrolet
13.	Brett Bodine	Ford
14.	Kevin Harvick	Chevrolet
15.	Bobby Hamilton	Chevrolet
16.	Ricky Craven	Ford
17.	Elliott Sadler	Ford
18.	Ron Hornaday Jr.	Pontiac
19.	Dale Earnhardt Jr.	Chevrolet
20.	Michael Waltrip	Chevrolet
21.	Matt Kenseth	Ford
22.	Kyle Petty	Dodge
23.	Kurt Busch	Ford
24.	Stacy Compton	Dodge
25.	Dorsey Schroeder	Dodge
26.	Dale Jarrett	Ford
27.	Jimmy Spencer	Ford
28.	Sterling Marlin	Dodge
29.	Johnny Benson	Pontiac
30.	John Andretti	Dodge
31.	Jerry Nadeau	Chevrolet
32.	Dave Blaney	Dodge
33.	Todd Bodine	Ford
34.	Mike Skinner	Chevrolet
35.	Buckshot Jones	Dodge
36.	Terry Labonte	Chevrolet
37.	Ken Schrader	Pontiac
38.	Ron Fellows	Chevrolet
39.	Jeremy Mayfield	Ford
40.	Steve Park	Chevrolet
41.	Casey Atwood	Dodge
42.	Brian Simo	Ford
43.	Kevin Lepage	Chevrolet

PEPSI 400

July 7
Daytona Beach, Florida
Time of Race: 2 hours, 32 minutes, 17 seconds
Average Speed: 157.601 mph
Margin of Victory: 0.123 seconds

FINISH	DRIVER	CAR
1.	Dale Earnhardt Jr.	Chevrolet
2.	Michael Waltrip	Chevrolet
3.	Elliott Sadler	Ford
4.	Ward Burton	Dodge
5.	Bobby Labonte	Pontiac
6.	Jerry Nadeau	Chevrolet
7.	Rusty Wallace	Ford
8.	Jeff Burton	Ford
9.	Brett Bodine	Ford
10.	Mike Wallace	Ford
11.	Dale Jarrett	Ford
12.	Todd Bodine	Ford
13.	Johnny Benson	Pontiac
14.	Ricky Rudd	Ford
15.	Ken Schrader	Ford
16.	Matt Kenseth	Ford
17.	Jeremy Mayfield	Ford
18.	Mark Martin	Ford
19.	Jimmy Spencer	Ford
20.	Steve Park	Chevrolet
21.	Dave Blaney	Dodge
22.	John Andretti	Dodge
23.	Robert Pressley	Ford
24.	Jason Leffler	Dodge
25.	Kevin Harvick	Chevrolet
26.	Tony Stewart	Pontiac
27.	Joe Nemechek	Chevrolet
28.	Casey Atwood	Dodge
29.	Kyle Petty	Dodge
30.	Kurt Busch	Ford
31.	Kevin Lepage	Chevrolet
32.	Stacy Compton	Dodge
33.	Ricky Craven	Ford
34.	Rick Mast	Chevrolet
35.	Bill Elliott	Dodge
36.	Dave Marcis	Chevrolet
37.	Jeff Gordon	Chevrolet
38.	Bobby Hamilton	Chevrolet
39.	Sterling Marlin	Dodge
40.	Terry Labonte	Chevrolet
41.	Mike Skinner	Chevrolet
42.	Jeff Purvis	Ford
43.	Andy Houston	Ford

TROPICANA 400

July 15
Joliet, Illinois
Time of Race: 3 hours, 18 minutes, 16 seconds
Average Speed: 121.200 mph
Margin of Victory: 0.649 seconds

FINISH	DRIVER	CAR
1.	Kevin Harvick	Chevrolet
2.	Robert Pressley	Ford
3.	Ricky Rudd	Ford
4.	Dale Jarrett	Ford
5.	Jimmy Spencer	Ford
6.	Mark Martin	Ford
7.	Matt Kenseth	Ford
8.	Kurt Busch	Ford
9.	Sterling Marlin	Dodge
10.	Bill Elliott	Dodge
11.	Dale Earnhardt Jr.	Chevrolet
12.	Rusty Wallace	Ford
13.	Dave Blaney	Dodge
14.	Todd Bodine	Ford
15.	Elliott Sadler	Ford
16.	Joe Nemechek	Chevrolet
17.	Jeff Gordon	Chevrolet
18.	Jeff Burton	Ford
19.	Brett Bodine	Ford
20.	Ward Burton	Dodge
21.	Ricky Craven	Ford
22.	John Andretti	Dodge
23.	Michael Waltrip	Chevrolet
24.	Jason Leffler	Dodge
25.	Terry Labonte	Chevrolet
26.	Stacy Compton	Dodge

FINISH	DRIVER	CAR
27.	Johnny Benson	Pontiac
28.	Casey Atwood	Dodge
29.	Ken Schrader	Ford
30.	Bobby Hamilton	Chevrolet
31.	Hut Stricklin	Ford
32.	Jeremy Mayfield	Ford
33.	Tony Stewart	Pontiac
34.	Kevin Lepage	Chevrolet
35.	Robby Gordon	Ford
36.	Jeff Green	Chevrolet
37.	Jerry Nadeau	Chevrolet
38.	Buckshot Jones	Dodge
39.	Bobby Labonte	Pontiac
40.	Ron Hornaday	Pontiac
41.	Steve Park	Chevrolet
42.	Mike Skinner	Chevrolet
43.	Andy Houston	Ford

NEW ENGLAND 300

July 22
Loudon, New Hampshire
Time of Race: 3 hours, 6 minutes, 28 seconds
Average Speed: 102.131 mph
Margin of Victory: 0.659 seconds

FINISH	DRIVER	CAR
1.	Dale Jarrett	Ford
2.	Jeff Gordon	Chevrolet
3.	Ricky Rudd	Ford
4.	Jimmy Spencer	Ford
5.	Tony Stewart	Pontiac
6.	Steve Park	Chevrolet
7.	Bobby Labonte	Pontiac
8.	Kevin Harvick	Chevrolet
9.	Dale Earnhardt Jr.	Chevrolet
10.	Mike Wallace	Ford
11.	Jeff Burton	Ford
12.	Casey Atwood	Dodge
13.	Brett Bodine	Ford
14.	Rick Mast	Chevrolet
15.	Todd Bodine	Ford
16.	Matt Kenseth	Ford
17.	Sterling Marlin	Dodge
18.	Mark Martin	Ford
19.	Robert Pressley	Ford
20.	Ward Burton	Dodge
21.	Bill Elliott	Dodge
22.	Ken Schrader	Ford
23.	John Andretti	Dodge
24.	Buckshot Jones	Dodge
25.	Robby Gordon	Ford
26.	Kyle Petty	Dodge
27.	Jason Leffler	Dodge
28.	Michael Waltrip	Chevrolet
29.	Bobby Hamilton	Chevrolet
30.	Kevin Lepage	Chevrolet
31.	Stacy Compton	Dodge
32.	Terry Labonte	Chevrolet
33.	Jerry Nadeau	Chevrolet
34.	Ron Hornaday	Pontiac
35.	Hut Stricklin	Ford
36.	Johnny Benson	Pontiac
37.	Dave Blaney	Dodge
38.	Ricky Craven	Ford
39.	Jeremy Mayfield	Ford
40.	Elliott Sadler	Ford
41.	Joe Nemechek	Chevrolet
42.	Kurt Busch	Ford
43.	Rusty Wallace	Ford

PENNSYLVANIA 500

July 29
Pocono, Pennsylvania
Time of Race: 3 hours, 42 minutes, 54 seconds
Average Speed: 134.590 mph
Margin of Victory: 1.680 seconds

FINISH	DRIVER	CAR
1.	Bobby Labonte	Pontiac
2.	Dale Earnhardt Jr.	Chevrolet
3.	Tony Stewart	Pontiac
4.	Bill Elliott	Dodge
5.	Johnny Benson	Pontiac
6.	Rusty Wallace	Ford
7.	Mark Martin	Ford
8.	Jeff Gordon	Chevrolet
9.	Robert Pressley	Ford
10.	Ricky Craven	Ford
11.	Ricky Rudd	Ford
12.	Jimmy Spencer	Ford
13.	Steve Park	Chevrolet
14.	Matt Kenseth	Ford
15.	Casey Atwood	Dodge
16.	Sterling Marlin	Dodge
17.	Ken Schrader	Ford
18.	Jeremy Mayfield	Ford
19.	Michael Waltrip	Chevrolet
20.	Kevin Harvick	Chevrolet
21.	Jason Leffler	Dodge
22.	Dave Blaney	Dodge
23.	Joe Nemechek	Chevrolet
24.	Jerry Nadeau	Chevrolet
25.	Mike Wallace	Ford
26.	Elliott Sadler	Ford
27.	John Andretti	Dodge
28.	Robby Gordon	Ford
29.	Bobby Hamilton	Chevrolet
30.	Ron Hornaday	Pontiac
31.	Kyle Petty	Dodge
32.	Stacy Compton	Dodge
33.	Brett Bodine	Ford
34.	Terry Labonte	Chevrolet
35.	Rick Mast	Chevrolet
36.	Jeff Burton	Ford
37.	Kurt Busch	Ford
38.	Ward Burton	Dodge
39.	Buckshot Jones	Dodge
40.	Hut Stricklin	Ford
41.	Dale Jarrett	Ford
42.	Kevin Lepage	Chevrolet
43.	Todd Bodine	Ford

BRICKYARD 400

August 5
Indianapolis, Indiana
Time of Race: 3 hours, 3 minutes, 30 seconds
Average Speed: 130.790 mph
Margin of Victory: .943 seconds

FINISH	DRIVER	CAR
1.	Jeff Gordon	Chevrolet
2.	Sterling Marlin	Dodge
3.	Johnny Benson	Pontiac
4.	Rusty Wallace	Ford
5.	Kurt Busch	Ford
6.	Ward Burton	Dodge
7.	Steve Park	Chevrolet
8.	Bill Elliott	Dodge
9.	Ricky Craven	Ford
10.	Dale Earnhardt Jr.	Chevrolet
11.	Kevin Harvick	Chevrolet
12.	Dale Jarrett	Ford
13.	Jimmy Spencer	Ford
14.	John Andretti	Dodge
15.	Bobby Labonte	Pontiac
16.	Jeff Burton	Dodge
17.	Tony Stewart	Pontiac
18.	Jeremy Mayfield	Ford
19.	Terry Labonte	Chevrolet
20.	Joe Nemechek	Chevrolet
21.	Jeff Green	Chevrolet
22.	Mark Martin	Ford
23.	Elliott Sadler	Ford
24.	Todd Bodine	Ford
25.	Michael Waltrip	Chevrolet

FINISH	DRIVER	CAR
26.	Jason Leffler	Dodge
27.	Bobby Hamilton	Chevrolet
28.	Ken Schrader	Pontiac
29.	Hut Stricklin	Ford
30.	Robby Gordon	Chevrolet
31.	Ryan Newman	Ford
32.	Rich Bickle	Chevrolet
33.	Stacy Compton	Dodge
34.	Ron Hornaday	Pontiac
35.	Robert Pressley	Ford
36.	Buckshot Jones	Dodge
37.	Brett Bodine	Ford
38.	Jerry Nadeau	Chevrolet
39.	Ricky Rudd	Ford
40.	Dave Blaney	Dodge
41.	Casey Atwood	Dodge
42.	Matt Kenseth	Ford
43.	Andy Houston	Ford

GLOBAL CROSSING AT THE GLEN

August 12
Watkins Glen, New York
Time of Race: 2 hours, 28 minutes, 31 seconds
Average Speed: 89.081 mph
Margin of Victory: 0.172 seconds

FINISH	DRIVER	CAR
1.	Jeff Gordon	Chevrolet
2.	Jeff Burton	Ford
3.	Jeremy Mayfield	Ford
4.	Ricky Rudd	Ford
5.	Todd Bodine	Ford
6.	Jerry Nadeau	Chevrolet
7.	Kevin Harvick	Chevrolet
8.	Boris Said	Ford
9.	Bobby Labonte	Pontiac
10.	Steve Park	Chevrolet
11.	Scott Pruett	Dodge
12.	Dale Earnhardt Jr.	Chevrolet
13.	Brett Bodine	Ford
14.	John Andretti	Dodge
15.	Mark Martin	Ford
16.	Johnny Benson	Pontiac
17.	Ron Hornaday	Pontiac
18.	Michael Waltrip	Chevrolet
19.	Ken Schrader	Pontiac
20.	Stacy Compton	Dodge
21.	Terry Labonte	Chevrolet
22.	Casey Atwood	Dodge
23.	Matt Kenseth	Ford
24.	Bill Elliott	Dodge
25.	Sterling Marlin	Dodge
26.	Tony Stewart	Pontiac
27.	Rick Mast	Pontiac
28.	Dave Blaney	Dodge
29.	Kurt Busch	Ford
30.	Elliott Sadler	Ford
31.	Joe Nemechek	Chevrolet
32.	Dale Jarrett	Ford
33.	Kevin Lepage	Chevrolet
34.	Anthony Lazzaro	Chevrolet
35.	Ricky Craven	Ford
36.	Bobby Hamilton	Chevrolet
37.	Brian Simo	Ford
38.	Jimmy Spencer	Ford
39.	Kyle Petty	Dodge
40.	Robby Gordon	Chevrolet
41.	Ward Burton	Dodge
42.	Ron Fellows	Ford
43.	Rusty Wallace	Ford

PEPSI 400

August 19
Brooklyn, Michigan
Time of Race: 2 hours, 18 minutes, 21 seconds
Average Speed: 140.513 mph
Margin of Victory: under caution

FINISH	DRIVER	CAR
1.	Sterling Marlin	Dodge
2.	Ricky Craven	Ford
3.	Bill Elliott	Dodge
4.	Matt Kenseth	Ford
5.	Johnny Benson	Pontiac
6.	Dave Blaney	Dodge
7.	Jeff Gordon	Chevrolet
8.	Mark Martin	Ford
9.	Steve Park	Chevrolet
10.	Casey Atwood	Dodge
11.	Jimmy Spencer	Ford
12.	Dale Earnhardt Jr.	Chevrolet
13.	Jeremy Mayfield	Ford
14.	Robert Pressley	Ford
15.	Elliott Sadler	Ford
16.	Jeff Burton	Dodge
17.	Rusty Wallace	Ford
18.	Mike Skinner	Chevrolet
19.	Bobby Labonte	Pontiac
20.	Ken Schrader	Pontiac
21.	Stacy Compton	Dodge
22.	Joe Nemechek	Chevrolet
23.	Todd Bodine	Ford
24.	Jason Leffler	Dodge
25.	Kyle Petty	Dodge
26.	John Andretti	Dodge
27.	Tony Stewart	Pontiac
28.	Bobby Hamilton	Chevrolet
29.	Terry Labonte	Chevrolet
30.	Ron Hornaday Jr.	Pontiac
31.	Andy Houston	Ford
32.	Hut Stricklin	Ford
33.	Ward Burton	Dodge
34.	Jerry Nadeau	Chevrolet
35.	Mike Wallace	Ford
36.	Michael Waltrip	Chevrolet
37.	Dale Jarrett	Ford
38.	Kevin Lepage	Chevrolet
39.	Rick Mast	Pontiac
40.	Brett Bodine	Ford
41.	Kevin Harvick	Chevrolet
42.	Ricky Rudd	Ford
43.	Kurt Busch	Ford

SHARPIE 500

August 25
Bristol, Tennessee
Time of Race: 3 hours, 7 minutes, 53 seconds
Average Speed: 85.106 mph
Margin of Victory: 0.487 seconds

FINISH	DRIVER	CAR
1.	Tony Stewart	Pontiac
2.	Kevin Harvick	Chevrolet
3.	Jeff Gordon	Chevrolet
4.	Ricky Rudd	Ford
5.	Rusty Wallace	Ford
6.	Dale Jarrett	Ford
7.	Steve Park	Chevrolet
8.	Bobby Labonte	Pontiac
9.	Sterling Marlin	Dodge
10.	Terry Labonte	Chevrolet
11.	Elliott Sadler	Ford
12.	Ward Burton	Dodge
13.	Kevin Lepage	Chevrolet
14.	Dale Earnhardt Jr.	Chevrolet
15.	Jeff Burton	Dodge
16.	Jeremy Mayfield	Ford
17.	Casey Atwood	Dodge
18.	Dave Blaney	Dodge
19.	Bill Elliott	Dodge
20.	Jerry Nadeau	Chevrolet
21.	John Andretti	Dodge
22.	Ken Schrader	Pontiac
23.	Bobby Hamilton	Chevrolet
24.	Joe Nemechek	Chevrolet
25.	Kurt Busch	Ford

26.	Brett Bodine	Ford
27.	Geoffrey Bodine	Ford
28.	Robert Pressley	Ford
29.	Ron Hornaday Jr.	Pontiac
30.	Jason Leffler	Dodge
31.	Mike Wallace	Ford
32.	Todd Bodine	Ford
33.	Matt Kenseth	Ford
34.	Mike Skinner	Chevrolet
35.	Jimmy Spencer	Ford
36.	Johnny Benson	Pontiac
37.	Mark Martin	Ford
38.	Ricky Craven	Ford
39.	Michael Waltrip	Chevrolet
40.	Andy Houston	Ford
41.	Rick Mast	Pontiac
42.	Jeff Green	Chevrolet
43.	Buckshot Jones	Dodge

MOUNTAIN DEW SOUTHERN 500

September 2
Darlington, South Carolina
Time of Race: 4 hours, 5 minutes
Average Speed: 122.773 mph
Margin of Victory: under caution

FINISH	DRIVER	CAR
1.	Ward Burton	Dodge
2.	Jeff Gordon	Chevrolet
3.	Bobby Labonte	Pontiac
4.	Tony Stewart	Pontiac
5.	Bill Elliott	Dodge
6.	Jeff Burton	Ford
7.	Ricky Rudd	Ford
8.	Kevin Harvick	Chevrolet
9.	Jerry Nadeau	Dodge
10.	Ken Schrader	Pontiac
11.	Terry Labonte	Chevrolet
12.	Mike Wallace	Ford
13.	Jeremy Mayfield	Ford
14.	Dale Earnhardt Jr.	Chevrolet
15.	Bobby Hamilton	Chevrolet
16.	Johnny Benson	Pontiac
17.	Sterling Marlin	Dodge
18.	Ricky Craven	Ford
19.	Dave Blaney	Dodge
20.	Mark Martin	Ford
21.	John Andretti	Dodge
22.	Rusty Wallace	Ford
23.	Matt Kenseth	Ford
24.	Mike Skinner	Chevrolet
25.	Casey Atwood	Dodge
26.	Kyle Petty	Dodge
27.	Brett Bodine	Ford
28.	Kevin Lepage	Chevrolet
29.	Elliott Sadler	Ford
30.	Rick Mast	Pontiac
31.	Jimmy Spencer	Ford
32.	Hut Stricklin	Ford
33.	Joe Nemechek	Chevrolet
34.	Dale Jarrett	Ford
35.	Buckshot Jones	Dodge
36.	Michael Waltrip	Chevrolet
37.	Ron Hornaday Jr.	Pontiac
38.	Robert Pressley	Ford
39.	Kurt Busch	Ford
40.	Todd Bodine	Ford
41.	Kenny Wallace	Chevrolet
42.	Stacy Compton	Dodge
43.	Jason Leffler	Dodge

CHEVROLET MONTE CARLO 400

September 8
Richmond, Virginia
Time of Race: 3 hours, 9 minutes, 11 seconds

Average Speed: 95.146 mph
Margin of Victory: 0.833 seconds

FINISH	DRIVER	CAR
1.	Ricky Rudd	Ford
2.	Kevin Harvick	Chevrolet
3.	Dale Earnhardt Jr.	Chevrolet
4.	Dale Jarrett	Ford
5.	Rusty Wallace	Ford
6.	Bobby Labonte	Pontiac
7.	Tony Stewart	Pontiac
8.	Jimmy Spencer	Ford
9.	Jeff Burton	Ford
10.	Johnny Benson	Pontiac
11.	Ricky Craven	Ford
12.	Ward Burton	Dodge
13.	Bobby Hamilton	Chevrolet
14.	Jerry Nadeau	Chevrolet
15.	Robert Pressley	Ford
16.	Joe Nemechek	Chevrolet
17.	Bill Elliott	Dodge
18.	Todd Bodine	Ford
19.	Mark Martin	Ford
20.	Michael Waltrip	Chevrolet
21.	Kenny Wallace	Chevrolet
22.	Stacy Compton	Dodge
23.	Ken Schrader	Pontiac
24.	Kurt Busch	Ford
25.	Kyle Petty	Dodge
26.	Dave Blaney	Dodge
27.	Casey Atwood	Dodge
28.	Jason Leffler	Dodge
29.	Jeremy Mayfield	Ford
30.	John Andretti	Dodge
31.	Elliott Sadler	Ford
32.	Sterling Marlin	Dodge
33.	Mike Skinner	Chevrolet
34.	Rick Mast	Pontiac
35.	Matt Kenseth	Ford
36.	Jeff Gordon	Chevrolet
37.	Buckshot Jones	Dodge
38.	Terry Labonte	Chevrolet
39.	Kevin Lepage	Chevrolet
40.	Jeff Green	Chevrolet
41.	Ron Hornaday Jr.	Pontiac
42.	Mike Wallace	Ford
43.	Brett Bodine	Ford

MBNA CAL RIPKEN JR. 400

September 23
Dover, Delaware
Time of Race: 3 hours, 56 minutes, 19 seconds
Average Speed: 101.559 mph
Margin of Victory: 1.576 seconds

FINISH	DRIVER	CAR
1.	Dale Earnhardt Jr.	Chevrolet
2.	Jerry Nadeau	Chevrolet
3.	Ricky Rudd	Ford
4.	Jeff Gordon	Chevrolet
5.	Tony Stewart	Pontiac
6.	Kevin Harvick	Chevrolet
7.	Joe Nemechek	Chevrolet
8.	Sterling Marlin	Dodge
9.	Casey Atwood	Dodge
10.	Bobby Hamilton	Chevrolet
11.	Rusty Wallace	Ford
12.	Dale Jarrett	Ford
13.	Jimmy Spencer	Ford
14.	Elliott Sadler	Ford
15.	Todd Bodine	Ford
16.	Kevin Lepage	Chevrolet
17.	Terry Labonte	Chevrolet
18.	Ken Schrader	Pontiac
19.	John Andretti	Dodge
20.	Mike Skinner	Chevrolet
21.	Jeff Burton	Ford

22.	Kenny Wallace	Chevrolet
23.	Mike Wallace	Ford
24.	Stacy Compton	Dodge
25.	Hut Stricklin	Ford
26.	Ricky Craven	Ford
27.	Hermie Sadler	Chevrolet
28.	Brett Bodine	Ford
29.	Matt Kenseth	Ford
30.	Bill Elliott	Dodge
31.	Johnny Benson	Pontiac
32.	Mark Martin	Ford
33.	Ward Burton	Dodge
34.	Ron Hornaday Jr.	Pontiac
35.	Dave Blaney	Dodge
36.	Bobby Labonte	Pontiac
37.	Robert Pressley	Ford
38.	Buckshot Jones	Dodge
39.	Michael Waltrip	Chevrolet
40.	Andy Houston	Ford
41.	Kurt Busch	Ford
42.	Jeremy Mayfield	Ford
43.	Kyle Petty	Dodge

PROTECTION ONE 400

September 30
Kansas City, Kansas
Time of Race: 3 hours, 37 minutes, 19 seconds
Average Speed: 110.576 mph
Margin of Victory: 0.413 seconds

FINISH	DRIVER	CAR
1.	Jeff Gordon	Chevrolet
2.	Ryan Newman	Ford
3.	Ricky Rudd	Ford
4.	Rusty Wallace	Ford
5.	Sterling Marlin	Dodge
6.	Mark Martin	Ford
7.	Robert Pressley	Ford
8.	Tony Stewart	Pontiac
9.	Kurt Busch	Ford
10.	Dave Blaney	Dodge
11.	Jeff Burton	Ford
12.	Jerry Nadeau	Chevrolet
13.	Kevin Lepage	Chevrolet
14.	Robby Gordon	Chevrolet
15.	Bobby Hamilton	Chevrolet
16.	Kevin Harvick	Chevrolet
17.	Kenny Wallace	Chevrolet
18.	Andy Houston	Ford
19.	Mike Wallace	Ford
20.	Joe Nemechek	Chevrolet
21.	Ricky Craven	Ford
22.	Jimmy Spencer	Ford
23.	Elliott Sadler	Ford
24.	Derrike Cope	Ford
25.	Brett Bodine	Ford
26.	Ken Schrader	Pontiac
27.	Terry Labonte	Chevrolet
28.	Jason Leffler	Dodge
29.	Bobby Labonte	Pontiac
30.	Dale Jarrett	Ford
31.	Buckshot Jones	Dodge
32.	Matt Kenseth	Ford
33.	Dale Earnhardt Jr.	Chevrolet
34.	Stacy Compton	Dodge
35.	Hut Stricklin	Ford
36.	Jeremy Mayfield	Ford
37.	Johnny Benson	Pontiac
38.	Michael Waltrip	Chevrolet
39.	John Andretti	Dodge
40.	Bill Elliott	Dodge
41.	Ward Burton	Dodge
42.	Todd Bodine	Ford
43.	Casey Atwood	Dodge

UAW-GM QUALITY 500

October 7
Concord, North Carolina

Time of Race: 3 hours, 36 minutes, 15 seconds
Average Speed: 139.006 mph
Margin of Victory: 6.002 seconds

FINISH	DRIVER	CAR
1.	Sterling Marlin	Dodge
2.	Tony Stewart	Pontiac
3.	Ward Burton	Dodge
4.	Dale Earnhardt Jr.	Chevrolet
5.	Jeff Burton	Ford
6.	Dale Jarrett	Ford
7.	Rusty Wallace	Ford
8.	Kevin Harvick	Chevrolet
9.	Mark Martin	Ford
10.	Bobby Labonte	Pontiac
11.	Jimmy Spencer	Ford
12.	Matt Kenseth	Ford
13.	Kevin Lepage	Chevrolet
14.	Ken Schrader	Pontiac
15.	Bill Elliott	Dodge
16.	Jeff Gordon	Chevrolet
17.	Todd Bodine	Ford
18.	Michael Waltrip	Chevrolet
19.	Ryan Newman	Ford
20.	Joe Nemechek	Chevrolet
21.	Ricky Rudd	Ford
22.	Kurt Busch	Ford
23.	Kenny Wallace	Chevrolet
24.	Casey Atwood	Dodge
25.	Robert Pressley	Ford
26.	John Andretti	Dodge
27.	Terry Labonte	Chevrolet
28.	Brett Bodine	Ford
29.	Carl Long	Dodge
30.	Hut Stricklin	Ford
31.	Bobby Hamilton	Chevrolet
32.	Stacy Compton	Dodge
33.	Bobby Hamilton Jr.	Chevrolet
34.	Mike Wallace	Ford
35.	Ricky Craven	Ford
36.	Johnny Benson	Pontiac
37.	Elliott Sadler	Ford
38.	Ron Hornaday	Pontiac
39.	Jimmie Johnson	Chevrolet
40.	Jerry Nadeau	Chevrolet
41.	Dave Blaney	Dodge
42.	Stuart Kirby	Ford
43.	Jason Leffler	Dodge

OLD DOMINION 500

October 15
Martinsville, Virginia
Time of Race: 3 hours, 28 minutes, 19 seconds
Average Speed: 75.750 mph
Margin of Victory: 0.141 seconds

FINISH	DRIVER	CAR
1.	Ricky Craven	Ford
2.	Dale Jarrett	Ford
3.	Ward Burton	Dodge
4.	Bobby Labonte	Pontiac
5.	Jeff Burton	Ford
6.	Johnny Benson	Pontiac
7.	Mark Martin	Ford
8.	Mike Wallace	Ford
9.	Jeff Gordon	Chevrolet
10.	Sterling Marlin	Dodge
11.	Ken Schrader	Pontiac
12.	Todd Bodine	Ford
13.	Bobby Hamilton	Chevrolet
14.	Jimmy Spencer	Ford
15.	Rusty Wallace	Ford
16.	Stacy Compton	Dodge
17.	Elliott Sadler	Ford
18.	Ron Hornaday Jr.	Pontiac
19.	Michael Waltrip	Chevrolet
20.	Kenny Wallace	Chevrolet
21.	Kevin Lepage	Ford

FINISH	DRIVER	CAR
22.	Kevin Harvick	Chevrolet
23.	Joe Nemechek	Chevrolet
24.	Jerry Nadeau	Chevrolet
25.	Casey Atwood	Dodge
26.	Hut Stricklin	Ford
27.	Dale Earnhardt Jr.	Chevrolet
28.	Hermie Sadler	Chevrolet
29.	Dave Blaney	Dodge
30.	Buckshot Jones	Dodge
31.	Rich Bickle	Chevrolet
32.	Dave Marcis	Chevrolet
33.	John Andretti	Dodge
34.	Terry Labonte	Chevrolet
35.	Kurt Busch	Ford
36.	Matt Kenseth	Ford
37.	Jason Leffler	Dodge
38.	Robby Gordon	Chevrolet
39.	Ricky Rudd	Ford
40.	Brett Bodine	Ford
41.	Tony Stewart	Pontiac
42.	Bill Elliott	Dodge
43.	Robert Pressley	Ford

EA SPORTS 500

October 21
Talladega, Alabama
Time of Race: 3 hours, 2 minutes, 45 seconds
Average Speed: 185.24 mph
Margin of Victory: 0.388 seconds

FINISH	DRIVER	CAR
1.	Dale Earnhardt Jr.	Chevrolet
2.	Tony Stewart	Pontiac
3.	Jeff Burton	Ford
4.	Matt Kenseth	Ford
5.	Bobby Hamilton	Chevrolet
6.	Kenny Wallace	Chevrolet
7.	Jeff Gordon	Chevrolet
8.	Joe Nemechek	Chevrolet
9.	Mark Martin	Ford
10.	Kevin Lepage	Ford
11.	Stacy Compton	Dodge
12.	Brett Bodine	Ford
13.	Terry Labonte	Chevrolet
14.	Bobby Hamilton Jr.	Chevrolet
15.	Jason Leffler	Dodge
16.	Rusty Wallace	Ford
17.	Sterling Marlin	Dodge
18.	Mike Wallace	Ford
19.	Robby Gordon	Chevrolet
20.	Bill Elliott	Dodge
21.	Ward Burton	Dodge
22.	Bobby Labonte	Pontiac
23.	Johnny Benson	Pontiac
24.	Ricky Craven	Ford
25.	Dale Jarrett	Ford
26.	Ricky Rudd	Ford
27.	Robert Pressley	Ford
28.	Buckshot Jones	Dodge
29.	Kurt Busch	Ford
30.	Dave Blaney	Dodge
31.	Ken Schrader	Pontiac
32.	Kevin Harvick	Chevrolet
33.	Kyle Petty	Dodge
34.	John Andretti	Dodge
35.	Jerry Nadeau	Chevrolet
36.	Hut Stricklin	Ford
37.	Michael Waltrip	Chevrolet
38.	Ron Hornaday	Chevrolet
39.	Casey Atwood	Dodge
40.	Elliott Sadler	Ford
41.	Todd Bodine	Ford
42.	Jeff Purvis	Ford
43.	Jimmy Spencer	Ford

CHECKER AUTO PARTS 500

October 28
Phoenix, Arizona

Time of Race: 3 hours, 2 minutes, 26 seconds
Average Speed: 102.613 mph
Margin of Victory: 2.645

FINISH	DRIVER	CAR
1.	Jeff Burton	Ford
2.	Mike Wallace	Ford
3.	Ricky Rudd	Ford
4.	Matt Kenseth	Ford
5.	Tony Stewart	Pontiac
6.	Jeff Gordon	Chevrolet
7.	Robby Gordon	Chevrolet
8.	Ricky Craven	Ford
9.	Dale Jarrett	Ford
10.	Johnny Benson	Pontiac
11.	Kenny Wallace	Pontiac
12.	Bobby Labonte	Pontiac
13.	Ward Burton	Dodge
14.	Casey Atwood	Dodge
15.	Rusty Wallace	Ford
16.	Buckshot Jones	Dodge
17.	Kevin Harvick	Chevrolet
18.	Ken Schrader	Pontiac
19.	Mark Martin	Ford
20.	Terry Labonte	Chevrolet
21.	Stacy Compton	Dodge
22.	Kurt Busch	Ford
23.	Michael Waltrip	Chevrolet
24.	Jerry Nadeau	Chevrolet
25.	Rick Mast	Chevrolet
26.	Brett Bodine	Ford
27.	Bill Elliott	Dodge
28.	Dave Blaney	Dodge
29.	Todd Bodine	Ford
30.	Ron Hornaday	Pontiac
31.	Jimmy Spencer	Ford
32.	Kevin Lepage	Chevrolet
33.	Elliott Sadler	Ford
34.	Sterling Marlin	Dodge
35.	Joe Nemechek	Chevrolet
36.	Bobby Hamilton	Chevrolet
37.	Dale Earnhardt Jr.	Chevrolet
38.	Bobby Hamilton Jr.	Chevrolet
39.	John Andretti	Dodge
40.	Ryan Newman	Ford
41.	Jason Leffler	Dodge
42.	Robert Pressley	Ford
43.	Kyle Petty	Dodge

POP SECRET MICROWAVE POPCORN 400

November 4
Rockingham, North Carolina
Time of Race: 3 hours, 5 minutes, 59 seconds
Average Speed: 128.941 mph
Margin of Victory: 6.285 seconds

FINISH	DRIVER	CAR
1.	Joe Nemechek	Chevrolet
2.	Kenny Wallace	Chevrolet
3.	Johnny Benson	Pontiac
4.	Dale Jarrett	Ford
5.	Jerry Nadeau	Chevrolet
6.	Ward Burton	Dodge
7.	Tony Stewart	Pontiac
8.	Ricky Rudd	Ford
9.	Bobby Labonte	Pontiac
10.	Matt Kenseth	Ford
11.	Sterling Marlin	Dodge
12.	Ricky Craven	Ford
13.	Robert Pressley	Ford
14.	Dave Blaney	Dodge
15.	Dale Earnhardt Jr.	Chevrolet
16.	Kevin Lepage	Ford
17.	Bobby Hamilton Jr.	
18.	Jeff Burton	Ford
19.	Ken Schrader	Pontiac
20.	Casey Atwood	Dodge
21.	Michael Waltrip	Chevrolet
22.	Bobby Hamilton	Chevrolet

23.	Elliott Sadler	Ford
24.	Rusty Wallace	Ford
25.	Jeff Gordon	Chevrolet
26.	Jimmy Spencer	Ford
27.	Kevin Harvick	Chevrolet
28.	Terry Labonte	Chevrolet
29.	John Andretti	Dodge
30.	Jason Leffler	Dodge
31.	Ron Hornaday	Chevrolet
32.	Mike Wallace	Ford
33.	Dick Trickle	Chevrolet
34.	Mark Martin	Ford
35.	Brett Bodine	Ford
36.	Stacy Compton	Dodge
37.	Robby Gordon	Chevrolet
38.	Buckshot Jones	Dodge
39.	Kurt Busch	Ford
40.	Bill Elliott	Dodge
41.	Todd Bodine	Ford
42.	Carl Long	Dodge
43.	Kyle Petty	Dodge

PENNZOIL FREEDOM 400

November 11
Homestead, Florida
Time of Race: 3 hours, 24 minutes, 36 seconds
Average Speed: 117.449 mph
Margin of Victory: 1.420 seconds

FINISH	DRIVER	CAR
1.	Bill Elliott	Dodge
2.	Michael Waltrip	Chevrolet
3.	Casey Atwood	Dodge
4.	Jeff Burton	Ford
5.	Sterling Marlin	Dodge
6.	Dave Blaney	Dodge
7.	Kevin Harvick	Chevrolet
8.	Bobby Labonte	Pontiac
9.	Jeff Green	Chevrolet
10.	Jason Leffler	Dodge
11.	Terry Labonte	Chevrolet
12.	Rusty Wallace	Ford
13.	Ward Burton	Dodge
14.	Kenny Wallace	Chevrolet
15.	Dale Earnhardt Jr.	Chevrolet
16.	Kyle Petty	Dodge
17.	Todd Bodine	Ford
18.	Jimmy Spencer	Ford
19.	Tony Stewart	Pontiac
20.	Johnny Benson	Pontiac
21.	Ricky Rudd	Ford
22.	John Andretti	Dodge
23.	Kurt Busch	Ford
24.	Mark Martin	Ford
25.	Jimmie Johnson	Chevrolet
26.	Mike Wallace	Ford
27.	Matt Kenseth	Ford
28.	Jeff Gordon	Chevrolet
29.	Kevin Lepage	Ford
30.	Ricky Craven	Ford
31.	Joe Nemechek	Chevrolet
32.	Brett Bodine	Ford
33.	Jerry Nadeau	Chevrolet
34.	Buckshot Jones	Dodge
35.	Bobby Hamilton Jr.	Chevrolet
36.	Elliott Sadler	Ford
37.	Geoffrey Bodine	Ford
38.	Rick Mast	Ford
39.	Bobby Hamilton	Chevrolet
40.	Robert Pressley	Ford
41.	Dale Jarrett	Ford
42.	Ken Schrader	Pontiac
43.	Stacy Compton	Dodge

NAPA 500

November 18
Atlanta, Georgia

Time of Race: 3 hours, 17 minutes, 53 seconds
Average Speed: 151.746 mph
Margin of Victory: 2.031 seconds

FINISH	DRIVER	CAR
1.	Bobby Labonte	Pontiac
2.	Sterling Marlin	Dodge
3.	Kevin Harvick	Chevrolet
4.	Jerry Nadeau	Chevrolet
5.	Ward Burton	Dodge
6.	Jeff Gordon	Chevrolet
7.	Dale Earnhardt Jr.	Chevrolet
8.	Dale Jarrett	Ford
9.	Tony Stewart	Pontiac
10.	Jeff Burton	Ford
11.	Hut Stricklin	Dodge
12.	Rusty Wallace	Ford
13.	Mike Wallace	Ford
14.	Bill Elliott	Dodge
15.	Bobby Hamilton Jr.	
16.	Todd Bodine	Ford
17.	Matt Kenseth	Ford
18.	Stacy Compton	Dodge
19.	Kevin Lepage	Ford
20.	Casey Atwood	Dodge
21.	Robert Pressley	Ford
22.	Mark Martin	Ford
23.	Johnny Benson	Pontiac
24.	Elliott Sadler	Ford
25.	John Andretti	Dodge
26.	Michael Waltrip	Chevrolet
27.	Bobby Hamilton	Chevrolet
28.	Kenny Wallace	Chevrolet
29.	Jimmie Johnson	Chevrolet
30.	Kyle Petty	Dodge
31.	Ken Schrader	Pontiac
32.	Terry Labonte	Chevrolet
33.	Buckshot Jones	Dodge
34.	Jeff Green	Chevrolet
35.	Ricky Rudd	Ford
36.	Brett Bodine	Ford
37.	Hermie Sadler	Chevrolet
38.	Ricky Craven	Ford
39.	Joe Nemechek	Chevrolet
40.	Jimmy Spencer	Ford
41.	Dave Blaney	Dodge
42.	Lance Hooper	Chevrolet
43.	Carl Long	Dodge

NEW HAMPSHIRE 300

November 23
Loudon, New Hampshire
Time of Race: 3 hours, 3 minutes, 50 seconds
Average Speed: 103.594 mph
Margin of Victory: 2.008 seconds

FINISH	DRIVER	CAR
1.	Robby Gordon	Chevrolet
2.	Sterling Marlin	Dodge
3.	Bobby Labonte	Pontiac
4.	Matt Kenseth	Ford
5.	Tony Stewart	Pontiac
6.	Jerry Nadeau	Chevrolet
7.	Robert Pressley	Ford
8.	Brett Bodine	Ford
9.	Mark Martin	Ford
10.	Dale Jarrett	Ford
11.	Dave Blaney	Dodge
12.	Johnny Benson	Pontiac
13.	Ricky Rudd	Ford
14.	Jimmy Spencer	Ford
15.	Jeff Gordon	Chevrolet
16.	Casey Atwood	Dodge
17.	Jeff Burton	Ford
18.	Rusty Wallace	Ford
19.	Elliott Sadler	Ford
20.	Joe Nemechek	Chevrolet

21.	Kurt Busch	Ford
22.	Bill Elliott	Dodge
23.	Kyle Petty	Dodge
24.	Dale Earnhardt Jr.	Chevrolet
25.	Kenny Wallace	Chevrolet
26.	Kevin Harvick	Chevrolet
27.	Terry Labonte	Chevrolet
28.	Rick Mast	Ford
29.	Bobby Hamilton	Chevrolet
30.	Jason Leffler	Dodge
31.	Todd Bodine	Ford
32.	Ron Hornaday	Pontiac
33.	Mike Wallace	Ford
34.	Stacy Compton	Dodge
35.	Kevin Lepage	Ford
36.	John Andretti	Dodge
37.	Bobby Hamilton Jr.	Chevrolet
38.	Ricky Craven	Ford
39.	Ken Schrader	Pontiac
40.	Michael Waltrip	Chevrolet
41.	Buckshot Jones	Dodge
42.	Ward Burton	Dodge

2002

DAYTONA 500

February 17
Daytona Beach, Florida
Time of Race: 3 hours, 29 minutes, 50 seconds
Average Speed: 142.971 mph
Margin of Victory: .193 seconds

FINISH	DRIVER	CAR
1.	Ward Burton	Dodge
2.	Elliott Sadler	Ford
3.	Geoffrey Bodine	Ford
4.	Kurt Busch	Ford
5.	Michael Waltrip	Chevrolet
6.	Mark Martin	Ford
7.	Ryan Newman	Ford
8.	Sterling Marlin	Dodge
9.	Jeff Gordon	Chevrolet
10.	Johnny Benson	Pontiac
11.	Bill Elliott	Dodge
12.	Jeff Burton	Ford
13.	Robby Gordon	Chevrolet
14.	Dale Jarrett	Ford
15.	Jimmie Johnson	Chevrolet
16.	Brett Bodine	Ford
17.	Ricky Craven	Ford
18.	Rusty Wallace	Ford
19.	Jeff Green	Chevrolet
20.	Terry Labonte	Chevrolet
21.	Mike Wallace	Chevrolet
22.	Robert Pressley	Dodge
23.	Mike Skinner	Chevrolet
24.	Shawna Robinson	Dodge
25.	Dave Blaney	Ford
26.	Ken Schrader	Pontiac
27.	Stacy Compton	Pontiac
28.	Jerry Nadeau	Chevrolet
29.	Dale Earnhardt Jr.	Chevrolet
30.	Kenny Wallace	Chevrolet
31.	Todd Bodine	Ford
32.	Bobby Hamilton	Chevrolet
33.	Matt Kenseth	Ford
34.	Bobby Labonte	Pontiac
35.	Casey Atwood	Dodge
36.	Kevin Harvick	Chevrolet
37.	John Andretti	Dodge
38.	Ricky Rudd	Ford
39.	Jeremy Mayfield	Dodge
40.	Joe Nemechek	Ford
41.	Kyle Petty	Dodge
42.	Dave Marcis	Chevrolet
43.	Tony Stewart	Pontiac

SUBWAY 400

February 24
Rockingham, North Carolina
Time of Race: 3 hours, 27 minutes, 40 seconds
Average Speed: 115.478 mph
Margin of Victory: Under caution

FINISH	DRIVER	CAR
1.	Matt Kenseth	Ford
2.	Sterling Marlin	Dodge
3.	Bobby Labonte	Pontiac
4.	Tony Stewart	Pontiac
5.	Ricky Craven	Ford
6.	Jeff Burton	Ford
7.	Jeff Gordon	Chevrolet
8.	Rusty Wallace	Ford
9.	Bobby Hamilton	Chevrolet
10.	Kenny Wallace	Chevrolet
11.	Bill Elliott	Dodge
12.	Kurt Busch	Ford
13.	Ward Burton	Dodge
14.	Ryan Newman	Ford
15.	John Andretti	Dodge
16.	Terry Labonte	Chevrolet
17.	Jeff Green	Chevrolet
18.	Ricky Rudd	Ford
19.	Kevin Harvick	Chevrolet
20.	Jimmy Spencer	Dodge
21.	Mark Martin	Ford
22.	Dave Blaney	Ford
23.	Johnny Benson	Pontiac
24.	Robby Gordon	Chevrolet
25.	Jerry Nadeau	Chevrolet
26.	Dale Earnhardt Jr.	Chevrolet
27.	Hut Stricklin	Dodge
28.	Jimmie Johnson	Chevrolet
29.	Jeremy Mayfield	Dodge
30.	Brett Bodine	Ford
31.	Elliott Sadler	Ford
32.	Todd Bodine	Ford
33.	Joe Nemechek	Ford
34.	Rick Mast	Ford
35.	Ken Schrader	Pontiac
36.	Mike Skinner	Chevrolet
37.	Kyle Petty	Dodge
38.	Mike Wallace	Chevrolet
39.	Casey Atwood	Dodge
40.	Michael Waltrip	Chevrolet
41.	Buckshot Jones	Dodge
42.	Dale Jarrett	Ford
43.	Stacy Compton	Pontiac

UAW-DAIMLERCHRYSLER 400

March 3
Las Vegas, Nevada
Time of Race: 2 hours, 55 minutes, 43 seconds
Average Speed: 136.754 mph
Margin of Victory: 1.163 seconds

FINISH	DRIVER	CAR
1.	Sterling Marlin	Dodge
2.	Jeremy Mayfield	Dodge
3.	Mark Martin	Ford
4.	Ryan Newman	Ford
5.	Tony Stewart	Pontiac
6.	Jimmie Johnson.	Chevy
7.	Dale Jarrett	Ford
8.	Bill Elliott	Dodge
9.	Jeff Burton	Ford
10.	Jimmy Spencer	Dodge
11.	Rusty Wallace	Ford
12.	Bobby Labonte	Pontiac
13.	Ricky Rudd	Ford
14.	Matt Kenseth	Ford
15.	Jerry Nadeau.	Chevy
16.	Dale Earnhardt Jr.	Chevy

17.	Jeff Gordon	Chevy
18.	Dave Blaney	Ford
19.	Joe Nemechek	Ford
20.	Kurt Busch	Ford
21.	Ward Burton	Dodge
22.	Michael Waltrip	Chevy
23.	Buckshot Jones	Dodge
24.	Hut Stricklin	Dodge
25.	Kevin Harvick	Chevy
26.	Ken Schrader	Pontiac
27.	Kenny Wallace	Chevy
28.	Elliott Sadler	Ford
29.	Todd Bodine	Ford
30.	Kyle Petty	Dodge
31.	Ricky Craven	Ford
32.	Johnny Benson	Pontiac
33.	Jeff Green	Chevy
34.	Mike Skinner	Chevy
35.	Brett Bodine	Ford
36.	John Andretti	Dodge
37.	Robby Gordon	Chevy
38.	Terry Labonte	Chevy
39.	Stacy Compton	Pontiac
40.	Rick Mast	Ford
41.	Casey Atwood	Dodge
42.	Shawna Robinson	Dodge
43.	Bobby Hamilton	Chevy

MBNA AMERICA 500

March 10
Hampton, Georgia
Time of Race: 3 hours, 22 minutes, 18 seconds
Average Speed: 148.443 mph
Margin of Victory: 0.376 seconds

FINISH	DRIVER	CAR
1.	Tony Stewart	Pontiac
2.	Dale Earnhardt Jr.	Chevrolet
3.	Jimmie Johnson	Chevrolet
4.	Matt Kenseth	Ford
5.	Ricky Craven	Ford
6.	Rusty Wallace	Ford
7.	Ward Burton	Dodge
8.	Mark Martin	Ford
9.	Sterling Marlin	Dodge
10.	Ryan Newman	Ford
11.	Kurt Busch	Ford
12.	Buckshot Jones	Dodge
13.	Dale Jarrett	Ford
14.	Terry Labonte	Chevrolet
15.	Kyle Petty	Dodge
16.	Jeff Gordon	Chevrolet
17.	Dave Blaney	Ford
18.	Robby Gordon	Chevrolet
19.	Elliott Sadler	Ford
20.	Ricky Rudd	Ford
21.	Jeff Burton	Ford
22.	Kenny Wallace	Chevrolet
23.	Jeremy Mayfield	Dodge
24.	Ken Schrader	Pontiac
25.	Joe Nemechek	Ford
26.	Jimmy Spencer	Dodge
27.	Johnny Benson	Pontiac
28.	Mike Skinner	Chevrolet
29.	Bobby Hamilton	Chevrolet
30.	Jerry Nadeau	Chevrolet
31.	Stacy Compton	Pontiac
32.	Casey Atwood	Dodge
33.	Rick Mast	Ford
34.	Shawna Robinson	Dodge
35.	Bill Elliott	Dodge
36.	John Andretti	Dodge
37.	Bobby Labonte	Pontiac
38.	Brett Bodine	Ford
39.	Kevin Harvick	Chevrolet
40.	Michael Waltrip	Chevrolet
41.	Jeff Green	Chevrolet
42.	Dick Trickle	Chevrolet
43.	Hut Stricklin	Dodge

CAROLINA DODGE DEALERS 400

March 17
Darlington, South Carolina
Time of Race: 3 hours, 10 minutes, 29 seconds
Average Speed: 126.070 mph
Margin of Victory: 3.581 seconds

FINISH	DRIVER	CAR
1.	Sterling Marlin	Dodge
2.	Elliott Sadler	Ford
3.	Kevin Harvick	Chevrolet
4.	Dale Earnhardt Jr.	Chevrolet
5.	Ryan Newman	Ford
6.	Jimmie Johnson	Chevrolet
7.	Rusty Wallace	Ford
8.	Matt Kenseth	Ford
9.	Jeff Gordon	Chevrolet
10.	Bill Elliott	Dodge
11.	Jeff Burton	Ford
12.	Ricky Rudd	Ford
13.	Bobby Hamilton	Chevrolet
14.	Kyle Petty	Dodge
15.	Michael Waltrip	Chevrolet
16.	Jeremy Mayfield	Dodge
17.	Joe Nemechek	Ford
18.	Jerry Nadeau	Chevrolet
19.	Buckshot Jones	Dodge
20.	Mike Skinner	Chevrolet
21.	Bobby Labonte	Pontiac
22.	John Andretti	Dodge
23.	Terry Labonte	Chevrolet
24.	Rick Mast	Ford
25.	Jeff Green	Chevrolet
26.	Casey Atwood	Dodge
27.	Stacy Compton	Pontiac
28.	Kurt Busch	Ford
29.	Mark Martin	Ford
30.	Dave Blaney	Ford
31.	Ward Burton	Dodge
32.	Hut Stricklin	Dodge
33.	Johnny Benson	Pontiac
34.	Robby Gordon	Chevrolet
35.	Ken Schrader	Pontiac
36.	Tony Stewart	Pontiac
37.	Jimmy Spencer	Dodge
38.	Brett Bodine	Ford
39.	Steve Park	Chevrolet
40.	Dale Jarrett	Ford
41.	Ricky Craven	Ford
42.	Shawna Robinson	Dodge
43.	Andy Hillenburg	Chevrolet

FOOD CITY 500

March 24
Bristol, Tennessee
Time of Race: 3 hours, 14 minutes, 20 seconds
Average Speed: 82.281 mph
Margin of Victory: 1.556 seconds

FINISH	DRIVER	CAR
1.	Kurt Busch	Ford
2.	Jimmy Spencer	Dodge
3.	Ricky Rudd	Ford
4.	Dale Earnhardt Jr.	Chevrolet
5.	Bobby Labonte	Pontiac
6.	Matt Kenseth	Ford
7.	Jimmie Johnson	Chevrolet
8.	Jerry Nadeau	Chevrolet
9.	Rusty Wallace	Ford
10.	Kevin Harvick	Chevrolet
11.	Mark Martin	Ford
12.	Kyle Petty	Dodge
13.	Ricky Craven	Ford
14.	Jeremy Mayfield	Dodge
15.	Tony Stewart	Pontiac
16.	Terry Labonte	Chevrolet

17.	Dave Blaney	Ford
18.	Casey Atwood	Dodge
19.	Sterling Marlin	Dodge
20.	Robby Gordon	Chevrolet
21.	Bill Elliott	Dodge
22.	Ken Schrader	Pontiac
23.	Mike Skinner	Chevrolet
24.	Steve Park	Chevrolet
25.	Ward Burton	Dodge
26.	Jeff Burton	Ford
27.	Jeff Green	Chevrolet
28.	Bobby Hamilton	Chevrolet
29.	Dale Jarrett	Ford
30.	Michael Waltrip	Chevrolet
31.	Jeff Gordon	Chevrolet
32.	Hermie Sadler	Chevrolet
33.	Rick Mast	Ford
34.	John Andretti	Dodge
35.	Hut Stricklin	Dodge
36.	Brett Bodine	Ford
37.	Ryan Newman	Ford
38.	Stacy Compton	Pontiac
39.	Johnny Benson	Pontiac
40.	Buckshot Jones	Dodge
41.	Elliott Sadler	Ford
42.	Dick Trickle	Chevrolet
43.	Joe Nemechek	Ford

SAMSUNG/RADIO SHACK 500

April 8
Fort Worth, Texas
Time of Race: 3 hours, 31 minutes, 3 seconds
Average Speed: 142.435 mph
Margin of Victory: .888 seconds

FINISH	DRIVER	CAR
1.	Matt Kenseth	Ford
2.	Jeff Gordon	Chevrolet
3.	Mark Martin	Ford
4.	Ricky Rudd	Ford
5.	Tony Stewart	Pontiac
6.	Jimmie Johnson	Chevrolet
7.	Sterling Marlin	Dodge
8.	Jimmy Spencer	Dodge
9.	Bill Elliott	Dodge
10.	Terry Labonte	Chevrolet
11.	Rusty Wallace	Ford
12.	Mike Skinner	Chevrolet
13.	Johnny Benson	Pontiac
14.	Ricky Craven	Ford
15.	Dave Blaney	Ford
16.	Jeff Green	Chevrolet
17.	Elliott Sadler	Ford
18.	Jeremy Mayfield	Dodge
19.	Stacy Compton	Pontiac
20.	Steve Park	Chevrolet
21.	Kyle Petty	Dodge
22.	John Andretti	Dodge
23.	Kurt Busch	Ford
24.	Dale Jarrett	Ford
25.	Kevin Harvick	Chevrolet
26.	Buckshot Jones	Dodge
27.	Hut Stricklin	Dodge
28.	Michael Waltrip	Chevrolet
29.	Rick Mast	Ford
30.	Bobby Labonte	Pontiac
31.	Bobby Hamilton	Chevrolet
32.	Jerry Nadeau	Chevrolet
33.	Frank Kimmel	Ford
34.	Ken Schrader	Pontiac
35.	Casey Atwood	Dodge
36.	Shawna Robinson	Dodge
37.	Jay Sauter	Chevrolet
38.	Brett Bodine	Ford
39.	Jeff Burton	Ford
40.	Ryan Newman	Ford
41.	Robby Gordon	Chevrolet
42.	Dale Earnhardt Jr.	Chevrolet
43.	Ward Burton	Dodge

VIRGINIA 500

April 14
Martinsville, Virginia
Time of Race: 3 hours, 33 minutes, 23 seconds
Average Speed: 73.951 mph
Margin of Victory: Under caution

FINISH	DRIVER	CAR
1.	Bobby Labonte	Pontiac
2.	Matt Kenseth	Ford
3.	Tony Stewart	Pontiac
4.	Dale Jarrett	Ford
5.	Dale Earnhardt Jr.	Chevrolet
6.	Terry Labonte	Chevrolet
7.	Ricky Rudd	Ford
8.	Mark Martin	Ford
9.	Jeff Burton	Ford
10.	Kurt Busch	Ford
11.	Jeremy Mayfield	Dodge
12.	Sterling Marlin	Dodge
13.	Michael Waltrip	Chevrolet
14.	Ward Burton	Dodge
15.	Hut Stricklin	Dodge
16.	Rusty Wallace	Ford
17.	Dave Blaney	Ford
18.	Stacy Compton	Pontiac
19.	Johnny Benson	Pontiac
20.	Kyle Petty	Dodge
21.	Jimmy Spencer	Dodge
22.	Jeff Green	Chevrolet
23.	Jeff Gordon	Chevrolet
24.	Steve Park	Chevrolet
25.	Mike Skinner	Chevrolet
26.	Brett Bodine	Ford
27.	Bobby Hamilton	Chevrolet
28.	Elliott Sadler	Ford
29.	Hermie Sadler	Chevrolet
30.	Ricky Craven	Ford
31.	Bill Elliott	Dodge
32.	Kenny Wallace	Chevrolet
33.	Buckshot Jones	Dodge
34.	Robby Gordon	Chevrolet
35.	Jimmie Johnson	Chevrolet
36.	Ken Schrader	Pontiac
37.	Rick Mast	Ford
38.	Casey Atwood	Dodge
39.	Jerry Nadeau	Chevrolet
40.	Frank Kimmel	Ford
41.	Ryan Newman	Ford
42.	John Andretti	Dodge
43.	Andy Hillenburg	Chevrolet

AARON'S 499

April 21
Talladega, Alabama
Time of Race: 3 hours, 8 minutes, 41 seconds
Average Speed: 159.022 mph
Margin of Victory: .060 seconds

FINISH	DRIVER	CAR
1.	Dale Earnhardt Jr.	Chevrolet
2.	Michael Waltrip	Chevrolet
3.	Kurt Busch	Ford
4.	Jeff Gordon	Chevrolet
5.	Sterling Marlin	Dodge
6.	Dale Jarrett	Ford
7.	Jimmie Johnson	Chevrolet
8.	Rusty Wallace	Ford
9.	Jeff Burton	Ford
10.	Kyle Petty	Dodge
11.	Hut Stricklin	Dodge
12.	Geoffrey Bodine	Ford
13.	Brett Bodine	Ford
14.	Ricky Rudd	Ford
15.	Ward Burton	Dodge

16.	Jeff Green	Chevrolet
17.	Jimmy Spencer	Dodge
18.	Ricky Craven	Ford
19.	Bill Elliott	Dodge
20.	Terry Labonte	Chevrolet
21.	Kenny Wallace	Chevrolet
22.	Bobby Hamilton	Chevrolet
23.	Mike Skinner	Chevrolet
24.	Ken Schrader	Pontiac
25.	Steve Grissom	Dodge
26.	Casey Atwood	Dodge
27.	Stacy Compton	Pontiac
28.	Kevin Harvick	Chevrolet
29.	Tony Stewart	Pontiac
30.	Matt Kenseth	Ford
31.	Dave Blaney	Ford
32.	Jerry Nadeau	Chevrolet
33.	Robby Gordon	Chevrolet
34.	Steve Park	Chevrolet
35.	Frank Kimmel	Ford
36.	Jeremy Mayfield	Dodge
37.	Mark Martin	Ford
38.	John Andretti	Dodge
39.	Johnny Benson	Pontiac
40.	Elliott Sadler	Ford
41.	Bobby Labonte	Pontiac
42.	Mike Wallace	Chevrolet
43.	Ryan Newman	Ford

NAPA AUTO PARTS 500

April 28
Fontana, California
Time of Race: 3 hours, 19 minutes, 53 seconds
Average Speed: 150.088 mph
Margin of Victory: .630 seconds

FINISH	DRIVER	CAR
1.	Jimmie Johnson	Chevrolet
2.	Kurt Busch	Ford
3.	Ricky Rudd	Ford
4.	Bill Elliott	Dodge
5.	Mark Martin	Ford
6.	Dale Jarrett	Ford
7.	Sterling Marlin	Dodge
8.	Rusty Wallace	Ford
9.	Dave Blaney	Ford
10.	Michael Waltrip	Chevrolet
11.	Jeff Green	Chevrolet
12.	Robby Gordon	Chevrolet
13.	Greg Biffle	Ford
14.	Ryan Newman	Ford
15.	Johnny Benson	Pontiac
16.	Jeff Gordon	Chevrolet
17.	Kyle Petty	Dodge
18.	Ward Burton	Dodge
19.	Jeff Burton	Ford
20.	Matt Kenseth	Ford
21.	Terry Labonte	Chevrolet
22.	Steve Park	Chevrolet
23.	Brett Bodine	Ford
24.	John Andretti	Dodge
25.	Joe Nemechek	Ford
26.	Jerry Nadeau	Chevrolet
27.	Jimmy Spencer	Dodge
28.	Casey Atwood	Dodge
29.	Tony Stewart	Pontiac
30.	Bobby Hamilton	Chevrolet
31.	Mike Skinner	Chevrolet
32.	Rick Mast	Ford
33.	Steve Grissom	Dodge
34.	Bobby Labonte	Pontiac
35.	Kevin Harvick	Chevrolet
36.	Dale Earnhardt Jr.	Chevrolet
37.	Ricky Craven	Ford
38.	Jeremy Mayfield	Dodge
39.	Elliott Sadler	Ford
40.	Hut Stricklin	Dodge
41.	Stacy Compton	Pontiac
42.	Shawna Robinson	Dodge
43.	Ken Schrader	Pontiac

PONTIAC EXCITEMENT 400

May 5
Richmond, Virginia
Time of Race: 3 hours, 27 minutes, 19 seconds
Average Speed: 86.824 mph
Margin of Victory: 1.484 seconds

FINISH	DRIVER	CAR
1.	Tony Stewart	Pontiac
2.	Ryan Newman	Ford
3.	Jeff Burton	Ford
4.	Mark Martin	Ford
5.	Jeremy Mayfield	Dodge
6.	Matt Kenseth	Ford
7.	Jeff Gordon	Chevrolet
8.	Steve Grissom	Dodge
9.	Ricky Craven	Ford
10.	Jimmy Spencer	Dodge
11.	Sterling Marlin	Dodge
12.	Joe Nemechek	Pontiac
13.	Jeff Green	Chevrolet
14.	Bill Elliott	Dodge
15.	Ken Schrader	Pontiac
16.	Hut Stricklin	Dodge
17.	Bobby Hamilton	Chevrolet
18.	Hermie Sadler	Chevrolet
19.	Brett Bodine	Ford
20.	John Andretti	Dodge
21.	Elliott Sadler	Ford
22.	Casey Atwood	Dodge
23.	Kyle Petty	Dodge
24.	Michael Waltrip	Chevrolet
25.	Rusty Wallace	Ford
26.	Stacy Compton	Pontiac
27.	Kurt Busch	Ford
28.	Mike Skinner	Chevrolet
29.	Dave Blaney	Ford
30.	Ward Burton	Dodge
31.	Jimmie Johnson	Chevrolet
32.	Bobby Labonte	Pontiac
33.	Terry Labonte	Chevrolet
34.	Steve Park	Chevrolet
35.	Rick Mast	Ford
36.	Dale Earnhardt Jr.	Chevrolet
37.	Robby Gordon	Chevrolet
38.	Dale Jarrett	Ford
39.	Ricky Rudd	Ford
40.	Kevin Harvick	Chevrolet
41.	Jerry Nadeau	Chevrolet
42.	Frank Kimmel	Ford
43.	Randy Renfrow	Dodge

COCA-COLA RACING FAMILY 600

May 26
Concord, North Carolina
Time of Race: 4 hours, 21 minutes, 23 seconds
Average Speed: 137.729 mph
Margin of Victory: .468 seconds

FINISH	DRIVER	CAR
1.	Mark Martin	Ford
2.	Matt Kenseth	Ford
3.	Ricky Craven	Ford
4.	Ricky Rudd	Ford
5.	Jeff Gordon	Chevrolet
6.	Tony Stewart	Pontiac
7.	Jimmie Johnson	Chevrolet
8.	Michael Waltrip	Chevrolet
9.	Bill Elliott	Dodge
10.	Rusty Wallace	Ford
11.	Sterling Marlin	Dodge
12.	Terry Labonte	Chevrolet
13.	Kyle Petty	Dodge
14.	Bobby Labonte	Pontiac
15.	John Andretti	Dodge

16.	Robby Gordon	Chevrolet
17.	Casey Atwood	Dodge
18.	Ken Schrader	Pontiac
19.	Dale Jarrett	Ford
20.	Jeff Green	Chevrolet
21.	Dave Blaney	Ford
22.	Hut Stricklin	Dodge
23.	Bobby Hamilton	Chevrolet
24.	Mike Skinner	Chevrolet
25.	Jimmy Spencer	Dodge
26.	Frank Kimmel	Ford
27.	Brett Bodine	Ford
28.	Jerry Nadeau	Pontiac
29.	Hermie Sadler	Ford
30.	Joe Nemechek	Chevrolet
31.	Kurt Busch	Ford
32.	Steve Grissom	Dodge
33.	Elliott Sadler	Ford
34.	Kevin Harvick	Chevrolet
35.	Dale Earnhardt Jr.	Chevrolet
36.	Ron Hornaday	Dodge
37.	Stacy Compton	Pontiac
38.	Steve Park	Chevrolet
39.	Jeremy Mayfield	Dodge
40.	Jeff Burton	Ford
41.	Ryan Newman	Ford
42.	Ward Burton	Dodge
43.	Kevin Lepage	Ford

MBNA PLATINUM 400

June 2
Dover, Delaware
Time of Race: 3 hours, 24 minutes, 10 seconds
Average Speed: 117.551 mph
Margin of Victory: .478 seconds

FINISH	DRIVER	CAR
1.	Jimmie Johnson	Chevrolet
2.	Bill Elliott	Dodge
3.	Jeff Burton	Ford
4.	Ryan Newman	Ford
5.	Dale Jarrett	Ford
6.	Jeff Gordon	Chevrolet
7.	Ricky Craven	Ford
8.	Robby Gordon	Chevrolet
9.	Bobby Hamilton	Chevrolet
10.	Elliott Sadler	Ford
11.	Tony Stewart	Pontiac
12.	Kurt Busch	Ford
13.	Sterling Marlin	Dodge
14.	Casey Atwood	Dodge
15.	Terry Labonte	Chevrolet
16.	Bobby Labonte	Pontiac
17.	Rusty Wallace	Ford
18.	Todd Bodine	Ford
19.	Ricky Rudd	Ford
20.	Kyle Petty	Dodge
21.	Michael Waltrip	Chevrolet
22.	Mike Skinner	Chevrolet
23.	Jimmy Spencer	Dodge
24.	Stacy Compton	Pontiac
25.	Steve Grissom	Dodge
26.	Hut Stricklin	Dodge
27.	Jerry Nadeau	Pontiac
28.	Kevin Harvick	Chevrolet
29.	Dave Blaney	Ford
30.	Dale Earnhardt Jr.	Chevrolet
31.	Tony Raines	Chevrolet
32.	John Andretti	Dodge
33.	Chad Little	Chevrolet
34.	Brett Bodine	Ford
35.	Jeremy Mayfield	Dodge
36.	Ken Schrader	Pontiac
37.	Ward Burton	Dodge
38.	Jeff Green	Chevrolet
39.	Steve Park	Chevrolet
40.	Matt Kenseth	Ford
41.	Mark Martin	Ford
42.	Dick Trickle	Dodge
43.	Joe Nemechek	Chevrolet

POCONO 500

June 9
Long Pond, Pennsylvania
Time of Race: 3 hours, 29 minutes, 10 seconds
Average Speed: 143.426 mph
Margin of Victory: Under caution

FINISH	DRIVER	CAR
1.	Dale Jarrett	Ford
2.	Mark Martin	Ford
3.	Jimmie Johnson	Chevrolet
4.	Sterling Marlin	Dodge
5.	Jeff Gordon	Chevrolet
6.	Jeff Burton	Ford
7.	Tony Stewart	Pontiac
8.	Michael Waltrip	Chevrolet
9.	Rusty Wallace	Ford
10.	Dave Blaney	Ford
11.	Casey Atwood	Dodge
12.	Dale Earnhardt Jr.	Chevrolet
13.	Kyle Petty	Dodge
14.	Ricky Craven	Ford
15.	Elliott Sadler	Ford
16.	Ken Schrader	Pontiac
17.	Ricky Rudd	Ford
18.	Todd Bodine	Ford
19.	Robby Gordon	Chevrolet
20.	Johnny Benson	Pontiac
21.	Jimmy Spencer	Dodge
22.	Hut Stricklin	Dodge
23.	Steve Park	Chevrolet
24.	Brett Bodine	Ford
25.	Steve Grissom	Dodge
26.	Bobby Labonte	Pontiac
27.	Bobby Hamilton	Chevrolet
28.	Stacy Compton	Pontiac
29.	Hermie Sadler	Ford
30.	Bill Elliott	Dodge
31.	John Andretti	Dodge
32.	Ryan Newman	Ford
33.	Ward Burton	Dodge
34.	Jeff Green	Chevrolet
35.	Matt Kenseth	Ford
36.	Jeremy Mayfield	Dodge
37.	Mike Skinner	Chevrolet
38.	Terry Labonte	Chevrolet
39.	Kevin Harvick	Chevrolet
40.	Kurt Busch	Ford
41.	Joe Nemechek	Chevrolet
42.	Carl Long	Dodge
43.	Frank Kimmel	Ford

SIRIUS SATELLITE RADIO 400

June 16
Brooklyn, Michigan
Time of Race: 2 hours, 35 minutes, 1 second
Average Speed: 154.822 mph
Margin of Victory: .131 seconds

FINISH	DRIVER	CAR
1.	Matt Kenseth	Ford
2.	Dale Jarrett	Ford
3.	Ryan Newman	Ford
4.	Michael Waltrip	Chevrolet
5.	Jeff Gordon	Chevrolet
6.	Johnny Benson	Pontiac
7.	Rusty Wallace	Ford
8.	Ricky Rudd	Ford
9.	Mark Martin	Ford
10.	Kurt Busch	Ford
11.	Bill Elliott	Dodge
12.	Kyle Petty	Dodge
13.	Dave Blaney	Ford
14.	Jimmie Johnson	Chevrolet
15.	Ricky Craven	Ford

16.	Tony Stewart	Pontiac
17.	Hut Stricklin	Dodge
18.	Jeff Green	Chevrolet
19.	Geoffrey Bodine	Ford
20.	Jeff Burton	Ford
21.	Sterling Marlin	Dodge
22.	Dale Earnhardt Jr.	Chevrolet
23.	John Andretti	Dodge
24.	Bobby Labonte	Pontiac
25.	Ken Schrader	Pontiac
26.	Elliott Sadler	Ford
27.	Kevin Harvick	Chevrolet
28.	Jimmy Spencer	Dodge
29.	Joe Nemechek	Chevrolet
30.	Mike Skinner	Chevrolet
31.	Terry Labonte	Chevrolet
32.	Steve Park	Chevrolet
33.	Robby Gordon	Chevrolet
34.	Brett Bodine	Ford
35.	Stacy Compton	Pontiac
36.	Jeremy Mayfield	Dodge
37.	Bobby Hamilton	Chevrolet
38.	Derrike Cope	Ford
39.	Casey Atwood	Dodge
40.	Steve Grissom	Dodge
41.	Jason Small	Dodge
42.	Ward Burton	Dodge
43.	Gary Bradberry	Ford

DODGE/SAVEMART 350

June 23
Sonoma, California
Time of Race: 2 hours, 42 minutes, 8 seconds
Average Speed: 81.007 mph
Margin of Victory: 2.487 seconds

FINISH	DRIVER	CAR
1.	Ricky Rudd	Ford
2.	Tony Stewart	Pontiac
3.	Terry Labonte	Chevrolet
4.	Kurt Busch	Ford
5.	Jeff Green	Chevrolet
6.	Elliott Sadler	Ford
7.	Mark Martin	Ford
8.	Bill Elliott	Dodge
9.	Ryan Newman	Ford
10.	John Andretti	Dodge
11.	Robby Gordon	Chevrolet
12.	Mike Skinner	Chevrolet
13.	Bobby Labonte	Pontiac
14.	Kevin Harvick	Chevrolet
15.	Dale Jarrett	Ford
16.	Johnny Benson	Pontiac
17.	Kyle Petty	Dodge
18.	Joe Nemechek	Chevrolet
19.	Ricky Craven	Ford
20.	Dave Blaney	Ford
21.	Casey Atwood	Dodge
22.	Michael Waltrip	Chevrolet
23.	Steve Park	Chevrolet
24.	Brett Bodine	Ford
25.	Ron Fellows	Chevrolet
26.	Todd Bodine	Ford
27.	Rusty Wallace	Ford
28.	Jeremy Mayfield	Dodge
29.	Jeff Burton	Ford
30.	Dale Earnhardt Jr.	Chevrolet
31.	Bobby Hamilton	Chevrolet
32.	Jim Inglebright	Chevrolet
33.	Hut Stricklin	Dodge
34.	Jerry Nadeau	Dodge
35.	Jimmie Johnson	Chevrolet
36.	Jimmy Spencer	Dodge
37.	Jeff Gordon	Chevrolet
38.	Ken Schrader	Pontiac
39.	Matt Kenseth	Ford
40.	Ward Burton	Dodge
41.	Boris Said	Ford
42.	Austin Cameron	Chevrolet
43.	Sterling Marlin	Dodge

PEPSI 400

July 6
Daytona Beach, Florida
Time of Race: 2 hours, 56 minutes, 32 seconds
Average Speed: 135.952 mph
Margin of Victory: Under caution

FINISH	DRIVER	CAR
1.	Michael Waltrip	Chevrolet
2.	Rusty Wallace	Ford
3.	Sterling Marlin	Dodge
4.	Jimmy Spencer	Dodge
5.	Mark Martin	Ford
6.	Dale Earnhardt Jr.	Chevrolet
7.	Todd Bodine	Ford
8.	Jimmie Johnson	Chevrolet
9.	Ward Burton	Dodge
10.	Geoffrey Bodine	Ford
11.	Kevin Harvick	Chevrolet
12.	Elliott Sadler	Ford
13.	Jeremy Mayfield	Dodge
14.	Terry Labonte	Chevrolet
15.	Ricky Rudd	Ford
16.	Bobby Hamilton	Chevrolet
17.	Bill Elliott	Dodge
18.	Stacy Compton	Pontiac
19.	Kyle Petty	Dodge
20.	Casey Atwood	Dodge
21.	Jeff Green	Chevrolet
22.	Jeff Gordon	Chevrolet
23.	Ricky Craven	Ford
24.	John Andretti	Dodge
25.	Ken Schrader	Pontiac
26.	Hut Stricklin	Dodge
27.	Ryan Newman	Ford
28.	Dave Blaney	Ford
29.	Robby Gordon	Chevrolet
30.	Matt Kenseth	Ford
31.	Kurt Busch	Ford
32.	Bobby Labonte	Pontiac
33.	Jeff Burton	Ford
34.	Steve Park	Chevrolet
35.	Dale Jarrett	Ford
36.	Joe Nemechek	Chevrolet
37.	Mike Skinner	Chevrolet
38.	Brett Bodine	Ford
39.	Tony Stewart	Pontiac
40.	Shawna Robinson	Dodge
41.	Mike Wallace	Chevrolet
42.	Kenny Wallace	Chevrolet
43.	Johnny Benson	Pontiac

TROPICANA 400

July 14
Joliet, Illinois
Time of Race: 2 hours, 55 minutes, 37 seconds
Average Speed: 136.832 mph
Margin of Victory: .812 seconds

FINISH	DRIVER	CAR
1.	Kevin Harvick	Chevrolet
2.	Jeff Gordon	Chevrolet
3.	Tony Stewart	Pontiac
4.	Jimmie Johnson	Chevrolet
5.	Ryan Newman	Ford
6.	Kurt Busch	Ford
7.	Bill Elliott	Dodge
8.	Robby Gordon	Chevrolet
9.	Mark Martin	Ford
10.	Dale Earnhardt Jr.	Chevrolet
11.	Dale Jarrett	Ford
12.	Jeff Green	Chevrolet
13.	Terry Labonte	Chevrolet
14.	Matt Kenseth	Ford
15.	Bobby Hamilton	Chevrolet

16.	Sterling Marlin	Dodge
17.	Dave Blaney	Ford
18.	Bobby Labonte	Pontiac
19.	Ricky Rudd	Ford
20.	Ricky Craven	Ford
21.	Elliott Sadler	Ford
22.	John Andretti	Dodge
23.	Mike Skinner	Chevrolet
24.	Kyle Petty	Dodge
25.	Rusty Wallace	Ford
26.	Todd Bodine	Ford
27.	Steve Park	Chevrolet
28.	Casey Atwood	Dodge
29.	Kenny Wallace	Chevrolet
30.	Brett Bodine	Ford
31.	Steve Grissom	Dodge
32.	Jimmy Spencer	Dodge
33.	Joe Nemechek	Chevrolet
34.	Jeremy Mayfield	Dodge
35.	Stacy Compton	Pontiac
36.	Hut Stricklin	Dodge
37.	Jerry Nadeau	Chevrolet
38.	Mike Wallace	Pontiac
39.	Jeff Burton	Ford
40.	Ken Schrader	Pontiac
41.	Ward Burton	Dodge
42.	Michael Waltrip	Chevrolet
43.	Stuart Kirby	Ford

NEW HAMPSHIRE 300

July 21
Loudon, New Hampshire
Time of Race: 3 hours, 26 minutes, 14 seconds
Average Speed: 92.342 mph
Margin of Victory: 3.230 seconds

FINISH	DRIVER	CAR
1.	Ward Burton	Dodge
2.	Jeff Green	Chevrolet
3.	Dale Jarrett	Ford
4.	Rusty Wallace	Ford
5.	Ryan Newman	Ford
6.	Todd Bodine	Ford
7.	Robby Gordon	Chevrolet
8.	Kurt Busch	Ford
9.	Kevin Harvick	Chevrolet
10.	Elliott Sadler	Ford
11.	Jimmy Spencer	Dodge
12.	Jeff Burton	Ford
13.	Bobby Labonte	Pontiac
14.	Sterling Marlin	Dodge
15.	Jimmie Johnson	Chevrolet
16.	Mark Martin	Ford
17.	Ricky Rudd	Ford
18.	Jerry Nadeau	Pontiac
19.	Jeremy Mayfield	Dodge
20.	Michael Waltrip	Chevrolet
21.	Ricky Craven	Ford
22.	Terry Labonte	Chevrolet
23.	Dale Earnhardt Jr.	Chevrolet
24.	Ken Schrader	Pontiac
25.	John Andretti	Dodge
26.	Bobby Hamilton	Chevrolet
27.	Brett Bodine	Ford
28.	Steve Grissom	Dodge
29.	Jeff Gordon	Chevrolet
30.	Stacy Compton	Pontiac
31.	Hut Stricklin	Dodge
32.	Steve Park	Chevrolet
33.	Matt Kenseth	Ford
34.	Bill Elliott	Dodge
35.	Dave Blaney	Ford
36.	Casey Atwood	Dodge
37.	Kyle Petty	Dodge
38.	Mike Skinner	Chevrolet
39.	Tony Stewart	Pontiac
40.	Morgan Shepherd	Ford
41.	Joe Nemechek	Chevrolet
42.	Kirk Shelmerdine	Ford
43.	Geoffrey Bodine	Ford

PENNSYLVANIA 500

July 28
Long Pond, Pennsylvania
Time of Race: 3 hours, 28 minutes, 39 seconds
Average Speed: 125.809 mph
Margin of Victory: 1.721 seconds

FINISH	DRIVER	CAR
1.	Bill Elliott	Dodge
2.	Kurt Busch	Ford
3.	Sterling Marlin	Dodge
4.	Dale Jarrett	Ford
5.	Ryan Newman	Ford
6.	Kevin Harvick	Chevrolet
7.	Tony Stewart	Pontiac
8.	Matt Kenseth	Ford
9.	Terry Labonte	Chevrolet
10.	Ricky Rudd	Ford
11.	Bobby Labonte	Pontiac
12.	Jeff Gordon	Chevrolet
13.	Mark Martin	Ford
14.	Ward Burton	Dodge
15.	Jimmie Johnson	Chevrolet
16.	Jeff Burton	Ford
17.	Ricky Craven	Ford
18.	Michael Waltrip	Chevrolet
19.	Bobby Hamilton	Chevrolet
20.	Ken Schrader	Pontiac
21.	Elliott Sadler	Ford
22.	Dave Blaney	Ford
23.	John Andretti	Dodge
24.	Joe Nemechek	Chevrolet
25.	Robby Gordon	Chevrolet
26.	Jeff Green	Chevrolet
27.	Kyle Petty	Dodge
28.	Casey Atwood	Dodge
29.	Mike Skinner	Chevrolet
30.	Johnny Benson	Pontiac
31.	Hut Stricklin	Dodge
32.	Jimmy Spencer	Dodge
33.	Brett Bodine	Ford
34.	Geoffrey Bodine	Ford
35.	Derrike Cope	Ford
36.	Jerry Nadeau	Pontiac
37.	Dale Earnhardt Jr.	Chevrolet
38.	Jeremy Mayfield	Dodge
39.	Mike Wallace	Pontiac
40.	Rusty Wallace	Ford
41.	Kirk Shelmerdine	Ford
42.	Morgan Shepherd	Ford
43.	Steve Park	Chevrolet

BRICKYARD 400

August 4
Indianapolis, Indiana
Time of Race: 3 hours, 11 minutes, 57 seconds
Average Speed: 125.033 mph
Margin of Victory: 1.269 seconds

FINISH	DRIVER	CAR
1.	Bill Elliott	Dodge
2.	Rusty Wallace	Ford
3.	Matt Kenseth	Ford
4.	Ryan Newman	Ford
5.	Kevin Harvick	Chevrolet
6.	Jeff Gordon	Chevrolet
7.	Steve Park	Chevrolet
8.	Robby Gordon	Chevrolet
9.	Jimmie Johnson	Chevrolet
10.	Dale Jarrett	Ford
11.	Bobby Labonte	Pontiac
12.	Tony Stewart	Pontiac
13.	Terry Labonte	Chevrolet
14.	Ken Schrader	Pontiac
15.	Dave Blaney	Ford

16.	Michael Waltrip	Chevrolet
17.	Hut Stricklin	Dodge
18.	Ricky Rudd	Ford
19.	Jeff Green	Chevrolet
20.	Joe Nemechek	Chevrolet
21.	Ted Musgrave	Dodge
22.	Dale Earnhardt Jr.	Chevrolet
23.	Bobby Hamilton	Chevrolet
24.	Jerry Nadeau	Dodge
25.	Kyle Petty	Dodge
26.	John Andretti	Dodge
27.	Sterling Marlin	Dodge
28.	Mark Martin	Ford
29.	Jeff Burton	Ford
30.	Ward Burton	Dodge
31.	Jimmy Spencer	Dodge
32.	Kenny Wallace	Chevrolet
33.	Ricky Craven	Ford
34.	Todd Bodine	Ford
35.	Elliott Sadler	Ford
36.	Mike Skinner	Chevrolet
37.	Johnny Benson	Pontiac
38.	Casey Atwood	Dodge
39.	Jeremy Mayfield	Dodge
40.	Geoffrey Bodine	Ford
41.	Kurt Busch	Ford
42.	Brett Bodine	Ford
43.	Mike Wallace	Pontiac

SIRIUS SATELLITE RADIO AT THE GLEN

August 11
Watkins Glen, New York
Time of Race: 2 hours, 40 minutes, 56 seconds
Average Speed: 82.208 mph
Margin of Victory: 1.636 seconds

FINISH	DRIVER	CAR
1.	Tony Stewart	Pontiac
2.	Ryan Newman	Ford
3.	Robby Gordon	Chevrolet
4.	P.J. Jones	Pontiac
5.	Ricky Rudd	Ford
6.	Scott Pruett	Dodge
7.	Jeff Burton	Ford
8.	Todd Bodine	Ford
9.	Michael Waltrip	Chevrolet
10.	Mark Martin	Ford
11.	John Andretti	Dodge
12.	Jeff Green	Chevrolet
13.	Boris Said	Ford
14.	Kevin Harvick	Chevrolet
15.	Jeremy Mayfield	Dodge
16.	Jimmie Johnson	Chevrolet
17.	Rusty Wallace	Ford
18.	Dave Blaney	Ford
19.	Bobby Hamilton	Chevrolet
20.	Ward Burton	Dodge
21.	Bill Elliott	Dodge
22.	Jeff Gordon	Chevrolet
23.	Bobby Labonte	Pontiac
24.	Tom Hubert	Dodge
25.	Johnny Benson	Pontiac
26.	Jerry Nadeau	Dodge
27.	Casey Atwood	Dodge
28.	Ken Schrader	Pontiac
29.	Kyle Petty	Dodge
30.	Sterling Marlin	Dodge
31.	Terry Labonte	Chevrolet
32.	Brett Bodine	Ford
33.	Matt Kenseth	Ford
34.	Ricky Craven	Ford
35.	Dale Earnhardt Jr.	Chevrolet
36.	Kenny Wallace	Chevrolet
37.	Dale Jarrett	Ford
38.	Joe Nemechek	Chevrolet
39.	Steve Park	Chevrolet
40.	Mike Skinner	Chevrolet
41.	Kurt Busch	Ford
42.	Joe Varde	Chevrolet
43.	Elliott Sadler	Ford

PEPSI 400

August 18
Brooklyn, Michigan
Time of Race: 2 hours, 50 minutes, 45 seconds
Average Speed: 140.555 mph
Margin of Victory: 2.285 seconds

FINISH	DRIVER	CAR
1.	Dale Jarrett	Ford
2.	Tony Stewart	Pontiac
3.	Kevin Harvick	Chevrolet
4.	Jeff Burton	Ford
5.	Mark Martin	Ford
6.	Sterling Marlin	Dodge
7.	Jimmie Johnsonx	Chevrolet
8.	Johnny Benson	Pontiac
9.	Jeff Green	Chevrolet
10.	Dale Earnhardt Jr.	Chevrolet
11.	Matt Kenseth	Ford
12.	Ricky Rudd	Ford
13.	Bobby Labonte	Pontiac
14.	Ken Schrader	Pontiac
15.	Michael Waltrip	Chevrolet
16.	Jeremy Mayfield	Dodge
17.	Ricky Craven	Ford
18.	Dave Blaney	Ford
19.	Jeff Gordon	Chevrolet
20.	John Andretti	Dodge
21.	Robby Gordon	Chevrolet
22.	Bill Elliott	Dodge
23.	Bobby Hamilton	Chevrolet
24.	Rusty Wallace	Ford
25.	Kyle Petty	Dodge
26.	Todd Bodine	Ford
27.	Elliott Sadler	Ford
28.	Mike Skinner	Chevrolet
29.	Ward Burton	Dodge
30.	Stacy Compton	Dodge
31.	Ryan Newmanx	Ford
32.	Jerry Nadeau	Dodge
33.	Terry Labonte	Chevrolet
34.	Jimmy Spencer	Dodge
35.	Joe Nemechek	Chevrolet
36.	Hut Stricklin	Dodge
37.	Derrike Cope	Ford
38.	Brett Bodine	Ford
39.	Kurt Busch	Ford
40.	Mike Wallace	Pontiac
41.	Steve Park	Chevrolet
42.	Casey Atwood	Dodge
43.	Tony Raines	Chevrolet

SHARPIE 500

August 24
Bristol, Tennessee
Time of Race: 3 hours, 27 minutes, 24 seconds
Average Speed: 77.097 mph
Margin of Victory: .502 seconds

FINISH	DRIVER	CAR
1.	Jeff Gordon	Chevrolet
2.	Rusty Wallace	Ford
3.	Dale Earnhardt Jr.	Chevrolet
4.	Kevin Harvick	Chevrolet
5.	Matt Kenseth	Ford
6.	Kurt Busch	Ford
7.	Sterling Marlin	Dodge
8.	Jimmy Spencer	Dodge
9.	Bobby Labonte	Pontiac
10.	Mike Wallace	Pontiac
11.	Bobby Hamilton	Chevrolet
12.	Johnny Benson	Pontiac
13.	Jeff Burton	Ford
14.	Ken Schrader	Pontiac
15.	Kyle Petty	Dodge
16.	Ricky Craven	Ford

17.	Bill Elliott	Dodge
18.	Casey Atwood	Dodge
19.	John Andretti	Dodge
20.	Robby Gordon	Chevrolet
21.	Jerry Nadeau	Dodge
22.	Michael Waltrip	Chevrolet
23.	Mark Martin	Ford
24.	Tony Stewart	Pontiac
25.	Jeremy Mayfield	Dodge
26.	Steve Park	Chevrolet
27.	Joe Nemechek	Chevrolet
28.	Dale Jarrett	Ford
29.	Mike Skinner	Chevrolet
30.	Terry Labonte	Chevrolet
31.	Lance Hooper	Ford
32.	Brett Bodine	Ford
33.	Dave Blaney	Ford
34.	Jimmie Johnson	Chevrolet
35.	Jeff Green	Chevrolet
36.	Ryan Newman	Ford
37.	Ward Burton	Dodge
38.	Hut Stricklin	Dodge
39.	Ricky Rudd	Ford
40.	Scott Wimmer	Dodge
41.	Derrike Cope	Dodge
42.	Elliott Sadler	Ford
43.	Todd Bodine	Ford

MOUNTAIN DEW SOUTHERN 500

September 1
Darlington, South Carolina
Time of Race: 4 hours, 13 minutes, 35 seconds
Average Speed: 118.617 mph
Margin of Victory: 1.734 seconds

FINISH	DRIVER	CAR
1.	Jeff Gordon	Chevrolet
2.	Ryan Newman	Ford
3.	Bill Elliott	Dodge
4.	Sterling Marlin	Dodge
5.	Dale Jarrett	Ford
6.	Ward Burton	Dodge
7.	Kurt Busch	Ford
8.	Tony Stewart	Pontiac
9.	Jimmie Johnson	Chevrolet
10.	Jeff Burton	Ford
11.	Mark Martin	Ford
12.	Jeff Green	Chevrolet
13.	Kyle Petty	Dodge
14.	Ricky Craven	Ford
15.	Bobby Labonte	Pontiac
16.	Dale Earnhardt Jr.	Chevrolet
17.	Robby Gordon	Chevrolet
18.	Jimmy Spencer	Dodge
19.	Elliott Sadler	Ford
20.	Jeremy Mayfield	Dodge
21.	Joe Nemechek	Chevrolet
22.	Rusty Wallace	Ford
23.	Bobby Hamilton	Chevrolet
24.	Michael Waltrip	Chevrolet
25.	Kenny Wallace	Dodge
26.	Ken Schrader	Pontiac
27.	Ted Musgrave	Dodge
28.	Casey Atwood	Dodge
29.	Dave Blaney	Ford
30.	Ricky Rudd	Ford
31.	Terry Labonte	Chevrolet
32.	Mike Wallace	Pontiac
33.	Todd Bodine	Ford
34.	Johnny Benson	Pontiac
35.	Tony Raines	Chevrolet
36.	Steve Park	Chevrolet
37.	Matt Kenseth	Ford
38.	Mike Skinner	Chevrolet
39.	Brett Bodine	Ford
40.	Kevin Harvick	Chevrolet
41.	Jerry Nadeau	Dodge
42.	John Andretti	Dodge
43.	Morgan Shepherd	Ford

CHEVROLET MONTE CARLO 400

September 7
Richmond, Virginia
Time of Race: 3 hours, 9 minutes, 54 seconds
Average Speed: 94.787 mph
Margin of Victory: 6.184 seconds

FINISH	DRIVER	CAR
1.	Matt Kenseth	Ford
2.	Ryan Newman	Ford
3.	Jeff Green	Chevrolet
4.	Dale Earnhardt Jr.	Chevrolet
5.	Todd Bodine	Ford
6.	Mark Martin	Ford
7.	Ricky Rudd	Ford
8.	Ward Burton	Dodge
9.	Dave Blaney	Ford
10.	Jeremy Mayfield	Dodge
11.	Steve Park	Chevrolet
12.	Mike Wallace	Pontiac
13.	Jimmie Johnson	Chevrolet
14.	Kenny Wallace	Dodge
15.	Rusty Wallace	Ford
16.	Bill Elliott	Dodge
17.	Kyle Petty	Dodge
18.	Kevin Harvick	Chevrolet
19.	Kurt Busch	Ford
20.	Brett Bodine	Ford
21.	Ricky Craven	Ford
22.	Mike Skinner	Chevrolet
23.	Hermie Sadler	Chevrolet
24.	Casey Atwood	Dodge
25.	Joe Nemechek	Chevrolet
26.	Ken Schrader	Pontiac
27.	Jerry Nadeau	Dodge
28.	Robby Gordon	Chevrolet
29.	John Andretti	Dodge
30.	Tony Stewart	Pontiac
31.	Dale Jarrett	Ford
32.	Bobby Labonte	Pontiac
33.	Greg Biffle	Chevrolet
34.	Elliott Sadler	Ford
35.	Johnny Benson	Pontiac
36.	Michael Waltrip	Chevrolet
37.	Tim Sauter	Chevrolet
38.	Geoffrey Bodine	Ford
39.	Jeff Burton	Ford
40.	Jeff Gordon	Chevrolet
41.	Terry Labonte	Chevrolet
42.	Jimmy Spencer	Dodge
43.	Sterling Marlin	Dodge

NEW HAMPSHIRE 300

September 15
Loudon, New Hampshire
Time of Race: 2 hours, 5 minutes, 3 seconds
Average Speed: 105.081 mph
Margin of Victory: Under caution

FINISH	DRIVER	CAR
1.	Ryan Newman	Ford
2.	Kurt Busch	Ford
3.	Tony Stewart	Pontiac
4.	Johnny Benson	Pontiac
5.	Bobby Labonte	Pontiac
6.	Ricky Craven	Ford
7.	Dale Jarrett	Ford
8.	Michael Waltrip	Chevrolet
9.	Jimmie Johnson	Chevrolet
10.	Matt Kenseth	Ford
11.	Dale Earnhardt Jr.	Chevrolet
12.	Ricky Rudd	Ford
13.	Ken Schrader	Pontiac
14.	Jeff Gordon	Chevrolet
15.	Jimmy Spencer	Dodge

16.	Mark Martin	Ford
17.	Robby Gordon	Chevrolet
18.	Kenny Wallace	Dodge
19.	Rusty Wallace	Ford
20.	Jeff Burton	Ford
21.	Sterling Marlin	Dodge
22.	John Andretti	Dodge
23.	Bill Elliott	Dodge
24.	Jeremy Mayfield	Dodge
25.	Dave Blaney	Ford
26.	Jeff Green	Chevrolet
27.	Greg Biffle	Chevrolet
28.	Jerry Nadeau	Dodge
29.	Steve Park	Chevrolet
30.	Terry Labonte	Chevrolet
31.	Mike Wallace	Pontiac
32.	Joe Nemechek	Chevrolet
33.	Kevin Harvick	Chevrolet
34.	Casey Atwood	Dodge
35.	Elliott Sadler	Ford
36.	Brett Bodine	Ford
37.	Hermie Sadler	Chevrolet
38.	Ward Burton	Dodge
39.	Kyle Petty	Dodge
40.	Kevin Lepage	Ford
41.	Morgan Shepherd	Ford
42.	Todd Bodine	Ford
43.	Mike Skinner	Chevrolet

MBNA AMERICAN HEROES 400

September 22
Dover, Delaware
Time of Race: 3 hours, 18 minutes, 40 seconds
Average Speed: 120.805 mph
Margin of Victory: .535 seconds

FINISH	DRIVER	CAR
1.	Jimmie Johnson	Chevrolet
2.	Mark Martin	Ford
3.	Dale Jarrett	Ford
4.	Matt Kenseth	Ford
5.	Tony Stewart	Pontiac
6.	Jeff Burton	Ford
7.	Kurt Busch	Ford
8.	Ryan Newman	Ford
9.	Ricky Craven	Ford
10.	Johnny Benson	Pontiac
11.	Dave Blaney	Ford
12.	Michael Waltrip	Chevrolet
13.	Jeff Green	Chevrolet
14.	Ricky Rudd	Ford
15.	Rusty Wallace	Ford
16.	Kyle Petty	Dodge
17.	Robby Gordon	Chevrolet
18.	Bill Elliott	Dodge
19.	Mike Skinner	Chevrolet
20.	Jeremy Mayfield	Dodge
21.	Sterling Marlin	Dodge
22.	Ken Schrader	Pontiac
23.	Joe Nemechek	Chevrolet
24.	Dale Earnhardt Jr.	Chevrolet
25.	Elliott Sadler	Ford
26.	Steve Park	Chevrolet
27.	Kenny Wallace	Dodge
28.	Mike Wallace	Pontiac
29.	John Andretti	Dodge
30.	Kevin Harvick	Chevrolet
31.	Tony Raines	Chevrolet
32.	Casey Atwood	Dodge
33.	Greg Biffle	Chevrolet
34.	Tim Sauter	Chevrolet
35.	Jimmy Spencer	Dodge
36.	Kevin Lepage	Dodge
37.	Jeff Gordon	Chevrolet
38.	Terry Labonte	Chevrolet
39.	Hideo Fukuyama	Ford
40.	Todd Bodine	Ford
41.	Bobby Labonte	Pontiac
42.	Jerry Nadeau	Dodge
43.	Ward Burton	Dodge

PROTECTION ONE 400

September 29
Kansas City, Kansas
Time of Race: 3 hours, 21 minutes, 16 seconds
Average Speed: 119.394 mph
Margin of Victory: .618 seconds

FINISH	DRIVER	CAR
1.	Jeff Gordon	Chevrolet
2.	Ryan Newman	Ford
3.	Rusty Wallace	Ford
4.	Joe Nemechek	Chevrolet
5.	Bill Elliott	Dodge
6.	Dale Earnhardt Jr.	Chevrolet
7.	Matt Kenseth	Ford
8.	Tony Stewart	Pontiac
9.	Jeremy Mayfield	Dodge
10.	Jimmie Johnson	Chevrolet
11.	Kevin Harvick	Chevrolet
12.	Terry Labonte	Chevrolet
13.	Robby Gordon	Chevrolet
14.	John Andretti	Dodge
15.	Kyle Petty	Dodge
16.	Kenny Wallace	Dodge
17.	Jeff Green	Chevrolet
18.	Elliott Sadler	Ford
19.	Mike Wallace	Pontiac
20.	Ricky Rudd	Ford
21.	Dave Blaney	Ford
22.	Bobby Labonte	Pontiac
23.	Johnny Benson	Pontiac
24.	Jimmy Spencer	Dodge
25.	Mark Martin	Ford
26.	Michael Waltrip	Chevrolet
27.	Jerry Nadeau	Dodge
28.	Ken Schrader	Pontiac
29.	Jeff Burton	Ford
30.	Steve Park	Chevrolet
31.	Kurt Busch	Ford
32.	Mike Skinner	Chevrolet
33.	Sterling Marlin	Dodge
34.	Todd Bodine	Ford
35.	Jack Sprague	Chevrolet
36.	Greg Biffle	Chevrolet
37.	Stuart Kirby	Dodge
38.	Ricky Craven	Ford
39.	Dale Jarrett	Ford
40.	Morgan Shepherd	Ford
41.	Tony Raines	Chevrolet
42.	Casey Atwood	Dodge
43.	Ward Burton	Dodge

EA SPORTS 500

Talladega, Alabama
Time of Race: 2 hours, 43 minutes, 22 seconds
Average Speed: 183.665 mph
Margin of Victory: .118 seconds

FINISH	DRIVER	CAR
1.	Dale Earnhardt Jr.	Chevrolet
2.	Tony Stewart	Pontiac
3.	Ricky Rudd	Ford
4.	Kurt Busch	Ford
5.	Jeff Green	Chevrolet
6.	Steve Park	Chevrolet
7.	Ryan Newman	Ford
8.	Michael Waltrip	Chevrolet
9.	Dale Jarrett	Ford
10.	Ward Burton	Dodge
11.	Jeff Burton	Ford
12.	Robby Gordon	Chevrolet
13.	Rusty Wallace	Ford
14.	Matt Kenseth	Ford
15.	Ricky Craven	Ford
16.	Kyle Petty	Dodge
17.	Scott Wimmer	Dodge

18.	John Andretti	Dodge
19.	Bill Elliott	Dodge
20.	Jeremy Mayfield	Dodge
21.	Jimmy Spencer	Dodge
22.	Stacy Compton	Dodge
23.	Todd Bodine	Ford
24.	Jerry Nadeau	Dodge
25.	Bobby Labonte	Pontiac
26.	Jamie McMurray	Dodge
27.	Kevin Harvick	Chevrolet
28.	Mike Skinner	Chevrolet
29.	Brett Bodine	Ford
30.	Mark Martin	Ford
31.	Dave Blaney	Ford
32.	Ron Hornaday	Chevrolet
33.	Kenny Wallace	Chevrolet
34.	Casey Atwood	Dodge
35.	Mike Wallace	Pontiac
36.	Elliott Sadler	Ford
37.	Jimmie Johnson	Chevrolet
38.	Terry Labonte	Chevrolet
39.	Joe Nemechek	Chevrolet
40.	Johnny Benson	Pontiac
41.	Ken Schrader	Pontiac
42.	Jeff Gordon	Chevrolet
43.	Jay Sauter	Chevrolet

UAW-GM QUALITY 500

October 13
Concord, North Carolina
Time of Race: 3 hours, 32 minutes, 19 seconds
Average Speed: 141.586 mph
Margin of Victory: .350 seconds

FINISH	DRIVER	CAR
1.	Jamie McMurray	Dodge
2.	Bobby Labonte	Pontiac
3.	Tony Stewart	Pontiac
4.	Jeff Gordon	Chevrolet
5.	Rusty Wallace	Ford
6.	Jimmie Johnson	Chevrolet
7.	Jeff Burton	Ford
8.	Ryan Newman	Ford
9.	Dale Earnhardt Jr.	Chevrolet
10.	Dave Blaney	Ford
11.	Michael Waltrip	Chevrolet
12.	Kurt Busch	Ford
13.	Jerry Nadeau	Dodge
14.	Dale Jarrett	Ford
15.	Steve Park	Chevrolet
16.	Mark Martin	Ford
17.	Mike Wallace	Pontiac
18.	Johnny Benson	Pontiac
19.	Elliott Sadler	Ford
20.	Kyle Petty	Dodge
21.	Terry Labonte	Chevrolet
22.	Kevin Harvick	Chevrolet
23.	John Andretti	Dodge
24.	Mike Skinner	Chevrolet
25.	Kenny Wallace	Dodge
26.	Brett Bodine	Ford
27.	Bobby Hamilton	Chevrolet
28.	Jeremy Mayfield	Dodge
29.	Jeff Green	Chevrolet
30.	Casey Atwood	Dodge
31.	Ken Schrader	Pontiac
32.	Jimmy Spencer	Dodge
33.	Ward Burton	Dodge
34.	Matt Kenseth	Ford
35.	Bill Elliott	Dodge
36.	Ricky Craven	Ford
37.	Todd Bodine	Ford
38.	Robby Gordon	Chevrolet
39.	Ricky Rudd	Ford
40.	Joe Nemechek	Chevrolet
41.	Hermie Sadler	Chevrolet
42.	Stacy Compton	Dodge
43.	Jason Hedlesky	Ford

OLD DOMINION 500

October 20
Martinsville, Virginia
Time of Race: 3 hours, 31 minutes, 23 seconds
Average Speed: 74.651 mph
Margin of Victory: .460 seconds

FINISH	DRIVER	CAR
1.	Kurt Busch	Ford
2.	Johnny Benson	Pontiac
3.	Ricky Rudd	Ford
4.	Dale Earnhardt Jr.	Chevrolet
5.	Ward Burton	Dodge
6.	Jimmie Johnson	Chevrolet
7.	Ricky Craven	Ford
8.	Dale Jarrett	Ford
9.	Rusty Wallace	Ford
10.	Mark Martin	Ford
11.	Tony Stewart	Pontiac
12.	Bobby Labonte	Pontiac
13.	John Andretti	Dodge
14.	Mike Bliss	Dodge
15.	Ryan Newman	Ford
16.	Steve Park	Chevrolet
17.	Jeff Burton	Ford
18.	Michael Waltrip	Chevrolet
19.	Matt Kenseth	Ford
20.	Dave Blaney	Ford
21.	Casey Atwood	Dodge
22.	Terry Labonte	Chevrolet
23.	Robby Gordon	Chevrolet
24.	Jimmy Spencer	Dodge
25.	Bobby Hamilton	Chevrolet
26.	Ken Schrader	Pontiac
27.	Mike Wallace	Pontiac
28.	Jeremy Mayfield	Dodge
29.	Ted Musgrave	Dodge
30.	Todd Bodine	Ford
31.	Kevin Harvick	Chevrolet
32.	Jeff Green	Chevrolet
33.	Mike Skinner	Chevrolet
34.	Elliott Sadler	Ford
35.	Hermie Sadler	Chevrolet
36.	Jeff Gordon	Chevrolet
37.	Kyle Petty	Dodge
38.	Brett Bodine	Ford
39.	Geoffrey Bodine	Dodge
40.	Steve Grissom	Dodge
41.	Joe Nemechek	Chevrolet
42.	Bill Elliott	Dodge
43.	Hideo Fukuyama	Ford

NAPA 500

October 27
Hampton, Georgia
Time of Race: 2 hours, 59 minutes, 42 seconds
Average Speed: 127.519 mph
Margin of Victory: Under caution

FINISH	DRIVER	CAR
1.	Kurt Busch	Ford
2.	Joe Nemechek	Chevrolet
3.	Dale Jarrett	Ford
4.	Tony Stewart	Pontiac
5.	Dale Earnhardt Jr.	Chevrolet
6.	Jeff Gordon	Chevrolet
7.	Jamie McMurray	Dodge
8.	Mark Martin	Ford
9.	Matt Kenseth	Ford
10.	Ryan Newman	Ford
11.	Michael Waltrip	Chevrolet
12.	Jeff Burton	Ford
13.	Bobby Labonte	Pontiac
14.	Kyle Petty	Dodge
15.	Steve Park	Chevrolet

16.	Ward Burton	Dodge
17.	Rusty Wallace	Ford
18.	Elliott Sadler	Ford
19.	Dave Blaney	Ford
20.	Robby Gordon	Chevrolet
21.	Ricky Craven	Ford
22.	Jimmie Johnson	Chevrolet
23.	Johnny Benson	Pontiac
24.	Jeff Green	Chevrolet
25.	Terry Labonte	Chevrolet
26.	Mike Skinner	Chevrolet
27.	Jeremy Mayfield	Dodge
28.	Ted Musgrave	Dodge
29.	Tony Raines	Chevrolet
30.	Jimmy Spencer	Dodge
31.	Mike Wallace	Pontiac
32.	Ricky Rudd	Ford
33.	Bill Elliott	Dodge
34.	Brett Bodine	Ford
35.	Bobby Hamilton	Chevrolet
36.	Kenny Wallace	Dodge
37.	Derrike Cope	Dodge
38.	Casey Atwood	Dodge
39.	Carl Long	Dodge
40.	Kevin Harvick	Chevrolet
41.	Todd Bodine	Ford
42.	Ken Schrader	Pontiac
43.	John Andretti	Dodge

POP SECRET 400

November 3
Rockingham, North Carolina
Time of Race: 3 hours, 6 minutes, 35 seconds
Average Speed: 128.526 mph
Margin of Victory: .261 seconds

FINISH	DRIVER	CAR
1.	Johnny Benson	Pontiac
2.	Mark Martin	Ford
3.	Kurt Busch	Ford
4.	Jeff Burton	Ford
5.	Jeff Gordon	Chevrolet
6.	Mike Skinner	Chevrolet
7.	Bobby Labonte	Pontiac
8.	Matt Kenseth	Ford
9.	Ricky Craven	Ford
10.	Jeff Green	Chevrolet
11.	Robby Gordon	Chevrolet
12.	Dale Jarrett	Ford
13.	Kenny Wallace	Dodge
14.	Tony Stewart	Pontiac
15.	Jamie McMurray	Dodge
16.	Elliott Sadler	Ford
17.	Dave Blaney	Ford
18.	John Andretti	Dodge
19.	Michael Waltrip	Chevrolet
20.	Ricky Rudd	Ford
21.	Jeremy Mayfield	Dodge
22.	Ken Schrader	Pontiac
23.	Ryan Newman	Ford
24.	Steve Park	Chevrolet
25.	Greg Biffle	Dodge
26.	Kevin Harvick	Chevrolet
27.	Rusty Wallace	Ford
28.	Joe Nemechek	Chevrolet
29.	Casey Atwood	Dodge
30.	Kyle Petty	Dodge
31.	Jimmy Spencer	Dodge
32.	Terry Labonte	Chevrolet
33.	Hank Parker Jr.	Dodge
34.	Dale Earnhardt Jr.	Chevrolet
35.	Jack Sprague	Chevrolet
36.	Brett Bodine	Ford
37.	Jimmie Johnson	Chevrolet
38.	Bobby Hamilton	Chevrolet
39.	Bill Elliott	Dodge
40.	Ward Burton	Dodge
41.	Hermie Sadler	Chevrolet
42.	Todd Bodine	Ford
43.	Mike Wallace	Pontiac

CHECKER AUTO PARTS 500

November 10
Avondale, Arizona
Time of Race: 2 hours, 44 minutes, 25 seconds
Average Speed: 113.857 mph
Margin of Victory: 1.344 seconds

FINISH	DRIVER	CAR
1.	Matt Kenseth	Ford
2.	Rusty Wallace	Ford
3.	Jeff Gordon	Chevrolet
4.	Mark Martin	Ford
5.	Dale Earnhardt Jr.	Chevrolet
6.	Kurt Busch	Ford
7.	Dave Blaney	Ford
8.	Tony Stewart	Pontiac
9.	Dale Jarrett	Ford
10.	Elliott Sadler	Ford
11.	Kenny Wallace	Dodge
12.	Jeff Burton	Ford
13.	Ricky Rudd	Ford
14.	John Andretti	Dodge
15.	Jimmie Johnson	Chevrolet
16.	Johnny Benson	Pontiac
17.	Kevin Harvick	Chevrolet
18.	Ryan Newman	Ford
19.	Ward Burton	Dodge
20.	Michael Waltrip	Chevrolet
21.	Steve Park	Chevrolet
22.	Todd Bodine	Ford
23.	Jimmy Spencer	Dodge
24.	Mike Skinner	Chevrolet
25.	Jeremy Mayfield	Dodge
26.	Terry Labonte	Chevrolet
27.	Robby Gordon	Chevrolet
28.	Mike Wallace	Pontiac
29.	Bobby Hamilton	Chevrolet
30.	Bill Elliott	Dodge
31.	Jason Leffler	Dodge
32.	Kyle Petty	Dodge
33.	Joe Nemechek	Chevrolet
34.	Ricky Craven	Ford
35.	Jeff Green	Chevrolet
36.	Ron Hornaday	Chevrolet
37.	Ken Schrader	Pontiac
38.	Derrike Cope	Dodge
39.	Bobby Labonte	Pontiac
40.	Jamie McMurray	Dodge
41.	Christian Fittipaldi	Dodge
42.	Scott Wimmer	Dodge
43.	Tony Raines	Chevrolet

FORD 400

November 17
Homestead, Florida
Time of Race: 3 hours, 26 minutes, 20 seconds
Average Speed: 116.462 mph
Margin of Victory: 2.070 seconds

FINISH	DRIVER	CAR
1.	Kurt Busch	Ford
2.	Joe Nemechek	Chevrolet
3.	Jeff Burton	Ford
4.	Mark Martin	Ford
5.	Jeff Gordon	Chevrolet
6.	Ryan Newman	Ford
7.	Bill Elliott	Dodge
8.	Jimmie Johnson	Chevrolet
9.	Elliott Sadler	Ford
10.	Bobby Hamilton	Chevrolet
11.	Mike Wallace	Pontiac
12.	Ward Burton	Dodge
13.	Johnny Benson	Pontiac
14.	Rusty Wallace	Ford
15.	Dale Jarrett	Ford

16.	Ted Musgrave	Dodge
17.	Steve Park	Chevrolet
18.	Tony Stewart	Pontiac
19.	Ricky Rudd	Ford
20.	Kevin Harvick	Chevrolet
21.	Dale Earnhardt Jr.	Chevrolet
22.	Jamie McMurray	Dodge
23.	Kenny Wallace	Dodge
24.	Ricky Craven	Ford
25.	Greg Biffle	Dodge
26.	Robby Gordon	Chevrolet
27.	Ken Schrader	Pontiac
28.	Terry Labonte	Chevrolet
29.	Bobby Labonte	Pontiac
30.	Jack Sprague	Chevrolet
31.	Kyle Petty	Dodge
32.	Geoffrey Bodine	Ford
33.	Jeremy Mayfield	Dodge
34.	Derrike Cope	Dodge
35.	Jason Leffler	Dodge
36.	Mike Skinner	Chevrolet
37.	Casey Atwood	Dodge
38.	Jeff Green	Chevrolet
39.	John Andretti	Dodge
40.	Matt Kenseth	Ford
41.	Michael Waltrip	Chevrolet
42.	Jimmy Spencer	Dodge
43.	Dave Blaney	Ford

APPENDIX A
RESOURCES

NASCAR ON FILM

Movies

The Big Wheel (1949) Old story retold fairly well. Mickey Rooney is a young son determined to travel in his father's tracks as a race car driver, even when dad buys the farm on the oval. Good acting and direction keep this a cut above average. **

Car Crash (1980) Organized crime hits stock car racing head on to produce crashing bore directed by Antonio Margheriti. *

Days of Thunder (1990) *Top Gun* in race cars! Tom Cruise follows the same formula he has followed for several years now (with the notable exception of *Born on the Fourth of July.*) Cruise and Robert Towne co-wrote the screenplay concerning a young kid bursting with talent and raw energy who must learn to deal with his mentor, his girlfriend, and eventually the bad guy. First film that featured cameras that were actually on the race cars. If you like Cruise or race cars then this is the movie for you. **

Eat My Dust (1976) Teenage son of a California sheriff steals the best stock cars from a race track to take the town's heartthrob for a joy ride. Subsequently he leads the town on a wild car chase. Brainless but fast-paced. **

Grandview U.S.A. (1984) A low-key look at low-rent middle America, centering on a foxy local speedway owner and the derby-obsessed boys she attracts. Pre-*Dirty Dancing* choreography from Patrick Swayze and wife Lisa Niemi. **

Greased Lightning (1977) The story of the first black auto racing champion, Wendell Scott, who had to overcome racial prejudice to achieve his success. Slightly-better-than-average Richard Pryor comedy vehicle. ***

The Last American Hero (1973) The true story of how former moonshine runner Junior Johnson became one of the fastest race car drivers in the history of the sport. Entertaining slice of life chronicling whiskey running and stock car racing, with Jeff Bridges superb in the lead. Based on a series of articles written by Tom Wolfe. ***

Red Line (1996) Stock-car racer Jim (Chad McQueen) loses his sponsorship, turns to petty crime to settle his debts, and winds up in trouble with the mob when he hooks up with a couple of hoods to steal some diamonds. *

Red Line 7000 (1965) High-stakes auto racers drive hot cars and date pretty women. Excellent racing footage in an otherwise routine four-wheel fest. **

Richard Petty Story (1972) The biography of race car driver Petty, played by himself, and his various achievements on the track. *

Six Pack (1982) The Gambler goes auto racing. Kenny Rogers, in his theatrical debut, stars as Brewster Baker, a former stock car driver. He returns to the racing circuit with the help of six larcenous orphans (the six-pack, get it?) adept at stripping cars. Kinda cute if you're in the mood for sugar-powered race car story. *

Speedway (1968) Elvis the stock car driver finds himself being chased by Nancy (Sinatra) the IRS agent during an important race. Will Sinatra keep to the business at hand? Or will the King melt her heart? Some cameos by real-life auto racers, including Richard Petty and Cale Yarborough. Watch for a young Terri Garr. Movie number 27 for Elvis. **

Stroker Ace (1983) Flamboyant stock car driver tries to break an iron-clad promotional contract signed with a greedy fried-chicken magnate. Off duty, he ogles blondes as dopey as he is. One of the worst from Burt Reynolds—and that's saying something. *

Documentaries

Darrell Waltrip: Quicksilver (ESPN–NASCAR)

Format: VHS
Description: A look back at Darrell Waltrip's nearly three-decade career racing at NASCAR's top level, first in the Grand National division, then in the Winston Cup.

Davey Allison Story

Release Date: 1994
Format: VHS
Description: A look at the life of Davey Allison.

Good to Go (ESPN–NASCAR)

Format: VHS
Description: A look at NASCAR racing from the perspective of a driver, a NASCAR legend, a car owner, a crew chief, and a race promoter.

Great Racing Legends—Bobby & Davey Allison

Release Date: 1994
Format: VHS
Description: A look back at one of the most successful sibling duos in NASCAR history.

Great Racing Legends—Michael & Darrell Waltrip

Release Date: 1994
Format: VHS
Description: A look back at the careers of "Old DW" and his brother Michael.

Great Racing Legends—Richard & Kyle Petty

Release Date: 1994
Format: VHS
Description: A review of the careers of the legendary father-son combination.

Great Racing Legends—Rusty & Kenny Wallace

Release Date: 1994
Format: VHS
Description: A career retrospective of brothers Rusty and Kenny Wallace.

The History of NASCAR

Release Date: 2004
Format: DVD
Description: A look back at the more than 50 years of NASCAR stock car racing, from Daytona to the Brickyard.

Jeff Gordon: One in a Million (ESPN–NASCAR)

Release Date: 1998
Format: VHS
Description: An up-close look at Jeff Gordon's 1997 championship season on the Winston Cup circuit, which was his second title.

Jeff Gordon—Wide Open

Release Date: 1996
Format: VHS
Run Time: 70
Description: Video biography of NASCAR Winston Cup's youngest champion.

Making of "Days of Thunder": NASCAR Goes to Hollywood

Release Date: 1991
Format: VHS
Run Time: 40
Description: See how the exciting race scenes were filmed in "Days of Thunder" in this fast-paced documentary.

NASCAR: Dale Earnhardt Jr.—Any Given Day

Release Date: 2004
Format: DVD
Description: Documentary on NASCAR star Dale Earnhardt Jr., son of the late Dale Earnhardt.

NASCAR: The Daytona Experience–1992

Format: VHS
Description: Covers the sights and sounds of the Daytona Speedway.

NASCAR: A Decade at the Brickyard

Release Date: 2003
Format: DVD
Description: A look back at the first 10 years of NASCAR racing at the legendary Indianapolis Motor Speedway.

NASCAR: Families In the Fast Lane

Release Date: 1997
Format: VHS
Description: Multigenerational and sibling relationships are common in NASCAR, and this video examines some of the sports leading families, such as the Pettys, Labontes, and Waltrips.

NASCAR for Kids: A Day at the Race Shop

Release Date: 1998
Format: VHS
Run Time: 30
Description: ESPN NASCAR commentator Dr. Jerry Punch gives children a look at how race cars are assembled.

NASCAR for Kids: A Day at the Races

Release Date: 1998
Format: VHS
Run Time: 30
Description: NASCAR world champion Benny Parsons gives children a look at race car maintenance and preparation.

NASCAR: Great Drivers Past Present & Future

Release Date: 1997
Format: VHS
Run Time: 55
Description: A look at some of the sports greatest drivers, including Richard Petty and Jeff Gordon.

NASCAR: Great Moments Early Years

Release Date: 1997
Format: VHS
Run Time: 45
Description: A look back at the early years of NASCAR, which was founded in Florida in 1948.

NASCAR: Great Moments The Modern Era

Release Date: 1997
Format: VHS
Run Time: 50
Description: A review of NASCAR racing in the 1970s and beyond, including the beginnings of the current Winston Cup circuit.

NASCAR Handbook: Behind The Scenes

Format: VHS
Description: Rules, strategies, racing terms and other NASCAR behind the scenes information is examined.

NASCAR: Road to Daytona 2003

Release Date: 2004
Format: VHS

The NASCAR Story, Volume One: From Thunder Road to Victory Lane: 1947–1958

Format: VHS

Run Time: 65

Description Covers the origins of stock car racing, from the early races on the beach at Daytona to the first NASCAR superstars, such as the Flock brothers and Lee Petty.

The NASCAR Story, Volume Two: Superstars and Superspeedways: 1959–1971

Format: VHS
Run Time: 65
Description Covers the birth of Daytona International Speedway, races at Darlington and Martinsville, and historical footage of NASCAR greats Junior Johnson, Bud Moore, Ned Jarrett, and Richard Petty.

The NASCAR Story, Volume Three: Four Star Battle for the Winston Cup: 1972–1979

Format: VHS
Run Time: 65
Description Covers the beginning of NASCAR's "Modern Era" in 1972 and highlights four of the best drivers of all-time: Richard Petty, David Pearson, Bobby Allison, and Cale Yarborough. Includes coverage of the famous Petty-Allison feud and Yarborough's record three straight Winston Cup championships.

The NASCAR Story, Volume Four: The Thunder Rolls On: 1980–1994

Format: VHS
Run Time: 65
Description Covers the start of Dale Earnhardt's career, Richard Petty's 200th career win, Bill Elliott's Winston Million, and the rise and tragic fall of Tim Richmond, Alan Kulwicki, and Davey Allison.

NASCAR: Tony Stewart—Smoke

Release Date: 2003
Format: DVD
Description: Profile of driver Tony Stewart, who won his first Winston Cup championship in 2002.

NASCAR Video: Alan Kulwicki: Champion of Dreams

Release Date: 1994
Format: VHS

Run Time: 30

Description: Tribute to Winston cup champion Kulwicki who died in May, 1993. Details the story of his career from his rookie of the year status in 1986 to his work with sponsors and other personal moments. Little on-the-track action.

The NASCAR Video: Collector's Series, Vol. 1

Release Date: 1991
Format: VHS
Run Time: 60
Description: This volume of the racing history series looks at Daytona's beginnings, profiles Richard Petty and Dale Earnhardt, offers driving tips, and much more.

The NASCAR Video: Collector's Series, Vol. 2

Release Date: 1991
Format: VHS
Run Time: 60
Description: Volume two of NASCAR's video magazine. This issue focuses on the top ten drivers of all time, profiles driver Ernie Irvan, and much more.

The NASCAR Video: Collector's Series, Vol. 3

Release Date: 1991
Format: VHS
Run Time: 60
Description: This volume of the series looks at what it means to own your own race car, profiles women drivers, looks at Joe Weatherly and Chad Little, offers racing tips, and much more.

NASCAR; Winston Cup 2002

Release Date: 2003
Format: DVD
Description: A review of the 2002 season, in which Tony Stewart won his first Winston Cup championship

NASCAR: Winston Cup 2003

Release Date: 2003
Format: DVD
Description: A review of the 2003 NASCAR season, in which Matt Kenseth won his first Win-

ston Cup (the last year before the series changed to the Nextel Cup).

NASCAR Year in Review: 1993

Format: VHS
Run Time: 70
Description: Recaps the 1993 Winston Cup season, including race footage from every race. Covers Dale Earnhardt's sixth Winston Cup title and the untimely deaths of Alan Kulwicki and Davey Allison.

NASCAR Year in Review: 1994

Format: VHS
Run Time: 70
Description Recaps the 1994 Winston Cup season, including race footage from every race. Covers Dale Earnhardt's record-tying seventh Winston Cup championship and the inaugural Brickyard 400.

NASCAR Year in Review: 1995

Format: VHS
Run Time: 70
Description Recaps the 1995 Winston Cup season, including race footage from every race. Covers Jeff Gordon's first Winston Cup Championship.

NASCAR Year in Review: 1996

Format: VHS
Run Time: 70
Description Recaps the 1996 Winston Cup season, including race footage from all 31 races. Covers Terry Labonte's second Winston Cup championship.

NASCAR Year in Review: 1997

Format: VHS
Run Time: 79
Description: Recaps the 1996 Winston Cup season, including footage of every race. Covers Jeff Gordon's second Winston Cup championship.

NASCAR Year in Review: 1998

Format: VHS
Run Time: 79

Description: Recaps the 1998 Winston Cup season, including Dale Earnhardt's win at the Daytona 500, Jeff Gordon tying Richard Petty's record of 13 wins in one season, and Mark Martin's win at the first Winston Cup event in Las Vegas.

NASCAR Year in Review: 1999

Format: VHS
Run Time: 79
Description: Recaps the 1999 Winston Cup season, including footage of every race. Covers Dale Jarrett's first Winston Cup championship.

NASCAR's 50th Anniversary: Fields & Towers

Format: VHS
Release Date: 1998
Description: Reviews the growth of NASCAR's tracks, from the small dirt tracks common in the 1950s to the gleaming superspeedways of the 1990s and beyond. One of a five-volume anniversary set.

NASCAR's 50th Anniversary: Good Old Gods

Format: VHS
Release Date: 1998
Description: A look back at the legends of NASCAR racing, including Richard Petty, Junior Johnson, David Pearson, Buck Baker, Fireball Roberts, and more. One of a five-volume anniversary set.

NASCAR's 50th Anniversary: Inherit the Win

Format: VHS
Release Date: 1998
Description: A look at some of the leading families in NASCAR history, including father and son driving combinations such as Ned and Dale Jarrett and Richard and Kyle Petty. One of a five-volume anniversary set.

NASCAR's 50th Anniversary: Sincerely, Bill France

Format: VHS
Release Date: 1998
Description: A look back at the life of Bill France Sr., the man who founded NASCAR in

Daytona Beach, Florida, in 1948. One of a five-volume anniversary set.

NASCAR's 50th Anniversary: Southern Exposure

Format: VHS
Release Date: 1998
Description: A chronology of the events that shaped NASCAR during its first 50 years, covering it's growth from a small regional sport in the 1950s to its spot as one of the leading spectator sports in America. One of a five-volume anniversary set.

NASCAR's Greatest Drivers (ESPN–NASCAR)

Format: VHS
Description: In-depth interviews with some of the legends of NASCAR racing, including Richard Petty, Dale Earnhardt, Jeff Gordon, and more.

NASCAR's Greatest Moments (ESPN–NASCAR)

Format: VHS
Description: Highlights of some of the historic moments in NASCAR history, including Richard Petty's 200th victory and the first Daytona 500.

NASCAR's Greatest Races (ESPN–NASCAR)

Format: VHS
Description: A look back at some of NASCAR's most memorable races, including the 1959 Daytona 500 and Richard Petty's last race.

NASCAR's Greatest Rivalries (ESPN–NASCAR)

Format: VHS
Description: A review of some of NASCAR's greatest personal battles, including Richard Petty and Bobby Allison, and more.

Pro Racing Video: The Race to Daytona

Release Date: 1997
Format: VHS
Run Time: 60
Description: Follows Kyle Petty as he builds, tests, and races a car in the Daytona 500.

Rusty Wallace: In the Driver's Seat

Format: VHS
Run Time: 70
Description Ride along with Rusty Wallace for an inside look at life in the high speed world of NASCAR. Includes exclusive behind-the-scenes looks at life in the pits and in a Winston Cup garage.

Terry Labonte: Turning Iron into Gold

Format: VHS
Run Time: 45
Description Covers Terry Labonte's 1996 championship season in complete detail, including interviews with Labonte and exclusive home movie footage. Also covers his memorable side-by-side victory lap with his brother Bobby in Atlanta.

The Top Ten Drivers of All Time

Format: VHS
Description: Part of the NASCAR Collector's Series, hosted by Benny Parson. Top ten drivers in the history of Stock Car racing talk about some of their greatest racing moments.

A Week in the Life of a Race Team

Format: VHS
Description: Part of the NASCAR Collector's Series. Highlights the teamwork and dedication needed by a race team to be successful in NASCAR Winston Cup Competition. Follows the activities of a Winston Cup racing team.

NASCAR IN PRINT

Books

Ahuja, Jay. *Speed Dreams: A Guide to America's 23 Nascar Tracks*. Citadel Press, March 2002.

Auto Racing Analysis. *2000 Auto Racing Analysis Stock Car Racing Racewinners and Champions: NASCAR and Other Stock Car Motorsport Series*. Auto Racing Analysis, 2000.

Assael, Shaun. *Wide Open: Days & Nights on the NASCAR Tour*. Ballantine Books, Inc., 1998.

Baker, Buddy and David Poole. *Flat Out and Half Turned Over: Tales from Pit Road with Buddy Baker.* Sports Publishing, Inc., October 2002.

Barber, Phil. *From Finish to Start: A Week in the Life of NASCAR Race Team.* Child's World, 2003.

Bledsoe, Jerry. *The World's Number One, Flat-Out, All-Time Great Stock Car Racing Book.* Down Home Press, February 1995.

Buchanan, Lee, and Don Coble. *Insiders' Guide to the NASCAR Tracks: The Unofficial, Opinionated, Fan's Guide to Where to Stay, Eat, and Enjoy the Circuit.* Globe Pequot Press, 2004.

Buckley, James Jr. *NASCAR: Speedway Superstars.* Random House, 2004.

Burt, William M. *Behind the Scenes of NASCAR Racing (Enthusiast Color Series).* Motorbooks International, 2003.

———. *NASCAR Transporters.* Motorbooks International, 2000.

———. *Stock Car Race Shop: Design and Construction of a NASCAR Stock Car.* Motorbooks International, 2001.

Canfield, Jack, Mark Victor Hansen, Matthew E. Adams, and Kirk Autio. *Chicken Soup for the Soul of NASCAR.* Health Communications, April 2003.

Cavin, Curt. *Under the Helmet: Inside the Mind of a Driver.* Child's World, 2003.

Center, Bill, and Bob Moore. *NASCAR 50 Greatest Drivers.* HarperCollins, December 1998.

Cerbone, John and Peter Monte. *Complete Idiot's Guide to Stock Car Racing.* Alpha Books, 2000

The Charlotte Observer. *Legends of NASCAR: Defying Time...Defining Greatness.* Triumph Books, February 2003.

———. *Powered by Faith: NASCAR Drivers Personal Testimonies and Devotions.* Triumph Books, 2004.

———. *Young Guns: Celebrating Nascar's Hottest Young Drivers.* Triumph Books, October 2002.

Cothren, Larry. *NASCAR'S Next Generation.* Motorbooks International, 2003.

Craft, John. *Chevy Stock Cars.* Motorbooks International, 2000.

Dale Earnhardt Jr.: The Driving Force Of A New Generation. Beckett Publications, April 2000.

Dutton, Monte. *At Speed : Up Close & Personal With The People, Places, & Fans of NASCAR.* Brasseys, Inc., 2000.

———. *Postcards from Pit Road: Inside NASCAR's 2002 Season.* Brasseys, Inc., March 2003.

———. *Rebel With a Cause: A Season With NASCAR Star Tony Stewart.* Brasseys, Inc., 2001.

Dutton, Monte, ed., and Jim Hunter. *Taking Stock: Life in NASCAR's Fast Lane.* Brasseys, Inc., October 2002.

Earnhardt Jr., Dale and Jade Gurss. *Driver #8.* Warner Books, January 2002.

Edelstein, Robert. *NASCAR Generations: The Legacy of Family in NASCAR Racing.* Harper Entertainment, 2000.

Ernsberger, Richard. *God, Pepsi, and Groovin' on the High Side: Tales from the NASCAR Circuit.* M. Evans & Co., March 2003.

Falk, Duane. *The Winston Cup.* Metro Books, 2000.

Gigliotti, Jim. *Fantastic Finishes: NASCAR's Great Races.* Child's World, 2003.

———. *NASCAR Official Handbook.* Regal Books, 2004.

Gillispie, Tom. *I Remember Dale Earnhardt: Personal Memories of and Testimonials to Stock Car Racing's Most Beloved Driver, As Told by the People Who Knew Him Best.* Cumberland House, September 2001.

Golenbock, Peter. *American Zoom: Stock Car Racing from the Dirt Tracks to Daytona.* Macmillan Publishing Company, Inc., September 1994.

———. *The Last Lap: The Life and Times of NASCAR's Legendary Heroes.* Macmillan General Reference, February 1998.

Golenbock, Peter. *NASCAR Confidential: Stories of the Men and Women Behind a Racing Empire.* Motema Music, 2004.

Golenbock, Peter and Ernie Irvan. *No Fear: The Hard Life and Fast Times of NASCAR Driver Ernie Irvan.* Hyperion, February 1999.

Golenbock, Peter, and Greg Fielden. *NASCAR Encyclopedia.* Motorbooks International, 2003.

————. *The Stock Car Racing Encyclopedia.* Macmillan Publishing Company, Inc., January 1997.

Gordon, Jeff. *Jeff Gordon: Racing Back to the Front—My Memoir.* Atria Books, 2003.

Green, David. *Heroes of NASCAR.* Carlton, May 2003.

Hagstrom, Robert G. Jr. *The NASCAR Way: The Business That Drives the Sport.* John Wiley & Sons, Inc., February 1998.

Hammond, Lee. *Draw NASCAR.* North Light Books, 2003.

Hembree, Michael. *NASCAR: The Definitive History of America's Sport.* Harper Entertainment, 2000.

Higgins, Tom. *NASCAR's Greatest Races: The 25 Most Thrilling Races in NASCAR History.* Harper Entertainment, 1999.

Higham, Peter. *International Motor Racing Guide: A Complete Reference from Formula One to NASCAR.* David Bull Publishing, 2003.

Houston, Rick. *Second To None: The History of the NASCAR Busch Series.* David Bull Publishing Inc., 2001.

Howell, Mark D. *From Moonshine to Madison Avenue: A Cultural History of the NASCAR Winston Cup Series.* Bowling Green University Popular Press, June 1997.

Huff, Richard M. *Behind the Wall.* Bonus Books, Inc., March 1997.

————. *The Insider's Guide to Stock Car Racing: NASCAR Racing: America's Fastest-Growing Sport.* Bonus Books, Inc., May 1997.

————. *Stock Car Champions: Running with NASCAR's Best.* Bonus Books, 2000.

Hunter, Don and Al Pearce. *The Illustrated History of Stock Car Racing.* Motorbooks International, Publishers & Wholesalers, September 1998.

Ingram, Jonathan. *NASCAR Fans Guide.* Carlton, February 2003.

————. *NASCAR in Photographs.* Carlton, September 2002.

Irvan, Ernie. *No Fear: Ernie Irvan: The NASCAR Driver's Story of Tragedy and Triumph.* Hyperion, 2000.

Jensen, Tom. *Cheating: An Inside Look at the Bad Things Good NASCAR Winston Cup Racers Do in Pursuit of Speed.* David Bull Publishing, September 2002.

Kirkpatrick, Rob. *Dale Earnhardt, Jr.: NASCAR Road Racer.* Powerkids Press, 2003.

McCullough, Bob. *My Greatest Day in NASCAR: The Legends of Auto Racing Recount Their Greatest Moments.* St. Martin's Press, 2000.

McLaurin, Jim. *NASCAR's Most Wanted : The Top 10 Book of Outrageous Drivers, Wild Wrecks, and Other Oddities.* Brasseys, Inc., 2001.

McReynolds, Larry and Bob Zeller. *Larry McReynolds, the Big Picture: My Life from Pit Road to the Broadcast Booth.* David Bull Publishing. October 2002.

Martin, Mark. *NASCAR for Dummies.* Hungry Minds, Inc., 2000.

Martin, Ronda J. *Stock Car Legends: The Laughs, Practical Jokes, & Fun Stories from Racing's Greats!* Premium Press America, March 1999.

Maurer, Tracy Nelson. *Stock Cars.* The Rourke Book Company, Inc., 2004.

Menzer, Joe. *The Wildest Ride: A History of NASCAR (or How a Bunch of Good Ol' Boys Built a Billion-Dollar Industry Out of Wrecking Cars).* Simon & Schuster, 2001.

Miller, G. Wayne. *Men and Speed: A Wild Ride Through NASCAR's Breakout Season.* PublicAffairs, April 2002.

Montville, Leigh. *At the Altar of Speed: The Fast Life and Tragic Death of Dale Earnhardt*. Doubleday, October 2001.

Moriarty, Frank. *The Encyclopedia of Stock Car Racing*. Michael Friedman/Fairfax Publishing, May 1998.

NASCAR Track and Travel Guide. Pit Stop Publishing, Inc. 2003.

NASCAR Yearbook & Press Guide. National Association for Stock Car Auto Racing. Annual.

NASCAR's Best Shots. DK Publishing, 2004.

The Official NASCAR Handbook: Everything You Want to Know About the NASCAR Winston Cup Series. HarperCollins, July 1998.

Official NASCAR Trivia: The Ultimate Challenge for NASCAR Fans. HarperEntertainment, 1998

On the Road With NASCAR Road Atlas 2003: United States/Canada/ Mexico. Lawrence Group, September 2002.

Owens, Tom. *Collecting Stock Car Racing Memorabilia*. Millbrook Press, 2001.

———. *Stock Car Racing*. Twenty First Century Books, 2000.

Pistone, Peter. *Official NASCAR Craftsman Series Handbook*. Harper Entertainment, December 2003.

Poole, David. *Race With Destiny: The Year That Changed NASCAR Forever*. Moyer Bell Ltd., 2004.

Rich, Rhonda and Childress, Richard. *My Life in the Pits: Living and Learning on the NASCAR Winston Cup Circuit*. Harper Entertainment, April 2002.

Sakkis, Tony. *A Fan's Guide to Circle Track Racing : Facts, Tracks, and Stats on NASCAR, Busch, Craftsman Truck, Arca, Asa, World of Outlaws, and Other Regional Racing*. H.P. Books, 2001.

Schaller, Bob. *Top Stars of NASCAR Volume II*. Crosstraining Publishing, 2000.

Skinner, Angela. *Turning Points: Defining Moments in the Lives of NASCAR Superstars*. Umi Publications, 2003.

Spencer, Reid. *NASCAR Fans Guide: The Essential Insider's Guide to Everything NASCAR*. Triumph Books, 2003.

The Sporting News. *NASCAR Record and Fact Book 2004*. McGraw-Hill/Contemporary Books, 2004.

Sports Illustrated. *Full Throttle: From Daytona to Darlington: The 2004 NASCAR Season*. Time Inc. Home Entertainment, 2004.

Stewart, Tony and Bones Bourcier. *True Speed: My Racing Life*. Harper Entertainment, April 2002.

Sullivan, Robert, ed. *American Speed: From Dirt Tracks to NASCAR*. Time Inc. Home Entertainment, October 2002.

White, Ben. Photos by Nigel Kinrade. *NASCAR Racers: Today's Top Drivers*. Motorbooks International, 2003.

Wood, Denise. *NASCAR Women: At the Heart of Racing*. David Bull Publishing, 2003.

Woods, Bob. *Earning a Ride: How to Become a NASCAR Driver*. Child's World, 2003.

———. *Live from the Racetrack: NASCAR on TV*. 2003.

———. *NASCAR: The Greatest Races*. Child's World, 2004.

Woody, Larry. *Along for the Ride: A Collection of Stories from the Fast and Furious World of NASCAR*. Sports Publishing Inc., 2003.

Wright, Jim. *Fixin' to Git: One Fan's Love Affair With NASCAR's Winston Cup*. Duke University Press, 2002.

Periodicals

Auto Racing Digest
Century Publishing Co.
990 Grove St.
Evanston, IL 60201-4370
Phone: (847)491-6440
Fax: (847)491-0459
Description: Magazine covering auto racing.

AutoWeek
Crain Communications, Inc.

1400 Woodbridge Ave.
Detroit, MI 48207-3187
Phone: (313)446-6000
Toll-free: 800-678-9595
Fax: (313)446-0347
Description: Magazine for car enthusiasts includes news coverage and features on vehicles, personalities, and events. Provides coverage of Formula One, CART, NASCAR, and IMSA races.

NASCAR Winston Cup Scene

Street & Smith's Sports Group
First Citizen Plaza
128 S. Tryon, Ste. 2200
Charlotte, NC 28202
Phone: (704)375-7404
Toll-free: 800-704-3757
Fax: (704)371-3299
Description: Trade paper covering the NASCAR Winston Cup and Busch Series circuits.

National Speed Sport News

National Speed Sport News
6509 Hudspeth Rd.
P.O. Box 1210
Harrisburg, NC 28075-1210
Phone: (704)455-2531
Fax: (704)445-2605
Description: Newspaper featuring auto racing, sport cars, and motors.

Road & Track

1499 Monrovia Ave.
Newport Beach, CA 92663
Phone: (949)720-5300
Fax: (949)631-2757
Description: Automotive magazine.

Southern MotoRacing

Southern Motor Racing
1049 Northwest Blvd.
P.O. Box 500
Winston-Salem, NC 27102
Phone: (336)723-5227
Fax: (336)722-3757
Description: Tabloid covering auto racing.

Speedway Scene

Hockomock Publishing
50 Washington St.
P.O. Box 300
North Easton, MA 02356
Phone: (508)238-7016
Fax: (508)230-2381
Description: Tabloid covering circle track racing from Winston Cup to local events.

Stock Car Racing

EMAP Petersen
3816 Industry Blvd.
Lakeland, FL 33811 USA
Phone: (863)607-5073
Fax: (863)648-1187
Description: Magazine covering stock car racing.

NASCAR ORGANIZATIONS

Associations

American Auto Racing Writers and Broadcasters Association (AARWBA)

c/o Dusty Brandel
922 N. Pass Ave.
Burbank, CA 91505
Phone: (818)842-7005
Fax: (818)842-7020
URL: http://www.aarwba.org
Contact: Dusty Brandel, Pres.
Description: Persons who write, broadcast, or photograph auto racing. Seeks to: upgrade coverage of auto racing; promote the stature of racing; secure better facilities for writers. Conducts contests for top race stories, photography, and broadcasts.

National Association for Stock Car Auto Racing (NASCAR)

P.O. Box 2875
1801 W. International Speedway Blvd.
PO Box 2875
Daytona Beach, FL 32120-2875
Phone: (386)253-0611
Fax: (386)258-7646
URL: http://www.nascar.com

Contact: Brian France, Pres.
Description: Sanctions and supervises stock car races. Compiles statistics and issues publications.

Fan Clubs

John Andretti Fan Club

http://www.jafanpage.com/

Johnny Benson Fan Club
http://www.johnnybenson.com/2004index.shtml

Dave Blaney Fan Club
http://www.4yourstyleracing.com/FanClubs/
   Drivers/blaney.htm

Jeff Burton Fan Club
http://www.roushracing.com/jeff_burton/
   default.asp

Ward Burton Fan Club
3475 Myer Lee Dr
Winston-Salem, NC 27101
http://www.wardburton.com

Kurt Busch Fan Club
http://www.kurtbusch.com

Ricky Craven Fan Club
18 Searsport Ave.
Belfast, ME 04915
http://www.rickycravenfans.com

Dale Earnhardt Jr. Club E Jr.
PO Box 5190
Concord, NC 28027
http://www.dalejr.com /

Bill Elliott Fan Club
PO Box 248
Dawsonville, GA 30534
http://www.billelliott.com/fans/fanclub.html

The Jeff Gordon Fan Club
PO Box 910
Harrisburg, NC 28075
http://www.jeffgordon.com/fancenter/fans.html

Robby Gordon Fan Club
201 Rolling Hills Rd.

Mooresville NC 28117
http://www.robbygordon.com/ROBBY/Fanzone/
   fanzone.htm

Jeff Green Fan Club
PO Box 268
Cornelius, NC. 28031
http://aolsvc.aolracing.sports.aol.com/fanzone/

Kevin Harvick Fan Club
PO Box 1491
West Monroe, LA 71294-1491
http://www.kevinharvick.com/fanclub.htm

Dale Jarrett Fan Club
PO Box 1269
Conover, NC 28613
http://www.dalejarrett.com/fanclub.asp

Jimmie Johnson Fan Club
PO Box 5599
Mooresville, NC 28027
http://www.motorsportsbymail.com/jjfanclub.htm

Kasey Kahne Fan Club
http://www.kaseykahne.com/fanclub.asp?target=

Matt Kenseth Fan Club
10 Water Street
Cambridge, WI 53523
http://www.roushracing.com/matt_kenseth/
   default.asp

Bobby Labonte Fan Club
PO Box 358
Trinity, NC 27370
http://www.bobbylabontefans.com

Terry Labonte Fan Club
PO Box 579
Harrisburg, NC 28075
http://www.terrylabonte.net/fanclub.shtml

Jamie McMurray Fan Club
P.O. Box 5034
Concord, NC 28027
http://www.havoline.com/racing/nascar/team/
   jm.html

Casey Mears Fan Club
http://www.caseymears.com/news30.html

The Sterling Marlin Fan Club
PO Box 1100
Pulaski, TN 38478
http://www.sterlingmarlinfanclub.com

Mark Martin Fan Club
http://www.roushracing.com/mark_martin/
default.asp

Jeremy Mayfield Fan Club
PO Box 2365
Cornelius, NC 28031
http://www.jeremymayfieldfan.com

Joe Nemechek Fan Club
https://coldfusion.hydrogenmedia.com/ssl/
joe_nemechek/fans/fan_club.cfm

Ryan Newman Fan Club
26425 Darden Road
South Bend, IN 46628
http://www.alltelracing.com/ryans_fan_club/

Steve Park Fan Club
PO Box 3062
Mooresville, NC 28117
http://www.steve-park.com/main/fanclub.php3

Kyle Petty Fan Club
135 Longfield Dr
Mooresville, NC 28115
http://www.pettyracing.com/current_season/
kyle_fan_club.html

Scott Riggs Fan Club
8904 Roxboro Road
Bahama, NC 27503
http://www.4yourstyleracing.com/FanClubs/
Drivers/riggs.htm

Ricky Rudd Fan Club
Attn: Membership Services
PO Box 4060
Mooresville, NC 28117
http://www.rickyrudd.com/fanclub.html

Elliott Sadler Fan Club
PO Box 32
Emporia, Virginia 23847
http://www.sadlerfanclub.com

Johnny Sauter Fan Club
641 N. Walnut St.
Reedsburg, WI 53959
http://www.rcrracing.com/Teams/Johnny_04.asp

Ken Schrader Fan Club
PO Box 5430
Concord, NC 28027
http://www.schraderracing.com/fanclub.htm

Jimmy Spencer Fan Club
PO Box 1626
Mooresville, NC 28115
http://www.jimmyspencer.net/fanclub/

Tony Stewart Fan Club
5671 W. 74th St. (Park 100)
Indianapolis, Indiana 46278
http://www.tonystewartstore.com/fanclubreg.asp

Brian Vickers Fan Club
http://www.brianvickers.com/

Rusty Wallace Fan Club
PO Box 515
Williams, AZ. 86046
http://www.RustyWallaceFanClub.com

Michael Waltrip Fan Club
PO Box 5065
Concord, NC 28027
http://www.michaelwaltrip.com/fancl.htm

Scott Wimmer Fan Club
1204 Starling Ln.
Wassau, WI 54401

NASCAR ON THE WEB

General Interest Sites

trackbytes.com
http://www.racecar.com/index.html

ESPN Auto Racing
http://rpm.espn.go.com/rpm/index

goracing.com
http://www.qvc.com/goracing.html

Hundreds of NASCAR Links
http://www.racinlinks.com

Indystar.com
http://www.indystar.com/sports/racing

Jayski.com
http://jayski.thatsracin.com/

Motor Racing Network Radio
http://www.mrnradio.com

Motorsports Hall of Fame
http://www.mshf.com

NASCAR Collectibles for Sale or Trade
http://www.angelfire.com/tn/harrygantcollector/
 index.html

NASCAR.COM
http://www.nascar.com/

ovaltrack.com
http://www.ovaltrack.com/

rec.auto.sports.nascar Image Archive
http://www2.msstate.edu/~rls3/rasn.html

That's Racin'.com
http://www.thatsracin.com

USA Today Sagarin's NASCAR Ratings
http://www.usatoday.com/sports/motor/smnajs.
 htm

Official Driver and Team Sites
The sites listed below are the official driver and
team sites only; for a list of fan club web sites,
please see the list of fan clubs that appears before
the "NASCAR On the Web" section of this chapter.

John Andretti
http://www.pettyracing.com/current_season/
 43_wc_driver.shtml

Greg Biffle
http://www.roushracing.com/greg_biffle/default.asp

Dave Blaney
http://www.daveblaney.com/

Brett Bodine
http://www.brettbodine.com/

Jeff Burton
http://www.roushracing.com/jeff_burton/
 default.asp

Ward Burton
http://www.wardburton.com

Kurt Busch
http://www.roushracing.com/kurt_busch/default.
 asp

Richard Childress Racing
http://www.rcrracing.com/

Derrike Cope
http://www.derrikecope.com

Ricky Craven
http://www.rickycraven.com/

Dale Earnhardt Jr.
http://www.dalejr.net

Bill Elliott
http://www.billelliott.com/

Jeff Gordon
http://www.jeffgordon.com

Robby Gordon
http://www.robbygordon.com/

Ron Hornaday
http://www.ronhornaday.com/

Dale Jarrett
http://www.dalejarrett.com/

Matt Kenseth
http://www.roushracing.com/matt_kenseth/
 default.asp

Bobby Labonte
http://www.bobbylabonte.com

Terry Labonte
http://www.terrylabonte.net

Chad Little
http://www.chadlittle.com

Sterling Marlin
http://www.sterlingmarlin.org

Mark Martin
http://www.roushracing.com/mark_martin/
  default.asp

Jeremy Mayfield
http://www.jeremymayfield.com

Jamie McMurray
http://www.jamiemcmurray

Jerry Nadeau
http://www.jerry-nadeau.com/

Joe Nemechek
http://www.joenemechek.com/

Ryan Newman
http://www.ryan12newman.com/welcome.htm

Steve Park
http://www.steve-park.com/

Penske Racing
http://www.penskeracing.com/

Kyle Petty
http://www.kylepetty.com/

Petty Racing
http://www.pettyracing.com/

Robert Pressley
http://www.robertpressley.com/

Roush Racing
http://www.roushracing.com

Ricky Rudd
http://www.rickyrudd.com

Elliott Sadler
http://www.sadlerfanclub.com/default.htm

Ken Schrader
http://www.ramppub.com/schraderracing/

Mike Skinner
http://www.mikeskinner.com/

Jimmy Spencer
http://www.jimmyspencer.net/

Tony Stewart
http://www.tonystewart.com/

Kenny Wallace
http://www.kennywallaceracing.com/

Rusty Wallace
http://www.rustywallace.com

Michael Waltrip
http://www.michaelwaltrip.com

Wood Brothers
http://www.woodbrothersracing.com

Official Track Sites

Atlanta Motor Speedway
http://www.atlantamotorspeedway.com/

Bristol Motor Speedway
http://www.bristolmotorspeedway.com/

California Speedway
http://www.californiaspeedway.com

Chicagoland Speedway
http://www.chicagolandspeedway.com/cgi-
  bin/r.cgi/index.html

Darlington Raceway
http://www.darlingtonraceway.com/

Daytona International Speedway
http://www.daytonaintlspeedway.com/

Dover International Speedway
http://www.doverspeedway.com

Homestead-Miami Speedway
http://www.homesteadmiamispeedway.com

Indianapolis Motor Speedway
http://www.brickyard.com

Infineon Raceway
http://www.infineonraceway.com

Kansas Speedway
http://www.kansasspeedway.com

Las Vegas Motor Speedway
http://www.lvms.com/

Lowe's Motor Speedway
http://www.lowesmotorspeedway.com

Martinsville Speedway
http://www.martinsvillespeedway.com

Michigan International Speedway
http://www.mispeedway.com

New Hampshire International Speedway
http://www.nhis.com

North Carolina Motor Speedway
http://www.northcarolinaspeedway.com/

Phoenix International Raceway
http://www.phoenixintlraceway.com

Pocono Raceway
http://www.poconoraceway.com

Richmond International Raceway
http://www.rir.com

Talladega Superspeedway
http://www.talladegasuperspeedway.com

Texas Motor Speedway
http://www.texasmotorspeedway.com

Watkins Glen International
http://www.theglen.com

APPENDIX B:
ALL-TIME LIST OF
CAR NUMBERS AND DRIVERS

0

John Andretti, Jeff Burton, Ward Burton, Irv Hoerr, Delmar Cowart, Doug Heveron, Clyde Dagit, Glen McDuffie, Jim Hurtubise, John Kennedy, Jason Leffler, Dick May, Steve Pfeifer, Ronnie Thomas, Roy Smith, Jim Hurlbert, Jeff McDuffie, George Altheide, Frank Warren, Eddie Bond, G. C. Spencer, Jim Inglebright, Jack Sprague, Johnny Sauter

00

Scott Gaylord, Buckshot Jones, Freddy Smith, John Utsman, Ed Sanger, Phil Barkdoll, Morgan Shepherd, Sterling Marlin, Jeff Krogh, Frank James, Bobby Mausgrover, Phil Good, Jerry Nadeau, Mike Skinner

01

Mickey Gibbs, Earle Canavan, Sonny Hutchins, Don Hall, George Behlman, Chuck Bown, Jim Insolo, Hershel McGriff, Geoff Bodine, David Pearson, Butch Lindley, Morgan Shepherd, Mark Martin, Dave Pletcher, Doug Heveron, Steve Grissom, Jeff Green, Bobby Hamilton Jr., Ron Hornaday Jr., P. J. Jones, Jason Leffler, Ted Musgrave, Dorsey Schroeder, Mike Skinner, Joe Nemechek, Jerry Nadeau, Jason Keller, Mike Wallace, Boris Said

02

T. W. Taylor, Rich Bickle, Mark Martin, Dick Bown, L. D. Ottinger, Jimmy Hensley, Jim Bown, Budd Hagelin, Dave Marcis, Chuck Bown, Darrell Waltrip, Donnie Allison, Dick May, Mike Potter, Jim Sauter, Tommy Gale, D. K. Ulrich, Rick Newsom, Frank Hill, Randy Baker, Dale Jarrett, Sam Ard, Ryan Newman, Hermie Sadler

03

Dave Pletcher, Bill Schmitt, Howard Mark, Chuck Bown, Ron McGee, Bill Seifert, Walter Ballard, Jimmy Finger, Bob Bondurant, Glen

Francis, David Pearson, Eddie Bierschwale, Alan Grice, Tommy Gale

04

Charles Meacham, Hershel McGriff, Andy Belmont, Bob Schacht, Ed Bradshaw, Gary Myers, Phil Finney, Rick Baldwin, Charles Rudolph, Pee Wee Wentz, Mel Larson, John Alexander, Harry Schilling, Johnny Miller

05

Charles Meacham, Ed Feree, David Sisco, Peter Knab, Lella Lombardi, Dick Brooks, Bill Elswick, Jim Sauter, Bruce Hill, Slick Johnson, Jabe Thomas

06

Terry Byers, Neil Castles, Harry Gant, Jim Lee, Jim Sauter, Ernie Cline, David Sisco, Dave Marcis, Mike Potter

07

Doug George, Larry Moyer, Dan Pardus, Sean Woodside, Randy LaJoie, Jerry Schild, Steve Moore, Steve Stolarek, Jeff McDuffie, Gene Thonsen, Bill Scott, Derrike Cope, Lance Hooper, Ivan Baldwin, Bobby Mausgrover, Jack McCoy, Geoff Brabham, Ted Musgrave

08

Rick McCray, Butch Miller, Johnny Rutherford, Ralph Jones, John Anderson, Bill Seifert, Joel Stowe, Bruce Jacobi, Donald Satterfield, Craig Spetman, Trevor Boys, Butch Miller, Bill Burns, Neil Castles, Donnie Allison, Bobby Poole, Dick May, Bob Whitlow

09

Roy Smith, Terry Fisher, A. J. Reno, Eddie Bradshaw, Nelson Oswald, Dick May, Cecil Gordon, Dick Trickle, Doug French, Carl Adams, Jody Ridley, Charles Barrett, Geoffrey Bodine, Mike Wallace, Scott Pruett, Buckshot Jones

1

Steve Park, Rick Mast, Terry Labonte, Donnie Allison, Sterling Marlin, Butch Miller, Dale Jarrett, Jim Bown, Darrell Waltrip, Morgan Shepherd, Jerry Nadeau, Bill Osborne, Johnny Rutherford, Pete Torres, Billy Scott, Neil Bonnett, John Banks, Don Hall, Bill Ward, Hershel McGriff, Steve Gray, Chuck Pittinger, Buddy Baker, Jim Insolo, Benny Parsons, Kyle Petty, Lake Speed, David Pearson, Ed Negre, Pancho Carter, Ron Bouchard, Davey Allison, Chuck Schroedel, Brett Bodine, Charles Poalillo, Dick Brooks, Cliff Garner, Lance Hooper, Harry Goularte, Joe Millikan, Dick Trickle, Clem Proctor, Kenny Wallace, John Andretti, Jeff Green, Ron Fellows

2

Rusty Wallace, Dale Earnhardt, Ernie Irvan, Jim Bown, Eddie Bierschwale, Rodney Combs, Kirk Bryant, Brett Bodine, Dave Marcis, Dick Trickle, John Martin, Dick May, Ed Negre, Richard White, Bobby Allison, David Pearson, Joe Ruttman, Robert Tartaglia, Tim Richmond, Morgan Shepherd, Mark Martin, Ken Rush, Ray Hendrick, Bill Seifert, Dick Bown, Elliott Forbes-Robinson, Roger McCluskey

3

Richard Childress, Ricky Rudd, Dale Earnhardt, Wally Dallenbach, Bobby Isaac, John Soares, Cale Yarborough, Jimmy Crawford, Alton Jones, Paul Felder

4

Bobby Hamilton, Sterling Marlin, Ernie Irvan, Rick Wilson, Phil Parsons, Jeff Purvis, Joe Nemechek, Lake Speed, Pee Wee Wentz, Hershel McGriff, Salt Walther, Gary Myers, James Hylton, Bobby Fisher, Connie Saylor, Gary Baker, Bob Riley, Mark Martin, D. K. Ulrich, Joe Ruttman, Dick Kranzler, John Sears, Lennie Pond, Tommy Ellis, Ed Negre, Jim Vandiver, Randy Myers, Rich Bickle, Robby Gordon, Bobby Hamilton Jr., Kevin Lepage, Mike Skinner, P. J. Jones, Johnny Miller, Stacy Compton, Johnny Sauter

5

Terry Labonte, Geoff Bodine, Ricky Rudd, Dick Simon, Doc Faustina, Neil Bonnett, Charles Blanton, John Martin, Jerry Sisco, Harry Gant, Earl Brooks, Neil Castles, Jim Thirkettle, James Hylton, Bruce Blodgett, Jimmy Means, Joe Ruttman, Clay Young, Sterling Marlin, Morgan Shepherd, Joe Millikan, Rodney Combs, Robin McCall, Jim Sauter, Greg Sacks, J. D. McDuffie, Wendell Scott, Ron Hornaday Sr. , Mel Larson, Todd Bodine, Ron Hornaday Jr.

6

Mark Martin, Trevor Boys, D. K. Ulrich, Richard Petty, Jim Sauter, Eddie Bierschwale, Rick Knoop, Joey Arrington, Sonny Easley, Tom Sneva, Rick Newsom, Harry Gant, Jim Hurtubise, Bobby Isaac, Neil Castles, Marty Robbins, Dick Whalen, Claude Ballot-Lena, Bob Senneker, Joe Ruttman, Stan Barrett, Terry Herman, Al Loquasto, Bob Jarvis, Randy Becker, Al Elmore, Tim Richmond, Ferrel Harris, Buddy Baker, Ron Esau, Connie Saylor, Ernie Irvan, Jerry Oliver, Charlie Glotzbach, Ray Johnstone, Bill Butts, Morgan Shepherd, Clark Dwyer, Doug Heveron, Jim Ingalls, Peter Gregg, Eddie Yarboro, Dick Brooks, Bobby Baker

7

Geoff Bodine, Alan Kulwicki, Jimmy Hensley, Tom Kendall, Kyle Petty, Jack McCoy, Dean Dalton, Frank Warren, Ivan Baldwin, Ed Negre, Jack Donohue, D. K. Ulrich, Al Holbert, Earl Brooks, Lake Speed, Tim Richmond, Dick Brooks, Ricky Rudd, Bruce Hill, Jeff McDuffie, Joey Arrington, Harry Goularte, Todd Bodine, Robby Gordon, Kevin Lepage, Ted Musgrave, Michael Waltrip, Mike Wallace, Casey Atwood, Jason Leffler

8

Bobby Hillin, Jeff Burton, Hut Stricklin, Rick Wilson, Sterling Marlin, Morgan Shepherd, Ed Negre, D. K. Ulrich, Dale Earnhardt, Dick May, Dean Dalton, Kevin Housby, James Hylton, Jimmy Means, Rick O'Dell, Kirk Shelmerdine, Dick Brooks, Ferrel Harris, Skip Manning, Ron Keselowski, Dale Earnhardt Jr.

9

Lake Speed, Jerry Nadeau, Bill Elliott, Chad Little, Greg Sacks, P. J. Jones, Stan Barrett, Butch Gilliland, Jeff Davis, Tony Bettenhausen, Mel Larson, John Kieper, Al Holbert, Terry Bivins, J. C. Danielson, Jim Vandiver, Frank Warren, Jim Insolo, Ramo Stott, Pete Hamilton, Dick Gulstrand, Carl Adams, Rich Bickle, Stacy Compton, Steve Grissom

10

Ricky Rudd, Bill Champion, Greg Sacks, Derrike Cope, Ken Bouchard, Jeff Swindell, Trevor Boys, Randy Hutchison, Elmo Langley, Don Puskarich, Leon Fox, Dean Dalton, Ed Negre, Tommy Gale, Dick May, Raymond Williams, John Ray, Bruce Jacobi, Clyde Lynn, Bill Elliott, Billy Smith, Tim Williamson, Jimmy Hindman, Clark Dwyer, Steve Gray, Jimmy Means, Doug Heveron, Dick

Trickle, Rodney Combs, Sterling Marlin, Johnny Benson, Jerry Nadeau, Mike Wallace

---

11

Darrell Waltrip, Cale Yarborough, Bill Elliott, Brett Bodine, Terry Labonte, Buddy Baker, Roy Smith

---

12

Jeff Purvis, Jeremy Mayfield, Bobby Allison, Mike Alexander, Hut Stricklin, Derrike Cope, Jimmy Spencer, Neil Bonnett, Davey Allison, Ted Fritz, Buck Simmons, Jack Ingram, Butch Lindley, Lennie Pond, Harry Gant, Donnie Allison, Buddy Baker, Tim Richmond, David Pearson, Tommy Ellis, Jim Insolo, Rodney Combs, Richard White, James Hylton, David Sosebee, Slick Johnson, Mark Martin, Larry Pollard, Jim Bown, Trevor Boys, Jeff Swindell, Brad Teague, Larry Caudill, Tom Hubert, Kyle Petty, Mike Wallace, Ryan Newman

---

13

Eddie Bierschwale, Jerry Nadeau, Ted Musgrave, Mike Skinner, Randy LaJoie, Gary Balough, Oma Kimbrough, Wally Dallenbach, Tom Hubert, Dennis Setzer, Don Puskarich, Jeff Halverson, Dick Brooks, Jack Ingram, Kevin Terris, Earle Canavan, Doug Wheeler, Eddie Yarboro, Johnny Coy, Stan Fox, Ted Christopher, Robby Gordon, P. J. Jones, Hermie Sadler

---

14

John Andretti, Bobby Labonte, Mike Chase, Terry Labonte, A. J. Foyt, Tracy Leslie, Steve Park, Coo Coo Marlin, Charlie Glotzbach, Sterling Marlin, Jimmy Means, Dick Kranzler, Harry Goulatre, Jeff Krogh, Jeff Green, Robby Gordon, Mike Bliss, Ron Hornaday Jr., Randy LaJoie,

---

Rick Mast, Dick Trickle, Boris Said, Stacy Compton, Mike Wallace, P. J. Jones, Larry Foyt

---

15

Ricky Rudd, Brett Bodine, Geoff Bodine, Morgan Shepherd, Lake Speed, Dick Trickle, Buddy Baker, Bobby Allison, Dale Earnhardt, Benny Parsons, Darrell Waltrip, Bobby Isaac, David Pearson, LeeRoy Yarbrough, Donnie Allison, Dick Brooks, George Follmer, Ted Musgrave, Derrike Cope, Michael Waltrip

---

16

Ted Musgrave, Wally Dallenbach, Kevin Lepage, Larry Pearson, Bob Schacht, Tom Rotsell, Gary Bettenhausen, Bobby Allison, George Follmer, Ed Negre, David Sisco, Richard Brickhouse, Rusty Wallace, Jim Bown, Chuck Bown, David Pearson, Raymond Williams, Glenn Jarrett, Mel Larson, Butch Lindley, Morgan Shepherd, Bill Osborne, Larry Pearson, Mark Donohue, Dave Marcis, Greg Biffle

---

17

Darrell Waltrip, Ron Hornaday Jr., Pancho Carter, Doug Heveron, Eddie Bierschwale, Lennie Pond, Jim Hull, Bobby Isaac, Roger Hamby, Gordon Johncock, Steve Pfeifer, Bill Elliott, Harry Goularte, Glenn Jarrett, Don Whittington, Lake Speed, Steve Spencer, John Anderson, Tommy Houston, Lowell Cowell, Harry Gant, Mike Potter, Sterling Marlin, Bosco Lowe, Phil Parsons, Ken Ragan, Jack McCoy, Bill Dennis, Clark Dwyer, Morgan Shepherd, Sarel Van der Merwe, Matt Kenseth

---

18

Ron Esau, Bobby Labonte, Greg Sacks, Dale Jarrett, Hut Stricklin, Brad Teague, Stan Barrett, Tom Kendall, Rick Jeffrey, Rick Hendrick,

Tommy Ellis, Glen Steurer, Joe Frasson, Jimmy Hailey, Jim Deneen, Harry Gant, G. C. Spencer, Buck Baker, Randy Ogden, Donnie Allison, Joe Booher, Donald Satterfield, J. D. McDuffie, Slick Johnson, James Hylton, Ed Negre, George Follmer, Leon Fox

---

19

Loy Allen, Chad Little, Phil Parsons, Ernie Cope, Jack Sellers, Bill Ingram, Tom Hubert, Gary Bradberry, Mike Skinner, Dick May, Henley Gray, Dale Earnhardt, Dave Marcis, Bob Burcham, Frank Warren, Bill Dennis, Cecil Gordon, Vince Giamformaggio, Billy Hagan, Glenn Jarrett, Steve Spencer, Steve Gray, Lennie Pond, Joe Fields, James Hylton, J. D. McDuffie, John Utsman, Ricky Rudd, John Anderson, Ronnie Sanders, Charlie Baker, Benny Parsons, Dennis Devea, Bobby Gerhart, Joey Arrington, Woody Fisher, Elmo Langley, Joe Booher, Derrike Cope, Dick Trickle, Mike Wallace, Jabe Thomas, Bill Cooper, Casey Atwood

---

20

Rob Moroso, Dave Mader III, Sammy Swindell, Bobby Hillin, Buddy Baker, Bobby Hamilton, Kim Campbell, Dirk Stephens, Joe Ruttman, Ricky Craven, Greg Sacks, Lance Hooper, Rick Newsom, Bob Burcham, Buck Peralta, G. T. Tallas, Richard White, Ron Esau, Ed Hale, Cecil Gordon, Elton Sawyer, George Althiede

---

21

Michael Waltrip, Morgan Shepherd, Kyle Petty, Neil Bonnett, Dale Jarrett, Tommy Ellis, Buddy Baker, Bobby Rahal, David Pearson, A. J. Foyt, Larry Pearson, Rick Wilson, Elliott Sadler, Ricky Rudd

---

22

Ward Burton, Sterling Marlin, Bobby Labonte, Randy LaJoie, Jimmy Hensley, Grant Adcox,

Rob Moroso, Steve Moore, Rodney Combs, Ricky Rudd, Bobby Allison, Jimmy Crawford, John Harkins, Jim Raptis, Larry Lemay, John Hamson, Richard White, Al Rudd Jr., Kevin Housby, Stan Barrett, Marty Robbins, Wally Dallenbach, Don Hume, Pete Hamilton, Dick Brooks, Rick Ware, Scott Wimmer

---

23

Jimmy Spencer, Eddie Bierschwale, Mike Chase, Butch Gilliland, Frank Kimmell, Michael Waltrip, Jim Hull, Roy Mayne, Earl Brooks, Charles Griffin, Larry LeMay, Louis Gatto, Charlie Glotzbach, Geoff Bodine, Elliott Forbes-Robinson, Morgan Shepherd, Dick May, Eldon Dotson, Mel Larson, Vic Elford, G. T. Tallas, Bill Dennis, James Cox, Henley Gray, Ed Hessert, Sterling Marlin, Gene Coyle, Connie Saylor, Boris Said, Scott Wimmer, Hut Stricklin, Kenny Wallace, Tom Hubert, Scott Wimmer

---

24

Butch Gilliland, Jeff Gordon, Mickey Gibbs, Dick Trickle, Jimmy Hensley, John McFadden, Kenny Wallace, Dorsey Schroeder, Gary Collins, Buddie Boys, Cecil Gordon, Larry Isley, D. K. Ulrich, Lake Speed, Lennie Pond, Morgan Shepherd, Steve Spencer, Ronnie Thomas, J. D. McDuffie, John Anderson, Tony Bettenhausen, Jim Vandiver, Junior Miller, Trevor Boys, Richard White

---

25

Ken Schrader, Ricky Craven, Todd Bodine, Jack Sprague, Tim Richmond, Jabe Thomas, Roy Mayne, Richie Panch, Jackie Rogers, Earl Brooks, Joe Ruttman, Ronnie Thomas, Ferrel Harris, Dean Dalton, Terry Bivins, Dick May, D. K. Ulrich, Charles Chamblee, Jim Reich, Bobby Gerhart, Rick Hendrick, Hermie Sadler, Jerry Churchill, Wally Dallenbach, Jerry Nadeau, Joe Nemechek, Brian Vickers

26

Ricky Rudd, Morgan Shepherd, Brett Bodine, Joe Ruttman, Dick Trickle, Steve Kinser, Johnny Benson, Hut Stricklin, Rich Bickle, Hershel Mc-Griff, Chuck Bown, Tiny Lund, Dick Bown, Carl Joiner, Jimmy Capps, Butch Lindley, Brad Teague, Ronnie Hopkins, Earl Brooks, Jimmy Spencer, Joe Nemechek, Frank Kimmel

27

Elton Sawyer, Cale Yarborough, Rusty Wallace, Buddy Baker, Greg Sacks, Bobby Hillin, Jimmy Horton, Gary Balough, Loy Allen, Hut Stricklin, Rick Wilson, Kenny Irwin, Bobby Isaac, Donnie Allison, Sam Sommers, Benny Parsons, Tim Richmond, Todd Bodine, Chuck Bown, Jim Paschal, Jeff McClure, Mike Bliss, Jeff Fuller, Rick Mast, Kenny Wallace, Scott Wimmer, Kirk Shelmerdine

28

Davey Allison, Ernie Irvan, Kenny Irwin, Dale Jarrett, Robby Gordon, Lake Speed, Kenny Wallace, Buddy Baker, Cale Yarborough, Chad Little, Charlie Glotzbach, Sam McQuagg, Bobby Isaac, A. J. Foyt, Donnie Allison, Gordon Johncock, Bobby Allison, Joe Ruttman, Jerry Jolley, Dave Dion, Fred Lorenzen, Earl Brooks, Carl Joiner, Ramo Stott, Ricky Rudd

29

Steve Grissom, Jeff Green, Andy Hillenburg, John Krebs, Gary Collins, Joe Ruttman, Brad Teague, Dale Jarrett, Cale Yarborough, Grant Adcox, George Follmer, Ross Surgenor, Bobby Isaac, Hershel McGriff, Roy Smith, Bill Hollar, Elliott Forbes-Robinson, Walter Ballard, Tim Williamson, Dave Dion, Junior Miller, Tim Richmond, Cecil Gordon, Eddie Bierschwale, Scott Autrey, Robert

Pressley, Greg Sacks, Chad Little, Butch Leitzinger, Bill Osborne, Connie Saylor, Dick May, Kerry Teague, Kevin Harvick, Kenny Wallace

30

Michael Waltrip, Derrike Cope, Johnny Benson, Willy T. Ribbs, Walter Ballard, Kenny Brightbill, Carl Van Horn, Terry Bivins, Dale Earnhardt, Tighe Scott, Roy Smith, Mike Bliss, Todd Bodine, Jeff Green, Salt Walther, Steve Park

31

Ward Burton, Mike Skinner, Neil Bonnett, Greg Sacks, Jimmy Hensley, Jim Sauter, Gary Bradberry, Brad Teague, Joe Ruttman, Butch Miller, Johnny Rutherford, Mike Dillon, Lee Faulk, Jim Vandiver, Jim Boyd, Chad Little, Billy McGinnis, John Rezek, Billy Harvey, John Anderson, Bobby Wawak, Slick Johnson, Steve Gray, Chet Fillip, Ron Shephard, Stewart Huffman, Jerry Jolly, Morgan Shepherd, Mike James, Robby Gordon

32

Jimmy Horton, Jimmy Hensley, Chuck Bown, Greg Sacks, Ed Berrier, Michael Ritch, Joe Ruttman, Ruben Garcia, Phillip Duffie, Lee Faulk, Jim Sauter, Alan Kulwicki, Dick Brooks, Ray Elder, Bobby Wawak, Gary Mathews, Jimmy Finger, Jim Ingram, Boscoe Lowe, Butch Lindley, Tommy Ellis, Tommy Houston, Jonathan Edwards, Kevin Terris, Johnny Halford, Randy Tissot, Ricky Craven, Scott Pruett, Mike Wallace

33

Ken Schrader, Harry Gant, Robert Pressley, Morgan Shepherd, Elmo Langley, Dick May, Jeff Handy, George Follmer, Glenn Francis, Earl Brooks, J. D. McDuffie, Buck Baker, John Anderson, Greg Sacks, Todd Bodine, Wayne Smith,

Baxter Price, Bobby Hamilton Jr., Scott Pruett, Joe Nemechek, Mike Wallace, Kenny Wallace, Christian Fittipaldi, Paul Menard

34

Dick Trickle, Rodney Combs, Jim Bown, Ted Kennedy, Connie Saylor, Todd Bodine, Jocko Maggiacomo, Ron Shepherd, Nestor Peles, Steve Peles, Darrell Busham, L. W. Wright, Jesse Samples, Eddie Bierschwale, Mike James, Wendell Scott

35

Darrell Waltrip, Todd Bodine, Bill Venturini, Jim Bown, Keith VanHoughten, Larry Gunselman, Alan Kulwicki, Dan Daughtry, Darel Dieringer, Jim Hurtubise, Pat Mintey, Dick May, Joe Millikan, Lynn Carroll, Louis Gatto, Bud Hickey, Benny Parsons, Morgan Shepherd, Gary Bradberry, Geoffrey Bodine, Bobby Hamilton Jr.

36

H. B. Bailey, Kenny Wallace, Butch Gilliland, Ernie Irvan, Ricky Craven, Derrike Cope, Bobby Wawak, Ron Hutcherson, Frank Warren, Marty Robbins, Dick May, Bill Green, Joe Nemechek, Dick Trickle

37

Rick Carelli, Loy Allen, John Andretti, Jeremy Mayfield, Patty Moise, Roy Hendrick, Joe Millikan, Bruce Jacobi, Chuck Wahl, Dave Watson, Don Sprouse, Bub Strickler, Tim Richmond, Mike Alexander, Tom Sneva, Donnie Allison, Neil Bonnett, Mark Martin, Curtis Markham, Ed Negre, Connie Saylor, Derrike Cope

38

Bobby Hamilton, Butch Gilliland, Dick Johnson, Mike Laws, Joe Fields, John Krebs, Jim Insolo,

Johnny Barnes, Walter Ballard, Tom Williams, Grant Adcox, Sandy Satullo, Don Waterman, Jerry Bowman, Laurant Rioux, Alan Kulwicki, Morgan Shepherd, Rich Woodland Jr., Phil Barkdoll, Joe Ruttman, Tony Bettenhausen, H. B. Bailey, Kevin Lepage, Elliott Sadler

39

Jim Sauter, Scott Lagasse, Dick Trickle, Chuck Bown, Paul Dean Holt, Vince Giamformaggio, Blackie Wangerin, Friday Hassler, Carl Adams

40

Dick Brooks, Kenny Wallace, Greg Sacks, Rich Bickle, Randy LaJoie, Joe Ruttman, Butch Leitzinger, Shane Hall, Ben Hess, Sterling Marlin, Robby Gordon, Wally Dallenbach, Joe Nemechek, Steve Park, D. K. Ulrich, Harry Schelling, Ed Negre, Tony Bettenhausen, Randy Bethea, Al Elmore, Lennie Pond, Stan Barrett, Mike Alexander, Dick Skillen, Ricky Rudd, Bill Whittington, Harry Dinwiddie, Tim Richmond, Dick May, Tommy Gale, Rick Baldwin, Don Hume, Cecil Gordon, Slick Johnson, Joe Booher, Ronnie Thomas, Jimmy Hensley, Joel Stowe, Tommy Houston, Ferrel Harris, Andy Hillenburg, Jonathan Edwards, Les Loeder, Frank Warren, Darin Brassfield, Jamie McMurray, Mike Bliss

41

Larry Pearson, Phil Parsons, Dick Trickle, Ricky Craven, Jim Bown, Ted Thomas, Joe Booher, David Green, Steve Grissom, Ronnie Thomas, Grant Adcox, Ernie Stierly, Dick Brooks, Stuart Huffman, Richard Childress, Sterling Marlin, Joe Millikan, Earle Canavan, Bobby Unser, A. J. Foyt, Gary Bradberry, Derrike Cope, Rick Mast, Jimmy Spencer, Scott Pruett, Casey Mears

42

Kyle Petty, Kenny Wallace, Tom Kendall, Bobby Hillin, Jack Pennington, Joe Nemechek, Phil Parsons, Dick Trickle, Richard White, Marty Robbins, Elmo Langley, Richard Petty, Ronnie Thomas, Lennie Pond, Tom Sneva, Jim Sauter, Larry Esau, Terry Schoonover, Jim Whitt, Kenny Irwin, Jamie McMurray

43

Kyle Petty, Richard Petty, John Andretti, Bobby Hamilton, Christian Fittipaldi, Jeff Green

44

Kyle Petty, Rick Wilson, Irv Hoerr, Jimmy Hensley, Jeff Purvis, Jim Sauter, Jack Sellers, Terry Labonte, Richard Brown, Gary Johnson, Earl Brooks, Robin Schildnecht, Sterling Marlin, Larry Dickson, Jim Whitt, Ed Negre, Bill Seifert, Steve Grissom, Buckshot Jones, Jerry Nadeau, Ted Musgrave, Greg Biffle, Christian Fittipaldi

45

Rich Bickle, Wally Dallenbach, Ron Hornaday Jr., Joe Ruttman, Patty Moise, Ken Ragan, Rick Newsom, Baxter Price, Larry LeMay, Walter Ballard, Roy Smith, Charles Chamblees, Jimmy Means, Joel Stowe, D. K. Ulrich, John McFadden, Rick McCray, Rick Baldwin, Vic Parsons, Bill Seifert, LeeRoy Yarbrough, Dick Brooks, Jeff Hooker, L. D. Ottinger, Ramo Stott, Steve Grissom, Adam Petty, Kyle Petty

46

Al Unser Jr., Greg Sacks, Jeff Green, Wally Dallenbach, Travis Tiller, Stacy Compton, Roy Mayne, Sam Stanley, Morgan Shepherd, Tommy Kendall, Vic Parsons, John Hren, Tod Bodine, Frank Kimmel

47

Rich Bickle, Greg Sacks, Billy Standridge, Jack Pennington, Alan Grice, Morgan Shepherd, Rob Moroso, Bruce Hill, Harry Gant, Geoff Bodine, Chuck Bown, Ron Bouchard, Satch Worley, Raymond Williams

48

James Hylton, Trevor Boys, Mickey Gibbs, Greg Sacks, Jimmy Crawford, Ronnie Thomas, Ken Ragan, Jerry Cranmer, Johnny Coy, Wayne Slark, Eddie Bierschwale, Ron Esau, Dan Gurney, D. K. Ulrich, Lennie Pond, Joe Millikan, Slick Johnson, Al Holbert, Hershel McGriff, Walter Ballard, Don Hume, Tony Spanos, Jerry Holden, Freddie Crawford, Jimmie Johnson

49

Roy Smith, James Hylton, Trevor Boys, Bill Flowers, G. C. Spencer, John Utsman, Bill Green, Glenn Jarrett, Kevin Housby, Claude Balot-Lena, Connie Saylor, Don Hume, Greg Sacks, Ron Esau, Shawna Robinson, Ron Hornaday, Derrike Cope, Stuart Kirby, Stacy Compton, Ken Schrader

50

Ricky Craven, Wally Dallenbach, Randy LaJoie, Andy Belmont, Mike Chase, Mickey Gibbs, Jim Sauter, Greg Sacks, Al Unser Sr. , A. J. Foyt, Jim Insolo, George Follmer, Terry Bivins, Darrell Bryant, Rusty Sanders, Bruce Hill, Baxter Price, Geoff Bodine, Joe Millikan, Jim Southard, Rich Bickle, Rick Mast, Larry Foyt

51

Jeff Purvis, Butch Miller, Bobby Hamilton, Hut Stricklin, Connie Saylor, Tom Rotsell, Jerry Hufflin, Bobby Fleming, Jack Donahue, Dick Simpson, Bob Whitlow, A. J. Foyt, Johnny Rutherford, Jim Insolo, Billy McGinnis, John Haver, Slick Johnson, Jim Thirkettle, Don Whittington, Scott Miller, Lennie Pond, Ron Hutcherson, Greg Sacks, Cecil Gordon, Jim Fitzgerald, David Simko, Dub Simpson, Jim Vandiver, Richard Brown, Vic Parsons, Rick Scribner

52

Jimmy Means, Bobby Hillin, Mike Wallace, Scott Gaylord, Mike Skinner, Odie Robertson, Earl Ross, Bill Elliott, Don Graham, Ed Hale, Lennie Pond, Jack Sprague, Gene Romero, Roy Smith, Bobby Wawak, Dale Jarrett, Sterling Marlin, Morgan Shepherd, Scott Sharp, Bob Keselowski

53

John Paul Jr., Bobby Hillin, Mike Potter, Ritchie Petty, Graham Taylor, Jimmy Means, Jerry O'Neill, Johnny Barnes, Jack Simpson, Keith Davis, Slick Johnson, Cecil Gordon, Tom Sneva, Ron Hutcherson, Jeff Hooker, Bill Scott, Don Paul, H. B. Bailey, Bill Ward, Dick May, Bobby Mausgrover,

54

Lennie Pond, Bob Schacht, Jim Derhaag, Eddie Bierschwale, Donnie Allison, David Simko, Bobby Wawak, Todd Bodine

55

Ted Musgrave, Phil Parsons, John Banks, Bill Osborne, Bill Baker, Larry Phillips, Sonny Easley, Wayne Watercutter, Bill Meazel, Don Whittington, Tommy Ellis, Benny Parsons, Tiny Lund, Bobby Chumley, Hut Stricklin, Tim Fedewa, Sam Beler, Ron Grana, Bobby Hamilton, Kenny Wallace, Greg Biffle, Ron Hornaday

56

Jerry Hill, Ron Esau, Howard Rose, Carl Adams, Jim Hurtubise, Jim Bray, Elmo Langley, Eddie Bradshaw, Bill Slawinski, John Callis, Ernie Irvan, Tiny Lund, Paul Jett, Bob Penrod, Ronnie Alderman

57

Bob Schacht, Hut Stricklin, Jimmy Spencer, Morgan Shepherd, Jody Ridley, Bob Burcham, George Wiltshire, Joey Arrington, Gary Mathews, Dick May, Robert Tartaglia, Jim Hopkinson, Steve Pfeifer, Janet Guthrie, Bill Elswick, Ken Ragan, David Ray Boggs, Derrike Cope, Bobby Hamilton Jr., Stuart Kirby, Kevin LePage, Brett Bodine

58

Jeff Purvis, Wayne Jacks, Brian Ross, Jimmy Means, Dick May, John Haver, Jerry Bowman, Rocky Moran, Robert Brown, Loy Allen, Ricky Craven, Hut Stricklin

59

David Sisco, Darel Dieringer, Buck Baker, Melvin Revis, Tighe Scott, Charles Blanton, Bobby Gerhart, Donnie Allison, Randy Renfrow, Jason Small, Carl Long

60

Mike Miller, Phil Parsons, Cliff Hucul, George Esau, Joe Mihalic, Jackie Rogers, Ramo Stott, David Sisco, Wayne Broome, Glen Ward, Bob Riley, Natz Peters, Ed Berrier, Bob Greeley, Jim Whitt, Maynard Troyer, Joe Bessey, Rick Bickle, Geoffrey Bodine, Ted Musgrave, Dick Trickle, Jack Sprague, Brian Vickers, David Green

61

Rick Carelli, Johnny Rutherford, Iggy Katona, Joe Mihalic, Bub Strickler, Wayne Broome, Baxter Price, Mike Potter, Jim Danielson, Jimmy Finger, Clarence Lovell, Scott Miller, Dick Brooks, Ed Szech, David Murry

62

Clay Young, Ron Esau, Joe Ruttman, Terry Petris, Rick Wilson, Jocko Maggiacomo, Steve Christman, Tru Cheek, Mark Thompson, Austin Cameron

63

Norm Benning, Randy LaJoie, Jocko Maggiacomo, Walt Price, Don Hoffman, Jimmy Hensley, Terry Bivins, Markey James, Bruce Jacobi, Dale Perry, Chuck Walton, Dick Trickle, Dick May, Robert Wales

64

Johnny Chapman, Mike Potter, Tommy Gale, Pancho Carter, Connie Saylor, Rick Baldwin, Bryan Baker, Jimmy Hensley, Clark Dwyer, Willy T. Ribbs, Elmo Langley, Bill Champion, Dean Dalton, Dick Brooks, Skip Manning, Don Whittington, John Gunn, Joe Fields, Mark Stahl, D. K. Ulrich, Randy Becker, Jerry Bowman, Jerry Cranmer, Rodney Combs, Rick McCray, Curtis Markham, Trevor Boys, Gary Mayeda, Ken Schrader, Joe Millikan

65

Dave Mader, Jerry O'Neill, Tommy Crozier, Carl Adams, Dick May, Ralph Jones, Bruce Jacobi, Gil Roth, Glenn Jarrett, Joe Booher, D. K. Ulrich, Walter Ballard, Roy Mayne, H. B. Bailey, Buck Baker

66

Janet Guthrie, Dick Trickle, Mike Wallace, Jimmy Hensley, Ben Hess, Lake Speed, Chuck Bown, Rick Mast, Derrike Cope, Randy LaJoie, Dorsey Schroeder, Bob Schacht, Don Pruitt, Terry Link, Jimmy Lee, Mike Potter, Lowell Cowell, Ron Esau, Phil Parsons, Harry Gant, Tom Sneva, John Krebs, Dick Brooks, Fred Drake, H. B. Bailey, Todd Bodine, Darrell Waltrip, Geoffrey Bodine, Hideo Fukuyama

67

Buddy Arrington, Mickey Gibbs, Brad Teague, Ken Schrader, Jimmy Hensley, Rick Jeffrey, Ron Esau, Dale Jarrett, Pee Wee Wentz, Larry Manning, Joey Arrington, Satch Worley, John Martin, Sonny Easley, Randy Becker, Eddie Bierschwale, Morgan Shepherd, Chet Fillip, Boris Said

68

Bobby Hamilton, Dorsey Schroeder, Greg Sacks, Loy Allen, Derrike Cope, Ron Fellows, Hut Stricklin, Jerry Holden, Mike Potter, Sonny Easley, Alton Jones, Janet Guthrie, Chuck Bown, Lennie Pond, John Greenwood, Ed Baugess, Jimmy Walker, Jerry Holden, Laurent Rioux, Anthony Lazzarro

69

Lee Raymond, Ronnie Thomas, Trevor Boys, Tommy Riggins, Hershel McGriff, Mike Kempton, Terry Bivins, Bill Polich, Henry Jones, Bob Bondurant, Bob Riley, Donny Paul, Denny Wilson, Brent Kaeding

70

J. D. McDuffie, Henley Gray, Dick May

71

Dave Marcis, Bobby Isaac, Buddy Baker, Terry Fisher, Ray Hendrick, Neil Bonnett, Joey Arrington, Bobby Wawak, Bobby Fisher, Mike Alexander, Bobby Gerhart, Lennie Pond, Kerry Earnhardt, Andy Hillenburg, Jay Sauter, Dick Trickle, Tim Sauter, Kevin LePage

72

Benny Parsons, Mark Reed, John Andretti, Dan Obrist, Tracy Leslie, Brent Elliott, Joe Millikan, Rusty Wallace, Sammy Swindell

73

Bill Schmitt, Joe Ruttman, Mike Wallace, Joe Nemechek, Jim Gilliam, Jerry Hansen, George England, Hugh Pearson, David Hobbs, Steve Moore, Ferrel Harris, Phil Barkdoll, Dick Brooks, Mel Larson, Tony Raines

74

Mike Potter, Randy LaJoie, Bobby Wawak, Jack Ely, Ray Kelly, Jim Fitzgerald, Randy Tissot, Roger McCluskey, Tim Williamson, Hal Callentine, Bobby Brack, Henry Jones, Junior Miller, Stuart Huffman, Bob Riley, Gary Kershaw, Roy Smith, Dick May, Joe Booher, Rick Wilson, Bill Shirey, Chad Little, Joe Varde, Tony Raines

75

Rick Mast, Todd Bodine, Joe Ruttman, Dick Trickle, Phil Parsons, Morgan Shepherd, Neil Bonnett, Rick Wilson, Lake Speed, Jody Ridley, Jim Sauter, Bobby Fleming, Ronnie Childress, Ernie Shaw, Walter Ballard, Johnny Barnes, Butch Hartman, Bill Elswick, Butch Mock, Joe Millikan, Harry Gant, John Anderson, Kyle Petty, Lennie Pond, Chuck Bown, Gary Balough, Dick May, Tim Richmond, Jim Insolo, Paul Dorrity,

Dave Marcis, Slick Gardner, Wally Dallenbach, Stuart Kirby, Ted Musgrave

76

Bill Sedgwick, Ron Hornaday, Tom Kendall, Phil Good, A. J. Reno, Hugh Pearson, Mike Potter, Junior Miller, Lowell Cowell, Hut Stricklin, Ben Arnold

77

Bobby Hillin, Robert Pressley, Gary Brooks, Mike Potter, Davy Jones, Ken Ragan, Morgan Shepherd, Rick Lach, Charlie Roberts, Neil Bonnett, Jan Opperman, Bill Champion, John Ray, Larry Esau, Johnny Rutherford, Dale Earnhardt, Bob Burcham, Jody Ridley, John Anderson, Dick May, Eddie Dickerson, Kenny Hemphill, Dean Combs, Lowell Cowell, Donnie Allison, Greg Sacks, Eddie Bierschwale, Nels Miller, Boris Said, Dave Blaney

78

Gary Bradberry, Jay Hedgecock, Pancho Carter, Jay Sommers, Tom Hubert, Jim Robinson, Dick Skillen, Hugh Pearson, Richard Brickhouse, Randy MacDonald, Billy Standridge, Clem Proctor, Vic Parsons

79

Roy Smith, Randy MacDonald, Derrike Cope, Jerry Grant, Frank Warren, Ed Negre, Joe Booher, Jim Hurlbert, Junior Miller, Joey Arrington, Marty Robbins, Jody Ridley, Tommy Gale, Travis Tiller, Dick May, Dick Skillen, Roy Smith, Lennie Pond, Jabe Thomas, David Ray Boggs

80

Joe Ruttman, Jimmy Horton, Gary Fedewa, Edward Cooper, Phil Finney, Terry Bivins, John

Callis, Bob Senneker, Wayne Morgan, Eddie Bierschwale, Dave Blaney, Mike Bliss

---

81

Kenny Wallace, Jeff Davis, Mike Potter, Chet Fillip, Dick Trickle, Warren Tope, Terry Ryan, John Borneman, Dave Marcis, David Sosebee, Jim Robinson, Ferrel Harris, Ed Negre, Jabe Thomas, Buddy Arrington, Eddie Bierschwale, Tom Rotsell, Slick Johnson, Glen Steurer, Jimmy Finger, A. J. Cox, Johnny Rutherford, John Andretti

---

82

Mark Stahl, Ferrel Harris, Hershel McGriff, Sumner McKnight, Skip Manning, Walter Ballad, Paul Fess, Dick May, Cecil Gordon, Janet Guthrie, Rick Jeffrey, Ron Gautsche, Sonny Hutchins, Bill Ward

---

83

Lake Speed, Rodney Combs, Joe Ruttman, Eddie Bierschwale, Ramo Stott, Kenny Brightbill, Johnny Rutherford, Bobby Isaac, Ron Hutcherson, Sumner McKnight, Lem Blankenship, Paul Tyler, Toby Tobias, David Ray Boggs, Ron Hornaday

---

84

Mike Alexander, Dick Trickle, J. C. Danielson, John Ray, Morgan Shepherd, Jody Ridley, Kenny Brightbill, Glenn Jarrett, Bobby Sands, Trevor Boys, Rick Baldwin, Harry Schilling, Bob Davis, Johnny Benson Sr. , Tony Bettenhausen, Shawna Robinson

---

85

Ken Bouchard, Bobby Fox, Tommy Crozier, Larry Richardson, Greg Heller, Wayne Watercutter, Mark Stahl, Bobby Wawak, Bobby Gerhart, Ronnie Daniels, Carl Long, Darrell Waltrip

---

86

Rick Jeffrey, Clay Young, Bobby Ore, Elliott Forbes-Robinson, Darryl Sage, John McFadden, Ronnie Sanders, Sonny Easley,

---

87

Randy Baker, Joe Nemechck, Gary Myers, Elliott Forbes-Robinson, Walter Wallace, Dick May, Gary Balough, Slick Johnson, Billy Harvey, Tom Hessert, J. C. Charbonneau, Jimmy Ingalls, Johnny Halford, Mike Stolarcyk, Patrick Latimer, Dave Marcis, Ron Fellows

---

88

Dale Jarrett, Darrell Waltrip, Bobby Allison, Donnie Allison, Jimmy Spencer, Joe Ruttman, Gary Bradberry, Greg Sacks, Buddy Baker, Larry Pearson, Morgan Shepherd, Rick Mast, Randy Baker, Al Unser, Mike Potter, Richard Childress, Jim Vandiver, Ricky Rudd, Geoff Bodine, Irv Hoerr, Ernie Irvan, Don Noel, Ed Hessert, Rusty Wallace, Ron Keselowski, Jeff Fuller

---

89

Jim Sauter, Rodney Combs, Michael Waltrip, Dennis Setzer, Gene Riniker, Don Reynolds, Jim Vandiver, Dean Roper, Sam Sommers, Patty Moise, Les Covey, Gerald Thompson, Johnny Barnes, Morgan Shepherd

---

90

Dick Trickle, Wally Dallenbach Jr., Mike Wallace, Bobby Hillin, Robby Gordon, Chad Little, Lennie Pond, Stanton Barrett, Ernie Irvan, Buddy Baker, Benny Parsons, Ken Schrader, Dick Brooks, Jody Ridley, Ricky Rudd, Christine Beckers, Jimmy Means, Dorsey Schroeder, Eddie Pettyjohn, Paul Radford, George Follmer, Bill Dennis, Richie Panch, Charlie Glotzbach, Jimmy Hensley, Bobby Isaac, Harry Gant, Jackie Oliver,

Fred Lorenzen, Max Berrier, LeeRoy Yarbrough, Ramo Stott, Bud Moore, Yvon DeHamel, Ray Hendrick, Terry Teague, Ron Hutcherson, Johnny Rutherford, Butch Hartman, Ed Berrier, Rick Mast, Morgan Shepherd, Brian Simo, Hut Stricklin, Hermie Sadler, Gary Bradberry, Lance Hooper, Jason Hedlesky, John Andretti, Ron Hornaday

91

Robert Sprague, Ken Pederson, J. T. Hayes, Todd Bodine, Kevin Lepage, Andy Hillenburg, Morgan Shepherd, Tommy Kendall, Mike Wallace, Greg Sacks, David Sosebee, Ed Negre, William Miller, Johnny Anderson, Marv Acton, Harold Miller, Terry Bivins, Roland Wlodyka, Bob Burcham, Dick May, Bill Osborne, John Krebs, Billy McGinnis, Ron Bouchard, Richard Brown, Steve Grissom, Dick Trickle, Hank Parker Jr., Casey Atwood

92

Jack Eley, Ralph Jones, David Sosebee, Elliott Sadler, Ron Barfield, Jonathan Edwards, Skip Manning, Bill Hagan, Sonny Easley, Chris Monoleos, Joe Fields, Bill Osborne, Mel Larson, Terry Labonte, Dick May, Larry Smith, Stacy Compton

93

Gary Bradberry, Charlie Baker, Troy Beebe, Jackie Rogers, Jody Ridley, Dick May, Earl Ross, Kenny Brightbill, Norm Palmer, Christine Beckers, Gene Felton, Buck Baker, Terry Bivins, Chuck Bown, Hershel McGriff, Don Whittington, Jim Bown, Maurice Randall, Mike Potter, Derrike Cope, Dave Blaney

94

Bill Elliott, Matt Kenseth, Terry Labonte, Sterling Marlin, Doug Heveron, Eddie Bierschwale, Trevor Boys, Morgan Shepherd, Bill Osborne,

Ron Esau, Mike Hiss, Steve Pfeifer, Bobby Wawak, Henry Jones, Cecil Gordon, Bob Riley, John Kennedy, John Soares, Tom Kendall, Todd Bodine, Dorsey Schroeder, Bobby Hillin, Rick McCray, David Green

95

Eddie Bierschwale, Brad Teague, Trevor Boys, Andy Hillenburg, Ed Berrier, Davey Allison, Darrell Waltrip, Harry Jefferson, Elmo Langley, Junior Miller, Gary Myers, Jerry Sisco, Jim Hurtubise, Ernie Shaw, Dave Dion, Ernie Cline, Tommy Houston, Derrike Cope, Slick Johnson, Ferrel Harris, Sterling Marlin, Chad Little, Mike Alexander, Chuck Bown, Gary Bradberry, Bob Kauf, Kerry Teague

96

David Green, Dana Patten, Mike Bliss, Robby Gordon, Ron Fellows, Hut Stricklin, Ted Musgrave, Steve Grissom, Todd Bodine, Jerry Bowman, Ray Elder, Richard Childress, Harry Jefferson, Ferrel Harris, Jerry Jolly, Jim Hurlbert, Mike Miller, Morgan Shepherd, Jimmy Walker, Elliott Forbes-Robinson, Jim Bown, Jim Sauter, Bobby Hillin, John Callis, Rick Baldwin, Kevin Lepage, Dale Earnhardt, Baxter Price, Eldon Dotson, Andy Houston

97

Chad Little, Tommy Ellis, Geoff Bodine, Morgan Shepherd, Rodney Combs, Joe Ruttman, Red Farmer, Bob Burcham, Harry Jefferson, Salt Walther, Jackie Rogers, Bill Osborne, Eddie Dickerson, Jim Osborne, Bob Schacht, Dean Combs, Ken Ragan, Ralph Jones, D. Wayne Strout, Kurt Busch

98

Joe Ruttman, John Andretti, Rich Bickle, Greg Sacks, Butch Miller, Jeremy Mayfield, Jimmy

Spencer, Derrike Cope, Ed Pimm, Brad Noffsinger, Ron Bouchard, Dale Jarrett, Jim Bown, Richie Panch, John Kieper, Roland Wlodyka, Dick May, Dave Marcis, Sam Sommers, Ralph Jones, Don Noel, Jimmy Means, Marv Acton, Hershel McGriff, Johnny Rutherford, Rusty Wallace, D. K. Ulrich, Morgan Shepherd, Dale Earnhardt, Jim Insolo, Trevor Boys, Mark Gibson, Dick Brooks, Bobby Isaac, L. D. Ottinger, Wayne Andrews, Mel Larson, Rick Newsom, Richard Brown, Geoffrey Bodine, Jeff Fuller, Rick Mast, Kenny Wallace, Jason Jarrett

99

Jeff Burton, Charlie Glotzbach, John Krebs, Brad Teague, Norm Benning, Connie Saylor, Dale Jarrett, Tom Bigelow, Ted Kennedy, Jim Hurtubise, Ron Keselowski, Jim Vandiver, Dick Trickle, Richie Panch, Don Noel, Dick May, Bill Hollar, D. K. Ulrich, Terry Herman, Bob McElwee, Elliott Forbes-Robinson, Tim Richmond, Sterling Marlin, Al Loquasto, Rick Knoop, Kevin Housby, Chuck Bown, Phillip Duffie, Blair Aiken, Don White, Danny Sullivan, Bobby Unser

APPENDIX C:
2004 NEXTEL CUP, BUSCH
GRAND NATIONAL, AND CRAFTS-
MAN TRUCK SERIES SCHEDULES

NEXTEL CUP

DATE	RACE	VENUE
February 7	Bud Shootout	Daytona International Speedway
February 12	Gatorade 125s	Daytona International Speedway
February 15	Daytona 500	Daytona International Speedway
February 22	Subway 400	North Carolina Motor Speedway
March 7	UAW/DaimlerChrysler 400	Las Vegas Motor Speedway
March 14	Golden Corral 500	Atlanta Motor Speedway
March 21	Dodge 400	Darlington Raceway
March 28	Food City 500	Bristol Motor Speedway
April 4	Radio Shack 500	Texas Motor Speedway
April 18	Advance 500	Martinsville Speedway
April 25	Aaron's 499	Talladega Superspeedway
May 2	Auto Club 500	California Speedway
May 15	Pontiac 400	Richmond International Raceway
May 22	Nextel All-Star Challenge	Lowe's Motor Speedway
May 30	Coca-Cola 600	Lowe's Motor Speedway
June 6	MBNA 400	Dover International Speedway
June 13	Pocono 500	Pocono Raceway
June 20	Michigan 400	Michigan International Speedway
June 27	Dodge 300	Infineon Raceway
July 3	Pepsi 400	Daytona International Speedway
July 11	Tropicana 400	Chicagoland Speedway
July 25	New England 300	New Hampshire International Speedway
August 1	Pennsylvania 500	Pocono Raceway
August 8	Brickyard 400	Indianapolis Motor Speedway
August 15	Sirius at the Glen	Watkins Glen International
August 22	Michigan 400	Michigan International Speedway
August 28	Sharpie 500	Bristol Motor Speedway
September 5	Pop Secret 500	California Speedway
September 11	Chevy 400	Richmond International Raceway

CHASE FOR THE CHAMPIONSHIP RACES (NEXTEL CUP)

September 19	Sylvania 300	New Hampshire International Speedway
September 26	MBNA 400	Dover International Speedway
October 3	EA Sports 500	Talladega Superspeedway
October 10	Banquet 400	Kansas Speedway

October 16	UAW-GM 500	Lowe's Motor Speedway
October 24	Subway 500	Martinsville Speedway
October 31	Bass Pro Shops 500	Atlanta Motor Speedway
November7	Checker 500	Phoenix International Raceway
November14	Mountain Dew	Darlington Raceway
November21	Ford 400	Homestead-Miami Speedway

BUSCH GRAND NATIONAL SERIES

DATE	RACE	VENUE
February 14	Hershey's Kisses 300	Daytona International Speedway
February 21	Rockingham 200	North Carolina Motor Speedway
March 6	Sam's Town 300	Las Vegas Motor Speedway
March 20	Darlingtonraceway.com 200	Darlington Raceway
March 27	Sharpie Professional 250	Bristol Motor Speedway
April 3	O'Reilly 300	Fort Worth Texas Motor Speedway
April 10	Pepsi 300 presented by Mapco	Nashville Superspeedway
April 24	Aaron'S 312	Talladega Superspeedway
May 1	1-800-PIT-SHOP.COM 300	California Speedway
May 8	Race TBA	Gateway International Raceway
May 14	NASCAR Busch Series 250	Richmond International Raceway
May 23	Race TBA	Nazareth Speedway
May 29	Carquest Auto Parts 300	Lowe's Motor Speedway
June 5	MBNA America 200	Dover International Speedway
June 12	Nashville 300	Nashville Superspeedway
June 19	Meijer 300	Kentucky Speedway
June 27	Race TBA	The Milwaukee Mile
July 2	Winn-Dixie 250 presented by PepsiCo	Daytona International Speedway
July 10	Twister 300	Chicagoland Speedway
July 24	New England 200	New Hampshire International Speedway
July 31	Pikes Peak Int'l Raceway	Pikes Peak International Raceway
August 7	Kroger 200	Indianapolis Raceway Park
August 21	Cabela's 250	Michigan International Speedway
August 27	Food City 250	Bristol Motor Speedway
September 4	Californiaspeedway.com 300	California Speedway
September 10	Funai 250	Richmond International Raceway
September 25	Stacker 200	Dover International Speedway
October 9	Mr. Goodcents 300	Kansas Speedway
October 15	Little Trees 300	Lowe's Motor Speedway
October 23	Sam's Town 250	Memphis Motorsports Park
October 30	Aaron's 312	Atlanta Motor Speedway
November 6	Bashas' Supermarkets 200	Phoenix International Raceway
November 13	South Carolina 200	Darlington Raceway
November 20	Ford 300	Homestead-Miami Speedway

CRAFTSMAN TRUCK SERIES

DATE	RACE	VENUE
February 13	Florida Dodge Dealers 250	Daytona International Speedway
March 13	Atlanta 200	Atlanta Motor Speedway
April 17	Martinsville 250	Martinsville Speedway
May 16	Ohio 250	Mansfield Motorsports Speedway
May 21	Hardee's 200	Lowe's Motor Speedway
June 4	MBNA America 200	Dover International Speedway
June 11	O'Reilly 400K	Texas Motor Speedway
June 19	O'Reilly 200	Memphis Motorsports Park
June 26	GNC 200	Milwaukee Mile
July 3	O'Reilly Auto Parts 250	Kansas Speedway
July 10	Built Ford Tough 225 presented by the Greater Cincinnati Ford Dealers	Kentucky Speedway
July 17	Missouri-Illinois Dodge Dealers Ram Tough 200	Gateway International Raceway
July 31	Michigan 200	Michigan International Speedway
August 6	Power Stroke Diesel 200	Indianapolis Raceway Park
August 14	Toyota Tundra 200	Nashville Superspeedway
August 25	O'Reilly 200 presented by Valvoline Maxlife	Bristol Motor Speedway
September 9	NASCAR Craftsman Truck Series 200	Richmond International Raceway
September 18	New Hampshire 200	New Hampshire International Speedway
September 25	Las Vegas 350	Las Vegas Motor Speedway
October 2	American Racing Wheels 200	California Speedway

October 16	Silverado 350K	Texas Motor Speedway
October 23	Martinsville 200	Martinsville Speedway
November 5	Chevy Silverado 150	Phoenix International Raceway
November 12	Craftsman 200	Darlington Raceway
November 19	Ford 200	Homestead-Miami Speedway

PHOTO AND ILLUSTRATION CREDITS

Images used in *The Unauthorized NASCAR Fan Guide 2004* were published courtesy of the following sources:

AP WideWorld: 3, 5, 8, 11, 19, 21, 24, 26, 29, 62, 79, 94, 99, 102, 114, 115, 117, 118, 120, 121, 122, 123, 124, 128, 129, 130, 131, 132, 134, 140, 142, 145, 149, 153, 157, 160, 163, 165, 168, 173, 179, 181, 184, 185, 208, 215

W. Dennis Winn: 13, 16, 31, 33, 35, 37, 39, 43, 45, 49, 50, 54, 55, 59, 67, 69, 75, 77, 81, 83, 92, 101, 106, 107, 109, 110, 133, 178, 188, 189, 191, 197, 199 (both), 201, 203, 204

Nextel Communications: All headshots in Chapter 3, the "Driver Register."

Toyota Motor Company: 90

INDEX

This index contains listings for all people, teams, races, and tracks listed in *The Unauthorized NASCAR Fan Guide 2004*. It also includes citations to major subjects and themes covered throughout the book. It does not cover names listed in race results, annual or career statistics, or in other material of a general statistical nature. Page references in italics refer to photographs, while page references in bold refer to main entries for that driver or race.

Bass Pro Shops/MBNA 500 (March 2003) **10–11**

Bass Pro Shops/MBNA 500 (October 2003) **35–36**

Baumgardner, Bill Jr. 64, 84

Bawel, Doug 48, 84–85

Beadle, Raymond 70, 176, 201

Beam, Herman 147

Beard, Tom 73, 76

Bearfinder 127

Beauchamp, Johnny *117,* 123, 147, 148

Bechtel, Gary 51, 65

Beckers, Christine 200

Bel-Car Racing 84

Belnavis, Sam 84

Benfield, Ron 70

Benson, Johnny 15, 20, 23, 38, **41–42,** 64, 75; 99–100, *106,* 108, 192, 196; Busch Grand National Series career 210, 211; Busch Grand National Series Rookie of the Year 42; in Craftsman Truck Series 210; Winston (Nextel) Cup Series Rookie of the Year 42, 183

Bernstein, Kenny 44, 65

Berrier, Todd 80

Bettenhausen, Gary 74

Beverly, Tim 42

Bias-ply tires *See* Tires

Bickford, John 50

Bickle, Rich 217

Biffle, Greg 20, 25, 27, 38, **42,** 45, 59, 60, 64, 108, 192, 196, 197, 200, 207, 209; Busch Grand National Series champion 42, 212; Busch Grand National Series Rookie of the Year 42; in Craftsman Truck Series 218, 219

Big Three automakers 218 *See also* Chrysler Corporation, Ford Motor Company, General Motors

Bill Davis Racing (BDR) 43, 46, 48, 80; in Craftsman Truck Series 216; switches to Toyota Tundras in the Craftsman Truck Series 88

Black boxes (in cars) 103

Blair, Bill 119, 137, 138, 140, 141

Blaney, Dave 8, 10, 15, *19, 42,* **42–43,** 48, 108, 188, 210

Bliss, Mike 200, 209, 218

Blown engines, in 2003 10

Blue Max Team 176

Bluebird (land-speed record car) 115

Bodine, Brett **43–44,** 108, 109, 177, 181, 196, 197; Busch Grand Na-

tional Series career 210; *See also* Brett Bodine Motorsports

Bodine, Geoffrey 44, 58, 74, 108, 109, 130, 171, 172, 175, 176, 177, 179, 180, 181, 183, 197, 201, 207; Busch Grand National Series career 210; in Craftsman Truck Series 219

Bodine, Todd *44,* 84, 108, 109, *178, 209;* Busch Grand National Series career 210

Bonifield, Phil 214

Bonnett, Neil 74, 80, 129, 130, 164, 166, 167, 168, 169, 170, 172, 175, 181, 205

Bonneville Salt Flats (Utah) 115

Books aboout NASCAR 534–537

Borland, Matt 12, 76

Boston Marathon 70

Bouchard, Ken 175

Bouchard, Ron 167, 168

Bowers, Nelson 42, 47, 60, 61, 73, 76

Bown, Chuck 211

Brack, Kenny 77, 89

Brasington, Harold 119, 138

Brasington's Folly 119

Brewco Motorsports 209

Brewer, Tim 74

Brickhouse, Richard 156

Brickyard 400 49, 95; importance of the inaugural 131

Brickyard 400 (1994) 44, 131, 180, 182, 205

Brickyard 400 (1996) 82

Brickyard 400 (1997) 65

Brickyard 400 (1998) 63

Brickyard 400 (2000) 55, 56

Brickyard 400 (2002) 38, 191

Brickyard 400 (2003) *21,* **23–24,** *24,* 31, 52, 59, 99

Briggs, Randy 214

Bristol Motor Speedway 124

Brooks, Dick 156, 160

Bud Moore Engineering 44, 125; *See also* Moore, Walter "Bud"

Budweiser 47, 76, 127, 209

Buesink, Julian 105

Buick Motor Company 83

Burdick, Bob 149

Burger King 127

Burke, Marvin 139

Burton, Jeff 4, 8, 9, 18, 20, 23, 25, 28, 38, *43, 44,* **44–45,** 46, 75, 85, 108, 109, 180, 184, 186, 187, 189, 190, 195, 197, *203;* Busch Grand National Series career

210; Winston (Nextel) Cup Rookie of the Year 181

Burton, Ward 36, 45, *46,* 71, 73, 80, 119, 181, 182, 189, 190, 191, 195, 197; Busch Grand National Series career 210;

Busch Grand National Series 4, 43, 44–45, 61, 110, 111, 196, 197, 198, 202, 205, 207–212; benefits of 210; career records in the 212; difference between Busch and Nextel Cup cars 212; growth of 210; name change from Sportsman Series 172

Busch, Kurt 7, 8, 10, 11, *11,* 12, 14, 15, 16, 18, 23, 26, 31, 32, 34, 36, *46,* **47,** 56, 85, 108, 132, 190, 192, 197, 209; fight with Jimmy Spencer, 25, 46, 67; in Craftsman Truck Series 219

Busch North Series 57

Bush, President George 83

Byron, Red 106, *117,* 119, 137, 138, 202

C

California Speedway 131, 184

Camp David 129

Campbell, Sir Malcolm 115

Car numbers 545–558

Car specifications, Busch Grand National 212

Car specifications, Nextel Cup 212

Carburetor restrictor plates *See* Restrictor plates

Cardon monoxide filters 103

Carey, Mariah 63

Carling Brewery 127, 143

Carolina Dodge Dealers 400 **10–11,** *11,*

CART *See* Championship Auto Racing Team (CART)

Carter, Larry 84

Carter, President Jimmy 76, 129, 162

Carter, Rosalyn 129

Carter, Travis 44, 61, 84

Castles, Neil 156, 158

Castroneves, Helio 74, 89

Caterpillar 80

CBS Television 124, 129, 166, 202; *CBS Sports Spectacular* 124

Central Park (New York) *133*

Chaffin, Chad 214

Chamberlain, Wilt 160

Champion, Bill 205

Champion Spark Plug Inc. 139

110, 197; first Winston (Nextel) Cup 38, *39;* in Craftsman Truck Series 214; *See also* Roush, Jack

RPM Team 65

Rubbermaid 85

Rudd, Ricky 8, *19,* 24, 28, **65,** 74, 79, 109, 129, 130, 131, 132, 162, 164, 166, 170, 171, 172, 174, 175, 176, 178, 179, 180, 183, 184, *185,* 186, 189, 190, 192, 195, 196, 200, 205, 207; consecutive races started streak 65; Winston (Nextel) Cup Rookie of the Year 65

Russ Togs 127

Rutherford, Johnny 151

Ruttman, Joe 202, 217, 218

Ruxer, Alvin

RYR *See* Robert Yates Racing (RYR)

S

Sabates, Felix 51, 57, 60, 61, 82

Sabco Racing 63

Sacks, Greg 85, 171

Sadler, Earl 59

Sadler, Elliott 10, 16, 31, *65,* **65–66,** 82, 109, 132, 187, 190, 195; Busch Grand National Series career 210

SAFER *See* Steel and foam energy reduction (SAFER) barriers

Said, Boris 20, 25

Sales, Leon 138

Samsung/Radio Shack 500 **12–13,**

Sanders, Rick 214

Sauter, Jay 66

Sauter, Jim 66

Sauter, Johnny 64, *66,* 68, 71, 81, 108; in Busch Grand National Series 207, 209

SCCA *See* Sports Car Club of America (SCCA)

Schanzer, Ken 1

Scheckter, Tomas 89–90

Schedules, all divisions 555–558

Schneider, Frankie 146

Schoonover, Terry 171

Schrader, Ken *66,* 74, 103, 108, 171, 175, 176, 179, 210; in Craftsman Truck Series 219; Winston (Nextel) Cup Rookie of the Year 66

Schrader, Ken 130, 132, 197, 207

Schwan Food Service 84

SCORE Desert Series 53, 89

SCORE Trophy 53

SCORE/HDRA Class 1 76

Scoring system, changes to 193

Scott, Wendell 152

Seagraves, Ralph 5, 6, 125

Sears, John 154, 155

Sears Point Raceway 196

Setzer, Dennis, controversial finish of the 2003 Craftsman season 213–214; in Craftsman Truck Series 213–214

7-Eleven 127

Shangri-La Speedway 205

Sharp, Scott 90

Sharpie 85

Sharpie 500 (2003) **26–27**

Shaw, Ben 116

Shelby, Carroll 88

Shepherd, Morgan 80, 84, 130, 167, 168, 172, 177, 180; in Craftsman Truck Series 214

Shoney's 127

Short-tracks, demise of 128–129. 158

Shuman, Buddy 117, 140

Sicking, Dr. Dean 98

Silver, Ronnie 211

Simpson, Banks 143

Sirius at the Glen (2003) **24–25,** *26*

Sirius Satellite Radio 67

Sirius Satellite Radio 400 (2003) **18–19,** *19,*

Skinner, Mike 18, 32, 81, 88 108, 196, 200, 202; Craftsman Truck Series champion 219; in Craftsman Truck Series 215, 217; Winston (Nextel) Cup Rookie of the Year 184

Skoal 127

SME *See* Sports Marketing Enterprises (SME)

Smith, Bruton 128, 183, 186

Smith, Geoff, on the France family 93

Smith, Jack 123, 144, 145, 146, 147, 148, 149, 150, 159

Smith, Jim 67, 70, 76; as Craftsman Truck owner 213, 214, 217, 218

Smith, Louise 200

Smith, Marlene, as Craftsman Truck owner 214

Smithsonian Institute 131

Snyder, Daniel 78

Soares, John 143

Soccer 2

SODA Winter Series 53

Sosebee, Gober 140, 143

Sospenzo, Peter 15, 80

South Carolina, dirt tracks in 122

Southeastern Mini-Stocks Series 61

Southern drivers in NASCAR 105–107

Southern 500 135, 138, 150, 171; *See also* Mountain Dew Southern 500

Southern 500 (1950) 119

Southern 500 (1954) *115*

Southern 500 (1995) 41

Spears, Wayne 214

Speed Channel 216

Speed, Lake *132,* 170, 171, 175

Speed Week 122, 123, 130

Spencer, G. C. 153

Spencer, Jimmy 23, 36, 60, *66,* **66–68,** *67,* 76, 84, 103, 108, 109, 177, 181, 196; Busch Grand National Series career 210; fight with Kurt Busch 25, 46, 67; IN Craftsman Truck Series 214

Sports Car Club of America (SCCA) 89

Sports Marketing Enterprises (SME) 5

Sportsman Division 209

Sprague, Jack 59, 73, 108, 200; in Craftsman Truck Series 213, 214, 217, 218

Stacker 2 80

Stacy, J. D. 168

Stacy, Nelson 149, 150

StaffAmerica 84

Staley, Gwyn 145

Stanford University 78

Starlite Speedway 205

Starr, David, in Craftsman Truck Series 213, 214

Stavola Brothers 45, 57

Steadman, Greg 83

Steel and foam energy reduction (SAFER) barriers 97–100, *99;* effectiveness of 98–99; installation of at Richmond International Raceway 98–99

Stewart, Cliff 70

Stewart, Tony 10, 15, 16, 17, 18, 21, 23, 30, 32, 33, 36, 38, *49,* 57, 58, 61, 66, *68,* 78, 107, 108, 111, 131, 132, *132,* 187, 189, 190, 191, 196, 200; Busch Grand National Series career 210; in Craftsman Truck Series 214; Indy car racng experience 68; Winston (Nextel) Cup champion 68, 78; Winston (Nextel) Cup Rookie of the Year 68

Stoddard, Frank 46, 80, *81*

207; in Craftsman Truck Series 216, 219

Waltrip, Michael 7, 9, 23, 28, 30–31, 36, 38, 41, 172*70*, 77, 80, 103, 108, 109, *189,* 190, 192, *197,* 197; in Busch Grand National Series 209, 210; success on restrictor-plate tracks 70

Ward Burton Wildlife Foundation 46

Washington, Joe 133

Washington Redskins 78, *79*

Watkins Glen International 145, 196

Weatherly, Joe 119, 123, 125, 146, 148, 149, 150, 151, 152, 196

Web sites about NASCAR, general 540–541

Web sites, team and driver 541–542

Web sites, track 543–544

Weinberg, Danny 139

Welborn, Bob 123, 143, 145, 146, 147

Wells, Cal III 47, 81–82, 89

Westminster Dog Show 131

Westmoreland, Hubert 119, 137, 138

Wheeler, H. A. "Humpy," 6, 165; on Brian France 95

White House, The 129

White, Jack 137

White, Rex 119, 146, 147, 148, 149, 150

Wide World of Sports 124

William & Mary, College of 78

Willingham, Haskell 205

Wilson, Shane 85

Wilson, Woody 148

Wimmer, Scott *45,* 64, 68, *71,* 80, 108; in Busch Grand National Series 207, 209

Win on Sunday, Sell on Monday 143

Wingo, Donnie 82

Winston All-Star Race 56, 70, 129

Winston Cup, birth of 128; Dodge's return to 197; inaugural 202; patriotism and *201*

Winston Cup Grand National (original name of Winston Cup) 128 *See also* Winston Cup

Winston 500 171

Winston 500 (1978) *165*

Winston 500 (1987) 174, 200, 203

Winston Million bonus 48, 129, 171, 184, 186

Winston Open 70

Winston West 48, 52, 111

Winston Western 500 (1978) *128*

Winston Western 500 (1981) *130*

Wood Brothers 52, 65, 70, 79, 125, 151, 160, 166, 196, 200 *See also* Wood, Glenn; Wood, Leonard

Wood, Eddie 80

Wood, Glen 79, 148, 151 *See also* Wood Brothers Racing; Wood, Leonard

Wood, Jon 214

Wood, Kim 80

Wood, Leonard 79; on the France family 93 *See also* Wood Brothers Racing; Wood, Glen

World Karting Association 207

World of Outlaws 43, 131

World 600 162, 163, 165, 171 *See also* Coca-Cola 600

World War II 203

Wrangler Jeans 127

Y

Yarborough, Cale 41, 52, 59, 79, 82, 83, 84, 120, 125, *128,* 129, 130, 147, 151, 153, 155, 156, 158, 160, 161, 162, 163, 164, *165,* 165, 166, 167, 169, 170–171, 176, 182, 196, 200, 202, 205, 210

Yarbrough, LeeRoi (LeeRoy's son) *153*

Yarbrough, LeeRoy 78, 122, 125, 152, *153,* 154, 155, 156, 158

Yates, Carolyn 82

Yates, Richard 82

Yates, Robert 53, 74, 82, 85, 186, 187

Yunnick, Smokey *115*

Z

Zanardi, Alex 82

Zervakis, Emanuel 149

Zipadelli, Greg 78